Mastering

Microsoft® Exchange
Server 2010

Mastering

Microsoft® Exchange Server 2010

Jim McBee

David Elfassy

WILEY

Wiley Publishing, Inc.

Acquisitions Editor: Agatha Kim
Development Editor: Lisa Bishop
Technical Editor: Ross Smith IV
Production Editor: Angela Smith
Copy Editor: Liz Welch
Editorial Manager: Pete Gaughan
Production Manager: Tim Tate
Vice President and Executive Group Publisher: Richard Swadley
Vice President and Publisher: Neil Edde
Book Designers: Maureen Forys, Happenstance Type-O-Rama; Judy Fung
Proofreader: Publication Services, Inc.
Indexer: Ted Laux
Project Coordinator, Cover: Lynsey Stanford
Cover Designer: Ryan Sneed
Cover Image: © Pete Gardner/DigitalVision/Getty Images

Dear Reader,

Thank you for choosing *Mastering Microsoft Exchange Server 2010*. This book is part of a family of premium-quality Sybex books, all of which are written by outstanding authors who combine practical experience with a gift for teaching.

Sybex was founded in 1976. More than 30 years later, we're still committed to producing consistently exceptional books. With each of our titles, we're working hard to set a new standard for the industry. From the paper we print on, to the authors we work with, our goal is to bring you the best books available.

I hope you see all that reflected in these pages. I'd be very interested to hear your comments and get your feedback on how we're doing. Feel free to let me know what you think about this or any other Sybex book by sending me an email at nedde@wiley.com. If you think you've found a technical error in this book, please visit http://sybex.custhelp.com. Customer feedback is critical to our efforts at Sybex.

Best regards,

Neil Edde
Vice President and Publisher
Sybex, an Imprint of Wiley

This book is dedicated to my father, Charles Roy McBee, the nicest and most decent person you could ever meet.

Acknowledgments

Congratulations to the Microsoft Exchange Server Team and their sixth release of the number one messaging system in the world. Each successive release has had both incremental and significant improvements. These improvements come as a result of hundreds of thousands of hours of interaction with their customers and taking their feedback into consideration in order to produce a superior product.

As we finish the last of this book and get it ready for the printers, I have already implemented several Exchange 2010 installations as well as been part of a large Exchange 2010 design. Even after reading many articles, email threads, newsgroup postings, and hundreds of pages of help files, I still learn new things about Exchange Server 2010 each and every day.

The task of writing a book that not only covers new and useful material but that is also reasonably easy to read is a daunting one. Fortunately, along the way, I have had a lot of help. Early on in this process I realized I would never be able to finish this book alone and invited David Elfassy to be my coauthor. David's guidance and knowledge has been invaluable.

I am indebted to Ross Smith. Ross agreed to be the technical editor for the book without realizing just how much of his time that would take and just how often he would need to steer us back on track.

The great folks at Wiley have been patient beyond belief when it comes to deadlines, content, and outline changes as well as last-minute ideas. They include acquisitions editor Agatha Kim, developmental editor Lisa Bishop, production editors Angela Smith and Dassi Zeidel, and copy editor Liz Welch.

Along the way, many other Exchange gurus out there have helped out, from writing entire chapters to providing just a few paragraphs. Throughout this book, you will find content written by Devin Ganger, Ken St. Cyr, John Rodriguez, Pat Richards, Doug Fidler, Michael B. Smith, Randy Williams, Martin Tuip, and Ilse van Criekinge. Each of these gurus helped me provide content that was outside of my area of specialization.

I would also like to acknowledge the many other Exchange and Windows gurus out there who have provided me with quick answers to my late-night questions. These heroes include the entire Exchange TAP list, Brian Tirch, David Espinosa, Melissa Travers, William Lefkovics, Paul Robichaux, John Fullbright, Peter O'Dowd, Scott Schnoll, Nino Bilic, Harold Wong, Evan Dodds, Rich Matheisen, Glen Scales, Missy Koslosky, Mark Arnold, and Bharat Suneja. My hat is also off to the hundreds of people I have talked to at conferences and events over the past year who have given me ideas for topics and how things can be better explained.

I would also like to thank my friends and coworkers, including Suriya Supatanasakul, Grace Tanaka, Clayton Kamiya, Michael Brown, Tyler Swartz, Jason Crawford, Ivan Baker, and Matt Cook.

About the Authors

Jim McBee is an MCT, MCSE, and Exchange MVP based in Honolulu, Hawaii. He has authored a number of previous books on Exchange Server, including the popular Exchange 24seven series. He speaks and consults on Exchange Server all over the world and is the founder of Ithicos Solutions. When not writing or working, he can either be found snowboarding or playing with his Siberian Husky, Luke.

David Elfassy, MCITP, MCT, and MVP: Exchange Server, is an international presenter and trainer; having presented on messaging technologies to thousands of Microsoft clients since the late 1990s. David collaborates with Microsoft on certification, courseware, and key development projects. As a senior technical advisor for two Microsoft Gold Certified Partners, including Netlogon Technologies where he specializes in large enterprise consulting and technical writing, and Kalleo where he specializes in small business network management (overseeing a team of consultants and network technicians), David is a project lead on many migrations and implementations of Microsoft infrastructure technologies for governmental and corporate organizations. Helping organizations migrate to the latest versions of Microsoft Exchange Server has always been a key focus of David's consulting commitments.

When David is not troubleshooting SMTP connections or working on Microsoft projects, he runs after his three young children, Zachary, Zoe, and Savannah, or hangs out with his lovely, supporting wife, Gillian.

Contents at a Glance

Contents

Introduction

Thank you for purchasing (or considering a purchase of) *Mastering Microsoft Exchange Server 2010*; this is the latest in a series of Mastering Exchange Server books that have helped thousands of readers to better understand Microsoft's excellent messaging system. Along the way, we hope that this series of books has made you a better administrator and allowed you to support your organizations to the best of your abilities.

When we started planning the outline of this book more than a year before its release, Exchange Server 2010 appeared to be simply a minor series of improvements over Exchange Server 2007. Of course, the further we explored the product, the more quickly we found that was not the case. Many of the improvements in Exchange Server 2010 were major improvements and sometimes even complete rewrites (such as in the case of Outlook Web App) of how the product worked previously.

Another challenge then presented itself. The market penetration of Exchange Server 2007 was fairly low, compared to the total number of Exchange Server deployments out there in the world. A large percentage of Exchange customers were still using Exchange Server 2003. Thus, we had to approach this book from two different viewpoints. We needed to explain the differences for not only the Exchange 2003 administrator but also for the Exchange 2007 administrator.

We took a step back and looked at the previous editions of the book to figure out how much of the previous material was still relevant. Some of the material from the Exchange 2007 book is still relevant but needed updating, but we could not just provide an update to Exchange Server 2007 material. We had to bring the Exchange 2003 administrators up to speed. We were faced with the challenge of not only explaining a completely new management interface, but also the new Exchange Management Shell command-line interface, new server roles, and new features.

We started working with the Exchange Server 2010 code more than a year before we expected to release the book. Much of the book was written using the code that was first made available in April 2009. As we finished various sections of the book, we immediately began thinking about topics we would like to add, such as SharePoint and email integration, as well as a more detailed description of archiving and virtualization. In writing this book, we had a few goals for both the book and the knowledge we wanted to impart to the reader:

- ◆ We want to provide you with some basic email administration skills that would help you regardless of which version of Exchange Server you are supporting.

- ◆ The book is designed to help you master the basics of Exchange Server 2010. We want you to get all of the basic skills necessary to install and manage an Exchange Server 2010 system.

- ◆ The skills and tasks covered in this book should be applicable to 80 percent of all organizations running Exchange Server.

◆ The book should educate not only "new to product" administrators, but those "new to version" administrators who are upgrading from a previous version.

◆ When explaining the differences between Exchange 2010 and prior versions, the book should focus on Exchange Server 2003 but also provide information for experienced Exchange Server 2007 administrators.

Despite the fact that many things have changed in Exchange Server 2010, if you are upgrading from a previous version you will still be comfortable with the concepts and principles of operation. Exchange Server 5.5 was one of the most powerful, extensible, scalable, easy-to-use, and manageable electronic-messaging back ends on the market. Exchange 2000 Server retained all of 5.5's best features and added new ones. Exchange Server 2003 went a step further, altering interfaces that didn't quite work in the 2000 flavor and adding some great new features.

Exchange Server 2007 then added features that improved dramatically on our ability to provide not only a highly available messaging environment but also site resiliency in case we needed to move our live data to an alternate site. Exchange 2007 also introduced integrated Unified Messaging capabilities directly into the product with the integration of the Unified Messaging server role.

Microsoft listened to the advice of many of its customers, its internal consultants at Microsoft Consulting Services (MCS), Microsoft Certified Systems Engineers (MCSEs), Most Valued Professionals (MVPs), and Microsoft Certified Trainers (MCTs) to find out what was missing from earlier versions of the product and what organizations' needs were. Much of this work started even before Exchange Server 2007 was released. Some common requests, feedback, and complaints that customers frequently provided about earlier versions of Exchange Server included the following:

◆ Simplify the management interface and make it easier to script all Exchange management functions.

◆ Allow for local or remote replicas of Exchange databases.

◆ Integrate archiving into the product and provide interfaces to allow the administrator to enforce corporate or organization messaging policies.

◆ Provide better antispam capabilities and update antispam configuration data and signatures more frequently.

◆ Provide better security for mobile devices and make them easier to manage.

◆ Provide better integration with voicemail solutions.

◆ Make resource scheduling simpler, more powerful, and better integrated.

◆ Reduce the burden on help desks by enabling clients to be configured automatically.

Improvements to Exchange Server 2010

Since most of the administrators reading this are probably going to be coming from an Exchange Server 2003 environment, let's look at the improvements that have been made to Exchange Server 2010 since that time.

Improvements to Exchange Server 2007 are not to any single component of Exchange Server. For starters, the management interface was completely revamped. The new Exchange Management Console simplifies Exchange Server administration with a totally redesigned interface that makes finding features and components much easier. The Exchange Management

Shell provides a powerful alternative to the Exchange Management Console; all administrative tasks can be performed via the Exchange Management Shell, including many advanced tasks that cannot be performed in the graphical user interface.

All mail-enabled recipient administration (mailboxes, groups, and contacts) is now performed through the Exchange Management Console utility, not the Active Directory Users and Computers utility; needless to say this was a bit of a controversial decision. The Exchange 2000/2003 extensions for Active Directory Users and Computers no longer work with Exchange Server 2010, and they should be removed from your administrators' desktops as soon as you start using Exchange Server 2010. Some features continue to work, but mail-enabled objects should not be created through Exchange System Manager, and once they have been moved to Exchange 2010 servers, they should not be managed using Exchange System Manager.

A controversial decision during the Exchange 2007 timeframe was the decision to support only x64 processor architecture. Exchange Server 2010 requires Windows 2008 SP2 x64 or Windows Server 2008 R2. The decision to support the x64 architecture was driven by the need for more RAM in larger organizations. Exchange Server 2010 has been tested heavily in environments with up to 64 GB of RAM. More RAM dramatically improves disk I/O performance.

Exchange Server 2010's tight integration with Active Directory has not changed; almost all of the Exchange configuration data and recipient email attributes are still stored in Active Directory, just as they were with Exchange 2000/2003/2007. A widespread misconception is that Exchange recipient configuration is no longer in Active Directory because the recipient management utility is no longer Active Directory Users and Computers.

To simplify installation of Exchange Server 2010 and to make it easier for organizations that split server functions across multiple servers, the setup program allows you to choose which functions (called roles) the server supports. These roles include the Mailbox server, the Client Access server, the Hub Transport server, the Unified Messaging server, and the Edge Transport server.

One of the most interesting new feature sets for Exchange Server 2007 was the continuous replication feature; in Exchange 2007 this feature was used for local continuous replication, clustered continuous replication, and standby continuous replication. In Exchange Server 2010, the continuous replication feature is now used with the database availability groups (DAGs) feature. DAGs allow you to group together two or more Exchange 2010 Mailbox servers into a single DAG; the databases on any of the DAG members can then be replicated to the other DAG members. At any given time the database is "active" on one of the DAG members, but is in "passive" mode on the other members and can be activated in the event of a failure. Failover is now at the database level rather than the entire server.

Though features such as sender filtering, recipient filtering, sender ID, and the real-time block list have been retained, antispam capabilities have been improved with additional methods of connection filtering, such as reputation filtering. An all-new version of the content filter (formerly known as the Intelligent Message Filter) is now included with Exchange Server 2010. Customers with Enterprise client access licenses (eCALs) can get daily updates to the reputation filter and the content filter. Antispam components can be installed on the Hub Transport servers, or they can be offloaded to dedicated Edge Transport servers in an organization's perimeter network. Enterprise client access licenses allow an organization to use Microsoft's Forefront Security for Exchange (formerly Sybari Antigen).

If you ever wanted to have better control of messages "in transit," the redesigned message transport and transport rules will have you dancing on tables. All messages are delivered through a Hub Transport server role, regardless of whether they are being delivered locally or remotely. Transport rules allow you to apply conditions to messages moving through the transport (such as sender/recipient, sender/recipient group memberships, message classification, and so on) and take an action on that message.

Calendaring and resource scheduling have been dramatically improved. The Free/Busy functions of earlier versions of Exchange have been completely replaced with a new web service. Resource mailboxes are now specific mailbox types rather than just a generic mailbox as with previous versions. The Calendar Concierge feature allows the administrator to configure automatic resource booking options.

Outlook Web App (formerly known as Outlook Web Access) is better than ever with a completely revamped interface that includes improved options, better scheduling integration, and the ability to manage mobile devices via the Outlook Web App interface. The Exchange Control Panel (ECP) is a new web application that allows users to manage their own Active Directory information and mail group memberships.

Another new web service is the Autodiscover service. The Autodiscover service works with Outlook 2007/2010 and Windows Mobile 6 devices to enable Outlook to automatically be configured to connect to the correct Exchange resources regardless of whether the client is on the internal network or the external network.

An entirely new Exchange server function is the Unified Messaging server role; this server role integrates with your Voice over IP (VOIP) phone system or legacy PBX via VOIP gateway. This allows Exchange Server to handle your automated call routing and inbound voicemail. Exchange users can call in to the Unified Messaging server to retrieve their voicemail, have their email read to them, listen to their calendar, or even move items around on their calendar.

With these and an impressive array of other features, Exchange Server 2010 can help your organization move smoothly and productively into the world of advanced, enhanced electronic messaging.

Windows Server 2008

Exchange Server 2010 requires either Windows Server 2008 SP2 x64 or Windows Server 2008 R2. Many IT organizations are now facing the same question. In many environments in which we work, Windows Server 2003 is still the de facto standard for any number of reasons. First and foremost, though, is that it is a known factor in the deployment; most of us have installed Windows Server 2003 many times by now, we are comfortable with it, and we know most everything we need to know to keep it running.

Exchange Server 2010 may be the driving factor that influences your organization to start using Windows Server 2008, but it does offer many improvements and security enhancements. There are some obstacles that you may need to overcome with respect to Windows Server 2008. Keep in mind also that either SP2 or R2 is required. Given a choice, since Windows Server 2008 R2 is a newer release, we recommend going ahead with that version. Under the hood, very few differences exist between Windows Server 2008 SP2 and Windows Server 2008 R2. You will find, though, that there are certain pieces of software that you may need to install or update if you are going to just use Windows Server 2008 SP2.

Many medium-sized and large organizations may have an information security policy or operational requirements that will prohibit you from deploying newer operating software until there is an officially sanctioned "build" or configuration. Thus you may face some hurdles when it comes to getting approval to deploy Windows Server 2008 SP2 or R2.

What You Need to Run Exchange Server

Exchange Server 2010 is a complex product, but the user interface has been completely revamped to be easier to administer Exchange. All of this complexity and parallel ease of use requires an industrial-strength computer. The minimum server requirement suggested here is for testing, learning about, and evaluating the product. It's also enough for a small, noncritical installation. However, as we discuss in the book, when the server moves into critical production environments, where it will be accessed by large numbers of users, you'll need to beef up its hardware and add a number of fault-tolerant capabilities. On the client side, with the broad range of clients available for Exchange, the machines in most organizations should be more than adequate.

At a minimum, to test, learn about, and evaluate Exchange Server, you need the following:

◆ Microsoft Exchange Server 2010, Windows Server 2008 SP2 x64 or R2.

◆ An AMD Athlon x64 or Intel x64 compatible processor with 4 GB of RAM and at least two 36 GB disk drives. This allows you to complete exercises involving a single Exchange server. The second disk can be used for Volume Snapshot Service (VSS) backups.

◆ Backup software that you plan to use in production and that is capable of taking VSS backups.

◆ A local area network (preferably connected to the Internet).

◆ At least a dual-core 1.6 GHz processor and 1 GB of memory running Windows XP Professional, Windows Vista, or Windows 7 for testing Outlook and other client-side functions. If you want to install the Exchange Management tools, you must use Windows Vista x64 or Windows 7 x64.

During the development of this book, we used a combination of Dell Xeon-based servers, HP Athlon-based servers, and lots and lots of virtual machines using VMware Server or Microsoft Windows Server 2008 HyperV.

How This Book Is Organized

This book consists of 30 chapters, divided into five broad topic areas. As you proceed through the book, you'll move from basic concepts to several increasingly complex levels of hands-on implementation.

This book won't work well for practitioners of the time-worn ritual of chapter hopping. Though some readers may benefit from reading one or two chapters, we recommend you read most of the book in order. If you have experience as an Exchange administrator, then you can skip Chapters 2 through 5 as much of this is going to be a review. Unless you already have considerable experience with these products, to get the maximum value out of this book, you need to track through the chapters in order. In later chapters, you will frequently find us referring to previous chapters to get more details on a specific topic.

If you are like most administrators, though, you like to get your hands on the software and actually see things working. Having a working system also helps many people as they read a book or learn about a new piece of software because this lets them test new skills as they are learning them. If this sounds like you, then start with Chapter 10, "Exchange Server 2010 Quick Start Guide." This chapter will take you briefly through some of the things you need to know to get Exchange running, though not necessarily in a lot of detail. As long as you're not planning to put your quickie server into production immediately, there should be no harm done. Before going into production, though, we strongly suggest that you explore other parts of this book. Here's a guide to what's in each chapter.

Part 1: Exchange Fundamentals

This part of the book focuses on concepts and features of Microsoft's Windows Server 2008, Exchange Server 2010, and some of the fundamentals of operating a modern client/server email system. It is designed to provide you with the underlying knowledge that you'll need when you tackle Windows and Exchange Server 2010 installation, administration, troubleshooting, and management later in this book.

Chapter 1, "Introducing Exchange Server 2010," is partially for administrators of Exchange Server 2003 or 2007, but also for people just getting started with email server administration. This chapter introduces the new features of Exchange Server 2010 as contrasted with previous versions.

Chapter 2, "Introduction to Email Administration," is for those administrators who have been handed an Exchange organization but who have never managed a previous version of Exchange or even another mail system. This will give you some of the basic information and background to help you get started managing Exchange Server and, hopefully, a little history and perspective.

Chapter 3, "Standards and Protocols," is intended as a primer for anyone who needs to manage an email system that relies on TCP/IP networking and that is connected to the Internet. Topics include some of the basics of the SMTP, POP, IMAP, DNS, and HTTP protocols and how they relate to an email system.

Chapter 4, "Understanding Availability, Recovery, and Compliance," helps even experienced administrators navigate some of the new hurdles that Exchange Server administrators must overcome, including providing better system availability, site resiliency, backup and restoration plans, and legal compliance.

Chapter 5, "Message Security and Hygiene," introduces Exchange administrators to technologies that can better help you protect your users from hostile content, viruses, and spam as well as message-level security and providing multilayer security for your messaging systems.

Chapter 6, "Introduction to PowerShell and the Exchange Management Shell," is a chapter that all Exchange administrators should read. This chapter introduces you to some of the basics of the new Microsoft PowerShell and how to use the new shell. The chapter focuses on and uses examples of features that are enabled in the PowerShell through the Exchange Server 2010 management extensions for the PowerShell. All administrations should have at least a basic familiarity with the Exchange Management Shell extensions for PowerShell even if you rarely use them. Though most Exchange management tasks can be performed from the graphical user interface (GUI), even people who do not script or use the command prompt frequently will find the Exchange Management Shell an attractive and useful alternative to many GUI-based tasks.

Chapter 7, "Exchange Autodiscover," helps you to come up to speed on the inner workings of Microsoft's new Exchange and Outlook 2007 (and later) feature that greatly simplifies the configuration of both internal and external Outlook clients. The user no longer has to remember the server name in order to configure Outlook 2007 and later.

Chapter 8, "Virtualizing Exchange Server 2010," helps bring you up to speed on this quickly evolving landscape of IT. Many organizations are virtualizing some or all of their Exchange servers. Should you virtualize some percentage of your servers? This chapter will help you answer that question.

Chapter 9, "Exchange Server, Email, and SharePoint 2007," helps to answer the nagging question that Exchange Server administrators are often asked: "How can I integrate SharePoint and Exchange Server?" SharePoint was certainly not designed with Exchange Server interoperability in mind, but this chapter will let you know where there are synergies between the two products.

Part 2: Getting Exchange Running

This section of the book is devoted to topics related to meeting the prerequisites for Exchange Server and getting Exchange Server installed correctly the first time. While installing Exchange Server correctly is not rocket science, getting everything right the first time will greatly simplify your deployment.

While Exchange Server 2010 runs on top of Windows Server 2008, this part covers the installation of Exchange 2010 and the prerequisites rather than doing a deep-dive into Windows Server 2008. We recommend that you refer to a dedicated Windows reference such as *Mastering Windows Server 2008 R2* by Mark Minasi (Sybex, 2010).

Chapter 10, "Exchange Server 2010 Quick Start Guide," is where everyone likes to jump right in and install the software. This chapter will help you quickly get a single server up and running for your test and lab environment. While you should not deploy an entire enterprise based on the content of this one chapter, it will help you get started quickly.

Chapter 11, "Understanding Server Roles and Configurations," covers the different Exchange Server role options, including Mailbox, Hub Transport, Edge Transport, Client Access, Unified Messaging, and combined function servers as well as the services and functions of each of those servers.

Chapter 12, "Exchange Server 2010 Requirements," guides you through the requirements (Windows Server, Active Directory, and earlier versions of Exchange) that you must meet in order to get Exchange Server 2010 successfully deployed.

Chapter 13, "Installing Exchange Server 2010," takes you through both the graphical user interface and the command-line setup for installing Exchange Server 2010.

Chapter 14, "Upgrades and Migrations," will help you decide what is the right migration or transition approach for your organization as well as recommending steps to take to upgrade your organization from Exchange Server 2003 to Exchange Server 2010. Also included in this chapter are recommendations for migration phases, co-existence, and reasons you would need to keep older Exchange servers in production.

Part 3: Recipient Administration

Recipient administration generally ends up being the most time-consuming portion of Exchange Server administration. Recipient administration includes creating and managing mailboxes, managing mail groups, creating and managing contacts, and administering public folders. Exchange 2007 and 2010 introduced improved resource mailbox management, which may also make your life a lot easier as well as providing some great new features for your users. Another new feature that was introduced in Exchange Server 2010 is the personal mailbox archive.

Chapter 15, "Management Permissions and Role-Based Administration (RBAC)," introduces one of the most powerful features of Exchange Server 2010: the roles-based administration control (RBAC) feature, which enables extremely detailed delegation of permissions for all Exchange administrative tasks. This feature will be of great value to large organizations.

Chapter 16, "Basics of Recipient Management," will undoubtedly consume most of your time as an administrator. This chapter introduces you to some concepts you should take into consideration before you start creating users, including how email addresses are generated and which domain names your Exchange servers will accept mail for. This chapter also includes mailbox policies that can be applied, such as ActiveSync and messaging records management.

Chapter 17, "Managing Mailboxes and Mailbox Content," is at the core of most Exchange administrators' jobs since the mailboxes represent our direct customer (the end user.) This chapter introduces the concepts of managing mailboxes (creating, updating, removing, and recovering) mailboxes. This chapter also introduces the messaging records management features of Exchange 2010, including creating managed custom folders, defining folder content settings, and configuring managed folder mailbox policies.

Chapter 18, "Managing Mail-Enabled Groups," covers management of mail-enabled groups, including creating groups, assigning e-mail addresses, securing groups, and allowing for self-service management of groups.

Chapter 19, "Managing Mail-Enabled Contacts and Users," covers mail-enabled contact management in your Exchange organization. A mail-enabled contact in your Active Directory can make it simple for your users to view external recipients via your global address list and easily send them mail. For external contacts to which your users must frequently send email, maintaining contacts of those external contacts provides a valuable service.

Chapter 20, "Managing Resource Mailboxes," introduces the new resource mailbox features of Exchange Server 2010. A resource can either be a room (such as a conference room) or a piece of equipment (such as an overhead projector.) Exchange Server 2010 makes it easy to allow users to view the availability of resources and request the use of these resources from within Outlook or Outlook Web App.

Chapter 21, "Public Folder Management," may either introduce you to the concept of public folders or update your skill set so that you know how to manage public folders using the Exchange Server 2010 tools. Though public folders are being deemphasized in many organizations, there are still other organizations that have massive quantities of data stored there. This chapter introduces the Exchange Public Folder Management Console, as well as the Exchange 2010 Exchange Management Shell cmdlets necessary to manage public folder properties.

Chapter 22, "Getting Started with Email Archiving," introduces not only the overall concepts of archiving and how the rest of the industry handles archiving, but also the exciting new Exchange Server 2010 personal archive mailbox feature. This feature is integrated into Exchange Server 2010 and requires no additional software.

Part 4: Server Administration

While recipient administration is important, administrators must not forget their responsibilities to properly set up the Exchange server and to maintain it. This section helps introduce you to the configuration tasks and maintenance necessary for some of the Exchange Server 2010 roles as well as safely connecting your server to the Internet.

Chapter 23, "Creating and Managing Mailbox Databases," will help familiarize you with the changes in Exchange Server 2010 with respect to mailbox database, storage, and basic sizing requirements. Many exciting changes have been made to support large databases and to allow Exchange to scale to support more simultaneous users.

Chapter 24, "Understanding the Client Access Server," introduces you to the critical Client Access server role and the components running on the Client Access server. While at first glance the CAS might seem to be an overgrown Exchange 2003 front-end server, that is far from the case. The Client Access server role provides Exchange Server 2010 with many essential services, not the least of which is Outlook Web App connectivity, mailbox access for Outlook clients via the RPC Client Access service, and the Exchange Control Panel.

Chapter 25, "Managing Connectivity with Hub Transport Servers," will bring you up to speed on the Hub Transport server role. This server is at the core of the message transport architecture. All messages transmitted and received within your Exchange Server 2010 architecture will traverse at least one Hub Transport server even if the message is sent from one recipient on a mailbox database to another recipient on the same mailbox database.

Chapter 26, "Managing Transport and Journaling Rules," introduces you to a feature set that was first introduced in Exchange Sever 2007 but has since been greatly improved upon. This is the transport rule feature and how to implement this feature. This chapter also discusses message journaling.

Chapter 27, "Internet and Email," concentrates on the Hub Transport and Edge Transport roles within an organization and how that organization interacts with the Internet. This includes configuring a Hub Transport server to send and receive email directly to and from the Internet or using the Edge Transport server role to provide antispam functions.

Part 5: Troubleshooting, Operations, and Monitoring

Troubleshooting and keeping a proper eye on how healthy your Exchange servers are often neglected tasks. We may not look at our Exchange servers until there is an actual problem. In this part we discuss some tips and tools that will help you proactively manage your Exchange environment, ensuring that you can track down problems as well as restore any potential lost data.

Chapter 28, "Troubleshooting Exchange Server 2010," introduces you not only to troubleshooting the various components of Exchange Server 2010, but also good troubleshooting techniques. This chapter also includes a discussion of using some of the Exchange Server 2010 built-in tools, such as the Exchange Management Shell test cmdlets and the Exchange Best Practices Analyzer.

Chapter 29, "Monitoring and Performance," introduces some key concepts that are useful in determining if a server has performance issues. Additional topics include troubleshooting tools and useful analysis tools. This chapter also includes information about security, auditing, tracking, and protocol logging.

Chapter 30, "Backing Up and Restoring Exchange Server," includes discussions on developing a backup plan for your Exchange Server 2010 servers as well as how backup has changed with Windows Server 2008 and Exchange Server 2008. For those of you transitioning from Exchange Server 2003, the biggest change that you may note is that you can no longer use streaming backups; you must now use Volume Shadow Copy Service (VSS)–based backups.

Conventions Used in This Book

The code continuation character is used on PowerShell commands to indicate that the line of text is part of a previous command line.

Many of the screen captures in this book have been taken from lab and test environments. However, sometimes you will screen captures that actually came from a working environment. We have obscured any information that would identify those environments.

Any examples that include IP addresses have had the IP addresses changed to private IP addresses even if we are referring to Internet addresses.

Remember, Exchange is designed to help your organization do what it does better, more efficiently, and with greater productivity. Have fun, be productive, and prosper!

Part 1

Exchange Fundamentals

- ◆ **Chapter 1: Introducing Exchange Server 2010**
- ◆ **Chapter 2: Introduction to Email Administration**
- ◆ **Chapter 3: Standards and Protocols**
- ◆ **Chapter 4: Understanding Availability, Recovery, and Compliance**
- ◆ **Chapter 5: Message Security and Hygiene**
- ◆ **Chapter 6: Introduction to PowerShell and the Exchange Management Shell**
- ◆ **Chapter 7: Exchange Autodiscover**
- ◆ **Chapter 8: Virtualizing Exchange Server 2010**
- ◆ **Chapter 9: Exchange Server, Email, and SharePoint 2007**

Chapter 1

Introducing Exchange Server 2010

Email clients used to be fairly simple and text based. Email servers had few connectivity options, no high-availability features, and no integrated directory. Then, beginning in the mid-1990s we saw a big push toward providing email service to most of our user communities. We also saw email go from an occasionally used convenience to a business-critical tool. Business management and users demanded more features, better availability, and more connectivity options as the email client and server evolved.

Microsoft released Exchange Server 4.0 (the first version of Exchange Server) in 1996 and the product has been evolving ever since. Exchange Server 2010 is the fifth major release of the Exchange Server family and represents a significant evolution of the product. The features and functions of this new release include not only feature requests from many thousands of Microsoft's customers, but also requirements shared internally at Microsoft by Microsoft Consulting Services and their own IT department, which supports nearly 100,000 mailboxes.

When we started planning this chapter, we considered discussing exclusively what was new in Exchange Server 2010 since the release of Exchange Server 2007. However, as of this writing most Exchange Server customers are still using Exchange Server 2003 rather than Exchange Server 2007. For this reason, we want to incorporate into this chapter a summary of the changes that have been made to Exchange Server since Exchange Server 2003.

In this chapter, you will learn to:

◆ Understand new high-availability options

◆ Understand new recipient management features

◆ Recognize Exchange architecture changes

Getting to Know Exchange Server 2010

It seems that we approach any new release of Exchange Server with a sense of both excitement and trepidation. We look forward to the new features and capabilities that are introduced with a newer version of a product. Certainly features such as the Exchange Management Shell, new database replication technology, antispam, resource management, and security features will allow us to deliver better, more reliable messaging services to our end users.

On the other side of the coin is the feeling that there is a whole new series of features that we have to learn inside and out so that we can better use them. Sure, we know Exchange

2003 or Exchange 2007 pretty well, but there will be new details to learn with Exchange 2010. Sometimes these implementation or management details are things that we have to learn the hard way — thus the trepidation associated with any new version of Exchange.

However, this next milestone in the evolution of Exchange Server is a good one. We can't help but be excited about learning about this new version and sharing what we have learned. We hope that you will feel the same sense of excitement. We have picked a top-ten list of new features that we like and hope that you will investigate further as you start to learn Exchange Server 2010. Some of these are summarized in this chapter while most of these you will find in more detail in later chapters. The new features are as follows:

- Powerful message transport rules applied and enforced at the server
- Continuously replicated Exchange databases and failover to a replicated database at the database level rather than the server level
- MAPI clients now able to communicate with the Client Access server rather than directly with the database engine
- Vastly improved antispam features
- Customizable ''over quota,'' nondelivery messages, and end-user informational messages
- Exchange Management Shell command-line and scripting interface
- Improved calendaring support via calendar concierge, the Availability service, and resource mailboxes
- Message routing now based on Active Directory site rather than Exchange administrator–configured routing groups
- Unified messaging technology that is now an integrated part of Exchange Server 2010
- Completely rewritten and vastly improved Outlook Web App (formerly known as Outlook Web Access)

This list could go on for the entire chapter, but this gives you a taste of a few of the features that excite Exchange administrators as well as administrators from other messaging systems when they talk about Exchange 2010.

LEARN THE EXCHANGE MANAGEMENT SHELL (AND WEAR SUNSCREEN!)

To those of you who have been around the Internet long enough to remember the ''Wear Sunscreen'' email that was supposedly the 1997 commencement address to MIT given by Kurt Vonnegut but was in reality a column written by the *Chicago Sun Tribune*'s Mary Schmich, I give you ''Learn the Management Shell'':

- If we could offer you one important tip when learning Exchange Server 2010, it would be that you should get to know the Exchange Management Shell (EMS). Sure, it looks intimidating and nearly everything you will ever need to do is in the Exchange Management Console. Many Exchange gurus will back us up on the value and usefulness of the new EMS, whereas they might not agree with us on things such as using real-time block lists, making full backups daily, and keeping lots of free disk space available.

- Make regular Exchange data backups.

◆ Document.

◆ Don't believe everything you read from a vendor; their job is to sell you things.

◆ Don't put off maintenance that might affect your up-time.

◆ If you get in trouble, call for help sooner rather than later. A few hundred dollars for a phone call to your vendor or Microsoft Product Support Services is better than a few days of downtime.

◆ Share your knowledge and configuration information with coworkers.

◆ Accept certain inalienable truths: disks will fail, servers will crash, users will complain, viruses will spread, and important messages will sometimes get caught in the spam filter.

◆ Get to know your users and communicate with them.

◆ SharePoint provides a good alternative for sharing many types of data you might find in public folders; get to know it.

◆ Make regular backups of your Active Directory.

◆ If a consultant is telling you something that you know in your gut is wrong, double-check his work or run his recommendation by another colleague. Second opinions and another set of eyes are almost always helpful.

◆ Be careful with RegEdit, Active Directory Service Interfaces Editor (ADSI Edit), and any advice you read on the Internet (or in books).

But trust us on the EMS.

In this chapter, we will cover the changes to Exchange 2010 not only to give experienced Exchange administrators the proper perspective on Exchange 2010, but also to educate newly minted Exchange administrators on just how powerful Exchange has become.

Exchange Server Architecture

Since Exchange Server 2003, a number of significant changes have been made to the architecture of Exchange Server. These changes positively improve the performance and scalability of Exchange Server, but they also make some pretty significant changes in the platform on which you support Exchange Server.

x64 Processor Requirement

For a long time, one of the most discussed (and perhaps the most controversial) enhancement to Exchange 2007 (and now Exchange Server 2010) was that Exchange 2007 Server used 64-bit extensions. That meant your production servers would have to have x64 architecture–based Intel Xeon and Pentium processes or AMD64 architecture–based AMD Opteron and Athlon processors. There was an x86 build of Exchange Server 2007 that could be used for evaluation, classroom, or lab purposes, but not in production. There is only an x64 build of Exchange Server 2010.

Although many people are thrilled with this change in the architecture, there are, no doubt, folks screaming, "What? I have to buy new hardware just to upgrade?" A good response to this concern is that on most messaging system upgrades, the hardware is usually replaced anyway.

Certainly this is true for hardware that has been in production for more than three or four years. Add to this the fact that there is no ''in-place'' upgrade from Exchange 2000, 2003, or 2007 to Exchange Server 2010.

The good news is that most server-class hardware that has been purchased since the end of 2005 or later probably already includes the x64 processor extensions that Windows 2008 x64 requires. If you have existing hardware you want to use with Exchange 2010, confirm with your vendor that it will run Windows 2008 x64.

Is the decision to move to the x64 memory architecture a bold move? Is the Exchange team forging the way to more robust applications? Well, to a certain degree, yes, but the move to the 64-bit architecture is more out of need than the desire to forge a bold, modern path. Anyone who has supported an older version of Exchange Server with a large number of mailboxes knows that Exchange is constrained by the amount of RAM that it can access and that Exchange significantly taxes the disk I/O system. Further, as Exchange Server scaled to support more connections, limitations in the x86 operating system kernel also began to surface.

The number one reason that the x64 processor extensions are required is to provide Exchange Server with access to more than just a few gigabytes of RAM. With more RAM available, Exchange caching is more efficient and thus reduces the I/O requirements that are placed on the disk subsystem. More RAM also helps provide the improved scalability and features that organizations require, such as improved high availability, larger mailboxes, messaging records management features, improved message content security, transport rules, unified messaging integration, and improved journaling. The bottom line: the x64 instruction set for processors means more RAM for applications.

If you are not sure whether your existing hardware supports the x64 extensions, you can check in a number of ways. One approach is to check with the hardware vendor regarding x64 for your server hardware. Another way, if the computer is already running Windows, is to get a handy little program called CPU-Z from www.cpuid.com. Figure 1.1 shows the CPU-Z program.

FIGURE 1.1
Using CPU-Z to identify the CPU type

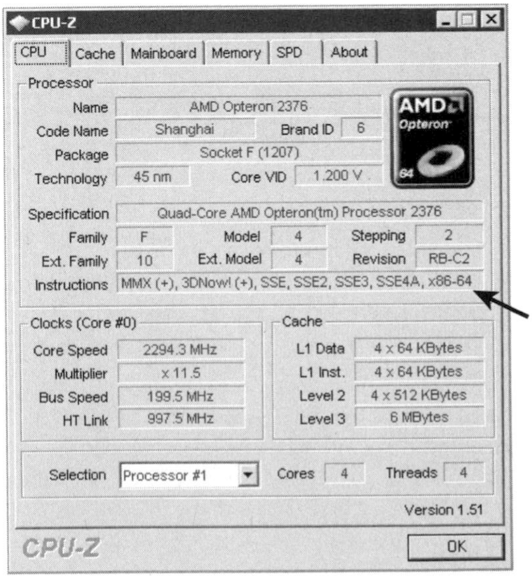

Notice in the Instructions line of CPU-Z that this particular chip supports x86-64. This means this chip will support the x64 instruction sets. Intel chips will report that they support the EM64T instruction set.

Windows Server 2008 x64

Because of some of the underlying requirements of Exchange Server 2010, you must run Windows Server 2008 x64 Service Pack 2 or Windows Server 2008 R2. Although many people are comfortable with Windows Server 2003, that operating system is fairly dated and does not have some of the components necessary for Exchange Server 2010. The following two editions of Windows 2008 will support Exchange Server 2010:

- Windows Server 2008 Standard x64 SP2 or R2

- Windows Server 2008 Enterprise x64 SP2 or R2

The Exchange Server 2010 management tools will run on the x64 version of Windows Vista Ultimate, Enterprise, and Business as well as Windows 7.

Installer, Service Pack, and Patching Improvements

The setup process in Exchange 2000/2003 had some serious annoyances; actually the whole process of getting a server up and running was pretty annoying. If a server did not meet the prerequisites, you had to close the Setup program, fix the problem, and then restart Setup. Once you got the release to manufacturing (RTM) or "gold" version installed, you had to install the most recent version of the Exchange service pack. Finally, you had to research all the post-service pack–critical fixes and apply them (sometimes in a specific order).

Microsoft has improved the setup process for Exchange Server 2010 as well as simplified patching. These improvements have been made in four key areas:

- The Exchange Server 2010 Setup program is good at finding missing prerequisites, letting you fix the missing prerequisite and then continue without starting over (unless a reboot is required after installing a prerequisite).

- The entire setup process can be performed from the command line using the `setup.com` program and EMS cmdlets.

- Service packs are now released as a complete installation pack; all updates are built into the service pack and you can install directly from the latest service pack. That means no more installing the RTM version and then applying the latest service pack.

- Rollup releases are now released approximately once every two months and contain a cumulative set of patches and critical fixes since the last service pack. So, rollup fix 4 (RU4) will contain all the updates contained in RU3 plus the other fixes released since RU3 was released.

Now all you have to do to get an Exchange Server completely built is to download the latest service pack, install Exchange Server 2010 from the latest service pack binaries, and then download the latest Exchange Server rollup fix and apply that fix. You can even simplify this process a bit more if you download the latest rollup fix MSP file and then copy it to the `Exchange 2010 setup \Updates` folder. Doing so greatly simplifies getting a server up and running as well as properly patched.

> **APPLYING SPECIAL HOTFIXES**
>
> If you get a rollup fix such as Exchange 2010 rollup fix 4 and then later you require an individual hotfix from Microsoft to address a specific issue, you may need to uninstall the post–rollup 4 hotfix prior to installing rollup fix 5. If you ever get a hotfix for Exchange 2010 to address a specific issue, always ask the Microsoft product support person if you will have to uninstall it prior to applying the next rollup.

Server Roles

In earlier versions of Exchange, once the Windows server was prepared to support Exchange, you simply installed an Exchange server. Then you customized the Exchange configuration, configured Internet Information Server (IIS), disabled unnecessary services, and prepared the server to assume the role you wanted it to assume, such as a Mailbox server, a bridgehead server, an Outlook Web Access front-end server, and so on.

Exchange 2007 officially introduced the concept of server roles at the point of setup; this continues with Exchange Server 2010. During the installation process, the Setup program (Figure 1.2) asks the installer which roles the server will be performing.

FIGURE 1.2
Specifying server roles

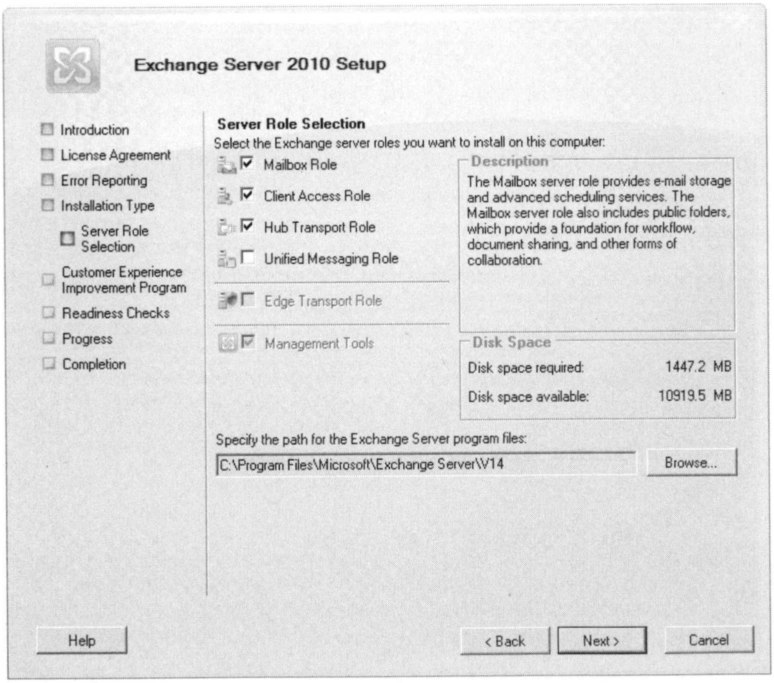

When running Setup, if you choose a custom installation, during setup you can specify the server roles by choosing from among the options in Table 1.1.

Once a role is selected, only the components necessary for that role are installed. This reduces the overhead on machines that are dedicated to a particular task (such as a Hub Transport server); ensures that no unnecessary executables, DLLs, or services are installed;

and makes creating dedicated server roles much easier. In a small organization with only one Exchange server, the same server may be assigned the Mailbox, Hub Transport, and Client Access server roles.

HIGH-AVAILABILITY DECISIONS

High-availability decisions do not need to be made at installation time. Unlike previous versions of Exchange Server, high availability for Exchange Server 2010 databases can be added incrementally *after* the initial deployment of the Mailbox server. There is no clustered mailbox server installation option.

TABLE 1.1:   Server Roles

SERVER ROLE	PURPOSE
Mailbox role	Supports mailboxes and public folders.
Client Access role	Supports functions such as Outlook, Outlook Web App, Outlook Anywhere (RPC over HTTP), Windows Mobile ActiveSync, POP3, and IMAP4, and supports web services such as Autodiscover, the Availability service, and calendar sharing.
Hub Transport role	Supports message transport functions such as delivering mail locally (to other Exchange servers in the organization) or externally (to an SMTP smart host such as an Exchange Edge Transport server). Using transport rules, the Hub Transport or Edge Transport roles can also help enforce messaging policies.
Unified Messaging role	Supports delivery of inbound voicemail and Outlook Voice Access features.
Edge Transport role	Supports separate antispam and antivirus functions for inbound and outbound messaging. The Edge Transport server is installed on a stand-alone machine usually in a perimeter network.

Edge Transport Services

The amount of spam and viruses that some organizations receive is staggering. Even small organizations are receiving tens of thousands of pieces of spam, dozens of viruses, and hundreds of thousands of dictionary spamming attacks each week. Some organizations estimate that more than 90 percent of all inbound email is spam or other unwanted content. Keeping as much of this unwanted content away from your Exchange servers as possible is important. A common practice for messaging administrators is to employ additional layers of message hygiene and security. The first layer is usually some type of appliance or third-party SMTP software package that is installed in the organization's perimeter network. The problem with these third-party utilities is that the administrator has to become an expert on an additional technology.

IS THE EDGE TRANSPORT SERVER ROLE REQUIRED?

A common misconception about Exchange 2010 is that the Edge Transport role is required for Exchange 2010. This is not the case. Inbound email can be sent directly to the Hub Transport role, or you can continue to use your existing third-party antispam/message hygiene system to act as an inbound message relay for Exchange Server.

Microsoft's solution to this dilemma is the Edge Transport server. The Edge Transport server is a stand-alone message transport server that is managed using the EMS and the same basic management console that is used to manage Exchange 2010. A server functioning in an Edge Transport role should not be a member of the organization's internal Active Directory.

Functions such as transport rules are identical to those that run on an Exchange 2010 Hub Transport server. Content filtering (formerly referred to as the Intelligent Message Filter, or IMF) and Microsoft Forefront Security for Exchange are implemented on the Edge Transport server.

An example of how an organization might deploy an Edge Transport server is shown in Figure 1.3. Inbound email is first delivered to the Edge Transport servers that are located in the organization's perimeter network, where the message is inspected by the content filter, Forefront Security for Exchange, and any message transport rules. The inbound message is then sent on to the internal Hub Transport servers. Additionally, the Exchange 2007 Hub Transport servers are configured to deliver mail leaving the organization to the Edge Transport servers rather than configuring the Hub Transport servers to deliver mail directly to the Internet.

FIGURE 1.3

Deploying an Edge Transport server

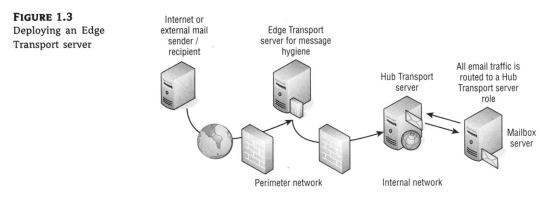

The Edge Transport server is a fully functional SMTP message hygiene system with many of the same features that are found in expensive message hygiene software packages and appliances. The following features are included:

◆ Per-user safe-sender, safe recipient, and blocked sender lists are automatically replicated from the user's mailbox to the Edge Transport server. For organizations using Exchange 2007, this represents a nice set of improvements.

◆ Recipient filtering is enabled when valid recipients are synchronized to the Edge Transport server's local Active Directory Application Mode (ADAM) database.

◆ Sender and recipient filtering can be configured via administrator-controlled lists.

◆ Integrated Microsoft content filter is included for spam detection. Spam can be rejected, deleted, quarantined, or delivered to the user's Junk E-mail folder.

◆ Multiple message quarantines allow messages that are highly likely to be spam to be quarantined and sent to a quarantine mailbox on your Exchange server. A separate quarantine exists in the form of the user's Junk E-mail folder for messages that are still tagged as spam but with a lower Spam Confidence Level (SCL).

◆ Microsoft Forefront Security for Exchange Server (formerly known as Antigen) is available for the Edge Transport server when Enterprise client access licenses are used.

◆ Daily content filter and virus signature updates are available for organizations using Microsoft Forefront Security for Exchange Server.

◆ Real-time block lists (RBLs) and IP Reputation Service allow an IP address to be checked to see if it is a known source of spam. Reputation filters can be updated on a daily basis.

◆ Sender ID filters allow for the verification of the mail server that sent a message and whether it is allowed to send mail for the message sender.

◆ Sender reputation filters allow a sender to be temporarily placed on a block list based on characteristics of mail coming from that sender, such as message content, Sender ID verification, and sender behavior.

Unified Messaging

The concept of unified messaging means that information from multiple sources is accessed in a single location. This concept is by no means a new one; third-party vendors have had fax and voicemail gateways for most major email systems. The Exchange 2010 Unified Messaging server role represents Microsoft's entrance into this market. This can make users more efficient by providing a single location for inbound information; voicemails can be read via Outlook Web App, Outlook, or Windows Mobile 6.5 or later devices. In addition, missed call information (someone who calls but does not leave a voicemail message) is sent to the user's mailbox.

An example of a voicemail that has been delivered to a user is shown in Figure 1.4. The form you see in the figure is in Outlook Web App 2010 and includes a player control for playing the message via the PC speakers.

The message also includes the ability to play the voice message on your desk phone. The Play On Phone option allows you to instruct the Unified Messaging server to call you at a specified extension (or optionally an external phone if the Unified Messaging dial-plan allows).

Further, the user can call the Unified Messaging server via the telephone and listen to their voicemail, have their email read to them, listen to their calendar, rearrange appointments, or look up someone in the global address book. Unified Messaging also allows the administrator to build a customized auto-attendant for call routing. In our experience, a typical voicemail (using the default MP3 codec) takes between 2 KB and 3 KB per second of message time, but this amount can be changed. However, with higher-quality recordings come higher message sizes.

The Unified Messaging server role functions as just another Exchange server in your organization, but this role includes components that allow IP-based phone systems and IP/PBX (public branch exchange) gateways to interface directly with Exchange over the network. This can take place provided the IP phone system or IP/PBX can communicate using Session Initiation Protocol (SIP) over TCP or Real-Time Transport Protocol (RTP) for voice communication.

FIGURE 1.4

Viewing a voicemail message sent via Unified Messaging

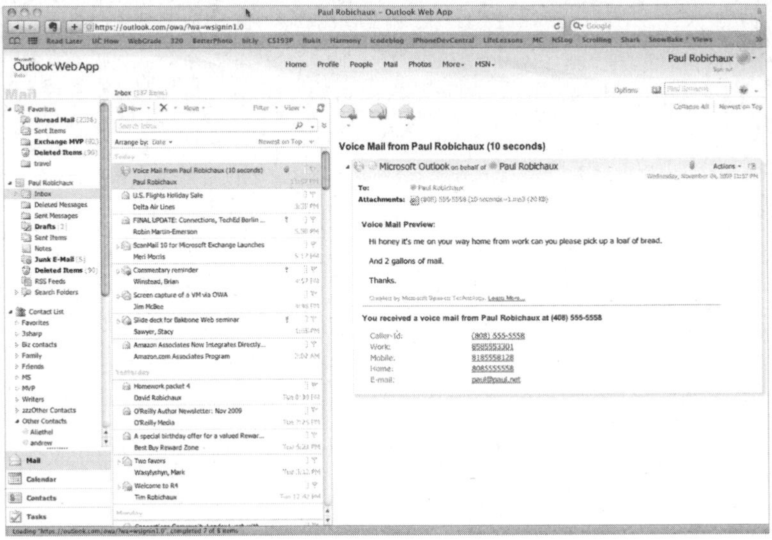

Not all voice systems are going to support this feature "right out of the box." More and more vendors (such as Cisco and Mitel) are tweaking their Voice over Internet Protocol (VoIP) systems to talk directly to Exchange Server 2010 Unified Messaging, but you may still require a VoIP gateway of some type. Many traditional "hard-wired" PBXs will require a PBX-to-VoIP gateway, but even some VoIP systems will require a VoIP-to-VoIP gateway.

If you are like us, you are more of a specialized network administrator. We have never managed a phone system in the past and are only slightly familiar with some of the phone terminology. We just assumed that VoIP was VoIP and that was that. Working with the folks who manage your telephone system will be a new and exciting experience. We were quite surprised to learn that there are more than 100 implementations of SIP on the market.

As of 2010, unified messaging solutions have only about a 10 to 15 percent market penetration — that is, of course, depending on whose survey you read and how you define unified messaging. Some vendors define it as delivering a voicemail to a user's computer and allowing them to play the voicemail over the PC speakers; this voicemail might have been delivered to the user's mailbox (on the server) or it might have been *pulled* by Outlook or another client application and stored in the user's PST file. Some vendors consider solely inbound faxing to be a unified messaging solution, though in our opinion that is not terribly unified.

EXCHANGE 2010 UNIFIED MESSAGING AND FAXING

The Exchange 2007 implementation of unified messaging implementation only supported inbound faxing. This feature has been removed from Exchange Server 2010. For a comprehensive faxing solution, we recommend you take a look at one of the many third-party faxing solutions. One of the reasons for this is that the Exchange 2007 solution only provided inbound faxing, but many third-party solutions on the market that integrate well with Exchange provide both inbound and outbound faxing.

Microsoft has decided to get into the unified messaging market for a number of reasons, including the fact that unified messaging has a fairly low market penetration thus far.

Customers are often reluctant to deploy unified messaging solutions due to the complexity, administrative overhead, schema changes, client-side deployment requirements, and cost. Microsoft is determined to make their unified messaging implementation less expensive than competing products and much better integrated with Active Directory.

When the Exchange 2010 Unified Messaging role is integrated with an IP-based phone system or a PBX with an IP/PBX gateway, the following additional functions may be possible:

◆ Inbound voicemail is delivered directly to the user's mailbox.

◆ Users can call in to the phone system to have their email read to them, to listen to their schedule, or to move appointments around on their schedule and notify attendees.

◆ Users can call in to the phone system to look up users from the Global Address List.

UNIFIED MESSAGING MESSAGE SIZES

A typical voicemail uses the default MP3 between 2 KB and 3 KB per second of message time, but this amount can be changed. The Exchange Server 2010 Unified Messaging server supports the MP3, WMA, G.711 PCM, and GSM codecs. However, with higher-quality recordings come larger message sizes.

Improved High-Availability Features

One of the biggest enemies of high availability is slow restoration times. As mailbox databases get larger and larger, restore times get longer and longer. Often this is used as a rationale for limiting user's mailbox sizes to less than what they need to do their jobs effectively.

As mentioned earlier, when Microsoft released Exchange Server 2007, they introduced a new technology called continuous replication. This technology allowed Microsoft to introduce three new features to improve high availability: the Local Continuous Replication (LCR), Cluster Continuous Replication (CCR), and Standby Continuous Replication (SCR) features. These features allowed a database to be initially seeded with another copy and then the log files to be replicated in near real time and replayed to the copy of the database. The database copy could then be restored quickly (in the case of LCR) or brought online in the event of a server failure.

Exchange 2007 CCR leveraged Windows Failover Clustering so that in the event of a server failure the server could automatically be recovered. SCR was used so that even a single database failure could be recovered by being brought online (manually) on a remote Exchange server. CCR was designed as a high-availability solution, whereas SCR was designed to provide resiliency.

Exchange Server 2010 has taken the continuous replication and clustering technologies even further so that the lines between high availability and resiliency have been blurred. Windows Failover Clustering is now used much differently than it was in the past and the complexities of clustering are better hidden from the Exchange Server administrator. The Exchange 2010 high-availability technology is easy to incorporate with existing Exchange 2010 Mailbox servers. Individual databases can now be replicated to multiple servers, and failover can automatically occur, not at the server level but at the database level.

Exchange 2010 makes building a failover cluster so much simpler than with past versions that the technology will be easy to implement even for small organizations with no clustering expertise.

CONTINUOUS REPLICATION BASICS

If we had to pick a single technology that is the most compelling in Exchange Server 2010, it would be the continuous replication technology. This new technology supports the ability to replicate a database to one or more additional Exchange Mailbox servers within your organization.

Unlike many tools from third-party vendors, which replicate data either at the disk block level or by taking snapshots of the disk and replicating changes, Exchange continuous replication is more similar to the SQL Server *log shipping* technology. This is considered similar to a *pull* model, but it is the active copy of the database that does the work. The replication service managing the passive copy of the database communicates with the active copy and indicates which logs the passive copy needs to keep the database in sync. The active source Exchange database, logs, and database engine do not even realize they are being copied. The Microsoft Exchange Replication Service (`Microsoft.Exchange.Cluster.ReplayService.exe`) handles copying the logs and managing the passive databases.

Initially (as when continuous replication is set up or reconfigured) the current copy of the database is copied to the passive location; this is called *seeding*. As an Exchange transaction log is filled up and renamed, (that is, when the `E00.LOG` file is filled and then renamed to `E000000001.LOG`), the renamed and closed log file is then copied to the passive location. The information store service then verifies the log file and commits it to the passive copy of the database. So the actual database file is not replicated at all, but it is kept in sync by copying the log files and replaying them.

You will probably understand this concept better with an illustration. Figure 1.5 shows an example of how this process works. The Exchange database engine is run by the Microsoft Exchange Information Store; transactions fill up the current transaction log (`E00.LOG`). The transaction log file (`E00.LOG`) is renamed to the next available transaction log filename (in this case `E0000000001.LOG`). All of this is handled by the Information Store service.

FIGURE 1.5
How continuous
replication works

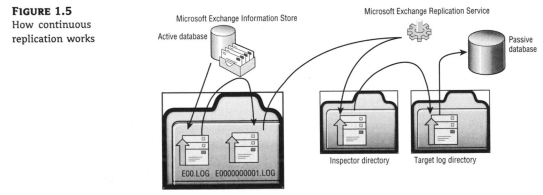

Active database transaction logs

If continuous replication is enabled, the Microsoft Exchange Replication Service copies the `E0000000001.LOG` file to the Inspector directory. This folder exists on any server within the database availability group (DAG) that has a copy of the database.

The service performs an intensive verification of the log files in the Inspector directory to ensure they are not corrupted. Once the log files are verified as not being corrupted, they are checked to ensure that they are in the correct sequence. Once this is verified, the replication service copies the log file (E0000000001.LOG) to the target log file directory. The Information Store service then replays the transactions found in the E0000000001.LOG file and the transactions are committed to the passive copy of the database.

At any given time, the most out-of-sync passive copy of the database will be approximately 15 minutes. The 15-minute lag time would be in a worst-case scenario such as in the dead of night when there is absolutely no activity on the mailbox database. During a normal workday in which users are actually using the database, the passive copy of the database will be no more than a few minutes behind.

If a database is dismounted or the Information Store service is stopped, the data is all committed to the active database and the log files are pulled over to the servers that hold a passive copy of the database. If the administrator has to manually switch over to the passive copy of the database, the passive copy should be completely synchronized with the active copy of the database.

Mailbox Database Mobility

Exchange 2010 introduces the concept of *database mobility*. Database mobility is a set of technologies and features that allow a mailbox database to be replicated to more than one Exchange server in an organization and that database to be brought online if the active copy of the database is no longer available. High availability is no longer tied to a specific server but rather to individual databases.

A mailbox database can be replicated to any Exchange 2010 Mailbox server within the same DAG. The DAG is a collection of one to 16 Exchange 2010 Mailbox servers that can be configured to host a set of databases. The DAG is the boundary of database replication and can span multiple Active Directory sites and geographic locations.

Figure 1.6 shows a simplified example of a DAG. This group has three Exchange Mailbox servers as members and each of the servers has a single "active" mailbox. The server in Tokyo has an active mailbox database called Executives, but a copy of this database is replicated to the Denver and Honolulu servers. The database can be replicated to one or more servers in the DAG.

In the event of a failure on the Tokyo Mailbox server or a problem with the Executives database on the Tokyo Mailbox server, the database on either the Denver or the Honolulu server will be made active and users will be redirected to the new "active" location.

Database mobility replaces the SCR, CCR, LCR, and single-copy cluster features that were available in previous versions of Exchange.

 **Real World Scenario**

High Availability and Resiliency

XYZZY Corporation has their headquarters office in South Florida as well as regional offices on the East Coast and in Colorado. The Colorado office has a small data center. Most data services are handled in the Florida office. In recent years, the South Florida office has had several instances where they had to close the office and shut down their data center because of hurricanes. This means not only does the South Florida office lose Exchange services but it also loses all users in the eastern United States.

XYZZY requires a high-availability solution that not only provides email access in the event of an Exchange server failure in the local office, but also provides a contingency in case their headquarters office has to be shut down. Email should be hosted in the Colorado office in the event the Florida office has to be closed. The solution that switches active email services over to Colorado must be smooth and simple.

The company decided to implement Exchange Server 2010 database availability groups (DAGs). The Eastern US DAG has three Mailbox servers: two Mailbox servers are in South Florida and one in Colorado. The databases assigned to the two South Florida servers will first fail-over to one or the other of those servers. In the event that both servers in Florida must be shut down, the databases will be switched over to the Mailbox server in Colorado.

MAPI and Directory on the Middle Tier

Previously, in all versions of Outlook and Exchange Server, the Outlook client (using MAPI over RPC, not RPC over HTTP) had to be configured to connect to a specific Exchange server. A traditional MAPI client-to-Exchange configuration is shown in Figure 1.7. First, the Outlook MAPI client would connect to a process the Exchange server's System Attendant service runs to get a referral to a global catalog server (for the Global Address List) or possibly to handle directory lookups on behalf of the Outlook client.

FIGURE 1.6
Simple database
availability group

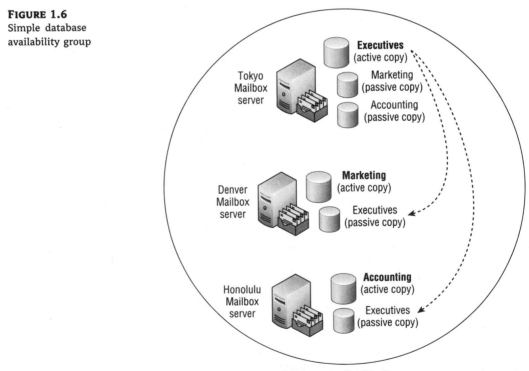

Database Availability Group

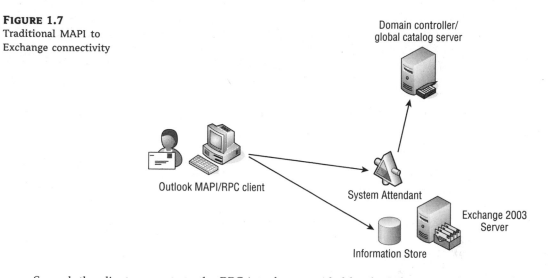

Second, the client connects to the RPC interface provided by the Information Store service (`store.exe`). This means that the Outlook RPC client is connected directly to the information store on the Exchange server on which their mailbox database resides.

Although this works just fine for earlier versions of Exchange Server, this makes building a version of Exchange that allows failover at the database level rather than the server level much more difficult. The Exchange developers had to find a new way to allow Outlook clients to connect both to their mailbox database and to the directory. Rewriting how Outlook works was not an option since Exchange 2010 has to be backward compatible with earlier versions of Outlook such as Outlook 2003 and 2007.

The solution is to "abstract" the MAPI interface out of the Mailbox server's System Attendant and Information Store services. Rather than having the Outlook MAPI client connect directly to the Mailbox server, the Outlook client connects to a service that proxies the connections to the server on which the active mailbox database currently resides. The mailbox store access and directory access functions are being moved out to the "middle tier." The middle tier is a software/service layer that is designed to sit between the client and the actual data source.

Abstracting the directory referrals or directory access out of the System Attendant is called the Address Book Service (or sometimes called *directory* on the middle tier) while abstracting the MAPI access layer out is called the RPC Client Access Service (or sometimes called *MAPI* on the middle tier). These abstracted functions are now part of the Exchange Server 2010 Client Access server role. Figure 1.8 shows an example of how this might work. A user whose mailbox database is on the Marketing database opens Outlook. For directory and mailbox database access, Outlook connects to a Client Access server. The Client Access server acts as the endpoint for Outlook global address lookups. This is a change from previous versions of Exchange where the server might provide the Outlook client with a referral to the nearest global catalog server. In Figure 1.8, the Client Access servers are load balanced for redundancy.

The Microsoft Exchange RPC Client Access service then looks up the Exchange server on which the user's mailbox database (the Marketing database in this case) is active and proxies MAPI requests for mail data to that server. If the mailbox database is in a DAG and fails over to another server, the connection will automatically be established with the new active server.

One Outlook client connectivity component that remains the same in Exchange Server 2010 is public folder server connectivity. Outlook continues to connect directly to the Exchange

Mailbox server on which a public folder replica is located. The RPC Client Access Service does not handle connectivity for public folders.

FIGURE 1.8
A client using MAPI on the middle tier

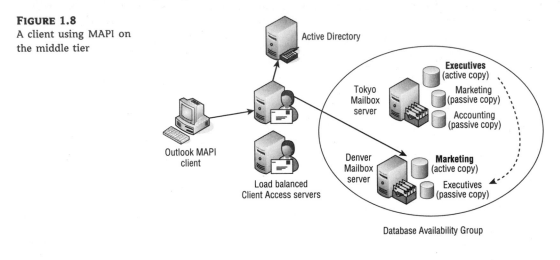

Content Storage Improvements

As we mentioned earlier, email systems have evolved not only in their complexity but also in the complexity (and size!) of the messages and mailbox content being sent and stored. Users' demands for improved searching and indexing of their mailboxes have stretched the limits of most server hardware. The following list includes some of the improvements with respect to data storage and recoverability:

◆ Support for recovering moved or deleted mailboxes using a recovery storage group

◆ Volume Shadow Copy restoration to recovery databases on alternate servers

◆ Lost log resilience that allows a database to be recovered even if the last few log files are missing and a new underlying technology that allows for incremental resynchronization

MAILBOX DATABASES

Even in a small or medium-sized organization, mailbox-size constraints are often based solely on the ability to restore a certain amount of data given a specified maximum amount of time. To scale to larger mailboxes, the administrator must create more mailbox stores. While in Exchange Server 2003 Enterprise Edition administrators could create 20 mailbox database spread across four storage groups, Exchange Server 2010 changes this paradigm by not only removing storage groups but also by increasing the number of databases available. The Exchange 2000/2003 term mailbox store has been replaced simply with the term mailbox database.

To allow a server to scale to support larger mailbox sizes or more mailboxes, Exchange Server 2010 Enterprise Edition allows up to 100 mailbox databases of up to 16 TB each. Exchange Server 2010 Standard Edition supports a maximum of five databases of up to 16 TB each.

MAXIMUM NUMBER OF DATABASES AND DATABASE AVAILABILITY GROUPS

Exchange Server 2010 Standard Edition permits a maximum of five mailbox databases on each Mailbox server. Exchange Server 2010 Enterprise Edition permits a maximum of 100 mailbox databases per Mailbox server. The maximum number of mailbox databases includes both the active and the passive copies. You must take this into consideration when planning database availability groups.

SMALLER TRANSACTION LOGS

Experienced Exchange 2000/2003 administrators will immediately recognize an Exchange transaction log because they are always 5,120 KB in size. Exchange 2010 transaction logs, however, are a bit smaller. In fact, the transaction log files are quite a bit smaller — 1,024 KB to be exact.

The transaction log files are smaller because Exchange 2010 includes continuous replication, which allows log files to be copied to another location and replayed into a backup copy of their corresponding database. Reducing the log file sizes ensures that data is copied more quickly to the target.

IMPROVED SEARCH FEATURES

Content indexing has been completely rewritten in Exchange 2010 so that it is far more efficient than in previous versions and is more closely integrated with the Information Store service. Improvements have been made so that the indexing process is throttled back during peak loads and does not affect client use of the Exchange server. By default, each mailbox database automatically has a full-text index associated with it. Messages are indexed upon arrival rather than on a fixed schedule; the index is up-to-date and immediately available to clients.

Full-text search capabilities are available from both Outlook clients as well as Outlook Web App and Windows Mobile devices. Searches can be done by word, phrase, or sentence, and in addition to the message bodies, attachments such as Word documents, Excel spreadsheets, text files, and HTML files can be searched. Where previously the content index could consume between 20 and 40 percent of the size of the database, Exchange Server 2010 content indexing (enabled by default) usually consumes between 5 and 10 percent of the total size of the mailbox database.

Exchange Server Management

Server management with Exchange 2010 becomes increasingly complex as administrators try to make Exchange work within their organizations, particularly in larger organizations. Exchange 2000/2003 management of mail recipients was performed through the Active Directory Users and Computers console, while management of Exchange Server–related tasks and global recipient tasks is performed through the Exchange System Manager console. In Exchange 2010, all recipient administration tasks are now performed through the Exchange Management Console (EMC) or the EMS.

With previous versions of Exchange Server, such as 5.5, 2000, or 2003, medium-sized and large organizations often had specific needs to perform bulk changes to Exchange data, manage Exchange servers from the command line or scripts, and access or manipulate data stored in Exchange databases. Although making bulk changes or manipulating Exchange servers might seem like a simple task (after all, Windows, Active Directory, and Exchange Server are all from the same company), the truth of the matter is that these tasks were not that simple to perform via script. That has all changed with Exchange Server 2010 (and also with Exchange Server 2007).

Bulk recipient tasks, such as creating multiple mailboxes, changing many email addresses, and configuring bulk properties, can be performed through an application programming interface (API) or scripting interface such as Active Directory Services Interface (ADSI). However, the EMS provides a vastly simpler way to manage all Exchange Server and email recipient properties.

Manipulation of Exchange Server operations, such as mounting and dismounting of databases, queue management, diagnostics logging, and tracking log management, should be handled through the EMS interface.

Finally, accessing or manipulating data stored in an Exchange database is also more complex than it might seem. A popular tool for Exchange 2003 administrators was the Exchange Merge (ExMerge) tool that allowed data to be exported out of an Exchange mailbox and into a personal store (PST) file. Exchange Server 2010 can still use ExMerge, but it can only be used from a client that has the Exchange 2003 administrative tools installed on it. Exchange Server 2007 SP1 introduced a new EMS function that allows the import and export of mailbox data to a PST file via the command line; this feature is also available in Exchange Server 2010, but it does require the x64 version of Outlook 2010.

Clearly, for any organization that is interested in customized management of Exchange (small, medium-sized, or large organizations), Exchange 2003 and earlier versions left a lot to be desired, and required tasks could often not even be performed because of their difficulty. In the minds of many experienced Exchange administrators, this is a gaping hole in the Exchange management architecture.

FIGURE 1.9
The new and improved EMC

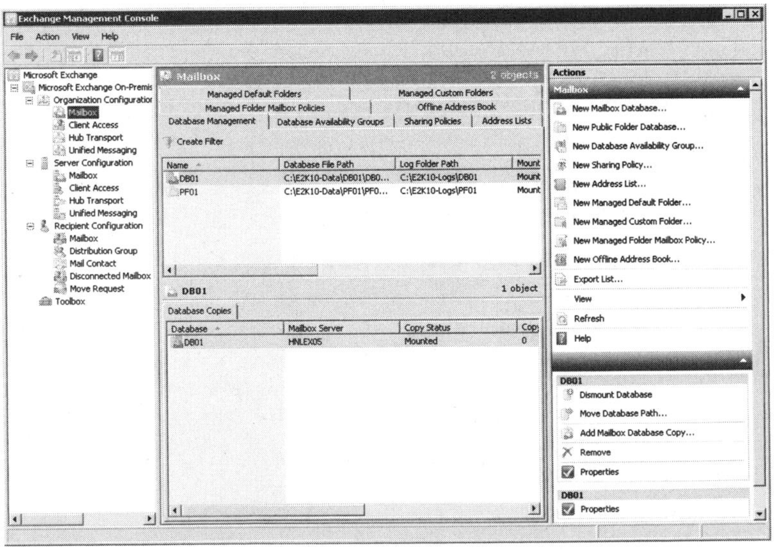

With Exchange 2010, the management interface has been completely rewritten from the ground up. All management operations related to Exchange management — whether they are performed against an Exchange server, Active Directory, the Registry, or the Internet Information Server (IIS) metabase — have been broken up into unique tasks. All Exchange tasks can be performed from the EMS (command-line interface); a subset of these tasks can be performed from the EMC graphical user interface. Anything that can be performed from the EMC can be performed via the EMS; there are advanced administrative tasks that can be performed only from the EMS.

The EMC (shown in Figure 1.9) has been completely redesigned to make it easier to use, to better organize Exchange management tasks, to reduce the complexity, and to make administrative tasks more discoverable.

The new console is built on top of an entirely new scripting technology called PowerShell and a set of Exchange-specific extensions called the EMS.

Improved Message and Content Control

All messaging system administrators can relate to challenges, such as adequately managing the content that is stored on their mail servers, keeping business-essential information available when it is required, removing content that is no longer necessary, controlling the flow of messaging information, and preventing disclosure of information. If one or more of these challenges has been a problem for you, then Exchange 2010 has solutions.

Messaging Records Management

Messaging records management was initially introduced in Exchange Server 2007and brings about a new concept in the control of messaging content. Messaging records management allows administrators to more closely control the life of message content (email, voicemail, calendar entries, and so on) from the moment the information is created on the Exchange server until the point at which that information no longer has business or legal value. This helps the organization maintain important records as long as necessary but discard unnecessary information in a timely fashion. These are configured at the organization level so they will affect all Mailbox server roles.

To a certain extent, some of the features of messaging records management are distantly related to the Exchange 2000/2003 Mailbox Manager. There are a number of components to messaging records management, as shown in Table 1.2.

TABLE 1.2:   Messaging records management features

COMPONENT	FUNCTION
Managed default folders	Default folders are found when an Outlook MAPI client uses its mailbox, including Calendar, Contacts, Deleted Items, Inbox, Junk E-mail, Sent Items, RSS Feeds, and so on.
Managed custom folders	Managed custom folders are folders that are created by the Exchange server administrator for users who are included in a managed folder mailbox policy. Storage limits and managed content settings can be applied to these folders.
Managed folder mailbox policies	Managed folder policies define which folders are included in a particular policy. Managed folder mailbox policies are then assigned to mailboxes.
Managed content settings	Managed content settings define retention settings and message journaling features for content, such as messages and voicemail.

Once a user has been assigned to a managed folder mailbox policy, any additional custom folders that must be created in that user's mailbox will show up in the Managed Folders folder in the root of the user's mailbox, such as those shown in Figure 1.10. You can now configure message journaling based on a specific type of content or folder.

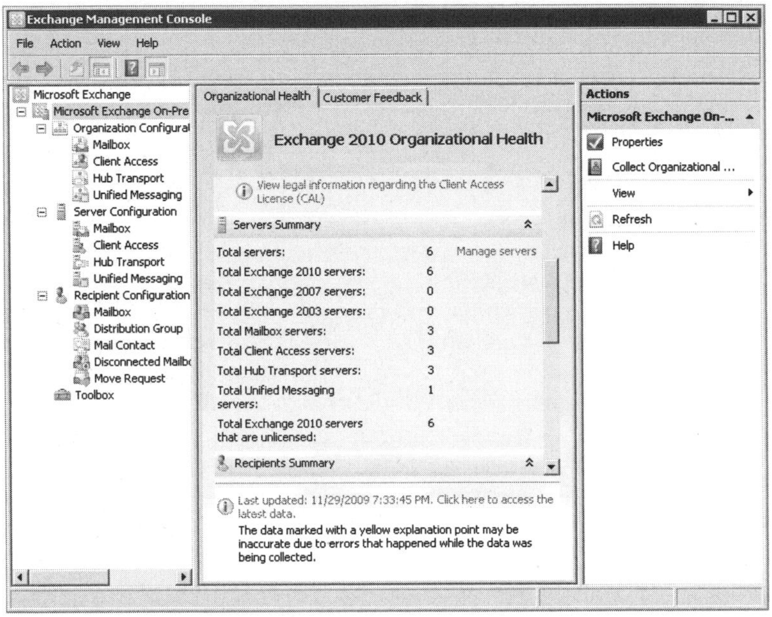

FIGURE 1.10
Managed folders assigned by the managed folder mailbox policy

Normally, content in these folders will be managed by the end user. Moving relevant content into these folders is their responsibility. In certain situations, a user can specify managed content settings that can accurately identify content types such as messages or voicemail and can move them into the appropriate custom-managed folders. A user can also build client-side rules that move content into their managed folders. Let's take a quick look at some of things that you can do with messaging records management:

◆ Control the length of time and the content types in users' folders.

◆ Define additional folders that should be created in a user's folder that the user can use for message retention. Differing retention policies can be defined for the custom folders that you create for your users.

◆ Automatically send copies of messages that users place in a managed folder to another email address each time the managed mailbox assistant runs.

◆ Move messages from a specified folder based on content type (email, contact, calendar, voicemail, etc.) to another managed folder.

The first time you look at messaging records management, it is a bit confusing until you realize that it must be configured in a few different steps, such as the following:

◆ Create managed folder mailbox policies to define which managed default and managed custom folders will be managed.

◆ Assign the managed folder mailbox policy to one or more users. A user does not need a managed folder mailbox policy. Only a single managed folder mailbox policy can be assigned to a user at one time.

◆ Create managed content settings for default folders (Inbox, Sent Items, etc.) to control the length of time that messages should remain in these folders and types of content that are allowed. This step is optional.

◆ Create managed custom folders that will appear in the user's Managed Folders folder in their mailbox. This step is optional.

◆ Create managed content settings for managed custom folders to control how content is managed or retained in the folders that will be created in the user's mailbox. This step is optional.

One confusing point with respect to messaging records management is that on the surface it is documented as a premium feature of Exchange 2010 and thus requires an Enterprise Client Access License for each user who will have their mailbox managed by it. However, Microsoft makes an exception if you are using messaging records management features to simply clean up message items in the folders in the same way you would have used the Exchange 2000/2003 mailbox management feature.

Built-In Archiving

The market for third-party tools to support Exchange Server has grown rapidly since the release of Exchange Server 2003. At one point, there were more than 60 third parties providing email archive solutions for Exchange Server. The sheer volume of email that users receive and the users' demand that they be able to keep their historical email has made these tools very attractive.

Exchange Server 2010 introduces a new premium feature that allows for the integration of email archiving. The email archiving feature is actually a series of features that interact directly with the user's mailbox:

Archive Mailbox   Defined on a user-by-user basis since all users might not need an archive mailbox. The content in the archive mailbox can be accessed by users using the Outlook 2010 client or Outlook Web App 2010.

Retention Policies   Define the types of mail and how long the mail can be retained within the user's primary mailbox. Retention policies can be defined that control when items are permanently deleted or when they are moved in to the archive mailbox. With Outlook 2010, end users can participate in the retention process by applying retention tags to messages or an entire folder.

Multi-mailbox Search   Allows an authorized user to search for content across multiple mailboxes (both the user's "active" mailbox as well as their "personal archive mailbox") within an organization. This would be useful during a lawsuit and an electronic discovery action became necessary.

Legal Hold   Allows the administrator to place a "hold" on a user's mailbox so that deleted and edited items are held during the hold period. This would be necessary in the event of legal action or an investigation regarding the conduct of one or more of your users.

Ultimately, the new Exchange 2010 archiving and retention policies are intended to replace the messaging records management features that were introduced in Exchange Server 2007.

More information on the archive and retention policy features can be found in Chapter 22, "Getting Started with Email Archiving."

Message Transport Rules

Message transport rules are quite similar to Outlook rules and are even created using a wizard similar to one used to create Outlook rules. However, these rules are quite a bit more powerful and are executed on the Hub Transport servers. Since all messages are processed by a Hub Transport server whether they are inbound, outbound, or for local delivery, you can build powerful policies to control the messages and data that flows within your organization. Transport rules can also be defined at your organization's perimeter by using an Edge Transport server.

Although we will cover a lot more about transport rules in Chapter 26, "Managing Transport and Journaling Rules," just to give you a taste of what you can do with transport rules, it is useful to highlight some of the cool things you can do with them:

- Append disclaimers to outgoing messages
- Implement message journaling based on recipients, distribution lists, message classification, or message importance
- Prevent users or departments from sending email to another by creating an ethical wall (a.k.a. a Chinese wall)
- Intercept messages based on content or text patterns using regular expressions (REGEX) found in the message subject or message body
- Apply message classifications to messages based on sender or message content
- Take action on a message with a certain attachment or attachment type or an attachment size that exceeds a specified limit
- Examine and set message headers or remove data from the message header
- Redirect, drop, or bounce messages based on certain criteria
- Apply Microsoft Rights Management Service (RMS) encryption-based transport rule conditions

Every transport rule has three components: conditions, actions, and exceptions. The conditions specify under what conditions the rule applies whereas the exceptions specify under what conditions it will not apply. The actions are the interesting part of the transport rule. Figure 1.11 shows the Conditions page of the Transport Rule wizard; this screen has two parts. The first part is simply checking the actions to take, and the second part specifies more details about the action.

For the transport rule you see in Figure 1.11, previously on the Conditions page, we selected a condition From People in Step 1, but in Step 2, we have to specify the list of people (or groups). In this case, we selected the group VIPs. On the Actions page (shown in Figure 1.11), we selected the Log An Event With Message, Apply Message Classification, and Blink Carbon Copy (BCC) The Message To Addresses options.

In the Step 2 box, we then have to specify the text of the event to log, the classification to apply, and to whom the BCC message should be sent.

FIGURE 1.11
Examining a transport rule

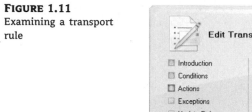

Per-User Journaling

Journaling a message is the process of keeping a message from one or more senders based on long-term storage, legal, regulatory, or human resources requirements. Exchange 2000/2003 essentially had one option for message journaling: create an additional mailbox store and move any mailboxes that must be kept to that mailbox store. Note that a true journaling solution happens before the user has any input into the process; a message is intercepted prior to or at the time of delivery via transport rules or by rules set on the mailbox database. A true message journaling feature produces a message envelope header that exposes the sender and recipient information as well as containing the original message. Exchange 2010 has many new options with respect to retaining messages; however, only the first two are considered true message journaling features:

◆ Messages can still be retained based on the journal settings on the mailbox database.

◆ Messages can be retained using a new hub transport feature called a journaling rule that allows messages to be retained based on a single sender or distribution group membership.

◆ Messages can be retained based on folder or content type using managed content settings; note that this is not considered true journaling because it is merely moving mail from one folder to another after the fact.

◆ Messages can be retained using transport rules by examining sender, recipient, message priority, message classification, or message content. This solution does not create a true journaling message.

◆ Messages can also be retained using transport rules by keeping only internal or only external messages.

◆ Messages can be sent to an SMTP address that is external to the Exchange organization, such as a Microsoft Office SharePoint Server 2007 server or a third-party service provider.

Figure 1.12 shows an example of a transport rule that applies to the Executives group. Any mail sent to members of the Executives group has a copy of that message sent to the Executives Journal Mailbox. While the journal rule shown in Figure 1.11 shows an internal Exchange mailbox in the Send Journal Reports To E-mail Address box, this could be any valid mail-enabled recipient (such as a mailbox-enabled user, mail-enabled user, or mail-enabled contact).

FIGURE 1.12
Creating a journaling rule

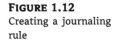

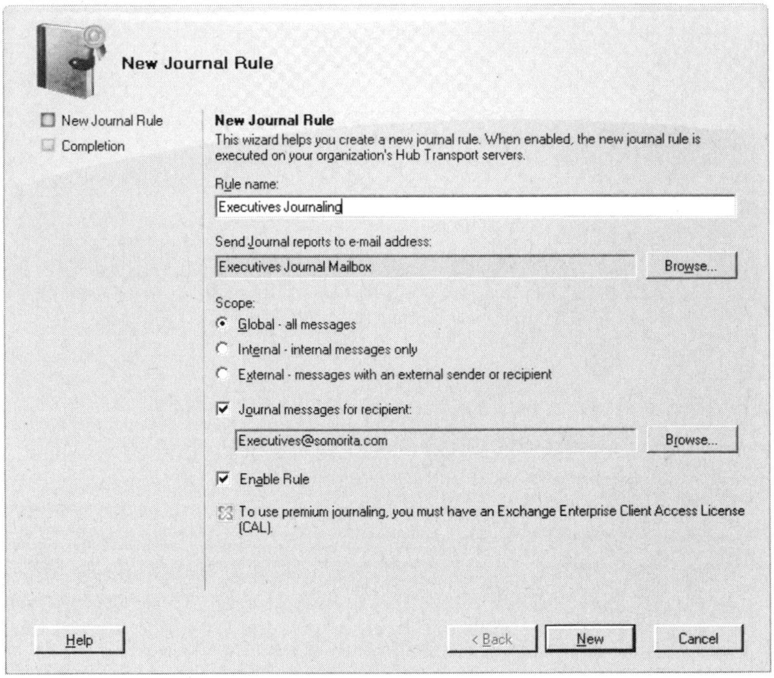

New Journal Rule

	New Journal Rule
☐ New Journal Rule	This wizard helps you create a new journal rule. When enabled, the new journal rule is executed on your organization's Hub Transport servers.
☐ Completion	

Rule name:
Executives Journaling

Send Journal reports to e-mail address:
Executives Journal Mailbox   Browse...

Scope:
⦿ Global - all messages
○ Internal - internal messages only
○ External - messages with an external sender or recipient

☑ Journal messages for recipient:
Executives@somorita.com   Browse...

☑ Enable Rule

To use premium journaling, you must have an Exchange Enterprise Client Access License (CAL).

Help   < Back   New   Cancel

Journaling is a premium feature and thus requires an Exchange Server 2010 Enterprise Client Access License for each user who will have their mail journaled.

Message Classifications

Organizations that send confidential, proprietary, or classified information via email often implement message classification templates. However, these client-side templates display the message classification only for the sender and the recipients; in previous versions of Exchange there was nothing within the message transport that could take action on or evaluate a classified message.

Exchange 2010 allows a message to enforce rules based on the classification of a message, such as Do Not Forward, Partner Mail, Attachment Removed, Company Confidential, Company Internal, Attorney/Client Privilege, and customized classification levels. The sender can assign the classification using Outlook 2007, Outlook 2010, or Outlook Web App 2010, or message transport rules can assign a classification based on sender, recipient, message content, importance, and so on. Figure 1.13 shows an example of a message that is being composed in Outlook Web App and has had the built-in Attorney/Client Privilege classification assigned to it; the classification text is shown just above the address list. The server administrator can create additional classifications and customize the text strings.

FIGURE 1.13
Classifying a message using Outlook Web App

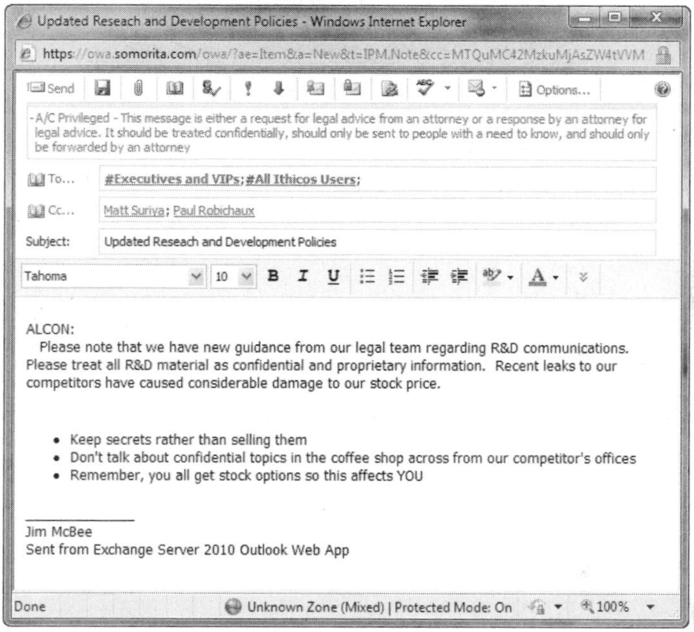

Rights Management Service Message Protection

If you are concerned about message content protection, one of the cool new features of Exchange Server 2010 is its integration with the Microsoft Active Directory Rights Management Services (RMS). While RMS has been integrated with the Outlook client for quite a few years now, Exchange Server 2010 introduces significantly better integration. Features include the following:

◆ Hub Transport server transport rules can now apply rights management protection to messages and attachments based on rule conditions.

◆ The Hub Transport service can be configured to allow decryption of information rights management (IRM) protected messages in transit in order to apply messages policies to the message.

◆ IRM provides protection for Unified Messaging voicemail messages.

◆ IRM protection is now integrated with Outlook Web App 2010.

New Programming Interfaces

Much of the underlying infrastructure of Exchange 2010 has been completely rewritten since Exchange Server 2000/2003. As a result, many of the APIs used to access Exchange data and to manage Exchange components have been replaced with new APIs.

EXCHANGE MANAGEMENT

Management of Exchange-related components and recipient objects is now performed with the new management API. All operations that can be performed have been defined as tasks. The management API provides access to all management functions via the EMS tasks, also known as cmdlets (pronounced "command-lets"). The EMS is a set of extensions for the Windows PowerShell. Exchange management functionality can be extended and accessed via managed code, and custom scripts can integrate with and use .NET objects.

TRANSPORT AGENTS

All messages and message content traveling through the message transport system (on a Hub Transport server or Edge Transport server) can be manipulated using transport agents. Transport agents are written using managed code. They replace Exchange 2000/2003 transport sinks.

EXCHANGE-MANAGED APIS

Exchange-Managed APIs extend the Microsoft .NET Framework by providing classes and data structures that allow custom programs to access and manipulate different parts of email message content. Functions include accessing MIME content; filtering email body content; converting message content between plaintext, HTML, and RTF formats; and reading or writing calendar items.

WEB SERVICES

One of the most exciting new APIs is the Web Services API. Using Web Services, developers can write applications that can remotely access mailboxes, folders, and message content. Many of the new Exchange services — such as the Autodiscover service, Availability service, and messaging records management — use the Web Services API. Services can be developed that can send notifications to client applications and provide synchronization of mailbox folders and items. The Web Services API provides these features:

- Ability to manage folders in a user mailbox, including creating, deleting, copying, changing, searching, viewing, and moving folders

- Ability to manage messages in a user mailbox, including creating, deleting, copying, changing, searching, viewing, moving, and sending messages as well as accessing message content

- Ability to enumerate distribution group memberships

Client-Side Features

There are a number of improvements that in Exchange Server 2010 that will directly affect the end user. These are improvements that did not exist in Exchange Server 2000/2003.

Schedulable and Internal/External Out-of-Office Messages

A very nice improvement from the user's perspective is the ability to schedule when out-of-office messages start and finish and the ability to specify a separate message for internal users than you have for external users. For this feature to work properly, you need either Outlook Web App 2010 or Outlook 2007/2010. Figure 1.14 shows an example of the Out Of Office Assistant in Outlook Web App.

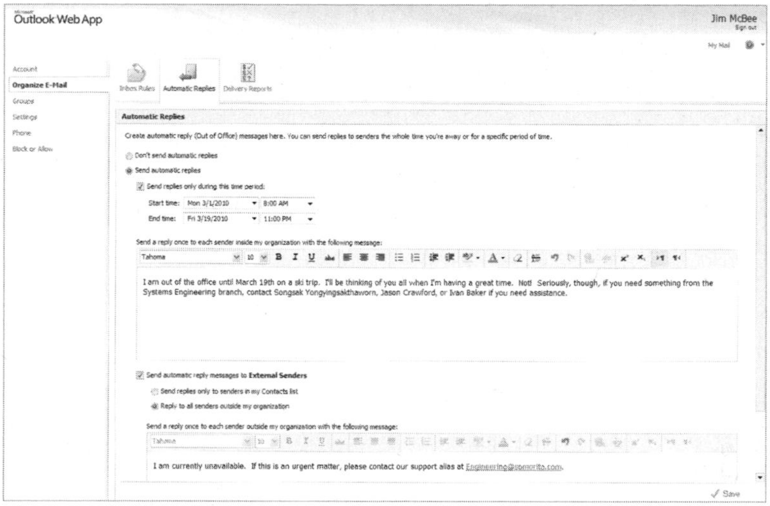

FIGURE 1.14
Scheduling out-of-office
messages for internal
and external recipients

When setting up an out-of-office message for external recipients, the user can specify that the response go only to senders whose address is in their Contacts folder or to any sender.

Improved Calendaring and Resource Management

Calendaring, resources, and out-of-office features were not as complete as most of today's sophisticated email users require. Exchange 2010 and Outlook 2007 have improved each of these with new features and functions. For many of the calendaring and resource management features to work properly, Outlook 2007 or later or Outlook Web App 2010 is required. The Availability service now works between multiple Exchange Server 2010 organizations provided the cross-organization features are enabled.

RESOURCE MANAGEMENT

One of the biggest hurdles that messaging system managers have had to overcome with Exchange is how to manage resource calendars. In earlier versions of Exchange, a resource calendar was nothing more than a mailbox whose calendar was shared with other users or a mailbox that had scripts or event sinks that allowed for automatic acceptance and processing of meeting requests for a particular resource. Exchange 2010 improves on the concept of resource mailboxes. At mailbox creation time (see Figure 1.15), the administrator designates the type of resource that is being created (room or equipment).

Administrators can then set custom properties, such as room capacity or audiovisual capabilities, for this resource. This information can be viewed within Outlook 2007/2010 when a user is looking for a resource that suits the user's requirements. The Resource Booking attendant provides features that control who can book a resource, for how long, and during which hours, and it also provides conflict information.

CALENDAR CONCIERGE

As users have become more sophisticated, their calendaring requirements have increased. The Calendar Concierge is a collection of features that allow for better management of user and resource mailboxes. The Exchange 2010 Calendar Assistant helps to keep out-of-date meeting requests from disturbing the user by ensuring that they are presented with only the most recent meeting request. The Calendar Assistant also reduces the amount of unnecessary messages relating to meeting requests, such as a Tentative response followed soon after by a Decline or Accept response. The user sees only the most recent message.

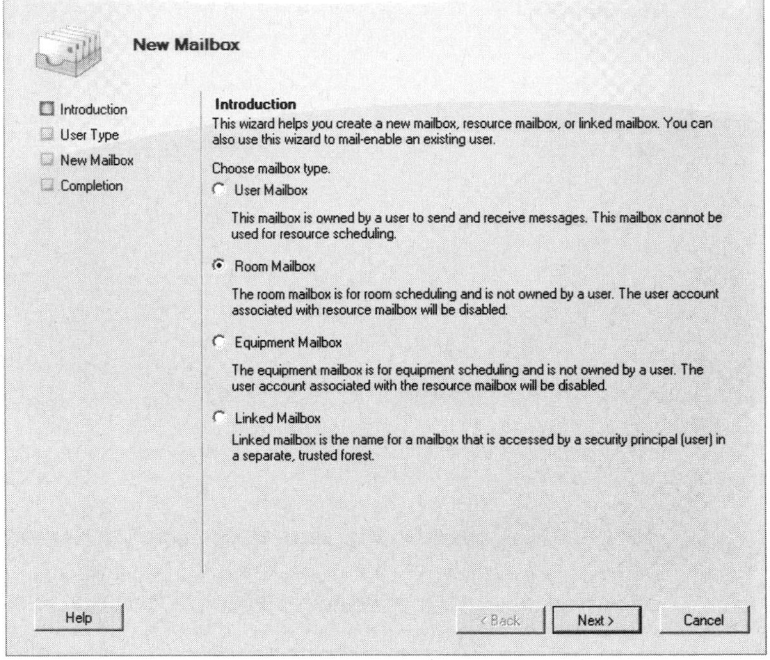

FIGURE 1.15
Resource type is designated when the mailbox is created.

The Scheduling Assistant makes the process of scheduling a meeting using either Outlook or Outlook Web App much simpler and recommends best meeting times based on requested attendees.

AVAILABILITY SERVICE

Earlier versions of Exchange used a system public folder for publishing a user's free/busy information. Periodically, the Outlook client had to connect to this public folder and update the user's free/busy times. Exchange 2010 supports a new Web Service that runs on the Client Access server role and provides an interface to all users' free and busy times. Outlook 2007/2010, the Outlook Web App 2010, and Entourage clients are able to use this new Web Service, so the Availability service ensures that free and busy times published by older clients are accessible via the Web Service and free and busy times published by Outlook 2007 and later are available via the system public folder.

AUTODISCOVER

One of the most time-consuming things that an Exchange administrator has to do is to help configure Outlook clients to connect to the Exchange server. In the past, profiles had to be created via scripting or profile utilities. Exchange 2010 introduces a feature called Autodiscover that makes configuration of Outlook 2007 (or later) profiles much simpler. Once the user provides their name and their email address, Outlook 2007 (or later) automatically discovers the correct server and updates the server if the mailbox moves (even if the original server is no longer online).

New and Improved Outlook Web App

Those of us who gushed when we saw the Outlook Web Access interface in Exchange 2003 thought a web interface could not get much better. For Outlook Web App in Exchange 2010, the Exchange team started over from scratch to build a much more functional interface than ever before. Here are some of the new features in Outlook Web App 2010:

◆ Ability to browse the Global Address List (GAL)

◆ Ability to manage and remotely wipe Windows mobile devices

◆ Improved meeting booking features

◆ Ability to perform full-text searches on mailbox content

◆ Selectable message format (HTML or plaintext) when composing a message

◆ Ability to set out-of-office messages, define them as internal or external, and schedule when they start

◆ Ability to manage voicemail features such as their greeting, reset their voicemail PIN, and turn on missed call notifications

◆ Conversation view, which provides threaded views of email conversations

◆ Exchange Control Panel (ECP), which allows an end user to update their own directory information as well as manage their own group membership

Windows Mobile and Improved Security

Windows Mobile and ActiveSync device support are certainly not new features to Exchange Server 2010. Exchange Server 2003 had good support for Windows Mobile devices, and you could even support mobile devices using Microsoft Mobile Information Server and Exchange 2000.

If you have supported Windows Mobile devices or other types of mobile devices, you realize how important centralized policies and security can be for your organization and your users. The latest versions of Exchange ActiveSync (EAS) have been improved greatly over the years. The newest features can be assigned to users based on the ActiveSync policy that is assigned to the user. Figure 1.16 shows two of the advanced properties pages.

FIGURE 1.16
Examples of ActiveSync policies

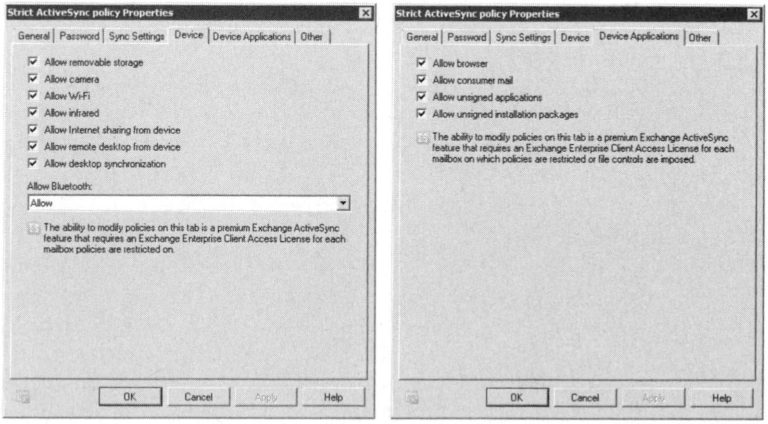

Of course, you have to have the corresponding version of Windows Mobile that will take advantage of all the newest features. Windows Mobile 5 with the Microsoft Security and Feature Pack (MSFP) uses EAS v2.5, Windows Mobile 6 uses EAS v12, and Windows Mobile 6.1 uses EAS v12.1. Table 1.3 shows a comparison of some features of various versions of EAS and the versions of Exchange Server.

TABLE 1.3: Exchange ActiveSync Features

SETTING/RESTRICTION	E2K3 SP2 EAS v2.5	E2K10 EAS 12	E2K10 STANDARD CAL EAS v12.1	E2K10 ENTERPRISE CAL EAS v12.1
Password Required	✓	✓	✓	✓
Min Password Length	✓	✓	✓	✓
Alphanumeric Pwd	✓	✓	✓	✓
Inactivity Timeout	✓	✓	✓	✓
Max Failed Password Attempts	✓	✓	✓	✓
Policy Refresh Interval	✓	✓	✓	✓
Allow Non-provisionable Devices	✓	✓	✓	✓
Attachments Enabled		✓	✓	✓
Storage Card Encryption		✓	✓	✓
Password Recovery Enabled		✓	✓	✓
Allow Simple Device Password		✓	✓	✓
Max Attachment Size		✓	✓	✓
WSS Access Enabled		✓	✓	✓
UNC Access Enabled		✓	✓	✓
Password Expiration		✓	✓	✓
Password History		✓	✓	✓
Require Manual Sync When Roaming			✓	✓
Min Device Pwd Complex Characters			✓	✓
Max Calendar Age Filter			✓	✓
Allow HTML Email			✓	✓
Max Email Age Filter			✓	✓
Max Email Body Truncation Size			✓	✓

TABLE 1.3: Exchange ActiveSync Features *(CONTINUED)*

SETTING/RESTRICTION	E2K3 SP2 EAS v2.5	E2K10 EAS 12	E2K10 STANDARD CAL EAS v12.1	E2K10 ENTERPRISE CAL EAS v12.1
Max Email HTML Body Truncation Size			✓	✓
Require Signed SMIME Messages			✓	✓
Require Encrypted SMIME Messages			✓	✓
Require Signed SMIME Algorithm			✓	✓
Require Encryption SMIME Algorithm			✓	✓
Allow SMIME Encryption Algorithm Negotiation			✓	✓
Allow SMIME Soft Certs			✓	✓
Require Device Encryption			✓	✓
Allow Storage Card				✓
Allow Camera				✓
Allow Unsigned Applications				✓
Allow Unsigned Installation Packages				✓
Allow Wi-Fi				✓
Allow Text Messaging				✓
Allow POP/IMAP Email				✓
Allow Bluetooth				✓
Allow IrDA				✓
Allow Desktop Sync				✓
Allow Browser				✓
Allow Consumer Email				✓
Allow Remote Desktop				✓
Allow Internet Sharing				✓
Unapproved InROM Application List				✓
Approved Application List				✓

Note that some of the advanced device configuration features require the use of an Exchange Server 2010 Enterprise Client Access License (CAL) for the device. This does not mean that the Exchange 2010 server requires the Enterprise Edition of Exchange Server, though.

Now, Where Did That Go?

As new and better functions and APIs have been introduced, naturally some functions are no longer emphasized or supported. There has been a lot of confusion surrounding what will continue to be supported in Exchange 2010 and what will no longer work. The phrase "no longer supported" itself tends to also generate a lot of confusion because a function may actually continue to work because it has not truly been removed. These functions and APIs fall into two unique categories: functions that have been deemphasized and functions that are no longer available.

Deemphasized Functions

When Microsoft says that in Exchange 2010 certain functions or APIs are no longer emphasized, this means that the company will not continue to enhance these features. The features will continue to be supported, and if there are bugs with these features, the bugs will be fixed. However, if something is being deemphasized, the writing is on the wall; you should consider replacing your use of this technology with something else.

The following is a list of some of the APIs and functions that are being deemphasized:

◆ Public folders are still supported in Exchange 2010, but their use is being deemphasized as newer collaborative technologies have been introduced, such as SharePoint and other portal technologies.

◆ Collaborative Data Objects technologies such as CDOSYS, CDO 1.2.1, and CDOEXM have been removed completely. Applications using these APIs should be rewritten using the Transport Agents API or Exchange Web Services API.

◆ Functions provided by Exchange WebDAV extensions are now provided by the Web Services API. If you have applications that require WebDAV, you will have to either update them or keep an Exchange 2003/2007 server running.

◆ The Exchange Object Linking and Embedding Database (ExOLEDB) API functionality is now provided via the Web Services API.

◆ Store events were removed from Exchange Server 2010 and should be replaced with functions written using the Web Services API.

Features No Longer Included

As Exchange Server has evolved into its current form, the code has experienced significant changes. This includes many of the new features we have discussed in this chapter, but there have also been features and programming interfaces that have been removed because it just no longer makes sense to support outdated technologies.

Some features and APIs have been completely removed from the Exchange 2010 product. If you require any of these features or APIs, you may need to keep an Exchange 2003 server in operation. If you still require features provided by the Exchange 2000 Server platform, you are not even going to be able to transition to Exchange Server 2010 until you can replace that particular feature requirement with newer software.

EXCHANGE SERVER 2003 FEATURES REMOVED FROM EXCHANGE SERVER 2010

Since the release of Exchange Server 2003, a number of Exchange Server 2003 (and Exchange 2000) features have been removed. Although most of these features will not affect the majority of the Exchange deployments out there, you should keep them in mind and thoroughly evaluate your existing messaging environment to make sure you are not dependent on a feature that has no equivalent in Exchange Server 2010. Here are some of the Exchange Server 2003 features and functionality that have been removed from the product:

◆ Exchange 5.5 and Exchange Server 2000 interoperability is no longer available and there is no transition path between these legacy versions and Exchange Server 2010. You cannot install an Exchange 2010 server until your Exchange organization is in native Exchange mode.

◆ Outlook Mobile Access, the lightweight browser-based access for WAP-based mobile phones, is not available. Nor are Exchange ActiveSync Always Up-to-Date notifications.

◆ Non-MAPI public folder hierarchies are no longer available.

◆ Public folder access via NNTP and IMAP4 is no longer available.

◆ Network News Transport Protocol (NNTP) features have been cut from Exchange 2010 completely.

◆ Routing groups and routing group connectors are no longer required once you have completely migrated to Exchange Server 2010. In a native Exchange 2010 organization, the message routing topology is determined using the Active Directory sites in which the Exchange servers are located. Message delivery between Exchange 2010 servers in different Active Directory sites is handled automatically.

◆ Mailbox databases no longer have a streaming database file (STM file). All mail, regardless of its original source, is stored in the EDB database file.

◆ The Recipient Update Service functionality has been replaced. Email proxy addresses and address list membership is set on a mail recipient object at the time of creation. They can be updated from the EMS.

◆ X.400 connectors are no longer available.

◆ ExMerge can no longer be run from the Exchange 2010 server console; it can continue to be run against Exchange 2007 mailboxes, but it must be run from a computer with Outlook installed.

◆ Mail recipient management using the Active Directory Users and Computers console extensions no longer works. All recipient management must be performed through the EMC. A few exceptions exist, of course, but using the EMC or the EMS is preferred. This will also keep you from accidentally doing something that is not supported.

◆ Administrative groups are no longer available. All permissions delegation is handled via either a series of built-in groups or via the new role-based authorization control (RBAC) feature.

◆ Development APIs and tools, such as CDO v1.2, CDO for Workflow, CDOEXM, Exchange WMI classes, Exchange Web Forms, Workflow Designer, ExOLEDB, store events, and transport event sinks, are no longer available.

◆ The Exchange installable file system (ExIFS), which was also known as the M:\ drive, is no longer available.

◆ The GroupWise, cc:Mail, and Microsoft Mail connectors are no longer available.

EXCHANGE SERVER 2007 FEATURES REMOVED FROM EXCHANGE 2010

Although Exchange Server 2007 did not enjoy wide deployment, there will be organizations that will be transitioning from Exchange Server 2007 to Exchange Server 2010. A number of features have been removed from Exchange since Exchange Server 2007; this list is in addition to the features that were removed since Exchange Server 2003. The following Exchange Server 2007 features are no longer available:

◆ Local Continuous Replication (LCR)

◆ Single Copy Clustering (SCC)

◆ Cluster Continuous Replication (CCR)

◆ Standby Continuous Replication (SCR)

◆ Unified Messaging inbound faxing functions

◆ Streaming backups

◆ SharePoint document library and network share access via Outlook Web Access

◆ 32-bit management tools

Clearing Up Some Confusion

We mentioned earlier that Exchange has certainly been hyped a lot during the design and beta-testing process. This has generated a lot of buzz in the information technology (IT) industry, but this buzz has also generated a lot of confusion and some misinformation. We want to take this opportunity to clear up some of this confusion by answering a few of the common questions that have generated misconceptions about Exchange 2010.

Do I have to have three or four separate servers to run each of the server roles? In a small environment, a single server can host all four primary server roles (Mailbox, Client Access, Hub Transport, and Unified Messaging), though Microsoft recommends against hosting the Unified Messaging role on the same server. Unlike Exchange Server 2007, an Exchange 2010 server can host the Mailbox, Client Access, Hub Transport, and Unified Messaging roles. The Edge Transport role must be installed on a separate server.

Is there a 32-bit version of Exchange? No, no 32-bit version of Exchange 2010 is available.

Is the Edge Transport server required? No, Edge Transport servers are not required. You can use any third-party message hygiene system in your perimeter network, or you can direct inbound and outbound mail through your Hub Transport servers, or both.

Does Exchange 2010 use a SQL database for mailboxes and public folders? Although there has been debate for years about using SQL Server for the Exchange databases, Exchange 2010 uses the Extensible Storage Engine (ESE), also known as the JET database engine.

Is EMS knowledge required? Do I have to learn scripting? Most common administrative tasks can be performed through the EMC graphical interface. Command-line management and scripting for Exchange 2010 has been greatly improved through the use of the EMS. Many tasks are simplified or more powerful through the EMS, but it is not necessary to learn scripting in order to start working with Exchange 2010. We strongly encourage you to get to know many of the powerful features of the EMS as you get comfortable with Exchange 2010. A number of advanced administration tasks do not have a graphical user interface option.

What is happening with public folders?   The use of public folders with Exchange 2010 is still available and supported, but their use is being deemphasized as newer collaborative technologies such as websites and portals have become commonplace. We urge you to examine your public folder applications with an eye toward migrating them to systems such as Microsoft Office SharePoint Server 2007.

Is there still a 32 KB limitation on folder rules?   For power users, the 32 KB limit on the size of rules for a folder was a serious annoyance. This limit is no longer a constraint for users whose mailbox is on an Exchange 2010 mailbox server.

Do I need to use every Exchange 2010 server role to have a functional Exchange 2007 system? To build a completely functional Exchange 2010 system, you need the Mailbox, Hub Transport, and Client Access server roles.

Can I run 32-bit applications with the 64-bit version of Exchange 2010?   Most 32-bit Windows applications will generally run on Windows 2008 x64, but applications that integrate with Exchange (such as message hygiene or backup applications) should be 64-bit.

The Bottom Line

Understand new high-availability options.   Exchange Server now provides replication technology that keeps databases synchronized between an active copy of the database and one or more passive copies. In the event of failure of the active database, one of the passive copies can be brought online. Storage groups have been eliminated and now each Exchange database has its own set of transaction logs.

An Exchange Mailbox server can belong to a database availability group (DAG). Exchange databases can be synchronized to one or more members of a DAG. Failovers between servers can now be handled at the database layer rather than a single database failure having to cause an entire cluster node to fail over.

Master It   You have been asked to provide a high-availability solution for your organization's 1,000 mailboxes. Describe the Exchange Server 2010 feature that will allow you to provide high availability for your Exchange 2010 mailboxes.

Understand new recipient management features.   The underlying management components for all Exchange server and mail recipient administration have been completely rewritten from scratch. All management tools are built on top of the Windows PowerShell and are included in the EMS. Exchange administration can now be performed from either a graphical user interface (the EMC) or the EMS. The EMS often includes functions that are not available from the management interface.

Master It   You support 8,000 mailboxes in your Exchange Server 2010 organization. You have been asked to perform a management task on mailbox-enabled users in your organization. This task consists of setting the Outlook Web App policy to a new policy name. What is the quickest way to assign all of your users the new policy?

Recognize Exchange architecture changes.   Significant changes were made to the Exchange Server 2010 architecture to improve the scalability, security, and stability. This includes providing only an x64 edition of Exchange Server 2010. Requiring an x64-based operating system and hardware dramatically improves the scalability and performance of Exchange Server 2010. The x64 architecture means that Exchange Server 2010 can now access more than 3 GB of physical memory. Microsoft has tested server configurations with up to 64 GB of physical memory. The additional physical memory means that data can be cached and written to disk more efficiently. This greatly improves the Exchange Server 2010 disk I/O profile over previous versions.

Unlike Exchange Server 2003 and earlier where a server's roles and functions were configured after installation, Exchange Server roles allow the Exchange administrator to define the functions of the server during installation.

Master It   You are planning your Exchange Server 2010 infrastructure to provide basic messaging functionality (email, shared calendars, and Windows Mobile phones). Which Exchange Server roles will you need to deploy?

Chapter 2

Introduction to Email Administration

Congratulations! You may have just stepped into the most important job in your entire organization. No, it's not the CEO, the number one salesperson, the janitor, the person who makes sure fresh coffee is made, or even the one who prints out the monthly TPS reports. We are talking about the person who keeps the email system running.

Now, do we honestly believe the email system is the most important component of an organization's information technology services? On a dollar-per-dollar basis, an organization's line-of-business applications (such as order entry, accounting, customer relationship management, shipping, billing, and others) are probably the most important types of applications when it comes to the actual value provided. However, email is often one of the most visible services (if not *the* single most visible service) that IT professionals provide; most organizations have become dependent on "soft" information to run their business. As a result, users have in turn developed an attachment to email that goes beyond the hard value of the information it contains. If there's a problem with email, it affects users' confidence in their ability to do their jobs — and their confidence in IT.

There is not much in this chapter that is specific to Exchange Server 2010, so an experienced email administrator may want to proceed on to more technical chapters such as Chapter 3, "Standards and Protocols," Chapter 10, "Exchange Server 2010 Quick Start Guide," or Chapter 12, "Exchange Server 2010 Requirements." However, everyone needs to start somewhere, and if you are new to the job or need a refresher, this chapter is for you!

In this chapter, we attempt to provide a primer on some of the issues that you'll need to know to maximize the coverage of Exchange provided in the rest of the book. We hope that this chapter will serve as a good introduction to email administration and prepare you to put Exchange Server 2010 in to the proper context.

In this chapter, you will learn to:

◆ Understand email fundamentals

◆ List email administration duties

◆ Explain Exchange Server history

Introducing Email

Okay, we agree that "Introducing Email" does seem like a pretty silly header, because most everyone within 50 miles of an Internet connection has an email address. Does a simple concept such as sending text and attachments from one person to another really need an explanation? Well, no, but "What Does Email Do for Your Users, or for Your Organization for That Matter?" is a bit too long.

Sure, sending simple text email and file attachments is the most basic function, but email systems (the client and/or the server) may also perform the following important functions:

◆ Act as a personal information manager, providing storage for and access to personal calendars, personal contacts, to-do and task lists, personal journals, and chat histories.

◆ Provide the user with a single "point of entry" for multiple types of information, such as voicemail, faxes, and electronic forms.

◆ Provide shared calendars, departmental contacts, and other shared information.

◆ Enable users to send faxes from their desktop to outside their organization.

◆ Receive notifications of workflow processes, such as finance/accounting activities, IT events (server status information), and more.

◆ Allow users to access their "email data" through a variety of means, including clients running on Windows computers, Apple computers, Unix systems, web browsers, mobile phones, and even a regular telephone.

◆ Perform records management and enable long-term storage of important information or information that must be archived.

◆ Enables near-time communication of sales and support information with vendors and customers.

These are just a few of the types of things that an email system may provide to the end user either via the client interface or as a result of some function running on the server.

A Brief History of Email

If you're currently responsible for electronic messaging in your organization, no one has to tell you about the steadily expanding use of e-messaging. You know it's happening every time you check the storage space on your disk drives or need an additional tape to complete the backup of your mail server. This section discusses some aspects of electronic mail and the ever-changing nature of email. Even experienced Exchange Server administrators may want to review this section to better understand how their users and requirements are evolving.

Over the past ten years, the number of email addresses has grown significantly. The technology research company International Data Corporation (IDC) estimated that in 2002, the number of email boxes worldwide was more than 500 million. The Radicati Group estimated that by 2006 there were more than 1.5 billion email accounts worldwide, accounting for more than 135 billion email messages per day.

SLOW INITIAL ADOPTION

When early adopters said "email" to their friends, the friends probably said "e-what"? Organizations considered early email systems a luxury or an option rather than an important part of a company's daily work processes.

Email systems began to take hold in the corporate world around 1988. More rapid adoption started in the mid-1990s as the number of email and directory access standards began to converge on some clear winners. In particular, the introduction of the Simple Mail Transfer Protocol (SMTP), used on the Internet, allowed the isolated silos of internal email functionality to interoperate with wildly different systems.

What happened to change these organizations' minds? Well, a few things:

◆ Electronic information processing for even small and medium-sized businesses became more affordable.

◆ More and more organizations moved from mainframe-based systems to PC-based systems. As a result, email applications became "just another program" that ran on the increasingly common desktop PC. Instead of mainframe access that was given to a relatively small number of people, it became more feasible for "regular" workers to profit from an email account.

◆ Email clients and email servers included more and more features and capabilities that were attractive to users and management. As the capabilities grew, the user interface became more accessible, allowing nontechnical users to compose and receive electronic messages.

◆ In the mid-to-late '90s, the Internet became accessible to corporations. The Internet served as an ideal (and relatively inexpensive) way to link organizations, especially when compared to existing wide area networking technologies such as X.25 or Frame Relay. As more organizations became connected to the Internet, people had more options for who they communicated with.

IMPROVING THE INTERFACE

Certainly email systems have come a long, long way since the first mainframe and minicomputer systems from more than 30 years ago. Even the primitive text-based systems like cc:Mail, Microsoft Mail, WordPerfect Office, and DaVinci eMail that first appeared on LANs in the late 1980s are almost unrecognizable ancestors when compared with a modern system based on Exchange Server 2010 and the Outlook client. Early email clients were text based and usually did not have any features other than the ability to read and send email (in other words, no personal information management). Looking at an early version of Microsoft Mail (see Figure 2.1), it seems downright sparse.

FIGURE 2.1
Early email clients had few features.

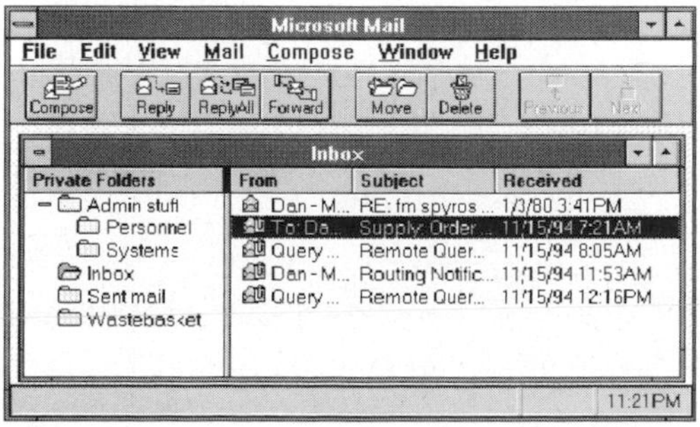

Modern email clients are much more feature rich than their predecessors. One interesting evolution is the features available when creating a message. New clients allow for the creation of much more complex email messages than in the past. What does "more complex" mean?

Well, take as an example the message shown in Figure 2.2. This Outlook 2007 message is formatted with fonts, a numbered list, a substantial message signature/disclaimer, and a corporate logo in the signature; all of this is formatted using HTML or rich text so that the message is viewable by any web-based mail system or HTML-compatible client. Finally, the message is digitally signed and authenticated with a digital signature.

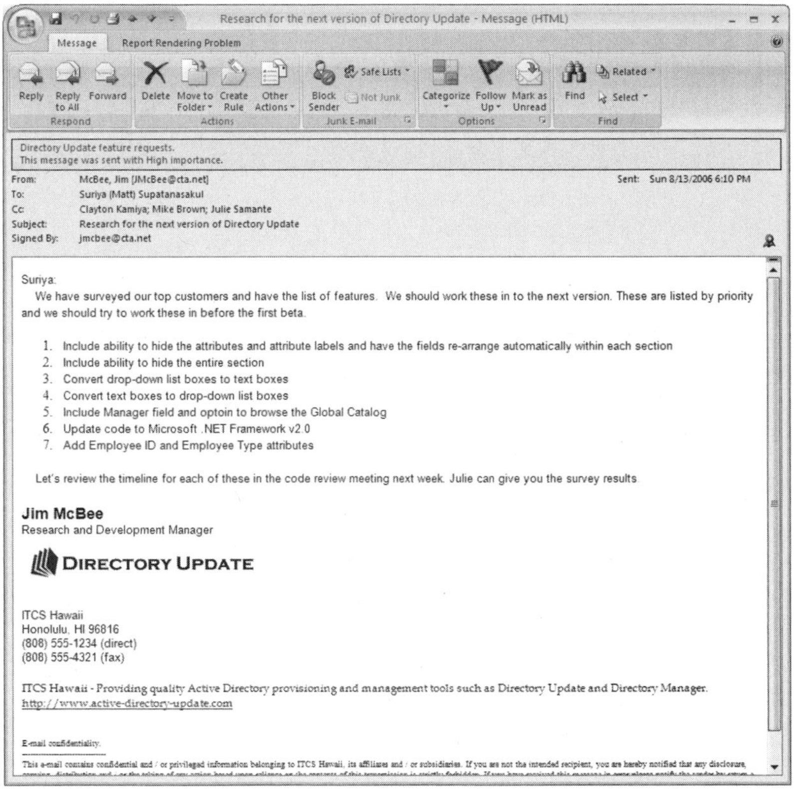

FIGURE 2.2
A typical modern email message

Messages formatted with rich text or HTML, containing disclaimers, digital signatures, and digital rights management controls, can help us communicate more effectively. Therefore, organizations depend far more on email today than they did even five years ago, and their users send even more mail than in the past.

In addition to regular email messages, users are sending scheduling requests, contact items, forms-enabled email messages, and more. Each of these increases the complexity of the messaging system as well as an organization's dependency on it.

The message shown in Figure 2.2 is 30KB in size, but has only a few hundred bytes of actual message content, including the recipient information.

ATTACHMENTS

As if that weren't complex enough, many email messages contain attachments — word processing, spreadsheet, and other files that you can attach to messages. Using attachments is a simple way to move files to the people who need to see them. They also gobble up disk space extremely fast!

Sure, you could send your files on disk or tell people where on the network they can find and download them. But email attachments let you make the files available to others with a click of their mouse buttons. Recipients just double-click an icon and the attachment opens in the original application that produced it (always assuming your correspondent has access to an application or software compatible with the attachment). Using attachments offers the added advantage of putting the files and accompanying messages right in the faces of those who need to see them. This leaves less room for excuses such as "I couldn't find/open that network folder" or "My Siberian Husky ate the disk."

As great as attachments can be, they have one real weakness: the minute an attachment leaves your Outbox, it's out of date. If you do further work on the original file, the work is not reflected in the copy that you sent to others. If someone then edits a copy of the attached file, it's totally out of sync with the original and all other copies. Getting everything synchronized again can involve tedious hours or days of manually comparing different versions and cutting and pasting them to create one master document.

SHARED FILES

Modern office productivity application suites such as Office 2007 offer two neat ways to avoid this problem. First, they let you insert a link to a file. When you open the file, you're opening the file the link points to. If the file is changed, you see the changed file. Second, Office lets you attach a file to a message and to set a shared folder where an updatable version of the file is stored. When the copy attached to the user's email is updated, these updates can be incorporated into the shared copy of the file. This option allows broader access to the file than a link.

The use of portals, such as Microsoft Office SharePoint Server, is becoming increasingly commonplace in organizations as they look for better ways to store, find, and manage the data that their users are producing. As new versions of Outlook offer better integration with SharePoint and provide an alternative to using email for attachments, messaging administrators may start to reduce or even remove the use of attachments in email.

About Messaging Services

Electronic messaging is now far more than email. Together, Exchange Server 2010 and its clients perform a variety of messaging-based functions. These functions include email, unified messaging, message routing, scheduling, and support for several types of custom applications. Together these features are called messaging services.

HOW MESSAGING SERVICES ARE USED

Certainly, email is a key feature of any messaging system, and the Outlook Calendar is far better than previous versions of Microsoft's appointment and meeting-scheduling software. Outlook 2007 together with Exchange 2010 or 2007 introduces even more improvements. Figures 2.3 and 2.4 show the Outlook 2007 client Inbox and Calendar in action.

Figure 2.5 shows the new Outlook Web App 2010 web browser client that you can use with Exchange Server 2010. For the first time, Outlook Web App 2010 provides the full premium user experience for browsers other than Internet Explorer; it also supports Mac OS X Safari 3.1 on Mac Leopard, Firefox 3.0+ on Windows, and Chrome on Windows.

Email clients are exciting and sexy, but to get the most out of Exchange Server 2010, you need to throw away any preconceptions you have that messaging systems are only for email and scheduling. The really exciting applications are not those that use simple email or scheduling, but those that are based on the routing capabilities of messaging systems. These applications bring people and computers together for improved collaboration.

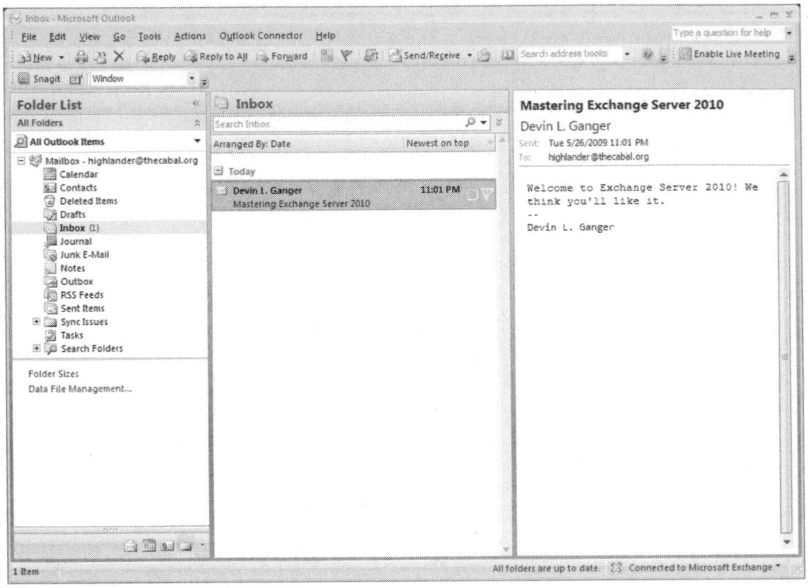

FIGURE 2.3
The Outlook 2007 client Inbox on an Exchange 2010 mailbox

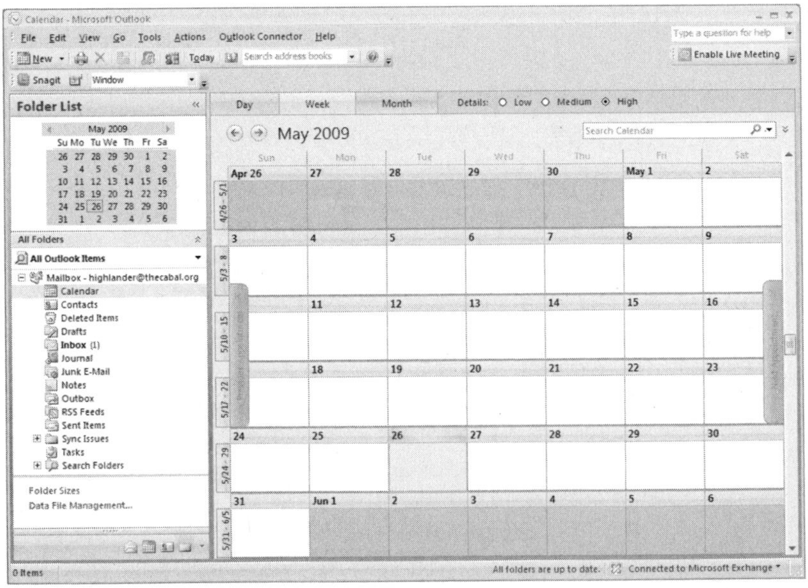

FIGURE 2.4
The Outlook 2007 client Calendar on an Exchange 2010 mailbox

FIGURE 2.5

Outlook Web App on an Exchange 2010 mailbox

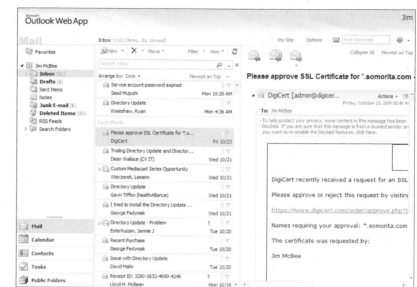

HOW MESSAGING SERVERS WORK

At the core of any messaging system, you will find a common set of basic functions. These functions may be implemented in different ways depending on the vendor or even the version of the product. Exchange Server has evolved dramatically over the past 13 years and its current architecture is almost nothing like the Exchange Server 4.0 from 1996. Common components of most messaging systems include the following:

◆ A message transport system that moves messages from one place to another. Examples include the Simple Mail Transport Protocol (SMTP) or remote procedure calls (RPCs).

◆ A message storage system that stores messages until a user can read or retrieve them. Messages may be stored in a client/server database, a shared file database, or even in individual files.

◆ A directory service that allows a user to look up information about the mail system's users, such as a user's email address.

◆ A client access interface on the server that allows the clients to get to their stored messages. This might include a web interface, a client/server interface (such as RPCs), or the Post Office Protocol (POP).

◆ The client program that allows users to read their mail, send mail, and access the directory. This may include Outlook, Outlook Web App, or iPhones.

Working in tandem with real-time interactive technologies, electronic messaging systems have already produced a set of imaginative business, entertainment, and educational applications with high payoff potential. All of this action, of course, accelerates the demand for electronic messaging capabilities and services.

Most organizations that deploy an email system usually deploy additional components from their email software vendor or third parties that extend the capabilities of the email system or provide required services. These include the following:

- Integration with existing phone systems or enterprise voice deployments to pull voice messages into the mailbox

- Message hygiene systems that help reduce the likelihood of a malicious or inappropriate message being delivered to a user

- Backup and recovery, disaster recovery, and business continuity solutions

- Message archival software to allow for the long-term retention and indexing of email data

- Electronic forms routing software that may integrate with accounting, order entry, or other line-of-business applications

- Mail gateways to allow differing types of mobile phones, such as BlackBerry devices or Palm-based mobile phones, to access the mail server

- Email security systems that improve the security of email data either while being transferred or while sitting in the user's mailbox

Application Networking Models

The technology industry has overused the term *client/server* to the point where it is almost meaningless. To put it simply, there are two kinds of networked applications: shared-file and client/server. The typical Exchange Server and Outlook deployment is a client/server messaging system and always has been. However, for people just getting involved in Exchange Server deployments, these concepts should be reviewed. It is also helpful to note that Exchange Server and Outlook are completely separate components. Although Outlook is the most popular (and feature-rich) client for Exchange Server, some organizations deploy Exchange Server entirely for web or POP3 clients.

SHARED-FILE APPLICATIONS

Early networked applications were all based on shared-file systems. The network shell that let you load your word processor from a network server also allowed you to read from and write to files stored on a server. At the time, this was the easiest and most natural way to grow networked applications.

Microsoft's first email product, Mail for PC Networks, was a shared-file application. You ran a Windows, OS/2, DOS, or Macintosh client application, which sent and received messages by accessing files on a Microsoft Mail for PC Networks post office that resided on a network file server. The front-end application and your PC did all the work; the server was passive. Figure 2.6 shows a typical Microsoft Mail for PC Networks setup.

Easy as it was to deploy, this architecture leads to some serious problems in today's networked computing world:

- Changing the underlying structure of the server file system is difficult because you have to change both the server and the client.

- System security is always compromised because users must have read and write permissions for the whole server file system, which includes all other users' message files. Things are so bad that in some cases a naive or malicious user can actually destroy shared-file system databases.

FIGURE 2.6
Microsoft Mail for PC
Networks is a typical
shared-file electronic
messaging system.

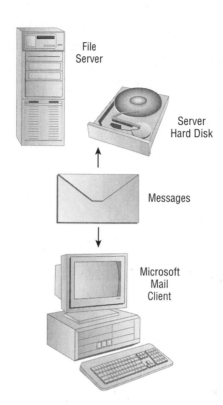

File
Server

Server
Hard Disk

Messages

Microsoft
Mail
Client

◆ Network traffic is high because the client application must constantly access indexes and hunt around the server's file system for user messages.

◆ Because the user workstation writes directly to shared files, the server-based files can be destroyed if workstation hardware or software stops functioning for some unexpected reason.

◆ Often the client program opens these shared files and locks them for use. This frequently prevents important data files from being backed up.

While they are still around (an Access database is a shared-file database, for example), shared-file applications are in decline. Plenty of *legacy* (that is, out-of-date) applications will probably live on for the data-processing equivalent of eternity, but client/server systems have quickly supplanted the shared-file model. This is especially true in the world of electronic messaging.

CLIENT/SERVER APPLICATIONS

Although they have some limitations of their own, client/server applications overcome the shortcomings of shared-file apps. So today, networked applications increasingly are based on the client/server model. The server is an active partner in client/server applications. Clients tell servers what they want done using some common protocol, and if security requirements are met, servers do what they are asked.

Processes running on a server find and ship data to processes running on a client. When a client process sends data, a server receives it and writes it to server-based files. Server processes can do more than simply interact with client processes. For example, they can compact data files on the server or — as they do on Exchange Server — automatically reply to incoming messages to let people know, for instance, that you're going to be out of the office for a period of time.

A simplified example of this is shown in Figure 2.7. In step 1, the client requests a specific email message from the server. Then, in step 2 the server responds by opening the appropriate database, searching through the database, retrieving the message, and sending it back to the client in step 3. Although the database might be hundreds of gigabytes in size, this operation usually takes less than a second.

FIGURE 2.7
A simple client/server messaging system

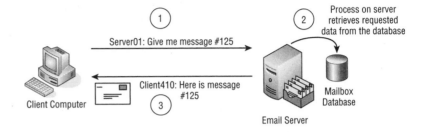

Client/server applications are strong in all the areas in which shared-file apps are weak:

♦ Changing the underlying structure of the server file system is easier than with shared-file systems because only the server processes access the file system.

♦ System security can be much tighter, again because only the server processes access the file system.

♦ Network traffic is lighter because all the work of searching and data access is done by the server, on the server.

♦ Because server processes are the only ones that access server data, breakdowns of user workstation hardware or software are less likely to spoil data. With appropriate transaction logging features, client/server systems can even protect data against server hardware or software malfunctions.

As good as the client/server model is, it does have some general drawbacks. Client/server apps require more computing horsepower, especially on the server side. With Exchange, therefore, you should plan to start with very fast machines, lots of RAM, and plenty of hard disk and tape backup capacity or disk snapshot capability — and expect to grow from there.

Client/server applications are more complex than shared-file apps. This is partly because of the nature of the client/server model and partly because client/server apps tend to be newer and thus filled with all kinds of great capabilities that you won't find in shared-file applications. Generally, you're safe in assuming that you'll need to devote more — and more sophisticated — human resources to managing a client/server application than to tending a similar application based on shared files.

The good news is that Microsoft has done a lot to reduce the management load and to make it easier for someone who isn't a computer scientist to administer an Exchange system. We have looked at many client/server messaging systems, and we can say without any doubt that Exchange is absolutely the easiest to administer. Exchange Server 2010 includes both a graphical user interface (GUI) and a management shell that organizes the processes of management very nicely. With these interfaces, you can do everything from adding users to assessing the health of your messaging system.

Things Every Email Administrator Should Know

The information in this section is something that we often find even our own email administrators and helpdesk personnel are not aware of. Sometimes the most important skill any technology administrator has is not a specific knowledge of something, but generic knowledge that they can use to quickly find the right answer.

Finding Answers

This topic deserves special attention. One of our jobs is working in Tier 3 support for a large organization. The thing we respect the most about the administrators who actually run the system and handle the trouble tickets is if they have done their homework prior to coming to us with a problem.

Too often techies make up an answer when they are not sure about something. Don't do that! When you are asked a question that you don't know the answer to, it is okay to say you don't know the answer. But follow that up by indicating that you will find the answer. Knowing the right resources (where to get answers) is therefore just as important as the technical knowledge it takes to implement the answer.

HELPFUL RESOURCES

Exchange has to be one of the most documented and discussed products (short of maybe Windows) that Microsoft produces. This means that most of the questions that we have about Exchange Server we can usually answer with the right search or by looking in the right place. The most obvious place to start when you have a problem or a question is to perform an Internet search, but many other resources are available:

Exchange Server Documentation   There is a world of free information on the Internet, but let's start right on the local hard disk of your Exchange Server or any place you have installed the admin tools. Microsoft has done an excellent job of providing better and better documentation for Exchange Server over the past few years. The Exchange Server 2010 documentation is comprehensive and so readable you will wonder if it is really from Microsoft. Figure 2.8 shows an example of the Exchange 2010 documentation. Look for the following file:

```
C:\Program Files\Microsoft\Exchange Server\v14\Bin\ExchHelp.chm
```

or run it from the Microsoft Exchange Server 2010 folder on the Start menu.

You can also download updated versions of ExchHelp.chm from the following URL:

```
http://technet.microsoft.com/en-us/exchange/bb456976.aspx
```

Exchange Server Release Notes   Another good resource for "I wish I had known that" types of things is the release notes. You should be able to find a link to the release notes here:

```
C:\Program Files\Microsoft\Exchange Server\v14\
```

Exchange Server TechNet Forums   If you have a question on which you have done your due diligence in searching and researching the problem but you don't have an answer, it is time to ask the world. A good place to start is the Microsoft TechNet forums. You can find the Exchange server section here:

```
http://forums.microsoft.com/technet/default.aspx?siteid=17
```

When you post your question, please take a moment to think about what information the other readers are going to need to answer your question. While you can post a question like

"Exchange is giving me an error," doing so is only going to result in (at best) delays while other forum participants have to request specific information from you. Instead, post the exact error message and any error codes you are seeing. Also indicate, at minimum, what version of the software you are using (including service pack), the role of the server, and what operating system.

FIGURE 2.8
Viewing the Exchange 2010 documentation

http://msexchangeteam.com   You Had Me at Ehlo is the Microsoft Exchange Team's blog. This is the best site on the Internet for getting the inside scoop on how Exchange works, best practices, and the future of Exchange Server. You can read articles written by Exchange developers and Customer Support Services engineers.

MSExchange.Org Website   One of the best sites on the Internet for free, easy-to-access content about Exchange Server is www.msexchange.org. The articles are written by Exchange gurus from all over the world and are usually in the form of easy-to-read and easy-to-follow tutorials. There is also a forums section where you can post questions or read other people's questions.

CALLING FOR SUPPORT

If your system is down or your operations are seriously hindered and you don't have a clue what to do next, it is time to call in the big guns. Sure, you should do some Internet searches to try to resolve your problem, but Internet newsgroups and forums are not the place to get support for business-critical issues.

Microsoft Product Support Services (PSS) is Microsoft's technical support organization. Its home page is http://support.microsoft.com. Professional support options (ranging from peer-to-peer support to telephone support) can be found at the following URL:

    http://support.microsoft.com/select/?LN=en-us&target=assistance&x=13&y=15

If you do not have a Microsoft Premier agreement, Microsoft telephone support may seem to be a bit expensive, but believe us, when an Exchange server is down and the users are burning you in effigy in the company parking lot, a few hundred dollars for business hours support is cheap.

When you call and get a support technician on the phone, don't be surprised or offended if they start at the beginning and ask you a lot of elementary questions. They have to double-check everything you have done before they can look into more advanced problems. Frequently, one of these basic questions will help you locate a problem that you were convinced was more complicated than it really was.

We always encourage people to call PSS if they truly need assistance. But PSS engineers are not mind-readers, nor do they know every bit of Exchange code. You will do both yourself and the PSS engineer a big favor if you have all of your ducks in a row before you call. Do the following before you call:

◆ Attempt a graceful shutdown and restart of the server in question, if applicable.

◆ Perform a complete backup if possible.

◆ Have a complete, documented history of everything you have done to solve the problem. At the first sign of trouble, you should start keeping a chronological log of the things you did to fix the problem.

◆ Find out if you are allowed to initiate support sessions with remote support personnel through a tool like Live Meeting or WebEx.

◆ Be at a telephone that is physically at the server's console, or be in a place where you can access the server remotely via the Remote Desktop Client. Your support call will be very brief if you cannot immediately begin checking things for the PSS engineer.

◆ Have the usernames and passwords that will provide you with the right level of administrative access. If you don't have those, have someone nearby who can log you in.

◆ Save copies of the System and Application event logs. Be prepared to send these to PSS if requested.

◆ Download a copy of MPSReports (for more information see `http://support.microsoft` `.com/kb/818742`) and run it on your Exchange server. Be prepared to send the resulting report to PSS if requested.

◆ Know the location of your most recent backup and how to access it when needed.

◆ Keep copies of all error messages. Don't paraphrase the message. Screen captures work great in this case. Pressing Alt+Print Scrn and pasting into a WordPad document works great, too. We usually create a document with screen captures along with notes of what we were doing when we saw each message.

Be patient; telephone support is a terribly difficult job. A little kindness, patience, and understanding on your part will most certainly be returned by the PSS engineer.

A Day in the Life of the Email Administrator

We know and work with a lot of email administrators and we can honestly say that no two people have the same set of tasks required of them. Your CEO, director of information technology, or even your supervisor is going to ask you to pull rabbits out of your hat, so don't expect each day to be the same as the last one. (And invest in some rabbits.) Keep up with your technology and supporting products so that you can be ready with answers or at the very least intelligent responses to questions.

DAILY ADMINISTRATIVE TASKS

So, what are some typical tasks that you may perform as part of your duties as an email administrator? These tasks will depend on the size of your organization, the number of administrators you have running your Exchange organization, and how administrative tasks are divided up.

Recipient Management Tasks   These are certainly the biggest day-to-day tasks that most Exchange administrators in medium and large organizations will experience. Recipient management tasks may include:

◆ Assigning a mailbox to a user account

◆ Creating mail-enabled contacts

◆ Creating and managing mail groups

◆ Managing mail-enabled object properties such as users' phone numbers, assigning more email addresses to a user, or adding/removing group members

Basic Monitoring Tasks   These ensure that your Exchange servers are healthy and functioning properly:

◆ Checking queues for stalled messages

◆ Verifying that there is sufficient disk space for the databases and logs

◆ Making sure that the message hygiene system is functioning and up-to-date

◆ Running and verifying daily backups

◆ Reviewing the System and Application event logs for unusual activity, errors, or warnings

Daily Troubleshooting Tasks   These include the following:

◆ Reviewing nondelivery report messages and figuring out why some mail your users are sending might not have been delivered

◆ Looking up errors and warnings that show up in the Application and System event logs to determine if they are serious and warrant corrective action

Security-Related Tasks   These are sometimes performed daily while others are performed only weekly or monthly:

◆ Looking at server and service up-times to ensure that servers are not rebooting unexpectedly

◆ Reviewing the event logs for warnings that may indicate users are inappropriately accessing other users' data

◆ Saving the Web and SMTP and connectivity logs

Email Client Administration Tasks   These include the following:

- Helping users get Outlook connected and configured properly

- Diagnosing problems with Windows Mobile devices, BlackBerry devices, or iPhones

Application Integration Tasks   These are performed on an as-needed basis and may include the following:

- Establishing and diagnosing SMTP connectivity with email-enabled third-party applications such as web servers

- Configuring, testing, and troubleshooting unified messaging interoperability with voice and SIP systems

COMMUNICATING WITH YOUR USERS

Communicating with your users is probably one of the most important things you do. Keeping your users informed and delivering good customer service are almost as important as delivering the IT service itself. Keeping users informed of full or partial service outages such as mobile or BlackBerry support or web connectivity may not score any immediate points, but users appreciate honest, forthright information. Remember how you felt the last time you were waiting for an airplane to arrive that kept on being delayed and delayed and all the airline could do was be evasive?

Also remember to have multiple avenues of communication available to your users. For example, you may need to get out to your users the message that you will be having downtime on the weekend. Postings on your company intranet or even the bulletin board in the cafeteria or on the wall of the elevator are good ways to keep your users informed.

PREPARING REPORTS

Maybe we have just worked in a large IT environment for too long now, but it seems to us that information technology is more and more about reports and metrics and less about delivering technological capabilities to the users. We are frequently asked to provide reports, statistics, and information on usage — not necessarily information on performance (how well the system performed for the users), but other types of metrics. Depending on your management, you may be asked to provide:

- Total number of mailboxes and mailbox sizes

- Top system users and top source/destination domains

- Antispam and message hygiene statistics

- Disk space usage and growth

- System availability reports indicating how much unscheduled downtime may have been experienced during a certain reporting period

Exchange does not provide you with a way to easily access most of this data. The mailbox statistics can be generated using the Exchange Management Shell, but many of these will actually require an additional reporting product.

Something that you can do to prepare for a reporting requirement is to ensure that you are keeping two to four weeks' worth of message tracking and protocol logs.

SCHEDULED DOWNTIME, PATCHES, AND SERVICE PACKS

No one likes downtime, whether it is scheduled or not. Management may actually be holding you to a specific service level agreement (SLA) that requires you to provide so many hours of up-time per month or to provide email services during certain hours. Unscheduled downtime is anything that happens during your stated hours of operation that keeps users from accessing their email.

Even a small organization can provide very good availability for its mail services, and without large investments in hardware. Good availability begins with the following:

◆ Server hardware should always be from a reputable vendor and listed in the Microsoft Server Catalog.

◆ Server hardware should be installed using the vendor recommended procedures and updated regularly. Problems with servers are frequently caused by outdated firmware and device drivers.

◆ Once the server is in production it should not be used as a test bed for other software. Keep an identically configured server that uses the same hardware for testing updates.

Don't underestimate the importance of training and documentation. In general, the industry formula for providing better availability for any system is to spend more money to purchase redundant servers and build fail-over clusters. But often better training for IT personnel and a simple investment in system documentation as well as system policies and procedures can improve availability as well, and for less money.

🌐 Real World Scenario

INTERNAL STAFF TRAINING IS JUST AS IMPORTANT AS YOUR INFRASTRUCTURE

Company MNOP invested hundreds of thousands of dollars in their infrastructure to improve server up-time. Three months into the operation of the new system, an untrained operator accidentally brought down a 15,000-mailbox cluster simply because he had been asked to do a task he had never done before and there was no documentation on how to proceed. So keep in mind that documentation, training, and procedures are very important in improving up-time.

Even the biggest fail-over clusters and most highly available systems need some scheduled downtime. Even if it is scheduled in the wee hours of the morning, undoubtedly someone, somewhere, somehow will need access when you are working on the system. Therefore, your scheduled downtime should be documented as part of your operational plans and your user community should know about these plans. The specific time window for maintenance should always be the same; for some organizations, this might be 6:30 p.m.–10:30 p.m. on Thursday once per month, whereas other organizations might schedule downtime 11:00 p.m. until 4:00 a.m. every Sunday.

The number one reason for downtime is to apply updates and fixes to the operating system or to the applications running on the server. Microsoft releases monthly security updates for the operating system and applications if vulnerabilities are discovered. Every few months, Microsoft releases roll-up (RU) fixes for Exchange Server 2010 that fix bugs or that may even add functionality.

Microsoft's updates are usually downloaded to your servers shortly after they are released. The server can download them directly from Microsoft, or they can be downloaded from Windows Software Update Service (WSUS), Microsoft Systems Center Configuration Manager, or another third-party server inside your network. Whichever you choose, it is important that you make sure that the machine is a server and not a workstation. For example, make sure the automatic updates component of Windows Server is configured correctly. Figure 2.9 shows the Change Settings options for Windows Updates.

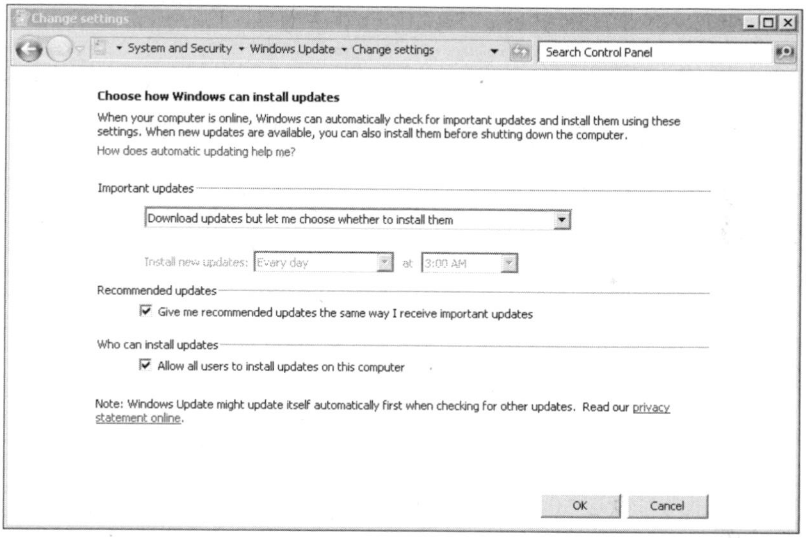

FIGURE 2.9
Configuring automatic updates

For production Exchange servers, you should configure the server with the option Download Updates But Let Me Choose Whether to Install Them. This is an important setting because if you choose the Install Updates Automatically (Recommended) option, the server will automatically apply any update within a day or so of downloading the update. This is not a desirable result for a production mail server. Instead, you want the server to download the updates and notify you via the updates icon in the system tray. You can then investigate the updates and schedule appropriate downtime to apply them manually.

Tools You Should Know

Out of the box, Exchange Server is an excellent product, but sometimes the base software that you install can use some assistance. Some of these tools are actually installed with Exchange Server whereas you may need to download other tools.

PowerShell and the Exchange Management Shell   Even here in the very first chapters, we are extolling the virtues of the new Windows management shell (or command line and scripting interface) called PowerShell. PowerShell enables some basic Windows management functions, such as managing event logs and services, to be performed via a command-line interface. This interface is simple to use and easy to learn, even for a GUI guy like this author. The Exchange team pioneered the adoption of PowerShell when they built the entire Exchange Server 2007 management interface, known as the Exchange Management Shell (EMS), as an extension to PowerShell. Exchange 2010 continues to follow this pattern.

Although almost every chapter in this book will include at least some information about using EMS to perform Exchange management tasks, we have dedicated all of Chapter 6, "Introduction to PowerShell and the Exchange Management Shell," to helping you learn your way around EMS.

Exchange Management Shell Test Cmdlets   The Exchange Management Shell (EMS) has a series of command-line tools that are very for testing and diagnosing problems. These include tools for testing Outlook Web App connectivity, Unified Messaging connectivity, Outlook connectivity, and even mail flow. They are installed when you install the Exchange Server 2010 Management Tools. For more information, at the EMS prompt type `Get-Excommand test*`.

Exchange Analyzers and Troubleshooters   In the Exchange Management Console under the Toolbox section (shown in Figure 2.10), you can find a series of troubleshooting wizards and analysis tools, including the Exchange Best Practices Analyzer, and the Performance Troubleshooting wizard.

FIGURE 2.10
Viewing the Exchange Management Console Toolbox

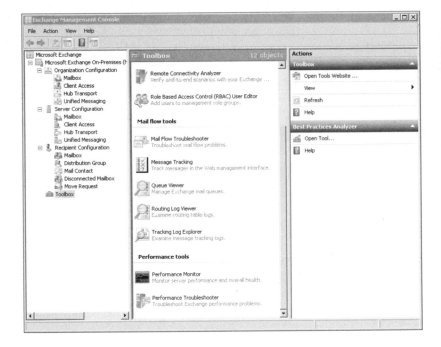

One of the most essential things that you can learn is how to use the Exchange Best Practices Analyzer (ExBPA) to run Health Check reports and determine if there is something that might not be configured properly within your organization. Check at www.exbpa.com for the release of a version of the ExBPA that supports Exchange 2010.

ADModify.NET   If you need to make bulk changes to Active Directory Objects such as users, groups, contacts, or even public folders, then you need ADModify.NET (shown in Figure 2.11). This powerful and free tool allows you to find and select objects from the Active Directory and then use a simple interface to modify one or more attributes of the selected objects. You can even use other attributes of that object to build a new attribute.

FIGURE 2.11
The main search screen of ADModify.NET

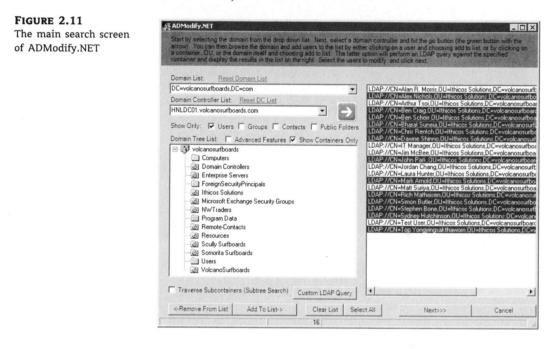

There are a few important things to note about ADModify. You must run it from your local hard disk, and the Microsoft .NET Framework v2.0 is required. Another important item to note is that it has an "undo" feature; you can back out a bulk change that you made if it turns out to be wrong. You can download ADModify from www.codeplex.com/admodify.

Quest ActiveRoles Management Shell for Active Directory   Quest Software is giving away one of the most useful add-in tools for Microsoft PowerShell that we have ever used. Its Management Shell for Active Directory allows you to manage users and groups using PowerShell even if you don't yet have Exchange Server 2010. We use this tool almost daily in organizations that have not yet migrated to Exchange Server 2007. You can download this free tool from Quest at

    www.quest.com/powershell/activeroles-server.aspx

PowerGUI   If you like the Quest ActiveRoles Management Shell, you will also like Power-GUI. PowerGUI is a graphical interface that "wraps itself" around PowerShell and allows you to see the results of PowerShell cmdlets. It will help you in writing scripts utilizing the PowerShell and other extensions to PowerShell. A sample of PowerGUI is shown in Figure 2.12.

You can download PowerGUI from http://powergui.org.

FIGURE 2.12
Using the PowerGUI tool

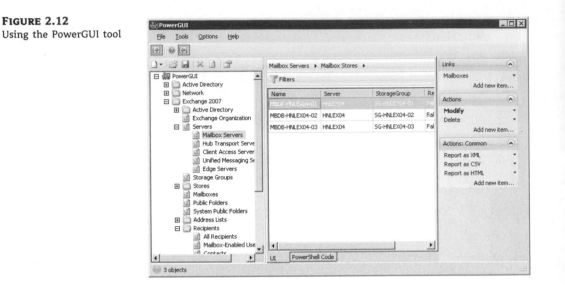

What Is Exchange Server?

In its simplest form, Exchange Server provides the underlying infrastructure necessary to run a messaging system. Exchange Server provides the database to store email data, the transport infrastructure to move the data from one place to another, and access points to access email data via a number of different clients.

However, Exchange Server, when used with other clients such as Outlook or Outlook Web App, turns the "mailbox" into a point of storage for personal information management such as your calendar, contacts, task lists, and personal journal. Users can share some or all of this information in their own mailbox with other users on the message system and start to collaborate.

The Outlook and Outlook Web App clients also provide access to public folders. Public folders look like regular mail folders in your mailbox, except that they are in an area where they can be shared by all users within the organization. A folder can have specialized forms associated with it to allow the sharing of contacts, calendar entries, or even other specialized forms. Further, each public folder can be secured so that only certain users can view or modify data in that folder.

The Unified Messaging role in Exchange Server 2010 further extends the functions of the Exchange Server in your organization by allowing your Exchange Server infrastructure to also act as your voicemail system and direct voicemails and missed call notifications automatically to the user's mailbox. Figure 2.13 shows a voicemail message that arrived in a mailbox and can be checked via Outlook Web App.

While integrated voicemail solutions are nothing new for Exchange customers, Microsoft is now providing these capabilities out of the box rather than relying on third-party products.

Exchange 2007 tightened the integration of collaborative tools with its integration with Office Communication Server 2007 and the Communicator client. OCS provided a core set of SIP-based enterprise voice capabilities that allowed it to act as a PBX in many cases. With Exchange, OCS, Outlook, and the Communicator client, users enjoyed full Unified Messaging with software-based telephony from their computer, including the new voicemail and missed call notification provided by Exchange and Outlook. Furthermore, Communicator could log chat and instant message conversation logs to a folder in the user's mailbox. Exchange

2010 further pushes this integration with OCS 2007 R2, embedding basic IM and presence capabilities into the Outlook Web App premium experience.

The capabilities of the client can be extended with third-party tools and forms-routing software so that electronic forms can be routed through email to users' desktops.

FIGURE 2.13

Checking your voicemail from Outlook Web App

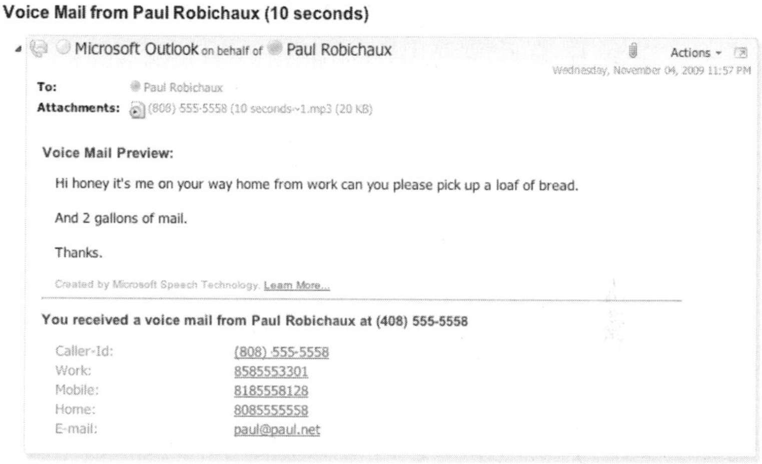

History of Exchange
=======================

History of Exchange

The original version of Exchange Server that debuted in 1996 was called Exchange Server 4.0 because the previous version of Microsoft's email offering was Microsoft Mail v3.2. However, Exchange Server 4.0 was nothing like Microsoft Mail v3.2 in any way, shape, or form. Exchange Server v4.0 included client/server database technology, a much more comprehensive directory service, and built-in connectors for connectivity with the Internet (SMTP), as well as cc:Mail and Microsoft Mail.

Exchange continued to evolve with Exchange 5.0 and 5.5 as new capabilities, such as improved Internet access, web-based email, database engine optimizations, additional messaging connectors, and better scalability were included with the product.

Exchange Server 2000 represented a big jump forward with even more scalability improvements, such as more databases on a single server. Exchange Server 2000 also moved from a dedicated directory service over to using Active Directory to store the Exchange configuration as well as recipient information. Internet connectivity and client interface improvements were also introduced in both Exchange 2000 as well as Exchange Server 2003.

Microsoft's Exchange Server products have played, and will continue to play, a key role in electronic messaging. Exchange Server 2007 was one of the most powerful, extensible, scalable, easy-to-use, and manageable electronic messaging back ends currently on the market. Combined with Microsoft's excellent Outlook clients, Internet-based clients from Microsoft and other vendors, mobile devices that use ActiveSync, and third-party or home-grown applications, Exchange Server 2007 offered a dramatic step into the future of messaging.

Exchange Server 2010 continues this trend, following many of the improvements begun with Exchange 2007. The I/O improvements realized by the Exchange 2007 64-bit architecture have been extended in Exchange 2010 by continued work on the underlying Extensible Storage Engine (ESE) database system, optimizing the database schema, and changing the characteristic Exchange I/O patterns to better match the performance and capacity of modern hard drives. The native continuous replication features have been improved while the configuration and management of highly available configurations has been simplified, making the design, deployment, and operation of high-performance, highly available Exchange systems even easier and more cost-effective than ever before. At the same time, users and administrators can enjoy the ability to grow mailboxes to vastly larger sizes while still maintaining and improving their ability to control their messaging data.

The Universal Inbox

Email systems are converging with their voicemail and faxing cousins. The concept of unified messaging is nothing new to email users. For at least the past 10 years, third-party vendors have included email integration tools for voicemail and network faxing solutions. However, for most organizations, integrated voicemail and faxing solutions remain the exception rather than the rule. Exchange 2007 introduced integrated voice, which Exchange Server 2010 improves upon.

Organizations with IP-based telephone systems or telephone systems with an IP gateway can now easily integrate a user's voicemail with the Exchange user's mailbox. The Exchange 2010 Unified Messaging server handles the interaction between an organization's telephone system and Exchange mailboxes. Inbound voicemail is transferred into the user's mailbox as a cross-platform-friendly MP3 file attachment; this message includes an Outlook or OWA form that allows the user to play the message. Because the default format has been changed to MP3 in Exchange 2010 (it was a Windows Media file in Exchange 2007, using a custom codec), this file can be easily played on mobile devices from any manufacturer, allowing easy on-the-go access to voicemail. A short voicemail message may be anywhere from 40 KB to 75 KB in size, whereas longer voicemail messages may be 200 KB to 500 KB in size. One estimate that is frequently used for the size of a voicemail message is around 5 KB per second of message.

With Outlook Voice Access, users can now dial into the Exchange 2010 Unified Messaging server and access their mailbox, have email read to them, have appointments read to them, and move or cancel appointments. If an appointment is changed, Outlook Voice Access will automatically notify attendees of scheduling changes; this is very useful if you are sitting in traffic on the freeway with nothing but your cell phone (using your headset of course)!

Inbound voicemail increases the demands on your Exchange server from the perspective of required disk space and possibly additional server hardware, though. This needs to be considered. Outlook Voice Access will increase the potential number of connections and usage of your Exchange mailbox servers and Unified Messaging servers.

JUST THE FAX, MA'AM

In Exchange Server 2007, the Unified Messaging role included the out-of-the-box capability to capture incoming facsimile (fax) messages. There were some limitations, but it provided good basic functionality. For outbound fax capability, organizations had to deploy some other solution, typically a third-party fax package.

For Exchange Server 2010, Microsoft made the decision to cut this feature. When talking with the product group, it's not hard to figure out why; the inbound-only fax functionality wasn't enough for the customers who needed fax integration. Exchange 2010 needed to either add outgoing fax capability and beef up its feature set (and lose other desired functionality), or drop the existing functionality since the majority of Exchange 2007 customers were going to need a third-party product anyway. While it's always disappointing to lose a feature, most of the organizations we've talked to didn't use it to begin with. We think that Microsoft definitely made the right call, if you'll pardon the pun.

Many Modes of Access

For years, the only way to access your email system was to use a Windows, Macintosh, or Unix-based client and access the email system directly. In the case of Outlook and Exchange, this access was originally in the form of a MAPI client directly against the Exchange server. As Exchange has evolved, it included support for the POP3 and IMAP4 protocols, then web-based email access, and finally mobile device access. Exchange Server 2010 doesn't offer any radically new modes of mailbox access like Exchange Server 2007 did, but it does provide ongoing support and refinement of existing Exchange 2007 technologies, such as Exchange Web Services, that can provide additional mechanisms for accessing data in mailboxes.

Outlook Web App (OWA) has evolved quickly and in Exchange 2010 bears almost no resemblance to the original version found in Exchange 5.0 in terms of features, functions, and the look of the interface. Exchange 2010 OWA is even a radical step beyond Exchange 2007; it offers first-class support for Firefox and the Mac OS X Safari web browsers, allowing non-Windows users to have a rich, Outlook-like experience. It also expands the previous option configuration experience into the full-featured Exchange Control Panel (ECP), which gives users a much greater degree of control over their mailbox, contacts, and group memberships. Using ECP, end users can create and join distribution groups (where permissions have been assigned), track their own messages throughout the own organization, and perform other functions that previously required helpdesk or IT professional intervention.

Users are more frequently asking for integration of mobile devices with email. The Radicati Group estimated that in 2006 there were 14 million wireless email users but by 2010 that number will grow to 228 million. You can bet that your users will want to be included! Mobile device access was first provided to Exchange 2000 using Microsoft Mobile Information Server and then later included as part of Exchange 2003. Mobile device functionality was further improved in Exchange 2007 with a major revision of the Exchange ActiveSync (EAS) protocol. With Exchange Server 2010, EAS continues to offer significant partnerships with and control over mobile devices. Many vendors have licensed EAS to provide their mobile devices with a high-performance, full-featured push mobile synchronization experience.

Unified Messaging and Outlook Voice Access allow users with nothing but a telephone to access their email and calendar and even make changes via the telephone.

With all of these mechanisms for retrieving and sending email, it is not unusual for users to access their mailbox using more than one device. In some cases, we have seen a single user accessing her mailbox from her desktop computer, her notebook computer using Outlook Anywhere (formerly known as RPC over HTTPS), and her Windows Mobile device.

In medium and large organizations, the fact that users are now accessing their mailbox from more than one device or mechanism will affect not only hardware sizing but also, potentially, your licensing costs.

WHAT'S GONE?

When Exchange 2007 was released, Microsoft introduced new core APIs (including Web Services, the new management API based on the .NET Framework), intended to replace existing Exchange APIs. Several of those legacy APIs were completely removed, while others were *deprecated* — while they still worked, developers were encouraged to port their applications over to the new APIs. The deprecated APIs were not guaranteed to be continued in future versions of Exchange.

> Well, the future's here and those deprecated APIs are now gone. One of the biggest is Web-
> DAV, which was the previous HTTP-based access protocol prior to Exchange Web Services.
> WebDAV calls are somewhat simpler to develop, but are more fundamentally limited in what
> they can do. Exchange 2007 was the transition version for application developers; Exchange
> 2010 moves forward into the bright new world of Web Services.

Architecture Overview

Understanding a bit about how Exchange Server works from an architectural perspective will
help make you a better administrator. You don't have to be able to reproduce or write your
own client/server messaging system, but it helps to know the basics.

EXCHANGE AS A CLIENT/SERVER MAIL SYSTEM

Since Exchange Server 4.0, Exchange has been a client/server messaging system. Remember
back in Figure 2.7, how the client sends a request to the Exchange server, the Exchange server
does the work, and then sends back only the response to the client? Well, that is how Exchange
Server works; the mechanism that the Outlook client uses is the messaging application
programming interface (MAPI); the data is sent using remote procedure calls (RPCs). The
underlying network infrastructure uses whatever the network transport is to move the RPC
request from the client to the server. In years past, this might have been IPX/SPX or even
NetBEUI, but it is rare that you will find any network transport today other than TCP/IP.
MAPI clients, such as Outlook 2003, 2007, or 2010, directly access an Exchange server Client
Access server using MAPI over RPCs, as shown in Figure 2.14.

FIGURE 2.14
Client Access server
architecture

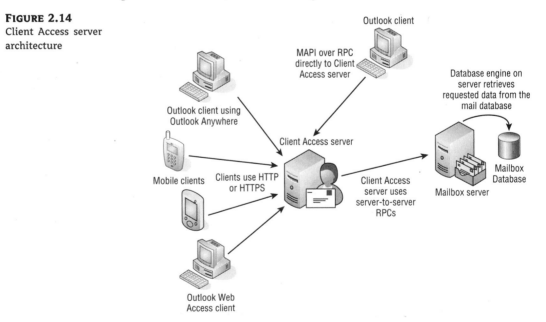

The client/server architecture does not just stop at Outlook clients, though; Internet clients
such as Outlook Web App, Outlook Anywhere, POP3, IMAP4, Windows Mobile devices, the

iPhone, and several other mobile devices all go through a middle tier to get to their data. In the case of Exchange Server 2010, all client access has been abstracted from the mail storage system and is run by a server role called the Client Access server. Figure 2.14 shows a simple diagram of how this works.

THE EXTENSIBLE STORAGE ENGINE (ESE)

The Exchange Server database uses a highly specialized database engine called the Extensible Storage Engine (ESE). Generically, you could say it is almost like SQL Server, but this is technically not true. It is a client/server database and is somewhat relational in nature, but it is designed to be a single-user database (the Exchange server itself is the only component that directly accesses the data). Further, the database has been highly tuned to store hierarchical data such as mailboxes, folders, messages, and attachments.

Without going into a lot of techno-babble on the database architecture, it is important that you understand the basics of what the database is doing. Figure 2.15 shows conceptually what is happening with the ESE database as data is sent to the database. In step 1, an Outlook client sends data to the Exchange Server (the information store service); the information store service places this data in memory and then immediately writes the data out to the transaction log files associated with that database.

FIGURE 2.15
Exchange data and
transaction logs

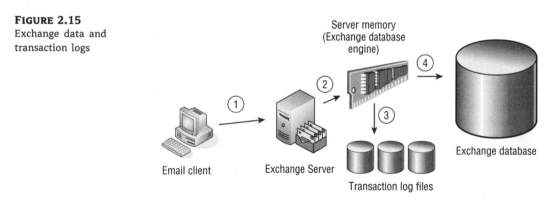

The transaction log that is always written to is the current transaction log for that particular database (e00.log, for example). Each transaction log file is exactly 1 MB in size, so when the transaction log is filled up, it is renamed to the next sequential number. For example, an old transaction log file might be named like this: e000004032.log.

The data is retained in RAM for some period of time (maybe as little as 5 seconds or maybe even 60 seconds or more) before it is then flushed to the database file. The actual period that data is retained in memory will depend on how much cache memory is available, what types of operations are happening in the data, and how busy the server is. The important operation, though, is to make sure that as soon as the data is sent to the Exchange server it is immediately flushed to the transaction log files. If the server crashes before the data is written to the database file, the database engine (the information store service) will automatically read the transaction log files once the server is brought back up and compare them with the data that's stored in the corresponding mailbox databases. Any inconsistency is resolved by replaying the missing data operations from the transaction logs back into the database, assuming that the entire transaction is present; if it's not, the operations are not written (and you can be confident that the operation wasn't completed at the time the crash happened). This helps ensure that the integrity of the mailbox database is preserved and that half-completed data operations aren't written back into the database and allowed to corrupt good data.

The transaction log files are important for a number of reasons. They are used by Microsoft replication technologies (as you'll learn in Chapter 23, "Creating and Managing Databases"), but they can also be used in disaster recovery. The transaction logs are not purged off the log disk until a full backup is run; therefore, every transaction that occurred to a database (new data, modifications, moves, deletes) is stored in the logs. If you restore the last good backup to the server, Exchange Server can replay and rebuild all the missing transactions back in to the database — provided you have all the transactions since the last full backup.

In previous versions of Exchange, you had two separate mail store objects: the *storage group*, which was a logical container that held an associated set of transaction logs, and the *mailbox database*, a set of files that held the actual permanent copies of user mailboxes. In old legacy versions, you often had multiple mailbox databases per storage group, meaning that one set of transaction logs contained interwoven transaction data for multiple databases (which could have detrimental effects on performance, space, and backups). In Exchange 2007, the recommendation changed; while you could still assign mailbox databases to a storage group in a many-to-one ratio, Microsoft encouraged you to assign them 1:1. In fact, to use the continuous replication features in Exchange 2007, you had to do so.

In Exchange Server 2010, you still have mailbox databases. However, storage groups have been removed; each mailbox database has its own integral set of transaction log files. In fact, mailbox databases — which were once tightly coupled with specific servers — can now have copies on multiple servers in the organization, even spread across multiple sites. The *database availability group* container is now available to contain servers that participate in the replication of mailbox databases with each other.

EXCHANGE AND ACTIVE DIRECTORY

We could easily write two or three chapters on how Exchange Server interacts with the Active Directory, but the basics will have to do for now. Exchange Server relies on the Active Directory for information about its own configuration, user authentication, and email-specific properties for mail-enabled objects such as users, contacts, groups, and public folders. Look at Figure 2.16 to see some of the different types of interactions that occur between Exchange and the Active Directory.

FIGURE 2.16
Active Directory and Exchange

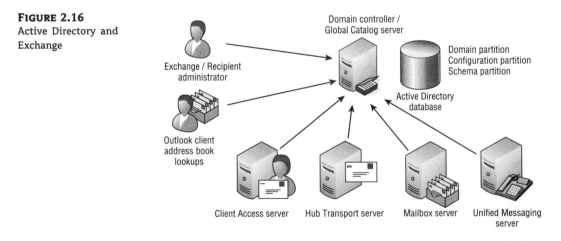

Because most of the Exchange configuration data for an Exchange server is stored in the Active Directory, all Exchange server roles must contact a domain controller to request its configuration data; this information is stored in a special partition of the Active Directory database called the configuration partition. The configuration partition is replicated to all domain controllers in the entire Active Directory forest.

Each of the individual Exchange Server roles uses the Active Directory for different things. Here is a list of some of those functions:

Mailbox Servers   Exchange Mailbox servers must query the Active Directory to authenticate users, enumerate permissions on mailboxes, look up individual mailbox limits, and determine which mailboxes are on a particular server. The Mailbox server may also support public folder database.

Hub Transport Servers   Exchange Hub Transport servers require access to global catalog servers to look up email addressing information, home server information, distribution list membership information, and other data related to message routing.

Client Access Servers   Exchange Client Access servers require access to the Active Directory to look up information about home servers for users, ActiveSync, and Outlook Web App user restrictions, as well as provide proxy connections to Active Directory for clients. One of the biggest architectural changes in Exchange Server 2010 is that now MAPI clients connect to the Client Access server for mailbox access rather than directly to the Mailbox server.

Unified Messaging Servers   Unified Messaging servers require access to the Active Directory to retrieve and play the user's personalized outgoing message as well as to retrieve email address information so that voicemail and faxes can be delivered to the user.

Exchange Management Tools   The Exchange Server management tools must connect to the Active Directory to make configuration changes to Exchange server objects and to create, update, manage, or delete mail-enabled objects such as mailbox-enabled users or mail-enabled groups.

Outlook Clients   Outlook clients require access to Active Directory global catalog servers to retrieve information about the global address lists as well as individual recipient information. In Exchange 2010, this access is now proxied through the Client Access server role (but is still required). Outlook clients connect to Exchange Client Access servers for mailbox access.

Controlling Mailbox Growth

As users have become more savvy and competent at using Outlook and the features of Exchange, and email messages themselves have become more complex, the need for email storage has grown. Back in the days of Exchange 4.0, an organization that gave its users a 25 MB mailbox was considered generous. With Exchange 2003, a typical user's mailbox may have a storage limit of 300 to 500 MB, with power users and VIPs requiring even more. At TechEd 2006, Exchange gurus were tossing about the idea that in the future a default mailbox limit would be closer to 2 GB as users start incorporating Unified Messaging features. Current discussions now look forward to and assume 10 GB mailboxes within the next few years.

We all see users with mailbox sizes in the gigabyte range, but is your organization prepared for a typical user with a 2 GB mailbox size limit? What sort of concerns will you face when your average user has 5 GB or even 10 GB of content (not just email!) in his mailbox?

Certainly the need for more disk storage will be the first factor that organizations need to consider. However, disk storage is reasonably cheap, and many larger organizations that are supporting thousands of mailbox users on a single mailbox server already have more disk space than they can practically use. This is due to the fact that they require more disk spindles to accommodate the number of simultaneous I/Os per second (IOPS) that are required by a large number of users. While previous versions of Exchange were primarily *performance-bound*, meaning that they would require more drive performance before they required more disk capacity, Exchange 2007 and now Exchange 2010 have solidly pushed that to being *capacity-bound*. With the performance characteristics and capacities of modern drives, it becomes feasible to economically provision Exchange storage in support of large mailboxes.

For more administrators with large amounts of mail storage, the primary concern they face is the ability to quickly and efficiently restore data in the event of a failure. These administrators are often faced with service level agreements that bind them to maximum restoration times. In even the most optimal circumstances, a 300 GB mailbox database will take some time to restore from streaming backup media

As mailbox sizes and database sizes continue to grow, streaming backups are going to become impractical both from the perspective of time to perform a backup but also from the time it would take to restore a backup from a tape. Snapshot or Volume Shadow Copy services (VSS) backups are going to become a more attractive option to streaming backups. Depending on what you use backups for, it may even be possible and cheaper to simply create multiple copies of the mailbox databases using continuous replication and move away from the traditional backup schedule.

Microsoft recommends that you do not allow an Exchange mailbox database to grow larger than 200 GB unless you are implementing continuous replication technologies in Exchange 2010. If you use Exchange Server 2010 database availability groups to replicate databases to multiple severs, the maximum database size recommendation goes up (way up) to 2 TB. However, the maximum supported database size is actually 64 TB. If you require more than the maximum recommend database storage, Exchange 2010 Standard Edition allows you to have up to 5 mailbox databases and Exchange 2010 Enterprise Edition allows you to have up to 100.

The solution in the past was to restrain the user community by preventing them from keeping all of the mail data that they might require on the mail server. This was done by imposing low mailbox limits, implementing message archival requirements, keeping deleted items for only a few days, and keeping deleted mailboxes for only a few days.

However, as Unified Messaging data now starts to arrive in a user's mailbox and users have additional mechanisms for accessing the data stored in their mailbox, keeping mail data around longer is going to be a demand and a requirement for your user community. The Exchange 2010 archive mailbox feature will also drive the need for more storage.

Personal Folders or PST Files

The Outlook personal folder or PST file can be the very bane of your existence. Outlook allows users to create a local database in which they can create folders and archive email. Although this seems like a good feature on the surface, there are a few downsides:

◆ Once data is in a user's PST file, you, as the server administrator, have lost control of it. If you ever had to find all copies of a certain message, perhaps for a lawsuit, you would be out of luck. PSTs can become a management and security nightmare as data is suddenly distributed all over your network.

◆ The data in PST files take up more space than the corresponding data on the server.

◆ The default location for a PST is the local portion of the user's profile; this means it is stored on the local hard disk of their computer and is not backed up.

◆ PST files can get corrupted, become misplaced, or even lost entirely. PSTs are not designed for access over a network connection; they're meant to be on the local hard drive, which wastes space as well as complicates the backup and management scenarios.

◆ For older versions of Outlook, performance when accessing PST files is not very good once a PST file is around 1 GB or larger. For Outlook 2007 SP2 and later, PST files up to 5 GB provide a good performance but may suffer as the file size increases above 5 GB.

Email Archiving

Sometimes, managing a mail server seems like a constant race between IT and users to keep users from letting their mailbox run out of space. Users are pack rats and generally want to keep everything. If there is a business reason for them to do so, you should look at ways to expand your available storage to accommodate them.

However, as databases become larger and larger, the Exchange server will be more difficult to manage. You might start requiring hundreds and hundreds of gigabytes (or even terabytes) of storage for email databases. Worse still, backups and data recovery take longer.

This is where email archiving becomes useful. The last time we counted, there were several dozen companies in the business of supplying email archiving tools and services. Archiving products all have a lot of functions in common, including the ability to keep data long term in the email archival, to allow the users to search for their own data, and to allow authorized users to search the entire archive.

If you look at how email is archived, archive systems generally come in one of three flavors:

◆ Systems that depend on journaling to automatically forward every email sent or received by specified users on to the archive system.

◆ Systems that perform a scheduled MAPI "crawl" of specified mailboxes, looking for messages that are eligible to be moved or copied to the archive.

◆ Systems that move data to the archive by copying the log files from the production mailbox servers and then replaying the logs in to the archive. This is called log shipping.

Each of these methods has its advantages and disadvantages with respect to using storage, providing a complete archive, and dealing with performance overhead.

Microsoft has introduced a new email archiving feature in Exchange Server 2010 that follows a different approach from third-party archive tools. For any user who require email archival, an archive mailbox is created for that user. As email ages past a certain point, the mail is moved from the active mailbox to the archive mailbox. The user can still access and search the archive mailbox from Outlook Web App or Outlook, though. The email data remains on the Exchange server and thus does not require an additional email archival infrastructure.

DOES IT MATTER HOW YOU ARCHIVE?

Every archival vendor is going to tell you how their product is best and give you long technical reasons why their approach is so much better than the competition's. The dirty little secret is that all three approaches have their pros and cons:

Journaling is based on SMTP. If content doesn't run across SMTP, it won't get journaled and thus won't get archived. Journaling is great for capturing messaging and calendaring traffic that involve multiple parties or external entities, but it won't capture what happens to messages and other mailbox data once they're in the mailbox. Journaling can also place additional load on the Hub Transport servers, depending on the amount and type of messaging traffic your users generate.

MAPI crawling can only capture changes at certain intervals; it can't capture every single change, even though it overcomes many of the limitations of journaling. For example, if one user sends a message to another in violation of policy and both hard delete their copy of the message before the next crawl interval, that message won't be detected and archived. The more often you schedule the crawl, the more of a performance impact your mailbox servers will suffer.

Log shipping is the best of all options; it captures every transaction and change, allowing you to capture the entire history of each object while offloading the performance hit from your Exchange servers. However, the Exchange product team does not like the concept of log shipping and tries to discourage its use — mainly because there are vendors who try to inject data back into Exchange by modifying logs. This, needless to say, results in mailbox data that won't be supported by Microsoft. Microsoft does not support Exchange servers that are using any type of third-party log shipping solution.

Messaging-Enabled Applications

Microsoft Office enables messaging in many word processing and spreadsheet applications. For example, when you install the Outlook client on your computer, Microsoft's Office products such as Word and Excel are enabled for electronic messaging. Let's say you want to send a Word document. You can select the Routing Recipient option from the application's File ➤ Send To menu. An electronic routing slip pops up. You then add addresses to the slip from your Exchange address books or from your Outlook contacts, select the routing method you want to use, and set other attributes for the route. Finally, you add the routing slip to the document with a click of the Add Slip button and ship it off to others using options on the File ➤ Send To menu.

FIGURE 2.17
Microsoft Word
messaging integration

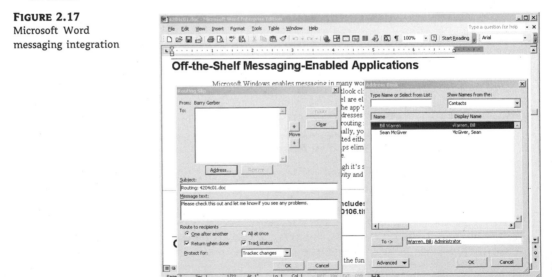

As you can see in Figure 2.17, a file can be routed either sequentially or all at once to each address you selected. Routing sequentially helps eliminate problems associated with multiple users editing the same file at the same time. With applications such as Microsoft Word that keep track of each person's comments and changes, once the document has been routed, the original author can read the comments and incorporate or not incorporate them as she sees fit.

Although it's simple, application-based messaging can significantly improve user productivity and speed up a range of business processes.

Objects

Object embedding and linking further enhance the functionality of the Exchange messaging system. Take a close look at Figure 2.18. Yes, the message includes an Excel spreadsheet and chart. The person who sent the message simply selected Object from the Insert menu that appears on every Exchange message. Then he specified a file with an existing spreadsheet as the source of the object to be inserted into the message. The Outlook client then inserted the file into the message as an object.

FIGURE 2.18
Object embedding permits sophisticated messaging-enabled applications.

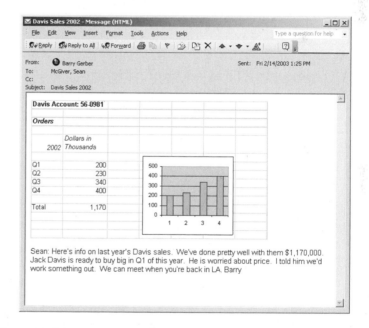

The recipient can see the spreadsheet as a graphic image in the message, as shown in the figure. When the recipient double-clicks the graphic image, Excel is launched inside the message, and Excel's menus and toolbars replace those of the message (see Figure 2.19). In essence, the message becomes an Excel document.

The Excel spreadsheet is fully editable if Excel is available to the recipient. Without Excel, the recipient can only look at the spreadsheet in graphic image form. The graphic image changes when someone else edits the spreadsheet in Excel.

You can also insert in a message an object that is a link to a file that was created by an application such as Word or Excel. As with other kinds of object insertion, your recipient sees a graphic picture of the contents of the file and can edit the file by double-clicking the graphic picture. Links are a bit more flexible, because they allow users to work with files stored on a shared disk. With inserted objects, users work with a file embedded in the message itself.

FIGURE 2.19
An embedded Excel
spreadsheet object

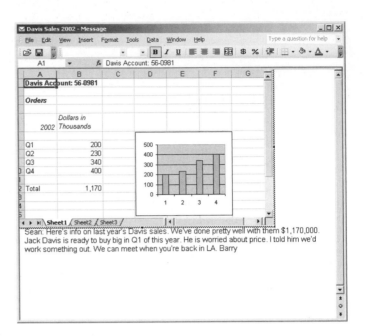

Technically, this capability is provided not by the Exchange server but by the Outlook client. However, OWA includes some of this same rich functionality, and the Exchange database and protocols are certainly built to support it, so many users consider it a feature of the Exchange system.

Public Folders

Public folders are for common access to messages and files. Files can be dragged from file-access interfaces, such as Windows Explorer, and dropped into public folders. The whole concept of public folders has many organizations in a quandary as they try to figure out the best place for these collaborative applications. Increasingly, applications that were once "best suited" for a public folder are now better suited for web pages or portals such as SharePoint workspaces. Although the whole concept of public folders is perceived as being deemphasized in Exchange 2007 and Exchange 2010, Microsoft continues to support public folders and many organizations will continue to find useful applications for public folders for the foreseeable future.

You can set up sorting rules for a public folder so that items in the folder are organized by a range of attributes, such as the name of the sender or creator of the item or the date that the item was placed in the folder. Items in a public folder can be sorted by conversation threads. Public folders can also contain applications built on existing products such as Word or Excel or built with Exchange or Outlook Forms Designer, client or server scripting, or the Exchange API set. You can use public folders to replace many of the maddening paper-based processes that abound in every organization.

For easy access to items in a public folder, you can use a *folder link*. You can send a link to a folder in a message. When someone navigates to the folder and double-clicks a file, the file opens. Everyone who receives the message works with the same linked attachment, so everyone reads and can modify the same file. As with document routing, applications such as Microsoft Word can keep track of each person's changes to and comments on file contents.

Of course, your users will have to learn to live with the fact that only one person can edit an application file at a time. Most modern end-user applications warn the user when someone else is using the file and if so allow the user to open a read-only copy of the file, which of course can't be edited.

Electronic Forms

Exchange Server 2010 continues to support forms created with the Outlook Forms Designer (OFD). You can use OFD to build information-gathering forms containing a number of the bells and whistles that you're accustomed to in Windows applications. These include drop-down list boxes, check boxes, fill-in text forms, tab dialog controls, and radio buttons (see Figure 2.20).

FIGURE 2.20
Electronic forms

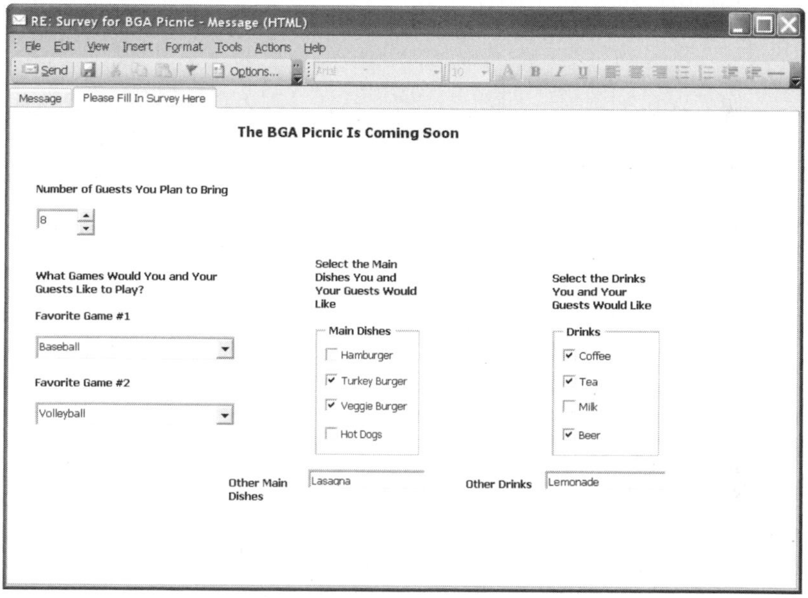

OFD, which is easy enough for nontechnical types to use, includes a variety of messaging-oriented fields and actions. For example, you can choose to include a preaddressed To field in a form so that users of the form can easily mail it off to the appropriate recipient. (The preaddressed To field for the form shown in Figure 2.20 is on the page with the tab marked Message, which is not visible in this figure.) When you've designed a form, you can make it available to all users or only to select users; users can access the completed form simply by selecting it while in an Outlook client.

The Bottom Line

Understand email fundamentals.   To gain the best advantage from Exchange Server 2010, you should have a good grounding in general email applications and principles.

Master It   What two application models have email programs traditionally used? Which one does Exchange Server use? Can you name an example of the other model?

List email administration duties. Installing an Exchange Server system is just the first part of the job. Once it's in place, it needs to be maintained. Be familiar with the various duties and concerns that will be involved with the care and feeding of Exchange.

Master It What are the various types of duties that a typical Exchange administrator will expect to perform?

Explain Exchange Server history. Exchange Server 2010 is the seventh and latest version of Exchange, starting from Exchange 4.0 in 1996. Although it introduces some new concepts and makes some radical changes from previous versions, several core concepts have stayed the same.

Master It The Extensible Storage Engine (ESE) is the heart of Exchange mailbox storage. Describe its basic architecture. Describe one past feature of the ESE that is no longer present in Exchange Server 2010.

Chapter 3

Standards and Protocols

Email didn't just spring forth one day from the heads of the founders of the Internet fully formed and fully functional. Although few people wholly appreciate it, the global email system we take for granted every day is in a constant state of evolution. Countless numbers of systems participate in millions of daily connections, with no two the same.

Every day, you and other people around the world effortlessly send and receive email. By this point in time there have been hundreds, perhaps thousands, of email clients and servers that have been, are being, and will be used, each with different design philosophies, features, and underlying programming languages.

For these servers and clients to interoperate, some level of standardization must exist. Although modern email systems are overwhelmingly based on Simple Mail Transfer Protocol (SMTP) and a handful of related protocols and technologies, that wasn't always the case.

In this chapter, you will learn to:

◆ Understand the components of an email system

◆ Identify the three major components of Active Directory

◆ Understand common protocols and standards used by Microsoft Exchange

Components of an Email System

In Chapter 2, "Introduction to Email Administration," we discussed the two general application models used by email systems. No matter the specifics of application and server, a handful of components and roles, shown in Figure 3.1, are involved in any email transmission:

Mail User Agent (MUA) This is the component that the user directly interacts with. If we were to use a postal metaphor, the MUA is roughly the equivalent of your local mailbox at the end of the driveway. Traditionally, the MUA has been a stand-alone client application such as Outlook; however, a web-based client such as Outlook Web App also offers MUA functionality, even though it is technically a server-side application.

Mail Retrieval Agent (MRA) The MRA, closely related to the MUA, is the component that handles retrieving messages from the main mail store. Depending on which protocols you are using, such as the Post Office Protocol (POP) or Internet Mailbox Access Protocol (IMAP), you can't just rely on new messages to be pushed to your MUA; something needs to pull them down for you. Typically, the MRA is not a separate component in modern systems, but a set of additional routines in the MUA that supports message retrieval. In an Exchange 2010 system, this functionality is supplied either by the Outlook client or by Outlook Web App when configured to pull mail from an external account into the mailbox. Outlook Web App leaves all mail on the server and merely serves as an interface for reading or sending email, so nothing is really being pulled off the server. Outlook can either manipulate mail directly on the mail server or make a copy of the mail on to the local hard drive of the client (in the case of Outlook, in local cache mode.)

FIGURE 3.1
Components of an email system

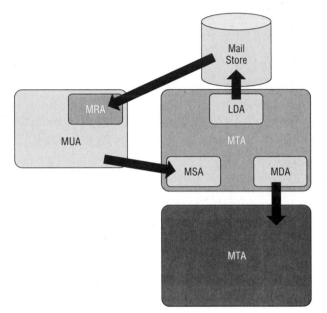

Mail Transport Agent (MTA)   If the MUA is the local mailbox, the mail transport agent (MTA) is the Post Office infrastructure connecting different towns and cities with one another. The MTA is responsible for accepting messages from other systems such as MUAs and MTAs, routing them, and ensuring their delivery to their recipients. Messages typically travel though two MTAs — the sender's and the recipient's (unless, of course, they share an MTA). In an Exchange 2010 system, the Hub Transport and Edge Transport roles fill the MTA role.

Mail Submission Agent (MSA)   Just as the MRA is a variant role often performed by the MUA, the mail submission agent (MSA) is a specialized form of the MTA. It's adapted to accept mail submissions from the MUA, introduce them into the mail flow, and handle any specialized processing that may be required. In Exchange 2010, this function is handled both in the Client Access server role via messaging application programming interfaces (MAPIs) and remote procedure calls (RPCs) — when receiving messages from Outlook, Outlook Web Access, Exchange Web Services, or mobile devices using Exchange ActiveSync — as well as through SMTP via the client receive connector on the Hub Transport role — when receiving messages from third-party clients.

Mail Delivery Agent (MDA)   What's missing from this picture? In this case, it's the equivalent of the local Post Office (or, if you prefer, the mailroom in the big corporation) — the mail delivery agent (MDA) or local delivery agent (LDA). Once the incoming message has been delivered to the proper collection of systems, the MDA/LDA is responsible for ensuring it's been put into the correct mailbox. In an Exchange system, this functionality is handled by a component of the Hub Transport role as messages are passed to the various Mailbox roles.

Each email system can use a wide variety of solutions to implement these functions. Some applications, such as Exchange, incorporate all these functions into a single end-to-end offering, whereas others provide just one piece of the puzzle, relying on other applications to provide the missing functionality. Even when using a complete solution, however, you can always mix and match pieces to provide functionality (such as using a third-party client for MUA functionality, or an edge mail appliance as an MTA to other mail systems). To ensure that these implementations work together, a series of standards have been developed over time.

Defining the Standards

When you have this many moving parts in a system — especially when they can be created, implemented, and configured by anyone — it helps if you define how the various parts work together. Although trying to create a true central authority for the Internet has proven to be a futile exercise, over the years the Internet community has evolved a method for describing, proposing, discussing, and documenting the various protocols that are in use across the world: a document known as the request for comment (RFC).

RFCs began as informal memos among members of the academic teams that invented and programmed the hardware and software used to develop the Advanced Research Projects Agency Network (ARPANET), which was an early predecessor of the Internet. Whenever a team member wanted to suggest a new feature or protocol to the rest of the team, they'd write up an RFC describing their idea as a formal invitation for feedback. Over the years, as the ARPANET grew into the core of the Internet, RFCs expanded in scope to become more formal definitions and descriptions, sometimes retroactive.

Taken in total, the RFC archives provide a fascinating history of the Internet, although not all of the various technologies that have been used were documented through RFCs. Many of these alternatives, such as the X.400 standard for message handling systems, were much more complicated and harder to implement than the systems described in the RFCs. In the end, the commercially developed X.400 standard and accompanying X.500 directory service protocols lost to SMTP, Lightweight Directory Access Protocol (LDAP), and Domain Name System (DNS). The latter protocols were all freely available in RFCs, allowing anyone with the time and interest to develop their own implementations.

LIVING DOCUMENTS

RFCs are not static; they can contain errors or even just erroneous assumptions. As the world has changed, older RFCs are often updated, modified, or even superseded by newer RFCs. You can examine any of the RFCs online at www.rfc-editor.org.

As you read through the RFCs, you will see many prescriptive statements. You may even find configurations or software functions that are dictated (or forbidden) but that your organization is using. Sometimes you will have good reasons for a specific congiuration, but sometimes a non-standard configuration may be set through ignorance. However, before you blindly make the changes in order to be RFC compliant, you should remember the ultimate rule: local policy trumps RFC.

For example, one common spam-fighting mechanism is to check the DNS records for remote SMTP servers that connect to your servers to see if the reverse and forward DNS lookups

> match. If not, many systems choose to regard that message source as a potential spam source and refuse to accept messages from those systems. Strictly speaking, this behavior violates RFCs. Practically, it can be a valuable spam-reduction technique, depending on your traffic patterns and characteristic mail partners. If the reason behind a particular recommendation doesn't meet your needs, don't use it; if you don't know the reason, ask.

Active Directory: The Foundation of Exchange 2010

Now that you understand the components of a typical messaging system and how they are defined, let's talk about the single biggest dependency that Exchange 2010 has: Windows Active Directory. Although the first several versions of Exchange used their own integrated directory service, modern Exchange implementations rely on the unified Active Directory implementation provided by Windows Server.

Active Directory is a big topic with lots of moving parts, so we're only going to skim the surface here. There are three key protocols, however, that you need to know about, far more than we have room to talk about here:

- The Domain Name System (DNS), which Exchange uses to look up other servers and services within the Active Directory domains and forests in the organization

- The Lightweight Directory Access Protocol (LDAP), which Exchange uses to find key configuration information for organization-wide objects, as well as to discover users and other mail-enabled objects

- Authentication protocols (such as Kerberos), which provide a central and secure mutual authentication mechanism not just for users, but for each machine in the Active Directory domains and forests

To be an effective Exchange administrator, you'll need to have a good working understanding of Active Directory. We recommend the following resources:

Active Directory Cookbook, 3rd Edition, by Laura Hunter and Robbie Allen (O'Reilly, 2008)

Mastering Active Directory for Windows Server 2008 by John A. Price, Brad Price, and Scott Fenstermacher (Sybex, 2008)

Finding Messaging Hosts with the Domain Name System

In the early days of the Internet, all of the hosts on the network were maintained in a single file called HOSTS. If you wanted to add a new computer to the Internet, you called the guy who maintained the file and asked him to add your computer's name and IP address. Periodically, everyone on the Internet downloaded the latest version of the HOSTS file.

You can see how that would be a bit difficult today; the file would be huge, slow to search, and changing constantly. Plus it would require a massive team of people to maintain it. In 1984, a standard was proposed and adopted to allow name resolution by creating a hierarchical namespace where different owners of the namespace would be responsible for maintaining their own hosts.

The hierarchy of this name resolution system is based on domains. The top of the hierarchy is the root and is defined by "`.`" Beneath the root domain are zones, such as `.com`, `.net`, `.edu`, and so forth. Root servers would provide referrals to clients so that they could contact the correct servers that held the information. So, for example, if you own a domain called somorita.com, you can control any hosts in that particular domain. The root servers on the Internet provide referrals to other servers on the Internet and point them to the servers that hold the somorita.com data.

As you may have guessed by now, we are talking about the Domain Name System (DNS); this is documented in RFC 1034. You may be wondering how DNS directly (or indirectly) affects mail servers, though. One obvious way that DNS and Exchange are related is through Active Directory; an Active Directory domain incorporates and relies on DNS. Because Exchange is in turn integrated with Active Directory, it too depends on DNS for name resolution of directory information and mail routing information.

A full discussion of DNS can consume an entire book, but we wanted to discuss a few key DNS record types and terms you should be familiar with.

FULLY QUALIFIED DOMAIN NAMES

Each machine can be referred to by one of at least two names: the short hostname, which is typically the same as the NetBIOS name, and the *fully qualified domain name* (FQDN), which is the hostname plus the full DNS domain suffix. The FQDN uniquely identifies the host on the Internet or within a private intranet.

AN EXAMPLE FQDN

The DNS server for the somorita.com domain has the hostname of dnsserver1 and a FQDN of dnsserver1.somorita.com.

CANONICAL ADDRESSES

Canonical address or hostname records (also called *A* records) are DNS entries that resolve the hostname to a corresponding IP address. A given hostname can have more than one IP address, in the case of a shared hostname or a host with multiple interfaces, and one IP address can have multiple A records pointing to it.

For more information on A records and an overview of the various types of DNS records, see http://en.wikipedia.org/wiki/A_record.

AN EXAMPLE A RECORD

The mail server for the somorita.com domain has the hostname of exch01.somorita.com and an IP address of 192.168.254.117:

```
$ORIGIN somorita.com.
exch01  IN  A     192.168.254.117
```

ALIASES

An alias record (also called a *CNAME*) usually points to a canonical address record. This gives you the ability to define an alias hostname for one or more systems (perhaps a user-friendly name such as mail for a farm of Client Access servers so users don't know about or have to remember the individual hostnames of the servers in the farm).

While you can point a CNAME to another CNAME, chaining aliases in this fashion can quickly get confusing and is generally discouraged.

For more information, see http://en.wikipedia.org/wiki/CNAME_record.

AN EXAMPLE CNAME RECORD

The mail server for the somorita.com domain has the hostname of exch01.somorita.com but has an alias of mail.somorita.com:

```
$ORIGIN somorita.com.
exch01  IN   A     192.168.254.117
mail    IN   CNAME exch01.somorita.com.
```

AREN'T THOSE BACKWARD?

We have talked with many people who are confused by DNS terminology for canonical addresses and aliases. It can be counterintuitive and hard to remember which record is supposed to point to an IP address and which one points to a hostname. The key thing to remember is that the DNS resource record is listed from left to right and that it's listing an attribute the domain name *has*, not an attribute the domain name *is*:

```
$ORIGIN somorita.com.
exch01  IN   A     192.168.254.117
mail    IN   CNAME exch01.somorita.com.
```

If we were reading these records aloud, we would say, "The domain name exch01.somorita .com has an IP address of 192.168.254.117, and the domain name mail.somorita.com has a canonical name of exch01.somortia.com." We have heard it said other ways, but doing so is what causes the confusion. Remember: the left-hand side of the record is the domain label, and that label *has* one or more types of records associated with it. Keep that difference in mind, and DNS will become a lot less confusing to you.

REVERSE POINTERS

A pointer record (PTR), also known as a reverse lookup, maps a given IP address back to a corresponding domain name. PTR records are not added specifically to your domain, but rather to a domain name that represents an IP subnet. PTR records allow clients to take the IP address of an Internet host and look up the name associated with the IP address.

All of these reverse domains are found in DNS in the in-addr.arpa domain; portions of this domain are delegated to companies that have been assigned blocks of IP addresses. PTR records are usually created and managed by the owner of the IP subnet block, not the manager for a domain like somorita.com.

It's not as commonly known, but PTR records can point to a CNAME record instead of an A record. This allows the maintainer of a reverse DNS zone to delegate the pointer lookup to a zone under someone else's control. Many ISPs, for example, use this technique to allow customers with only a handful of addresses to maintain control over both the forward and reverse DNS lookup information of their hosts without returning to the ISP helpdesk to update the PTR records when hostnames change. This type of solution can be helpful if you have external systems that refuse to accept messages from your system because your reverse DNS is not in order.

For more information, see http://en.wikipedia.org/wiki/Reverse_DNS_lookup.

AN EXAMPLE PTR RECORD

The IP address 192.168.254.117 has been assigned to the mail server for the somorita.com domain, exch01.somorita.com:

```
$ORIGIN 254.168.192.in-addr.arpa.
117    IN    PTR    exch01.somorita.com.
```

MAIL EXCHANGERS

The Mail Exchanger (MX) record is the DNS entry for your domain that allows mail servers on the Internet to look up the hostnames of systems that accept mail for your domain. These DNS records point to public address (A) records of the SMTP servers that accept mail for your organization; this may be your Hub Transport or Edge Transport server, a third-party message hygiene system, a simple SMTP relay server, or even a third-party managed provider. To provide some degree of redundancy and availability, you can define multiple MX records for each domain, and you can assign a priority value to each of them.

You can use the nslookup command to look up and validate MX records for your domain. Here is an example of looking up the servers that accept mail for apple.com:

```
nslookup -q=mx apple.com
Server:   dnsserver1.somorita.com
Address:  192.168.254.71
Non-authoritative answer: apple.com
MX preference = 100, mail exchanger = mail-in3.apple.com apple.com
MX preference = 10, mail exchanger = mail-in11.apple.com apple.com
MX preference = 10, mail exchanger = mail-in12.apple.com apple.com
MX preference = 20, mail exchanger = mail-in1.apple.com apple.com
MX preference = 20, mail exchanger = mail-in2.apple.com
```

Notice in the MX records that the preference values are different for different records.

Mail servers are always supposed to choose the record with the lowest preference value first and then only use the records with the higher preference values if the lower ones do not respond. If two or more records are equal, the sending mail server is supposed to rotate between them to provide a degree of load balancing. This is covered in Chapter 27, "Internet and Email."

For more information, see http://en.wikipedia.org/wiki/MX_record.

AN EXAMPLE MX RECORD

The administrator for the somorita.com domain wishes all incoming mail to be handled by the exch01.somorita.com host:

```
$ORIGIN somorita.com.
@       IN   MX 10 exch01.somorita.com.
exch01  IN   A     192.168.254.117
```

SENDER POLICY FRAMEWORK

Sender Policy Framework (SPF) records are special DNS records that help a receiving mail server determine whether the mail server that originally sent a message is authorized to send mail for that domain. These records are used both by SPF and Sender ID–compliant systems. Although the SPF system proposes a separate record type (SPF, or type 99), the standards also permit the use of the common text (TXT) records. Most organizations that publish SPF or Sender ID policies use TXT records to do so. SPF is often billed as an antispam system, but it is better defined as an antispoofing system.

For more information on the SPF system and records, see www.openspf.org.

AN EXAMPLE SPF RECORD

The administrator for the somorita.com domain has defined the following SPF policy:

```
$ORIGIN somorita.com.
@       IN   TXT   "v=spf1 mx -all"
```

SERVICE LOCATION

Service location records (SRV) records are DNS records that help a client locate a specific service type that is provided for a domain, including service-specific information such as which specific protocol and network port it is using.

Active Directory publishes SRV records for a number of different services, including enumerating Active Directory sites and locating global catalog servers. Since Exchange relies on global catalog servers and domain controllers for proper function, it will regularly perform lookups to determine which controllers exist in its local AD site. There might be multiple global catalog SRV records for a particular domain, as well as a separate listing of domain controllers by site.

Another good example of the use of an SRV record is the option to use SRV records with Outlook 2007 Service Pack 1 to publish an Autodiscover URL on a nonstandard hostname. If you don't know what we're talking about, don't worry; it'll all become clear in Chapter 7, "Namespaces and the Autodiscovery Service."

For more information, see http://en.wikipedia.org/wiki/SRV_record.

SPLIT BRAIN DNS

Split brain DNS systems are systems that have two or more different views of the same DNS namespace. This, in turn, requires two or more sets of DNS servers that host the same DNS namespace (or a DNS server that can handle multiple versions of the same namespace).

Usually one set of DNS servers hosts the domain name for an internal network and is used to resolve the hostnames to internal IP addresses, while the other set is used to resolve IP addresses for hosts on the Internet. This configuration is commonly used when the organization's public and private domain name are the same and the organization does not want internal host information available to Internet users. It is also commonly used to provide a fast, limited view of specific DNS information to servers in a perimeter network.

Real World Scenario

IMPLEMENTING SPLIT BRAIN DNS

Company BCDE implemented their Active Directory DNS domain name so that it matched exactly their Internet domain name: bcde.com. This seemed both convenient and logical.

The company used the same DNS servers for both their Internet name resolution (such as www.bcde.com) as well as their internal server and domain resolution. Sometime after the Active Directory domain was initially deployed a security consultant pointed out several flaws in this design. These included:

◆ The public facing DNS included internal host names and internal infrastructure information such as Active Directory sites and domain controller information.

◆ If the DNS servers were ever compromised by a denial-of-service attack the attack would also affect functionality of the internal servers and workstations.

To address this issue, the company implemented a split brain DNS with two different sets of DNS servers. In their perimeter network, they configured two Internet-facing DNS servers; these servers hosted only the DNS records required by Internet users such as the web server host name (www.bcde.com), mail servers, mail exchanger (MX) records, and sender protection framework (SPF) records.

Internally, the Active Directory domain controllers host the Windows DNS server software; all internal clients and domain controllers use these DNS servers. The DNS manager has to make sure that "external" records such as the company's web server record are also created on the internal network so that internal clients can also access the web server.

DISJOINT DNS NAMESPACE

Machines joined to an Active Directory domain by default are configured with a primary DNS suffix, which is by default the same domain name as the Active Directory domain and its corresponding DNS zone. When the primary DNS suffix for a machine does not match the DNS domain of the Active Directory domain, it is said to have a *disjoint namespace*. While disjoint namespaces are supported under some circumstances, they can cause problems, so be sure these configurations are thoroughly tested. For more information, see

```
http://technet.microsoft.com/library/cc773264.aspx
```

A HOST BY ANY OTHER NAME

These days many servers — especially those that exchange a lot of traffic with the Internet (such as your trusty Exchange servers) — have more than one hostname. For example, an Exchange 2007 Client Access server may be autodiscover.somorita.com, mail.somorita.com, and cas01.somorita.com. These names may point to separate IP addresses, or they may point to the same IP address. They may all be A records; one or more of them may be CNAME records. We regularly see improperly configured DNS records, typically with one of the following errors:

Missing PTR Records   For each A record mapping a FQDN to an IP address, there should be a corresponding PTR record mapping that IP address back to the same FQDN. You can (and should) do this even if that means one IP address has multiple PTR records; this configuration is not only permitted but is best practice. It's not so important to do this for internal transactions between Exchange servers in the same organization, but it is critical to do so to ensure the proper acceptance of your external messages to other organizations.

Improper CNAME Records   DNS aliases are one of the most confusing DNS records types because they have a number of restrictions on their use. They are typically used to make human-friendly hostnames. A CNAME record should always resolve to an A record, *not* a bare IP address or another CNAME record. Also, if you have an existing A record or MX record for a domain name, you can't configure a CNAME record for it. Again, this isn't so important to Exchange servers within the organization, but when you configure CNAMEs externally be aware that if there are any other records for the domain, adding a secondary name will require you to add another A record (and corresponding PTR record) instead of a CNAME.

Improper MX Records MX records are not used within the Exchange organization for intra-Exchange communications; they're present solely for other messaging systems. An MX record should be pointed to an A record, not an IP address and *definitely* not a CNAME record. Doing so can cause embarrassing mail loops on external systems that are trying to send mail to you.

Finding People and Services with Directory Services

One important aspect of messaging systems is how they look up message senders and recipients. Modern Exchange systems rely on Active Directory for this functionality. However, early messaging systems used simple flat-file lookups — typically out of the same files that listed user accounts, such as the passwd files on a Unix system. Flat files quickly got unwieldy for a large number of users, though, so various systems began using alternatives:

♦ Sun's Unix variants offered the Network Information Services (NIS), which provided a shared directory service, including messaging aliases and delivery information, across hundreds or even thousands of hosts within an organization.

♦ Early versions of Windows NT offered the local SAM database — their equivalent of the Unix passwd file — as well as Windows NT domains. NT domains allowed multiple Windows machines to share the same user information, including email addresses.

Other messaging systems often provided tight integration with a corresponding directory service. The OSI networking stack (which, if you remember, included the X.400 messaging transport and system) provided the X.500 directory service. X.500 was a behemoth, requiring a lot of effort to implement, deploy, and maintain.

Although the concept of X.500 was interesting and useful, it was far too complicated to implement in conjunction with SMTP systems. Not even the original versions of Exchange used a full X.500 implementation, but they used many of the same concepts in their built-in proprietary directory service. Messaging systems such as Exchange were not, however, the only systems in need of a fast, flexible, and extensible directory service to provide centralized authentication and configuration lookups for users and applications.

The University of Michigan had an X.500 deployment, but found that there was too much overhead for application developers to use it. At the same time, this central directory implementation proved to have many useful concepts. They took these concepts and the directory service as a back-end store and created a lightweight X.500-like front-end service, offering a simplified API. Thus was born the prototype of what would eventually become known as the Lightweight Directory Access Protocol (LDAP).

LDAP, which provided an extensible and hierarchical data access model that was less rigid (and more customizable) than X.500, proved to be a good complement for a variety of applications, including messaging systems. Today, almost all modern MUAs and MTAs provide the ability to look up contacts, users, and other configuration information from an LDAP-based directory service. Windows Server Active Directory, Novell's Novell Directory Service, and eDirectory products are direct adaptations and extensions of the LDAP standard.

Unlike many of the other common Internet protocols developed through the IETF RFC process, LDAP queries and responses are defined using the ASN.1 grammar. ASN.1 is commonly used in International Telecommunication Union (ITU)-developed protocols as a fundamental building block for structured character encoding, allowing a common definition for data interchange between systems that may use different internal byte orders for representing data. Although LDAP was originally developed outside the RFC process, it has since been described and codified by RFCs, as shown in Table 3.1.

TABLE 3.1:   Core RFCs for LDAP

RFC	TITLE	DESCRIPTION
4510	LDAP: Technical Specification Road Map	An overview of the various RFCs that define LDAP version 3, the current version of LDAP. Released in June 2006; obsoletes all previous versions.
4511	LDAP: The Protocol	The core protocol and data encodings using ASN.1 for programmatic use. Released in June 2006; obsoletes all previous versions.
4512	LDAP: Directory Information Models	The X.500 Directory Information Model, which establishes the directory tree and hierarchy. Released in June 2006; obsoletes all previous versions.
4513	LDAP: Authentication Methods and Security Mechanisms	How LDAP uses SASL and TLS to provide a common framework for authentication and session encryption. Released in June 2006; obsoletes all previous versions.
4514	LDAP: String Representation of Distinguished Names	How LDAP DNs are represented as text strings for human readability. Released in June 2006; obsoletes all previous versions.
4515	LDAP: String Representation of Search Filters	How LDAP search filters are represented as text strings for human readability. Released in June 2006; obsoletes all previous versions.
4516	LDAP: Uniform Resource Locator	How to format LDAP URLs and extension mechanisms. Released in June 2006; obsoletes all previous versions.
4517	LDAP: Syntaxes and Matching Rules	Comparison rules and matching rules for syntax validation of LDAP objects and values. Released in June 2006; obsoletes all previous versions.
4518	LDAP: Internationalized String Preparation	Rules for performing consistent string matching. Released in June 2006; obsoletes all previous versions.
4519	LDAP: Schema for User Applications	A basic schema intended for use with multiple directory services. Released in June 2006; obsoletes all previous versions.

LDAP objects are organized in a hierarchical fashion. The distinguished name (DN) is the key identifier for LDAP objects; it uniquely identifies the position of any object within a specific directory store and provides a unique fully qualified name for that object. The DN is in turn built up from comma-separated substrings derived by each level of the directory hierarchy, moving in order from most specific to least specific, as shown in Table 3.2.

ALL I WANT IS LDAP!

By using LDAP, a distributed mail system can efficiently route and process millions of messages with minimal administrative overhead. Exchange Server relies heavily on Active Directory to do its work. However, Active Directory isn't just an application-generic directory service; it includes the overhead of specific objects and schemas that are useful to run an Active Directory forest or domain, but may clutter or be a security risk in specific situations.

Microsoft Active Directory Lightweight Directory Services (AD-LDS), formerly known as Active Directory Application Mode (ADAM), is an application-focused LDAP implementation designed to allow easy integration with existing Active Directory implementations while limiting the scope and type of information. Exchange Server 2007 and 2010 use AD-LDS to provide a secure LDAP implementation for the Edge Transport role.

TABLE 3.2:   Common LDAP DNs from an Active Directory Domain

DN	OBJECT
CN=Users, DC=somorita, DC=com	The built-in Users container
CN=Administrator, CN=Users, DC=somorita, DC=com	The Administrator user
OU=Domain Controllers, DC=somorita, DC=com	The Domain Controllers OU
CN=DC01, OU=Domain Controllers, DC=somorita, DC=com	The server DC01

Kerberos

Kerberos is the third key technology for Active Directory, which is funny if you know where Kerberos got its name: from Cerberus, the giant three-headed dog that kept watch over Hades. Just like Cerberus, Kerberos helps ensure that only the people who are supposed to can access Active Directory resources.

Kerberos was initially developed during the 1980s at MIT as part of Project Athena, an educational-focused distributed computing environment. (Another technological offspring of Project Athena, known as the X Window System, provides Unix systems with the framework for a graphical user interface.) The first public version of Kerberos was v4, published by MIT in 1987. The current version, Kerberos v5, was published in September 1993 in RFC 1510.

Kerberos was designed to allow the various workstations and servers in this environment to securely function and to allow users to securely pass credentials to network resources over an untrusted network:

◆ Unlike other authentication mechanisms such as the legacy Windows NTLM, Kerberos provides *mutual authentication* between all computers in a transaction; NTLM assumes that the servers are trustworthy and never explicitly allows the initiating system to verify that the server it has connected to is in fact genuine. This is a weakness an attacker can exploit under certain conditions.

◆ Each computer, user, and network-aware application participating in a Kerberos-enabled network is represented by a *security principal*. These principals request tokens from a central Key Distribution Center (KDC) and can then pass those tokens on to other systems. The practical upshot is that each principal must only have a trust relationship with the KDC.

◆ Another core Kerberos principal is that credentials must never be passed over the network. The KDC and all associated principals are known as the *realm*; every principal in the realm can leverage its trust relationship with the KDC to securely authenticate itself to other resources in the realm without sending credentials over the network. In Active Directory, each domain controller acts as a KDC, preventing the KDC from being a single point of failure. Additionally, each server can validate a given token without calling a domain controller to validate the token.

◆ Kerberos realms can form trust relationships with other realms, allowing principals in one realm to access resources in another realm. In Windows Active Directory, the forest is equivalent to the Kerberos realm. Multiple Active Directory forests can be linked through forest trusts, and third-party Kerberos implementations can also be linked through Kerberos realm trusts. This allows interoperability with non-Windows environments and operating systems.

◆ Kerberos allows the concept of *delegation*, where applications and services can access other network resources on behalf of a client within the client's security context, without having to have the client's credentials. This is not possible with legacy authentication protocols and helps prevent the dissemination and proliferation of client credentials.

This is all well and good, but why do we care about Kerberos in Exchange 2010? The answer is simple: it's the default authentication mechanism in Active Directory. Depending on how complex you make your Exchange 2010 deployment (and how many forests you need to join into a single organization), you will be relying more heavily on proper Kerberos functionality than in previous versions of Exchange. Even mailbox access protocols like POP3 and IMAP have been made Kerberos aware ("Kerberized"). Exchange servers within the organization use Kerberos-authenticated SMTP to securely transmit all traffic by default, falling back to NTLM only when there is a problem that prevents the use of Kerberos and when security policies permit.

PREVENTING REPLAY ATTACKS

While Kerberos presents a robust design, there's one potential weakness that could allow an attacker to record a network session and later replay the relevant parts to gain illicit access to resources. This type of attack, known as a *replay attack*, is prevented by using an *authenticator* in the network packets. This authenticator is tied to the current network time and is only valid for a short window — by default, five minutes.

One of the consequences of this is that all of the computers in the Active Directory forest, as well as those in any other trusted forests or third-party Kerberos realms, must share the same time source and be configured to be within five minutes of each other. Computers whose clocks are not in synchronization are said to be *skewed*. Within a domain, the Windows Time

> Synchronization service will usually take care of time skew, although use of a more robust protocol such as the Simple Network Time Protocol (SNTP) or Network Time Protocol (NTP) is preferred, especially when coordinating time between multiple realms.
>
> If you need to change the acceptable level of time skew, refer to Microsoft Knowledge Base article 837361, "Kerberos Protocol Registry Entries and KDC Configuration Keys in Windows Server 2003," at http://support.microsoft.com/kb/837361.

Other Key Technologies Used by Exchange

We next turn our attention to several fundamental technologies that Exchange 2010 relies on. You don't have to be an expert on every single one of the following technologies, but you should have some idea of how they work and how they fit together.

Moving Messages with the Simple Mail Transport Protocol

Although you could argue that the mailbox is the most important part of a mail system — that's where messages are stored, after all — we have always held a different opinion. Without the ability to send and receive messages, a messaging system is worthless. To us, the message transfer agent (MTA) is the living heart and soul of any email system. With modern systems, the key inter-system transport is the Simple Mail Transport Protocol (SMTP), and Exchange 2010 is no different.

The original versions of Exchange were built around the International Telecommunication Union (ITU) X.400 standard as part of the OSI network protocol family. While Exchange used X.400 over TCP/IP as the primary transport to other organizations, internally it used a variant optimized for Exchange-to-Exchange server communications. These first versions of Exchange offered SMTP as a foreign connector service for messaging systems on the Internet, requiring messages to be converted from OSI message formatting to the equivalent Internet formats. These conversions were complicated and often a source of problems, because the various properties didn't map exactly.

With Exchange 2000, Microsoft made crucial changes to the architecture of Exchange organizations, including a switch from the proprietary X.400 variant to SMTP. There are two advantages to using SMTP as the internal transport:

- As the name SMTP implies, SMTP is a simple protocol. It is less complicated, and therefore much easier to implement, than X.400. As organizations started using Exchange 2000, the vast majority of Exchange organizations were transmitting messages with other Internet-connected organizations using SMTP, so in most cases, there was a performance advantage for removing the layers of message conversion.

- SMTP is an open framework that allows additional vendor extensions to be easily added. This was important, because Exchange still required a large amount of additional information and functionality not present in standard SMTP. Exchange 2000 servers, therefore, speak standard SMTP to other mail servers, but a special superset of SMTP to other Exchange servers in the organization.

The X.400-based transport wasn't totally removed at this time, however; it still existed as the X.400 connector, intended to allow connections both to external X.400 organizations as well as legacy Exchange organizations. Since Exchange internally tracked both sets of properties, these connectors no longer required the same degree of message conversion.

In each successive release of Exchange, additional work has been done to implement more of the standard SMTP extensions and remove dependency on the X.400 transport code except for interoperability with previous versions. In Exchange 2007, the legacy X.400 transport code was removed, as were many of the legacy Exchange-specific SMTP extensions. Exchange 2007 and 2010 use standard technologies such as Transport Layer Security (TLS) and Kerberos to secure SMTP sessions.

Table 3.3 summarizes some of the important mail transport RFCs you should know as an Exchange 2010 administrator or professional.

Part of what makes SMTP so relatively simple is that it isn't based on any complicated transport schemes; at its heart, it is a *store-and-forward* system. Once an SMTP system accepts responsibility for a message, it attempts to deliver it to the next best hop that it knows about. An SMTP connection, in its simplest form, is easy to understand. It involves just two systems: the client, which opens the connection so that it can submit email, and the server, which accepts inbound connections and determines if it can accept the message that has been submitted.

This is what a typical session, sending a message from `sender@client.tld` to `recipient@server.tld`, would look like:

```
   {The client connects to the server}
01 S: 220 smtp.server.tld ESMTP mail system ready
   C: HELO desktop.client.tld
   S: 250 Hello desktop.client.tld, I am glad to meet you
02 C: MAIL FROM:<sender@client.tld>
   S: 250 Sender ok
03 C: RCPT TO:<recipient@server.tld>
   S: 250 Recipient ok
04 C: DATA
   S: 354 End data with <CR><LF>.<CR><LF>
05 C: From: "Client Sender" <sender@client.tld>
   C: To: Another User <another@otherdomain.tld>
   C: Date: Wed, 22 Oct 2008 01:13:22 -0800
   C: Subject: Test message 06
   C:
   C: Isn't SMTP easy?
07 C: .
   S: 250 Ok: queued as 918273645
08 C: QUIT
   S: 221 Bye
   {The server closes the connection}
```

This sample conversation uses a simple subset of SMTP; there is no authentication, no session security — none of the extensions you would see in a real session. Having said that, though, there are still eight key points of note in this conversation:

1. The initial greeting from the server, combined with the HELO or EHLO ("hello") response from the client.

2. The client begins sending the SMTP envelope information that tells who the actual sender is. If the message is rejected or bounced, this envelope sender is the person who will receive the notification — not necessarily the person in the "From:" header.

TABLE 3.3:   Common RFCs for SMTP

RFC	TITLE	DESCRIPTION
821	Simple Mail Transfer Protocol	Defines how clients and servers transmit messages to each other using a simple, text-based conversational model. Released in August 1982; modified by 974 and 1869 among others; obsoleted by 2821.
822	Standard for the Format of ARPA Internet Text Messages	Defines the format and some of the standard headers used in messages passed by SMTP. Released in August 1982; modified by 1123 among others; obsoleted by 2822.
974	Mail Routing and the Domain System	Introduces the MX record into DNS and explains how it affects mail routing to remote systems. Released in January 1986; obsoleted by 2821.
1123	Requirements for Internet Hosts — Application and Support	An attempt to codify best practices and identify (and fix) errata for a variety of protocols; Chapter 5, "Message Security and Hygiene," focuses on SMTP. Released in October 1989; updated by 5321.
1869	SMTP Service Extensions	Defines the EHLO mechanism for Extended SMTP (ESMTP), allowing new features to be easily added to SMTP without requiring a complete updated RFC. Critical for certain features we now take for granted, such as SMTP authentication, TLS support, and streamlined data transfers of binary messages. Released in November 1995; obsoleted by 2821.
2554	SMTP Service Extension for Authentication	One of the main SMTP extensions, used to allow clients and servers to provide authentication before message submission. Provided an alternative to an open relay configuration. Released in March 1999; obsoleted by 4954.
2821	Simple Mail Transfer Protocol	This update ties SMTP, Extended SMTP, and many of the updates and fixes into a single document. It was the operational standard for systems such as Exchange 2007. Released in April 2001; obsoleted by 5321.
2822	Internet Message Format	An update to 822, published as a companion to 2821. Released in April 2001; obsoleted by 5322.
4954	SMTP Service Extension for Authentication	Provides several minor updates to the existing SMTP AUTH mechanism. Released in July 2007.
5321	Simple Mail Transfer Protocol	The third (and current) release of SMTP, intended to be the standard for future messaging systems such as Exchange 2010. Addresses several lingering operational prohibitions and loopholes that make it hard for messaging administrators to fight spam within strict RFC compatibility. Released in October 2008.
5322	Internet Message Format	An incremental update to the message format used by SMTP messages; the current release that goes hand-in-hand with 5321. Released in October 2008.

3. The client continues the envelope by listing one or more recipients. Like the envelope sender, these recipients don't have to match the ones listed in the actual message. In fact, having an envelope recipient not listed in the message is precisely how Blind Carbon-Copy works.

4. The envelope is done; the client now begins submitting the actual message. Unless it uses modern SMTP extensions, this is just simple text.

5. First come the message headers. Note that these recipients don't match the ones in the envelope. Though these headers may be used for filtering, they won't be used for routing.

6. When the headers are finished, the client sends a blank line and continues with the message body starting on the next line.

7. When the message body is done, the client sends the End of Data sequence. The server now accepts or rejects the message; if the message is accepted, the server reports the associated queue information (much like a receipt).

8. The client indicates that it's finished with the connection. If it had another message to send to recipients on this system, it could reset this connection and reuse it for one or more following messages.

If the server were not the final destination for this message — perhaps it's just an edge mail system, handling all interaction with the Internet and performing message hygiene functions before routing accepted messages further into the organization — it would pass the system on to the next hop. Note that SMTP only handles message flow from the MUA through the MTA or MSA, and from one MTA to another MTA; it is not used to transfer messages to an MDA or LDA, or from the user's mailbox database back to the MUA or MRA.

HANDOFF, NOT ROUTING

You should also be clear on another important point: the SMTP RFCs, for the most part, have very little to say about how messages are routed, especially within multiple systems making up an organization. The RFCs simply define the standard for how two systems talk to each other to hand off messages; they say nothing about how to pick which system the message will be handed off to. We'll cover how Exchange makes these routing decisions between Internet-connected systems in Chapter 27; it's up to each organization to make its own rules. There are some existing options out there that the majority of people use; the most popular one requires the Domain Name System.

Accessing Mailboxes with Message Access Protocols

As we just mentioned, SMTP is designed for message transport — getting a message from one system to another. Once the message has been received and delivered to a mailbox store, there's one final hop that needs to happen: to the user's MUA. SMTP would be a poor protocol to handle this function — it has no concept of mailboxes or folders — so alternate protocols must be used.

THE MESSAGING APPLICATION PROGRAMMING INTERFACE

The Messaging Application Programming Interface (MAPI) is a programming interface that allows a developer to more easily write an application that accesses email or directory functions and services. Though often considered an industry standard, MAPI was developed by Microsoft in the early 1990s and the API set is published so that anyone can use it.

Outlook, for example, uses MAPI to access data on the Exchange server as well as accessing directory information that is stored in the Active Directory. An underlying directory service provider and email service provider allows MAPI to access these systems. Outlook includes an underlying service provider for Exchange Server as well as a service provider that allows access to PST files and IMAP4/POP3 servers. Third parties have developed service providers that will allow Outlook to access other messaging systems such as Lotus Notes, HP OpenMail, Hotmail, and even Zimbra.

A number of variations and versions of MAPI have been released over the years as new messaging functionality has been developed. To communicate with a client/server messaging system such as Exchange Server, MAPI relies on remote procedure calls (RPCs) to transport MAPI requests and data between the client and the server. These RPCs by default travel over a native TCP stream to form the MAPI-RPC protocol and use the User Datagram Protocol (UDP) to provide notifications of new mail. This protocol is used by Outlook when it is on the local network and not configured to use Outlook Anywhere. When Outlook Anywhere is used, MAPI is encapsulated within HTTP/HTTPS and transported from the Outlook client to the Client Access server.

MAPI-RPC over TCP has several characteristics that make it less than suitable for use outside of firewalls, or in networks that are heavily segmented. To understand why, you need to understand a bit about how RPCs work. A single Windows server may have many different services that all use RPCs and each listen on a different. One example of this is the Client Access server's Microsoft Exchange RPC Client Access service. This is the service to which an Outlook client connects in order to access mailbox data. When this service starts, it dynamically allocates an unused TCP port above 1,024 for that function.

If the port is dynamic, how does the Outlook client discover to which port it should connect for mailbox access? Well, the Microsoft Exchange RPC Client Access service also registered a particular application identifier with the RPC End Point Mapper service along with the port that it is using. The Outlook client first contacts the RPC End Point Mapper (always on TCP port 135) and inquires as to which port the information store service is listening. Once the information store port is determined, Outlook can connect to the correct port number. This is, of course, simplified, but it gives you an idea of how Outlook determines the correct port numbers to which it must connect on the Client Access server.

MAPI-RPC over TCP uses the same RPC framework (MS-RPC) as several other Microsoft protocols, including many of the management protocols used by various MMC administration consoles and the SMB file sharing protocol. As a consequence, opening the firewall to allow MAPI-RPC also opens many other protocols for access.

While there are several well-known ports used for initial connections, the actual connections are negotiated on the fly using an upper port range. Without a well-known port for all traffic, firewalls must either understand the protocol and perform application-level proxying or be configured to open the entire dynamic port range.

To securely deploy MAPI-RPC outside of the firewall, you need to tunnel the RPCs over another transport protocol. The Outlook Anywhere protocol uses Secure Hypertext Transport Protocol (HTTPS) as a secure, single-port transport for the RPC connection between Outlook and the Exchange servers. If you would like detailed information on how RPC is encapsulated in HTTP, take a look at this article:

```
http://msdn.microsoft.com/en-us/library/aa379169(VS.85).aspx
```

HTTP and Exchange Server

The HTTP component has gone from being almost an afterthought in early versions of Exchange to a critical component for all Exchange servers. It provides web clients with access to their mailbox and to the directory, as well as a number of additional Exchange Server components. The following is a list of services and functionality that are now provided via HTTP:

◆ Outlook Web App provides web browser clients with access to mailbox data (email, calendar, contacts, tasks), public folders, and address lists.

◆ Exchange ActiveSync provides ActiveSync-enabled mobile phones, such as Windows Mobile phones and the iPhone, with access to mailbox data (email, calendar, contacts) and access to the global address list.

◆ Outlook MAPI clients can encapsulate MAPI requests into HTTP and send them to the Client Access server, where they are de-encapsulated and sent on to Mailbox servers or the Active Directory.

◆ HTTP provides the PowerShell with the connectivity it needs between Exchange servers to use the Remote PowerShell.

◆ The Exchange Web Services API is used for services such as Autodiscover and downloading the offline address book as well as being used to access, manage, and manipulate Exchange data.

POP3 and IMAP

POP3, the third version of the Post Office Protocol, is intended to be a simple, no-frills mailbox retrieval protocol. A POP3 client connects to the Client Access server, provides the user's credentials, gets a list of messages that have arrived in the user's Inbox folder, and downloads one or more of them to the local client. POP3 is simple and lightweight to implement, ensuring that just about every email client application supports it, but it has two main flaws in a traditional business setting:

◆ POP3 doesn't understand the concept of folders. POP3 will only pull messages from the Inbox; if you have server-side rules that move messages to alternate folders (or have moved them manually, perhaps through a web-based mail client), they will not be visible to POP3. Once messages have been downloaded to the MUA, they can be filed in any local folders.

◆ Both POP3 and IMAP are supported by Exchange 2010 out of the box, but they're not configured by default. Also, both require the users to have access to an SMTP server to submit any new messages or replies to; neither POP3 nor IMAP handles submitting new messages back from the MUA to the server. They're strictly pull protocols and require a push protocol like SMTP to ensure new messages get delivered.

Ensuring that clients have access to a suitable SMTP port in modern organizations can be a substantial challenge, especially when your users are outside of your network and traveling. Many ISPs block outbound connections on TCP port 25, the port used by SMTP, unless these connections come from their own mail servers. Additionally, because of SPF and Sender ID policies, regulatory compliance policies, or even message hygiene regimes that require all outbound traffic from the domain to be scanned through specific gateways, you may need to ensure that all message clients send their outgoing messages through your Exchange servers only.

There are three main solutions for these problems:

Use clients that don't require SMTP.   We are compelled by union regulations (that's a joke) to point out that Outlook in Exchange mode, Outlook Anywhere (formerly known as RPC over HTTPS), Outlook Web App, and Exchange ActiveSync all receive and submit messages over the same non-SMTP connections and thus avoid these problems. If you can restrict your users to using one of these options, or something that uses a similar transport (such as Exchange Web Services over HTTPS or the latest version of Microsoft Entourage for Mac OS X), then you can sidestep the whole issue. We like this solution because we think that Exchange users, by and large, are going to have the best user experience with one of these clients, especially in Exchange 2010. However, there are times where you have to support other clients.

Use a virtual private network.   By requiring your clients to use a VPN connection to access their messages, you can ensure (and enforce) that they are connecting to your Exchange servers. This approach also has the advantage of allowing you to not publish POP3 or IMAP services outside of your firewall. However, traveling users may be on networks that don't support VPNs, leaving them without reliable email access.

Use the client submission port.   Starting with many Unix messaging systems, administrators began to separate server-to-server mail traffic from client-to-server mail traffic. They did this by reserving TCP 25 for standard server-to-server SMTP sessions as well as opening TCP 587 for clients to submit messages to their mail servers, as shown in Figure 3.2. By the time Exchange 2007 came about, the submission port was a de facto standard and was supported out of the box. Exchange 2010 continues supporting this standard.

FIGURE 3.2
The client submission port

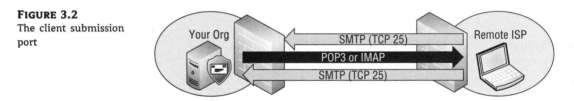

Securing Network Sessions with TLS and SSL

The final notable protocol you need to understand at more than a basic level helps keep your network sessions secure through the use of sophisticated cryptography. Transport Level Security (TLS) and its little brother Secure Socket Layer (SSL) are client-server protocols that provide encrypted transport sessions for network connections, as well as X.509 digital certificate-based authentication of the server identity through a trusted certificate authority. Optionally, they also allow for mutual authentication, enabling both the server and client to authenticate each other's identity.

Most of us are familiar with at least the basics of how SSL operates from years of using web browsers with HTTPS. For the most part, TLS and SSL are indistinguishable, certainly from the level of detail you'll need for day-to-day operations deploying, managing, and troubleshooting Exchange issues. Here is the big difference between TLS and SSL:

A SSL session is negotiated and established at the beginning of the connection, before the actual application or service responds to the client.   In order to offer both a secured and non-secured version of a given protocol using SSL, you must expose two ports: the insecure version (HTTP on TCP 80) and the secure version (HTTPS on TCP 443).

A TLS session is negotiated and established after the server has responded to the client, as an in-band option within the protocol being exchanged. This allows you to offer the secure session as a protocol-level option over a single port, while still using application-level configuration options to enforce how that security will be used.

This distinction is illustrated in Figure 3.3, which shows the difference between SMTP using TLS and SMTPS (Secure SMTP).

FIGURE 3.3
SMTP using TLS versus SMTPS

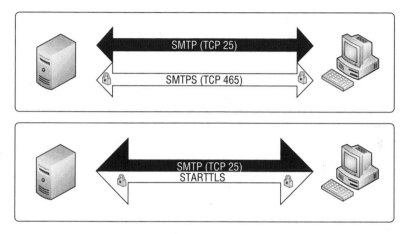

Although we'll go into quite a bit more detail about TLS and SSL in Chapter 5, and cover digital certificates in Chapter 7, there are two key facts you should keep in mind for now:

TLS and SSL are used by default for almost all connections in Exchange 2010. Out of the box, all Exchange servers use TLS to protect SMTP connections and SSL to protect HTTP connections between systems. They also offer these mechanisms for client connections and in the default configuration require TLS/SSL connections before allowing potentially risky operations (such as the use of Basic plaintext authentication). Expect a much deeper dive into TLS and SSL in Chapter 5.

TLS and SSL require a working knowledge of (and proficiency with) digital certificates. Although Exchange 2010 follows the example of Exchange 2007 and includes self-signed certificates, these self-signed certificates are only trusted by other Exchange servers in the organization that have other authentication mechanisms such as Kerberos at their disposal. The principals and mechanisms of request and deploying certificates are fairly simple; the complexity comes only in trying to figure out which names you need. We'll demystify much of this in Chapter 7 and teach you how to handle certificates for Exchange.

The Bottom Line

Understand the components of an email system. As we begin to take a deeper look at the Exchange 2010 system, we examine how the different roles and components work together. To understand these pieces, it is necessary to understand the purpose each one fulfills.

Master It How many components are in an email system? What are they called and how could they be described in an analogy to the traditional postal system?

Identify the three major components of Active Directory. Exchange depends heavily on the Windows Active Directory service. Many Exchange design, deployment, and administrative tasks depend on a mastery of Active Directory concepts and technologies.

Master It There are three major components and technologies that make up Active Directory. What are they, and what purpose do they serve?

Understand common protocols and standards used by Microsoft Exchange. Exchange doesn't just depend on Microsoft standards and technologies. There's a whole range of protocols and standards that are used by multiple applications, and Exchange Server 2010 provides support for them in order to allow interoperability.

Master It What are the major standard protocols used by Exchange to interact with other mail servers and clients, and what are they commonly used for?

Chapter 4

Understanding Availability, Recovery, and Compliance

The modern business world is getting more complex, not less; email in turn evolves to keep up. As an Exchange administrator or implementer, you need to know more about a wider variety of topics without losing your core competency in Exchange.

In this chapter, you will learn to:

◆ Distinguish between availability, backup and recovery, and disaster recovery

◆ Determine the best option for your disaster recovery

◆ Distinguish between the different types of availability meant by the term *high availability*

◆ Implement the four pillars of compliance and governance activities

Changing from a Technology to a Business Viewpoint

You've probably heard the old adage that "every cloud has a silver lining." It can often be a comfort to know that we can usually find some good when bad things happen to us. When the mailbox database server's RAID controller goes bad and corrupts the drive array with the executive mailboxes, we have the opportunity to validate our backup strategy and show that it works perfectly under pressure.

However, the often unacknowledged corollary is that for every good thing that happens (or that you make happen), a number of potential pathways for complication are opened. If you think for a moment about the spread of email and how it has changed from a luxury to a utility, you can see that electronic messaging administrators have become victims of their own success.

Gone are the days where you simply had to worry about editing and publishing the correct DNS records, provisioning and configuring your T1 lines, and wrestling with your server hardware. Today's challenges revolve around meeting more goals, meeting business requirements, and analyzing risks such as the following common scenarios:

◆ Ensuring that your mailbox servers have the proper storage back-end design to allow your backups to happen within the defined window

◆ Ensuring that your users continue to have access to their mailboxes even when a server fails, a flaky router takes a site offline, or power fails for an entire rack or storage array

- Ensuring that you have a plan for enabling dial-tone mailbox functionality for your users after a major storm takes out the region for several days

- Ensuring that the messages your users send to external clients are in compliance with the various policies and regulations that apply to your business

- Determining the risks associated with failing to provide disaster recovery plans and the risks associated with various service level agreements

- Balancing the business costs associated with providing recovery, ensuring compliance, and providing a specified level of service

What's in a Name?

Backup and recovery, *high availability*, *disaster recovery*, and *compliance and governance*. You may have heard of these once or twice; each plays a role in the overall protection strategy of your organization's data.

All four of these topics must be at least considered by every modern Exchange administrator and professional, even if they are not actively addressed in each deployment of Exchange 2010. Even when you do need to address them in your planning, Exchange 2010 provides a variety of options to ensure that your deployment meets your own particular needs and situation. One size does not fit all. To best use the tools that Exchange gives you, though, you must clearly understand the problems they are designed to solve. It doesn't do to use a screwdriver as a hammer — and you can't solve a disaster recovery problem by using the wrong continuous replication option.

In this section, we'll establish a shared vocabulary for discussing these topics so that you get the most from our discussions of the new features and functionality in Exchange 2010 that you'll find in later chapters. We want you to clearly understand how Microsoft intended Exchange 2010's features to be deployed and used, so that you have confidence that they will meet your goals.

Backup and Recovery

Let's start with a topic that is arguably one of the core tasks for any IT administrator, let alone Exchange administrators: backup and recovery.

Backup is the process of preserving one or more point-in-time copies of a set of data, regardless of the number of copies, frequency and schedule, or media type used to store them. In Exchange backups, there are four main types:

Full Backups Full backups capture an entire set of target data; in legacy versions of Exchange, this is a storage group with the transaction log files and all the associated mailbox databases and files. In Exchange 2010, each mailbox database is a separate backup target, since there is now an enforced 1:1 relationship between mailbox databases and transaction logs (it was merely strongly recommended in previous versions). Full backups take the most time to perform and use the most space, but they must be regularly performed on Exchange mailbox databases so that the Exchange Information Store knows that transaction logs have been preserved and can be safely deleted.

Incremental Backups Incremental backups capture only a partial set of the target data — specifically, the data that has changed since either the last full backup or the last incremental backup. For Exchange, this means any new transaction logs. Incremental backups are designed to *minimize how often* you have to perform full backups as well as *minimize the space used* by any particular backup set. As a result, a backup set that includes incremental backups can be more time-consuming and fragile to restore; successful recovery includes first recovering the latest full backup, then each successive incremental backup. Incremental backups also instruct Exchange Server to purge the transaction logs after they are backed up.

Differential Backups   Differential backups also capture only a partial set of the target data — specifically, the data that has changed since the last full backup. All other backups (incremental and differential) are not considered. For Exchange, this means any transaction logs generated since the last full backup plus a new copy of the mailbox database files. Differential backups are designed to *minimize how many* recovery operations you have to perform in order to fully restore a set of data. In turn, differential backups use more space than incremental backups, but they can be recovered more quickly and with fewer opportunities for data corruption; successful recovery includes first recovering the latest full backup, then the latest differential backup.

Recovery   Also known as restoration, recovery is the process of taking one or more sets of the data preserved through backups and making it once again accessible to administrators, applications, or end users. Most recovery jobs require the restoration of multiple sets of backup data, especially when incremental and differential backups are in use. Two metrics are used to determine if the recovery time and the amount of data recovered are acceptable:

> **Recovery Time Objective (RTO)**   RTO is a metric commonly used to help define successful backup and restore processes. The RTO defines the time window in which you have to restore Exchange services and messaging data after an event. You may have multiple tiers of data and service, in which case it could be appropriate to have a separate RTO for each tier. Often, the RTO is a component of (ideally, an input into, but that's not always the case) your service level agreements. As a result, the RTO is a critical factor in the design of Exchange mailbox database storage systems; it's a bad idea to design mailbox databases that are larger than you can restore within your RTO.

> **Recovery Point Objective (RPO)**   RPO is a metric that goes hand in hand with the RTO. While the RTO measures a timeframe, the RPO sets a benchmark for the maximum amount of data (typically measured in hours) you can afford to lose. Again, multiple tiers of service and data often have separate RPOs. The RPO helps drive the backup frequency and schedule. It's worth noting that this metric makes an explicit assumption that all data within a given category is equally valuable; that's obviously not true, which is why it is important to properly establish your categories. Remember, though, if you have too many classes or categories, you'll just have confusion.

One thing to note about Exchange 2010 is that it only supports online backups and restores created through the Windows Volume Shadow Copy Service (VSS). While previous versions allowed the use of an online streaming backup, this option is no longer available. VSS provides several advantages, including the ability to integrate with third-party storage systems to speed up the backup and recovery process. The most important benefit VSS gives, though, is that it ensures that the Exchange Information Store flushes all pending writes consistently, ensuring the backup data set can be cleanly recovered.

HOW MUCH DATA GETS COPIED?

One thing that Volume Shadow Copy Service (VSS) does not natively provide is the ability to reduce the amount of data that must be copied during a backup operation. VSS simply creates either a permanent or temporary replica (depending on how the invoking application requested the replica be created) of the entire disk volume; it's then up to the application to sort out the appropriate files and folders that make up the data set. Many Exchange-aware backup applications simply copy the various transaction log files and mailbox database files to the backup server.

Some applications, however, are a bit more intelligent; they keep track of which blocks have changed in the target files since the last backup interval. These applications can copy just those changed blocks to the backup data set — typically some percentage of the blocks in the mailbox database file as well as all the new transaction log files — thus reducing the amount of data that needs to travel over the network and be stored. Block-level backups help strike a good balance between storage, speed, and reliability. As you go forward with VSS-aware Exchange-compatible backup solutions, be sure to investigate whether they offer this feature.

Disaster Recovery

Regular backups are important; the ability to successfully restore them is even better. This capability is a key part of your extended arsenal for problem situations. Restoring the occasional backup is fairly straightforward but assumes that you have a functional Exchange server and dependent network infrastructures. What do you do if an entire site or datacenter goes down and your recovery operations extend beyond just an Exchange mailbox database? The answer to this question is a broad topic that can fill a large number of books, blog postings, and websites of its own.

Disaster recovery (DR) is the practice of ensuring that you can restore critical services when some disaster or event causes large-scale or long-term outage. A successful DR plan requires you to identify your critical services and data, create documentation that lists the necessary tasks to re-create and restore them, and modify the suitable policies and processes within your organization to support your plan.

It's not enough to consider how to rebuild Exchange servers and restore Exchange mailbox databases. Exchange is a complicated application with a large number of dependencies, so your plans need to accommodate the following issues:

Network Dependencies This topic includes subnets, IP address assignments, DHCP services, and router configurations. Are you rebuilding your services to have the same IP addresses or new ones? Whatever you decide, you'll need to make sure that other services and clients can reach the Exchange servers.

Active Directory Services This topic includes associated DNS zones and records. Exchange cannot function without reliable access to global catalog servers and domain controllers. Which forests and domains hold objects Exchange will need to reference? Does your existing replication configuration meet those needs?

Third-Party Applications This topic includes monitoring, backup, archival, or other programs and services that require messaging services or interact with them. Don't just blindly catalog everything in production; be sure these systems are also being provided as part of the disaster recovery plan.

There's a blurry line between disaster recovery and the associated concept of *business conti-nuity* (also called *business continuance* by some). Business continuity (BC) is the ability of your organization to continue providing at least the minimum set of operations and services neces-sary to stay in business during a large-scale outage, such as during a regional event or natural disaster. In a business continuity plan, you will identify and prioritize the most critical services and capabilities for which you need to provide at least some level of operational capacity as soon as possible, even without full access to data or applications.

It's important to note that the business continuity plan is designed and implemented alongside your disaster recovery efforts. In many organizations, they will be maintained by two separate groups of professionals; it goes without saying that these groups should have good lines of communication in place.

🌐 Real World Scenario

DRAWING THE LINE BETWEEN DISASTER RECOVERY AND BUSINESS CONTINUITY

There's a lot of confusion over exactly how disaster recovery and business continuity relate to each other. We have good news and bad news: the good news is that it's a simple relationship. The bad news is, "It depends."

Both types of plans are ultimately aimed at the goal of repairing the damage caused by extended outages. The biggest difference is the scope; many business continuity plans focus very little on technology and look instead at overall business processes. In contrast, disaster recovery plans of necessity have to be concerned with the finer details of IT administration. The reality is that both levels of focus are often needed — and must be handled in parallel, with coordination, and in support of any additional ongoing crisis management.

Let's try to clarify the difference by providing an example. Acme Inc. is a national manufac-turer and supplier of various goods, mainly to wholesale distributors but with a small and thriving mail-order retail department for the occasional customer who needs quality Acme products but has no convenient retail outlet in their locale. Acme's main call center has a small number of permanent staff but a large number of contract call center operators.

Unfortunately, Acme's main order fulfillment center — for both bulk wholesale orders as well as the relatively small amount of mail order traffic — gets hit by a large fragment in a meteor shower, causing a fire that rapidly transforms the entire site into smoking rubble even as all personnel are safely evacuated. The call center and supporting datacenter are completely destroyed and, conservatively, will take several months to fully rebuild. Obviously, Acme is going to suffer some sort of setback, but with proper planning they can minimize the effects. What types of actions would Acme's BC and DR plans each be taking?

◆ Acme's BC plan is concerned with getting the minimum level of operational function back online as quickly as possible. In this case, it's going to take a while before they can resume call center operations. Their immediate needs are to establish at least some level of messag-ing support for the temporary call center workers the BC plan brings in. Their BC plan does not assume that they will have in-house capability, so makes provisions — if required — to use hosted Exchange services as a short-term stopgap so that communications with customers and wholesalers will proceed until Acme's IT staff can bring up sufficient Exchange servers to switch back to on-premise services.

◆ Acme's DR plan is concerned with rebuilding critical structures. In addition to restoring critical network infrastructure services, Acme's Exchange administrators are tasked with first rebuilding sufficient Exchange servers in their DR location to recover the mailbox databases for the call center's permanent staff. They also need to then create sufficient Exchange servers to allow the recovery of operator mailbox databases to extract message data pertaining to currently open cases that need investigation. Once the datacenter is rebuilt, they can build the rest of the Exchange servers and restore operations from the DR site.

Location, Location, Location

One factor tends to consistently blur the line between regular backups, disaster recovery, business continuity, and even high availability: where your solution is located. We have talked to many administrators who have the false assumption that once a recovery activity moves off-site, that automatically makes it disaster recovery (or business continuity, or high availability). This is an understandable misconception — but it's still not true.

In reality, the question of "where" is immaterial. If you're taking steps to protect your data, it's backup and recovery. If you're taking steps to rebuild services, it's disaster recovery. If you're taking steps to ensure you can still do business, it's business continuity. This is obviously an oversimplification, but it'll do for now unless we start looking at all the ways the lines can blur. We do want to touch on one of those complications now, however: where you deploy your recovery operations. There are three overall approaches: on-premise, off-premise, or a combination of the two.

ON-PREMISE SOLUTIONS

Most of what we do as Exchange administrators, especially in the backup and restore problem space, is *on-premise*. In an on-premise solution, you have one or more sites where your Exchange servers are deployed, and those same sites host the backup and disaster recovery operations. Note that this definition of "on-premise" differs somewhat from traditional disaster recovery terminology, which talks about *dedicated disaster recovery sites*. These sites are still part of your premises and so are still "on-premise" for our purpose.

Many organizations can handle all their operations in this fashion through the use of Exchange, storage and networking devices, and third-party applications. Some, however, can use additional help. When you need on-premise help in the Exchange world, there are two broad categories:

Appliances Appliances are self-contained boxes or servers, usually a sealed combination of hardware and software, placed into the network. They are designed to interface with or become part of the Exchange organization and provide additional abilities. Appliances are useful for smaller organizations that want sophisticated options for disaster recovery but don't have the budget or skill level to provide their own. Appliances can be used to provide services such as cross-site data replication, site monitoring, or even additional services aimed at other types of functionality.

On the plus side, appliances are typically easy to install. On the downside, they can quickly become a single point of failure. The temptation to place an appliance and treat it as a "fire-and-forget" solution is high. In reality, most appliances need to be tested, monitored, and upgraded on a regular basis.

Remote Managed Services Remote managed services (or remote management) are service offerings. Instead of buying a sealed black box, the customer purchases a period of service from a vendor. The service provider provides design, deployment, and ongoing maintenance services as part of the offering for the customer — sometimes as a package, sometimes as a set of a la carte offerings. Like appliances, these offerings can extend beyond traditional disaster recovery offerings.

These types of service providers are able to provide trained Exchange expertise on a scale that is typically only available to very large organizations. They can do this through economies of scale; by using these highly trained personnel to monitor, maintain, and troubleshoot many disparate customer organizations of all sizes and types, they can both afford this type of staff and offer them the kind of challenges necessary to retain them.

Some solutions exist that combine these two approaches; customers purchase both an appliance as well as a managed service offering.

OFF-PREMISE SOLUTIONS

Some problems are easier to solve — or more efficient to solve — if you let someone else deal with them. In the Exchange world, this translates to *hosted services* — services or offerings provided by a third party. Hosted services provide a large variety of functionality to an Exchange organization, ranging from backup, disaster recovery, and business continuity to such services as message hygiene, archival, and compliance and governance.

There's a close similarity between hosted services and remote managed services. Both are provided by an external service model. They can both offer a combination of features, performance, and convenience that makes them attractive to small and medium-sized organizations. The difference is that with hosted services, messaging traffic is diverted — whether externally or internally — to the hosting provider, which then performs specific actions. Depending on the specific service, traffic can then be rerouted back to the organization.

Most hosted services charge on a per-user or per-mailbox basis, which is part of the reason why they tend to be favored by smaller organizations, or for specific portions of a larger enterprise. They can also require a large amount of bandwidth, depending on the overall amount of messaging traffic your organization is sending to the service. This can drive the costs higher than just the up-front per-mailbox price.

One of the main differences between hosted services and remote managed services is that a hosted service provider commonly (but not always) has an internal Exchange deployment that is designed to host multiple tenants. For many years, the retail version of Exchange Server has assumed that each deployment will be used for a single organization or corporate entity. In fact, legacy versions of Exchange have been difficult to manage in the cases where one organization splits into two, or multiple organizations are merged or joined into one. However, there have been hosted versions of Exchange that were made available to specific Microsoft partners, allowing them to create and host multitenant Exchange deployments.

With Exchange 2010, Microsoft specifically worked on implementing their own hosted solution to gain operational experience with multitenant architectures and fix Exchange design features that caused problems with those architectures. As a result of this work, Exchange Server 2010 now explicitly recognizes off-premise hosted services that are based on the Exchange 2010 platform. As a result, the Exchange 2010 management tools are designed to work both on on-premise deployments as well as those hosted services. As more service providers move to support Exchange 2010, be sure to investigate their integration with the native Exchange 2010 tools.

Management Frameworks

There's a lot of great guidance out there (including fine books such as this one) on the technical aspects of designing, installing, configuring, and operating Exchange servers and organizations. There's a lot less material that provides a coherent look at the issues of the entire lifecycle of IT management in general, let alone Windows or Exchange deployments in particular. There may be, however, more than you think: every organization of every size struggles with common nontechnical issues and needs a good defined framework for managing IT resources. Having this type of framework in place makes it easier to properly plan for disaster recovery and business continuity concerns as well as other common management tasks.

There are several frameworks you may wish to examine, or with which you are already familiar in some fashion:

The *Information Technology Infrastructure Library (ITIL)* is the 900-pound gorilla of the IT management framework world. ITIL provides a generic set of tools for IT professionals to use as template concepts and policies when developing their own management processes of their IT infrastructure and operations.

Microsoft has developed the *Microsoft Operations Framework (MOF)*, a detailed framework based on the concepts and principles of ITIL. MOF takes the generic framework offered by ITIL and provides greater detail optimized for Windows and other Microsoft technologies.

Like Microsoft, IBM offers its own ITIL-centric framework: the *IBM Tivoli Unified Process (ITUP)*. ITUP provides guidance on taking generic ITIL concepts and processes and linking them into real-world processes and tasks that map to real IT objectives.

The *Control Objectives for Information and Related Technologies (COBIT)* best practices framework was initially created as a way to help organizations develop IT governance processes and models. While COBIT is typically thought of as optimized for IT audits, it offers a number of supplemental practices suitable for IT management.

While a deep dive into any of these alternatives is out of scope for this book, we do want to take a short peek at two of them: first ITIL, then MOF. Although you don't have to know anything about these subjects to be a low-level Exchange administrator, Microsoft has begun introducing exposure to these concepts into the training for their high-level Exchange certifications.

ITIL

The best way to learn about ITIL is to go through one of the training and certification events. Outside such classes, ITIL is in essence a collection of best practices in the discipline of IT service management. IT service management is just what it sounds like: effective and consistent management of IT services. IT management is in many respects nonintuitive and offers several specific challenges that are not common to many other management disciplines; most people need specific training to learn how to manage IT in the most effective way. ITIL represents the most accepted IT management approach in the world.

ITIL was developed by the British Standards Institution in an attempt to develop a centralized management standard for IT throughout the various British government agencies. This effort was not successful — in part due to the change from mainframe-based computing to personal computers and networks and the resulting lowering of barriers to server acquisition and deployment. However, it did allow the formation of existing best practices and thoughts on IT service management into a single collection of best practices and procedures, supported by tasks and checklists IT professionals can use as a starting point for developing their own IT governance structures. ITIL is supported and offered by a wide variety of entities, including many large enterprises and consulting firms, with training and certification available for IT professionals.

ITIL has been through several iterations. The most current version, ITIL v3, became available in mid-2007 and consists of five core texts:

Service Strategy   Demonstrates how to use the service management discipline and develop it as both a new set of capabilities as well as a large-scale business asset

Service Design   Demonstrates how to take your objectives and develop them into services and assets through the creation of appropriate processes

Service Transition   Demonstrates how to take the services and assets previously created and transition them into production in your organization

Service Operation   Demonstrates the processes and techniques required to manage the various services and assets previously created and deployed

Continual Service Improvement   Demonstrates the ongoing process of improving on the services and assets that already exist to increase value to your customers

While ITIL provides a reasonably coherent management approach, it is not without its flaws. There are four main common criticisms:

- ITIL is by no means complete. In particular, it doesn't map into definitive, prescriptive guidance. By concentrating on best practices and concepts, it can be rather generic and sometimes vague. It doesn't offer instrumentation or benchmarking to measure the impact of ITIL adoption on your organization's management practices. If you adopt ITIL, be prepared to spend time adapting its guidance to your organization, identifying gaps, and coming up with processes to fill those gaps.

- ITIL is focused solely on service management and, as result, fails to address related issues such as enterprise architecture design. While at first this focus seems reasonable, in practice it can cause long-term problems; ITIL does not have a way to detect problems or flaws in the design, let alone a mechanism to fold feedback gathered from ITIL-aligned management practices back into the design process (or vice versa).

- The ITIL process can be somewhat expensive. Between the acquisition cost of the core texts, the training, and the certification, organizations can spend a fair amount of money without any specific mechanism for gauging their return on that investment. Additionally, the quality of the books (aside from the overall holes in the ITIL guidance) is reported by many to be spotty and uneven.

- ITIL's limitations are not always well understood even by those who have gone through certification, leading to a common attitude that ITIL is not a solution for all IT governance problems. In particular, many ITIL practitioners can lose sight of the practical benefits and flaws of the discipline and tend instead toward a dogmatic pursuit of ITIL.

For more information on ITIL, see its official website at `www.itil-officialsite.com/`.

MOF

Microsoft has worked with ITIL for more than 10 years, beginning in 1999. As ITIL has developed and grown in popularity, Microsoft saw that its customers needed more specific guidance for using the principles and concepts of ITIL in the context of Microsoft technologies and applications. As a result, they created the *Microsoft Operations Framework*, which they describe in the following manner:

> *The Microsoft strategy for IT service management is to provide guidance and software solutions that enable organizations to achieve mission-critical system reliability, availability, supportability, and manageability of the Microsoft platform. The strategy includes a model for organizations and IT pros to assess their current IT infrastructure maturity, prioritize processes of greatest concern, and apply proven principles and best practices to optimize performance on the Microsoft platform.*

MOF is not a replacement for ITIL; it is one specific implementation of ITIL, optimized for environments that use Microsoft products. It's specifically designed to help IT professionals align business goals with IT goals and develop cohesive, unified processes that allow the creation and management of IT services throughout all portions of the IT lifecycle. It is currently on version 4.0, which aligns with ITIL v3.

MOF defines four stages of the IT service management lifecycle:

Plan   Plan is the first stage of the cycle: new IT services are identified and created, or necessary changes are identified in existing IT services that are already in place.

Deliver   Deliver is the second stage: the new service is implemented for use in production.

Operate   Operate is the final stage of the cycle: the service is deployed and monitored. It feeds back into the Plan stage in order to effect incremental changes as necessary.

Manage   Manage stage is not a separate stage; instead, it is an ongoing set of processes that take place at all times throughout the cycle to measure and monitor the effectiveness of your efforts. This is illustrated in Figure 4.1.

FIGURE 4.1
The four stages of the
Microsoft IT service
management lifecycle

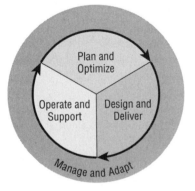

For more information on MOF, see `http://technet.microsoft.com/en-us/solutionaccelerators/dd320379.aspx`.

WHAT ARE YOU MEASURING?

So, how necessary are management frameworks in real deployments? Why are we wasting valuable space talking about ITIL and MOF when we could be cramming in a couple more nuggets of yummy Exchange 2010 technical goodness? The answer is simple: we can't include everything. No matter how thorough (and long) the book, there will always be more technical details that you can't include. Instead, we wanted to include at least an introduction to some of the nontechnical areas that can give you an advantage.

Let's demonstrate the practical value of some of this ITIL mumbo-jumbo by tackling a hot topic of discussion: availability and uptime. We've heard a lot of executives talk about "five nines of availability" — but what, exactly, does that mean? You can't have a meaningful discussion about availability without knowing exactly what kind of availability you're talking about (which we'll get to later in this chapter), and without knowing that, you can't measure it, let alone to the ludicrous degree of detail that five nines represents.

Now let's discuss uptime. Uptime has a pretty well-defined meaning; you just need to know what scope it applies to. Are you talking server uptime, mailbox uptime, or service uptime? Once you have that defined, you can take measurements and apply numbers for quantitative comparisons.

ITIL and MOF give you not only the conceptual framework for agreeing on what you're measuring, but also guidance on how to put the process of measurement into place. That kind of discipline can give you a lot of long-term advantages and help keep your Exchange deployment better managed than you could do on your own. The thing to remember is that these frameworks are starting points; they're not cast in stone, and they're not laws you must rigidly obey. If you find some aspect that doesn't work for your organization, you should first make sure you understand what the purpose of that feature is and how it's intended to work. Once you're sure that it doesn't apply as is, feel free to make documented changes to bring it into alignment with your needs.

A Closer Look at Availability

We've already talked about disaster recovery and how it can be confused with general data protection (backup and recovery) and business continuity. Perhaps an even more common confusion, though, is the distinction between high availability and disaster recovery. This is a common enough error that we felt it was worth devoting a separate section of this chapter.

High availability (HA) is a design strategy. The strategy is simple: try to ensure that users keep access to services, such as their Exchange mailboxes or Unified Messaging servers, during periods of outage or downtime. These outages could be the result of any sort of event:

- Hardware failure, such as the loss of a power supply, a memory module, or the server motherboard

- Storage failure, such as the loss of a disk, disk controller, or data-level corruption

- Network failure, such as the cutting of a network cable or a router or a switch losing configuration

- Some other service failure, such as the loss of an Active Directory domain controller or a DNS server

HA technologies and strategies are designed to allow a given service to continue to be available to users (or other services) in the event of these kind of failures. No matter which technology is involved, there are two main approaches, one or both of which is used by each HA technology and strategy:

Fault Tolerance and Redundancy   This involves placing resources into a pool so that one can take up the load when another member of the pool fails. This strategy removes the presence of a single point of failure. Fault tolerance needs to be accompanied by some mechanism for selecting which of the redundant resources is to be used. These mechanisms are either *round-robin* or *load balancing*. In the former, each resource in the pool is used in turn, regardless of the current state or load. In the latter, additional mechanisms are used to direct users to the least loaded member of the resource pool. Many higher-end hardware systems use redundant parts to make the overall server system more redundant to many common types of hardware failures. Exchange Server 2010 can use database availability groups (DAGs) to replicate copies of data from one Mailbox server to another and to provide failover in the event the node where the data resides fails.

Replication   This process involves making copies of critical data between multiple members of the resource pool. If replication happens quickly enough and with a small enough time interval, when one member of the resource pool becomes unavailable another member can take over the load. Most replication strategies, including Exchange's database replication features, are based on a *single master* strategy, where all updates happen to the master (or active) copy and are replicated to the additional copies. Some technologies such as Active Directory are designed to allow *multimaster replication*, where updates can be directed to the closest member.

To achieve complete availability with Exchange, you'll use both strategies. However, you also need to think of the different levels of availability that you'll need to ensure.

MEASURING AVAILABILITY

It is not uncommon to find that availability of a system is measured differently depending on the organization. Typically, to report the percentage of availability, you take the amount of time during a measurement period and then subtract the total downtime during that period. Finally, you divide that number by the total elapsed time.

So, let's say that during a 30-day period of time, there was no *scheduled* downtime, but there was a 4-hour period of time when patches were applied to the system. So, 30 days − .17 days = 29.8 days of total uptime, and 29.8/30 = 99.3 percent availability.

This is just a sample calculation, of course. In the real world, you would probably have a maintenance window during your operations that would not count against your availability numbers. You want to do your very best to minimize the amount of unplanned downtime, but you also have to take in to consideration scheduled maintenance and planned downtime.

SERVICE AVAILABILITY

When we have discussions with people about high availability in Exchange organizations, we find that the level of high availability that most of them are actually thinking about is *service availability*. That is, they think of the Exchange deployment as an overall service and think of how to ensure that users can get access to the whole shebang (either that, or they think solely of hardware clusters, storage replication, and the other low-end technologies). It is important to note that when discussing service availability, this term may mean different things to different people.

Service availability is an important consideration for your overall availability strategy. It doesn't make a lot of sense to plan for redundant server hardware if you forget to deploy sufficient numbers of those servers with the right Exchange roles in the appropriate locations. (We'll discuss the proper ratios and recommendations for role and server placement in Chapter 11, "Understanding Server Roles and Configurations.") To ensure true service availability, you need to consider all the other levels of availability.

The other aspect of service availability is to think about what other services Exchange is dependent on:

◆ The obvious dependency is Active Directory. Each Exchange server requires access to a domain controller as well as global catalog services. The more Exchange servers in the site, the more of each Active Directory role that site requires. If your domain controllers are also DNS servers, you need enough DNS servers to survive the loss of one or two. If you lose DNS servers or domain controllers in a site, Exchange will fail.

◆ What type of network services do you need? Do you assign static IP addresses and default gateways or do you use DHCP and dynamic routing? Do you have extra router or switching capacity? What about your firewall configurations — do you have only a single firewall between different network zones, or are those redundant as well?

◆ What other applications do you deploy as part of your Exchange deployment? Do you rely on a monitoring system such as Microsoft System Center Operations Manager? What will occur if something happens to your monitoring server; is there a redundant or backup system that takes over, or will additional faults and failures go unnoticed and be allowed to take down the Exchange system? Do you have enough backup agents and servers to protect your mailbox servers?

Service availability typically requires a combination of redundancy and replication strategies. For example, you deploy multiple Active Directory domain controllers in a site for redundancy, but they replicate the directory data between each other.

NETWORK AVAILABILITY

The next layer we want to talk about is network availability. By this, we don't mean the types of network services we mentioned in the previous section. Instead, what we mean is the ability to ensure that you can receive new connections from clients and other servers, whether your organization uses Exchange servers, PBX systems and telephony gateways, or external mail servers. Network availability is a key part of your Exchange infrastructure and should therefore be considered part of your overall service availability.

The typical strategy for network availability is load balancing. This is network-level redundancy. Simple network load balancers use a round-robin mechanism to alternately and evenly (on the basis of numbers) distribute incoming connections to the members of the resource pool. Other solutions use more sophisticated mechanisms, such as monitoring each member of the pool for overall load and assigning incoming connections to the least-loaded member.

For larger organizations and complex Exchange deployments, it's common to use hardware load balancers. Hardware systems are typically more expensive and represent yet more systems to manage and maintain, so they add a degree of complexity that is often undesirable to smaller organizations. Smaller organizations prefer to use software-based load-balancing solutions likes Windows Network Load Balancing (WNLB).

Unfortunately, WNLB isn't generally suitable for Exchange 2010 deployments. This is the official recommendation of both the Exchange product group and the Windows product group, the folks who develop the WNLB component. WNLB has a few characteristics that render it unsuitable for use with Exchange in any but smaller deployments or test environments:

◆ WNLB simply performs round-robin balancing of incoming connections. It doesn't detect whether members of the load-balance cluster are down, so it will keep sending connections to the downed member. This could result in intermittent and confusing behavior for clients and loss or delay of messages from external systems.

◆ WNLB is incompatible with the Windows Failover Clustering components. This means that small shops can't deploy a pair of servers with the Mailbox, Client Access, and Hub Transport roles; use WNLB to balance the Client Access and Hub Transport roles; or use continuous replication to replicate the mailbox databases. They'd have to deploy four servers at a minimum.

Even when using hardware network load-balancing, there are a number of things to remember and best practices to follow.

DATA AVAILABILITY

We've seen many Exchange organization designs and deployment plans. Most of them spend a lot of time ensuring that the mailbox data will be available.

In versions of Exchange prior to Exchange 2007, data availability meant using failover clustering. Failover clustering used a feature of Enterprise Edition Windows, the Windows Cluster Service (now called Windows Failover Clustering in Windows Server 2008), to create groups of servers that shared a single storage source. Within this cluster, one or more clustered Exchange server instances are activated and control the corresponding mailbox databases. When one underlying hardware node fails, the active virtual server instance fails over to another node.

Failover clustering is a common HA strategy and Windows clustering is a proven technology. This turned out to be a good strategy for many Exchange organizations. However, failover clustering has some cons. For clusters that relay on a shared quorum, the biggest is the reliance on shared storage — typically a storage area network. Shared storage increases the cost and complexity of the clustering solution, but it doesn't guard against the most common cause of Exchange outage: data corruption.

Exchange Server 2007 used failover clustering when implementing the Single Copy Cluster (SCC) feature, but a new data availability solution was introduced called *continuous replication* to help overcome some of the weaknesses associated with failover clustering and allow more organizations to take advantage of highly available deployments. Continuous replication, also known as log shipping, copies the transaction logs corresponding to a mailbox database from one Mailbox server to another. The target then replays the logs into its own separate copy of the database, re-creating the latest changes.

Exchange 2007 offered three types of continuous replication:

Local Continuous Replication (LCR) Protects a server from local data corruption and disk failure by creating a second copy of mailbox databases on separate disks. Because these copies are on the same server, it doesn't protect from server or site failure; activation is manual, making it less than ideal for availability designs.

Clustered Continuous Replication (CCR)   Protects against server failure (and site failure if the CCR cluster is stretched across sites) by using log shipping and Windows failover clustering components to copy mailbox databases to a second server known as the passive node.

Standby Continuous Replication (SCR)   Protects from site failure by allowing one or more copies of mailbox databases to be created. One target can host replicated copies from multiple servers, making SCR ideal for disaster recovery strategies. SCR isn't really an availability option because it requires not only manual activation, but also the activation of dependent services.

Exchange 2010 makes some sweeping changes in the data availability offerings. First, the bad news is the SCC feature is gone. Yes, that's correct; Exchange 2010 no longer supports SCC clusters. The LCR feature was discontinued as well. These features have been replaced with a solution that provides significantly better service and data availability.

What Microsoft has done instead is combine CCR and SCR into a single continuous replication offering. You now join servers into a *database availability group (DAG)*; members of that group can replicate one or more of their mailbox databases with the other servers in the group. Each database can be replicated separately from others and have one or more replicas. A DAG can cross Active Directory site boundaries, thus providing site resiliency. And activation of a passive copy is automatic, avoiding some of the pitfalls of the Exchange 2007 SCR solution.

We'll go into more detail about DAGs and continuous replication in Exchange 2010 in Chapter 23, "Creating and Managing Databases."

HA vs. DR: Not the Same

We'll provide a quick comparison between the typical Exchange HA deployment and DR deployment. If you think that by having disaster recovery you have availability, or vice versa, think again.

In an HA Exchange environment, the focus is usually on keeping mailboxes up and running for users, mail transferring with external systems, and Exchange services up. In a DR environment, the focus is usually on restoring *a bare minimum* of services, often for a smaller portion of the overall user population. In short, the difference is that of *abundance* vs. *triage*.

For Exchange, an HA design can provide several advantages beyond the obvious availability goals. A highly available Exchange environment often enables server consolidation; the same technologies that permit mailbox data to be replicated between servers or to keep multiple instances of key Exchange services also permit greater user mailbox density, or force the upgrading of key infrastructure (like network bandwidth) so that greater number of users can be handled. This increased density can make proper DR planning more difficult by increasing the requirements for a DR solution and making it harder to identify and target the appropriate user populations.

That's not to say that HA and DR are incompatible. Far from it; you can and should design your Exchange 2010 deployment for both. To do that effectively, though, you need to have a clear understanding of what each technology and feature actually provides you, so you can avoid design errors. For example, if you have separate groups of users who will need their mailboxes replicated to a DR site, set them aside in separate mailbox databases, rather than mingling them in with users whose mailboxes won't be replicated.

Storage Availability

Many administrators and IT professionals immediately think of storage designs when they hear the word *availability*. While storage is a critical part of ensuring the overall service availability of an Exchange organization, the impact of storage design is far more than just availability; it directly affects performance, reliability, and scalability.

An Overview of Exchange Storage

In medium-sized and large organizations, the Exchange administrator is usually not also responsible for storage. Many medium-sized and large organizations use specialized storage area networks (SANs) that require additional training to master. Storage is a massive topic, but we feel it is important that you at least be able to speak the language of storage.

From the very beginning, messaging systems have had a give-and-take relationship with the underlying storage system. Even on systems that aren't designed to offer long-term storage for email (such as ISP systems that offer only POP3 access), email creates demands on storage:

◆ The transport (MTA) components must have space to queue messages that cannot be immediately transmitted to the remote system.

◆ The MDA component must be able to store incoming messages that have been delivered to a mailbox until users can retrieve them.

◆ The message store, in systems like Exchange, permits users to keep a copy of their mailbox data on central servers.

◆ As the server accepts, transmits, and processes email, it keeps logs with varying levels of detail so administrators can troubleshoot and audit activities.

Though you'll have to wait for subsequent chapters to delve into the details of planning storage for Exchange, the following sections go over the two broad categories of storage solutions that are used in modern Exchange systems: direct attached storage (DAS) or storage array networks (SAN). The third type of storage, network-attached storage (NAS), is generally not supported with either Exchange 2007 or Exchange 2010.

Direct attached storage is the most common type of storage in general. DAS disks are usually internal disks or directly attached via cable. Just about every server, except for some high-end varieties such as blade systems running on boot-over-SAN, uses DAS at some level; typically, at least the boot and operating system volumes are on some DAS configuration. DAS, however, has drawbacks for use with Exchange storage: it doesn't necessarily scale as well for either capacity or performance. Further organizations that have invested significant amounts of money in their SANs may still require that Exchange use the SAN instead of DAS.

To solve these problems, people looked at NAS devices as one of the potential solutions. These machines — giant file servers — sit on the network and share their disk storage. They range in price and configuration from small plug-in devices with fixed capacity to large installations with more configuration options than most luxury cars (and a price tag to match). Companies that bought these were using them to replace file servers, web server storage, SQL Server storage — why not Exchange?

For many years, Exchange Server wasn't compatible with NAS devices; Microsoft didn't support moving Exchange storage to NAS, and vociferously argued against the idea. But ultimately Microsoft supported NAS devices for Exchange 2003.

Apparently, despite all the people asking for NAS support in Exchange 2003, it didn't turn out to be a popular option, because NAS devices were no longer supported for Exchange Server 2007 and beyond. Instead, the push switched to reducing the overall I/O requirements so that DAS configurations become practical for small to midsized organizations. Exchange 2007 moved to a 64-bit architecture to remove memory management bottlenecks in the 32-bit Windows kernel, allowing the Exchange Information Store to use more memory for intelligent mailbox data caching and reduce disk I/O. Exchange 2010 in turn makes aggressive changes to the on-disk mailbox database structures, such as moving to a new database schema that allows pages to be sequentially written to the end of the database file rather than randomly throughout the file. The schema updates improve indexing and client performance, allowing common tasks such as updating folder views to happen more quickly while requiring fewer disk reads and writes. These changes help improve efficiency and continue to drive mailbox I/O down.

The premise behind SAN is to move disks to dedicated storage units that can handle all the advanced features you need — high-end RAID configurations, hot-swap replacement, on-the-fly reconfiguration, rapid disk snapshots, tight integration with backup and restore solutions, and more. This helps consolidate the overhead of managing storage, often spread out on dozens of servers and applications (and their associated staff), into a single set of personnel. Then, dedicated network links connect these storage silos with the appropriate application servers. Yet this consolidation of storage can also be a serious pitfall since Exchange is usually not the only application placed on the SAN. Applications such as SharePoint, SQL, archiving, and file services may all be sharing the same aggregated set of spindles and cause disk contention.

Direct Attached Storage

When early versions of Exchange Server came on the market, DAS was just the way you did things. As used for legacy Exchange storage, DAS historically displays two main problems: performance and capacity. As mailbox databases got larger and traffic levels rose, pretty soon people wanted to look for alternatives; DAS storage under Exchange 2000 and Exchange 2003 required a lot of disks, because Exchange's I/O profile was optimized only for the 32-bit architecture that Windows provided at the time. Quite simply, with a fixed amount of RAM available for caching, the more simultaneous users there were on an Exchange 2003 server, the less cache per user was available.

To get more scalability on logical disks that support Exchange databases, you can always try adding more disks to the server. This gives you a configuration known as Just a Bunch of Disks (JBOD).

Although JBOD can usually give you the raw disk storage capacity you need, it has three flaws that render it unsuitable for all but the smallest legacy Exchange deployments:

JBOD forces you to partition your data   Because each disk has a finite capacity, you can't store data on that disk if it is larger than the capacity. For example, if you have four 250 GB drives, even though you have approximately one terabyte of storage in total, you have to break that up into separate 250 GB partitions. Historically, this has caused some interesting design decisions in messaging systems that rely on file system–based storage.

JBOD offers no performance benefits   Each disk is responsible for only one chunk of storage, so if that disk is already in use, subsequent I/O requests will have to wait for it to free up before they can go through. A single disk can thus become a bottleneck for the system, which can slow down mail for all your users (not just those whose mailboxes are stored on the affected disk).

JBOD offers no redundancy   If one of your disks dies, you're out of luck unless you can restore that data from backup. True, you haven't lost all your data, but the one-quarter of your users who have just lost their email are not likely to be comforted by that observation.

Several of the Exchange 2010 design goals have focused on building in the necessary features to work around these issues and make a DAS JBOD deployment a realistic option for more organizations. However, legacy versions of Exchange contain no mechanisms to work around these issues. Luckily, some bright people came up with a great generic answer to JBOD that also works well for legacy Exchange: the Redundant Array of Inexpensive Disks (RAID).

The basic premise behind RAID is to group the JBOD disks together in various configurations with a dedicated disk controller to handle the specific disk operations, allowing the computer (and applications) to see the entire collection of drives and controller as one very large disk device. These collections of disks are known as arrays; the arrays are presented to the operating system, partitioned, and formatted as if they were just regular disks. The common types of RAID configurations are shown in Table 4.1.

TABLE 4.1: RAID Configurations

RAID LEVEL	NAME	DESCRIPTION
None	Concatenated drives	Two or more disks are joined together in a contiguous data space. As one disk in the array is filled up, the data is carried over to the next disk. Though this solves the capacity problem and is easy to implement, it offers no performance or redundancy whatsoever, and makes it more likely that you're going to lose all your data, not less, through a single disk failure. These arrays are not suitable for use with legacy Exchange servers.
RAID 0	Striped drives	Two or more disks have data split among them evenly. If you write a 1 MB file to a two-disk RAID 0 array, half the data will be on one disk, half on the other. Each disk in the array can be written to (or read from) simultaneously, giving you a noticeable performance boost. However, if you lose one disk in the array, you lose all your data. These arrays are typically used for fast, large, temporary files, such as those in video editing. These arrays are not suitable for use with Exchange; while they give excellent performance, the risk of data loss is typically unacceptable.
RAID 1	Mirrored drives	Typically done with two disks (although some vendors allow more), each disk receives a copy of all the data in the array. If you lose one disk, you've still got a copy of your data on the remaining disk; you can either move the data or plug in a replacement disk and rebuild the mirror. RAID 1 also gives a performance benefit; reads can be performed by either disk, because only writes need to be mirrored. However, RAID 1 can be one of the more costly configurations; to store 500 GB of data, you'd need to buy two 500 GB drives. These arrays are suitable for use with legacy Exchange volumes, depending on the type of data and the performance of the array.
RAID 5	Parity drive	Three or more disks have data split among them. However, one disk's worth of capacity is reserved for parity checksum data; this is a special calculated value that allows the RAID system to rebuild the missing data if one drive in the array fails. The parity data is spread across all the disks in the array. If you had a four-disk 250 GB RAID 5

TABLE 4.1: RAID Configurations *(CONTINUED)*

RAID LEVEL	NAME	DESCRIPTION
		array, you'd only have 750GB of usable space. RAID 5 arrays offer better performance than JBOD, but worse performance than other RAID configurations, especially on the write requests; the checksum must be calculated and the data + parity written to all the disks in the array. Also, if you lose one disk, the array goes into degraded mode, which means that even read operations will need to be recalculated and will be slower than normal. These arrays are suitable for use with legacy Exchange mailbox database volumes on smaller servers, depending on the type of data and the performance of the array. Due to their write performance characteristics, they are usually not well matched for transaction log volumes.
RAID 6	Double parity drive	This RAID variant has become common only recently, and is designed to provide RAID 5 arrays with the ability to survive the loss of two disks. Other than offering two-disk resiliency, base RAID 6 implementations offer mostly the same benefits and drawbacks as RAID 5. Some vendors have built custom implementations that attempt to solve the performance issues. These arrays are suitable for use with Exchange, depending on the type of data and the performance of the array.
RAID 10 RAID 0+1 RAID 1+0	Mirroring plus striping	A RAID 10 array is the most costly variant to implement because it uses mirroring. However, it also uses striping to aggregate spindles and deliver blistering performance, which makes it a great choice for high-end arrays that have to sustain a high-level of I/O. As a side bonus, it also increases your chances of surviving the loss of multiple disks in the array. There are two basic variants. RAID 0+1 takes two big stripe arrays and mirrors them together; RAID 1+0 takes a number of mirror pairs and stripes them together. Both variants have essentially the same performance numbers, but 1+0 is preferred because it can be rebuilt more quickly (you only have to regenerate a single disk) and has far higher chances of surviving the loss of multiple disks (you can lose one disk in each mirror pair). These arrays have traditionally been used for high-end highly loaded legacy Exchange mailbox database volumes.

Note that several of these types of RAID arrays may be suitable for your Exchange server. Which one should you use? The answer to that question depends entirely on how many mailboxes your servers are holding, how they're used, and other types of business needs. Beware of anyone who tries to give hard-and-fast answers like, "Always use RAID 5 for Exchange database volumes." To determine the true answer, you need to go through a proper storage sizing process, find out what your I/O and capacity requirements are really going to be, think about your data recovery needs and service level agreements (SLAs), and then decide what storage configuration will meet those needs for you in a fashion you can afford. There are no magic bullets.

In every case, the RAID controller you use — the piece of hardware, plus drivers, that aggregates the individual disk volumes for you into a single pseudo-device that is presented to Windows — plays a key role. You can't just take a collection of disks, toss them into slots in your server, and go to town with RAID. You need to install extra drivers and management software, you need to take extra steps to configure your arrays before you can even use them in Windows, and you may even need to update your disaster recovery procedures to ensure that you can always recover data from drives in a RAID array. Generally, you'll need to test whether you can move drives in one array between two controllers, even those from the same manufacturer; not all controllers support all options. After your server has melted down and your SLA is fast approaching is not a good time to find out that you needed to carry a spare controller on hand.

If you choose the DAS route (whether JBOD or RAID), you'll need to think about how you're going to house the physical disks. Modern server cases don't leave a lot of extra room for disks; this is especially true of rack-mounted systems. Usually, this means you'll need some sort of external enclosure that hooks back into a physical bus on your server, such as SAS or eSATA disks. Make sure to give these enclosures suitable power and cooling; hard drives pull a lot of power and return it all eventually as heat.

Also make sure that your drive backplanes (the physical connection point) and enclosures support hot-swap capability, where you can easily pull the drive and replace it without powering the system down. Keep a couple of spare drives and drive sleds on hand, too. You don't want to have to schedule an outage of your Exchange server in order to replace a failed drive in a RAID 5 array, letting all your users enjoy the performance hit of a thrashing RAID volume because the array is in degraded mode until the replacement drives arrive.

RAID CONTROLLERS ARE NOT ALL CREATED EQUAL

Beware! Not all kinds of RAID are created equal. Before you spend a lot of time trying to figure out which configuration to choose, first think about your RAID controller. There are three kinds of them, and unlike RAID configurations, it's pretty easy to determine which kind you need for Exchange:

Software RAID   Software RAID avoids the whole problem of having a RAID controller by performing all the magic in the operating system software. If you convert your disk to dynamic volumes, you can do RAID 0, RAID 1, and RAID 5 natively in Windows 2008 without any extra hardware. However, Microsoft strongly recommends that you not do this with Exchange, and the Exchange community echoes that recommendation. It takes extra memory and processing power, and inevitably slows your disks down from what you could get with a simple investment in good hardware. You will also not be able to support higher levels of I/O load with this configuration, in our experience.

BIOS RAID   BIOS RAID attempts to provide "cheap" RAID by putting some code for RAID in the RAID chipset, which is then placed either directly on the motherboard (common in workstation-grade and low-end server configurations) or on an inexpensive add-in card. The dirty little secret is that the RAID chipset isn't really doing the RAID operations in hardware; again it's all happening in software, this time in the associated Windows driver (which is written by the vendor) rather than an official Windows subsystem. If you're about to purchase a RAID controller card for a price that seems too good to be true, it's probably one of these cards. These RAID controllers tend to have a smaller number of ports, which limits their overall utility. Although you can get Exchange to work with them, you can do so only with very low numbers of users. Otherwise, you'll quickly hit the limits these cards have and stress your storage system. Just avoid them; the time you save will more than make up for the up-front price savings.

Hardware RAID This is the only kind of RAID you should even be thinking about for your Exchange servers. This means good-quality, high-end cards that come from reputable manufacturers that have taken the time to get the product on the Windows Hardware Compatibility List (HCL). These cards do a lot of the work for your system, removing the CPU overhead of parity calculations from the main processors, and they are worth every penny you pay for them. Better yet, they'll be able to handle the load your Exchange servers and users throw at them.

If you can't tell whether a given controller you're eyeing is BIOS or true hardware RAID, get help. Lots of forums and websites on the Internet will help you sort out which hardware to get and which to avoid. And while you're at it, spring a few extra bucks for good, reliable disks. We cannot stress enough the importance of not cutting corners on your Exchange storage system; while Exchange 2010 gives you a lot more room for designing storage and brings back options you may not have had before, you still need to buy the best components that you can to make up the designed storage system. The time and long-term costs you save will be your own.

Storage Area Networks

Initial SAN solutions used fiber-optic connections to provide the necessary bandwidth for storage operations. As a result, these systems were incredibly expensive and were used only by organizations with deep pockets. The advent of Gigabit Ethernet over copper and new storage bus technologies such as SATA and SAS, however, has moved the cost of SANs down into the realm where midsized companies can now afford both the sticker price and the resource training to become competent with these new technologies.

Over time, many vendors have begun to offer SAN solutions that are affordable even for small companies. The main reason they've been able to do so is the iSCSI protocol; block-based file access routed over TCP/IP connections. Add iSCSI with ubiquitous Gigabit Ethernet hardware, and SAN deployments have become a lot more common.

Clustering and high availability concerns are the other factors in the growth of Exchange/SAN deployments. Exchange 2003 supported clustered configurations but required the cluster nodes to have a shared storage solution. As a result, any organization that wanted to deploy an Exchange cluster needed some sort of SAN solution (apart from the handful of people who stuck with shared SCSI configurations). A SAN has a certain elegance to it; you simply create a virtual slice of drive space for Exchange (called a LUN, or logical unit number), use Fibre Channel or iSCSI (and corresponding drivers) to present it to the Exchange server, and away you go. Even with Exchange 2007 — which was reengineered with an eye toward making DAS a supportable choice for Exchange storage in specific CCR and SCR configurations — many organizations still found that using SAN for Exchange storage was the best answer for their various business requirements. By this time, management had seen the benefits of centralized storage management and wanted to ensure that Exchange deployments were part of the big plan.

However, SAN solutions don't fix all problems, even with (usually because of) their price tag. Often, SANs make your environment even more complex and difficult to support. Because SANs cost so much, there is often a strong drive to use the SAN for all storage and make full use of every last free block of space. The cost per GB of storage for a SAN can be between three and ten times as expensive as DAS disks. Unfortunately, Exchange's I/O characteristics are very different than those of just about any other application, and few dedicated SAN administrators really know how to properly allocate disk space for Exchange:

◆ SAN administrators do not usually understand that total disk space is only one component of Exchange performance. For day-to-day operations, it is far more important to ensure enough I/O capacity. Traditionally, this is delivered by using lots of physical disks (commonly referred to as "spindles") to increase the amount of simultaneous read/write operations supported. It is important to make sure the SAN solution provides enough I/O capacity, not just free disk space, or Exchange will crawl.

◆ Even if you can convince them to configure LUNs spread across enough disks, SAN administrators immediately want to reclaim that wasted space. As a result, you end up sharing the same spindles between Exchange and some other application with its own performance curve, and then suddenly you have extremely noticeable but hard-to-diagnose performance issues with your Exchange servers. Shared spindles will kill Exchange.

◆ Although some SAN vendors have put a lot of time and effort into understanding Exchange and its I/O needs so that their salespeople and certified consultants can help you deploy Exchange on their products properly, not everyone does the same. Many vendors will shrug off performance concerns by telling you about their extensive write caching and how good write caching will smooth out any performance issues. Their argument is true . . . up to a point. A cache can help isolate Exchange from effects of transient I/O events, but it won't help you come Monday morning when all your users are logging in and the SQL Server databases that share your spindles are churning through extra operations.

The moral of the story is simple: don't believe that you need to have a SAN. This is especially true with Exchange 2010; there have been a lot of under-the-hood changes to the mailbox database storage to ensure that more companies can deploy a 7200 RPM SATA JBOD configuration and be able to get good performance and reliability from that system.

If you do find that a SAN provides the best value for your organization, get the best one you can afford. Make sure that your vendors know Exchange storage inside and out; if possible, get them to put you in contact with their on-staff Exchange specialists. Have them work with your SAN administrators to come up with a storage configuration that meets your real Exchange needs.

Needless to say, the hints we've scattered here should have given you clues that storage and the Mailbox role have undergone some radical changes in Exchange 2010. We'll go into more details about Exchange storage in Chapter 23, "Creating and Managing Databases."

Compliance and Governance

Quite simply, today's legal system considers email to be an official form of business communication just like written memos. This means that any type of legal requirement or legal action against your organization (regarding business records) will undoubtedly include email. Unless you work in a specific vertical market such as healthcare or financials, the emergence of compliance and governance as topics of import to the messaging administrator is a relatively recent event. The difference between compliance and governance can be summarized simply:

Governance is the process of defining and enforcing policies, while compliance is the process of ensuring that you meet external requirements.

However, both of these goals share a lot of common ground:

◆ They require thorough planning to implement, based on a detailed understanding of what behaviors are allowed, required, or forbidden.

◆ Though they require technical controls to ensure implementation, they are at heart about people and processes.

◆ They require effective monitoring in order to audit the effectiveness of the compliance and governance measures.

In short, they require all the same things you need in order to effectively manage your messaging data. As a result, there's a useful framework you can use to evaluate your compliance and governance needs: Discovery, Compliance, Archival, and Retention, also known as the DCAR framework.

DCAR recognizes four key pillars of activity, each historically viewed as a separate task for messaging administrators. However, all four pillars involve the same mechanisms, people, and policies; all four in fact are overlapping facets of messaging data management. These four pillars are described in the following list:

Discovery   Finding messages in the system quickly and accurately, whether for litigation, auditing, or other needs. There are generally two silos of discovery: *personal discovery*, allowing users to find and monitor the messages they send and receive, and *organizational discovery*, which encompasses the traditional litigation or auditing activities most messaging administrators think about. It requires the following:

◆ Good storage design to handle the additional overhead of discovery actions

◆ The accurate and thorough indexing of all messaging data that enters the Exchange organization through any means

◆ Control over the ability of users to move data into and out of the messaging system through mechanisms such as personal folders (PSTs)

◆ Control of the user's ability to delete data that may be required by litigation

Compliance   Meeting all legal, regulatory, and governance requirements, whether derived from external or internal drivers. Although many of the technologies used for compliance also look similar to those used by individual users for *mailbox management*, compliance happens more at the organization level (even if not all populations within the organization are subject to the same regimes). It requires the following:

◆ Clear guidance on which behaviors are allowed, required, or prohibited, as well as a clear description of which will be enforced through technical means

◆ The means to enforce required behavior, prevent disallowed behavior, and audit for the success or failure of these means

◆ The ability to control and view all messaging data that enters the Exchange organization through any means

Archival   The ability to preserve the messaging data that will be required for future operations, including governance tasks. Like discovery, archival happens on two broad levels: the *user archive* is a personal solution that allows individual users to retain and reuse historical personal messaging data relevant to their job function, while the *business archive* is aimed at providing immutable organization-wide benefits such as storage reduction, eDiscovery, and knowledge retention. It requires the following:

◆ Clear guidance on which data must be preserved and a clear description of procedural and technical measures that will be used to enforce archival

◆ The accurate and thorough indexing of all messaging data that enters the Exchange organization through any means

◆ Control over the ability of users to move data into and out of the messaging system through mechanisms such as personal folders (PSTs)

Retention   The ability to identify data that can be safely removed without adverse impact (whether immediate or delayed) on the business. Although many retention mechanisms are defined and maintained centrally in the organization, it is not uncommon for many implementations to either depend on voluntary user activity for compliance or allow users to easily define stricter or looser retention policies for their own data. It requires the following:

◆ Clear guidance on which data is safe to remove and a clear description of the time frames and technical measures that will be used to enforce removal

◆ The accurate identification of all messaging data that enters the Exchange organization through any means

◆ Control over the ability of users to move data into and out of the messaging system through mechanisms such as personal folders (PSTs)

If many of these requirements look the same, good; that emphasizes that these activities are all merely different parts of the same overall goal. You should be realizing that these activities are not things you do with your messaging system so much as they are activities that you perform while managing your messaging system. The distinction is subtle, but important; knowing your requirements helps make the difference between designing and deploying a system that can be easily adapted to meet your needs and one that you will constantly have to fight. Many of these activities will require the addition of third-party solutions, even for Exchange 2010, which includes more DCAR functionality out-of-the-box than any other previous version of Exchange.

What makes this space interesting is that many of these functions are being filled by a variety of solutions, include both on-premise and hosted solutions, often at a competitive price. Also interesting is the tension between Microsoft's view of how to manage messaging data in the Exchange organization versus the defined needs of many organizations to control information across multiple applications. More than ever, no solution will be one-size-fits-all; before accepting any vendor's assurance that their product will meet your needs, first make sure that you understand the precise problems you're trying to solve (instead of just the set of technology buzzwords that you may have been told will be your magic bullet) and know how their functionality will address the real needs.

WHERE JOURNALING FITS INTO DCAR

In our discussion of DCAR, we deliberately left out a common keyword that you inevitably hear about. *Journaling* is a common technology that gets mentioned whenever compliance, archival, and discovery are discussed. However, it often gets over-discussed. Journaling is not the end goal; it's simply a mechanism for getting data out of Exchange into some other system, which provides the specific function that you really want or need.

Very simply, journaling allows Exchange administrators to designate a subset of messaging data that will automatically be duplicated into a *journal report* and sent to a third party — another mailbox in the Exchange organization, a stand-alone system in the organization, or even an external recipient such as a hosted archival service. The journal report includes not only the exact, unaltered text of the original message, but additional details that the senders and recipients may not know, such as any BCC recipients, the specific SMTP envelope information used, or the full membership list and recipient distribution lists (as they existed at the time of message receipt). These reports are commonly used for one of two purposes: to capture data into some other system for archival, or to provide a historical record for compliance purposes.

We don't know a single Exchange administrator who has ever come up to us and said, "I want to journal my data." Instead, they say, "I need to archive my data and I have to use journaling to get it to my archival solution." Journaling isn't the end goal; it's the means to the end. If journaling is a potential concern for you, you should stop and ask yourself why:

◆ What information am I trying to journal?

◆ What do I want the journaled information for?

◆ Perhaps most important, what am I going to do with the journaled information?

Understanding why you need journaling will give you the ammunition you need to effectively design your Exchange organization, journaling requirements, and appropriate add-on applications and hosted solutions. It will also help you identify when journaling may not be the answer you need to solve the particular business problems you're facing.

You should also understand the impact that journaling will have on your system, as well as know what limitations journaling has. There are certain types of data that never get journaled, and if you need that data, you'll have to at a minimum supplement your solution with something that captures that data.

We will discuss Exchange 2010's journaling features in greater detail in Chapter 26. For now, just be aware that journaling is merely a tool that helps you solve some other problem.

The Bottom Line

Distinguish between availability, backup and recovery, and disaster recovery　When it comes to keeping your Exchange 2010 deployment healthy, you've got a lot of options provided out of the box. Knowing which problems they solve is critical to deploying them correctly.

Master It You have been asked to select a backup type that will back up all data once per week but on a daily basis will ensure that the server does not run out of transaction log disk space.

Determine the best option for your disaster recovery When creating your disaster recovery plans for Exchange 2010, you have a variety of options to choose from. Exchange 2010 includes an improved ability to integrate with external systems that will widen your recovery possibilities.

Master It What are the different types of disaster recovery?

Distinguish between the different types of availability meant by the term *high availability* The term high availability means different things to different people. When you design and deploy your Exchange 2010 solution, you need to be confident that everyone is designing for the same goals.

Master It What types of availability are there?

Implement the four pillars of compliance and governance activities Ensuring that your Exchange 2010 organization meets your regular operational needs means thinking about the topics of compliance and governance within your organization.

Master It What are the four pillars of compliance and governance as applied to a messaging system?

Chapter 5

Message Security and Hygiene

Security and email go together like peanut butter and chocolate. When your users are sending vital business information through email, you can bet that they're going to want some way to ensure that information can't be intercepted or exposed. Although the basics of securing email haven't radically changed in Exchange Server 2010 since Exchange 2007, the new version gives you many new options over Exchange 2003 that will make your life as an IT professional much easier.

Message hygiene goes hand-in-hand with the topic of security. Email is one of the primary vectors that malicious people use to attack organizations and people. Their goal could be to get users to expose valuable information that can be exploited for financial gain — whether personal or corporate information. Or they may want your users to open unsafe messages and attachments and load your organization's desktops and servers with malware, in the process subverting firewalls and allowing them to use your computing resources as their own.

In this chapter, you will learn to:

◆ Secure messages through the transport protocols

◆ Secure messages from end to end

◆ Ensure the email hygiene of your organization

Transport Security

When it comes to securing your organization's email, there are a number of good general guidelines to follow:

◆ Use well-tested security mechanisms. Closed, proprietary mechanisms are more likely to contain serious flaws and are harder to fix when those flaws are found.

◆ Reuse the same mechanisms whenever you can. This helps minimize administrative complexity and reduces the amount of code that must be patched to distribute a fix.

◆ Go for as much coverage for as little effort as you can. You want to reduce the amount of work you need to do and maximize your bang for the buck.

With these guidelines firmly in mind, we'll start our discussion of email security by talking about transport security — the art of securing messages that are in transit or moving from one location to another, such as from your client to your mailbox server, between Exchange servers in your organization, or between organizations (whether or not both are using Exchange).

If you deploy no security measures with Exchange 2010 other than Secure Socket Layer (SSL) and Transport Layer Security (TLS), you will have done more to ensure transport security for your organization's message traffic than any other single step you can do. Exchange 2010 even makes it ridiculously easy for you to do so; the SSL and TLS protocols are enabled and configured out of the box.

SSL: Pick Your Port

Everyone who has used a web browser sometime in the last five years should be familiar with the basics of what SSL is. Unfortunately, all most people know is that "it's that little padlock on some websites." A few more know that SSL has something to do with digital certificates, although most people don't know what a digital certificate is in turn. All they know is that SSL is what makes secure web transfers possible.

Developers through the years have spent a lot of time and energy developing security protocols. SSL is perhaps the best known and most popular, in part because it piggybacked on the exploding success of the World Wide Web. As a result, SSL has become firmly linked with HTTP — which is a shame, because it can be used to secure just about any TCP-based protocol. It has, however, gone through multiple revisions and additions. In fact, SSL version 1 was never actually released.

SSL v2.0 was developed and released in November 1994 by Netscape Communications. While it incorporated several advanced features — such as support for per-session negotiation of a number of specific cryptographic algorithms — and provided a decent level of security for HTTP sessions, it wasn't perfectly secure. It had several flaws and weaknesses that left it vulnerable to determined attackers and allowed the risk of data exposure, including the ability to force weaker algorithms to be used. At this time, SSL was not an open standard that was part of the IETF standards process.

Privacy Communication Technology (PCT) v1.0 was Microsoft's 1995 attempt to do two things: first, fix the weaknesses present in SSL v2.0; second, either supplant or replace Netscape's proprietary security protocol with a competitor or, at the very least, pressure Netscape to open up control of SSL. Although PCT incorporated several new features, history bears the record of the result: PCT was never widely adopted and is not used in the modern Web. However, SSL was revised and the resulting standard was opened up to the IETF standards process.

SSL v3.0 was released as an IETF draft in November 1996, once again by Netscape. It both addressed most of the weaknesses in SSL v2.0 and incorporated many features of PCT to strengthen the overall protocol. Because the standard was released as an Internet draft, implementers could freely include support for SSL v3.0 in their code. This version of SSL is still widely used on the Internet today — a testament to its flexibility and robust design.

How SSL Works

Let's dive beneath the hood and take a deeper look at how SSL works. We'll need the following objects:

A Web Server Although SSL can be used to protect a variety of protocols, we'll use HTTP for our example.

An X.509v3 Digital Certificate for the Web Server We haven't talked about what digital certificates are in depth, and we won't go into the details until Chapter 7, "Namespaces and the Autodiscovery Service." For the time being, just know that a digital certificate is essentially a document that consists of multiple properties and values. Some of the important properties and values we'll look at include:

◆ The SubjectName property describes the hostname associated with the certificate. In our example, the hostname is `www.somorita.com`.

◆ The SubjectAlternateName property is optional, and describes one or more hostnames that are also associated with the certificate. For our example, we won't use this property.

◆ The Thumbprint property provides a cryptographic hash that is used to uniquely identify a certificate. When you have multiple certificates on your Exchange server, this can be a valuable shortcut for uniquely identifying which one you want to work with. For our example, this property isn't important.

◆ The PublicKey property describes a cryptographic public key that is associated with the certificate. The public key is intended for use by any remote server (or user). Data that is encrypted using the public key cannot be decrypted using that key.

◆ The Private Key is not part of the certificate but is nonetheless important. When the certificate is installed on the server and is intended for the server to use for authentication, an associated private key is securely stored on the server. The private key is never associated with the certificate or stored as one of the server properties. Our example certificate has a public key and private key; the specific values are unimportant.

◆ The certificate also contains one or more digital signatures from the issuing certificate authorities. These signatures are essential to verify the validity of the certificate. Without these signatures, malicious people could easily forge a certificate. However, the chain of trust is only as strong as the amount of security around the issuing certificates of the upstream certificate authorities. Our example certificate has a signature from the enterprise root CA installed on `ca.somorita.com`.

◆ The certificate may also contain other metadata fields that define information such as the length of time the certificate is valid, the valid uses for the certificate, and other information. Not all of these fields are required for every certificate, but flexibility with certificates makes the certificates a generic useful tool rather than a specialized tool for one or two narrow uses. For our example, these aren't important.

A Web Client   Typically a web browser, although it could be any program that speaks HTTP. In this example, you can imagine we're using whichever browser you're happy with.

A URL for the Client to Contact   This URL contains the hostname of the server. The client will resolve this hostname back to an IP address through the usual mechanisms. Our example URL is `https://www.somorita.com/` — which specifies the HTTPS (HTTP + SSL) protocol.

A Dedicated TCP Port for the Server to Listen for HTTP and SSL Traffic   Traditionally, HTTP is on TCP port 80 while HTTPS is on TCP port 443.

With this configuration in mind, let's look at Figure 5.1. What we see is a multistep process. It looks complicated, but it's not.

1. The client contacts the `www.somorita.com` server on TCP port 443. Since the browser knows that the URL protocol is HTTPS, it knows it must first negotiate the SSL layer and sends the *ClientHello* message. This message includes several important pieces of

information, such as the highest SSL protocol version the client supports, a list of cipher suites, a list of supported compression methods, and a random number.

FIGURE 5.1
The SSL protocol exchange

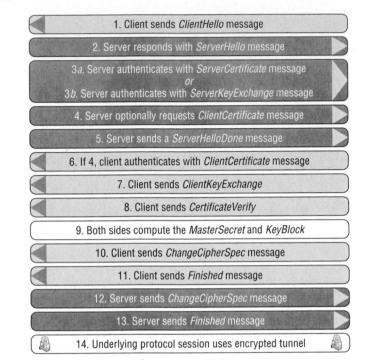

1. Client sends *ClientHello* message

2. Server responds with *ServerHello* message

3*a*. Server authenticates with *ServerCertificate* message
or
3*b*. Server authenticates with *ServerKeyExchange* message

4. Server optionally requests *ClientCertificate* message

5. Server sends a *ServerHelloDone* message

6. If 4, client authenticates with *ClientCertificate* message

7. Client sends *ClientKeyExchange*

8. Client sends *CertificateVerify*

9. Both sides compute the *MasterSecret* and *KeyBlock*

10. Client sends *ChangeCipherSpec* message

11. Client sends *Finished* message

12. Server sends *ChangeCipherSpec* message

13. Server sends *Finished* message

14. Underlying protocol session uses encrypted tunnel

2. The server responds with the *ServerHello* message. Based on the information contained in the *ClientHello*, the server can pick which protocol version to use (typically the highest version mutually supported). This allows backward compatibility. The *ServerHello* message tells the client which protocol version was chosen, which cipher suite will be used (again, the most secure suite supported by both sides), the chosen compression method, and the server's random number. This message may also contain a session ID, which allows the client to later establish additional connections to the server and participate in the existing SSL session without having to perform the associated re-negotiation.

3. Depending on how it is configured and which cipher suite was chosen, the server will send either the *ServerCertificate* message, which contains the entire digital certificate, or the *ServerKeyExchange* message, which contains a public key used by those cipher suites that don't use a full digital certificate.

4. If the server is configured to require client authentication using digital certificates, it sends a *ClientCertificate* request message. This is an optional step.

5. The server sends the *ServerHelloDone* message. This indicates that it has completed its portion of the SSL handshake negotiation process.

6. The first client response is optional. If it received a *ClientCertificate* request, it responds with the corresponding *ClientCertificate* message containing its digital certificate and public key.

7. The client examines the digital certificate presented by the server and validates it. The specifics of how that validation is performed depend on the particular client application and configuration, but it typically includes validating the certificate metadata, such as the expiration date; the digital signatures of the issuing CAs; and whether the certificate has been revoked using the CA's certificate revocation list (CRL).

8. At this point, the client generates a master secret key that is based on random numbers generated during the *ClientHello* and *ServerHello*.

9. In any event, the client then sends the *ClientKeyExchange* message. This message contains specific information required by the selected cipher suite; a secret value, a public key, or even no value at all. The secret key will be encrypted with the server's public key so that it is protected when it is sent back.

10. The client and server now need to establish a shared secret. They can't just pass it over the wire — communications to this point are in the clear and could be intercepted. Instead, they use the random numbers and other cryptographic elements previously passed in steps 1, 2, and 7 to compute a common valued called the *master secret*. This master secret cannot be validated by an eavesdropper, which doesn't possess the private key data necessary to decrypt specific values. Using private key encryption would be slower and more CPU-intensive than using a symmetric key cipher, so the server and client both use the master secret to generate the *session key block*. This key will be used for the actual session encryption algorithm.

11. The client sends the *ChangeCipherSpec* message to the server. This signals the server that all further client communications will use the selected cipher suite, encrypted with the mutually generated session key block.

12. The client sends a final *Finished* message. This message is authenticated and encrypted, so only the server can decrypt it and respond appropriately.

13. The server now responds to the encrypted *Finished* message from the client with its own *ChangeCipherSpec* message. This signals that the server is also switching to authenticated, encrypted communication.

14. The server sends its final *Finished* message. Again, this message is authenticated and encrypted, so the client can trust it is actually the server (and not some man-in-the-middle attacker) that has sent the message.

At this point, the SSL handshake is complete. All further application traffic sent over this SSL session will be encrypted and authenticated according to the parameters established during the handshake.

So that's how SSL works, and it works well enough to be the backbone of our entire modern web-based commerce system. However, SSL v3.0 does have drawbacks:

◆ As we said before, each SSL handshake picks a cipher suite from the list of suites mutually supported by the client and server. These cipher suites allow an almost modular support for a variety of special-purpose cryptographic algorithms, each one specialized for a specific use and strength. Each organization can then prevent the use of any specific algorithm without crippling the SSL protocol as a whole. However, using a poor or weak cipher can result in an SSL that can be easily broken. Many of the algorithms included in SSL v3.0 are now considered cryptographically obsolete, or at least only suitable for use in conjunction with newer algorithms that are not supported by the SSL protocol.

♦ The certificate private key lengths and cryptographic algorithm key lengths become an important factor. Longer keys take longer to generate and process but provide greater security, because it makes it harder for an attacker to brute-force or mathematically break the key. With modern computer resources, older 40-bit keys should be avoided and SSL should always be configured to require 128 bits unless otherwise required. Additionally, new certificates should be at least 1024 bits, and you should seriously consider 2048 bits or higher.

♦ Certificate validation is a huge part of SSL. Depending on your application, some very strict measures can be taken to validate not just the server certificate, but also the entire certificate chain. Typically, each server that hosts the certificate (including any reverse proxies or firewalls that terminate the SSL session) should be configured with the appropriate intermediate CA and root CA certificates as well. As part of the SSL negotiation, the server can pass intermediate certificates in the signing chain on to the client, allowing the client to validate the chain as long as it trusts the root CA certificate. The trick is to pick a CA that has appropriate safeguards for validating the identity of the entity requesting the certificate.

♦ Traditionally, SSL required a separate IP address for every hostname. With wildcard certificates and certificates that make use of the Subject Alternate Name (SAN) property, this restriction is somewhat eased. However, if you're trying to offer both secured and nonsecured versions of the same protocol, you must do so over two separate ports. SSL cannot discriminate between an incoming connection that requires a secure tunnel and those that do not; it's all or nothing.

TROUBLESHOOTING CERTIFICATE ISSUES

If you are ever trying to troubleshoot protocol problems in your Exchange organization, and that protocol uses SSL or TLS, the very first thing that you should do is use a browser to connect to the appropriate resource. Modern browsers will generate warnings about the SSL session when there is an issue with the certificate, such as a name mismatch, an expired certificate, a revoked certificate, or a certificate signed by a CA whom you do not trust. When you can connect without errors, you know that you've got your certificate issues worked out and can move on to the next stage.

Often, clients like Outlook or other Exchange servers will not tell you exactly what is wrong with your certificate configuration without a lot of extra diagnostic logging. Simply knowing how to use a browser can be a lot faster and easier.

Enter Transport Layer Security

As SSL began to be widely adopted and the nature of laws of cryptographic exports changed how computer science was able to research and publish new algorithms, the IETF pushed forward with continuing to improve SSL into a fully open standard. Their result, published in January 1999 as RFC 2246, introduced Transport Layer Security (TLS) v1.0. The current version of TLS, v1.2, is described by RFC 5246.

While TLS is clearly based on SSL, it is not meant to be 100 percent backward compatible, although compatibility concerns were minimized by including an SSL v3.0 fallback mode. However, the IETF replaced some internal calculations with stronger variants, improved the cipher suites, and made other housekeeping changes. These details are minor, though, and TLS and SSL are generally (as protocols) considered equally strong. TLS can be configured to be stronger because it supports stronger component algorithms in its supported cipher suites — but that's a reflection on those algorithms, not on TLS as a whole.

The biggest difference between SSL and TLS is that the latter is specifically designed to be invoked in-band in a nonsecure protocol connection, allowing the client and server to establish a protocol session, create the secure tunnel, and then move on with their protocol session. This difference has one very real benefit that has made TLS of great benefit to SMTP in particular: it allows a single well-known listener at TCP port 25 to offer both nonsecure SMTP sessions from non-TLS SMTP mailers as well as secure SMTP + TLS sessions from servers that are configured to take advantage of the additional security. If some error such as certificate validation prevents the secure tunnel from being established, the client and server applications can continue to use the existing session, albeit with whatever limitations each has locally configured. As an example, an SMTP mailer can offer strong authentication options such as NTLM to every connection, but restrict the offering of Basic text authentication to only those machines that first establish TLS.

Let's take a look at this in action with this sample Exchange SMTP protocol log:

```
   {The client connects to the server}
01 S: 220 ex2010.somorita.com ESMTP ready at Sun, 31 May 2009 22:37:28 -0700
   C: EHLO desktop.somorita.com
   S: 250-ex2010.somorita.com Hello desktop.somorita.com
   S: 250-SIZE
   S: 250-PIPELINING
   S: 250-DSN
   S: 250-ENHANCEDSTATUSCODES
02 S: 250-STARTTLS
   S: 250-X-ANONYMOUSTLS
03 S: 250-AUTH NTLM
   S: 250-X-EXPS GSSAPI NTLM
   S: 250-8BITMIME
   S: 250-BINARYMIME
   S: 250-CHUNKING
   S: 250-XEXCH50
   S: 250 XRDST
04 C: STARTTLS
   S: 250 2.0.0 Ready to start TLS
05 C: <starts TLS negotiation>
   C & S: <negotiate a TLS session>
   C & S: <check result of negotiation>
06 S: 220 ex2010.somorita.com ESMTP ready at Sun, 31 May 2009 22:37:30 -0700
   C: EHLO desktop.somorita.com
   S: 250-ex2010.somorita.com Hello desktop.somorita.com
   S: 250-SIZE
   S: 250-PIPELINING
   S: 250-DSN
   S: 250-ENHANCEDSTATUSCODES
   S: 250-X-ANONYMOUSTLS
07 S: 250-AUTH NTLM LOGIN PLAIN
   S: 250-X-EXPS GSSAPI NTLM
   S: 250-8BITMIME
```

```
S: 250-BINARYMIME
S: 250-CHUNKING
S: 250-XEXCH50
S: 250 XRDST
{The client continues the session}
```

There are seven key points of note in this conversation:

1. The server sends an initial greeting from the server to the client; the client responds with the EHLO response .

2. The server advertises its support for the STARTTLS verb, which allows the client to begin the TLS handshake.

3. The server is also advertising SMTP AUTH. In this case, it only offers the NTLM authentication mechanism. This is prudent security; it prevents the transmission of user credentials in clear text over a nonsecured connection.

4. The client begins the TLS negotiation process and the server responds with the status code, indicating that it will allow the negotiation to begin.

5. The client and server walk through the TLS negotiation process (refer to Figure 5.1 if you're rusty on the overall details).

6. The server accepts the results and resets the SMTP session. This is explicitly mandated by the STARTTLS RFC (RFC 2487); the only state information the client and server are allowed to keep after the TLS session is established is the information gathered during the TLS handshake. Any knowledge of SMTP verbs offered or hostnames used is explicitly forbidden to be kept. The client must effectively begin the SMTP session again.

7. This time, however, the results are a little different. First, STARTTLS is not offered again — that would be redundant and could cause some interesting bugs and denial-of-service conditions. The interesting part, though, is that this time, SMTP AUTH is also offering Basic authentication methods. Because the connection is now secure, the server configuration permits the use of this less secure authentication technique.

While TLS and SSL aren't exactly the same, we will use them interchangeably for the rest of this book. If we mean one specifically, we'll be sure to point that out.

CHECK YOUR CIPHER SUITE CONFIGURATION

Windows Server 2008 made some changes to the default cipher suites that it supports and the order in which it offers these ciphers. For the most part, these changes are good — they introduce newer, stronger algorithms, such as AES and SHA-1, and retire older, nonsecure algorithms, such as RC4 and MD5. In some rare cases, you may find that these changes prohibit interoperability with external systems and programs.

These cipher suites specify three sets of algorithms: a *key exchange* algorithm to transfer the public key information needed to ensure authenticity, a *streaming cipher* that allows encryption of the session data using the derived symmetric key, and a *message digest* algorithm that provides a secure cryptographic hash function.

In Windows Server 2003, this is the default list of cipher suites:

```
TLS_RSA_WITH_RC4_128_MD5 (RSA certificate key exchange, RC4 streaming session
cipher with 128-bit key, and 128-bit MD5 HMAC; a safe, legacy choice of
protocols, although definitely aging in today's environment)
TLS_RSA_WITH_RC4_128_SHA (RSA certificate key exchange, RC4 streaming session
 cipher with 128-bit key, and 160-bit SHA-1 HMAC; a bit stronger than the above,
thanks to SHA-1 being not quite as brittle as MD5 yet)
TLS_RSA_WITH_3DES_EDE_CBC_SHA (you can work out the rest)
TLS_DHE_DSS_WITH_3DES_EDE_CBC_SHA
TLS_RSA_WITH_DES_CBC_SHA
TLS_DHE_DSS_WITH_DES_CBC_SHA
TLS_RSA_EXPORT1024_WITH_RC4_56_SHA
TLS_RSA_EXPORT1024_WITH_DES_CBC_SHA
TLS_DHE_DSS_EXPORT1024_WITH_DES_CBC_SHA
TLS_RSA_EXPORT_WITH_RC4_40_MD5
TLS_RSA_EXPORT_WITH_RC2_CBC_40_MD5
TLS_RSA_WITH_NULL_MD5
TLS_RSA_WITH_NULL_SHA
```

In Windows Server 2008, you get the following default configuration (new suites are bold-faced):

```
TLS_RSA_WITH_AES_128_CBC_SHA (Using AES 128-bit as a CBC session cipher)
TLS_RSA_WITH_AES_256_CBC_SHA (Using AES 256-bit as a CBC session cipher)
TLS_RSA_WITH_RC4_128_SHA
TLS_RSA_WITH_3DES_EDE_CBC_SHA
TLS_ECDHE_ECDSA_WITH_AES_128_CBC_SHA_P256 (AES 128-bit, SHA 256-bit)
TLS_ECDHE_ECDSA_WITH_AES_128_CBC_SHA_P384(AES 128-bit, SHA 384-bit)
TLS_ECDHE_ECDSA_WITH_AES_128_CBC_SHA_P521(AES 128-bit, SHA 521-bit)
TLS_ECDHE_ECDSA_WITH_AES_256_CBC_SHA_P256(AES 256-bit, SHA 256-bit)
TLS_ECDHE_ECDSA_WITH_AES_256_CBC_SHA_P384(AES 256-bit, SHA 384-bit)
TLS_ECDHE_ECDSA_WITH_AES_256_CBC_SHA_P521(AES 256-bit, SHA 521-bit)
TLS_ECDHE_RSA_WITH_AES_128_CBC_SHA_P256 (you can work out the rest)
TLS_ECDHE_RSA_WITH_AES_128_CBC_SHA_P384
TLS_ECDHE_RSA_WITH_AES_128_CBC_SHA_P521
TLS_ECDHE_RSA_WITH_AES_256_CBC_SHA_P256
TLS_ECDHE_RSA_WITH_AES_256_CBC_SHA_P384
TLS_ECDHE_RSA_WITH_AES_256_CBC_SHA_P521
TLS_DHE_DSS_WITH_AES_128_CBC_SHA
TLS_DHE_DSS_WITH_AES_256_CBC_SHA
TLS_DHE_DSS_WITH_3DES_EDE_CBC_SHA
TLS_RSA_WITH_RC4_128_MD5
SSL_CK_RC4_128_WITH_MD5 )
SSL_CK_DES_192_EDE3_CBC_WITH_MD5
TLS_RSA_WITH_NULL_MD5
TLS_RSA_WITH_NULL_SHA
```

Note that key lengths are not an Exchange-specific issue; they are controlled by the underlying operating system. If you have Exchange 2007 servers deployed on Windows 2008, they're benefiting from the same changes and can be affected by the same issue.

Opportunistic TLS

We hammered home the point in the previous section about how the certificates you use must be trusted and validated. Now, normally in Exchange and Outlook, this validation is pretty strict. Sometimes neither Exchange nor Outlook will give you any nice errors if validation fails — they just won't work. However, when Exchange 2010 (and Exchange 2007, while we're at it) is acting as an SMTP client and connecting to another SMTP server, Exchange performs no certificate validation. Exchange's SMTP client (the Send connectors, if you like) will *always* accept whatever certificate the server offers during TLS handshakes.

Now, your initial reaction may be something like "You've got to be kidding! That's so unsecure!" Well, yes and no. It's arguably less secure than the ideal case of being and enforcing certification validation. However, one of the most common reasons why certificate validation fails is that the server is using a CA the client doesn't trust. This is reasonably common; many organizations deploy certificates using an internal PKI. Their clients are given the correct root CA certificates; all other systems won't validate it and will use regular SMTP. No biggie, right? In this case, we actually *gain security* by using the certificate anyway — we'll take advantage of the opportunity to encrypt the session.

But what if there's a genuine spoofed or "self-signed" certificate in place? Here's the thinking: so what? Consider the options. You either refuse to use the certificate (and send the message in the clear where anyone can be listening to it), or you use the untrusted certificate and send the message anyway — and only expose the message to the person who provided the untrusted certificate. If they have the level of access to be able to create and install an untrusted certificate, they have the level of access to get administrator access to the server and intercept your communications anyway.

When an SMTP client or server goes ahead and allows a TLS session to be initiated even if the certificate is untrusted, this is called *opportunistic TLS*. If the remote system offers TLS, the client will then try to negotiate with the server to use TLS without being specifically configured to. This is a direct contrast to legacy Exchange (2000 or 2003) behavior, which only used TLS when configured to (and then *only* used TLS). The benefit here is that the certificates on the Hub Transport server do not have to be trusted in order to use TLS and the SMTP data transfer between your Exchange Hub Transport server and a remote SMTP server that supports opportunistic TLS will be encrypted.

Domain Security

Opportunistic TLS gives you the ability to automatically encrypt the SMTP message flow between an SMTP client and an SMTP server that supports opportunistic TLS, but without any type of certificate validation. This gives you an additional level of security when email is being sent between your servers and the Internet. However, as we pointed out in the previous section, there is no validation of the sender's certificate (or even yours).

The *Domain Security* feature allows you to configure one or more remote domains on the Internet (or your intranet) for which you want a secure SMTP connection, and you also want to validate that the connection did indeed come from one of their mail servers. Domain Security requires that the certificates that you are using as well as the remote systems be trusted.

Both you and the administrator of the remote system have to configure the transport configuration's TLSReceiveDomainSecureList and TLSSendDomainSecureList properties for Exchange 2010 server (or Exchange 2007 server). Both organizations must be using Exchange Server 2007 or 2010, and those servers must be the servers that both send and receive email. You cannot go through a third-party message hygiene system and use Domain Security. Exchange Server (a Hub Transport or an Edge Transport) must be the source server as well as the target end-point.

If both the sender's system as well as the recipient's system are configured to use Domain Security and if the certificates on both sides are trusted, the recipient of messages from the trusted remote domain will see a special icon on the message in Outlook 2007 or 2010 that indicates the message was received from a trusted source.

For more information on Domain Security, read this article:

`http://technet.microsoft.com/en-us/library/bb266978.aspx`

Message-Level Security

While transport security is the low-hanging fruit of messaging security, it's not appropriate for all situations. The big problem with transport security is that it only covers hop-to-hop security. Within your Exchange organization, you can assume that all your message traffic will be handled securely. Once you hand off a message to an external system, though, you lose all control over it. Even if they use TLS, you have no guarantee that some party isn't intercepting messages within the server process.

If you need to ensure that your messages are secure from endpoint to endpoint, you have two options with Exchange 2010: the Secure Multimedia Internet Mail Extensions (S/MIME) standard, or rights-managed messages using the built-in integration with the Windows Rights Management (RMS) service.

S/MIME

The S/MIME standard was originally developed in 1995 by a consortium of security vendors amidst a number of competing standards. In 1998, the S/MIME group submitted a draft of S/MIME v2 to the IETF standard process. This change helped propel S/MIME to the leading message security contender. S/MIME v3 followed in 1999 to provide additional enhancements that had been identified. S/MIME v3 is described in three RFCs: RFC 2632, RFC 2633, and RFC 2634. This version of S/MIME is widely accepted and supported by a number of products, including previous versions of Exchange Server.

Although Exchange 2007 allowed the use of S/MIME with Outlook clients at RTM, it required SP1 to permit S/MIME support in OWA. In Exchange 2010, the necessary OWA support is present in the release version — although because it relies on ActiveX, you can only use it with Internet Explorer, not any of the other browsers that are otherwise supported by the premium version of OWA.

S/MIME in Exchange doesn't involve a lot of server-side configuration on the Exchange side of things. The bulk of administrative work for S/MIME is tied up in your PKI and client operations. You need to be able to issue S/MIME certificates, and you must place those certificates where clients can access them. For Exchange and Outlook, this typically means some sort of Active Directory–integrated PKI. You can, of course, issue S/MIME certificates using the Windows Certificate Services (as it's known in Windows Server 2003; in Windows Server 2008, it's renamed Active Directory Certificate Services). However, you can use any other X.509v3 standards-compliant PKI solution that you wish (or already have in place).

S/MIME provides two security services:

Digital Signatures   These allow the sender to perform a signing operation on the email message. The recipient can then validate this signature. Digital signatures provide the benefits of *authentication* (the recipient can be certain the sender is who they claim to be), *nonrepudiation* (the sender cannot claim that they did not sign the message), and *integrity* (by ensuring the message contents have not been altered, which would cause the signature to no longer match).

Message Encryption   This allows the sender to ensure that the message contents cannot be viewed by anyone who does not possess the private key that corresponds to the recipient's digital certificate. While a regular email message can be read by anyone who can access it in transit or in storage, an encrypted message is not so vulnerable. Encryption provides the benefits of *confidentiality* (the contents of the messages remain confidential even through untrusted systems and hops) and *integrity*.

When users choose to use S/MIME, they can apply either digital signatures or message encryption, or both. They are neither mutually exclusive nor automatically combined.

 **Real World Scenario**

TRUST ME, I'M A PKI ADMINISTRATOR

Company CDEF experienced a small-scale phishing attack where their customers were solicited via email by an outside (and unauthorized) party to visit a website and provide customer information. The executives of this company wanted a way that anyone receiving an email from one of their users could verify the authenticity of the message.

A rather hastily prepared plan involved standing up a Windows Certificate Server and issuing S/MIME certificates to all of their users. They then required their users to digitally sign messages that they sent to their customers.

While the messages arrived at the customer and were digitally signed, there was one drawback. The certificate authority that issued the certificates was not trusted by the customers and thus the authenticity of the sender could not truly be authenticated.

While this might have worked if Company CDEF were only concerned with sending to a single, external organization it did not work in this case. They could ask the remote organization to "trust" their own certificate authority.

A better and more trustworthy way to issue S/MIME certificates is to get them from a trusted certificate authority.

Typically, Exchange 2010 does not directly handle S/MIME certificates, perform S/MIME signing or encryption functions, or otherwise interact with the PKI; it leaves these activities to the client applications. In an Exchange system, there are three main types of clients:

◆ The Outlook application is a member of the Office application family and provides a rich set of functionality when used with any email system, including support for the S/MIME standards. If user certificate enrollment is automatic (such as through the use of Group Policy or logon scripts) and stored in Active Directory, Outlook can automatically look up user certificates for other users in the organization. For external users, the certificates must be saved and applied to the contact object.

◆ The Outlook Web App client is part of Client Access role of the Exchange Server system and is the only Exchange component that directly interacts with S/MIME. As stated previously, OWA requires a separate ActiveX control to handle S/MIME certificates, restricting it to users who use the Premium OWA client on Internet Explorer.

◆ The Pocket Outlook application on Windows Mobile 6.1 clients can make use of S/MIME when connecting to Exchange using the Exchange ActiveSync protocol. All current Windows Mobile devices that run versions 6.1 and above should support the S/MIME functionality.

In addition, many other third-party clients also support S/MIME. Check with your vendor for details.

Rights-Managed Email

Windows has provided a Rights Management Service for several years now, and with Windows Server 2008, it's been folded into the Active Directory as Active Directory Rights Management Service (AD-RMS). RMS provides a native Windows information rights management (IRM) capability. RMS-enabled applications such as the Office family of applications give their users the ability to create and apply certificate-based protection policies to their documents or email messages. These policies go beyond the binary "read/don't read" functionality provided by S/MIME and give you a far more granular set of permissions and abilities:

◆ You can control the specific actions recipients and readers can take with the protected content, including reading, modifying, printing, and forwarding.

◆ You can define expirations and revocations for any rights-managed content.

◆ You can easily define different levels of permissions for different users or groups.

◆ You can create and manage RMS policies to define standard categories of information, such as Company Confidential.

With Exchange 2010, you can integrate your Exchange servers into your RMS deployment using the new ControlPoint integration with the Windows Server 2008 AD-RMS role. In addition to your Outlook users being able to apply RMS policies and rights to their own messages, you can also define transport rules in your organization that automatically apply specified RMS policies to matching email messages. With the new RMS federation functionality in Windows Server 2008, you can even federate your RMS deployment with other Windows organizations, allowing your contents to be delivered externally and still be protected to the same degree. AD-RMS also provides the ability to interoperate with a per-individual Windows Live–based RMS service, giving you the ability to designate any recipient who has a Windows Live account.

Exchange 2010 includes one RMS template out of the box: the Do Not Forward template permits only the designated recipient to decrypt and access the message contents. The RMS client (and either Outlook or OWA) prevents the end user from forwarding the protected message to other recipients, copying the contents of the message into a new message, or printing out the message. Of course, RMS cannot prevent the user from re-typing the message or telling someone over the phone what he or she has read. RMS cannot completely stop bad behavior.

Additionally, the Exchange 2010 Unified Messaging role provides RMS integration to protect voice mail messages. We'll cover the specifics of the RMS integration in later chapters.

WHAT IF I JUST WANT PRETTY GOOD?

There's another option for message security that is common in environments that run a combination of Windows and other platforms: the Pretty Good Privacy (PGP) package. Originally an end-user solution for performing ad hoc encryption of files, several mail clients provided support and allowed the same technology to be used to protect email messages. While PGP gained adherents, the technology was encumbered by some of the RSA algorithm patents, so the open source community wrote an independent implementation called Gnu Privacy Guard (GPG). For more information about GPG, see www.gnugp.org. GPG uses the same basic mechanisms and can be compiled to use the proprietary RSA algorithms if the organization owns a license (or wants to pay for one), but GPG uses unencumbered protocols and code.

Over time, the commercial PGP solution added the type of centralized policy control and key management functions that large organizations need. You can't deploy a solution to thousands of mailboxes and clients if you can't keep track of encryption keys in a coherent, centralized manner. It interoperates with major mail clients, providing the kind of message security functionality equivalent to S/MIME but without the reliance on X.509v3 digital certificates. Many organizations view PKIs with alarm and would rather not have to deploy one if they can avoid it; PGP seems to be a great solution.

However, this seeming simplicity may not be what you think. In reality, PGP is a PKI — it's just not one based on the X.509v3 standard. What this means is that if you ever need an X.509v3 PKI deployed, you'll be managing two PKIs, not one. It also means that interoperability with other organizations can't be assumed; you have to ensure they also support and use PGP and make provisions for your PGP keys to be available. With S/MIME and X.509v3, you need to make provisions to publish your CA certificates and your CRL, but after you do so, any other organization that has deployed S/MIME can easily start taking advantage of message security to your organization.

In the end, it comes down to your business needs. If you have partners that use PGP and you need to interoperate with them, PGP may be the right solution for you. But for most organizations these days looking for comprehensive message security, we think they're better off looking at the other two options we've discussed.

Mail Hygiene

The SMTP protocol that allows us to easily send an email to any email server in the world is simple, but it is also very nonsecure. Essentially, for your mail server to be able to send email to, say, obama@washington.gov, the SMTP server at washington.gov needs to be able to accept the mail from you anonymously. If SMTP required authentication, washington.gov would need to have a user account and password for anyone who was going to send them email.

Due to the open nature of Internet mail, it is easy for unscrupulous people to send unsolicited commercial email (UCE), hereafter known as spam. It is also easy for mail to be spoofed so that it appears to come from a credible source (such as your bank) and encourages you to take an action, such as logging on to a fake URL and providing your banking credentials; this is known as phishing.

It is easy for these unscrupulous people to send emails with malicious attachments that might spread a virus, load a program onto your computer that will further spread itself (such programs are called worms), load a program that will then generate spam to send to others (this is a bot), or load a monitoring or remote control program on your computer that a malicious hacker can then use. These viruses, worms, and Trojan horse–type programs are collectively known as malware.

Finally, email is such an easy way to send information back and forth that your users may misuse it by sending inappropriate information to their friends and colleagues. Inappropriate use of email can open an organization up to bad publicity and even potential lawsuits, not to mention getting the senders and recipients into big trouble.

Blocking Unsolicited Messages

Collectively, the science of scanning messages for inappropriate content is known as message hygiene. All mail systems today should include some type of message hygiene system that, at a minimum, protects against viruses and reduces the amount of spam that makes its way into the user's mailbox.

Out of the box, a full Exchange Server 2010 deployment provides a high level of protection against spam through the antispam agents that are deployed on the Edge Transport role. These agents can also be manually deployed on your servers with the Hub Transport role. However, you will need additional software for protection against viruses. Customers who have Enterprise Client Access Licenses (eCALs) for all users can use Microsoft's Forefront Security for Exchange Server product (`www.microsoft.com/forefront`) or the Exchange Hosted Services Filtering offering.

You may choose to implement your own message hygiene system, in which case you have your own servers performing the message hygiene functions. Figure 5.2 shows a multilayer message hygiene system.

FIGURE 5.2
Implementing your own multilayer message hygiene system

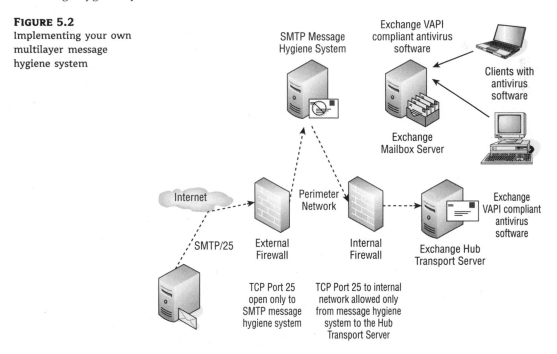

The message hygiene system in Figure 5.2 is a multilayer system; this system has more than one place that may stop an email-borne threat. Ideally, the majority of spam and malicious email will be stopped by the message hygiene system in the perimeter network; this could be the Microsoft Exchange Edge Transport server or it could be one of the dozens of available SMTP-based message security systems available from third parties. The point of the hygiene system in the perimeter is to keep as much undesirable content as possible from reaching your production mail system and to protect the internal mail servers from possible attempts to compromise them.

Once a message is scanned in the perimeter network, it is then passed on to the Exchange servers on your internal network. There, additional scanning takes place either when the message is moving through the message transport system or when the message is placed in the user's Inbox. Ideally, the scanning system (or scanning engine) on the inside of the network should be a different scanning engine from the one that is used on the perimeter.

The final layer of protection is implemented at the client. The client has a file and memory virus/malware scanner that looks at any content as it is opened, whether that content is in the user's Inbox or something downloaded from the Internet or something on a CD-ROM in the CD drive. Once again, ideally the software running on the client will be from a different vendor than the software running on the server. Running multiple types of scanning software improves the likelihood that newer threats will be stopped.

Some organizations decided that they don't want to have to maintain perimeter-based message hygiene systems, so they use a third-party vendor that provides Internet-based scanning for them. These are usually known as managed providers, and they have SMTP-based scanning systems that will scan messages coming to your mail system before they are delivered to your Exchange servers. Figure 5.3 shows an example of using a managed provider.

FIGURE 5.3
Using a managed provider

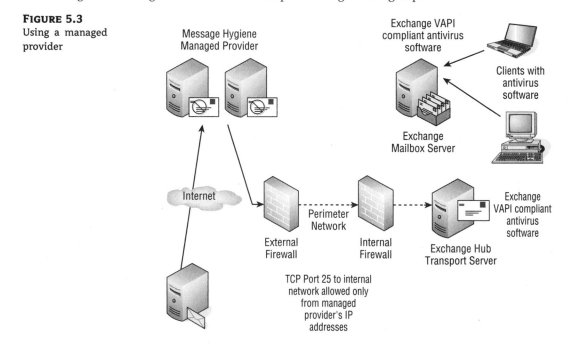

The additional cost of using a managed provider is offset by the fact that you don't have to maintain your own perimeter-based scanning system and that most malicious or unwanted email content can be stopped prior to entering your network in the first place. Some third-party managed providers can also provide additional message security, disaster recovery, and message archival functions.

Levels of Inspection

There are a lot of ways that your message hygiene system can determine whether something is spam or it's being sent by an unauthorized sender. Though each of these topics deserves in-depth treatment, our intent here is merely to familiarize you with the concepts.

Content Inspection   The most common way that a message is determined to be spam or a phishing message is through content inspection. The software opens the message and looks for characteristics of spam messages, such as a message with nothing but a URL or image, messages that mention certain words or phrases, and so on. Based on the content, the software ranks the message with a number (usually called the Spam Confidence Level [SCL]) from 0 to 9, with 0 being likely the message is not spam and 9 being very spammy. Internal messages and messages that are sent by an authenticated connection are set to an SCL level of negative one (−1). The message transport can then be configured with your tolerance level for spam and can reject, delete, or quarantine messages with higher SCL values. Arguably, content inspection is considered the most accurate method of detecting spam.

Quarantines   Most message hygiene systems offer a quarantine feature that allows the administrator to temporarily move inbound messages that are marginally suspicious or that may require some level of additional inspection. Quarantines may work okay for a small organization, but they can quickly consume valuable manpower in medium-sized and large organizations.

Block Lists   Block lists are lists that either you or a third party maintains. The lists contain IP addresses of known spammers, dial-up IP addresses, DHCP IP addresses, or IP addresses of systems that will allow spammers to send through. The third-party lists are often known as real-time block lists (RBLs) and are maintained (usually by volunteers).

Tarpitting   An SMTP tarpit is frequently used to combat dictionary spammers or bots that go through a list of common names and prepend those to your domain name. They can attempt to send a million messages to your mail server and will probably guess correctly on at least some recipients' names. A tarpit tells the SMTP server to wait some number of seconds (such as 30 seconds) prior to responding to invalid names. This makes dictionary spamming much more difficult.

Sender Protection Framework/Sender ID   The Sender Protection Framework (SPF) and Sender ID are initiatives that are backed by Microsoft. These require that all known senders on the Internet register the addresses of mail servers that will send mail on their behalf. The registration is in the form of a DNS record that defines the mail servers that will send mail for a specific domain.

Domain Keys   The Domain Keys initiative (DKIM) is backed by Yahoo! and requires that a sending system include a calculation in the header of each outgoing message that the receiving system then verifies. Both of these initiatives are more directly "antispoofing" systems than they are "antispam" systems, but they are useful in helping ensure that messages are coming from the stated sender — which can help reduce spam. It is important to note that Exchange 2010 does not natively provide support for DKIM.

DNS Name and IP Verification   Though Exchange Server cannot do some of these verifications, some SMTP systems will verify things such as whether your public IP address has a valid pointer (PTR) record and whether the DNS domain name you are using is valid. This can help reduce spam but also increases the probability of false positives. (A false positive occurs when the message hygiene mistakenly tags a legitimate message as spam and quarantines, deletes, or rejects it.)

Recipient Filtering   Recipient filtering allows you to configure servers so that they reject mail sent to specific users. While filtering to individual addresses is not particularly useful, you can configure Exchange so that it rejects inbound mail sent to unknown recipients. This prevents the message hygiene system from having to process it further before the message is rejected.

Sender Inspection   Sender inspection or sender filtering is the least useful method of blocking spam because it requires maintaining lists of senders' SMTP addresses or lists of domains from which you will not accept inbound mail. The problem with this approach is that spammers usually do not use the same sender address twice.

Why Is My Mail Being Rejected?

Naturally, if you put a system in place that scans and possibly rejects email based on the characteristics or the sender of the message, you are occasionally going to end up with false positives. These false positives will always be in the form of an important email that is being sent to your CEO or one that she is waiting to receive. Take a look at the nondelivery report (NDR) shown in Figure 5.4; this message was rejected by the receiving mail system.

FIGURE 5.4
Examining the report of a rejected message

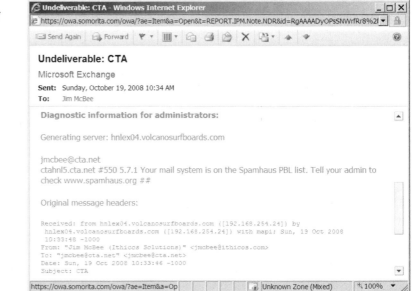

Exchange Server 2010's message transport system does a pretty good job of examining rejection codes and letting you know why a message was rejected, but you may still have to do some detective work. A remote mail system might reject mail from your users for a number of reasons:

◆   The public IP address from which you send mail is on a real-time block list (RBL) provider.

- Your public IP address is registered as a DHCP IP address on some RBLs; your Internet service provider (ISP) must correct this.

- You do not have Sender ID records registered in DNS for your public IP addresses, or the records are incorrect.

- The message has content that makes it look like spam such as suspicious words (mortgage, Viagra, enlargement, free) or the messages is very short (one sentence, for example).

- Your public IP address does not have a DNS PTR record; your ISP or the owner of the IP address must fix this.

- Your mail server is sending out the wrong mail domain name when it connects to a remote mail system. For example, your mail domain is `somorita.com` but it is saying your domain name is `somorita.local`.

The Bottom Line

Secure messages through the transport protocols   Some of the easiest and most effective email security measures you can take involve keeping the various protocols secure. Rather than use a separate security mechanism for each protocol, Exchange uses two versatile, standards-based security protocols that can protect virtually all client-to-server and server-to-server traffic from hop to hop.

> **Master It**   What is the major difference between SSL and TLS?
> What type of certificate does Exchange use to secure transport protocols out of the box?
> Which Exchange protocol is not secured by SSL or TLS?

Secure messages from end to end   While transport security has become more ubiquitous and suffices for many organizations, there are times when messages must be secured every step of the way, from the sender's client to the recipient's client — no intermediate systems or entities must be able to read or open the message, even if they are trusted entities used to transport the message.

> **Master It**   What options does Exchange 2010 provide for end-to-end message security?
> Why don't these options include the common PGP suite?

Ensure the email hygiene of your organization   Ensuring that your messaging system doesn't accept improper messages, such as spam, phish, and virus messages, improves the health of the overall organization and makes each user's mail experience better.

> **Master It**   What options do you have for deploying a mail hygiene solution with Exchange 2010?

Chapter 6

Introduction to PowerShell and the Exchange Management Shell

Microsoft PowerShell is a new, extensible, object-oriented command-line interface for the Windows operating system. The Exchange Management Shell (EMS) is a set of Exchange-specific extensions to Microsoft's PowerShell. The EMS was introduced with Exchange Server 2007 and has been further enhanced with Exchange Server 2010, including the ability to use the EMS against remote servers.

In this chapter, we introduce you to both PowerShell and the EMS. Introducing a concept like PowerShell or the EMS in just a few pages is difficult, but we hope to give you a basic idea of some of the capabilities and encourage you to learn more.

Is knowledge of the EMS required? Some administrators will manage their Exchange servers for years and rarely use the EMS, whereas others will use it daily. However, we think it is safe to say that at least limited knowledge of the EMS will be required by all administrators because some specialized configuration options can be set only from the EMS.

We hope that this chapter will provide you with enough of an introduction to PowerShell so that you won't dread getting to know it.

In this chapter, you will learn to:

◆ Use PowerShell command syntax

◆ Understand object-oriented use of PowerShell

◆ Employ tips and tricks to get more out of PowerShell

◆ Get help with using PowerShell

Why Use PowerShell?

Based on discussions in Internet newsgroups, web forums, and classrooms about the decision to put the management architecture of Exchange 2007 on top of PowerShell, you would think that this was one of the most controversial decisions that Microsoft has ever made. Indeed, there has been enthusiastic debate (and name-calling) on both sides of the fence. Depending on who you ask, some experienced Exchange administrators will tell you that the Exchange Management Shell (EMS) is the best improvement Microsoft has made after Exchange 2003.

We have to admit to becoming big supporters of the EMS. All it took was spending a bit of time with it and getting to know some of the basic functionality. The biggest fear that many administrators have is that they will have to learn not only some of the shell's commands (called cmdlets) but also a scripting language just to manage Exchange Server 2010. That is not the case.

The intent of the EMS is to provide a consistent interface for performing management tasks for Exchange 2010 servers, whether performing automation tasks, writing scripts, or extending the management capabilities. Tasks or operations that once required multiple programming APIs and hundreds of lines of scripting can now be accomplished in a single command. Single commands can be joined together — the output of one command can be piped to another command as input — to perform extremely powerful functions.

The base PowerShell provides more than 120 built-in cmdlets; PowerShell v2 and Windows Server 2008 and Windows Server 2008 R2 add even more cmdlets. In total, there are over 600 additional Exchange-related cmdlets that you can use in the EMS; the goal is to cover all Exchange-related administrative tasks. You will find cmdlets that manipulate other data in the Active Directory (such as cmdlets for managing user accounts) and control Exchange-related data in the Registry or Internet Information Services, but the cmdlets will only manipulate or manage data related to Exchange. The Exchange team is expecting other internal Microsoft teams such as the Active Directory or Internet Information Server team to provide their own extensions to the management shell.

There are a lot of very good reasons for Microsoft to create this management layer across all its products. It provides a consistent management and scripting interface for all server products, develops a secure method for remote scripting, improves batching, and provides you with an easy way to automate and repeat anything you can do in the GUI.

Understanding the Command Syntax

The problem with a lot of scripting languages and command shells is that as they get more complex and powerful, the command syntax gets more and more cryptic. PowerShell and the EMS seek to make using the command-line interface and scripting more intuitive. To this end, most of PowerShell and EMS cmdlets consist of two components: a verb and a noun.

JUST IN CASE

PowerShell cmdlets and the EMS extensions for PowerShell are case insensitive. That means that you can type everything in uppercase, everything in lowercase, or mix and match the case of the letters in your commands.

For readability and per suggestions from folks on the Exchange team at Microsoft, we are using Pascal casing in this book. When you use Pascal casing, the first character of each word is in uppercase; if the cmdlet has more than one word, the first letter in each word is in uppercase. All other letters in the cmdlet are in lowercase. So the cmdlet that is used to retrieve mailbox statistics is written as `Get-MailboxStatistics`.

Verbs and Nouns

The verb identifies the action that is being taken, and the noun indicates the object on which the action is being taken. The verb always comes first, and the verb and noun are separated by a hyphen (such as `Get-Mailbox`). Table 6.1 shows some of the common verbs you'll use in the EMS; some of these are specific to the EMS, but most are generic to the Windows PowerShell.

TABLE 6.1: Common EMS Cmdlet Verbs

VERB	DESCRIPTION
Get	Get is probably the most common verb that you will use. Get retrieves information about the specified object and outputs information about the object.
Set	Set is probably the second most common verb that you will use. Set allows you to update properties of the object specified in the noun.
New	New creates new instances of the object specified in the noun.
Enable	Enable activates or enables a configuration on the object specified, such as enabling an existing user account.
Add	Add can be used to add items to an object, or to add properties of an object.
Remove	Remove deletes an instance of the object specified in the noun.
Disable	Disable disables or deactivates the object specified in the noun. An example of this is removing a mailbox from an existing user (but not deleting the user account).
Mount	Mount is used to mount an Exchange 2007 mailbox or public folder database.
Dismount	Dismount is used to dismount an Exchange 2007 mailbox or public folder database.
Move	Move can be used to activate a database copy on a mailbox server.
Test	Test performs diagnostic tests against the object specified by the noun and the identity option.
Update	Update is used to update specified objects.

The actual nouns that are used in conjunction with these verbs are too numerous to mention in even a few pages of text. Table 6.2 lists some of the common nouns; later in this chapter you'll learn how to use the online help to find more cmdlets that you need. The nouns in Table 6.2 can be used in conjunction with verbs, such as the ones in Table 6.1, to manipulate the properties of Exchange-related objects. However, not all verbs work with all nouns, and unfortunately it sometimes requires some trial and error to determine what works and what doesn't.

CMDLETS WORK ONLY WITHIN POWERSHELL

One important thing to keep in mind with cmdlets is that they are not individual executables, but rather .NET classes that are only accessible from within PowerShell and only if the Exchange extensions to PowerShell are loaded.

TABLE 6.2:   Common EMS Cmdlet Nouns

NOUN	DESCRIPTION
ActiveSyncMailboxPolicy	Properties of ActiveSync policies that can be assigned to a mailbox
CASMailbox	Properties of a mailbox relating to client features such as OWA and MAPI
ClientAccessServer	Properties specific to an Exchange Client Access server role
DistributionGroup	Properties relating to mail-enabled distribution groups.
DynamicDistributionGroup	Properties relating to a dynamic distribution group
EmailAddressPolicy	Properties relating to the policies that are used to define email addresses
ExchangeServer	Properties related to Exchange servers
Mailbox	Properties related to user mailboxes
MailboxDatabase	Properties related to mailbox databases
MailboxServer	Properties specific to an Exchange Mailbox server role
MailContact	Properties relating to mail-enabled contact objects
MailPublicFolder	Properties relating to mail-enabled public folder objects
MailUser	Properties relating to a user that has an email address but not a mailbox
MoveRequest	Properties and actions related to move mailbox requests
ReceiveConnector	Properties relating to Receive connectors
SendConnector	Properties relating to Send connectors
TransportServer	Properties specific to an Exchange Hub Transport server role
UMMailbox	Properties relating to Unified Messaging
UMServer	Properties specific to an Exchange Unified Messaging server role
User	Properties relating to user objects

Help

There is a more detailed section near the end of this chapter titled "Getting Help"; however, as you start your journey into learning PowerShell and the EMS, you should know how to get quick and basic help. At any time you can use the Get-Help cmdlet to show what parameters any cmdlet takes. This is much like the man command on Linux systems:

```
Get-Help Get-Mailbox
```

The -Identity Parameter

For cmdlets that require input, usually the first parameter provided is the -Identity parameter. For example, if you want to retrieve information about a mailbox called Tyler Swartz in the Corporate Organizational Unit (OU), you would type this:

```
Get-Mailbox -Identity 'ithicos.local/Corporate/Tyler Swartz'
```

However, you will quickly find that the -Identity parameter is not required. And, if your aliases or account names are unique, even the domain and organizational unit (OU) information is not required. For example, this command would yield the same result:

```
Get-Mailbox 'fourthcoffee.com/Corporate/Tyler Swartz'
```

As long as there is only one Tyler Swartz in the Active Directory, you can even drop the domain and the OU name and this cmdlet will yield the same result:

```
Get-Mailbox 'Tyler Swartz'
```

YOU CAN QUOTE ME ON THAT . . .

Anytime the identity you are using has a space in it, you must use quotes. Either single or double quotes will work as long as you are consistent.

The -Identity parameter is optional by design. As you will find shortly, the input for one cmdlet can even be piped in from the output of another cmdlet.

If you are not sure what input can be specified for the identity parameter, you can easily look up this information either in the Exchange online help or by using the EMS command-line help (more on this later in this chapter). For now, let's look at one small piece of the Get-Mailbox help screen that shows the different values that can be used to identify a mailbox:

```
-Identity <MailboxIdParameter>
    The Identity parameter identifies the mailbox. You can use one of the
following values:
    * GUID
    * Distinguished name (DN)
    * Domain\Account
    * User principal name (UPN)
    * LegacyExchangeDN
    * SmtpAddress
    * Alias

    Required?                    false
    Position?                    1
    Default value
    Accept pipeline input?       True
    Accept wildcard characters?  true
```

There, you can see that the -Identity parameter will take the mailbox GUID, the user's distinguished name, the domain name and account, the UPN name, the legacy Exchange distinguished name, the SMTP address, or the Exchange alias.

Cmdlet vs. Command

You will notice that sometimes we use "command" and sometimes we use "cmdlet" when talking about PowerShell. There is a subtle difference:

◆ A cmdlet is the verb-noun combination that performs a specific task; it is the base Power-Shell object that takes input, does something to it, and produces some output.

◆ A complete command is the cmdlet along with any necessary options that the task might require. The command necessary to retrieve information about a specific mailbox looks like this:

```
Get-Mailbox "JulieR.Samante"
```

Cmdlet Parameters

PowerShell and EMS cmdlets also support a number of command-line parameters that are useful. Parameters can be categorized as mandatory or not, and as positional or not. When a parameter is *mandatory*, PowerShell will require you to add the parameter with a given cmdlet and specify a value for it. If the use of a parameter is not mandatory, you are allowed to include it, but you don't have to. The cmdlet New-Mailbox illustrates this behavior nicely. When creating a new mailbox-enabled user, you have to include the parameter UserPrincipalName, but you are free to include the parameter OrganizationalUnit. The EMS will prompt you for the value of any mandatory parameter you forgot to specify. Next to being mandatory or not, it is not always necessary to include the parameter name. When a parameter is so-called positional, you can just add the value and leave out the parameter name. The cmdlet Get-Mailbox has no mandatory parameters, but does have a positional parameter, namely -Identity. If we run the following EMS line, the shell will return the properties of a mailbox-enabled user whose Exchange alias is Michael.Brown:

```
Get-Mailbox Michael.Brown
```

Name	Alias	ServerName	ProhibitSendQuota
Michael.Brown	Michael.Brown	hnlmbx01	unlimited

which is the same as running this:

```
Get-Mailbox -Identity Michael.Brown
```

Name	Alias	ServerName	ProhibitSendQuota
Michael.Brown	Michael.Brown	hnlmbx01	unlimited

However, if we run the following line, the shell will complain that it doesn't know any mailbox-enabled user by the name of hnlmbx01, because the parameter Server is not positional.

```
Get-Mailbox hnlmbx01
The operation couldn't be performed because object 'hnlmbx01' couldn't be
found on 'dc01.exchange.local'.
    + CategoryInfo    : NotSpecified: (:) [Get-Mailbox],
ManagementObjectNotFoundException
    + FullyQualifiedErrorId : 3FEDEA30,Microsoft.Exchange.Management.
RecipientTasks.GetMailbox
```

as opposed to

```
Get-Mailbox -Server HNLMBX01
```

Name	Alias	ServerName	ProhibitSendQuota
Administrator	Administrator	hnlmbx01	unlimited
DiscoverySearchMailbox...	DiscoverySearchMa...	hnlmbx01	unlimited
Clayton Kamiya	Clayton.Kamiya	hnlmbx01	unlimited
Jordan Chang	JordanChang	hnlmbx01	unlimited
Tyler M. Swartz	Tyler.Swartz	hnlmbx01	unlimited
Anita Velez	AnitaVelez	hnlmbx01	unlimited
John Rodriguez	JohnRodriguez	hnlmbx01	unlimited
Jonathan Core	JonathanCore	hnlmbx01	unlimited
Kevin Wile	KevinWile	hnlmbx01	unlimited
John Park	JohnPark	hnlmbx01	unlimited
Julie R. Samante	JulieR.Samante	hnlmbx01	unlimited
David Elfassy	DavidElfassy	hnlmbx01	unlimited
Chuck Swanson	ChuckSwanson	hnlmbx01	unlimited
Kelly Siu	KellySiu	hnlmbx01	unlimited
Gerald Nakata	GeraldNakata	hnlmbx01	unlimited

Table 6.3 shows some of the parameters that cmdlets accept. Not all cmdlets will accept all of these parameters; these are usually optional, and, of course, some of them will not be relevant.

If you are piping output of one cmdlet into another, the parameters must be within the cmdlet that you want the parameter to affect.

Tab Completion

In order to be descriptive and helpful, some of the cmdlets are actually pretty long. Consider if you had to type **Get-DistributionGroupMember** several times! However, PowerShell includes a feature called tab completion. If we type part of a command and then press the Tab key, PowerShell will complete the cmdlet with the first matching cmdlet it can find. For example, if we type **Get-Distri** and press Tab, PowerShell will automatically fill out Get-DistributionGroup. If we press Tab again, PowerShell will move on to the next matching cmdlet, or in this case Get-DistributionGroupMember.

The tab completion feature also works for cmdlet parameters. If you type a cmdlet followed by a space and a hyphen, such as **Get-Mailbox -**, and then press Tab, you will cycle through all the parameters for that particular cmdlet. When you include parameters with your cmdlet, it is not necessary to specify their full names. It is sufficient to enter enough letters to make sure the EMS can figure out which parameter you meant to define. For example, if you enter **Get-Mailbox -Se server1** you will be given a list of all mailboxes homed on server server1. But tab completion can be useful to help you keep an overview of your EMS lines.

Alias

PowerShell and the EMS also include aliases that allow you to invoke cmdlets using a familiar synonym. A typical example here is entering **Dir** to get a list of all files in the directory that you are in and all subdirectories after that directory, which is in fact an alias for the cmdlet Get-ChildItem. Table 6.4 shows some common aliases that are built into PowerShell.

TABLE 6.3: PowerShell Cmdlet Parameters

PARAMETER	DESCRIPTION
-Identity	-Identity specifies a unique object on which the cmdlet is going to act. The -Identity parameter is a positional parameter, which means that it does not necessarily have to be on the command line; PowerShell will prompt you for the identity if it is not specified. As noted previously, in most cases you do not need to specify the -Identity parameter but just the unique object name.
-WhatIf	-WhatIf tells the cmdlet to simulate the action that the cmdlet would actually perform, but not actually make the change.
-Confirm	-Confirm asks the cmdlet to prompt for confirmation prior to starting the action. This option type is Boolean so you need to include either $True or $False. Some cmdlets (such as New-MoveRequest-) ask for confirmation by default, so you could specify -Confirm:$false if you did not want the confirmation request to occur.
-Validate	-Validate will check the prerequisites of the cmdlet to verify that it will run correctly and let you know if the cmdlet will run successfully.
-Credential	-Credential allows you to specify alternate credentials when running a PowerShell command.
-DomainController	-DomainController allows you to specify the FQDN of a specific domain controller that you want to perform a PowerShell task against.
-ResultSize	The -ResultSize option allows you to specify a maximum number of results when working with Get- cmdlets.
-SortBy	The -SortBy option allows you to specify a sorting criteria when outputting data that is usually the result of a Get- cmdlet.
-Verbose	-Verbose instructs Get- cmdlets to return more information about the execution of the cmdlet.
-Debug	-Debug instructs the cmdlet to output more information and to proceed step by step through the process of performing a task. -Debug returns more information than a typical administrator needs to perform daily tasks.

But it is important to remember that entering an alias in the end is like entering a cmdlet, thus imposing some constraints that do not apply when entering the listed aliases in Table 6.4 in a command prompt. If you would like to get a list of all files, and files located in subdirectories, you would be inclined to enter **dir /s**, but when doing so in you will be faced with the following error message:

```
dir /s
Get-ChildItem : Cannot find path 'C:\s' because it does not exist.
At line:1 char:4
+ dir  <<<< /s
```

TABLE 6.4:   PowerShell Common Aliases

ALIAS	DEFINITION
Dir	Get-ChildItem
Ls	Get-ChildItem
Type	Get-Content
Cat	Get-Content
Write	Write-Output
Echo	Write-Output
cd	Set-Location
sl	Set-Location
cls	Clear-Host

Using the PowerShell, you know you need to include any parameter by adding a hyphen followed by the parameter name.

```
dir -Recurse:$True
```

or

```
dir -r
```

Object-Oriented Use of PowerShell

PowerShell is even more flexible because the output of commands is not text-based, but rather object-based. PowerShell uses an object model that is based on the Microsoft .NET Framework. PowerShell cmdlets accept and return structured data. Don't let the terms "object model" or "object oriented" scare you, though. This is really quite simple. For example, Figure 6.1 shows the output of the Get-Mailbox cmdlet.

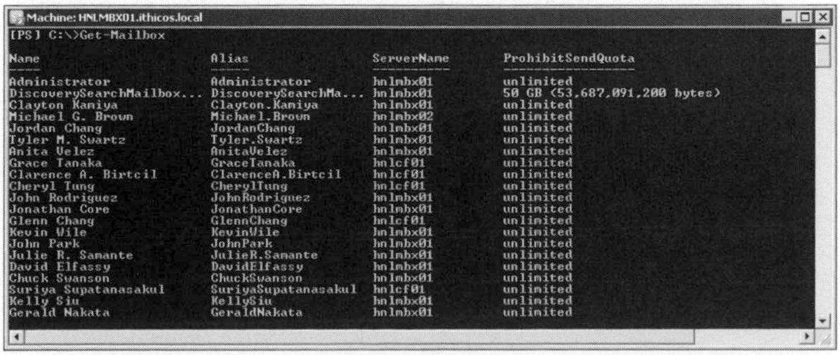

FIGURE 6.1
Output of the
Get-Mailbox cmdlet

What you see on the screen is text to the user interface, but to PowerShell it is really a list of objects. You can manipulate the output to see the properties you want, filter the output, or pipe the output (the objects) to another cmdlet.

Filtering Output

In Figure 6.1, you can see that the cmdlet we used (Get-Mailbox) outputs every mailbox in the entire organization. There are a number of ways that you can filter or narrow the scope of the output that you are looking for from a specific cmdlet. In the case of Get-Mailbox and other cmdlets, you can specify just the identity of the mailbox that you are looking for.

PowerShell includes two options that can be used specifically for filtering the output. These are the Where-Object (or Where alias) and the Filter-Object (or Filter) objects. The Where clause can be used on most cmdlets and the filter is applied at the client. The Filter clause is only available on a subset of the commands because this filter is applied by the server.

```
Get-Mailbox | Where-Object {$_.MaxSendSize -gt 25000000}
```

In the preceding command, the output of the Get-Mailbox cmdlet is piped to the Where clause, which filters the output. In this case, the output is any mailbox whose -MaxSendSize parameter is greater than 25,000,000 bytes. Did you notice the portion of the Where statement $_.MaxSendSize? The $_ portion represents the current object that is being piped to the Where-Object cmdlet, and .MaxSendSize represents the MaxSendSize property of that object.

For nonprogrammers, this might seem a little difficult at first, but we promise it gets much easier as you go along. The operators are also simple to remember. Table 6.5 shows a list of common operators that can be used in clauses such as Where-Object or just the Where alias.

TABLE 6.5: Shell Values and Operators

SHELL VALUE	OPERATOR	FUNCTION
-eq	Equals	The object.property value must match exactly the specified value.
-ne	Not equals	The object.property value must not match the specified value.
-gt	Greater than	-gt works when the object.property value is an integer.
-ge	Greater than or equal to	-ge works when the object.property value is an integer.
-lt	Less than	-lt works when the object.property value is an integer.
-le	Less than or equal to	-le works when the object.property value is an integer.
-like	Contains	-like is used when the object.property value is a text string. The matching string can either match exactly or contain wildcards (*) at the beginning or end of the string.
-notlike	Does not contain	-notlike is used when the object.property value is a text string and you want to see if the values do not match the string. The matching string can contain wildcards (*) at the beginning or end of the string.

Sometimes, finding all of the properties that can be used with a particular cmdlet can be difficult. There are a couple of tips that we would like to share that will help illustrate or discover these properties. Let's take the Set-Mailbox cmdlet as an example. First, you can simply use the available online help such as this:

```
set-mailbox -?

NAME
    Set-Mailbox

SYNOPSIS
    Use the Set-Mailbox cmdlet to modify the settings of an existing
mailbox. You can use this cmdlet for one mailbox at a time. To perform bulk
management, you can pipeline the output of various Get- cmdlets (for
example, the Get-Mailbox or Get-User cmdlets) and configure several
mailboxes in a single-line command. You can also use the Set-Mailbox cmdlet
in scripts.


SYNTAX
    Set-Mailbox -Identity <MailboxIdParameter> [-AcceptMessagesOnlyFrom
<RecipientIdParameter[]>] [-AcceptMessagesOnlyF
    romDLMembers <RecipientIdParameter[]>]
[-AcceptMessagesOnlyFromSendersOrMembers  <RecipientIdParameter[]>]
[-Alias <String>]
[-AntispamBypassEnabled <$true |
$false>] [-ApplyMandatoryProperties <SwitchParameter>] [-Arbitration
<SwitchParameter>] [-ArbitrationMailbox <MailboxIdParameter>] [-ArchiveName
<MultiValuedProperty>] [-ArchiveQuota <Unlimited>] [-ArchiveWarningQuota
<Unlimited>] [-BypassModerationFromSendersOrMembers <RecipientIdParameter[]>]
[-CalendarRepairDisabled <$true | $false>] [-CalendarVersionStoreDisabled <$true
| $false>] [-Confirm [<SwitchParameter>]] [-CreateDTMFMap <$true | $false>]
[-CustomAttribute1 <String>] [-CustomAttribute10 <String>] [-CustomAttribute11
<String>] [-CustomAttribute12 <String>] [-CustomAttribute13 <String>]
[-CustomAttribute14 <String>] [-CustomAttribute15 <String>] [-CustomAttribute2
<String>] [-CustomAttribute3 <String>] [-CustomAttribute4 <String>]
[-CustomAttribute5 <String>] [-CustomAttribute6 <String>] [-CustomAttribute7
<String>] [-CustomAttribute8 <String>] [-CustomAttribute9 <String>] [-Database
<DatabaseIdParameter>] [-DeliverToMailboxAndForward <$true | $false>]
[-DisplayName <String>] [-DomainController <Fqdn>]
[-DowngradeHighPriorityMessagesEnabled <$true | $false>] [-EmailAddresses
<ProxyAddressCollection>] [-EmailAddressPolicyEnabled <$true | $false>]
[-EndDateForRetentionHold <Nullable>] [-ExternalOofOptions <InternalOnly |
External>] [-Force <SwitchParameter>] [-ForwardingAddress
<RecipientIdParameter>] [-GrantSendOnBehalfTo
<MailboxOrMailUserOrMailContactIdParameter[]>]
[-HiddenFromAddressListsEnabled <$true | $false>] [-IgnoreDefaultScope
<SwitchParameter>] [-IssueWarningQuota <Unlimited>] [-Languages
<MultiValuedProperty>] [-LinkedCredential <PSCredential>] [-LinkedDomainController
```

```
<String>] [-LinkedMasterAccount <UserIdParameter>] [-LitigationHoldEnabled
<$true | $false>] [-MailboxPlan <MailboxPlanIdParameter>] [-MailTip <String>]
[-MailTipTranslations <MultiValuedProperty>] [-ManagedFolderMailboxPolicy
<MailboxPolicyIdParameter>] [-ManagedFolderMailboxPolicyAllowed <SwitchParameter>]
[-MaxBlockedSenders <Nullable>] [-MaxReceiveSize <Unlimited>] [-MaxSafeSenders
<Nullable>] [-MaxSendSize <Unlimited>] [-MessageTrackingReadStatusEnabled <$true
| $false>] [-ModeratedBy <MultiValuedProperty>] [-ModerationEnabled <$true
| $false>]
[-Name <String>] [-Office <String>] [-OfflineAddressBook
<OfflineAddressBookIdParameter>] [-Password <SecureString>]
[-Pop3AggregationEnabled <$true | $false>] [-PrimarySmtpAddress <SmtpAddress>]
[-ProhibitSendQuota <Unlimited>] [-ProhibitSendReceiveQuota <Unlimited>]
[-QueryBaseDNRestrictionEnabled <$true | $false>] [-RecipientLimits <Unlimited>]
[-RecoverableItemsQuota <Unlimited>] [-RecoverableItemsWarningQuota <Unlimited>]
[-RejectMessagesFrom <RecipientIdParameter[]>] [-RejectMessagesFromDLMembers
<RecipientIdParameter[]>] [-RejectMessagesFromSendersOrMembers
<RecipientIdParameter[]>] [-RemoteAccountPolicy <RemoteAccountPolicyIdParameter>]
[-RemoveManagedFolderAndPolicy <SwitchParameter>] [-RemovePicture
<SwitchParameter>]
 [-RemoveSpokenName <SwitchParameter>] [-RequireSecretQA <$true | $false>]
[-RequireSenderAuthenticationEnabled <$true | $false>] [-ResetPasswordOnNextLogon
<$true | $false>] [-ResourceCapacity <Nullable>] [-ResourceCustom
<MultiValuedProperty>] [-RetainDeletedItemsFor<EnhancedTimeSpan>] [-
RetainDeletedItemsUntilBackup <$true | $false>] [-RetentionComment <String>]
[-RetentionHoldEnabled <$true | $false>] [-RetentionPolicy
<MailboxPolicyIdParameter>] [-RetentionUrl <String>] [-RoleAssignmentPolicy
<MailboxPolicyIdParameter>]
[-RssAggregationEnabled <$true | $false>] [-RulesQuota <ByteQuantifiedSize>]
[-SamAccountName <String>] [-SCLDeleteEnabled <Nullable>] [-SCLDeleteThreshold
<Nullable>] [-SCLJunkEnabled <Nullable>] [-SCLJunkThreshold <Nullable>] [-
SCLQuarantineEnabled <Nullable>] [-SCLQuarantineThreshold <Nullable>]
[-SCLRejectEnabled <Nullable>] [-SCLRejectThreshold <Nullable>]
[-SecondaryAddress <String>] [-SecondaryDialPlan <UMDialPlanIdParameter>]
[-SendModerationNotifications <Never | Internal | Always>] [-SharingPolicy
<SharingPolicyIdParameter>] [-SimpleDisplayName <String>]
[-SingleItemRecoveryEnabled <$true | $false>] [-StartDateForRetentionHold
 <Nullable>] [-ThrottlingPolicy <ThrottlingPolicyIdParameter>] [-Type
<Regular | Room | Equipment | Shared>] [-UMDtmfMap <MultiValuedProperty>]
[-UseDatabaseQuotaDefaults <Nullable>] [-UseDatabaseRetentionDefaults <$true
| $false>] [-UserCertificate <MultiValuedProperty>] [-UserPrincipalName
<String>] [-UserSMimeCertificate <MultiValuedProperty>] [-WhatIf
[<SwitchParameter>]] [-WindowsEmailAddress <SmtpAddress>] [-WindowsLiveID
<SmtpAddress>] [<CommonParameters>]
```

The Set-Mailbox -? command generates a lot of output to the screen, and it is compressed into a hard-to-read format. Since the Set-Mailbox cmdlet is manipulating the same object as the Get-Mailbox cmdlet, you could also use the following command to view all the properties that have been set on a particular mailbox (Matt.Cook in this example):

```
Get-Mailbox Matt.Cook | Format-List
```

```
RunspaceId                           : ba5c4d2d-ada0-43a5-a3fa-
b19af7d7e3cd
Database                             : DB01
DeletedItemFlags                     : DatabaseDefault
UseDatabaseRetentionDefaults         : True
RetainDeletedItemsUntilBackup        : False
DeliverToMailboxAndForward           : False
LitigationHoldEnabled                : False
SingleItemRecoveryEnabled            : False
RetentionHoldEnabled                 : False
EndDateForRetentionHold              :
StartDateForRetentionHold            :
RetentionComment                     :
RetentionUrl                         :
ManagedFolderMailboxPolicy           :
RetentionPolicy                      :
CalendarRepairDisabled               : False
ExchangeGuid                         : ad903a00-0ab3-453d-925d-
5218c5e8ad48
ExchangeSecurityDescriptor           :
System.Security.AccessControl.RawSecurityDescriptor
ExchangeUserAccountControl           : None
MessageTrackingReadStatusEnabled     : True
ExternalOofOptions                   : External
ForwardingAddress                    :
RetainDeletedItemsFor                : 14.00:00:00
IsMailboxEnabled                     : True
Languages                            : {en-US}
OfflineAddressBook                   :
ProhibitSendQuota                    : unlimited
ProhibitSendReceiveQuota             : unlimited
RecoverableItemsQuota                : unlimited
RecoverableItemsWarningQuota         : unlimited
DowngradeHighPriorityMessagesEnabled : False
ProtocolSettings                     : {}
RecipientLimits                      : unlimited
IsResource                           : False
IsLinked                             : False
IsShared                             : False
```

This example is a partial listing since a full listing would include a few pages of information you can easily look up yourself. Further, note that some of the properties you see as a result of a Get- cmdlet cannot be set since they are system-controlled properties or they are manipulated using other cmdlets, such as ExchangeGuid or Database.

The third way to view all of the properties associated with an object is to simply use the Get-Member cmdlet. Here is an example where the Get-Mailbox cmdlet pipes its output to the Get-Member cmdlet and filters only the members that are properties. Again, the output is a partial output listing only.

```
Get-Mailbox | Get-Member -MemberType Property


    TypeName: Microsoft.Exchange.Data.Directory.Management.Mailbox


Name                              MemberType Definition
----                              ---------- ----------
AcceptMessagesOnlyFrom            Property
Microsoft.Exchange.Data.MultiValuedProperty'1[[Microsoft.Exchange....
AcceptMessagesOnlyFromDLMembers Property
Microsoft.Exchange.Data.MultiValuedProperty'1[[Microsoft.Exchange....
AddressListMembership             Property
Microsoft.Exchange.Data.MultiValuedProperty'1[[Microsoft.Exchange....
Alias                             Property    System.String Alias
{get;set;}
{get;set;}
ArbitrationMailbox                Property    Microsoft.Exchange.Data.Directory
ArbitrationMailbox {g...
ArchiveGuid                       Property    System.Guid ArchiveGuid {get;}
ArchiveName                       Property
Microsoft.Exchange.Data.MultiValuedProperty'1[[System.String, msco...
ArchiveQuota                      Property
Microsoft.Exchange.Data.Unlimited'1[[Microsoft.Exchange.Data.ByteQ...
ArchiveWarningQuota               Property
Microsoft.Exchange.Data.Unlimited'1[[Microsoft.Exchange.Data.ByteQ...
BypassModerationFromSendersOrMembersProperty
Microsoft.Exchange.Data.MultiValuedProperty'1[[Microsoft.Exchange....
CalendarRepairDisabled            Property    System.Boolean
CalendarRepairDisabled {get;set;}
CalendarVersionStoreDisabled      Property    System.Boolean
CalendarVersionStoreDisabled {get;set;}
CustomAttribute1                  Property    System.String CustomAttribute1
{get;set;}
CustomAttribute10                 Property    System.String CustomAttribute10
{get;set;}
CustomAttribute11                 Property    System.String CustomAttribute11
{get;set;}
CustomAttribute12                 Property    System.String CustomAttribute12
{get;set;}
CustomAttribute13                 Property    System.String CustomAttribute13
{get;set;}
CustomAttribute14                 Property    System.String CustomAttribute14
{get;set;}
```

Formatting Output

If you look at the output of the Get-Mailbox cmdlet shown in Figure 6.1, you might be tempted to think that the output capabilities of PowerShell are limited, but this is far from the truth. The output shown in Figure 6.1 was the default output for the Get-Mailbox cmdlet. The programmer decided that the output should be in a formatted table with the name, alias, home server, and ProhibitSendQuota properties as columns. However, you can select on your own the properties you want by merely piping the output of the Get-Mailbox cmdlet to either the Format-Table (FT for short) or Select cmdlet:

```
Get-Mailbox | FT Name,ProhibitSendQuota,ProhibitSendReceiveQuota
```

Figure 6.2 shows the output of the preceding command.

FIGURE 6.2
Formatting output
to a formatted table

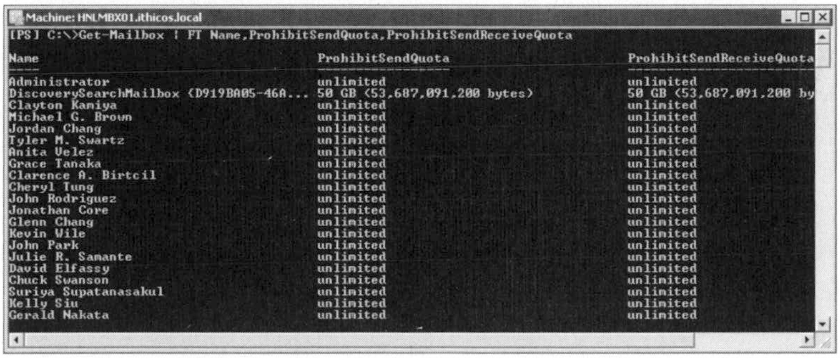

The output of the Get-Mailbox cmdlet was directed to the Format-Table or FT cmdlet; the result was columns for the Name, ProhibitSendQuota, and ProhibitSendReceiveQuota limits.

You may be wondering how you can learn all the properties of an object. The default output of the Get-Mailbox cmdlet, for example, is probably not the most useful for your organization. We discuss getting help in PowerShell and Exchange Management Shell later in this chapter, but here is a simple trick to see all the properties of an object: just direct the output of a Get- cmdlet to the Format-List (FL for short) cmdlet instead of the default Format-Table output.

When you direct the output of a cmdlet such as Get-Mailbox to the Format-List cmdlet, you will see *all* the properties for that object. Figure 6.3 shows an example where we have directed the output of a Get-Mailbox cmdlet to the FL (Format-List) cmdlet. You will notice in Figure 6.3 that the properties filled up more than one screen. However, you will find that outputting all the properties of an object using the Format-List cmdlet is very useful if you need to know specific property names.

The command we used is as follows:

```
Get-Mailbox "Clayton Kamiya" | Format-List
```

Directing Output to Other Cmdlets

You have already seen a couple of examples where we used the pipe symbol (|) to direct the output of one command to be used as input for the next command, such as Get-Mailbox |

Format-Table. You can do this because PowerShell commands act on objects, not just text. Unlike with other shells or scripting languages, you don't have to use string commands or variables to pass data from one command to another. The result is that you use a single line to perform a query and complex task — something that might have required hundreds of lines of programming in the past.

One of our favorite examples would be making specific changes to a group of people's mailboxes. Let's say you need to ensure that all executives in your organization should be able to send and receive a message that is up to 50 MB in size rather than the default 10 MB to which the system limits the user. Earlier we showed you how you could get the properties of the mailbox that you were interested in, such as the MaxSendSize and MaxReceiveSize properties.

FIGURE 6.3
Formatting output to a formatted list

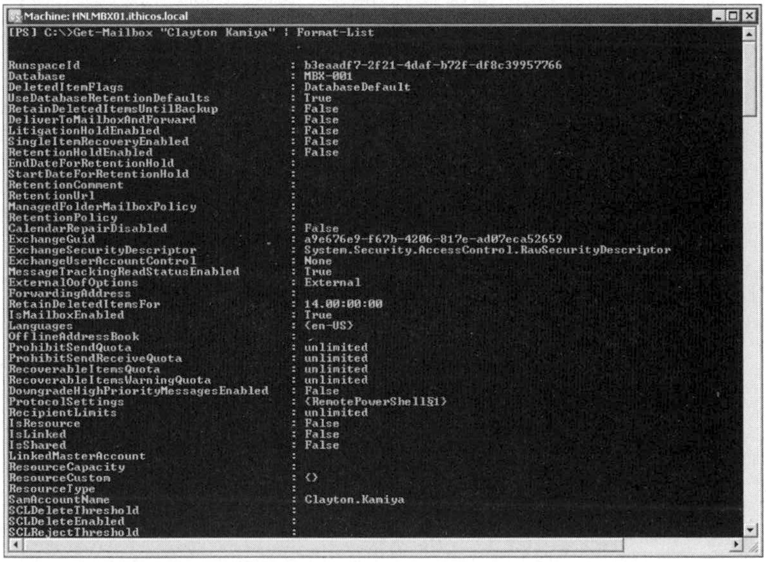

First, let's use the Get-DistributionGroupMember cmdlet to retrieve the members of the Executives distribution group:

```
Get-DistributionGroupMember "Executives"
Name                                    RecipientType
----                                    -------------
Mark Watts                              MailboxUser
David Elfassy                           MailboxUser
Brian Tirch                             MailboxUser
Paul Robichaux                          MailboxUser
Devin Ganger                            MailboxUser
Julie Samante                           MailboxUser
Cynthia Wang                            MailboxUser
```

Remember that though you see the text listing of the group members, what is actually output are objects representing each of the members.

It is important to note that while piping the output of one cmdlet as input for another cmdlet works frequently, it does not work all the time. Piping input to a cmdlet will always work when the noun used by the two cmdlets is the same, such as this:

```
Get-Mailbox -Server HNLMBX01 | Set-Mailbox -CustomAttribute1 "I am on a ↵
great server!"
```

For cmdlets that do not support piping between them, you can usually use a trick such as using the `foreach` cmdlet to process the data.

So, now let's pipe the output of that cmdlet to the `Set-Mailbox` cmdlet and do some real work! To change the maximum incoming and outgoing message size for the members of the Executives group, you would type the following command:

```
Get-DistributionGroupMember "#Executives" | Set-Mailbox ↵
-MaxSendSize:50MB -MaxReceiveSize:50MB  ↵
-UseDatabaseRetentionDefaults:$False
```

Notice that the `Set-Mailbox` cmdlet did not require any input because it will take as input the objects that are output from `Get-DistributionGroupMember`. When you run these two commands, there will be no output unless you have specified other options. But you can easily check the results by requesting the membership of the Executives group, piping that to the `Get-Mailbox` cmdlet, and then piping that output to the `Format-Table` cmdlet, as shown here:

```
Get-DistributionGroupMember "#Executives" | Get-Mailbox | Format-Table ↵
Name,MaxSendSize,MaxReceiveSize
Name                    MaxSendSize                MaxReceiveSize
----                    -----------                --------------
Clarence A. Birtcil  50 MB (52,428,800 bytes)  50 MB (52,428,800 bytes)
Cheryl Tung          50 MB (52,428,800 bytes)  50 MB (52,428,800 bytes)
Jonathan Core        50 MB (52,428,800 bytes)  50 MB (52,428,800 bytes)
Kevin Wile           50 MB (52,428,800 bytes)  50 MB (52,428,800 bytes)
Julie R. Samante     50 MB (52,428,800 bytes)  50 MB (52,428,800 bytes)
Gerald Nakata        50 MB (52,428,800 bytes)  50 MB (52,428,800 bytes)
```

Pretty cool, eh? After just a few minutes working with PowerShell and the EMS extensions, we hope that you will be as pleased with the ease of use as we are.

PowerShell v2

Exchange 2010 uses PowerShell v2, whereas Exchange 2007 used the power of PowerShell v1 (or also v2 with E2K7 SP2). PowerShell v2 includes some amazing new features, like remoting and eventing, which enable it to manage any IT environment even better than before.

Integrated Scripting Environment

Next to a lot of new cmdlets that are added to PowerShell and EMS, there is now a graphical user interface available called the Integrated Scripting Environment (ISE), which also includes a debugging tool. In Windows 2008 R2, Windows PowerShell ISE is an optional feature that you need to install using the Add Features Wizard, as opposed to Windows Vista and Windows Server 2008, where installing PowerShell v2 includes ISE by default.

To launch the new graphical user interface, you just need to type **ISE** in your Shell. Figure 6.4 shows you the ISE when launched.

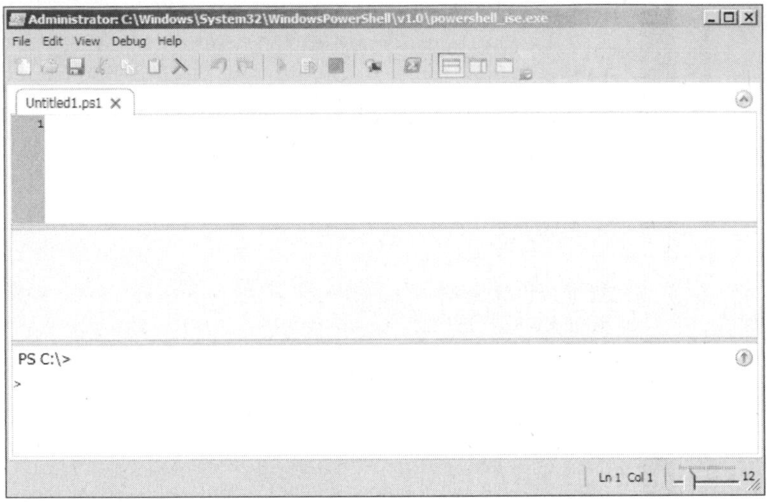

FIGURE 6.4
Integrated Scripting Environment

Using ISE you can enter cmdlets in the bottom pane, watch the result of running that cmdlet in the middle pane, and start scripting in the top pane, as shown in Figure 6.5.

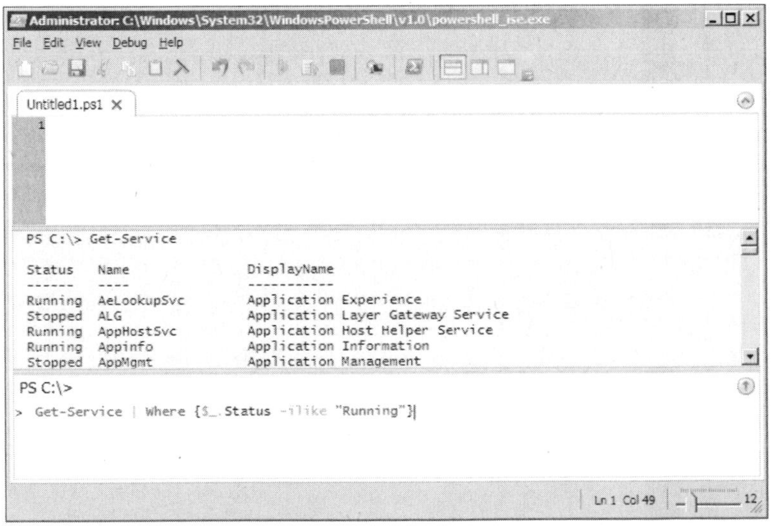

FIGURE 6.5
Working in ISE

Before you can start managing Exchange using ISE, you will need to connect to an Exchange Server. First, we create a new persistent connection to an Exchange 2010 Client Access server in our environment by initializing a variable, such as $Session:

```
$Session = New-PSSession -ConfigurationName Microsoft.Exchange ↵
-ConnectionUri http://<ExchangeServerName>/PowerShell/ ↵
-Authentication Kerberos -Credential $SkipCertification
```

which we import then into the client-side session using the cmdlet Import-PSSession:

```
Import-PSSession $Session
```

And then we are ready to use PowerShell ISE to manage Exchange 2010, as shown in Figure 6.6.

FIGURE 6.6
Configuring ISE to manage Exchange

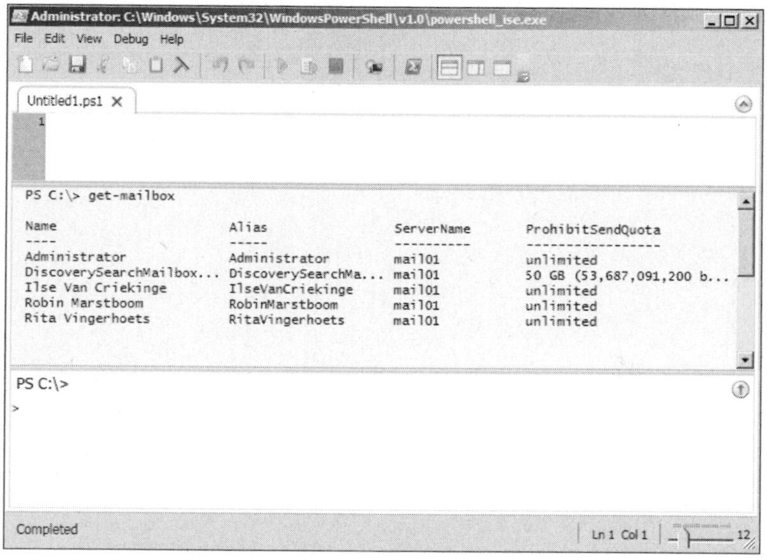

In the example in Figure 6.7, we're creating a function called MailboxPerServer, and after pressing F5 we can test the created function.

FIGURE 6.7
Creating a function in ISE

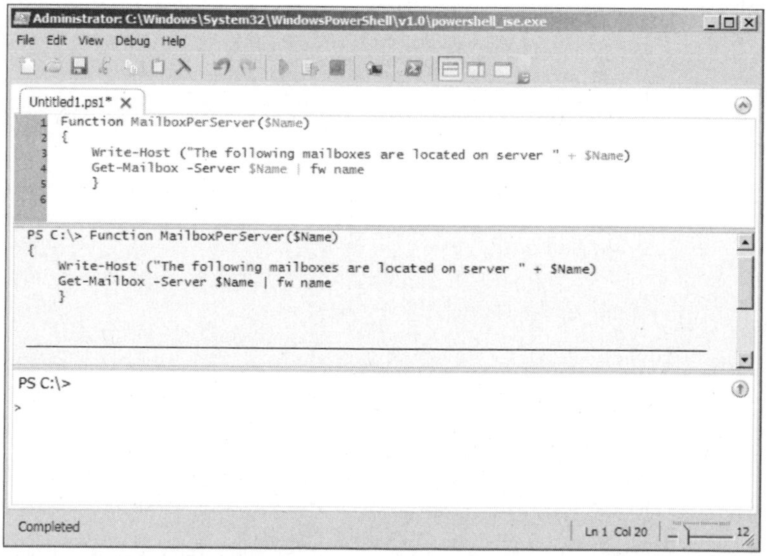

And as Figure 6.8 shows, running the Shell line MailboxPerServer("e2010chm1") will give us an overview of all mailboxes homed on a server called E2010CHM1.

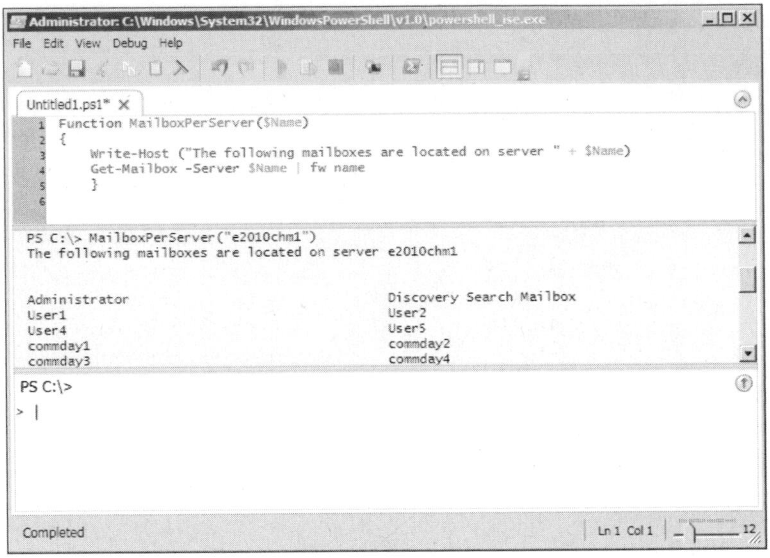

FIGURE 6.8
Running
`MailboxPerServer`
(`"e2010chm1"`) to see
all mailboxes homed
on a server called
E2010CHM1

Remote PowerShell

Exchange 2010 doesn't use local PowerShell anymore, except for the Edge Transport server role, but relies on remote PowerShell to manage its other roles (Hub Transport, Client Access, Mailbox, and Unified Messaging).

You won't see any difference between using remote or local shell to manage Exchange; except for Edge Transport servers, the local shell is no longer even available. When you click the Shell shortcut, Windows PowerShell connects to the closest Exchange 2010 Client Access server using Windows Remote Management 2.0, performs an authentication check, and then creates a remote session for you to use. It's thanks to Remote PowerShell that role-based access control (RBAC) can be fully implemented. (For more information about RBAC, refer to Chapter 15, "Management Permissions and Role-Based Administration").

Another advantage of introducing Remote PowerShell is the ability to launch the Shell and manage your Exchange servers by connecting to an Exchange 2010 Client Access server, without requiring you to install the management tools locally on that machine, which was a requirement in Exchange 2007.

Since Windows Server 2008 x64 is required for installing and running the Exchange binaries, remote PowerShell includes another nice benefit: the ability to manage Exchange 2010 using a 32-bit remote PowerShell client.

Tips and Tricks

In this section we discuss handling data output, sending output to a file, sending email from the PowerShell, and debugging.

Managing Output

Let's start by exploring how to massage or manipulate the output of PowerShell and EMS cmdlets. In this section, we are going to focus on the `Get-MailboxStatistics` cmdlet; we are using this cmdlet in our example because in our opinion its default output format is the least desirable of *all* the EMS cmdlets. Whoever set the defaults for this cmdlet's output clearly expected the user to be proficient at manipulating the output.

If you are coming from an Exchange Server 2007 environment, you may be used to running the `Get-MailboxStatistics` cmdlet with no parameters. Exchange Server 2010 expects you to either specify a mailbox name, server name (`-Server`), or mailbox database (`-Database`) in the command line. Here is an example of the `Get-MailboxStatistics` cmdlet's output specifying a mailbox server:

```
Get-MailboxStatistics -Server HNLMBX01

DisplayName              ItemCount StorageLimitStatus    LastLogonTime
-----------              --------- ------------------    -------------
John Park                7         BelowLimit
SystemMailbox{21db5e47... 1        BelowLimit
Chuck Swanson            6         BelowLimit
Online Archive - Tyler... 0        NoChecking
Microsoft Exchange       1         BelowLimit
Microsoft Exchange App... 1        BelowLimit
Jordan Chang             7         BelowLimit
Administrator            2         BelowLimit   8/9/2009 1:24:44 AM
David Elfassy            6         BelowLimit
Discovery Search Mailbox 1         BelowLimit
Clayton K. Kamiya        27        NoChecking 7/24/2009 12:17:44 AM
Microsoft Exchange App... 1         BelowLimit
Tyler M. Swartz          6          BelowLimit
Julie R. Samante         6          BelowLimit
Michael G. Brown         9          BelowLimit
Jonathan Core            6          BelowLimit
SystemMailbox{94c22976... 1         BelowLimit
Kevin Wile               8          BelowLimit
John Rodriguez           6          BelowLimit
Anita Velez              6          BelowLimit
```

Obviously this output is not very useful for most of us.

OUTPUT TO LISTS OR TABLES

Keep in mind that internally, when PowerShell is retrieving data, everything is treated as an object. However, when you are displaying something to the screen, you see just the textual information. Most cmdlets output data to a formatted table, but you can also output the data to a formatted list using the `Format-List` cmdlet or FL alias. Here is an example of piping a single mailbox's statistics to the `Format-List` cmdlet:

```
[PS] C:\>Get-MailboxStatistics "Clayton K. Kamiya" | Format-List


RunspaceId            : 3a8e6797-44a5-4c71-8a21-3022b379cb57
AssociatedItemCount   : 16
DeletedItemCount      : 0
```

```
DisconnectDate          :
DisplayName             : Clayton K. Kamiya
ItemCount               : 27
LastLoggedOnUserAccount : ITHICOS\Clayton.Kamiya
LastLogoffTime          : 7/24/2009 9:54:13 AM
LastLogonTime           : 7/24/2009 12:17:44 AM
LegacyDN                : /O=ITHICOS SOLUTIONS LLC/
OU=EXCHANGE ADMINISTRATIVE GROUP (FYDIBOHF23SPDLT)/
CN=RECIPIENTS/CN=CLAYTON K. KAMIYA
MailboxGuid             : a9e676e9-f67b-4206-817e-ad07eca52659
ObjectClass             : Mailbox
StorageLimitStatus      : NoChecking
TotalDeletedItemSize    : 0 B (0 bytes)
TotalItemSize           : 949.5 KB (972,245 bytes)
Database                : MBX-001
ServerName              : HNLMBX01
DatabaseName            : MBX-001
MoveHistory             :
IsQuarantined           : False
IsArchiveMailbox        : False
Identity                : a9e676e9-f67b-4206-817e-ad07eca52659
MapiIdentity            : a9e676e9-f67b-4206-817e-ad07eca52659
OriginatingServer       : hnlmbx01.ithicos.local
IsValid                 : True
```

This example shows you all the properties that can be displayed via the
Get-MailboxStatistics cmdlet.

The following are the default results of filtering the command through the Format-Table
or FT alias:

```
Get-MailboxStatistics "Clayton K. Kamiya" | FT

DisplayName       ItemCount  StorageLimitStatus  LastLogonTime
-----------       ---------  ------------------  -------------
Clayton Kamiya    1063       BelowLimit          8/9/2008 1:33:31 PM
```

However, the Format-Table and Format-List cmdlets allow you to specify which properties you want to see in the output list. Let's say that you want to see the user's name, item
count, and total item size. Here's the command you would use:

```
Get-MailboxStatistics "Clayton Kamiya" | FT DisplayName, ↵
ItemCount,TotalItemSize

DisplayName               ItemCount TotalItemSize
-----------               --------- -------------
Clayton K. Kamiya              1063 4.00 MB (4,190,207 bytes)
```

There we go — that is a bit more useful. It's not perfect, mind you, but the output format is
getting better.

SORTING AND GROUPING OUTPUT

Any output can also be sorted based on any of the properties that you are going to display. If you are using the Format-Table command, you can also group the output by properties. First, let's go back and look at the original example where we are outputting all the mailbox statistics for the local mailbox server. Let's say we are interested in sorting by the maximum mailbox size. To do so, we can pipe the output of Get-MailboxStatistics to the Sort-Object cmdlet. Here is an example:

```
Get-Mailbox | Get-MailboxStatistics -Server HNLMBX01 | Sort-Object ↵
TotalItemSize -Descending | Format-Table DisplayName, ↵
ItemCountTotalItemsize
```

```
DisplayName            ItemCount        TotalItemSize
-----------            ---------        -------------------
Mike Brown                   306        22.92 MB (24,030,192 bytes)
Clayton Kamiya              1063        21.34 MB (22,376,612 bytes
Simon Butler                   2        221.3 KB(226,596 bytes)
Omar Droubi                    2        71.75 KB (73,469 bytes)
Brian Tirch                    2        50.00 KB(51,200 bytes)
```

This example used the command Sort-Object TotalItemSize -Descending, but we could also have used the -Ascending option. There are several far more sophisticated examples in PowerShell help.

We can take this a step further when using the Format-Table cmdlet by adding a -GroupBy option. Here is an example where we are exporting this data and grouping it using the StorageLimitStatus property:

```
Get-Mailbox | Get-MailboxStatistics | Sort-Object TotalItemSize ↵
-Descending | Format-Table DisplayName, ItemCount, Totalitemsize ↵
-GroupBy StorageLimitStatus
```

```
    StorageLimitStatus: MailboxDisabled

DisplayName            ItemCount        Total Item Size
-----------            ---------        ---------------
Mike Brown                   314        21.25 MB (21,763 bytes)


    StorageLimitStatus: ProhibitSend

DisplayName            ItemCount        Total Item Size
-----------            ---------        ---------------
Clayton Kamiya              1066        5.02 MB (5,145 bytes)


    StorageLimitStatus: BelowLimit

DisplayName            ItemCount        Total Item Size
-----------            ---------        ---------------
Omar Droubi                    8        1.09 MB (1,119 bytes)
Andy Webb                      6        286 B (286 bytes)
```

OUTPUT TO FILE

Outputting data to the screen is great, but it does not help you with reports. You can also output data to CSV and XML files. Two cmdlets make this easy to do:

◆ Export-Csv exports the data to a CSV file.

◆ Export-Clixml exports the data to an XML file.

Simply direct the output you want sent to a file and these cmdlets will take care of converting the data to the proper format. Let's take our earlier example where we want a report of all mailboxes and their ProhibitSend and ProhibitSendAndReceive limits. We can't use the Format-Table cmdlet in this instance; we have to use the Select-Object or Select cmdlet to specify the output because we will be directing this output to another cmdlet. Here is an example of the Get-Mailbox cmdlet when using the Select command:

```
Get-Mailbox | Select Name, ProhibitSendQuota, ProhibitSendReceiveQuota
```

The output of this cmdlet is shown here:

```
Name               ProhibitSendQuota      ProhibitSendReceiveQuota
----               -----------------      ------------------------
Janie Nimetz       unlimited                  unlimited
Josh Kostick       unlimited                  unlimited
Daniel Petri       unlimited                  unlimited
Matt Paleafei      unlimited                  unlimited
Mike Brown         unlimited                  unlimited
Dan Holme          unlimited                  unlimited
Russ Zimmer        unlimited                  unlimited
Tyler Swartz       unlimited                  unlimited
Chris Pfennig      unlimited                  unlimited
```

To direct this output to the C:\report.csv file, we simply pipe it to the Export-Csv cmdlet as shown here:

```
Get-Mailbox | Select Name, ProhibitSendQuota, ProhibitSendReceiveQuota | ↵
Export-Csv c:\report.csv
```

If you want to export the report to an XML file, simply use the Export-Clixml cmdlet instead of Export-Csv.

Finally, just as when working with the DOS prompt, you can redirect output of a command to a text file. To send the output of the Get-Mailbox to the file c:\mailboxes.txt, you would type this:

```
Get-Mailbox > c:\mailboxes.txt
```

Out-GridView

PowerShell v2 introduces a new cmdlet that enables you to display the information in a data grid as opposed to a table or list. The PowerShell grid not only gives you the ability to resize the given columns, but also enables you to filter data, and much more.

The following PowerShell line will request a list of mailboxes and create a grid view, as you can see in Figure 6.9.

FIGURE 6.9
Out-GridView

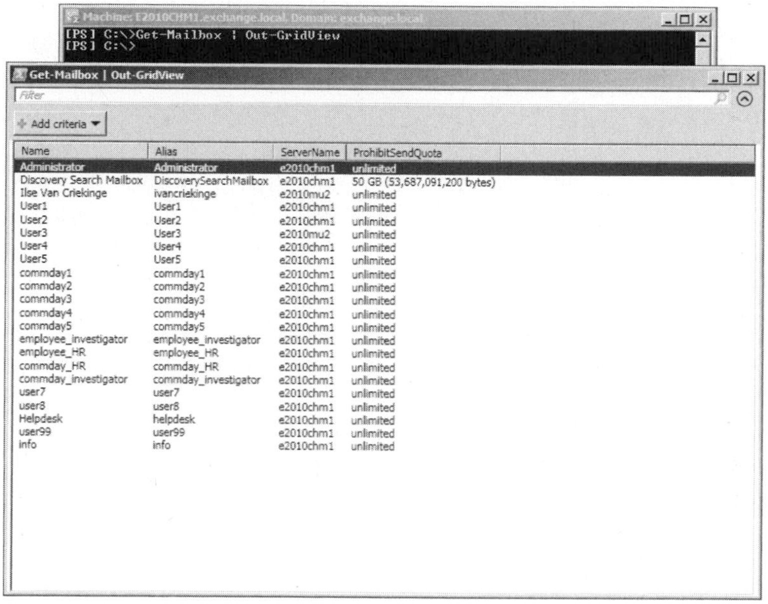

And with some filtering, you can change the grid view without having to play around with cmdlets like `Where-Object`, `Sort-Object`, and so on, as shown in Figure 6.10.

FIGURE 6.10
Filtering with
Out-GridView

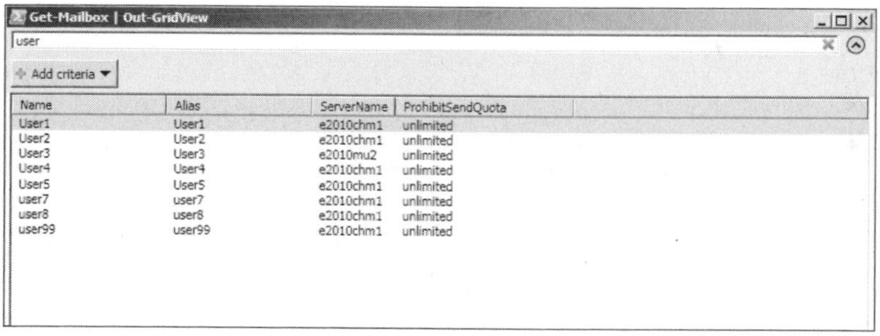

You can also add some criteria to get just the list of objects you want to retrieve, as shown in Figure 6.11.

FIGURE 6.11
Criteria and
Out-GridView

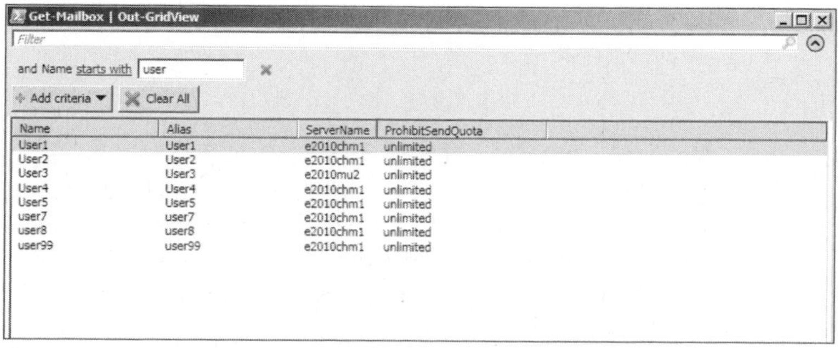

Even though it is impossible to save data from the grid itself, you can bypass this limitation by importing saved data first. The example in Figure 6.12 will first export the mailbox statistics data to an XML file, and then show the imported results in a data grid view.

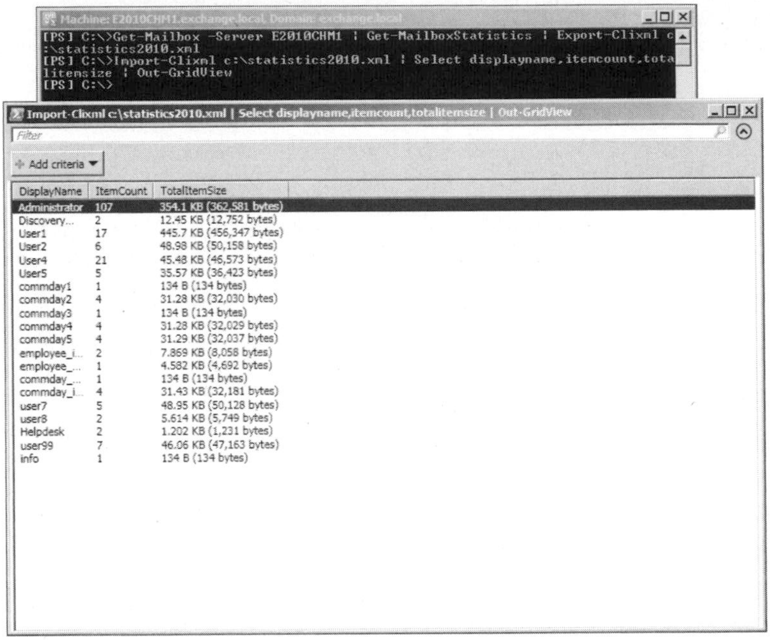

FIGURE 6.12
Import-CliXML,
Export-CliXML,
and Out-GridView

PUTTING IT ALL TOGETHER

Let's consider one more example of Get-MailboxStatistics piping. Hopefully this will be an example that you can use in the future. We will create a report of the mailbox statistics using the Get-MailboxStatistics cmdlet. Then we will export the mailbox statistics for a specific server. We will limit the output by using the Where-Object command, choose the properties to output using the Select command, and finally pipe that output to the Export-Csv cmdlet:

```
Get-MailboxStatistics -Server HNLEX04 | Sort-Object TotalItemSize ↵
-Descending | Select-Object DisplayName,ItemCount,TotalItemSize ↵
| Export-CSV c:\StorStats.csv
```

If you are thinking that this looks a bit sticky to implement, you are probably right. Getting this syntax together took the better part of an afternoon, and arguably, you should be able to perform common tasks like exporting mailbox storage statistics from the GUI. However, on the bright side, now we have the command we need to run each time we want to generate this report; further, the knowledge to do this particular type of report within PowerShell carries over into many other tasks.

Running Scripts

PowerShell scripts are easy to build and to run, but there are a few things you need to know to write your own scripts and/or to read others' scripts:

◆ The file extension for a PowerShell script is `.PS1`.

◆ You can't run the script from the source directory. You actually have to preface the script name with the path.

Say we have a script called `c:\scripts\Report.ps1`. We can't just change it to the `c:\reports` directory and run `report.ps1`, so we would have to type `.\report.ps1`.

◆ PowerShell (and scripts) use variables preceded with a $ symbol. You can set a variable within a script or just by typing it at the command line. The PowerShell variable is an object, so we can associate an object or an entire list of objects with a single variable.

For example, the following command associates the variable `$Matt` with the entire object for the user Matt Suriya:

```
$Matt = Get-User "Matt Suriya"
```

We could then use just specific properties of that object. For example, if we want to just output Matt's display name, we could type this:

```
$Matt.DisplayName
```

Even better, we could then set Matt's display name to a variable called `$MattDisplayName` by doing this:

```
$MattDisplayName = $Matt.DisplayName
```

We can set a single variable to a lot of objects and then manipulate them all at once via a script. Here is an example where we set the `$AllUsers` variable to all the users in the domain:

```
$AllUsers = Get-Users
```

Now here are some interesting things we can do with that variable. We could obtain a count of how many objects it contains:

```
$AllUsers.Count
944
```

Further, each of the 944 objects contained in the `$AllUsers` variable is treated as an item in an array, so we can retrieve individual ones, such as object number 939:

```
AllUsers[939] | FL samAccountName,DisplayName,WindowsEmailAddress,Phone,↵
Office


        SamAccountName      : Andrew.Roberts
        DisplayName         : Andrew Roberts (Operations)
```

```
WindowsEmailAddress : andrew.roberts@ithicos.com
Phone               : 011-77-8484-4844
Office              : Tokyo
```

Though this is certainly not a comprehensive briefing on PowerShell scripting or variables, we hope it will give you a quick introduction to a few things that we found interesting and helpful when we got started.

SENDING EMAIL FROM THE EXCHANGE MANAGEMENT SHELL

Sometimes the smallest new features are among the best features. In this particular case, we are talking about a new PowerShell v2.0 cmdlet called Send-MailMessage that allows you to easily send an email from within the PowerShell. While you could accomplish this in Exchange 2007 and PowerShell v1.0, accomplishing it was a bit cumbersome.

For example, if you want to send an email message from the alias SystemMessages@ithicos.local to HelpDesk@ithicos.local, it would look something like this:

```
Send-MailMessage -To HelpDesk@ithicos.local -Subject "This is a test ↵
message" -From SystemMessages@ithicos.local -BodyAsHtml -Body "This ↵
is the body of the message" -SmtpServer hn1ht01
```

Note that you must specify an SMTP server that will either accept this connection or relay the message for you.

Running Scheduled PowerShell Scripts

Frequently PowerShell advocates will extol the virtues of creating simple PowerShell scripts (PS1 files) that you can schedule to perform routine tasks. There are quite a few articles and newsgroup postings about how easy this is to do. However, running the PS1 script using a scheduled task is a bit trickier. You can't just run a PS1 script from the DOS command prompt or the Task Scheduler. Before a PS1 script can be run, PowerShell has to be run, the Exchange Management Extensions have to be loaded, and then the script or command can be called.

The PowerShell executable (powershell.exe) is found in the C:\Windows\System32 \WindowsPowerShell\v1.0\ folder. PowerShell needs to be told from which Exchange Server it will need to import the Exchange session from (using the Import-PSSession cmdlet).

Finally, we need the name and the location of the script we are going to run, so let's say we are going to execute this command:

```
Get-Mailbox | Select Name, ProhibitSendQuota, ProhibitSendReceiveQuota ↵
| Export-Csv c:\report2.csv
```

Rather than pasting all this into the job scheduler, we can create a simple batch file that looks like this:

```
@echo off
cls
C:\Windows\System32\WindowsPowerShell\v1.0\PowerShell.exe ↵
-command "& { c:\scripts\Report1.ps1 }"
```

Now we need to create the Report1.ps1 script that will run once PowerShell is opened:

```
$Session = New-PSSession -ConfigurationName Microsoft.Exchange ↵
-ConnectionUri http://hnlmbx01/PowerShell/
Import-PSSession $session
Get-Mailbox | Select Name, ProhibitSendQuota, ProhibitSendReceiveQuota↵
| Export-Csv c:\report2.csv
```

Debugging and Troubleshooting from PowerShell

PowerShell has a lot of features that will help you test your scripts and one-line commands.

Set-PSDebug   The cmdlet Set-PSDebug is designed to allow you to debug PowerShell scripts. To use this, add this command to your script: Set-PSDebug -Trace 1. This will allow you to examine each step of the script. You can enable more detailed trace logging by setting the trace level to 2: Set-PSDebug -Trace 2. If you add the -Step option to the command line, you will be prompted for each step. To turn off trace logging, use this command Set-PSDebug -Off.

-WhatIf   Most cmdlets support the -WhatIf option. If you add the -WhatIf option to the command line, the cmdlet will run and tell you what will happen without actually performing the task. This is useful for checking to make sure the command you are about to run will really do what you want.

-Confirm   Most cmdlets support the -Confirm option and many cmdlets that perform more destructive types of options, such as those that begin with Remove-, Move-, Dismount-, Disable-, and Clear-, have the -Confirm option turned on by default. If this is turned on, the cmdlet will not proceed until you have confirmed it is okay to proceed. For cmdlets that confirm by default, you can include the -Confirm:$False option if you do not want to be prompted.

-ValidateOnly   The -ValidateOnly option is a bit more powerful than -WhatIf. The -ValidateOnly option will perform all the steps the cmdlet is specifying without actually making any changes and then will summarize what would have been done and if this would have caused any problems.

Getting Help

We have shown you a few simple yet powerful examples of how to use PowerShell and the EMS. Once you dig in and start using the EMS, you will need some references to help you figure out all the syntax and properties of each of the cmdlets.

Exchange Server 2010 Help File

A great starting place for just reading about the cmdlets is in the Microsoft Exchange Server 2010 help file. The help file documents explain how to do most common operations both through the graphical user interface as well as through the EMS. Figure 6.13 shows the online help for how to create a new mailbox. After the procedures for creating the mailbox through the GUI are shown, you will also see the procedures for using the EMS.

After the example for creating the mailbox, you see a link to the New-Mailbox cmdlet that will take you to much more detailed information on that specific cmdlet. The New-Mailbox help topic (shown in Figure 6.14) will provide you with a great amount of detail about the use of the cmdlet. We strongly recommend you take advantage of the Exchange help file that is included with Exchange Server. In fact, you might want to even copy the file and save it to your workstation. The filename is ExchHelp.chm.

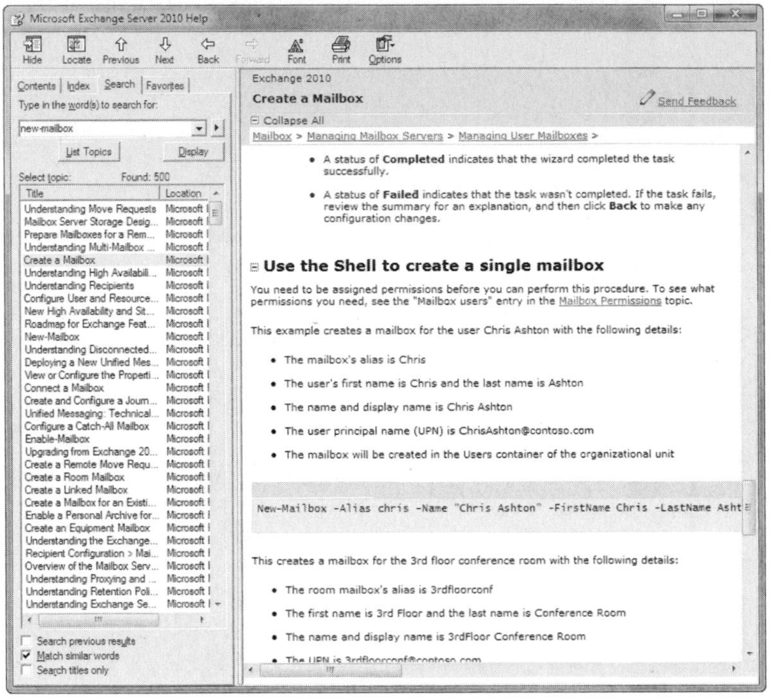

FIGURE 6.13
Referring to the online help for creating a new mailbox

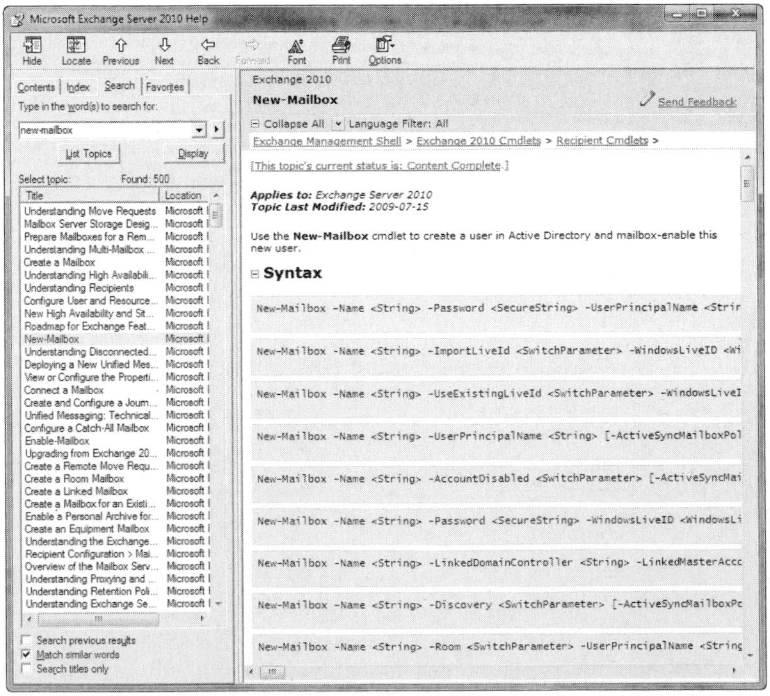

FIGURE 6.14
Online help for creating a new mailbox using the Exchange Management Shell

---

HELP FILES AND OTHER DOCUMENTATION UPDATED REGULARLY

Microsoft tends to update the help file more frequently than it updates the service packs. Visit the Exchange Server downloads site to make sure you have the latest help file at http://technet.microsoft.com/en-us/exchange/bb456976.aspx. The online documentation is updated even more frequently than the help file, so visit http://technet.microsoft.com/en-us/library/aa996058.aspx for the latest documentation.

Help from the Command Line

Information is also available on the cmdlets from within PowerShell. For a good starting point, you can just type the help command and this will give you a good overview of using PowerShell and how to get more help. Table 6.6 summarizes common methods of getting help on PowerShell and Exchange Management Shell cmdlets.

TABLE 6.6:   Methods of Getting Help Within the EMS

ACTION	DESCRIPTION
help	Provides generic PowerShell help information.
help *Keyword*	Lists all cmdlets that contain the keyword. For example, if you want to find all PowerShell v2 cmdlets that work with the Windows event log, you would type **help *EventLog***. To find all Exchange cmdlets that work with mailboxes, type **Get-ExCommand *mailbox***. You cannot use the help alias to locate all available Exchange cmdlets.
Get-Command *Keyword*	Lists all PowerShell cmdlets and files (such as help files) that contain the keyword.
Get-Command	Lists all cmdlets (including all PowerShell extensions currently loaded such as the EMS cmdlets).
Get-ExCommand	Lists all Exchange cmdlets.
Get-PSCommand	Lists all PowerShell cmdlets.
Help *Cmdlet* or Get-Help *Cmdlet*	Lists online help for the specified cmdlet and pauses between each screen. Provides multiple views of the online help (such as detailed, full, examples, and default).
Cmdlet -?	Lists online help for the specified cmdlet.

When working with help within PowerShell, help topics are displayed based on the view of help that you request. In other words, you can't just type Get-Help and see everything about that cmdlet. The Get-Help cmdlet includes four possible views of help for each cmdlet. Table 6.7 explains the four primary views along with the parameters view.

TABLE 6.7:   Possible Output Views for the Get-Help Cmdlet

VIEW OPTION	EXPLANATION
Default	Lists the minimal information to describe the function of the cmdlet and shows the syntax of the cmdlet
Example	Includes a synopsis of the cmdlet and some examples of its usage
Detailed	Shows more details on a cmdlet, including parameters and parameter descriptions
Full	Shows all the details available on a cmdlet, including a synopsis of the cmdlet, a detailed description of the cmdlet, parameter descriptions, parameter metadata, and examples
Parameters	Allows you to specify a parameter and get help on the usage of just that particular parameter

The Full option for Get-Help includes in its output each parameter's metadata. The metadata is shown in Table 6.8.

TABLE 6.8:   Metadata Output by the Get-Help Cmdlet

OPTION	PURPOSE
Required?	Is the parameter required? This value is either true or false.
Position?	Specifies the position of the parameter. If the position is named, the parameter name has to be included in the parameter list. Most parameters are named. However, the -Identity parameter is 1, which means that it is always the first parameter and the -Identity tag is not required.
Default value	Specifies what a value will be for a parameter if nothing else is specified. For most parameters this is blank.
Accept pipeline input?	Specifies if the parameter will accept input that is piped in from another cmdlet. The value is either true or false.
Accept wildcard characters?	Specifies if the parameter accepts wildcard characters such as the asterisk or question mark character. This value is either true or false.

Still not clear about what each view gives you? Perhaps Table 6.9 can shed some further light on the issue. This table shows you the various sections that are output when using each view option.

TABLE 6.9: Information Output for Each Get-Help View

	DEFAULT VIEW	EXAMPLE VIEW	DETAILED VIEW	FULL VIEW
Synopsis	✓	✓	✓	✓
Detailed description	✓		✓	✓
Syntax	✓		✓	✓
Parameters			✓	✓
Parameter metadata				✓
Input type				✓
Return type				✓
Errors				✓
Notes				✓
Example		✓	✓	✓

To use these parameters, you would use the following `Get-Help` cmdlet and the view option. For example, to see the example view for the `Get-Mailbox`, you would type the following:

```
Get-Help Get-Mailbox -Example
```

We feel it is important for administrators to understand the available online help options, so let's look at a couple more detailed examples for the `Get-MailboxStatistics` cmdlet. We are picking a cmdlet (`Get-MailboxStatistics`) that we feel is pretty representative of the EMS cmdlets but that also does not have a huge amount of help information. First, let's look at the default view:

```
Get-Help Get-MailboxStatistics

NAME
    Get-MailboxStatistics

SYNOPSIS
    Use the Get-MailboxStatistics cmdlet to obtain information about a mailbox,
such as the size of the mailbox, the number of messages it contains, and the
last time it was accessed. In addition, you can get the move history or a move
report of a completed move request.
SYNTAX
    Get-MailboxStatistics -Identity <GeneralMailboxIdParameter> [-Archive
<SwitchParameter>] [-DomainController <Fqdn>] [-IncludeMoveHistory
<SwitchParameter>] [-IncludeMoveReport <SwitchParameter>] [<CommonParameters>]
```

```
    Get-MailboxStatistics -Database <DatabaseIdParameter> [-DomainController
<Fqdn>] [<CommonParameters>]

    Get-MailboxStatistics -Server <ServerIdParameter> [-DomainController <Fqdn>]
[<CommonParameters>]
```

DESCRIPTION
    On Mailbox servers only, you can use the Get-MailboxStatistics cmdlet
without parameters. In this case, the cmdlet returns the statistics for all
mailboxes on all databases on the local server.
    The Get-MailboxStatistics cmdlet requires at least one of the following
parameters to complete successfully: Server, Database, or Identity.
    You can use the Get-MailboxStatistics cmdlet to return detailed move history
and a move report for completed move requests to troubleshoot a move request.
To view the move history, you must pass this cmdlet as an object. Move histories
are retained in the mailbox database and are numbered incrementally, and the last
executed move request is always numbered 0. For more information, see "EXAMPLE 6,"
"EXAMPLE 7," and "EXAMPLE 8" later in this topic.
    You can only see move reports and move history for completed move requests.
    You need to be assigned permissions before you can run this cmdlet. Although
all parameters for this cmdlet are listed in this topic, you may not have access
to some parameters if they're not included in the permissions assigned to you.
To see what permissions you need, see the "Recipient Provisioning Permissions"
section in the Mailbox Permissions topic.

RELATED LINKS
    Online Version http://technet.microsoft.com/EN-US/library/cec76f70-941f-
4bc9-b949-35dcc7671146(EXCHG.140).aspx

REMARKS
    To see the examples, type: "get-help Get-MailboxStatistics -examples".
    For more information, type: "get-help Get-MailboxStatistics -detailed".
    For technical information, type: "get-help Get-MailboxStatistics -full".

The default view (as you could have predicted from Table 6.9) includes the synopsis, syntax, and detailed description sections. Let's change our approach and look at the example view:

```
[PS] C:\>Get-Help Get-MailboxStatistics -Examples
```

NAME
    Get-MailboxStatistics

SYNOPSIS
Use the Get-MailboxStatistics cmdlet to obtain information about a mailbox,
such as the size of the mailbox, the number of messages it contains, and
the last time it was accessed. In addition, you can get the move history or
a move report of a completed move request.

```
------------------------ EXAMPLE 1 ------------------------
```

This example retrieves the mailbox statistics for all mailboxes on the local server. You can use the Get-MailboxStatistics cmdlet without parameters only on a Mailbox server, and it defaults to the local mailbox database.

```
Get-MailboxStatistics
```

```
------------------------ EXAMPLE 2 ------------------------
```

This example retrieves the mailbox statistics for all mailboxes on the server MailboxServer01.

```
Get-MailboxStatistics -Server MailboxServer01
```

```
------------------------ EXAMPLE 3 ------------------------
```

This example retrieves the mailbox statistics for the specified mailbox.

```
Get-MailboxStatistics -Identity contoso\chris
```

```
------------------------ EXAMPLE 4 ------------------------
```

This example retrieves the mailbox statistics for all mailboxes in the specified mailbox database.

```
Get-MailboxStatistics -Database "Mailbox Database"
```

```
------------------------ EXAMPLE 5 ------------------------
```

This example retrieves the mailbox statistics for all disconnected mailboxes. This example uses a WHERE clause. The $_ variable is used to specify the object passed on the pipeline. The -ne operator means not equal.

```
Get-MailboxStatistics | Where {$_.DisconnectDate -ne $null}
```

```
------------------------ EXAMPLE 6 ------------------------
```

This example returns the summary move history for the completed move request for Ayla Kol's mailbox. If you don't pipeline the output to the Format-List cmdlet, the move history doesn't display.

```
Get-MailboxStatistics -Identity AylaKol -IncludeMoveHistory | Format-List
```

```
------------------------- EXAMPLE 7 -------------------------


This example returns the detailed move history for the completed move
request for Ayla Kol's mailbox. This example uses a temporary variable
to store the mailbox statistics object. If the mailbox has been moved
multiple times, there will be multiple move reports. The last move
report is always MoveReport[0].

$temp=Get-MailboxStatistics -Identity AylaKol -IncludeMoveHistory
$temp.MoveHistory[0]



------------------------- EXAMPLE 8 -------------------------


This example returns the detailed move history and a verbose detailed
move report for Ayla Kol's mailbox. This example uses a temporary
variable to store the move request statistics object and outputs
the move report to a CSV file.

$temp=Get-MailboxStatistics -Identity AylaKol -IncludeMoveReport
$temp.MoveHistory[0] | Export-CSV C:\MoveReport_AylaKol.csv
```

The example view does not have as much data, but a lot of techies learn by looking at examples so we find this view particularly useful. Next let's look at the detailed view; because this view includes the parameters, it will have quite a bit more information:

```
[PS] C:\>Get-Help Get-MailboxStatistics -Detailed

NAME
    Get-MailboxStatistics

SYNOPSIS
    Use the Get-MailboxStatistics cmdlet to obtain information about
a mailbox, such as the size of the mailbox, the number of messages it
contains, and the last time it was accessed. In addition, you can get
the move history or a move report of a completed move request.

SYNTAX
    Get-MailboxStatistics -Identity <GeneralMailboxIdParameter>
[-Archive <SwitchParameter>] [-DomainController <Fqdn>]
[-IncludeMoveHistory <SwitchParameter>] [-IncludeMoveReport
<SwitchParameter>] [<CommonParameters>]

    Get-MailboxStatistics -Database <DatabaseIdParameter>
[-DomainController <Fqdn>] [<CommonParameters>]

    Get-MailboxStatistics -Server <ServerIdParameter>
[-DomainController <Fqdn>] [<CommonParameters>]
```

DESCRIPTION
    On Mailbox servers only, you can use the Get-MailboxStatistics
cmdlet without parameters. In this case, the cmdlet returns the
statistics for all mailboxes on all databases on the local server.
    The Get-MailboxStatistics cmdlet requires at least one of the
following parameters to complete successfully: Server, Database,
or Identity.
    You can use the Get-MailboxStatistics cmdlet to return detailed
move history and a move report for completed move requests to
troubleshoot a move request. To view the move history, you must pass
this cmdlet as an object.
    Move histories are retained in the mailbox database and are numbered
incrementally, and the last executed move request is always numbered 0.
For more information, see "EXAMPLE 6," "EXAMPLE 7," and "EXAMPLE 8"
later in this topic.
    You can only see move reports and move history for completed move
requests. You need to be assigned permissions before you can run this
cmdlet. Although all parameters for this cmdlet are listed in this
topic, you may not have access to some parameters if they're not
included in the permissions assigned to you. To see what permissions
you need, see the "Recipient Provisioning Permissions" section in
the Mailbox Permissions topic.

PARAMETERS
    -Database <DatabaseIdParameter>
        The Database parameter specifies the name of the mailbox
database. When you specify a value for the Database parameter,
the Exchange Management Shell returns statistics for all the mailboxes
on the database specified.
        You can use the following values:
        * GUID
        * Server\Database
        * Database
        This parameter accepts pipeline input from the Get-MailboxDatabase
cmdlet.

    -Identity <GeneralMailboxIdParameter>
        The Identity parameter specifies a mailbox. When you specify
a value for the Identity parameter, the command looks up the mailbox
specified in the Identity parameter, connects to the server where the
mailbox resides, and returns the statistics for the mailbox. You can
use one of the following values:
        * GUID
        * Distinguished name (DN)
        * Domain\Account
        * User principal name (UPN)
        * Legacy Exchange DN
        * SMTP address
        * Alias

```
-Server <ServerIdParameter>
    The Server parameter specifies the server from which you
want to obtain mailbox statistics. You can use one of the following values:
    * Fully qualified domain name (FQDN)
    * NetBIOS name
    When you specify a value for the Server parameter, the command
returns statistics for all the mailboxes on all the databases, including
recovery databases, on the specified server. If you don't specify this
parameter, the command returns logon statistics for the local server.

-Archive <SwitchParameter>
    The Archive switch parameter specifies whether to return
mailbox statistics for the archive mailbox associated with the
specified mailbox. You don't have to specify a value with this parameter.

-DomainController <Fqdn>
    The DomainController parameter specifies the fully qualified
domain name (FQDN) of the domain controller that retrieves data from
Active Directory.

-IncludeMoveHistory <SwitchParameter>
    The IncludeMoveHistory switch specifies whether to return
additional information about the mailbox that includes the history of
a completed move request, such as status, flags, target database, bad
items, start times, end times, duration that the move request was in
various stages, and failure codes.

-IncludeMoveReport <SwitchParameter>
    The IncludeMoveReport switch specifies whether to return a
verbose detailed move report for a completed move request, such as
server connections and move stages.
    Because the output of this command is verbose, you should
send the output to a .CSV file for easier analysis.

<CommonParameters>
    This cmdlet supports the common parameters: Verbose, Debug,
    ErrorAction, ErrorVariable, WarningAction, WarningVariable,
    OutBuffer and OutVariable. For more information, type,
    "get-help about_commonparameters".

-------------------------- EXAMPLE 1 --------------------------

This example retrieves the mailbox statistics for all mailboxes on the
local server.  You can use the Get-MailboxStatistics cmdlet without
parameters only on a Mailbox server, and it defaults to the local mailbox
database.

Get-MailboxStatistics
```

Notice in the previous output we left out most of the examples just to save some page space and because we had already shown them to you earlier. We did so with the full view as well since it contains even more information than the detailed view. The full view includes the meta-data for each parameter as well as examples:

```
Get-Help Get-MailboxStatistics -Full

NAME
    Get-MailboxStatistics

SYNOPSIS
    Use the Get-MailboxStatistics cmdlet to obtain information
about a mailbox, such as the size of the mailbox, the number of
messages it contains, and the last time it was accessed. In
addition, you can get the move history or a move report of a
completed move request.

SYNTAX
    Get-MailboxStatistics -Identity <GeneralMailboxIdParameter>
[-Archive <SwitchParameter>] [-DomainController <Fqdn>]
[-IncludeMoveHistory <SwitchParameter>] [-IncludeMoveReport
<SwitchParameter>] [<CommonParameters>]

    Get-MailboxStatistics -Database <DatabaseIdParameter>
[-DomainController <Fqdn>] [<CommonParameters>]

    Get-MailboxStatistics -Server <ServerIdParameter>
[-DomainController <Fqdn>] [<CommonParameters>]

DESCRIPTION
    On Mailbox servers only, you can use the Get-MailboxStatistics cmdlet
without parameters. In this case, the cmdlet returns the statistics for all
mailboxes on all databases on the local server.
    The Get-MailboxStatistics cmdlet requires at least one of the following
parameters to complete successfully: Server, Database, or Identity.
    You can use the Get-MailboxStatistics cmdlet to return detailed move
history and a move report for completed move requests to troubleshoot a move
request. To view the move history, you must pass this cmdlet as an object.
Move histories are retained in the mailbox database and are numbered
incrementally, and the last executed move request is always numbered 0.
For more information, see "EXAMPLE 6," "EXAMPLE 7," and "EXAMPLE 8" later
in this topic.
    You can only see move reports and move history for completed move
requests. You need to be assigned permissions before you can run this
cmdlet. Although all parameters for this cmdlet are listed in this topic,
you may not have access to some parameters if they're not included in the
permissions assigned to you.
To see what permissions you need, see the "Recipient Provisioning
Permissions" section in the Mailbox Permissions topic.
```

PARAMETERS
   -Database <DatabaseIdParameter>
      The Database parameter specifies the name of the mailbox
database. When you specify a value for the Database parameter, the
Exchange Management Shell returns statistics for all the mailboxes
on the database specified.
      You can use the following values:
      * GUID
      * Server\Database
      * Database
      This parameter accepts pipeline input from the Get-MailboxDatabase
cmdlet.

Required?	true
Position?	Named
Default value	
Accept pipeline input?	True
Accept wildcard characters?	false

   -Identity <GeneralMailboxIdParameter>
      The Identity parameter specifies a mailbox. When you specify
a value for the Identity parameter, the command looks up the mailbox
specified in the Identity parameter, connects to the server where the
mailbox resides, and returns the statistics for the mailbox. You can
use one of the following values:
      * GUID
      * Distinguished name (DN)
      * Domain\Account
      * User principal name (UPN)
      * Legacy Exchange DN
      * SMTP address
      * Alias

Required?	true
Position?	1
Default value	
Accept pipeline input?	True
Accept wildcard characters?	false

   -Server <ServerIdParameter>
      The Server parameter specifies the server from which you
want to obtain mailbox statistics. You can use one of the following
values:
      * Fully qualified domain name (FQDN)
      * NetBIOS name
      When you specify a value for the Server parameter, the
command returns statistics for all the mailboxes on all the databases,
including recovery databases, on the specified server. If you don't

specify this parameter, the command returns logon statistics for
the local server.

Required?	true
Position?	Named
Default value	
Accept pipeline input?	True
Accept wildcard characters?	false

-Archive <SwitchParameter>
      The Archive switch parameter specifies whether to return
mailbox statistics for the archive mailbox associated with the
specified mailbox. You don't have to specify a value with this parameter.

Required?	false
Position?	Named
Default value	
Accept pipeline input?	False
Accept wildcard characters?	false

-DomainController <Fqdn>
      The DomainController parameter specifies the fully
qualified domain name (FQDN) of the domain controller that
retrieves data from Active Directory.

Required?	false
Position?	Named
Default value	
Accept pipeline input?	False
Accept wildcard characters?	false

-IncludeMoveHistory <SwitchParameter>
      The IncludeMoveHistory switch specifies whether to
return additional information about the mailbox that includes
the history of a completed move request, such as status, flags,
target database, bad items, start times, end times, duration that
the move request was in various stages, and failure codes.

Required?	false
Position?	Named
Default value	
Accept pipeline input?	False
Accept wildcard characters?	false

-IncludeMoveReport <SwitchParameter>
      The IncludeMoveReport switch specifies whether to return
a verbose detailed move report for a completed move request, such
as server connections and move stages. Because the output of this

command is verbose, you should send the output to a .CSV file for easier analysis.

```
            Required?                 false
            Position?                 Named
            Default value
            Accept pipeline input?    False
            Accept wildcard characters?  false
```

    <CommonParameters>
        This cmdlet supports the common parameters: Verbose,
Debug, ErrorAction, ErrorVariable, WarningAction, WarningVariable,
OutBuffer and OutVariable. For more information, type,
"get-help about_commonparameters".

INPUTS

OUTPUTS

TERMINATING ERRORS
    (Category:)

    Type:
    Target Object Type:
    Suggested Action:

NON-TERMINATING ERRORS
    (Category:)

    Type:
    Target Object Type:
    Suggested Action:

```
------------------------- EXAMPLE 1 -------------------------
```

    This example retrieves the mailbox statistics for all
mailboxes on the local server. You can use the Get-MailboxStatistics
cmdlet without parameters only on a Mailbox server, and it defaults
to the local mailbox database.

    Get-MailboxStatistics

Yes, that's a lot of text for examples of one cmdlet, but we hope that these examples will make it easier for you to quickly learn the capabilities of all cmdlets and how you can use them.

The EMS help system also gives you some options with respect to getting help on parameters. For example, here is an example if you want help on just the -`Database` parameter of the `Get-MailboxStatistics` cmdlet:

```
Get-Help Get-MailboxStatistics -Parameter Database
```

```
-Database <DatabaseIdParameter>
     The Database parameter specifies the name of the mailbox database.
When you specify a value for the Database parameter, the Exchange
Management Shell returns statistics for all the mailboxes on the
database specified.
     You can use the following values:
     * GUID
     * Server\Database
     * Database
     This parameter accepts pipeline input from the
Get-MailboxDatabase cmdlet.


     Required?                 true
     Position?                 Named
     Default value
     Accept pipeline input?    True
     Accept wildcard characters? false
```

The -`Parameter` option also accepts the asterisk (*) wildcard. Here is an example if you want to see help on all the parameters that contain SCLQuarantine for the `Set-Mailbox` cmdlet:

```
[PS] C:\>Get-Help Set-Mailbox -Parameter *SCLQuarantine*
```

```
-SCLQuarantineEnabled <Nullable>
     The SCLQuarantineEnabled parameter specifies whether messages
that meet the SCL threshold specified by the SCLQuarantineThreshold
parameter are quarantined. If a message is quarantined, it's sent
to the quarantine mailbox where the messaging administrator can
review it. You can use the following values:
     * $true
     * $false
     * $null


     Required?                 false
     Position?                 Named
     Default value
     Accept pipeline input?    False
     Accept wildcard characters? false


-SCLQuarantineThreshold <Nullable>
```

The SCLQuarantineThreshold parameter specifies the SCL
at which a message is quarantined, if the SCLQuarantineEnabled
parameter is set to $true. You must specify an integer from 0 through 9
inclusive.

```
Required?                      false
Position?                      Named
Default value
Accept pipeline input?         False
Accept wildcard characters?    false
```

Getting Tips

You may have noticed a useful tip each time you launched the Exchange Management Console. Figure 6.15 shows the Tip of the Day text that you see each time you launch the EMS. There are more than 70 of these tips.

FIGURE 6.15
Viewing the Tip
of the Day

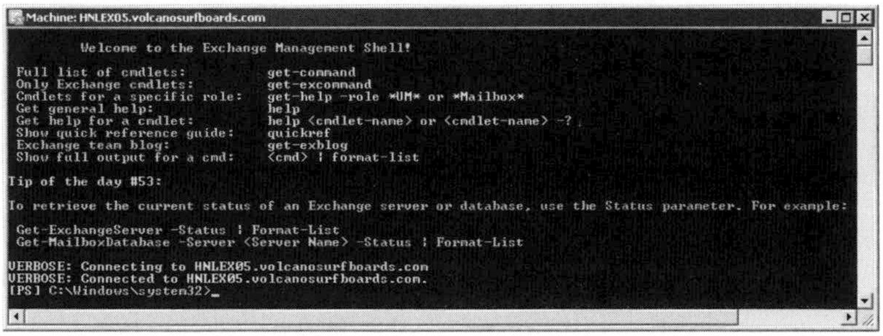

If you want to view additional tips, just type **Get-Tip** at the Exchange Management Shell prompt. You can also visit the following URL if you want to see more:

http://technet.microsoft.com/en-us/library/bb397216(EXCHG.80).aspx

You can even add your own tips if you don't mind editing an XML file; the tips for English are found in C:\program files\Microsoft\Exchange Server\v14\bin\extips.xml.

Learning from the Graphical User Interface

If you are like most Windows administrators, during your tenure as a Windows administrator you have come to rely almost entirely on the graphical user interface for most of the administration that you need to do. The advent of the PowerShell did not really worry too many of us in the "GUI boat" until we found that Exchange Server 2007/2010 relies so heavily on the underlying Exchange Management Shell.

As we mentioned earlier, there are even some Exchange functions and management settings that you can only perform from the EMS. However, even a hard-core GUI administrator can quickly learn some powerful new tricks by learning the EMS. Microsoft has tried to provide you with a few powerful tools for learning more about how the EMS functions. The first of these tools is the Completion page of most wizards that you find in the Exchange Management Console. An example appears in Figure 6.16.

The Completion page shows you the command or commands that were executed to complete the task you created in the Exchange Management Console wizard. In the example in Figure 6.16, we created a new mailbox for user Jason.Crawford and assigned it to database DB01. By simply pressing Ctrl+C on the Completion wizard page, we can copy the entire text of the page to the paste buffer. From there, we can easily grab the command that was executed; in this case it is as follows:

```
New-Mailbox -Name 'Jason R. Crawford' -Alias 'Jason.Crawford' ↵
-OrganizationalUnit 'volcanosurfboards.com/Scully Surfboards' ↵
-UserPrincipalName 'Jason.Crawford@volcanosurfboards.com' ↵
-SamAccountName 'Jason.Crawford' -FirstName 'Jason' -Initials 'R' ↵
-LastName 'Crawford' -Password 'System.Security.SecureString' ↵
-ResetPasswordOnNextLogon $false -Database 'DB01' ↵
-ActiveSyncMailboxPolicy 'Strict ActiveSync policy' -Archive
```

This type of output is available for the wizards, but what about making simple changes to something like a user account? The Exchange 2010 Management Console includes an option that you might not even notice unless you were looking for it. In Figure 6.17, we're editing the user account for John.Rodriguez. Look in the lower-left corner of this screen for a small icon; the icon is not even available until you have actually made a change.

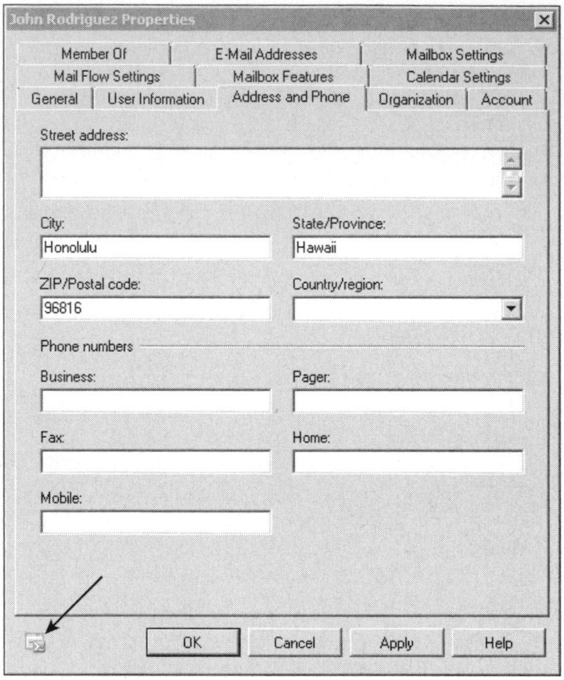

FIGURE 6.17
Editing a user's
properties in the
Exchange Management
Console

In Figure 6.17, we changed the city, state, and zip code; as soon as we make the first change on this screen, the icon in the lower left can now be clicked. When we click this icon, we see a dialog box showing the EMS command necessary to make these changes. An example is shown in Figure 6.18.

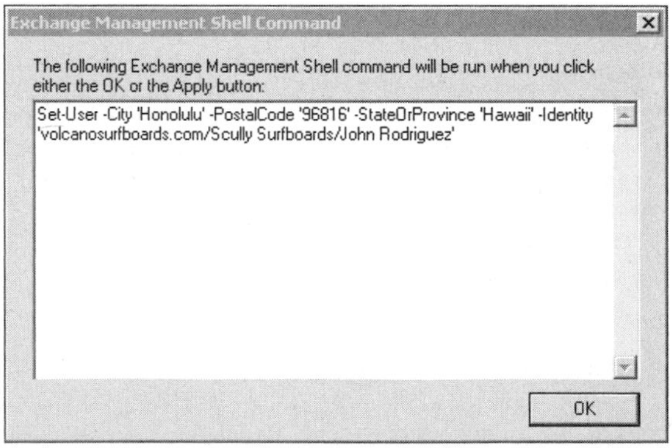

FIGURE 6.18
Viewing the command
necessary to make
account changes

We can then copy the text in this dialog box and use that as an example for making similar changes in the future. In this particular example, the cmdlet necessary to make these changes looks like this:

```
Set-User -City 'Honolulu' -StateOrProvince 'Hawaii' -PostalCode ↵
'96816' -Identity 'volcanosurfboards.com/Scully ↵
Surfboards/John Rodriguez'
```

This feature is pretty clever; we tried to trick it by changing two properties that require separate cmdlets, but it detected those correctly. Here is an example of changing the phone number (`Set-User`) and a custom attribute (`Set-Mailbox`):

```
Set-Mailbox -CustomAttribute1 'Marketing' -Identity ↵
'volcanosurfboards.com/Scully Surfboards/John Rodriguez'
Set-User -Phone ' (808) 555-1234' -Identity ↵
'volcanosurfboards.com/Scully Surfboards/John Rodriguez'
```

🌐 Real World Scenario

CAN'T GET ENOUGH POWERSHELL

The Exchange Management Shell was first introduced in Exchange Server 2007. Early in the initial betas of Exchange 2007 (then known as Exchange 12), one of the authors was a Shell-phobic. He griped and whined each time he had to use the shell to do even the simplest task. He finally invested a few hours learning the basics of using the EMS and some of the basics of piping output of one cmdlet into another. Then he found that the online help had not only good documentation but also examples! The author found out how to use the help from the shell itself.

After seeing some examples and one-liners online and at TechEd, the author was sold on the concept. When he had to start working with Exchange 2007 in production (rather than the lab), though, is when he finally became an EMS evangelist.

Third-party vendors are coming out with their own PowerShell extensions and we could not be happier. One of the most noteworthy extensions to PowerShell is Quest's ActiveRoles Management Shell for Active Directory (www.quest.com/powershell). This is a great extension for PowerShell that you can even use with your Windows 2003 domain controllers and Exchange 2003 servers.

Other noteworthy free add-ins and PowerShell sites include the PowerGUI (www.powergui.org), PoshConsole (www.codeplex.com/PoshConsole), as well as other PowerShell projects at Microsoft's CodePlex (www.codeplex.com). These extensions allow you to take advantage of your newfound knowledge of PowerShell to perform tasks other than just Exchange Server tasks and maintenance.

The Bottom Line

Use PowerShell command syntax. The PowerShell is an easy-to-use, command-line interface that allows you to manipulate many aspects of the Windows operating system, Registry, and file system. The Exchange Management Shell extensions allow you to manage all aspects of an Exchange organization and many Active Directory objects.

PowerShell cmdlets consist of a verb (such as `Get`, `Set`, `New`, or `Mount`) that indicates what is being done and a noun (such as `Mailbox`, `Group`, `ExchangeServer`) that indicates on which object the cmdlet is acting. Cmdlet options such as `-Debug`, `-Whatif`, and `-ValidateOnly` are common to most cmdlets and can be used to test or debug problems with a cmdlet.

Master It   You need to use the Exchange Management Shell cmdlet `Set-User` to change the telephone number (the `phone` property) to (808) 555-1234 for user Matt.Cook, but you want to first confirm that that the command will do what you want to do without actually making the change. What command should you use?

Understand object-oriented use of PowerShell.   Output of a cmdlet is not simple text but rather objects. These objects have properties that can be examined and manipulated.

Master It   You are using the `Set-User` cmdlet to set properties of a user's Active Directory account. You need to determine the properties that are available to use with the `Set-User` cmdlet. What can you do to view the available properties?

Employ tips and tricks to get more out of PowerShell.   The PowerShell (as well as extensions for PowerShell, such as the Exchange Management Shell) is a rich, powerful environment. Many daily administrative tasks can be performed via the PowerShell as well as tasks that previously may have been difficult to automate.

One of the most powerful features of the PowerShell is the ability to pipe the output of one cmdlet to another cmdlet to use as input. While this is not universally true, cmdlets within the same family can usually be used, such as cmdlets that manipulate or output mailbox information.

Master It   You need to set the custom attribute 2 to have the text "Marketing" for all members of the Marketing department. There is a distribution group called Marketing that contains all of these users. How could you accomplish this using a single command (a one-liner)?

Get help with using PowerShell.   Many options are available when you are trying to figure out how to use a PowerShell cmdlet, including online help and the Exchange documentation. PowerShell and the EMS make it easy to "discover" the cmdlets that you need to do your job.

Master It   How would you locate all the cmdlets available to manipulate a mailbox? You are trying to figure out how to use the `Set-User` cmdlet and would like to see an example. How can you view examples for this cmdlet?

Chapter 7

Exchange Autodiscover

Being an Exchange administrator is rewarding and, at times, frustrating. One of the most common sources of frustration we've encountered is managing the interactions between our Exchange servers and the Outlook desktop client. In a large organization, two separate groups maintain these pieces of the common puzzle. In smaller organizations, though, the same people can handle both the server and the client. It's in organizations like these that you learn the truth of the fact that Exchange and Outlook were developed by two separate product groups.

Many Outlook client issues are the result of mismatches between the Outlook profile settings and the actual server configurations. In Exchange 2007, Microsoft introduced the Autodiscover service, a component of the Client Access role, which was intended to allow both clients (such as Outlook, Windows Mobile, and Entourage) and other Exchange servers to automatically discover how your Exchange organization is configured and determine the appropriate settings without direct administrator involvement.

Many Exchange 2007 organizations ran into two main problems getting Autodiscover properly configured and deployed: understanding the concepts and getting the certificates properly deployed.

In this chapter, you will learn to:

◆ Work with Autodiscover

◆ Configure site affinity

◆ Manage Exchange certificates

Autodiscover Concepts

Let's share an unpleasant truth that a lot of Exchange 2007 administrators have not yet learned: the Autodiscover service is *not an optional component* of an Exchange organization. It may seem as if it's optional, especially if you haven't yet deployed a version of Outlook, Windows Mobile, or Entourage that takes advantage of it. More than that, you can't get rid of it — Autodiscover is on from the moment that you install the first Client Access role in the organization. You can't shut it off, you can't disable it, and you can't keep clients and Exchange servers from trying to contact it (although you can cause problems by not properly configuring Autodiscover, breaking features, and forcing fallback to older, more error-prone methods of configuration).

We know several Exchange 2007 organizations that limped along seemingly just fine with Autodiscover improperly configured or just plain ignored. However, when Autodiscover has been neglected this inevitably signals an Exchange organization with other problems — and this is even truer in Exchange 2010 than in Exchange 2007. Autodiscover is more than just a way to ease administration of Outlook client profiles. Other Exchange components, servers, and services also use Autodiscover to find the servers and settings they need to communicate with. In order for the Outlook 2007 or Outlook 2010 client to leverage many of the advanced features of Exchange 2010, including the new high availability features, the client depends on a functional Autodiscover service. And if you want to use the external calendar sharing or Office Communications Server integration, you'd better get Autodiscover squared away.

The good news, though, is that in order to properly plan and deploy Autodiscover, you have to work through some of the most potentially confusing aspects of an Exchange 2010 deployment. Once you've got these issues solved, you will have headed off some confusing and annoying errors that might otherwise cause problems down the road. These issues include namespace planning and certificate management. Trust us that getting these issues sorted will make your client access deployment and your overall management tasks a lot easier.

What Autodiscover Provides

We made the point that Autodiscover is a necessary part of your Exchange deployment. It is necessary for far more reasons than that it makes configuring your Outlook 2007 and 2010 clients easier. In Exchange 2007, the clients did benefit a great deal, which is part of the reason why many people did not see the point of learning about the service. In Exchange 2010, the non-client benefits get better, but the client benefits do, too. Some of the information provided by Autodiscover includes the following:

◆ Client Access server names that Outlook should use to access a user's mailbox

◆ Configuration URLs for the offline address book (OAB)

◆ Configuration URLs for free and busy information

◆ Outlook profile configuration information

CLIENT BENEFITS

Exactly what benefits you get from Autodiscover depend on which client you're using:

◆ Outlook 2007 (SP2 recommended) and Outlook 2010 fully supports Autodiscover. Outlook 2010 will support Autodiscover when it's released. Outlook versions prior to 2007 do not use Autodiscover, but they don't support many of the other cool features of Exchange 2010 — so why are you still using them?

◆ Windows Mobile 6.1 and later support Autodiscover for the most part; they don't support the use of DNS SRV records, instead reverting to the baseline Outlook 2007 behavior. Earlier versions of Windows Mobile, sadly, don't support Autodiscover, but they also support down-level versions of the Exchange ActiveSync protocol, which means you've already lost some cool functionality.

◆ Entourage 2008 for the Macintosh, which still relies on the WebDAV protocol for mailbox access, supports some limited Autodiscover benefits, but the forthcoming update to Entourage 2008 that fully supports Exchange Web Services will also take full advantage of Autodiscover. If you're a Mac user, this new version of Entourage is the only way to integrate with Exchange.

Although these are the main Autodiscover-aware clients, they're not the only ones. For example, the Microsoft Office Communicator client and devices use Autodiscover and Exchange Web Services. The behavior of Autodiscover has been clearly documented by Microsoft, so other third-party clients and devices may also make use of it. Features that Outlook and Windows Mobile will leverage include the following:

Support for DNS A Records   By default, external clients attempt to find the Autodiscover service through DNS lookups against well-known hostname (A) records. While CNAME records can be used, they cause a nonconfigurable security warning to be displayed that some organizations find provides a less than desirable user experience. The CNAME warnings can be disabled via the Registry, though. See this Microsoft Knowledgebase article for more information: `http://support.microsoft.com/?id=956528`.

Support for DNS SRV Records   Due to popular demand, the Exchange and Outlook teams provided support for the use of Service Locator (SRV) records for organizations that couldn't use A records and didn't want to use CNAMEs. Unfortunately, use of the SRV record also results in a warning dialog, so it's still not the best approach (though it can be disabled via the Registry).

Support for Active Directory Service Connection Point Objects   Domain-joined clients that can contact Active Directory — effectively any Windows machine running Outlook 2007 or greater — can make use of an Active Directory feature called service connection points (SCPs). SCPs provide a number of benefits that aren't available with plain DNS lookups. SCPs allow internal clients to locate resources via SCP objects within the Active Directory.

Internal Organization Settings   Services on Exchange 2010 and Exchange 2007 Client Access servers have both internal URLs for clients within the firewall (such as Outlook and Communicator on domain-joined Windows machines) and external URLs for pretty much everything else. Internal settings use the appropriate Exchange server FQDNs by default, unless you modify them (such as when using load balancers).

External Organization Settings   External settings allow services to be reached through Internet-available hostnames and FQDNs. For some reason, many organizations don't like publishing the internal FQDNs of their Exchange servers. Using external settings may also ensure that connections are load balanced or sent through firewalls, such as ISA Server 2006 or Forefront Threat Management Gateway.

Location of the User's Mailbox Server   The location of the user's mailbox server is in Active Directory, stamped on the user object. However, with the use of Exchange 2010 high availability features and the RPC Client Access service on the Client Access server, Outlook may connect to one of several Client Access servers. With the RPC Client Access Array feature, the Client Access server that Outlook is using may change quickly. Autodiscover can get this information, which allows the client to quickly reconnect to the correct Client Access server.

Location of the Availability Service   Calendar items are stored in each user's mailbox. However, their free/busy information has historically been placed in a system public folder, which could suffer from latency due to replication lag. The Exchange Availability Service allows current information to be quickly looked up by clients (both in the organization and in federated organizations) as they need it, rather than having them dependent on stale data in public folders.

Location of the Exchange Unified Messaging Service   Although voicemail messages created by Exchange Unified Messaging are placed in the mailbox, additional controls and features are available to users through this Exchange Web Service.

Location of the Offline Address Book Service If you have taken advantage of the ability to publish your OABs to web virtual directories, your clients can use HTTP to download them in the background (using the Windows Background Internet Transfer Service, or BITS) instead of having to connect to a system public folder.

Outlook Anywhere settings Having the external URL information is a good start for clients outside your corporate firewall, but more settings are necessary for a successful Outlook Anywhere session to be established, such as the certificate validation name.

Later in this chapter, we'll walk through a typical Outlook 2007 Autodiscover session and show how all this information is used. For now, just be aware that the value of many of these options can be user dependent (such as the mailbox location) or site dependent. As a result, the Autodiscover service is a vital part of spreading load throughout the entire organization, minimizing traffic over WAN links between sites and branches, and ensuring that your users are connecting to the best servers they can reach at the time.

SERVER BENEFITS

Autodiscover isn't just useful for clients connecting to the Exchange server infrastructure; it's also useful for other servers, both within the organization and without:

◆ Servers within the same organization and Active Directory forest use Autodiscover to locate various services on a user's behalf. For example, when a user performs a logon to Outlook Web Access, the CAS role handling the OWA session needs several of the pieces of information provided by Autodiscover. Using Autodiscover reduces the load on Active Directory domain controllers and global catalog servers and removes reliance on cached information. This is true whether you're in a mixed Exchange 2010/2007 organization or are deploying Exchange 2010 fresh.

◆ Servers within the same organization but in a different Active Directory forest depend on cross-forest service connection points and internal Autodiscover to cross the forest boundaries and discover the appropriate servers to use. In this situation, one CAS server in the source forest will often act as a proxy for the appropriate services in the target forest, or it may simply redirect the client. In multiple forest deployments, the use of Autodiscover is pretty much mandatory to ensure that Exchange servers in separate forests can interoperate properly.

◆ Servers within separate federated organizations require the use of the external Autodiscover information to reach federated Availability services. This, plus the relevant authentication information, allows users to securely share calendar and free/busy information with their counterparts in federated Exchange 2007 and 2010 organizations. To share availability information with a federated Exchange 2007, you have to jump through a number of hoops. With other Exchange 2010 organizations, the new Windows Live–based Federation Gateway greatly simplifies the configuration and management of these types of operations.

So, let's take a look at the nitty-gritty of how Autodiscover works.

How Autodiscover Works

Don't be fooled by the seeming complexity you're about to see. Autodiscover is pretty simple to understand. The biggest complications come from certificates and namespace planning, which we'll get to in a bit.

THE SERVICE CONNECTION POINT OBJECT

The first piece of the Autodiscover puzzle lies with the Service Connection Point (SCP) object. As each CAS role instance is installed into your organization, it creates an SCP object in the Configuration-naming partition of the Active Directory domain to which it is joined, at the following location:

```
CN=<CAS Server NetBIOS Name>, CN=Autodiscover, CN=Protocols, CN=<CAS Server
NetBIOS Name>, CN=Servers, CN= Exchange Administrative Group
(FYDIBOHF23SPDLT), CN=Administrative Groups, CN=<Organization Name>,
CN=Microsoft Exchange,CN=Services
```

Here's what a typical SCP object looks like when dumped from the LDP (LDP.EXE) tool:

Expanding base 'CN=HNLEX05,CN=Autodiscover,CN=Protocols,CN=HNLEX05,CN=Servers,
CN=Exchange Administrative Group (FYDIBOHF23SPDLT),CN=Administrative Groups,
CN=Ithicos Solutions,CN=Microsoft Exchange,CN=Services,CN=Configuration,
DC=ithicos,DC=com' ...
Getting 1 entries:
Dn: CN=HNLEX05,CN=Autodiscover,CN=Protocols,CN=HNLEX05,CN=Servers,
CN=Exchange Administrative Group (FYDIBOHF23SPDLT),CN=Administrative
Groups,CN=Ithicos Solutions,CN=Microsoft Exchange,CN=Services,
CN=Configuration,DC=ithicosDC=com
cn: HNLEX05;
distinguishedName: CN=HNLEX05,CN=Autodiscover,CN=Protocols,CN=HNLEX05,
CN=Servers,CN=Exchange Administrative Group (FYDIBOHF23SPDLT),
CN=Administrative Groups,CN=Ithicos Solutions,CN=Microsoft Exchange,CN=Services,
CN=Configuration,DC=ithicos,DC=com;
dSCorePropagationData: 0x0 = (   );
instanceType: 0x4 = (WRITE);
keywords (2): Site=Redmond; 77378F46-2C66-4aa9-A6A6-3E7A48B19596;
name: HNLEX05;
objectCategory: CN=Service-Connection-Point,CN=Schema,CN=Configuration
DC=ithicos,DC=com;
objectClass (4): top; leaf; connectionPoint; serviceConnectionPoint;
objectGUID: ce804393-df59-4152-9cc2-d2701d069479;
serviceBindingInformation:
https://HNLEX05.ithicosithicos.com/Autodiscover/Autodiscover.xml;
serviceClassName: ms-Exchange-AutoDiscover-Service;
serviceDNSName: HNLEX05;
showInAdvancedViewOnly: TRUE;
systemFlags: 0x40000000 = (CONFIG_ALLOW_RENAME);
uSNChanged: 7754800;
uSNCreated: 7754800;
whenChanged: 6/7/2009 2:48:22 PM Pacific Daylight Time;
whenCreated: 6/7/2009 2:48:10 PM Pacific Daylight Time;

There are a few key properties of these entries you should take note of:

◆ The objectClass property includes the serviceConnectionPoint type. This identifies the entry as an SCP, allowing it to be easily searched.

◆ The `serviceClassName` property identifies this particular SCP as an `ms-Exchange-AutoDiscover-Service` entry. The computers searching for Autodiscover records can thus determine that this is an entry pertaining to Autodiscover and that they should pay attention to it. The client searches the configuration-naming context for any objects that have a `serviceClassName= ms-Exchange-Autodiscover-Service`. Using the combination of `objectClass` and `serviceClassName` allows computers to efficiently find all relevant SCP entries (through an indexed search from a domain controller) without knowing any computer names ahead of time.

◆ The `serviceBindingInformation` points to the actual Autodiscover XML file that the client should access in order to retrieve the current Autodiscover information.

◆ The `keywords` property holds additional information that the clients use. Specifically, take note of the `Site=` value. This value helps you control site affinity, ensuring that clients and servers aren't using servers in far-off sites to provide their Exchange services.

The rest of the properties on an SCP object are fairly standard for Active Directory objects, so we won't discuss them further.

Now that you know what a service connection point is and where they're located, you're mostly set. The distinguished name of each SCP object uniquely identifies the host associated without that object. If the client search returns multiple SCP objects that the client will use, it will select between them according to alphabetic order.

Note also that a CAS role instance only publishes its corresponding SCP object to Active Directory when it is installed. If you change something about the CAS — such as which site it's located in — it will not update its SCP object. You have to do that manually. The best way is to use Exchange Management Shell. Here is a sample command:

```
Set-ClientAccessServer -Identity ↵
"<CAS Server NetBIOS Name>" -AutodiscoverServiceInternalURI ↵
"https://<CAS Server FQDN>/autodiscover/autodiscover.xml" ↵
-AutoDiscoverSiteScope "<Site Name 1>", "<Site Name 2>"
```

DNS OPTIONS

The SCP is used when the client or server is joined to an Active Directory domain and can retrieve the search from the domain controllers. When the discovering computer is external or not domain joined, another mechanism is used: DNS lookups.

The following list describes the DNS lookups that are performed for the Autodiscover service in a given domain. For this example, let's use the user `devin@somorita.com`. The client (or server) takes the domain portion (`somorita.com`) of this address and performs the following lookups in order until it finds a match:

1. A DNS A record (or CNAME record) for `somorita.com` that points to a web server that responds to the HTTPS URL `https://somorita.com/Autodiscover/Autodiscover.xml`

2. A DNS A record (or CNAME record) for `autodiscover.somorita.com` that points to a web server that responds to the HTTPS URL `https://autodiscover.somorita.com/Autodiscover/Autodiscover.xml`

3. A DNS A record (or CNAME record) for `somorita.com` that points to a web server that responds to the HTTP URL `http://autodiscover.somorita.com/Autodiscover/Autodiscover.xml` (note that this URL should be configured to redirect to the actual HTTPS location of the Autodiscover service)

4. A DNS SRV record for `autodiscover._tcp.somorita.com` (this record should contain the port number 443 and a hostname such as `mail.somorita.com`, allowing the client to try the HTTPS URL `https://mail.somorita.com/Autodiscover/Autodiscover.xml`)

If the requested hostname is returned through either a CNAME record or an SRV record, then be aware that your clients (Outlook in particular) will display a warning dialog with the following text:

`Allow this website to configure devin@somorita.com server settings?`
`https://mail.somorita.com/autodiscover/autodiscover.xml`
`Your account was redirected to this website for settings.`
`You should only allow settings from sources you know and trust.`

This warning will appear every time the client performs Autodiscover unless you check the Don't Ask Me About This Website Again check box. You can also pre-populate the Registry key to prevent this warming. See the Knowledge Base article at `http://support.microsoft.com/?id=956528`.

Note that Autodiscover expects the use of SSL. Don't publish it over insecure HTTP and expect clients to be happy about it. You have a lot of sensitive information going through Autodiscover, including user credentials. As a result, SSL certificate considerations will play a large part in your Autodiscover configuration.

 **Real World Scenario**

WHICH DNS OPTIONS SHOULD I CHOOSE?

In the end, the DNS option you choose is up to you and your business needs. However, you should consider these points to see how they align with your business objectives. Again, let's consider the case of `somorita.com`.

◆ Publishing Autodiscover under `https://somorita.com` doesn't require you to have an extra DNS name. If you have HTTPS published on this hostname already, you don't need to use an extra certificate or hostname as long as you can ensure that the Autodiscover virtual directory can be published under the existing website. Most organizations will probably already have this namespace published in their DNS, but it could result in name-resolution collisions if the URL that it points to does not have the Autodiscover information.

◆ Publishing Autodiscover under `https://autodiscover.somorita.com` requires you to have an extra DNS name, but it's a hostname that isn't likely to be used by any other servers. However, you'll need to have a Subject Alternative Name (SAN) certificate or a wildcard certificate, or use multiple certificates and a second virtual website. Publishing a second website is quite a bit more complicated than simply using the defaults, so keep that in mind.

◆ Publishing Autodiscover under the HTTP redirect not only requires you to have an extra DNS name, but also invokes the security warning for each user. You'll need to configure the appropriate redirect, and you'll need to have a SAN certificate or a wildcard certificate, or use multiple certificates and a second virtual website. This option may make sense for organizations that are hosting multiple servers or SMTP namespaces within a single Exchange organization.

> ◆ Publishing Autodiscover under an SRV redirect requires you to have external DNS servers that handle the SRV type. Most modern DNS servers should handle this, but some DNS hosting services do not. Additionally, this redirect invokes the security warning for each user. Finally, you'll need to have a SAN certificate or a wildcard certificate, or use multiple certificates and a second virtual website.
>
> In our experience, the second option (`https://autodiscover.somorita.com`) is the best combination of simplicity and control. It's the one that most organizations we've worked with have used. When Exchange 2007 was first introduced, certificate authorities that could provide SAN certificates were rare and the certificates themselves were expensive, making the alternative more palatable. Now, however, that is no longer the case. If you hesitate to deploy SAN certificates, there is a lot of good guidance out there to help you — including the section "Deploying Exchange Certificates" later in this chapter — and Exchange 2010 gives you better tools to manage them.

TWO STEP-BY-STEP EXAMPLES

Enough theory. Let's dive into our example with the `ithicos.com` domain and show you a walkthrough of a common scenario: a domain-joined Outlook 2007 SP2 client performing Autodiscover behind the organization firewall. To illustrate this scenario, we'll use a tool every Exchange administrator should know well: the Outlook Test E-mail AutoConfiguration tool, shown in Figure 7.1. As shown in this example, when using this tool be sure to uncheck the Use Guessmart and Secure Guessmart Authentication options.

FIGURE 7.1
Using the Test E-mail
AutoConfiguration tool

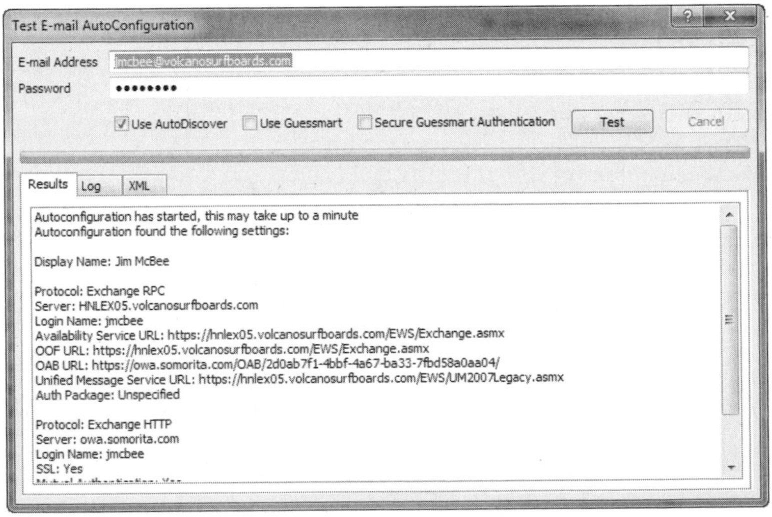

You can access this tool from Outlook 2007 and later by holding down the Ctrl key while right-clicking the Outlook icon in the notification area on the taskbar. This opens the menu shown in Figure 7.2. From this menu, select the Test E-mail AutoConfiguration option.

FIGURE 7.2
Accessing the Test
E-mail AutoConfigura-
tion tool

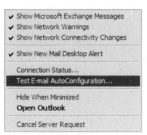

When a domain-joined machine performs Autodiscover, it steps through the following process:

1. It first performs an LDAP search for all SCP objects in the forest. Outlook enumerates the returned results based on the client's Active Directory site by sorting the returned SCP records using the keywords attribute; if there are no SCP records that contain a matching site value, all nonmatching SCP records are returned. If there are multiple matching SCP objects, Outlook simply chooses the oldest SCP record as the list is not sorted in any particular order. In our case, we return three SCP objects for our Redmond site: HNLEX05 (an Exchange 2007 server), HNLEX05 (an Exchange 2010 server), and HNLEX06 (an Exchange 2010 server), so Outlook picks the HNLEX05 SCP object.

2. Outlook attempts to connect to the configured URL specified in the SCP record's ServiceBindingInformation attribute: https://hnlex05.ithicos.ithicos.com/Autodiscover/Autodiscover.xml. It can do so.

3. In this case, because our user is on an Exchange 2010 mailbox server and this is an Exchange 2007 CAS instance, Autodiscover provides an HTTP 302 redirect to an Exchange 2010 CAS instance: https://HNLEX05.ithicos.com/Autodiscover/Autodiscover.xml.

4. Outlook attempts to connect to the new URL, the XML file is generated based on the client request, and the client successfully receives the XML file shown in Listing 7.1.

LISTING 7.1:   An Autodiscover XML Response

```
<?xml version="1.0" encoding="utf-8"?>
<Autodiscover xmlns="http://schemas.microsoft.com/exchange/autodiscover
/responseschema/2006">
    <Response xmlns="http://schemas.microsoft.com/exchange/autodiscover
/outlook/responseschema/2006a">
01    <User>
        <DisplayName>Luke Husky</DisplayName>
        <LegacyDN>/o=Ithicos Solutions/ou=First
Administrative Group/cn=Recipients/cn=LukeH</LegacyDN>
        <DeploymentId>a8203546-03b5-4050-af6d-394b71048a6c</DeploymentId>
      </User>
      <Account>
        <AccountType>email</AccountType>
        <Action>settings</Action>
```

```
              <Protocol>
02                <Type>EXCH</Type>
                  <Server>HNLEX05.ithicos.com</Server>
                  <ServerDN>/o=Ithicos Solutions/ou=Exchange
Administrative Group (FYDIBOHF23SPDLT)/cn=Configuration/cn=Servers/cn=HNLEX05
</ServerDN>
                  <ServerVersion>73808259</ServerVersion>
                  <MdbDN>/o=Ithicos Solutions/ou=Exchange
Administrative Group (FYDIBOHF23SPDLT)/cn=Configuration
/cn=Servers/cn=HNLEX05/cn=Microsoft Private MDB</MdbDN>
                  <AD>hnldc03.ithicos.com</AD>
                  <ASUrl>https://HNLEX05.ithicos.com/EWS/Exchange.asmx</ASUrl>
                  <EwsUrl>https://HNLEX05.ithicosithicos.com/EWS
/Exchange.asmx</EwsUrl>
                  <EcpUrl>https://HNLEX05.ithicos.com/ecp</EcpUrl>
                  <EcpUrl-um>?p=customize/voicemail.aspx&amp;exsvurl=1</EcpUrl-um>
                  <EcpUrl-aggr>?p=personalsettings/EmailSubscriptions.slab&amp;
exsvurl=1</EcpUrl-aggr>
                  <EcpUrl-mt>PersonalSettings/DeliveryReport.aspx?exsvurl=1&amp;
IsOWA=&lt;IsOWA&gt;&amp;MsgID=&lt;MsgID&gt;&amp;Mbx=
&lt;Mbx&gt;&amp;Sender=&lt;Sender&gt;</EcpUrl-mt>
                  <EcpUrl-sms>?p=sms/textmessaging.slab&amp;exsvurl=1</EcpUrl-sms>
                  <OOFUrl>https://HNLEX05.ithicos.com/EWS/Exchange.asmx</OOFUrl>
                  <UMUrl>https://HNLEX05.ithicos.com/EWS/UM2007Legacy.asmx</UMUrl>
                  <OABUrl>https://HNLEX05.ithicos.com/OAB/
78903a8b-af16-4a1d-b87e-17002b926ba1/</OABUrl>
                  <ServerExclusiveConnect>off</ServerExclusiveConnect>
              </Protocol>
              <Protocol>
03                <Type>EXPR</Type>
                  <Server>mail.ithicos.com</Server>
                  <SSL>On</SSL>
                  <AuthPackage>Basic</AuthPackage>
                  <ASUrl>https://mail.ithicos.com/EWS/Exchange.asmx</ASUrl>
                  <EwsUrl>https://mail.ithicos.com/EWS/Exchange.asmx</EwsUrl>
                  <EcpUrl>https://mail.ithicos.com/ecp</EcpUrl>
                  <EcpUrl-um>?p=customize/voicemail.aspx&amp;exsvurl=1</EcpUrl-um>
                  <EcpUrl-aggr>?p=personalsettings/EmailSubscriptions.slab&amp;
exsvurl=1</EcpUrl-aggr>
                  <EcpUrl-mt>PersonalSettings/DeliveryReport.aspx?exsvurl=1&amp;
IsOWA=&lt;IsOWA&gt;&amp;MsgID=&lt;MsgID&gt;&amp;Mbx=
&lt;Mbx&gt;&amp;Sender=&lt;Sender&gt;</EcpUrl-mt>
                  <EcpUrl-sms>?p=sms/textmessaging.slab&amp;exsvurl=1</EcpUrl-sms>
                  <OOFUrl>https://mail.ithicos.com/EWS/Exchange.asmx</OOFUrl>
                  <UMUrl>https://mail.ithicos.com/EWS/UM2007Legacy.asmx</UMUrl>
                  <OABUrl>https://mail.ithicos.com/OAB/
78903a8b-af16-4a1d-b87e-17002b926ba1/</OABUrl>
                  <ServerExclusiveConnect>on</ServerExclusiveConnect>
              </Protocol>
```

```
           <Protocol>
04             <Type>WEB</Type>
               <Internal>
                  <OWAUrl AuthenticationMethod="Basic,
Ntlm, WindowsIntegrated">https://HNLEX05.ithicos.com
/owa/</OWAUrl>
                  <OWAUrl AuthenticationMethod="Basic,
Ntlm, WindowsIntegrated">https://red-exch02.ithicos.com
/owa/</OWAUrl>
                  <OWAUrl AuthenticationMethod="Basic,
Ntlm, WindowsIntegrated">https://red-msg01.ithicos.com
/owa/</OWAUrl>
                  <Protocol>
                    <Type>EXCH</Type>
                    <ASUrl>https://HNLEX05.ithicos.com/EWS/Exchange.asmx</ASUrl>
                  </Protocol>
               </Internal>
               <External>
                  <OWAUrl AuthenticationMethod="Fba">https://legacy.ithicos.com
/owa/</OWAUrl>
                  <OWAUrl AuthenticationMethod="Fba">https://mail.ithicos.com
/owa/</OWAUrl>
                  <Protocol>
                    <Type>EXPR</Type>
                    <ASUrl>https://mail.ithicos.com/EWS/Exchange.asmx</ASUrl>
                  </Protocol>
               </External>
           </Protocol>
        </Account>
      </Response>
    </Autodiscover>
```

There are five key sections to note in Listing 7.1:

◆ The User and Account sections list the user information for the authenticated user.

◆ The EXCH protocol section (identified by the EXCH tag) is MAPI RPC over TCP, or traditional MAPI connections. These settings control how Outlook will connect inside the firewall, over a VPN, or in other situations where direct connectivity via MAPI is possible. The URLs provided in this section are based on the InternalURL values.

◆ The EXPR protocol section (identified by the EXPR tag) is Outlook Anywhere — RPC over HTTPS. These settings control how Outlook connects over slow connections or when a direct MAPI connection is not possible. The URLs provided in this section are based on the InternalURL values.

◆ The WEB protocol section (identified by the WEB tag) is used for OWA and other types of clients. The URLs provided in this section are for clients and are based on the ExternalURL values.

If the client had been outside the firewall, it would have followed a similar process, but instead steps through the hostnames and URLs as described in the previous section on DNS names. An external client (for the domain `somorita.com`) using Autodiscover goes through these steps:

1. The client tries to connect to the Active Directory SCP, but is unable to do so.

2. The client performs a DNS query for either `somorita.com` or `autodiscover.somorita.com` and tries to connect to the Autodiscover URL.

3. The client retrieves `autodiscover.xml` from the Autodiscover HTTPS host.

4. The client parses through the `WEB` sections of the `autodisover.xml` file in order to determine the correct URL to which it should connect.

5. The client initiates a connection to the appropriate external URL.

To help step through and troubleshoot external connectivity, you should be aware of the Exchange Remote Connectivity Analyzer tool, available online from `http://testexchangeconnectivity.com/`. This Microsoft tool provides a secure, reliable suite of tests to help diagnose problems with not only Autodiscover but all of the web-based Exchange remote client access protocols.

Advanced Autodiscover Concepts

If you're reading this far, you've gotten through the basics of Autodiscover. There are some advanced concepts we need to share with you: how site affinity works (and how to manage it) and how to configure Autodiscover to work with multiple forests.

SITE AFFINITY

To understand the point of site affinity, consider an organization that has multiple locations — we'll say in Seattle, Washington (code SEA); Toledo, Ohio (code TOL); and New Orleans, Louisiana (code MSY). There are Exchange servers and users in each of these locations. The links between these locations run over WAN links from Seattle to Toledo and Toledo to New Orleans; it is neither optimal nor desired to allow users in Seattle to use Client Access servers in New Orleans (or vice versa). Using site affinity, we can use the following commands to help ensure this does not happen:

```
Set-ClientAccessServer -Identity "sea-cas01" ↵
-AutodiscoverServiceInternalURI "https://sea-cas01.somorita.com/↵
autodiscover/autodiscover.xml" -AutodiscoverServiceSiteScope ↵
"Site-SEA","Site-TOL"

Set-ClientAccessServer -Identity "sea-cas02" ↵
-AutodiscoverServiceInternalURI "https://sea-cas02.somorita.com/↵
autodiscover/autodiscover.xml" -AutodiscoverServiceSiteScope ↵
"Site-SEA","Site-TOL"

Set-ClientAccessServer -Identity "tol-cas01" ↵
-AutodiscoverServiceInternalURI "https://tol-cas01.somorita.com/↵
autodiscover/autodiscover.xml" -AutodiscoverServiceSiteScope ↵
"Site-SEA","Site-TOL","Site-MSY"
```

```
Set-ClientAccessServer -Identity "tol-cas02" ↵
-AutodiscoverServiceInternalURI "https://tol-cas02.somorita.com/↵
autodiscover/autodiscover.xml" -AutodiscoverServiceSiteScope ↵
"Site-SEA","Site-TOL","Site-MSY"

Set-ClientAccessServer -Identity "msy-cas01" ↵
-AutodiscoverServiceInternalURI "https://msy-cas01.somorita.com/↵
autodiscover/autodiscover.xml" -AutodiscoverServiceSiteScope ↵
"Site-TOL","Site-MSY"

Set-ClientAccessServer -Identity "msy-cas02" ↵
-AutodiscoverServiceInternalURI "https://msy-cas02.somorita.com/↵
autodiscover/autodiscover.xml" -AutodiscoverServiceSiteScope ↵
"Site-TOL","Site-MSY"
```

When clients perform Autodiscover, they will only match the records for those Client Access servers that match the site they are currently in.

Clients in Seattle will only match the SEA-CAS01, SEA-CAS02, TOL-CAS01, and TOL-CAS02 SCP objects. Because there are multiple objects, they will perform their initial discovery to TOL-CAS01 (this was the last server configured), which will then return URLs for the servers in the Seattle site.

Likewise, clients in New Orleans will only match the MSY-CAS01, MSY-CAS02, TOL-CAS01, and TOL-CAS02 SCP objects. Because there are multiple objects, they will perform their initial discovery to MSY-CAS01, which will then return URLs for the servers in the New Orleans site.

Clients in Toledo will match all six SCP objects. Because there are multiple objects, they will perform their initial discovery to MSY-CAS01, which will then return URLs for the servers in the Toledo site.

If these are not the required behaviors, you should take a close look at the Exchange 2007 Autodiscover white paper, which can be found on the Microsoft website at http://technet.microsoft.com/en-us/library/bb332063.aspx. Although this paper is for Exchange 2007, the concepts transfer to Exchange 2010 without much damage.

Planning Certificates for Autodiscover

The other hard part for Autodiscover is managing the required SSL certificates. After working with a number of Exchange 2007 deployments, we began to realize that the biggest difficulty with Autodiscover certificates was inevitably the need to use a SAN certificate. While other scenarios are possible (such as creating a separate Autodiscover website on a separate IP address and using a second single-name certificate) as outlined in the Exchange 2007 Autodiscover white paper, these options ended up being far more complicated to run.

So what's so hard about SAN certificates? We think that for most people, they don't understand what certificates really are or how they work. Certificates and PKIs are black magic — stark naked voodoo — mainly because they've traditionally been complicated to deploy and play with. Getting even an internal PKI like the Windows Server 2008 Active Directory Certificates Services in place and running can be hard to manage unless you already know what to do and what the results should look like. Add to that the difficulty of managing certificates with the built-in Windows tools, and most Exchange administrators we know want to stay far away from TLS and SSL.

Although Exchange 2010 follows the lead of Exchange 2007 and installs self-signed certificates on each new server, these certificates are not meant to take you into production for all scenarios. You won't be able to use them to secure client access for any of your users who are connecting remotely, even though Outlook will bypass its certificate validation checks when it detects an Exchange self-signed certificate as long as it is connecting from within the domain. Internal Outlook clients *can* use the self-signed certificates, but Outlook does not ignore improperly matched names or expired certificates. Internal Outlook clients will just ignore the fact that the certificate is from an untrusted certificate authority.

External or web-based clients won't accept a self-signed certificate without you manually importing the certificate — which is a huge administrative burden for mobile clients. For externally facing deployments, you either need to have a well-managed PKI deployment or use a third-party commercial certificate authority. Make sure that you use one whose root and intermediate CA certificates are well supported by the operating systems and devices that will be connecting to your network.

The X.509 Certificate Standard

As mentioned in Chapters 3 and 5, the digital certificates that Exchange and other SSL/TLS-aware systems use are defined by the X.509 v3 certificate standard. This standard is documented in RFC 2459. The X.509 certificates were originally developed as part of the X.500 family of standards from the OSI, but proved to be useful enough that they were adopted by other standards organizations.

The X.509 certificates are based on the concept of *private key cryptography*. In this system, you have an algorithm that generates a pair of cryptographic keys for each entity that will be exchanging encrypted message traffic: a *private key* that only that entity knows, and a corresponding *public key* that can be freely transmitted. As long as the private keys are kept safe, the system can be used to not only securely encrypt messages but also to prove that messages were sent from the claimed sender. The exclusivity of the private key provides authentication as well as security.

If Jim and Devin want to exchange encrypted messages using a private key system, here's how it works:

1. Both Jim and Devin ensure that they have secure private keys. They have exchanged their corresponding public keys — maybe through email, by publishing them on their websites, or even through a mutual friend.

2. Jim, when sending a message to Devin, will use Jim's public key and Devin's public key to encrypt the message. This ensures that only Devin will be able to decrypt the message.

3. Devin receives the encrypted messages and uses his private key and Jim's public key to decrypt the message. This ensures that the message actually came from Jim.

   When Devin receives the message, he uses his own private key to decrypt the message. If Devin wants to send a message to Jim in return, he simply reverses the process: he uses his public key and Jim's public key to encrypt, and Jim uses his private key. If Devin later needs to open the message in his Sent Items folder, he would use his private key to decrypt.

Digital certificates help streamline this process and expand it for more uses than just message encryption by providing a convenient wrapper format for the public keys plus some associated metadata. For our purposes, though, we're concerned about using certificates for server authentication and establishing the symmetric shared session key for the TLS session.

In Windows, you can view digital certificates, examine their properties, and validate the certificate chain through the MMC. Although Windows doesn't include a preconfigured

Certificate console, it does include a Certificate snap-in. Open a generic MMC and add the Certificate snap-in, configured for the local machine as shown in Figure 7.3. You can now view and manage the server certificates that will be used by Exchange.

FIGURE 7.3
The Certificates MMC snap-in

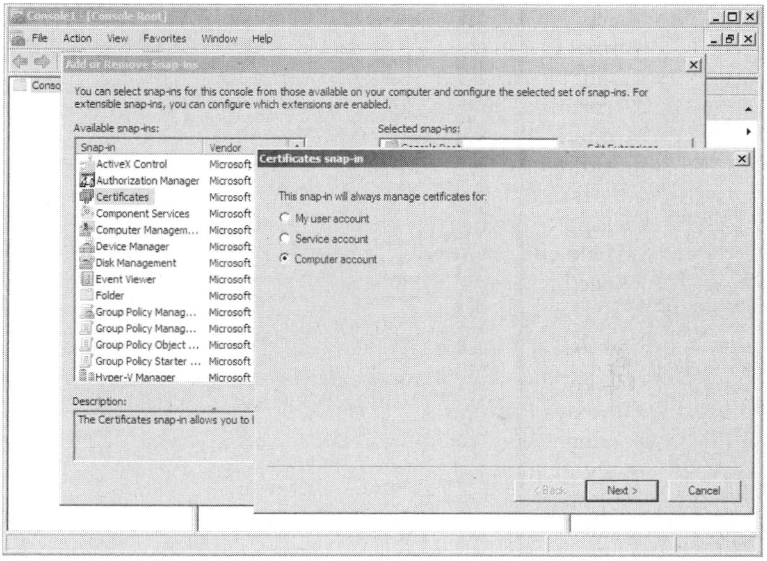

While you can view the properties of a certificate using the certificates console, all certificates that are used by Exchange (for HTTPS, SMTP, IMAP, or POP) should be managed using either the Exchange Management Console or the Exchange Management Shell.

Let's take a look at the typical properties of an X.509v3 digital certificate as provisioned for Exchange, shown in Figure 7.4:

Subject Name This property provides the identity of the entity the certificate applies to. This can be in X.500 format, which looks like LDAP, or in DNS format if intended for a server.

Subject Alternate Name This is an optional property that lists one or more additional identities that will match the certificate. If the hostname in the URL that the client attempts to connect to doesn't match the subject name or subject alternate name properties, the certificate will not validate. Without this property, a certificate can only match a single hostname.

Common Name Also known as the friendly name, this property provides a useful text tag for handling and managing the certificate once you have a collection of them.

Issuer This property lists the identity of the issuing certificate authority (CA). This can be a root CA or an intermediate CA. Combined with the digital signature from the CA's own digital signature, this property allows establishment of the certificate chain of trust back to the root CA. What distinguishes a root CA? The fact that this property (plus signature) is self-signed.

Serial Number This property allows the certificate to be easily published on a certificate revocation list (CRL) by the certificate authority if the certificate has been expired. The location of the CRL is usually included on the issuer's certificate. Many systems, including Outlook, attempt to check the CRL to verify the certificate has not expired.

Thumbprint This property (and the corresponding thumbprint algorithm) is a cryptographic hash of the certificate information. This thumbprint is commonly used by Exchange as an easy identifier for certificates.

Valid From and Valid To These properties define the effective length of the certificate. They are evaluated as part of the certificate validation.

Public Key This property contains the entity's associated cryptographic public key. The corresponding private key is never associated with the certificate.

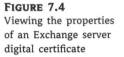

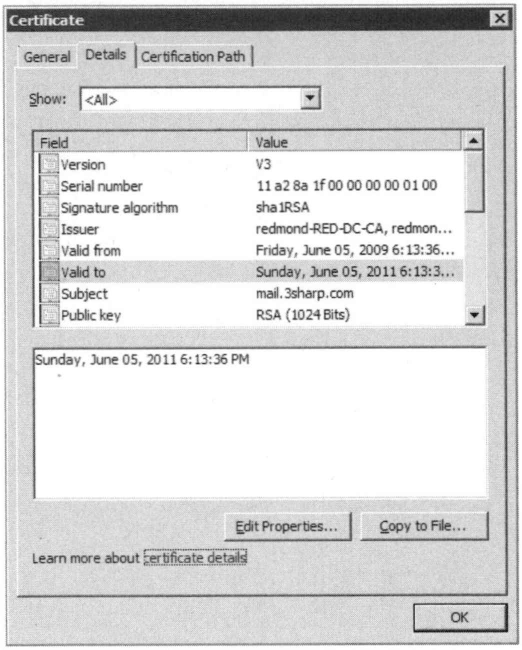

FIGURE 7.4
Viewing the properties of an Exchange server digital certificate

In Figure 7.5, we can see the certificate trust chain and verify that we have the proper CA certificates installed.

Deploying Exchange Certificates

Now that we've talked about certificates in general, let's dive into the issues of getting them deployed on your Exchange 2010 servers.

PLANNING CERTIFICATE NAMES

The first part of creating digital certificates for your Exchange 2010 servers is deciding on which names you need. For a Client Access server, it's highly recommended that you accept the need for a SAN certificate. Although SAN certificates are more expensive than single-name certificates, you can often configure them so that you can reuse them on multiple servers. Otherwise, you need to use a lot of single-name certificates — possibly with multiple websites and virtual directories on your CAS instances. And since HTTPS requires a dedicated IP address for each hostname, this can become an overwhelming amount of operational overhead.

Sure, you can use wildcard certificates for some scenarios such as Outlook and Windows Mobile 6.0 and later. The wildcard certificate is a certificate that is issued for an entire domain, such as `*.somorita.com`. This certificate could then be used by multiple servers and sites. Naturally, wildcard certificates are usually more expensive than certificates issued for a single host. Be aware, also, that not all clients (such as Windows Mobile 5 and earlier) will recognize wildcard certificates.

FIGURE 7.5

Viewing a certificate
trust chain

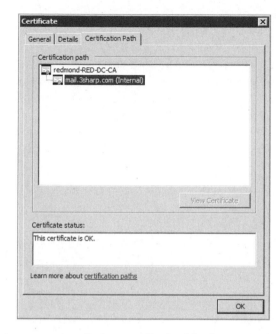

Let's take the three-site `somorita.com` example from earlier in this chapter and some of the factors to consider when requesting certificates:

◆ We've already established that we don't want Seattle clients using New Orleans Client Access servers and vice versa, so for Internet connectivity, the Toledo site makes sense as the gateway to the Internet. This will need the domain name `autodiscover.somorita.com`.

◆ We'll use the domain name `mail.somorita.com` as our generic external access domain name. We don't need to use a separate domain name for this — we could easily use `autodiscover.somorita.com`, but users are accustomed to an easier-to-understand domain name.

◆ Having two domain names means either multiple IP addresses and websites or a SAN certificate. We don't want to incur the overhead of multiple certificates and websites, so we will use a SAN certificate; we can issue a single certificate for all the Client Access servers in the Toledo site. We'll include the FQDNs of each of the servers, bringing our total number of names to four. Most commercial CAs have a price increase after five domain names on a SAN certificate, so we're within our limit. But always consider all the places you may want to use a certificate such as on Hub Transport servers for SMTP.

Our certificate will therefore need four domain names: `mail.somorita.com`, `autodiscover` `.somorita.com`, `tol-cas01.toledo.somorita.com`, and `tol-cas02.toledo.somorita.com`. We don't need to include the NetBIOS names of our servers — Exchange and its clients don't use them unless we choose to configure them otherwise.

It is important to note as you start requesting certificates that poor namespace planning or separate internal namespaces (such as `somorita.com` for external clients but `somorita.local` for internal clients) will result in more complex certificate requirements. If possible, ensure that you have carefully thought out the internal and external URL requirements as you are planning your Exchange Server 2010 deployment.

ISSUING AND ENABLING CERTIFICATES WITH EMC

In Exchange 2007, you had to do all your certificate requests and imports either through the Certificate MMC snap-in (which was a pain) or through the EMS. In Exchange 2010, if you click on the Server Configuration node in the EMC, you can view, manage, and even request new certificates for your Exchange 2010 servers. Figure 7.6 shows the tasks that are available in the Actions pane for the server HNLEX05 (selected in the Results pane) as well as for a specific certificate that is selected in the Work pane).

FIGURE 7.6
Certificate options
available in the EMC

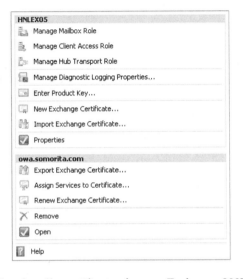

Note that you cannot use this tool to handle certificates for any Exchange 2007 servers you may have in your organization; certificate handling typically must be done on the server. This interface is the only Windows-based certificate management tool we have seen that allows creation and management of certificates on remote Exchange Server 2010 servers — all thanks to the magic of Remote PowerShell. To create a new certificate, you use the New Exchange Certificate wizard; when you launch this wizard, you will first be asked on the Introduction page for a friendly name for the certificate. While this name can be anything, we recommend you name it something that describes the use of the certificate.

On the Domain Scope page of the wizard, you need to specify the scope of the certificate, such as if it should be enabled for all subdomains. This is sometimes called a wildcard certificate; your certificate issuer must support wild card certificates. Wild card certificates can be considerably more expensive than single-name certificates.

On the Exchange Configuration page of the wizard, you will see the different types of services that you can enable for a certificate (such as OWA, ActiveSync, SMTP, etc.) From this page of the wizard, you can enter the names as fully qualified domain names of the services.

Note in Figure 7.7 that this server's internal OWA name is hnlex05.volcanosurfboards.com and the external name is owa.somorita.com. For some of these fields, the New Exchange Certificate wizard is making a "best guess" at the correct names, but you will need to fill in some of the others manually. The fields that are populated on the Exchange Configuration page are the ones that will appear in the certificates subject alternate name field.

In Figure 7.8, you can see the Certificate Domains page; this page allows you to specify additional fully qualified domain names that will show up in the certificate request. The wizard is making another "best guess" for this certificate request by adding all of the accepted domains as well as adding the host name autodiscover to each of these domain names.

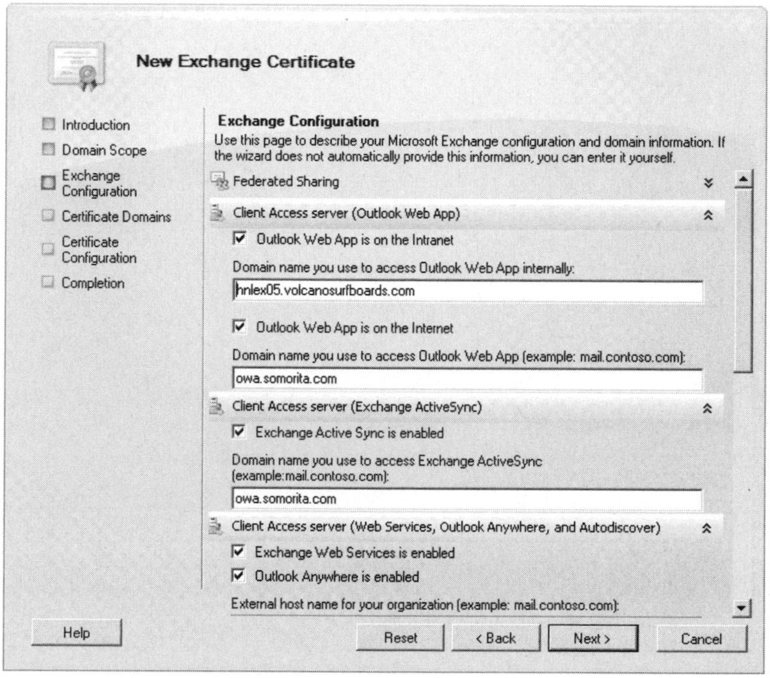

FIGURE 7.7
Viewing the Exchange
Configuration page
of the New Exchange
Certificate wizard

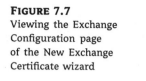

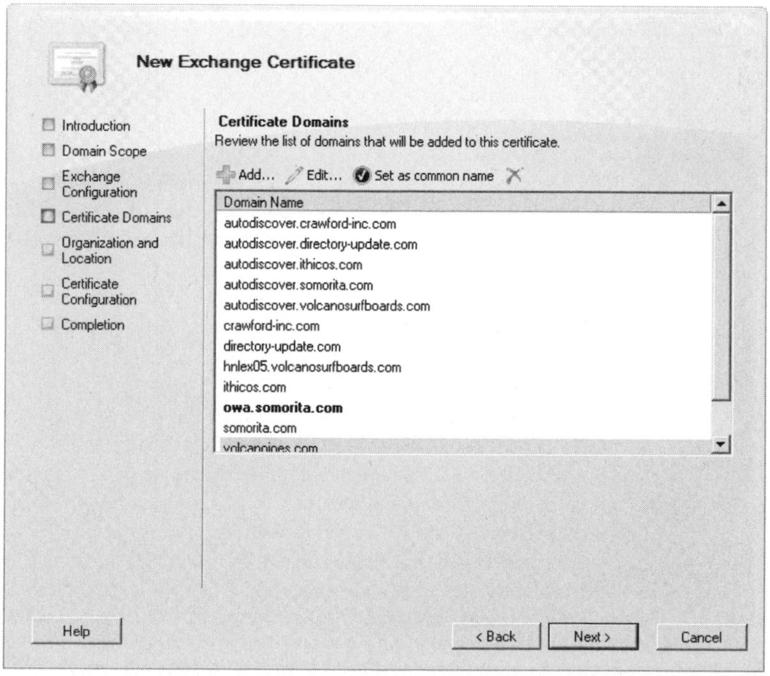

New Exchange Certificate

- Introduction
- Domain Scope
- Exchange Configuration
- Certificate Domains
- Certificate Configuration
- Completion

Exchange Configuration

Use this page to describe your Microsoft Exchange configuration and domain information. If the wizard does not automatically provide this information, you can enter it yourself.

Federated Sharing

Client Access server (Outlook Web App)

☑ Outlook Web App is on the Intranet

Domain name you use to access Outlook Web App internally:

`hnlex05.volcanosurfboards.com`

☑ Outlook Web App is on the Internet

Domain name you use to access Outlook Web App (example: mail.contoso.com):

`owa.somorita.com`

Client Access server (Exchange ActiveSync)

☑ Exchange Active Sync is enabled

Domain name you use to access Exchange ActiveSync (example:mail.contoso.com):

`owa.somorita.com`

Client Access server (Web Services, Outlook Anywhere, and Autodiscover)

☑ Exchange Web Services is enabled

☑ Outlook Anywhere is enabled

External host name for your organization (example: mail.contoso.com):

Help   Reset   < Back   Next >   Cancel

FIGURE 7.8
The Certificate Domains
wizard page

New Exchange Certificate

- Introduction
- Domain Scope
- Exchange Configuration
- Certificate Domains
- Organization and Location
- Certificate Configuration
- Completion

Certificate Domains

Review the list of domains that will be added to this certificate.

➕ Add...   ✏ Edit...   ✅ Set as common name   ✖

Domain Name
autodiscover.crawford-inc.com
autodiscover.directory-update.com
autodiscover.ithicos.com
autodiscover.somorita.com
autodiscover.volcanosurfboards.com
crawford-inc.com
directory-update.com
hnlex05.volcanosurfboards.com
ithicos.com
owa.somorita.com
somorita.com
volcanopines.com

Help   < Back   Next >   Cancel

The Organization and Location page of the wizard (shown in Figure 7.9) is requesting information that most administrators who have configured a certificate request before will recognize. This includes the organization information, department, city, state, and country. At the bottom of the Organization and Location page you must provide a name and path where the certificate request file will be created.

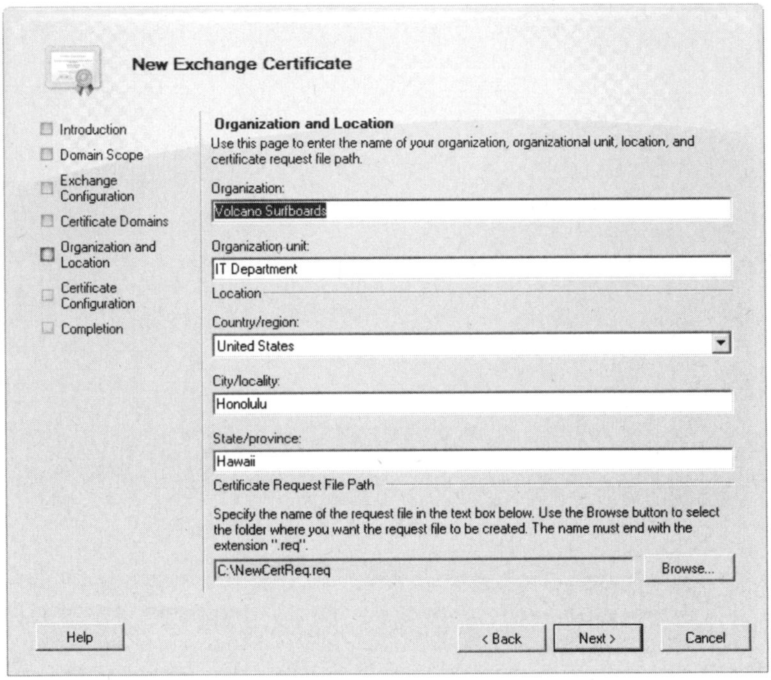

FIGURE 7.9
Specifying organization, department, city, and country information for a certificate request

The Certificate Configuration page allows you to review the information about the certificate request that you are generating prior to actually creating the request. Once you are sure that the certificate request is correct, you can click the New button to actually generate the request and store it in the certificate request file.

Like all EMC wizards, the Completion page of the wizard will include the actual EMS command that was executed in order to generate the certificate request. Here is the EMS command that was generated for this particular example:

```
New-ExchangeCertificate -FriendlyName 'smtp.somorita.com' ↵
-GenerateRequest -PrivateKeyExportable $true -KeySize '2048' ↵
-SubjectName 'C=US,S="Hawaii",L="Honolulu",O="Volcano ↵
Surfboards",OU="IT Department",CN=owa.somorita.com' ↵
-DomainName 'hnlex05.volcanosurfboards.com', ↵
'owa.somorita.com','somorita.com', ↵
'autodiscover.volcanosurfboards.com', ↵
'autodiscover.directory-update.com', ↵
'autodiscover.somorita.com', ↵
```

```
'autodiscover.ithicos.com', ↵
'autodiscover.crawford-inc.com','volcanosurfboards.com', ↵
'directory-update.com','volcanojoes.com', ↵
'ithicos.com','crawford-inc.com' -Server 'HNLEX05'
```

You can now take the contents of the file that was created and submit it to a certificate authority to issue the certificate. Once you have received back a signed certificate, you use the Complete Pending Request wizard to complete the process. This wizard will load the signed certificate in to the certificate store on the appropriate server.

The final process after the certificate is fully loaded is to assign the certificate to be used by the appropriate services (such as SMTP or IIS). Select the certificate in the work pane and then select the Assign Services to Certificate wizard. On the Select Services page of the wizard (shown in Figure 7.10) select the appropriate services. When you select Internet Information Services, that includes OWA, the Exchange Control Panel (ECP), Exchange Web Services (EWS), and ActiveSync. Note that a service can only be assigned to one certificate at a time.

FIGURE 7.10
Selecting services that
will use the certificate

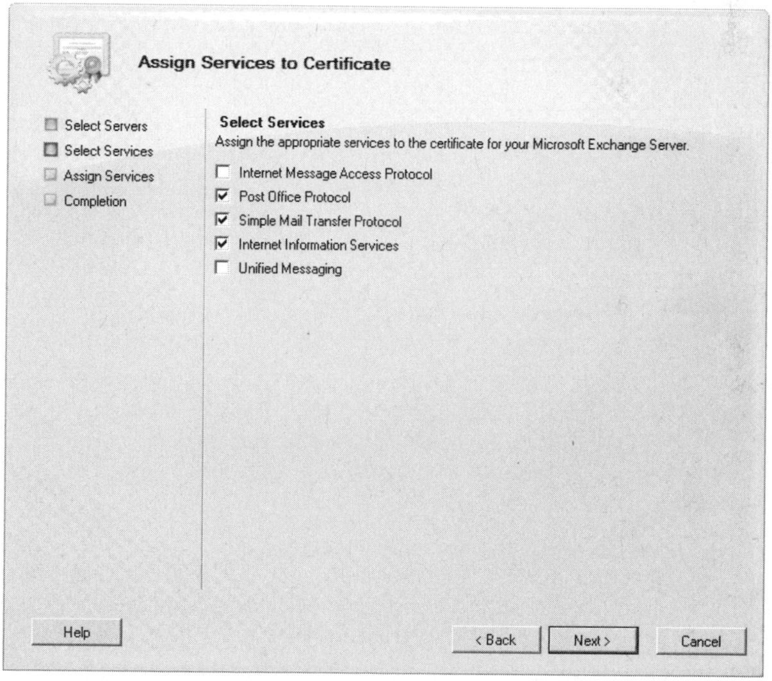

The only other note of caution we give you is that whichever tool you use to request certificates should be the tool you use to import them. Although you should be able to mix and match them in theory, we've seen odd results. Also, don't use the certificate wizard in IIS to request Exchange certificates, especially if you need SAN certificates.

ISSUING AND ENABLING CERTIFICATES WITH EMS

Although Exchange 2010 provides an Exchange Management Console interface for managing certificates, you can still manage certificates in Exchange 2010 (and 2007) through the EMS.

If you have done this in the past with Exchange Server 2007, you will have to learn a few new tricks in order to work with certificates from the EMS. Due to the remote PowerShell, you can no longer specify a path for certificate request file. Instead, the certificate request is output to the shell, so you must capture that to a variable. Here's the command you would issue to generate a certificate request for the URL mail.somorita.com and capture it to the $Data variable:

```
$Data = New-ExchangeCertificate -GenerateRequest -SubjectName "c=US, ↵
o=Somorita Surfboards, cn=mail.somorita.com" -DomainName somorita.com ↵
-PrivateKeyExportable $true
```

Next we need to take the value stored in the $Data variable and output that to the file c:\CertRequest.req using this command:

```
Set-Content -path "C:\Docs\MyCertRequest.req" -Value $Data
```

Here are the details of the New-ExchangeCertificate cmdlet command:

GenerateRequest   This parameter tells Exchange to generate a certificate request. Had we left it off, the command would have generated a new self-signed certificate. That's usually not what you want. This request is suitable for either an internal PKI or a commercial CA.

PrivateKeyExportable   This parameter is extremely important and is the cause of most certificate headaches we've seen. When a certificate request is generated, it includes the public key, but the private key stays in the secure Windows certificate store. If the CA is configured to allow export of the private key, the request must explicitly ask for the private to be exportable. If this parameter wasn't included or was set to $false, we wouldn't be able to export the certificate's private key to import to the other Toledo CAS instance, or on to the external firewall.

FriendlyName   This parameter is set for administrative convenience. If we have multiple certificates issued to the machine, it allows us to identify which certificate we're dealing with.

DomainName   This parameter allows us to set one or more domain names. If we specify more than one, Exchange will automatically create and populate the SAN property with all the requested hostnames and set the subject name of the certificate to the first hostname in the list. Although the cmdlet provides additional parameters to explicitly set the subject and alternate names, *you don't need them.*

A successful run of the cmdlet will generate the request output and a thumbprint of the request. Submit the request to your CA, download the corresponding certificate, and then import the certificate back on the same machine:

```
Import-ExchangeCertificate -FileData $(Get-Content ↵
-Path c:\ \CertImport.pfx -Encoding byte) ↵
-Password:(Get-Credential).password
```

This cmdlet will import the saved certificate if it matches a pending request, and print out the thumbprint of the newly imported certificate. You can now view the certificate in MMC or from the certificate management functionality in the Exchange Server 2010 Management Console.

The final step is to enable Exchange services against the certificate:

```
Enable-ExchangeCertificate -Thumbprint <certificate thumbprint> ↵
-Services <services>
```

`<services>` is a comma-separated list of one or more of the following values, depending on the protocols you have enabled and the roles you have installed:

SMTP   For use with SMTP + TLS on Hub Transport and Edge Transport servers

UM   For use with Unified Messaging servers

IIS   For use with Client Access servers, including Autodiscover

IMAP   For use with Client Access servers that are serving the IMAP client protocol

POP   For use with Client Access servers that are serving the POP3 client protocol

The Bottom Line

Work with Autodiscover.   Autodiscover is a key service in Exchange 2010, both for ensuring hassle-free client configuration as well as keeping the Exchange servers in your organization working together smoothly. Autodiscover can be used by Outlook 2007, Outlook 2010, Entourage, and Windows Mobile 6.1 and later.

Master It   You are configuring Outlook 2007 to connect to Exchange server and you want to diagnose a problem that you are having when connecting. What tool can you use?

Configure site affinity.   In a large organization with multiple Active Directory sites, it is important to consider the question of which CAS instances will receive Autodiscover traffic.

Master It   What is a method you can use to set site affinity on an Autodiscover SCP object?

Manage Exchange certificates.   Exchange 2010 servers rely on functional X.509v3 digital certificates to ensure proper SSL and TLS security.

Master It   Which tools will you need to create and manage Exchange certificates?

Chapter 8

Virtualizing Exchange Server 2010

Virtualization of computers has been around for a long time. Users have been virtualizing servers on mainframe computers for more than 15 years. It has only been in the past 5 years or so that nonmainframe computers have gained the capability to perform virtualization. Only in the past couple of years have they gotten good at virtualization. In this chapter, we will discuss virtualizing Microsoft Exchange 2010.

In this chapter, you will learn to:

◆ Evaluate the possible virtualization impacts

◆ Evaluate the existing Exchange environment

◆ Determine which roles to virtualize

Virtualization Overview

Virtualization gives you the ability to host multiple independent instances of operating systems on a single server. The virtualized instances ''borrow'' physical resources from the host system. You are able to configure the virtual machines to provide the required amount of physical resources to the virtual machine. Here are some of the resources you can manage and present to your virtual machines:

◆ Processors

◆ RAM

◆ Number and type of hard drives

◆ Network interface card(s)

Virtualization of servers is becoming popular in many organizations. There are compelling reasons to consider virtualization for your infrastructure, although some situations will not lend themselves to a positive virtualization experience. Some of these reasons will be covered a bit later in the chapter. You may even encounter *both* positive and negative experiences.

Technology continues to evolve, and we have seen great strides in the virtualization world over the past few years. There are multiple vendors in the virtualization game. Microsoft and VMware both have hypervisors that are at the top of the pile for virtualization technologies. They are not the only companies offering virtualization solutions, but they are the most popular. Figure 8.1 gives a virtualization overview. More details about virtualization will be covered throughout this chapter.

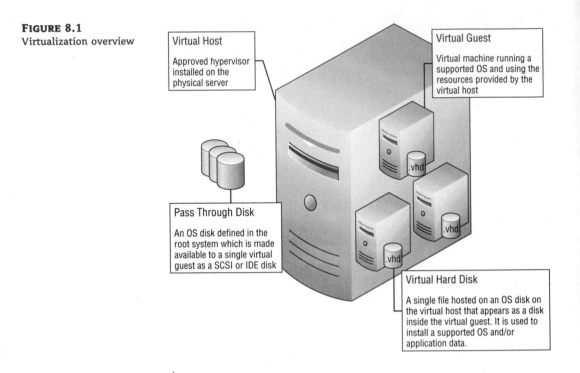

FIGURE 8.1
Virtualization overview

Virtual Host

Approved hypervisor installed on the physical server

Virtual Guest

Virtual machine running a supported OS and using the resources provided by the virtual host

Pass Through Disk

An OS disk defined in the root system which is made available to a single virtual guest as a SCSI or IDE disk

Virtual Hard Disk

A single file hosted on an OS disk on the virtual host that appears as a disk inside the virtual guest. It is used to install a supported OS and/or application data.

Terminology

Table 8.1 contains terms you need to be familiar with as you move through this chapter and the virtualization world.

TABLE 8.1: Virtualization Terms

TERM	DEFINITION
Virtual host	The server that is running the virtualization product. This is the computer that is sharing its physical resources to the virtual guests. Also referred to as the *parent*.
Virtual guest	Virtual machine running a supported OS and using the resources provided by the virtual host.
Database availability group (DAG)	A group of Mailbox servers that host a set of databases and provide automatic database-level recovery from failures.
Virtual hard disk (VHD)	The virtual hard disks are the files that will hold the operating system, data, application, and so forth for the virtual guests.
BIN	This is the temporary memory storage. It is the same size as the virtual guest RAM size. The BIN file is located on the virtual host file system and is used to dump memory during a system save or planned migration from one node to another node in a cluster.

TABLE 8.1:   Virtualization Terms (*CONTINUED*)

TERM	DEFINITION
VSV	This is the virtual save state file. It is also stored on a virtual host file system. It is used to save the virtual guest state during save operations or a planned failover to another node.
Fixed VHD	Presented to the virtual host as a predetermined size for virtual guests to use. When this disk is presented to the virtual host, it is at its maximum size.
Dynamic VHD	Presented to the virtual host; dynamic VHD has been set with a maximum size. This disk is initially only a fraction of the maximum size and will grow as data is written. There is a performance hit as the disk grows.
Differencing VHD	This is linked to a fixed or dynamic VHD. Changes are written to the differencing VHD and not to the fixed or dynamic VHD. Any changes can be rolled back to a previous state. Differencing VHD would be used for testing purposes only.

Understanding Virtualized Exchange

Microsoft started supporting Exchange as a supported, virtualized application with Exchange 2003. Support for virtualizing Exchange and the desire to virtualize Exchange has grown since then. With Exchange 2007, the virtualization platform moved from Virtual Server to one of the approved hypervisors. This moved Exchange into the mainstream for applications that could take advantage of the benefits of virtualization.

Microsoft's stance on virtualizing Exchange has not changed between Exchange 2007 and Exchange 2010. Windows Server 2008 SP2 and Windows Server 2008 R2 are the only supported operating systems for the virtualization of Exchange 2010. Supported roles include the Mailbox, CAS, Hub Transport, and Edge Transport roles. The Unified Messaging role is not supported because it has too much voice codec processing for it to be a viable candidate for virtualization. Visit http://technet.microsoft.com/en-us/library/cc794548.aspx to learn the details of Microsoft's support policy. The virtualized instances of Exchange must still meet the basic Exchange requirements.

MICROSOFT RECOMMENDATIONS

Make sure you have read and are familiar with the "Microsoft Support Policies and Recommendations for Exchange Servers in Hardware Virtualization Environments," which you'll find at http://technet.microsoft.com/en-us/library/cc794548.aspx.

Here are some of the unsupported technologies:

◆ The combination of virtual host clustering and Exchange Mailbox high availability

◆ Snapshots of the virtual machines

◆ Differencing disks

◆ Virtual-to-logical processor ratios greater than 2:1

◆ Any applications running in the root partition

Understanding Your Exchange Environment

Before virtualizing your Exchange environment, you must define your current environment. The better you understand your environment, the more prepared you will be to define the virtualized environment. Here is some of the information you need to gather:

◆ Number of users

◆ User profiles

◆ Number of messages sent/received per day, per user

◆ Server CPU utilization

◆ Server memory utilization

◆ Server network utilization

◆ Database sizes

◆ Storage patterns

◆ Storage type

◆ Current high availability model

◆ Concurrently connected users

◆ Number and types of clients accessing the system

◆ Exchange connectors

◆ Administration model

As you gather this information, you will be painting a picture of your Exchange environment. This information will be placed into various calculations throughout the process to ensure that you have done a complete evaluation before moving forward with virtualization. This information will have a significant impact on the Exchange system moving forward. For example, 500 users who have *heavy* profiles (see Table 8.2) will utilize storage much differently than 500 users who have *average* profiles.

TABLE 8.2:   Exchange User Profiles

USER PROFILES	MESSAGES SENT/RECEIVED PER DAY
Light	5 sent/20 received
Average	10 sent/40 received
Heavy	20 sent/80 received
Very heavy	30 sent/120 received

Each bit of the information you gather will add another piece to the puzzle. As you put the puzzle together, you will have a good idea whether virtualization will meet your needs. You also will be able to validate whether you will get the performance from the virtualized environment that your users require.

Benefits of Virtualization

Virtualization brings a number of impacts that you should consider. Some of the impacts are positive and some are negative, as you'll learn in this section.

Environmental Impact

For most people, the environmental impact is a positive one. The amount of power saved by reducing the number of physical servers can be significant. This number is a completely fluid number and is dependent on the environment that you want to virtualize. An organization with 100 servers will see a much different impact than a company with only 15 servers. Figure 8.2 provides a basic cost reduction calculation.

FIGURE 8.2
Hyper-Green
virtualization savings

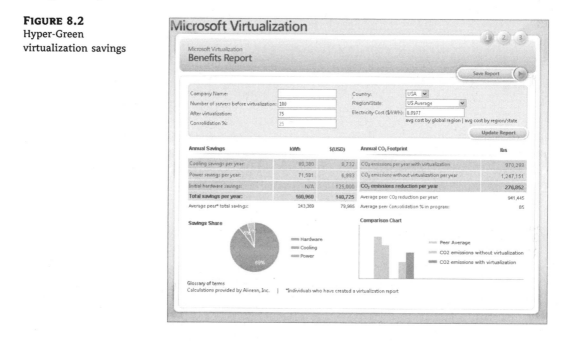

This information was gathered from the Microsoft Hyper-Green tool located at www.hyper-green.com. As you can see, this organization started with 100 servers and only virtualized 25 percent. The power and cooling savings alone were over $15,000 per year — that is after virtualizing only 25 servers. Take into account the CO_2 emissions and you are looking at a savings of 276,852 pounds per year.

The VMware Virtualization Tangible CapEx and OpEx Cost Savings tool can be found at www.vmware.com/solutions/cost-savings.

Datacenter Impact

As with the environmental impact, you will also have an impact in the server room or datacenter. Your organization may or may not feel this impact. Affected organizations are the ones that have a company host their physical servers for them. If your company has all its servers in a facility that they own and maintain, then chances are that you will not enjoy any savings. Companies that host their servers at a hosting facility pay a price for each server that is put into that datacenter. This cost is above and beyond the initial purchase cost of the server. This cost includes the following:

◆ Rental of the space for the physical server

◆ Power

◆ Network connectivity

◆ Cooling

These are the minimal costs associated with the hosting. They usually cover the redundancy for power, network, and cooling. There may be other optional costs associated with your servers, such as the following:

◆ Monitoring of the hardware

◆ Additional firewall capabilities

◆ Out-of-band access to the servers

You can potentially save money by building servers virtually instead of physically. If you currently have ten servers and you are able to virtualize them into three physical servers, you have just saved the cost of seven physical servers and the space, power, cooling, and network for them. Now, there is a trade-off involved. Depending on the workload of the servers before you virtualized them, you may have needed to deploy larger servers for the virtual hosts. In a datacenter, larger servers will bring a higher cost for the space. Be sure to do the math before deciding that this approach will save you money.

One of the ways companies are saving money is by virtualizing the underused servers. By doing this, they reduce the power and cooling footprints that we have talked about. An underused server is thought to use less than 20 percent of its physical hardware. If your current Exchange environment has been sized properly, the servers should not fall into the underused category. This does not mean that you will not benefit from virtualizing Exchange; you need to do your research. Microsoft, with the support of HP, has published a white paper called "Comparing the Power Utilization of Native and Virtual Exchange Environments," available at `http://technet.microsoft.com/en-us/library/dd901773.aspx`. This white paper was written for Exchange 2007, but the information gives you a good background on the impact that virtualization can have. The study shows a reduction of 50 percent in power utilization for the servers used in the study. The total power reduction for the servers and storage was between 34 and 37 percent depending on the storage solution.

Virtualization Requirements

Just as with any software you deploy, there are hardware and software requirements that you need to meet when you virtualize.

Hardware Requirements

For the newer virtualization technologies, make sure that your hardware supports virtualization. Most of the market-leading servers do have the proper BIOS, motherboard, and CPU support. If you are building a server from scratch, review the hardware requirements for the hypervisor you will be using to make sure the server you are building will perform the way you intend it to perform.

You will find that there are different pitfalls for the virtual host than you normally see with physical servers. Since you will be sharing the virtual hosts' physical resources, you need to make sure that you have an idea what servers will be virtualized on the host. This will allow you to verify that you have enough RAM, processors, and network connections. Knowing what is going to be virtualized will also enable you to plan the proper storage for the virtual guests. No matter how many servers you will be virtualizing, make sure you have gathered the physical requirements of the virtual guest. Knowing what your virtual guests will need before you enter the planning stages for virtualization will put you in a better position for success.

No matter what roles or how many servers you will be virtualizing, you need to plan. The virtual host will require resources before the virtual guests are even started. Once you have started the virtual machines, your resources can deplete very quickly. Make sure that you have enough system resources to go around and that you have some breathing room. Plan for your virtual hosts to see an overhead of roughly 10 percent. This will differ from installation to installation, but it is a good number to use when sizing your equipment and laying out your virtual guests.

Storage is another major design point for virtualizing Exchange. As you know, Exchange has always been sized for performance and for capacity. That will not change for any roles that are virtualized. Always design your servers for performance, reliability, and capacity. You need to leverage the storage calculator and size your storage appropriately. Also make sure that you follow the reference processor and memory recommendations and server ratios that are posted on TechNet. These recommendations will always be your first stop for the supported guidance.

Make sure that you have separated your LUNs. You don't want to have spindle contention between your virtual host OS and the storage for your virtual guest OS or application data. Since you are a good system administrator or engineer, you already know that you should have the LUNs on a RAID disk. The level of RAID that you choose is up to you and depends on the project requirements. There is an exception to this rule: the DAG. If you are deploying your Exchange Mailbox servers with at least three copies of the database in the DAG, then you can go RAID-less.

When you are creating your virtual guest OS VHD, make sure that you have included enough space for the page file. Use the following calculation to determine the minimum VHD size that will be needed for the virtual guest:

OS Requirement + Virtual Guest RAM = Minimum OS VHD Size

20 GB + 8 GB = 28 GB

When you start laying out the disk requirements for the Exchange roles, be sure to include space for the .vsv file. The .vsv file is used by the virtual host to save data about the virtual guest in case of a failover or a server suspension. It dumps the contents of the virtual guest memory and process information from the guest to the .vsv file so that it can be brought up to the same state when the failover has completed. Each Exchange role will require a different amount of space. The following examples give you an idea of the minimum requirements. Your environment will differ, so go through the math to allocate enough space for your servers.

CAS VHD = Minimum OS VHD Size + Virtual Guest RAM

HUB VHD = Minimum OS VHD Size + Virtual Guest RAM + Queues

Mailbox VHD = Minimum OS VHD Size + Virtual Guest RAM + Database + Transaction Logs

In addition to the normal storage requirements, make sure you have the appropriate bandwidth for all your virtual guests to access your storage subsystem. The requirements for your storage have not changed since Exchange 2007. Storage should be fixed VHDs, SCSI pass-through, or iSCSI disks. Microsoft recommends that you use SCSI pass-through disks to host the databases, transaction logs, and mail queues.

Make sure you have planned your network bandwidth. You are going to be sharing a limited number of physical network ports on your virtual host with your virtual guests. Depending on your virtual guest layout and requirements, you will exhaust your physical network ports in short order. You may end up needing to install multiple quad-port network interface cards (NICs) to give you the port density required to support your Exchange design. Keep in mind that you may need several NICs per virtual guest. Depending on the role of the server, there may be replication traffic as well as client traffic.

You are not locked into one type of physical server for the virtual host. You can use a standard server, or you may choose to use blade servers. Blade servers require a bit more planning than standard servers. Since you are sharing resources before you start your virtualization, be sure you have carved out your disks, network traffic, and storage traffic adequately.

Software Requirements

Now we are ready to install the host operating system (OS) and at some point the guest operating system(s). Your software requirements for the host OS will differ depending on which hypervisor you have decided to use. Check with your hypervisor provider to ensure that you have all the required software before you begin. There are differences in the base OSs that may preclude you from loading any hypervisor without a complete reload of the server. Although this is not a huge deal, it is time consuming, and if you purchased the incorrect version, it is also expensive. Make sure that you know how many servers will be virtualized on the host servers as well. This may have an impact on what version of the OS you need to install. Make certain that you have completed the virtual guest configuration before you start to load Exchange.

For the virtual guest, installation is pretty straightforward. Once you have made the initial configurations for the virtual guest, load the appropriate OS. There are no requirements from a virtualization perspective as to what OS you need to load. The guest OS will be driven by the business requirements for the server or application that you will be virtualizing. This is where your requirements gathering will guide you to the correct OS and application versions. For example, if you are going to be using DAGs in your virtual guests, you must install the Enterprise version of Windows and Exchange.

Make sure that no matter what hypervisor you use, you stay within the licensing agreement of all software components:

Windows Server Standard Edition   Allows for one virtual instance of Windows Server

Windows Server Enterprise Edition   Allows for four virtualized Windows servers

Windows Server Datacenter Edition   Allows for an unlimited number of virtualized Windows servers

These requirements are only relevant for the Windows Server OS and not any of the Exchange server licenses. Each of the Exchange servers will need to be licensed. So will any applications that you load on your Exchange servers.

You also must ensure that the hypervisor you're using is included in the Windows Server Virtualization Validation Program (SVVP); information is available at www.windowsservercatalog.com/svvp.aspx. If you install Exchange on any hypervisors that are not in the SVVP, you will not be supported by Microsoft if you have any problems.

Operations

Operations include many factors, such as the patching and monitoring of the OS and application, daily maintenance, and troubleshooting. A popular misconception is that your operating costs will decrease when you start to virtualize. Nothing could be further from the truth. Chances are that your costs will actually increase. The reason for the potential increase is from the addition of virtualization. Virtualization does bring in an additional skill set requirement for the organization. While virtualization is not rocket science, it is pretty close. Being able to balance the needs of the virtual guests against the resources of the host against the requirements of the users can be a daunting task. The size of your IT organization and the number and location of servers will affect the cost of operations. If you have enough staff to learn the virtualization technology, there may not be a huge impact to the bottom line. If you don't have that staff, you will most likely be looking for additional personnel to support your virtualization efforts. The benefit to getting someone who knows about virtualization is the virtualization experience that they bring to the table. On top of learning the ins and outs of the virtualization platform, you now have an additional OS to patch and maintain. You may need to increase your IT staff to account for the virtualization component. Your staff does not need to consider the virtual hosts as just other servers. You must be cautious when you perform routine maintenance on your virtual host. It is easy to perform what is considered routine maintenance and then end up harming the virtual guest.

When you virtualize your Exchange servers, you still have to take care of an OS and the application. The virtualized guests still have 100 percent of the daily operations that their physical counterparts have. The only savings result from the operational cost of the physical hardware.

You still have to test and patch your systems. You still have systems that will experience issues, and you need to spend time troubleshooting. On top of that, you now have added the hypervisor layer. This layer may or may not be familiar to your support and engineering staff. You can't just reboot a virtual host because you feel like it is the best solution for a situation. You now have to expand your thought process to include the Exchange servers that are virtualized on that host and take these factors into consideration:

- What Exchange services will be affected by shutting down this host?

- Exchange virtual guests are on the virtual host, and how will the users be affected when they are shut down?

- Do the affected services have a redundant nature?

- Are the redundant services located on the same virtual host or on a different host? (If they are on the same virtual host, are they really redundant?)

Deciding What to Virtualize

No matter how many Exchange servers you plan to virtualize, you must do your research as you are planning the architecture for your environment. Plan your virtual guests just as though they are physical servers. Then include the additional overhead for the virtual host. Make sure that you are thinking about the end product that you will deliver to your users. Consider the possible differences between the physical and virtualized environment. Will your user base be as happy with a virtualized environment if it means a decrease in performance? If you set the expectations, size the environment appropriately, and test appropriately, there should not be a noticeable difference for your end users.

As with any architecture, things that you do can make positive or negative impacts. With Exchange 2003 and earlier versions, Exchange and the OS were limited to only 4 GB of physical

RAM. By using the /3gb switch, you can have Exchange take advantage of 3 GB of RAM. Starting with Exchange 2007, Microsoft changed the Extensible Storage Engine (ESE). The part of the change that we are concerned about for this discussion was brought on by the 64-bit nature of Exchange 2007. This allowed Exchange 2007 to utilize over 32 GB of RAM if needed. This change allowed the ESE to grab as much RAM as needed to make the Exchange server more efficient. Since RAM is much faster to access than regular disk drives, ESE places as much information as possible in memory. Keep this in mind as you design your virtual guests. Some applications will use RAM and then release it back to the operating system after processes are done. Exchange memory allocation is dynamic. ESE will use all available memory in the system and then return the memory as other processes need it. If you have a server that has 16 GB of memory, you can expect that ESE will consume roughly 14 GB of it until other processes need the resources. The Dynamic Buffer Allocation (DBA) will manage the cache by comparing the amount of I/O generated by the databases to the system I/O in terms of hard page faults. If Exchange is producing more I/O and hitting hard page faults, it will increase the cache. If Exchange is producing less I/O than the hard page faults, Exchange will decrease the amount of cache. The primary goal is to keep ESE cache in balance with the disk cache to reduce the amount of paging.

Implementing virtualization involves bringing in new technologies to make the applications operate smoothly. One popular technique is the ability to overallocate the physical resources of the virtual host. For example, say your virtual host has 64 GB of physical RAM. You are going to put six virtual guests on the server, each with 16 GB of RAM. This is allowed in some hypervisors, but Microsoft does not recommend it. By doing this, you have told the virtual guests that they can potentially have a total of 96 GB of RAM in use. Obviously, this cannot happen since you don't have that much RAM available. But, since all six of your virtual guests will not utilize this much RAM under normal workloads, it may not impact you. With this scenario in mind and the fact that the Exchange store.exe process will use any RAM that has been advertised to the guest OS, you will run out of RAM.

Overallocation happens most often with the amount of RAM and/or the number of processors that are configured for the virtual guest. Be extremely careful when you are planning your systems and avoid enabling overallocation of any physical resources on the virtual host. Be sure to leave your virtual guest enough resources to handle the processing of the OS and the hypervisor.

While you are planning your virtualization environment, remember that just because a solution would be supported by Microsoft does not necessarily mean that it would be a recommended solution. There are plenty of situations in which it would make sense to virtualize Exchange, and there are just as many cases in which virtualization would not make sense. Don't get pushed into virtualization because it is the "new kid on the block." There is always a new technology that is the best thing since sliced bread, but that does not mean that it is the right solution for your environment.

At some point you will have to decide on your high availability solution. Exchange High Availability is the automatic switchover of the application services and does not compromise the integrity of the data. Exchange will automatically detect the best location for the target of the switchover. If Exchange determines that there is a healthy copy of the database(s) and a quorum, Exchange will make the switch to one of the other database(s).

Microsoft will not support a mixture of high availability solutions. What this means is that you must choose to either use the replication that is built into Exchange or use the hypervisor's high availability capabilities. With the introduction of DAGs, you have a good story for both high availability and site resilience in the application. Since DAGs are application aware, your servers are always in control of any Exchange data. Since the Exchange servers are in constant "discussion" about the status of a database in the DAG, there should be minimal impact if a server or database goes down for any reason.

You also have the opportunity to utilize the virtual host replication. If you decide to implement your hypervisor's replication, you cannot leverage DAGs on those virtual hosts. The downside to using virtual host replication is that Exchange has no clue what is happening with the data and resources. Although it is technically possible to install Exchange and configure the DAG on a cluster virtual host, there is a huge potential for data corruption at the Exchange level. This is why the Exchange team at Microsoft has chosen not to support this type of deployment. In Table 8.3, you will see a breakdown of the differences in clustering technology. The table compares the major differences between the two technologies.

TABLE 8.3:   Virtual Host Clustering and Failover vs. Exchange High Availability

FEATURE	VIRTUAL HOST CLUSTERING HIGH AVAILABILITY	EXCHANGE MAILBOX HIGH AVAILABILITY
OS heartbeat	Yes	Yes
Exchange heartbeat	No	Yes
Copies of the Exchange data	1	Minimum of 2
Shared storage requirement	Yes	No
Machine or role failover granularity	No	Yes, down to the database level
Support hardware VSS	No	Yes
Support backup from passive copy	No	Yes

Third-party applications can have a direct impact on your virtualization design. When planning your environment, be sure that you have included any applications that will be coming into the Exchange organization and what impact they will have. Some applications will hit the CAS or Hub Transport roles, while others may stress the storage subsystem.

Exchange Roles

As stated earlier, the ability is there to virtualize any Exchange 2010 roles except the Unified Messaging role. You also have the ability to combine Exchange roles. You may find a need to virtualize the CAS and Hub Transport roles on the same virtual guest. This is a supported solution by Microsoft. Your environment may benefit from having the CAS, Hub Transport, and Mailbox roles virtualized.

We have already said this, but make sure you do your due diligence when creating the architecture for your virtualized environment. This is one of the key factors you have to make sure of before moving forward in virtualizing Exchange successfully. At the end of the day, you will be measured by the happiness of your users. It does not matter if you felt the Exchange deployment was a success if your users are not 100 percent satisfied.

Performance Counters

To put yourself in the best possible position for success, gather some information about your current environment. If you are currently using Exchange, you can get information from counters like the ones shown in Table 8.4 for Exchange 2007. If you have Exchange 2003 in your environment, then check out Table 8.5. These counters are not a hard-and-fast rule but guidance on what to look for. If you see that your systems are much higher than the recommendations, test your system thoroughly with a simulated user load before you put your production users on the virtualized systems.

TABLE 8.4: Exchange 2007 Counters

CATEGORY	OBJECT\COUNTER	EXPECTED VALUE
Common Performance Counters (All Exchange Servers)	Processor\% Total	Should be less than 40% average.
	System\Processor Queue Length (All Instances)	Should be less than 5 (per processor).
	Network Interface(*)\Bytes Total/Sec	For a 1000-Mbps network adapter, should be below 30–35 Mbps.
Mailbox Server-Specific Performance Counters	MSExchangeIS Client (*)\RPC Average Latency	Should be less than 30 milliseconds (ms) on average.
	Process(Microsoft.Exchange.Search. ExSearch)\% Processor time	Should be less than 1% of overall CPU typically and not sustained above 3%
	MSExchange Store Interface(_Total)\RPC Latency average (msec)	Should be less than 100 ms at all times.
	MSExchange Store Interface(_Total)\RPC Requests Outstanding	Should be 0 at all times.
CCR, LCR and SCR Mailbox Server-Specific Performance Counters	MSExchange Replication(*)\CopyQueueLength	Should be less than 10 at all times for CCR and SCR. Should be less than 1 at all times for local continuous replication (LCR).
CAS Server - Availability	MSExchange Availability Service\Average Time To Process A Free Busy Request	Should always be less than 5.
CAS Server - OWA	MSExchange OWA\Average Response Time	Should be less than 100 ms at all times.

TABLE 8.4: Exchange 2007 Counters (*CONTINUED*)

CATEGORY	OBJECT\COUNTER	EXPECTED VALUE
Hub Transport - Disk	Logical/Physical Disk(*)\Avg. Disk Sec/Read Logical/Physical Disk(*)\Avg. Disk Sec/Write	Should be less than 20 ms on average.
Hub Transport - Transport Database	MSExchange Database ==> Instances(edgetransport/Transport Mail Database)\Version Buckets Allocated	Should be less than 200 at all times.
Hub Transport - Transport Database	MSExchange Database ==> Instances(edgetransport/Transport Mail Database)\Log Record Stalls/Sec	Should be less than 10 per second on average.
Hub Transport - Transport Database	MSExchange Database ==> Instances(edgetransport/Transport Mail Database)\Log Threads Waiting	Should be less than 10 threads waiting on average.

Source: Monitoring Without System Center Operations Manager, http://technet.microsoft.com/en-us/library/bb201720.aspx

TABLE 8.5: Exchange 2003 Counters

CATEGORY	OBJECT\COUNTER	EXPECTED VALUE
Mailbox Server - Memory	Free System Page Table Entries/All	Always greater than 8000 pages. Never less than 3500 pages available.
Mailbox Server - Processor	% Processor Time/All	Average less than 75%.
Mailbox Server - Log Record Stalls/Sec	Information Store/<Storage Group>	Should be less than 10 per second.
Mailbox Server - Log Threads Waiting	Information Store/<Storage Group>	Average should be less than 10.
Front-End Server - Outlook Mobile Access	Last response time	Should be less than 60 seconds.
Routing Group Connector Bridgehead - SMTP Virtual Server	Categorizer Queue Length	Average should be less than 3, spikes less than 10.
Routing Group Connector Bridgehead - SMTP Virtual Server	Remote Queue Length	Should be less than 1000.

These counters are not 100 percent hardened counters. Use them as a guide to help you figure out whether your organization could benefit from virtualization. You need to make sure that any servers you are planning to virtualize are underutilized. If they are overutilized, you are only going to see a negative impact once you virtualize.

You must also keep your user profiles in mind during your planning. You can use profile size information to help answer the questions about the estimated load on your virtual guests. This way is much more fluid, but it should put you in the ballpark.

Testing

As with any engineering effort, you need to make sure that you have a testing plan for the virtualized guests and host. Part of your plan needs to include testing all your virtual guests at the same time. One of the worst things you can do is to test only a single server at a time. If you test only one server at a time, you will probably have very good numbers. Think about what happens when you turn on all your virtual guests; the performance will probably head south in a hurry. The bottom line is to test the entire solution and not pieces of the solution. The solution should include any third-party applications that are in the environment as well. Anything that you leave out of the testing cycle could come back to haunt you when you move to production.

You should use both Exchange Server Jetstress and Exchange Load Generator to validate your configuration. Jetstress is used to test the performance of the disk subsystem. The information that Jetstress gives you should line up with your performance requirements that were gathered early in the project. Load Generator will simulate the different client connections that will be in your environment. You will be able to define the number of each client connection and how much email traffic they will send and receive. When using the testing tools, try to emulate the user base that is currently in the environment. If none of your users use OWA, then don't put OWA in the test cases. If your organization includes heavy users of Windows Mobile, make sure that you have included the correct information to heavily test for Windows Mobile.

Remember: in the virtualized environment, you should do everything you would normally do in a physical environment. Don't fall into the trap of thinking that because this is a virtualized environment, it is a different solution. You are the only one who will know that these servers are virtualized. The end users and the first line of the help desk will think these are physical servers.

Also, please keep in mind that with the change from Exchange 2007 to Exchange 2010 you will need to change the focus of the client access services to the Client Access servers only. You can refer to the Exchange 2010 TechCenter, `http://technet.microsoft.com/en-us/library/bb124558(EXCHG.140).aspx`, for up-to-date information on server processor and RAM recommendations.

You don't want to be caught off guard when you get to production. If you start your pilot and you have not tested the solution, you will find out pretty quickly. Part of the project will be to set the expectations of the virtualized environment. Obviously you will be monitoring your environment closely as you deploy. As you deploy more users to the virtualized systems, you may find that there is more of a hit on the systems than testing showed. If this is the case, you may need to add more virtual guests and virtual hosts to your environment. There is nothing wrong with this, but make sure that you have informed management of the possibility before you get in this situation.

Possible Times to Virtualize

Once you start testing your environment, you may find that in some situations physical servers are the best route. In this section we will look at several scenarios that could lead to a positive virtualization experience. These scenarios are not guarantees for success, but examples of what *may* work. We will not be looking at the physical specifications for the virtual hosts and storage. There will be discussions about the possible hardware for both the virtual host and virtual guest, but this is just an estimation of hardware that may be needed. These scenarios have not been tested in a lab for performance. They are merely examples of what could be virtualized.

Small Office/Remote or Branch Office

In this scenario, our office has a relatively small number of users and we need to provide email services to them. We have determined that users would be better off by using local Exchange servers instead of pulling email across the WAN. We want to provide redundancy and high availability where possible.

As we start to build this solution, we must determine which virtual guest roles will have to be placed on which virtual hosts. We see that there will be a need for the following:

- Two CAS server roles
- Two Hub Transport server roles
- Two Mailbox server roles
- Two domain controllers

Because the users are in a remote office, we will be supplying directory services as well. It has been determined, through research, interviews with staff members, and data collection, that our users are light email users. The CAS and Hub Transport roles will be combined, and we will be providing high availability via DAG. We have also found a requirement for site resilience. We will be fulfilling the requirement by adding a server at the main datacenter into the DAG.

We can put this solution together with only three physical servers and storage. Again, the exact specifications on the servers and storage are not being discussed. When we create the DAG, it will automatically place the file share witness, but in our solution we will have to specify the correct location for the file share witness. We need to ensure that we do not create an issue where the file share witness ends up being on the same virtual host as a Mailbox server in the DAG. If this were to happen and we created the file share witness on virtual host 2, then we'd have two voting members of the DAG on the same physical hardware. This is not a recommended solution. We can move the file share witness from the Exchange Management Console (EMC) or the Exchange Management Shell (EMS).

Virtual Host 1 will have the following virtual guests:

- Domain Controller 1
- CAS and Hub Transport 1

Virtual Host 2 will have the following virtual guests:

- Domain Controller 2
- Mailbox Server 1

Virtual Host 3 will have the following virtual guests:

◆ CAS and Hub Transport 2

◆ Mailbox Server 2

As you can see, the physical servers would probably not be overutilized with the current workloads that we have placed on them. If you add a file server cluster into the mix, make sure that the virtual host has enough resources to perform the additional work. So instead of having six servers in use, you will have three servers, or a 50 percent reduction in servers for this location.

Site Resilience

In this scenario, we are going to be setting up a second location for site resilience. We are assuming that the primary datacenter is fully functional with Exchange 2010 physical servers. We have been handed a new requirement that states we will be providing site resilience for all users in our organization. We have also been told that we will need to provide the same level of performance and reliability as the primary datacenter. Our primary datacenter information is listed here:

◆ Four Mailbox servers in a DAG (four processors and 16 GB of RAM each)

◆ Three CAS servers (four processors and 8 GB of RAM each)

◆ Two Hub Transport servers (four processors and 8 GB of RAM each)

So to meet the requirements we will be deploying four physical servers to host 11 virtual guests. These 11 guests include four domain controllers. We are using four domain controllers to keep the number of virtual processors and RAM down on each domain controller.

We will need five physical servers for the solution. For ease of ordering, we will order all servers with the same hardware specifications. They will have four quad-core processors and 32 GB of RAM for each virtual host. A breakdown of virtual guests and the virtual host to which they belong follows. Since we have to provide the same level of performance as the primary datacenter, we will leave the CAS and Hub Transport servers separated. If we didn't have the requirement to meet performance for the primary datacenter, we could have combined the CAS and Hub Transport roles and possibly met the performance needs on four physical servers.

Virtual Host 1 will have the following virtual guests:

◆ Domain Controller 1 (four processors and 4 GB of RAM)

◆ Mailbox Server 1 (four processors and 16 GB of RAM)

◆ CAS Server 1 (four processors and 8 GB of RAM)

Virtual Host 2 will have the following virtual guests:

◆ Mailbox Server 2 (four processors and 16 GB of RAM)

◆ CAS Server 2 (four processors and 8 GB of RAM)

Virtual Host 3 will have the following virtual guests:

◆ Mailbox Server 3 (four processors and 16 GB of RAM)

◆ Hub Transport Server 1 (four processors and 8 GB of RAM)

Virtual Host 4 will have the following virtual guests:

◆ Mailbox Server 4 (four processors and 16 GB of RAM)

◆ Hub Transport Server 2 (four processors and 8 GB of RAM)

Virtual Host 5 will have the following virtual guests:

◆ Domain Controller 2 (four processors and 4 GB of RAM)

◆ CAS Server 3 (four processors and 8 GB of RAM)

You are probably wondering where we are going to put the file share witness since there is a Mailbox server on each of the virtual hosts. In this scenario, it is fine to let Exchange place the file share witness. You may recall that the file share witness is only used when there is an even number of servers in the DAG. We do have that here, but there are enough servers to separate the witness without putting the DAG in jeopardy.

By separating the virtual guests across four virtual hosts, we have accomplished the task at hand. If we had chosen to mirror the production environment and use physical servers, we would have needed nine servers plus the domain controllers. At a minimum, we cut our servers by 50 percent if not more with the inclusion of the domain controllers. The flip side of this is that we probably increased the number of processors and RAM in the virtual hosts. By doing this, we also increased the cost of the virtual hosts. It may have not been much, but that is something you would calculate before implementing this solution.

Mobile Scenario

For the mobile solution, we are going to look at a customer that has a requirement to react to an emergency quickly. They need to have their entire infrastructure physically with them. They do not need to tie back into a corporate environment, but they will be connecting to the Internet and must be able to send and receive email and surf the Internet. They also require a database server, file/print capabilities, and collaboration. There will be an external appliance to provide firewall protection. This is also considered a short-term solution. Once the disaster is over or a permanent datacenter has been established, the mobile solution will be decommissioned. This solution brings in several different technologies in addition to Exchange.

The customer has only 50 users, but they will be sending and receiving a large amount of email. With this number of users, there will not be a huge draw on any of the servers. Knowing this, we are able to pull back on some of the server requirements. We can keep the file share witness separated from the Mailbox servers and stay within the recommendations of Microsoft. We will place a node of the database cluster on the same virtual host as one of the Mailbox servers. This is not a recommended solution, but since we are looking at a temporary solution with limited users, we should be fine with the layout.

Virtual Host 1 will have the following virtual guests:

◆ Domain Controller 1 (two processors and 4 GB of RAM)

◆ Mailbox Server 1 (four processors and 8 GB of RAM)

◆ CAS and Hub Transport 1 (four processors and 8 GB of RAM)

◆ Database Server Node 1 (four processors and 8 GB of RAM)

Virtual Host 2 will have the following virtual guests:

◆ Domain Controller 2 (two processors and 4 GB of RAM)

◆ Mailbox Server 2 (four processors and 8 GB of RAM)

◆ Collaboration Server 2 (four processors and 8 GB of RAM)

◆ File and Print Node 1(two processors and 8 GB of RAM)

Virtual Host 3 will have the following virtual guests:

◆ File and Print Node 2 (two processors and 8 GB of RAM)

◆ CAS and Hub Transport 2 (four processors and 8 GB of RAM)

◆ Database server node 2 (four processors and 8 GB of RAM)

◆ Collaboration server 2 (four processors and 8 GB of RAM)

We are able to meet the requirements for the customer with only three physical servers. Each server will have four dual-core processors and 32 GB of RAM. If during testing we decide that we would need an additional server, we can add another server. Looking at the numbers, you can see that we have decreased the number of servers from twelve to three, which is a 75 percent reduction.

🌐 Real World Scenario

VIRTUALIZE THE LAB

You will find that there are plenty of times for you to virtualize Exchange. One of the times to virtualize is in the lab. When you virtualize your lab, you can either do an equal virtualization to what is going to be in production, or you can have a different layout. There are benefits to both.

If you are able to duplicate the lab and production, you can include performance testing. Duplicating the lab to production does not only mean matching the number of servers and role designations, but also determining whether or not they will be physical servers. If you are going to virtualize in production, this test will give you accurate results and a baseline for the production environment. You will also increase the hardware requirement for the virtual hosts and the storage that you will be using.

If you are not able to duplicate the lab, you must prepare yourself and management that the lab is for functional testing only. If you were to do any performance testing, the results would not be accurate. By using this method, you will save on hardware for the virtual hosts and storage.

Both scenarios will give you a good base for testing your virtualized Exchange environment. One gives you the ability to test performance and functionality with an added hardware cost, while the other gives you the ability to do a functionality test with minimal hardware costs.

The Bottom Line

Evaluate the possible virtualization impacts.   Knowing the impacts that virtualization brings to the table will help you make the virtualization a success. Failure to realize how virtualization will impact your environment can end up making virtualization a poor choice.

Master It   What kind of impact would be caused by virtualizing Exchange in your environment?

Evaluate the existing Exchange environment.   Before you can determine the feasibility of a virtualized Exchange environment, you must first know how your current systems are performing.

Master It   Are your Exchange servers good candidates for virtualization?

Determine which roles to virtualize.   There are going to be times when virtualization of one or more roles would be successful and there are going to be times when virtualization of roles is not going to be successful.

Master It   What roles will you virtualize?

Chapter 9

Exchange Server, Email, and SharePoint 2007

In only its third version, the adoption of SharePoint has taken off in many organizations. And it's no surprise. Organizations commonly struggle with managing their overwhelming volume of data, information, and knowledge. Quite often workers use Microsoft Exchange as both a transport and a repository for content.

This solution can frustrate users with defining current and authoritative content sources. SharePoint addresses these and other challenges.

In this chapter, you will learn to:

◆ Connect to SharePoint using Outlook as a client

◆ Configure outgoing and incoming email in SharePoint

◆ Set up SharePoint to enable searching on an Exchange public folder

SharePoint Overview

Information workers desperately need to collaborate. They need to quickly find content relevant to their job and a way to publish new content. The flexibility of Outlook and Exchange together make it a powerful communication tool. Everyone knows how easy it is to send emails and attachments. However, this flexibility can be a hindrance. Many develop an overreliance on it and are quickly inundated with content buried in a mountain of messages. The problem stems from the fact that these emails and their attachments are not easy to classify, version, or search.

The overreliance on email also creates its own set of IT challenges as well, with soaring mailbox sizes and the known difficulty of recovering individual messages. SharePoint addresses these and other challenges by delivering on a number of fundamental areas:

◆ Document management that provides versioning, check-in/check-out, and security controls

◆ Easy and flexible website creation that helps organize content

◆ Flexible branding options to customize the look and feel

◆ Portals to both organize and centralize the storage of content that needs to be published across the organization

◆ A search engine to ensure content and people resources can be quickly found using simple keywords

◆ Business intelligence to ensure staff at all levels can make better, faster decisions

The most common form of a SharePoint deployment is within an organization. This is usually termed an intranet. However, just like email, which is no longer internal anymore, SharePoint can extend outside the company walls as an extranet. This facilitates collaboration between organizations, which is growing in importance. There are also a growing number of public-facing websites that are built using SharePoint.

SharePoint comes delivered in two products: Windows SharePoint Services and Microsoft Office SharePoint Server. Windows SharePoint Services is licensed as part of Windows Server 2003 or Windows Server 2008. Assuming licenses for the server and clients are in place and in effect, it is free. Windows SharePoint Services provide much of the foundational technology and is quite a powerful offering for no additional cost.

Microsoft Office SharePoint Server is a separately licensed product. It comes in two forms: Standard and Enterprise. Microsoft Office SharePoint Server Standard Edition builds on top of the Windows SharePoint Services infrastructure by providing a wealth of additional improvements. This includes enterprise-capable searching, enterprise content management, records management, social networking, and other improvements. Enterprise builds on Standard by improving business intelligence features and delivering a powerful electronic forms engine. Contrary to what you might guess, Microsoft Office SharePoint Server is not always targeted at larger organizations, and many organizations under 100 users find it adds significant value.

As of this writing, the latest version of Windows SharePoint Services is 3.0 and the latest version of Microsoft Office SharePoint Server is 2007. A new version of SharePoint will be out around the time the next version of Microsoft Office is released. This is expected sometime in the first half of 2010. The feature set covered in this chapter is based on the 3.0 and 2007 versions.

Speaking of Office, it's certainly one big reason for the success of SharePoint. SharePoint integrates very nicely with Office 2007 and makes a number of operations, such as check-in and check-out, a snap. Integration with Office 2003 and prior versions is not as seamless, but you have some options, as you will learn in this chapter.

Outlook Integration

Even though web-based technologies are very popular, the power and richness are still not up to par with Windows desktop applications. Performance, ease of use, and offline access to data are some of the reasons why desktop applications are still going strong. In fact, SharePoint is often referred to as Office Server to make clear its important relationship with the Office client applications, such as Microsoft Word, Excel, and Outlook.

How many people do you know say that they "live in Outlook"? It's no surprise. Email is the lifeblood for most organizations, and while SharePoint might be a better repository for some forms of email correspondence, people are wedded to their Outlook client. Fortunately, one of the many aspects where Outlook excels as a universal tool is by integrating with Share-Point. Outlook integration as described in this section is fully supported on both Windows SharePoint Services and Microsoft Office SharePoint Server.

Integration Overview

As you'll see, Outlook is a rich client to SharePoint in managing a number of content forms. When working with Outlook and SharePoint, you will mostly be connecting to SharePoint lists and libraries. Outlook will then cache a local copy of the list or library into a local PST file. If you are using Outlook 2007, you have full read and write operations. SharePoint integration with Outlook 2003 is less capable and will be covered at the end of this section.

Connecting from Outlook to any list or library involves the same initial steps. The first step is to access the SharePoint list or library from the browser. From the Actions menu, select the Connect To Outlook option, as shown in Figure 9.1.

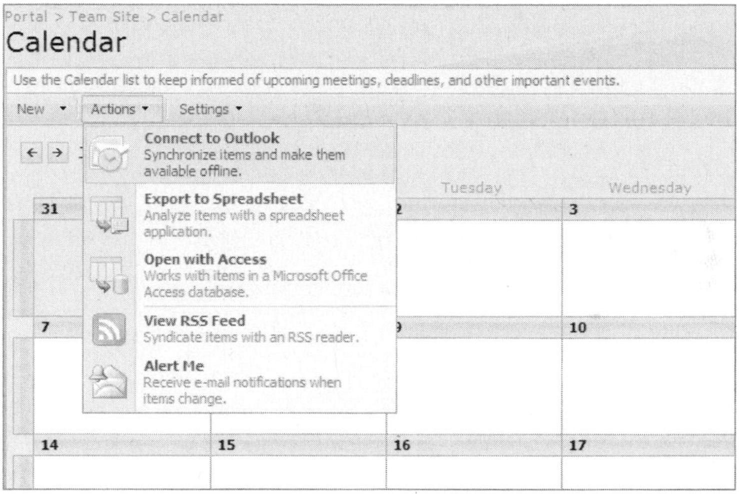

FIGURE 9.1
Connecting a list to Outlook

At this point, Outlook should start if it is not running already. Inside Outlook, you will receive a prompt asking you to confirm the operation (see Figure 9.2).

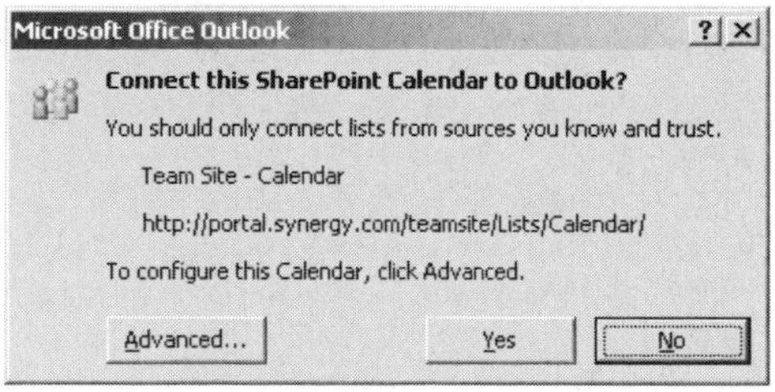

FIGURE 9.2
Confirming the connection

This prompt is given to prevent websites from establishing rogue or unwanted connections in Outlook. You must select Yes to connect to the list or library. Selecting Advanced allows you to change the folder name and description you see in Outlook. The default folder name is the name of the SharePoint website followed by the name of the list or library. For example, if your SharePoint website is named Team Site and your list is named Calendar, the default name in Outlook is "Team Site - Calendar."

To disconnect from any list or library, you can right-click the name in the navigation panel and select Delete. Doing so does not delete the list or library from SharePoint; it only deletes the Outlook connection. You will lose any changes made in Outlook that haven't been sent up to SharePoint.

You can also see all your connected lists and libraries by selecting Tools ➢ Account Settings, and then clicking the SharePoint Lists tab. From this screen, you can also edit or remove connections.

The first time you connect to any SharePoint list or library from Outlook, a new local PST file is created in your mail profile. This file is named `SharePoint Lists.pst`, and it's where all SharePoint-connected lists and libraries are locally cached.

Permissions that you have in SharePoint will carry over to Outlook. For example, if you only have read permissions to a tasks list, you will not be able to create new tasks in this list from Outlook.

The rest of this section will walk through how to work with many list and library types from Outlook. You'll start by learning how to manage calendars and create meeting workspace sites in SharePoint. You'll then see how to manage contacts, tasks, alerts, and document libraries.

In addition to what is covered in this chapter, Outlook lets you manage other SharePoint content, such as SharePoint discussion libraries and RSS-generated feeds. Not all lists and libraries can be connected, however. For example, announcements, surveys, links, custom lists, and a few others offer no direct integration with Outlook.

USING MICROSOFT ACCESS

Microsoft Access can also be used as a client when working with SharePoint lists and libraries. It supports many list types that Outlook does not, such as custom lists, but it does not offer the rich offline editing that Outlook does.

Calendar Integration

Shared calendars are a great way to schedule team meetings, reserve resources such as a projector, or just document milestones for a project. Shared calendars have been around for many years with Outlook and Exchange, but times have changed and many now store these shared calendars within SharePoint websites. One advantage to a SharePoint calendar is that you can locate it with other related department or project resources (contacts, documents, tasks, and so forth).

Outlook displays calendars from SharePoint in the same way that it shows personal and public folder calendars. With Outlook 2007, this integration is two way, meaning that not only can you see SharePoint calendar entries from Outlook, but you can also create, edit, and delete them.

Once the SharePoint calendar is connected in Outlook, it is visible from the Calendar view from the navigation pane (by default on the left). You work with a SharePoint calendar just like any other calendar. For example, you can search calendar entries, or create, change, and delete entries. All changes made using Outlook are automatically synched with the SharePoint calendar on the server. Whether you are working with it through Outlook or the SharePoint browser interface, you are working with the same set of calendar entries.

Let's see how some of this works. We'll start by first connecting a SharePoint calendar, as shown in Figures 9.1 and 9.2 earlier. With the connection in place, let's take a look at side-by-side calendars, which is a handy way to see how meetings overlap, allowing you to spot potential conflicts. From the calendar view, we have selected both a personal and a project calendar. Figure 9.3 shows how they look side by side.

FIGURE 9.3
Viewing side-by-side
calendars

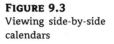

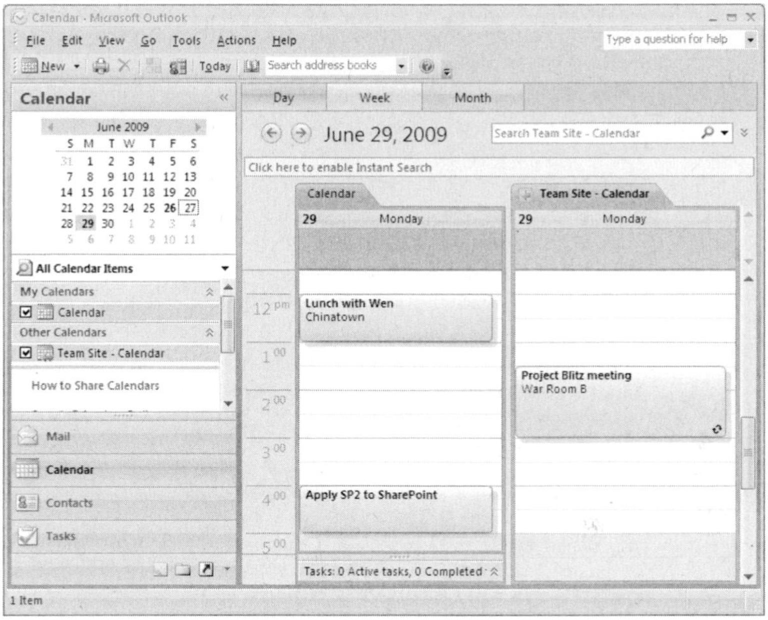

Outlook also has a great overlay mode that allows you to see all the entries within one unified view. Each calendar's entries will show in a different color, allowing you to spot the calendar from which an entry originates (see Figure 9.4).

FIGURE 9.4
Calendars in overlay
mode

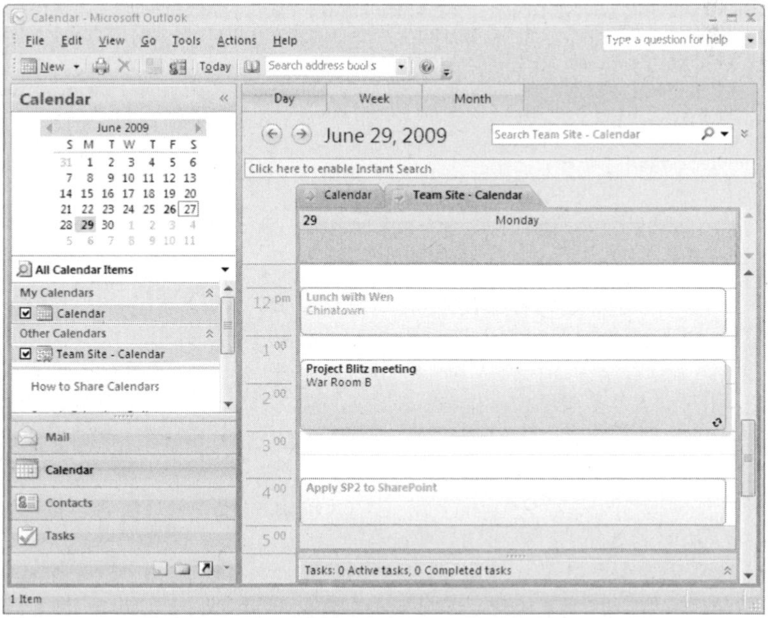

To activate overlay mode, you simply click the left-arrow icon in the calendar's tab at the top. You return to side-by-side view by clicking the right-arrow icon in the same tab.

To include a SharePoint calendar on a meeting request, you must enable incoming email on it. We will explain how to do this in the next section.

Unlike Outlook, SharePoint doesn't allow you to have a meeting reminder for appointments. Nonetheless, you can still use reminders for SharePoint calendar entries provided that you have connected the calendar into Outlook as we just covered. All you need to do is double-click the entry and manually add a reminder setting. The reminder setting will not be sent back to the SharePoint calendar. This means that it is only a personal reminder and will not apply to other users of this calendar.

Having a locally, cached copy of the calendar is a great advantage and allows you to work with this content while you are offline. For example, while you are traveling or just offline, you can still read and edit calendar entries. When you are connected, these will automatically be synchronized. Local changes from Outlook are sent to the server and changes on the server are downloaded. Of course, there is always the chance of a conflict, but Outlook is quite smart at handling this.

For example, let's say that you have a SharePoint calendar entry that is scheduled to start at 10 a.m. While offline, you change the start time to 11 a.m. Meanwhile, another user changes it through the browser to 9 a.m. When you sync, Outlook will detect that the item changed on the server and will not overwrite it. At this point, the meeting time reflected in Outlook is 9 a.m. However, if you open up the item, Outlook will inform you about what happened and allow your changes to override what's on the server. If you do this, the meeting would be changed to 11 a.m.

A final calendar integration option between Outlook and SharePoint involves not connecting to a calendar, but opening a single SharePoint calendar entry in Outlook. When viewing a SharePoint calendar item through the browser, you have the option of downloading this into an .ics file. Outlook recognizes this file type and then stores this entry into your personal calendar. This is convenient if you only want to store a copy of one or more calendar entries. You can do this by first clicking the Export Event link when viewing a single calendar entry. Figure 9.5 shows how the screen looks in the browser.

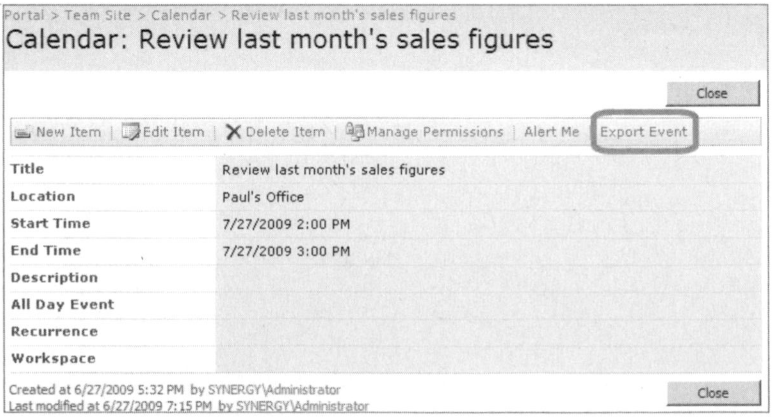

FIGURE 9.5
Exporting a calendar entry into Outlook

From here, you will be prompted to download the .ics file type that Outlook automatically recognizes. Figure 9.6 shows what the dialog looks like.

FIGURE 9.6
Download the `.ics`
calendar entry.

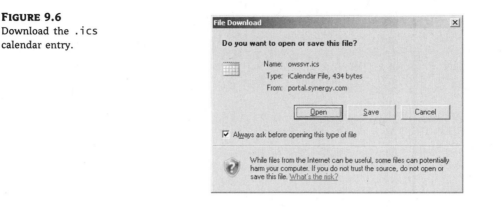

The item will then show up within Outlook. At this point, you must save it; once you do, it will be stored in your personal calendar.

 **Real World Scenario**

MANAGING TIME ZONES

Company XYZ has two offices, one in New York City and one in San Francisco. Despite the separation, many projects get executed by staff in both offices. To organize documents, tasks, and scheduled events, they use SharePoint websites. However, time zones can be tricky to manage, especially with managing calendar entries.

Each SharePoint website has its own regional settings that define, among other things, the time zone in which calendar entries are displayed. By default, when working with SharePoint using the browser, all dates and times shown are based on this time zone setting defined for the website. In other words, SharePoint does not read and use the time zone from the local computer.

To help eliminate confusion, for all project websites that use resources from both offices, Company XYZ has standardized on using Eastern Standard Time (EST), the time zone for the New York office.

For the users based in San Francisco, they override these default settings and specifically tell SharePoint what their local time zone is. This allows them to view dates and times that are correct for them. To do this, they click their name (by default located in the upper-right corner) and select My Settings. From here, they click My Regional Settings and adjust the time zone.

In most cases, this works just fine for them, but what about when someone is traveling? For example, a user normally based in New York is now working out of the San Francisco office. Again, by default, SharePoint will continue to display calendar entries in New York time. This may be what makes most sense to the user but maybe not. The bottom line is that there is no right answer, and it has become an important training issue in the company.

Fortunately, when linking the SharePoint calendar into Outlook, everything is displayed properly. This is because Outlook is able to translate all entries into the local time zone of the computer, something the browser cannot do. Company XYZ has found that using Outlook this way is the best strategy to solve this time zone problem.

Creating a Meeting Workspace

Related to calendar integration, Outlook also has the ability to create a SharePoint meeting workspace site when creating a meeting request. This makes it easy for a team to centralize agenda files, tasks, meeting attendees, and other details. This option appears as a button on the Outlook ribbon when you create a meeting request, as shown in Figure 9.7.

FIGURE 9.7
Creating a meeting workspace

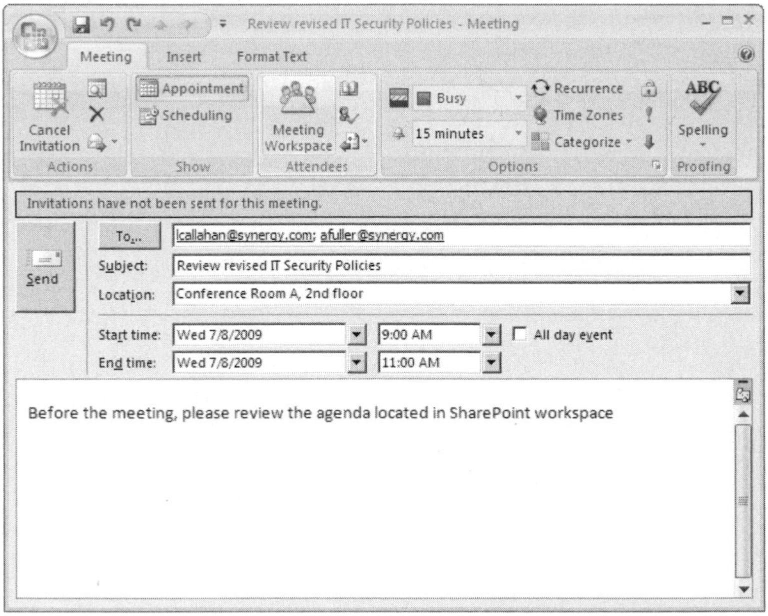

After you click the Meeting Workspace button, a new area will appear on the right side of the meeting request. The first time you create a workspace this way, you will need to provide the URL to the parent website where you want the workspace created. You specify this by first clicking the Change Settings link and then clicking in the Select A Location drop-down list and choosing Other. You should be presented with an interface that looks like Figure 9.8.

FIGURE 9.8
Specifying the parent URL

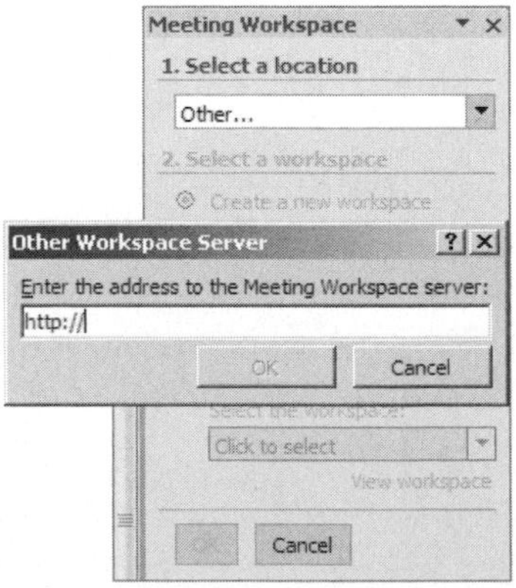

For you to create a SharePoint meeting workspace from Outlook, you must have the Manage Hierarchy or Full Control permission in the parent site. If you do not have permissions, Outlook will let you know.

If the URL is valid and you have permissions to create a new website at this location, you are then asked for the new site's language and template. Windows SharePoint Services and Microsoft Office SharePoint Server both support five different templates for meetings. After you choose the desired template, click OK. Outlook will not only create the new site, but will also automatically grant site permissions to each meeting recipient that it recognizes. It will also store each recipient in an attendee list that you can see in the workspace site. In addition, it will put the URL of the workspace site in the body of your email message so all meeting attendees can find the new site. Figure 9.9 shows how it looks just after creation.

FIGURE 9.9

The newly created meeting workspace

At this point, the workspace site is ready for you to populate with agenda items and other meeting artifacts. In case you're wondering, if you make any changes to the meeting request, such as adding additional attendees or changing the scheduled date, it will also update these changes inside the workspace.

The title of the new site is based on the subject in the meeting request. Thus, it's best to set meeting request details first and then create the workspace. If you do not have a subject, Outlook will tell SharePoint to create the workspace as "untitled." If you'd like, you can always rename it inside SharePoint from the Site Settings screen (off the Site Actions menu).

You can also link to an existing SharePoint workspace site when creating a meeting. This is useful if you schedule several separate but related meetings and don't want to create and maintain multiple workspace sites. To do this, just click the Link To An Existing Workspace radio button and select an existing website in the drop-down list.

One final point: if you delete a meeting workspace site in SharePoint, Outlook cannot correct this and will link to a nonexistent site. This is not a big problem, but it may be confusing for users. Likewise, if you delete or cancel a meeting request, Outlook will not automatically delete the SharePoint site. In cases where you want to reschedule the meeting, it's best to just update the original meeting request rather than deleting it and creating a new one. If you really want to delete the meeting, it's best to delete the meeting request and then also delete the workspace site.

Contact Integration

SharePoint includes a built-in list template that allows you to create and manage contacts within a website. Columns that are part of this list are all the expected ones, such as First Name, Last Name, Email Address, Company, and Notes. In general, these are the same columns that you find for a contact record within Outlook.

There are many advantages to having SharePoint manage contacts. Having a centrally stored set of contacts for a department or a team site saves staff from having to maintain individual contact lists. Since the list is stored in SharePoint, as opposed to a contact entry within Active Directory, users can easily add, update, and remove contacts as needed. It's also much easier to store separate contact lists with only those contact records that are relevant. For example, you may want to store a single set of contacts that are relevant to a project and keep these separate from other contact lists.

Of course, storing the list in SharePoint offers all the SharePoint list benefits, such as versioning, item-level security, and creating multiple views (such as showing all contacts grouped by a region). Figure 9.10 shows how a populated contact list looks inside SharePoint.

FIGURE 9.10
SharePoint contact list

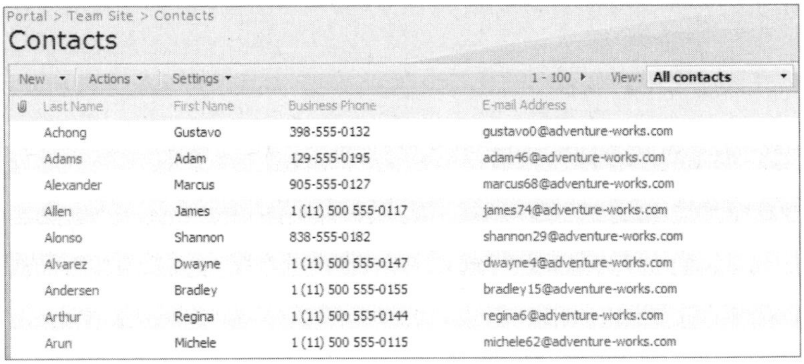

As with all lists and libraries, you use the Action menu in SharePoint to connect to a contact list. After confirming the connection in Outlook, the contact list will be created and cached inside your SharePoint Lists.pst file. You can find it along with your other contact lists when you click the Contacts link in the navigation pane.

Since this appears in Outlook as just another contact list, you have all the benefits of a regular contact list. For example, you can quickly copy or move entries between contact lists, contacts can be searched, and you can customize how you want to view the contacts in Outlook.

Another key benefit is that the contact list by default is marked as an Outlook address book. This allows you to easily send an email to a contact by simply using the contact's name. The name should resolve to the contact's email address. If you want to turn off this behavior, right-click the Contact list in Outlook and choose Properties. Click the Outlook Address Book tab and clear the check box, as shown in Figure 9.11.

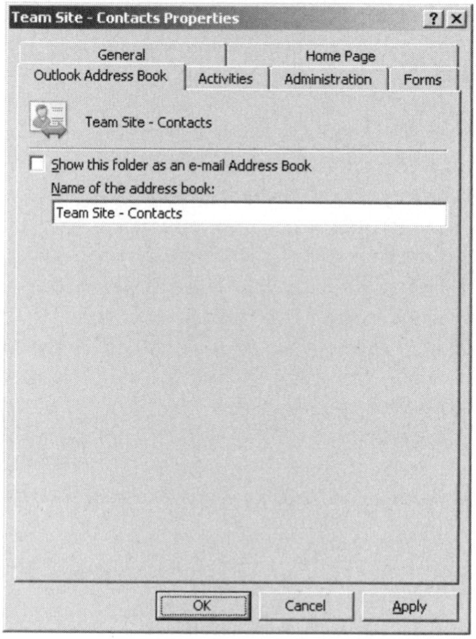

FIGURE 9.11
Disabling a contact list as an Outlook address book

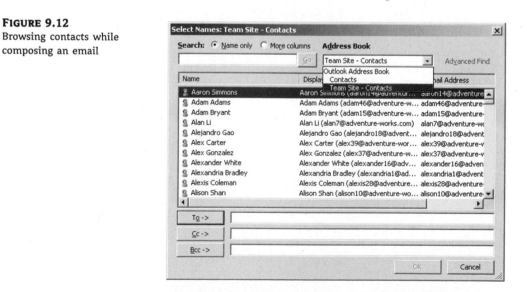

A related feature is to search or browse contacts from a single list. For example, suppose you are composing a new message and can't recall the name of a contact. If you click the To button in the New Message dialog, you can select the desired contact list in the Address Book drop-down and just scroll through the list of names, as shown in Figure 9.12.

FIGURE 9.12
Browsing contacts while composing an email

Task Integration

Tasks play an important role in SharePoint and can be used in a variety of ways. Tasks help project teams and business units centrally manage to-do items. They help ensure these items do not fall through the cracks, increasing accountability. Since they can be centrally managed and are visible within SharePoint, they also provide interested parties with an easy status update. The goal here is to decrease the number inquiries such as "What is the status of your TPS report?"

SharePoint tasks are also the fundamental way that SharePoint-based workflow tells someone to perform some action. For example, if I submit an expense report to a SharePoint document library that has a workflow associated with it, my manager can automatically be assigned a task informing him to review and (hopefully) approve it. After manager approval, a new task can be assigned to someone in the accounting department to cut a check.

One drawback to SharePoint tasks is that they may be scattered across numerous lists in various websites. This makes it difficult for a user to have a single view of all tasks they may have. This is one area where Outlook can assist, as we will see shortly.

As with other SharePoint lists we have discussed, you can also connect to a SharePoint task list from Outlook. This allows you to view, create, edit, and delete tasks right from the comfort of your favorite client.

Let's first look at how a series of tasks looks in a SharePoint list. In Figure 9.13 we have created a series of tasks for a server consolidation project.

FIGURE 9.13
SharePoint tasks

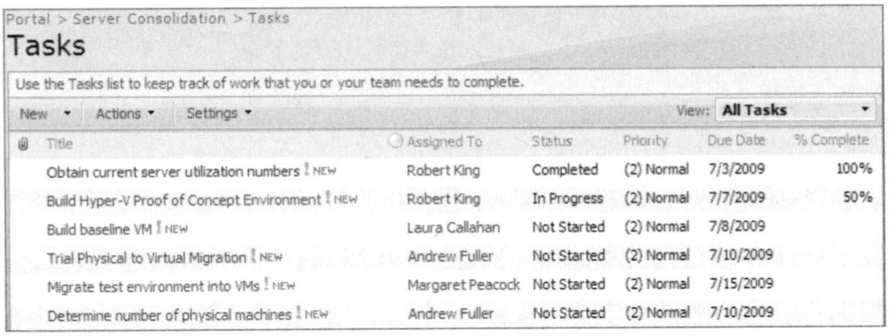

SharePoint also supports certain project management-like views. For example, you may want to represent these tasks in a familiar Gantt chart to get a sense of the project schedule (Figure 9.14).

FIGURE 9.14
SharePoint tasks in Gantt view

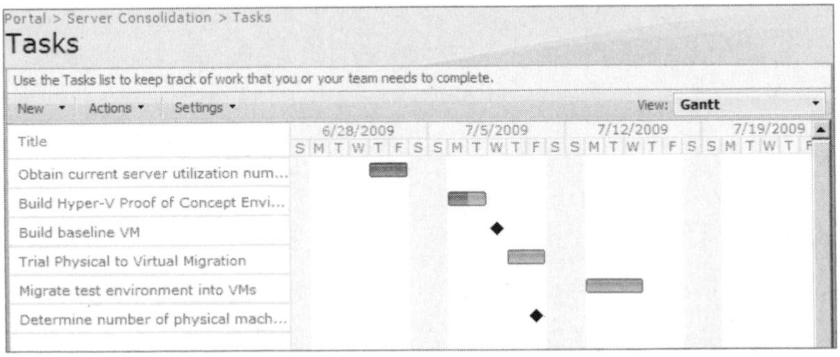

As you can see, this is a great way to get a project-level view of the current status. Of course, you can drill into each task to get a more detailed understanding.

Now that you grasp the basics of SharePoint tasks, let's look at how Outlook can augment their value. As before, we connect to the list from Outlook by selecting the Connect To Outlook option in the SharePoint Actions menu. After confirming the connection within Outlook, you should be greeted with the initial view shown in Figure 9.15.

From here you can change this to any of the out-of-the-box or custom views that Outlook supports. You'll see these listed in the navigation pane on the left in Figure 9.15. Note that these views are unique to Outlook and separate from any SharePoint views (such as the Gantt view) that may exist.

FIGURE 9.15
Viewing SharePoint tasks in Outlook

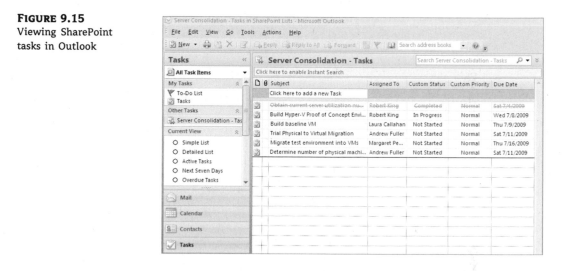

Of course, you can connect to multiple task lists, and you may want to do this as you'll probably have a number of tasks assigned to you from different lists in different SharePoint websites. As mentioned earlier, this is where Outlook really shines in that you can have a consolidated view of all your tasks in one area. To demonstrate, we have connected Outlook to two separate SharePoint task lists. In addition, we have created a couple of tasks in our personal task list. When we click on the To-Do List in the Outlook navigation pane, we see all tasks that have been assigned to us. One such view can be seen in Figure 9.16.

FIGURE 9.16
Showing all tasks using To-Do view

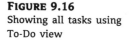

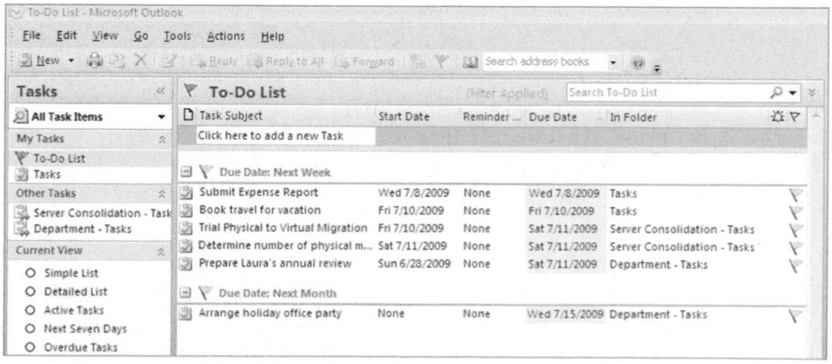

As you can see, the origin of the task is shown in the In Folder column, easily allowing you to sort and organize all your task items. When you complete a task and would like to cross it off your list, you can simply click the flag icon that is shown on the right edge of a task. If you do this from your To-Do List, it immediately drops out of sight since it's no longer active. To view or edit the task again, click on the originating task list to see it. When viewing tasks for a list, the completed tasks are displayed with the strikethrough text, as shown in the first task in Figure 9.15 earlier.

Some tasks may be worked on gradually, so it's common to just open up the task and update any particular task field as needed. Figure 9.17 shows how a single task appears if opened in Outlook.

Saving the task will then synchronize changes you made with the task stored in SharePoint. In Figure 9.17, you'll notice that you can also set a reminder for this task. As with meeting reminders, reminders are not saved in SharePoint. This feature still provides a useful way to set personal reminders for those more critical tasks.

FIGURE 9.17
Editing a task's
properties in Outlook

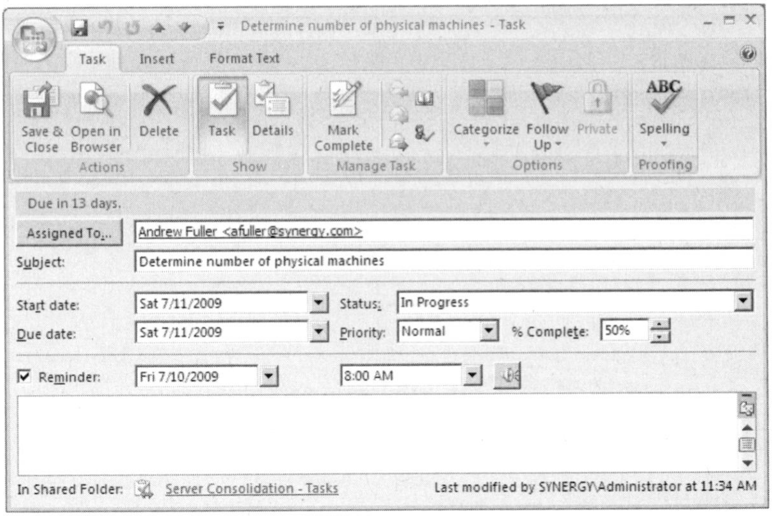

Alert Integration

A SharePoint alert is a notification that will send you an email when some type of change occurs within a SharePoint list or library. This is quite helpful when you consider the vast amount of information that SharePoint can amass. Unless you check regularly, you have no way of knowing that tasks were marked as complete, or that a new project document was just uploaded into a library.

Users can create alerts on individual lists or libraries, such as a tasks list or a document library. The alert can be created by selecting the Alert Me option in the Actions menu of a list or library, as shown in Figure 9.18.

From here, you are presented with a new screen where you have the option of defining the criteria that determines what triggers alert messages to you. The available criteria will vary depending on what list type the alert is based on. Figure 9.19 shows the settings when you add an alert on a tasks list.

Portal > Server Consolidation > Tasks
Tasks
Use the Tasks list to keep track of work that you or your team needs to complete.
New
Actions
Settings
Title
Obtain
Build H
Build b
Trial P
Migrat
Detern
Edit in Datasheet
Bulk edit items using a datasheet format.
Connect to Outlook
Synchronize items and make them available offline.
Export to Spreadsheet
Analyze items with a spreadsheet application.
Open with Access
Works with items in a Microsoft Office Access database.
View RSS Feed
Syndicate items with an RSS reader.
Alert Me
Receive e-mail notifications when items change.

FIGURE 9.18
Creating an alert on a tasks list

Alert Title
Enter the title for this alert. This is included in the subject of the e-mail notification sent for this alert.
Tasks
Send Alerts To
This alert will be sent to the e-mail address indicated.
E-mail address:
lcallahan@synergy.com
Change Type
Specify the type of changes that you want to be alerted to.
Only send me alerts when:
All changes
New items are added
Existing items are modified
Items are deleted
Send Alerts for These Changes
Specify whether to filter alerts based on specific criteria. You may also restrict your alerts to only include items that show in a particular view.
Send me an alert when:
Anything changes
A task is assigned to me
A task becomes complete
A high priority task changes
Someone else changes a task assigned to me
Someone else changes a task
Someone else changes a task created by me
Someone else changes a task last modified by me
Someone changes an item that appears in the following view:
My Tasks

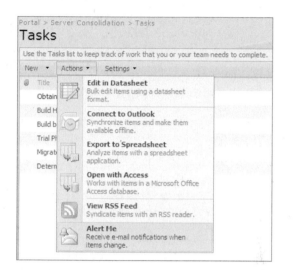

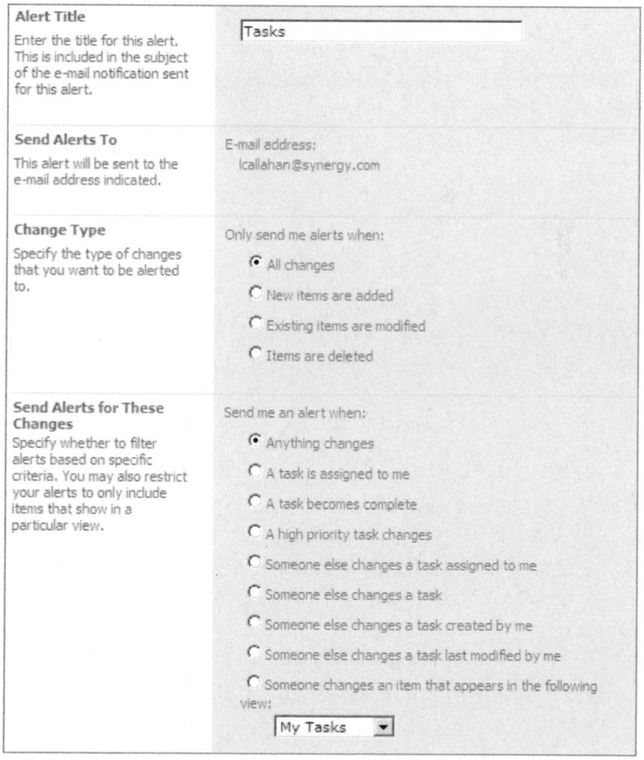

FIGURE 9.19
Defining alert criteria

In addition to the criteria, you can specify the desired frequency when creating an alert. For some alerts you might want to be notified immediately, whereas for others a daily or weekly summary is more suitable. For users who have the Manage Hierarchy or Full Control permission in a website, you can create alerts for other users as well. You will see this option when you create a new alert.

For each alert you create, you will receive a single registration-like email that provides you with the address of the website and the list on which the alert was created. However, SharePoint does not offer a single view that lets you see all the alerts you have across a multitude of websites. This is where Outlook can help.

Outlook is able to provide a consolidated view of all your SharePoint alerts. It also offers an easy way to delete alerts. You can access this from Outlook by selecting Tools ➤ Rules And Alerts, and clicking the Manage Alerts tab. The initial screen will look like Figure 9.20.

Since your existing alerts may be scattered among dozens of lists in various SharePoint websites, Outlook is not able to automatically find them all. What you must do is provide Outlook with the address of each website where you have alerts configured. From here, it will allow you to edit, delete, or add new ones.

To create a website address for Outlook, you must select the New Alert toolbar button shown in Figure 9.20. Even though you may not want to create a new alert, this is the only screen where you can enter a website address. After you click New Alert, you are presented with the dialog shown in Figure 9.21.

FIGURE 9.20
Managing SharePoint alerts

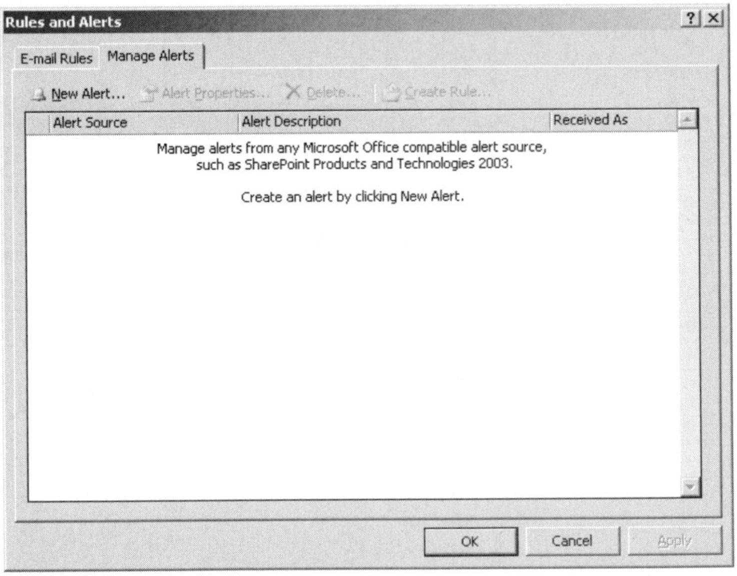

Enter the website address and click Open. At this time, a SharePoint browser window will open, prompting you to create a new alert. If you intend on creating an alert at this time, choose a list or library and click Next. If you only want Outlook to find all the existing alerts on this website, you can just close the browser window. In my case, we have added the address of three separate SharePoint websites (Document Center, SharePoint Consolidation, and Team Site). Outlook is now able to find all the alerts that have been configured (Figure 9.22).

FIGURE 9.21
Adding a website URL for a new alert

FIGURE 9.22
Active SharePoint alerts

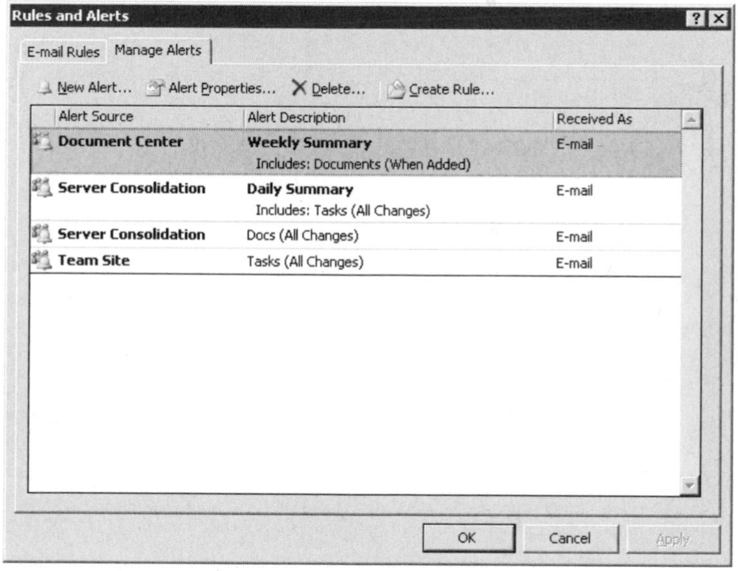

SYNCHING WITH SHAREPOINT

For Outlook to pull down all your alerts, you must either wait for the next re-sync or force it to sync immediately by pressing F9. This hot key will synchronize all your connected lists and libraries.

Once Outlook finds all your alerts, you can edit them. However, editing an alert simply takes you to the SharePoint web page, so you cannot edit them offline or directly in Outlook.

Creating an alert works the same, so you must also do it through SharePoint. Deleting an alert is a bit more seamless. When you delete it from Outlook, it will automatically delete it in Share-Point for you.

Document Library Integration

While Outlook works best when working with lists, there are some benefits to connecting Outlook to a document library. Document libraries allow users to store files (Word, Excel, PDF, etc.) in SharePoint. As with lists, libraries support check-in, check-out, versioning, and security controls. In addition to just storing a file, libraries also allow metadata to be attached to it. This then yields greater organization, classification, and searching for the files stored.

Figure 9.23 shows a SharePoint document library that has been populated with a number of documents, along with some corresponding metadata.

FIGURE 9.23
SharePoint document library

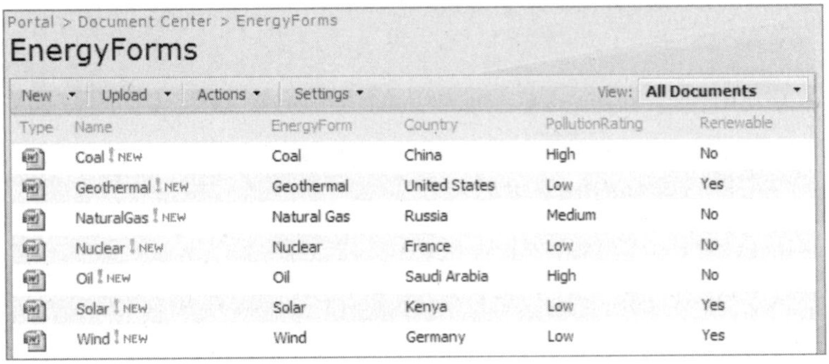

You connect a document library into SharePoint the same way as with all the lists we have covered. This is how the same document library is displayed after being connected to Outlook (Figure 9.24).

FIGURE 9.24
Document library connected to Outlook

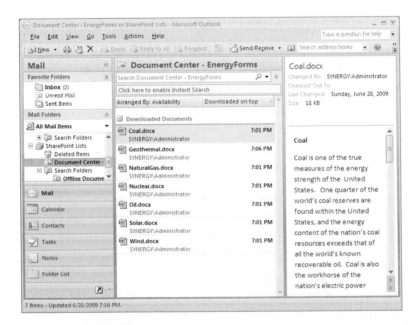

If you are using folders in your connected document library, these will also be shown within Outlook. You'll also notice that you have a preview pane on the right for easily reading many Office file formats, including pictures. Document libraries that are connected from Outlook can be found in your SharePoint Lists container. By default, this is located underneath your mail folders in the navigation pane.

All the documents in the library are automatically downloaded and stored in your `SharePoint Lists.pst` file. This may be good or bad. It's convenient since all content is now available in an offline state; however, for large libraries, the total size of the content may take a long time to download and will cause the PST file to balloon in size. In general, you don't want to be connecting to large document libraries this way.

After downloading all content in the library, you have the option of removing offline copies of large files, which would help decrease the size of your PST file. To do this, just right-click any document in Outlook and select Remove Offline Copy. Figure 9.25 shows how the list looks after performing this task on two files.

FIGURE 9.25
Documents taken offline

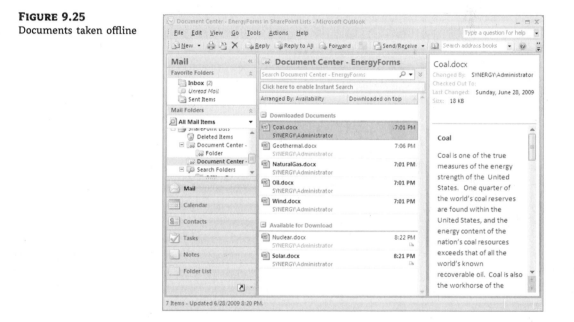

You do have the ability to edit downloaded files, but Outlook will neither check out nor check in the file for you. If you open a document from Outlook, it will store a separate editable copy in your SharePoint Drafts folder (inside your My Documents folder). To update the file back on the server, you must open the document again while online. Only then will the file be uploaded to SharePoint.

USING MICROSOFT GROOVE

If you are in need of a more complete offline solution for managing your document libraries, consider using Microsoft Office Groove. It is much better at synching document libraries and allows you to automatically upload all documents back into SharePoint in one operation.

Outlook 2003 Integration

As you might expect, Outlook 2003 does not deliver the same number of features as you have with Outlook 2007. The primary difference with Outlook 2003 is that your connected lists are entirely read-only. That is, you only have a one-way sync from SharePoint into Outlook.

The other major difference is that Outlook 2003 does not allow you to connect to the variety of list and library types. Unfortunately, you are limited to calendars and contacts only.

With these and other limitations in other Office applications, organizations that are investing in SharePoint are strongly encouraged to upgrade their Office clients to the newer release.

Email Integration

SharePoint relies on outgoing email messages as the primary notification method to SharePoint users. SharePoint also allows you to send email to lists or libraries. Both Windows Share-Point Services and Microsoft Office SharePoint Server support these outgoing and incoming messages.

In this section, you'll learn how to configure SharePoint to enable outgoing and incoming email.

Configuring Outgoing Email

SharePoint sends email messages for a number of reasons. One is for the alert engine with SharePoint. For example, if a user is assigned a new task, they will automatically receive a new message. Related to this, users can also create an alert that allows them to be notified when an item in a list or library has changed. We covered how to do this using Outlook in the previous section.

SharePoint also sends out other notifications from time to time. These may go to SharePoint administrators informing them that a user is requesting access to a particular website. Another common example is when a quota warning in a site collection has been exceeded. Users can also receive an email notification if they have been granted access to a website.

Configuring the SharePoint portion of outgoing email is fairly simple and can be done using Central Administration. When configuring outgoing email settings, you have the option of configuring it for all SharePoint web applications or individual ones. To configure outgoing email for all web applications, first click the Operations tab, and then select the Outgoing Email Settings link in the Topology and Services category. To configure a single web application, click the Application Management tab, and then select Web Application Outgoing Email settings. In either case, the settings screen will look like Figure 9.26.

As you can see, the settings are straightforward. For Outbound SMTP Server, you can specify an IP address or any name that can be resolved to an IP address. For the email to be encoded in a different language, you can adjust the character set, and this is one reason why you might want different settings per web application.

To list all the SMTP servers that you are using for outgoing email, you can select the Operations tab and choose Servers In Farm. On the resulting screen, you'll see all the servers in your farm and their services. Among the list, you'll see each server that you have configured as an outgoing email server.

SHAREPOINT FARM

Within SharePoint, the term "farm" is used frequently and has a specific meaning. A farm consists of all the SharePoint servers that share a single configuration database stored in SQL Server. Servers in the farm communicate with each other using this configuration database.

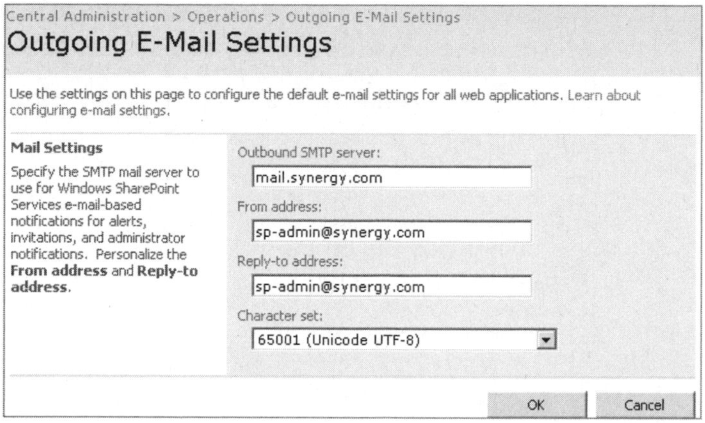

FIGURE 9.26
Configuring outgoing email

While these settings look easy to configure, there are some important implications you should be aware of. First, since you can specify only one SMTP server per web application, you may have a single point of failure in delivering email. That is, if the SMTP server is down or if SharePoint cannot deliver to TCP port 25 for any reason (for example, a firewall is blocking), all outgoing mail for this web application will fail. If email delivery is critical, consider a load balancer for your SMTP services.

Another consideration is that SharePoint does not have the ability to authenticate to the SMTP server. This means the SMTP server must allow anonymous connections. Assuming that SharePoint is pointing to an Exchange server for mail delivery, the best solution is to create a new connector in Exchange that allows anonymous connections. The new connector should then be configured to only accept connections from the SharePoint web servers.

If your security policy does not permit you to configure your existing Exchange server to allow anonymous connections, there is a workaround. On one of your SharePoint web servers, you can install and use the SMTP service that is part of IIS. You configure your outgoing email settings to deliver to this server, and this server would then authenticate to your Exchange server and forward the messages.

One final item is that you must ensure that your Exchange server (or designated SMTP server) allows relaying from your SharePoint web servers. Since a message may originate from any web server in your SharePoint farm, you must ensure that all these hosts are marked as valid.

Configuring Incoming Email

SharePoint's incoming email delivery is a convenient way to send a message and its attachments to a list or library. This email could originate from within the organization or outside it. Let's look at a few examples of how you can use this feature.

A Human Resources department would like to have all resumes that are emailed to the company be automatically stored in a Resumes document library. (An added bonus is that you can also start a workflow when a new resume is received!)

SharePoint has a list type called a discussion board that allows you to have threaded discussions. However, most teams just use email since it's so much easier and faster. The drawback with this is trying to organize and track all the emails in a thread. Having an email message automatically stored in a discussion board gives you the best of both worlds.

When you send a meeting request from Outlook, you can include a SharePoint calendar as one of the attendees. When SharePoint receives the message, it will nicely store it as a new calendar entry, ensuring that your Outlook and SharePoint calendars are consistent.

Archiving email is a challenge in many organizations. Using a document policy in Share-Point, you can define and apply retention rules to items in a list or library. This policy can then archive the items in a records management system. By simply including the document library as a recipient in an email message, you ensure that SharePoint will store and manage the message as a record.

Now that you have an idea of the value of having SharePoint receive incoming messages, let's look at how this works at a high level. When Exchange receives a message intended for SharePoint, a send connector forwards it to a SMTP service running on a SharePoint web server. From here, SharePoint matches it up to the corresponding list or library and creates a new item for it.

Configuring incoming email is a four-step process:

1. Enable incoming email in SharePoint.

2. Install the SMTP service on one of the SharePoint web servers.

3. Configure Exchange to forward messages to SharePoint.

4. Specify which lists and libraries will be email enabled.

To enable incoming email in SharePoint, select the Operations tab and click Incoming Email Settings. You will then be prompted with the screen shown in Figure 9.27.

FIGURE 9.27
Configuring incoming email

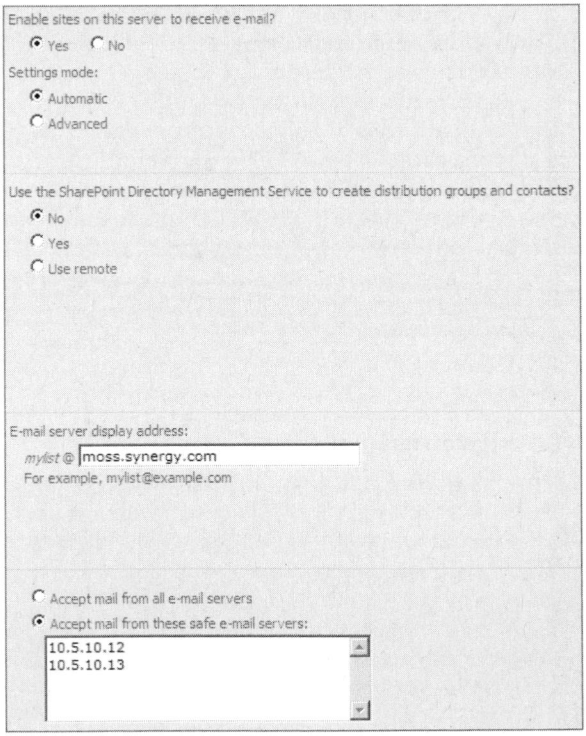

ARE YOU AN ADMINISTRATOR?

To configure incoming email, you must be logged in using an account that is a member of the local administrators group on the SharePoint server hosting the central administration website. If you do not see this link on the Operations tab, this is the most likely reason.

On this screen, you have several options. In most cases, you'll want to use Automatic settings, which means that SharePoint will work with an SMTP service.

Directory Management Service is not required for basic incoming email, so you can set this option to No if you prefer. This will be covered in more detail later.

You then specify what the fully qualified domain name should be. We recommend that you prefix a subdomain name to your current domain. For example, if your domain is synergy.com, use moss.synergy.com. There are two primary reasons for this:

◆ In the event you have multiple SharePoint farms and want to keep each with separate settings

◆ To simplify the routing of the message from Exchange to SharePoint

The final setting allows you to define safe email servers. The purpose of this is to set designated SMTP servers (in this case Exchange) that are able to route to SharePoint. This helps ensure that spam or other rogue messages cannot be delivered into SharePoint. This section requires one or more IP addresses, and you should specify the Exchange server(s) that are able to forward mail to SharePoint.

The second step is to install the SMTP service on at least one your SharePoint web servers. If you have multiple web servers using network load balancing for your web applications, you can load-balance the SMTP service as well. For each server where you have installed the service, make sure you create an SMTP domain that matches the fully qualified domain name that SharePoint will be using (for example, moss.synergy.com). In most cases, you can just edit the Local (Default) domain entry that's created for you.

The third step is to configure Exchange to forward messages on to SharePoint. This is where we use a send connector. The send connector is responsible for identifying those messages that are destined for SharePoint and forwarding them to a designated SMTP server. Here is how to set it up:

1. In Exchange Management Console, expand through Organization Configuration and select Hub Transport.

2. In the Actions pane, click New Send Connector. This will launch a wizard.

3. Give the connector an appropriate name — for example, **SharePoint**.

4. For Address Space, click Add. In the dialog box, enter in the fully qualified domain name that you configured for SharePoint — for example, **moss.synergy.com**.

5. For Network Settings, select Route Mail Through The Following Smart Hosts and click Add. Enter either the IP address or a resolvable fully qualified domain name that directs Exchange to SharePoint's SMTP server.

6. For Smart Host Authentication, accept the default of None.

7. For Source Server, ensure that your Exchange server name is listed.

The final settings should resemble the summary screen shown in Figure 9.28.

FIGURE 9.28
Exchange send
connector summary

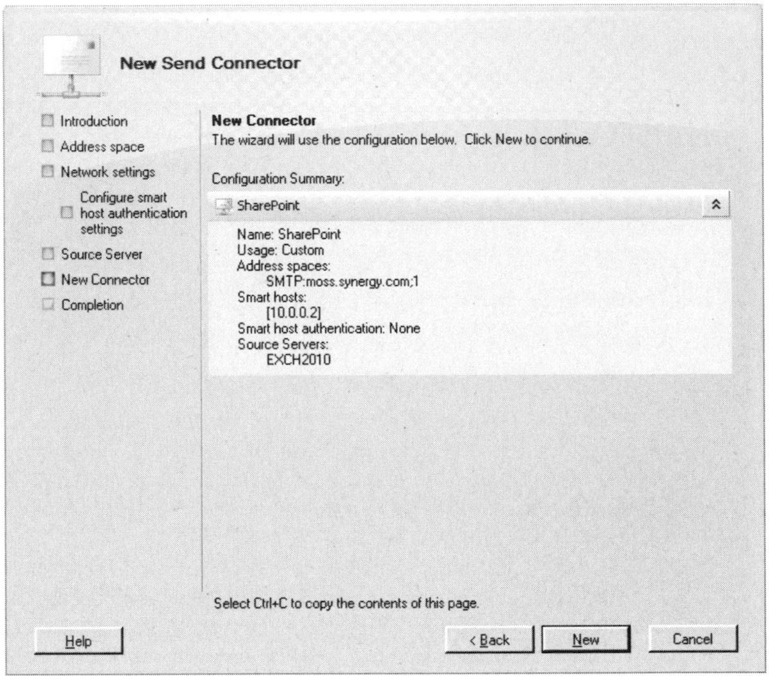

CREATING MX RECORDS

When delivering email to SharePoint, you can also create a new MX record in your DNS server. The record would point to the SharePoint SMTP server. The result is that all email would now go directly to SharePoint, bypassing Exchange. While this may sound easier, doing this would cause you to lose all the great Exchange benefits, such as spam filtering, antivirus protection, and logging. Thus, it is best to have Exchange be the routing agent for all email.

The fourth and final step is to define which list or libraries are configured to receive incoming mail. You set this by going to the list or library settings from the Settings menu, as shown in Figure 9.29.

On the Settings screen, click the Incoming Email Settings link in the Communications group in the upper-right part of the screen. If you do not see this link, this means either you did not enable incoming email as shown earlier or this type of list or library does not support incoming email. Contacts, tasks, custom lists, and a few others do not support incoming email.

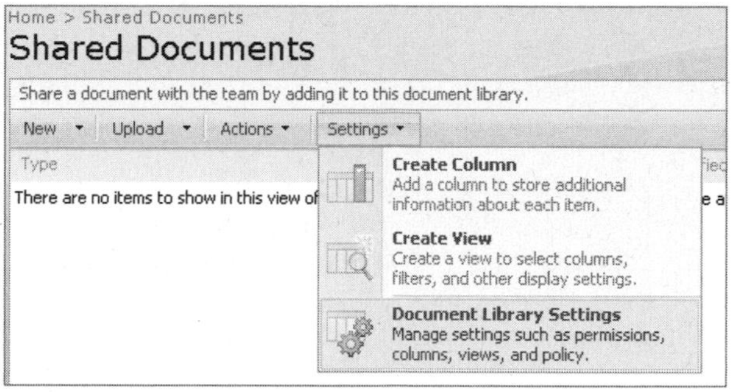

FIGURE 9.29
Document library
settings menu

Figure 9.30 shows the incoming email configuration screen for a document library.

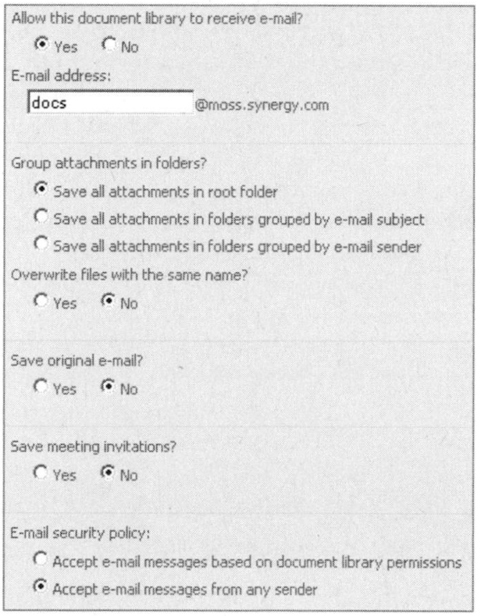

FIGURE 9.30
Incoming email settings
for a document library

You may have slightly different settings depending on the type of list or library. Let's walk through some of the settings for a document library.

The email address is where you specify the alias for this one list or library. You'll notice that it automatically adds the domain name you specified when you enabled incoming email in Central Administration.

When the message and/or attachments are stored in this list or library, you have some options. For a document library, you can store all attachments in the root folder, group them in folders based on the subject, or group them in folders by the sender. Storing attachments in the root folder works fine for small libraries but is ill-suited for heavily used ones. Grouping by subject works well, but if there is no subject specified in the email, the folder name will become a random GUID. Grouping by sender will create a folder based on the name and email address of each unique sender.

For all three choices, you can specify whether or not you want to overwrite files with the same filename. If you choose to not overwrite, and the same filename exists, a random number will be appended to the filename to make it unique.

If you save the original email, the message is stored in an `.eml` file that will be saved in the same folder as the attachment. This allows you the open the original message using Outlook Express.

In your email security policy, you can restrict access to only users who have permissions to add files to the document library. (In SharePoint, this is granted with the Contribute permission.) Restricting access this way is the default setting and SharePoint will check to see if the sender has permission. If not, the email and its attachments are not stored.

These are the basic settings to configure incoming email and have it delivered to a list or library. Let's now discuss some more advanced options using the Directory Management Service.

DIRECTORY MANAGEMENT SERVICE

Based on what we have covered already, users can send email to lists or libraries, but there is one problem: how will the users actually know or be able to find the email address for an emailed enabled list or library? Of course, you can just provide it to them, but a better solution might be to add it as a mail-enabled contact within Active Directory. This would allow it to appear in the Global Address List (GAL), which should enable users to find it much easier.

Of course, you can always manually add contacts directly through Exchange, and for a small number of lists or libraries, this is the best choice. However, if you have a large number and don't want to be burdened with having to create new contacts, an automated option is available: the Directory Management Service.

With Directory Management Service enabled, when a list or library is enabled for incoming email, SharePoint will automatically create a mail-enabled contact for you. Figure 9.31 shows the configuration options when you enable this service.

The first text box asks you for the organizational unit (OU) in Active Directory. This becomes the container for these newly created contacts. As shown in Figure 9.31, we're using an OU named SharePoint. To keep your SharePoint contacts separate, do not use a container that is used for non-SharePoint contacts or user accounts.

FIGURE 9.31
Configuring Directory
Management Service

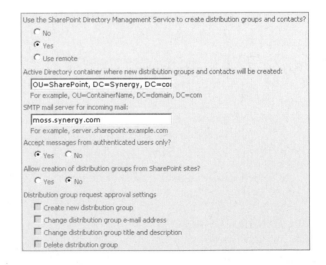

For SMTP server, just enter the fully qualified domain name for the SharePoint SMTP server.

In addition to creating contacts, Directory Management Service can also create and synchronize distribution groups in Active Directory. This would allow you to keep SharePoint group membership and distribution group membership consistent. Note that these groups in Active Directory are not automatically created and must still be individually approved by a SharePoint farm administrator.

With these settings in place, when a user specifies that a new list or library is to be email enabled, SharePoint will create the contact in Active Directory. Before this works, there is one additional configuration step that must be done. The Windows account that creates the contact is the identity account that is running the Central Administration v3 application pool. This account must be granted read, write, and create permissions to this OU in Active Directory.

To identify the proper account, start IIS Manager on the web server that is running the Central Administration website. Expand down through the server name and click Application Pools. In the list of application pools, select the one named SharePoint Central Administration v3. In the Actions pane, select Advanced Settings. You will be presented with a Settings dialog like the one shown in Figure 9.32.

FIGURE 9.32
Retrieving Application
Pool identity

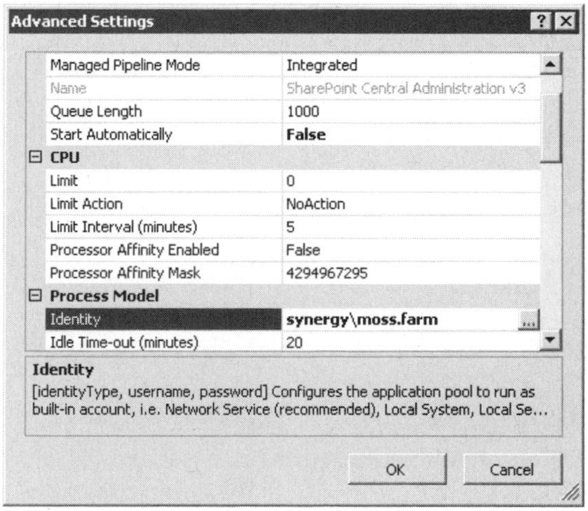

The account is the one listed next to Identity. Note that these steps are for Windows Server 2008. If you're running Windows Server 2003, the steps are similar.

With the account known, you can finally delegate (or grant) permissions to it within Active Directory. To do this, start Active Directory Users and Computers. If the OU container that you specified earlier has not been created, create it now. Then, right-click the container and select Delegate Control from the context menu. A wizard should start.

◆ For Users And Groups, enter the account name.

◆ For Tasks To Delegate, select Create A Custom Task To Delegate.

◆ For Active Directory Object Type, accept the default setting.

For Permissions, check Read, Write, and Create All Child Objects. The screen should look like the one shown in Figure 9.33.

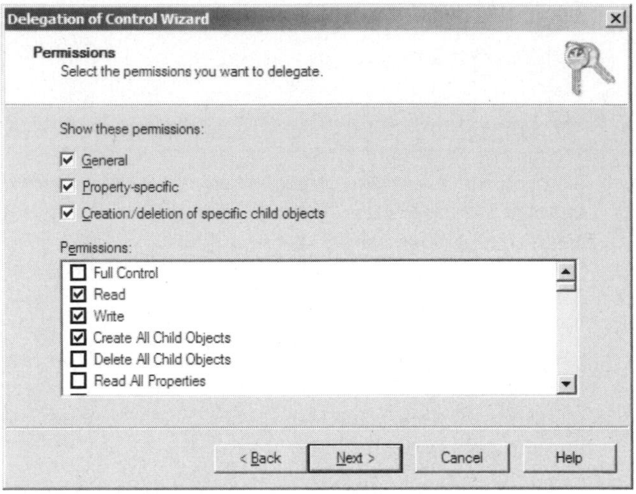

FIGURE 9.33
Delegating AD permissions for SharePoint

CONCERNS WITH DIRECTORY MANAGEMENT SERVICE

There is a drawback to Directory Management Service that you should be aware of. In most cases, it will be your end-users who are probably configuring their lists and libraries to be email enabled, and they can specify any name they want. With Directory Management Service enabled, this name will automatically be published as a contact and be visible by everyone in the organization. Whether unintentional or malicious, this may be an unsuitable name. You must weigh the risks here and determine whether you want complete control over the names that are published.

TROUBLESHOOTING INCOMING EMAIL

As you can see, configuring incoming email can be complex. Here are a few troubleshooting tips that may help you solve why incoming mail is not working properly.

◆ To identify whether the problem is with SharePoint or Exchange, take a look at the SMTP service's drop folder (by default, `C:\Inetpub\mailroot\Drop`) on the SharePoint web server. If you see files in here, Exchange routing is working properly, and the problem is most likely with SharePoint.

◆ The program that picks up and processes the messages from this Drop folder is the Windows SharePoint Services Timer service. This is a regular Windows service and should be running under the same account that is the identity for the Central Administration application pool. This account will need the Modify NTFS permission to the Drop folder to ensure that it can read and then delete these files.

◆ Enable logging for the SharePoint SMTP Service.
Review the SharePoint logs. By default, these are stored here:

```
C:\Program Files\Common Files\Microsoft Shared\web server extensions\12\LOGS
```

Indexing Exchange Public Folders

One of the major strengths of SharePoint is its ability to index (or crawl) a variety of content sources. This index can then be searched using keywords, enabling users to find the information they seek wherever it lives.

When it comes to search, the capabilities will vary depending on whether you are running Windows SharePoint Services or Microsoft Office SharePoint Server. With Windows Share-Point Services, only content stored within SharePoint (for example, lists and libraries) can be searched. With Microsoft Office SharePoint Server, searched content can include additional content sources such as file shares, regular websites, and Exchange Public Folders, which is the area of focus for this section. This section assumes you are using Microsoft Office SharePoint Server 2007.

USING MICROSOFT SEARCH SERVER 2008

Search Server 2008 integrates with SharePoint, and it supports the ability to search Exchange Public Folders. One advantage is that you can enhance the Windows SharePoint Services search engine without having to upgrade to Microsoft Office SharePoint Server. There is also an Express edition of Search Server 2008 that supports this at no additional licensing cost.

Configuring search in Microsoft Office SharePoint Server is done through a designated Shared Services Provider (SSP). To access your SSP, click on the SSP name in the left-hand navigation menu in Central Administration. Inside the SSP, click the Search Settings link, which you'll find in the Search category.

It is important to note that crawling public folders from SharePoint is not supported in a native Exchange 2010 environment due to the lack of WebDAV support. Organizations wishing to use this feature must keep an Exchange 2003 or 2007 server in their environment that houses the public folder store. If you use Exchange 2007, at least Service Pack 1 (SP1) must be applied. Also, you must ensure that you have applied at least SP1 for your SharePoint farm.

Defining a Content Source

The first step in indexing Exchange Public folders is to create a content source. Each content source defines a certain type of content, such as Exchange Public Folders, SharePoint Sites, and so forth. You can have multiple content sources of the same type. To create a content source, click the Content Sources And Crawl Schedules link on the Configure Search Settings screen.

On this screen, the current content sources will be listed. Click the New Content Source button to create a new one. On the Add Content Source screen, choose Exchange Public Folders. SharePoint crawls public folders via their web address using the `http://<exchangeserver>/public/<folderpath>` syntax. Enter one or more addresses that you want to include in this content source. You'll notice that you can specify whether you want to recursively crawl this folder and all subfolders or just the folder itself.

You can also specify a full and incremental crawl schedule. As you would guess, a full crawl must be completed before incremental crawls can run. The crawl schedule is configured a little differently than other scheduling systems you may have worked with. Figure 9.34 shows what the schedule interface looks like.

The Repeat Within The Day setting at the bottom allows you to repeat the schedule throughout the day. When setting this option, you'll need to do a little math to calculate the ending time. Based on the settings shown in Figure 9.34, the schedule will repeat every hour between 6:00 a.m. and 6:00 p.m. Due to the strain this places on both Exchange and SharePoint, carefully plan your crawl schedules.

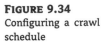

FIGURE 9.34
Configuring a crawl schedule

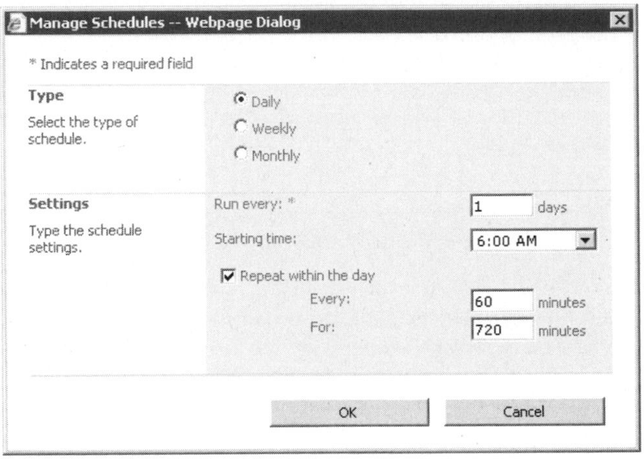

Figure 9.35 gives the full settings for an Exchange Public Folder content source.

Each content source can only have one set of crawl settings and schedules. Thus, if you need different settings based on different sections of your public folders, you should create additional Exchange Public Folder content sources.

For SharePoint to properly crawl your public folders, the crawler account must be granted Reviewer permissions to the folders it will crawl. By default, SharePoint uses a single account called the Default Content Access account when crawling all content sources. You can view and change this account by clicking the Default Content Access Account link on the Configure Search Settings screen.

Even though SharePoint has read access to all Exchange public folders, it doesn't mean that all users will. SharePoint's search engine is security trimmed, which means that it only shows results that the user has at least Reviewer permissions on. SharePoint is able to do this by also reading the folder's permissions and storing them within its index.

If you expect SharePoint to index non-Microsoft file formats, you may need to install an appropriate IFilter on your SharePoint index servers. This will apply to files found in any content source, including public folders. For PDF files, which is the most common need, you can install Adobe's free PDF IFilter (http://adobe.com/support/downloads/detail.jsp?ftpID=2611) or a third-party one from FoxIt (www.foxitsoftware.com/pdf/ifilter). If you'll be indexing a heavy amount of files, consider FoxIt as it performs much better.

CREATING A SHAREPOINT SCOPE

To help users narrow the breadth of a search, SharePoint supports the use of scopes. A scope is a set of rules that allows you to set logical boundaries around indexed content. These rules can be based on a content source, a file type (such as Excel documents), and even metadata on the content (such as Author). Without scopes, users would search everything in the index — which can result in far too many hits to be useful. One idea is to create a scope that allows users to search only Exchange public folders.

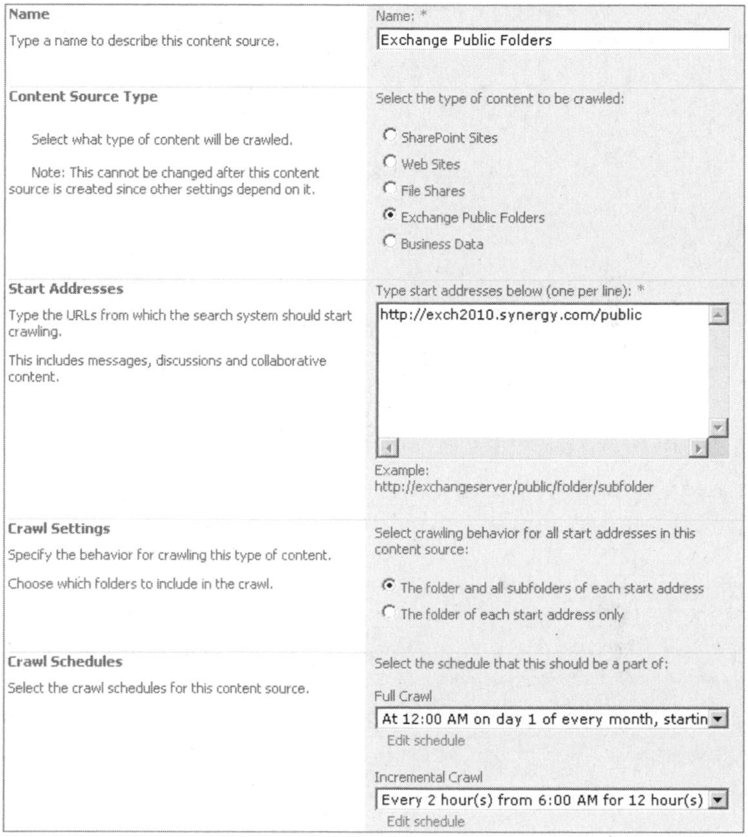

FIGURE 9.35
Configuring an Exchange Public Folder content source

The Bottom Line

Connect to SharePoint using Outlook as a client.   Outlook lets you connect to SharePoint and manage its content while either connected or offline. When using Outlook, working with SharePoint calendars, contacts, tasks, alerts, and document libraries is usually faster and more intuitive for users. You can also create new meeting workspace websites right from Outlook.

Master It   Outlook is not able to connect to all types of SharePoint lists. Name a few list types that cannot be connected.

Configure outgoing and incoming email in SharePoint.   Outgoing email from SharePoint is how SharePoint notifies users that content they are monitoring has changed in some way. It is also used to notify users that they have been granted permissions to a new area of SharePoint. Configuring it is as easy as telling SharePoint which SMTP server to use.

Incoming email allows internal or external users to email messages and documents directly to SharePoint. Configuring incoming email involves two steps: enabling incoming email in Central Administration and then enabling email on the desired lists and libraries.

> **Master It**   You are a consultant and one of your customers is an insurance company. They want to have their third-party agents email new policy contracts directly into a document library within SharePoint. The insurance company's mail routing plan is to create an MX record in their external-facing DNS server that points to the IP address of their internal SharePoint server. What are some of the advantages and disadvantages of this design?

Set up SharePoint to enable searching on an Exchange public folder.   By configuring SharePoint to crawl Exchange public folders, users can more easily find content located here. This also helps unify content regardless of where it is located. Keep in mind that your public folder store must be located on an Exchange 2003 or 2007 server. To enable searching, you need to create an Exchange Public Folder content source in SharePoint and supply the web URL to the path where you want the crawl to start.

> **Master It**   You are setting up SharePoint and Exchange to crawl public folders. How can you find the account SharePoint will use when crawling this source? Also, what minimum permission level to the public folder store will this account need?

Part 2

Getting Exchange Running

## Chapter 10

Exchange Server 2010 Quick Start Guide

Going through a Mastering book just to figure out how to get a quick installation of Exchange 2010 up and running may seem like a daunting task — especially if all you want to do is get a look at Exchange and play around. This chapter should help with that. We'll present the steps for getting a lab or test server up and running quickly.

The purpose of building a test server is to learn and optimize the installation and configuration experience. Exchange is a feature-rich application and, as such, has many different ways to configure settings for optimization, performance, and stability. Using a test server to try various scenarios provides for a better production deployment — and a better prepared administrator.

We won't cover every little detail on every setting or extensive design and best practices in this chapter. That's what the rest of this book is for. But we will discuss the requirements for getting a typical Exchange 2010 server up and running. A typical Exchange server is one that holds the three roles required in an Exchange 2010 organization: the Mailbox role, where user mailboxes reside; the Client Access role, which handles how users connect to Exchange; and the Hub Transport role, which deals with mail flow and routing. Other roles, such as Unified Messaging (voice) and Edge Transport (message hygiene), are optional roles, and outside what we'll accomplish in this chapter.

In this chapter, you will learn to:

◆ Quickly size a typical server

◆ Install the necessary Windows Server 2008 R2 prerequisites

◆ Install a multifunction Exchange Server 2010 server

◆ Configure Exchange to send and receive email

◆ Configure recipients, contacts, and distribution groups

Server Sizing Quick Reference

Although properly sizing a server for production is extremely important, sizing for a lab or test server is somewhat less involved if you're only interested in pushing some buttons and "kicking the tires" of Exchange 2010. For instance, a lab server might have enough storage for a few users, but a production server might be configured for many hundreds or thousands.

But we do have some basics that you should pay attention to when building a test server.

Hardware

In this section, we'll take a look at the hardware required to quickly setup a lab server. Among the resources we need to focus on are memory, processors, storage, Operating System, and virtualization considerations. First, let's look at memory.

MEMORY

You'll enjoy some substantial improvements when using a 64-bit server, not the least of which is better memory management, including the ability to handle much more memory. This works to your advantage with Exchange.

For an Exchange server running multiple roles such as Mailbox, Client Access, and Hub Transport, like our typical server, consider 8 GB plus 5 MB per mailbox a good starting point.

PROCESSORS

Server hardware that will host Exchange 2010 requires 64-bit processors. This includes either x64 Intel or AMD64 CPUs. Itanium IA64 processors are not supported for Exchange 2010. The minimum recommended number of processor cores for a typical Exchange server is two, and the maximum recommend number of cores is 24. For a well-performing server, use four–eight processor cores. For this configuration, two dual-core or two quad-core processors will work just fine.

DISK SPACE

Basic Exchange 2010 storage requirements include space for the Exchange binary files, message tracking logs, transaction logs, and mail databases. A typical installation requires at least the following:

- 1.2 GB available on the installation drive for binaries
- 200 MB available on the system drive (typically C:)
- 500 MB available on the installation drive for the transport queue
- Space for mailbox databases and transaction logs

Using these guidelines, two 72 GB hard drives in RAID Level 1 should suffice for a small test server. Larger hard drives can be used, but these should be considered the minimum. Hard drives must be formatted with NTFS for Exchange 2010 due to security permissions.

NETWORK

The server for Exchange should have at least one 1 GB Ethernet network interface card. Additional cards can be used but aren't required.

SERVER VIRTUALIZATION

A growing trend is to use virtualization technologies to get a higher return on investment (ROI), which allows an organization to get more out of the same hardware. Virtualization also reduces hardware server sprawl. This helps reduce power consumption, cooling needs, and so forth, and reduces the total cost of ownership (TCO). Microsoft's virtualization effort with Windows Server 2008, Hyper-V, is an excellent virtualization platform from which to deploy Exchange. With Exchange 2010, all roles of a typical Exchange server are supported in Microsoft Hyper-V. Only the Unified Messaging (UM) role is not supported in Hyper-V. Due to the 64-bit hardware requirement, Exchange Server 2010 is not supported in Microsoft Virtual Server 2005.

Microsoft supports Exchange Server 2010 in production on hardware virtualization software only when all the following conditions are true:

◆ The hardware virtualization software is running:

  ◆ Windows Server 2008 with Hyper-V technology

  ◆ Windows Server 2008 R2 with Hyper-V technology

  ◆ Microsoft Hyper-V Server 2008

  ◆ Microsoft Hyper-V Server 2008 R2

  ◆ Any third-party hypervisor that has been validated under the Windows Server Virtualization Validation Program

◆ When the Exchange Server guest virtual machine:

  ◆ Is running Microsoft Exchange Server 2010.

  ◆ Is deployed on the Windows Server 2008 Service Pack 2 (SP2) or Windows Server 2008 R2 operating system.

Virtual Storage   Virtual storage can consist of fixed virtual hard drives (VHDs), SCSI pass-through storage, or iSCSI-based storage.

VHDs cannot exceed 2 TB (2,040 GB) in Hyper-V. Dynamically expanding virtual disks are not supported. Differencing VHDs, or those that use differencing or delta mechanisms, are not supported in Exchange 2010.

SCSI pass-through storage is configured at the host level and dedicated to one virtual guest. Pass-through volumes must be presented as block-level storage to the hardware virtualization software.

When you're using iSCSI, the use of jumbo frames is not supported. Exchange Server 2010 does not support network-attached storage (NAS).

Guest Virtual Machine Storage   When you are using virtualization, the OS volume minimum is 15 GB and the memory. For example, for a guest provisioned with 16 GB of memory, a minimum volume for a virtualization-based server would be 15 GB + 16 GB = 31 GB OS volume.

Operating System

Like its predecessor Exchange 2007, Exchange 2010 requires a 64-bit operating system for installation. Operating systems that Exchange 2010 is supported on include the following:

◆ 64-bit edition of Windows Server 2008 Standard Service Pack 2

◆ 64-bit edition of Windows Server 2008 Enterprise Service Pack 2

◆ 64-bit edition of Windows Server 2008 Standard R2

◆ 64-bit edition of Windows Server 2008 Enterprise R2

Trial versions of each of these operating systems are available for download from Microsoft's website. They will provide months of use, and can be installed over and over for testing.

Although Exchange 2007 did have a 32-bit version you could use for testing and installing the Exchange management tools on your workstation, that is not the case with Exchange 2010. Exchange 2010 is only available in 64 bit. This means that any administrative workstations for Exchange will need to be 64 bit as well.

Windows Server 2008 R2 is the latest version of the Windows operating system, and includes many stability, performance, and security related updates from its predecessors. Why not use the non-R2 version of Windows Server 2008? When looking at a new mail platform, it makes sense to use the latest operating system because of all the enhancements available. Building a test server is a perfect time to get some experience with the new operating system. Additionally, it makes sense to deploy an operating system that will still be in mainstream support during the typical lifecycle of a newly deployed server. While Exchange Server 2010 is supported on Windows Server 2008, Windows Server 2008 R2 does include some of the prerequisites required for Exchange. Thus, deployment is quicker and easier.

Since we are focusing on getting an Exchange server up and running quickly in this chapter, we aren't spending time focusing on some things. In this chapter, we assume the following:

◆ The server is joined to an Active Directory domain, and the Active Directory domain is isolated from any production domains.

◆ The server has a static IP address assigned.

◆ Test Active Directory user accounts have been created.

◆ You have an administrative account that is a member of the Schema Admins, Domain Admins, and Enterprise Admins security groups.

◆ The server is not a domain controller.

◆ There are no other Exchange servers in the domain.

◆ There is a domain controller in the same Active Directory site that the Exchange server will reside in.

Based on these assumptions, we should be able to go through this chapter and build a functioning Exchange 2010 server quickly.

Configuring Windows Server 2008 R2

In this section, we'll look at prerequisites. This includes those for Active Directory as well as the server and its operating system. We'll start with Active Directory.

ACTIVE DIRECTORY REQUIREMENTS

It's important to keep your test environment isolated from your production environment. Exchange 2010 requires many changes to Active Directory through schema updates. Exchange 2010 introduces new objects and adds many parameters to existing objects. Additionally, Exchange 2010 has some other Active Directory requirements:

◆ Domain controllers and global catalogs in the same site are Windows Server 2003 Service Pack 2 (SP2) or higher.

◆ Read Only Domain Controllers and Read Only Global Catalogs in the same Active Directory site are ignored by Exchange 2010. Because of this, a conventional Domain Controller and Global Catalog must exist in the AD site.

We also need to look at the domain and forest functional levels. Active Directory forest and domain functionality modes must be at least Windows Server 2003 to install Exchange 2010. To verify, follow these steps:

1. Log on to a domain controller as a domain administrator.

2. Click Start ➢ All Programs ➢ Administrative Tools ➢ Active Directory Domains And Trusts.

3. Right-click on the domain in the left pane and choose Properties.

4. On the General tab of the properties dialog box, look for Domain Functional Level and Forest Function Level; both appear in the lower half of the screen, as shown in Figure 10.1.

FIGURE 10.1
Checking the domain and forest functional level

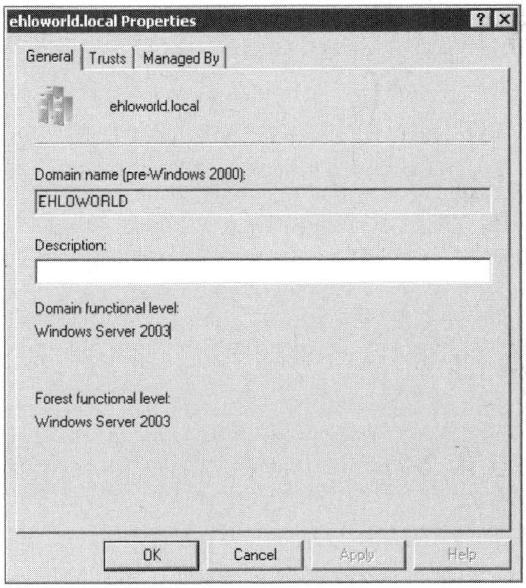

If the forest or domain is not Windows Server 2003 or higher, it must be raised before Exchange can be installed.

Although installing Exchange Server 2010 on a domain controller is a supported scenario, performance and security are enhanced when Exchange Server 2010 is installed on a member server. Once Exchange is installed, that server cannot be promoted to a domain controller or demoted to a member server.

OPERATING SYSTEM PREREQUISITES

Log onto the server as an administrator and install the 2007 Office System Converter: Microsoft Filter Pack. With features like transport rules, this filter pack adds support for inspection of Office files. You may be familiar with transport rules from Exchange 2007; Exchange 2010 adds the ability to inspect files and take action accordingly. An example is keyword matching. Files added for inspection via the filter pack include those with the extensions .docx, .docm, .pptx, .pptm, .xlsx, .xlsm, .xlsb, .zip, .one, .vdx, .vsd, .vss, .vst, .vdx, .vsx, and .vtx. The filter pack is available for download at www.microsoft.com. Later, after installing Exchange 2010, we'll register the file formats for Exchange to index. We can now move on to operating system roles and features within Windows Server 2008 R2.

An excellent component of Windows Server 2008 and Windows Server 2008 R2 is Server Manager. Server Manager is a framework that allows an administrator to add, review, or remove Windows features and roles from a server. We will use some Server Manager features to install our prerequisites. First, we must enable the commands. Doing this is straightforward:

1. Open PowerShell by clicking on its icon in the taskbar.

2. Type **Import-Module ServerManager** and press Enter.

   This enables the following PowerShell commands in Windows Server 2008 R2:

   ◆ Add-WindowsFeature

   ◆ Get-WindowsFeature

   ◆ Remove-WindowsFeature

For Windows Server 2008 R2, only a few components must be installed before you can install Exchange. These include features such as the .NET Framework and IIS components.

There are several ways in which they can be installed. The first is to open the Server Manager GUI on the server via Start ➢ All Programs ➢ Administrative Tools ➢ Server Manager and select the required check boxes. The next method is much faster. Simply use the PowerShell Add-WindowsFeature cmdlet to install all the roles and features in one step. To do so, return to the PowerShell window opened earlier and type the following:

```
Add-WindowsFeature NET-Framework,RSAT-ADDS,Web-Server,Web-Basic-Auth, ↵
Web-Windows-Auth,Web-Metabase,Web-Net-Ext,Web-Lgcy-Mgmt-Console, ↵
WAS-Process-Model,RSAT-Web-Server,Web-ISAPI-Ext,Web-Digest-Auth, ↵
Web-Dyn-Compression,NET-HTTP-Activation,RPC-Over-HTTP-Proxy -Restart
```

Once you press Enter, the server will install the required roles and features, and then automatically restart. Note that it is normal to see yellow warning text scroll by while this code is running, as shown in Figure 10.2. These are merely warnings that a reboot is required.

But wait — there's an even faster method. Instead of typing that long line of roles and features to be installed, Microsoft included a method that uses XML files to specify which roles and features to install. This method uses the ServerManagerCmd.exe program, which was first introduced in Windows Server 2008. While it is deprecated in Windows Server 2008 R2, it still works fine.

ServerManagerCmd.exe has an optional switch, -ip, which can be used to take action based on XML configuration files. The command syntax looks like this: ServerManagerCmd -ip <name of XML file>. An additional switch, -restart, will force the server to restart upon completion, if a restart is required.

Microsoft has included Exchange Server 2010 prerequisite configuration files on the Exchange DVD. Located in the \scripts folder, are some XML files, among others. The XML configuration files appear in Table 10.1.

FIGURE 10.2
Add-WindowsFeature
installing features
and roles

TABLE 10.1:   Exchange 2010 XML Configuration Files

CONFIGURATION FILE	PURPOSE
exchange-all.xml	All server roles
exchange-base.xml	Base installation for any role
exchange.cadb.xml	CentralAdmin database
exchange-cas.xml	Client Access Server role
exchange-eca.xml	CentralAdmin
exchange-edge.xml	Edge Transport Server role
exchange-hub.xml	Hub Transport Server role
exchange-mbx.xml	Mailbox Server role
exchange-typical.xml	Mailbox/Client Access/Hub Transport Server roles
exchange-um.xml	Unified Messaging Server role

For our typical Exchange 2010 server, we'll use the exchange-typical.xml file. To use
this method, return to the PowerShell window and navigate to the location of your Exchange
Server 2010 files, and then to the \scripts subfolder. For example, if your Exchange DVD is
drive D:, navigate to D:\Scripts and type **ServerManagerCmd -ip Exchange-Typical.xml
-restart**. Entering this command will install all necessary roles and features defined in
Exchange-Typical.xml and then automatically restart the computer.

Regardless of which method you use, once you reboot the server you can verify the installation of the various roles and features by opening a command prompt or PowerShell window and typing **ServerManagerCmd -q**. This will list all roles and features available in Windows Server 2008 R2, and indicate in green which are installed.

There is one more setting that needs to be completed before we start the actual installation program for Exchange. The Client Access Server role requires the Net TCP Port Sharing service be set to start automatically. We can do this quickly within PowerShell.

1. Log on to the server as an administrative user.

2. Open PowerShell once again and type **Set-Service NetTcpPortSharing -StartupType Automatic**.

Installing Exchange Server 2010

The installation of Exchange 2010 does require an account with some specific permissions. Installation must be performed with an account that has membership in the following groups:

♦ Domain Admin

♦ Schema Administrators (first server)

♦ Enterprise Administrators (first server)

During the installation, the Active Directory schema will be extended with attributes necessary for Exchange 2010, which is why the Schema Administrators group membership is required.

At this point, we're ready to install Exchange Server 2010. We can use the GUI to install Exchange, or we can use the command line. Each approach has its advantages. First, let's look at the GUI-based installation.

GUI-Based Installation

Insert the Exchange 2010 DVD in your server's DVD-ROM drive. If the DVD doesn't automatically start the setup program, navigate to the Exchange DVD and run `setup.exe` in the root folder. You will be presented with the start screen shown in Figure 10.3.

As you can see, previously installed components are grayed out. This should include Steps 1 and 2.

On the start screen, click Step 3: Choose Exchange Language Option. The language options will appear below this. Choose Install Only Languages From The DVD. Choosing this option will install only English (US) language support. You can install language bundles at a later time to provide support for additional languages if needed.

Once Step 3 is complete, click Step 4: Install Microsoft Exchange. Setup will then copy the setup files locally to the computer on which you are installing Exchange Server 2010. Once the files are copied and the setup program initializes, you'll see the Introduction screen. Click Next.

On the License Agreement screen, read the license agreement, select I Accept The Terms In The License Agreement, and click Next.

On the Error Reporting page, select No. This is a test server and the whole purpose is to get used to Exchange. During testing, you may attempt some tasks that will yield errors or unexpected results. If this were a production server, then you could answer differently. Click Next.

On the Installation Type page, click Typical Exchange Server Installation, as shown in Figure 10.4. Typical includes the Hub Transport, Client Access, and Mailbox roles, and also includes the Exchange Management Tools. These are the minimal roles required in an Exchange organization.

If you want to change the path for the installation, click Browse, specify the appropriate folder, and then click OK. Click Next.

Since this is the first Exchange Server 2010 server in your organization, you are presented with the Exchange Organization screen. Type a name for your Exchange organization (see Figure 10.5). This can be any name, such as your company name. The Exchange organization name can contain only the following characters:

◆ Letters A through Z

◆ Letters a through z

◆ Numbers 0 through 9

◆ Space (not leading or trailing)

◆ Hyphen or dash

The organization name can't be more than 64 characters long. The organization name also can't be blank. When you've finished typing the name, click Next.

FIGURE 10.5
Organization name

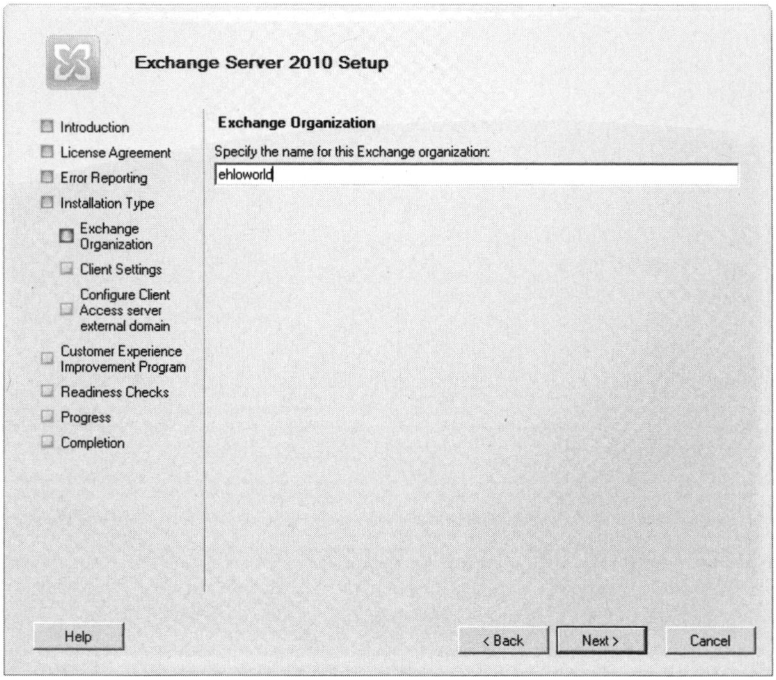

If you will have legacy versions of Outlook, such as anything prior to Outlook 2007, or any non-Exchange Web Services version of Entourage that will be connecting to this Exchange organization, click Yes at the Client Settings screen. This will cause the installation to create a public folder database for use with Free/Busy (calendar) information. If you will only be using Outlook versions from 2007 and later, choose No. This can be changed later if your needs change. Click Next.

If the Client Access Server role being installed is intended to be an Internet-facing server, check the box The Client Access Server Roles Will Be Internet-Facing. Enter the domain name you will use for external client access (for example, `mail.ehloworld.com`). Then click Next.

Since the purpose of this chapter is to set up a quick Exchange Server 2010 box for testing and evaluation, there is no need to join the Customer Experience Improvement Program.

On the Customer Experience Improvement page, choose I Don't Wish To Join The Program At This Time, and then click Next.

On the Readiness Checks screen, the setup routine will inspect the system to verify that Exchange can be successfully installed. This is based on the settings you've chosen, the rights of the user account, and the operating system prerequisites, as shown in Figure 10.6.

FIGURE 10.6
Readiness checks

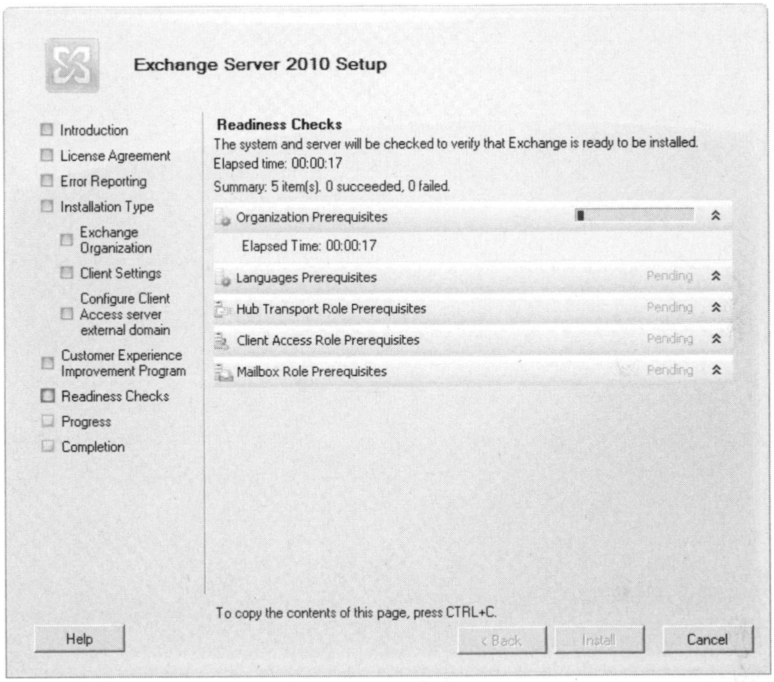

The Organization Prerequisites section will display a warning (as shown in Figure 10.7) that reads as follows:

> Setup is going to prepare the organization for Exchange Server 2010 by using 'Setup /PrepareAD'. No Exchange 2007 server roles have been detected in this topology. After this operation, you will not be able to install any Exchange 2007 server roles.

This is expected; it's simply a notice that legacy versions of Exchange can't be installed after Exchange Server 2010 is installed into an organization.

View the status of the remaining items to determine if the organization and server role prerequisite checks completed successfully. If they have not completed successfully, you must resolve any reported errors before you can install Exchange Server 2010. For most, there is no need to exit Setup while attempting to resolve them. After resolving an error, click Retry to rerun the prerequisite checks.

If all the other readiness checks have completed successfully, click Install to install Exchange Server 2010. The Setup program will display the Progress screen, which will show you each step of the process, as well as the outcome.

On the Completion page, shown in Figure 10.8, click View Setup Log. Take a few minutes to look through this log file and notice any issues. When finished, close the log file.

FIGURE 10.7
Warning about legacy
versions of Exchange

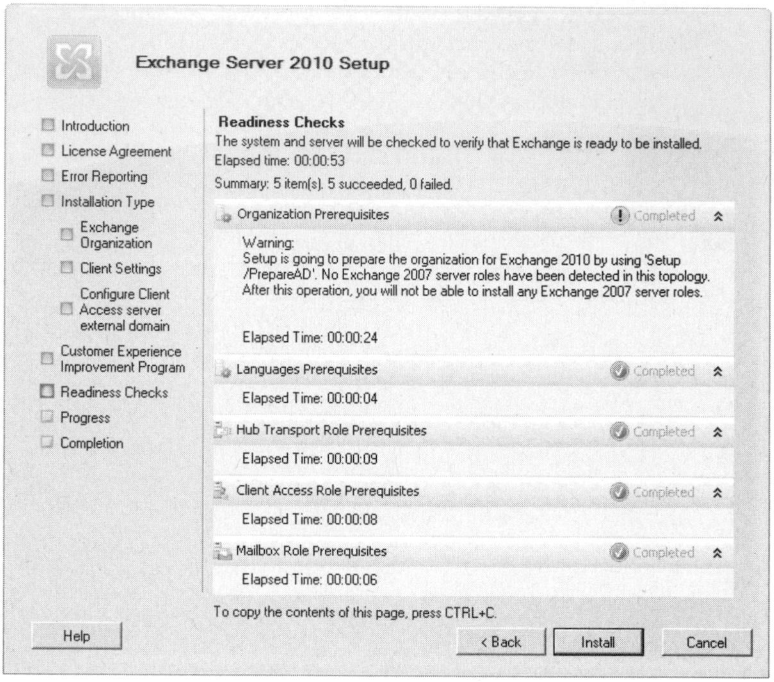

FIGURE 10.8
Completion screen

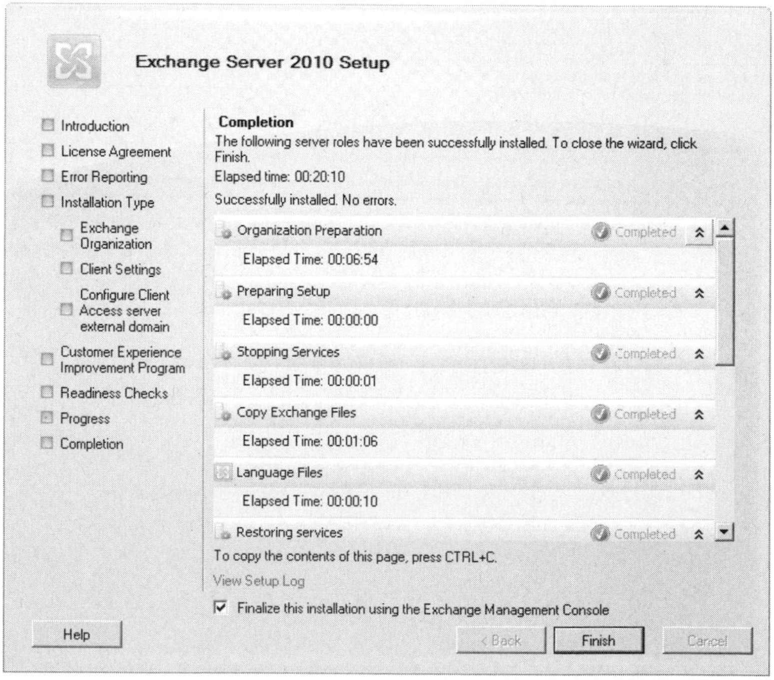

Ensure that the Finalize This Installation Using The Exchange Management Console check box is not selected, and then click Finish.

Return to the Setup program and click Close. When prompted to confirm exiting, as shown in Figure 10.9, click Yes and install any critical updates.

FIGURE 10.9
Click Yes to confirm that you want to exit.

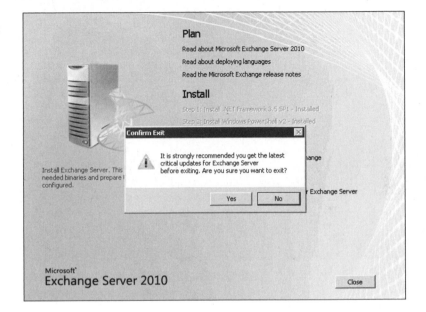

Even if you are not prompted, reboot the server to complete installation of Exchange Server 2010.

Unattended Installation

As mentioned earlier, you can also install Exchange 2010 from the command line. The setup routine allows you to specify all necessary parameters in one line, and thus avoid having to click on things through a GUI. To achieve the same end result as in the previous steps but through a command line, open a command prompt and navigate to the DVD drive. From there, use the following format:

```
Setup.com /r:"c,h,m" /on:"<organization name>" ↵
/ExternalCASServerDomain:"<CAS Server domain>"
```

Here's an example:

```
Setup.com /r:"c,h,m" /on:"First Organization" ↵
/ExternalCASServerDomain:"mail.ehloworld.com"
```

When the setup routine finishes, reboot the server as prompted. Once these steps are completed, continue with the rest of the configuration, as explained in the next section.

Post Installation Configuration Steps

Once the server has rebooted, take a few minutes and verify that things are working the way they should. If you didn't look at the setup log at the end of the installation, review it now. It's located at <system drive>\ExchangeSetupLogs\ExchangeSetup.log. Look for errors and warnings.

Remember the FilterPack installed as part of the prerequisites? Now that Exchange is installed, we need to register the file formats we wish Exchange to include when indexing. This requires editing the registry of the Exchange server. Fortunately, Microsoft has provided some shell code to perform this task. A complete copy of the script, called RegisterMicrosoftFilterPack.ps1, is available at http://technet.microsoft.com/en-us/library/ee732397%28EXCHG.140%29.aspx but is also listed below:

```
# Copyright (c) 2009 Microsoft Corporation. All rights reserved.
# THIS CODE IS MADE AVAILABLE AS IS, WITHOUT WARRANTY OF ANY KIND. THE ENTIRE RISK
    OF THE USE OR THE RESULTS FROM THE USE OF THIS CODE REMAINS WITH THE USER.
# This is a filter registration script to configure Exchange Server 2010 to
    index Office 2007 file formats.
$DLLPath = $env:CommonProgramFiles + "\Microsoft Shared\Filters"
$CLSIDKey = "HKLM:\SOFTWARE\Microsoft\ExchangeServer\V14\MSSearch\CLSID"
$FiltersKey = "HKLM:\SOFTWARE\Microsoft\ExchangeServer\v14\MSSearch\Filters"

# Filter DLL Locations
$officeFilterLocation = $DLLPath + "\offfiltx.dll"
$onenoteFilterLocation = $DLLPath + "\ONIFilter.dll"
$visioFilterLocation = $DLLPath + "\VISFilt.DLL"

# Filter GUIDs
$docxGuid    ="{5A98B233-3C59-4B31-944C-0E560D85E6C3}"
$pptxGuid    ="{DDFE337F-4987-4EC8-BDE3-133FA63D5D85}"
$xlsxGuid    ="{F90DFE0C-CBDF-41FF-8598-EDD8F222A2C8}"
$zipGuid     ="{20E823C2-62F3-4638-96BD-90F4F6784EBC}"
$xlsbGuid    ="{312AB530-ECC9-496E-AE0E-C9E6C5392499}"
$onenoteGuid ="{B8D12492-CE0F-40AD-83EA-099A03D493F1}"
$vsdGuid     ="{FAEA5B46-761B-400E-B53E-E805A97A543E}"

# Create CLSIDs
Write-Host "Creating CLSIDs..."

New-Item -Path $CLSIDKey -Name $docxGuid -Value $officeFilterLocation -Type String
New-Item -Path $CLSIDKey -Name $pptxGuid  -Value $officeFilterLocation -Type String
New-Item -Path $CLSIDKey -Name $xlsxGuid  -Value $officeFilterLocation -Type String
New-Item -Path $CLSIDKey -Name $zipGuid   -Value $officeFilterLocation -Type String
New-Item -Path $CLSIDKey -Name $xlsbGuid -Value $officeFilterLocation -Type String
New-Item -Path $CLSIDKey -Name $onenoteGuid -Value $onenoteFilterLocation ↵
   -Type String
New-Item -Path $CLSIDKey -Name $vsdGuid   -Value $visioFilterLocation -Type String

# Set Threading model
Write-Host "Setting threading model..."
```

```
New-ItemProperty -Path "$CLSIDKey\$docxGuid" -Name "ThreadingModel" ↵
   -Value "Both" -Type String
New-ItemProperty -Path "$CLSIDKey\$pptxGuid" -Name "ThreadingModel" ↵
   -Value "Both" -Type String
New-ItemProperty -Path "$CLSIDKey\$xlsxGuid" -Name "ThreadingModel" ↵
   -Value "Both" -Type String
New-ItemProperty -Path "$CLSIDKey\$zipGuid" -Name "ThreadingModel" ↵
   -Value "Both" -Type String
New-ItemProperty -Path "$CLSIDKey\$xlsbGuid" -Name "ThreadingModel" ↵
   -Value "Both" -Type String
New-ItemProperty -Path "$CLSIDKey\$onenoteGuid" -Name "ThreadingModel" ↵
    -Value "Both" -Type String
New-ItemProperty -Path "$CLSIDKey\$vsdGuid" -Name "ThreadingModel" ↵
   -Value "Both" -Type String

# Create Filter Entries
Write-Host "Creating Filter Entries..."

# Uncomment these if you wish to index these uncommonly exchanged formats
#New-Item -Path $FiltersKey -Name ".docm" -Value $docxGuid -Type String
#New-Item -Path $FiltersKey -Name ".pptm" -Value $pptxGuid -Type String
#New-Item -Path $FiltersKey -Name ".xlsm" -Value $xlsxGuid -Type String
#New-Item -Path $FiltersKey -Name ".vss" -Value $vsdGuid   -Type String
#New-Item -Path $FiltersKey -Name ".vst" -Value $vsdGuid   -Type String
#New-Item -Path $FiltersKey -Name ".vsx" -Value $vsdGuid   -Type String
#New-Item -Path $FiltersKey -Name ".vtx" -Value $vsdGuid   -Type String

# These are the entries for commonly exchange formats
New-Item -Path $FiltersKey -Name ".docx" -Value $docxGuid -Type String
New-Item -Path $FiltersKey -Name ".pptx" -Value $pptxGuid -Type String
New-Item -Path $FiltersKey -Name ".xlsx" -Value $xlsxGuid -Type String
New-Item -Path $FiltersKey -Name ".xlsb" -Value $xlsbGuid -Type String
New-Item -Path $FiltersKey -Name ".zip" -Value $zipGuid   -Type String
New-Item -Path $FiltersKey -Name ".one" -Value $onenoteGuid -Type String
New-Item -Path $FiltersKey -Name ".vsd" -Value $vsdGuid   -Type String

Write-Host "Registry subkeys created."
Write-Host "Please restart Microsoft Search  (Exchange) service from the Services
   console, or by running stop-service msftesql-Exchange -Force ; start-service
   MSExchangeSearch "
```

Save that code as c:\RegisterMicrosoftFilterPack.ps1. Open Exchange Management Shell. Click Start➢ All Programs➢ Microsoft Exchange Server 2010➢ Exchange Management Shell. The first time this is started, it will take a couple of minutes to complete some post installation initialization.

Change to c:\ and type **.\RegisterMicrosoftFilterPack.ps1** and press Enter. The script will run, registering any file formats that aren't already registered. Once registered, we restart the Exchange Search service using the following command in the Exchange Management Shell:

```
stop-service msftesql-Exchange -Force ; start-service MSExchangeSearch
```

Next, use the `Get-ExchangeServer` cmdlet to get the information about installed roles. An example would be:

```
Get-ExchangeServer | FT Name,ServerRole -auto
```

The output of this command will list verify installed roles for the Exchange server. You should see `Mailbox`, `ClientAccess`, and `HubTransport` listed under `ServerRole`.

Next, let's take a look using Event Viewer for any signs of problems. Click Start ➤ All Programs ➤ Administrative Tools ➤ Event Viewer. Navigate to Windows Logs and then Application. Look for errors and warnings that may indicate a problem. It's common to see a warning such as the one shown in Figure 10.10.

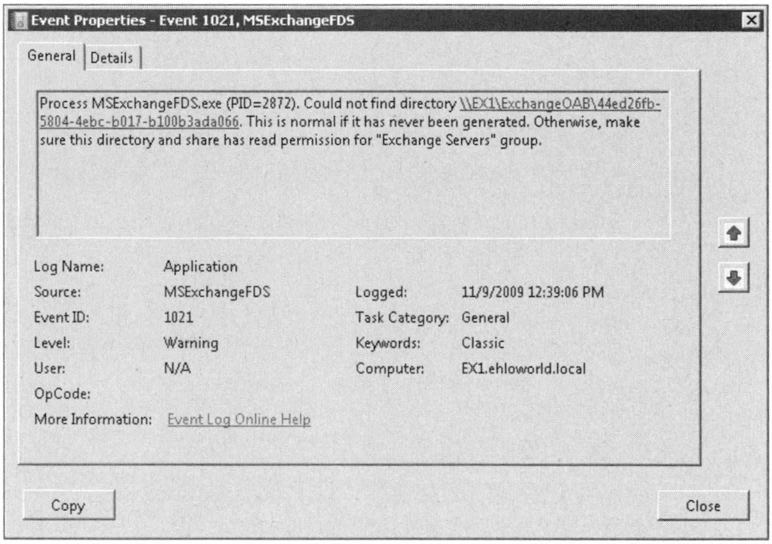

FIGURE 10.10
Event log error about
the offline address book

The error appears because the Offline Address Book (OAB) has yet to be generated. This error can be safely ignored for now, and you can close Event Viewer.

When you're sure that the installation has been successful, you can move on to post-installation configuration. We'll start with the Exchange Management Console. To open that, click Start ➤ Exchange Management Console. As with the Exchange Management Shell, the first time this is started, the program will take a minute or two to finish configuration.

You will be presented with a popup box that lists any unlicensed Exchange servers, and how much time is left in the trial period. Click OK on the message. We are now ready to use the Exchange Management Console.

Configuring the Mailbox Role

Next, we'll set an OAB on mailbox databases (see Figure 10.11). The OAB, which is used by Outlook when running in cached mode, contains a copy of the Global Address List.

1. On the left, expand Microsoft Exchange – On-Premises (server) ➤ Organization Configuration ➤ Mailbox.

2. Click the Database Management tab.

3. Right-click the mailbox database listed in the upper pane, and click Properties. Click the Client Settings tab.

4. Click Browse next to Offline Address Book.

5. Select Default Offline Address Book, as shown in Figure 10.12, and click OK twice.

FIGURE 10.11
Setting an OAB on mailbox databases

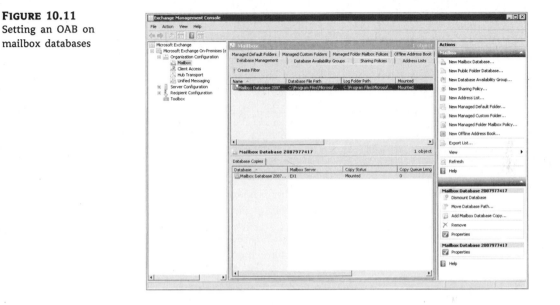

FIGURE 10.12
Offline Address Book

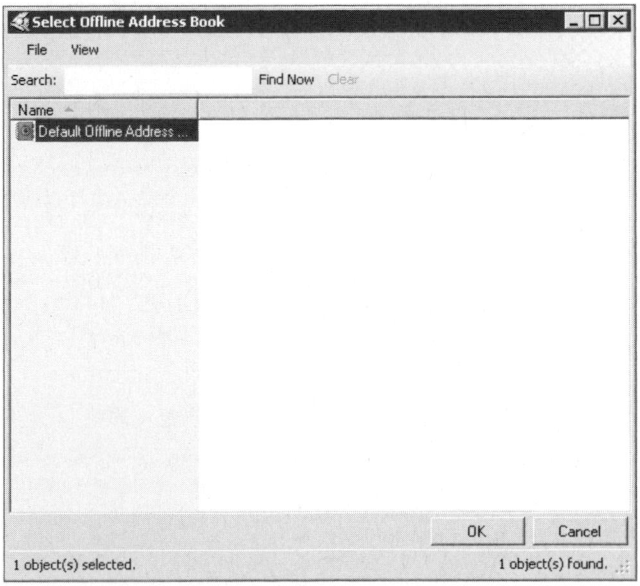

You can do the same in the Exchange Management Shell using both the `Get-MailboxDatabase` and `Set-MailboxDatabase` cmdlets together:

```
Get-MailboxDatabase | Set-MailboxDatabase -OfflineAddressBook ↵
"\Default Offline Address Book"
```

Configuring the Hub Transport Role

For the Hub Transport role, we'll configure accepted domains, which are domains for which Exchange is responsible:

1. On the left, navigate to Microsoft Exchange – On-Premises (server) ➤ Organization Configuration ➤ Hub Transport.

2. Click the Accepted Domains tab in the center pane.

3. In the Actions pane on the far right, click New Accepted Domain.

4. Give the accepted domain a name, such as **ehloworld.com**, and enter the domain name for which Exchange will receive email, such as **ehloworld.com**.

5. Click Authoritative Domain to indicate that Exchange is responsible for delivering email for that domain in the Exchange organization.

6. Click New, then click Finish.

7. Right-click the newly created accepted domain and choose Set As Default, as shown in Figure 10.13. Click Yes when you see the confirmation message.

FIGURE 10.13
Setting the accepted domain as the default

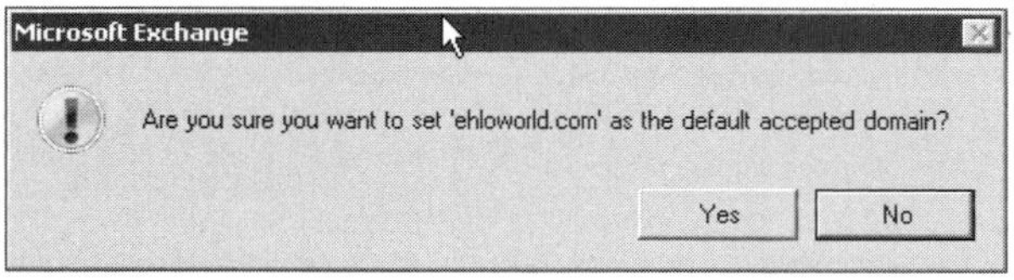

You can accomplish the same thing in the Exchange Management Shell using the `New-AcceptedDomain` cmdlet and the `Set-AcceptedDomain` cmdlet together:

```
New-AcceptedDomain -Name ehloworld.com ↵
-DomainName *.ehloworld.com ↵
-DomainType authoritative | ↵
Set-AcceptedDomain -MakeDefault $true
```

CONFIGURING EMAIL ADDRESS POLICIES

Email address policies define how email addresses are assigned to recipients within the organization. We'll configure one for our domain, ehloworld.com, using these steps in the Exchange Management Console:

1. Navigate to Microsoft Exchange – On-Premises (server) ➤ Organization Configuration ➤ Hub Transport ➤ E-mail Address Policies.

2. In the Actions pane, click New E-mail Address Policy.

3. Enter a name for the policy, such as **ehloworld.com**. Leave the Recipient Container and Recipient Type options at their default settings, and click Next.

4. Since we'll apply this policy to all users, we don't need to define conditions. At the Conditions screen, click Next.

5. On the E-Mail Addresses page, click Add. Make sure that the E-mail Address Local Part check box is selected, and choose a format for the email addresses. The options are as follows:

- Use Alias

- First Name.Last Name (John.Smith)

- First Name Initial And Last Name (Jsmith)

- First Name And Last Name Initial (Johns)

- Last Name.First Name (Smith.John)

- Last Name Initial And First Name (Sjohn)

- Last Name And First Name Initial (Smithj)

6. Check the option Select The Accepted Domain For The E-mail Address, click Browse, and choose the domain added in the accepted domains process earlier, such as ehloworld.com, as shown in Figure 10.14.

FIGURE 10.14
Email address format

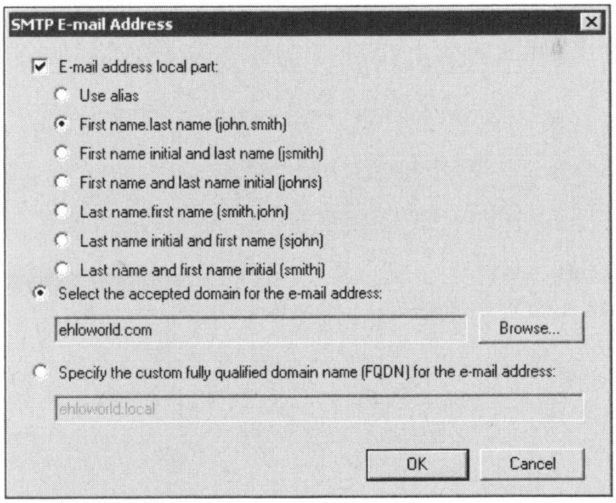

7. Click OK twice, and then click Next.

8. On the Schedule screen, choose Immediately and click Next. This will apply the policy to all current recipients immediately.

9. On the New E-mail Address Policy summary screen, click New.

10. When the wizard completes, click Finish.

As with all the previous configuration settings we've made, we can use the Exchange Management Shell to make these changes using both the New-EmailAddressPolicy and Update-EmailAddressPolicy cmdlets together:

```
New-EmailAddressPolicy -Name ehloworld.com ↵
-EnabledPrimarySMTPAddressTemplate "SMTP:%g.%s@ehloworld.com" ↵
-IncludedRecipients AllRecipients -Priority 1 | ↵
Update-EmailAddressPolicy
```

To verify that the policy has been applied, navigate to Microsoft Exchange On-Premises (server) ➤ Recipient Configuration ➤ Mailbox. Right-click the Administrator account and choose Properties. Click the E-Mail Addresses tab, and you'll see that the list includes the newly added address.

SEND CONNECTORS

A send connector is an object that holds configuration information on how Exchange can send email out of the organization. This can include to the Internet as well as to partner email systems. Exchange has no send connectors configured by default. We'll use the Exchange Management Console to create one for sending mail to the Internet:

1. Navigate to Microsoft Exchange – On-Premises (server) ➤ Organization Configuration ➤ Hub Transport.

2. In the Actions pane, click New Send Connector.

3. On the Introduction screen, give the send connector a name, such as **Outbound to Internet**.

4. Under Select The Intended Use For This Send Connector, choose Internet and click Next.

5. On the Address Space page, click Add.

6. In the Address field, enter *.

7. Check the box Include All Subdomains, as shown in Figure 10.15, click OK.

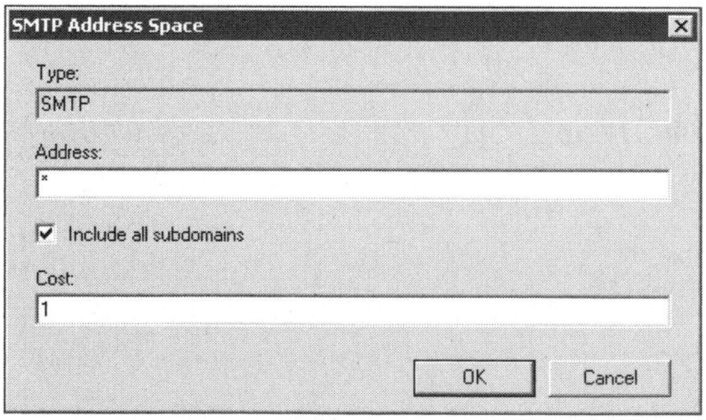

FIGURE 10.15
Send connector settings

8. Click Next.

9. On the Network Settings screen, click Use Domain Name System (DNS) "MX" Records To Route Mail Automatically, and click Next.

10. On the Source Server screen, verify that the local server is listed, and click Next.

11. On the New Connector screen, click New, then click Finish.

To accomplish this in the Exchange Management Shell, use the `New-SendConnector` cmdlet:

```
New-SendConnector -name "Outbound to Internet" ↵
-AddressSpaces "*" -DNSRoutingEnabled $true ↵
-FQDN "mail.ehloworld.com" -Usage Internet
```

RECEIVE CONNECTORS

A receive connector is just the opposite of a send connector. Receive connectors hold configuration for how Exchange will receive mail. This can include mail from client machines as well as from the Internet and other servers.

When Exchange Server 2010 is installed, two receive connectors are created. The first is called Client (server), such as Client EX1. This connector receives mail on TCP port 587, and is used for receiving email from client computers.

The second receive connector is called Default (server), such as Default EX1. This connector receives mail on TCP port 25, and is designed for receiving mail from other servers within your organization that use authentication.

By default, there is no receive connector configured to receive email from the Internet. Creating one is fairly straightforward with these steps:

1. Open the EMC and navigate to Microsoft Exchange – On-Premises (server) ➢ Server Configuration ➢ Hub Transport.

2. In the Actions pane, click New Receive Connector.

3. On the Introduction screen, give the receive connector a name, such as **Inbound from Internet**.

4. Under Select The Intended Use For This Receive Connector, choose Internet, and click Next.

5. On the Local Network settings screen, highlight the (All Available IPv4) entry and click Edit.

6. Click Specify An IP address, and enter the IP address of the server, as shown in Figure 10.16.

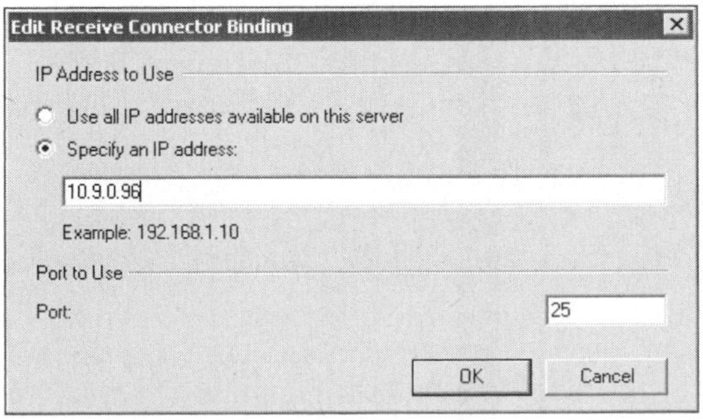

FIGURE 10.16
Receive connector
settings

7. Click OK.

8. Enter the FQDN name that will be used, such as **mail.ehloworld.com**, and click Next.

9. On the New Connector page, click New, and then click Finish.

In the Exchange Management Shell, you can create the same receive connector using the New-ReceiveConnector cmdlet:

```
New-ReceiveConnector -name "Inbound from Internet" ↵
-Usage Internet -Bindings "10.9.0.96:25" ↵
-FQDN "mail.ehloworld.com"
```

INSTALLING ANTISPAM AGENTS

Like its predecessor, Exchange Server 2010 comes with some robust antispam agents. These agents are installed by default on servers with the Edge Transport role installed, but can also be installed on servers with the Hub Transport role. These agents can be useful when you're testing Exchange or in organizations that don't have Exchange servers with the Edge Transport role installed.

Installation of the antispam agents is accomplished in the Exchange Management Shell:

1. Close the Exchange Management Console.

2. Click Start ➢ All Programs ➢ Microsoft Exchange Server 2010 ➢ Exchange Management Shell.

3. Navigate to the \scripts folder (which by default is c:\Program Files\Microsoft\ Exchange Server\V14\scripts).

4. Type .**Install-AntispamAgents.ps1** and press Enter, as shown in Figure 10.17.

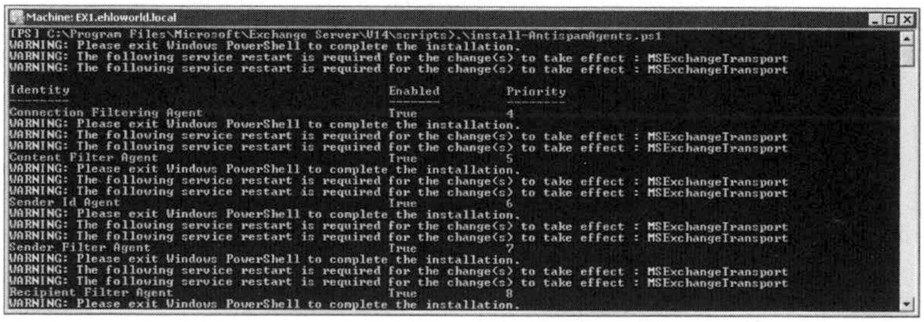

FIGURE 10.17
Installing antispam agents

5. Restart the Exchange Transport service from within the Exchange Management Shell using the Restart-Service cmdlet and specifying the name of the service, as shown here:

```
Restart-Service MSExchangeTransport
```

6. Close the Exchange Management Shell.

7. Restart the EMC and navigate to Microsoft Exchange ➢ Microsoft Exchange On-Premises (server) ➢ Organization ➢ Hub Transport. You should notice an Anti-spam tab now that allows for configuration of the various agents. All the agents should be enabled.

TESTING THE CONFIGURATION

You now have a significant amount of configuration finished in Exchange. You can test Exchange using some built-in PowerShell cmdlets. To begin, start the Exchange Management Shell and type **Test-mailflow**. Check the results in the `TestMailflowResult` column. It should say Success.

Next, test MAPI client connectivity using `Test-MAPIConnectivity`. You should see Success under Result for each database.

You can verify that all necessary Exchange-related services are running by using `Test-ServiceHealth`. The output of this cmdlet breaks down the services needed for each of the installed server roles. If everything is running correctly, you should see True for each of the `RequiredServicesRunning` results.

Configuring Recipients

There are various types of recipients in Exchange Server 2010, including Mailbox, Distribution Group, and Mail Contact. Mailboxes can be further broken down, and that is explained elsewhere in this book. We'll focus on creating the three types mentioned earlier.

Mailbox-enabled users are Active Directory accounts that have a mailbox located in Exchange. To create a mailbox-enabled user:

1. Open the EMC and navigate to Microsoft Exchange ➢ Microsoft Exchange On-Premises (server) ➢ Recipient Configuration ➢ Mailbox. You will notice that the Administrator is already listed, as is the Discovery Search Mailbox.

2. To create a new mailbox, go to the Actions pane on the right side and click New Mailbox.

3. Choose User Mailbox, and click Next.

4. To create a mailbox for a user that does not yet exist in Active Directory, click New User and then click Next. To create a mailbox for a user that already exists in Active Directory, click Existing User.

5. Click Add.

6. Highlight the users you want to mailbox-enable, as shown in Figure 10.18.

7. Click OK, then click Next.

8. On the Mailbox Settings screen, enter an alias for the user. All the other fields can be left blank. Click Next. Note that if you select multiple users, aliases are automatically generated for each.

9. Click Next.

10. On the New Mailbox screen, shown in Figure 10.19, click New, and then click Finish. Mailbox-enabled users are now visible.

Creating mailbox-enabled users in the Exchange Management Shell is quite simple using the Enable-Mailbox cmdlet. An example would be:

```
Enable-Mailbox -Identity Abby.Smith
```

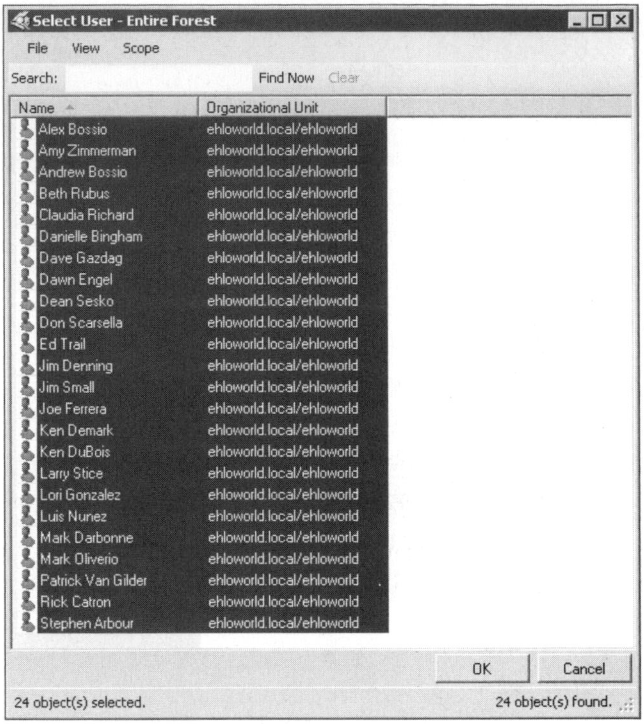

FIGURE 10.18
Creating a mailbox for
an existing user

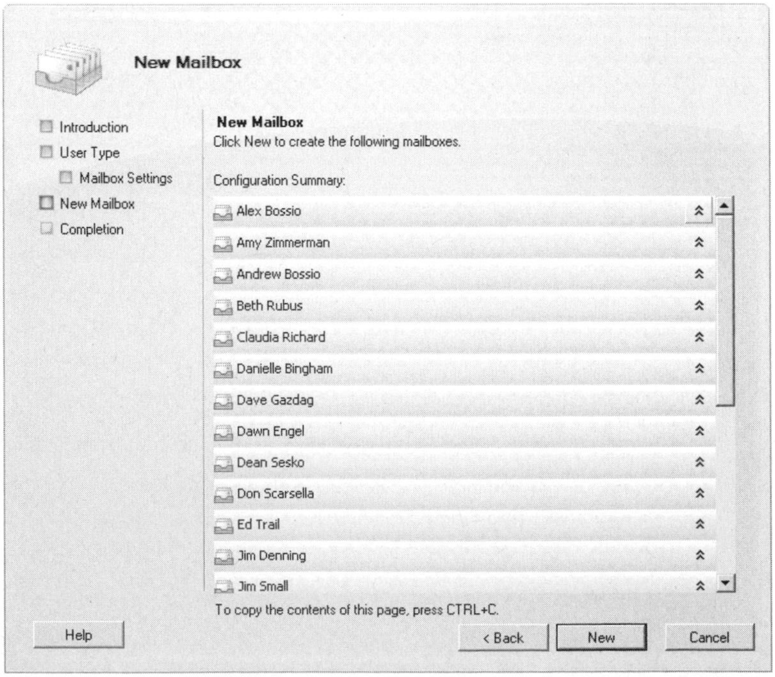

FIGURE 10.19
Mailbox summary
settings

Mail-enabled contacts are objects in the Global Address List that represent external recipients. These can be vendors or clients. To create a new mail-enabled contact:

1. In the Exchange Management Shell, navigate to Microsoft Exchange ➤ Microsoft Exchange On-Premises (server) ➤ Recipient Configuration ➤ Mail Contact.

2. In the Actions pane, click New Mail Contact.

3. Click New Contact and click Next.

4. If the Specify An Organizational Unit Rather Than Using A Default One option is left blank, the mail contact will be placed in the Users OU.

5. Fill out the fields for the name and alias, as shown in Figure 10.20.

FIGURE 10.20
Creating a mail contact

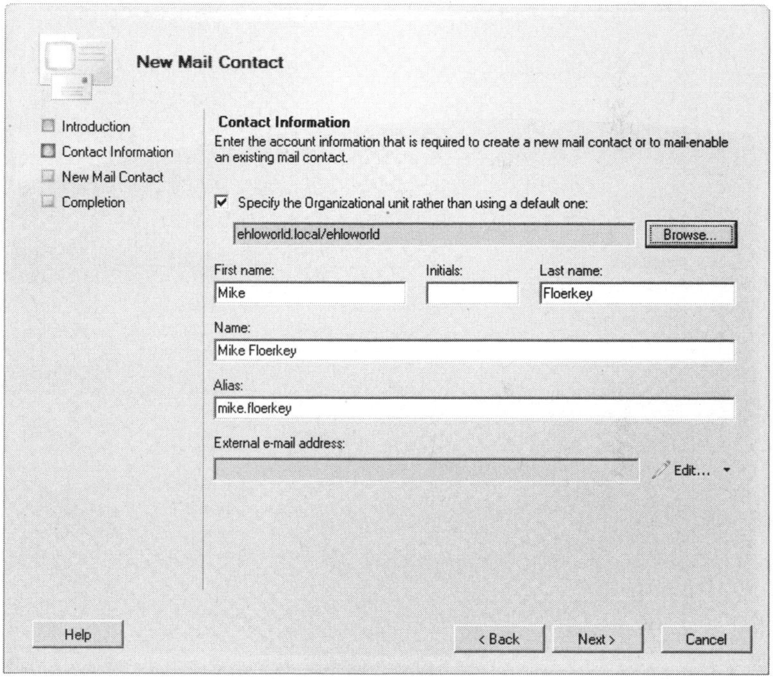

6. Under External E-mail Address, click Edit.

7. Enter an email address and click OK; then click Next.

8. On the New Mail Contact screen, click New, and then click Finish.

Creating a mail contact in the Exchange Management Shell is quite simple using the New-MailContact cmdlet:

```
New-MailContact -Name "Claudia Richard" -ExternalEmailAddress "crichard@contoso.com"
```

Creating Distribution Groups

To create a distribution group in the EMC:

1. Navigate to Microsoft Exchange ➢ Microsoft Exchange On-Premises (server) ➢ Recipient Configuration ➢ Distribution Group.

2. In the Actions pane, click New Distribution Group.

3. Click New Group, and click Next.

4. Choose Distribution/Security.

5. (Optional) Select an organizational unit.

6. Enter a name and alias, and then click Next.

7. On the New Distribution Group screen, click New.

8. Highlight Distribution Group, and then click Properties in the Actions pane.

9. Click the Members tab, and then click Add.

10. As you can see in Figure 10.21, you can add mailboxes, mail contacts, and even other distribution groups. Highlight those you'd like to add to the distribution group, and click OK. Then click OK again.

FIGURE 10.21
Creating a distribution group

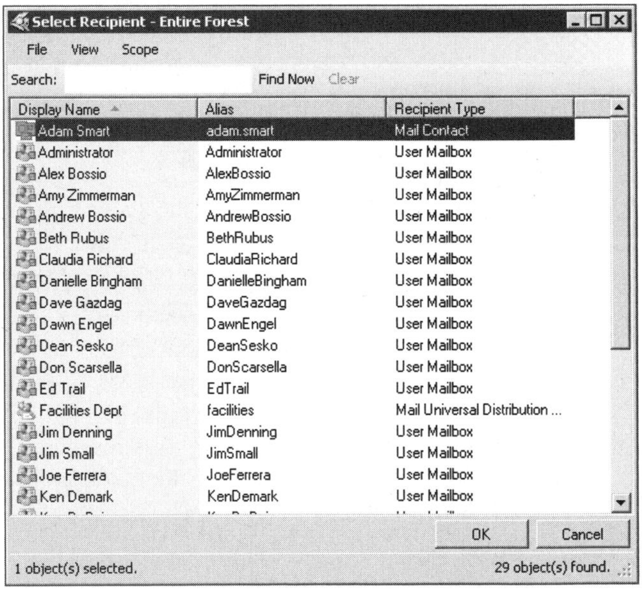

You can accomplish both the task of creating a distribution group as well as adding members in one line of code in the Exchange Management Shell using something like this:

```
New-DistributionGroup -name "Program Managers" | ↵
Add-DistributionGroupMember -member "Amy Zimmerman"
```

Organizational Health

Now that you've configured some settings in Exchange Server 2010, we can look at a high-level overview called Organizational Health. This view shows us some statistical data about the Exchange organization, such as the number of licenses required, number of servers, databases, and recipients. This is a great snapshot of Exchange that is collected as needed. To collect and view this information in the Exchange Management Console:

1. Navigate to Microsoft Exchange ➢ Microsoft Exchange On-Premises (server).

2. In the Actions pane, click Collect Organizational Health Data.

3. On the Introduction screen, choose Immediately, and then click Next.

4. On the Collect Organizational Health Data screen, click Collect.

5. When completed, click Finish, and review the data presented in the center pane as shown in Figure 10.22.

FIGURE 10.22
Organizational Health

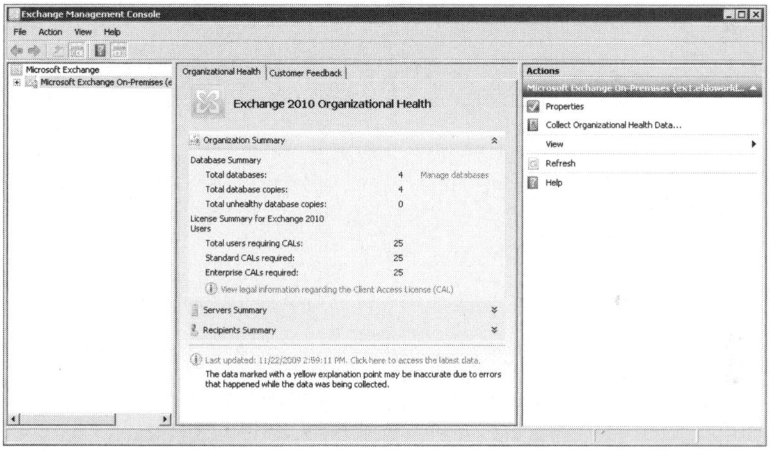

Configuring a Postmaster Address

A postmaster address is needed for the sending of non-delivery reports (NDRs) and other related messages to recipients outside the Exchange organization and is required by RFC 2821. Configuring your environment takes two steps. First, either create a new mailbox for the postmaster, or assign the address to an existing mailbox, such as Administrator. Second, use the Exchange Management Shell to set the external postmaster address in Exchange. To do so, open the Exchange Management Shell and use the `Set-TransportConfig` cmdlet and the `-ExternalPostmasterAddress` parameter, using the following format:

```
Set-TransportConfig -ExternalPostmasterAddress ↵
<ExternalPostmasterSMTPAddress>
```

Here's an example:

```
Set-TransportConfig -ExternalPostmasterAddress ↵
postmaster@ehloworld.com
```

SSL Certificate

In a production environment, using a third-party trusted SSL certificate to security communications is highly recommended. When Exchange 2010 is installed, Exchange installs a self-signed certificate valid for five years. This is perfectly fine for testing in a lab environment. When testing Exchange using Outlook Web App, for example, you will be presented with a screen indicating that the security certificate was not issued by a trusted certificate authority (see Figure 10.23). You can ignore these warnings during testing.

FIGURE 10.23
SSL warning about the self-signed certificate

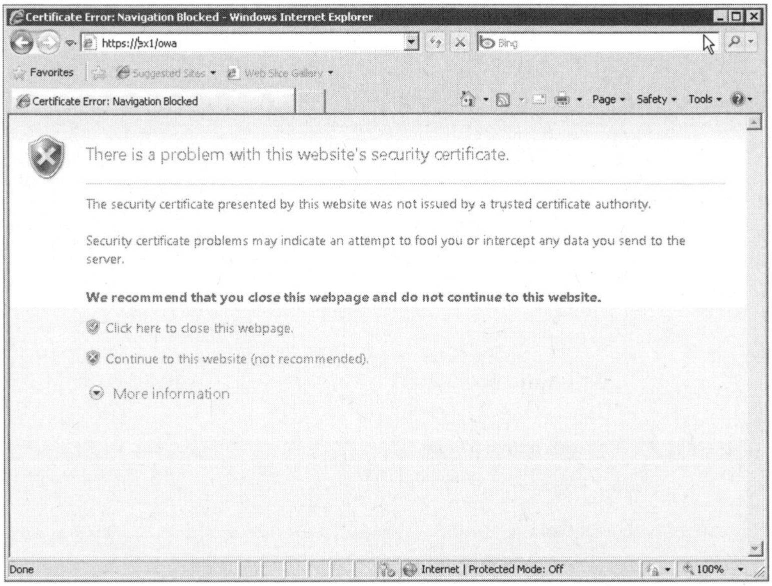

Entering the Product Key

You don't have to enter a product key in order to test Exchange Server 2010. However, if you do have a product key and would like to enter it into the server, it's very simple using these steps:

1. Open the Exchange Management Console and navigate to Microsoft Exchange ➢ Microsoft Exchange On-Premises (server) ➢ Server Configuration.

2. In the center pane, highlight the server.

3. In the Actions pane on the far right, click Enter Product Key.

4. Enter the digits for the product key. Hyphens are automatically entered. When finished, press Enter, and then click Finish.

As with any other configuration, you can set the product key using the Exchange Management Shell with the `Set-ExchangeServer` cmdlet and the `-ProductKey` parameter:

```
Set-ExchangeServer -identity '<server>' -ProductKey <product key>
```

Here's an example:

```
Set-ExchangeServer -identity 'ex1' -ProductKey AAAAA-BBBBB-CCCCC-DDDDD-FFFFF
```

TESTING OUTLOOK WEB APP

You can now also test Outlook Web App (OWA), the web-based email client for Exchange 2010:

1. Open a web browser and type `https://<servername>/owa`.

2. Click Continue To This Website (Not Recommended) at the certificate prompt.

3. Enter the domain and username for a user that was mailbox-enabled previously, and enter a password. Click OK.

4. Set your language and time zone, and click OK.

You will now be logged into Outlook Web App, and you can test some functionality. As mentioned earlier, since we're using an internal certificate, features that require a certificate will yield a certificate prompt first. This includes viewing the address book. In all cases, you can click Continue To This Website (Not Recommended) to continue testing. For more information on security and certificates in Exchange Server 2010, see Chapter 5, ''Message Security and Hygiene.''

The Bottom Line

Quickly size a typical server. Having a properly equipped server for testing can yield a much more positive experience. Taking the time to get the right hardware will avoid problems later.

> **Master It** What parameters must be kept in mind when sizing a lab/test server?

Install the necessary Windows Server 2008 R2 prerequisites. Certain configuration settings must be performed before installing Exchange 2010.

> **Master It** What is involved in installing and configuring the prerequisites?

Install a multi-function Exchange Server 2010 server. You should provide a basic, bare-bones server for testing and evaluation.

> **Master It** What installation methods are available for installing Exchange 2010?

Configure Exchange to send and receive email.

> **Master It** What are the configuration requirements for sending and receiving email?

Configure recipients, contacts, and distribution groups. Add mailboxes, distribution groups, resource accounts, and mail contacts to Exchange.

> **Master It** How are recipients created, and what's the difference between them?

Chapter 11

Understanding Server Roles and Configurations

Exchange Server 2010 allows you to specify only the components necessary for a specific server function during installation of the server rather than reconfiguring the server after software installation. You can install all components on a server or only the components necessary, for example, to support message transport functions.

In this chapter, you will learn to:

- ◆ Understand the importance of server roles
- ◆ Understand the Exchange Server 2010 server roles
- ◆ Explore possible role configurations

The Importance of Server Roles

The concept of an Exchange server role is not really a new concept. Microsoft officially introduced the concept in Exchange Server 2007, but in Exchange Server 2003 we did have server roles, such as a Mailbox server, a front-end server, or a bridgehead server.

What was different is that for an Exchange 2003 front-end server, you installed the entire Exchange Server 2003 installation package, including the database engine, the message transport (SMTP), and other Exchange server functions.

Once all the Exchange Server 2003 software was installed, you then had to make configuration changes and disable services to make the server provide only the services you required of that specific "role."

Exchange administrators may want to know why server roles are so important and why the change from the way we used to configure servers. Granted, the architecture of Exchange Server 2003 was fairly monolithic, but the process of securing and configuring an Exchange 2003 bridgehead or front-end server was fairly well understood.

Now, during installation, we are prompted to choose which server roles a particular Exchange server will be providing. Figure 11.1 shows the screen that you will see if you choose a custom setup of Exchange Server 2010. You are prompted for which server roles you need to install.

FIGURE 11.1
Selecting the Exchange
Server 2010 roles

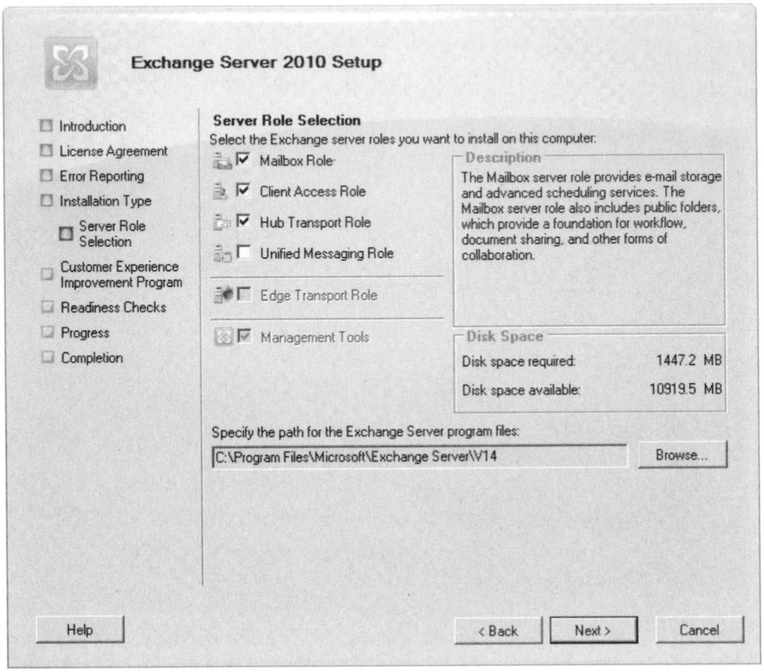

There are some clear and important advantages to this approach, such as the following:

◆ Server configuration complexity is reduced.

◆ Unnecessary components are no longer installed. Additional steps to disable services or lock down a component are not necessary.

◆ Server security is improved because now unnecessary components are not even installed, thus reducing a server's potential attack surface.

◆ Servers that have only the specific components necessary for their required role are more scalable.

Exchange 2010 Server Roles

Now let's take a look at the specific Exchange Server 2010 roles that you may find in your organization:

◆ Mailbox server

◆ Client Access server

◆ Hub Transport

◆ Unified Messaging

◆ Edge Transport

If you have worked with Exchange Server 2007, you may be wondering where the active clustered mailbox and passive clustered mailbox server roles are. They are no longer necessary: clustering can be achieved after installation because the concept of a clustered mailbox server no longer exists as it did in previous versions.

Mailbox Server

The Mailbox server role is at the center of the Exchange Server 2010 universe. The Mailbox server role hosts Exchange mailbox and public folder databases. Figure 11.2 shows the interaction with other messaging system components. Outlook MAPI clients still connect to the Exchange server but only for public folder access; for mailbox access, Outlook MAPI clients now connect to the Client Access server. Public Folder server referrals are provided by the Client Access server, though.

FIGURE 11.2
Messaging components interacting with a Mailbox server

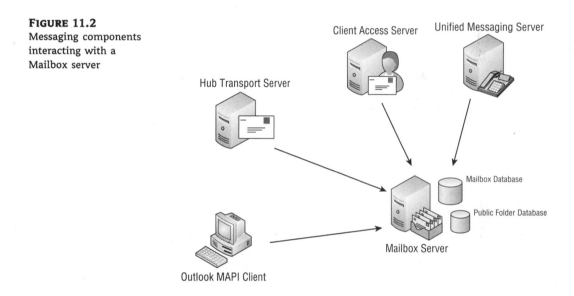

Mail delivery (even mail going from one mailbox on a local database to another mailbox on the same database) is routed through the Hub Transport server. The Unified Message server role connects directly to the Exchange Mailbox server to retrieve a user's outgoing voicemail message.

On the Mailbox server role, the Microsoft Information Store service will almost always be the number one consumer of systems resources; this is especially true of RAM usage. In Figure 11.3, this service shows up as `store.exe`. Don't be alarmed if you see this service consuming 90 percent of the RAM on a server; it is not uncommon for `store.exe` to use 24 GB of RAM on a server that has a total of 32 GB. This RAM usage enables the database to cache more data and interact with the disk subsystem more efficiently.

On an Exchange 2010 server that is dedicated to providing only Mailbox server functionality, you will still find quite a few Exchange services running. The Exchange 2010 Mailbox server services are listed in Table 11.1.

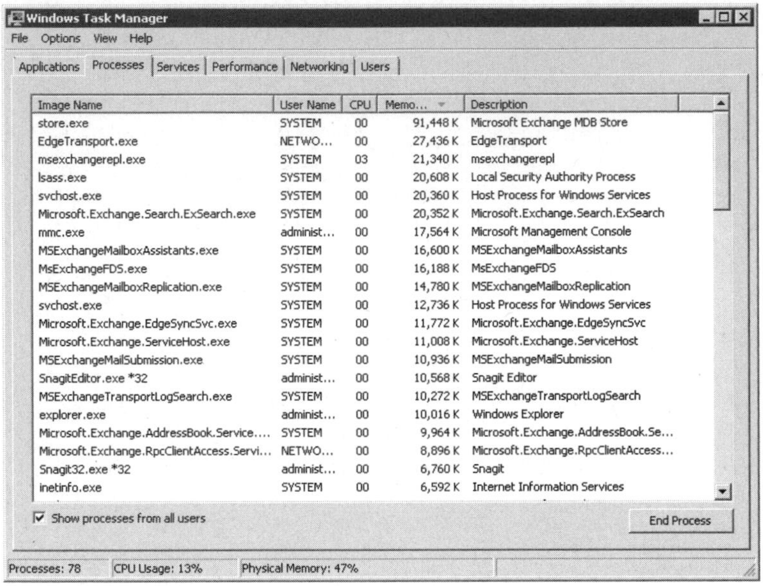

FIGURE 11.3
Viewing store.exe in
Task Manager

TABLE 11.1: Exchange Server 2010 Mailbox Server Services

SERVICE DISPLAY NAME, SHORT NAME, AND EXECUTABLE	FUNCTION
Microsoft Exchange Active Directory Topology/ MSExchangeADTopology/ ADTopologyService.exe	Locates Active Directory domain controllers and global catalog servers, and provides Active Directory topology information to Exchange services. Most Exchange services depend on this service; if it does not start, the Exchange server will probably not function.
Microsoft Exchange Information Store/ MSExchangeIS/store.exe	The information store is the actual Exchange database engine (also known as ESE). This service manages the mailbox and public folder databases. If the store.exe service does not start, databases will not be mounted.
Microsoft Exchange Mail Submission/ MSExchangeMailSubmission/ MSExchangeMailSubmission.exe	Handles message submission to the Exchange message transport service running on Exchange servers handling the Hub Transport role. If this service is stopped, email will not flow.
Microsoft Exchange Mailbox Assistants/ MSExchangeMailboxAssistants/ MSExchangeMailboxAssistants.exe	Handles background processing functions for Exchange mailboxes.

TABLE 11.1:   Exchange Server 2010 Mailbox Server Services *(CONTINUED)*

SERVICE DISPLAY NAME, SHORT NAME, AND EXECUTABLE	FUNCTION
Microsoft Exchange Monitoring/ MSExchangeMonitoring/ `Microsoft.Exchange.Monitoring.exe`	Handles the interaction between management and troubleshooting tools and the Exchange server. Used by tools such as the Exchange Management Shell diagnostic cmdlets.
Microsoft Exchange Replication/ MSExchangeRepl/`msexchangerepl.exe`	Provides the continuous replication service to copy log files from an active database to a server that hosts a passive copy of the database and handles log replay on passive servers.
Microsoft Exchange RPC Client Access/ MSExchangeRPC/`Microsoft.Exchange. RpcClientAccess.Service.exe`	Handles the interaction between Outlook MAPI clients and public folder databases.
Microsoft Exchange Search Indexer/MSExchangeSearch/`Microsoft. Exchange.Search.ExSearch.exe`	Handles content indexing for mailbox data.
Microsoft Exchange Server Extension for Windows Server Backup/ wsbexchange/`wsbexchange.exe`	Allows the Windows Server Backup utility to back up and restore Exchange Server data.
Microsoft Exchange Service Host/ MSExchangeServiceHost/`Microsoft. Exchange.ServiceHost.exe`	Provides a service host for Exchange components that do not have their own service. These include components such as configuring Registry and virtual directory information.
Microsoft Exchange System Attendant/MSExchangeSA/`mad.exe`	Provides general management tasks for the Exchange server, including generating offline address books, updating free/busy information, and maintaining group memberships for the server's computer account.
Microsoft Exchange Throttling/ MSExchangeThrottling/ `MSExchangeThrottling.exe`	Handles the limits on the rate of user operations to prevent any single user from consuming too many server resources.
Microsoft Exchange Transport Log Search/ MSExchangeTransportLogSearch/ `MSExchangeTransportLogSearch.exe`	Handles the remote search capabilities for the Exchange server transport log files.
Microsoft Search (Exchange)/msftesql-Exchange/`msftesql.exe`	Handles full-text creation for mailbox content and properties.

Hub Transport Server

If a message is delivered in an Exchange 2010 organization, at least one Hub Transport server touched the message. This is true even if the message is sent from a mailbox to another mailbox on the same database; the message is routed through a Hub Transport server.

There is a very important reason for that: a Hub Transport server must "touch" all email messages; the Exchange 2010 transport rules and journaling features need to be able to process every message that is sent by a user so that the rules can be applied consistently. However, if a message must pass through more than one Hub Transport server, the transport rules only "fire" one time on the message; the transport rules fire only on the first Hub Transport server that the message passes through.

Figure 11.4 shows the placement of the Hub Transport role within an Exchange organization. There must be at least one Hub Transport server role in each Active Directory site that contains a Mailbox server.

FIGURE 11.4
Hub Transport server
role placement

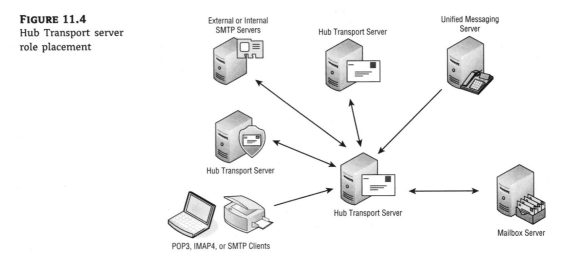

Looking at things from a high-level overview, the Hub Transport server provides the message transport function for all email. However, there is quite a bit more to the Hub Transport server's functions, which include:

◆ Picking up and delivering email for Mailbox servers in the local Active Directory site

◆ Routing email to Hub Transport servers in other Active Directory sites

◆ Sending mail to or receiving mail from an Edge Transport server

◆ Sending mail to or receiving mail from a third-party SMTP server, an external SMTP server, or an external (hosted) message hygiene system

◆ Sending to or receiving mail directly from the Internet (depending on your configuration)

◆ Receiving email from POP3 or IMAP4 clients and routing those messages on to Mailbox servers or outside the organization

◆ Receiving email from network-enabled scanners or photocopiers and routing those messages on to Mailbox servers or outside the organization

- ◆ Expanding distribution list membership

- ◆ Executing transport rules

- ◆ Performing mailbox-level journaling functions

- ◆ Processing antispam or antivirus scanning functions depending on your organization's configuration

- ◆ Receiving voicemail messages from Unified Messaging servers in the local Active Directory site that should be delivered to the destination mailbox

If you examine the service console on an Exchange 2010 server that has the Hub Transport server running, you will see a number of services related to Exchange Server. The service display name, short name, and the executable name as well as the service function are shown in Table 11.2.

TABLE 11.2:   Exchange Server 2010 Hub Transport Server Services

SERVICE DISPLAY NAME, SHORT NAME, AND EXECUTABLE	FUNCTION
Microsoft Exchange Active Directory Topology/ MSExchangeADTopology/ ADTopologyService.exe	Locates Active Directory domain controllers and global catalog servers, and provides Active Directory topology information to Exchange services. Most Exchange services depend on this service; if it does not start, the Exchange server will probably not function.
Microsoft Exchange Anti-spam Update/ MSExchangeAntispamUpdate/Microsoft. Exchange.AntispamUpdateSvc.exe	Handles the antispam automated signature and configuration updates.
Microsoft Exchange EdgeSync/ MSExchangeEdgeSync/Microsoft.Exchange. EdgeSyncSvc.exe	Synchronizes configuration, recipient, and safe-sender information between the Hub Transport and the Edge Transport Active Directory Application Mode (ADAM) instance.
Microsoft Exchange Monitoring/ MSExchangeMonitoring/Microsoft. Exchange.Monitoring.exe	Handles the interaction between management and troubleshooting tools and the Exchange server. Used by tools such as the Exchange Management Shell diagnostic cmdlets.
Microsoft Exchange Protected Service Host/ MSExchangeProtectedServiceHost/Microsoft. Exchange.ProtectedServiceHost.exe	Provides a service host for Exchange components that need to be protected from one another.
Microsoft Exchange Service Host/ MSExchangeServiceHost/Microsoft. Exchange.ServiceHost.exe	Provides a service host for Exchange components that do not have their own service. These include components such as configuring Registry and virtual directory information.

TABLE 11.2: Exchange Server 2010 Hub Transport Server Services *(CONTINUED)*

SERVICE DISPLAY NAME, SHORT NAME, AND EXECUTABLE	FUNCTION
Microsoft Exchange Transport/ MSExchangeTransport/ MSExchangeTransport.exe	Handles message transport between Hub Transport servers, Edge Transport servers, and external SMTP servers.
Microsoft Exchange Transport Log Search/ MSExchangeTransportLogSearch/ MSExchangeTransportLogSearch.exe	Handles the remote search capabilities for the Exchange server transport log files.
Microsoft Search (Exchange)/ msftesql-Exchange/msftesql.exe	Handles full-text creation for mailbox content and properties.

Client Access Server

The Exchange Server 2010 Client Access server provides most of the interface for accessing email data. The Exchange 2010 iteration of the Client Access server is the latest development as Microsoft abstracts the messaging database from end-user applications.

As you can see in Figure 11.5, the Client Access server, rather than the Mailbox server, now sits at the center of the client's universe.

FIGURE 11.5
Placement of the Client Access server

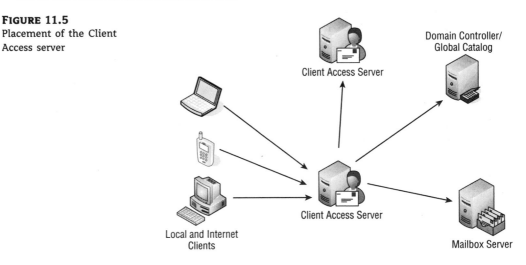

The Client Access server coordinates all communication between clients except for Outlook MAPI client connectivity with Mailbox servers that host public folder databases. Some of the functions of the Client Access server include the following:

◆ Supporting connections from Outlook MAPI clients

◆ Supporting connections from Outlook Anywhere (RPC over HTTP)

- Supporting connections from mobile devices using Microsoft ActiveSync technology

- Supporting connections from POP3 and IMAP4 clients

- Supporting connections from other Exchange Web Services (EWS) applications

- Proxying connections from various email clients to the relevant Exchange Mailbox server

- Acting as an endpoint for Outlook and Windows Mobile clients by proxying connections for directory lookups to a global catalog server in the local Active Directory site.

- Proxying connections from external Outlook Anywhere, Outlook Web App, or Windows Mobile clients to Client Access servers (CASs) in other Active Directory sites. The actual mechanics of the connection depends on the client that is being used and the location of the mailbox:

  - If an OWA user's mailbox is on an E2K3 server, then the E2K10 CAS silently redirects the user to the E2K3 front-end or E2K7 CAS using single sign-on.

  - If an OWA user's mailbox is on an E2K2 server and is located in same site as the E2K10 CAS, then the CAS silently redirects the user to the E2K7 CAS using single sign-on.

  - If an OWA user's mailbox is on an E2K7 server and is located in a different Active Directory site and there are no externally facing E2K7 CASs present in that Active Directory site, then the E2K10 CAS proxies the session to the E2K7 CAS in the target Active Directory site.

  - If an OWA user's mailbox is on an E2K7 server and is located in a different Active Directory site and there are externally facing E2K7 CASs present in that Active Directory site, then the E2K10 CAS performs a manual redirect, requiring the user to utilize the target Active Directory site's external URL link.

  - If an ActiveSync user's mailbox is on an E2K3 server, then the E2K10 CAS directly connects over TCP 80 to the E2K10 Mailbox server.

  - If an ActiveSync user's mailbox is on an E2K7 server and the ActiveSync version of the device is 12.1 or higher, and the target E2K7 CAS is externally facing, then the E2K10 CAS issues a 451 redirect with the external URL of the E2K7 CAS.

  - If an ActiveSync user's mailbox is on an E2K7 server, and the ActiveSync version of the device is less than 12.1, then the E2K10 CAS server proxies the session to the E2K7 CAS.

  - If an Outlook Anywhere user's mailbox is an E2K3 or E2K7 server, then the E2K10 CAS directly connects to the E2K3 or E2K7 Mailbox server.

When the hardware is properly sized, a Client Access server can accept thousands and thousands of simultaneous connections from different types of clients and connect on behalf of those clients to the Mailbox server. The Client Access server does not require one active connection for each active client between the CAS and the Mailbox server. The CAS and each Mailbox server share a pool of 100 RPC connections even if there are far more CAS clients using a particular Client Access server. This allows the Mailbox server to host more simultaneous clients by simply scaling upward on the number of CASs in the Active Directory site.

CLIENT ACCESS SERVERS IN THE PERIMETER NETWORK

If an organization is going to allow external clients (Outlook Web App, mobile phones, Outlook Anywhere) to connect to your Exchange servers from the Internet, a common question is whether or not the Client Access server should be in the perimeter or DMZ (demilitarized zone) network. We can tell you that the answer to this question is an unequivocal "no."

There are simply too many TCP and UDP ports that have to be open on the firewall between the internal Mailbox servers, domain controllers, global catalog servers, and DNS servers to make this practical. In addition, by putting a Windows server with domain membership in your perimeter network, you are increasing your risk factor for external exploitation. Great care should be taken when considering which servers located in a perimeter network should be domain members and which should not, and evaluate the reasons for each. Client Access and Hub Transport servers should not be in the perimeter network, but there are advantages to putting a server such as an ISA server into the perimeter network and making it a domain member.

While some security-conscious organizations may have a policy stating that no web-accessible server can be on the internal network, you can remediate that concern by using a reverse proxy in the perimeter network that handles inbound HTTP/HTTPS security and proxies requests from the perimeter into the internal Client Access servers.

Each Active Directory site that contains an Exchange 2010 Mailbox server must have at least one Client Access server. Microsoft recommends a ratio of three Client Access processor cores for each four Mailbox server processor cores and that the Client Access server have 2 GB of RAM for processor core. This is, of course, a generic recommendation and your actual mileage may vary depending on the number of simultaneous clients and the types of users (light, medium, heavy). You should keep up with Microsoft's current recommendations for sizing as they may change over time.

When you look in the service console on an Exchange 2010 Client Access server, you will see a number of services that may or may not be familiar to you. The Client Access server is dependent on many of the Internet Information Server web services so they are also required. The services found on an Exchange 2010 Client Access server are listed in Table 11.3.

TABLE 11.3:   Exchange Server 2010 Client Access Server Services

SERVICE DISPLAY NAME, SHORT NAME, AND EXECUTABLE	FUNCTION
Microsoft Exchange Active Directory Topology/ MSExchangeADTopology/ ADTopologyService.exe	Locates Active Directory domain controllers and global catalog servers, and provides Active Directory topology information to Exchange services. Most Exchange services depend on this service; if it does not start, the Exchange server will probably not function.
Microsoft Exchange Address Book Service/ MSExchangeAB/Microsoft.Exchange. AddressBook.Service.exe	Manages client address book connections.

TABLE 11.3:   Exchange Server 2010 Client Access Server Services *(CONTINUED)*

SERVICE DISPLAY NAME, SHORT NAME, AND EXECUTABLE	FUNCTION
Microsoft Exchange File Distribution/ MSExchangeFDS/MSExchangeFDS.exe	Replicates the offline address book files to other Client Access servers.
Microsoft Exchange Forms-Based Authentication service/MSExchangeFBA/ExFBA.exe	Handles forms-based authentication for applications such as Outlook Web Access and the Exchange Control Panel.
Microsoft Exchange IMAP4/ MSExchangeImap4/Microsoft.Exchange. Imap4Service.exe	Provides IMAP4 clients with access to Exchange mailboxes. This service is set to manual by default.
Microsoft Exchange Mailbox Replication/ MSExchangeMailboxReplication/ MSExchangeMailboxReplication.exe	Handles move mailbox requests submitted by New-MoveRequest.
Microsoft Exchange Monitoring/ MSExchangeMonitoring/Microsoft.Exchange. Monitoring.exe	Handles the interaction between management and troubleshooting tools and the Exchange server. Used by tools such as the Exchange Management Shell diagnostic cmdlets.
Microsoft Exchange POP3/ MSExchangePop3/Microsoft.Exchange. Pop3Service.exe	Provides POP3 clients with access to Exchange mailboxes. This service is set to manual by default.
Microsoft Exchange Protected Service Host/ MSExchangeProtectedServiceHost/ Microsoft.Exchange. ProtectedServiceHost.exe	Provides a service host for Exchange components that need to be protected from one another.
Microsoft Exchange RPC Client Access/ MSExchangeRPC/Microsoft.Exchange. RpcClientAccess.Service.exe	Handles the interaction between Outlook MAPI clients and mailbox databases.
Microsoft Exchange Service Host/ MSExchangeServiceHost/Microsoft.Exchange. ServiceHost.exe	Provides a service host for Exchange components that do not have their own service. These include components such as configuring Registry and virtual directory information.

Unified Messaging Server

The Unified Messaging server role was introduced in Exchange Server 2007 and is reasonably similar in Exchange Server 2010. There are a few useful new features such as voicemail preview, protected voicemail, and the personal auto-attendant. One notable change is that the inbound faxing function is no longer supported. This server role integrates voicemail with Exchange mailboxes and provides voice auto-attendant functions and phone access to email and calendar. The Unified Messaging server requires an IP-based telephone switch or a traditional public branch exchange (PBX)-to-IP gateway.

The Unified Messaging server role integrates into your environment, as shown in Figure 11.6. This server must be in the same Active Directory site as a Hub Transport server and preferably the same site as the Mailbox servers that hold the mailboxes it is supporting. Further, the Unified Messaging server roles should sit on the same subnet as the IP-based PBX or PBX-to-IP gateway.

FIGURE 11.6
Integrating a Unified
Messaging server role

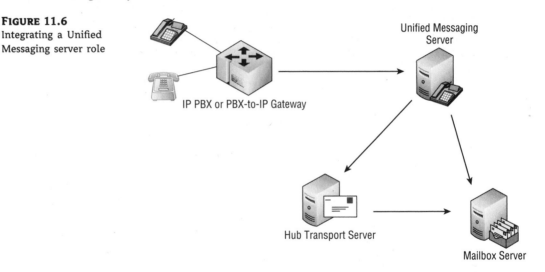

The following functions are handled by the Unified Messaging server role:

◆ Accepts inbound VOIP phone calls for users if they do not answer their voice line in the same way that a traditional voicemail system accepts calls. The VOIP system or PBX-to-IP gateway passes along identifying information to Unified Messaging, indicating which phone extension had been called.

◆ Identifies which user mailbox a phone call is intended for and retrieves the user's outgoing message from their mailbox.

◆ Provides voicemail for users of the IP-based phone system or through the PBX-to-IP gateway; includes voicemail greetings and options. Inbound voicemail is recorded as a Windows Media Audio (WMA) file and stored as a message in a user's Inbox.

◆ Allows users to dial into the Unified Messaging server to retrieve voicemail, listen to email messages, review their calendar, or change appointments

◆ Provides voice menus and prompting call menus acting as an auto-attendant system.

UNIFIED MESSAGING AND VOICEMAIL MESSAGE SIZE

Many administrators are concerned about the size of a user's mailbox once their voicemail starts to be directed to the user's Inbox. Visions of 30-second messages being stored as 1 MB attachments flash through people's heads.

In reality, it is not that bad, though. Granted, your mail storage requirements will rise just a bit because there will be additional content stored in the user's mailbox. However, voice-mail messages are not as large as you might think. Unified Message supports three codecs (coder/decoders) when recording a voice mail message. These are the MP3 code (the default for Exchange Server 2010), Windows Media Audio (WMA), Group System Mobile (GSM), and G.711 Pulse Code Modulation (PCM). You can pick these on a systemwide basis or override them on a user-by-user basis. Each of these has advantages and disadvantages, of course.

The MP3 codec requires about 2 KB per second so a 30-second message would be about 60 KB. The WMA codec requires about 7 KB per message plus 1 KB for each second. So a 30-second message would be about 37 KB. The GSM codec requires about 1.6 KB per second. The PCM codec records a much higher quality voice message but at a cost of approximately about 16 KB per second of voice. The MP3 codec is probably your best bet for most users as it is almost universally compatible with most mobile devices, including the iPhone.

If you look in the service console on a server with the Unified Messaging role installed, you will see the services shown in Table 11.4.

TABLE 11.4: Exchange Server 2010 Unified Messaging Server Services

SERVICE DISPLAY NAME, SHORT NAME, AND EXECUTABLE	FUNCTION
Microsoft Exchange Active Directory Topology/ MSExchangeADTopology/ ADTopologyService.exe	Locates Active Directory domain controllers and global catalog servers, and provides Active Directory topology information to Exchange services. Most Exchange services depend on this service; if it does not start, the Exchange server will probably not function.
Microsoft Exchange File Distribution/ MSExchangeFDS/MSExchangeFDS.exe	Replicates the offline address book files to other Client Access servers.
Microsoft Exchange Monitoring/ MSExchangeMonitoring/Microsoft. Exchange.Monitoring.exe	Handles the interaction between management and troubleshooting tools and the Exchange server. Used by tools such as the Exchange Management Shell diagnostic cmdlets.
Microsoft Exchange Service Host/ MSExchangeServiceHost/Microsoft. Exchange.ServiceHost.exe	Provides a service host for Exchange components that do not have their own service. These include components such as configuring Registry and virtual directory information.

TABLE 11.4: Exchange Server 2010 Unified Messaging Server Services *(CONTINUED)*

SERVICE DISPLAY NAME, SHORT NAME, AND EXECUTABLE	FUNCTION
Microsoft Exchange Speech Engine Service/MSSpeechService/SpeechService.exe	Handles text-to-speech processing for Unified Messaging.
Microsoft Exchange Unified Messaging/MSExchangeUM/umservice.exe	Handles processing of inbound voice calls, records voicemail messages, implements auto-attendant functions, and provides end users with access to their voicemail, email, and calendar via the phone.

Edge Transport Server

The Edge Transport functionality is another new feature that was included with Exchange Server 2007. The Edge Transport server provides a slimmed-down version of the Exchange message transport functionality that requires neither Active Directory nor components such as the information store.

The Edge Transport server is usually placed in an organization's perimeter network rather than the internal network, as shown in Figure 11.7.

IS THE EDGE TRANSPORT ROLE REQUIRED?

One common misconception about the Edge Transport server role is that it is required; it is not. An Exchange 2010 Hub Transport server can send and receive email directly with the Internet or it can use any third-party SMTP relay or message hygiene system.

FIGURE 11.7
Implementing an Edge Transport server role

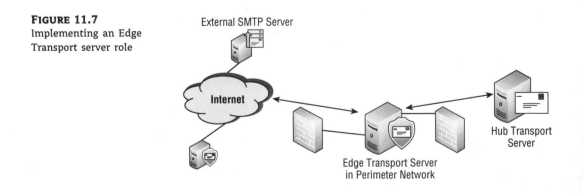

External SMTP Server

Internet

Edge Transport Server in Perimeter Network

Hub Transport Server

There are a number of reasons that the Edge Transport role has advantages over using an Exchange 2003 server in your perimeter network:

◆ To process delivery reports, nondelivery reports, and address rewrites, the information store service must be running and the default mailbox database must be mounted.

◆ Placing an Exchange 2000/2003 server in the perimeter network requires many ports to be opened on the firewall from the perimeter network to the internal network.

◆ Allowing inbound email directly to an Exchange server could jeopardize both Exchange and Active Directory.

For these reasons, a server role was developed that has many of the advantages of an Exchange 2010 server. However, it can be made much more secure because it can run in the perimeter network as a stand-alone computer and does not require Active Directory membership. Here are some of the characteristics of the Edge Transport server role:

◆ It should be deployed in the perimeter network.

◆ It can be managed with Exchange Management Shell scripts and the Exchange Management Console in much the same way a regular Exchange server is managed.

◆ The Edge Transport server receives LDAP updates from an internal Hub Transport that updates information such as valid SMTP domains, recipients, and safe sender and blocked sender lists for each user.

◆ The only components required to run the Edge Transport role are the message transport system and an instance of the Active Directory Lightweight Directory Services database.

◆ Features such as transport rules can be implemented in the perimeter network and provide message policy enforcement for messages entering or leaving the organization that is separate from that provided on the internal network.

◆ Connectivity between internal Hub Transport servers and Edge Transport servers is authenticated and the data stream encrypted.

◆ The content filter functionality and other antispam and message security tools are built in, as is the ability to add third-party content filtering/message hygiene tools.

◆ Microsoft Forefront Security for Exchange Server can be employed on the Edge Transport server role for virus detection and quarantine.

For medium and large organizations, higher availability comes in the form of installing multiple Edge Transport servers and providing load balancing using multiple DNS Mail Exchanger (MX) records, network load balancing, DNS round-robin, or failover using multiple Internet connections.

If you look at the service console on an Exchange Server 2010 Edge Transport server, you will find the services in Table 11.5.

TABLE 11.5: Exchange Server 2010 Edge Transport Server Services

SERVICE DISPLAY NAME, SHORT NAME, AND EXECUTABLE	FUNCTION
Microsoft Exchange ADAM/ADAM_MSExchange/dsamain.exe	Runs the Active Directory Lightweight Directory Services (ADLDS) database also known as the ADAM service. This service stores the Edge Transport configuration and recipient information.
Microsoft Exchange Anti-spam Update/ MSExchangeAntispamUpdate/Microsoft. Exchange.AntispamUpdateSvc.exe	Handles the antispam automated signature and configuration updates.
Microsoft Exchange Credential Service/ MSExchangeEdgeCredential/Microsoft. Exchange.EdgeCredentialSvc.exe	Handles the Edge Transport credential service.
Microsoft Exchange Monitoring/ MSExchangeMonitoring/ Microsoft.Exchange.Monitoring.exe	Handles the interaction between management and troubleshooting tools and the Exchange server. Used by tools such as the Exchange Management Shell diagnostic cmdlets.
Microsoft Exchange Service Host/ MSExchangeServiceHost/ Microsoft.Exchange.ServiceHost.exe	Provides a service host for Exchange components that do not have their own service. These include components such as configuring Registry and virtual directory information.
Microsoft Exchange Transport/ MSExchangeTransport/ MSExchangeTransport.exe	Handles message transport between Hub Transport servers, Edge Transport servers, and external SMTP servers.
Microsoft Exchange Transport Log Search/ MSExchangeTransportLogSearch/ MSExchangeTransportLogSearch.exe	Handles the remote search capabilities for the Exchange server transport log files.

Possible Role Configurations

There are many possible configurations for Exchange Server 2010; unfortunately, there is no "magic formula" that will help you determine the exact number of servers you need and the roles those servers should host — well, at least not a simple formula. Knowing exactly when to scale Exchange Server 2010 from a single combined function server to multiple dedicated server roles depends on a lot of factors:

- Server roles that your organization requires. Note that all Exchange organizations require at least one Mailbox, Hub Transport, and Client Access server; the Unified Messaging and Edge Transport roles are optional.

- The number of simultaneous users that will be using the system and their usage profile (light, average, heavy).

- The number of messages sent and received per hour and the average size of those messages.

- An organization's high availability requirements.

- The distribution of your users (across various offices) as well as the WAN link speeds and latency between the offices.

- The number of transport rules, journaling rules, daily messaging records management events, daily archiving, and other Exchange features that are required.

- Any third-party products that place additional transport, mailbox, or I/O load on the server, such as discovery, compliance, antivirus, antispam, archiving, or mobile devices.

You might need to segment server roles in a situation where you need to simplify server configuration by ensuring that only specific server roles reside on a single Windows server.

Combined Function Server

For many companies, a single Windows Server 2008 R2 or SP2 running Exchange Server 2010 with the Mailbox, Hub Transport, and Client Access server roles will be just fine depending on their usage patterns and number of simultaneous users. A company with only a few hundred users will fit perfectly well on a single server. Figure 11.8 shows a combined function server and some of the typical components that will interact with the server.

FIGURE 11.8
Implementing a combined function server

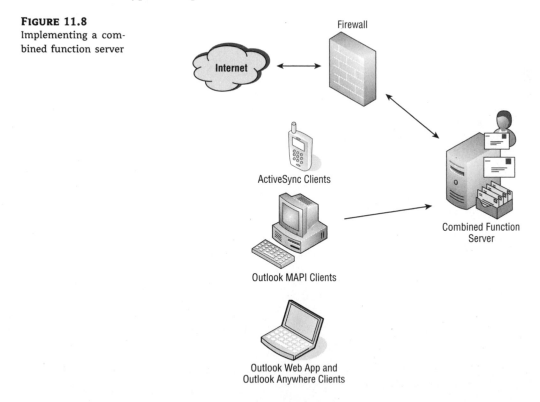

Firewall

Internet

ActiveSync Clients

Outlook MAPI Clients

Combined Function Server

Outlook Web App and Outlook Anywhere Clients

When properly configured with sufficient memory, disk capacity, and CPU resources, the combined function server or multirole server can easily support upward of 500 users. This is, of course, taking into consideration that these are mostly light to medium users; 500 simultaneous users all sending and receiving hundreds of messages per day would probably not fit well on a single machine. The combined function server is an economical solution provided you don't overload the server and provided you have good disaster recovery documentation. The disaster recovery documentation is important since all server roles are on a single server, so if it ever has to be rebuilt, all server roles have to be recovered at the same time.

Picking the right server hardware configuration is especially important when using a combined function server. We recommend using a server with a minimum of dual quad-core CPUs, Gigabit Ethernet adapter, and 8 GB of RAM plus 5 and 10 MB additional RAM per mailbox. So, for a server that will support 500 medium profile mailboxes, it would need approximately 12 GB of RAM. Whatever you do, do not skimp on the RAM.

Real World Scenario

EXCHANGE 2010 AND DOMAIN CONTROLLERS COEXISTING

In almost no circumstances do your authors recommend installing Exchange Server 2010 on the same machine as a domain controller. Too many problems have arisen in every previous version of Exchange. Troubleshooting one or the other becomes more difficult when both Exchange Server and Active Directory are hosted on the same Windows server. We certainly see the logic that can be applied when buying server hardware, though.

For a company that is only supporting 50 mailboxes (and does not want to use Small Business Server), it seems foolish to purchase two separate physical machines that will both be very lightly loaded.

Company QRS had a total of 72 users; at any given time only about 60 of those users were actually using the email server. With the help of their consultant, they decided to use a host Windows Server 2008 x64 operating system and run a domain controller in one Hyper-V virtual machine and the Exchange 2010 Server in a different Hyper-V virtual machine. This kept the applications separated on different operating systems, but did not require the purchase of two physical servers. A third Hyper-V machine was configured to run SharePoint, an additional web application, and to act as their file/print server.

The actual physical machine running these three guest operating systems had a dual quad-core processor and 24 GB of physical memory.

Scaling Exchange Server 2010 Roles

If you have determined that you are unable to host all your Exchange server roles on a single physical machine, you will need to start splitting the roles off to multiple Windows servers. This is usually because you need to scale to support a larger user load than a single server can provide, or you may be trying to build in high availability and fault tolerance.

The first example here in Figure 11.9 is an organization that, for example, needs to support a single Mailbox server with 1,500 mailboxes. In this environment, ensuring that the Mailbox server has sufficient capacity to handle that many mailboxes is important, but the Client Access and Hub Transport servers must also be properly configured.

FIGURE 11.9
Moving the Client Access and Hub Transport roles off the Mailbox server

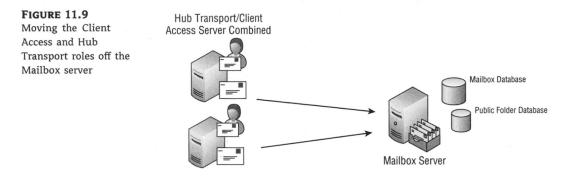

In this particular example, the Client Access and Hub Transport server roles have been combined on a single Windows server, and then two of this particular combination have been used. This provides higher availability for the access and transport functions while still using only two additional Windows servers. And this particular server combination can be virtualized. However, additional Hub Transport and Client Access servers will not provide you with Mailbox server redundancy; for that you need to use database availability groups (DAGs) and multiple Mailbox server roles.

You may still need to scale even further. For example, take an organization that needs to support 4,000 mailboxes and desires a high availability for the Mailbox server role as well as fault tolerance for the Hub Transport and Client Access servers. At this number of users, it probably makes sense to split the Hub Transport and Client Access servers off to separate Windows servers.

If you are trying to achieve high availability on the Mailbox server side, you will probably also want to take advantage of Exchange Server 2010 DAGs. In Figure 11.10, you can see that there are two Mailbox servers in a single DAG; the database on one server would be configured to replicate to the second server.

In this type of configuration, the public folder databases can be split off to separate Windows servers or each member of the DAG can hold a public folder replica. High availability for the public folder content can be achieved by replicating the public folder content between the two servers.

The Bottom Line

Understand the importance of server roles For medium-sized and large organizations, server roles allow more flexibility and scalability by providing you with the ability to isolate specific Exchange Server 2010 functions on different Windows servers. By installing only the necessary Exchange server roles on a Windows server, there is less likelihood that one set of functions will consume all the server's resources and interfere with the operation of the other functions.

Installing less actual Exchange server binaries reduces the amount of software running on the Windows server and thereby reduces the attack surface of the server.

FIGURE 11.10
Distributing server roles
even further

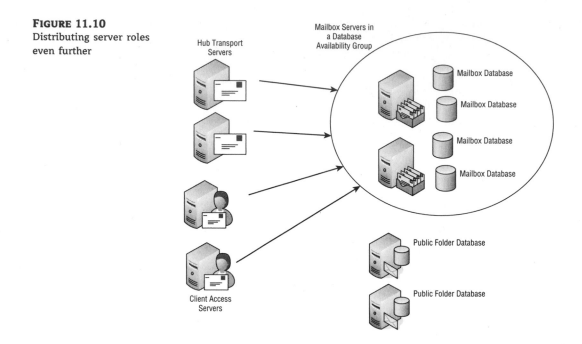

Server complexity is reduced since only specific functions must be configured on servers hosting segmented server roles.

> **Master It** You are the administrator for an Exchange organization with 1,700 mailboxes. Your design calls for a dedicated Mailbox server. Your boss has asked you to explain some of the reasons why you need to segment the Mailbox role to a dedicated server.

Understand Exchange Server 2010 server roles Exchange Server 2010 supports five unique server roles.

The Mailbox server hosts the Exchange server database engine, which in turn provides access to mailbox and public folder databases.

The Client Access server provides access to email data for Outlook MAPI clients, POP3, IMAP4, Outlook Web App, and ActiveSync (mobile) clients.

The Hub Transport server moves messages between the sender and the recipient (even if they are on the same server), routes mail to Hub Transport servers in other Active Directory sites, interacts with the Edge Transport server role, and can even send or receive Internet mail. The Hub Transport server is also responsible for message journaling and transport rules.

The Unified Messaging server acts as an organization's voicemail system by recording voicemail and delivering it to the user's mailbox (via the Hub Transport servers). Users can call the Unified Messaging server (via VOIP access) and listen to their voicemails, have their emails read, review their calendar, or even make changes to their calendar.

The Edge Transport server role is similar to the Hub Transport server, but resides in the perimeter network and requires no connectivity to the Active Directory. The Edge Transport server provides message hygiene (antispam and possible antivirus functions) was well as Internet message routing.

Master It   Which Exchange server role provides access to the mailbox database for Outlook Web App and Outlook clients?

Explore possible server role configurations   Server roles can be mixed and matched to meet most configuration requirements. Roles can be mixed and matched as necessary depending on an organization's requirements.

For small organizations, a combined function server that hosts the Mailbox, Client Access, and Hub Transport roles will suffice provided it has sufficient hardware even if it needs to support 500 or more mailboxes.

We do not recommend installing Exchange Server 2010 on a domain controller.

Scalability, fault tolerance, and high availability can be achieved by adding additional Windows servers and splitting server roles across many servers.

Client Access, Hub Transport, and Unified Messaging servers can be virtualized. Depending on the client load, Mailbox servers may also be virtualized as long as you remain within Microsoft's support boundaries.

Master It   Your company has approximately 400 mailboxes. Your users will only require basic email services (email, shared calendars, Outlook, and Outlook Web App). You already have two servers that function as domain controllers / global catalog servers. What would you recommend to support the 400 mailbox?

Chapter 12

Exchange Server 2010 Requirements

When you get ready to start installing Exchange Server 2010, one of the things that may slow you down the most is getting to the point where you meet all the necessary prerequisites. Depending on your expertise with Exchange Server, Active Directory, and Windows Server 2008, it may take hours or even days before you are ready to install Exchange Server 2010.

Some of the things that can slow you down include operating system and Active Directory prerequisites (software versions, patches, updates) as well as having the required permissions. If you are upgrading from a previous version of Exchange, you must make sure you are at the right version and service pack for all your existing servers.

In this chapter, we will make sure you are aware of all these prerequisites so that when you are ready to install Exchange Server 2010 you will breeze through the installation quickly and without interruption.

In this chapter, you will learn to:

- ◆ Use the right hardware for your organization

- ◆ Configure Windows Server 2008 to support Exchange Server 2010

- ◆ Confirm that Active Directory is ready

- ◆ Verify that previous versions of Exchange can interoperate with Exchange Server 2010

Getting the Right Server Hardware

One of the things that you can always depend on when looking at any manufacturer's hardware specifications is that the specs will always provide the minimum recommendations necessary to run the specified product. Microsoft has learned from their customers that recommending a minimum configuration often yields unhappy customers.

Minimum hardware configuration works just fine if you are building a test lab or a classroom environment. But for production environments you want to make sure that your hardware can support a typical everyday workload plus a bit more. In this section, we will make some recommendations that are partially based on our own experiences and partially based on Microsoft's best practices.

Note that hardware configuration can vary quite a bit depending on the server's role and its workload. You may be supporting a single server with 100 mailboxes or a multiserver site with 100,000 mailboxes. You should plan to comfortably support your maximum expected load along with some room to grow.

CHOOSING THE RIGHT HARDWARE

There are three key factors to ensuring that your Exchange servers function reliably and efficiently: stable hardware, correctly configured software, and proper management. If you fail to get any one of these right, the result will be poor performance, downtime, data loss, and unhappy users.

Windows hardware compatibility is probably the most important part of your choice for a server platform. This includes not only the server model itself, but also the components you will be using, such as network adapters and any third-party software.

Pick a server vendor that offers local support. Choose a server model that will provide you with the card slots and available disk drives. When evaluating server models, ensure that the server model is near the beginning of its model life rather than near the end. It is not uncommon to purchase a server through a discount outlet that is near or at the end of its model life.

As you build your Windows servers, ensure that you are running reasonably recent versions of all supporting software, such as device drivers, and that the operating system is patched.

The Typical User

If you have worked with more than one organization, you have probably reached the same conclusion that we have: no two Exchange organizations are exactly alike. Even businesses within the same industry can have dramatically different usage patterns based on slightly different business practices.

Where does this put the poor hapless person in charge of figuring out how much hardware to buy and how much capacity that hardware should have? If you are currently running an earlier version of Exchange Server, at least you have a leg up over other people.

You can use tools such as Performance Monitor to measure the number of messages sent and received per day and disk I/O capacity. You can use a tool such as the Exchange 2003 System Manager to report on mailbox sizes. You can enable message tracking and use tools such as the Exchange Server Profile Analyzer or Promodag Reports (www.promodag.com) to report how much mail each user sends and receives per day (and more).

Microsoft has done a lot of research in this area and has published some statistics on what they consider to be light, average, heavy, very heavy, and extra heavy Outlook users. They have also calculated that the average email message size is 50 KB in size. Table 12.1 shows how Microsoft has defined each type of user.

Just relying on emails sent and received may not be the best judge of the hardware capacity required. We will talk about these other factors throughout the book, but here are some factors that can adversely affect performance:

◆ Email archiving

◆ Mobile device user (the Blackberry can place a load four times higher on a server than a typical Outlook user)

◆ Antivirus scanning

◆ Messaging records management

◆ Transport rules

◆ Database replication

TABLE 12.1:   Microsoft's Outlook User Types

USER TYPE	MESSAGES SENT PER DAY	MESSAGES RECEIVED PER DAY
Light	5	20
Average	10	40
Heavy	20	80
Very heavy	30	120
Extra heavy	40	160

CPU Recommendations

Exchange Server 2010 only runs on Windows Server 2008 x64 and therefore only on hardware (physical or virtualized hardware) that is capable of supporting the x64 processor extensions. The processor should be at least 1.6 GHz, though you will certainly benefit from processors faster than 2 GHz and multicore processors. The processor must be one of the following:

◆ Intel Xeon or Intel Pentium x64 that supports the Intel Extended Memory 64 Technology (EM64T)

◆ AMD Opteron 64-bit processor that supports the AMD64 platform

The Intel Itanium IA64 processor family is not supported.

Table 12.2 shows the processor recommendations from Microsoft for different Exchange Server 2010 roles.

TABLE 12.2:   Processor Recommendations Based on Server Role

EXCHANGE 2010 SERVER ROLE	MINIMUM	RECOMMENDED	RECOMMENDED MAXIMUM
Edge Transport	1 × processor core	4 × processor cores	12 × processor cores
Hub Transport	1 × processor core	4 × processor cores	12 × processor cores
Client Access	2 × processor core	8 × processor cores	12 × processor cores
Unified Messaging	2 × processor core	4 × processor cores	12 × processor cores
Mailbox	2 × processor core	8 × processor cores	12 × processor cores
Combined function (combinations of Hub Transport, Client Access, and Mailbox server roles)	2 × processor core	8 × processor cores	16 × processor cores

This may seem like a lot of processor horsepower, and in some ways it sure is. But remember that an Exchange 2010 server is doing a lot more than an Exchange 2003 server. For example, on a combined-function server that is running the Mailbox, Client Access, and Hub Transport server roles, not only are the database engine, web components, and message transport running, but new components such as transport rules, messaging records management, mailbox archival, and RPC client access functions are also running.

If you have worked with Exchange Server 2007 in the past, you may also note that the CPU recommendations for the Exchange 2010 Client Access server are for more capacity than in Exchange 2007. This is because all Outlook MAPI RPC traffic has been abstracted out of the Information Store service and is now handled by the RPC client access service.

If you are planning to use existing server hardware, consult your manufacturer's documentation for specific information on the processors and cores.

If you are not sure whether your existing hardware supports the x64 extensions, you can check this in a number of ways, including confirming it with the hardware vendor. If the computer is already running Windows, you can get a handy little program called CPU-Z from www.cpuid.com that will check your processor. Figure 12.1 shows the CPU-Z program.

FIGURE 12.1
Using CPU-Z to identify the CPU type

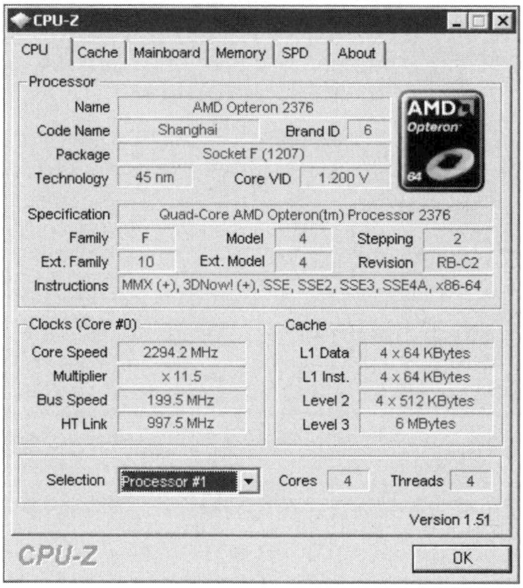

Notice in the Instructions line of CPU-Z that this particular chip supports x64–86. This means that this AMD chip will support the x64 instruction sets. Intel processors will report that they support the EMT64T instruction set.

HUB TRANSPORT CPU CONSIDERATIONS

We don't have a specific formula that you should use when planning for the CPU requirements on a Hub Transport server. For organizations that are small enough to support all roles on a single, combined-function server, you just want to make sure that the server has sufficient CPU cores for all the tasks that all the different Exchange roles must perform.

As you start to scale your organization to the point that you are putting specific server roles on dedicated server hardware, consider the factors that utilize the CPU on a Hub Transport server. The number one factor, of course, is the number of messages transported per hour. Four processor cores will probably be sufficient for a server that transports 1,000 messages per hour, but factors that might require more CPU capacity on a Hub Transport server include the following:

- Integrating Windows Rights Management
- Enabling transport rules
- Using message journaling
- Antivirus and/or antispam scanning
- Processing lots of large messages
- Enabling additional transport agents

CLIENT ACCESS SERVER CPU CONSIDERATIONS

All access to mailbox content is now handled through the Client Access server; this was not necessarily true in previous versions of Exchange. Now, mobile devices, web clients, Outlook MAPI clients, POP3, and IMAP4 clients *all* go through the Client Access server.

Although this is a good thing for the Mailbox server, it means that the Client Access server has more work to do. A Client Access server in an environment with a few hundred mailboxes can probably use a two-CPU core processor, but as the number of simultaneous users climbs, the processor power required will also climb. These additional factors may affect CPU requirements:

- Implementing SSL (secure sockets layer) access on the Client Access server
- Supporting larger numbers of POP3, IMAP4, Outlook Web Access, or Windows Mobile clients (since these clients require messages to be converted)

MAILBOX SERVER CPU CONSIDERATIONS

The number of processors required on a Mailbox server mostly depends on the total number of simultaneous users. According to Microsoft, a dedicated Mailbox server with sufficient memory and a four-processor core server should be able to support 2,000+ mailboxes. Microsoft estimates a factor for calculating CPU requirements is one CPU core for each 1,000 mailboxes; this guideline is based on some assumptions about the usage profiles of those 1,000 users. In this case, they assume that 750 of those are active and heavy usage mailboxes. Sizing your mailbox servers for 10 to 20 percent more capacity than you think you are going to need is a good practice.

A number of factors affect CPU requirements, including the usage profile of the typical user and the concurrency rate (the percentage of your users who are accessing the server at any given time). If you are planning to support 2,000 very heavy users who use Outlook 90 percent of the day, you may need more CPU capacity. Factors that affect mailbox server CPU requirements include the following:

- Number of simultaneous users and usage profile
- Email archiving processes
- Mobile device usage

SCALING TO DEDICATED SERVERS ROLES

For an awful lot of Exchange Server administrators, we never have to worry about more than a single server because our entire user community can fit nicely on to a single, combined function server. At some point, though, you may be required to add dedicated Exchange Server 2010 server roles to your organization. Here are some scenarios that may require dedicated server roles:

◆ The Active Directory site has more than one Mailbox server role.

◆ The Hub Transport, Client Access, or Unified Messaging functions place too much overhead on a single server.

◆ The requirements for high availability and/or load balancing demand more than one point of failure.

Exactly how many Client Access or Hub Transport servers do you require? As with almost everything related to an Exchange Server configuration, this depends largely on your user community and the load they place on the server. Microsoft has a guideline based on the number of processor cores that the Mailbox server has versus the number of supporting Client Access or Hub Transport server processor cores.

For Hub Transport servers, this ratio will be different depending on whether or not the Hub Transport has antivirus software on it. For Hub Transport servers without antivirus software, you should plan to have one Hub Transport processor core for every seven Mailbox server cores. If the Hub Transport server has antivirus software scanning enabled, that ratio changes to one Hub Transport processor core for every five Mailbox server cores.

The ratio is different for Client Access servers partially because of the additional load placed on the Client Access server by the RPC client access component. A typical environment should have three Client Access CPU cores for every four Mailbox server cores.

If you have a dedicated Mailbox with eight CPU cores, a dedicated Hub Transport server (with antivirus scanning enabled) should have two CPU cores. The Client Access server should have six CPU cores. This configuration provides no redundancy and does not take into consideration any additional factors that might increase processing load, such as enabling SSL, or many transport rules.

Memory Recommendations

As mentioned previously, the advantage that Exchange Server gets out of the x64 architecture is the ability to access more physical memory. Additional physical memory improves caching, reduces the disk I/O profile, and allows for the addition of more features.

Microsoft recommends a minimum of 4 GB of RAM in each Exchange 2010 server. This amount will depend on the roles that the server is supporting. Table 12.3 shows the minimum, recommended, and maximum memory for each of the server roles.

Although Microsoft's minimum RAM recommendation for any server hosting the Mailbox role is 4 GB, we strongly recommend a minimum of 6 GB. Once you have calculated the minimum amount of RAM that you require for the server, if you are configuring a Mailbox server, you will need to add some additional RAM for each mailbox. This amount will depend on either your user community's estimated message profile or the mailbox size. You should calculate the memory requirement based on not only the usage profile of your users but also the mailbox size; then you will need to take the larger of these two calculations. So, let's start with the amount of memory required based on usage profiles. Table 12.4 shows the additional memory required based on the number of mailboxes supported. The user profiles were defined previously in Table 12.1.

TABLE 12.3:   Minimum and Recommended RAM for Exchange Server 2010 Roles

SERVER ROLE	MINIMUM	RECOMMENDATION	MAXIMUM
Mailbox	4 GB	4 GB of base memory plus per mailbox calculation (generally 2 to 10 MB per mailbox)	64 GB
Hub Transport	4 GB	1 GB per CPU core	16 GB
Client Access	4 GB	2 GB per CPU core	16 GB
Unified Messaging	4 GB	1 GB per CPU core	8 GB
Edge Transport	4 GB	1 GB per CPU core	16 GB
Multiple roles	10 GB	16 GB for combination Hub Transport, Client Access, plus the per-mailbox calculation*	64 GB

For more information, see http://technet.microsoft.com/en-us/library/dd346700.

TABLE 12.4:   Additional Memory Factor for Mailbox Servers

USER PROFILE	PER MAILBOX MEMORY RECOMMENDATION
Light	Add 2 MB per mailbox
Average	Add 4 MB per mailbox
Heavy	Add 6 MB per mailbox
Very Heavy	Add 8 MB per mailbox
Extra Heavy	Add 10 MB per mailbox

Next, let's look at the recommendations based on the mailbox size. Table 12.5 shows Microsoft's per mailbox memory recommendations for mailboxes of different sizes.

So for example, a server handling a Mailbox server role should have 4 GB of memory plus the additional RAM per mailbox shown in Table 12.4 or the memory shown in Table 12.5 (whichever is larger). Let's do the calculations for a simple organization. If the Mailbox server is supporting 1,000 mailboxes and it is estimated that 500 of the users are average (1.75 GB of RAM if assuming 4 MB per mailbox) and 500 are heavy users (2.5 GB of RAM if assuming 6 MB per mailbox), the server should have about 9 GB of RAM. For good measure, we would recommend going with 10 or 12 GB of RAM so that there is additional RAM just in case it is required.

However we perform the additional calculation based on mailbox size, we may arrive at a different amount of RAM. Of the 1,000 mailboxes that this server supports, 400 of these users have an average mailbox size that is in excess of 10 GB, whereas the remainder of the mailboxes average around 6 GB. That would require 4 GB of RAM (400 times 10 MB per mailbox) for the extra large mailboxes and about 5 GB of RAM (600 times 8 MB per mailbox) for the very large mailboxes. That is a total of about 9 GB of RAM.

TABLE 12.5: Memory Required Based on Mailbox Size

MAILBOX SIZE	PER MAILBOX MEMORY RECOMMENDATION
Small (0 to 1 GB)	Add 2 MB per mailbox
Medium (1 to 3 GB)	Add 4 MB per mailbox
Large (3 to 5 GB)	Add 6 MB per mailbox
Very Large (5 to 10 GB)	Add 8 MB per mailbox
Extra Large (10 GB+)	Add 10 MB per mailbox

So in this case, going with at least 10 GB to 12 GB of extra RAM for mailbox caching will definitely be a good design decision. Remember that these RAM estimates are just that: estimates. Additional factors (message hygiene software, continuous replication, email archiving, and so on) may require more or less RAM (usually more) than the calculations and recommendations here. For example, antivirus and antispam software on Mailbox servers can place a significant burden on RAM. Microsoft publishes a storage calculator that can be useful when estimating RAM requirements; see this article on the Exchange Team blog for more information:

`http://msexchangeteam.com/archive/2009/11/09/453117.aspx`

Network Requirements

With previous versions of Exchange Server, recommending network connectivity speeds was often a gray area because of the variety of networking hardware that most organizations were using. Essentially, not everyone had a Gigabit Ethernet backbone for their servers. Today, however, Gigabit Ethernet is present in most data centers at least for the data center backbone.

So, the recommendation is pretty simple. All Exchange Server 2010 servers should be on a Gigabit Ethernet backbone. Will Exchange 2010 work on a 100 Mb or even 10 Mb network? Sure, it will, but you will get the best results in even a medium-sized network if you are using Gigabit Ethernet.

In organizations that have put their Exchange server roles onto different Windows servers (physical or virtual), a lot of communication is taking place between the Client Access servers and the Mailbox servers and a lot of communication between the Hub Transport servers and the Mailbox servers. All Exchange server roles should be Gigabit Ethernet.

The majority of the "client-to-server" communication traffic now takes place between the client (usually Outlook) and the Client Access server. But you will still see some MAPI traffic between Outlook clients and Mailbox servers that are hosting public folders (if, of course, you are using public folders).

If you are planning to implement database availability groups (DAGs) between two or more Exchange 2010 Mailbox servers, each server will need a second network adapter installed. The first network adapter will be used for MAPI and MAPI.NET connections while the second adapter will be used for replication. The replication network will be on its own IP subnet and should also have Gigabit Ethernet connectivity to the physical network. In large environments with multiple servers and dozens of databases in a DAG, consider adding additional network adapters that act as replication or MAPI network connections.

If you are planning to put DAG members on a separate physical network (such as across the WAN), the maximum network latency between members cannot exceed 250 milliseconds (ms) and there must be sufficient bandwidth to keep up with the volume of replication traffic.

Disk Requirements

When calculating disk requirements for some applications, it is easy to decide that a single 500 GB hard disk will solve your storage needs. You might be tempted to think the same thing about Exchange Server.

With earlier versions of Exchange, getting the disk requirements sized correctly could be a bit tricky. That is not to say that doing so cannot still be tricky with Exchange Server 2010. This is because sizing a disk is not just a matter of figuring out how much storage you need. Physical storage requirements are a big part of the sizing, of course, because if you don't get large enough disks to support your users, you will be going back to the boss for more money to buy more disks.

But, asking the boss to buy more physical disk drives because the user's mailboxes are full is at least something tangible you can ask for. The other side of the sizing requirement is ensuring that the disk I/O capacity will keep up with the database engine. The more users using the Exchange Server, the greater the disk I/O capacity required by the disk subsystem. Try explaining to your boss that the disks have plenty of storage available but can't keep up with the database load.

The disk subsystem that you choose has to be able to support not only the *amount* of storage required but also the I/O load that the users will place on the disk subsystem. Therefore, understanding the I/O profile as well as the amount of storage required is important.

A full discussion of all the factors you may need to take into consideration when calculating disk storage is beyond the scope of a single chapter in this book. Fortunately, Microsoft has already done a lot of the legwork for us in the form of the Storage Requirements Calculator. See this article on the Exchange Team blog for more information:

`http://msexchangeteam.com/archive/2009/11/09/453117.aspx`

IMPROVED CACHING AND REDUCED I/O PROFILES

By and large, Client Access and Hub Transport servers require far less disk I/O capacity than Mailbox servers, though Hub Transport servers in very large messaging environments may need more I/O than most organizations. The information in this section applies to servers that are hosting the Mailbox server role.

If you are coming from the Exchange Server 2000/2003 world, you already know that even on a server with only a few hundred mailboxes, Exchange Server 2000/2003 quickly reaches the maximum amount of RAM available for caching (1.2 GB maximum). As more and more users vie for the same physical memory for caching, Exchange Server quickly becomes constrained by the amount of I/O operations that the Exchange server's disk subsystem can support.

Hundreds of pages of material have been written on the concept of optimizing Exchange Server for maximizing performance by improving I/O performance with Exchange — and we certainly can't do the concept justice in just a few paragraphs — but understanding the basic input/output per second (IOPS) requirements of users is helpful. Microsoft and hardware vendors have done much research on I/O requirements based on the mailbox size and the average load that each user places on the server. A good starting point is this information from TechNet:

`http://technet.microsoft.com/en-us/library/dd351197(EXCHG.140).aspx`

Remember the user profile table shown previously in Table 12.1? Well, Table 12.6 takes that and includes the estimated IOPS given a user type and an estimated mailbox size for Exchange 2003. We are including this information because we want you to see the database performance improvements since Exchange Server 2003. IOPS requirements climb as the number of messages sent and received increases and as the mailbox size increases.

TABLE 12.6:   User Type, Database IOPS, Messages Sent and Received, and Mailbox Size Estimates for Exchange 2003

USER TYPE	DATABASE VOLUME IOPS	MESSAGES SENT/RECEIVED PER DAY*	MAILBOX SIZE
Light	.5	20 sent/50 received	50 MB
Average	.75	30 sent/75 received	100 MB
Heavy	1.0	40 sent/100 received	200 MB
Large	1.5	60 sent/150 received	500 MB

Assumes average message size is approximately 50 KB.

For an Exchange 2003 server that is supporting 3,000 heavy mailbox users, the disk subsystem would have to support at least 3,000 IOPS. A typical SCSI or SAS disk drive supports between 100 and 150 IOPS (depending on the disk drive model). To meet this requirement, the disk subsystem may require more disks (from an I/O capacity perspective) than are required from a disk space perspective; thus, the disk subsystem may have far more disk space than is actually necessary to support the IOPS profile. Failure to plan for sufficient IOPS capacity on the disk subsystem will significantly hurt performance.

When Exchange Server 2007 entered the market, the 64-bit architectural improvements allowed the operating system and Exchange Server 2007 to access more physical memory. With additional physical memory available for caching, disk I/O is significantly reduced. Microsoft estimates that I/O requirements are reduced by approximately 70 percent provided the Exchange 2007 server has the recommended amount of RAM. Table 12.7 shows the estimated IOPS requirements for Exchange 2007 Mailbox servers. Please keep in mind that these are estimates and may change over time. These numbers are also calculated when the Mailbox server is configured with more than the recommended amount of RAM.

With this significant improvement in caching Exchange data, the Extensible Storage Engine (ESE) database engine needs to read and write from the disk less frequently and thus reduces the IOPS requirements. When the IOPS requirements are reduced, fewer disks are required to support the I/O load. Notice an Exchange Server 2007 "heavy" user requires only 0.32 IOPS as opposed to an Exchange 2003 "heavy" user that requires 1.0 IOPS.

The Exchange database team has been hard at work further improving the I/O performance of Exchange Server 2010 Mailbox. One of the key factors that the database team focused on with Exchange Server 2010 is to further improve the I/O performance so that most types of affordable disk drive can be used (such as SATA, SAS, or SCSI). They have done this by further optimizing the use of cache memory, increasing database page sizes, changing the database schema, and optimizing how the database arranges data to be written to the disk.

The resulting improvements to the Exchange Server 2010 database engine further reduce the I/O requirements for the standard usage profiles. Table 12.8 shows the disk I/O recommendations based on usage profiles for Exchange Server 2010. Note that the estimates in Table 12.8 are based on the release-to-manufacturing version of Exchange Server 2010 and Microsoft may refine these further in the future.

TABLE 12.7: User Type, Database Volume IOPS, and Messages Sent and Received Per Day for Exchange 2007

USER TYPE	DATABASE VOLUME IOPS	MESSAGES SENT/RECEIVED PER DAY*
Light	.11	5 sent/20 received
Average	.18	10 sent/40 received
Heavy	.32	20 sent/80 received
Very Heavy	.48	30 sent/120 received
Extra Heavy	.64	40 sent/160 received

Assumes average message size is approximately 50 KB.

TABLE 12.8: User Type, Database Volume IOPS, and Messages Sent and Received per Day For Exchange 2010

USER TYPE	DATABASE VOLUME IOPS	MESSAGES SENT/RECEIVED PER DAY*
Light	.10	5 sent/20 received
Average	.14	10 sent/40 received
Heavy	.20	20 sent/80 received
Large	.29	30 sent/120 received

Assumes average message size is approximately 50 KB.

The I/O requirements, of course, are just estimates, but they generally provide a pretty good guideline for the IOPS requirements for the disks that will host Exchange databases. The disks that will host the Exchange transaction logs will require approximately 10 to 20 percent of the IOPS requirements for their corresponding database.

Real World Scenario

IMPROVEMENTS IN DISK I/O AND HOW THIS AFFECTS STORAGE COSTS

In many environments with more than a few hundred mailboxes, the storage subsystem becomes the most expensive part of the Exchange infrastructure.

Company XYZ had a single Exchange 2003 server that supported approximately 1,500 users. Using Performance Monitor, they estimated that the average IOPS requirement was approximately 0.75 IOPS per second. The disk subsystem that held the database therefore had to support approximately 1,125 IOPS. To give themselves some room to grow and to accommodate unusual spurts in activity, the company used an estimated value of 1,500 IOPS.

Based on the architecture of the physical server they were using for their Exchange 2003 Mailbox server role, the company could not achieve this IOPS requirement using direct attached storage (DAS). Therefore, they had to use a fiber channel storage area network (SAN) to accommodate the Exchange data. The cost per gigabyte for the SAN storage was approximately $38.

During their planning for Exchange Server 2010, the company estimated that the typical user was somewhere between an average user and a heavy user. They further estimated that the IOPS requirement for each user would be approximately 0.20 IOPS per user, or a total of 300 IOPS. This represented a significant drop in the IOPS requirements from Exchange Server 2003. With their proposed server architecture, they could accommodate this IOPS requirement with DAS for a cost of approximately of $5 per gigabyte.

Granted that a SAN can often provide more features (scalability, snapshots, replication, and so forth) than just raw storage, but this company had to weigh the costs for those additional features against their relative value to the company. In this case, they chose to use DAS instead of the SAN and saved a considerable amount of money.

Mailbox Storage

Exchange servers holding the Mailbox server role consume the most disk space. Exchange system designers often fall short in their designs by not allowing sufficient disk space for mail storage, transaction logs, and extra disk space. Often the disk space is not partitioned correctly, either. Here are some important points to keep in mind when planning your disk space requirements:

◆ Transaction log files should be on a separate set of physical disks (spindles) from their corresponding Exchange database files if you are only deploying a single database copy. RAID 1 or RAID 0+1 arrays provide better performance for transaction logs.

◆ Allow for at least 7 to 10 days' worth of transaction logs to be stored for each database. The estimated amount of transaction logs will vary dramatically from one organization to another, but a good starting point is about 4 GB of transaction logs per day per 1,000 mailboxes. This is just one estimate of a specific usage profile, though, and your actual mileage may vary. Tools like the Exchange Storage Calculator can be used to assist in disk space requirements.

◆ If you frequently move mailboxes from one mailbox database to another, take this into consideration. When a mailbox is moved in Exchange 2010, the mailbox's dumpster is moved with the mailbox.

◆ Allow for whitespace estimates in the maximum size of each of your database files. (The whitespace is the empty space that is found in the database at any given time.) The size of the whitespace in the database can be approximated by the amount of mail sent and received by the users with mailboxes in that database. For example, if you have one hundred 2 GB mailboxes (a total of 200 GB) in a database where users send and receive an average of 10 MB of mail per day, the whitespace is approximately

1 GB (100 mailboxes × 10 MB per mailbox). See this article for more information: http://technet.microsoft.com/en-us/library/bb738147.aspx.

◆ Factor in 5 to 10 percent additional disk space for the content index databases. You will have one content index database for each production database.

◆ Allocate enough free space on the disk so that you can always make a backup copy of your largest database and still have some free disk space. A good way to calculate this is to take 110 percent of the largest database you will support because that also allows you to defragment the database using Eseutil if necessary.

◆ Consider additional disk space for message tracking, message transport, RPC Client Access, HTTP protocol, POP3 protocol, and IMAP4 protocol log files if you have combined function servers.

◆ Always have recovery in mind and make sure you have enough disk space to be able to restore a database to a recovery database.

Microsoft has a number of excellent guidelines for estimating disk space requirements and database sizing, including the Storage Calculator. Here is another article that is worth reading:

http://technet.microsoft.com/en-us/library/bb738147.aspx

Let's move on to an example of a server that will support 1,000 mailboxes. We are estimating that we will provide the typical user with a Prohibit Send size warning of 500 MB and a Prohibit Send And Receive limit of 600 MB. In any organization of 1,000 users, you have to take into account that 10 percent will qualify as VIPs who will be allowed more mail storage than a typical user; in this case, let's allow 100 VIP users to have a Prohibit Send And Receive limit of 2GB.

These calculations result in 540 GB of mail storage requirements (600 MB × 900 mailboxes) for the first 900 users plus another 200 GB (2 GB × 100 mailboxes) for the VIP users. This results in a maximum amount of mail storage of 740 GB. However, this estimate does not include estimates for deleted items in a user's mailbox and deleted mailboxes, so we want to add an additional overhead factor of about 15 percent, or about 111 MB, plus an additional overhead factor of another 15 percent (another 111 MB) for database whitespace.

So at any given time, for these 1,000 mailboxes we can expect mail database storage (valid email content, deleted data, and empty database space) to consume approximately 962 GB, but because we like round numbers, we'll average that up to 1,000 GB, or 1TB.

In this example, let's say that we have decided the maximum database size we want to be able to back up or restore is 100 GB. This means that we need to split the users' mailboxes across 10 mailbox databases.

For the transaction logs, we estimate that we will generate approximately 5 GB of transaction logs per day. We should plan for enough disk space on the transaction log disk for at least 50 GB of available disk space.

Next, because full-text indexing is enabled by default, we should allow enough disk space for the full-text index files. In this case, we will estimate that the full-text index files will consume a maximum of about 10 percent of the total size of the mail data, or approximately 100 GB. If we combine the full-text index files on the same disk drive as the database files, we will need about 1.3 TB of disk space.

Anytime you are not sure how much disk space you should include, it is a good idea to plan for more rather than less. Although disk space is reasonably inexpensive, unless you have sophisticated storage systems, adding additional disk space can be time consuming and costly from the perspective of effort and downtime.

PLANNING FOR MAIL GROWTH

Growth? You may be saying to yourself, "I just gave the typical user a maximum mailbox size of 600 MB and the VIPs a maximum size of 2 GB! How can my users possibly need more mailbox space?" Predicting the amount of growth you may need in the future is a difficult task. You may not be able to foresee new organizational requirements or that you might be influenced by future laws that require specific data retention periods.

In our experience, though, mailbox limits, regardless of how rigid you plan to be, are managed by exception and by need. In the preceding example, we calculated that we would need 1.3 TB of disk space for our 1,000 mailboxes. Would we partition or create a disk of exactly that size? Probably not.

Instead of carving out exactly the amount of disk space you anticipate needing, add a "fluff factor" to your calculations. We recommend adding approximately 20 to 25 percent additional capacity to the anticipated amount of storage you think you will require, but this is just a wild guess. In this example, though, we might anticipate using 1.3 TB of disk space if we added 25 percent to our expected requirements. Here are some factors that you may want to consider when deciding how much growth you should expect for your mailbox servers:

◆ Average annual growth in the number of employees

◆ Acquisitions, mergers, or consolidations that are planned for the foreseeable future

◆ Addition of new mail-enabled applications such as Unified Messaging features or electronic forms routing

◆ Government regulations that require some types of corporate records (including email) to be retained for a number of years

Conversely, potential events in your future could reduce the amount of mailbox storage you require. Many organizations are now including message archival and long-term retention systems in their messaging systems. These systems archive older content from a user's mailbox and move it to some type of external storage such as disk, storage area network (SAN), network-attached storage (NAS), optical, or tape storage.

EMAIL ARCHIVING AND MAIL STORAGE

Email has emerged as the predominant form of business communications. Sales, marketing, ordering, human resources, legal, financial and all other types of information are now disseminated via email.

An emerging trend in the email business is email archiving. As of this writing, more than 60 companies provide archiving solutions for email systems. Some of these companies provide in-house solutions whereas some are hosted solutions. There are just about as many reasons to implement an email archive system as there are archive vendors. Some of the reasons to implement email archiving include:

◆ Reduces the size of mailbox databases and mailboxes (smaller databases and smaller mailboxes improve disaster recovery response times and improve performance)

◆ Provides long-term retention of email data

◆ Provides users with a searchable index of their historical email data

- Allows for eDiscovery of email (message content, attachments, as well as email metadata) that often must be indexed for legal proceedings

- Eliminates the use of Outlook personal folder (PST) files

Third-party archive systems are great for organizations that must retain much of the information in their mailboxes but want to move it to external storage. However, depending on the system, you don't want to archive everything older than five days, because that may prevent the user from accessing it via Outlook Web Access or mobile devices. Further, once the content is archived and no longer residing in the user's mailbox, it will no longer be accessible from a user's desktop search engine, such as the Google Desktop or the Windows Desktop search engine. So keeping a certain amount of content in the user's mailbox will always make sense.

Microsoft has introduced an email archive system for Exchange Server 2010. Microsoft's approach in this version is to establish an extra archive mailbox for each user who requires archiving. The email archive mailbox must reside on the same mailbox database as the user's mailbox. This approach does serve the goal of reducing the size of the user's primary mailbox, but it does not reduce the size of the database.

If you are planning to use the Exchange Server 2010 mailbox archive feature, you will need to take this into account and plan for additional storage as needed.

Software Requirements

After you have the right hardware chosen to support Exchange Server 2010, you now need to make sure that the software is ready. This includes getting the right version and edition of the operating system, software updates, and any prerequisite Windows roles or functions.

Operating System Requirements

The operating system requirements for Exchange Server 2010 are pretty cut and dried. Windows Server 2008 or Windows Server 2008 R2 is the only operating system supported and only in one of the following configurations:

- Windows Server 2008 Standard Edition x64 with Service Pack 2

- Windows Server 2008 Enterprise Edition x64 with Service Pack 2

- Windows Server 2008 R2 Standard Edition x64

- Windows Server 2008 R2 Enterprise Edition x64

You may be a fan of the Server Core installation, but Exchange Server 2010 does not run on Server Core.

NAME THE SERVER QUICKLY!

Once you have installed Windows Server 2008, make sure that the server is assigned the correct name before you proceed. During installation, the Windows Server setup assigns a random name to the server. More than likely, this name will not be the one you want to use. Once Exchange Server 2010 is installed, you cannot change this name.

If you are planning on using the database availability group (DAG) high availability feature, you must use Windows Server 2008 Enterprise x64.

Additional Software

There are a few additional pieces of software that you will need to ensure are installed on Windows Server 2008 SP2 or R2 in addition to Exchange Server 2010:

◆ Internet Information Server

◆ .NET Framework v3.5 Service Pack 1

◆ Office 2007 System Converter Filter Pack for Mailbox servers

Do not install the version of PowerShell or Windows Remote Management software that ships with Windows Server 2008; use the version that you download. During installation, you will be asked which features are required (Figure 12.2).

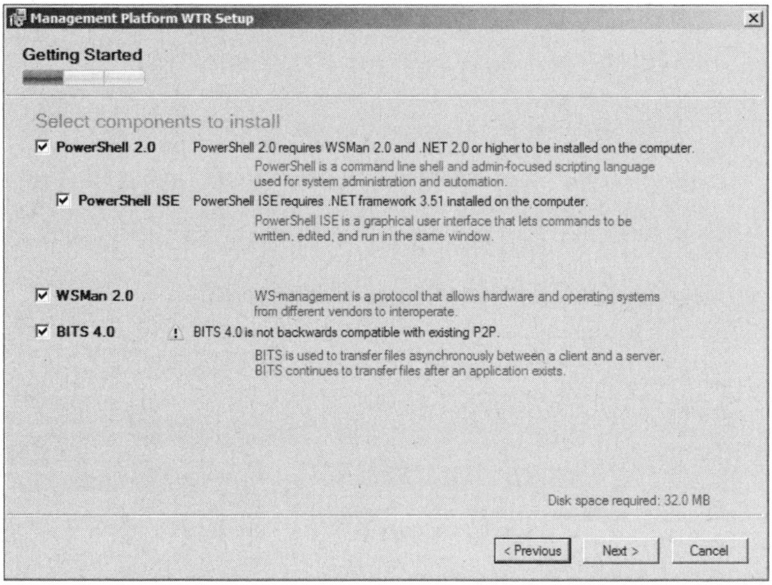

FIGURE 12.2
Installing the Windows PowerShell and Remote Management features

Windows Server Roles and Features

Windows Server 2008 breaks down the additional Windows components into roles and features. Depending on the Exchange 2010 roles, Windows Server 2008 will require additional Windows Server roles and features to be installed. These can be installed using the Windows 2008 Server Manager console, as shown in Figure 12.3.

Installing the server roles and features required is pretty easy to do using the Server Manager interface, but installing them is even easier using the ServerManagerCmd.exe command-line utility. You can use ServerManagerCmd with the -Query option to see which roles are already installed (see Figure 12.4), or you can use ServerManagerCmd -Install to install additional roles if you know the short name of the role or feature.

FIGURE 12.3
Viewing the server roles
and features

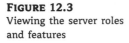

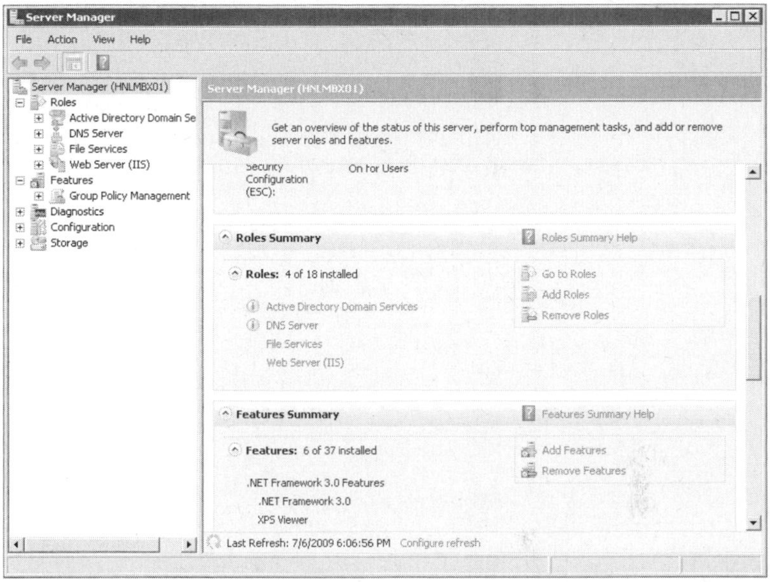

FIGURE 12.4
Using ServerManagerCmd
to view the roles and
features that are
installed

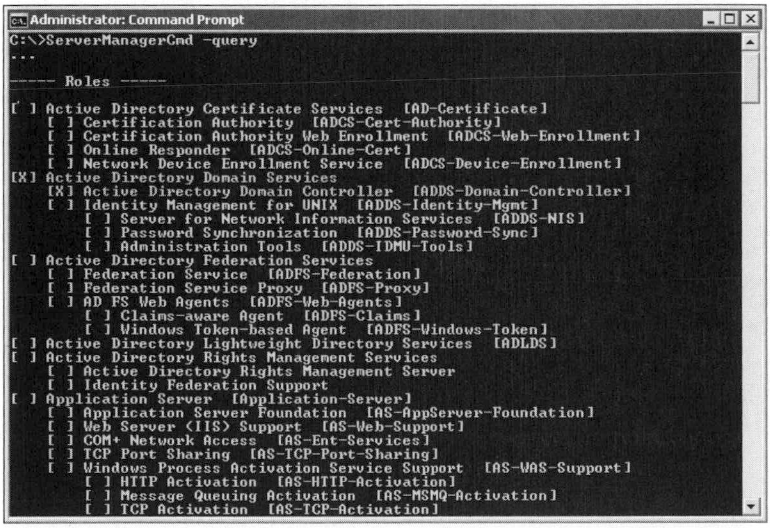

Table 12.9 shows the roles and features that are installed for the Exchange server roles. You should install the required roles in the order found in the table.

The ServerManagerCmd.exe program is smart enough that if you select a role that has prerequisites or additional features, it will install the required software. For example, in Figure 12.5 we are installing the Web Server role; notice that the required functions are automatically installed.

TABLE 12.9: Windows Roles and Features Required for Exchange Roles

Component	Mailbox	Hub Transport	Client Access	Unified Messaging	Edge Transport
Active Directory Domain Services Tools (RSAT-ADDS)	✓	✓	✓	✓	
Web Server (IIS) (Web-Server)	✓	✓	✓	✓	
ISAPI Extensions (Web-ISAPI-Ext)			✓		
IIS 6 Metabase Compatibility (Web-Metabase)	✓	✓	✓	✓	
IIS 6 Management Console (Web-Lgcy-Mgmt-Console)	✓	✓	✓	✓	
Basic Authentication (Web-Basic-Auth)	✓	✓	✓	✓	
Digest Authentication (Web-Digest-Auth)			✓		
Windows Authentication (Web-Windows-Auth)	✓	✓	✓	✓	
.NET Extensibility (Web-Net-Ext)	✓	✓	✓	✓	
Dynamic Content Compression (Web-Dyn-Compression)			✓		
HTTP Activation (NET-HTTP-Activation)			✓		
RPC over HTTP Proxy (RPC-over-HTTP-proxy)			✓		
Desktop Experience (Desktop-Experience)				✓	
Active Directory Lightweight Directory Services (ADLDS)					✓

PREPARING WINDOWS 2008 FOR THE MAILBOX ROLE

If you are preparing a Windows Server 2008 SP2 server to support the Exchange 2010 Mailbox server role, here are the steps you should take:

1. Download or install via Microsoft Update the .NET Framework v3.5 Service Pack.

2. Download and install the Office 2007 System Converter filter pack.

3. Run ServerManagerCmd -Install RSAT-ADDS and then reboot.

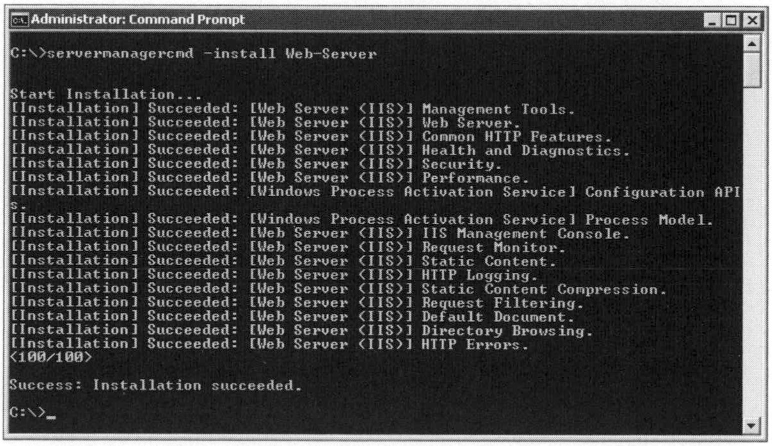

FIGURE 12.5
Required features
are installed by
ServerManagerCmd

4. Run ServerManagerCmd -Install Web-Server.

5. Run ServerManagerCmd -Install Web-Metabase.

6. Run ServerManagerCmd -Install Web-Lgcy-Mgmt-Console.

7. Run ServerManagerCmd -Install Web-Basic-Auth.

8. Run ServerManagerCmd -Install Web-Windows-Auth.

9. Run ServerManagerCmd -Install Web-Net-Ext.

Note that if you like "one-liners," you can install all the necessary components from a single command. For example, to install the necessary features and roles for a Hub Transport or Mailbox server, you could type this:

```
ServerManagerCmd -i Web-Server Web-Metabase Web-Lgcy-Mgmt-Console ↵
Web-Basic-Auth Web-Windows-Auth Web-Net-Ext RSAT-ADDS -restart
```

PREPARING WINDOWS 2008 FOR THE HUB TRANSPORT ROLE

If you are preparing a Windows Server 2008 SP2 server to support the Exchange 2010 Hub Transport server role, here are the steps you should take:

1. Download or install via Microsoft Update the .NET Framework v3.5 Service Pack 1.

2. Run ServerManagerCmd -Install RSAT-ADDS and then reboot.

3. Run ServerManagerCmd -Install Web-Server.

4. Run ServerManagerCmd -Install Web-Metabase.

5. Run ServerManagerCmd -Install Web-Lgcy-Mgmt-Console.

6. Run ServerManagerCmd -Install Web-Basic-Auth.

7. Run ServerManagerCmd -Install Web-Windows-Auth.

8. Run ServerManagerCmd -Install Web-Net-Ext.

These steps can all be accomplished in a single command:

```
ServerManagerCmd -i Web-Server Web-Metabase Web-Lgcy-Mgmt-Console ↵
Web-Basic-Auth Web-Windows-Auth Web-Net-Ext RSAT-ADDS -restart
```

PREPARING WINDOWS 2008 FOR THE CLIENT ACCESS ROLE

If you are preparing a Windows Server 2008 SP2 server to support the Exchange 2010 Client Access server role, here are the steps you should take:

1. Download or install via Microsoft Update the .NET Framework v3.5 Service Pack.
2. Run ServerManagerCmd -Install RSAT-ADDS and then reboot.
3. Run ServerManagerCmd -Install Web-Server.
4. Run ServerManagerCmd -Install Web-Metabase.
5. Run ServerManagerCmd -Install Web-Lgcy-Mgmt-Console.
6. Run ServerManagerCmd -Install Web-Basic-Auth.
7. Run ServerManagerCmd -Install Web-Windows-Auth.
8. Run ServerManagerCmd -Install Web-Digest-Auth.
9. Run ServerManagerCmd -Install Web-Net-Ext.
10. Run ServerManagerCmd -Install Web-Dyn-Compression.
11. Run ServerManagerCmd -Install Net-HTTP-Activation
12. Run ServerManagerCmd -Install RPC-over-HTTP-proxy.

These commands can be consolidated into a single ServerManagerCmd as follows:

```
ServerManagerCmd -i Web-Server Web-Metabase Web-Lgcy-Mgmt-Console ↵
Web-Basic-Auth Web-Windows-Auth Web-Net-Ext RSAT-ADDS -restart
```

PREPARING WINDOWS 2008 FOR THE UNIFIED MESSAGING ROLE

If you are preparing a Windows Server 2008 SP2 server to support the Exchange 2010 Unified Messaging role, here are the steps you should take:

1. Download or install via Microsoft Update the .NET Framework v3.5 Service Pack. 1.
2. Run ServerManagerCmd -Install RSAT-ADDS and then reboot.
3. Run ServerManagerCmd -Install Web-Server.
4. Run ServerManagerCmd -Install Web-Metabase.
5. Run ServerManagerCmd -Install Web-Lgcy-Mgmt-Console.
6. Run ServerManagerCmd -Install Web-Basic-Auth.
7. Run ServerManagerCmd -Install Web-Windows-Auth.
8. Run ServerManagerCmd -Install Web-Net-Ext.
9. Run ServerManagerCmd -Install Desktop-Experience.

These steps can be consolidated into the following command:

```
ServerManagerCmd -i Web-Server Web-Metabase Web-Lgcy-Mgmt-Console ↵
Web-Basic-Auth Web-Windows-Auth Web-Net-Ext Desktop-Experience RSAT-ADDS ↵
-restart
```

PREPARING WINDOWS 2008 FOR A COMBINED FUNCTION SERVER

If you are preparing a Windows Server 2008 SP2 server to support a combined function Exchange 2010 server role, here are the steps you should take:

1. Download or install via Microsoft Update the .NET Framework v3.5 Service Pack.

2. Download and install the Office 2007 System Converter filter pack.

3. Run ServerManagerCmd -Install RSAT-ADDS and then reboot.

4. Run ServerManagerCmd -Install Web-Server.

5. Run ServerManagerCmd -Install Web-Metabase.

6. Run ServerManagerCmd -Install Web-Lgcy-Mgmt-Console.

7. Run ServerManagerCmd -Install Web-Basic-Auth.

8. Run ServerManagerCmd -Install Web-Windows-Auth.

9. Run ServerManagerCmd -Install Web-Digest-Auth.

10. Run ServerManagerCmd -Install Web-Net-Ext.

11. Run ServerManagerCmd -Install Web-Dyn-Compression.

12. Run ServerManagerCmd -Install Net-HTTP-Activation.

13. Run ServerManagerCmd -Install RPC-over-HTTP-proxy.

14. Run ServerManagerCmd -Install Desktop-Experience.

PREPARING WINDOWS 2008 FOR THE EDGE TRANSPORT ROLE

If you are preparing a Windows Server 2008 SP2 server to support the Exchange 2010 Edge Transport server role, here are the steps you should take:

1. Download or install via Microsoft Update the .NET Framework v3.5 Service Pack 1.

2. Download and install the Windows PowerShell v2.

3. Download and install Windows Remote Management v2.

4. Add Active Directory Lightweight Directory Service (AD LDS) feature using this command: ServerManagercmd -I ADLDS.

Additional Requirements

In addition to making sure that the hardware and server software can support Exchange Server 2010, there are a few infrastructure requirements that you need to consider. These include making sure that your Active Directory infrastructure can support Exchange 2010 and that you have the necessary permissions to prepare the forest and domain.

Active Directory Requirements

The actual Active Directory domain controller requirements to install Exchange Server 2010 into your forest can be a bit confusing. We are going to simplify this for you but also raise the minimum bar just a bit. Here are some tips that you should follow when ensuring that your Active Directory infrastructure will properly support Exchange Server 2010:

◆ All domain controllers in each Active Directory site where you plan on deploying Exchange 2010 must be running Windows Server 2003 SP2 at a minimum.

◆ The Active Directory forest must be in Windows Server 2003 Forest Functional level.

◆ Each Active Directory site in which you will install Exchange 2010 servers should contain at least two global catalog servers to ensure local global catalog access and fault tolerance.

◆ For organizations using domain controllers running x86 Windows, each Active Directory site that contains Exchange servers should have one domain controller processor core for each four Exchange mailbox server processor cores.

◆ For organizations using domain controllers running x64 Windows and having enough RAM installed for the entire NTDS.DIT to be loaded into memory, each Active Directory site that contains Exchange servers should have one domain controller processor core for each eight Exchange Mailbox server processor cores.

◆ Always take into account that domain controllers may not be dedicated to just Exchange Server. They may be handling authentication for users logging into the domain and for other applications.

◆ Read-only domain controllers and global catalog servers are not used by Exchange Server 2010, so do not include their presence in your domain controller planning.

Installation and Preparation Permissions

It might seem that the easiest possible way to get Exchange Server 2010 installed is to log on to a Windows Server 2008 computer as a member of Domain Admins, Schema Admins, and Enterprise Admins. Indeed, using a user account that is a member of all three of those groups will give you all the rights you need.

In some larger organizations, though, getting a user account that is a member of all three of these groups is an impossible request. In some cases, the Exchange administrator may have to make a request from the Active Directory forest owner to perform some of the preparation tasks on behalf of the Exchange team. For this reason, it is important to know the permissions that are required to perform the different setup tasks, as shown in Table 12.10.

Coexisting with Previous Versions of Exchange Server

Exchange Server is fairly widely deployed in most organizations, so it is likely that you will be transitioning or migrating your existing Exchange organization over to Exchange Server 2010. For some period of time (hopefully short), your Exchange 2010 servers will be interoperating with either Exchange 2007 or Exchange 2003 servers. For this reason, you must know the factors necessary to ensure successful coexistence.

The recommended order for installing Exchange 2010 servers and transitioning messaging services over to those new servers is as follows:

1. Install Client Access servers and decide how you will handle legacy OWA clients (either via proxying, redirection, or direct connections). Outlook Web Access, Windows Mobile, Outlook Anywhere, POP3, and IMAP4 clients to the new Client Access servers.

TABLE 12.10:   Task Permissions

TASK	GROUP MEMBERSHIP
PrepareLegacyExchangePermissions	Enterprise Admins group membership or be delegated the Exchange Full Administrator role and Domain Admins membership in each domain that has had Exchange 2003/DomainPrep executed against it
PrepareSchema	Schema Admins and Enterprise Admins
PrepareAD	Enterprise Admins
PrepareDomain	Domain Admins
Install Exchange Server 2010	Administrators group on the Windows Server and Exchange Organization Management

2. Install Hub Transport servers and have the new Hub Transport servers take over as much of the messages transport function as possible.

3. Install Mailbox servers and begin to transition mailboxes and public folders from the legacy servers to the new servers.

4. Install the Edge Transport servers if required and transition inbound/outbound mail through the Edge Transport servers.

5. Install Unified Messaging servers if required.

COEXISTENCE WITH EXCHANGE SERVER 2003

Prior to installing your first Exchange Server 2010 server in an organization that is running Exchange Server 2003, you must make sure that the current organization meets some minimum software and configuration requirements:

◆ All Exchange 2003 servers must be running a minimum of Exchange 2003 Service Pack 2.

◆ Each Active Directory site must have at least one global catalog server running Windows Server 2003 SP2 or later.

◆ The Active Directory forest must be at the Windows Server 2003 Forest Functional level.

◆ The SuppressStateChanges Registry key should be set on all Exchange 2003 servers to suppress minor state link state version changes.

◆ The Exchange organization must be in native mode, which means that the Exchange 5.5 Active Directory Connector and Site Replication Service must be removed.

◆ All Exchange Server 2000 servers must be removed from the organization.

COEXISTENCE WITH EXCHANGE SERVER 2007

If you are currently using Exchange Server 2007, prior to installing the first Exchange 2010 server ensure that you meet the following prerequisites:

◆ All Exchange 2007 Client Access and Unified Messaging servers in the organization must be at Exchange Server 2007 Service Pack 2.

◆ All Exchange 2007 servers within the Active Directory where you are planning to introduce Exchange Server 2010 must be running a minimum of Exchange Server 2007 Service Pack 2.

◆ The Active Directory forest must be at the Windows Server 2003 Forest Functional level.

◆ Each Active Directory site must have at least one global catalog server running Windows Server 2003 SP2 or later.

The Bottom Line

Use the right hardware for your organization.   Properly sizing the hardware that will support your Exchange servers is one of the most important decisions you will make with respect to ensuring the stability of your Exchange organization and the satisfaction of your end users.

Size the memory required for Exchange Mailbox server roles based on the number of active mailboxes and the usage profile. Estimate the amount of RAM required based on your user community's usage profiles or the mailbox sizes so that your server has sufficient memory.

Ensure that the processor core ratio for Hub Transport and Client Access servers to Mailbox servers is adequate to keep up with the load clients will place on these servers. For Hub Transport servers, use a ratio of five Hub Transport processor cores for each Mailbox server. For Client Access servers, use a ratio of three processor cores for every four mailbox processor cores.

> **Master It**   You must estimate the minimum amount of RAM required for an Exchange 2010 Mailbox server that will support 1000 mailboxes that have been designated as heavy users and 500 mailboxes that are designated as average users. What is the minimum amount of RAM this server should have?

Configure Windows Server 2008 to support Exchange Server 2010.   Windows Server 2008 requires that additional software be downloaded and installed as well as adding some roles and features. You should always start with at least Windows Server 2008 Service Pack 2 or Windows Server 2008 R2 plus the latest updates and patches.

> **Master It**   How would you use the `ServerManagerCmd.exe` command-line utility to quickly add the necessary additional roles and features.

Confirm that Active Directory is ready.   Avoid frustration during installation or potential problems in the future that may result from domain controllers or global catalog servers running older versions of the software.

> **Master It**   You must verify that your Active Directory meets the minimum requirements to support Exchange Server 2010. What should you check?

Verify that previous versions of Exchange can interoperate with Exchange Server 2010. Exchange Server 2010 will only interoperate with specific previous versions of Exchange.

> **Master It**   You must verify that the existing legacy Exchange Servers in your organization are running the minimum versions of Exchange required to interoperate with Exchange Server 2010. What should you check?

## Chapter 13

Installing Exchange Server 2010

People who install Exchange Server 2010 fall into two camps. The first — and probably most fall into this camp — are those who simply run the Setup program with no command-line options and choose the default roles. The second camp consists of those who want to install specific Exchange Server roles on different servers and who may need the command-line options to successfully install those servers.

Regardless of which camp you fall into, getting the prerequisites out of the way first will ensure a smooth installation. Further, knowing your setup options will help to make sure you get everything right the first time.

In this chapter, you will learn to:

◆ Implement important steps before installing Exchange Server 2010

◆ Prepare the Active Directory forest for Exchange Server 2010 without actually installing Exchange Server

◆ Use the graphical user interface to install Exchange Server 2010

◆ Determine the command-line options available when installing Exchange

Before You Begin

When you run the Exchange Server 2010 Setup program, there are a number of things that the setup program checks to ensure that not only the Windows Server but also the Active Directory and your specific permissions all meet the necessary prerequisites. Some missing prerequisites are easy to resolve whereas others may take hours or even days.

You don't want these missing pieces and prerequisites to slow you down. If you have not already reviewed Chapter 12, "Exchange Server 2010 Requirements," you should do so. Let's review the prerequisites and best practices:

◆ If you have existing Exchange servers in your environment, run the Exchange Best Practices Analyzer (ExBPA). Make sure that you correct any serious problems that the ExBPA finds.

◆ The Active Directory forest should be at least Windows 2003 Forest Functional mode.

◆ The Active Directory Schema Master role must be on a Windows 2003 SP2 domain controller or later.

◆ Each Active Directory domain in which you will install an Exchange 2010 server must have at least one domain controller running at least Windows 2003 SP2.

◆ Existing Exchange 2007 Client Access and Unified Messaging servers must be running at least Exchange Server 2007 SP2 to install the first Exchange 2010 server into the organization. To install the first Exchange 2010 server into an Active Directory site, upgrade all Exchange 2007 Mailbox, Client Access, and Edge Transport servers in that site to Exchange Server 2007 SP2.

◆ Existing Exchange 2003 servers must be running at least Exchange Server 2003 SP2.

◆ All Active Directory sites in which you plan to install Exchange 2010 servers should have at least one global catalog server running at least Windows server 2003 SP2.

◆ Ensure that the server has at least 4 GB of RAM and 10 GB of hard disk space free. For Mailbox servers, ensure that you have performed the proper disk space and memory requirement calculations and that you are providing the right amount of disk space and physical memory.

◆ For Client Access servers, make sure that the Net.TCP Port Sharing Service is set to start automatically.

◆ Windows Server 2008 SP2 or Windows Server 2008 R2 must be the operating system used on any server that is going to run Exchange Server 2010.

◆ If you have storage area networks (SANs), get your device drivers configured, storage connected, and logical units (LUNs) connected ahead of time. Don't mix Exchange troubleshooting with SAN troubleshooting.

◆ If you are using database availability groups (DAGs), you must get the DAG/replication network configured ahead of time.

◆ Install the required Windows 2008 roles and features.

◆ Confirm that you have the Exchange installation files (including any additional language packs above and beyond English) that you require. We recommend that you copy them onto a network share so that they are easily accessible.

Preparing for Exchange 2010 Ahead of Time

In some large organizations, you may find it necessary to prepare your Active Directory prior to installing Exchange Server 2010. You may need to do this for a number of reasons. Remember that the various steps to prepare the forest require membership in the Schema Admins and Enterprise Admins groups as well as Domain Admins membership in each of the forests' domains.

In a small or medium-sized business, you may be the person where the proverbial buck stops. You may have a user account that has all of these permissions, and you can run everything easily by yourself. In that case, simply log on as a user with the necessary permissions and run Setup.

However, large organizations are a bit different. Here are a few points you should consider:

◆ Large organizations may have configuration control and change management in place. Configuration management and change control are best practices that should be followed. You may need to document the steps that you will take, request permissions to proceed, and schedule the forest preparation.

◆ Large Active Directories may have many Active Directory sites and domain controllers.

◆ Organizations that are distributed across large geographic areas may have replication delays on their domain controllers of anywhere from 15 minutes to seven days. Replication of schema and domain changes may need to be completed prior to proceeding with Exchange server installations.

◆ Permissions to update the schema, configuration partition, and child domains are sometimes spread across a number of different individuals or departments. You may need to have another administrator log in for you to run various preparation steps.

If you have to prepare the Active Directory forest ahead of time, there are a few steps you will need to take. The number of steps will vary depending on the following factors:

◆ Whether or not you have a previous version of Exchange Server running

◆ The number of domains that you have in your forest

◆ The permissions you have within the forest root domain and the child domains

---

IMPORTANT STEPS PRIOR TO PREPARING ANY DOMAIN

Before running any of the Active Directory preparation steps, make sure that the machine from which you are running the `setup.exe` program is in the same Active Directory site as the Schema Master and has good connectivity to the Schema Master as well as a domain controller from each domain within the forest. The Windows 2008 R2 or SP2 server must meet all of the Exchange Server 2010 prerequisites. Further, ensure that you have installed the Active Directory management tools on your Windows 2008 SP2 or R2 server by running `ServerManagerCmd -I RSAT-ADDS`.

Existing Exchange Organizations

If you have any Exchange 2003 servers in your organization, you must first prepare each domain so that Exchange Server 2010 can properly communicate with Exchange 2003 and so that Exchange 2003 can access certain newly created attribute sets in Active Directory. This must be done for each domain that has Exchange 2003 servers or that was prepared for Exchange 2003. You can determine this by searching the domain for the Exchange Domain Servers or Exchange Enterprise Servers groups.

The process of preparing the legacy Exchange permissions gives the Exchange Enterprise Servers and Exchange Domain Servers groups read and write permissions to the attributes in the Active Directory `Exchange-Information` property set. It also provides authenticated users with the ability to read information in the `Exchange-Information` property set.

To prepare a specific domain, use an account that is a member of that domain's Domain Admins group. For example, to configure the legacy Exchange permissions for the domain `somorita.local` from the Exchange installation files folder, run the following command:

```
setup.com /PrepareLegacyExchangePermissions:somorita.local
```

If you are logged on as an account that is a member of the Enterprise Admins group, you can run `setup.com` one time and prepare all the domains in the forest by running this command:

```
setup.com /PrepareLegacyExchangePermissions
```

Preparing the Schema

Next is the step that usually scares Active Directory administrators the most: extending the Active Directory schema. Essentially the schema is the set of rules that define the structure (the objects and the attributes of those objects) for Active Directory. This operation requires the user account running this operation to have both Enterprise Admins and Schema Admins group memberships.

This scares Active Directory administrators for a couple of reasons. First, schema changes cannot be undone. Ever. Second, once the schema changes are made, they replicate to every domain controller in the entire forest.

Naturally, schema changes are not done to an Active Directory forest very often. When schema changes are performed, often the Active Directory administrators do want to know exactly what is being changed. This is a bit more difficult to document for Exchange due to the sheer number of changes. The number of changes will depend on whether you are running any previous version of Exchange and which particular version. An Active Directory that has never been prepped for Exchange will have more than 3,000 changes made to the schema, including new classes (object types), new attributes, new attributes being flagged for the global catalog replication, and existing attributes being flagged to replicate to the global catalog. If you want to point your Active Directory administrators to a specific list of changes, this document is helpful:

www.microsoft.com/downloads/details.aspx?displaylang=en&FamilyID=3d44de93-3f21-44d0-a0a1-35ff5dbabd0b

If you, or your Active Directory administrators, are curious about what is being changed, take a look at the LDF files in the \Setup\Data folder within the Exchange 2010 setup files. For the most part, you probably don't have to worry about this unless you have done something nonstandard with your Active Directory, such as defining your own classes or attributes without giving them unique names and unique object identifiers.

To extend the schema effectively, the server from which you are running the schema preparation must be in the same Active Directory site as the Schema Master domain controller. You can locate the schema master domain controller using the Schema Management console; the console is not available by default, so you first must register it. At the command prompt, type **regsvr32.exe schmmgmt.dll**; you will see a message indicating the schmmgmt.dll registration succeed.

Then you can run the management console program (mmc.exe) and add the Active Directory Schema snap-in. This snap-in will not appear unless the schmmgmt.dll registered properly. Once you have the Active Directory Schema console open, right-click on Active Directory Schema and choose Operations Master. The Change Schema Master dialog (shown in Figure 13.1) will show you which server currently holds the Schema Master role.

To extend the schema, run the following command from within the Exchange 2010 setup folder:

Setup.com /PrepareSchema

Note that this can take between 15 and 30 minutes depending on the speed of the computer on which you are running Setup, the speed of the Schema Master domain controller, and the network connection between the computers. If Setup detects that the forest has Exchange 2003, it will automatically perform the /PrepareLegacyExchangePermissions step if it has not already been done.

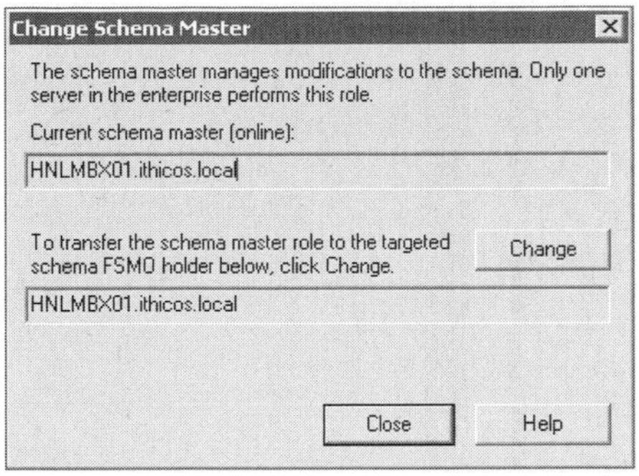

FIGURE 13.1
Determining which
domain controller holds
the Schema Master role

Preparing the Active Directory Forest

The next step is to prepare the Active Directory forest to support an Exchange organization. Although this process does not make as many changes to the forest, it does make quite a few more noticeable changes, such as creating the various Exchange configuration containers and creating Exchange security groups. An example of the configuration containers that are created is shown in Figure 13.2.

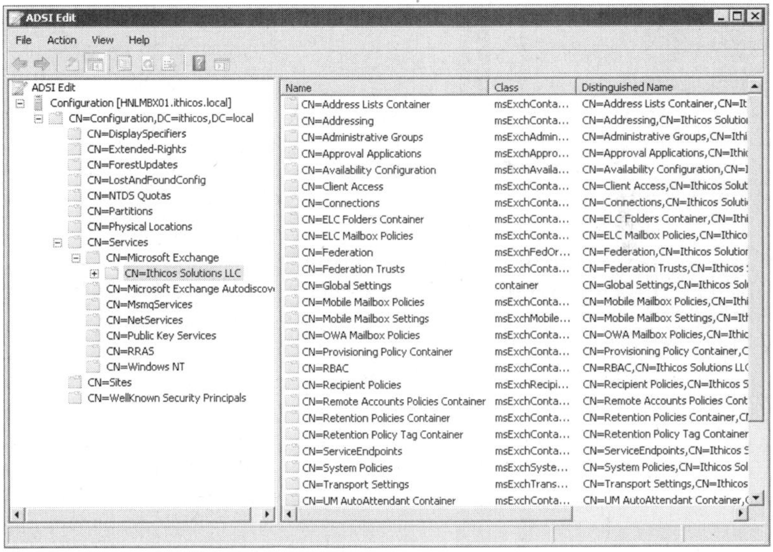

FIGURE 13.2
Exchange configura-
tion containers that
are found in the Active
Directory configuration
partition

Here are some tasks that the Active Directory preparation process includes:

◆ Defining the Exchange organization name if it does not exist already in the Microsoft Exchange container under the Services container of the Active Directory configuration partition

◆ Creating configuration objects and containers under the Exchange organization container (see Figure 13.2)

- Creating the Microsoft Exchange Security Groups organizational unit in the forest root domain and then creating the Exchange universal security groups:
  - Delegated Setup
  - Discovery Management
  - Exchange All Hosted Organizations
  - Exchange Servers
  - Exchange Trusted Subsystem
  - Exchange Windows Permissions
  - ExchangeLegacyInterop
  - Help Desk
  - Hygiene Management
  - Organization Management
  - Public Folder Management
  - Recipient Management
  - Records Management
  - Server Management
  - UM Management
  - View-Only Organization Management
- Importing new Exchange-specific extended Active Directory rights and assigning the necessary permissions in Active Directory
- Creating the Microsoft Exchange System Objects container in the forest root domain
- Preparing the forest root domain for Exchange Server 2010

To run the forest preparation, you must be logged on with a user who is a member of the Enterprise Admins group. Further, you should run the forest preparation process from a server that is in the same Active Directory site and domain that holds the schema master flexible single master of operations (FSMO) role. The setup /PrepareAD option is used to prepare the Active Directory.

You have two options when running /PrepareAD; the option you choose will depend on whether you have an existing Exchange organization. For example, to prepare a forest that has never supported any version of Exchange Server and to use the organization name SomoritaSurfboards, you would run the following command from the Exchange 2010 setup folder:

```
Setup /PrepareAD /OrganizationName:SomoritaSurfboards
```

CHOOSING AN EXCHANGE ORGANIZATION NAME

In previous versions of Exchange Server, choosing the right organization name was often a source of great anxiety. With Exchange 5.5 and earlier, when you built an Exchange site, if you did not pick the right organization name, you could not replicate that site's global address list to the rest of the organization.

Even with Exchange 2000/2003, the organization name was visible at the top of the global address list and within the Exchange System Manager administrative console. And once the organization name is set, it cannot be changed. Fears of acquisitions, mergers, and company name changes still drive people to be concerned about this name.

Although we still recommend naming your organization something descriptive, the actual name is not as important because it is not going to be seen by the end users and is rarely (if ever) seen by the administrators. You can always set the organization name to something generic like ExchangeOrganization if you want something that would not be affected by a reorganization.

When you pick an organization name, use a name that is 64 characters or less and uses only valid Active Directory characters for a container name. We recommend you stick to the basics:

◆ A–Z

◆ a–z

◆ 0–9

◆ Spaces and hyphens

However, if the forest already supports a previous version of Exchange Server, the /OrganizationName option is not necessary. You can simply run this command:

```
Setup /PrepareAD
```

When the /PrepareAD process runs, it will check to see if the /PrepareLegacyExchange Permissions or /PrepareSchema steps need to be run. If so, Setup will check to see if you have the necessary permissions to run them, and Setup will run these steps as well. However, if the other steps are necessary and you do not have the necessary permissions, you will see an error and Setup will fail.

Preparing Additional Domains

If you have only a single domain in your Active Directory forest, the Setup option /PrepareAD will prepare that domain and you will be ready to proceed with your first Exchange server installation.

However, if you have additional domains in your Active Directory forest, you may have to prepare these additional domains if they are going to contain mail-enabled recipients or if they will contain Exchange servers. To prepare these domains, use the /PrepareDomain or /PrepareAllDomains Setup options. Some of the things this process does include the following:

◆ Assigning to the domain container various permissions to the Authenticated Users and Exchange universal security groups that are necessary for viewing recipient information and performing recipient management tasks.

◆ Creating a Microsoft Exchange System Objects container in the root of the domain; this container holds mail-enabled recipient information for organization objects such as Exchange databases.

To prepare a single domain, you must be logged on as a member of that domain's Domain Admins group, and there should be a domain controller for that domain in the same site as the server from which you are running Setup. The domain controller should be running a minimum of Windows Server 2003 SP2. To prepare a domain called eu.somorita.local, type this command:

```
Setup /PrepareDomain:eu.somorita.local
```

If you have a user account that is a member of the Enterprise Admins group, you can run this command and prepare all domains in the entire forest:

```
Setup /PrepareAllDomains
```

Graphical User Interface Setup

The simplest way to install Exchange Server 2010 is to use the graphical user interface (GUI). The GUI will be sufficient for most Exchange Server installations. We recommend first copying the Exchange Server 2010 installation files to the local hard disk or using a locally attached CD/DVD from which to run the Exchange installation. Copying the Exchange binaries to the local hard disk will speed up the installation time.

From the Exchange Server installation folder, run Setup.exe to see the main setup screen (shown in Figure 13.3). The main setup screen will show you some of the components that are missing, such as the PowerShell v2 or the .NET Framework v3.5 SP1 (if you are running Windows Server 2008 SP2 instead of R2).

FIGURE 13.3
Main Exchange 2010
graphical setup screen

If you meet the prerequisites for installation, the next step is to select which languages you are going to install. Your selection will depend on whether you have downloaded the entire language bundle or only want to use the specific language(s) included with the installer.

You can usually just click Step 3: Choose Exchange Language Option and then click Install Only Languages from the DVD. Once you have selected the correct language option, proceed to Step 4: Install Microsoft Exchange. This will launch the Exchange Server installer wizard.

The first page of the Exchange Server 2010 Setup wizard is simply the Introduction page. You can click Next to proceed. On the next page, you will see the license agreement screen. Select the I Accept The Terms In The License Agreement radio button and then click Next.

The third page of the setup wizard is the Error Reporting screen. Here you can specify whether or not you want to send reports of problems or errors automatically to Microsoft. The server will send information back to Microsoft via HTTPS; this information may prove valuable for Microsoft in identifying errors in their software. Passing along this information also provides you (the customer) with good value because it means that Microsoft can more quickly identifying bugs and software issues. The report sent back to Microsoft does not usually contain any information specific to your organization or to your server, but some organization's Information Security departments will want you to block this anyway. If you are concerned about this, select No. You can read more about the Microsoft Online Crash Analysis program at `http://oca.microsoft.com/en/dcp20.asp` and read about Microsoft's privacy statement and what information might be collected. When you have made your choice, click Next.

The next page on the wizard is the Installation Type screen and the path for the Exchange program files, as shown in Figure 13.4. On this screen, you can select a typical installation or a custom installation, or change the path for the Exchange program files.

FIGURE 13.4
Choosing the Exchange installation type

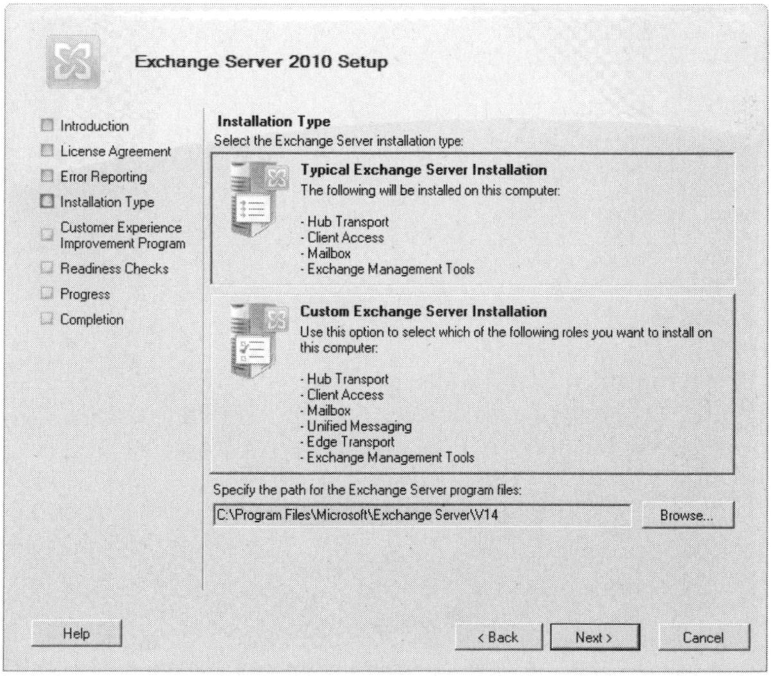

When specifying a path for the Exchange program files, remember that by default this is where all Exchange databases and log files will be stored. Most of these you can (and should) move after the installation, but you want to make sure that the disk on which the Exchange program files are stored has at least 5 GB of free space.

If you are deploying a single Exchange 2010 server and you are not using unified messaging, you can choose the Typical Exchange Server Installation selection and click Next. The Typical Exchange Server Installation will install the Mailbox, Client Access, and Hub Transport server roles as well as the Exchange management tools.

However, as the old joke goes, real computer geeks *always* pick Custom; this allows you to specify which Exchange server roles are installed. Figure 13.5 shows the Server Role Selection page of the Exchange setup wizard.

FIGURE 13.5
Selecting the Exchange server roles

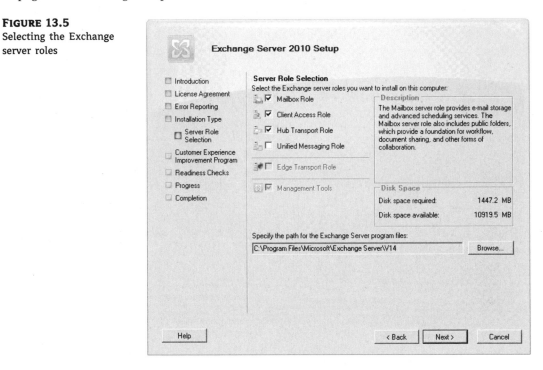

Once you click Next, if you have selected the Mailbox role and this is a newly created Exchange organization, you will be asked if you want to maintain compatibility with Outlook 2003 and earlier clients. You should select this option as doing so will create a MAPI public folder tree and a public folder database on this server. All subsequent Exchange 2010 Mailbox servers will not ask you this question since there is already an Exchange Mailbox server that holds a MAPI public tree in the organization.

If you have selected the Hub Transport server role and this is the first Hub Transport server in an organization with only Exchange 2003 servers, you must specify an Exchange 2003 server to use as a bridgehead server for routing mail between Exchange 2003 and Exchange 2010. This step will not be required if you have Exchange 2007 servers.

If you have selected the Client Access server role, you will be asked if this Client Access server is Internet facing and what the external URL will be that will be used by clients connecting to this server. This setting is optional and can be configured later.

Configure Client Access server external domain

Enter a domain name to use to configure your Client Access servers for Internet-facing services (for example, Exchange ActiveSync, Outlook Web App, Outlook Anywhere). This will allow clients to connect to your Exchange deployment from outside of your domain.

☐ The Client Access server role will be Internet-facing.

Enter the domain name you will use with your external Client Access servers (for example, mail.contoso.com):

The next page of the wizard is the Customer Experience Improvement Program; on this screen you can specify that you want to join the Microsoft Exchange Customer Experience Improvement Program (CEIP) — well, actually, not "you" specifically, but this server. Periodically, the server will upload usage and configuration data that helps Microsoft when designing future versions of Exchange Server. The program is completely anonymous and will not be used to gather information about your organization. We recommend selecting Join The Exchange Customer Experience Improvement Program (CEIP), but this is entirely a decision that each person installing Exchange must make. For more information on the CEIP, visit www.microsoft.com/products/ceip/en-us/default.mspx.

Once you have clicked Next on the CEIP page, the Setup program launches the Readiness Check to make sure that all the server features and roles, hotfixes, and other services are available.

Readiness Checks

The system and server will be checked to verify that Exchange is ready to be installed.
Elapsed time: 00:00:28
Summary: 4 item(s). 2 succeeded, 0 failed.

Languages Prerequisites   ✅ Completed ⌃
   Elapsed Time: 00:00:17

Hub Transport Role Prerequisites   ✅ Completed ⌃
   Elapsed Time: 00:00:08

If you find anything about the configuration that should be changed, you must resolve before continuing.

Client Access Role Prerequisites   ❌ Failed ⌃

Error:
The start mode for the Net.Tcp Port Sharing service must be set to Automatic before Setup can continue.

Elapsed Time: 00:00:06

One of the nice things about the Exchange Server 2010 Setup wizard is that if it detects a missing component or something that must be done prior to starting the Exchange setup, you can fix the issue and then click the Retry button. The Setup program will recheck the prerequisites and pick up where it left off.

Once the prerequisites have all been met and the Readiness Check is complete, you must then click the Install button to initiate the installation.

Command-Line Setup

The Exchange Server 2010 Setup program includes a powerful set of command-line options that can help you completely automate an Exchange server setup or perform custom setup options that you could not do through the GUI. The command-line setup options are broken into seven categories of setup:

◆ Installing Exchange server roles

◆ Removing Exchange server roles

◆ Recovering an existing Exchange server

◆ Preparing the Active Directory to support Exchange

◆ Creating delegated or pre-provisioned servers

◆ Adding or removing Unified Messaging language packs

◆ Adding or removing Exchange language packs

All of these options are used by running the `setup.com` program, not `setup.exe`.

⊕ Real World Scenario

THE USEFULNESS OF COMMAND LINE INSTALLATIONS

A lot of Exchange Administrators wonder why the command line setup options even exist since the graphical user interface is so easy to use and has most of the same options. Consider the case of organization JCE that is installing 30 Mailbox servers, 18 Client Access servers, and 12 Hub Transport servers.

Due to their organization's requirements for certifying a production IT system, all server builds have to be thoroughly documented prior to being deployed. By generating the installation scripts ahead of time, their Exchange team can ensure that each server is built exactly to the design specifications and with the necessary options. This speeds up the overall installation and ensures that nothing is overlooked.

Command-Line Installation Options

By and large, the server role installation options are probably the most useful for a typical person installing or configuring Exchange. They are certainly the most numerous. If you use some of these `setup.com` options, they will have some required parameters. For example, if you use the `/mode:install` option, you will also have to specify which server role or roles you are installing. Table 13.1 lists the installation options.

ABBREVIATIONS AND SHORTCUTS

Most of the command-line switches and options have a long and short option. For example, the following two commands accomplish exactly the same thing (installing the Mailbox role):

◆ `setup /m:install /r:m`

◆ `setup /m:install /r:mb`

◆ `setup /m:install /r:Mailbox`

In this chapter, we have chosen to spell out the options completely to more clearly illustrate the commands and in the hope that you will remember them more easily. However, once you learn the long version of the options, you will probably find it easier to use the shorter versions. They are just a bit cryptic when you are learning.

TABLE 13.1: Exchange Server 2010 Installation Options

OPTION	OPTIONAL (O) OR REQUIRED (R)	EXPLANATION
/mode or /m	R	Specifies whether the Setup program is installing a new role or removing it. Valid options are: /mode:install /mode:uninstall /mode:upgrade
/roles or /r	R	Specifies which roles are being installed. Valid role types are: Client Access, CA, C Edge Transport, ET, E Hub Transport, HT, E Mailbox, MB, M ManagementTools, MT, T Unified Messaging, UM, U
/OrganizationName	O	Allows you to specify an organization name; this is only necessary if this is the first server being installed in the Active Directory forest and the /PrepareAD step has not previously been done.
/TargetDir	O	Allows you to specify an optional path for the Exchange program files rather than the default location on the C:\ drive.
/SourceDir	O	Specifies the location for the Exchange installation files.
/UpdatesDir	O	Specifies a path to look for updates from after the installation is completed.
/DomainController	O	Allows you to specify the NetBIOS name or the FQDN of a domain controller.
/AnswerFile	O	Allows you to specify a text file that contains answers to some of the advanced setup parameters.
/DoNotStartTransport	O	Tells Setup to not allow the transport service on a Hub Transport or Edge Transport server.

TABLE 13.1:   Exchange Server 2010 Installation Options *(CONTINUED)*

OPTION	OPTIONAL (O) OR REQUIRED (R)	EXPLANATION
/EnableLegacyOutlook	O	Tells Setup to create a public folder tree and public folder database on a mailbox. This is only valid for the first Mailbox server role that is being installed in a new organization.
/LegacyRoutingServer	O	Tells Setup to create a routing group connection to an Exchange 2003 bridgehead server. This option is only valid for the first Hub Transport server that is being installed in an Exchange 2010 organization.
/EnableErrorReporting		Configures Exchange Server to report errors automatically to Microsoft. All server roles can use this option. The default is not to enable this feature.
/CustomerFeedbackEnabled	O	Configures Exchange Server to report usage information to Microsoft automatically. All server roles can use this information. This is used with the /Industry switch.
/Mdbname	O	Specifies the name of the default mailbox database when installing a Mailbox server.
/DbFilePath	O	Specifies the path and name to the default database file. This is used in conjunction with the /Mdbname and the /LogFolderPath switches.
/LogFolderPath	O	Specifies the path for the log files for the default database when installing a Mailbox server role.
/ExternalCASServerDomain	O	Allows to you to specify the external URL that will be used by Internet clients accessing the Client Access server. This is only used for Client Access servers.
/NoSelfSignedCertificates	O	Instructs Setup not to create self-signed certificates for the Client Access or Unified Messaging server roles.
/AdamLdapPort	O	Specifies the LDAP port number to be configured for an Edge Transport server's ADAM database.
/AdamSslPort	O	Specifies the LDAPS port number to be configured for an Edge Transport server's ADAM database.

Command-Line Server Recovery Options

There may come a time when you have to recover an Exchange server from a backup. This process will involve rebuilding the Windows server, then reinstalling Exchange Server using the Recover Server mode. This option will read most of the configuration of the server from the Active Directory rather than installing the server from scratch. Several options are available when recovering a server, as shown in Table 13.2.

TABLE 13.2:   Exchange Server 2010 Server Recovery Setup Options

OPTION	OPTIONAL (O) OR REQUIRED (R)	EXPLANATION
/mode:RecoverServer	R	Specifies that the installation mode is to be the Recover Server option.
/TargetDir	O	Allows you to specify an optional path for the Exchange program files rather than the default location on the C:\ drive.
/UpdatesDir	O	Specifies a path to look for updates after the installation is completed.
/DomainController	O	Allows you to specify the NetBIOS name or the FQDN of a domain controller.
/DoNotStartTransport	O	Tells Setup to not allow the transport service on a Hub Transport or Edge Transport server. This is useful during a recovery if you do not want messages to start flowing until you are sure the server is fully recovered.
/EnableErrorReporting	O	Configures Exchange Server to report errors automatically to Microsoft. All server roles can use this option. The default is not to enable this feature.

Command-Line Delegated Server Installation

In some large organizations, the person who is installing the Exchange servers may not have an account with sufficient Active Directory permissions to create the server objects in the Active Directory. For this reason, someone else may have to create the necessary server objects and the installer can then set up the servers.

TABLE 13.3:   Exchange Server 2010 Delegated Setup Options

OPTION	OPTIONAL (O) OR REQUIRED (R)	EXPLANATION
/NewProvisionedServer	O	Creates a new provisioned server with the name specified on the command line, such as this: Setup.com /NewProvisionedServer:HNLMBX
/RemoveProvisionedServer	O	Removes a server that was previously configured with the /NewProvisionedServer option

This is where the delegated server installation is handy. The person with the necessary rights to set the servers up can "prestage" the servers in the Active Directory. Table 13.3 shows a list of the options available for delegated server setup.

Installing Language Packs

If you are supporting an Exchange 2010 Server for only English-speaking users and administrators, you do not need to worry about installing additional language packs. Exchange Server 2010 automatically includes the US English (en-US) messaging language pack (and it can't be removed). Depending on your environment and users, you should know how to install additional language packs or Unified Messaging language packs.

Table 13.4 shows the valid options for installing language packs. Note that the Unified Messaging language pack options are only available on servers that already have the Unified Messaging role installed.

TABLE 13.4:   Exchange Server 2010 Language Pack Options

OPTION	OPTIONAL (O) OR REQUIRED (R)	EXPLANATION
/AddUmLanguagePack	O	Adds the specified Unified Messaging language pack. You must specify the language pack name that you want to install; for French, you would use this command: Setup /AddUmLanguagePack:fr-fr
/RemoveUmLanguagePack	O	Removes the specified Unified Messaging language pack.
/SourceDir	O	Specifies the source folder for the Unified Messaging language pack.
/UpdatesDir	O	Specifies the path for updates for the Unified Messaging language pack.
/LanguagePack	O	Specifies the path to the language pack bundle. Must be used in conjunction with the /mode:install option.

The Bottom Line

Implement important steps before installing Exchange Server 2010.   One of the things that slows down an Exchange Server installation is finding out you are missing some specific Windows component, feature, or role. Reviewing the necessary software and configuration components will keep your installation moving along smoothly.

Server hardware should match the minimum requirements, including at least 10 GB of free space and 4 GB of RAM for most server roles. Ensure that you are using Windows Server 2008 SP2 or R2 with the most recent updates. Install the Windows Server 2008 roles and features necessary for the Exchange server's role requirements.

Master It   You are working with your Active Directory team to ensure that the Active Directory is ready to support Exchange Server 2010. What are the minimum prerequisites that your Active Directory must meet in order to support Exchange Server 2010?

Prepare the Active Directory forest for Exchange Server 2010 without actually installing Exchange Server.   In some organizations, the Exchange administrator or Exchange installer may not have the necessary Active Directory rights to prepare the Active Directory schema, the forest, or a child domain.

◆ A user account that is a member of the Schema Admins group is necessary to extend the Active Directory schema.

◆ A user account that is a member of the Enterprise Admins group is necessary to make all the changes and updates necessary in the forest root.

◆ A user account that is a member of the Enterprise Admins group or the child domain's Domain Admins group is necessary to prepare a child domain.

◆ The Exchange Server 2010 `setup.com` program allows the schema to be prepared without installing Exchange by using the `/PrepareSchema` command-line option.

◆ The Exchange Server 2010 `setup.com` program allows the forest root domain and the Active Directory configuration partition to be prepared without installing Exchange by using the `/PrepareAD` command-line option.

Master It   You have provided the Exchange 2010 installation binaries to your Active Directory team so that the forest administrator can extend the Active Directory schema. She wants to know what she must do in order to extend only the schema to support Exchange Server 2010. What must she do?

Use the graphical user interface to install Exchange Server 2010.   The graphical user interface can be used for most Exchange Server installations that do not require specialized prestaging or nonstandard options. The GUI will provide all the necessary configuration steps, including Active Directory preparation.

The GUI allows you to install the Mailbox, Client Access, Hub Transport, Unified Messaging, or Edge Transport roles on a server.

Master It   You are using the GUI for the Exchange Server 2010 installation program to install the Hub Transport and Client Access server roles onto the same Windows Server R2 system. You must install both of these roles. Which setup option must you choose?

Determine the command-line options available when installing Exchange.   The Exchange 2010 command-line installation program has a robust set of features that allow all installation options to be chosen from the command line exactly the same as if you were installing Exchange Server 2010 using the graphical user interface.

Master It   You are attempting to use the command line to install an Exchange Server 2010 Mailbox server role. What is the command line necessary to install this role?

Chapter 14

Upgrades and Migrations

According to Ferris Research, if Exchange Server were a stand-alone software business, it would be the ninth-largest software company in the world. It is a solid bet that a lot of existing Exchange customers will be looking to move to Exchange Server 2010.

Depending on the software, you may be used to *in-place upgrades,* where you have an existing version of the software on the computer, run the installer, and end up with the new version of the software. Some of the previous versions of Exchange have supported an in-place upgrade process for at least one previous version back, but the Exchange 2010 upgrade process doesn't.

There is no in-place upgrade path for organizations running either Exchange 2003 or Exchange Server 2007. Life is not all gloom and doom, however, and this seeming complication will make the new Exchange servers more stable and ease interoperability during the migration.

In this chapter, you will learn to:

- ◆ Choose between an upgrade and a migration
- ◆ Determine the factors you need to consider before doing your upgrade
- ◆ Coexist with legacy Exchange servers
- ◆ Perform an interorganization migration

Upgrades, Migrations, or Transitions

Let's take a moment to clear up a matter of terminology and distinguish between *upgrading* and *migrating.*

Exchange 2000/2003 cannot be "upgraded" to Exchange 2007. You must perform a migration. The process of moving from Exchange 2003 to Exchange 2010 or from Exchange 2007 to Exchange 2010 is often referred to as an upgrade, but technically it is not. An upgrade occurs *in-place*; that is, it involves taking an existing server and installing the newer version of the software on *that* server. The server installation process then performs whatever changes it needs to in order to convert the old software (and database) to the newest version.

> **IS IT A MIGRATION OR A TRANSITION?**
>
> If you search through the Microsoft documentation and then read books and articles on Exchange 2007 migration, you will see the term *transition* tossed around a lot. A transition is a type of migration that occurs when you install new Exchange servers in the same organization; the servers interoperate for some period of time, you move services and data over to the new servers, and then you shut down the old servers and remove them.
>
> Most Exchange migrations are really transitions, because you usually install new servers and move the data over. However, we are using the term *migration* in a more generic sense.

Just to make things less straightforward, you will often see migration guidelines that give you two upgrade strategies:

◆ Upgrade your existing organization, which Microsoft sometimes calls an *upgrade*, though in places we will refer to it as a *transition*.

◆ Create a new organization and move your messaging data over. This is called a *migration*. Be aware that this use of *migration* refers only to the act of moving your data between the two organizations.

To be consistent with Microsoft usage and minimize confusion, we will use the term *upgrade* to refer to the process of moving from an existing Exchange 2003 organization to Exchange 2010, no matter the strategy you use to get there. Actual migrations from messaging systems other than earlier versions of Exchange (or from Exchange 5.5) are outside the scope of this book.

When we need to refer to moving data between organizations, we will explicitly say *migration strategy*. This helps us be clear and stay consistent with the excellent documentation provided for Exchange 2010.

Exchange 2003 Migration Overview

Again, Exchange 2003 cannot be "upgraded" in-place to Exchange Server 2010; the services and data on Exchange 2003 must be migrated or moved to Exchange Server 2010. There are a number of reasons for this:

◆ Exchange 2003 runs only on Windows 2003 x32.

◆ Exchange Server 2010 runs only Windows Server 2008 x64 or Windows Server 2008 R2.

◆ Exchange Server 2010's database architecture is radically different. Exchange 2010 uses 1 MB transaction logs, a different database page size, and a single EDB file rather than Exchange 2003 EDB and STM files.

◆ Exchange Server 2010's message transport and client access components are very different from those of Exchange 2010.

What you must do instead of an in-place upgrade is to install new Exchange Server 2010 servers in the existing Exchange organization. To the existing Exchange 2003 servers, these new servers will appear similar to other Exchange 2003 servers. Once you start installing new Exchange 2010 servers in the organization, you can start transitioning messaging services over to these new services. We will revisit this topic in more detail later in the section "An Overview of Transition."

Real World Scenario

EXCHANGE 2000 MIGRATIONS

Company WXYZ used Exchange Server 2000 for nearly eight years before they needed to upgrade. Their Exchange 2000 server supports just over 750 mailboxes. They decided to wait until the release of Exchange Server 2010, but there is no direct migration path between Exchange 2000 and Exchange Server 2010, nor can the two systems be in the same Exchange organization.

WXYZ had several options available, including upgrading to either (an in-place upgrade) Exchange Server 2003 or migrating to Exchange Server 2007 first. One option that was briefly considered was exporting all the mailboxes out to PST, and then removing Exchange 2000 entirely, installing Exchange 2010, re-creating the mailboxes, and importing the data into Exchange Server 2010. That option was quickly discarded because of the amount of disruption to the end users and the time it would take for the import and export.

It was determined that the Exchange 2000 server could be upgraded in-place to Exchange Server 2003 and continue to be operated for some period of time afterward. The sequence for this "upgrade and migration" was as follows:

◆ Performed an in-place upgrade of the Exchange 2000 server to Exchange 2003

◆ Tested that Exchange 2003 still functioned properly with mail clients and for transferring mail

◆ Installed two Exchange 2010 servers that each held the Hub Transport and Client Access server roles

◆ Directed inbound to the Hub Transport servers and created a send connector to deliver outbound mail using the Hub Transport servers

◆ Installed two Exchange 2010 servers holding the Mailbox server role and added both servers to a single DAG

◆ Created four Exchange mailbox databases and placed a copy of the database on both DAG members

◆ Created two public folder databases (one on each of the Mailbox servers) and replicated all the public folder content to these two public folder instances

◆ Moved mailboxes to one of the four mailbox databases

Most of the upgrade and migration took place over a single weekend.

MIGRATION TO NEW SERVER HARDWARE

Many organizations planning to replace Exchange 2003 will just about be ready for an Exchange server hardware refresh. If you have new servers, here are the services that need to be transitioned, in roughly this order:

1. Transitioning Outlook Web App, POP3, IMAP4, and Exchange ActiveSync to Exchange Server 2010 Client Access servers

2. Messaging routing (Internet inbound/outbound) as well as routing between routing groups handled by Exchange Server 2010 Hub Transport servers

3. Replicating public folders to Exchange Server 2010 Mailbox servers

4. Moving mailboxes to Exchange Server 2010 Mailbox servers

5. Transitioning antispam services to Edge Transport services (optional)

6. Deploying Unified Messaging and other new features

LEAPFROG MIGRATION

If you just bought brand-new Exchange Server hardware for your 2003 servers, you are in more of a bind. You will still need at least one or two unused servers, but you can do a "leapfrog" migration to reuse existing hardware. Those steps might look like this:

1. Use a new server to deploy an Exchange 2010 Client Access server.

2. Redirect all Outlook Web App (OWA), POP3, IMAP4, and ActiveSync clients to the new Client Access server.

3. Remove one of the Exchange 2003 front-end servers from production. If you only have one front-end server, OWA clients will not be able to use OWA during the upgrade.

4. Rebuild the Exchange 2003 front-end server as an Exchange Server 2010 Hub Transport server.

5. Redirect all Exchange 2003 message-routing functions from existing bridgehead servers to new Exchange 2010 Hub Transport servers.

6. Remove the Exchange 2003 bridgehead server from production.

7. Rebuild the Exchange bridgehead server as an Exchange Server 2010 Mailbox server.

8. Move mailboxes to the new Mailbox server role. Replicate public folders to the new Mailbox server.

9. Remove public folder replicas from the old Exchange 2003 Mailbox server.

10. Remove the old Exchange 2003 Mailbox server from the organization and reuse the hardware as necessary.

The leapfrog migration is by no means a simple one due to the constant shuffling of servers that you must do. If you can avoid this approach, we recommend doing so. For more information, read this article from the Microsoft Exchange Team blog:

```
http://msexchangeteam.com/archive/2009/11/20/453272.aspx
```

Exchange 5.5 Migrations

The number of questions that pop up in the newsgroups and web support forums with respect to Exchange 5.5 is surprising. We know of a few organizations that run Exchange 5.5 on the theory that "it works so we don't want to replace it." One of the cosmic laws of software, though, is that sooner or later it must be upgraded. Exchange Server is no exception.

Unfortunately, like with Exchange 2000 there is no direct upgrade or migration path from Exchange 5.5 to Exchange Server 2010. You have options, but they are by no means simple or cheap.

If you have a small number of users and only one or two locations, you might consider "leapfrogging" through Exchange 2003. This means that you perform a migration to Exchange 2003 and then shortly thereafter perform another migration to Exchange Server 2010. This leapfrog process might be the smoothest transition for most of your users. It ensures that public folders, shortcuts, folder rules, permissions delegations, and Outlook profiles do not need to be modified. If you have the extra server hardware and you can use Exchange Server 2003 licenses temporarily, this is a good approach. However, it means that you must endure the pain of the Active Directory Connector (ADC) that synchronizes data between the Exchange 5.5 directory and the Active Directory.

The other approach is to use a third-party migration utility such as the Quest Software Exchange Migration Wizard (`www.quest.com`). Although third-party tools usually represent a significant cost on your part, for larger organizations these utilities can ensure a smooth transition if you are migrating from Exchange 5.5 or performing an interorganization migration.

AVOID HEADACHES — DON'T DEPLOY NEW FEATURES DURING MIGRATIONS

We have mentioned this before, but it bears repeating: do not deploy new features of Exchange Server 2010 while you are still migrating mailboxes.

We know that you will be tempted to start using features such as messaging records management, Unified Messaging, improved Exchange ActiveSync features, per-mailbox journaling, or transport rules before the migration is finished. If there are features that you must deploy during your migration, just ensure that they will not interfere with your support of the users who are migrating.

The exception to this is features such as database availability groups that are deployed at the server level. DAGs can be configured and tested before the first mailbox is ever moved.

A good rule of thumb is to avoid deploying any feature that will require additional user support or training. Such features distract the help desk and the migration team from getting the migration completed in a timely fashion.

Considering Messaging Connectors

Another area for you to consider as you're getting ready to upgrade to Exchange 2010 is your connectors. In legacy Exchange organizations, you have four basic types of connectors: routing group connectors, SMTP connectors, X.400 connectors, and other foreign connectors to specialized messaging systems such as Lotus Notes and Novell GroupWise. In general, you'll want to treat these connectors in the following fashion:

Routing Group Connectors Routing group connectors still exist in Exchange 2010 but are meant solely as a means of interoperability with legacy Exchange servers. They will be naturally phased out as you convert your Exchange infrastructure over to Exchange 2010, decommission your legacy Exchange servers, and remove the legacy administrative and routing groups from your organization.

SMTP Connectors SMTP connectors provide connections to external SMTP-speaking systems and the Internet. In Exchange 2010, connectors are divided into two types: receive connectors, which are configured on a per-server basis, and send connectors, which are configured and maintained throughout the organization. As with the routing group connectors, these legacy SMTP connectors will be phased out as you move your message-routing functions off your legacy Exchange servers to your new Exchange 2010 Hub Transport and Edge Transport servers.

> **ABOUT LEGACY EXCHANGE SERVERS**
>
> We will use the phrase *legacy Exchange servers* in this chapter to refer to the existing Exchange Server 2003 machines in your organization. This might cause a slight bit of cognitive dissonance for those of you used to thinking of Exchange 2000 or Exchange 5.5 servers as legacy servers.

X.400 Connectors X.400 connectors are finally gone in Exchange 2010. With the decline and fall of X.400 as a messaging standard, almost all the X.400 connectors used in legacy Exchange organizations today are used to connect to the MTA service in Exchange 5.5 sites. Because you can't have Exchange 5.5 sites and servers in an organization with Exchange 2010, you'll need to remove these sites and connectors before beginning your upgrade. If you have a non–Exchange X.400 system that you connect to, maintain your legacy Exchange 2003 bridgehead servers until you can arrange some sort of alternate connection supported natively by Exchange 2010.

Foreign Connectors Foreign connectors are dramatically different in Exchange 2010. The new foreign connectors don't try to implement a specific non-SMTP protocol; instead, they require you to define a drop directory on the Hub Transport server or network file share. When messages are routed through this connector, they will be written to the drop directory and the remote gateway software can then pick them up and process them appropriately.

You'll need to consider your current routing topology, especially if you have a single routing group in your legacy organization. By default, legacy Exchange servers route messages directly out of their local SMTP virtual server. This default Exchange 2003 behavior means that, out of the box, Exchange Server 2003 servers directly attempt to deliver external messages based on DNS MX record lookups instead of forwarding messages to bridgehead servers. For many small organizations, this behavior is acceptable, and as a result many Exchange administrators never get around to creating an SMTP connector and defining bridgehead servers for their organization.

If you are moving from Exchange Server 2007, by default there are no outbound SMTP connections until you create your first send connectors. These send connectors can be switched to use Exchange Server 2010 Hub Transport servers as their source servers.

When you install the first Exchange 2010 Hub Transport instance into your Exchange 2003 organization, it creates its own routing group and associated routing group connector, as discussed in Chapter 13, ''Installing Exchange Server 2010.'' It also creates a default set of SMTP connectors that are enough to send and receive authenticated SMTP to/from other Exchange servers in the organization.

By default, Exchange Server 2010 does not have any send connectors to deliver email outside the organization. An Exchange 2010 server will rely on legacy SMTP connectors on Exchange 2003 or send connectors created on Exchange 2007 servers, if they exist. To allow Exchange 2010 to deliver mail to the Internet, you have three solutions from which to choose:

◆ Create an outbound SMTP send connector on your Exchange 2010 Hub Transport server. This may be suboptimal in some instances, but if you're already using an external mail gateway, you can simply configure Exchange 2010 to pass outbound mail to the appropriate smarthost.

◆ Deploy an Exchange 2010 Edge Transport server to handle your outbound traffic. If you're upgrading to Exchange 2010 to take advantage of its advanced message hygiene capabilities, we recommend this option; it gets your incoming and outgoing mail going through Exchange 2010 sooner rather than later.

◆ Create an SMTP connector with the default address space in your legacy Exchange organization before you begin installing Exchange 2010. This option has the advantage that it keeps mail flow in your organization going through a known and trusted set of bridgehead servers until you have your Hub Transport and Edge Transport servers configured and tested. If you have existing legacy Exchange servers configured with mail hygiene solutions, this is probably what you're going to want to select for the short term.

USING LEGACY EXCHANGE SERVERS AS BRIDGEHEADS DURING UPGRADE

Don't be afraid or hesitant to continue using your legacy Exchange servers as bridgeheads to the Internet while you're working your way through your Exchange 2010 migration. Although we firmly believe that configuring and troubleshooting message flow and routing is much easier with Exchange 2010, you still have a lot of material to learn and master as you begin to put Exchange 2010 into play. Choose your battles.

Legacy Exchange and Third-Party Services

Another factor you need to consider is whether you're using additional legacy Exchange services that are no longer present in Exchange 2010. We've already covered the case of the foreign connectors that are no longer part of Exchange 2010, but those aren't the only services and features for which you need to watch out.

Previous versions of Exchange included several services that are now supplied by either Windows Server 2008 components or other Microsoft applications. If your organization depends on them, you'll need a migration strategy to get off these services before you can proceed with your Exchange Server 2010 migration. These services include the following:

◆ Exchange 2000 Conferencing Server

◆ Exchange 2000 Instant Messaging Server

◆ Exchange 2000 Key Management Server

◆ Exchange 2000 Chat Server

The first Exchange Server 2010 server cannot be installed until the last Exchange 2000 server is removed.

You may also have third-party services that are essential to your organization. Examples of such services include, but are by no means limited to, the following:

◆ Message hygiene add-ins such as spam filters and virus scanners (both for transport and store)

◆ Fax services

◆ Message discovery, compliance, archival, and retention solutions

◆ Geo-clustering, mailbox snapshot, and other storage-related solutions

◆ Transport event sinks, whether commercial or custom (a common event sink is a module to stamp disclaimers on all outbound email)

◆ Conference room and shared resource booking management software

◆ Mailbox database backup and restore agents

🌐 Real World Scenario

OOPS, I FORGOT ABOUT THE...

Company EFGH experienced one of the most common causes of a delay when migrating from Exchange Server 2003 to Exchange 2010. They neglected to consider all the components necessary to make Exchange Server 2010 work in their environment. They were using a third-party backup software package to perform streaming backups of their Exchange databases.

Early in the planning process for their Exchange 2010 migration, they neglected to consider their current backup methodology and how that would have to change for Exchange Server 2010. The streaming backup API no longer exists in Exchange Server 2010. Not only did this mean that the company would need to upgrade their existing backup software, but they had to upgrade their backup infrastructure to support snapshot software.

The lesson to take away from this example is to never assume that all your existing third-party software will work with a new version of the server software, or that a simple software upgrade will make something start working properly.

Of course, there are many other possibilities. The point is that you need to ensure that these products are going to work with Exchange 2010. Some products may work directly with Exchange 2010 already, whereas others may require an upgrade of their own. In some cases, you may need to switch software packages if your current vendor' product isn't compatible with Exchange 2010 and you require that functionality.

There's always the possibility that you no longer need a given third-party package because new functionality in Exchange 2010 allows you to perform the same task natively.

Factors to Consider Before Upgrading

Are you ready to upgrade? Not so fast! Before you pull the trigger and pop the Exchange 2010 installation media into the drive, you must take into account a few factors. Let's take some time to go over them in more detail so that your upgrade is successful.

Prerequisites

Before you can begin upgrading your Exchange organization, you have to ensure that it meets the necessary prerequisites. We've gone over some of these in previous chapters from the context of a fresh installation of Exchange 2010, but let's look at them again, this time keeping in mind how your existing Exchange deployment may affect your ability to meet them.

HARDWARE AND OPERATING SYSTEM

For production use, you must have x64-compatible hardware — systems with one of the following types of processors:

- The Opteron processor line, made by AMD, found in high-end server hardware
- Athlon 64 processors, also by AMD, meant for inexpensive servers and high-end workstations

◆ Intel Xeon and Pentium line of processors with the Extended Memory 64 Technology (EM64T) extensions

The Xeon family is typically found in high-end servers, whereas the Pentiums are found in low-end servers and workstations.

The Intel Itanium processor line is not compatible with Exchange 2010. Unlike some other Microsoft restrictions, this isn't just a case of being an unsupported configuration; the Itanium processors are not compatible with the x64 specification and Exchange 2010 has not been compiled to run on the Itanium family of CPUs.

Nowadays, multicore processors are increasingly common — both Intel and AMD. Although Windows recognizes multiple cores as separate processors when managing processes and threads, Microsoft licensing does not make a distinction between single-core and dual-core processors. This fact is to your benefit because Exchange will certainly benefit from additional cores.

You can run Exchange 2010 on any of the following versions of Windows Server 2008 SP2 or R2:

◆ Windows Server 2008 x64 Standard Edition with SP2 or R2

◆ Windows Server 2008 x64 Enterprise Edition with SP2 or R2

When Microsoft first began releasing the requirements for Exchange 2007 deployments, no single revelation drew greater attention than the requirement for 64-bit hardware. Even now, many people insist that the lack of support for 32-bit hardware will dramatically increase the final cost of upgrades to Exchange 2010. Microsoft makes the valid argument that most of the servers sold these days already have 64-bit support. Because the x64 hardware platform (initially introduced by AMD for its Opteron and Athlon 64 processors, then supported by Intel with the EM64T extensions to its Xeon and Pentium 4 processors) is backward compatible with 32-bit hardware and operating systems, many server manufacturers switched to offering 64-bit hardware regardless of which operating system their customers order.

This doesn't mean you're completely off the hook on the hardware front, however. Even if your current Exchange 2003 servers are running on 64-bit hardware, you can't just pop the Exchange 2010 DVD in and do an in-place upgrade. Why not, you may ask?

◆ Previous versions of Exchange are all 32-bit only and can't be run on Windows Server 2003 x64. Note that this is not a matter of support; Exchange 2003 simply will not run on 64-bit Windows — period, end of story.

◆ You can't upgrade from Windows Server 2003 x86 to Windows Server 2008 x64. You have to perform a clean installation.

◆ There is no x32 bit version of Exchange Server 2010.

All this means that to reuse existing server hardware, you're going to have to have at least one spare server and be prepared to reinstall Windows and Exchange on your servers as you go. We discuss this topic in more detail in the section "An Overview of Transition" later in this chapter.

ACTIVE DIRECTORY

Because Exchange 2010 depends on Active Directory, you should take a good look at the domain controllers and global catalog servers in your Active Directory forest before starting the upgrade process.

Unlike Exchange 2003, which could use domain controllers running either Windows 2000 Server with the appropriate service pack or Windows Server 2003, Exchange 2010 requires that all of the following domain controllers be running Windows Server 2003 + SP1:

◆ The schema master domain controller, which is usually the first domain controller that you installed in the forest — unless you have moved the schema master flexible single master of operations (FSMO) role to another domain controller

◆ At least one global catalog server in each Active Directory site in your forest where you will be installing an Exchange 2002 server

Our recommendation is to upgrade all your domain controllers to at least Windows Server 2003 SP2, especially if you still have Windows 2000 Server domain controllers. The Active Directory improvements in Windows Server 2003 can vastly reduce the bandwidth required for Active Directory replication, and several Exchange 2010 features (such as address book browsing in OWA) rely on features in Windows Server 2003 SP1. By making sure you've upgraded all your domain controllers, you increase the redundancy and resiliency of your Exchange/Active Directory integration.

CHECK THE HEALTH OF YOUR ACTIVE DIRECTORY SITE BEFORE UPGRADING

It is extremely important that Active Directory be healthy before you upgrade to Exchange 2010. Exchange 2010 relies directly on your Active Directory site structure for message-routing information. In previous versions of Exchange (2000 or 2003), the Active Directory site design could become decoupled from the Exchange Server routing design. Microsoft introduced this tight coupling between the internal message-routing architecture and the Active Directory site architecture in Exchange Server 2007.

Whether you upgrade all your domain controllers or just the minimum number, you need to list all the domains in which you will either install Exchange 2010 or create Exchange 2010 recipient objects such as users, contacts, and mail-enabled groups. For each of these domains, ensure that the domain functional level is set to the Windows Server 2003 native level or higher. Doing so ensures that you have no lingering Windows NT 4.0 servers acting as down-level domain controllers via the primary domain controller (PDC) emulator. The Active Directory forest must be Windows Server 2003 Forest Functional mode or higher.

Officially, you need to have only a single Windows Server 2003 SP1 global catalog server in each site, but Windows Server 2003 SP1 domain controllers offer many advantages to your organization above and beyond their benefits to Exchange Server 2010.

For Windows 2003 Active Directory forests, the minimum forest functional level must be Windows Server 2003.

A few additional caveats exist:

◆ If you plan on using OWA and any of your domain controllers are using a non-English version of Windows 2003 SP1, you must install the hotfix in Knowledge Base article 919166 on each non-English domain controller.

◆ You may want to use 64-bit Windows Server 2003 or 2008 on your domain controllers for performance benefits; however, doing so is not required.

◆ Assuming similar speeds and models of processor, you should still plan to meet the long-standing recommendation of ensuring a proper ratio of Exchange Mailbox processor cores to global catalog processor cores in a given site. If you are using x86 domain controllers, the ratio is 4:1; while using x64 domain controllers, the ratio is 8:1. Note that the x64 ratio is assuming that you have enough RAM on the domain controllers to cache the entire NTDS.DIT database. This helps ensure that global catalog lookups happen quickly enough to keep Exchange responding in a timely fashion.

◆ Avoid installing Exchange 2010 on a domain controller. Although it is technically possible, such a combined server is much less resilient to service outages or configuration changes and is much harder to restore in the event of a disaster. If you do go this route, you will have to uninstall Exchange if you ever want to demote the machine from being a domain controller; you cannot run the dcpromo command once Exchange is installed.

EXCHANGE VERSION

The final prerequisite you must consider is what mode your legacy Exchange organization is in. By default, these versions of Exchange install in mixed mode even when you did not upgrade from Exchange 5.5. You must upgrade the organization to Exchange 2000/2003 native mode. Note that in order to do this, you must ensure the following points:

◆ No Exchange 5.5 or Exchange 2000 servers remain in the organization.

◆ No legacy Exchange Site Replication Service (SRS) instances remain in the organization.

◆ No configured connection agreements in the Active Directory Connector (ADC) remain in the organization. In fact, if you still have the ADC in your organization and you have no more Exchange 5.5 servers or legacy Exchange SRS instances, remove the ADC from the organization.

Once you have verified that your Active Directory domains and forest and Exchange organization meet these prerequisites, you can begin the process of installing Exchange 2007 by preparing Active Directory.

Setting the Legacy Routing Server Parameter

Chapter 13 briefly mentioned the /LegacyRoutingServer installation option (see Table 13.1). We will now discuss why it exists and what problems it solves.

When you install Exchange 2010 in an existing legacy Exchange organization, you should address some architectural differences. We said earlier that Exchange 2010 doesn't use administrative groups or routing groups, and that's almost completely true. Although Exchange 2010 servers don't make use of them, the legacy Exchange servers do require them; in a mixed organization, you're going to have the administrative groups and routing groups created for the older Exchange servers. So far, so good; the Exchange 2010 servers use the new Active Directory site-based architecture and the legacy Exchange servers use the administrative groups and routing groups. Under these conditions, everything is happy until the new Exchange 2010 server tries to interact with a legacy Exchange server.

To deal with this, the Exchange 2010 installer takes several actions to ensure compatibility with legacy Exchange servers:

◆ To facilitate communication with legacy Exchange servers, the Exchange 2010 installer creates a special administrative group the first time it is run in a legacy organization. All Exchange 2010 servers are placed into this special administrative group, which is named Exchange Administrative Group (FYDIBOHF23SPDLT). If you have previously installed Exchange 2007, this administrative group will already exist. The Exchange 2010 servers don't use this group, but it will show up, along with all the Exchange 2010 servers, in the legacy Exchange System Manager.

◆ The installer also creates a special routing group for Exchange 2010 servers, named Exchange Routing Group (DWBGZMFD01QNBJR). As with the administrative group, all Exchange 2007 servers are placed into this routing group, even though they use the native Exchange 2010 and Active Directory site-based routing mechanisms; the group and servers are visible in the legacy Exchange System Manager. The only purpose of this routing group is to force the legacy Exchange servers to use a routing group connector to communicate with Exchange 2010 servers.

◆ The installer also creates a universal security group named ExchangeLegacyInterop in Active Directory. Exchange 2010 servers use this group to determine which legacy servers are permitted to submit messages to the default SMTP receive connectors on the Exchange 2010 Hub Transport instances. By default, these connectors require successful authentication and permit message submission only from legacy servers whose computer accounts are in this group, such as the legacy Exchange bridgehead server.

◆ When the first Exchange 2010 Hub Transport role is installed, the installer creates a two-way routing group connector between the Exchange 2010 routing group and a user-selected legacy Exchange bridgehead server. If you use the command-line installer, you use the /LegacyRoutingServer switch to specify which legacy Exchange server to use. You can add additional bridgehead servers to these routing group connectors after the installation is complete, and we talk about that in more detail later in this chapter. As with the administrative and routing groups, this connector is visible in the legacy Exchange System Manager.

TABLE 14.1:   Comparison of Exchange 2010 Upgrade Strategies

POINT OF COMPARISON	MIGRATION STRATEGY	UPGRADE STRATEGY
Tools	You will need a combination of free Microsoft tools to manage the multiple sets of data that need to be migrated (Active Directory user information and third-party tools to manage/migrate the Exchange mailbox data at a minimum). These tools usually result in at least some minor information loss.	You can use the built-in tools in Exchange 2010 and Windows Server to control all aspects of the transition, including building the new servers, reconfiguring Active Directory, or moving mailbox data.
Hardware	You will usually require a significant amount of new hardware. You may not need to have a complete spare set of replacement hardware, but you'll need enough to have the basic infrastructure of your new Exchange 2010 organization in place.	You can accomplish this strategy, but you must ensure that you have sufficient hardware in place to handle loads such as the additional load placed on the Exchange 2010 Client Access servers. For example, the Client Access server handles both direct MAPI clients as well as Outlook Anywhere clients. The recommendation is three Client Access server processor cores for each four Mailbox processor cores.

TABLE 14.1:   Comparison of Exchange 2010 Upgrade Strategies *(CONTINUED)*

POINT OF COMPARISON	MIGRATION STRATEGY	UPGRADE STRATEGY
Active Directory and DNS	You must create a new Active Directory forest. Typically, this means that you cannot reuse the same AD and DNS domain names (although you will be able to share the same SMTP domain names).	You can make use of your existing Active Directory and DNS deployment; however, you will first need to upgrade your existing domain controllers and global catalogs to meet the prerequisites.
User accounts	You must migrate your user accounts to the new AD forest or re-create them.	Your users will be able to use their existing accounts without any changes.
Message routing	Your SMTP domains must be split between your legacy organization and your new organization; one of them must be configured to be nonauthoritative and to route to the other. This configuration may need to change during the course of the migration. Additionally, you must set up explicit external SMTP connectors between the two organizations or play tricks with name resolution.	Your organization continues to be a single entity, with full knowledge of all authoritative domains shared among all Exchange servers. Message flow between organizations can be controlled by the simple addition of bridgehead servers to the default legacy routing group connector or the creation of additional legacy routing group connectors to meet the needs of your topology.
Outlook profiles	You will need either to create new Outlook profiles (manually or using the tools found in the matching version of the Microsoft Office Resource Kit) or to use third-party tools to migrate them over to the new organization. This may cause loss of information.	As long as you keep the legacy mailbox servers up and running during an appropriate transition phase, Outlook will transparently update your users' profiles to their new Mailbox server the first time they open it after their mailbox is moved to Exchange 2010.

At first these changes may seem overwhelming, especially if your current Exchange organization consists of only one or two administrative and routing groups. The thought of adding another administrative group and routing group to the mix initially strikes many people as counterintuitive; after all, the point of the move away from them is to simplify things, not clutter them up! Consider for a moment an organization that consists of the following elements:

◆ A single Active Directory forest and domain

◆ Two sites, imaginatively named Site A and Site B

◆ A domain controller and global catalog server in each site, for a total of four domain controllers

◆ An Exchange 2003 organization, consisting of a separate administrative group and routing group for each site (for the sake of argument, we'll say that this administrative and routing group design is a legacy of an earlier upgrade from Exchange 5.5)

◆ Four Exchange 2003 servers in each site: two Mailbox servers, a front-end server, and a bridgehead server, for a total of eight Exchange 2003 servers

---

ABOUT EXCHANGE 2007/2010 ADMINISTRATIVE AND ROUTING GROUPS

The names of the Exchange 2007/2010 administrative and routing groups are designed to be unique, something that is not likely to be already present in any legacy organization. Do not rename these groups!

The Exchange 2007/2010 administrative group and routing group are intended only for Exchange 2007/2010 servers. Do not place legacy Exchange servers in these groups thinking that it will somehow improve interoperability or remove the need for the routing group connector. You will break mail flow because there is no other mechanism for translating between the legacy Exchange routing mechanism and the Exchange 2010 routing mechanism.

Now, this organization wants to install Exchange 2010. The goal is to end up with a total of six Exchange 2010 servers: one Mailbox instance, one Client Access instance, and one Hub Transport instance for each AD site. As shown in Figure 14.1, things certainly look messy while they're in the middle of their upgrade.

FIGURE 14.1
Logical structures present when Exchange 2010 coexists in a legacy organization

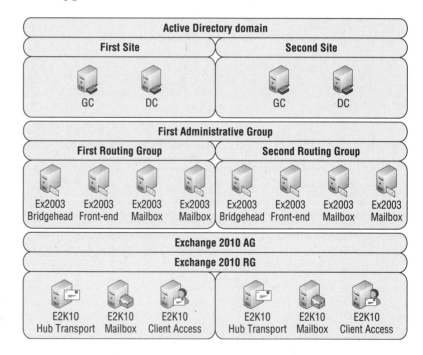

Although this is not a terribly complicated organization if you compare it to an organization with 100,000 users, it is nonetheless a handful for a small or medium-sized company. They've got administrative groups, multiple routing groups, and Active Directory infrastructure spread out. Even with at most a total of 18 servers to handle, tracking the multiple overlapping memberships gets ugly.

Ah, but when they've completed their upgrade, things are a lot calmer, as shown in Figure 14.2. They've got their two Active Directory sites, a single deprecated Exchange administrative group, and a single deprecated Exchange routing group.

FIGURE 14.2
Logical structures simplified when only Exchange 2010 remains

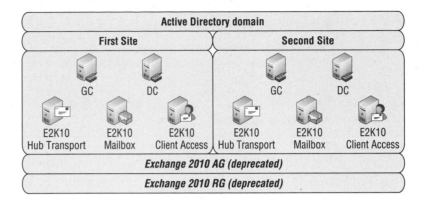

Once you've specified the legacy bridgehead server and successfully added the first Exchange 2010 Hub Transport instance to the organization, you can later configure the default routing group connector with additional legacy Exchange bridgehead servers or even create new routing group connectors to simplify the message routing paths in your organization. However, you're going to have to perform these tasks from the Exchange Management Shell; you won't see the legacy routing group connectors listed in the Exchange Management Console.

To see the existing legacy routing group connectors, use the `Get-RoutingGroupConnector` cmdlet. Its output is shown in Figure 14.3.

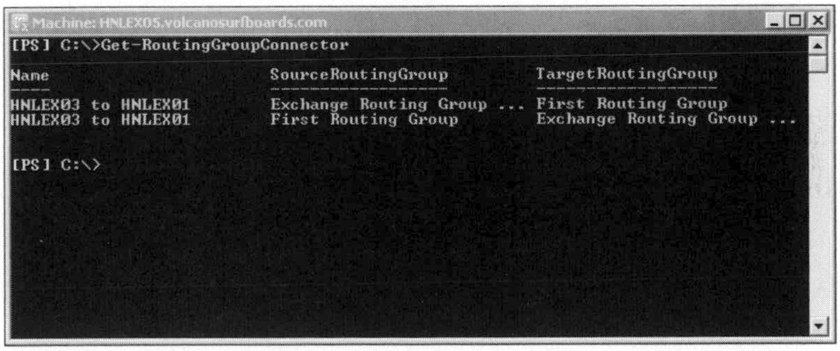

FIGURE 14.3
Output from the Get-RoutingGroup Connector cmdlet

```
Machine: HNLEX05.volcanosurfboards.com                                    _ □ X
[PS] C:\>Get-RoutingGroupConnector

Name                    SourceRoutingGroup          TargetRoutingGroup

HNLEX03 to HNLEX01      Exchange Routing Group ...  First Routing Group
HNLEX03 to HNLEX01      First Routing Group         Exchange Routing Group ...


[PS] C:\>
```

To add a new legacy bridgehead to an existing legacy routing group connector, use the `Set-RoutingGroupConnector` cmdlet. Here is an example where we are adding Exchange 2003 servers hnlbh01.somorita.int and hnlbh02.somorita.int and Exchange 2007 servers hnlht03.somorita.int and hnlht04.somorita.int to a routing group connector called E2K7 to E2K3 RGC:

```
Set-RoutingGroupConnector -Name "E2K7 to E2K3 RGC" ↵
-SourceTransportServers "hnlht03.somorita.int", ↵
"hnlht04.somorita.int" -TargetTransportServers ↵
"hnlbh01.somorita.int", "hnlbh02.somorita.int"
```

This cmdlet ensures that the legacy servers are automatically added to the ExchangeLegacy-Interop security group so that SMTP authentication will take place and messages will flow properly.

SUPPRESSING LINK STATE UPDATES

One of the interesting features included with Exchange Server 2000/2003 was link state updates. This feature allowed an Exchange 2000/2003 server to notify other bridgehead servers in the organization in the event of a connector failure. The intent was to ensure that messages did not get bounced back and forth between connectors and bridgehead servers. Exchange Server 2010 does not use or require link state updates, so this feature should be disabled on all Exchange 2003 servers.

To create a new routing group connector, use the `New-RoutingGroupConnector` cmdlet. Here is an example of creating a new routing group connector called E2K7 to Hawaii RG using the Exchange 2003 server hnlbh01.somorita.int and the Exchange 2007 server hnlht01.somorita.net as bridgehead servers:

```
New-RoutingGroupConnector –Name "E2K7 to Hawaii RG" ↵
-SourceTransportServers "hnlht01.somorita.int" ↵
-TargetTransportServers "hnlbh01.somorita.int" ↵
-Cost 100 –Bidirectional $True -PublicFoldersEnabled $True
```

When you use the `New-RoutingGroupConnector` and `Set-RoutingGroupConnector` cmdlets to specify the `TargetTransportServers` and `SourceTransportServers` parameters, you need to specify all the servers you wish to be bridgeheads for the connector. Each invocation of the cmdlet will overwrite the existing parameter.

Choosing Your Strategy

Now that you've considered the various factors that could affect your upgrade, you need to figure out which strategy you're going to use. As mentioned earlier, you have two main choices: *migration* or *transition*, as Microsoft calls them. Although neither option gives you the relative ease of the traditional in-place upgrade, each option has its pros and cons. In the following sections, we review them briefly and then move on to a more in-depth discussion.

Comparing the Strategies

If you're like many readers, you probably have at least some preference for your upgrade strategy already in mind. Before you set that choice in stone, though, read through this section and see whether there are any surprises (good or bad) that might allow you to address some aspect of the upgrade that you hadn't previously considered. If, on the other hand, you're not sure which strategy would be best for you, this section should give you enough information to begin making a well-informed decision.

Let's start with an overview of how the two strategies stack up. Table 14.1 lists several points of comparison between the migration and transition strategies.

For the most part, Table 14.1 speaks for itself; if any point requires more in-depth discussion, we address it properly during the detailed sections that follow.

MIGRATING YOUR EXCHANGE ORGANIZATION

From the overview given in Table 14.1, it may seem as if we have a grudge against upgrading to Exchange 2010 by using the migration strategy. Although we have to admit it's not our favorite strategy, we'll hasten to say that migration offers many advantages that a transition upgrade doesn't offer:

◆ It is the only realistic way to consolidate two or more separate Exchange organizations into a single organization. This kind of consolidation can happen as the result of a major reorganization inside one company or as the result of merger or acquisitions.

◆ It allows you to set up a *greenfield* (a term used to denote the ideal state of implementation) deployment of Exchange 2010. No matter how conscientious you are as an admin, any real network is the product of a number of design compromises. After a while, the weight of those compromises and workarounds add up; the design and structure of your network can reflect imperatives and inputs that no longer exist, or are no longer relevant, in your organization. It's nice to be able to wipe the slate clean, especially if that ends up being less work than trying to start with your current mess and clean it up.

◆ It permits you to move your Exchange servers out of your existing Active Directory forest and establish them in their own forest. If you're in an environment that separates administrative control between Active Directory and the Exchange organization, having a separate forest for Exchange can make it a lot easier to accomplish many of the day-to-day management tasks on your servers. (We don't know about you, but we'd much prefer to have control of the OU structure and Group Policy Objects that affect our Exchange servers.) If the benefits of a multiforest deployment outweigh the drawbacks, this configuration may improve the efficiency of the split between directory/account administration and Exchange administration.

◆ It gives you the chance to easily define new policies and procedures that apply equally to everyone, from account provisioning to server-naming conventions. With the importance of regulatory compliance and strong internal IT controls and auditing rising on a daily basis, this can be a strong motivator.

◆ It allows you to perform additional configuration and testing of your new organization before you move the bulk of your live data and users to it. Being able to perform additional validation, perhaps with a pilot group of users, gives you additional confidence in the strength of your design and affords you extra opportunities to spot problems and correct them while you can.

Now that we've said that, we should point out that a migration strategy usually involves more work, more money, or both. Sometimes, though, it's what you have to do.

Here's what a migration might look like:

1. Deploy a new Active Directory forest and root domain, as well as any additional domains. These will probably be named something different from the domains in use in your current network so that you can operate in both environments (and your users can as well). You could be using this forest as an Exchange resource forest, or you could be moving all your servers and desktops as well. Because migrations don't happen overnight, you'll probably need some sort of forest trust between your forests so that accounts and permissions will work properly while the migration is in progress. This step is outside the scope of this book; for more information see *Mastering Microsoft Windows Server 2008 R2* by Mark Minasi, et al (Sybex: 2010).

2. Migrate a suitable set of user accounts to the new forest. Perhaps you're concentrating on one site at one time to minimize confusion; if so, you need to migrate each user account

in the site to the corresponding site in the new Active Directory forest. Again, this step is outside the scope of this book.

3. Install Windows Server 2008 x64 SP2 or R2 and Exchange 2010 on a suitable number of 64-bit servers to form the core of your new Exchange 2010 organization. You don't need to have new servers for everything, but you usually should have at least a site's worth of equipment on hand. You'll need to configure SMTP connectors between the two organizations, and you must have some sort of directory synchronization going on between the two forests. That way, as users get moved into the new forest, each Global Address List (GAL) is properly updated to ensure that internal mail is delivered to the right Exchange organization. You'll probably need to configure public folder synchronization so that free-busy data is shared between the two organizations as well.

4. Move the mailbox data for the site from the legacy Exchange mailbox servers to the new Exchange 2010 mailbox servers. Update your users' Outlook profiles so that they can get to their mailboxes, and ensure that the GAL information is updated so that mail follows these users to their new mailbox servers. Once everything is working, you can remove the legacy Exchange servers from this site.

5. Don't forget that you may have to join your users' desktops, as well as any other Windows member servers (such as file/print, database, and web servers) to the new forest if it isn't being used exclusively as an Exchange resource forest. This step is outside the scope of this book.

6. Continue this process one site at a time until you've moved all your user accounts and mailbox data into the Exchange 2010 organization and have decommissioned the remaining legacy Exchange servers.

Now you can see why we consider the migration strategy to be the labor-intensive route. You don't have the luxury of accepting your existing Active Directory structure and accounts. Although you can move message data over to a new organization, more effort is involved in making sure users' profiles are properly updated. Alternatively, you can rebuild your users' profiles and accept some data loss. If you're upgrading the desktop clients to Outlook 2007 or Outlook 2010, you have the additional worry of whether you need to move the desktop machines into a new forest.

On the other hand, if you have an Active Directory deployment with serious structural problems (whether through years of accumulation or the results of previous mistakes), if you need to extract your Exchange servers into a separate Active Directory forest, or if there is some other reason transitioning your existing organization isn't going to work for you, migration has a lot to offer.

Migrations require you to keep track of a lot of details and separate types of information. Although you can migrate all the important information — mailboxes, public folders, GAL data — using the freely available Microsoft tools, you'll have a harder time migrating some of the smaller details that aren't mission critical but nonetheless can add up to a negative user experience if omitted. If users' first experience on the new messaging system is having to reconfigure Outlook with all their preferences, they're going to be less than happy about the experience. The cost of third-party migration tools may well prove to be a good investment that saves you time, reduces complexity, and gains you the goodwill of your users.

UPGRADING YOUR EXCHANGE ORGANIZATION

The process of transitioning your legacy Exchange organization to Exchange 2010 in many ways resembles the process required to upgrade from Exchange 5.5 to Exchange 2000 or

Exchange 2003. If you have experience in that particular upgrade, relax; transitioning to Exchange 2010 is much easier. You're using Active Directory, so no directory upgrade or synchronization is required. You're not multiplying the number of organizational structures required, as did the transition from Exchange 5.5 sites to Exchange 2000 administrative groups and routing groups. You're not changing from the X.400-based MTA protocol to SMTP. All you're doing is moving mailboxes and public folder information, so it's easy — well, as easy as these types of projects get.

Let's take a closer look at the average transition to Exchange 2010.

AN OVERVIEW OF TRANSITION

Imagine that you have an Exchange 2003 organization that has eight mailbox servers, two front-end servers, and two bridgehead servers that handle all SMTP traffic with the Internet. For the sake of illustration, say that all your existing Exchange servers are already on 64-bit hardware; you have spares that you plan on using during the transition to keep your new hardware costs to a minimum.

In this organization, the transition process would look something like this:

1. Ensure that your organization meets all the prerequisites, including upgrading at least one Active Directory domain controller in each Active Directory site to Windows Server 2003 SP1 if they're not already at that level. Run the Active Directory preparation to upgrade the forest schema with the Exchange 2010 extensions and to create the proper objects in the domains.

2. Install the first Exchange 2010 Client Access instance into your organization. Once it is configured, you can bring it into production use and decommission the first Exchange 2003 front-end server provided you have an additional Exchange 2003 front-end server to handle OWA clients. You can then reuse this hardware to install the second Exchange 2010 Client Access instance and decommission the second Exchange 2003 front-end server.

3. Install the first Exchange 2010 Hub Transport instance into your organization. This instance could be on the same 64-bit machine as one of the Client Access instances (or as an intended Mailbox server) or on a separate machine; however, both the Client Access and Hub Transport roles need to exist before you install your first Exchange 2010 Mailbox instance. You also install an Exchange 2010 Edge Transport server on a separate machine. You configure the Edge Subscription connection between the Edge Transport server and the Hub Transport server and establish the Send connector.

4. Install the second Exchange 2010 Hub Transport instance. You can either install a second Edge Transport server or live with the existing one. Once the second Hub Transport instance (and second Edge Transport server, if deployed) is in production, you reconfigure your SMTP connectors so that your Edge Transport servers are now handling all external SMTP traffic.

5. Install Windows Server 2008 x64 SP2 or R2 on your spare 64-bit mailbox server hardware. Install Exchange 2010 on it as the first Exchange 2010 Mailbox instance in the organization.

6. Reconfigure Exchange Server 2010 to handle the offline address book distribution. Be sure to consider Outlook 2003 clients and the need to replicate this information to the public folder database on Exchange Server 2010.

7. Replicate public folders to the Exchange 2010 public folder servers. Once replication is complete and you no longer need the replicas on the Exchange 2003 servers, remember to remove the replicas from Exchange Server 2003.

8. Move the mailboxes from the first Exchange 2003 mailbox server onto the first Exchange 2010 Mailbox server. Remove the first Exchange 2003 mailbox server from the organization.

9. Perform a clean installation of Windows Server 2003 x64 SP2 or R2 on this server and then install the Exchange 2010 Mailbox instance. Move the mailboxes from the second Exchange 2010 server onto this new Mailbox instance.

10. Continue the process in Step 9 one server at a time until you have moved all mailboxes onto Exchange 2010 Mailbox instances and you have no remaining Exchange 2003 mailbox servers left in the organization. At this point, you will have the same number of spare servers you started with. If they are 64-bit machines, you can install some other Exchange 2010 role on them.

11. Once all Exchange 2003 mailboxes have been moved to Exchange Server 2010, you can then retire the Exchange 2003 front-end, bridgehead, and Mailbox servers.

It sounds like a lot of work, but many people have favored this kind of approach even in previous upgrades to Exchange. It gives you the advantage of having a clean installation of Windows to work with and allows you to configure the operating system exactly the way you want it.

ORDER OF INSTALLATION FOR EXCHANGE 2010 ROLES

Microsoft makes some specific recommendations on the order in which you should install the various roles. Technically, you can install your roles in any order you like. However, following Microsoft's recommendations allows you to minimize the deployment of new server hardware and get the most reuse value from your existing servers if that's a major consideration in your upgrade plans.

Microsoft's recommended order ensures that as each role is installed it can locate the prerequisite roles it depends on for proper function. You do not, however, have to install all instances of a particular role before beginning to deploy instances of the next role. You can always go back and install additional instances of any role as you scale up a site.

CLIENT ACCESS SERVERS

The Client Access role should be the first Exchange 2010 instance you install into a legacy Exchange organization. The reason for this is simple: once you actually have mailboxes on Exchange 2010 servers and your users attempt to access them using any protocol other than MAPI over RPC, you will need to have an Exchange 2010 Client Access instance to provide that protocol access. The Exchange 2010 Client Access role can also provide access to legacy Exchange 2003 or 2007 mailboxes. This potentially allows you to switch client and web protocol access to Exchange 2010 and decommission your legacy front-end servers. This will depend on the client version, protocols in use, mailbox version, and whether or not you are configured to proxy or redirect OWA requests to legacy versions. In contrast, a legacy Exchange server cannot provide front-end or client protocol access to a server running a newer version of Exchange. For more information, see Chapter 24, "Understanding the Client Access Server."

In smaller organizations, it is common to deploy the Client Access, Hub Transport, and Mailbox roles on the same physical server. In fact, this is the standard Exchange 2010 installation option when you use the GUI setup.

CLIENT ACCESS ROLE REQUIREMENTS AND BEST PRACTICES

Upgrading the front-end servers first has long been an Exchange best practice; even when applying service packs, you always want the front-end server running the most recent version of Exchange. Although the Client Access role isn't exactly the same thing as a front-end server, this rule of thumb still applies in Exchange 2010.

When you are determining the number of Client Access instances you need, remember that you must have at least one Client Access instance in each Active Directory site where you will have an Exchange 2010 mailbox. Although any Client Access instance can answer an incoming request, if the requested resource is on a Mailbox server that is not in the same site as the initial Client Access instance, it will redirect the request to an available Client Access instance in the Mailbox server's Active Directory site.

This role is mandatory in an Exchange 2010 organization even if you do not plan to support Outlook Web App, ActiveSync, POP, or IMAP clients. Outlook MAPI clients must use the Microsoft Exchange RPC Client Access service to access mailbox data; Outlook 2007/2010 use the Client Access server for Autodiscover as well as accessing free/busy information and downloading the offline address book.

HUB TRANSPORT SERVERS

The Hub Transport role is the next logical role to install. Under the new Exchange 2010 architecture, Mailbox servers are no longer responsible for transporting messages directly. This task is now handled by the Hub Transport role. Likewise, all SMTP traffic with other routing groups and external systems is routed through Hub Transport instances. Even if you installed Exchange 2010 Mailbox servers first, they would literally be unable to communicate with any other Exchange servers until an Exchange 2010 Hub Transport instance was installed in the same site. If multiple Hub Transport instances are available in the same site, Exchange 2010 will automatically load-balance SMTP traffic across the available instances.

In smaller organizations, it is common to deploy the Client Access, Hub Transport, and Mailbox roles on the same physical server. In fact, this is the standard Exchange 2010 installation option when you use the GUI setup.

When you are planning the number of Hub Transport instances you need, remember that you must have at least one Hub Transport instance in each Active Directory site where you will have an Exchange 2010 Mailbox server. As messages are routed to recipients in the organization, the Hub Transport instance that is processing the message looks up the mailbox data in Active Directory. If the mailbox is in the same site, the Hub Transport instance will directly pass the message along; if the recipient's mailbox is in a different site, the Hub Transport instance will transmit the message to an available Hub Transport instance in the recipient's Active Directory site.

The Hub Transport role is mandatory in an Exchange 2010 organization.

MAILBOX SERVERS

After you have suitable Client Access and Hub Transport roles in a given site, you can begin deploying the Mailbox role. Until you have mailboxes hosted on Exchange 2010, the advanced features of Exchange 2010, such as Unified Messaging, cannot be used.

When moving mailboxes to Exchange 2010 Mailbox servers, only use the Exchange 2010 Exchange Management Console Mailbox Move Wizard or the Exchange Management Shell Move-Mailbox cmdlet. In particular, do not use the wizard in legacy versions of Exchange or you could break the mailboxes.

The Mailbox role is mandatory in an Exchange 2010 organization. Well, we suppose that technically it's not — but if you're not going to have mailboxes, why bother to upgrade?

EDGE TRANSPORT SERVERS

The Edge Transport server role can be deployed once you have a Hub Transport instance in your organization. Because the Edge Subscription process is initiated and controlled by Hub Transport instances, and Edge Transport servers should not be part of the same Active Directory forest as the rest of the Exchange organization, there are no requirements for site affinity.

The Edge Transport role must be placed on its own physical server and cannot be co-located with any other roles.

The Edge Transport role is designed to be placed in perimeter networks with limited connectivity to the internal network. Although there are no requirements for where you place the Edge Transport server, for best performance it should be placed so that it has a low-latency, high-bandwidth connection to the Internet, as well as one or more Hub Transport instances, through the appropriate firewalls.

UNIFIED MESSAGING SERVERS

Although the Unified Messaging role is not within the scope of this book, we can make a few general observations about deploying it. This is probably the last role to deploy in your organization; it requires working Hub Transport and Mailbox instances in the organization; it also requires a Hub Transport instance to be placed in the same Active Directory site that the Unified Messaging server will be placed in. This Hub Transport instance will transmit messages created by the Unified Messaging server instance to recipient mailboxes in the organization.

Depending on the number of recipients and the hardware configuration, you can combine the Unified Messaging role with any (or all) of the Client Access, Hub Transport, or Mailbox roles on the same physical server.

The Unified Messaging role is, of course, optional.

For your users to make use of the Unified Messaging functionality, you must have sufficient Enterprise Client Access Licenses (CALs) for those users.

Management Consoles

As you install Exchange 2010 on your servers, you may or may not wish to install the sixth role — the management tools. You can instead place the management tools role on a separate server or workstation and use it as a management console. One slight road bump for the Exchange 2010 management tools is that there is not a 32-bit version of these; therefore, users must either be running Windows Vista x64 or Windows 7 x64. The other option for remote administration is to install the tools on a terminal server and allow the administrators to perform management tasks via terminal server.

You cannot install the legacy Exchange 2003 System Manager on an Exchange 2010 server; legacy versions of Exchange are not supported on 64-bit Windows, and the IIS SMTP component required by the legacy System Manager would conflict with the Exchange 2010 transport components.

So, under what conditions would you want to have the legacy System Manager management console available for your users?

◆ You still have existing legacy Exchange servers during the duration of your transition.

◆ You have legacy Exchange servers with features that are not supported in Exchange 2010. As long as you use these features, you will need to keep the legacy System Manager.

◆ You have public folders in your organization. Though you can manage them using the Exchange Management Shell or the Public Folder Management Console, it is frankly easier to do it using the System Manager. If you have a large public folder infrastructure, we would say that keeping the System Manager is mandatory — unless, of course, you don't value your sanity. Note, though, that Exchange 2010 does not support WebDAV so the Exchange System Manager must have an Exchange 2003 or Exchange 2007 public folder store to which it connects.

ABOUT THE MOVE MAILBOX FEATURE

In legacy versions of Exchange, the creation of user accounts and provisioning of Exchange features all took place with extensions to the Active Directory Users and Computers MMC snap-in. In Exchange 2010, you can only use the management tools to provision existing users or create new mail-enabled objects. You may be tempted to continue using the Active Directory Users and Computers MMC snap-in to provision mailboxes and other recipients on your Exchange 2010 servers. However, these recipients are in mixed mode and cannot use most of the new Exchange 2010 features until you use the Exchange 2010 management tools to update them. When you move mailboxes to an Exchange 2010 Mailbox server using the Exchange 2010 Management Console's New Local Move Request Wizard or New-MoveRequest cmdlet, the user object is automatically upgraded.

Coexistence

As you proceed with your Exchange 2010 upgrade, you will almost certainly have a period of time during which your Exchange 2010 servers will be required to coexist with legacy Exchange. During this time, there are several points you should consider:

◆ If you have multiple routing group connectors with legacy Exchange routing groups, especially so that there are multiple paths between a legacy Exchange routing group and the Exchange 2010 routing group, you must suppress the propagation of minor state version changes in link state. Link state is not used by Exchange 2010, but the presence of multiple paths can cause message routing loops in the legacy Exchange servers. The Exchange 2010 documentation contains instructions on performing this task under the topic "How to Suppress Link State Updates."

◆ Legacy Exchange servers use the X-EXCH50 SMTP extension to pass Exchange-specific properties with message data within the organization. Although Exchange 2010 no longer uses this connection, any routing group connectors created with legacy routing groups in the organization are automatically configured to support this extension. If you have a multiple-forest configuration where Exchange 2010 and legacy Exchange servers are communicating but in separate forests, you must enable this extension manually.

- The Edge Transport role can be used as a smart host for an Exchange 2003 organization without requiring the Active Directory preparation steps. However, because Edge Transport cannot synchronize with a legacy Exchange organization, you lose much of the advanced functionality that it offers.

- The Unified Messaging role cannot offer services for recipients whose mailboxes are on Exchange 2003 servers.

Performing an Interorganization Migration

If you have been digging through the Microsoft Exchange Server 2010 documentation, you may be a bit confused due to a slightly different use of terminology. Most of the rest of the world refers to moving to a new system of any type as a migration, and that is why we keep using that word. Earlier in this chapter, we covered a migration type where you move existing services and data to Exchange 2010 servers from Exchange 2000/2003 servers in the same organization. This is what Microsoft refers to as an *upgrade*.

The last part of this chapter focuses on migrating from either an Exchange 2003 organization into a new or separate Exchange 2010 organization. This type of migration is somewhat more difficult than an intraorganization migration, may be more disruptive for your users, and often leaves you with fewer options than a transition migration. However, you may be faced with an organizational configuration that leaves you no choice.

Is Interorganization Migration the Right Approach?

An interorganization migration is quite a bit more complex for both the person handling the migration and also for the users. The "upgrade" migration is by far the simplest type of Exchange 2010 migration. Before you choose an interorganization migration over an upgrade migration, you want to make sure you are choosing the right (and simplest) migration path.

Most organizations that are moving to Exchange Server 2010 will not need to perform an interorganization migration. If the following checklist sounds like your organization, you will need to perform an "upgrade":

- You have a single Active Directory forest and no resource forests.

- You are running Exchange 2003.

- Your Exchange 2003 organization is part of your existing Active Directory.

Does this sound like you? If so, go back and read the first part of this chapter because performing a transition migration is what you are going to need to do. Because you already have Exchange 2003 in your Active Directory, there is no need for the extra effort for an interorganization migration.

So, who needs to perform an interorganization migration? You might need to perform an interorganization migration for a number of reasons:

- You are consolidating one or more separate Exchange 2003 organizations.

- You are moving Exchange resources from a resource forest into your accounts forest.

- You are moving from Exchange 5.5 or Exchange 2000 to Exchange 2010.

- You are moving from a different messaging system to Exchange 2010.

If you have multiple organizations that you need to consolidate or some other type of migration, you have no choice but to proceed down the interorganization migration path. Proceeding down this path means different things to different organizations, but most of these interorganization migrations face a number of challenges:

◆ Finding the tools necessary to perform the migration based on your needs

◆ Moving mail data between two systems

◆ Moving directory data between two systems

◆ Maintaining directory synchronization and messaging between two systems during some period of interoperability

◆ Ensuring that email flows correctly between the email systems during the transition

◆ Figuring out how and when to transition services such as public folders, MX records, mobile phones, and web mail

CHOOSING THE RIGHT TOOLS

When you're planning an interorganization migration, it is important to pick the right tools to help you create accounts, move data, synchronize directories, create forwarders, and perform other migration tasks. Naturally, the most powerful and flexible of these tools are all provided by third parties rather than by Microsoft. However, Microsoft does provide some basic tools that you can use to perform Exchange 2003 to Exchange Server 2010 interorganization migration.

Active Directory Migration Tool If the user accounts have not yet been created or migrated into your target Active Directory, consider migrating the accounts from their original Active Directory rather than creating new user accounts. The Active Directory Migration Tool is a free tool from Microsoft that will help you migrate users, groups, and computers from one Windows domain or Active Directory to another. The big advantages of this tool are that it preserves the source domain's security identifier (SID) in the target account's SID history attribute and that it preserves group membership.

You can download the Active Directory Migration Tool (ADMT) v3 from the Tools section of Microsoft's TechNet website at `http://technet.microsoft.com/en-us/windowsserver/bb405947.aspx`.

New-MoveRequest Cmdlet The Exchange 2010 `New-MoveRequest` cmdlet has options that allow you to migrate mailbox data from a separate Exchange 2003, 2007, or 2010 organization, and it will even create a disabled account for you if one does not exist. We cover this tool in more detail later in this chapter in the section "Moving Mailboxes Using the New-MoveRequest Feature."

ExMerge and Import-Mailbox Cmdlet If you have a small number of users (fewer than 50), you might opt to export all their mail out from their old mail server using a tool like ExMerge (or even Outlook, yikes!) and then use the Exchange 2010 `Import-Mailbox` cmdlet to import mail data from these PST files into the user's new mailbox. This is a basic solution, but it saves you from having to get to know the `New-MoveRequest` cmdlet, and you still get to move your user's mail data. Keep in mind, though, that if you use this method you will lose things like folder rules and delegates that users have assigned to their folders.

Exchange 2003 Mail Migration Wizard   Exchange 2003 has an awesome migration utility called the Mail Migration Wizard that exports mail from Exchange 5.5, Exchange 2000, Exchange 2003, cc:Mail, Lotus Notes, and other mail systems. Exchange 2010 has no such tool, unfortunately. If you think you might need such functionality, you will need to install this tool on an Exchange 2003 server. If you are building a brand-new Exchange 2010 organization, you will need to install an Exchange 2003 server before you install your first Exchange 2010 server. Then you can migrate the mail temporarily to Exchange 2003 and move it on to Exchange 2010. This process may be more trouble than it is worth, and you may find it worthwhile to invest in a third-party migration tool.

Third-Party Tools   If you have more than a few hundred users, a lot of public folder data, or very large mailboxes, or if you will need to maintain some level of interoperability between your old Exchange 2003 or Exchange 2007 system and your new Exchange 2010 system for a long period of time (longer than a few weeks), you should consider a third-party tool. These are often a tough sell after an organization has invested a lot of money in a new mail system, but they can make your migration much easier and allow for better, long-term interoperability.

Maintaining Interoperability

During either a true migration or a transition migration from one messaging system to another, the period of interoperability is always one of the biggest headaches. One of the first factors we always want to take into consideration when faced with an interorganization migration is developing a plan that will minimize the time during which the old system and the new system must coexist.

The transition type of migration is the simplest type if you are going to need two systems to coexist for some period of time. However, this approach is not always an option. In that case, you need to figure out if you can perform an "instant" or light-switch migration, or if you must have some period of interoperability.

Light-Switch Migrations

For a smaller number of users (fewer than 1,000 mailboxes, for example), we try to find a way to perform a "light-switch" migration. On Friday afternoon when the user leaves work, she is using the old system. On Monday morning when she returns to work, she is using the new system. This is a light-switch migration; from the user's perspective the transition occurs very quickly.

We like the light-switch migration strategy because it usually does not require you to perform any sort of destructive migration on the source system, and everything is migrated all at once. We have performed successful light-switch migrations for 20-user organizations all the way up to 1,500-user organizations. A number of factors will determine if a light-switch migration is possible in your organization. Here are some of the factors that we had to consider:

◆ Can all of the data be moved in a short period of time?

◆ Can users' Outlook clients and ActiveSync devices be directed or reconfigured to use the new servers effectively and accurately?

◆ Are there sufficient Help Desk and Information Technology resources to support the user community on "the morning after"?

◆ If new accounts have to be created for users, can the old passwords be synchronized or can new passwords be distributed to the users?

If you can properly support the light-switch migration, it is best for minimizing interoperability between two systems. The first goal has to be minimizing disruption for the user community, but a long transition between two mail systems can often be more disruptive if the interoperability issues are not properly addressed.

A lot of factors are involved in planning any interorganization migration strategy, but here is a list of major factors and roughly the order in which they should be done:

◆ Deploy the new messaging system and test all components including inbound/outbound mail routing and web components.

◆ Develop a plan for migrating Outlook profiles such as using Outlook 2007/2010 Autodiscover or a script that creates a new profile.

◆ Create mailboxes and establish email addresses that match the existing mailboxes on the source system.

◆ Move older data (mailboxes and public folders) if possible.

◆ Restrict user access to older mail system and start migration.

◆ Switch inbound email to the new mail system.

◆ Switch Outlook profiles to new servers.

◆ Switch over inbound HTTP/HTTPS access to mailboxes.

◆ Replicate public folder data.

◆ Move mailbox data; if using a third-party migration tool, try to replicate older mailbox data prior to migration day.

◆ Keep the old mail system up and running for a month or two just in case you need to retrieve something.

Interoperability Factors

In every migration in which we have been involved, we try to avoid keeping two mail systems operating in parallel for very long. Without the right tools, interoperability is a royal pain in the neck. That being said, you are probably wondering what some of the issues of interoperability are. Here is a partial list of some things you need to be concerned about or that your migration utilities should address:

◆ Email forwarding between domains should work seamlessly; email should be delivered to the right location regardless of whether someone has been migrated.

◆ Directory/address book synchronization should work seamlessly; users should be able to continue to use the GAL and it should accurately reflect the correct address of the user.

◆ Mail distribution groups should continue to work properly regardless of where the member is located.

◆ Replying to email messages that were migrated to the new system should still work.

◆ Public folder data and free/busy data should be synchronized between the two systems.

◆ You should have a plan that includes how to transition from one web-based mail system and mobile device system to another.

◆ Your plan should include migrating users in groups or by department if possible.

◆ Your plan or migration utilities should also include a mechanism to migrate (or help the user to reproduce) rules, folder permissions, and mailbox delegate access.

Preparing for Migration

You can do some things to get ready for your interorganization migration; these tasks will make things go more quickly for you. This preparation includes gathering information about what you have to migrate as well as preparing for the actual steps of migration. Here is a partial list:

◆ Because you are migrating your users from an existing Exchange organization to a new Exchange 2010 organization, have all the target systems' Exchange 2010 servers installed, tested, and ready to use before starting the migration.

◆ Document everything relevant about your source organization, including connectors, email flow, storage/message size limits, mail-enabled groups, and web access configuration (OWA, ActiveSync, IMAP4, POP3).

◆ Ensure that DNS name resolution between the two Active Directories is working correctly. You may need to configure conditional forwarders or zone transfers to achieve this.

◆ Ensure that WINS name resolution between all resources in both domains works properly. This step may not be necessary, but it never hurts.

◆ Make sure there are no firewalls between the two systems; if there are, ensure that the necessary ports are open between the systems.

◆ Configure trust relationships between the two systems.

◆ Ensure that you have Domain Administrator and Exchange Administrator permissions in both the source and target systems.

◆ If you are planning to use the Active Directory Migration Tool (ADMT) to migrate user accounts, you must establish name resolution, a trust relationship, and admin accounts in both domains.

Moving Mailboxes Using the New-MoveRequest Feature

Exchange Server 2010 includes the new New-MoveRequest cmdlet, which can be used to move either mailboxes within an organization or between two different Exchange organizations. For interorganization migrations, New-MoveRequest can be used whether the source server is running Exchange 2000/2003 or Exchange 2007; the target server must always be running Exchange 2010.

The New-MoveRequest cmdlet is a powerful tool with a lot of parameters and options. In this section, we focus just on its use when moving mail data between one Exchange organization and another. Keep in mind that one requirement for using the New-MoveRequest cmdlet is that the global catalog servers in both the source and target forest must be running Windows Server 2003 Service Pack 1 or later.

MIGRATING USER ACCOUNTS

When you use the New-MoveRequest cmdlet, this cmdlet requires a mail-enabled user account with a matching msExchMailboxGuid in the target forest. For more information, see this article:
http://technet.microsoft.com/en-us/library/ee633491(EXCHG.140)

Rather than creating the accounts manually or importing the accounts, we strongly recommend that you find some method to migrate user accounts, security groups, and distribution groups prior to running `New-MoveRequest`. This will make the migration to the new forest and Exchange organization more seamless and easier for your users as well as yourself. Even a free tool such as the Active Directory Migration Tool v3 is powerful enough to help you to perform these tasks.

PERMISSIONS REQUIRED

When you are using `New-MoveRequest`, you need to have accounts in both the source and destination forests that will give you the necessary permissions to move mailbox data between the two organizations. Usually, the accounts you use for the source and target organizations will *not* be the same account. Don't worry, though; `New-MoveRequest` makes it easy to move to different accounts. In the source organization, you need the following:

◆ For Exchange 2003 source servers, the account you are using must have been delegated the Exchange Administrator role for the organization or the administrative group in which the mailboxes are located.

◆ If the source server is an Exchange 2007 or Exchange 2010 server, the account you are using must have the Exchange Recipient Administrator role.

◆ The account you are using must be a member of each Exchange server's local administrators group.

Naturally, in the target organization, the account you are using with `New-MoveRequest` must also have a special permission:

◆ The account must be delegated the Recipient Management role in the target organization.

Finally, regardless of the credentials that you are using for the source and target organizations, the account with which you are logged into the Exchange management tools must be delegated the Recipient Management role for the server on which you are running `New-MoveRequest`.

NEW-MOVEREQUEST REQUIRED PARAMETERS

Let's start with the basic `New-MoveRequest` parameters that are required to move a mailbox from one organization to another, and then move on to some "nice to have" options. We'll share some of these options and then some examples of how to use them.

-Remote   Using the `-Remote` switch tells the Exchange Mailbox Replication service that the move you are performing is outside the current forest. This switch is required for cross-organization moves.

-RemoteGlobalCatalog   The `-RemoteGlobalCatalog` switch allows you to specify the fully qualified domain name of a domain controller in the remote organization.

-RemoteHostName   The `-RemoteHostName` switch specifies the name of the server in the remote organization.

-RemoteCredential   This option allows you to specify the credentials that the Mailbox Replication Service will use to connect to the remote server.

-TargetDatabase   The `-TargetDatabase` parameter allows you to specify the database to which the mailbox will be moved. This information is optional, but if you do not include it in the Move-Mailbox command line the mailbox will be randomly placed on a mailbox database within the Active Directory site where the cmdlet was executed. The target mailbox database name can be in the format of -TargetDatabase "Mailbox Database", -TargetDatabase "ServerName\Mailbox Database". You must specify a target database name that is unique within the organization.

-DomainController   The -DomainController parameter allows you to specify a domain controller in the target forest that you can use. This parameter is optional unless you are specifying target credentials via the command line, in which case it is required. When specifying this parameter, you must use the fully qualified domain name of the global catalog server; here is an example: -DomainController hnldc01.somorita.local.

A NEW-MOVEREQUEST EXAMPLE

Now that you know the basic parameters, let's take a look at how you would use these to perform a basic account migration. Here are the criteria for the migration:

◆ Target global catalog is duke.alohasurf.local

◆ Source user/mailbox is Brenda.Johnson

◆ Target credentials are VolcanoSurfb\Administrator

◆ Target mailbox database is HNLEX04\MBDB-HNLEX04-01

The first thing you need to do is set the target credentials. We mentioned earlier that you can't just specify the credentials in the command line because of the format that the -RemoteCredential parameters are expecting the credentials to be in. But you can use the PowerShell Get-Credential cmdlet to prompt you for each of these credentials and set them as a variable that you can use in the New-MoveRequest cmdlet. We are creating a variable called $TargetUser and will set that to the credentials of the source forest. Here is the cmdlet you would type:

```
$TargetUser = Get-Credential
```
When you type this cmdlet, you are going to get a dialog that prompts you for the username and password.

Once you enter the source forest's username and password and click OK, the dialog goes away. Then type **$TargetUser** and see the properties of that variable. Here is an example:

```
$TargetUser | FL
UserName : volcanosurfb\administrator
Password : System.Security.SecureString
```
Now you are ready to move a user's mailbox. Here is an EMS command that will move Brenda Johnson's mailbox:

```
New-MoveRequest brenda.johnson -TargetDatabase MBDB-HNLEX04-01 ↵
-RemoteGlobalCatalog duke.alohasurf.local ↵
-RemoteCredenentials $TargetUser
```
Notice that you left out the -DomainController and your own local credentials. If you leave these out, the credentials of the currently logged-on user will be used. The EMS is going to prompt to make sure that this is what you want to do; once you confirm that you do want to move the mailbox, the move will begin. This particular mailbox was 19 MB in size and took approximately 5 minutes to move.

Once the `New-MoveRequest` is complete, you will get a report telling you about the move operation and how long it took to move.

Importing Data from PST

A nice new feature of Exchange Server 2010 is the addition of the `Import-Mailbox` cmdlet and the option to import data from a PST. There is a small limitation to this feature, though: it can only be run on a server or workstation that has the 64-bit version of Outlook 2010 installed. As of this writing, Outlook 2010 is still in beta.

Before you begin trying to import PST data into an existing mailbox, make sure that you have the necessary permissions. By default, just because you are an Exchange Server administrator does not mean you can import data. Use the EMS `New-ManagementRoleAssignment` cmdlet to give your account the necessary permissions. Here is an example where we give user Rena.Dauria permission to user import or export data from mailboxes

```
New-ManagementRoleAssignment -Role "Mailbox Import Export" ↵
-User "Rena.Dauria"
```

One you have the necessary permissions to the mailbox and you have a computer with Outlook 2010 as well as the Exchange Management Tools installed, you can proceed. Here is an example of importing a PST file called `ARoberts.PST` into the mailbox Andrew.Roberts:

```
Import-Mailbox Andrew.Roberts -PSTFolderPath c:\ARoberts.PST
```

You can also import just a specific date range of data into a user's folder using the `Import-Mailbox` cmdlet's `-StartDate` and `-EndDate` options. Here is another example:

```
Import-Mailbox Grace.Tanaka -PSTFolderPath ↵
  c:\RDauria.PST -StartDate 03/01/2006 -EndDate 03/01/2008
```

The Bottom Line

Choose between an upgrade and a migration.   The migration path that you take is going to depend on a number of factors, including the amount of disruption that you can put your users through and the current version of your messaging system.

Master It   Your company is currently running Exchange Server 2003 and is supporting 3,000 users. You have a single Active Directory forest. You have purchased new hardware to support Exchange Server 2010. Management has asked that the migration path you choose have minimal disruption on your user community. Which type of migration should you use? What are the high-level events that should occur?

Determine the factors you need to consider before doing your upgrade.   Organizations frequently are delayed in their expected deployments due to things that they overlook when preparing for their migration.

Master It   You are planning your Exchange Server 2010 migration from an earlier version. What are some key factors that you must consider when planning the migration?

Coexist with legacy Exchange servers.   Coexistence with earlier versions if Exchange Server is a necessary evil unless you were able to migrate all your Exchange data and functionality at one time. Coexistence means that you must keep your old Exchange servers running for one of a number of functions, including message transfer, email storage, public folder storage, or mailbox access. One of the primary goals of any transition migration should be to move your messaging services (and mailboxes) over to new servers as soon as possible.

Master It   You are performing a transition migration from Exchange 2003 to Exchange Server 2010. Your desktop clients are a mix of Outlook 2003 and Outlook 2007. You quickly moved all your mailbox data and public folder data to Exchange Server 2010. Why should you leave your Exchange 2003 mailbox servers online for a few weeks after the mailbox moves have completed?

Perform an interorganization migration.   Interorganization migrations are by far the most difficult and disruptive migrations. These migrations move mailboxes as well as other messaging functions between two separate mail systems. User accounts and mailboxes usually have to be created for the new organization; user attributes such as email addresses, phone numbers, and so forth must be transferred to the new organization. Metadata such as "reply-ability" of existing messages as well as folder rules and mailbox permissions must also be transferred.

Although simple tools are provided to move mailboxes from one Exchange organization to another (such as the `New-MoveRequest` Exchange Management Shell cmdlet), large or complex migrations may require third-party migration tools.

Master It   You have a business subsidiary that has an Exchange 2003 organization with approximately 2,000 mailboxes; this Exchange organization is not part of the corporate Active Directory forest. The users all use Outlook 2003. You must migrate these mailboxes to Exchange Server 2010 in the corporate Active Directory forest. What options are available to you to move email to the new organization?

Part 3

Recipient Administration

## Chapter 15

Management Permissions and Role-Based Administration (RBAC)

In Exchange Server 2010, a new methodology is used for managing access permissions to user and administrative functionality. This technology, called role-based access control (RBAC), provides more powerful and granular control over what people can do than what was available in earlier versions of Exchange.

This approach to permissions is completely new for Exchange, so to use it effectively, we'll need to first take an in-depth look at how RBAC works and how it differs from the permission model in previous versions of Exchange. Then we'll examine the tools and processes for configuring and managing RBAC. After that, we can dig deeper into the topic of roles and how to assign them to users and administrators.

In this chapter, you will learn to:

◆ Determine what built-in roles and role groups provide you with the permissions you need

◆ Manage RBAC through both the Exchange Management Shell and the Exchange Control Panel

◆ Assign permissions to administrators using roles and role groups

◆ Grant permissions to end users for updating their address list information

◆ Create custom administration roles and assign them to administrators

RBAC Basics

Since role-based access control (RBAC) is a new concept for most Exchange administrators, we're going to start with an overview of the technology. The goal in this section is to give you a broad and high-level understanding of what RBAC is and how it works. As we discuss these various topics throughout the remainder of this chapter, we will build on this knowledge and you will gain deeper insights into RBAC. This will help you learn what RBAC can do for you and how you can use it.

Differences from Previous Exchange Versions

In the most basic sense, RBAC is the new permissions model for Exchange Server 2010. Anyone who has had to customize permissions in previous versions of Exchange can understand the inconvenience of making permission changes in Active Directory and keeping track of what permission modifications were made. Permissions in previous Exchange versions used access control lists (ACLs) on various Active Directory objects. Each object to which you wanted to delegate permissions had its own ACL. Each ACL was further composed of multiple access control entries (ACEs) that defined what permissions each user or group had on that object. To make this process a bit more manageable, Exchange used property sets. A *property set* is a group of attributes that can share a common ACE. For example, instead of setting an ACE on 15 different attributes, those attributes could be added to a property set so that applying the ACE to the property set would update the ACLs on each of the attributes.

RBAC is a significantly different approach to solving this problem. Since the management of Exchange Server 2010 is brokered through PowerShell cmdlets, it makes more sense to apply the permissions at the administrative level instead of on the Active Directory object. RBAC does this by using roles to define which Exchange cmdlets can be run and what parameters can be used with those cmdlets. By moving these permissions to the cmdlet level, you ensure that access control is enforced by PowerShell. This allows Exchange to do some really powerful things, such as presenting administrators only with the cmdlets that they have permissions to run. If an administrator doesn't have access to run the `Set-Mailbox` cmdlet, the cmdlet will not even be available to that administrator when the Exchange Management Shell (EMS) is used. Not only will the cmdlet not be found if the administrator tries to run it, but it won't even be a part of tab completion in the EMS.

How RBAC Works

To illustrate how RBAC works, let's look at an example. Suppose that in your Exchange infrastructure, you have a group of people who provide support for your end users. This group is primarily responsible for creating new accounts, mail-enabling users, configuring mailbox properties, and similar tasks. To enable this group of people to do their job, you could assign the Mail Recipients role to their accounts. When these users are assigned this role, they gain the permissions to run the Exchange cmdlets that this role allows. In this example, the users will have access to cmdlets such as `Enable-Mailbox`, `Set-Mailbox`, and `Get-MailboxStatistics`.

The previous example illustrates only one aspect of RBAC: the ability to assign roles to various levels of Exchange administrators. But there is another aspect of RBAC that allows you to assign roles to end users. The types of roles that end users would have are different than the roles that an Exchange administrator would have. Whereas the Exchange administrator's roles are geared toward managing Exchange, the end user's roles are geared toward managing the end-user's contact information, mailbox settings, and distribution groups. For example, if you want your users to be able to update their own phone numbers in the Global Address List (GAL), you can assign them the MyContactInformation role.

To understand how RBAC defines and distributes roles, you will need to become familiar with a few new terms:

Management Role   A management role, also referred to as a *role*, represents a grouping of Exchange cmdlets that can be run by people who are assigned the role. These cmdlets are also referred to as management role entries.

Management Role Entry   A management role entry, also known as a *role entry*, is the term used to refer to each Exchange cmdlet that is defined on a role. There is also a special type of role that allows your role entries to be PowerShell scripts or non-Exchange cmdlets.

Scope   The scope defines the boundary of objects that a role can be applied to. By default, the scope of impact on roles is not very restrictive. However, you can create custom scopes that make the scope of impact for a role more restrictive, such as restricting a role to only an organizational unit (OU) of recipients.

Role Group   A role group is a security group in Active Directory that defines who gets which roles applied to them. Along with the specific roles, a role group can also define the scope to which those roles are applied. An administrator can create a role group that contains a collection of common roles that are grouped together in a related job function. For example, there is a built-in role group in Exchange called Help Desk. This role group contains the roles that help desk personnel would need to perform their job function. Rather than assigning management roles directly to Active Directory accounts, we recommend that you add the account to the appropriate role group.

Role Assignment Policy   A role assignment policy is similar to a role group, because it is a representation of a collection of management roles. However, the role assignment policy is used for distributing roles to end users, whereas the role group is used for assigning roles to Exchange administrators.

Management Role Assignment   Management role assignments, also known as *role assignments*, are what pull everything together. RBAC defines who (the role group or user account) has what permissions (the roles) and where (the scope) those permissions are in effect. The role assignment pulls this together by assigning a management role to a role group, a user account, or a role assignment policy. Each time a role is assigned to a unique role group, user account, or role assignment policy, a different role assignment is created. Each role assignment assigns only one role to one role group, user account, or role assignment policy.

Two different processes define how the RBAC components interact with one another. The process for assigning permissions to Exchange administrators is different than the process used to assign permissions to end users, though there is some overlap. In both instances, management roles are used to define what the assignee can do. Management roles contain management role entries. The difference, however, is in how management roles are assigned.

RBAC FOR ADMINISTRATORS

When assigning roles to administrators, management role groups are the basic method used for defining which roles administrators have. These groups are universal security groups in Active Directory. When you want to give an administrator a group of roles, you would add the administrator's Active Directory account to the right management role group. Each of these groups is assigned one or more management roles.

Management role assignments allow you to assign one or more management roles to management role groups. For example, the Organization Management role group has several roles associated with it. Each of these roles is associated with the role group by using a unique management role assignment. Within this management role assignment, you can also define the scope of the role. Suppose you want to create a group of administrators who can only manage the mailboxes belonging to the users in the Baltimore OU. You can create a role group called Baltimore Mailbox Administrators and use a management role assignment to assign the Mail Recipients role to that group for only users in the Baltimore OU.

To better illustrate how these components come together, see Figure 15.1. Management role entries are defined on management roles. Management role assignments tie a management role to a management role group. Administrator accounts are added as members of the role group. Once in the group, those administrators have access to the functionality defined by the roles that are assigned to the group.

FIGURE 15.1
The interaction among
the RBAC components
for granting permissions
to administrators

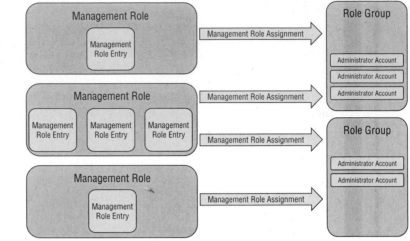

RBAC for End Users

The process for assigning roles to end users is different than the process for assigning roles to administrators. End users still use management roles and management role entries. However, the roles are assigned to user accounts using a role assignment policy. The role assignment policy has management roles assigned, just as role groups do. The difference is that role assignment policies aren't groups to which users can be added. Therefore, a user cannot have multiple role assignment policies. Like other types of policies in Exchange, user accounts can only have one role assignment policy assigned to it. The roles that users have in Exchange are defined by that policy.

Figure 15.2 describes how this process takes place for user accounts. Contrasting this with Figure 15.1, you can see that each end-user account gains its roles by specifying the policy that takes effect on it, but each administrator account gains its roles by being a part of the role group.

FIGURE 15.2
How RBAC is used to
grant permissions to
end users

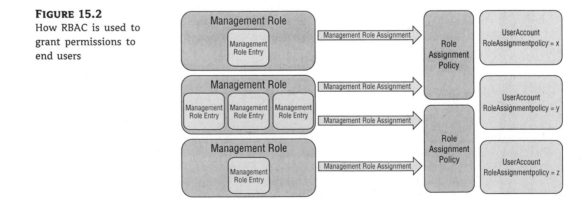

Managing RBAC

As you are managing RBAC, multiple areas need your attention. When you deploy Exchange, you have to manage the various RBAC components. This work consists of assigning the roles, modifying role groups, setting role assignments, and much more. You will also have to manage the role distribution, which consists of managing the role groups and the role assignment policies. And before anyone can manage those things, you must delegate the RBAC management permissions to the appropriate people.

There are primarily two tools you can use to manage these various aspects of RBAC. In this section, we'll look at these tools and discuss what they enable you to do at a high level. Throughout the remainder of this chapter, we will be using these tools and examining them in more detail.

Exchange Control Panel

The first tool that we will look at is the Exchange Control Panel (ECP). The ECP is a web application that is hosted on your Client Access servers along with Outlook Web App. Using the ECP, administrators and end users can modify certain Exchange settings and mailbox settings over the Web.

When you log into the ECP and use the My Organization management interface, you should see the Users & Groups category on the left side of the interface. If you select this category, you should see some tabs across the top of the UI. Notice the two tabs Administrator Roles and User Roles, as shown in Figure 15.3. If you don't have these tabs available, you likely don't have the appropriate permissions to manage the roles.

FIGURE 15.3
Managing Administrator Roles and User Roles in the ECP

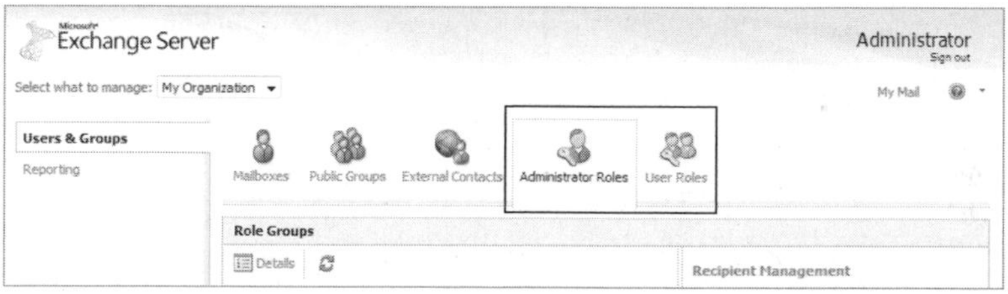

When you click the Administrator Roles tab, the Role Groups list is populated with all the role groups that are defined. This list includes both the built-in role groups and any custom role groups that you may have created. If you select a role group, the panel to the right of the list displays the description of the role group, the roles that the group is assigned, and the members of the group. This is shown in Figure 15.4.

Aside from viewing the role groups and looking at the roles and memberships, you can also add and remove members from the role group. The steps for doing this are described in the "Distributing Roles" section later in this chapter.

When you click the User Roles tab in the ECP, you are presented with a list of role assignment policies that exist in your organization. In a manner similar to the Administrator Roles tab, you can select the role assignment policy from the list and view the details of the policy in the pane on the right. You can also edit the user roles that are assigned to this policy. This is covered later in the section "Distributing Roles." Figure 15.5 shows the information available on the User Roles tab of the ECP.

FIGURE 15.4
Viewing role group
details in the ECP

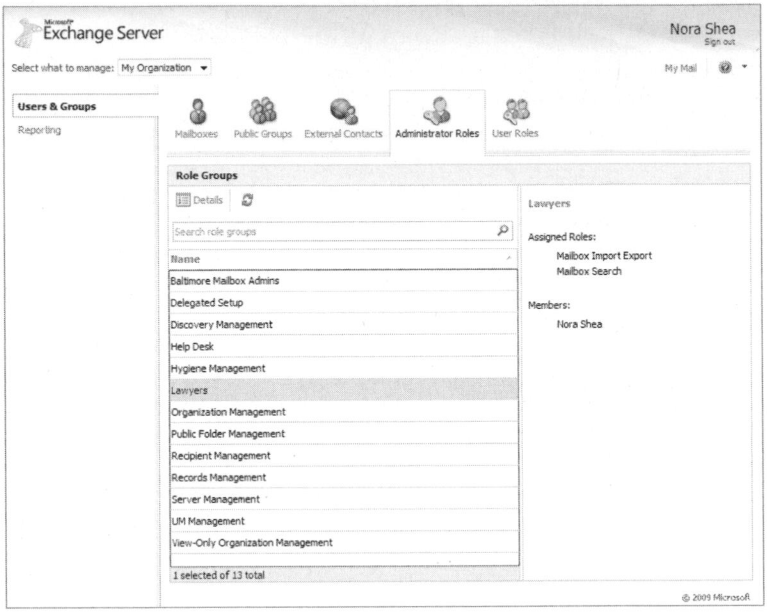

FIGURE 15.5
Viewing the user role
information in the ECP

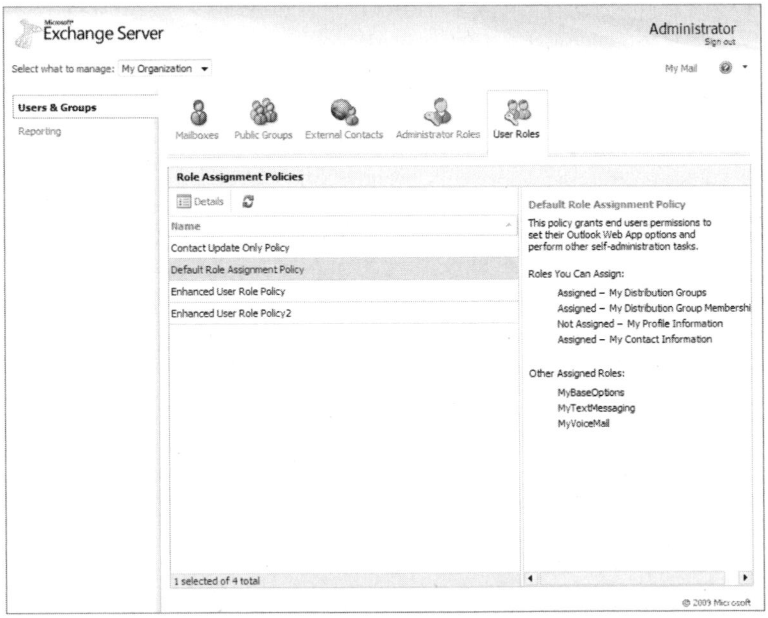

This is the extent to which you can manage RBAC inside the ECP. Therefore, most of the tasks required to set up RBAC and configure it will require you to use the EMS.

Exchange Management Shell

The EMS is probably the tool where you will be spending most of your time when you are managing RBAC. Unlike in the ECP, the EMS provides you access to the cmdlets necessary to manage the various RBAC components. Several cmdlets are provided for managing each of the components. Table 15.1 lists which cmdlets are available for managing each RBAC component. These cmdlets are further discussed and used throughout the remainder of this chapter.

TABLE 15.1:   Cmdlets for Managing the RBAC Components

COMPONENT	CMDLET	DESCRIPTION
Management role	New-ManagementRole	Creates a new role
	Get-ManagementRole	Gets the list of roles or the properties of a specific role
	Remove-ManagementRole	Deletes a role
Management role entry	Add-ManagementRoleEntry	Adds a role entry to an existing role
	Get-ManagementRoleEntry	Retrieves the list of role entries on a role
	Remove-ManagementRoleEntry	Removes a role entry from a role
	Set-ManagementRoleEntry	Sets the parameters on an already defined role entry
Role group	Get-RoleGroup	Gets the list of role groups or the properties of a specific role group
	New-RoleGroup	Creates a new role group
	Remove-RoleGroup	Deletes a role group
	Set-RoleGroup	Changes the properties of the role group
	Add-RoleGroupMember	Adds an administrator to a role group
	Get-RoleGroupMember	Lists the members of a role group
	Remove-RoleGroupMember	Removes an administrator from a role group
	Update-RoleGroupMember	Modifies the role group membership in bulk

TABLE 15.1:   Cmdlets for Managing the RBAC Components *(CONTINUED)*

COMPONENT	CMDLET	DESCRIPTION
Role assignment policy	`Get-RoleAssignmentPolicy`	Retrieves the list of role assignment policies or retrieves the details of a specific role assignment policy
	`New-RoleAssignmentPolicy`	Creates a new role assignment policy
	`Remove-RoleAssignmentPolicy`	Deletes a role assignment policy
	`Set-RoleAssignmentPolicy`	Configures the properties of a role assignment policy, including whether the policy is the default policy for the domain
Management role assignment	`Get-ManagementRoleAssignment`	Retrieves the list of role assignments or the details of a specified role assignment
	`New-ManagementRoleAssignment`	Creates a new role assignment
	`Remove-ManagementRoleAssignment`	Deletes a role assignment
	`Set-ManagementRoleAssignment`	Configures the properties of the role assignment, including the scope that the assignment uses

Defining Roles

The management role is the key component of RBAC. This section will go into a little more detail about roles and show you how to choose an existing role to assign and how to create a custom role if it's necessary.

What's in a Role?

At the most basic level, a management role is a grouping of Exchange cmdlets and parameters. Anyone who is assigned the management role has permissions to execute those cmdlets with those parameters. To illustrate this more clearly, let's take a management role and examine it more closely. The Mailbox Import Export role is a built-in role in Exchange, meaning that Exchange created this role by default during setup. There are many built-in roles, but we'll look at Mailbox Import Export in particular for this example.

The Mailbox Import Export role has three cmdlets that it allows assignees to run:

◆ `Import-Mailbox`

◆ `Get-Mailbox`

◆ `Export-Mailbox`

Having the `Get-Mailbox` cmdlet as a part of this role is especially important. If you don't have any `Get-*` cmdlets defined in your roles, the assignee cannot retrieve the data they are modifying. With each one of these cmdlets, the role defines which parameters can be used by the assignee. If the parameter isn't in this list, it can't be used. For example, the Mailbox Import Export role doesn't specify that the assignees can use the `Database` parameter with the `Get-Mailbox` cmdlet. Because of this, the assignee can't list all the mailboxes on a database, unless they are assigned another role that has those permissions.

Since PowerShell is the underlying command execution engine in Exchange, you can see how this level of granularity is very powerful. In RBAC terms, these cmdlets are referred to as management role entries. There is another type of management role that allows you to use PowerShell scripts and non-Exchange cmdlets as management role entries, but we'll look at that a little later in the section "Unscoped Top-Level Roles — The Exception." The relationship between management roles and management role entries is illustrated in Figure 15.6.

FIGURE 15.6

The relationship between a management role and its management role entries

As discussed earlier in this chapter, the RBAC data is stored in Active Directory. Each management role has an associated object in Active Directory of the object type `msExchRole`. The role objects are stored in the Configuration Naming Context inside the following container: `Services\Microsoft Exchange\Org Name\RBAC\Roles`. If you were to examine this in ADSI Edit, you would see something similar to Figure 15.7.

FIGURE 15.7

The role objects in Active Directory

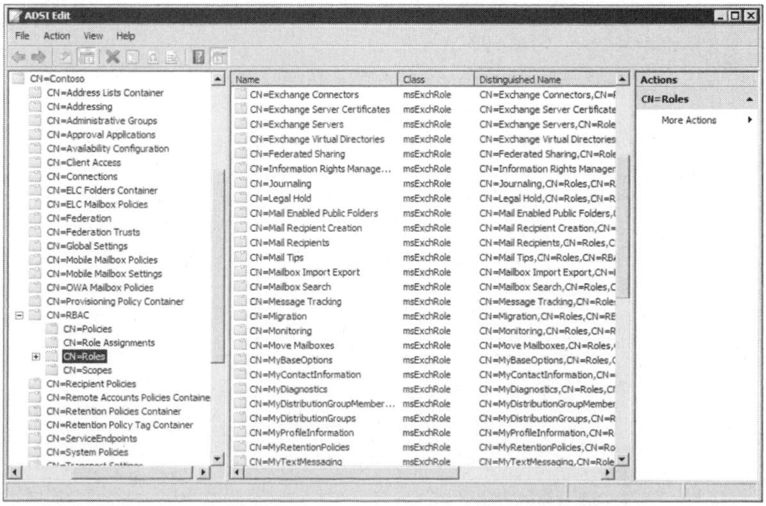

If you were to open up the Mailbox Import Export role object (CN=Mailbox Import Export), you would see the properties dialog in Figure 15.8.

FIGURE 15.8

The properties for the Mailbox Import Export role object

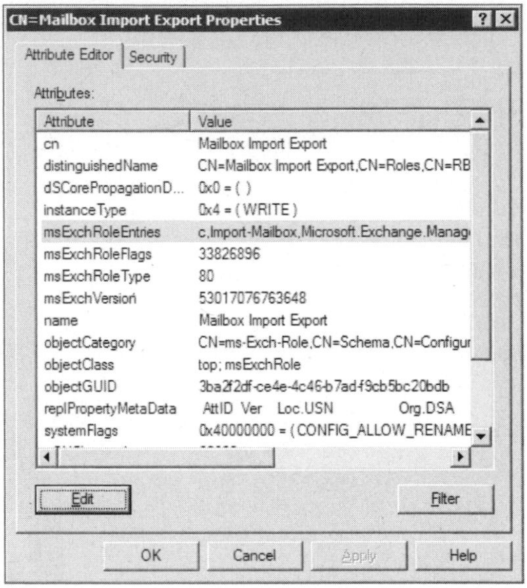

You will notice that one of the attributes on this object is the msExchRoleEntries attribute. This is a multivalued string attribute that lists each management role entry and the parameters that role assignees can run. Figure 15.9 shows the values that the Mailbox Import Export object has for its msExchRoleEntries attributes, as viewed in ADSI Edit.

FIGURE 15.9

The management role entries for the Mailbox Import Export role as seen in ADSI Edit

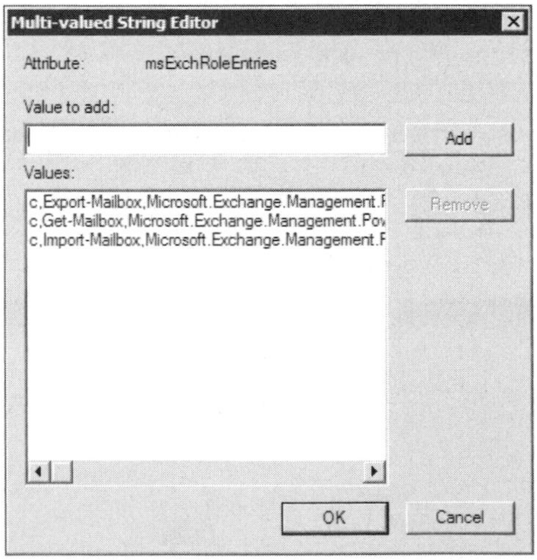

So as you can see, management role entries are added to management roles as an attribute of the management role. The management role itself is its own object. Each of these management role entries defines an Exchange cmdlet that an assignee can run.

Choosing a Role

Exchange already has several management roles defined out of the box. These defined roles give you a great degree of flexibility without having to create and customize your own management roles. For the sake of simplicity and manageability, these built-in roles should be used whenever possible.

But how do you know which built-in role to use? Let's pretend that you didn't know the Mailbox Import Export role existed. However, you have an ongoing legal investigation and you need to give your lawyer, Nora, the ability to export mail from people's mailboxes. To determine which role you need to assign to Nora, you can use the `Get-ManagementRoleEntry` cmdlet. With this cmdlet, you can specify wildcards to determine the following:

◆ What management role contains a particular management role entry

◆ Which management role entries are allowed for a particular Management Role

To determine which role allows Nora to run the `Export-Mailbox` cmdlet, you can run the following EMS command:

```
Get-ManagementRoleEntry "*\Export-Mailbox"
```

Name	Role	Parameters
Export-Mailbox	Mailbox Import Export	{AllContentKeywords...

As you can see from the command's output, the `Export-Mailbox` cmdlet is only added to the Mailbox Import Export role. There are no other options by default in Exchange. If you want to use the built-in roles, you must assign the Mailbox Import Export role to Nora.

You will also notice that in the command, we specified `*\Export-Mailbox` as the management role entry that we were looking for. When working with management role entries, the identity of each entry is in the following format: *management role\management role entry*. By specifying a wildcard character (*) in place of the *management role* portion, we told the cmdlet to retrieve every management role that has the `Export-Mailbox` cmdlet defined on it. You can use wildcards in different places and retrieve different results.

For example, let's pretend that you stumbled across the Mailbox Import Export role and you want to find out what management role entries this management role allows. Again, you can use the `Get-ManagementRoleEntry` cmdlet to find this information. However, this time you will place the wildcard at the end of the role entry's identity instead of the beginning. The following command retrieves the management role entries that the Mailbox Import Export Management Role allows:

```
Get-ManagementRoleEntry "Mailbox Import Export\*"
```

Name	Role	Parameters
Import-Mailbox	Mailbox Import Export	{AllContentKeywords...
Get-Mailbox	Mailbox Import Export	{Anr, Credential, D...
Export-Mailbox	Mailbox Import Export	{AllContentKeywords...

By using `Mailbox Import Export\*` in the command, we told the cmdlet to retrieve every management role entry that is defined on the Mailbox Import Export management role. When deciding which roles you need to assign to administrators, it's very important to look at not only what role allows the administrator to do their job but also what other permissions the administrator will gain when using one of the built-in roles.

Customizing Roles

You should always turn to the built-in management roles first and determine if you can use what's already there before attempting to customize your own roles. However, there may be times when the built-in roles offer you too much access. To illustrate this, let's continue with the scenario of your legal struggles. In the previous section, we determined that to give Nora, your lawyer, the ability to export mail from people's mailboxes, you could assign her the Mailbox Import Export role. This role allows her to run three cmdlets: `Import-Mailbox`, `Get-Mailbox`, and `Export-Mailbox`.

Now let's suppose that you run a very tight ship. When you examined the Mailbox Import Export role, you noticed that not only does the role give Nora the ability to export mail, but it also gives her the ability to import it. Knowing this, you've decided that you don't want your lawyer to be able to import mail into people's mailboxes. In this case, you can create a custom management role.

HOW A CUSTOM ROLE WORKS

To create a new custom management role, you must first start with an existing management role. You cannot create a custom management role from scratch (however, there is one exception that we will discuss shortly in the section "Unscope Top-Level Roles — The Exception"). Each custom role that you create must inherit properties from an existing management role that is already in place. This forms a parent/child relationship between an existing role (the parent) and the custom role (the child). Let's take a closer look at the Mailbox Import Export role to understand this more clearly.

To fulfill the scenario that we just discussed of only allowing Nora to export mail, you would have to create a custom role that was similar to the Mailbox Import Export role but that doesn't have the ability to import mail. Since every custom role has to have a parent management role that already exists, we can make the Mailbox Import Export role the parent to our new custom role. We'll call this new role Mailbox Export Only.

When we create the custom role, it will only be able to use the same management role entries that the parent role uses. This will give the Mailbox Export Only role access to the `Import-Mailbox`, `Get-Mailbox`, and `Export-Mailbox` cmdlets when it is created, since those are the management role entries defined on its parent role, Mailbox Import Export. We cannot add any role entries to our new custom role that aren't already included in the Mailbox Import Export role. This restriction not only applies to the cmdlets, but also to the parameters on the cmdlets. Because of this, the role entries that the child role can have are limited to the role entries defined on the parent. Even though we don't have the ability to add role entries to the Mailbox Export Only role, we do have the ability to remove them. In this case, you would remove access to the `Import-Mailbox` cmdlet. This can be accomplished with the following command:

```
Remove-ManagementRoleEntry "Mailbox Export Only\Import-Mailbox"
```

This leaves the Mailbox Export Only role with only two role entries: `Get-Mailbox` and `Export-Mailbox`. Figure 15.10 illustrates the relationship between the parent and child roles.

DEFINING CUSTOM ROLES

To create custom roles, you must use the EMS. The ECP does not give you the ability to manage custom roles. When defining these roles, you will use the cmdlets specified in Table 15.2.

FIGURE 15.10
The relationship
between a parent role
and a child role

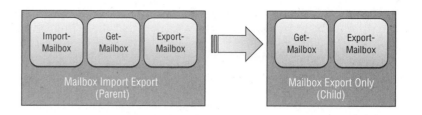

Mailbox Import Export
(Parent)

Mailbox Export Only
(Child)

TABLE 15.2: EMS Cmdlets for Defining Custom Roles

CMDLET NAME	PURPOSE
New-ManagementRole	Creates a new custom role
Remove-ManagementRole	Deletes a custom role that you previously created
Add-ManagementRoleEntry	Adds a role entry onto an existing role
Remove-ManagementRoleEntry	Removes a role entry that you previously added
Set-ManagementRoleEntry	Adjusts the parameters that can be used on a role entry that has already been added to a role

To continue with the legal scenario, let's create the Mailbox Export Only role using the New-ManagementRole cmdlet. When using the cmdlet, you specify the name of the new role and the parent from which the role is inheriting its management role entries. The following example creates the Mailbox Export Only role that we've been discussing:

```
New-ManagementRole "Mailbox Export Only" -Parent "Mailbox Import Export"

Name                                    RoleType
----                                    --------
Mailbox Export Only                     MailboxImportExport
```

You can run the Get-ManagementRoleEntry cmdlet on this newly created role to see that, by default, the custom role defines all the same role entries that the parent role has:

```
Get-ManagementRoleEntry "Mailbox Export Only\*"

Name                Role                        Parameters
----                ----                        ----------
Export-Mailbox      Mailbox Export Only         {AllContentKeywords...
Get-Mailbox         Mailbox Export Only         {Anr, Credential, D...
Import-Mailbox      Mailbox Export Only         {AllContentKeywords...
```

Now that the role is created, you can remove the Import-Mailbox cmdlet from the list of role entries. To do so, you run the Remove-ManagementRoleEntry cmdlet and specify the role entry that you want to remove. When you run this command, you will be prompted with a confirmation message that asks you if you are sure that you want to remove the role entry. You can bypass this message by adding the -Confirm:$False parameter to the command. The following example demonstrates the command that you would use to remove the `Import-Mailbox` role entry from the Mailbox Export Only role, bypassing the confirmation message:

```
Remove-ManagementRoleEntry "Mailbox Export Only\Import-Mailbox" ↵
-Confirm:$False
```

To verify that the role entry was removed, you can run the `Get-ManagementRoleEntry` cmdlet again to retrieve the management role entries on the management role. You will notice that the Mailbox Export Only role now only has two management role entries defined on it.

```
Get-ManagementRoleEntry "Mailbox Export Only\*"
```

Name	Role	Parameters
Export-Mailbox	Mailbox Export Only	{AllContentKeywords...
Get-Mailbox	Mailbox Export Only	{Anr, Credential, D...

UNSCOPED TOP-LEVEL ROLES: THE EXCEPTION

Earlier in this section, we stated that there was an exception to the fact that custom management roles require an existing management role to be the parent. That exception is a special type of management role called the unscoped top-level role. This type of role does not have a parent. The unscoped top-level role is a type of role that allows you to define both PowerShell scripts and non-Exchange cmdlets as its role entries. This type of role is highly customized, so it can't effectively have a parent role because there is no starting point for it. You would typically want to use an unscoped top-level role when you want to strictly limit what an administrator can do, such as only giving them access to predefined scripts.

By default, no one has permissions to create unscoped top-level roles. If you want to grant these permissions to an administrator, you will need to assign the role called Unscoped Role Management to the administrator who needs to create unscoped top-level roles.

To create the unscoped top-level role, use the `New-ManagementRole` cmdlet with the `UnscopedTopLevel` parameter. If the `UnscopedTopLevel` parameter isn't available, that means you have not been assigned the Unscoped Role Management role. The following example creates an unscoped top-level role called Run Custom Scripts:

```
New-ManagementRole "Run Custom Scripts" -UnScopedTopLevel
```

Name	RoleType
Run Custom Scripts	UnScoped

After the role is created, you can use the `Add-ManagementRoleEntry` cmdlet to add custom scripts or non-Exchange cmdlets as role entries on the role. When you run this cmdlet, specify the script with the syntax of *Management Role\Script*. Also specify the type of role entry that you are adding (script or cmdlet), and use the `UnScopedTopLevel` parameter. You can also use the `Parameters` parameter to specify what parameters can be used with the script. For example, to add the custom script called `CheckServerHealth.ps1` to the Run Custom Scripts role, you would use the following command:

```
Add-ManagementRoleEntry "Run Custom Scripts\CheckServerHealth.ps1" ↵
-UnScopedTopLevel -Type Script -Parameters CheckServices, CheckLogs
```

Distributing Roles

After you have defined the roles you want to use in your RBAC implementation, you must distribute those roles to administrators and end users. This section will discuss the important aspects of role distribution and show you how to distribute roles to both administrators and end users.

Determining Where Roles Will Be Applied

When distributing roles, one important detail that should not be overlooked is where those roles apply. In RBAC, this is referred to as the role's *scope*. The scope defines what objects (such as recipients or servers) the role can impact. As you'll see throughout this section, scopes are extremely flexible. They allow roles to be applied throughout the organization, or even restricted to just a particular OU of recipients in Active Directory.

INHERITED SCOPES

Every role has a scope. When a role is created, it has a default scope, also known as an *implicit* scope. There are two types of implicit scopes: a recipient scope and a configuration scope. The recipient scope defines which recipients the role can impact. The configuration scope defines which configuration components the role can impact. To illustrate how this applies to a role, let's look at our example of the Mailbox Import Export role. We can use the `Get-ManagementRole` cmdlet to view the implicit scope defined on this role:

```
Get-ManagementRole "Mailbox Import Export" | fl *scope*


ImplicitRecipientReadScope  : Organization
ImplicitRecipientWriteScope : Organization
ImplicitConfigReadScope     : OrganizationConfig
ImplicitConfigWriteScope    : OrganizationConfig
```

The first thing you will notice is that there are four scope attributes on the role. Each type of scope (recipient and configuration) has both a read scope and a write scope associated with it. In most cases, the read and write scope is the same. However, there are a few roles where they are different. If you run the following command, you can see the roles that have different read and write scopes defined. As you can tell from the output of the command, the cases where the read and write scope differs make sense. For example, the View-Only Configuration role can read the configuration of Exchange, but not write to it.

```
Get-ManagementRole | where { ↵
$_.ImplicitRecipientReadScope -ne $_.ImplicitRecipientWriteScope -or ↵
$_.ImplicitConfigReadScope -ne $_.ImplicitConfigWriteScope} | ↵
fl Name, *scope*

Name                        : Legal Hold
ImplicitRecipientReadScope  : Organization
ImplicitRecipientWriteScope : Organization
ImplicitConfigReadScope     : OrganizationConfig
ImplicitConfigWriteScope    : None

Name                        : View-Only Configuration
ImplicitRecipientReadScope  : Organization
```

```
ImplicitRecipientWriteScope : None
ImplicitConfigReadScope     : OrganizationConfig
ImplicitConfigWriteScope    : None

Name                        : View-Only Recipients
ImplicitRecipientReadScope  : Organization
ImplicitRecipientWriteScope : None
ImplicitConfigReadScope     : OrganizationConfig
ImplicitConfigWriteScope    : None

Name                        : MyDistributionGroups
ImplicitRecipientReadScope  : MyGAL
ImplicitRecipientWriteScope : MyDistributionGroups
ImplicitConfigReadScope     : OrganizationConfig
ImplicitConfigWriteScope    : None
```

You will also notice that there are different values in some of the scope parameters, such as `Organization` or `OrganizationConfig`. Table 15.3 describes what each of these values mean.

TABLE 15.3:   Implicit Scope Values

SCOPE	APPLIES TO RECIPIENT SCOPE	APPLIES TO CONFIGURATION SCOPE	DESCRIPTION
MyDistributionGroups	Yes	No	If in the read scope, allows read access to distribution groups owned by the user. If in the write scope, allows users to create or modify distribution lists that they own.
MyGAL	Yes	No	View the properties of recipients in the GAL. Only valid with the read scope.
None	Yes	Yes	Disallows access to the scope that it's applied to.
Organization	Yes	No	If in the read scope, gives users read access to all recipients in the organization. If in the write scope, gives users the ability to create or modify recipients in the organization.
OrganizationConfig	No	Yes	If in the read scope, allows the user to view the configuration of any server in the organization. If in the write scope, the user can modify configuration settings on any server.
Self	Yes	No	If in the read scope, users can only view their own properties. If in the write scope, users can modify their properties.

The implicit scope that is defined on a role cannot be changed. When you define a custom role, the same implicit scopes on the parent role also apply to the custom role, and they also cannot be changed. However, the implicit scopes defined on the roles can be overwritten. To overwrite the implicit scopes, you can set an explicit scope on the role assignment, instead of configuring it on the role. *Explicit* scopes are scopes that you apply, as opposed to the implicit scopes that Exchange has already applied. Explicit scopes come in two forms: predefined scopes and custom scopes.

OVERWRITING THE WRITES

Explicit scopes only overwrite the write scopes associated with the role. The read scopes will always apply, regardless of any explicit scope defined in the role assignment. Because of this, you can't specify an explicit write scope that is larger than a read scope. For example, if the read scope on a role is `Self`, you can't specify a write scope of `Organization`.

USING PREDEFINED SCOPES

Predefined scopes are explicit scopes that Exchange makes available to you by default. These predefined scopes only apply to the recipient scope type. The following predefined scopes are created by Exchange:

MyDistributionGroups   Allows users to create distribution groups and modify the properties of distribution groups where they are defined as the owner.

Organization   Allows users that hold the role to modify recipients in the entire organization. For example, if the role allows users to change the recipient display name, this scope would allow the role holders to change it for any recipient in the organization.

Self   Allows users to modify only their own properties. For example, if the role allows users to change the recipient display name, this scope would allow the role holder to only change his or her own display name.

CREATING CUSTOM SCOPES

Aside from using an existing predefined scope, you can create a custom scope that offers more flexibility. Custom scopes are extremely useful because they allow you to narrow the scope of a role down to a very granular level. For example, you can narrow the scope of recipients down a specific OU or only recipients with a specific attribute set on their accounts. For servers, you can narrow the configuration scope down to a specific site or even name the servers themselves.

Like predefined scopes, custom scopes are applied to the role assignments, and not the roles themselves. However, unlike with predefined scopes, you can specify a configuration scope as well as a recipient scope. You can create a custom scope using the `New-ManagementScope` cmdlet. When you create the scope, you have several options that give you the ability to narrow the scope as granularly as you want. Table 15.4 shows you what options you have available when creating the scope.

To illustrate how this works, let's create a couple of custom scopes. For our first example, we'll say that you want to create a scope that allows you to confine certain roles to only servers in Baltimore. To accomplish this, we'll use the `New-ManagementScope` cmdlet with the `ServerRestrictionFilter` parameter. In this parameter, we'll create a filter that specifies only servers in the Baltimore Active Directory site. The following command would be used:

```
New-ManagementScope "Baltimore Servers" -ServerRestrictionFilter { ↵
ServerSite -eq "CN=Baltimore,CN=Sites,CN=Configuration,DC=contoso,DC=com"}
```

TABLE 15.4: Options for Creating Custom Scopes

CMDLET PARAMETER	DESCRIPTION
ServerList	Allows you to specify a list of servers that this scope applies to.
ServerRestrictionFilter	Allows you to define a filter based on server attributes to which that the scope applies. For example, you can filter out the servers based on the Active Directory site that they are in.
RecipientRestrictionFilter	Gives you the ability to define a filter based on attributes on the recipient. For example, you can define a scope whose recipients include only the people on the 4th floor of a specific building.
RecipientRoot	Allows you to restrict the scope to an OU in Active Directory.

For the next example, we'll build a custom recipient scope that applies only to users in the Accounting OU in Active Directory. Referring to Table 15.4, you can see that you will need to use the RecipientRoot parameter. You are also required to specify a RecipientRestrictionFilter, but you can set this to be all accounts that are user mailboxes. This command creates a scope that includes all user mailboxes in the Accounting OU:

```
New-ManagementScope "Accounting Only" -RecipientRoot ↵
"OU=Accounting,DC=contoso,DC=com" -RecipientRestrictionFilter ↵
{RecipientType -eq "UserMailbox"}
```

You can also create a custom recipient scope based only on a filter. The following command creates a scope that only includes mailboxes that are considered Discovery Mailboxes:

```
New-ManagementScope "Discovery Mailboxes" -RecipientRestrictionFilter ↵
{RecipientTypeDetails -eq "DiscoveryMailbox"}
```

After the scope is created, you can apply the role assignment. This is discussed in more detail in the next section.

⊕ Real World Scenario

GEOGRAPHIC ROLES VS. TIERED ROLES

RBAC gives you great flexibility in designing the access model for your Exchange implementation. There are many models that you can use when defining your roles. The rule of thumb is that the RBAC model you adopt should mirror how you manage your Exchange organization.

There are two models in particular that we've frequently encountered in various Exchange organizations.

The Geographic management model divides the management of Exchange into different physical regions. One of the authors of this book recently worked with an organization that wanted to have central control of the Exchange organization maintained from one region, but also allow other regions to manage their own Exchange servers and recipients. This organization could use RBAC to define server scopes based on sites and recipient scopes based on regional OUs.

Another organization that one of the authors recently worked with uses a Tiered management model in their organization. In this model, the lower tier (Tier 1 in this case) handles basic recipient management tasks. Higher tiers (Tier 2 and Tier 3) handle more advanced tasks. As you get to higher tiers of support, the permissions get less and less restrictive. Eventually you would reach the top tier of support, who would have rights to administer anything in the Exchange organization. This organization could also use RBAC to their benefit by creating different role groups for each tier of support and assigning the necessary roles to the appropriate tiers. In this case, the scope of management is the entire organization, so there would be no need to specify an explicit scope.

Assigning Roles to Administrators

The process for assigning roles to administrators is different than the process for assigning roles to end users. The roles that administrators are assigned are inherently different than the roles that users are assigned. Administrators need to have the permissions to manage and configure Exchange. Before going further and showing you how to assign roles to administrators, you should first understand how role assignments work for administrators.

How Roles Are Assigned to Administrators

When assigning roles to administrators, you have two options. The first option is to assign the role to a management role group and then add the administrator to the role group. This is the easiest and preferred method of assigning roles to administrators. The second option is to assign the role directly to the administrator's account using a direct role assignment.

Regardless of which method you use, management roles are assigned to either the management role group or the administrator's account using a management role assignment. In Active Directory, an msExchRoleAssignment object is created that represents the role assignment between the account and the role. These role assignment objects are stored in the Configuration Naming Context under the container Services\Microsoft Exchange\<Org Name>\RBAC\Role Assignments.

When these role assignments are created, the default name of the assignment object is the name of the role, followed by a hyphen, followed by the name of the object that it's being assigned to. Figure 15.11 shows an example of a role assignment. Here, the Mail Recipients role is assigned to the Organization Management role group.

If you were to take a closer look at the role assignment object, you would see that the msExchRoleLink attribute corresponds to the Mail Recipients role's AD object and the msExchUserLink attribute corresponds to the distinguished name of the Organization Management security group (Figure 15.12). This is how a role is united with the assignee.

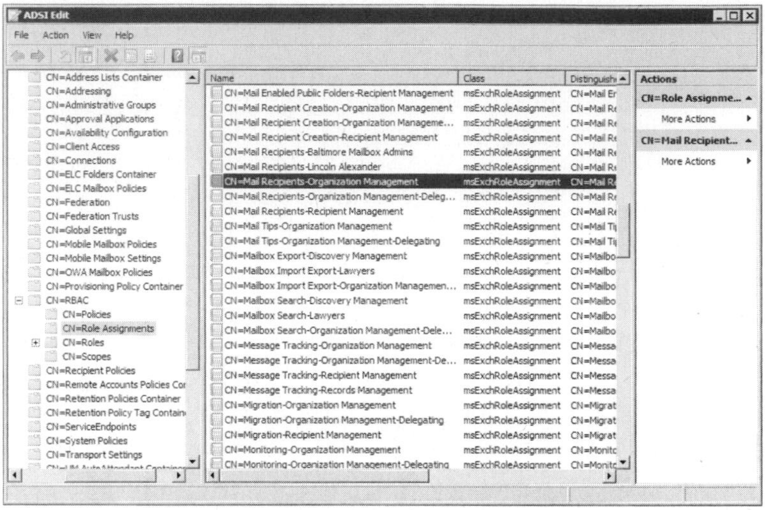

FIGURE 15.11
A role assignment object is created in Active Directory when assigning roles.

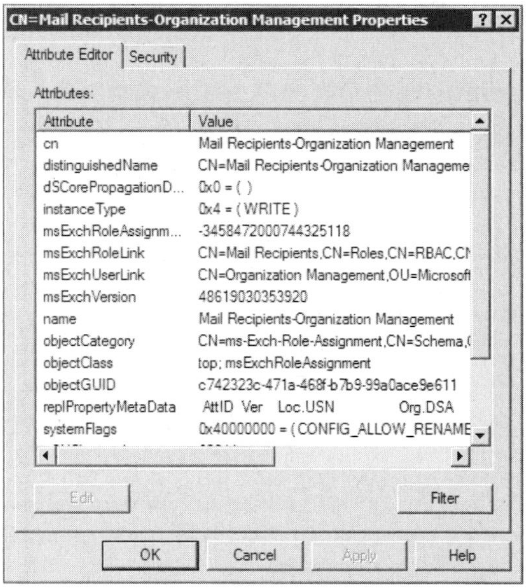

FIGURE 15.12
A deeper look at the role assignment object in Active Directory

You can retrieve a list of the role assignments in the EMS by running the `Get-ManagementRoleAssignment` cmdlet with no parameters. Several role assignments are created by default. The following example is only a partial listing:

```
Get-ManagementRoleAssignment
```

Name	Role	RoleAssig neeName	RoleAssig neeType	Assignmen tMethod	Effectiv eUserNam e
----	----	---------	---------	---------	--------
View-Only Configuratio...	View-O...	Delega...	RoleGroup	Direct	All G...
Legal Hold-Discovery M...	Legal ...	Discov...	RoleGroup	Direct	All G...

```
Mailbox Search-Discove... Mailbo... Discov... RoleGroup Direct   All G...
User Options-Help Desk    User O... Help Desk RoleGroup Direct   All G...
View-Only Recipients-H... View-O... Help Desk RoleGroup Direct   All G...
ApplicationImpersonati... Applic... Hygien... RoleGroup Direct   All G...
Receive Connectors-Hyg... Receiv... Hygien... RoleGroup Direct   All G...
Transport Agents-Hygie... Transp... Hygien... RoleGroup Direct   All G...
Transport Hygiene-Hygi... Transp... Hygien... RoleGroup Direct   All G...
View-Only Configuratio... View-O... Hygien... RoleGroup Direct   All G...
View-Only Recipients-H... View-O... Hygien... RoleGroup Direct   All G...
Active Directory Permi... Active... Organi... RoleGroup Direct   All G...
Active Directory Permi... Active... Organi... RoleGroup Direct   All G...
...
```

Figure 15.13 illustrates the relationship between management role assignments, scopes, management roles, and management role groups. This figure shows that a management role assignment object is used to assign a role to a role group.

FIGURE 15.13
The relationship between management role assignments, scopes, management roles, and management role groups

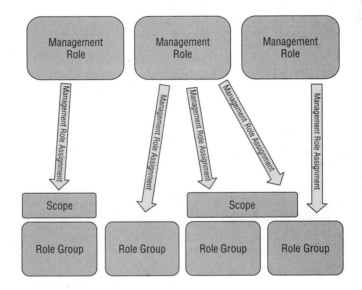

ADDING ADMINISTRATORS TO A ROLE GROUP

You can add an administrator's account to a management role group using the EMS or the ECP, or by adding the account directly to the group in Active Directory using a tool such as Active Directory Users and Computers. The Exchange Management Console cannot be used to manage RBAC settings. When you add an administrator's account to a management role group, the account gains every role that is specified on the role group. Roles are added cumulatively, so if an administrator's account is a member of another role group, the account will retain those permissions in addition to the permissions assigned by the roles of the new role group.

To add an administrator to a management role group, use the Add-RoleGroupMember cmdlet. To use the cmdlet, specify the name of the management role group and the administrator's account in the command. The following example shows the command for adding lawyer

Nora Shea's account to the Lawyers role group, which only has permissions to export mail from a mailbox:

```
Add-RoleGroupMember "Lawyers" -Member "Nora Shea"
```

After you execute this command, you can verify that the administrator was added to the group by enumerating the group membership using the `Get-RoleGroupMember` command and specifying the name of the management role group:

```
Get-RoleGroupMember "Lawyers"

Name                                              RecipientType
----                                              -------------
Administrator                                     UserMailbox
Nora Shea                                         UserMailbox
```

If you look in the Active Directory security group that represents the Lawyers group, you will also notice that Nora Shea's account has been added as a member (Figure 15.14).

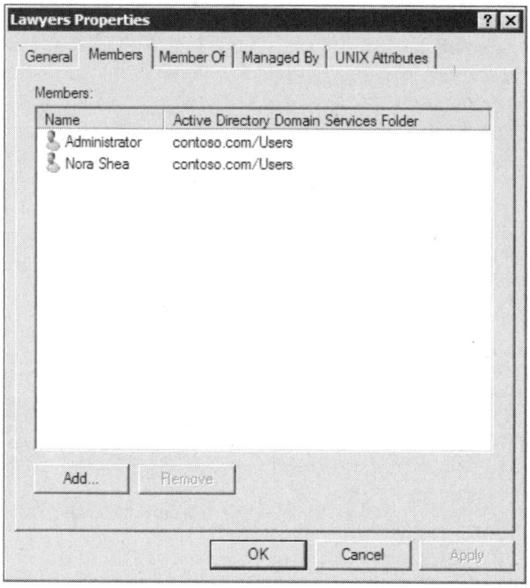

FIGURE 15.14
Administrator accounts are added to the AD group that represents management role groups.

You can also add the administrator's account to the role group through the ECP. This provides a convenient method for modifying permissions without having to open a remote PowerShell connection. You can use the following steps to add an administrator account to a management role group in the ECP:

1. On your client computer, open Internet Explorer and browse to the ECP URL. This URL should be the name of your Client Access server with **/ecp** appended to the end. If you don't know the URL for ECP, you can use the Outlook Web App URL and specify **/ecp** instead of **/owa** at the end of the URL. For example, for Contoso, the ECP URL might be `https://mail.contoso.com/ecp`.

2. When prompted with the authentication page, type in your name and password and log in.

3. In the ECP, ensure that the My Organization option is selected in the Select What To Manage list at the upper-left of the browser. See Figure 15.15 for an example.

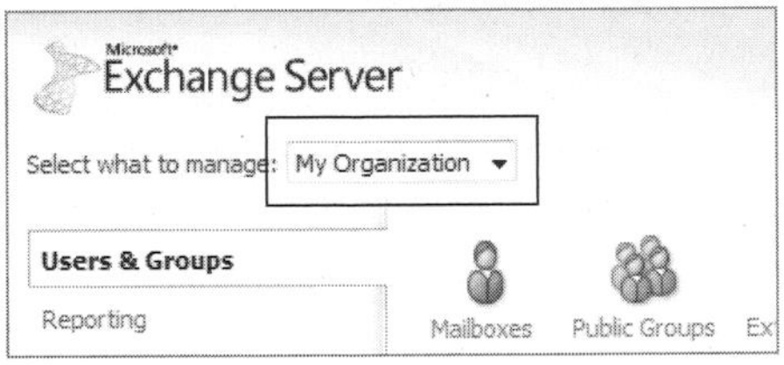

FIGURE 15.15
Ensure that My Organization is selected in the ECP.

4. In the left column of the ECP, select Users & Groups.

5. In the toolbar across the top of the ECP, select the Administrator Roles tab. The role groups are populated in the list in the center of the ECP, as shown in Figure 15.16.

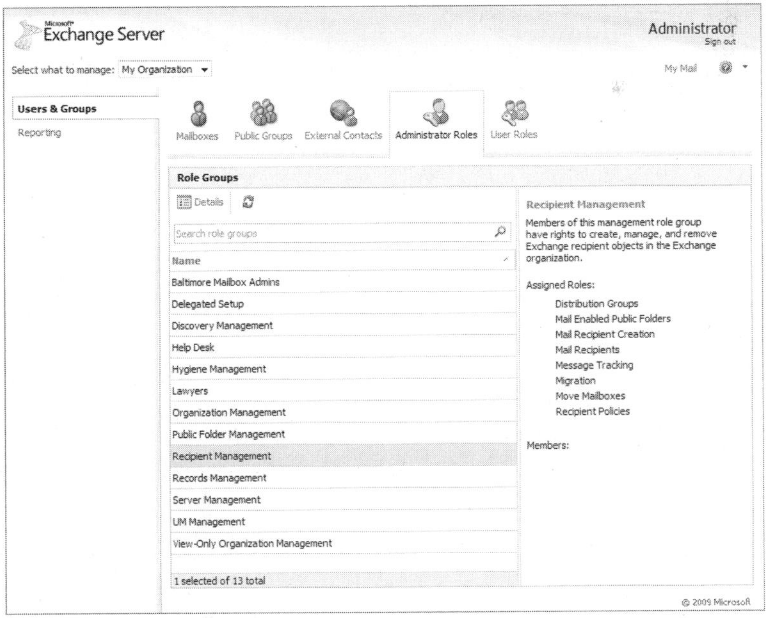

FIGURE 15.16
The list of management role groups is populated into the ECP.

6. Double-click on the role group to which you want to add the administrator's account.

The management role group's details will be displayed in a separate Internet Explorer dialog.

7. In the role group's dialog, click the Add button under the Members list, as shown in Figure 15.17.

8. The Select Members dialog will be displayed, listing the accounts that can be added to the role group. Select the accounts that you want to add one at a time and click the Add button to add them to the list. After you have added all the accounts in the Select Members dialog, click OK.

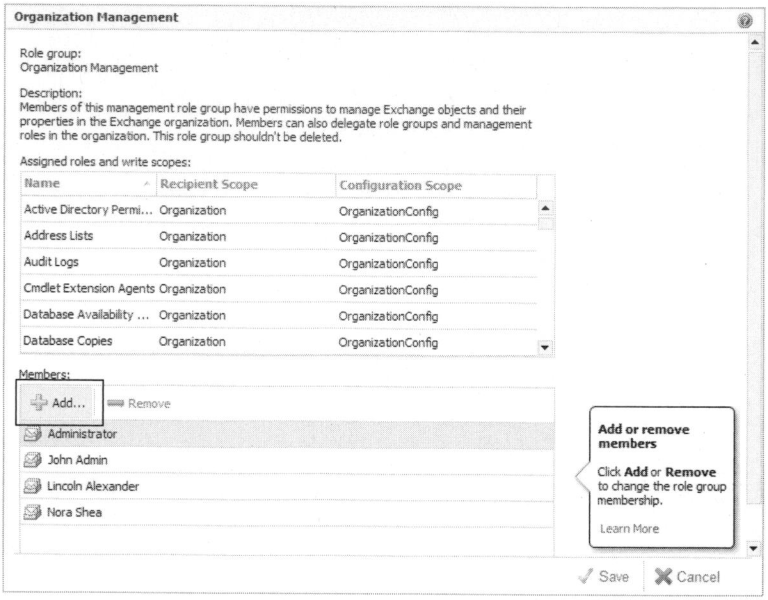

FIGURE 15.17
Click the Add button
to add a member of a
role group in the ECP.

9. When you are returned to the details dialog for the role group, the accounts that you added are displayed in the Members list. Click the Save button to close this dialog and return to the ECP.

Whether you decide to use the ECP to add administrator accounts to management role groups or you use the EMS cmdlets, the end results are the same: the administrators gain the permissions they need to do their job.

MODIFYING ROLE GROUPS

You may find that a role you want to assign is not available on any of the existing role groups. You can modify the existing role groups or even create your own custom role groups to assign the management roles that you want to use. To add a role to an existing role group, you have to create a role assignment for the group.

For example, let's suppose your legal team is a member of the Discovery Management role group. The Discovery Management role group is assigned the roles Legal Hold and Mailbox Search. The legal team discovers that they can't export mail from searches that they've completed. You need to give the legal team the ability to export messages from the discovery mailbox. To do this, you can modify the Discovery Management role group and add the Mailbox Export Only role to the group.

To modify an existing role group, use the New-ManagementRoleAssignment cmdlet to create the role assignment between the Mailbox Import Export role and the Discovery Management role group. When running the command, specify the SecurityGroup parameter to indicate that the role is being assigned to a group, and to identify the group that the role is being assigned to. The following command demonstrates adding the Mailbox Import Export role to the Discovery Management role group:

```
New-ManagementRoleAssignment -Role "Mailbox Export Only" -SecurityGroup ↵
"Discovery Management"
```

Name	Role	RoleAssig neeName	RoleAssig neeType	Assignmen tMethod	Effectiv eUserNam e
----	----	---------	---------	---------	--------
Mailbox Export Only-Di...	Mailbo...	Discov...	RoleGroup	Direct	

When assigning a role to a role group, you have the ability to specify the scope that the role impacts. Earlier in this chapter, we showed you how to use explicit scopes and how to create your own custom scopes. If you want to apply a custom scope that you created, specify the `CustomConfigWriteScope` and `CustomRecipientWriteScope` parameters. For example, if you want to apply the Mailbox Export Only role to only discovery mailboxes, you can use the custom scope called Discovery Mailboxes that we created earlier in this chapter. The following command would apply this:

```
New-ManagementRoleAssignment -Role "Mailbox Export Only" -SecurityGroup ↵
"Discovery Management" -CustomRecipientWriteScope "Discovery Mailboxes"
```

If there isn't an existing role group that you want to use, you can create your own role group and then use the previous command to create the role assignment to assign the necessary roles to it. To create a role group, use the `New-RoleGroup` cmdlet. Specify the name of the role group that you are creating and at least one role that will be assigned to the role group. In the following example, we're creating the role group called Lawyers and assigning the Mailbox Import Export role to the role group:

```
New-RoleGroup "Lawyers" -Roles "Mailbox Export Only"
```

Name	DisplayName	AssignedRoles	RoleAssignments	ManagedBy
----	-----------	-------------	---------------	---------
Lawyers		{Mailbox Exp...	{Mailbox Exp...	{contoso.com...

After the role group is created, you can manage it just like any existing role group. For steps on adding administrator accounts to this role group, see the previous section.

DIRECTLY ASSIGNING ROLES TO ADMINISTRATORS

Instead of adding administrator accounts to management role groups, you can assign management roles directly to the administrator's account. Although this method is available, it's not necessarily preferred. When you use this method of assigning permissions, it's harder to track the roles that you delegate to administrators and it's more difficult to manage the access. With direct role assignments, access management is no longer just a matter of adding an account to a role group.

When you use direct role assignment, a management role assignment is created that ties that role directly to the administrator's account. You can assign roles directly to administrator accounts using the `New-ManagementRoleAssignment` cmdlet in the EMS. When running the command, specify the `User` parameter to tell the command to which account you want to assign the role. Also specify the `Role` parameter to tell the command what role you want to assign. The following example command directly assigns the Mailbox Export Only role to Nora Shea's account:

```
New-ManagementRoleAssignment -User "Nora Shea" -Role "Mailbox Export Only"
```

You can verify that the administrator account has the role assigned by running the Get-ManagementRoleAssignment cmdlet and specifying the role for which you want to see the assignments. This command will display each assignment for that role, including the nondirect assignments:

```
Get-ManagementRoleAssignment -Role "Mailbox Export Only" | ↵
ft Name, RoleAssigneeName

Name                                    RoleAssigneeName
----                                    ----------------
Mailbox Export Only-Nora Shea           Nora Shea
Mailbox Export Only-Discovery Manage... Discovery Management
Mailbox Export Only-Lawyers             Lawyers
```

Assigning Roles to End Users

When you are assigning roles to end users, the process is a little different than when assigning roles to administrators. User roles serve a different purpose than do administrator roles. Whereas administrators will need permissions assigned to manage Exchange, users only need to be assigned permissions to modify settings on their mailbox or distribution groups. Not only is the scope different between the administrators and users, but users will be managing their own mailboxes instead of other people's mailboxes.

HOW ROLES ARE ASSIGNED TO END USERS

As discussed in the previous section, administrators are assigned to roles by either adding the administrator's account to a management role group that contains the necessary roles or by assigning the management role directly to the administrator's account. This process is quite different for end users.

Roles are assigned to end users using a role assignment policy. Each mailbox can have only one role assignment policy attached to it. Management roles are tied to the role assignment policy with management role assignments. Exchange creates a management role assignment object in Active Directory that links the management role with the management role assignment policy. If you are browsing the management role assignment objects in Active Directory, you will notice that among the assignments that link roles to role groups, you will also find assignments that link roles to assignment policies. In Figure 15.18, you will see that the MyBaseOptions role is assigned to the Default role assignment policy using a role assignment object.

DEFAULT USER ROLES

Every mailbox gets a role assignment policy by default when the mailbox is created. The role assignment policy called Default is created when Exchange is installed and is set to be the default policy for new mailboxes. On this default policy, five roles are assigned by default, as shown in Table 15.5.

The Default role assignment policy doesn't have to remain as the default policy. You can designate a different role assignment policy that you created to be the default policy. When you do this, new mailboxes will use the new policy that you defined instead of the one that Exchange created. The existing mailboxes that were using the Default role assignment policy will remain with that policy.

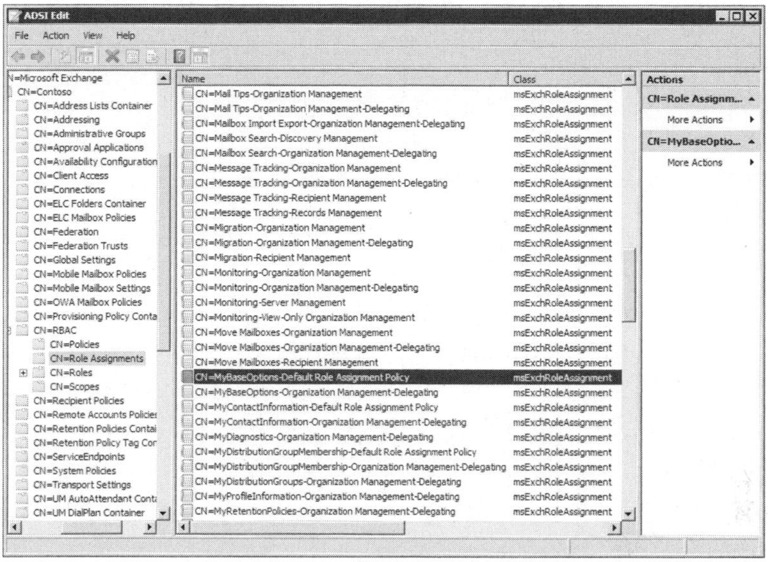

FIGURE 15.18
Role assignment objects
are also used for
assigning roles to role
assignment policies.

TABLE 15.5:   Default Roles That Are Assigned to End Users

ROLE	DESCRIPTION
MyBaseOptions	Allows users to modify basic mailbox settings for their own mailbox. This includes settings for managing their ActiveSync device, inbox rules, spell check settings, and so on.
MyContactInformation	Gives users the ability to update their contact information in Active Directory.
MyVoiceMail	Allows users to change their voicemail settings, which includes the ability to do things like changing their pin number.
MyTextMessaging	Allows users to manage their text messaging settings.
MyDistributionGroupMembership	Gives users the ability to change their own distribution group memberships. They can use this role to add or remove themselves from distribution groups.

To change the Default role assignment policy, use the Set-RoleAssignmentPolicy cmdlet with the IsDefault parameter. The following EMS command changes the default role assignment policy to a different policy:

```
Set-RoleAssignmentPolicy "Contact Update Only Policy" -IsDefault
```

WORKING WITH ROLE ASSIGNMENT POLICIES

Role assignment policies can be managed using either the ECP or the EMS. In the ECP, you can add and remove certain user-specific roles to and from the role assignment policy. You can do this by performing the following steps:

1. On your client computer, open Internet Explorer and browse to the ECP URL. This URL should be the name of your Client Access server with /ecp appended to the end. If you don't know the URL for ECP, you can use the Outlook Web App URL and specify **/ecp** instead of **/owa** at the end of the URL. For example, for Contoso, the ECP URL might be https://mail.contoso.com/ecp.

2. When prompted with the authentication page, type in your name and password and log in.

3. In the ECP, ensure that the My Organization option is selected in the Select What To Manage option at the upper left of the browser.

4. In the left column of the ECP, select Users & Groups.

5. In the toolbar across the top of the ECP, select the User Roles tab. The role assignment policies are populated in the list in the center of the ECP.

6. Select the role assignment policy on which you want to assign or unassign roles.

    When you select the role assignment policy, the panel to the right of the list will display some information about the policy. There are two categories there: Roles You Can Assign and Other Assigned Roles. You cannot use the ECP to modify the list of roles under the Other Assigned Roles category.

7. After you have selected the role assignment policy that you want to modify, click the Details button at the top of the list of policies.

8. The Default Role Assignment Policy dialog will open. In the section labeled Roles You Can Assign, you can check or uncheck existing roles for end users. The list of roles for the Default role assignment policy is displayed in Figure 15.19.

9. After you have chosen the roles that you want to be assigned to the policy, click the Save button at the bottom of the dialog.

    If you are prompted with a Warning dialog indicating that this policy change will affect many users, click Yes to tell it that you want to continue.

Although you can assign roles to role assignment policies, this option does not give you a lot of flexibility because you can't create or configure role assignment policies. To do this, you must use the EMS to manage the role assignment policies.

To start off, you can view a list of the role assignment policies that are currently in existence by running the Get-RoleAssignmentPolicy cmdlet. No parameters are needed to run this command. With a fresh Exchange organization, you should only see the Default role assignment policy. The following example demonstrates the use of this command and the output:

```
Get-RoleAssignmentPolicy

RunspaceId      : c0d14883-58e8-41dd-bf51-3edc4fdf666e
IsDefault       : True
```

```
Description         : This policy grants end users permissions to set their
                      Outlook Web App options and perform other self-
                      administration tasks.
AdminDisplayName    :
ExchangeVersion     : 0.11 (14.0.509.0)
Name                : Default Role Assignment Policy
DistinguishedName   : CN=Default Role Assignment Policy,CN=Policies,CN=RBAC,
                      CN=Contoso,CN=Microsoft Exchange,CN=Services,
                      CN=Configuration,DC=contoso,DC=com
Identity            : Default Role Assignment Policy
Guid                : c91480a0-3369-4441-91bf-6e1b18072bc7
ObjectCategory      : contoso.com/Configuration/Schema/ms-Exch-RBAC-Policy
ObjectClass         : {top, msExchRBACPolicy}
WhenChanged         : 10/17/2009 12:33:06 AM
WhenCreated         : 10/17/2009 12:33:06 AM
WhenChangedUTC      : 10/17/2009 4:33:06 AM
WhenCreatedUTC      : 10/17/2009 4:33:06 AM
OrganizationId      :
OriginatingServer   : CONTOSO-EX01.contoso.com
IsValid             : True
```

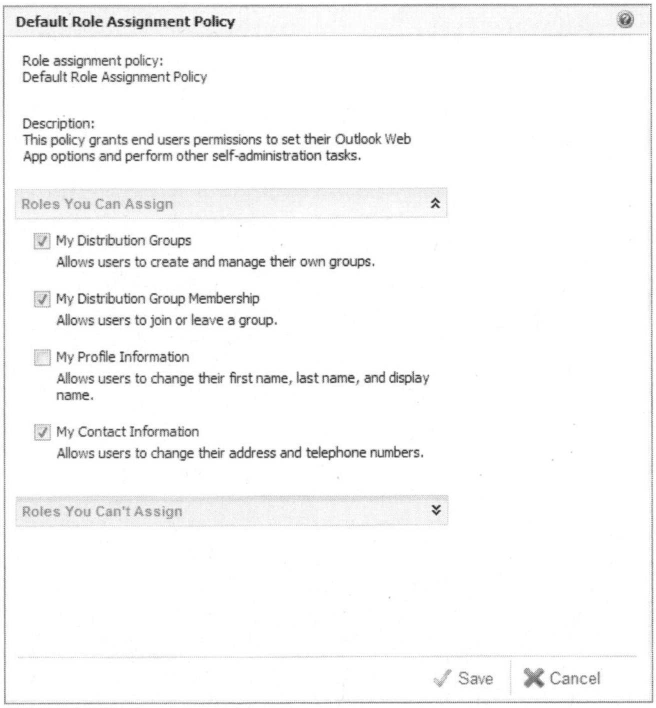

FIGURE 15.19
Check and uncheck the roles that you want to add to or remove from the role assignment policy.

You can view the roles that are tied to the policy by using the Get-ManagementRoleAssignment cmdlet with the RoleAssignee parameter. Just specify the name of the policy and the roles will be enumerated for you. The following command demonstrates this by listing all the roles in the Default role assignment policy:

```
Get-ManagementRoleAssignment -RoleAssignee "Default Role Assignment ↵
Policy" | ft Name, Role

Name                                      Role
----                                      ----
MyBaseOptions-Default Role Assignment Policy MyBaseOptions
MyContactInformation-Default Role Assignm... MyContactInformation
MyVoiceMail-Default Role Assignment Policy   MyVoiceMail
MyTextMessaging-Default Role Assignment P... MyTextMessaging
MyDistributionGroupMembership-Default Rol... MyDistributionGroupMembership
```

If you can't use an existing role assignment policy, you can create a custom policy and add your own set of roles to it. To create the policy itself, use the `New-RoleAssignmentPolicy` cmdlet. The following example creates a new role assignment policy that is similar to the default policy, but removes some of the functionality in the `MyBaseOptions` role:

```
New-RoleAssignmentPolicy "Limited Assignment Policy"
```

You can add a role to an existing policy by creating a new management role assignment. This is serviced by the `New-ManagementRoleAssignment` cmdlet in the EMS. Specify the role that you are adding to the role assignment policy along with the name of the role assignment policy itself. Let's say that you don't want users to have access to the message-tracking features that come with the `MyBaseOptions` role. Therefore, you've created a custom role based on `MyBaseOptions` called `MyLimitedBaseOptions` and removed the message-tracking role entries from the role. The following command adds the `MyLimitedBaseOptions` role to the policy that we just created:

```
New-ManagementRoleAssignment -Role "MyLimitedBaseOptions" -Policy ↵
"Limited Assignment Policy"
```

After the role assignment policy is created and configured with the management roles that you want to use, you can start applying that policy to end users. To apply a role assignment policy to end users, use the `Set-Mailbox` cmdlet in the EMC. When you use this cmdlet, specify the name of the mailbox to which you are applying the policy as well as the name of the policy that you are applying. The following example sets the role assignment policy on Lincoln's account to the Limited assignment policy that we created previously:

```
Set-Mailbox "Lincoln Alexander" -RoleAssignmentPolicy "Limited Assignment Policy"
```

The Bottom Line

Determine what built-in roles and role groups provide you with the permissions you need.
Exchange Server 2010 includes a vast amount of built-in management roles out of the box. Many of these roles are already assigned to role groups that are ready for you to use. To use these built-in roles, figure out which roles contain the permissions that you need. Ideally, determine which role groups you can use to gain access to these roles.

Master It   As part of your recent email compliance and retention initiative, your company hired a consultant to advise you on what you can do to make your Exchange implementation more compliant. The consultant claims that he needs escalated privileges to your existing journal rules so he can examine them. Since you tightly control who can make changes to your Exchange organization, you don't want to give the consultant the ability to modify your journal rules, though you don't mind if he is able to view the configuration details of Exchange. What EMS command can you run to find out what role the consultant can be assigned to view your journal rules but not have permissions to modify them or create new ones? What role do you want to assign to the consultant?

Manage RBAC through both the Exchange Management Shell and the Exchange Control Panel.   Exchange provides you with the ability to manage RBAC through both the EMS and the ECP. The ECP is a less powerful interface than the EMS, but it has a visual layout that could be useful when browsing roles, and it gives you the ability to manage a subset of the RBAC features through a web browser.

Master It   One of your junior administrators on staff isn't as well versed in Exchange Server 2010 as you are. He is refusing to learn how to use the EMS because he claims that he can just use the ECP to manage RBAC. To convince your junior administrator that he needs to learn to use the EMS, you should come up with three things that you can't do in the ECP that you need the EMS for.

Assign permissions to administrators using roles and role groups.   When assigning permissions to administrators, the preferred method is to use assign management roles to role groups and then add the administrators account to the appropriate role group. However, Exchange allows you to assign management roles directly to the administrator's account if you want.

Master It   Earlier in the day, you determined that you need to assign a certain role to your email compliance consultant. You've created a role group called Email Compliance Evaluation and you need to add your consultant to this role group. What command would you use in the EMS to add your consultant, Sam, to this role group?

Grant permissions to end users for updating their address list information.   RBAC doesn't just apply to Exchange administrators. You can also use RBAC to assign roles to end-user accounts, so users can have permissions to update their personal information, Exchange settings, and their distribution groups.

Master It   You've decided that you want to give your users the ability to modify their contact information in the Global Address List. You want to make this change as quickly as possible and have it apply to all existing users and new users coming into your Exchange organization immediately. You determine that using the ECP would be the easiest way to make this change. What would you modify in the ECP to make this change?

Create custom administration roles and assign them to administrators.   If you can't find an existing role that meets your needs, don't worry! You can create a custom role in Exchange Server 2010 and assign the permissions you need to the custom role.

Master It   Your company's legal team is asking you for permissions to export mail from people's mailboxes. However, you operate a highly secure environment and want to ensure that they only have the ability to export mail and not import it as well. You've decided that you need to create and assign a custom role to your legal team that only grants them the ability to export mail. What are the high-level steps for making this happen?

## Chapter 16

Basics of Recipient Management

The term "Exchange recipient" is used to define any mail or mailbox-enabled object in Active Directory used to send or receive email within an Exchange organization.

Depending on the size of your organization, recipient management (handling the user accounts, groups, contacts, public folders, and other resources that can receive email) may consume the vast majority of Exchange administration time. In a small organization, you may be responsible for every aspect of your Exchange server, including creating and managing recipients. In a larger organization with lots of changes, new users, and users leaving the organization, recipient administration will probably be handled by a person or team that is separate from the person who actually manages the Exchange Server infrastructure (message routing, backups, server maintenance, and so on).

This chapter discusses the basics of recipient management. It examines the environment configurations that must exist to support recipient management and the tools you use to manage recipients. It also examines Exchange address lists and how email addresses are defined.

In this chapter, you will learn to:

◆ Identify the various types of recipients

◆ Use the Exchange management tools to manage recipients

◆ Configure accepted domains and define email address policies

Exchange Recipients

There are different types of users in your organization, as well as different types of needs for messaging delivery. To account for those differences, Exchange provides various types of recipients. Each recipient type fills a specific need within your messaging environment. In this section, we will first outline the various recipient types and then describe their purpose.

Mailbox-Enabled Users (Mailbox)

A mailbox-enabled user has an account in Active Directory and a mailbox on an Exchange server. A mailbox-enabled user can send and receive email messages within the Exchange organization and through the Internet. A mailbox-enabled user also has access to a personal calendar, contact list, and other services provided by the Exchange servers. In most organizations, all corporate users have mailboxes, and therefore store all emails on the Exchange servers.

Users who have a mailbox can use various client applications to access mailbox content or send emails. For example, they can use Office Outlook, Outlook Web App, or Exchange ActiveSync to access all mailbox content.

When you create a mailbox-enabled user, there are multiple types of mailboxes that can be created. For example, you can create a standard mailbox that is associated with a user and then used by a company employee to send and receive emails; or you can create a resource mailbox that can be used to represent a company's resources, such as a conference room. More detailed information about mailbox-enabled users is available in Chapter 17, "Managing Mailboxes."

Mail-Enabled User

At first glance, it just looks like a few letters are missing to have a mailbox-enabled user, but a mail-enabled user is quite different. A mail-enabled user has a user account in Active Directory and an *external* email address associated with the account. The mail-enabled user has *no* mailbox on an Exchange server inside your organization.

All mail-enabled users appear in the corporate global address list and can be used as a delivery recipient by any user inside your organization (assuming that there are no restrictions in place to prevent delivery).

So why would a company *not* create a mailbox for a user; why would they only associate an external email address with their user accounts? Well, the answer is that mail-enabled users are used to fill a specific need: the need to make an external *contact* appear in the internal address list. Yes, but there is already an object that fills that need, the *mail-enabled contact* (more on that recipient type later in this section). Well, the caveat here is that the external *contact* needs access to internal network resources, by using an Active Directory user account. An example of this would be an onsite contract employee who requires access to the network but needs to continue receiving email through their existing email address. As a result, the mail-enabled user appears in the global address list and other users can easily locate and send email to the address, even though the user does not have a mailbox in the Exchange organization. Note also that a mail-enabled user *cannot* send or receive email by using the internal Exchange servers.

More information about mail-enabled users is available in Chapter 19, "Managing Mail-Enabled Contacts."

Mail-Enabled Contacts

Mail-enabled contacts are exactly that: *contacts* for individuals that are external to your organization. A mail-enabled contact is an individual who has neither a security principal in Active Directory nor a mailbox on an internal Exchange server. Mail-enabled contacts are visible in the global address list, but they receive all email on an external messaging system. Any internal user can send an email message to a contact simply by selecting the contact from an address list.

So what is the real-world purpose of a mail-enabled contact? Well, imagine a company that has a large number of suppliers or customers, with whom many internal users regularly communicate. You may want to make it very easy for your internal users to locate and identify these external contacts; by adding these contacts to Active Directory, you are making them available from a central location and accessible to all internal users. This also provides you with a way to include the suppliers in distribution groups that are used for mass mailings.

In Table 16.1, you can find a matrix that shows the core differences between the recipient types.

TABLE 16.1:   Mailbox-Enabled Users, Mail-Enabled Users, and Mail-Enabled Contacts

RECIPIENT	NEEDS ACCESS TO INTERNAL RESOURCES?	NEEDS A MAILBOX IN EXCHANGE?
Mailbox-enabled user	Yes	Yes
Mail-enabled user	Yes	No
Mail-enabled contact	No	No

Contacts can be created in Active Directory without an Exchange infrastructure in place, but in that case, they are essentially useless. More information about mail-enabled users is available in Chapter 19.

CONTACTS: USED IN A SYNCHRONIZATION SCENARIO

We certainly don't want to oversimplify or minimize the purpose of mail-enabled contact objects. These seemingly minimal objects, which have no access rights, are key elements of some of the most complex Exchange environments. Organizations that establish long-lasting business relationships with other organizations may want to maintain a *somewhat* unified address list. They may want to have all users from both companies appear in a single address list.

To achieve this goal, your company will create contact objects for all users in the other company, and vice versa. Though this doesn't actually result in a *single* global address list, it is a way to make both address lists look identical.

You can imagine that in such a scenario, the information in both address lists will become stale quickly, as new users are added and removed in both companies. At this point, to synchronize both lists you need to use a software solution, such as Microsoft Identity Lifecycle Manager (ILM) Feature Pack 1 or later. This article describes the steps necessary to synchronize address lists by using ILM: http://technet.microsoft.com/en-us/library/aa998597.aspx. (Note that this article describes the process for synchronizing address lists in an Exchange Server 2007 organization. The process is identical for Exchange Server 2010.)

Mail-Enabled Groups

A mail-enabled group is an Active Directory group that has been tagged with all the appropriate exchange mail attributes, including an email address. Once a group has been mail-enabled, any internal or external user can send mail to the group (assuming that there are no restrictions preventing message delivery to the group). The membership of the group can then be modified to configure who receives emails that are sent to the group.

An Active Directory forest that does not include any Exchange organization already uses groups to manage access to resources and permissions. With the integration of an Exchange organization into Active Directory, the same groups (security groups) can be mail-enabled or new groups (distribution groups) that will only be used as a *distribution list* can be created and then mail-enabled.

Active Directory contains two types of groups: distribution and security groups. Some organizations may decide to only mail-enable distribution groups to prevent the likelihood of mistakenly adding users to a group and assigning them access to secured resources. This decision point should be made early on in an Exchange deployment to ensure consistent use of groups.

A mail-enabled group can contain any type of Exchange recipients, including other mail-enabled groups. In Exchange Server 2010, you can only mail-enable universal groups.

More information about mail-enabled groups is available in Chapter 18, "Managing Mail-Enabled Groups."

Mail-Enabled Public Folders

A public folder is an electronic version of a bulletin board. Public folders can be used to store messages, contacts, or calendars that must be accessed by multiple users in your organization. Users can create public folders by using Microsoft Outlook, and administrators can create public folders by using the Exchange management tools.

A mail-enabled public folder is a public folder that has been tagged with all the appropriate Exchange mail attributes. Mail-enabled public folders have an email address and can receive email from any internal or external user from your organization (assuming that the appropriate permissions have been configured for the folder).

Mail-enabled public folders are particularly useful if you need to have a "virtual" shared mailbox between multiple users. For example, you may want to have multiple individuals of the HR department review the job applications that are sent to your company. You can mail-enable a public folder and provide an email address of hr@yourcompany.com. As a last step, you would then provide the necessary permissions to individuals in the HR department to review the contents of the folder, without having a large number of emails polluting their inboxes.

More information about mail-enabled public folders is available in Chapter 21, "Public Folder Management."

Defining Email Addresses

Before we discuss how to create mail-enabled users, groups, or contacts, we'll first discuss how these objects get their email addresses. Those of you who are familiar with Exchange 2000/2003 probably remember that email addresses were defined by a recipient policy. Once the recipient policy was defined, the Microsoft Exchange System Attendant's Recipient Update Service (RUS) would establish email addresses for any mail-enabled recipient at some point in the future (hopefully just a minute or two).

This process is just a bit different in Exchange 2007 and Exchange 2010. Email addresses are generated for the object at the time the mail-enabled recipient is created, and they are generated by an Exchange Management Shell (EMS) task or the Exchange Management Console (EMC) — still with a background EMS task, though. Recipient policies from Exchange 2000/2003 have been broken up into two separate concepts:

◆ Email domains for which your organization will accept mail

◆ Email address policies for your users

For addresses that will be assigned to mailboxes on your Exchange 2010 servers, you define both an accepted domain and an email address policy.

Accepted Domains

An accepted domain is an SMTP domain name (aka SMTP namespace) for which your Exchange 2010 servers will accept mail. The servers will either deliver the mail to Exchange 2010 mailboxes or relay it on to internal or external SMTP mail servers. If you are in the middle of a migration from Exchange 2000/2003, the accepted domains list will include the SMTP domains for your Exchange 2000/2003 mailboxes. Accepted domains must be defined for all email addresses that will be routed into your organization by your Hub Transport servers.

Most small and medium-sized organizations will have only a single accepted domain.

SETTING UP AN ACCEPTED DOMAIN USING THE EMC

Accepted domains are found within the Organization Configuration work center under the Hub Transport subcontainer. When you choose the Accepted Domains tab in the Results pane, you will see a list of the accepted domains that have been defined for your organization, such as those shown in Figure 16.1.

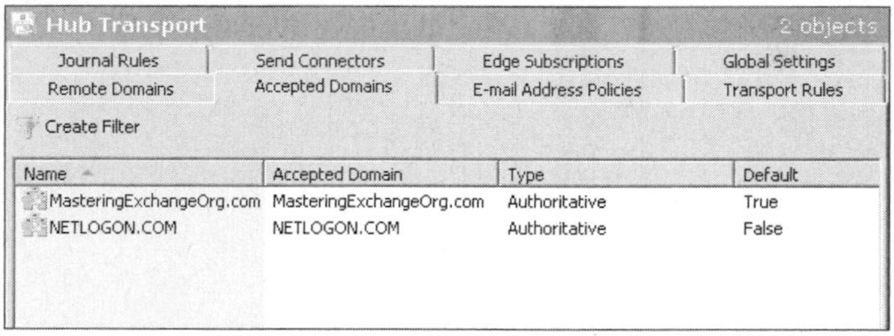

FIGURE 16.1
List of accepted domains

When you create an Exchange organization, a single accepted domain is automatically created and given a name. This is the name of the Active Directory forest root domain; for many organizations this will not be correct because the naming convention for Active Directory domain names and SMTP domain names may be different. For example, your Active Directory name may be `Netlogon.local` whereas your public domain name for email is `Netlogon.com`.

Accepted domains are simple to create and require little input. To create a new accepted domain using the EMC, click the New Accepted Domain task in the Actions pane to launch the New Accepted Domain Wizard (shown in Figure 16.2). You only need to provide a descriptive name for the accepted domain, the SMTP domain name, and how messages for this domain should be treated when messages are accepted by Exchange 2010.

Keep in mind that you cannot change the domain name of an accepted domain once it is created. (You can change the domain type, however.)

SETTING UP AN ACCEPTED DOMAIN USING THE EMS

You can also manage accepted domains using the following EMS cmdlets:

◆ `New-AcceptedDomain`

◆ `Set-AcceptedDomain`

◆ `Get-AcceptedDomain`

◆ `Remove-AcceptedDomain`

FIGURE 16.2
Creating a new
accepted domain

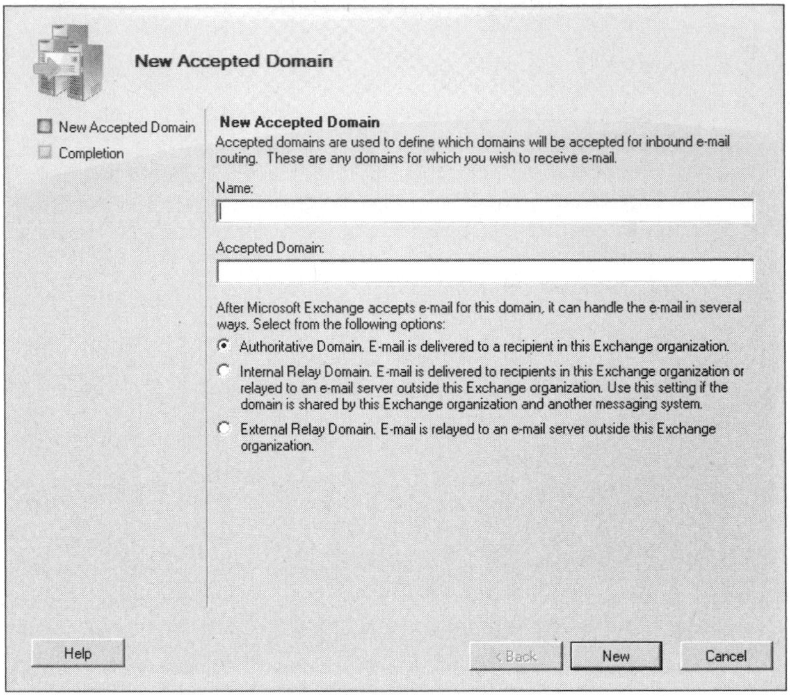

For example, to create a new accepted domain for a Canadian division of Leigh Enterprises, use the following EMS command:

```
New-AcceptedDomain -Name "Leigh Enterprises Canada" -DomainName "leigh-inc.ca"↵
-DomainType "Authoritative"
```

About Domain Types

One tricky thing about defining an accepted domain is that you must define how Exchange is to treat a message for it. You can choose from three types of domains when creating an accepted domain:

Authoritative Domains   These are SMTP domains for which you accept the inbound message and deliver it to an internal mailbox within your Exchange organization.

Internal Relay Domains   These are SMTP domains for which your Exchange server will accept inbound SMTP mail. The Exchange server must have mail-enabled contacts or mail-enabled users who specify forwarding addresses for users in those domains. The Exchange server then relays the message on to another internal mail system. Internal relay domains are used when two Exchange organizations are doing global address list synchronization.

External Relay Domains   These are SMTP domains for which your Exchange organization will accept inbound SMTP mail and then relay that mail on to an external SMTP mail server, usually one that is outside of the organization's boundaries. If Edge Transport servers are used, the Edge Transport server handles external relay domains.

Email Address Policies

Exchange email address policies are the configuration objects used by Exchange management tasks when new mail objects are created. Each policy's conditions are examined to see if the policy's conditions apply to the object that is being created; if they do, the new mail-enabled object's email address policies are generated based on the email address generation rules.

Using the EMC, email address policies are found in the Organization Configuration work center under the Hub Transport subcontainer. Once you have highlighted the Hub Transport subcontainer, select the Email Address Policies tab to see a list of the email address policies in the organization. In Figure 16.3, we only have the default policy assigned by the Exchange Server 2010 installation.

FIGURE 16.3
Email address policies for an Exchange 2010 organization

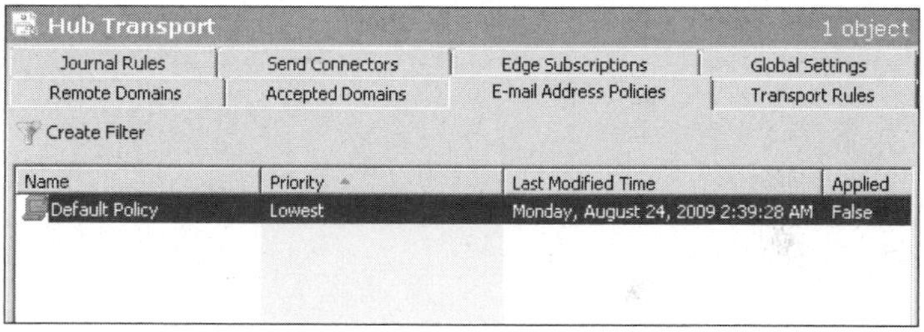

The default policy is the lowest-priority policy and applies if no other policies above it apply. This is just like having multiple recipient policies in Exchange 2000/2003.

CHANGING AN EXISTING POLICY

The default email address generation rule uses the object's Exchange alias and the domain name of the Active Directory forest root. Suppose you want to make two changes to the email address policy:

♦ You want to change the SMTP domain name that is on the default policy to something else.
For example, this is relevant when the default domain name for the Active Directory forest root is different from the public domain name used for SMTP and you need to fix this.

♦ You want all email addresses to be generated using the first name, followed by a period, then the last name, and then the domain name.

To perform those tasks, follow these steps:

1. Define an accepted domain. If the default accepted domain is not correct for your organization, you need to create a new accepted domain because Exchange 2007 does not allow you to change an accepted domain. Let's say that your Active Directory forest root is called `fourthcoffee.com` but your public SMTP domain is `volcanocoffee.com`. First, under the Accepted Domains tab of the Organization Configuration work center's Hub Transport subcontainer, create a new authoritative accepted domain for `volcanocoffee.com`.

2. Change the default email address policy so that it uses the new domain name and generates an address using the *firstname.lastname* format, such as `josh.maher@volcanocoffee.com`.

Locate the default policy in the Organization Configuration work center (found under the Hub Transport subcontainer by clicking the Email Address Policies tab), highlight the default policy, and click the Edit task in the Actions pane. Click Next until you reach the Email Addresses page. In the Email Addresses page, you see the list of all domain names used to generate Email addresses. On the page you would then click on the domain name you want to modify, in this case @fourthcoffee.com, and then click the Edit button to see the SMTP Email Address dialog box (shown in Figure 16.4). When you first see this box, the Email Address Local Part check box is not checked. This means that the object's Exchange alias will be used when creating the SMTP address. You want to change that, so enable the Email Address Local Part check box; once it's selected, you will be able to enable the First Name.Last Name (John.Smith) radio button. We selected that check box in Figure 16.4 so that you can easily see the available choices.

FIGURE 16.4
Changing how the SMTP address is generated

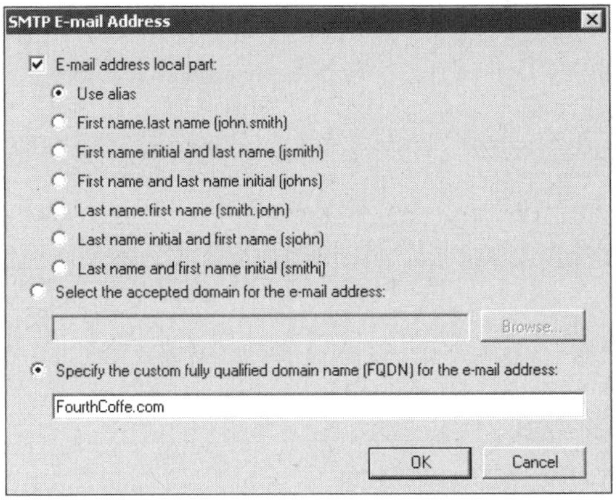

3. Next, you can either click the Browse button to select from the list of available accepted domains or type in the SMTP domain you want to use to generate email addresses. To better illustrate the options, we typed the **VolcanoCoffee.com** domain in the dialog box. When you are done here, you would then click OK.

4. You have now modified the default policy; just click Next on the Email Addresses page to finish the modification.

5. Next you will see the Schedule page of the wizard (see Figure 16.5). This might be a bit confusing at first because on the surface it doesn't seem as if there is anything to schedule. However, remember that in Exchange 2000/2003, the Exchange Recipient Update Service (RUS) took care of adding SMTP addresses to mail-enabled objects. There is no equivalent for Exchange 2007 mail-enabled recipients. Thus, some process or task has to be kicked off that will do this. If you choose Immediately, this will kick off the `Update-EmailAddressPolicy` cmdlet with the `-Identity:'Default Policy'` option and immediately update any email addresses.

If you don't choose Immediately, you have additional options:

◆ Do Not Apply skips the `Update-EmailAddressPolicy` cmdlet phase altogether. If you have just updated the default policy, you can always run the `Update-EmailAddressPolicy "Default Policy"` command from the EMS at a later point.

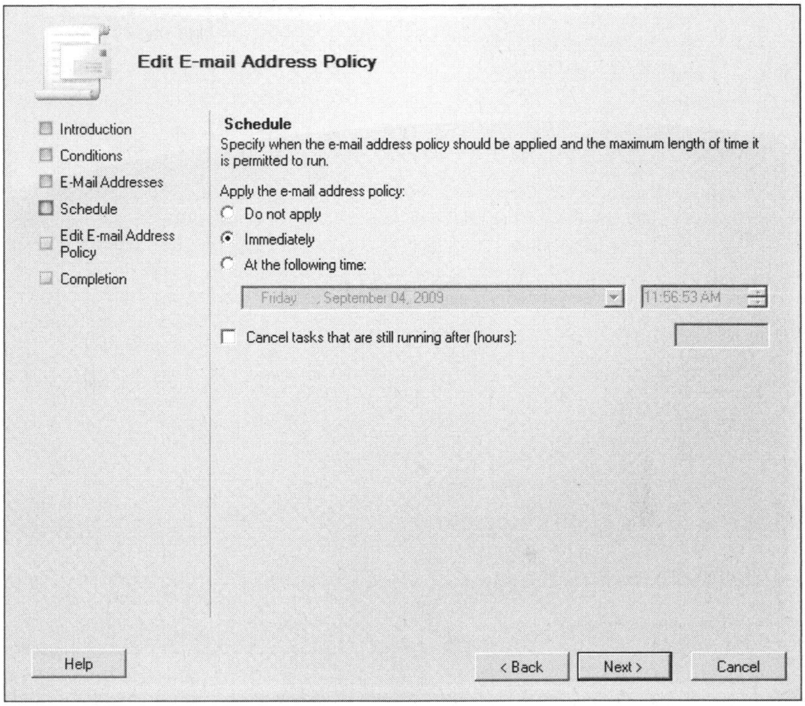

FIGURE 16.5
Scheduling an update to
the email address policy

- At The Following Time allows you to schedule the `Update-EmailAddressPolicy` cmdlet to run later. This is useful if you know that it will have to update thousands of mail-enabled objects in your Active Directory and you don't want it affecting usage during the business day. This option, when selected, allows you to specify that the task be canceled if it is still running after a certain number of hours.

Of course, you can also create email address policies using the EMS; the following is an example of an EMS command that would create an email address policy for the domain `Kalleo.ca`:

```
New-EmailAddressPolicy –Name 'Kalleo Solutions' –IncludedRecipients↵
'MailboxUsers' –ConditionalCustomAttribute1 'test' –Priority '1'↵
–EnabledEmailAddressTemplates 'SMTP:%g.%s@Kalleo.ca'
```

So getting back to our example of VolcanoCoffee.com, one thing we want to point out is what happens to existing email addresses once you change to a new default address. Figure 16.6 shows the Email Addresses property page for the mailbox of a user whose address was updated; notice that this user has three email addresses now. He has the old email addresses `Lcohen@masteringexchangeorg.com` and `Lcohen@fourthcoffee.com` and his newly created SMTP address `Larry.cohen@volcanocoffee.com`. The process of updating email addresses never removes existing addresses; it creates the new address and makes it the Reply To address.

Although this example was done entirely in the graphical user interface, you could use the EMS to perform the same steps. The EMS cmdlets you would use to create, delete, modify, and update email address policies are shown in Table 16.2.

FIGURE 16.6
Newly created SMTP
address for an existing
user

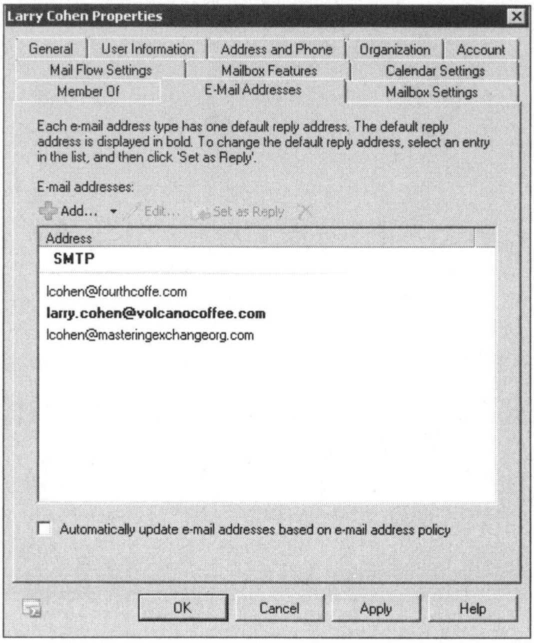

TABLE 16.2: EMS Cmdlets Used to Manipulate Email Address Policies

EMS CMDLET	DESCRIPTION
New-EmailAddressPolicy	Creates a new email address policy
Set-EmailAddressPolicy	Changes properties of the email address policy specified
Update-EmailAddressPolicy	Updates mail-enabled objects in the Active Directory if the conditions of the policy specified apply to those objects
Get-EmailAddressPolicy	Retrieves a list of email address policies and their properties
Remove-EmailAddressPolicy	Deletes the specified email address policy

Finally, of course, if you want to see the email addresses that have been applied to a mail-enabled object, you can also use an EMS cmdlet to retrieve that information. You would use Get-Mailbox, Get-MailContact, or Get-DistributionGroup. To retrieve the email addresses for a mailbox whose alias is Julie.Samante, you could type the following command and see output similar to this:

```
Get-Mailbox "julie.samante" | Format-List DisplayName,EmailAddresses
DisplayName    : Julie Samante
EmailAddresses : {smtp:Julie.Samante@fourthcoffee.com,
SMTP:Julie.Samante@volcanocoffee.com}
```

CREATING A NEW EMAIL ADDRESS POLICY

If you have a small or medium-sized organization, you probably support only a single SMTP domain for your users. However, even companies with a handful of mailboxes can sometimes require two or three SMTP domain names. Let's take as an example an organization that has two divisions, each of which requires its own unique SMTP addresses.

Previously, you changed the default policy for an organization so that all users would get an SMTP address of @volcanocoffee.com. Let's extend that example a bit further. Let's say that this organization has another division called Volcano Surfboards and its SMTP domain is @volcanosurfboards.com. Anyone whose company attribute in the Active Directory contains *Volcano Surfboards* should have an SMTP address of firstname.lastname@volcanosurfboards.com and that address should be set as its default reply address.

🌐 Real World Scenario

CREATING A NEW ADDRESS POLICY OR MODIFYING THE DEFAULT ADDRESS?

This is one of the questions we hear the most often: Should I create a new address list when I need to add a new SMTP domain, or should I simply modify the default address list?

To answer that question, we usually tell our clients or students that there is no *single* answer for this question that applies to all scenarios. One of us once had a customer experience that should illustrate when you need to use one or the other. First, keep in mind that only *one* email address policy can be applied to a new user that is created in your organization. When you create a new user, Exchange checks to see which policy matches the new recipient, based on conditions and filters. If multiple policies apply to the user, it will only apply the policy with the highest priority and then ignore all others. If no custom policies apply to the user, then the default policy is applied. (A policy must always be applied when you create a mailbox-enabled user, which is why you cannot remove or delete the default email address policy.)

So now to the customer. One of us was called in because "The Internet was broken and not sending emails" (We love those descriptions!). We'll spare you the initial troubleshooting steps, but we soon noticed that the organization had five different email address policies. Each address policy had a different SMTP domain and was configured to apply to *all users*. So, you now know that when a new user was created in their company, the user only received the highest priority email address policy, and was therefore only assigned a single SMTP address that matched that policy. (That policy was created for a separate business unit that was not even launched yet.) There was an easy fix to this: simply remove all the custom email address policies, and then add the SMTP domains to the default email address policy. Then reapply the policy and all users were assigned correct addresses.

So now to answer the initial question: Create a custom email address policy when you need to assign a separate SMTP domain to a *subset* of your users. Modify the default email address policy when you want to add domains to *all users* in your organization.

The first thing you need to do is define volcanosurfboards.com as an authoritative accepted domain. If you don't define the accepted domain, you can still define the email address policy, but your organization will reject any emails sent to the @volcanosurfboards.com addresses.

Next, you want to create the email address policy. In the EMC, select the Hub Transport subcontainer of the Organization Configuration work center, and then select the Email Address Policies tab in the Results pane.

To create a new email address policy, click the New Email Address Policy task in the Actions pane. On the first page (see Figure 16.7) of the New Email Address Policy wizard, you will be prompted for the name of the policy and what type of objects this policy applies to.

In this example, the policy is being created for the Volcano Surfboards company users and you want the policy to apply only to mailboxes, so you will provide that information on the screen shown in Figure 16.7. When you have provided this information, click Next to move on through the wizard.

FIGURE 16.7

Naming the email address policy and defining the objects to which it applies

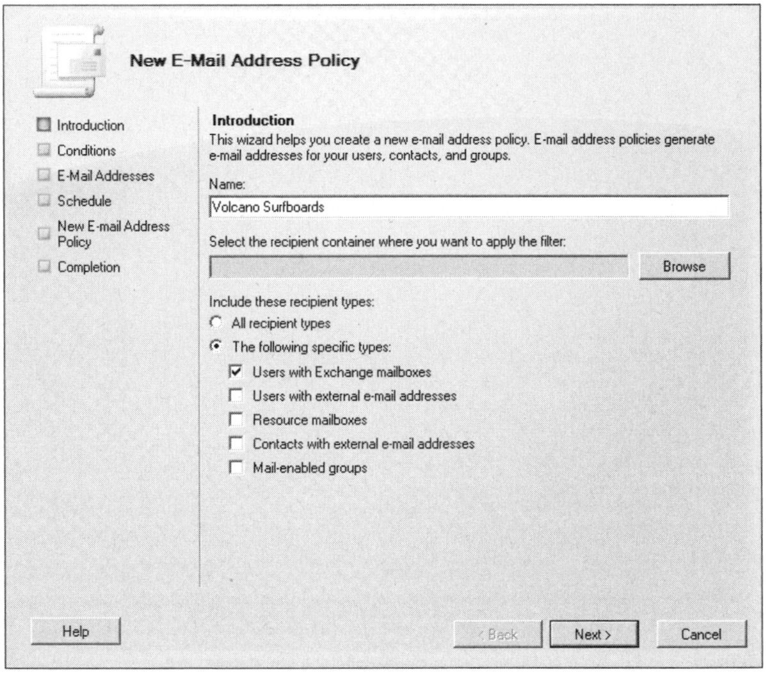

The next screen, Conditions, is where you define the conditions under which this policy will be applied. There are two steps to the Conditions page. First, you need to narrow the scope to a specific condition, such as the State or Province attribute, Department attribute, or Company Name attribute of the object. Second, you need to provide values for the attributes you have selected.

In this example, you want this policy to apply to anyone whose company name attribute contains *Volcano Surfboards*. Figure 16.8 shows the Conditions page after filling in the necessary information.

Once you select the condition Recipient Is In A Company, that option shows up in the Step 2 portion of the dialog box as Users With Exchange Mailboxes In The *specified* Company(s). The word *specified* appears very much like a hyperlink; it is blue and underlined. If you click that link, a dialog box appears that allows you to edit or specify one or more company names. (See Figure 16.8.)

When you have entered the necessary company information (in this case, just a single company called Volcano Surfboards), you click OK to close the Specify Company dialog box.

You can verify that the conditions are defined correctly by clicking the Preview button on the Conditions page of the wizard. The Preview button displays the Email Address Policy Preview dialog box; you should see users with mailboxes and whose company name is Volcano Surfboards.

FIGURE 16.8
Defining conditions for an email address policy

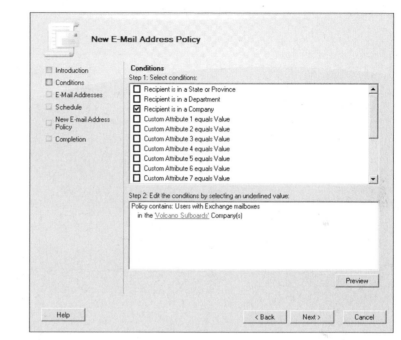

The Preview button is also helpful in confirming that attributes are being entered correctly in Active Directory. Administrators may not recognize if everyone in a 10,000-user company exists in the Preview window, but hopefully it will give them an idea that the information is being entered correctly. In this case, if a user's company name does not contain exactly *Volcano Surfboards*, the policy conditions will not be met and the user's mailbox will have the email addresses from the default policy.

The next step is to define the SMTP address or addresses that will be generated when the conditions of this policy apply. The default action for the Add button is to create a new SMTP address, but if you need to create a custom address, click the drop-down arrow to the right of the Add button to see a list that provides an option to create a Custom Address type. (See Figure 16.9.)

On the Email Addresses page, you need to click the Add button to create a new SMTP address. You will then type the SMTP Email Address domain name (in this example, **volcanocoffee.com**) in the Email Address Domain dialog box and click the First Name.Last Name (John.Smith) radio button option. (See Figure 16.10.)

If you have created an accepted domain for volcanosurfboards.com, you can also select it by clicking the Browse button.

The next page of the New Email Address Policy wizard is the Schedule page; if you want the addresses to appear immediately, you must click the Immediately radio button and click Next. If there are many thousands of addresses to be created, you may want to schedule the task to run during off-hours. Once you click Next on the Schedule page, you will see the Summary page. Here you can see the tasks that will be performed once you click the New button.

FIGURE 16.9
Adding a custom address type

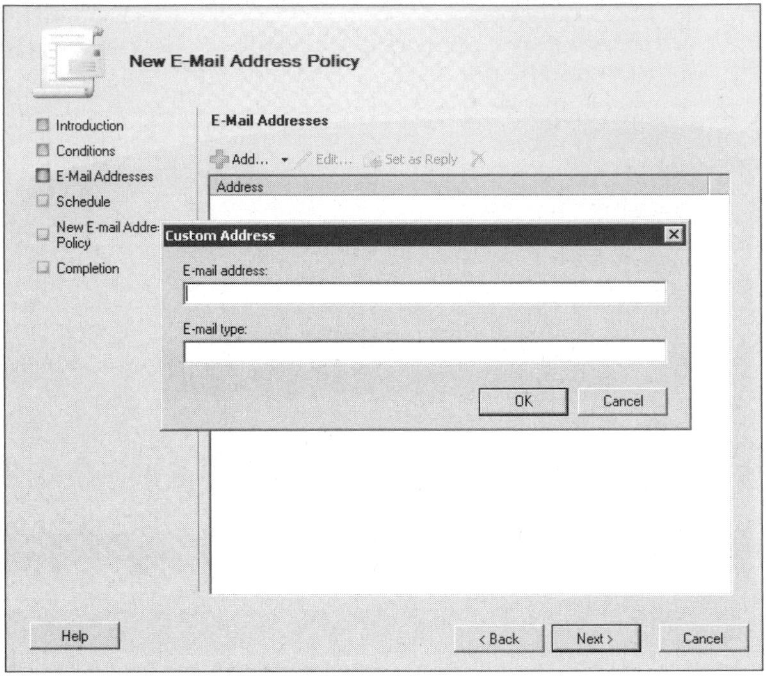

FIGURE 16.10
Adding an SMTP address and specifying the local part of the email address

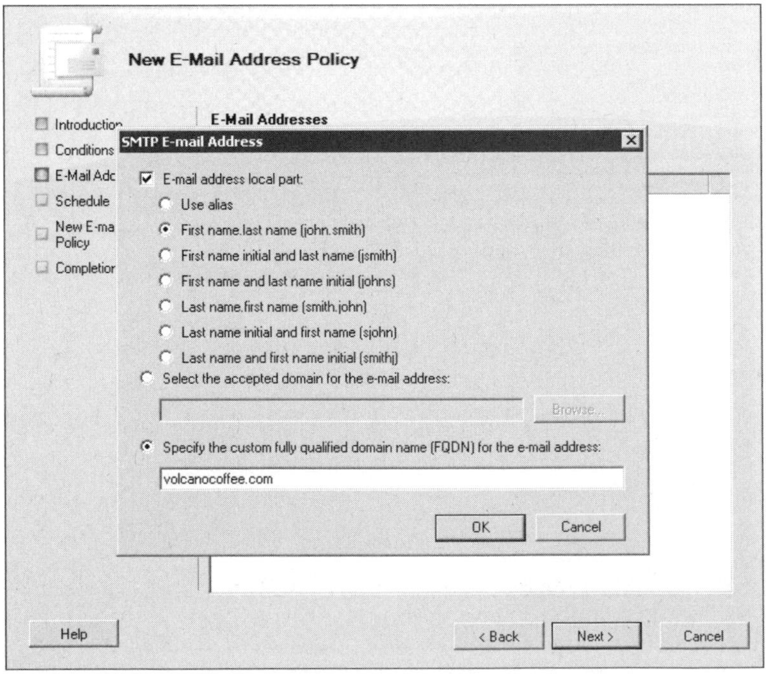

The final phase of email address policy creation is the Completion page. Though no actual operations or input are required here (other than clicking the Finish button), this page is useful because it provides you with the cmdlets and commands that were used to perform this particular task. In the case of creating a new email address policy, the task used two cmdlets (`New-EmailAddressPolicy` and `Update-EmailAddressPolicy`). The Completion page is shown in Figure 16.11.

FIGURE 16.11
Completion page of the New Email Address Policy Wizard

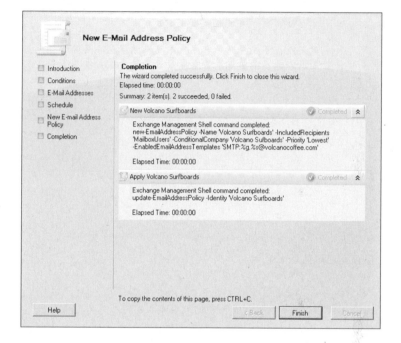

The Bottom Line

Identify the various types of recipients   Most recipient types that we find today in Exchange Server 2010 have been around since the early days of Exchange. Each serves a specific different purpose and all have objects that reside in Active Directory.

Master it   Your company has multiple Active Directory domains that exist in a single forest. You must make sure that the following needs for your company are met:

◆ Group managers cannot, by mistake, assign permissions to a user by adding someone to a group.

◆ Temporary consultants for your company must not be able to access any internal resource.

Use the Exchange management tools to manage recipients   Historically, Exchange administrators mainly used a combination of Active Directory tools and Exchange-native tools to manage Exchange servers and objects. That all changed with Exchange 2007 and Exchange

2010, mainly with the advent of the Exchange Management Shell, but also with the now more powerful Exchange Management Console.

Master It   You are responsible for managing multiple Exchange organizations and you need to apply identical configurations to servers in all organizations. Since you are just starting out with Exchange Server 2010 and you are not yet familiar with the Exchange Management Shell, you need some guidance regarding the commands that must be used. What should you do?

Configure accepted domains and define email address policies   The concept of accepted domains and email address policies was once a single concept in Exchange Server 2000/2003, the recipient policy. Now that this concept has been broken up, it gives us more flexibility in managing email address suffixes and SMTP domains that will be accepted by your Hub Transport servers.

Master It   You plan to accept mail for multiple companies inside your organization. Once accepted, the mail will be rerouted to the SMTP servers responsible for each of those companies. What do you need to create in your organization?

## Chapter 17

Managing Mailboxes and Mailbox Content

In a small or medium-sized business, you may be the sole person responsible for all Exchange tasks, such as backing up the server, checking the queues, reviewing event logs, and managing mailboxes. In other organizations, you might have a specific task, such as running backups or managing mobile devices.

In most Exchange organizations, the single biggest day-to-day administration task is the management of end-user mailboxes. The majority of mailbox management tasks involve the creation of mailboxes, moving them to the correct database, setting mailbox properties or policies, and management of email addresses. Mailbox management also may entail the management of the actual content, such as purging the Deleted Items folder, moving content to other folders, or removing content from a user's mailbox.

In this chapter, you will learn to:

◆ Create and delete user mailboxes

◆ Manage mailbox permissions

◆ Move mailboxes to another database

◆ Perform bulk manipulation of mailbox properties

◆ Use messaging records management to manage mailbox content

Managing Mailboxes

This first section on mailbox management tackles the most common tasks: creating, managing, and deleting mailboxes associated with a real user account. If you are upgrading from Exchange Server 2003 to Exchange Server 2010, the most important thing you need to learn up-front and immediately is that mailbox management tasks are no longer performed via extensions to Active Directory Users and Computers.

Real World Scenario

CLEAN UP THE EXCHANGE 2003 MANAGEMENT CONSOLES

An organization, STUV, had user account and Exchange mailbox administrators spread out across eight different offices in North America. After they completed their upgrade to Exchange Server 2010 and removed their Exchange 2003 servers, they frequently found that they were having problems with new users accessing their mailboxes.

A new user would be created, but the user was never able to access her mailbox. The user did not appear in the Global Address List (GAL), nor did she get email addresses. The problem continued to escalate to the corporate help desk but the "solution" they found was to move the mailbox to another database.

After much investigation, the corporate email administrator found that some of the remote user account administrators were still using the Exchange 2003 extensions to Active Directory Users and Computers (ADUC). The Recipient Update Service (RUS) that took care of stamping a user account with email address and address list membership information no longer exists in Exchange Server 2010. The Exchange Server 2010 Management Console and the Exchange Management Shell take care of all these tasks the instant that the object is created rather than the RUS taking care of this a few seconds or minutes later. Thus, the ADUC extensions provided with Exchange 2003 no longer worked.

Rather than moving the mailboxes to another database, this issue could also have been fixed using the Exchange Management Shell and the Set-Mailbox cmdlet. The Set-Mailbox cmdlet has an -ApplyMandatoryProperties option that would fix this as well.

As administrators' areas of responsibility are moved from Exchange 2003 to Exchange 2010, their management tools should immediately be upgraded. The Exchange Server 2003 management tools must be removed, and administrators should be provided with a way to use the Exchange 2010 management tools, such as upgrading their desktop systems to an x64 operating system or accessing the tools via Remote Desktop to a Windows 2008 x64 Terminal Server.

Don't confuse user mailboxes with mailboxes that are associated with a resource, such as a conference room or an overhead projector; user and resource mailboxes are almost identical, but we cover resource mailboxes in Chapter 20, "Managing Resource Mailboxes."

The Exchange Management Console (EMC) allows you to associate a mailbox with an existing user in the Active Directory, or you can create the user account (if you have the necessary permissions). All mailbox management–related tasks handled within the Exchange Management Console are performed within the Mailbox subcontainer of the Recipient Configuration container, as shown in Figure 17.1. By default, all mailboxes in the entire organization are shown in this container.

The rules for mailbox ownership and associating an account with a mailbox have not changed since Exchange 2000. There are a few important things to keep in mind with respect to user account and mailbox management:

◆ A user account can own only a single mailbox or a single mailbox and an archive mailbox associated with that mailbox.

◆ A user account can be given permissions to other mailboxes.

◆ Each mailbox must be associated with a user account that is in the same Active Directory forest as the Exchange server.

◆ A single user account from another Active Directory forest can own a mailbox, but a user account in the Exchange server's home forest must still exist and be associated with the mailbox.

FIGURE 17.1
The Mailboxes subcontainer in the Exchange Management Console

Using the EMC to Assign a Mailbox

Let's start with a common task: assigning a mailbox to an existing user. You may also hear this process referred to as "mailbox-enabling" a user or simply creating a mailbox. In this example, there is a user in the ithicos.local Active Directory whose account is Bharat.Suneja. His unique location and distinguished name are as follows:

```
ithicos.local/Corporate/Bharat Suneja
CN=Bharat Suneja,OU=Corporate,DC=ithicos,DC=local
```

To assign this user a mailbox, you must use either the EMS or the EMC; remember that extensions for Active Directory Users and Computers from Exchange 2000/2003 do not work for Exchange 2010.

A WIZARD BY ANY OTHER NAME

We are usually only describing one way to launch a wizard, such as the New Mailbox wizard. However, for most wizards and tasks within the Exchange Management Console, there are three different ways to launch the wizard. The New Mailbox wizard can be launched by clicking New Mailbox in the Actions pane, by right-clicking on the Mailboxes (or Recipient Configuration) container and choosing New Mailbox, or by choosing New Mailbox from the Actions pull-down menu (while the Mailbox or Recipient Configuration container is selected in the EMC tree).

Launch the EMC and navigate to the Mailboxes subcontainer of the Recipient Configuration work center. From here, click the New Mailbox task in the Actions pane. This will launch the New Mailbox wizard. The first screen in this wizard (shown in Figure 17.2) introduces some entirely new concepts for administrators of previous versions of Exchange. This screen asks you to define what type of mailbox you are creating.

FIGURE 17.2
Defining the type of mailbox you want to create

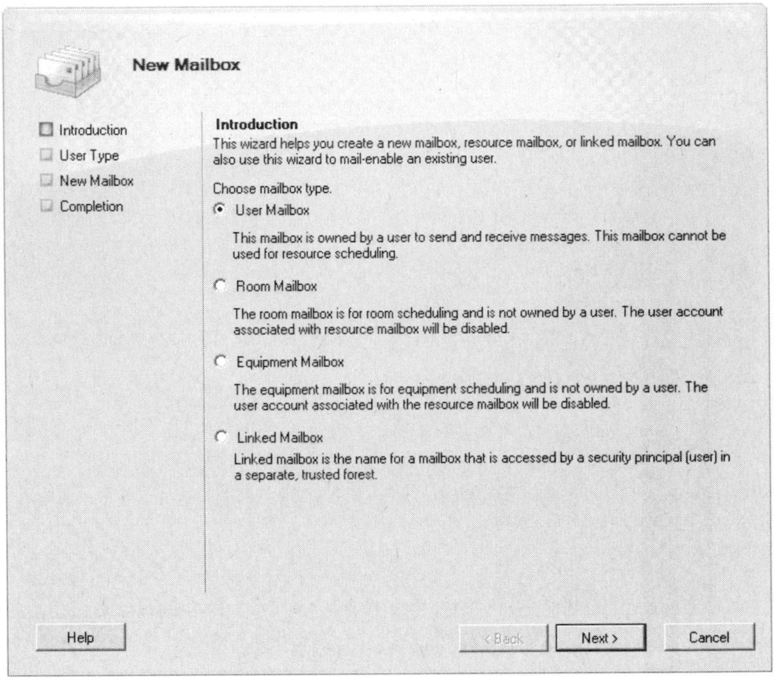

You have four possible choices for mailbox types (see Table 17.1). For all of them, there *must* be a user account in the same Active Directory in which the Exchange servers are located.

TABLE 17.1: The Four Types of Exchange 2010 Mailboxes

MAILBOX TYPE	PURPOSE
User mailbox	Assigns a mailbox to an existing user account in the same Active Directory forest in which the Exchange server is located. This is the most common type of mailbox that most administrators will create.
Room mailbox	Creates a disabled user account and assigns a mailbox to that user. The ResourceType property of the mailbox is set to Room, the RecipientTypeDetails property is set to ConferenceRoomMailbox, and the IsResource property is set to True.
Equipment mailbox	Creates a disabled user account and assigns a mailbox to that user. The ResourceType property of that mailbox is set to Equipment, the RecipientTypeDetails property is set to EquipmentMailbox, and the IsResource property is set to True.

TABLE 17.1: The Four Types of Exchange 2010 Mailboxes *(CONTINUED)*

MAILBOX TYPE	PURPOSE
Linked mailbox	Creates a disabled user account, assigns it a mailbox, and prompts the administrator to provide a user account in a separate, trusted forest. The account in the other forest is considered the owner of this mailbox and has the Associated External Account permissions to the mailbox. This is used in organizations that install Exchange in a resource forest. If you are creating Linked mailboxes, the user account in your forest must remain disabled.

In this first example, you are creating a simple mailbox-enabled user account, so you would choose the User Mailbox radio button and then click the Next button.

On the next screen, you are asked whether you are creating a new user account or using an existing user account (Figure 17.3). Notice that you can create mailboxes for more than one user at a time.

FIGURE 17.3

User Type screen

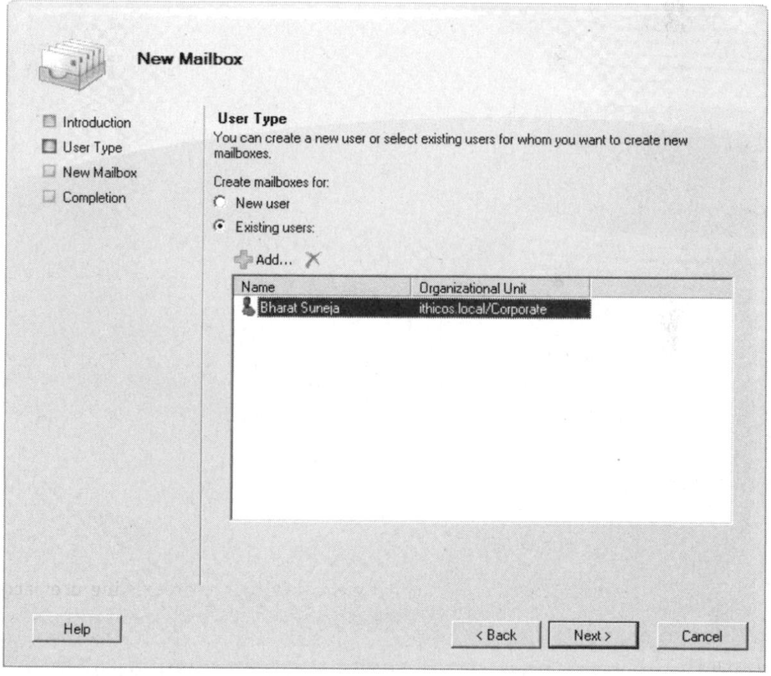

Since we are going to use an existing user account, when we click the Add button, we are presented with the Select User dialog (Figure 17.4). Here, you can narrow down the scope of your search using the Search option. Note that only user accounts that are enabled and that do not already have a mailbox will show up in this list.

After you select from the Active Directory a user that does not already have a mailbox assigned to it, the Mailbox Settings page allows you to specify the user's Exchange alias, define the mailbox database on which the mailbox will be hosted (or allow Exchange to automatically select one for you), and specify the managed folder and the ActiveSync policies. Much of the information requested on the Mailbox Settings page (shown in Figure 17.5) will look familiar to Exchange 2000/2003 administrators. Note that the managed folder policy and the ActiveSync policy are optional; you can always add them later. Note that if you assign a managed folder policy to this mailbox you cannot assign an archive retention policy.

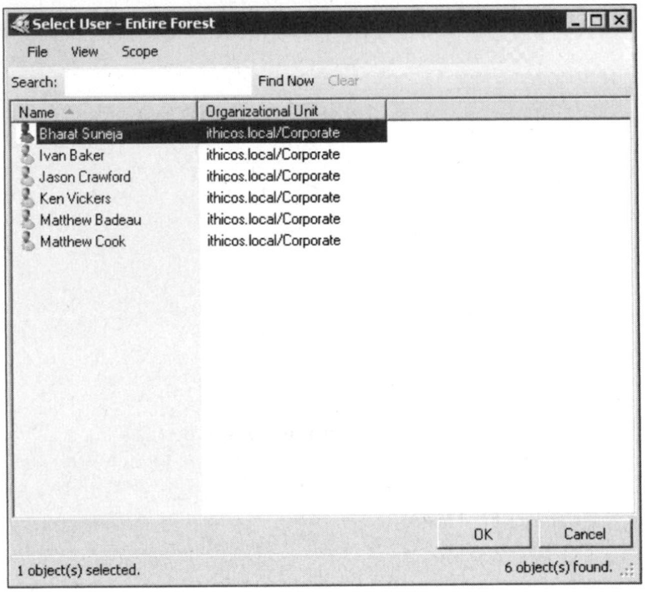

FIGURE 17.4
Select User dialog box

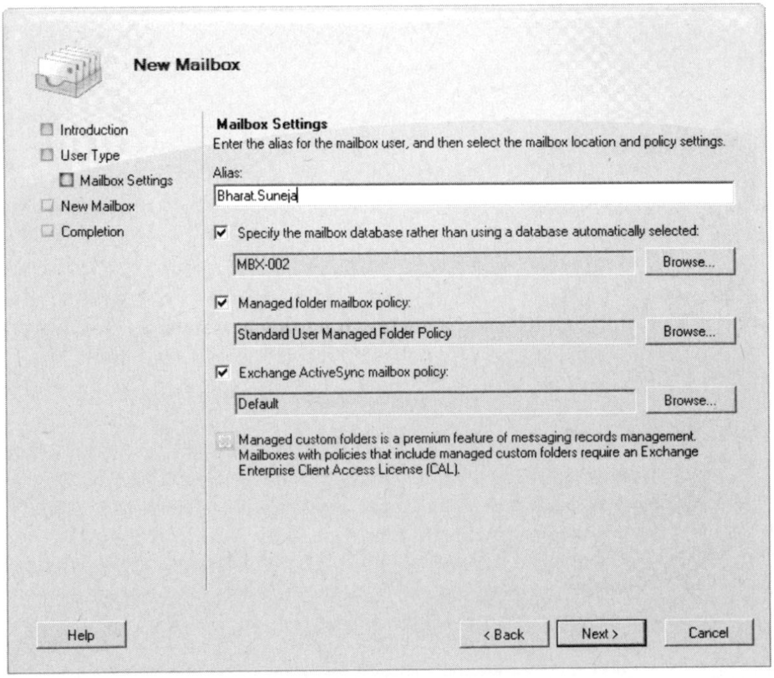

FIGURE 17.5
Assigning a mailbox database, managed folder policy, and ActiveSync policy

AUTOMATICALLY ASSIGNING A MAILBOX TO A DATABASE

Exchange Server 2010's management tools include a great new feature that will automatically assign a user to a mailbox database. This is a great feature for organizations that have trouble balancing mailboxes on mailbox databases; frequently a mailbox administrator will always select the first mailbox database in the list.

Exchange 2010 has some load-balancing provisioning logic built into mailbox moves and new mailbox creation. You don't need to specify a database name when doing a mailbox creation or mailbox move. The logic is as follows:

1. Gather all databases in the organization.

2. Exclude any databases that are marked to be excluded for mailbox load.

3. Exclude any that are not in the same Active Directory site as the provisioning server (such as those that reside where the cmdlet is running).

4. Pick a database at random; check if it's "up" according to Active Manager. If yes, use it. If no, repeat step 4.

If you want to use the load-balancing logic, keep in mind that specifying in the database name the mailbox type or profile type won't be successful as mailboxes will be randomized eventually across all databases. Microsoft has always recommended that you equalize distribution of the mailbox population and not scope stores with specific classes of users, so this feature helps you follow this recommendation.

Given that, there are scenarios where you may have defined specific databases on which you do not want automatic distribution of mailboxes (such as when you're defining journaling based on the database). You can exclude these databases from the provisioning logic by changing the properties on the database via the Set-MailboxDatabase cmdlet. You have two options: IsExcludedFromProvisioning and IsSuspendedFromProvisioning.

The two options have the same net effect (causing the database to be excluded from the load balancer algorithm), but one is intended to be short term and the other long term. The scenario for "off" (IsExcludedFromProvisioning) is used when you have a mailbox database that you want to have off for provisioning always. Let's say it's "full" or it's a special "VIP" database. The scenario for "temporarily off" (IsSuspendedFromProvisioning) is used when you are temporarily taking a server out of rotation for new mailboxes. The reason why this distinction is interesting is that you might wish to identify databases that are "off" from those that are "temporarily off" if you are trying to manage the load balancing via automation. If you're turning on and off load balancing to particular databases, you want to make sure you're only doing this for the subset of databases that you would not want to keep permanently excluded.

From the Mailbox Settings page, you specify the information shown in Table 17.2.

The next screen provides the configuration summary; part of the configuration summary wizard screen is shown in Figure 17.6. Here you can review the configuration of the mailbox you are creating or assigning.

When you are convinced that the parameters for the mailbox you are creating are correct, click the New button on the New Mailbox summary screen. The EMC then launches an EMS cmdlet that enables the mailbox in the Active Directory. If you have selected a managed folder mailbox policy, you will see a warning dialog that will remind you that clients prior to Outlook

2007 will not have all the features available and that clients older than Outlook 2003 SP2 are not supported (Figure 17.7).

TABLE 17.2:   Mailbox Settings Page Options

OPTION	DESCRIPTION
Alias	The alias is used to generate the default SMTP addresses as well as other internal Exchange functions, such as the legacy Exchange distinguished name. The alias defaults to be the same as the user account name, but it can be changed if you need it to conform to another standard.
Mailbox Database	This browse list will consist of mailbox databases found in the organization.
Managed Folder Mailbox Policy	The Managed Folder Mailbox Policy selection allows you to define which managed folder policy affects this particular mailbox. Once this has been assigned, the next time the messaging records management process is run, the managed folders specified by this policy will be created.
Exchange ActiveSync Mailbox Policy	The Exchange ActiveSync mailbox policy defines the ActiveSync parameters for the user.

FIGURE 17.6
The configuration summary

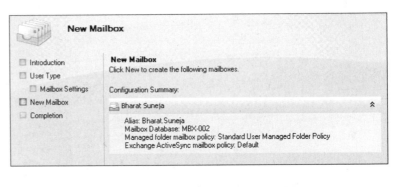

FIGURE 17.7
Managed folder mailbox policy warning message

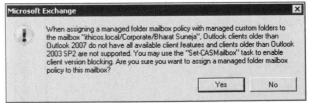

The last page of the wizard is the Completion page, which tells you if the operation was successful or not and shows you the EMS cmdlet and options that were used to perform the operation. Figure 17.8 shows part of the Completion page for the mailbox that was just created.

The Completion page also allows you to copy the output of the screen to the paste buffer so that you can then paste that output into a text editor. If you are just learning PowerShell and the EMS, this makes it simple to learn what cmdlets do and how to use them — which is helpful if you want to mailbox-enable user accounts using the EMS.

FIGURE 17.8
Successfully completing the assignment of a mailbox to an existing user

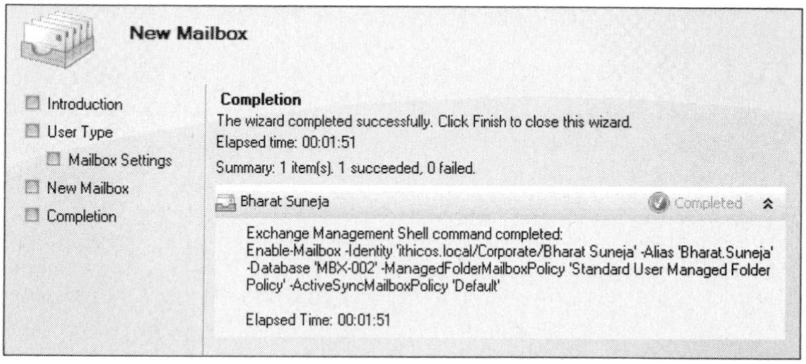

Assigning a Mailbox to More than One User

For most administrators, user accounts and mailboxes are created a few at a time rather than one at a time. The procedure for doing this using the EMC is almost identical to the procedure for assigning a mailbox to a single user. When configuring the mailbox settings (shown in Figure 17.9), the alias for each user is automatically configured; the alias will be the same as the user's Active Directory user account. The mailbox database must also be the same for all the users selected.

FIGURE 17.9
Assigning more than one user a mailbox

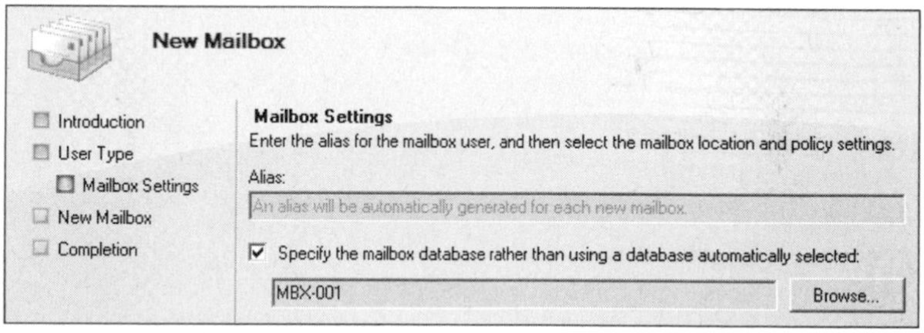

The configuration summary (shown in Figure 17.10) will show you all the users selected and what will be configured for each user.

FIGURE 17.10
Reviewing the configuration summary for more than one user

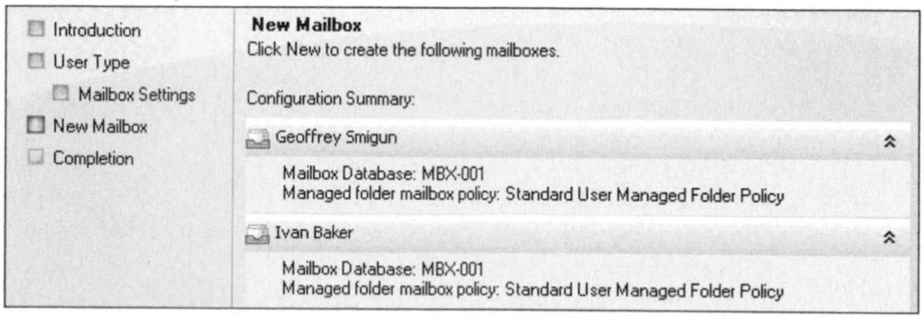

One annoyance that you will experience when configuring more than one user is that if you assign a user a managed folder policy, the legacy clients confirmation box (shown previously in Figure 17.6) will pop up for each user that you are configuring. You can avoid this by using the Exchange Management Shell, but that may be more than many administrators are prepared to deal with.

Finally, the Completion screen that shows you the EMS cmdlet(s) that were executed is a bit different. In Figure 17.11 you can see the EMS cmdlets that were executed to mailbox-enable two user accounts. Note that in this case the unique name of the user account was piped to the Enable-Mailbox cmdlet.

FIGURE 17.11
Mailbox-enabling more than one user

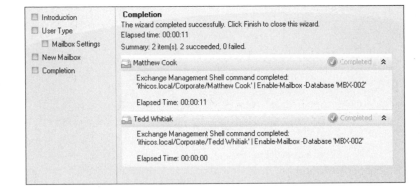

Assigning a Mailbox to a User from the EMS

In a larger organization, you will probably want to streamline or script the creation of new mailboxes and/or user accounts. The EMS allows you to do this easily. For now, though, let's look at the example you just completed from the EMC graphical user interface. You enabled a mailbox for an existing user, assigned that user a mailbox on the MBX-002 mailbox database, and assigned that user the Standard User Managed folder policy and the Default ActiveSync policy. The cmdlet executed is as follows:

```
Enable-Mailbox -Identity 'ithicos.local/Corporate/Bharat Suneja' -Alias ↵
'Bharat.Suneja' -Database 'MBX-002' -ManagedFolderMailboxPolicy 'Standard ↵
User Managed Folder Policy' -ActiveSyncMailboxPolicy 'Default'
```

The Exchange Management Console created this command and used object names to identify the user and the home mailbox database in explicit terms. However, we want to show you another example and simplify it just a bit. In this case, you have another existing user whose account is Luke.Husky and he is in the ITHICOS Active Directory domain. We will simplify this command as much as possible and here is the result:

```
Enable-Mailbox ithicos\luke.husky -Alias:Luke.Husky -Database:MBX-002
```

Name	Alias	ServerName	ProhibitSendQuota
Luke Husky	Luke.Husky	hnlmbx01	unlimited

This command works because there is only a single mailbox database in the entire organization called MBX-002. If you have not established a naming standard for databases so that each database name is not only readable but also unique, you need do so. Unique database names are required for Exchange Server 2010. When considering database names, we recommend against including the server name since a database may move from one server to another if you are using database availability groups.

ASSIGNING PERMISSIONS TO A MAILBOX USING THE EMS

On some occasions, you may need to assign a user the permission necessary to access another user's mailbox. This was easy enough to do in Exchange 2000/2003 using Active Directory Users and Computers. With Exchange 2010, you can perform the same task using the Manage Full Access Permission task in the Actions pane of the Exchange Management Console. The tasks available for a selected mailbox are shown in Figure 17.12; this includes the Manage Send As Permission and the Manage Full Access Permission tasks.

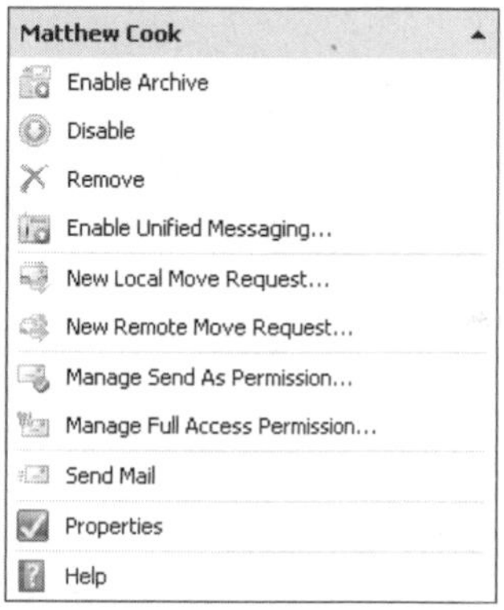

FIGURE 17.12
Mailbox management
tasks available

Matthew Cook
- Enable Archive
- Disable
- Remove
- Enable Unified Messaging...
- New Local Move Request...
- New Remote Move Request...
- Manage Send As Permission...
- Manage Full Access Permission...
- Send Mail
- Properties
- Help

In Exchange 2010, there are two types of mailbox permissions:

◆ Full Access permission lets another user open the mailbox and view any message or folder within it.

◆ Send As permission lets another user send a message that appears to be coming from the user whose mailbox it is.

FULL ACCESS VS. SEND AS PERMISSION

Giving a user full access to another user's mailbox will allow the user to open the other user's mailbox and view any folder or message within the user's mailbox. However, if the user needs to be able to send a message as another user, full mailbox permission is not sufficient. Third-party products such as the Research in Motion BlackBerry Enterprise Server's (BES) service account may require Receive As permissions to the mailboxes that it manages. And the BES service account must have Send As permissions on the Active Directory object. Receive As mailbox permissions can be added through the EMC or using the Add-MailboxPermission cmdlet. Send As permissions can be added through the EMC or using the Add-ADPermission cmdlet.

If you have been managing Exchange Server organizations for some time, you may remember a time when giving users full mailbox rights would allow them to see all the messages and folders as well as send messages that would originate from that mailbox's address. However, that changed with an Exchange Server 2003 post–Service Pack 2 hotfix. Now Send As permissions must be assigned separately.

ASSIGNING FULL ACCESS PERMISSION

To assign Full Access permissions, simply select the mailbox to which you want to add more permissions and click the Manage Full Access Permission task. This launches the Manage Full Access Permission wizard shown in Figure 17.13. In this example, we are adding users Clayton.Kamiya and Chris.Eanes to the list of users who have full access for this mailbox.

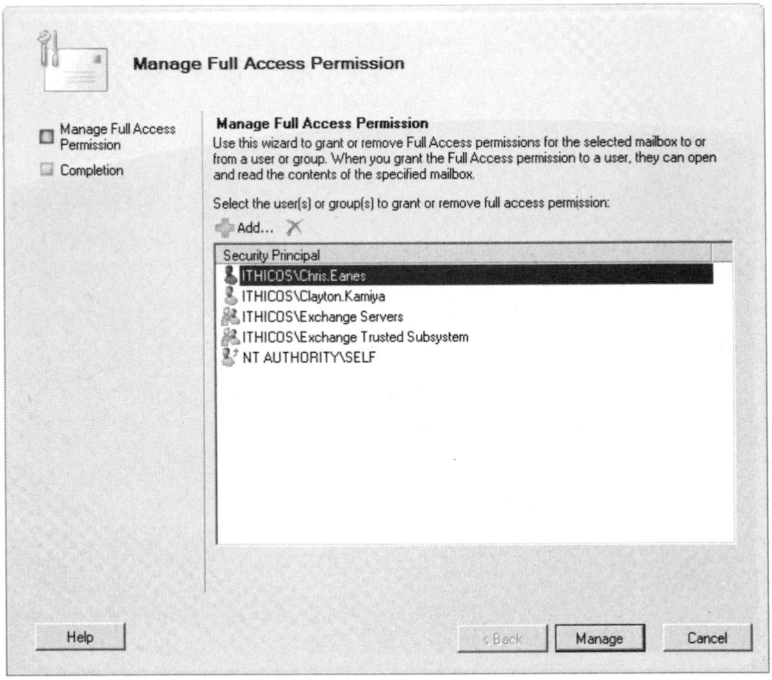

FIGURE 17.13
Adding full mailbox access permissions

This could also be done using the EMS cmdlet Add-MailboxPermission. In this example, we are assigning user Clayton.Kamiya permissions to access Betty McBee's mailbox:

```
Add-MailboxPermission Betty.McBee -User volcanosurfb\Clayton.Kamiya ⏎
-AccessRights FullAccess
```

If you want to assign an administrator permissions to access all mailboxes (such as to import or export mailbox content), you can use the Role-Based Access Control (RBAC) management role called Mailbox Import Export. For example, if we want to assign user Clayton.Kamiya the role that would allow him to open all mailboxes, we could use this command:

```
New-ManagementRoleAssignment -Role "Mailbox Import Export" ⏎
-User Clayton.Kamiya
```

ASSIGNING SEND AS PERMISSION

To assign Send As permissions, you need to run the Manage Send As Permission task in the Actions pane. Figure 17.14 shows the Manage Send As Permission wizard; here we are assigning user Peter.ODowd the Send As permissions to Betty's user account.

FIGURE 17.14
Assigning Send As permissions for a user

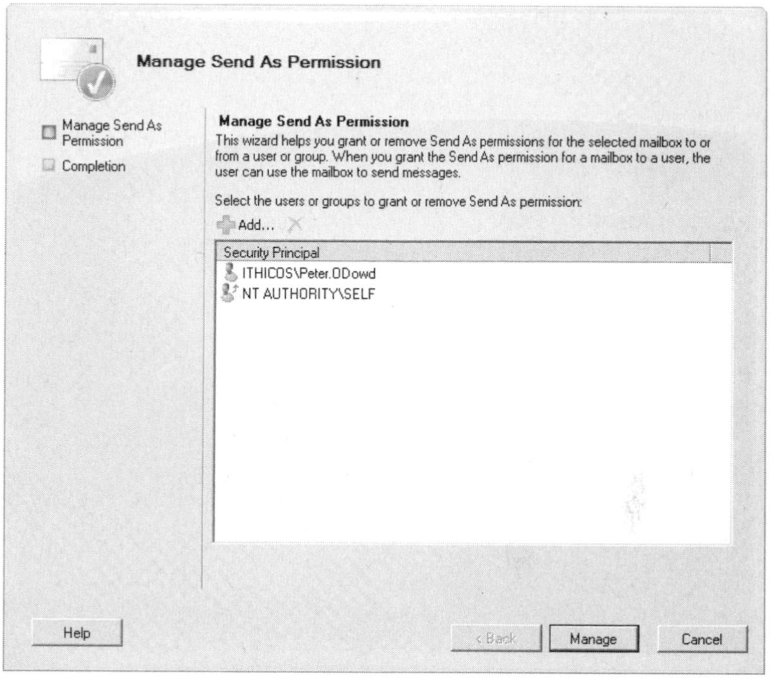

You can perform the same task using the EMS; here is an example of giving user volcanosurfb\Peter.ODowd Send As permissions to Betty McBee's user account:

```
Add-ADPermission 'CN=Betty McBee,OU=VolcanoSurfboards, ↵
DC=volcanosurfboards,DC=com' -User 'VOLCANOSURFB\Peter.ODowd' ↵
-ExtendedRights'Send-as'
```

You can also remove the permissions you have assigned via the EMS with the following command:

```
Remove-ADPermission 'CN=Betty McBee,OU=VolcanoSurfboards, ↵
DC=volcanosurfboards,DC=com' -User 'VOLCANOSURFB\PeterODowd' ↵
-InheritanceType 'All' -ExtendedRights 'send-as' -ChildObjectTypes $null ↵
-InheritedObjectType $null -Properties $null
```

Creating a New User and Assigning a Mailbox Using the EMC

Previously, you saw that the EMC's New Mailbox wizard would allow you to create a new user account at the same time you enable the mailbox. It is true that the new EMC has some rudimentary user creation and management tasks. On the User Type page of the New Mailbox wizard, if you select the New User radio button and click Next, you are prompted for the user account information on the User Information screen (shown in Figure 17.15).

On the User Information screen, you provide some basic account information such as the first name, middle initials, last name, UPN name, pre–Windows 2000 account name, and the password. You must also specify the organizational unit (OU) in which the user account will be created, and you must have the Active Directory permissions necessary to create user accounts in that OU.

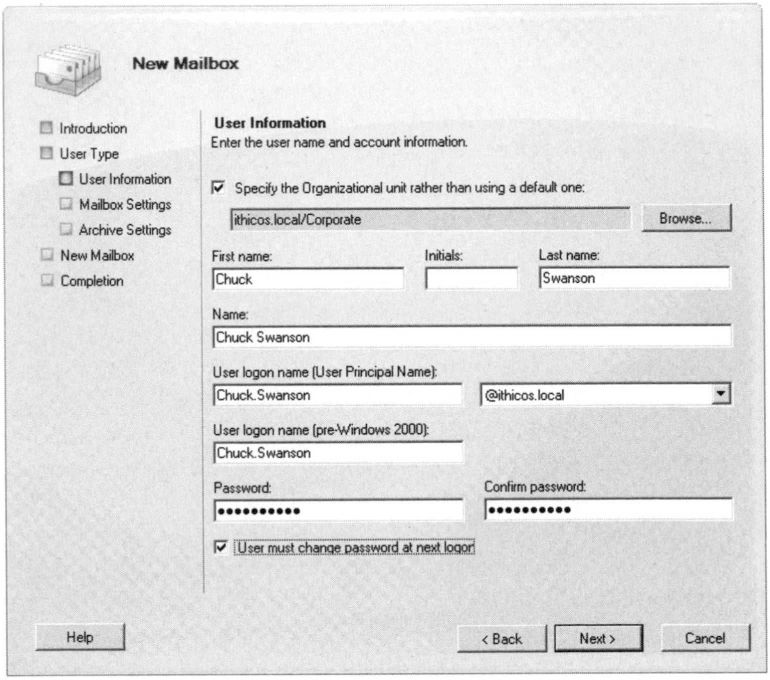

FIGURE 17.15

Creating a user account from the Exchange Management Console

The rest of the wizard is exactly the same as if you were enabling a mailbox for an existing user. On the Completion page, though, you will notice some small differences in the cmdlet and the cmdlet's parameters. To create a user named Chuck.Swanson in the Corporate OU, assign his mailbox to the MBX-003 mailbox database, and assign him an archive mailbox, here is the command that the EMC performed:

```
New-Mailbox -Name 'Chuck Swanson' -Alias 'Chuck.Swanson' ↵
-OrganizationalUnit 'ithicos.local/Corporate' -UserPrincipalName ↵
'Chuck.Swanson@ithicos.local' -SamAccountName 'Chuck.Swanson' -FirstName ↵
'Chuck' -Initials '' -LastName 'Swanson' -Password ↵
'System.Security.SecureString' -ResetPasswordOnNextLogon $true -Database ↵
'MBX-003' -Archive
```

Because the MBX-003 mailbox database is unique for the Exchange organization, no additional identifying information is necessary.

When you include the -Password:'System.Security.SecureString' option, you are prompted to enter the password for the user; this helps prevent the password from being compromised. Notice that the cmdlet is not Enable-Mailbox as it was in the earlier section "Assigning a Mailbox to a User from the EMS." The Enable-Mailbox cmdlet is used to assign a mailbox to an existing user account. The cmdlet used here is New-Mailbox; this cmdlet creates the user account as well as enables the mailbox. Notice there is an -OrganizationalUnit parameter that allows you to specify the domain and the OU name in canonical name format such as ithicos.local/Corporate.

The New-Mailbox cmdlet also has parameters for setting the password, pre–Windows 2000 account name, and UPN.

Managing User and Mailbox Properties

Many of the user account properties that can be managed through the Active Directory Users and Computers console can now also be managed through the EMC or the EMS. Naturally, using the EMC is a little easier than using the command line, but the EMS is much more flexible and powerful once you learn how to use it. And with the tips feature of the EMS that allows you to easily see the EMS cmdlet and syntax necessary to update an object, learning the EMS is even easier.

Using the EMC to Manage User and Mailbox Properties

Let's start with managing user and mailbox properties using the EMC. We want to take a look at a few of the things that you can do and some of the user property pages. We'll begin by taking a look at the mailbox's General properties page, shown in Figure 17.16. The General page has some interesting information on it, including the user ID of the last person to access the mailbox, the mailbox size, and the mailbox database name.

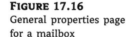

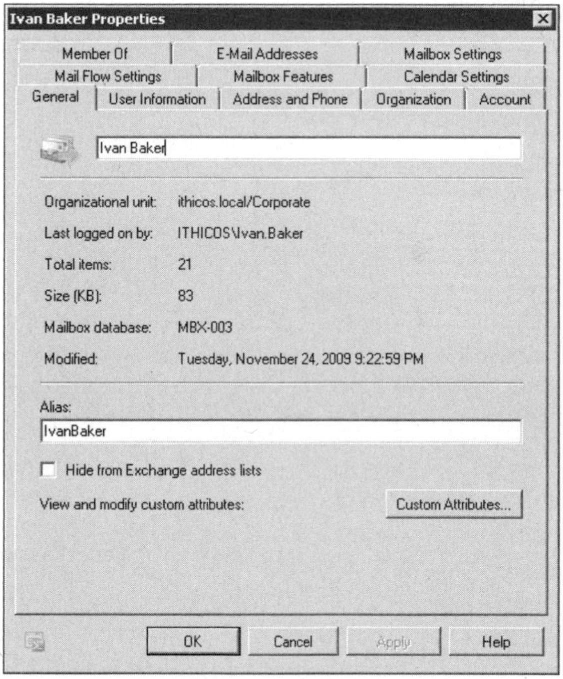

FIGURE 17.16
General properties page for a mailbox

Ivan Baker Properties

Member Of	E-Mail Addresses	Mailbox Settings
Mail Flow Settings	Mailbox Features	Calendar Settings
General	User Information	Address and Phone	Organization	Account

Ivan Baker

Organizational unit: ithicos.local/Corporate
Last logged on by: ITHICOS\Ivan.Baker
Total items: 21
Size (KB): 83
Mailbox database: MBX-003
Modified: Tuesday, November 24, 2009 9:22:59 PM

Alias:
IvanBaker

☐ Hide from Exchange address lists

View and modify custom attributes: [Custom Attributes...]

[OK] [Cancel] [Apply] [Help]

On the General page you'll notice the Hide From Exchange Address Lists check box. This setting prevents the mailbox from appearing in address lists such as the GAL. The General page also includes a Custom Attributes button that allows you to access all 15 custom attributes (extension attributes).

The field that is not clearly labeled is the Display Name field; this is the field that is next to the mailbox icon in the upper-left corner of the General page. The display name is what users see in the GAL.

The next page of interest is E-Mail Addresses, shown in Figure 17.17. Here you can manage the SMTP addresses (and other address types) that are assigned to this particular mailbox. Notice in Figure 17.17 that this user has multiple SMTP addresses that can be used to send messages to this mailbox.

FIGURE 17.17
E-Mail Address properties of a mailbox

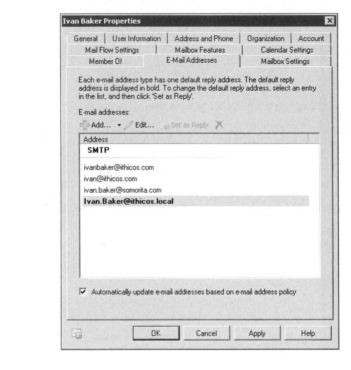

Regardless of how many email addresses are assigned to this mailbox, when an Exchange user clicks the reply button to reply to a message sent to any of these addresses, the Set As Reply address is the one that is always used as the Reply To address. In Figure 17.17, this is the address shown in bold. This can be changed by selecting another address and clicking the Set As Reply button.

If an email address policy that affects this mailbox is updated with new email address generation rules and then reapplied, additional email addresses will be created. If a policy that affects the default SMTP address is changed, the email address policy can change a user's primary email address. However, the user will retain the previous SMTP addresses.

If you clear the Automatically Update E-mail Addresses Based On E-mail Address Policy check box, any changes to the email address policy that affects this mailbox will not be made.

If you try to change the Reply To email address of an address that is based on an email address policy by either selecting a different Reply To address or editing the existing email address, you must first clear the Automatically Update E-mail Addresses Based On E-mail Address Policy check box. Otherwise, the Set As Reply button is not available. You will receive an error if you try to update the Reply To address, as shown in Figure 17.18.

Notice in Figure 17.17 that user Ivan Baker has multiple email addresses, including addresses from two different domains. He has an ivan.baker@ithicos.local and an ivan.baker@somorita.com address. All inbound email for both email addresses will be directed to his mailbox; this is a useful feature for organizations that have more than one domain; however, any email to which he replies will have the `Ivan.Baker@ithicos.local` address. Exchange does not allow a user to select which address will be used in the From field of a message.

FIGURE 17.18
Changes to the Reply To address may not be allowed.

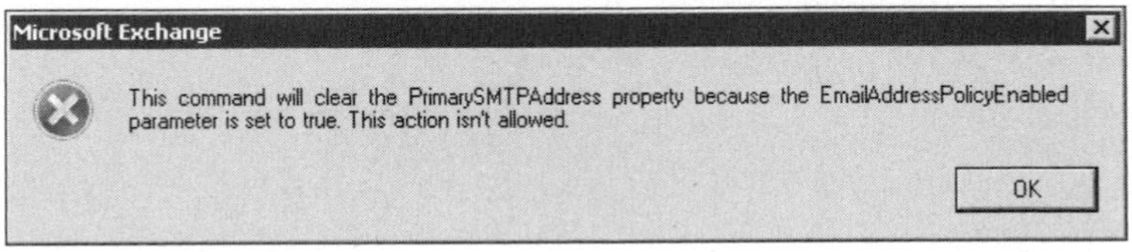

On the Mailbox Settings property page, there are four configuration items that are of interest depending on your environment and the features of Exchange Server that you are using. The first of these is Messaging Records Management, shown in Figure 17.19. Figure 17.19 shows that the user has been assigned a messaging records management (MRM) policy called Standard User Managed Folder Policy.

FIGURE 17.19
MRM features for a mailbox

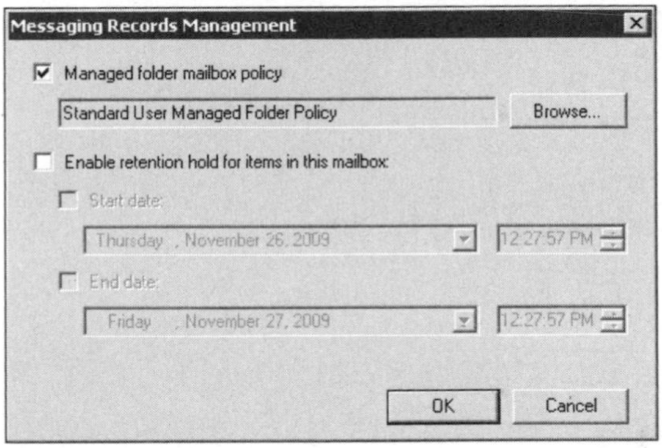

On the Messaging Records Management properties page for each user you'll find an option to turn off the MRM feature for some period of time. This is called enabling a retention hold, and can be useful for times such as when the user has an extended period of absence. Enabling this option will prevent action from being taken on items that might ordinarily be deleted, archived, expired, or moved.

MRM AND CLIENT ACCESS LICENSES

If you are using MRM only for features equivalent to the Exchange 2000/2003 mailbox management features such as purging the Deleted Items folder or deleting messages older than a certain number of days, standard Exchange client access licenses (CALs) can be used. However, if you use MRM to perform tasks such as management of custom folders, you need an Exchange enterprise client access license (an eCAL) for users who use those features. ECALs are required for each mailbox that uses the personal archive mailbox, MRM, transport journaling, advanced features of ActiveSync, and Unified Messaging features.

The next Mailbox Settings property set is the Federated Sharing feature; this is, of course, only useful if you have configured the federated sharing features of Exchange 2010 to share calendars and contacts across multiple Exchange 2010 organizations. Figure 17.20 shows the Federated Sharing properties for the user in question and the sharing policy that has been applied.

FIGURE 17.20
Assigning a federated sharing policy

All users are automatically assigned the default sharing policy, which enables users in a remote organization to view the free and busy information for your users. Keep in mind, though, that the remote organization must be first configured to allow for sharing.

The next Mailbox Settings property set is for storage quotas. The Storage Quotas dialog is shown in Figure 17.21. Storage quotas allow you to override mailbox database storage quotas for individual users. This is helpful for VIPs who need more mailbox storage than a typical user or for users who should have lower mailbox quotas.

FIGURE 17.21
Applying individual storage quotas

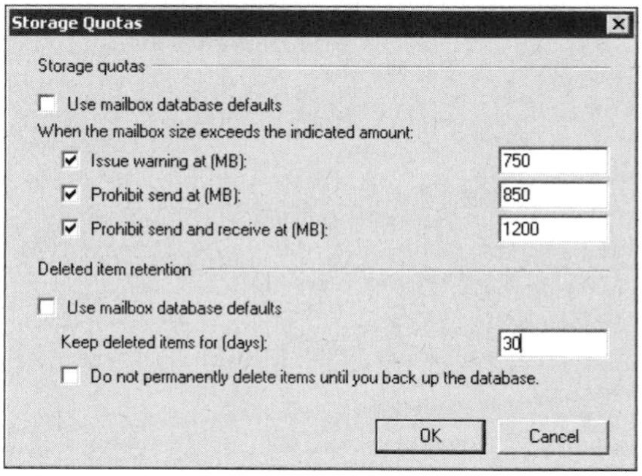

On the bottom of the Storage Quotas dialog is the individual deleted item retention times. By default, each Exchange mailbox database will keep a user's data that has been emptied from the Deleted Items folder or "hard deleted" for 14 days. Although this does somewhat increase the size of the mailbox database, it also greatly helps reduce the necessity of restoring single items or folders that a user may have accidentally deleted. If you have a user who is frequently coming back to you after deleting something for more than two weeks past and "has to have it restored right away," you could increase their individual deleted item retention time.

The final Mailbox Setting property set that you should note are the Archive Quota settings, shown in Figure 17.22. These settings allow you to specify an archive size at which a warning message will be generated; by default, the archive quota is not configured.

Note that the Archive Quota properties will only be available if the user has been configured with an archive mailbox. Each mailbox that has Exchange 2010 archiving configured for it will require an Exchange 2010 eCAL.

The Mail Flow Settings properties page for the mailbox shows mailbox settings that most experienced Exchange administrators will already be familiar with. They are now just located in slightly different places. The properties found on the Mail Flow Settings properties page are grouped into Delivery Options, Message Size Restrictions, and Message Delivery Restrictions sections. You merely need to highlight one of them and click the Properties button to see them.

FIGURE 17.22
Applying an archive size
limit warning

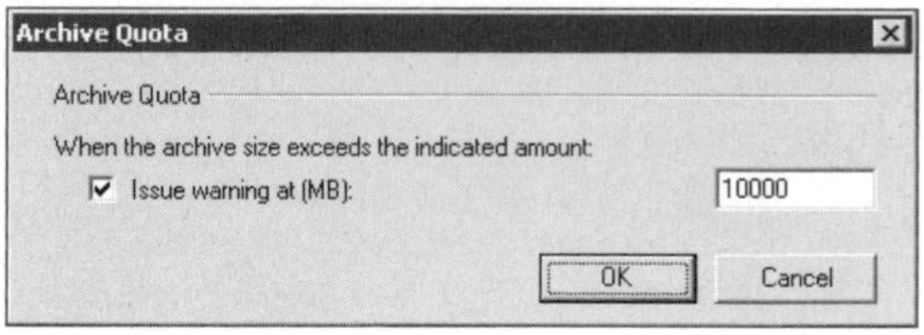

The Delivery Options properties (shown in Figure 17.23) include a couple of important options. The first is the Send On Behalf permission; this allows anyone who has been assigned this permission to send a message on behalf of this user. For example, in Figure 17.23, users Grace Tanaka and John Rodriguez can now send a message on behalf of this mailbox.

For example, if John Rodriguez sends a message on behalf of this mailbox, when the message arrives, it will say it is from John Rodriguez on behalf of the specified mailbox. This implies, at least, a tacit authorization on the part of the mailbox owner that the message should have been sent by John Rodriguez. This is a bit different than the Send As permission, which does not indicate that the message was sent on behalf of a user.

FIGURE 17.23
A mailbox's
delivery options

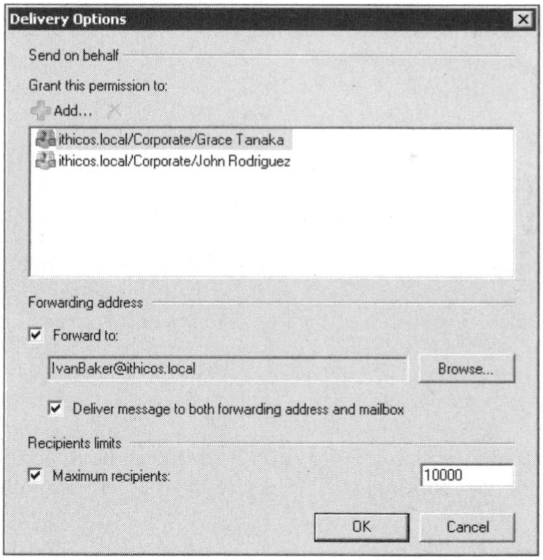

Also on the Delivery Options page is the option to deliver messages to an alternate recipient (known as forwarding address). The recipient that you specify must be a mailbox in your organization or a mail-enabled contact that you find within your GAL. If you select a mail-enabled contact that you have created in your global address list, this would let you forward all of this user's mail to an external mail system. That can be useful if someone has left the organization and wants to keep getting his or her mail. It could also be a disaster if that person has left your organization and gone to work for a competitor, so use this feature with caution.

If the Deliver Message To Both Forwarding Address And Mailbox check box is enabled, the message is delivered to both places. This is useful when "the boss" wants her assistant to receive all her mail but she wants to see the mail as well.

Finally, the bottom part of the Delivery Options page allows you to specify the maximum number of recipients to which this person can send a message. The global default is 5,000, but some organizations want to reduce this figure and allow only the VIPs or authorized users such as Human Resources users to send messages to large numbers of users.

The Message Size Restrictions options (shown in Figure 17.24) allow you to specify the maximum size of messages the user can send or receive. If they are not specified, the user is limited by the global defaults or the connector defaults.

FIGURE 17.24

Overriding the maximum inbound and outbound message sizes a user can send

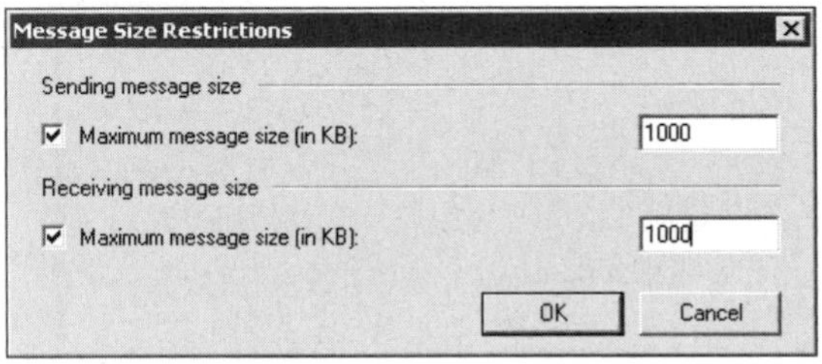

The final selection of settings found on the Mail Flow Settings properties page is Message Delivery Restrictions. With these options, you can restrict who is allowed to send mail to this particular mailbox. For example, if this is a VIP, you might want to restrict who can send to this mailbox to only a subset of users within the organization. Conversely, you could configure a mailbox to reject mail from a specific set of users. Figure 17.25 shows the Message Delivery Restrictions settings for a VIP's mailbox; the VIP wants to receive mail only from the other members of the #Executives group, the $All Corporate Users group, and user Matthew Badeau.

If you select the Require That All Senders Are Authenticated check box, this will cut down on the spam that mailbox receives, but it also means that no anonymous Internet mail will be received. By default, all mail received from the Internet is received anonymously.

If you have spent a lot of time troubleshooting nondelivery reports and error messages that your users have received in the past, you will be happy to hear that the Exchange team has worked hard to make the error messages more descriptive and helpful. When users send a message to someone they are not allowed to send to, they receive a nondelivery report (NDR) message in return. Figure 17.26 shows an example of an NDR message that a user received when they tried to send to someone to which they were not authorized to send.

The next mailbox properties page of interest to email administrators is Mailbox Features (shown in Figure 17.27). Here you can enable or disable additional features of the mailbox, such as Outlook Web App, Exchange ActiveSync, Unified Messaging, MAPI access, POP3, IMAP4, and Archive.

Some of these features can only be enabled or disabled, whereas others (such as the POP3 and IMAP4 features) have additional properties:

◆ Outlook Web App allows you to specify an Outlook Web App mailbox policy.

◆ The Exchange ActiveSync selection has a Properties option that allows you to configure the Exchange ActiveSync policy for this user.

◆ You can now disable MAPI clients.

- The Unified Messaging option allows you to specify the user's Unified Messaging properties if you have Unified Messaging server roles installed.

- The Archive option allows you to change the display name of the archive mailbox.

FIGURE 17.25
Restricting who can send mail to a mailbox

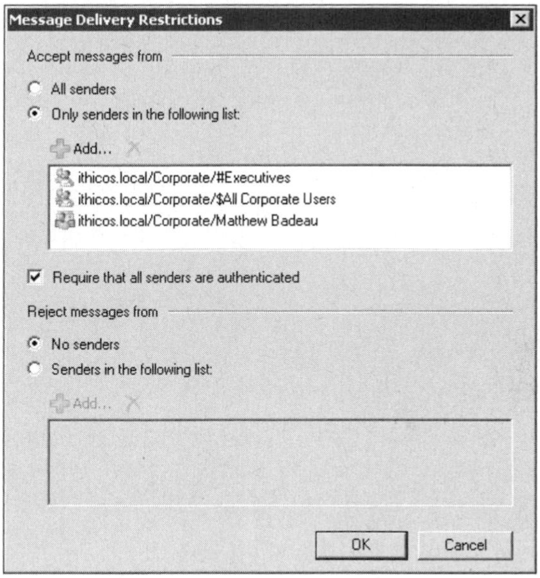

FIGURE 17.26
NDR message sent when sender is not authorized to send to the intended recipient

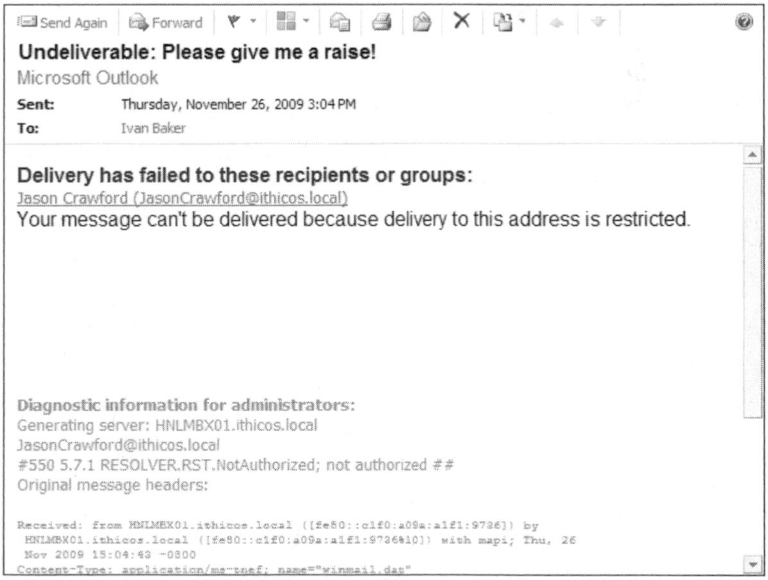

FIGURE 17.27
Mailbox Features
properties page

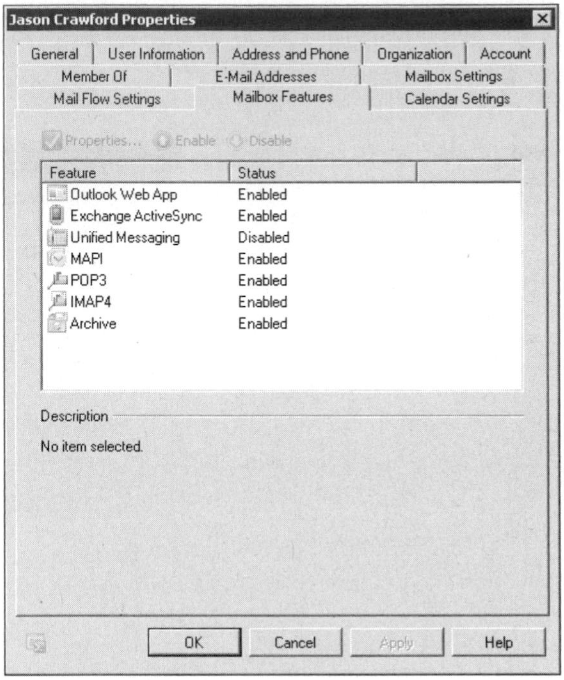

FIGURE 17.28
Configuring automated
calendar processing

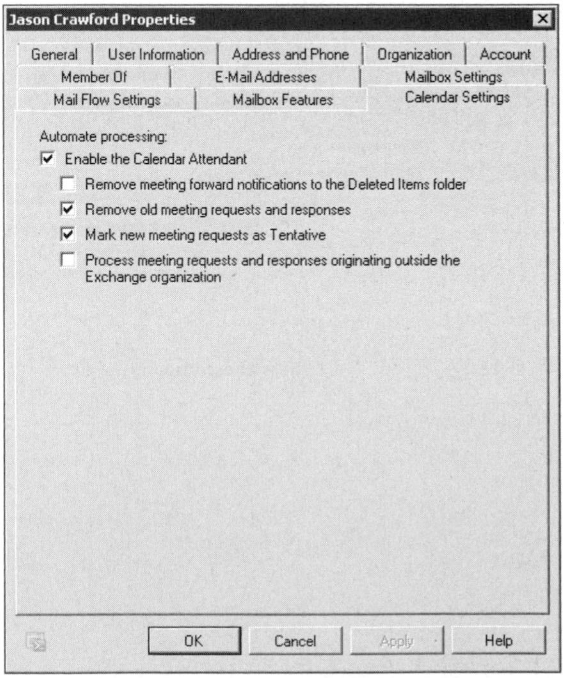

The final mailbox properties page that is of interest to Exchange administrators is Calendar Settings. The default calendar settings for an Exchange 2010 mailbox are shown in Figure 17.28. Here you can configure how the server-based calendar attendant handles meeting notifications, meeting requests, meeting responses, and external requests.

USING THE EMS TO MANAGE USER PROPERTIES

You can also manage mailbox and user properties from the EMS. For doing any type of mailbox administration "in bulk," you will definitely want to learn how to use the EMS. There are three cmdlets that you should know about in order to manage most of the properties: the `Set-User`, `Set-Mailbox`, and `Set-CasMailbox` cmdlets.

Let's start with the `Set-User` cmdlet; this cmdlet manages user account properties that are unrelated to Exchange Server. Say that we want to update user Stan.Reimer's mobile phone number. We would type this:

```
Set-User Stan.Reimer -MobilePhone "(808) 555-1234"
```

The `Set-User` cmdlet has quite a few useful parameters. Table 17.3 lists many of these options. You can retrieve them from within the EMS by typing `Set-User -?` or `Help Set-User`.

TABLE 17.3:   Some Set-User Cmdlet Parameters

PARAMETER	FUNCTION
PostalCode	Sets the zip or postal code.
Manager	Sets the name of the user's manager; the input value must be a distinguished name in canonical name format, such as fourthcoffee.com/Corporate/Ben Craig.
DisplayName	Updates the user's display name, which appears in the GAL.
MobilePhone	Sets the mobile/cell phone number.
City	Sets the city or locality name.
FirstName	Specifies the given or first name.
LastName	Specifies the surname or last name.
Company	Sets the company name.
Department	Sets the department name.
Fax	Specifies the facsimile number.
HomePhone	Sets the home phone number.
Phone	Sets the business phone number.
StateOrProvince	Sets the state or province.
StreetAddress	Sets the street address.
Title	Sets the title or job function.

You can retrieve the list of properties for Set-User by using the Get-User cmdlet, specifying a username, and then piping the output to the Format-List cmdlet. Piping the output of a Get- cmdlet to Format-List is a great way to enumerate of the properties of an object and to also learn the property names. Here is an example of some of the properties that are returned; we removed some properties to save space.

```
Get-User Matthew.Cook | FL

IsSecurityPrincipal       : True
SamAccountName            : Matthew.Cook
SidHistory                : {}
UserPrincipalName         : Matthew.Cook@ithicos.local
ResetPasswordOnNextLogon  : False
CertificateSubject        : {}
RemotePowerShellEnabled   : True
NetID                     :
OrganizationalUnit        : ithicos.local/Corporate
AssistantName             :
City                      : Honolulu
Company                   : Somorita Surfboards
CountryOrRegion           :
Department                : Surfboard Design
DirectReports             : {}
DisplayName               : Matthew Cook
Fax                       : (808) 555-6657
FirstName                 : Matthew
HomePhone                 :
Initials                  :
LastName                  : Cook
Manager                   :
MobilePhone               : (808) 555-7777
Notes                     :
Office                    : Honolulu Surfboard Design
OtherFax                  : {}
OtherHomePhone            : {}
OtherTelephone            : {}
Pager                     : (808) 555-5545
Phone                     : (808) 555-1234
PhoneticDisplayName       :
PostalCode                : 96816
PostOfficeBox             : {}
RecipientType             : UserMailbox
RecipientTypeDetails      : UserMailbox
SimpleDisplayName         : Matt Cook (Honolulu)
StateOrProvince           : Hawaii
StreetAddress             : 550 Kalakaua Avenue, Suite 201
Title                     : Senior Systems Engineer
UMDialPlan                :
UMDtmfMap                 : {emailAddress:62884392665,
lastNameFirstName:26656288439, firstNameLastName:62884392665}
```

```
AllowUMCallsFromNonUsers : SearchEnabled
WebPage                   :
TelephoneAssistant        :
WindowsEmailAddress       : MatthewCook@ithicos.local
UMCallingLineIds          : {}
IsValid                   : True
ExchangeVersion           : 0.10 (14.0.100.0)
Name                      : Matthew Cook
DistinguishedName         : CN=Matthew Cook,OU=Corporate,
DC=ithicos,DC=local
OriginatingServer         : HNLMBX01.ithicos.local
```

Not only does the Get-User cmdlet allow you to view this information about a user account, but it also allows you to see all the property names. For example, if you did not know what the property name was for the State, you could look in the output listing and see that it is -StateOrProvince. You could then change the user's state by typing the following EMS command:

```
Set-User vlad.mazek -StateOrProvince "Florida"
```

You can pipe the output of one cmdlet together with another one in order to perform bulk administration. Let's say that we want to set the Office name of all users who are in Honolulu. We can use a combination of Get-User and Set-User to accomplish this:

```
Get-User | Where-Object {$_.city -eq "Honolulu"} | ↵
Set-User -Office "Main Office"
```

In this example, we piped the output of the Get-User cmdlet to a local filter (using the Where-Object cmdlet). This provided us with a subset of only the users whose city property is equal to Honolulu; the output of that was then piped to the Set-User cmdlet and the office property was updated. That was not too difficult once you saw it the first time, was it?

Using the EMS to Manage Mailbox Properties

The Set-User and the Get-User cmdlets helped you with non-Exchange-specific properties of a user account, but the Get-Mailbox and the Set-Mailbox cmdlets will help you view and set the properties of a mailbox-enabled user account. In fact, you have already seen these cmdlets earlier in this book when we talked about setting mailbox storage limits. Let's take a quick look at some ways you can use these cmdlets. For example, if you want to change the user Cheyne.Manalo's rules quota, you would type this:

```
Set-Mailbox cheyne.manalo -RulesQuota:128KB
```

You can set a lot of properties through the EMS and the Set-Mailbox cmdlet. A few of the more useful ones are found in Table 17.4.

Table 17.4 shows just a few of the parameters that can be used by the Set-Mailbox cmdlet or that can be viewed using the Get-Mailbox cmdlet. If you want to look up these parameters, from the EMS type **Set-Mailbox -?,** or type **Help Set-Mailbox.** As we showed you previously with Get-User, you can pipe the output for a mailbox to the Format-List (or FL) cmdlet and see all the properties for that mailbox. Following Table 17.4, you will see some examples of some of the properties; we did trim out a few of the properties to save space. You may notice that there are some properties that you will find by issuing the Get-User cmdlet also. That is expected; remember many of these properties for both Get-User and Get-Mailbox are stored as properties on the same Active Directory user object.

TABLE 17.4:   Some Set-Mailbox Properties

PARAMETER	FUNCTION
RulesQuota	Specifies the maximum amount of rules a user can have in a folder. Note that having more than 32 KB of rules per folder requires the Outlook 2007 client.
SCLDeleteThreshold	Specifies the SCL (spam confidence level) value at and above which messages flagged as spam should be deleted.
SCLDeleteEnabled	Specifies if messages above the value of the SCLDeleteThreshold property should be deleted. There are additional SCL threshold options that are not listed in this table.
RecipientLimits	Specifies the maximum number of recipients per message that a user can send to.
EmailAddressPolicyEnabled	Specifies whether or not this mailbox should have its email addresses updated by email address policies.
MaxSendSize	Specifies the maximum size for messages that can be sent by this mailbox.
MaxReceiveSize	Specifies the maximum size for messages that can be received into this mailbox.
ForwardingAddress	Specifies an address to which mail sent to this mailbox will be forwarded. The value must be in canonical name format, such as volcanosurfboards.com/Corporate/Mike Brown.
HiddenFromAddressListsEnabled	If set to True, this mailbox will not appear in any of the Exchange address lists. The default is False.
CustomAttribute1	Specifies the value for Custom Attribute 1 (Extension Attribute 1). Fifteen custom attributes can be set through the EMS; simply change 1 to 2, 3, and so on.
ProhibitSendQuota	Specifies the mailbox size above which the user will not be able to send any new messages.
ProhibitSendReceiveQuota	Specifies the mailbox size above which the mailbox will reject new mail and the user will not be able to send any messages.
IssueWarningQuota	Specifies the mailbox size above which users will receive a warning message indicating they are over their mailbox quota.
AntispamBypassEnabled	If set to True, this specifies that this mailbox should not have its mail filtered by the Exchange 2007 content filtering component on the Edge Transport or Hub Transport server. The default is False.
UseDatabaseQuotaDefaults	If set to False, the mailbox uses the storage quotas set on the mailbox. If set to True (the default), the mailbox uses the mailbox storage quotas that are defined for the mailbox database on which the mailbox is located.

```
Get-Mailbox matthew.cook | Format-List

Database                             : MBX-003
DeletedItemFlags                     : DatabaseDefault
UseDatabaseRetentionDefaults         : True
RetainDeletedItemsUntilBackup        : False
DeliverToMailboxAndForward           : False
LitigationHoldEnabled                : False
SingleItemRecoveryEnabled            : False
RetentionHoldEnabled                 : False
EndDateForRetentionHold              :
StartDateForRetentionHold            :
RetentionComment                     :
RetentionUrl                         :
ManagedFolderMailboxPolicy           :
RetentionPolicy                      :
CalendarRepairDisabled               : False
ExchangeUserAccountControl           : None
MessageTrackingReadStatusEnabled     : True
ExternalOofOptions                   : External
ForwardingAddress                    :
RetainDeletedItemsFor                : 14.00:00:00
IsMailboxEnabled                     : True
OfflineAddressBook                   :
ProhibitSendQuota                    : unlimited
ProhibitSendReceiveQuota             : unlimited
RecoverableItemsQuota                : unlimited
RecoverableItemsWarningQuota         : unlimited
DowngradeHighPriorityMessagesEnabled : False
ProtocolSettings                     : {}
RecipientLimits                      : unlimited
IsResource                           : False
IsLinked                             : False
IsShared                             : False
ResourceCapacity                     :
ResourceCustom                       : {}
ResourceType                         :
SamAccountName                       : Matthew.Cook
SCLDeleteThreshold                   :
SCLDeleteEnabled                     :
SCLRejectThreshold                   :
SCLRejectEnabled                     :
SCLQuarantineThreshold               :
SCLQuarantineEnabled                 :
SCLJunkThreshold                     :
SCLJunkEnabled                       :
AntispamBypassEnabled                : False
ServerName                           : hnlmbx01
```

```
UseDatabaseQuotaDefaults              : True
IssueWarningQuota                     : unlimited
RulesQuota                            : 64 KB (65,536 bytes)
Office                                :
UserPrincipalName                     : Matthew.Cook@ithicos.local
UMEnabled                             : False
MaxSafeSenders                        :
MaxBlockedSenders                     :
RssAggregationEnabled                 : True
Pop3AggregationEnabled                : True
WindowsLiveID                         :
ThrottlingPolicy                      :
RoleAssignmentPolicy                  : Default Role Assignment Policy
SharingPolicy                         : Default Sharing Policy
RemoteAccountPolicy                   :
MailboxPlan                           :
ArchiveGuid                           : 00000000-0000-0000-0000-
000000000000
ArchiveName                           : {}
ArchiveQuota                          : unlimited
ArchiveWarningQuota                   : unlimited
QueryBaseDNRestrictionEnabled         : False
MailboxMoveTargetMDB                  :
MailboxMoveSourceMDB                  :
MailboxMoveFlags                      : None
MailboxMoveRemoteHostName             :
MailboxMoveBatchName                  :
MailboxMoveStatus                     : None
IsPersonToPersonTextMessagingEnabled  : False
IsMachineToPersonTextMessagingEnabled : False
UserSMimeCertificate                  : {}
UserCertificate                       : {}
CalendarVersionStoreDisabled          : False
Extensions                            : {}
HasPicture                            : False
HasSpokenName                         : False
AcceptMessagesOnlyFrom                : {}
AcceptMessagesOnlyFromDLMembers       : {}
AcceptMessagesOnlyFromSendersOrMembers : {}
AddressListMembership                 : {\Mailboxes(VLV),
\All Mailboxes(VLV),\All Recipients(VLV), \Default Global
Address List, \All Users}
Alias                                 : MatthewCook
ArbitrationMailbox                    :
BypassModerationFromSendersOrMembers  : {}
OrganizationalUnit                    : ithicos.local/Corporate
CustomAttribute1                      :
CustomAttribute2                      :
```

```
DisplayName                            : Matthew Cook
EmailAddresses                         : {SMTP:MatthewCook@ithicos.local}
GrantSendOnBehalfTo                    : {}
HiddenFromAddressListsEnabled          : False
LegacyExchangeDN                       : /o=Ithicos Solutions LLC
/ou=Exchange Administrative Group (FYDIBOHF23SPDLT)/cn=Recipients
/cn=Matthew Cook
MaxSendSize                            : unlimited
MaxReceiveSize                         : unlimited
ModeratedBy                            : {}
ModerationEnabled                      : False
PoliciesExcluded                       : {}
EmailAddressPolicyEnabled              : True
PrimarySmtpAddress                     : MatthewCook@ithicos.local
RecipientType                          : UserMailbox
RecipientTypeDetails                   : UserMailbox
RejectMessagesFrom                     : {}
RejectMessagesFromDLMembers            : {}
RejectMessagesFromSendersOrMembers     : {}
RequireSenderAuthenticationEnabled     : False
SimpleDisplayName                      :
SendModerationNotifications            : Always
UMDtmfMap                              : {emailAddress:62884392665,
  lastNameFirstName:26656288439, firstNameLastName:62884392665}
WindowsEmailAddress                    : MatthewCook@ithicos.local
MailTip                                :
MailTipTranslations                    : {}
ExchangeVersion                        : 0.10 (14.0.100.0)
Name                                   : Matthew Cook
DistinguishedName                      : CN=Matthew Cook,OU=Corporate,DC=ithicos,
DC=local
```

When you look at these properties, please keep in mind that not all properties can be modified, even using the EMS. Many of these properties are system properties and are either created or managed by the system.

Properties specific to the mailbox using a Client Access server are viewed and set using the Get-CasMailbox and Set-CasMailbox cmdlets. These include properties related to ActiveSync, Outlook Web App, POP, IMAP, and MAPI. Here are some of the attributes that can be set using the Set-CasMailbox cmdlet:

```
Get-CASMailbox Matthew.Cook | Format-List

EmailAddresses                 : {SMTP:MatthewCook@ithicos.local}
LegacyExchangeDN               : /o=Ithicos Solutions LLC/ou=Exchange
Administrative Group (FYDIBOHF23SPDLT)/cn=Recipients/cn=Matthew Cook
LinkedMasterAccount            :
PrimarySmtpAddress             : MatthewCook@ithicos.local
SamAccountName                 : Matthew.Cook
ServerLegacyDN                 : /o=Ithicos Solutions LLC/ou=Exchange
```

```
Administrative Group (FYDIBOHF23SPDLT)/cn=Configuration/cn=Servers
/cn=HNLMBX01
ServerName                            : hnlmbx01
DisplayName                           : Matthew Cook
ActiveSyncAllowedDeviceIDs            : {}
ActiveSyncBlockedDeviceIDs            : {}
ActiveSyncMailboxPolicy               : Default
ActiveSyncMailboxPolicyIsDefaulted    : True
ActiveSyncDebugLogging                : False
ActiveSyncEnabled                     : True
HasActiveSyncDevicePartnership        : False
OwaMailboxPolicy                      :
OWAEnabled                            : True
ECPEnabled                            : True
EmwsEnabled                           : False
PopEnabled                            : True
PopUseProtocolDefaults                : True
PopMessagesRetrievalMimeFormat        : BestBodyFormat
PopEnableExactRFC822Size              : False
PopProtocolLoggingEnabled             : False
ImapEnabled                           : True
ImapUseProtocolDefaults               : True
ImapMessagesRetrievalMimeFormat       : BestBodyFormat
ImapEnableExactRFC822Size             : False
ImapProtocolLoggingEnabled            : False
MAPIEnabled                           : True
MAPIBlockOutlookNonCachedMode         : False
MAPIBlockOutlookVersions              :
MAPIBlockOutlookRpcHttp               : False
IsValid                               : True
ExchangeVersion                       : 0.10 (14.0.100.0)
Name                                  : Matthew Cook
DistinguishedName                     : CN=Matthew Cook,OU=Corporate,
DC=ithicos,DC=local
```

Moving Mailboxes

Moving mailboxes from one mailbox database to another is a pretty common task for most Exchange administrators. Often mailbox databases need to be "smoothed out" because too many large mailboxes are created on a single mailbox database. You may also need to decommission a server or database and thus move all the mailboxes to a new mailbox database.

If you are an experienced Exchange Server administrator and you are transitioning to Exchange Server 2010 from any previous version of Exchange, you are in for a bit of a surprise with respect to how mailboxes are moved. In all previous versions — the Exchange System Manager, Exchange Management Console, or the Exchange 2007 — the Move-Mailbox cmdlet operated in the foreground and moved the mailbox in real time. If a user was in the middle of working in their mailbox, they would get an error during a move.

EXCHANGE SERVER 2010 AND MOVING MAILBOXES

You must always use the Exchange 2010 Management Console or the New-MoveRequest cmdlet to move mailboxes to or between Exchange 2010 mailboxes. Do not use the old Exchange 2003 system manager or Exchange 2007 Move-Mailbox cmdlet to do this. The new process for moving mailboxes to Exchange 2010 databases is significantly different than it was in the past.

Mailboxes are now moved in the background by the Microsoft Exchange Mailbox Replication Service running on a Client Access server. The process is as follows:

1. The administrator submits a new move mailbox request.

2. The New-MoveRequest request updates the Active Directory and adds the mailbox to be moved to a queue by adding a message to the system mailbox on the target mailbox database. The status of the request at this point is queued.

3. An instance of the Mailbox Replication Service (MRS) on one of the Client Access servers in the Active Directory site that contains the target mailbox will see the move request. The MRS services on each CAS periodically query the system mailbox on each database within the local site.

4. The MRS begins to move the mailbox data from the source database to the target database and updates the queue status to InProgress.

5. Near the end of the move, the mailbox is locked, a final synchronization occurs, and the status is changed to CompletionInProgress.

6. When the move is completed, the Active Directory attributes are updated, the old mailbox on the source database is deleted, and the new mailbox is activated. The status is changed to Completed. Client accesses to this mailbox will now be directed to the new mailbox database.

7. The administrator can clear the move request via the Remove-MoveRequest cmdlet or via the Exchange Management Console.

Move statistics for the last two mailbox moves are retained within the mailbox metadata and can be retrieved using the Get-MailboxStatistics cmdlet. Exchange Server 2010 completely changes how mailboxes are moved from one database to another. The Exchange Management Console or the New-MoveRequest cmdlet merely submits requests to move mailboxes to a queue that is managed by a new service running on the CAS. This service is called the Microsoft Exchange Mailbox Replication Service, and it is now responsible for the moving of the mailboxes. There are a number of advantages to this change, including that the mailbox is always available during the move and the actual move is handled server-to-server rather than through a computer running the admin tools. Further, items in the dumpster are also retained.

Mailbox move operations are certainly not instantaneous and can be quite lengthy depending on a number of factors, including bandwidth between servers, server speed, available RAM, and disk I/O. For typical servers on LAN-speed network segments, we estimate you can move from 3 GB per hour to 5 GB per hour. For better or worse, your results may vary. Depending on your Active Directory infrastructure and replication times, Outlook Web App users might not be able to reconnect to their mailboxes for up to 15 minutes because the home mailbox database attribute must replicate to all domain controllers.

As with all Exchange management tasks, you can perform move mailbox operations using the Exchange 2010 Management Console or the Exchange Management Shell using New-MoveRequest.

MOVING MAILBOXES USING THE EMC

Mailboxes can be moved via the GUI using the Exchange Management Console (EMC). To move mailboxes using the EMC, open the Recipient Configuration work center of the EMC and select the Mailboxes subcontainer. Here, you can select one or more mailboxes and then select the New Local Move Request task in the Actions pane.

This launches the New Local Move Request wizard. The most important information to be provided is found on the Introduction page (see Figure 17.29). Here you define the destination mailbox database for the mailboxes you are about to move. In previous versions of Exchange, you also had to select a server and a storage group, but this step is no longer necessary.

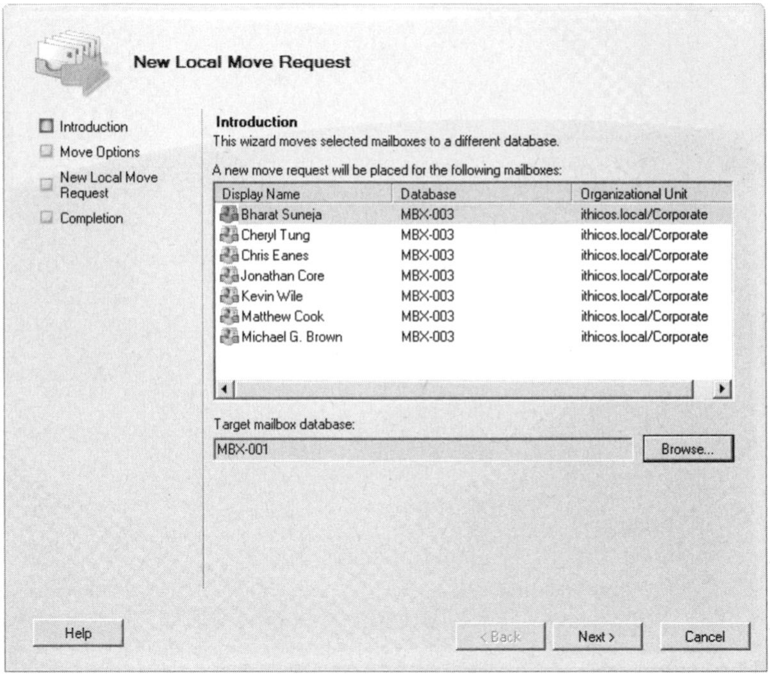

FIGURE 17.29
Defining the destination
mailbox database

Once you have selected the destination mailbox database or specified that the wizard should automatically select a mailbox database, click Next. The Move Options page is displayed (see Figure 17.30). On this screen you can specify whether or not to ignore corrupted messages.

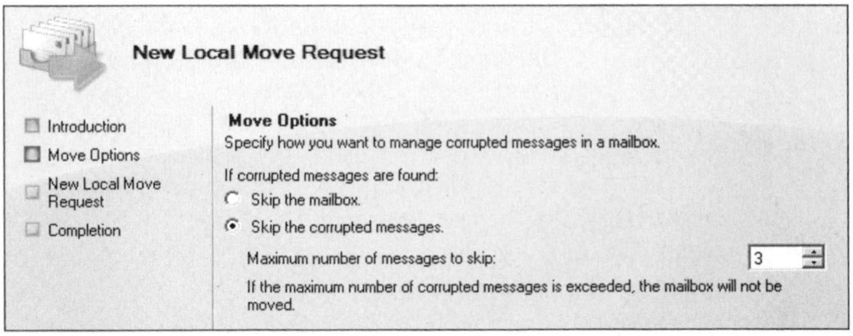

FIGURE 17.30
Options for moving
a mailbox

Normally mailboxes don't have corrupted messages (otherwise your telephone will be ringing), but occasionally the properties of a message get corrupted. This often happened with previous versions of Exchange if a pointer between one table and another table got corrupted. Corrupted messages are much less likely in Exchange 2010 since the single instance storage (SIS) feature has been removed from this version. If a mailbox has more than the maximum number of corrupted messages specified, that particular mailbox will be skipped.

WHY IS THE NEW LOCAL MOVE REQUEST TASK NOT AVAILABLE?

You may notice that sometimes you highlight a mailbox, but the New Local Move Request task option is not available in the Actions pane. If you look carefully at the mailbox icon in the EMC, you'll notice it has a small green arrow on it. The reason for this is that the mailbox already has a previously scheduled or completed task request. Before you can move the mailbox again, you must ensure that the previous move task has completed and remove it. You can accomplish this via the Clear Move Request task found under the Move Request subcontainer or via the Remove-MoveRequest cmdlet.

The next page is a confirmation page that allows you to review the mailboxes you are about to move as well as the destination mailbox database. When you are confident you are moving all the mailboxes you are supposed to move, you can click the New button.

After you click the Next button, the wizard will begin operations. If the wizard seems to have run very quickly, this is because it was merely updating a property of each mailbox in the Active Directory and setting an option on the system mailbox in the target mailbox database. The wizard did not actually move any data; that task will now be the responsibility of one or more of your Client Access servers.

After all the move mailbox requests have been submitted, the final screen shows you a summary of which mailboxes submitted. As with many other wizards in the EMC, the actual Exchange Management Shell (EMS) command that was necessary to submit the request is included in the report. In Figure 17.31 we have collapsed a few of the trident controls so that you can see more of the summary page. Notice for mailbox Glenn Chang the EMS cmdlet New-MoveRequest and the parameters that were used to move the mailbox (see Figure 17.31).

If you want to keep a copy of the move mailbox report, you can use the Ctrl+C keyboard combination to copy the information on the Completion page to the Clipboard, where you can then paste it in to Notepad or Word. When you are finished with the Completion page, just click Finish to close it.

To see if the actual move request has completed, you can either view this information via the Move Request subcontainer in the EMC or via the EMS. Figure 17.32 shows the Move Request subcontainer that is found under the Recipient Configuration container. Here, you can see all pending and completed move requests.

Additional information on a specific move request is available by selecting the mailbox in question and then choosing Properties from the Actions menu. One example of this is shown in Figure 17.33.

Once you have confirmed that a mailbox has been moved, we recommend that you clear completed move requests.

Moving Mailboxes Using the EMS

We have just showed you how easy it is to move mailboxes using the EMC; you just select the mailbox you want to move and click Next through the wizard to specify any other options. The EMC then generates the necessary cmdlet to move the mailbox or mailboxes selected.

In the previous example, one of the mailboxes moved belonged to a user named Glenn Chang. We decided that his mailbox should be moved to a mailbox database called MBX-001. The EMS generated the following command parameters for the New-MoveRequest cmdlet:

```
'ithicos.local/Corporate/Glenn Chang' | New-MoveRequest -TargetDatabase ↵
'MBX-001' -BadItemLimit '2'
```

FIGURE 17.31
New Local Move Request
Completion report

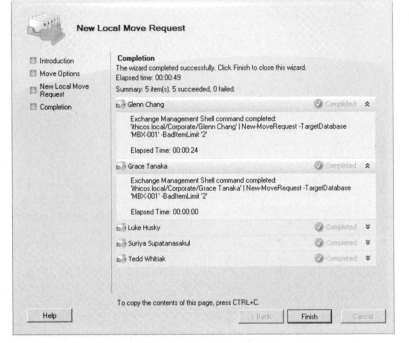

FIGURE 17.32
Viewing all move
requests

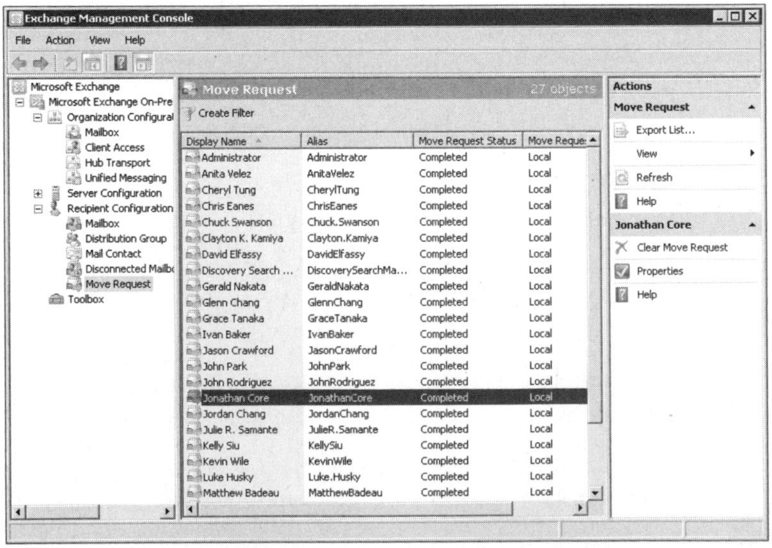

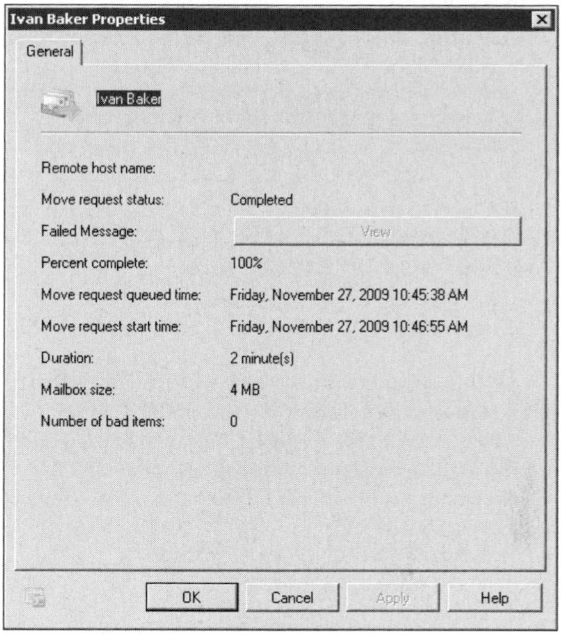

FIGURE 17.33
Viewing information
about a specific move
request

This command would also have moved the mailbox:

```
New-MoveRequest "Glenn Chang" -TargetDatabase 'MBX-001' -BadItemLimit '2'
```

If you wanted to include the bad item count, you could include the parameter
-BadItemLimit:'2' in the command. Notice that this cmdlet asks you to confirm that
you want the mailbox to be moved. To avoid the confirmation prompt, you can include in
the command line -Confirm:$False and the cmdlet will not prompt you. That command line
would look like this:

```
New-MoveRequest Grace.Tanaka -TargetDatabase "mbdb-laxmb01-15" ↵
-Confirm:$False -BadItemLimit:"2"
```

A few other tricks may prove useful for you when you are using the New-MoveRequest
cmdlet. Let's look at a couple of quick examples. In this first example, you want to move everyone who is a member of the Executives group to the mailbox database called MBX-001. You
would type this command, which uses the Get-DistributionGroupMember cmdlet to enumerate the membership of the Executives group, and pipes that output to the New-MoveRequest
cmdlet:

```
Get-DistributionGroupMember "#Executives" | New-MoveRequest ↵
-TargetDatabase "MBX-001" -Confirm:$False
```

Another useful set of cmdlets enumerates everyone whose mailbox is located on one mailbox database and then moves them to another database. You need to use the Get-Mailbox
cmdlet and narrow the scope of the search using the -Database parameter so that you only

output the objects for mailboxes located on a specific database. Here is another example that includes the output of the New-MoveRequest:

```
Get-Mailbox -Database mbx-001 | New-MoveRequest -TargetDatabase MBX-003

DisplayName     Status   TotalMailboxSize      TotalArchiveSize PercentComplete
-----------     ------   ----------------      ---------------- ---------------
Michael Brown   Queued   59.54 KB (60,966 bytes)                0
Grace Tanaka    Queued   59.19 KB (60,610 bytes)                0
Cheryl Tung     Queued   80.89 KB (82,831 bytes)                0
Jonathan Core   Queued   59.4 KB (60,822 bytes)                 0
Glenn Chang     Queued   59.13 KB (60,547 bytes)                0
```

With a little creativity, you can probably figure out a number of other ways to accomplish this task or tasks similar to it.

Once you have submitted move requests, you have a few ways you can check on the status of the moves to see if they are completed. The simplest way is to use the Get-MoveRequest cmdlet to see a list of all the move requests that have been submitted:

```
Get-MoveRequest

DisplayName             Status          TargetDatabase
-----------             ------          --------------
Tyler M. Swartz         Queued          MBX-001
Grace Tanaka            Queued          MBX-001
Cheryl Tung             Queued          MBX-001
Julie R. Samante        Queued          MBX-001
Suriya Supatanasakul    Queued          MBX-001
Clayton K. Kamiya       InProgress      MBX-001
Michael G. Brown        InProgress      MBX-001
Jordan Chang            InProgress      MBX-001
```

If you want to see details of the move and how far along a move request is, you can use the Get-MoveRequestStatistics cmdlet to view a specific move request. Here is an example of Ivan Baker's mailbox performing an intraorganization move. We have piped this to the Format-List cmdlet so that you can see all the properties.

```
Get-MoveRequestStatistics ivan.baker | Format-List

UserIdentity            : ithicos.local/Corporate/Ivan Baker
DistinguishedName       : CN=Ivan Baker,OU=Corporate,
DC=ithicos,DC=local
DisplayName             : Ivan Baker
Alias                   : IvanBaker
ArchiveGuid             :
Status                  : InProgress
StatusDetail            : CreatingInitialSyncCheckpoint
SyncStage               : CreatingInitialSyncCheckpoint
Flags                   : IntraOrg, Pull
```

```
MoveType                            : IntraOrg
Direction                           : Pull
IsOffline                           : False
Protect                             : False
Suspend                             : False
SuspendWhenReadyToComplete          : False
IgnoreRuleLimitErrors               : False
SourceVersion                       : Version 14.0 (Build 639.0)
SourceDatabase                      : MBX-001
TargetVersion                       : Version 14.0 (Build 639.0)
TargetDatabase                      : MBX-003
RemoteHostName                      :
RemoteGlobalCatalog                 :
BatchName                           :
RemoteCredentialUsername            :
RemoteDatabaseName                  :
RemoteDatabaseGuid                  :
TargetDeliveryDomain                :
BadItemLimit                        : 0
BadItemsEncountered                 : 0
QueuedTimestamp                     : 11/27/2009 10:45:38 AM
StartTimestamp                      : 11/27/2009 10:46:55 AM
LastUpdateTimestamp                 : 11/27/2009 10:47:16 AM
InitialSeedingCompletedTimestamp    :
FinalSyncTimestamp                  :
CompletionTimestamp                 :
SuspendedTimestamp                  :
MoveDuration                        : 00:01:42
TotalFinalizationDuration           :
TotalSuspendedDuration              :
TotalFailedDuration                 :
TotalQueuedDuration                 : 00:01:13
TotalInProgressDuration             : 00:00:29
TotalStalledDueToCIDuration         :
TotalStalledDueToHADuration         :
TotalTransientFailureDuration       :
MoveServerName                      : HNLMBX01.ithicos.local
TotalMailboxSize                    : 4.355 MB (4,566,443 bytes)
TotalMailboxItemCount               : 44
TotalArchiveSize                    :
TotalArchiveItemCount               :
BytesTransferred                    : 22.55 KB (23,089 bytes)
BytesTransferredPerMinute           : 56.31 KB (57,657 bytes)
ItemsTransferred                    : 0
PercentComplete                     : 15
PositionInQueue                     :
FailureCode                         :
Message                             :
```

```
FailureTimestamp            :
IsValid                     : True
ValidationMessage           :
```

You can also pipe the output of all move requests currently queued, in progress, or completed using this command:

```
Get-MoveRequest | Get-MoveRequestStatistics
```

DisplayName	Status	TotalMailbox Size	TotalArchiv eSize	PercentComplete
Grace Tanaka	Queued	115.4 KB ...		0
Clarence A. ...	Queued	59.74 KB ...		0
Clayton K. K...	InProgress	3.895 MB ...		29
Michael G. B...	Completed	116.1 KB ...		100
Jordan Chang	CompletionInProg...	401.6 KB ...		95
Tyler M. Swartz	InProgress	272.5 KB ...	3.427 KB (3	89
Anita Velez	Completed	59.24 KB ...		100

You can also request use the `Get-MoveRequest` cmdlet to retrieve information about a specific user's remove request. Here is one example:

```
Get-MoveRequest "Ivan Baker" | FL
```

```
RunspaceId                  : 49ca8abe-886f-4203-82f5-c3cf750f5d1b
ExchangeGuid                : e8c489ba-3513-4133-a046-aeab6139a325
SourceDatabase              : MBX-003
TargetDatabase              : MBX-001
Flags                       : IntraOrg, Pull
RemoteHostName              :
BatchName                   :
Status                      : Completed
MoveType                    : IntraOrg
Direction                   : Pull
IsOffline                   : False
Protect                     : False
Suspend                     : False
SuspendWhenReadyToComplete  : False
Alias                       : IvanBaker
DisplayName                 : Ivan Baker
RecipientType               : UserMailbox
RecipientTypeDetails        : UserMailbox
IsValid                     : True
ExchangeVersion             : 0.10 (14.0.100.0)
Name                        : Ivan Baker
DistinguishedName           : CN=Ivan Baker,OU=Corporate,DC=ithicos,DC=local
```

```
Identity                          : ithicos.local/Corporate/Ivan Baker
Guid                              : e48f79c2-af8d-4ef1-9641-2e23b70e23d3
OrganizationId                    :
OriginatingServer                 : HNLMBX01.ithicos.local
```

The mailbox object does have some specific information about the mailbox's move request as well. Here is an example of how to retrieve that information using the Get-Mailbox cmdlet:

```
Get-Mailbox Ivan.Baker | FL Displayname,*move*
```

```
DisplayName               : Ivan Baker
MailboxMoveTargetMDB      : MBX-001
MailboxMoveSourceMDB      : MBX-003
MailboxMoveFlags          : IntraOrg, Pull
MailboxMoveRemoteHostName :
MailboxMoveBatchName      :
MailboxMoveStatus         : Completed
```

The Get-MailboxStatistics cmdlet also includes some interesting information with respect to the move history, but you have to include the -IncludeMoveHistory option in the command line. Look at the MoveHistory property in this example:

```
Get-MailboxStatistics ivan.baker -IncludeMoveHistory | Format-List
```

```
AssociatedItemCount     : 12
DeletedItemCount        : 0
DisconnectDate          :
DisplayName             : Ivan Baker
ItemCount               : 32
LastLoggedOnUserAccount : ITHICOS\Ivan.Baker
LastLogoffTime          :
LastLogonTime           : 11/27/2009 1:34:31 PM
ObjectClass             : Mailbox
StorageLimitStatus      : BelowLimit
TotalDeletedItemSize    : 0 B (0 bytes)
TotalItemSize           : 4.356 MB (4,568,055 bytes)
Database                : MBX-003
ServerName              : HNLMBX01
DatabaseName            : MBX-003
MoveHistory             : {(11/21/2009 10:48:01 AM: TargetMDB=MBX-003,
Size=4.355 MB (4,566,443 bytes), Duration=00:02:18), (11/26/2009
11:31:02 PM: TargetMDB=MBX-001, Size=4.301 MB (4,510,383 bytes),
Duration=00:02:03)}
IsQuarantined           : False
IsArchiveMailbox        : False
```

Once you are sure that you no longer need the information about a move request, you can remove the completed or queued move requests using the Remove-MoveRequest cmdlet. This removes the move status information from Active Directory but does not remove the move history from the mailbox statistics. To remove user Ivan.Baker's move request information, use this command:

```
Remove-MoveRequest Ivan.Baker -Confirm:$False
```

We can also remove all move requests that completed successfully using this command:

```
Get-MoveRequest | Where {$_.Status -eq "Completed"} | Remove-MoveRequest
```

Retrieving Mailbox Statistics

Frequently Exchange mailbox administrators need to run a report and list the amount of storage that each mailbox is consuming. With previous versions of Exchange, this information was available via the GUI, but now it is available via the EMS cmdlet `Get-MailboxStatistics`. The `Get-MailboxStatistics` cmdlet requires one of three parameters:

-Identity   Retrieves the mailbox statistics for a specific mailbox

-Database   Retrieves statistics for all mailboxes on a specific mailbox database

-Server   Retrieves statistics for all mailboxes on a specific server

Here are two examples using this cmdlet with either a single mailbox or for all mailboxes on the database MBX-003:

```
Get-MailboxStatistics Clayton.Kamiya
```

DisplayName	ItemCount	StorageLimitStatus	LastLogonTime
Clayton K. Kamiya	35	NoChecking	11/27/2009 1:34:31 PM

```
Get-MailboxStatistics -Database MBX-003
```

DisplayName	ItemCount	StorageLimitStatus	LastLogonTime
Suriya Supatanasakul	4	BelowLimit	11/25/2009 9:55:28 AM
Online Archive - Chuck...	0	NoChecking	12/15/2009 7:47:41 AM
Michael G. Brown	4	BelowLimit	11/26/2009 9:01:12 AM
Chuck Swanson	9		
Jason Crawford	5	BelowLimit	11/27/2009 3:53:09 PM
Jordan Chang	11	BelowLimit	
Luke Husky	4	BelowLimit	12/21/2009 5:23:48 PM
Clayton K. Kamiya	35	NoChecking	12/23/2009 6:48:12 AM
Ivan Baker	32	BelowLimit	12/13/2009 7:13:38 PM

Not a real attractive report, is it? However, keep in mind that what is being output to the PowerShell are objects (and those objects' properties) so that provides us with the building blocks to produce a report that contains the information we require.

There are a few useful properties that are part of the objects that output when you use the `Get-MailboxStatistcs` cmdlet. These properties can be used to constrain the output that is sent to the screen (or a file) as well as the output if you redirect this information to a file. Table 17.5 shows some of the properties of the objects that are output when you use the `Get-MailboxStatistcs` cmdlet.

TABLE 17.5:   Properties of Objects Output Using Get-MailboxStatistics

PROPERTY	DESCRIPTION
DisplayName	Name of the mailbox.
ItemCount	Total number of items stored in the entire mailbox.
TotalItemSize	Total size of all of the items in the mailbox except for items in the deleted item cache.
TotalDeletedItemsSize	Total size of items that are in the deleted item cache.
StorageLimitStatus	Status of the mailbox storage limits; the limits you may see are as follows: -BelowLimit — Mailbox is below all limits. -IssueWarning — Mailbox storage is above the issue warning limit. -ProhibitSend — Mailbox is above the prohibit send limit. -MailboxDisabled — Mailbox is over the prohibit send and receive limit.
Database	Name of the database, such as MBX-002, on which the mailbox is located.
ServerName	Name of the mailbox server on which the database is active.
LastLogoffTime	Date and time of the last time someone logged off the mailbox.
LastLogonTime	Date and time of the last time someone logged on to the mailbox.
LastLoggedOnUserAccount	Domain name and username of the last person to access the mailbox.
DisconnectDate	Date and time when the mailbox was deleted or disconnected.
IsArchive	Indicates if this is an archive mailbox (True) or not (False).
IsQuarantined	Indicates if this mailbox has been flagged as having problems and has been quarantined (True).
MoveHistory	Includes the history (date/time/mailbox database) of mailbox moves if the -IncludeMoveHistory parameter is used.

So, perhaps you only want to look at a mailbox report that includes the display name, total size of the mailbox, the total number of items, and the storage limit status. Further, you can include the where clause and filter out any mailbox whose name contains the word *system*. The following example shows what this would look like:

```
Get-MailboxStatistics -Database MBX-003 | where {$_.displayname -notlike ↵
"*System*"} | FT displayname, @{expression={$_.totalitemsize.value.ToKB()}; ↵
width=20;label="Mailbox Size(kb)"},ItemCount,StorageLimitStatus
```

DisplayName	Mailbox Size(kb)	ItemCount	StorageLimitStatus
Julie R. Samante	114	4	BelowLimit
Suriya Supatanas...	117	4	BelowLimit
Ken Vickers	114	4	BelowLimit
John Park	402	11	BelowLimit
Online Archive -...	1	0	NoChecking
Michael G. Brown	117	4	BelowLimit
Chuck Swanson	184	9	
Online Archive -...	3	0	NoChecking
Clarence A. Birtcil	115	4	BelowLimit
Jonathan Core	117	4	BelowLimit
Matthew Badeau	115	4	BelowLimit
Kevin Wile	116	4	BelowLimit
Jason Crawford	145	5	BelowLimit

Did you notice that we threw in some new features of PowerShell? This includes taking the output and reformatting it using the Expression feature and converting the mailbox size to kilobytes. Depending on the size of your typical mailbox, you might want to convert the mailbox size report to megabytes or gigabytes. Here is an example of the expression necessary to convert to megabytes:

```
expression=($_TotalItemSize.Value.ToMB()}
```

You can redirect the output to a text file using the > character and a filename:

```
Get-MailboxStatistics -Database MBX-003 | where {$_.displayname -notlike ↵
"*System*"} | FT displayname, @{expression={$_.totalitemsize.value.ToKB()}; ↵
width=20;label="Mailbox Size(kb)"},ItemCount,StorageLimitStatus ↵
> c:\Mailbox.txt
```

You could also pipe the output to the Export-Csv, Export-Clixml, or ConvertTo-Html cmdlets and send the data to a comma-separated value, XML, or HTML file. Take a look at Chapter 6, "Introduction to PowerShell and the Exchange Management Shell," for more detailed examples of how to "tune" the output of Get-MailboxStatistics.

Here are a few more useful examples of things that you can do with the Get-Mailbox Statistics cmdlet. This command lets you report on mailboxes that have not been accessed in the last 30 days; it uses the PowerShell cmdlet Get-Date, but subtracts 30 days from the current date.

```
Get-MailboxStatistics -Database MBX-003 | where {$_.LastLogonTime -lt ↵
(Get-Date).AddDays(-30)} -And $_DisplayName -notlike "*System*"} | ↵
Format-Table displayName,lastlogontime, ↵
lastloggedonuseraccount,servername
```

Here is a command that will let you see a list of all the mailboxes that have been disconnected over the last seven days on server HNLMBX01:

```
Get-MailboxStatistics -Server HNLMBX01 | Where-Object {$_.DisconnectDate ↵
-gt (Get-Date).AddDays(-7)} | Format-Table displayName,ServerName, ↵
DatabaseName,TotalItemSize -Autosize
```

Deleting Mailboxes

Deleting mailboxes might not seem like such a complicated task until you look at the Actions pane once you have selected a mailbox in the Recipient Configuration work center. There are few options with respect to deleting a mailbox, including simply disconnecting the mailbox from a user account, deleting both the account and the mailbox, and purging a previously deleted mailbox.

In the section of the Actions pane (shown in Figure 17.34) that reflects the mailbox that is currently selected in the Results pane, you will see both a Disable and a Remove option.

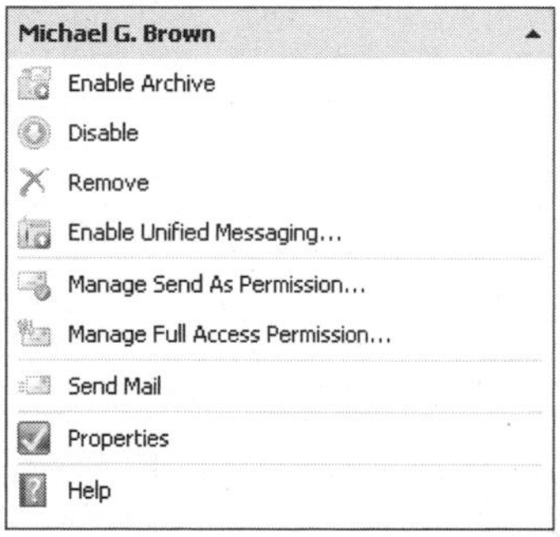

FIGURE 17.34
Management tasks for Michael Brown's mailbox

Both the Remove and the Disable options will delete the mailbox; it's just how they go about doing it that is the difference. The Disable option deletes the mailbox but not the user. The Remove option deletes both the mailbox and the user.

DELETING THE MAILBOX BUT NOT THE USER

If you choose the Disable option, the mailbox is disconnected from the user account but the user account remains in the Active Directory. This is the equivalent of using the EMS cmdlet Disable-Mailbox. For example, to remove a mailbox from an existing user, you could type this:

```
Disable-Mailbox Damion.Jones -Confirm:$False
```

All this command does is disconnect the mailbox from the user account; the user account remains in the Active Directory. After the deleted mailbox recovery time expires, the mailbox will be permanently removed from the mailbox database.

DELETING BOTH THE USER AND THE MAILBOX

If you choose the Remove option, the mailbox is disconnected from the user account *and* the user account is deleted from the Active Directory. You can accomplish the same thing from the EMS using the Remove-Mailbox cmdlet. Here is an example:

```
Remove-Mailbox Cheyne.Manalo
```

This command will prompt you to verify that you want to remove the mailbox; you can avoid the confirmation prompt by including the -Confirm:$False parameter. If you want to delete the mailbox and the account and prevent the mailbox from being recovered, you can include the -Permanent:$True parameter. Here is another example that automatically confirms the deletion and permanently removes the mailbox:

```
Remove-Mailbox Jonathan.Long -Permanent:$True -Confirm:$False
```

PERMANENTLY PURGING A MAILBOX

By default, after the deleted mailbox recovery time has expired, the mailbox will be permanently purged from the mailbox database. If you have already deleted the mailbox and want to permanently purge the mailbox from the mailbox database, you can also do that, but it requires two lines. The first line is going to set a variable ($Temp) that retrieves the mailbox object for a mailbox whose display name is Martha Lanoza. The second line uses that variable along with the MailboxGuid property of that mailbox to remove that mailbox from the VIP Mailboxes database. Here are the two commands that would need to be executed:

```
$Temp = Get-User "Martha Lanoza" | Get-MailboxStatistics
Remove-Mailbox -Database "VIP Mailboxes" -StoreMailboxIdentity ↵
$Temp.MailboxGuid
```

This example assumes there would only be a single mailbox whose display name is Martha Lanoza and that there is only a single mailbox database named VIP Mailboxes. With a little creativity, you can permanently purge mailboxes in other ways, but this is a basic EMS method for doing so.

Reconnecting a Deleted Mailbox

Exchange Server allows you to "undelete" a mailbox that you may have accidentally disconnected from a user account. The simplest way to do this is to use the EMC, but you can also do it using the EMS.

RECONNECTING A MAILBOX USING THE EMC

In the Recipient Configuration work center you will find the Disconnected Mailbox subcontainer (shown in Figure 17.35).

Click the Connect To Server task in the Actions pane to see a mailbox listing; otherwise, deleted mailboxes may not show up in the Results pane.

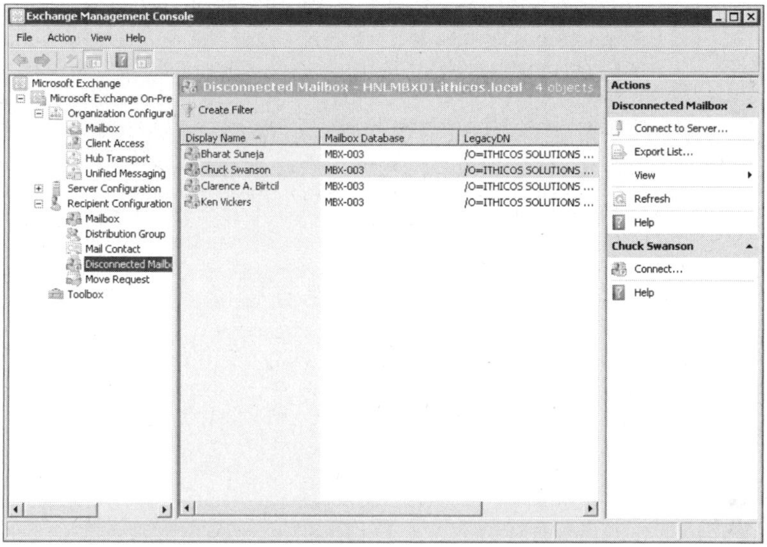

FIGURE 17.35

Reconnecting mailboxes
that have been deleted

FIGURE 17.35

Reconnecting mailboxes that have been deleted

The disconnected mailbox listing you see in Figure 17.35 is a list of the mailboxes on the Mailbox server to which you are currently connected. You can view other mailbox servers by choosing the Connect To Server option in the Actions pane.

You could generate the same list using the `Get-MailboxStatistics` command and filter based on viewing only objects whose `DisconnectDate` property contains data:

```
Get-MailboxStatistics -Server HNLMBX01 | Where {$_.DisconnectDate ↵
-ne $null} | Format-Table DisplayName,DisconnectDate
```

```
DisplayName          DisconnectDate
-----------          --------------
Micah Hoffmann       12/10/2009 3:13:37 AM
David Elfassy        12/02/2000 3:13:23 AM
Paul Agamata         11/25/2009 3:13:55 AM
Brian Tirch          11/20/2009 3:13:47 AM
Clayton Kamiya       11/16/2009 3:13:01 AM
```

If you have removed one of these mailboxes from its user account accidentally, you can still reconnect it back to a user account. In the EMC's Disconnected Mailbox subcontainer, highlight the mailbox that you want to reconnect and choose the Connect task on the Actions pane. This will launch the Connect Mailbox wizard. The main page of the Connect Mailbox wizard looks a lot like the main page of the New Mailbox wizard.

FORCING A MAILBOX TO DISCONNECT

If a mailbox was deleted after the cleanup process has been run, it will not show up in the list of disconnected mailboxes. You may have to force Exchange to realize that the mailbox and its corresponding Active Directory user account have been disconnected. You can do this with the `Clean-MailboxDatabase` cmdlet.

On the Connect Mailbox Introduction screen, you are asked what type of mailbox you are connecting. Choices include a User mailbox, Room Resource mailbox, Equipment Resource mailbox, and a Linked mailbox. Select the type of mailbox that you are working with and click the Next button.

The next page of the wizard is where we reconnect the mailbox with a user account. The deleted mailboxes can only be connected to a user account that does not have a mailbox already associated with it.

On the Mailbox Settings page of the Connect Mailbox wizard (shown in Figure 17.36), you must select the user account to which you want to connect this mailbox. The user account must not already have a mailbox associated with it. There are two different ways that you can locate the user account. If you choose the Matching User radio button and then click the Browse button, the EMC will make its "best guess" at finding the right user account in the Active Directory.

FIGURE 17.36
Mailbox Settings page of the Connect Mailbox wizard

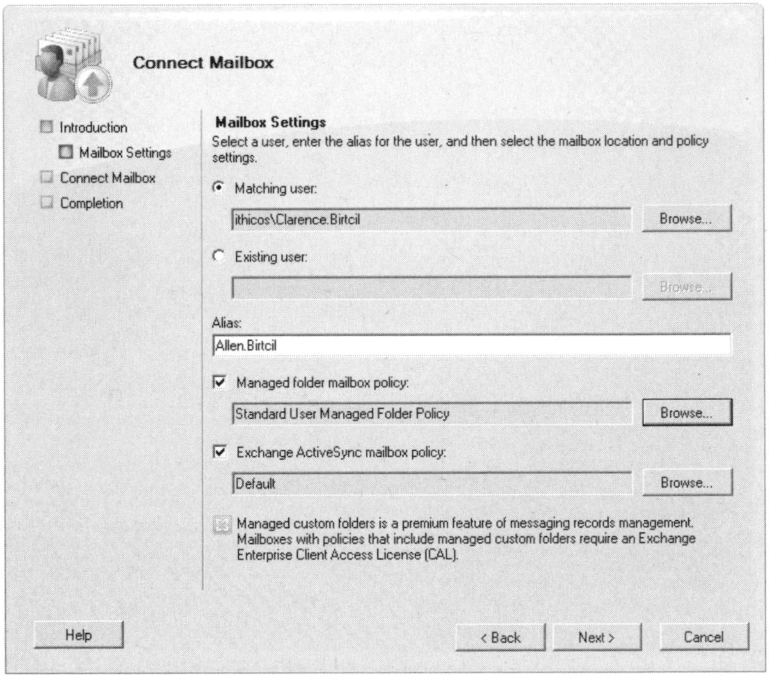

If you choose the Existing User radio button and then click the Browse button, you will be presented with a browse list of all users in the Active Directory. This list will include users that have been mailbox-enabled and those that do not have mailboxes. If you select a user that already has a mailbox, you will see an error message.

Regardless of whether you use the Matching User or the Existing User selection, the Exchange Alias value will be displayed and you can override it if necessary.

Note that you may also specify a managed folder mailbox policy and an ActiveSync policy for this mailbox. They can always be assigned later, but you have the option of reassigning them at the time when you are reconnecting the mailbox to the account. Remember that if you assign a managed folder mailbox policy you will be reminded that clients older than Outlook 2007 will not support all features of managed folder policies.

Once you have completed the information required on the Mailbox Settings page of the wizard, click Next to move on to the Connect Mailbox page. From here you can verify everything you are about to do and then click the Connect button.

RECONNECTING A MAILBOX USING THE EMS

To reconnect a deleted mailbox using the EMS, you use the `Connect-Mailbox` cmdlet. This cmdlet takes an identifier for the mailbox you are trying to connect to using the unique mailbox GUID, the display name, or the legacy Exchange distinguished name. The display name of the mailbox is by far the easiest to use. You also must provide the name of the database on which the mailbox is located and the user account to which you are connecting the account.

Before you do this, let's take a quick look at another iteration of the `Get-MailboxStatistics` cmdlet and how to enumerate the information you need to reconnect a mailbox. This output is displaying just the database name and the display name:

```
Get-MailboxStatistics -Server HNLMBX01 | Where {$_.DisconnectDate ↵
-ne $null} | Format-Table DisplayName,Database

DisplayName                      Database
-----------                      --------
Aran Hoffmann                    MBX-001
Paul Agamata                     MBX-002
Donny Shimamoto                  MBX-003
Clayton Kamiya                   MBX-003
```

Let's say you have accidentally deleted user Clayton Kamiya's mailbox from the Executives mailbox database; this user also had a managed folder policy and an ActiveSync policy. To reconnect this user's mailbox to user account volcanosurf\Clayton.Kamiya, here is the command you would execute:

```
Connect-Mailbox "Clayton Kamiya" -Database:"MBX-003" -Alias:"Clayton.Kamiya" ↵
-User:"volcanosurf\Clayton.Kamiya" -ManagedFolderMailboxPolicy: ↵
"All Employees"-MobileMailboxPolicy:"Standard User ActiveSync ↵
Policy"
```

In the previous section where we used the EMC to connect the mailbox back to the user, the `Connect-Mailbox` command was a bit more complex, but this is done to ensure uniqueness when a mailbox is being connected. Here is the command that was executed by the EMC:

```
Connect-Mailbox -Identity '9bca86e4-2a57-4784-9bf6-23931436b6ea' -Database ↵
'MBX-003' -User 'ithicos\Clarence.Birtcil' -Alias 'Allen.Birtcil' ↵
-ManagedFolderMailboxPolicy 'Standard User Managed Folder Policy' ↵
-ActiveSyncMailboxPolicy 'Default'
```

Bulk Manipulation of Mailboxes Using the EMS

Probably the most useful feature of the PowerShell and the EMS is the ability to perform bulk manipulation of objects.

Managing Mailbox Properties with the EMS

Let's say we want to do something like turn off OWA for all users. This is set using the Set-CASMailbox cmdlet, not Set-Mailbox. We could do this with a one-liner, though, by retrieving a list of all mailboxes in the organization and then piping each mailbox to the Set-CASMailbox cmdlet. Here is one way to do this:

```
Get-Mailbox | Set-CASMailbox -OWAEnabled:$False
```

Does this look powerful? Does this look dangerous? We say yes on both counts. You can easily do something you did not intend to do, so take great care when using the EMS if you are performing any type of bulk administration.

You are probably not interested in making mass changes to every mailbox or user account in your organization, at least not usually. That is why group membership comes in so handy. A few cmdlets are useful when it comes to using the membership of a group. The Get-DistributionGroup cmdlet will list all of the distribution groups in the organization, but it does not provide you with a membership list:

```
Get-DistributionGroup
```

Name	DisplayName	GroupType	PrimarySmtpAddress
$Operations Group	$Operations Group	Global, Security...	OperationsGroup@...
$Executives and ...	$Executives and ...	Global, Security...	ExecutivesandVIP...
DirectoryUpdateS...	!Directory Updat...	Universal	DirectoryUpdateS...
Executives	Executives	Universal	Executives@somor...
VIPs	VIPs	Universal, Secur...	VIPs@somorita.com
Executives	Somorita Executives	Universal, Secur...	SomoritaExecutiv...
Somorita Sales a...	Somorita Sales a...	Universal, Secur...	SomoritaSalesand...

To retrieve a list of objects that are members of a distribution group, you need the Get-DistributionGroupMember cmdlet. Here is the output (remember that this is not text within the PowerShell environment; these are unique objects that can be piped as input to another cmdlet):

```
Get-DistributionGroupMember "Executives"
```

Name	RecipientType
Goga Kukrika	UserMailbox
Pavel Nagaev	UserMailbox
Ryan Tung	UserMailbox
George Cue	UserMailbox
Chris Eanes	UserMailbox
Bthaworn Thaweeaphiradeemaitree	UserMailbox
Jason Sherry	UserMailbox

Do you remember a cmdlet we used to override the mailbox quotas for one mailbox? Well, let's expand on that and set that quota for all members of the Executives group. Here is an example:

```
Get-DistributionGroupMember "Executives" | Set-Mailbox ↵
-ProhibitSendQuota:250MB -IssueWarningQuota:200MB ↵
-UseDatabaseQuotaDefaults:$False -ProhibitSendReceiveQuota:300MB
```

This cmdlet retrieves the membership list for the Executives distribution group and then passes those objects as input to the `Set-Mailbox` cmdlet.

How about another common task? Let's say we need to move all of the mailboxes in the Executives group to a mailbox database called Executives. Here is the command to do that:

```
Get-DistributionGroupMember "Executives" | New-MoveRequest -BadItemLimit:2 ↵
-TargetDatabase:Executives
```

We could extend that and move all mailboxes on a specific server by using the `-Server` option of the `Get-Mailbox` cmdlet to help us narrow our listing of mailboxes:

```
Get-Mailbox -Server:HNLEX04 | New-MoveRequest -TargetDatabase:MBX-003
```

What if you only want to move the mailboxes on a specific database? Here is another example:

```
Get-Mailbox -Database MBX-004 | New-MoveRequest ↵
-TargetDatabase "MBX-003" -Confirm:$False
```

With a little creativity, you can probably figure out a number of other ways to accomplish this or similar tasks.

Scripting Account Creation

In some organizations, many accounts are created at one time. The EMS and PowerShell give you the ability to automate this process by reading the data in from a text or CSV file. Though you could probably automate the process if you created a massive one-liner, it is much easier to create a simple PowerShell script. First, let's look at a CSV input file of new user accounts:

```
Name,Database,OrganizationalUnit,UserPrincipalName
Saul Tigh,MB-DB1,colonialfleet.int/Military,Saul.Tigh@fleet.int
Helena Cain, MB-DB1,colonialfleet.int/Military,Helena.Cain@fleet.int
Felix Gaeta, MB-DB1,colonialfleet.int/Military,Felix.Gaeta@fleet.int
Tory Foster, MB-DB1,colonialfleet.int/Civilians,Tory.Foster@fleet.int
Tom Zarek,MB-DB1,colonialfleet.int/Civilians,Tom.Zarek@fleet.int
Samuel Anders,MB-DB1,colonialfleet.int/Civilians,Samuel.Anders@fleet.int
Hera Agathon,MB-DB1,colonialfleet.int/Civilians,Hera.Agathon@fleet.int
```

This CSV file has four columns; they represent the absolute minimum columns necessary to create an account and assign it a mailbox. Naturally, in real life you would have more columns (first name, last name, SAM account name, Exchange alias, and so on). Also, the OUs in the Active Directory must exist for these users.

Here is the script for creating these mailboxes:

```
# Read the c:\demo\newaccounts.csv file. The first line is the header.
# Each additional line represents a user object.
# Read all of these in to the $Users variable.
$Users = Import-Csv C:\Demo\newaccounts.csv
# Output the contents of the $Users variable.
# This command is not necessary as it only outputs the list to the screen.
$Users
```

```
# Prompt the person running the script for a password.
# This password will be assigned to each user created.
$Password = Read-Host "Please enter a password" -AsSecureString

# A simple Foreach loop to create the new users
# For each line in the $Users variable, run the New-Mailbox cmdlet.
# $User.Database represents the value of the Database field for user.
Foreach ($User in $Users) {
  New-Mailbox -Name $User.Name -Database $User.Database -OrganizationalUnit ↵
$User.OrganizationalUnit -UserPrincipalName $User.UserPrincipalName↵
-Password $Password
}
```

Managing Mailbox Content

The need to control mailbox content and size is often due to limited disk space for mailbox databases, but it may also be due to company security policies, archiving, electronic discover (eDiscovery) requirements, or regulatory compliance. Or you may just want to help your users clean the junk out of their mailboxes. Over the years, a lot of solutions for managing mailbox and folder content have come and gone.

Seasoned Exchange Server administrators are probably familiar with the Exchange 2000/2003 Mailbox Manager function or may even be familiar with the Exchange 5.5 Mailbox Cleanup Agent. These tools gave the administrator some control over how long content was kept in a user's mailbox folder. The administrator could configure these tools to delete information in a mailbox if it was older than the specified number of days or larger than a specified size.

Many organizations are now employing archival solutions that will remove content from users' mailboxes and store it in long-term storage such as tape, optical, network-attached storage (NAS), or storage area networks (SANs). In some cases, archival solutions are put in place merely to reduce the size of the Exchange databases but still allow users long-term access to their old mail data. In other cases, an organization is required to keep certain types of message content such as financial data, official company communications, and healthcare-related data.

Mailbox archiving has raised new issues and challenges not only for the Exchange administrator but for management and users as well. Some types of messages may need to be retained for long periods of time, but not necessarily one copy of each message in each mailbox. There has to be some method of determining which messages should be retained or archived, and sometimes that task may fall on the user.

Organizations that are concerned about meeting regulatory requirements with respect to message archiving and long-term retention of certain types of messages may also be interested in keeping a journaled copy of messages.

Understanding the Basics of Messaging Records Management

Before diving into how you would set up and implement MRM, let's discuss some basics. We'll explore possible usage scenarios, what the user would see, and the basics of getting started.

First and foremost, let's get some terminology out of the way. Messaging records management encompasses management of email content "at rest." This means that you are managing the content while it is sitting in a folder in someone's mailbox. Don't get this concept confused with transport rules, which are discussed in more detail in Chapter 26, "Managing Transport and Journaling Rules."

MESSAGING RECORDS MANAGEMENT AND LICENSING

There has been a lot of confusion regarding the licensing requirements for the MRM features of both Exchange Server 2007 and 2010. In general, this feature is considered an Enterprise feature and thus requires an Exchange enterprise client access license (eCAL) for each user that will be "managed."

However, there are exceptions. Any operation that you could have used the Exchange 2000/2003 Mailbox Manager feature to perform can be done with Exchange Server 2010 with only a standard CAL. This includes automatically deleting folder content or moving folder content to a System Cleanup folder or the Deleted Items folder.

USER PARTICIPATION

It is important to keep in mind that MRM does not include "important message pixie dust." A popular misconception is that content that should be retained will automatically be moved to the appropriate managed folder. Messages do not get organized automatically. Users must participate in MRM by moving their relevant content into the appropriate managed folders.

There are two different perspectives on what we can implement with MRM. We can do certain tasks without user intervention, such as purging mail in existing folders or moving mail to a message archive.

However, the real mission of MRM is to get the user to participate in the process. We can use the MRM process to create custom folders in the user's mailbox, but it is up to the user to determine which types of messages belong in which folder.

Figure 17.37 shows a set of custom folders that were created inside a folder called Managed Folders. These are called managed custom folders.

FIGURE 17.37
Managed custom folders created by a managed folder mailbox policy

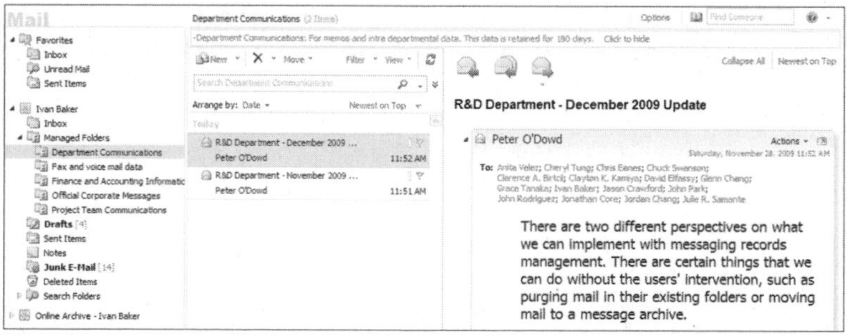

The administrator decides what the managed custom folder names will be and assigns a managed folder mailbox policy to the mailbox to ensure that the folders are created. The administrator can do additional things with these folders, but for now let's stick with the basics.

The users are trained to categorize their mailbox content based on the folders you make available to them. This will allow the administrator to then purge folders such as the Inbox or Sent Items every 60, 90, or 180 days without worrying about purging important information.

You can journal the data that you find in Managed Folders, or you can leave it on the server for a longer period of time based on the users' or the organization's requirements.

ARCHIVE MAILBOXES AND MESSAGING RECORDS MANAGEMENT

If you are planning on using the Exchange 2010 archive mailbox feature, you cannot implement MRM. A mailbox can either have a managed folder policy assigned to it or a retention policy assigned to it, but not both.

The most important thing to realize is that, as we mentioned previously, the user must participate in the process.

POSSIBLE SCENARIOS

After you finish reading this chapter, you will probably find a lot of potentially useful scenarios for MRM. This is true even if your organization does not perform mailbox archiving or has to deal with regulatory compliance. So, what are some possible uses for MRM?

◆ Creating custom folders that are used by users to categorize or organize information that must be retained

◆ Defining content settings that purge certain types of content from either custom folders or the default folders

◆ Defining for managed custom folders content settings that automatically copy specified content types (or all content types) that are moved into the folder

◆ Defining content settings for managed default folders

◆ Defining maximum folder sizes for managed custom folders

◆ Using managed content settings to expire items in a folder so they are eligible for archiving

These are just a few of the possible uses for MRM.

Getting Started with Messaging Records Management

Messaging records management folders, content settings, and policies can be defined in the EMC or the EMS. For most of the actions we will be describing, we will show you the EMC interface and follow up with EMS commands as necessary.

The MRM content settings, policies, and folders are found in the Organization Configuration work center of the EMC under the Mailbox subcontainer. This work center is shown in Figure 17.38. You can see the Managed Default Folders tab in the Results pane.

You cannot set up MRM using a single dialog or wizard. A couple of steps are involved in getting started. We go into more detail later in the chapter on how to do each of these steps, but let's start with a basic outline of how you would get started with a policy:

1. Create managed custom folders (if applicable).

2. Define managed content settings for the managed custom folders.

3. Optionally create managed content settings for default folders.

4. Create managed folder mailbox policies that include managed custom folders and/or managed default folders.

5. Assign the managed folder mailbox polices to users.

6. Configure the mailbox servers to run the Managed Folder Assistant on a schedule.

FIGURE 17.38
Viewing the MRM components in the EMC

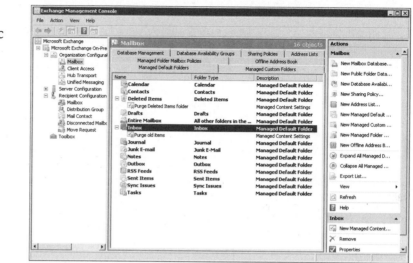

Managing Default Folders

Let's start by talking about a mailbox's default folders; these are the folders that the Outlook client automatically creates the first time the mailbox is accessed. The default folders list is found under the Managed Default Folders tab in the Results pane shown in Figure 17.38.

List of Default Folders

The Managed Default Folder list is static; you cannot create additional default folders either through the EMC or the EMS. The following is a list of the folders that are considered default folders:

- Calendar
- Contacts
- Deleted Items
- Drafts
- Entire Mailbox
- Inbox
- Journal
- Junk E-mail
- Notes
- Outbox

- ◆ RSS Feeds

- ◆ Sent Items

- ◆ Sync Issues

- ◆ Tasks

Depending on the client version you are using, you may not see all of these folders. For example, if you have never opened your mailbox using the Outlook 2007 client, you will not see the RSS Feeds folder in your mailbox.

Creating Managed Content Settings

Although you cannot define new default folders, you can manage the content in the existing folders. Managed content settings can be defined for each folder (and also for the entire mailbox). In many ways, the managed content settings work the same way that they did in the Exchange 2000/2003 Mailbox Manager.

When creating a managed content setting, you must define what type of content it will be affecting; this means that you specify the message type. Table 17.6 shows the message types that you can define for managed content settings; this table includes the `MessageClass` property that would be used when creating managed content settings via the EMS and the `New-ManagedContentSettings` cmdlet.

TABLE 17.6:   Message Types for Managed Content Settings

MESSAGE TYPE	MESSAGE CLASS	EXPLANATION
All message content	`*` (or `AllMailboxContent`)	All content types in the folder
Calendar items	`IPM.Appointment`	Entries found on a calendar
Contacts	`IPM.Contact`	Contact items
Documents	`IPM.Document`	Message content that has been set as a document
Email message	`IPM.Note`	Standard email message of any format
SMIME message	`IPM.Note.SMIME`	Email message that has been digitally signed or encrypted
Faxes	`IPM.Note.Microsoft.Fax`	Faxes generated by the Exchange 2007 Unified Messaging server role or Exchange Server 2010 compatible third-party faxing applications
Journal items	`IPM.Activity`	Journal items
Meeting requests, responses, and cancellations	`IPM.Schedule`	Schedule requests, responses to schedule requests, cancellations, and so on
Missed calls	`IPM.Note.Microsoft.Missed.Voice`	Notices of telephone calls missed when using Exchange 2007 or 2010 Unified Messaging

TABLE 17.6: Message Types for Managed Content Settings *(CONTINUED)*

MESSAGE TYPE	MESSAGE CLASS	EXPLANATION
Notes	`IPM.StickyNote`	Note items usually found in the Outlook Notes folder
OCS Communicator conversation	`IPM.Note.Microsoft.Conversation`	Logs conversations generated by Office Communication Server's Communicator client
OCS Communicator Phone device call log	`IPM.Note.Microsoft.Conversation.Voice`	Call log messages that are generated when using Office Communication Server phone devices
Posts	`IPM.Post`	Post item types usually used for public folders
RSS items	`IPM.Post.RSS`	RSS feed data in the Outlook 2007 client RSS Feeds folder
Tasks	`IPM.Task`	Task items
Voicemail	`IPM.Note.Microsoft.Voicemail`	Voicemail messages generated by the Exchange 2007 Unified Messaging server or equivalent software

You can optionally specify a retention period for items that meet the conditions of the message content setting. The retention period is specified in days and the retention period starts from one of two points:

When Delivered, End Date For Calendar And Recurring Tasks   This selection allows you to specify that the starting point for the retention cycle is when the message arrives in the mailbox. Alternately, if the item is a calendar entry or recurring task, the retention cycle starts at the end date of the item.

When Item Is Moved To The Folder   This selection specifies that the retention date starts when the item is first placed into the folder.

Once the retention period expires, you have to take an action on any items that meet your criteria. Table 17.7 shows a list of the possible actions you can take on an item at the end of the retention period. The table also includes the `RetentionAction` value that would be used if you were creating managed content settings from the EMS instead of the EMC.

An additional option you have available when you are creating a managed content setting is to automatically copy the message to a mailbox or external location. We will look at an example of journaling using the managed content settings later in this chapter.

If you want to use the EMS to see the managed content settings that you have created, here is an example of using the `Get-ManagedContentSettings` cmdlet:

```
Get-ManagedContentSettings

Name                      MessageClass           ManagedFolderName
----                      ------------           -----------------
RecoverableItems_cs       *                      RecoverableItems
RecoverableCalendarIte... IPM.Appointment.*....  RecoverableCalendarItems
```

```
AutoGroup_cs                *        AutoGroup
ModeratedRecipients_cs      *        ModeratedRecipients
Personal 1 Year move t...   *        Personal 1 Year move t...
Default 2 year move to...   IPM.Note  Default 2 year move to...
Personal 5 year move t...   *         Personal 5 year move t...
Personal never move to...   *        Personal never move to...
Purge old items             *        Inbox
Purge Deleted Items fo...   *        Deleted Items
```

TABLE 17.7:   Actions That Can Be Taken on Items at the End of the Retention Period

ACTION	RETENTION ACTION	EXPLANATION
Move to the Deleted Items folder	MoveToDeletedItems	Moves the item to the Deleted Items folder; this setting is not valid if you are trying to create a managed content setting in the Deleted Items folder.
Move to a managed custom folder	MoveToFolder	Moves the item to a managed custom folder that you specify.
Delete and allow recovery	DeleteAndAllowRecovery	Deletes the item but allows a user to undelete the item before the item is removed from the deleted item cache.
Permanently delete	PermanentlyDelete	Deletes the item and does not allow it to be recovered from the deleted item cache.
Mark as past retention limit	MarkAsPastRetentionLimit	Marks the item as past the retention limit but takes no further action. At this point, message archival software could take over and archive just the messages that are past their retention limit.

Table 17.8 shows a number of cmdlets that you can use from within the EMS to create or manipulate managed content settings.

TABLE 17.8:   Exchange Management Shell Cmdlets for Manipulating Managed Content Settings

CMDLET	EXPLANATION
New-ManagedContentSettings	Creates a new managed content setting
Set-ManagedContentSettings	Changes the properties of an existing managed content setting object
Get-ManagedContentSettings	Retrieves managed content settings
Remove-ManagedContentSettings	Deletes a managed content setting object

Let's now look at some practical examples of managed content settings.

Keeping the Deleted Items Folder Clean

One pet peeve of many Exchange administrators is that users will delete messages from their Inbox or Sent Items folder but never empty the Deleted Items folder. It is not uncommon to find hundreds of megabytes of message content in a user's Deleted Items folder. In the following example, you set up conditions on the Deleted Items folder so that nothing older than 7 days is kept in the Deleted Items folder but users can recover the deleted message from the deleted item cache after you empty their Deleted Items folder.

Let's see how to create a new content setting to purge items from the Deleted Items folder that is older than seven days. To do this through the EMC, locate the Deleted Items folder in the Managed Default Folder list and select it. In the Actions pane, select New Managed Content Settings, which will launch the New Managed Content Settings wizard (shown in Figure 17.39). On the Introduction screen of the wizard, you specify the name of the managed content settings item, the type of message content it will apply to (in this case, all message content), the length of retention, when the retention period starts, and the action to take.

FIGURE 17.39
Configuring a managed content setting to delete items that have been in the Deleted Items folder longer than 7 days

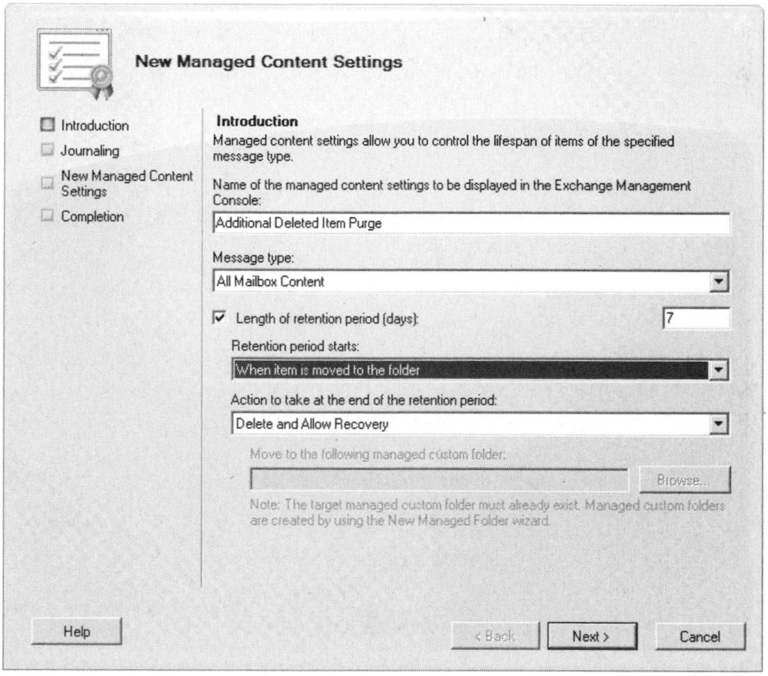

If you want to delete an item from a folder after a specified number of days, choose one of the following options from the Retention Period Starts drop-down list:

◆ When Item Is Moved To The Folder

◆ When Delivered, End Date For Calendar And Recurring Tasks

Because you are working on a default folder, not a custom folder, the option to specify a managed custom folder is not available. Once you click Next, you move to the Journaling page in the wizard, but you do not need anything from that page for this particular managed content setting. The New Managed Content Settings page allows you to review what you are about to configure, and then you click New. Like most EMC wizards, the Completion screen will include the EMS command that was executed to complete this task. Here is the EMS command that was necessary to define this managed content setting:

```
New-ManagedContentSettings -Name 'Additional Deleted Item Purge' ↵
-FolderName 'Deleted Items' -RetentionAction 'DeleteAndAllowRecovery' ↵
-AddressForJournaling $null -AgeLimitForRetention '7.00:00:00' ↵
-JournalingEnabled $false -MessageFormatForJournaling 'UseTnef' ↵
-RetentionEnabled $true -LabelForJournaling '' -MessageClass '*' ↵
-MoveToDestinationFolder $null -TriggerForRetention 'WhenMoved'
```

Note that although you have defined the managed content setting to this particular folder, it will not yet apply to anyone's mailbox, nor will any server enforce this content setting. The managed folder mailbox policies and scheduling the Managed Folder Assistant are covered later in this chapter.

MOVING CONTENT TO AN ALTERNATE LOCATION

A good use of managed content settings is to move content to an alternate location. However, we should note that this feature requires an eCAL for each mailbox that will be managed. In this example, you see how to mimic one of the functions of the Exchange 2000/2003 Mailbox Manager. It had the ability to move mail that was nearly ready to be deleted from the system in to a System Cleanup folder. Mail could then be purged from the System Cleanup folder after it had been in that folder for a specified number of days.

You are going to create a managed content setting that moves all items in the Inbox folder into a System Cleanup Folder. This is assuming that you have previously created a managed custom folder for the mailbox that is called System Cleanup Folder.

Before you carry out the instructions in this example, create a managed custom folder called System Cleanup Folder:

1. Locate and select the Inbox in the Managed Default Folder list. Then in the Actions pane, select New Managed Content Settings, which will launch the New Managed Content Settings wizard.

2. Specify a retention period of 180 days, specify that the action to take is Move To A Managed Custom Folder, and then in the section Move To The Following Managed Custom Folder, select System Cleanup Folder.

The EMS command that created this managed content setting is similar to the one used to purge the Deleted Items folder:

```
New-ManagedContentSettings -Name 'Move items older than 180 days ↵
to the System Cleanup Folder' -FolderName 'Inbox' ↵
 -RetentionAction 'MoveToFolder' -AddressForJournaling $null ↵
 -AgeLimitForRetention '180.00:00:00' -JournalingEnabled $false ↵
 -MessageFormatForJournaling 'UseTnef' -RetentionEnabled $true ↵
 -LabelForJournaling '' -MessageClass '*' ↵
 -MoveToDestinationFolder 'System Cleanup Folder' ↵
 -TriggerForRetention 'WhenDelivered'
```

If you now wanted to move items in the Sent Items folder that are older than 180 days into the System Cleanup Folder, you could do so by making a single modification to the managed content settings. The only change required is to the -FolderName parameter; its value must be changed to 'Sent Items':

```
New-ManagedContentSettings -Name 'Move items older than 180 days ↵
  to the System Cleanup Folder' -FolderName 'Sent Items' ↵
  -RetentionAction 'MoveToFolder' -AddressForJournaling $null ↵
  -AgeLimitForRetention '180.00:00:00' -MessageClass '*' ↵
  -MoveToDestinationFolder 'System Cleanup Folder' ↵
  -TriggerForRetention 'WhenDelivered'
```

Because you did not require the journaling settings, you can remove those from the New-ManagedContentSettings command line.

Creating and Managing Custom Folders

Managed custom folders are folders that you define as the administrator and then assign to users' mailboxes. As you see in Figure 17.40, the managed custom folders are created in the user's mailbox in the Managed Folders folder. Creating a managed custom folder is simple. While you are viewing the Managed Custom Folders tab, simply click the New Managed Custom Folder task in the Actions pane. Figure 17.40 shows the New Managed Custom Folder wizard.

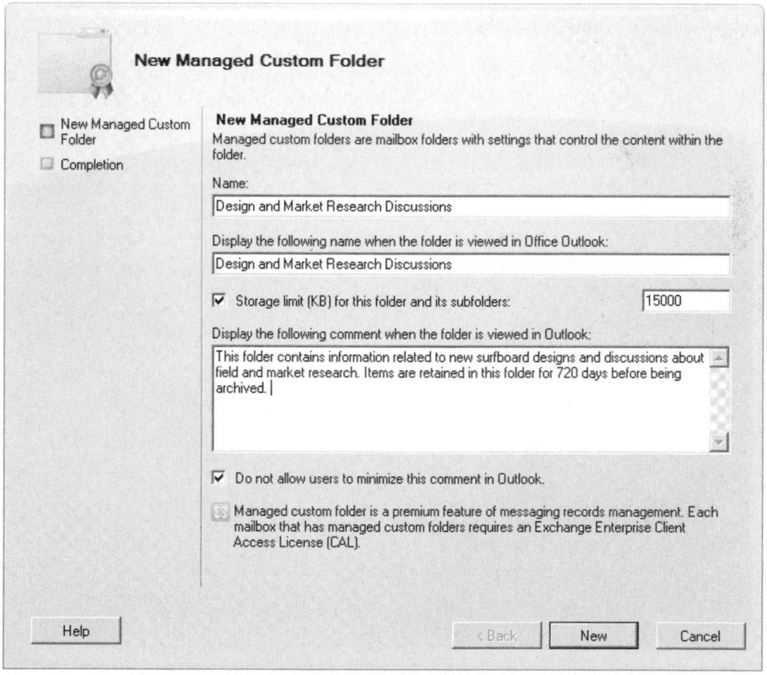

FIGURE 17.40
Creating a new managed custom folder

This wizard has only two pages. The Introduction page asks that you provide a name for the folder, the display name that is shown in Outlook, and a comment that is shown in Outlook. Optionally, you can specify a storage quota option (a maximum amount of data that the managed custom folder can contain). The EMS command that was used to generate this managed custom folder is as follows:

```
New-ManagedFolder -Name 'Design and Market Research Discussions' ↵
-FolderName 'Design and Market Research Discussions' -StorageQuota ↵
'14.65 MB (15,360,000 bytes)' -Comment 'This folder contains ↵
information related to new surfboard designs and discussions about ↵
field and market research. Items are retained in this folder for ↵
720 days before being archived. ' -MustDisplayComment $true
```

The command that you enter for the folder is useful in helping users to know what the folder is supposed to be for. This comment will be displayed at the top of the listing of messages in the folder if you are using Outlook Web App, Outlook 2007, or Outlook 2010. An example of this is shown in Figure 17.41. This information is not displayed with earlier versions.

FIGURE 17.41
Comment text for a custom folder

The storage quota option is useful if you are planning to restrict content for each of the managed folders. Once users reach the storage quota maximum for this folder, the folder name will turn red and users will see a dialog informing them that their mailbox needs to be cleaned up. This dialog (shown in Figure 17.42) is displayed only if you are using Outlook 2007 or 2010 as the client.

FIGURE 17.42
Users are prompted to clean up their mailbox if a managed custom folder is over its size limit.

The only problem with the dialog shown in Figure 17.42 is that it does not tell the user which folder is over its limit. The Get-ManagedFolder cmdlet allows you to retrieve a list of both the managed custom folders and the default folders:

```
Get-ManagedFolder
```

```
Name                      FolderName                Description
----                      ----------                -----------
Calendar                  Calendar                  ManagedDefaultFolder
Contacts                  Contacts                  ManagedDefaultFolder
Deleted Items             DeletedItems              ManagedDefaultFolder
Drafts                    Drafts                    ManagedDefaultFolder
Inbox                     Inbox                     ManagedDefaultFolder
Junk E-mail               Junk-Email                ManagedDefaultFolder
Journal                   Journal                   ManagedDefaultFolder
Notes                     Notes                     ManagedDefaultFolder
Outbox                    Outbox                    ManagedDefaultFolder
Sent Items                SentItems                 ManagedDefaultFolder
Tasks                     Tasks                     ManagedDefaultFolder
Entire Mailbox            All                       ManagedDefaultFolder
RSS Feeds                 RssSubscriptions          ManagedDefaultFolder
Sync Issues               SyncIssues                ManagedDefaultFolder
Finance and Accounting... Finance and Accounting... ManagedCustomFolder
Project Team Communica... Project Team Communica... ManagedCustomFolder
Fax and voice mail data   Fax and voice mail data   ManagedCustomFolder
Department Communications Department Communications ManagedCustomFolder
Official Corporate Mes... Official Corporate Mes... ManagedCustomFolder
Design and Market Rese... Design and Market Rese... ManagedCustomFolder
```

If you are a fan of the EMS, Table 17.9 shows the cmdlets that can be used for creating and managing managed custom folders.

TABLE 17.9:   Managed Folder Exchange Management Shell Cmdlets

CMDLET	EXPLANATION
New-ManagedFolder	Creates a new managed custom folder
Set-ManagedFolder	Sets properties for an existing managed custom folder
Get-ManagedFolder	Retrieves a list of the managed folders in the organization
Remove-ManagedFolder	Deletes a managed custom folder

Managed Folder Mailbox Policies

Creating managed custom folders and defining managed content settings are just part of the equation when implementing MRM. Now you have to assign those managed folders to mailboxes. You assign folders to mailboxes with the managed folder mailbox policy. Once you have created a managed folder mailbox policy, you can assign the policy to one or more mailboxes.

ONE MANAGED FOLDER POLICY PER MAILBOX

A mailbox can have only one managed folder policy assigned to it.

Creating Managed Folder Mailbox Policies

Managed folder mailbox policies are found in the Mailboxes subcontainer of the Organization Configuration work center. You find them under the Managed Folder Mailbox Policies tab; by default there are no managed folder mailbox policies. In a small organization, you may need only a single managed folder mailbox policy, whereas larger organizations may have many policies. The policies assign different managed folders or managed content settings to different users based on their departments, job functions, or company division.

A managed folder mailbox policy has few properties. When you launch the New Managed Folder Mailbox Policy wizard, you are asked to provide a name for the policy, and you must provide the folders (both custom and default) that will be managed by this policy. Figure 17.43 shows the New Mailbox Policy page of this wizard.

FIGURE 17.43
Creating a managed folder mailbox policy

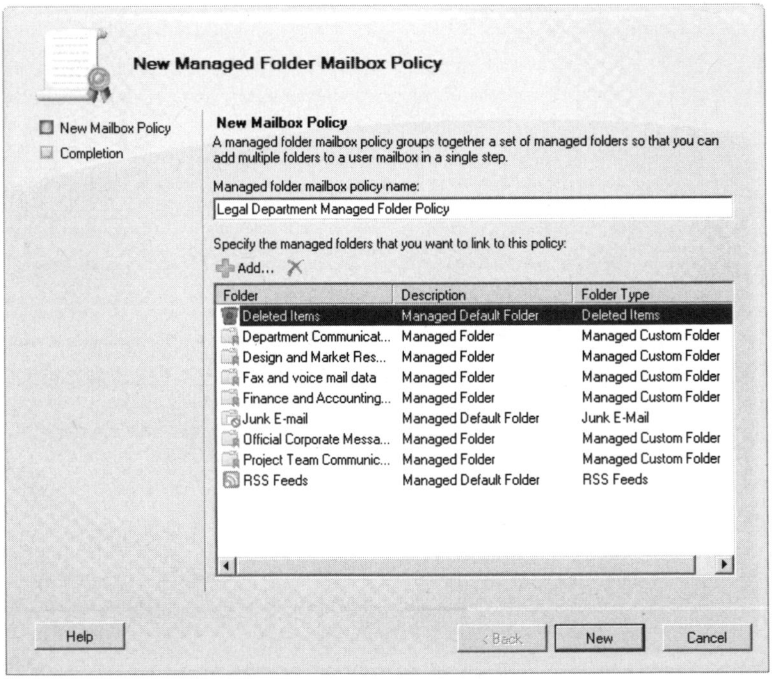

Note that the folders linked with this policy include both custom and default folders. A folder can be linked with more than one policy. The resulting EMS command that is executed to create this policy is as follows:

```
New-ManagedFolderMailboxPolicy -Name 'Legal Department Managed ↵
Folder Policy' -ManagedFolderLinks 'Deleted Items','Department ↵
```

```
Communications','Design and Market Research Discussions','Fax ↵
and voice mail data','Finance and AccountingInformation','Junk ↵
E-mail','Official Corporate Messages','Project Team ↵
Communications','RSS Feeds'
```

Assigning Managed Folder Mailbox Policies to Users

After a managed folder mailbox policy is defined, the next step is to assign it to a user. You can do this in one of two ways. The first way you can assign the policy to a user is during account creation; Figure 17.44 shows the Mailbox Settings page of the New Mailbox Wizard. You can check the Managed Folder Mailbox Policy check box and then browse for a listing of available managed folder mailbox policies in the organization.

FIGURE 17.44
Assigning a managed folder mailbox policy at account creation

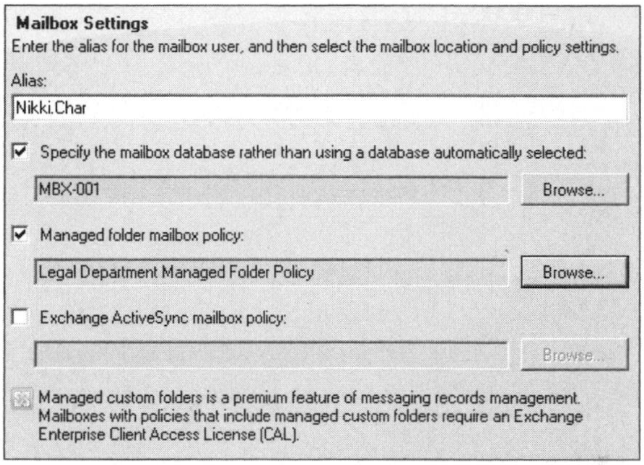

If your organization is supporting Outlook 2003 or earlier clients, you will see a warning message informing you that not all of the managed folder features may be available to the user. This dialog appears whenever you assign a managed folder mailbox policy to a user account.

The second way to assign a policy to a user is by using the Exchange Management Shell; you will notice an additional option in the Enable-Mailbox or New-Mailbox command line. This option, -ManagedFolderMailboxPolicy, sets the ManagedFolderMailboxPolicy property on the mailbox. Here is an example of an EMS command that would enable a mailbox and set the managed folder mailbox policy:

```
Enable-Mailbox 'volcanosurfboards.com/VolcanoSurfboards/Nikki Char' ↵
-Alias 'Nikki Char' -Database 'MBX-001' -ManagedFolderMailboxPolicy ↵
'Executives Managed Folder Mailbox Policy'
```

If someone created an account without defining the managed folder mailbox policy, you can assign a policy to the account using the EMC. Locate the mailbox in the Recipient Configuration work center, display the mailbox's properties, go to the Mailbox Settings properties page, select Messaging Records Management, and click the Properties button. This will display the Messaging Records Management properties for that mailbox (see Figure 17.45).

Using the Messaging Records Management properties, you can define which managed folder mailbox policy is assigned, and you can optionally specify a period of time during which the policy does not apply to the particular mailbox.

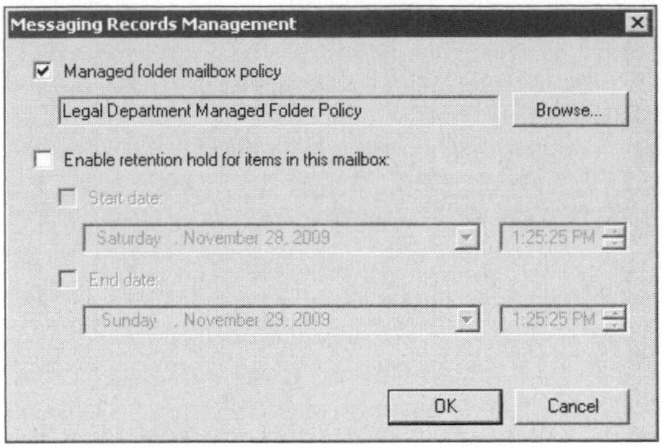

FIGURE 17.45
Messaging Records
Management properties
of a mailbox

If the mailbox already exists, you can assign the policy using the EMS. For example, if you want to assign user Supatana to the Executives Managed Folder Mailbox policy, you would type the following EMS cmdlet:

```
Set-Mailbox "Supatana" -ManagedFolderMailboxPolicy "Executives Managed ↵
Folder Mailbox Policy"
```

Actually, if you know that you have to assign a group of mailboxes to a specific policy, it is much easier to do using the EMS. For example, if you want to assign everyone in the Executives group to a managed folder mailbox policy, you can use a single EMS command to accomplish this. Before we show you the command, let's take apart the pieces.

First you want to enumerate the objects that are members of the Executives distribution group. You would use the Get-DistributionGroupMember cmdlet. Here is what that would look like:

```
Get-DistributionGroupMember "Executives"
Name                              RecipientType
----                              -------------
Saso Erdeljanov                   UserMailbox
Jordan Chang                      UserMailbox
Don Nguyen                        UserMailbox
Goga Kukrika                      UserMailbox
Pavel Nagaev                      UserMailbox
George Cue                        UserMailbox
Julie Samante                     UserMailbox
Chris Eanes                       UserMailbox
Bthaworn Thaweeaphiradeemaitree   UserMailbox
Cheyne Manalo                     UserMailbox
Jason Sherry                      UserMailbox
Konrad Sagala                     UserMailbox
```

Remember that when you retrieve information using PowerShell, what is actually output is the objects; you can pipe those objects to other cmdlets. You want to pipe this command to the Set-Mailbox cmdlet in order to assign the ManagedFolderMailboxPolicy property:

```
Get-DistributionGroupMember "Executives" | Set-Mailbox ↵
-ManagedFolderMailboxPolicy "Executives Managed Folder Mailbox Policy"
```

Another useful thing you can do from the EMS is to list the mailboxes that are already assigned to a particular policy. You just need to implement the `Where` cmdlet and filter only the objects whose `ManagedFolderMailboxPolicy` property starts with `Default`. Here is an example:

```
Get-Mailbox | Where {$_.ManagedFolderMailboxPolicy -like "*Default*"} ↵
| Format-Table Name,Managed*


Name                      ManagedFolderMailboxPolicy
----                      --------------------------
Nathan Nakanishi          Default Managed Folder Mailbox Policy
Lily Ebrahimi             Default Managed Folder Mailbox Policy
Aran Hoffmann             Default Managed Folder Mailbox Policy
Ryan Tung                 Default Managed Folder Mailbox Policy
```

Enabling Messaging Records Management on the Mailbox Server

The final piece of enabling MRM is to configure the mailbox servers to schedule and run the Managed Folder Assistant. Managed custom folders do not get created, nor do the content settings get enforced, unless the Managed Folder Assistant is run. The Managed Folder Assistant also processes retention policies for personal mailbox archives. Each Exchange server that has the Mailbox role assigned to it has a Messaging Records Management properties page (shown in Figure 17.46.) Here, you can define a schedule on which the Managed Folder Assistant runs; by default, the assistant is scheduled to run from 1:00 a.m. until 9:00 a.m. daily.

FIGURE 17.46
Viewing a Mailbox server's Messaging Records Management properties page

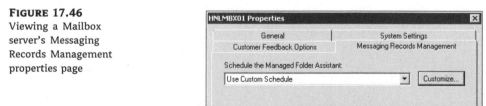

When you click the Customize button, you are presented with the Select schedule dialog (see Figure 17.47). The Detail View radio buttons allow you to specify if you are looking at the schedule in 15-minute increments or 1-hour increments.

As with other schedule dialogs that have a 1-hour view and a 15-minute view, be very careful when selecting a schedule. (If you use the 1-hour view and select an entire hour block, the Managed Folder Assistant will run four times per hour.) We recommend that you select the 15-minute view and then schedule times in 15-minute intervals. Further, unless you have a business requirement to run the Managed Folder Assistant more frequently, we recommend that you schedule it to run no more than two or three times per day.

If you want to kick off the Managed Folder Assistant manually, there is a cmdlet that lets you do this: the `Start-ManagedFolderAssistant` cmdlet. It will create any custom folders that need to be created and manage any folder content that is now eligible to be managed by MRM. This cmdlet is useful to know if you have just assigned a new policy to a group of users and want to make sure that any custom folders that need to be created are created immediately.

FIGURE 17.47
The Select Schedule
dialog for the Managed
Folder Assistant

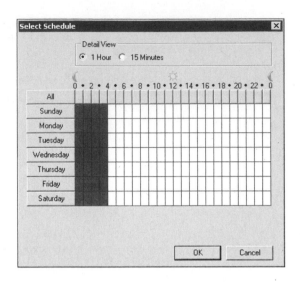

If you run `Start-ManagedFolderAssistant` from the EMS on a Mailbox server, no parameters are necessary. However, if you want to run it on a remote mailbox server, you would type this (substituting the name of your server):

```
Start-ManagedFolderAssistant hnlex03
```

You can also run the Managed Folder Assistant against a specific mailbox, as in this example:

```
Start-ManagedFolderAssistant -Mailbox Suriya.Supatanasakul
```

The Bottom Line

Create and delete user mailboxes.   Exchange Server 2010 supports the same types of mail-enabled users as previous versions of Exchange. These are mailbox-enabled users which have a mailbox on your Exchange server and the mail-enabled user account. The mail-enabled user account is a security principal within your organization (and would appear in your Global Address List), but their email is delivered to an external email system.

For mailbox-enabled user accounts, there are four different types of accounts: the User mailbox, a Room Resource mailbox, an Equipment Resource mailbox, and a Linked mailbox. Mailbox management tasks can either be performed via the Exchange Management Console or the Exchange Management Shell.

Master It   Your Active Directory forest has a trust relationship to another Active Directory forest that is part of your corporate IT infrastructure. The administrator in the other forest wants you to host their email. What type of mailboxes should you create for the users in this other forest?

Master It   You must modify user Nikki.Char's office name to say Honolulu. You want to do this using the Exchange Management Shell. What command would perform this task?

Master It   You need to change the maximum number of safe senders allows for user Jeff.Bloom's mailbox to 4096. You want to make this change using the Exchange Management Shell. What command would you use?

Manage mailbox permissions.   A newly created mailbox only allows the owner of the mailbox to access the folders within that mailbox. An end user can assign someone else permissions to access individual folders within their mailbox or to send mail on their behalf using the Outlook client. The administrator can assign permissions to the entire mailbox for other users. Further, the administrator can assign a user the Send As permission to a mailbox.

Master It   All executives within your organization share a single administrative assistant whose username is Chris.Rentch; all of the executives belong to a mail distribution group called #Executives. All of the executives want user Chris.Rentch to be able to access all of the folders within their mailboxes. What are some different ways you can accomplish this?

Move mailboxes to another database.   Exchange Server 2010 implements an entirely new way to move mailbox content from one mailbox database to another. The administrative tools (the Exchange Management Console and the New-MoveRequest cmdlet) are no longer responsible for moving mailbox data. The Microsoft Exchange Mailbox Replication service that runs on each Client Access server role handles mailbox moves.

Master It   You want to use the Exchange Management Shell to move mailbox Brian.Desmond from mailbox database MBX-001 to MBX-002. The move should ignore up to three bad messages before it fails. What command should you use?

Master It   You have submitted a move request for user Brian.Desmond. You want to check the status and statistics of the move request to see if it has completed; you want to use the Exchange Management Shell to do this. What command would you type?

Perform bulk manipulation of mailbox properties.   Perhaps the most powerful and useful feature of Exchange Server 2007 and 2010 has been the inclusion of the Exchange Management Shell. Even a new Exchange administrator can quickly take advantage of the basic shell features. As an administrator gains more experience, she can use piping to use the object(s) that are output from one cmdlet as input for another cmdlet.

By taking advantage of piping and the EMS, bulk manipulation of users and mailboxes can performed in a single command that previously might have taken hundreds of lines of scripting code.

Master It   You want to move all of your executives to a single mailbox database called MBX-004. All of your executives belong to a mail distribution group called #Executives. How could you accomplish this task with a single command?

Use messaging records management to manage mailbox content.   Messaging records management provides you with control over the content of user's mailbox. Basic MRM features allow you to automatically purge old content such as Deleted Items or Junk E-mail. You can create new managed folders within the user's mailbox as well as move content to these folders.

Master It   You are managing an Exchange organization that was transitioned from Exchange Server 2003. You have found that many of your users are not emptying the contents of their Deleted Items and Junk E-mail folders. You want to automatically purge any content in these folders after 14 days. What are the steps you should take to do this?

Master It   You have a newly created managed folder mailbox called E-mail Purge Policy. You now need to assign this to all 900 of your existing mailboxes. What is the quickest and most efficient way to perform this task?

Chapter 18

Managing Mail-Enabled Groups

We're now well into the discussion on Exchange recipients and you are aware of the different recipient types that are available to messaging administrators in Exchange Server 2010. (If you need a refresher, they are all conveniently located for you in Chapter 16, "Basics of Recipient Management.")

Mail-enabled groups are one type of recipient that makes things a bit more interesting for us — and by *interesting* we mean complex. Most administrators are familiar with the concept of groups, but starting in Exchange 2000 Server, with the integration of Active Directory and Exchange services, groups can now be mail enabled. This essentially provides the group with all the necessary attributes to be listed in the Exchange-specific directories and to be identified as a recipient object.

All the benefits of *groups*, as Active Directory objects, still apply to *mail-enabled groups*. They are objects that allow us to apply permissions in *bulk*, or allow us to send email messages in *bulk* — essentially making our lives as administrators and email users a little easier.

In this chapter, you will learn to:

◆ Choose the appropriate type and scope of mail-enabled groups

◆ Create and manage mail-enabled groups

◆ Explore the moderation features of Exchange Server 2010

Managing Mail-Enabled Groups

If your organization is like most organizations today, you make significant use of mail groups. You may refer to these as mail-enabled groups, distribution groups, or distribution lists. The official term for a mail group, though, is *mail-enabled group*. Within the Active Directory are two basic types of groups:

Security Groups   These are groups that can be assigned permissions to resources or rights to perform certain tasks. Security groups can be mail enabled and can be used for addressing mail by Exchange Server recipients.

Distribution Groups   These are groups that are not security principals; they have no security identifier and thus cannot be assigned any rights or permissions. Distribution groups are intended for use with a mail system that integrates with the Active Directory, such as Exchange Server.

Dynamic Distribution Groups   There is a subset of distribution groups called a dynamic distribution group (DDG). You will also see these referred to as query-based distribution groups (QBDGs). A DDG's membership list is dynamic, based on some criteria the administrator defines. DDGs are managed by using the Exchange Management Console or the Exchange Management Shell only.

When you create a new distribution group using the Active Directory Users and Computers interface, you will also notice that you must provide a scope for the group in addition to defining the group type (see Figure 18.1).

FIGURE 18.1
Creating a new group in
Active Directory

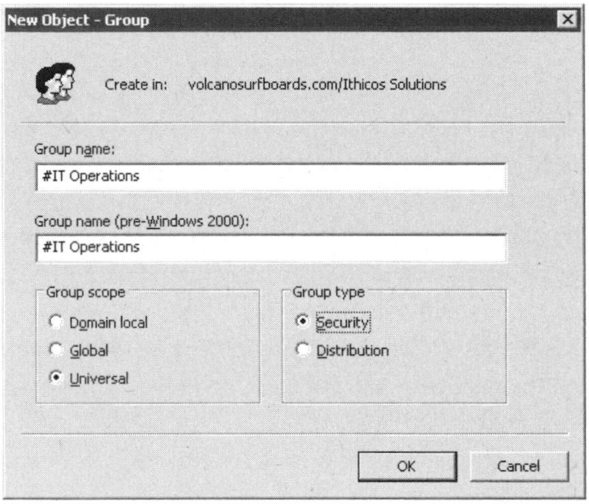

All groups utilized by Exchange Server 2010 must be set to the Universal scope. This tells the Active Directory that the membership list attribute for that group should be replicated to all global catalog servers in the organization. In previous versions of Exchange, you could mail-enable a global or domain local group. However, this could cause mail delivery problems in organizations that have multiple Active Directory domains, since the membership of a global group, for example, is not replicated to a global catalog server. In previous versions of Exchange this possibly resulted in lost emails.

In Exchange Server 2010, by default the only type of group that you can mail-enable using the Exchange Management Console is a universal group. However, if you have migrated from Exchange Server 2003, you may have domain local or global groups that were mail-enabled previously. The recipient type for these groups is MailEnabledNonUniversalGroup. We strongly recommend that you convert each of these domain local and global groups to a universal group. This ensures that you do not have group expansion problems in multi-domain environments.

Creating and Managing Mail-Enabled Groups

Let's first go through the process of defining a mail-enabled group and look at the steps necessary to create them. Groups can be created or mail-enabled using the EMC and the EMS command shell. If you are inclined to use the EMC, groups have their own subcontainer, called Distribution Group, which is found under the Recipient Configuration container. Figure 18.2 shows an example of the Distribution Group container in the EMS.

FIGURE 18.2
Viewing the Distribution
Group subcontainer

An important consideration when creating group names is to create a standard for mail-enabled group display names. This allows them to all be grouped together in the global address list. For example, in Figure 18.2 we have used special characters in front of the group names, mostly to illustrate how they will sort together in the global address list. Remember that special characters will be sorted before letters or numbers in the global address list.

When selecting a name for the groups, pick a standard that will work for your organization and that your users will clearly understand. We find that most companies differ in their naming convention for groups. There is no best or perfect naming convention. The key is to identify a naming convention that represents static units (based on geography or company-wide) and that is, therefore, less likely to have to be modified. Departmental groups are common, but again here, try to create a structure that makes sense for users and that is less likely to have to be modified.

⊕ Real World Scenario

MAIL-ENABLED GROUPS: WHAT NOT TO DO

There are many examples of companies misusing or overusing technology. Unfortunately, inappropriate management of group permissions, as well as the lack of a standard naming convention, can cause havoc for administrators and end users.

The most blatant representation of this problem became painfully obvious during a recent visit to a new customer. Their Active Directory infrastructure had lost all default and standard security provisions for minimizing administrative rights. This was one of those networks where everyone was a domain administrator. So beyond the obvious security implications, this issue had snowballed into a messaging issue where the global address list included more than 50,000 objects for a company of fewer than 200 users.

A large group of support users were in charge of creating mail-enabled groups for anyone who requested them. And requests came from everyone, with little more reason than "I need a group for Project X. Please add me and Jim to that group. We need to send emails to each other as well." The company did not have a standard group naming convention, so it was difficult to identify the purpose of each group. The groups were never purged from Active Directory and most of them had been stale for many years, and all were mail enabled.

This was a sad illustration of improper planning in implementing both Active Directory and Exchange. A large offline address book, a security risk (when mail-enabled security groups are mistaken for distribution groups), and an inefficient Active Directory structure are only some of the possible impacts of inadequate group management.

Creating Mail-Enabled Groups

The simplest way to create and manage mail-enabled groups is to use the EMC graphical interface. Previously, in Active Directory we created a group; the group's scope is universal and the type is a security group. However, just using Active Directory Users and Computers will not define any mail (Exchange) attributes.

To create a mail-enabled group:

1. Open the EMC, navigate to the Recipient Configuration work center, and find the Distribution Group subcontainer.

2. Click the New Distribution Group task in the Actions pane to launch the New Distribution Group wizard. The first screen in the wizard is the Introduction page, which prompts you to either create a new group or choose an existing group.

3. Because the group you want to mail-enable is already in the Active Directory, choose the Existing Group radio button and click the Browse button to locate and select the group (see Figure 18.3). The only group types that will appear in the Select Group dialog box will be universal groups that have not already been mail enabled.

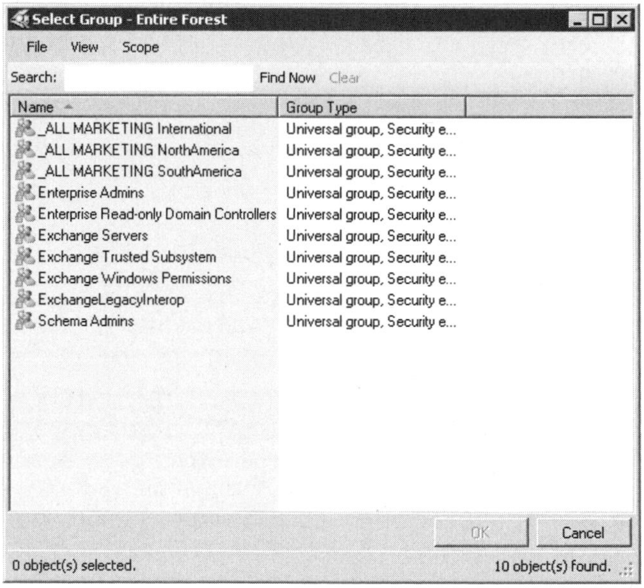

FIGURE 18.3
Selecting a group to mail-enable

4. Once you click Next on the Introduction page, the next page you see is the Group Information page (see Figure 18.4). The Group Information page will ask you to provide the display name for the group as well as the alias. By default, the alias is used to define the SMTP email address for the group and should not have any spaces in it.

5. When you click Next on the Group Information page, you will see the confirmation page that allows you to verify the actions you are about to take.

6. When you are sure that you have defined everything you need to define, you can click the New button and the group you have selected will be mail enabled.

FIGURE 18.4
Entering information
about the group

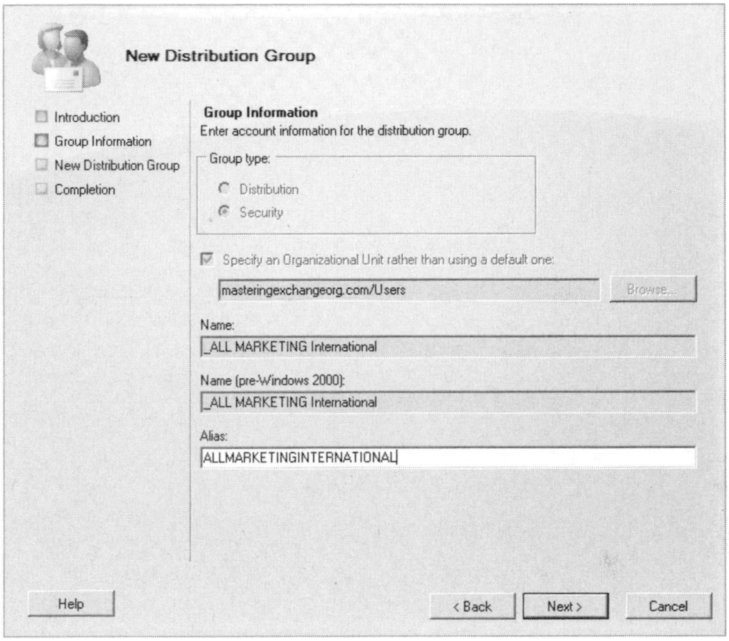

The resulting EMS command that performed the action is as follows:

```
Enable-DistributionGroup -Identity:'MasteringExchangeOrg.com/Corporate/ ↵
IT Operations' -DisplayName:'_ALL MARKETING International' ↵
-Alias:'ALLMARKETINGINTERNATIONAL'
```

The New Distribution Group wizard can be used to create new mail-enabled groups as well as to mail-enable existing ones. If you choose to create a new group on the Introduction page, you must provide a few additional pieces of information on the Group Information page, including the group type (Distribution or Security), the OU in which the group will be created, the group's name, the group's pre–Windows 2000 name, the display name, and the alias. The EMS command that is executed uses the `New-DistributionGroup` cmdlet rather than the `Enable-DistributionGroup` cmdlet.

Managing Mail-Enabled Groups

Once groups have been mail enabled, their properties can be configured to achieve advanced messaging results. Though the core function of a group is to facilitate the delivery of mail messages to multiple users, and its subsequent management, there are many specific group features that can be set. This next section describes many of those properties and the methods for applying them.

MANAGING GENERAL PROPERTIES OF MAIL-ENABLED GROUPS

You should be aware of some additional properties when you are creating mail-enabled groups. Let's start with the Mail Flow Settings properties page. This page includes two components you can configure: Message Size Restrictions and Message Delivery Restrictions.

If you select the Message Size Restrictions option and click the Properties button, you will see the Message Size Restrictions dialog box. Notice that we have restricted the maximum message size for this particular group to 100 KB; this can help prevent misuse of distribution groups or the accidental distribution of large files.

The Message Delivery Restrictions dialog box (shown in Figure 18.5) has a little more information. If you have looked at the message delivery restrictions for a single mailbox, you are already familiar with these settings and concepts. In the example in Figure 18.5, we have restricted who is allowed to send mail to this group. You can specify individuals and other groups. We recommend you always restrict who is allowed to send mail to large groups or groups that contain VIPs. This prevents accidents and keeps unwanted mail content from your VIPs.

FIGURE 18.5
A distribution group's Message Delivery Restrictions dialog box

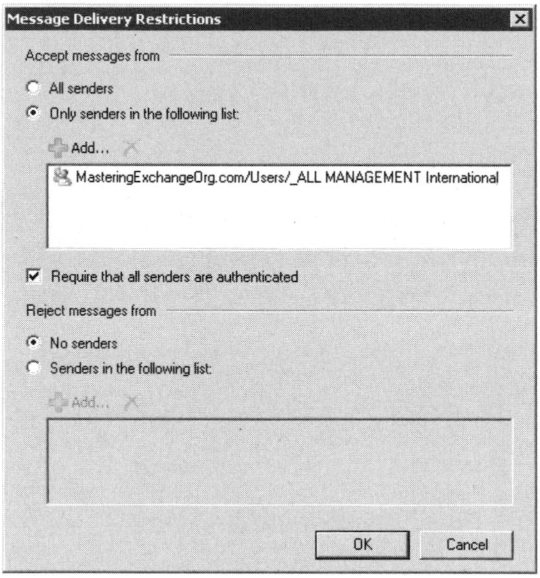

You may also notice the Require That All Senders Are Authenticated check box. For mail-enabled groups, this box is checked by default. We recommend you keep it set this way; after all, you probably don't want spammers or external salespeople to start sending mail to your Everyone@company.com or Executives@company.com addresses. However, you will have to uncheck this option if you have specific groups that need to receive email from unauthenticated users, such as users from unaffiliated companies on the Internet.

The E-Mail Addresses properties page (Figure 18.6) shows the email addresses that can be used to address a message to the group. You can edit the existing addresses or add new ones.

If a distribution list is used entirely within your organization, the Reply To address will not be particularly important. However, if you use lists both internally and externally, keep in mind that the Reply To address is the one that will be seen by people outside the organization. For example, if someone sends a message to your HelpDesk@company.com address and internal users reply to that message and courtesy copy (Cc) the distribution group, the original sender will see the Reply To address of the distribution group. You must also keep in mind that all addresses set on the E-mail Addresses properties page must have an associated accepted domain. Though the EMC will not prevent you from assigning an SMTP address for a nonauthoritative domain in your company, you should make sure that all necessary transport configurations have been set. (To verify your transport settings for an alternate SMTP domain, look at Chapter 26, "Managing Transport and Journaling Rules.")

Now let's look at the Advanced properties page, shown in Figure 18.7.

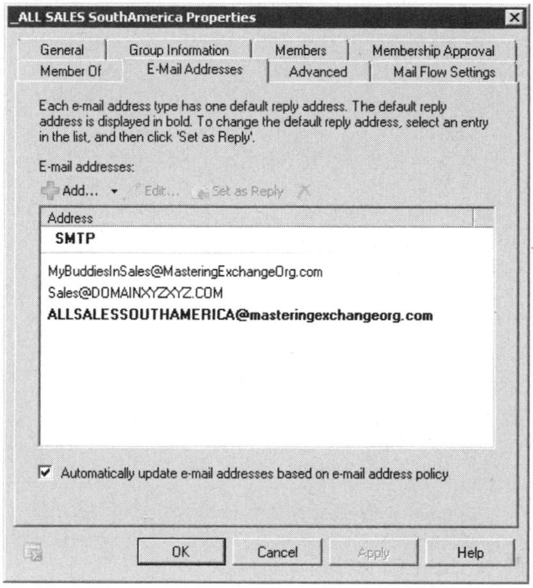

FIGURE 18.6
Email address properties
of a mail-enabled group

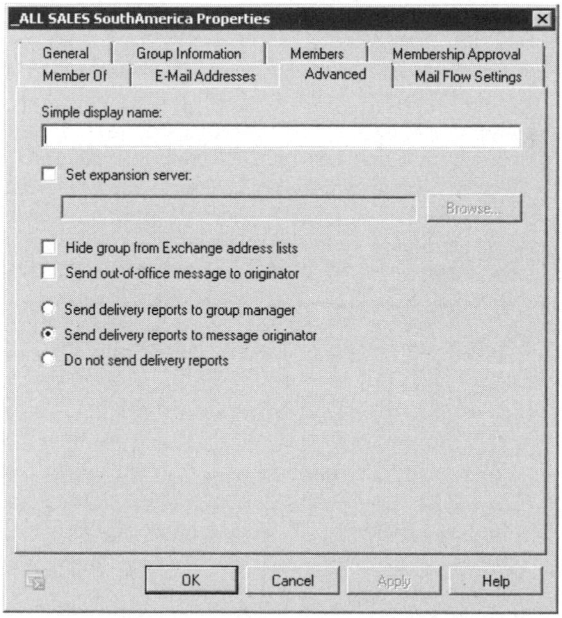

FIGURE 18.7
Advanced properties of
a mail-enabled group

You should be aware of several properties on this page, and you should know what they may mean to your organization and users:

Simple Display Name By default, when a message is sent from a recipient, the recipient's display name is included; in some organizations the display name can be quite long. Exchange also allows non-ASCII characters (Unicode characters) to be included in the display name. If you are connecting to older mail systems that do not support long display names or Unicode characters, you can include a simple display name that consists only of ASCII characters.

Set Expansion Server   Message expansion is the process of enumerating the members of a mail-enabled group and figuring out where each member is, either within your organization or externally. Expansion of large mail-enabled groups can be a pretty intensive process for a Hub Transport server as well as the Active Directory global catalog server that it is using.

The Expansion Server list provides you with a listing of all the Hub Transport servers in your organization. By default, Expansion Server is set to Any Server In The Organization. This means that the first Exchange Hub Transport server receiving the message is responsible for expanding the mail-enabled group. In some environments, you may want to manually specify which Hub Transport server handles expansion.

For example, if you have a mail-enabled group called Executives, and you know that all members of the Executives group are in the headquarters office, you could designate a Hub Transport server in the headquarters office to be responsible for expansion. But keep in mind that this solution provides no fault tolerance: if that Hub Transport server is down (or taken offline permanently), Exchange will not dynamically assign another server to handle expansion. We therefore recommend you keep the default settings and allow Exchange to determine the appropriate place to expand the group's membership. This setting is appropriate for most Exchange deployments.

EXPANSION SERVERS IN A COEXISTENCE SCENARIO BETWEEN EXCHANGE SERVER 2003 AND EXCHANGE SERVER 2010

Both Exchange Server 2003 and Exchange Server 2010 provide the ability to configure a specific server to expand mail-enabled groups. In an environment where you install Exchange Server 2010 servers into an Exchange Server 2003 organization, there are cases where you should ensure that you use only Exchange Server 2010 Hub Transport servers as expansion servers. Specifically, if you enable Exchange 2010 recipients for journaling, you should never configure Exchange Server 2003 servers as expansion servers. If a message is routed for expansion to an Exchange 2003 server, because the server cannot access journal rules, the message will not be journaled.

Hide Group From Exchange Address Lists   This check box (unchecked by default) allows you to prevent a mail-enabled group from being displayed in the address lists. This might be useful for specialized groups that are used just for mail distribution by an automated system or for users that know the SMTP address.

Send Out-Of-Office Message To Originator   This check box allows you to specify whether an out-of-office message will be returned to the sender of a message if someone's out-of-office rule is enabled. This option is unchecked by default. For small or departmental mail-enabled groups, it might be useful to turn it on, but for large or company-wide distribution groups, you should probably leave this disabled.

Delivery Reports   If messages are not properly delivered to the intended recipients of a message sent to a mail-enabled group, you can control how the delivery reports are generated. There are three options:

Send Delivery Reports To Group Manager   Will send the delivery reports to the person listed as the manager on the group's properties

Send Delivery Reports To Message Originator   Sends the delivery report back to the message sender.

Do Not Send Delivery Reports   Prevents delivery reports from being sent to anyone.

MANAGING MODERATION FOR DISTRIBUTION GROUPS

We're always gratified when an often-requested feature appears in a release of the product. Such is the case of moderated groups. The first release of this feature appears in Exchange Server 2010.

Now any group can be enabled for moderation. Once moderation is enabled, you can define one or more moderators, as well as exceptions to the moderation process. Though moderation is handled on the back end by the Hub Transport servers, you configure the moderation options in the properties of the moderated groups. Figure 18.8 shows the moderated group configuration options on the Message Moderation page. Note that you can also configure moderated groups from the Exchange Control Panel. A group owner, or an administrator who has been assigned the necessary RBAC role, can enable groups for moderation and add multiple moderators.

FIGURE 18.8
Configuration options
for moderated groups

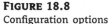

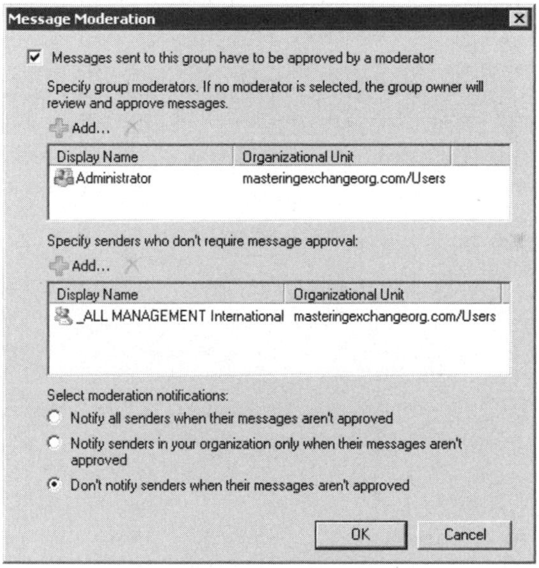

Message Moderation

☑ Messages sent to this group have to be approved by a moderator

Specify group moderators. If no moderator is selected, the group owner will review and approve messages.

✛ Add... ✕

Display Name	Organizational Unit	
Administrator	masteringexchangeorg.com/Users	

Specify senders who don't require message approval:

✛ Add... ✕

Display Name	Organizational Unit
_ALL MANAGEMENT International	masteringexchangeorg.com/Users

Select moderation notifications:

○ Notify all senders when their messages aren't approved

○ Notify senders in your organization only when their messages aren't approved

⦿ Don't notify senders when their messages aren't approved

[OK]   [Cancel]

Notice first that all groups have moderation disabled by default. The first feature you will immediately need to configure is the moderator(s) for the group. A moderator will be notified each time a message is sent to the group. The moderator will receive a copy of the message and will then be able to perform an action against the message. The moderator can accept or reject messages sent to the group. Messages are not delivered to the group until a moderator of the group has approved the message. You can define multiple moderators, but you can only assign users (not groups) as moderators.

An administrator can also exempt a specific user from being moderated. Users listed in the Specify Senders Who Don't Require Message Approval list are able to send email messages to the group without being moderated.

The Select Moderation Notifications settings provide the ability to notify or silently drop messages sent to the list. If you choose to notify senders of rejected messages, you can select to notify only internal senders or all senders.

Note that moderation is not limited to groups; an administrator can also moderate email sent to mailboxes or mail contacts, in the same way as mail sent to distribution groups. Email sent from a specific mailbox can be moderated by using a transport rule, which contains moderation as an action.

Creating Dynamic Distribution Groups

Do you have a problem keeping your distribution groups up-to-date? Dynamic distribution groups (DDGs) may be the solution you have been looking for. Mail is sent to users in a DDG based on one or more criteria, such as organizational unit, city, or department. As a user's Active Directory properties are changed or updated, the DDG membership changes automatically.

DDGs are created a little differently than a regular mail-enabled group because you have to define the filter settings and the conditions of the group. In the Distribution Group subcontainer of the Recipient Configuration work center, you can launch the New Dynamic Distribution Group wizard by clicking the New Dynamic Distribution Group task in the Actions pane. The Introduction page of the wizard shows some typical information required for creating a new group object. This page requires that you specify the organizational unit in which you want the object created, the display name (Name), and the Exchange alias of the group.

Once you have specified the information necessary on the Introduction page, the next page, Filter Settings (Figure 18.9), allows you to specify which recipient container (or the entire domain) you want to apply to the filter and which types of recipients you want to display.

FIGURE 18.9
Filter Settings for a dynamic distribution group

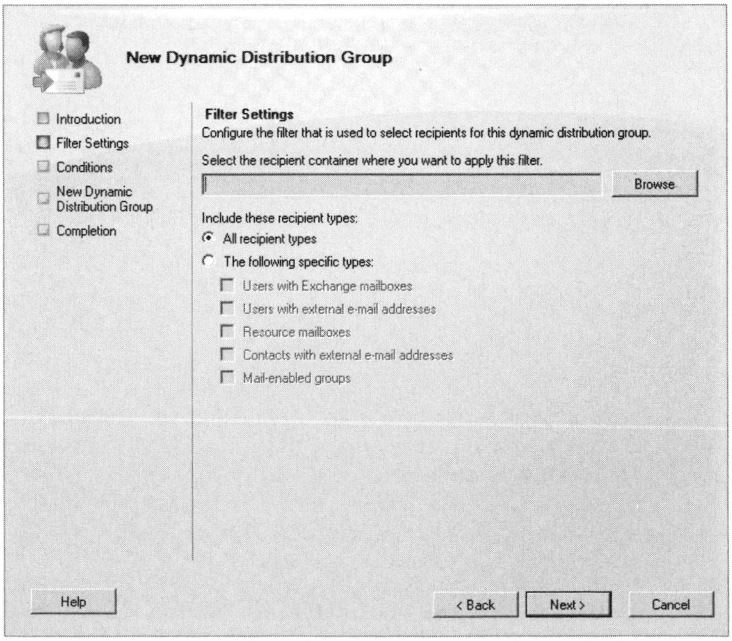

The following recipient types can be included in the filter settings:

◆ All Recipients Types

◆ Users With Exchange Mailboxes (mailbox-enabled user accounts)

◆ Users With External E-mail Addresses (mail-enabled user accounts)

◆ Resource Mailboxes (room and equipment)

◆ Contacts With External E-mail Addresses

◆ Mail-Enabled Groups

After selecting the recipient type and OU scope for the DDG and clicking Next, you will be able to further refine the scope of the group membership on the Conditions page. In the example shown in Figure 18.10, we have selected all users whose state or province is Quebec.

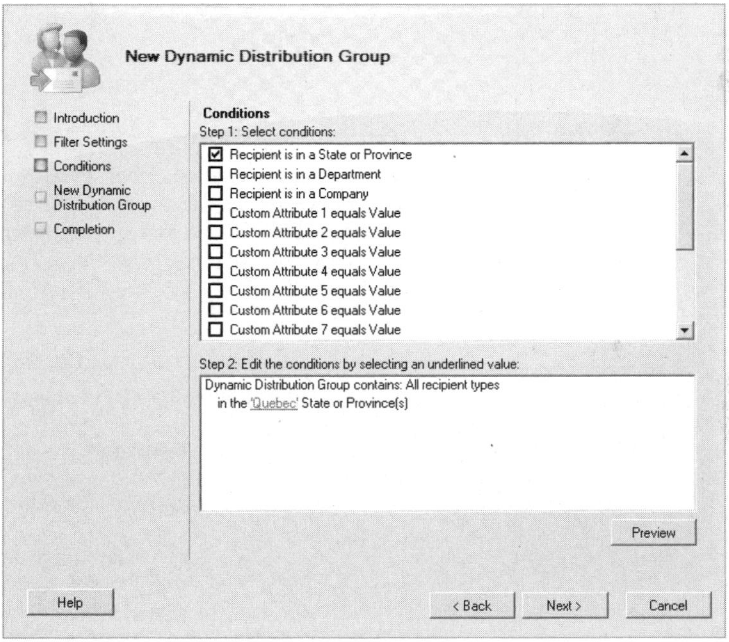

FIGURE 18.10
Narrowing the membership of a dynamic distribution group

The Conditions page of the DDG allows you to specify the following attributes for inclusion in the DDG:

◆ State or province

◆ Department

◆ Company

◆ Custom attribute 1 through 15

Using DDGs will help emphasize the importance of having accurate and consistent information in the Active Directory. Looking back to Figure 18.10 when the account was created, if there were users who misspelled their state name or used an abbreviation rather than spelling it out, the DDG would not include everyone we wanted it to include.

The Preview button on the Conditions properties page is helpful in confirming that your scope and conditions are defined properly. By clicking this button, you will see the Dynamic Distribution Group Preview dialog box. Here, you should verify that the membership appears to be what you expected.

The next screen after Conditions is the New Dynamic Distribution Group screen, where you confirm the configuration properties. When you are sure that the properties are correct, click the New button. As with most wizards in the EMC, the Completion screen will include the EMS command that was executed:

```
New-DynamicDistributionGroup -Name '#Everyone in Quebec ↵
-IncludedRecipients 'MailboxUsers, MailUsers' ↵
 -ConditionalStateOrProvince 'Quebec' ↵
 -OrganizationalUnit 'MasteringExchangeOrg.com/Users' ↵
 -Alias '_EveryoneINquebec' ↵
 -RecipientContainer 'MasteringExchangeOrg.com/Recipients'
```

Using the Exchange Management Shell to Manage Groups

If you are just getting started with Exchange Server 2010 and the EMS, managing groups is going to be a little tougher using the EMS than it will be if you use the EMC. However, we want to review the cmdlets that are available for managing and manipulating mail-enabled groups so that, as you learn more about the EMS, you will have these cmdlets in your management arsenal. Table 18.1 lists the EMS cmdlets you can use to manage groups and mail-enabled groups.

TABLE 18.1:   EMS and PowerShell Cmdlets for Group Management

CMDLET	FUNCTION
Get-Group	Retrieves information about all Active Directory groups.
Set-Group	Sets information about an Active Directory group; this will work for any Active Directory group, not just mail-enabled ones.
Get-DistributionGroup	Retrieves information related to mail-enabled groups.
Set-DistributionGroup	Sets properties of mail-enabled groups.
New-DistributionGroup	Creates a new group in the Active Directory and mail-enables that group.
Enable-DistributionGroup	Mail-enables an existing group that was previously created in the Active Directory.
Disable-DistributionGroup	Removes mail attributes from a mail-enabled group but does not remove the group from the Active Directory.

TABLE 18.1: EMS and PowerShell Cmdlets for Group Management *(CONTINUED)*

CMDLET	FUNCTION
Remove-DistributionGroup	Deletes the mail attributes of a mail-enabled group and removes the group from the Active Directory.
Get-DistributionGroupMember	Retrieves membership list information from a mail-enabled group.
Add-DistributionGroupMember	Adds members to a mail-enabled group.
Remove-DistributionGroupMember	Removes members from a mail-enabled group.
Get-DynamicDistributionGroup	Retrieves information about a dynamic distribution group.
Set-DynamicDistributionGroup	Sets properties for dynamic distribution groups.
New-DynamicDistributionGroup	Creates a new dynamic distribution group.
Remove-DynamicDistributionGroup	Removes mail properties from a dynamic distribution group and deletes the group from the Active Directory.

CREATING DISTRIBUTION GROUPS USING THE EMS

For our purposes in this chapter, we'll focus on only a few of the cmdlets listed in Table 18.1 and some of the more common properties that can be used with them. The best way to illustrate them is to use some examples. In the first example, let's say you have a universal group in the Corporate OU in the Active Directory. The group is called Raptor Pilots. You want to set up this group as a distribution group.

Because the group already exists in the Active Directory, you'll use the Enable-Distribution Group cmdlet. You need to assign the group an Exchange alias (the -Alias property) and you need to assign it a display name (-DisplayName). The following command would accomplish these tasks:

```
Enable-DistributionGroup "Raptor Pilots" -DisplayName:"Raptor Pilots" ↵
-Alias:"raptorpilots"
```

If the group does not yet exist in the Active Directory and you wanted to create it in addition to mail-enabling it, you would use the New-DistributionGroup cmdlet. The following example creates the Raptor Pilots group in the Corporate OU; the -OrganizationalUnit property is required. The -SamAccountName property is also required if the group will be a security group:

```
New-DistributionGroup -Name:'Raptor Pilots' -Type:'Distribution' ↵
-OrganizationalUnit:'MasteringExchangeOrg.com/Corporate' ↵
-SamAccountName:'RaptorPilots' -DisplayName:'Raptor Pilots' ↵
-Alias:'Raptor Pilots'
```

To add members to a group, you use the Add-DistributionGroupMember cmdlet. Conversely, you can use the Remove-DistributionGroupMember cmdlet to remove members. For example, if you want to add user Elizabeth.Owusu to the Raptor Pilots group, you would type the following command:

```
Add-DistributionGroupMember "Raptor Pilots" -Member "Elizabeth.Owusu"
```

To enumerate the members of a group, you use the Get-DistributionListMember cmdlet. Here is an example and the resulting output:

```
Get-DistributionGroupMember "Raptor Pilots"

Name              RecipientType
----              -------------
Elizabeth Owusu   UserMailbox
```

You can modify the properties of a distribution group by using the Set-DistributionGroup cmdlet. Specifically, you can modify the moderation properties with this cmdlet. The following example enables moderation for a group and then configures the moderators, along with the exceptions and the notification settings.

```
Set-DistributionGroup "Raptor Pilots" -ModerationEnabled $true ↵
-ModeratedBy "David@MasteringExchangeOrg.com","Jim@MasteringExchangeOrg.com" ↵
-ByPassModerationFromSendersOrMembers "Administrators" ↵
-SendModerationNotifications Internal
```

You can set many properties for a mail-enabled group, as you probably recall from seeing what you can set through the graphical user interface. To update the properties of a group from the EMS, you use the Set-DistributionGroup cmdlet. Table 18.2 lists some of the common properties that you can define for a mail-enabled group.

TABLE 18.2:   Common Mail-Enabled Group Properties

PROPERTY	FUNCTION
Alias	Sets the Exchange alias for the group. By default, the alias is used when SMTP addresses are generated.
CustomAttribute1 through CustomAttribute15	Sets 1 of the 15 custom attributes (a.k.a. extension attributes).
DisplayName	Sets the display name of the mail-enabled group; the display name is what is visible in address lists.
HiddenFromAddressLists Enabled	Sets whether or not the group will be displayed in address lists. The default is that the objects are visible. You can set this to $True and it will hide the lists.
MaxReceiveSize	Sets the maximum size message that can be sent to the group.
ModerationEnabled	Enables or disables moderation for a group.

You can view the group's properties using the EMS cmdlet Get-DistributionGroup. This cmdlet lets you view the properties of the group. Many of these you can modify using the Set-DistributionGroup cmdlet. Here is how to view the properties of a mail-enabled universal group named "_All Management International":

```
get-distributiongroup "_all management international" | fl
RunspaceId                            :
2ad487e7-aec0-464a-b7ea-1b48d0810292
GroupType                             : Universal
SamAccountName                        : _ALL MANAGEMENT International
BypassNestedModerationEnabled         : False
ManagedBy                             :
{MasteringExchangeOrg.com/Users/Administrator}
MemberJoinRestriction                 : Closed
MemberDepartRestriction               : Open
ExpansionServer                       :
ReportToManagerEnabled                : False
ReportToOriginatorEnabled             : True
SendOofMessageToOriginatorEnabled     : False
AcceptMessagesOnlyFrom                : {}
AcceptMessagesOnlyFromDLMembers       : {}
AcceptMessagesOnlyFromSendersOrMembers : {}
AddressListMembership                 : {\Groups(VLV), \All Groups(VLV),
 \All Recipients(VLV), \Default Global Address List, \All Groups}
Alias                                 : ALLMANAGEMENTINTERNATIONAL
ArbitrationMailbox                    : MasteringExchangeOrg.com/Users/
SystemMailbox{1f05a927-c78f-4458-87ab-1985e85bde9d}
BypassModerationFromSendersOrMembers  : {}
OrganizationalUnit                    : masteringexchangeorg.com/Users
CustomAttribute1                      :
CustomAttribute10                     :
CustomAttribute11                     :
CustomAttribute12                     :
CustomAttribute13                     :
CustomAttribute14                     :
CustomAttribute15                     :
CustomAttribute2                      :
CustomAttribute3                      :
CustomAttribute4                      :
CustomAttribute5                      :
CustomAttribute6                      :
CustomAttribute7                      :
CustomAttribute8                      :
CustomAttribute9                      :
DisplayName                           : _ALL MANAGEMENT International
EmailAddresses                        :
{SMTP:ALLMANAGEMENTINTERNATIONAL@masteringexchangeorg.com}
GrantSendOnBehalfTo                   : {}
HiddenFromAddressListsEnabled         : False
LegacyExchangeDN                      : /o=MasteringExchangeOrg/ou=Exchange
```

```
Administrative Group (FYDIBOHF23SPDLT)/cn=
                                     Recipients/cn=_ALL MANAGEMENT
International
MaxSendSize                         : unlimited
MaxReceiveSize                      : unlimited
ModeratedBy                         : {}
ModerationEnabled                   : False
PoliciesIncluded                    : {42c01b72-415f-444a-a545-725773ea787f,
{26491cfc-9e50-4857-861b-0cb8df22b5d7}}
PoliciesExcluded                    : {}
EmailAddressPolicyEnabled           : True
PrimarySmtpAddress                  :
ALLMANAGEMENTINTERNATIONAL@masteringexchangeorg.com
RecipientType                       : MailUniversalDistributionGroup
RecipientTypeDetails                : MailUniversalDistributionGroup
RejectMessagesFrom                  : {}
RejectMessagesFromDLMembers         : {}
RejectMessagesFromSendersOrMembers  : {}
RequireSenderAuthenticationEnabled  : True
SimpleDisplayName                   :
SendModerationNotifications         : Always
UMDtmfMap                           : {emailAddress:2556262436368468376 2846625,
lastNameFirstName:255626243636846837
                                      62846625,
firstNameLastName:2556262436368468376 2846625}
WindowsEmailAddress                 :
ALLMANAGEMENTINTERNATIONAL@masteringexchangeorg.com
MailTip                             :
MailTipTranslations                 : {}
PartnerObjectId                     : 00000000-0000-0000-0000-000000000000
IsValid                             : True
ExchangeVersion                     : 0.10 (14.0.100.0)
Name                                : _ALL MANAGEMENT International
DistinguishedName                   :
CN=_ALL MANAGEMENT International,CN=Users,DC=MasteringExchangeOrg,DC=com
Identity                            :
MasteringExchangeOrg.com/Users/_ALL MANAGEMENT International
Guid                                :
ed0fe70e-36f4-4fd5-b2d2-090ac51755a3
ObjectCategory                      :
MasteringExchangeOrg.com/Configuration/Schema/Group
ObjectClass                         : {top, group}
WhenChanged                         : 8/24/2009 10:54:03 PM
WhenCreated                         : 8/24/2009 10:54:03 PM
WhenChangedUTC                      : 8/25/2009 2:54:03 AM
WhenCreatedUTC                      : 8/25/2009 2:54:03 AM
OrganizationId                      :
OriginatingServer                   : MTL-EX2010.MasteringExchangeOrg.com
```

Finally, if you no longer need a group, you can use `Remove-Group` to get rid of it completely (including the group object in the Active Directory) or `Disable-Group` to simply remove the mail attributes from it.

CREATING DYNAMIC DISTRIBUTION GROUPS USING THE EMS

Let's now look at an example where you create and manage a dynamic distribution group using the EMS. Let's say that you need to create a group called All Research that consists only of mailbox-enabled users. You want to create the Active Directory object in the MasteringExchangeOrg.com domain and in the Research organizational unit. Further, let's say that the maximum receive size should be only 75 KB.

To create this DDG, you would use the following cmdlet:

```
New-DynamicDistributionGroup -Name "All Research" ↵
-IncludedRecipients 'MailboxUsers' ↵
-ConditionalDepartment 'Research' ↵
-OrganizationalUnit 'fourthcoffee.com/Research' ↵
-Alias 'AllResearch' ↵
-RecipientContainer 'fourthcoffee.com/Corporate'
```

After you create the group, you use the `Set-DynamicDistributionGroup` cmdlet to update the maximum receive size:

```
Set-DynamicDistributionGroup -Name "All Research" ↵
-MaxReceiveSize 75KB
```

CONVERTING GLOBAL OR LOCAL DISTRIBUTION GROUPS TO UNIVERSAL GROUPS

In multidomain environments, creating groups of type Global and Domain Local could cause problems with distribution list expansion. If the Exchange server that performed the group expansion pointed to a domain controller from a domain that did not contain the membership list for a domain local or global group, the group would not be expanded and the message would not be delivered. Worse, the message sender might not get a notification that there was a problem.

For this reason, Microsoft is now enforcing that all groups created for Exchange Server mail distribution be universal groups. If you create a domain local or global group using Active Directory Users and Computers and then try to mail-enable it using the Exchange Management Console, you will not even see the group in the list of available groups.

In an organization that was upgraded or transitioned from a previous version of Exchange to Exchange Server 2010, you may have some mail-enabled groups that are not universal groups. You can still manage those groups from either the Exchange Management Console or the Exchange Management Shell.

For groups that you want to change to universal groups, the group type can be changed using Active Directory Users and Computers, of course. On the General properties page for the group (shown in Figure 18.11), simply select the Universal radio button and click OK to convert the group.

You can also convert the group to a universal group from the EMS.

You can convert groups one at time with the `Set-Group` cmdlet like this:

```
Set-Group "Operations Group" -Universal
```

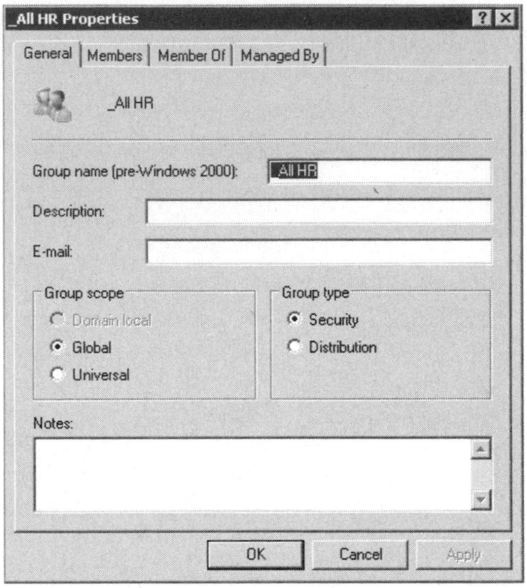

FIGURE 18.11
Converting a group to a universal group using Active Directory Users and Computers

However, one at a time is probably not the best use of your time. We recommend you convert all groups used for mail distribution, but not necessarily your non-mail groups. You can generate a list of just these groups with the `Get-DistributionGroup` cmdlet and a `Where-Object` filter; here is an example:

```
Get-DistributionGroup | Where {$_.RecipientType ↵
-eq "MailNonUniversalGroup"}
```

```
Name                DisplayName         GroupType           PrimarySmtpAddress
----                -----------         ---------           ------------------
$Operations Group   $Operations Group   Global, Security... OperationsGroup@...
$Executives and ...  $Executives and ...  Global, Security... ExecutivesandVIP...
Field Research G...  Field Research G...  Global, Security... FieldResearchGro...
Failure Analysis...  Failure Analysis...  Global                          FailureAnalysisT...
```

This outputs a list of all groups that are mail enabled and that are not universal groups. Converting them all at once is just a matter of piping this as input to the `Set-Group` cmdlet. Here is the command necessary to convert all of these groups to universal groups:

```
Get-DistributionGroup | Where {$_.RecipientType ↵
-eq "MailNonUniversalGroup"} | Set-Group -Universal
```

Note that this command does not change whether the group is a security group or a distribution group.

Allowing End Users to Manage Group Membership

A handy feature of Outlook is that when you locate a distribution group in the global address list and select its properties, if you have the right permissions you can add and remove users, contacts, or groups from the group's membership. Figure 18.12 shows the Outlook interface that allows you to manage the membership of a mail-enabled group.

Note that only mail-enabled groups can have their membership managed by an Outlook client. This feature is not available for dynamic distribution groups.

In the EMC, a distribution group's Group Information properties page includes a Managed By field that allows you to set the "manager" or "owner" of the group.

Disappointingly, this Managed By option alone does not allow the manager to manage the membership list; the ability to manage a distribution group membership is now delegated through the management roles. In addition to being designated as an owner, a user must be assigned a management role assignment policy that contains the My Distribution Groups and My Distribution Group Membership roles to manage the membership of the group. By default, all users are assigned the My Distribution Groups and My Distribution Group Membership roles in the default role assignment policy. You only need to add these roles to the policy if you previously removed them. (Management roles and role-based access control is covered in detail in Chapter 15, "Management Permissions and Role-Based Administration.") That takes an extra step (or two). In Active Directory Users and Computers, locate the group and then display its properties. On the Managed By properties page, you should see the option to define the manager and a Manager Can Update Membership List check box.

With the introduction of the Exchange Control Panel (or Outlook Web App) in Exchange Server 2010, administrators and users with permissions can modify the properties of groups by using a web-based administrative console. The Exchange Control Panel can be used, once permissions have been properly delegated, to create or manage groups and group memberships. Figure 18.13 shows how an administrator can modify the membership of an existing distribution group.

FIGURE 18.13
Modify the membership of a mail-enabled distribution group from the Exchange Control Panel

An administrator (or a user with elevated privileges) can also use the Exchange Management Console or the Exchange Management Shell to add a member to a distribution group. From the Exchange Management Console, simply locate the group in the group list and then modify the properties of the Member tab. From the Exchange Management Shell, you can use the `Add-DistributionGroupMember` cmdlet. For example, we used the following command to add four users to the distribution group named SnowBoard Masters:

```
Add-DistributionGroupMember -identity "SnowBoard Masters" ↵
 -Member " Gillian@Netlogon.com, Zachary@Netlogon.com, ↵
Zoe@Netlogon.com, Savannah@Netlogon.com"
```

The Bottom Line

Choose the appropriate type and scope of mail-enabled group   Though you can modify your group scope or group type at any time after the group has been created, it's always a best practice to create all groups as universal groups in an environment that contains Exchange servers.

> **Master It**   Your company needs to ensure that if an administrator adds a user to a distribution list, that user will not get any unnecessary access to resources on the network. How should you ensure that this type of administrative mistake does not impact the security of your networking environment?

Create and manage mail-enabled groups   Creating and managing distribution groups can mostly be done from the Exchange Management Console, with only limited options that require the Exchange Management Shell.

> **Master It**   You want to simplify the management of groups in your organization. You recently reviewed the functionalities of dynamic distribution groups and decided that this

technology can provide the desired results. You need to identify the tools that should be used to manage dynamic distribution groups. What tool should you identify?

Explore the moderation features of Exchange Server 2010   Moderation and moderated groups is one of the new features of Exchange Server 2010. As part of the new self-service focus of Exchange Server 2010, moderation allows a user to review messages sent to an email address on your server.

Master It   If you want to use moderated groups in a mixed organization that contains both Exchange Serve 2007 and an Exchange Server 2010 Hub Transport server, what group feature should you configure?

## Chapter 19

Managing Mail-Enabled Contacts and Users

After installing Active Directory on your network, you likely noticed a type of object that can be created, which sounded as though it belonged in a client email application rather than in a network resource management system. This object is the contact object.

In essence, there is really no use for a contact object but a lot of value in having mail-enabled contacts.

In this chapter, you will learn to:

◆ Create and mail-enable contact objects

◆ Manage mail-enabled contacts and mail-enabled users in a messaging environment

◆ Implement coexistence between on-premise Exchange deployments and Outlook Live deployments

Creating and Managing Contacts

So what is the use of a mail-enabled contact? Well, many organizations like to have their users' frequently used contacts in the organization's address lists, so they are accessible to all, rather than having users add the addresses to their individual contacts folders or address books. Making these addresses accessible to the organization is the intention of the mail-enabled contact. Mail-enabled contacts appear in your organization's address lists, but these contacts direct email to an external mail system. The email addresses of these external contacts are almost always SMTP, so we are going to limit our discussion to that type of contact.

In Exchange Server 2010, a contact object can be created in Active Directory, but it will not be mail-enabled and thus will not appear in the Exchange address lists. This is different from Exchange 2000/2003, where you could mail-enable a contact using the Active Directory Users and Computers snap-in. The process of mail-enabling the contact will have to occur as a second step, described later in the section "Managing Mail-Enabled Contacts and Users Using the EMS."

Creating a contact object in Active Directory requires minimal information; you can simply create a new contact and specify the contact's name information. Figure 19.1 illustrates the context options for creating contact objects from the Active Directory Users and Computers console.

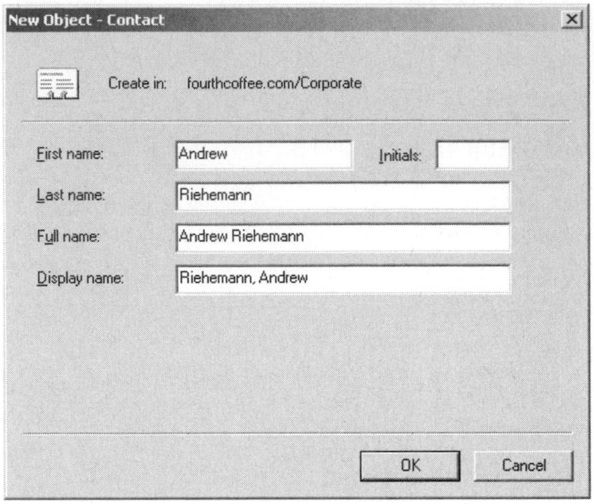

FIGURE 19.1
Creating a new
contact object in Active
Directory

However, you may notice that there is no way to provide email address information when you create a contact object from Active Directory Users and Computers. If you look at the contact's information (shown in Figure 19.2), you will see an email property, but Exchange will not include the contact information in the address lists with just this information populated. The complete mail attributes must be set on the contact.

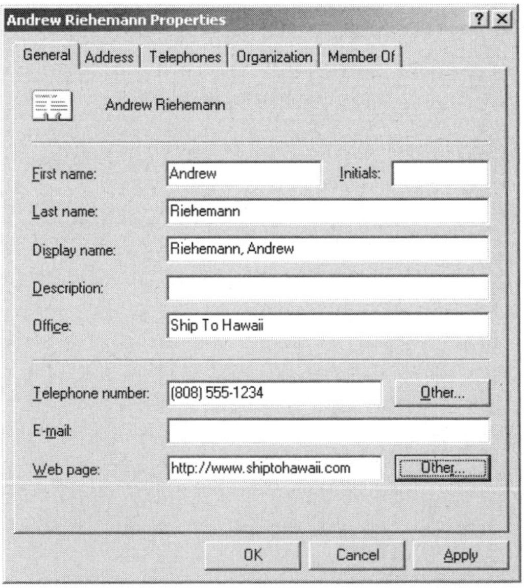

FIGURE 19.2
Contact information
in Active Directory

To properly mail-enable a contact for use with Exchange, you must use the EMC or the EMS tools.

Managing Mail-Enabled Contacts and Users Using the EMC

Let's start by examining how you would create and manage a mail-enabled contact using the EMC. In the Recipient Configuration work center of the EMC, you will find the Mail Contact subcontainer. If you highlight this container, you will see two new tasks in the Actions pane: the New Mail Contact and the New Mail User tasks.

The mail contact is an object that appears in the Active Directory and Exchange address lists, but it is not a security principal. You cannot put the mail contact into any security groups and assign it any permissions because it does not have a security identifier (SID). This type of contact is useful when you need to make an external email address appear in your address lists. However, the external user associated with the email address does not need any sort of permissions in your organization.

The mail user is a user account in your organization but not one for which you host a mailbox. For example, you might need to create a user account for an accounting auditor who will be working at one of your workstations for a few months. You want that person to appear in your Exchange address lists, but his mailbox is hosted somewhere else. This is also called a mail-enabled user. The easiest way to understand the difference between a mail-enabled user and a mailbox-enabled user is that you are *not* responsible for a mail-enabled user's email storage, but you are responsible for a *mailbox*-enabled user's e-mail storage. The mailbox-enabled user is the type of mailbox we covered in Chapter 16, "Basics of Recipient Management."

This short list describes the three principal recipients in Exchange Server 2010:

- Mailbox-enabled user
  - User exists *inside* your organization

◆ Mailbox exists *inside* your organization

◆ Recipient appears in your address lists by default or can be hidden

◆ Mail-enabled user

◆ User exists *inside* your organization

◆ Mailbox exists *outside* your organization

◆ Recipient appears in your address lists by default or can be hidden

◆ Mail-enabled contact

◆ User exists *outside* your organization

◆ Mailbox exists *outside* your organization

◆ Recipient appears in your address lists by default or can be hidden

Let's look at creating a mail-enabled contact. Simply click New Mail Contact in the Actions pane to launch the New Mail Contact wizard. The Introduction screen asks you if you want to create a new contact or mail-enable an existing contact in Active Directory. In this example, you will mail-enable an existing contact by completing the following steps:

1. Choose the Existing Contact radio button and click the Browse button to locate this contact in Active Directory.

2. On the next page (the Contact Information page shown in Figure 19.3), all you have to provide is the external email address. You cannot proceed if the object does not have an external email address.

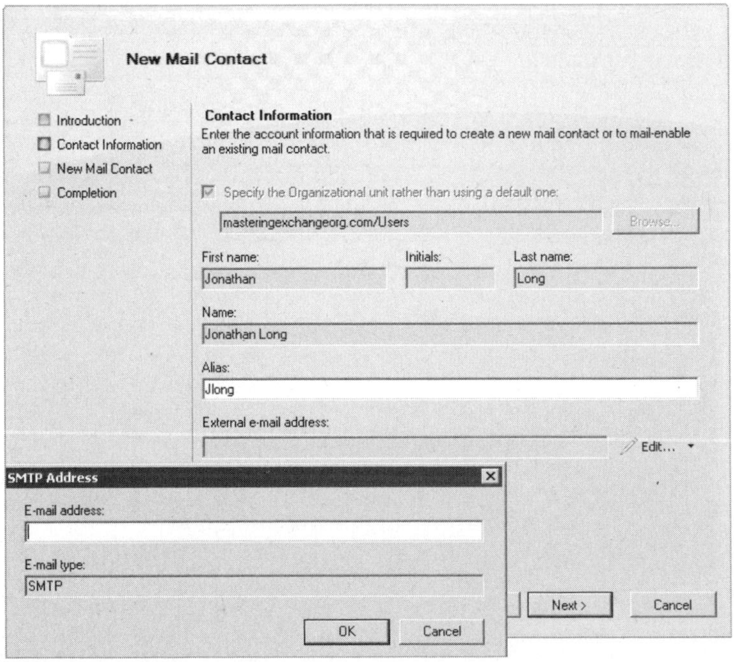

FIGURE 19.3
Creating a mail-enabled contact

After you confirm that this is what you want to do, the Completion screen will show you the EMS command that was used to enable this object:

```
Enable-MailContact -Identity 'MasteringExchangeOrg.com/Users/Jonathan Long' ↵
-ExternalEmailAddress 'SMTP:jlong@netlogon.com' -Alias 'Jlong'
```

Before we go on to look at the mail-related properties of a contact, let's look at the creation of a mail-enabled user. You run the New Mail User wizard and create a new user. On the Mail Settings properties page, all you need to specify is the External E-mail Address properties.

Once you confirm that the information is correct and complete the wizard, the Completion page will show the EMS command that was used to create the object:

```
New-MailUser -Name 'Gillian Katz' -Alias 'gkatz' -OrganizationalUnit ↵
'MasteringExchangeOrg.com/Users' ↵
-UserPrincipalName 'GKatz@MasteringExchangeOrg.com' ↵
-SamAccountName 'GKatz' -FirstName 'Gillian' -Initials '' -LastName 'Katz' ↵
-Password 'System.Security.SecureString' -ResetPasswordOnNextLogon $false ↵
-ExternalEmailAddress 'SMTP:gkatz@netlogon.com'
```

With respect to the properties of a mail-enabled contact or a mail-enabled user, most properties are similar to those you have seen in previous chapters for mail-enabled mailboxes, so we won't bore you with a lot of repetition. We want to remind you, though, that a mail-enabled user can be a member of a distribution group, have a telephone number attribute, and have an SMTP email address. The General properties page of the object does have something you may not have seen yet: notice in Figure 19.4 that there is a Use MAPI Rich Text Format drop-down list.

FIGURE 19.4
Contact object's General properties

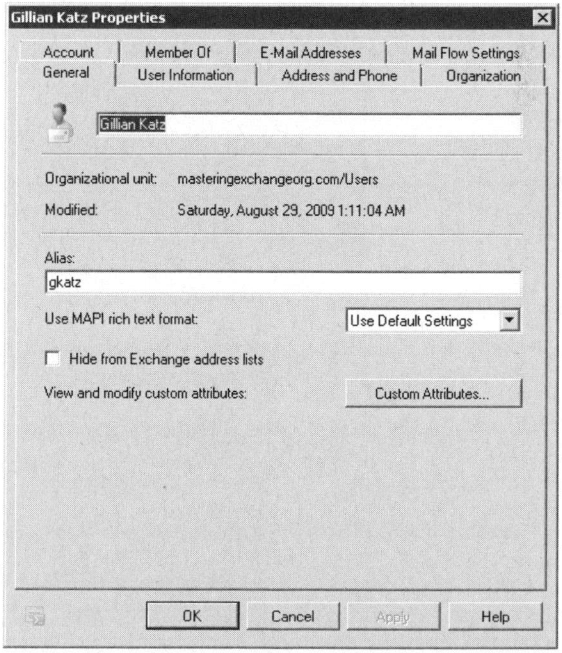

This setting determines whether the Exchange Hub Transport server will convert the message to a MIME or UUencode message when it leaves your organization. By default, all mail leaving your organization is converted into an Internet standards–based format; this is almost always MIME. In some cases, this may strip out some formatting or features that users who use Word as their email editor have put into the message. For just any recipient on the Internet, this is fine because there is no guarantee that they have a mail client that can read those messages. However, if you know for sure that the recipient will have a mail reader that is capable of reading a rich text–formatted message (Outlook, for example), then you can send the message to the recipient in that format. You have three possible settings in this drop-down list:

◆ Use Default Settings means that the message will be sent based on the global settings configured or on the remote domain's settings.

◆ Always means that regardless of the global settings, the message will be sent to this recipient in rich text formatting.

◆ Never means that regardless of the global settings, the message will always be converted to an Internet-standards message.

If someone sends a rich-text message and the recipient is not able to read it, the recipient will see attachments named `winmail.dat` or a MIME attachment called `application/tnef`. If you have remote organizations that need specific message formatting, the remote domains feature of Exchange Server allows you to specify formatting to be used for a specific SMTP domain. This can be found in the Organization Configuration under the Hub Transport subcontainer.

Managing Mail-Enabled Contacts and Users Using the EMS

Once you become proficient at the EMC, as with many other tasks, you may want to try your hand at creating mail-enabled contacts or mail-enabled users from the EMS instead of the GUI. Table 19.1 shows the cmdlets that can be used to manipulate mail-enabled contacts and users.

TABLE 19.1: Exchange Management Shell Cmdlets for Mail-Enabled Contacts and Users

CMDLET	DESCRIPTION
New-MailContact	Creates a new contact in the Active Directory and mail-enables that contact.
Enable-MailContact	Mail-enables a previously existing contact
Set-MailContact	Sets mail properties for a mail-enabled contact.
Get-MailContact	Retrieves properties of a mail-enabled contact
Remove-MailContact	Removes the mail properties from a contact and deletes that contact from the Active Directory.

TABLE 19.1: Exchange Management Shell Cmdlets for Mail-Enabled Contacts and Users *(CONTINUED)*

CMDLET	DESCRIPTION
Disable-MailContact	Removes the mail properties from a contact
New-MailUser	Creates a new user in the Active Directory and mail-enables that user
Enable-MailUser	Mail-enables a previously existing user.
Set-MailUser	Sets mail properties for a mail-enabled user
Get-MailUser	Retrieves properties of a mail-enabled user.
Remove-MailUser	Removes the mail properties from a user and deletes that user from the Active Directory
Disable-MailUser	Removes the mail properties from a user

The best way to learn how to use the EMS to create mail-enabled contacts and users is to look at some examples.

Let's say a user named Oliver Cohen is a contractor who works for your company occasionally. He requires a desk and a company logon, so you have already created his Oliver.Cohen user account in the Active Directory domain; the account is in an OU called Corporate. You want Oliver to appear in the address lists, but he should receive his email at an external address: Oliver.Cohen@IAMAHUMONGOUSSUPPLIER.COM. Here is the command you would use to mail-enable Oliver's user account. In this example, you are using his common name attribute instead of his username:

```
Enable-MailUser "Oliver Cohen" -Alias 'Oliver.Cohen' ↵
-ExternalEmailAddress 'SMTP:Oliver.Cohen@IAMAHUMONGOUSSUPPLIER.COM'
```

Let's extend this example now to a mail-enabled contact. You have a contact that you want to appear in your address lists, but this contact does *not* need to access any resources on your network. The contact does not yet exist, so you will create a mail-enabled contact in the Corporate OU for contact named Oren Pinto, whose external address will be Oren.Pinto@Netlogon.com:

```
New-MailContact ↵
-ExternalEmailAddress 'SMTP:Oren.Pinto@Netlogon.com' ↵
-Name 'OrenPinto' -Alias 'OrenPinto' ↵
-OrganizationalUnit 'Netlogon.com/Corporate' ↵
-FirstName 'Oren' -LastName 'Pinto'
```

When setting properties for the mail contact and mail user objects, you should keep in mind some useful properties. Table 19.2 shows some of the common properties that these two object types share.

TABLE 19.2: Useful Properties of Mail Contact and Mail User Objects

PROPERTY	DESCRIPTION
Alias	Sets the object's Exchange alias.
CustomAttribute1 through CustomAttribute10	Sets custom attributes 1 through 10; these are also known as the extension attributes.
DisplayName	Sets the display name of the object.
ExternalEmailAddress	Sets the address that is to be used to deliver mail externally to the user or contact.
HiddenFromAddressLists Enabled	Specifies whether or not the object is hidden from address lists. The default is $False, but it can be set to $True.
MaxSendSize	Sets the maximum size of a message that can be sent to this recipient.

Implementing Coexistence Between Exchange On-Premise and Outlook Live Deployments

By now, most of us are familiar with the concepts of "cloud computing." Company executives no longer raise their eyebrows in fear when a consultant suggests moving core IT services to the Internet. Of course, email solutions are following suit, and Microsoft now has multiple offerings to meet the demands of "cloud computing." Specifically, when comparing Exchange Server deployment solutions, companies have two options: Exchange on-premise and hosted solutions, which include Outlook Live.

However, with the introduction of Exchange Server 2010, companies can now opt for a hybrid solution, a solution that incorporates both on-premise and Exchange-hosted deployments. A hybrid can be a permanent solution, where some users are hosted in the "cloud" and other users are hosted on internal Exchange servers. Or, the hybrid solution can be a temporary solution implemented to support a migration to the "cloud."

BUSINESS DECISION POINTS REGARDING DEPLOYMENT CHOICES

We have worked with multiple companies in the past few years that have asked themselves, "Should we go online or should we stay in-house?" Unfortunately, there is no standard answer to this question that will fit all companies. The decision to go to an Exchange-hosted solution is usually based on a combination of the following internal motivating forces:

◆ An effort to reduce initial hardware and software costs

◆ An effort to reduce initial deployment costs

◆ A reduction of internal IT support personnel and resources

◆   A deployment solution for branch offices

◆   A part of an outsourced IT deployment

This list is not all-inclusive, but it is representative of the motivating forces for most companies. Whatever the factor that makes a company tip the scale toward an Exchange-hosted solution, you can be sure that the decision is never taken lightly.

Implementing a Single Global Address List in a Coexistence Scenario

A company that has decided to move to a hosted solution may choose a solution from Microsoft or, in the future, from a Microsoft partner. A company may choose, among the solutions offered by Microsoft today, Outlook Live or the Business Productivity Online Suite; both solutions are designed to suit the diverse needs of companies.

One of the first issues that comes up when a company decides to move to a hybrid (mixed solution) is maintaining a single, unified Global Address List. Outlook Live Directory Sync (OLSync), formerly known as GALSync 2010, is a directory synchronization tool that you use to replicate and synchronize user information between your on-premises Active Directory and Outlook Live. The goal of directory synchronization is to represent a single entity in different identity databases: one identity is your internal Active Directory domain and the other is the organization hosted in the cloud. Also, another goal is to keep the information about that entity consistent and up-to-date in both directories.

OLSync is designed to simplify the complex task of directory synchronization. Before you deploy OLSync, you need a high-level understanding about how directory synchronization works and some basic concepts behind Microsoft Identity Lifecycle Manager (ILM) 2007. OLSync relies on ILM 2007 Feature Pack 1 (FP1) as its directory synchronization engine.

OLSync pulls user, contact, group, and dynamic distribution group data from Active Directory and replicates and synchronizes it with an Outlook Live domain. OLSync can then create, manage, and delete accounts in Outlook Live. When OLSync runs, it completes a one-way synchronization from your directory to the Outlook Live datacenter that Microsoft operates. OLSync doesn't write information back to your directory.

Use the following steps to implement OLSync:

1. Deploy Outlook Live. Before you can deploy OLSync, the organization must have deployed an Outlook Live domain.

2. Prepare your on-premises organization. Install Microsoft Identity Lifecycle Manager (ILM) 2007 Feature Pack 1 (FP1) and all dependencies in the on-premise organization.

3. Configure Outlook Live authentication for OLSync. OLSync requires access to the Outlook Live domain to create mail user, mailbox, and external contact objects. You can configure OLSync to use a Windows Live ID service account or to use certificate-based authentication.

4. Create an on-premises OLSync service account. The on-premises OLSync service account is used by ILM FP1 to access the on-premises Active Directory. After you create the account, you need to grant it specific permission to initiate directory replication.

5. Run OLSync Setup. OLSync Setup installs the Outlook Live Management Agent (OLMA) configuration and other files in the appropriate ILM directories. OLSync Setup also imports the OLMA configuration and management agents.

6. Configure the OLSync Hosted management agent. The Hosted management agent manages the connection to Outlook Live.

7. Perform a full data synchronization. To perform the first data synchronization with Outlook Live, you must run synchronization operations from ILM FP1 in a specific order that is unique to a full data synchronization. Synchronization is actually triggered by PowerShell scripts that were installed as part of the OLMA installation.

The Bottom Line

Create and mail-enable contact objects   Mail-enabled contacts can be used to provide easy access to external email contacts by using your internal address lists. Mail-enabled users can be used to provide convenient access to internal resources for workers who require an externally hosted email account.

> **Master It**   You periodically update the email addresses for your Active Directory contacts. However, some users report that they are not seeing the updated contact address and that they receive NDRs when sending mail to some contacts. What should you do?

Manage mail-enabled contacts and mail-enabled users in a messaging environment   All Exchange-related attributes for mail-enabled users and contacts are not available from Active Directory Users and Computers. To manage all Exchange-related attributes, you must use the EMC or EMS tools.

> **Master It**   Whether you want to manage users in bulk, need to create multiple users in your domain or multiple mail-enabled contacts in your organization, or simply want to change the delivery restrictions for 5,000 recipients, what tool should you use?

Implement coexistence between Exchange on-premises and Outlook Live deployments   When an organization goes through the decision process of moving to a "cloud computing" solution, the design may involve moving the messaging infrastructure to the cloud. This decision may require coexistence and GAL synchronization.

> **Master It**   You have implemented OLSync and started synchronizing mailbox-enabled users to your Outlook Live domain. You notice that for each mailbox in your on-premises organization, a corresponding mailbox is created in the Outlook Live domain. You need to ensure that only mail-enabled users are created in the corresponding Outlook Live domain.

Chapter 20

Managing Resource Mailboxes

For some organizations, Resource mailboxes are unnecessary because shared resources are either managed manually or through some type of third-party software. However, in other organizations (even small ones), every conference room, plasma television, and projector is managed electronically. Exchange Server 2010, Outlook Web App, and Outlook give you the ability to schedule these resources and view their availability quite easily.

In some aspects, managing Resource mailboxes is the same as managing User mailboxes. But there are some unique features and settings that can enhance the use of Resource mailboxes. In this chapter, you will learn to:

◆ Understand how Resource mailboxes differ from regular mailboxes

◆ Create Resource mailboxes

◆ Configure Resource mailbox booking and scheduling policies

◆ Migrate Resource mailboxes

How Resource Mailboxes Differ from Regular Mailboxes

As mentioned in Chapter 17, "Managing Mailboxes and Mailbox Content," there are four possible choices for mailbox types: the User mailbox, a Room mailbox, an Equipment mailbox, and a Linked mailbox. We covered User and Linked mailboxes in Chapter 17; in this chapter, we'll focus on the other two: Room mailbox and Equipment mailbox:

Room Mailbox   A Room mailbox is simply a Resource mailbox assigned to a meeting location, such as conference and training rooms, and auditoriums. Room mailboxes can be included in meeting requests as a resource.

Equipment Mailbox   An equipment mailbox is a Resource mailbox assigned to a resource that is not generally location specific, such as a projector, specialty AV equipment, or even a company car. Like a Room mailbox, equipment mailboxes can be included in meetings requests as a resource.

Both room and equipment mailboxes are created as disabled mailbox enabled accounts in Active Directory. They are not intended to be logged into like a normal User mailbox. Additionally, certain attributes on the mailboxes are configured that allow them to be utilized as resources. They are otherwise the same as standard user accounts.

Exchange 2010 Resource Mailbox Features

Resource mailboxes are handy when it comes to booking resources, such as conference rooms, or equipment, such as projectors. With Exchange 2010, Resource mailboxes can accept or decline meeting requests, and provide capacity and feature information to those scheduling meetings. Different clients, including Outlook, Outlook Web App, and mobile clients, can all utilize Resource mailboxes to streamline the process of reserving resources quickly and easily. No longer needed are the paper schedules taped to conference room doors, or paper-based scheduling ledgers.

Myriad features are available for Resource mailboxes: from customization features to booking policy features that determine whether a meeting request is accepted or rejected. By utilizing Resource mailboxes, overbooking problems can be eliminated, while also enforcing some rules such as how long a resource can be reserved, who can reserve it, and what to do with certain information within requests.

Delegation of Resource room mailboxes provides for manual approval or rejection of meeting requests, while also allowing for some to reserve resources outside the defined policies.

Creating Resource Mailboxes

The process of creating Resource mailboxes isn't much different than creating standard mailboxes. We can use the Exchange Management Console (EMC) or the Exchange Management Shell (EMS). Both just require an added parameter to define the mailbox as a Resource mailbox.

Creating and Defining Resource Mailbox Properties

We'll begin with a single room Resource mailbox for a conference room called Conference Room South. We'll create it in the EMC just like we create standard user accounts. To do so, launch the New Mailbox wizard. On the Introduction screen, choose Room Mailbox, and then click Next. For User Type, click New User, and then click Next. Complete the information on the User Information screen (shown in Figure 20.1).

If an organizational unit (OU) is not defined, the Resource mailbox will be placed in the Users OU. If you would like it placed elsewhere, check the box and click the Browse button to specify the appropriate OU.

The rest of the mailbox settings are the same as when you're creating a standard User mailbox. Since we'll configure how the resource account will handle booking requests and other information later, there is no need to define a managed folder mailbox policy or an Exchange ActiveSync mailbox policy. On the Archive Settings screen, leave the check box unchecked. As the wizard completes, a disabled account is created for the Resource mailbox.

When we view the mailboxes in Exchange, we see that the icon is different, and the Recipient Type Details shows Room Mailbox. The other columns are similar to standard User mailboxes, as shown in Figure 20.2.

To create a room resource account using the EMS, we'll use the New-Mailbox cmdlet and specify the -Room parameter. Here's an example:

```
New-Mailbox -Name 'Conference Room East' -Alias 'cr_east' ↵
-OrganizationalUnit 'ehloworld.local/ehloworld/Resource Mailboxes' ↵
-UserPrincipalName 'cr_east@ehloworld.local' -SamAccountName 'creast' ↵
-FirstName 'Conference Room' -LastName 'East' -Database 'MB01SG01MS01' ↵
-Room
```

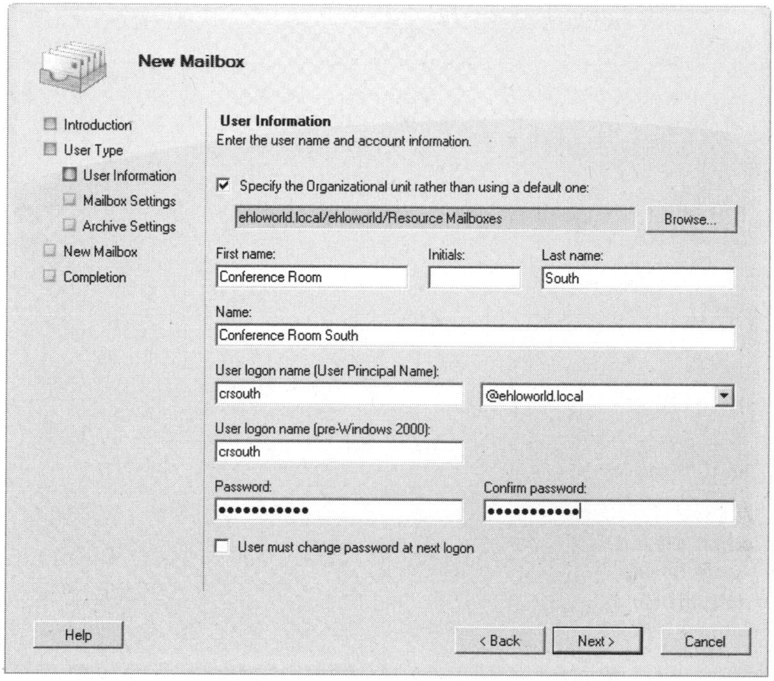

FIGURE 20.1
Defining user
information for a
conference room
mailbox

FIGURE 20.2
Viewing recipients
in the EMC

While the visible difference within the EMC might be fairly subtle, the differences behind the scenes are much more complex. In Exchange 2010, additional attributes are added to resource accounts. These include different values for `RecipientTypeDetails`, as well as use of the attributes `ResourceType`, `ResouceCapacity`, and `ResourceCustom`. We can see examples of these using the `Get-Mailbox` cmdlet. An example is shown here, along with sample output:

```
Get-Mailbox "Conference Room South" | Format-List Name, ↵
*recipient*, *resource*

Name                  : Conference Room South
RecipientLimits       : unlimited
RecipientType         : UserMailbox
RecipientTypeDetails : RoomMailbox
IsResource            : True
ResourceCapacity      :
ResourceCustom        : {}
ResourceType          : Room
```

Table 20.1 shows the details of these attributes when using Resource mailboxes.

TABLE 20.1:   Recipient-Related Attributes for Mailboxes

ATTRIBUTE	VALUE/PURPOSE
RecipientType	Set to UserMailbox, regardless of whether the mailbox is a standard User mailbox or Resource mailbox
RecipientTypeDetails	Set to either RoomMailbox or EquipmentMailbox
ResourceType	Set to either Room or Equipment
ResourceCapacity	For defining room capacity to assist in determining the correct room for the number of participants
ResourceCustom	For defining additional properties for a Resource mailbox

Having these additional attribute settings allows Exchange to enable specific handling of meeting requests for these accounts, as well as to provide for easier recognition of Resource mailboxes versus User mailboxes. An example is shown in Figure 20.3, where a user can choose the All Rooms address book to see just a list of room resource accounts.

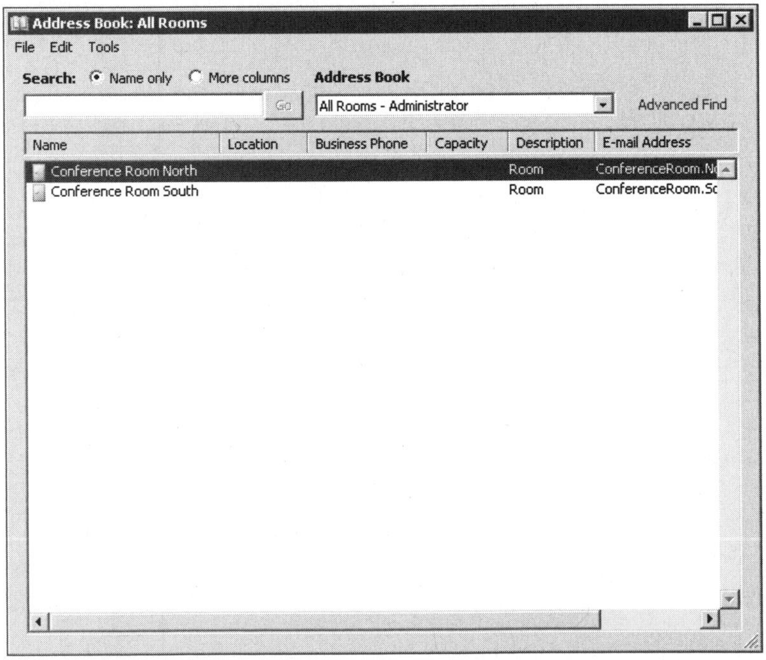

FIGURE 20.3
Viewing room resources
in the Address Book
using Outlook

As you can see, this simplifies locating and viewing rooms without the clutter of the entire Global Address List.

Defining Advanced Resource Mailbox Features

At this point, we've created a Resource mailbox. With Exchange 2010, we can now specify additional parameters for the mailbox to help make it more convenient for end users when they are scheduling meetings that may involve this resource. As shown previously, we see the ResourceCapacity and ResourceCustom attributes of a mailbox. ResourceCapacity allows us to define the capacity of a room, which can certainly help in finding the correctly sized room for an event.

To define the resource capacity of a Room mailbox, open the mailbox in the EMC and click the Resource General tab. Enter the room capacity in the appropriate field, as shown in Figure 20.4.

FIGURE 20.4

Entering room capacity for a Resource mailbox

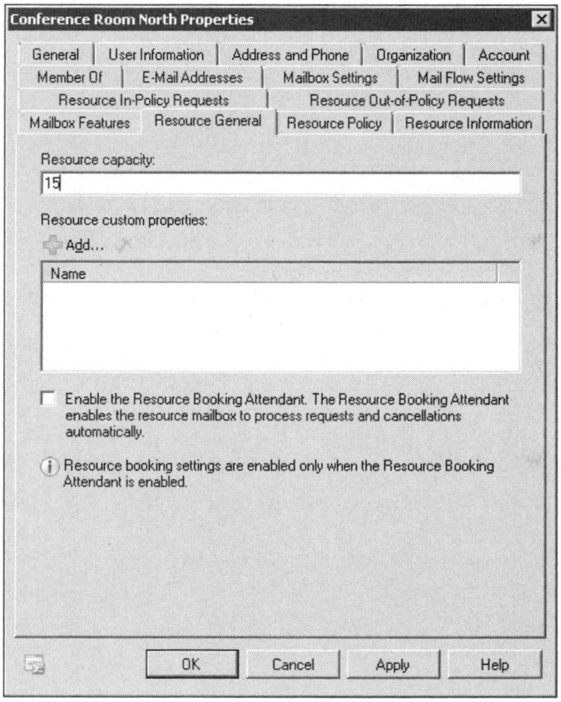

Resource capacity can be defined from the EMS as well, using the Set-Mailbox cmdlet. Let's say you want to define the room capacity of Conference Room North to 12 people. To do so, we use this:

```
Set-Mailbox "Conference Room North" -ResourceCapacity 15
```

What good is finding a conference room with the correct capacity if you can't find one with all the equipment or resources you need? Some organizations have certain conference rooms equipped with TVs, projectors, and so forth. This is where the ResourceCustom attribute comes into play.

To configure ResourceCustom for any Resource mailbox, the schema needs to be configured. You do this using the Set-ResourceConfig cmdlet. With Set-ResourceConfig, the attribute needed is `ResourcePropertySchema`. We can also use `Get-ResourceConfig` to see the current settings. An example of the default configuration is shown here:

```
Get-ResourceConfig | FL Name,ResourcePropertySchema

Name                    : Resource Schema
ResourcePropertySchema : {}
```

Notice that `Set-ResourceConfig` replaces the existing value with the new value, so make sure you include the existing properties when using `Set-ResourceConfig`. Let's say you want to define an additional type of resource property for TV, `Projector`, and `Speakerphone`. To set that, use the following example:

```
Set-ResourceConfig -ResourcePropertySchema("Room/TV", ↩
"Room/Projector", "Room/Speakerphone")
```

Once the resource property schema includes TV, `Projector`, and `Speakerphone`, we can assign them as resources of a particular room. To do so, open the appropriate Resource mailbox in the EMC and go to the Resource General tab. Under Resource Customer properties, click Add and pick from the list, as shown in Figure 20.5.

To set these attributes via the EMS, we use the Set-Mailbox cmdlet with the `-ResouceCustom` attribute. We can also specify the room capacity at the same time using the `-ResourceCapacity` attribute, as shown here:

```
Set-Mailbox "Conference Room North" -ResourceCustom ("TV", ↩
"Speakerphone", "Projector") -ResourceCapacity 15
```

This will configure both the capacity and custom properties of the Room mailbox. We can then verify the settings using the `Get-Mailbox` cmdlet, as shown here with sample output:

```
Get-Mailbox "Conference Room North" | FL Name, *resource*

Name             : Conference Room North
IsResource       : True
ResourceCapacity : 15
ResourceCustom   : {TV, Speakerphone, Projector}
ResourceType     : Room
```

Now that these have been defined, we can look in Outlook and see the properties when viewing the All Rooms list. As shown in Figure 20.6, we see not only the capacity but also the additional resources in the room.

Defining Resource Scheduling Policies

In some older versions of Exchange, configuring the system to automatically handle meeting requests could be cumbersome. Various methods had their pros and cons, and it was difficult to find the perfect mix.

In Exchange 2010, processing of meeting requests is much more streamlined and far more feature rich. Among the options are who can book automatically or via a delegate, how to handle conflicting requests, and when and for how long meetings can be scheduled.

FIGURE 20.5

Custom resources for a conference room

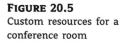

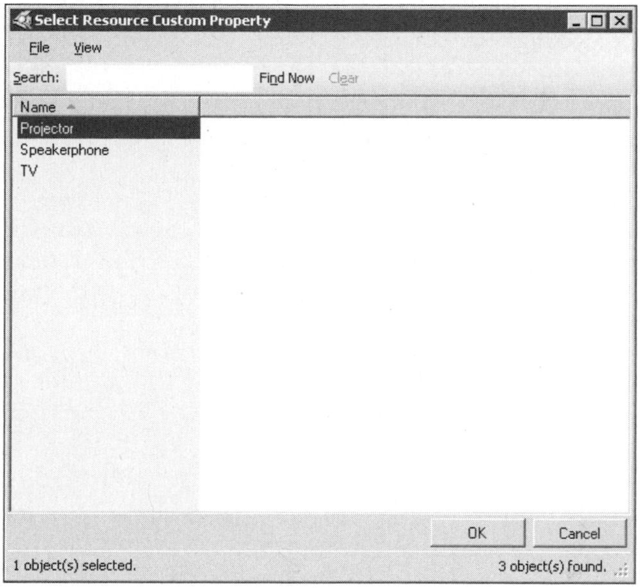

FIGURE 20.6

Viewing room resources and their respective capacity and features

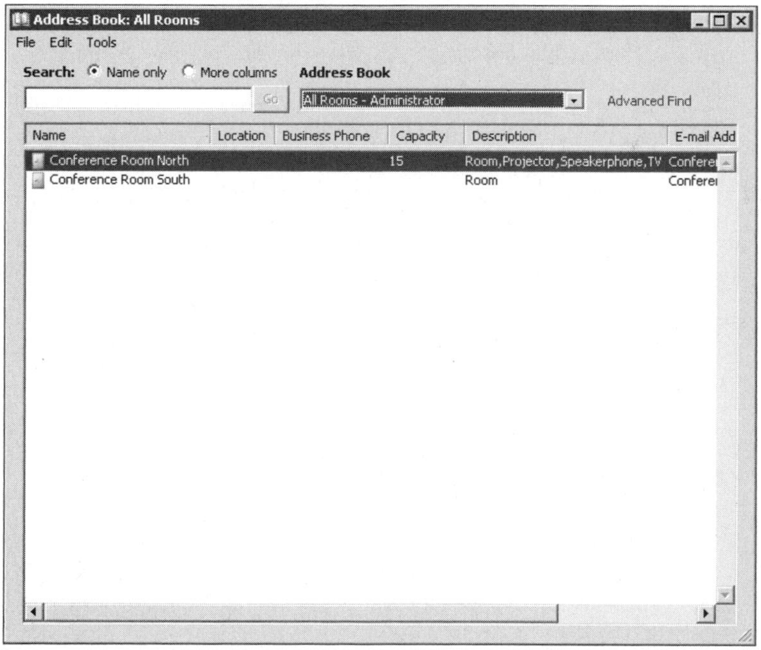

Exchange 2010 gives us three different interfaces for configuring these settings: Exchange Management Console, Exchange Management Shell, and Outlook Web App via the Exchange Control Panel (ECP). We'll look at all three here.

DEFINING RESOURCE SCHEDULING POLICIES USING THE EMC

When opening a Resource mailbox in the EMC, we can see that there are five tabs related to resource configuration. The purpose for each is detailed in Table 20.2.

TABLE 20.2:   Resource-Related Tabs and Their Purposes

TAB	PURPOSE
Resource General	Contains Resource Capacity, custom resource properties, and Booking Attendant settings
Resource Policy	Defines what meetings are accepted or declined, including recurring meetings, time frames, etc.
Resource Information	Settings for how information in meeting requests is handled
Resource In-Policy Requests	Defines who can automatically book resource rooms, and who can book them with approval from a delegate
Resource Out-Of-Policy Requests	Defines who can book resource rooms outside of the policy settings, such as after hours, recurring meetings, etc.

Let's take a look at each of the tabs. First is the Resource General tab. This is where we see the settings for Resource Capacity, the custom properties (such as TVs and Projectors), and the setting to enable the Resource Booking Attendant, as shown in Figure 20.7. We'll discuss this last setting a little later.

Next, click the Resource Policy tab to view the settings available. An example of some default settings is shown in Figure 20.8.

The list of options here includes settings to define what is acceptable for a meeting request to be approved. These include recurring and conflicting meeting requests, how long meetings can be, and how far in the future they can be booked. We've broken down the individual settings in Table 20.3, including how they are referenced in the EMC, Outlook Web App, and the EMS.

On the Resource Information tab of the mailbox, we have options to handle the information contained within the meeting request, such as attachments, comments, and subjects, as shown in Figure 20.9.

This tab helps you standardize how meeting requests appear in the Resource mailbox calendar. Those settings are listed in Table 20.4, along with their EMS equivalents.

Next is the Resource In-Policy Requests tab, which defines who can book the resource when it's available, according to the Resource Policy settings. This can be just a specific group of people, or everyone, as shown in Figure 20.10.

FIGURE 20.7
Resource General tab
for a Resource mailbox

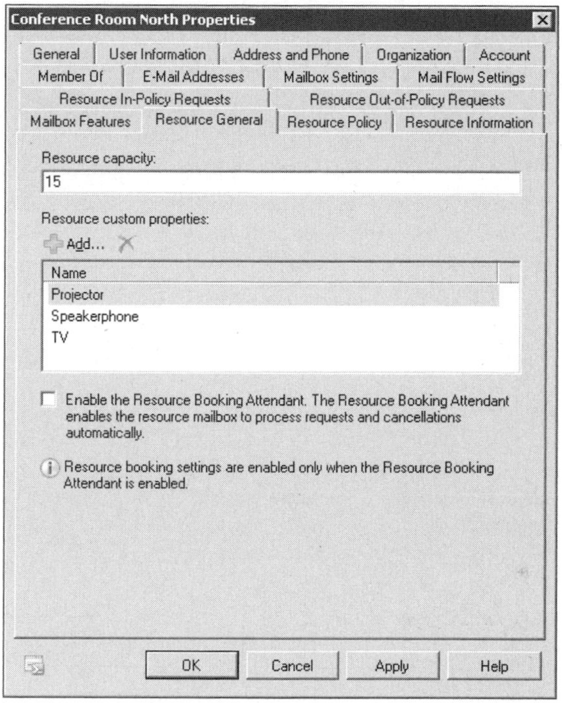

FIGURE 20.8
Resource Policy settings
for a Room mailbox

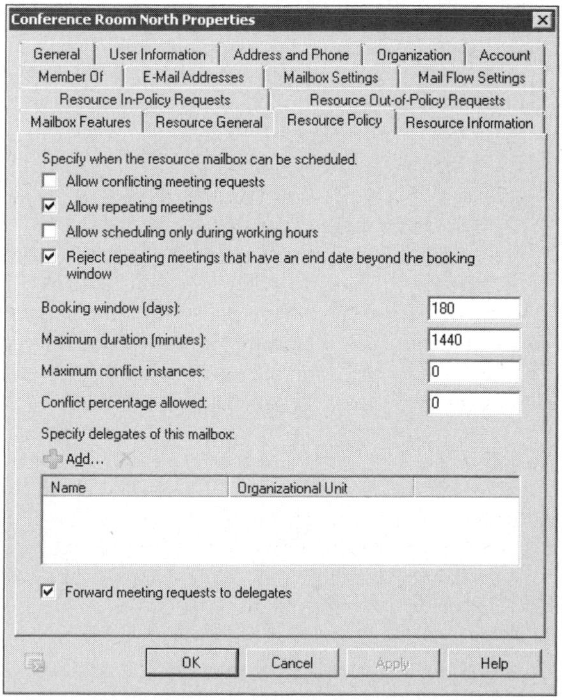

TABLE 20.3:   Resource Policy Tab Features, and Their OWA and
                    EMS Equivalents

EMC Parameter	OWA Parameter	EMS Parameter	Description
Allow Conflicting Meeting Requests	Allow Conflicts	`-AllowConflicts`	Specifies whether to allow conflicting meeting requests. If enabled, this will allow multiple meetings to be accepted for the same date and time.
Allow Repeating Meetings	Allow Repeating Meetings	`-AllowRecurring Meetings`	Specifies whether to allow recurring meetings. When enabled, recurring meeting requests, such as those for every Monday at 9 a.m., are accepted.
Allow Scheduling Only During Working Hours	Allow Scheduling Only During Working Hours	`-ScheduleOnly DuringWorkHours`	Specifies whether to allow meetings to be scheduled outside work hours. If checked, meeting requests for times outside the mailbox's working hours will be rejected.
Reject Repeating Meetings That Have An End Date Beyond The Booking Window	Always Decline If The End Date Is Beyond This Limit		Recurring meeting request is automatically declined if the end date is greater that the value specified by Booking Window (Days).
Booking Window (Days)	Maximum Number Of Days In Advance Resources Can Be Booked	`-BookingWindow InDays`	Specifies the maximum number of days in advance that the resource can be reserved. Maximum is 1080. When set to 0, the resource can be reserved at any date in the future.
Maximum Duration (Minutes)	Maximum Allowed Minutes	`-MaximumDuration InMinutes`	Specifies the maximum duration allowed for incoming meeting requests. Valid input is 0 through 2147483647. When set to 0, the maximum duration of a meeting is unlimited. This applies to individual meetings in the case of recurring meeting requests.

TABLE 20.3:   Resource Policy Tab Features, and Their OWA and
EMS Equivalents *(CONTINUED)*

EMC PARAMETER	OWA PARAMETER	EMS PARAMETER	DESCRIPTION
Maximum Conflict Instances	Allow Up To This Number Of Individual Conflicts	-MaximumConflict Instances	Specifies the maximum number of conflicts for new recurring meeting requests when the Allow Repeating Meetings parameter is checked. Valid input ranges from 0 through 2147483647. If a new recurring meeting request conflicts with existing reservations for the resource more than the number of times specified by Maximum Conflict Instances, the recurring meeting request is automatically declined. When set to 0, no conflicts are permitted for new recurring meeting requests.
Conflict Percentage Allowed	Allow Up To This Percentage Of Individual Conflicts	-Conflict PercentageAllowed	Specifies the maximum percentage of meeting conflicts for new recurring meeting requests. Valid input is 0 through 100. If a new recurring meeting request conflicts with existing reservations for the resource more than the percentage specified by the Conflict Percentage Allowed value, the recurring meeting request is automatically declined. When set to 0, no conflicts are permitted for new recurring meeting requests.
Specify Delegates Of This Mailbox		-Resource Delegates	Specifies a list of users who are Resource mailbox delegates. Resource mailbox delegates can approve or reject requests sent to this Resource mailbox.
Forward Meeting RequestsTo Delegates		-ForwardRequests ToDelegates	Specifies whether to forward incoming meeting requests to the delegate(s) defined for the mailbox.
		-Enforce SchedulingHorizon	Enforces an end date for recurring meetings based on the BookingWindowInDays setting.

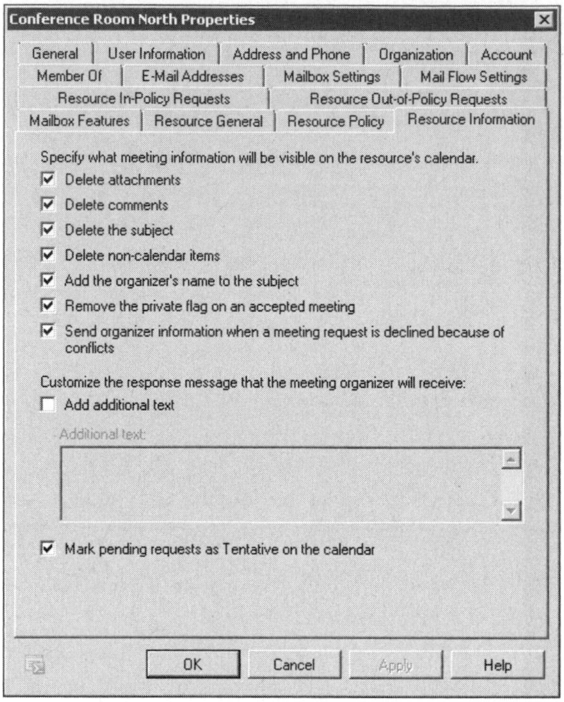

FIGURE 20.9
Resource Information
settings for Resource
mailboxes

TABLE 20.4: Resource Information Tab Settings, and Their EMS Equivalents

EMC PARAMETER	EMS PARAMETER	DESCRIPTION
Delete Attachments	-DeleteAttachments	Specifies whether to remove attachments from all incoming messages.*
Delete Comments	-DeleteComments	Removes any text in the message body of incoming meeting requests.*
Delete The Subject	-DeleteSubject	Removes the subject of incoming meeting requests.*
Delete Non-Calendar Items	-DeleteNonCalendarItems	Removes all noncalendar items received by the mailbox.
Add The Organizer's Name To The Subject	-AddOrganizerToSubject	Specifies whether the meeting organizer's name is used as the subject of the meeting request.
Remove The Private Flag Of An Accepted Message	-RemovePrivateProperty	Clears the private flag for incoming meeting requests.

TABLE 20.4:   Resource Information Tab Settings, and Their EMS Equivalents *(CONTINUED)*

EMC PARAMETER	EMS PARAMETER	DESCRIPTION
Send Organizer Information When A Meeting Request Is Declined Because Of Conflicts		Resource mailboxes send organizer information when a meeting request is declined because of conflicts.
Add Additional Text	-AdditionalResponse	Specifies the additional information to be included in responses to meeting requests.
Mark Pending Request As Tentative On The Calendar	-AllowNewRequests Tentatively	Specifies whether to mark pending requests as tentative on the calendar. If set to $false, pending requests are marked as free.
	-RemoveForwardedMeeting Notifications	Specifies whether meeting forwarding notifications are moved to Deleted Items after processing.
	-RemoveOldMeetingMessages	Specifies whether old and redundant updates and responses are removed.

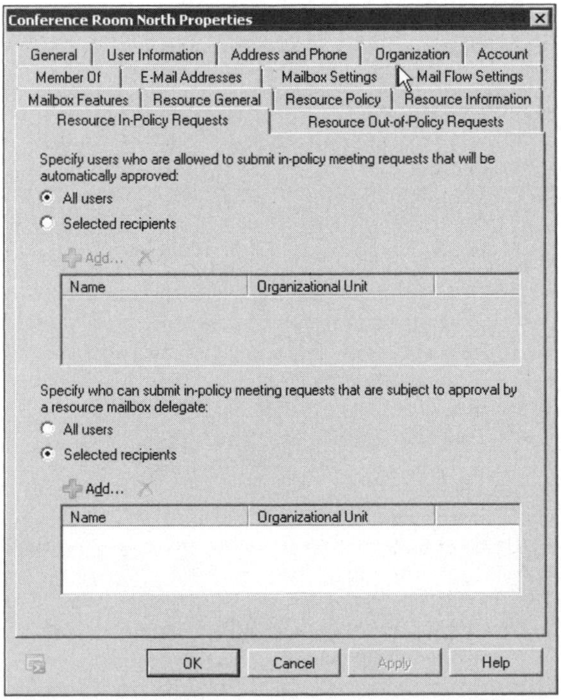

FIGURE 20.10

Resource In-Policy settings for Resource mailboxes

The difference between the two settings is who can book the resource automatically and who can request the resource, which requires approval from a Resource mailbox delegate. Those settings, and their EMS version, are listed in Table 20.5.

TABLE 20.5:   Resource In-Policy Request Features and Their EMS Equivalents

EMC PARAMETER	EMS PARAMETER	DESCRIPTION
Specify Users Who Are Allowed To Submit In-Policy Meeting Requests That Will Be Automatically Approved.	–BookInPolicy	Specifies a list of users who are allowed to submit in-policy meeting requests. These are automatically approved.
Specify Who Can Submit In-Policy Meeting Requests That Are Subject To Approval By A Resource Mailbox Delegate	–RequestInPolicy	Specifies a list of users who are allowed to submit in-policy meeting requests. These require approval from a Resource mailbox delegate.
	–AllBookInPolicy	Specifies whether to automatically approve in-policy requests from all users.
	–AllRequestInPolicy	Specifies whether to allow all users to submit in-policy requests. These would require approval from a Resource mailbox delegate.

The last tab, Resource Out-Of-Policy Requests, defines how requests are handled that are outside the resource policy. Requests by users defined here are sent to Resource mailbox delegates for approval. These can include requests for meetings outside of working hours, longer duration, and so forth, and are listed in Table 20.6.

TABLE 20.6:   Resource Out-Of-Policy Request Settings and Their EMS Equivalents

EMC PARAMETER	EMS PARAMETER	DESCRIPTION
Specify Users Who Are Allowed To Submit Out-Of-Policy Meeting Requests. Out-Of-Policy Meeting Requests Are Subject To Approval By A Resource Mailbox Delegate.	–RequestOutOfPolicy	Specifies a list of users who are allowed to submit out-of-policy requests. These require approval from a Resource mailbox delegate.
	–AllRequestOutofPolicy	Specifies whether to allow all users to submit out-of-policy requests. These require manual approval from a Resource mailbox delegate.

DEFINING RESOURCE SCHEDULING POLICIES USING THE EXCHANGE CONTROL PANEL

Another way to configure a resource's calendar scheduling policy is to use the Exchange Control Panel (ECP) or Outlook Web App. To access the mailbox via OWA, the account must be enabled, since it will initially be created as a disabled user account. Then, log in via Outlook Web App. Once logged in, click the Options button in the upper-right area of the OWA interface, and then click Settings on the left side and Resource at the top. (This option does not appear for a regular mailbox.) If you want to use the ECP, a user must be assigned as a delegate to the Resource mailbox. The user can open it via the Open Other Mailbox option.

The settings are broken down into three sections: those pertaining to scheduling options, those related to permissions, and the third for extra text in the response message. The first check box, Automatically Process Meeting Requests And Cancellations, enables or disables the in-policy processing of items for the Resource mailbox. An example is shown in Figure 20.11.

FIGURE 20.11
Resource configuration settings in Outlook Web App

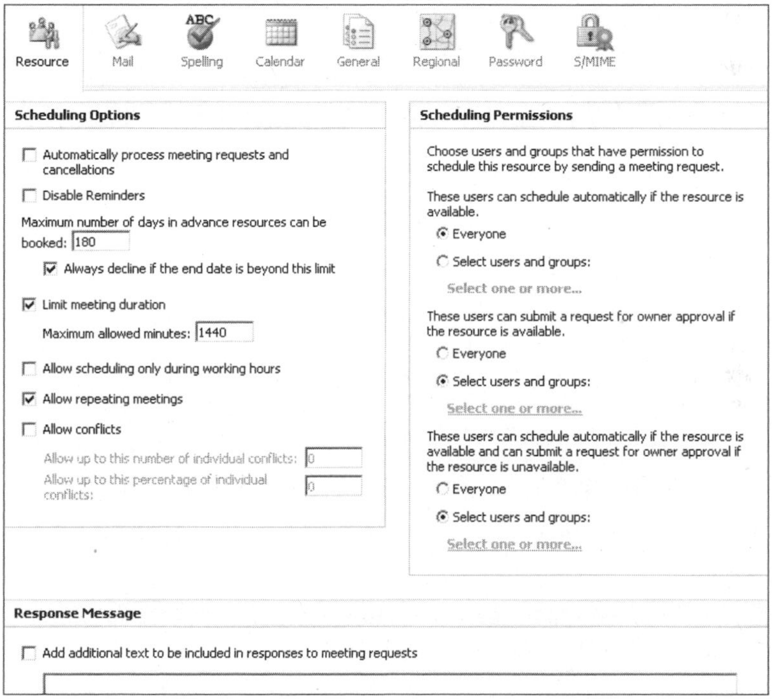

While OWA doesn't provide for setting all the options that the EMC and EMS do, the ease of a web interface makes it convenient. Those options that are available here work the same as in the EMC and EMS. Refer to the tables in the previous section for information on each setting. Options that are not available in OWA include defining delegate-related settings. Also, there is no provision in OWA for defining resource information settings, such as how to handle attachments, private meetings, and so forth. Those settings must be configured via the EMC or EMS.

Although many of these settings are exposed via the ECP and can be set per Resource mailbox, other configuration settings are usually viewed from an organizational perspective and are configured one way for all resources.

DEFINING RESOURCE SCHEDULING POLICIES USING THE EXCHANGE MANAGEMENT SHELL

While we can use EMC and/or OWA to configure the settings, we can also use the EMS. To view resource scheduling policies in the EMS, we turn to the Get-CalendarProcessing cmdlet, as shown along with its output:

```
Get-CalendarProcessing "Conference Room South" | Format-List

RunspaceId                            : 53135a92-3a51-4db4-
a0aa-7a45c231fb91
AutomateProcessing                    : AutoAccept
AllowConflicts                        : False
BookingWindowInDays                   : 180
MaximumDurationInMinutes              : 1440
AllowRecurringMeetings                : True
EnforceSchedulingHorizon              : True
ScheduleOnlyDuringWorkHours           : False
ConflictPercentageAllowed             : 0
MaximumConflictInstances              : 0
ForwardRequestsToDelegates            : True
DeleteAttachments                     : True
DeleteComments                        : True
RemovePrivateProperty                 : True
DeleteSubject                         : True
AddOrganizerToSubject                 : True
DeleteNonCalendarItems                : True
TentativePendingApproval              : True
EnableResponseDetails                 : True
OrganizerInfo                         : True
ResourceDelegates                     : {}
RequestOutOfPolicy                    :
AllRequestOutOfPolicy                 : False
BookInPolicy                          :
AllBookInPolicy                       : True
RequestInPolicy                       :
AllRequestInPolicy                    : False
AddAdditionalResponse                 : False
AdditionalResponse                    :
RemoveOldMeetingMessages              : True
AddNewRequestsTentatively             : True
ProcessExternalMeetingMessages        : False
RemoveForwardedMeetingNotifications   : False
Identity                              : ehloworld.local
/ehloworld/Resource Mailboxes/Conference Room South
```

Setting an attribute in EMS is straightforward using the `Set-CalendarProcessing` cmdlet. For example, let's say we want to add a resource delegate to our Conference Room South. We accomplish that in one line:

```
Set-CalendarProcessing "Conference Room South" -ResourceDelegates ↵
"Alex Bossio"
```

As with other EMS commands, we can supply multiple attributes together in one command. If we want to, say, add a delegate and also add the meeting organizer's name to the subject, we could use this:

```
Set-CalendarProcessing "Conference Room South" -ResourceDelegates ↵
"Alex Bossio" —AddOrganizerToSubject $true
```

A complete description of each of the attributes is listed in Tables 20.2, 20.3, and 20.4 earlier in this chapter.

SETTINGS THAT CAN ONLY BE CONFIGURED IN THE EMS

There are some settings that can only be configured using the Exchange Management Shell. They include working hours and days, such as time zone, and default reminder settings. We can see an example of these using the `Get-MailboxCalendarConfiguration` cmdlet:

```
Get-MailboxCalendarConfiguration "Conference Room South" | ↵
Format-List

RunspaceId               : 53135a92-3a51-4db4-a0aa-
7a45c231fb91
WorkDays                 : Weekdays
WorkingHoursStartTime    : 08:00:00
WorkingHoursEndTime      : 17:00:00
WorkingHoursTimeZone     : Pacific Standard Time
WeekStartDay             : Sunday
ShowWeekNumbers          : False
TimeIncrement            : ThirtyMinutes
RemindersEnabled         : True
ReminderSoundEnabled     : True
DefaultReminderTime      : 00:15:00
Identity                 :
IsValid                  : True
```

Setting options here is possible via the `Set-MailboxCalendarConfiguration` cmdlet. For example, if we need to change the `WorkingHoursTimeZone`, we can use this:

```
Set-MailboxCalendarConfiguration "Conference Room South" ↵
—WorkingHoursTimeZone "Eastern Standard Time"
```

A complete breakdown of the various attributes is shown in Table 20.7.

Automatic Processing: AutoUpdate vs. AutoAccept

Automatic processing of meeting requests is enabled by an attribute on Resource mailboxes called `AutomateProcessing`. By default, when a Resource mailbox is created, or an existing mailbox is converted to a Resource mailbox, the `AutomateProcessing` attribute is set to `AutoUpdate`. `AutoUpdate` processes requests automatically but doesn't validate the request against any booking policy settings. This is generally not ideal for an organization.

TABLE 20.7:   Set-MailboxCalendarConfiguration Attributes

PARAMETER	DESCRIPTION
Workdays	Specifies which days are defined as workdays in the OWA calendar
WorkingHoursStartTime	Specifies the start of the workday in hours, minutes, and seconds
WorkingHoursEndTime	Specifies the end of the workday in hours, minutes, and seconds
WorkingHoursTimeZone	Specifies the time zone used to determine start and end times
WeekStartDay	Specifies which day of the week is the start of the workweek
ShowWeekNumber	Specifies whether the OWA date picker shows the week number
TimeIncrement	Specifies in which increments the OWA calendar shows time frames
RemindersEnabled	Specifies whether OWA events trigger a reminder
DefaultReminderTime	Specifies the default time frame before a scheduled event that OWA displays the reminder

The alternative value available for `AutomateProcessing` is `AutoAccept`. When a Resource mailbox is configured for `AutoAccept`, the attendant validates the meeting request against the configured policy settings before determining whether the meeting request is accepted or rejected. For the settings in the resource policy to be effective, a Resource mailbox needs to be changed to `AutoAccept`. To change a Resource mailbox is simple, regardless of whether you use the EMC, EMS, or OWA.

In the EMC, open the Resource mailbox, go to the Resource General tab, and check the box that says Enable the Resource Booking Attendant. Then click OK. You see an example of this in Figure 20.12.

In OWA, go to Options ➢ Settings ➢ Resource, and check the box that reads Automatically Process Meeting Requests And Cancellations. Then click Save. This will change `AutomateProcessing` to `AutoAccept`, and future meeting requests will be validated against the policy settings for that mailbox.

In the EMS, set the `AutomateProcessing` attribute using the `Set-CalendarProcessing` cmdlet, like this:

```
Set-CalendarProcessing "Conference Room South" ↵
-AutomateProcessing AutoAccept
```

We can also use the EMS to make the change across all Resource mailboxes:

```
Get-Mailbox -filter {IsResource -eq $true} | ↵
Set-CalendarProcessing -AutomateProcessing AutoAccept
```

Using any of these methods will change the Resource mailbox to `AutoAccept`.

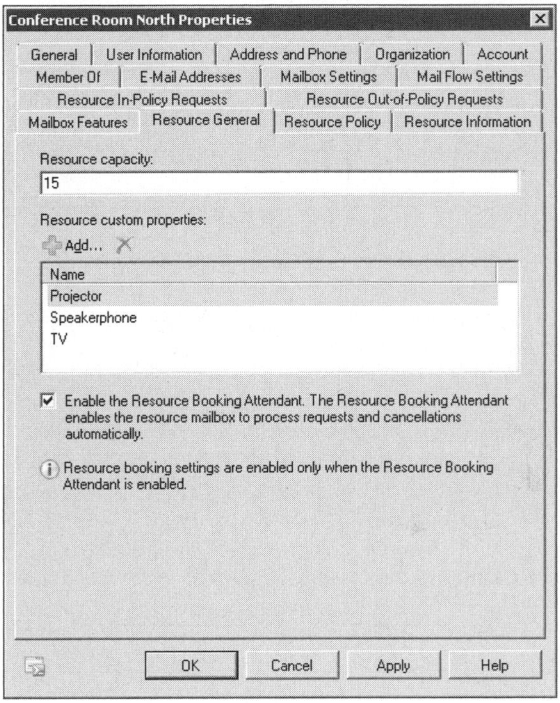

FIGURE 20.12

Setting processing on a Resource mailbox

Migrating Resource Mailboxes

Since versions of Exchange prior to Exchange 2007 used a different method to handle resource booking, moving Resource mailboxes to Exchange 2010 involves a few steps. Exchange is not intelligent enough to know that a mailbox called "Conference Room South" is a resource, and thus, make a Resource mailbox. We must tell Exchange this is the case.

- ◆ Document all Resource mailboxes that need to be moved, as well as any settings configured via third-party solutions or scripts.

- ◆ Disable any automatic processing configured via script or third-party solutions.

- ◆ Move the mailboxes to Exchange 2010 using either the EMC or the EMS. This process is detailed in Chapter 17.

- ◆ Use the EMS to convert the mailboxes from User mailboxes to Room mailboxes.

- ◆ Configure the appropriate policy settings for the Resource mailboxes.

Converting a standard User mailbox to a Resource mailbox is quick and simple using the `Set-Mailbox` cmdlet in the EMS and specifying the `Room` or `Equipment` attribute, as in this example:

```
Set-Mailbox "Conference Room South" -Type Room
```

You should then set the room Resource mailbox to automatically process appointments using a command like this:

```
Get-Mailbox "Conference Room South" | Set-CalendarProcessing -AutomateProcessing ↵
AutoAccept
```

Once this occurs, Exchange considers the mailbox a Room or Equipment mailbox, and the ability to configure them via the EMC, EMS, or OWA is enabled.

Real World Scenario

ELIMINATING CONFERENCE ROOM HIJACKING

Organization KLMN is a large community church; it is not like most churches. With more than 400 staff, volunteers, and interns, there is a constant level of meetings, conferences, and gatherings in the building's five conference rooms. And to make matters worse, the scheduling process for the conference rooms was antiquated and inconvenient. In the building's lobby were three-ring binders for each conference room. Each contained pages for each calendar day. Those wishing to reserve a conference room had to go to the lobby, look through the binder for the desired conference room, and try to decipher sometimes cryptic entries. Additionally, when meetings were cancelled, meeting organizers didn't always remove the entry in the binder to allow the conference room to be rescheduled. Since some of KLMN's staff worked outside the main building, the process was even more cumbersome when trying to find a conference room that was available. The process was so inconvenient that many would just hijack a conference room without scheduling it. This led to "musical conference rooms" sometimes, and a lot of user frustration.

When KLMN moved to Resource mailboxes in Exchange, users could immediately reserve conference rooms by merely adding the conference room to the meeting request. Additionally, since the resource Room mailboxes were configured with capacity and special features defined, finding a conference room that best fit the needs of the users was much easier. Remote users had the same experience as local users, and the number of conference room "hijackings" dropped to nearly zero.

This process has improved the adoption of using Outlook Meeting Requests, the Outlook Calendar in general, and the correct process for booking conference rooms. Users no longer have to walk to the other end of the building, or go up three floors just to find when a conference room may be reserved. They can simply open Outlook, OWA, or use a mobile device to schedule their meeting including all attendees, the conference room, and any necessary equipment.

The Bottom Line

Understand how Resource mailboxes differ from regular mailboxes. Resource mailboxes serve a different purpose in Exchange 2010 than standard User mailboxes, and thus have different features and capabilities. Understanding how Resource mailboxes are different, including what added features are provided, can help improve the end-user experience and increase adoption rate.

Master It   You are planning to create Resource mailboxes to support conference room and other resource scheduling. Identify how the Resource mailboxes are different from regular User mailboxes.

Create Resource mailboxes.   Creating Resource mailboxes is easy using various tools in Exchange. Users need Resource mailboxes for conference rooms and equipment like vehicles to allow for easier, more informative scheduling.

Master It   What tools are available to create Resource mailbox and to define additional schema properties for resource mailboxes?

Configure Resource mailbox booking and scheduling policies.   Properly configured resource mailboxes help users find the correct resource that is available when needed. When the resource mailbox is properly configured, users need to quickly and easily find conference rooms that have the proper capacity and features needed to hold a meeting.

Master It   You need to configure a resource mailbox to handle automatic scheduling. What tools can you use?

Migrate Resource mailboxes.   Moving Resource mailboxes from legacy versions of Exchange require proper planning an execution to ensure that Exchange 2010 features and capabilities for Resource mailboxes are available. Resource mailboxes in Exchange versions prior to 2007 were standard user accounts, and need to be migrated and converted to Resource mailboxes.

Master It   You have moved a resource mailbox from an Exchange 2003 mailbox server to an Exchange 2010 mailbox server. You need to convert this resource to an Exchange 2010 Resource mailbox. What steps should you take?

Chapter 21

Public Folder Management

For many companies, public folders are a major part of their Exchange Server deployments. Public folders are a powerful way to share knowledge and data throughout your organization, and they've been a staple of Exchange Server. They are a great way to share content and information with many users, and because they can be mail-enabled, they can also be an easy way for third-party application developers to hook into Exchange. All you have to do is use the MAPI libraries to connect to Exchange as a user with permissions to the specified public folder and you've got the ability to send and receive messages — and share them with multiple users — without having to do a lot of coding.

In Exchange Server 2010, the EMS cmdlets for handling public folders and the RBAC roles for administering permissions are definitely worth the price of admission.

In this chapter, you will learn to:

◆ Understand how public folders are supported in Exchange 2010

◆ Manage public folders

◆ Manage replication

Understanding Public Folder Support in Exchange 2010

Despite the rumors of their demise, public folders are alive and well, and in some ways they're even better in Exchange 2010 than they ever have been.

When Microsoft announced it was "deemphasizing" support for public folders in Exchange Server 2007, many Exchange administrators worried that the public folders would be completely removed from Exchange Server 2010. What was the future of public folders? Would Exchange Server 2010 continue to support them? Would they be forced to migrate all their Public Folders to SharePoint server?

Unfortunately, Microsoft's announcement initially caused a lot of worry and confusion. Combined with the lack of any GUI public folder management tools in the initial release of Exchange 2007, the announcement led a lot of people to the conclusion that you just can't use public folders anymore. If you've got a large public folder deployment in your organization, this is obviously an area of concern for you.

Happily, Microsoft has clarified its position on public folder support. Public folders are still fully supported in Exchange Server 2010 (and will be through 2019) and probably even beyond that point.

In the meantime, you can go forward with your Exchange 2010 migration secure in the knowledge that you will be able to continue using your public folder infrastructure.

THE FUTURE OF PUBLIC FOLDERS

Customers and students frequently ask if they should continue to support public folders on their network. Frankly, we're torn when answering that question. Though we really can't do much with SharePoint other than deploy it and make it available on the network, we can see the writing on the wall. SharePoint is the future of collaborative solutions in a Microsoft world.

Exchange Server public folders can still do some things that are hard (or impossible) to do with SharePoint. One such task is easily replicating content from one location to another and making it transparent to the end user. Still, the collaborative and information-sharing capabilities of SharePoint certainly seem to outweigh those of Exchange Server in most respects.

Now is the time to start looking to the future, especially if you have thousands (or tens of thousands) of public folders. If you are starting to deploy SharePoint, look at each of your public folders (and public folders that are being requested for future use) and decide if SharePoint is a better platform. Companies such as Quest Software provide migration tools that will help you move data and applications from public folders to SharePoint.

From a client's perspective, you should also start looking at Microsoft Office 2010 SharePoint Workspace (formally known as Groove), which provides great multiuser file-sharing capabilities.

Understanding Native Exchange 2010 Support

The Exchange Management Console (EMC) offers minimal support for public folders — just public folder databases actually. The Public Folder Management Console will offer some basic functionality for managing public folder properties. However, Exchange 2010 provides the bulk of its built-in support via Exchange Management Shell (EMS) cmdlets, including the RBAC administrative management. Don't worry; they're not difficult to use, even if you're not a script or command-line guru.

Before we show you how to use the public folder cmdlets, though, we'll cover what you can do in the EMC. Be warned that it isn't much: you can create and delete public folder databases on your Mailbox servers and manage the basic properties of these databases. The Public Folder Management Console includes some basic capabilities for viewing the public folder hierarchy, adding or deleting public folders, setting folder properties, and viewing and managing replication.

Public Folder Limitations

If you have been using public folders for years, you are probably already aware of these limitations. If that's the case, you can probably skip this section. The intent here is to make sure you understand that public folders are not necessarily a "fix all" solution for information sharing. Public folders have the following limitations:

◆ Although you can store files in public folders, Exchange is not designed to be a file repository, so you shouldn't use your public folders to store gigabytes and gigabytes of files.

◆ High availability and redundancy of public folder content is achieved by creating additional replicas of public folder content on other public folder databases.

- Though you can have public folder databases on Mailbox servers that are members of a database availability group (DAG), those databases cannot be replicated by Exchange's replication services.

- You must mail-enable user accounts or security groups to assign client permissions to any public folder.

- Client permissions to public folders must be assigned from Office Outlook clients or the Exchange Management Shell.

- IMAP and POP users cannot access public folders.

Moving the Public Folder Hierarchy to Exchange 2010

If you are migrating from Exchange 2003 to Exchange Server 2010 and you are planning to continue to use public folders, there is one important step you should take care of sooner rather than later. You need to move the public folder hierarchy from the Exchange 2003 administrative group into the Exchange Server 2010 administrative group. Notice in Figure 21.1 that there is a Folders container under First Administrative Group; this is where the public folder hierarchy is currently held on an Exchange Server 2003 organization.

FIGURE 21.1
Default location for the public folder hierarchy

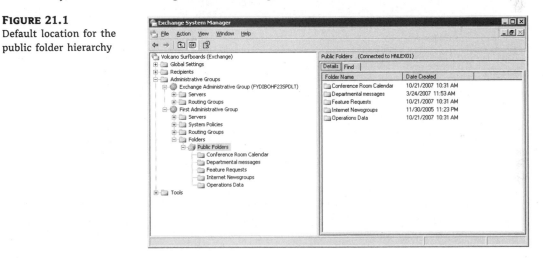

Although Exchange Server does not care which administrative group the hierarchy is located in, Outlook clients will break if you delete the administrative group without first moving the hierarchy. We have heard of several instances where someone removed all their legacy Exchange 2003 servers and then removed the administrative group that held the public folder hierarchy. As a result, Outlook 2003 clients could no longer access the public folders and they could no longer access system folders, such as the Free/Busy folders and the offline address book.

Do *not* delete the Exchange 2003 administrative groups without moving the public folder hierarchy. To be safe, you should just leave the old admin groups in place; you will not see them in the Exchange Server 2010 admin tools and it doesn't hurt anything to leave them there after all your Exchange 2003 servers are removed.

We strongly recommend that you move the public folder hierarchy to the Exchange 2010 administrative group — Exchange Administrative Group (FYDIBOHF23SPDLT) — as soon as you get Exchange Server 2010 running in your organization. Follow these steps to move the public folder hierarchy:

1. Using the Exchange 2003 System Manager, expand the Administrative Groups container, right-click the Exchange Administrative Group (FYDIBOHF23SPDLT), and choose New ➢ Public Folders Container.

2. Expand the Exchange 2003 administrative group that holds the public folder hierarchy.

3. Open the Folders container and drag the Public Folders container to the new Folders container in the Exchange Administrative Group (FYDIBOHF23SPDLT) container. When you release the mouse button, the public folder hierarchy will be moved to the new public folder container.

4. Don't forget to create the public folder databases and replicate the public folder and system folder content to Exchange Server 2010

Creating a Public Folder Database

As we mentioned earlier, public folder databases are not created by default on Exchange Server 2010 Mailbox servers unless you specify that Outlook 2003 users are available on your network. When you set up the first Mailbox server in the organization, you can include a public folder database.

Mailbox and public folder databases can be created from either the Exchange Management Console or the Exchange Management Shell. To create a public folder database from the Exchange Management Shell, simply use the `New-PublicFolderDatabase` cmdlet and remember to use the `Mount-Database` cmdlet to mount the database after it has been created. The commands look like this:

```
New-PublicFolderDatabase CoolStuff -Server Montreal-Server1 -EdbFilePath ↵
E:\Databases\CoolStuff\CoolStuff.edb -LogFilePath D:\Logs\CoolStuff
```

Note in this command that we specified the location of the database file for the public folder database named CoolStuff. We also defined the location of the log files. If we didn't specify those file folder locations, they would have been placed in the following default value locations:

Public Folder Database and Filename   In the Install folder V14\Mailbox\coolstuff\CoolStuff.edb

Public Folder Database Log File Path   In the Install folder V14\Mailbox\CoolStuff

In addition, because the database is not mounted after it is created, the following command can be used to mount the database:

```
Mount-Database CoolStuff
```

OOPS ... THE DATABASE WILL NOT MOUNT

Note that the task might not mount the database due to replication delays in Active Directory. Delays occur if the cmdlet connects to one domain controller to make the changes and Exchange Server is connected to another domain controller for its configuration. In this case, the `Mount-Database` cmdlet may display a message that Exchange Server 2010 can't mount a database that it does not even know exists yet. Alternately, wait a few minutes or force replication between domain controllers, and then attempt the mount command again.

Managing Public Folder Database Properties

Now that you have a public folder database created, let's look at the properties of that database that you can manage using the EMC as well as the EMS. We'll start with the EMC and look at some of the properties you can set.

On the General properties page, you can change the display name of the public folder database, specify whether the database should be mounted at startup, and specify whether the database can be overwritten by a restore from backup.

You also view statistical information about the public folder database, such as the database path, the date of the last full backup, the date of the last incremental backup, the status of the database, and the last time the database's properties were modified.

On the Replication properties page of the public folder database, you can specify the replication schedule (the default is Always), the Replicate Always Interval setting (the default is 15 minutes), and the maximum replication message size.

The Limits properties page allows you to set some of the same types of information for public folders that you can set for mailboxes. Figure 21.2 shows the Limits properties page for a newly created public folder database. These settings will affect any newly created folder on this particular public folder database.

FIGURE 21.2
Default limits for an
Exchange 2010 public
folder database

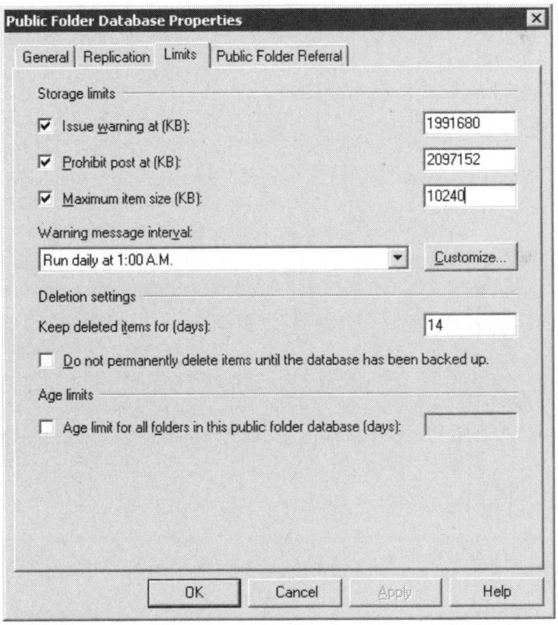

The Warning Message Interval option specifies the time of day that over-the-limit warning messages are generated and emailed to public folder contacts and owners.

Deleted items are retained for 14 days; during this time the folder owner can undelete items (or folders) that were inadvertently deleted. You can tell Exchange to keep deleted items after the expiration interval by clicking Do Not Permanently Delete Items Until The Database Has Been Backed Up.

Finally, the Age Limits property instructs the database to delete any item in any folder on this database that exceeds the age limit. This is useful if you want to delete or age out older content, but it is probably more useful to apply this property on a folder-by-folder basis.

The Public Folder Referral properties page (Figure 21.3) shows how to enable a feature that was first introduced in Exchange 2003. By default, when an Outlook client connects to its *home* public folder database, if the public folder it requires is not on that particular database, it is given a referral to another public folder server. The referral list has all public folders that contain a replica of the required folder and is sorted and gives preference to public folder servers in the local site (or routing group in Exchange Server 2003).

FIGURE 21.3
Public folder referral properties

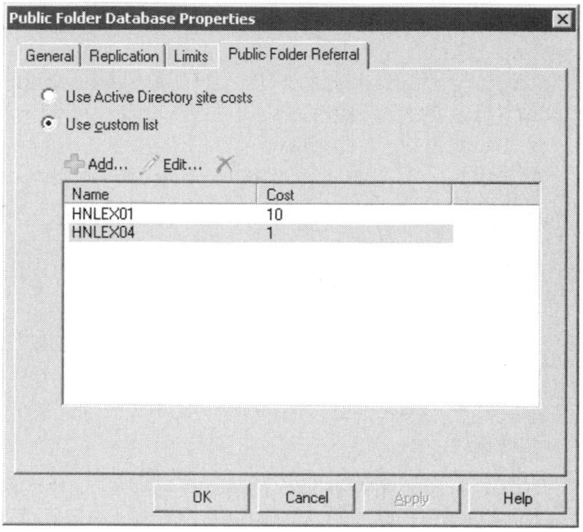

In Exchange 2010, the referral list is generated based on the Active Directory site that the public folder replicas are located in and is sorted based on the site link cost. This may not be desirable for public folder connectivity, so you can specify a custom list and a cost value that should be used to sort the list of public folder servers.

Although you can configure this manual list, keep in mind that when servers are decommissioned from the network, the servers will not be removed from that list and may cause some negative future effects.

All of the properties of public folder databases can be managed from the Exchange Management Shell. Table 21.1 contains a list of EMS cmdlets that can be used to manage public folder databases.

TABLE 21.1: EMS Cmdlets for Public Folder Databases

CMDLET	FUNCTION
New-PublicFolderDatabase	Creates a new public folder database
Set-PublicFolderDatabase	Sets properties of a public folder database
Get-PublicFolderDatabase	Retrieves a list of public folder databases and their properties
Remove-PublicFolderDatabase	Deletes a public folder database

Defining the Default Public Folder Server

When a user attempts to access a public folder, Outlook and Outlook Web App clients first look for a public folder server setting on the user's public folder database, which might or might not be the same Exchange server where the user's mailbox is located. The default public folder database is configured on the Client Settings tab of the properties dialog box for a mailbox database.

If a specific public folder doesn't exist in the default public folder database, the client is directed to a server where the public folder resides. As you can imagine, when many public folders are accessed over a lower-bandwidth network, server and network loads can get pretty heavy as users access public folders on one or a limited number of Exchange servers. If you need to, you can replicate folders on one Exchange server to other Exchange servers, therefore alleviating the load on a single server and creating redundancy for public folders.

Defining Public Folder Administrators

In a small or medium-sized organization, one or two administrators are going to be responsible for all Exchange Server administrative tasks, including managing the public folders. However, in very large organizations, you may need to delegate the public folder administration tasks to a different person or group. Exchange Server 2010 automatically creates a group in the Microsoft Exchange Security Groups OU called Public Folder Management. Members of this group can manage the Exchange public folder attributes in the public folder and perform public folder operations, including these tasks:

- Creating public folders

- Creating top-level public folders

- Modifying public folder permissions

- Modifying public folder administrative permissions

- Modifying public folder properties such as content expiration times, storage limits, and deleted item retention time

- Modifying public folder replica lists

- Mounting and dismounting public folder databases

- Mail-enabling/disabling public folders

Managing Public Folders

When you start working with public folders, setting permissions, creating replicas, and setting folder limits, you will find a number of tools available to you. As a matter of fact, you may need a couple of tools to accomplish everything you need to. For example, you might need the Exchange 2010 Public Folder Management Console to create a folder and to mail-enable it (assign it an email address) and then Outlook or the Exchange Management Shell to set permissions on the folder. That's right: the only way to configure client permissions for public folders is to use the Outlook client application or the Exchange Management Shell.

Using the Exchange 2010 Public Folder Management Console

Exchange Server 2010 contains the Public Folder Management Console; you can find it in the Toolbox work center of the Exchange Management Console. When you first launch this console, it will select an Exchange 2010 server with a public folder database, but you can change that if the server that is selected is not convenient. Figure 21.4 shows the Exchange 2010 Public Folder Management Console.

FIGURE 21.4
Exchange Public Folder Management Console

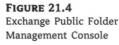

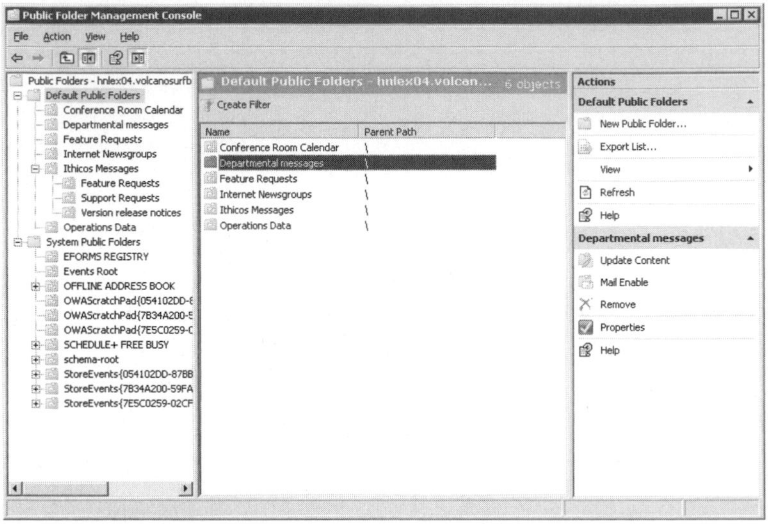

You will notice that the Public Folder Management Console looks a lot like the Exchange Management Console. The left side of the console shows the Console tree; this area is only for viewing the public and system folders. You cannot manipulate any folder properties in the tree view.

In the Results pane in the middle, you can see the public folders within the part of the public folder tree that you currently have selected. If you plan to manage any properties of a public folder, you must select that folder here in the Results pane. For example, we currently have the Departmental Messages folder highlighted. We can manage it by choosing Properties from the Actions pane (or just right-clicking and selecting Properties).

VIEWING THE PROPERTIES OF A PUBLIC FOLDER

Figure 21.5 shows the General properties of the Departmental Messages folder.

The General properties page shows the display name, path, total items, size, public folder database, and the date the folder's properties were last modified. In an environment with more than one public folder server, this information will not always be accurate, though. In some cases, the General properties page displays "Not available on this server." This means you are looking at a public folder database that does not have a local replica of this particular folder.

Next is the Replication properties page, which shows you the servers and public folder databases where you can find a replica (copy) of this particular public folder. The Replication properties page for the Departmental Messages folder is shown in Figure 21.6; this folder has two replicas.

Earlier in this chapter, we showed you how you can specify a global default for limits for a particular public folder database. The Limits properties page (shown in Figure 21.7) in an individual public folder allows you to override this per-database limit. Notice that by default the folder will use the limits set for it on its public folder database, but you can override that.

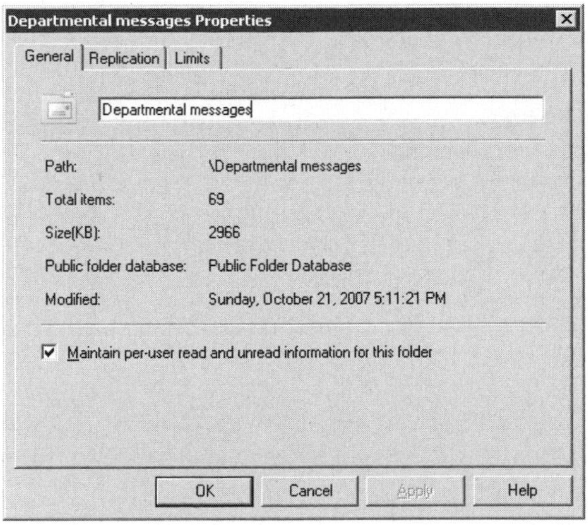

FIGURE 21.5
Viewing a public folder's
General properties page

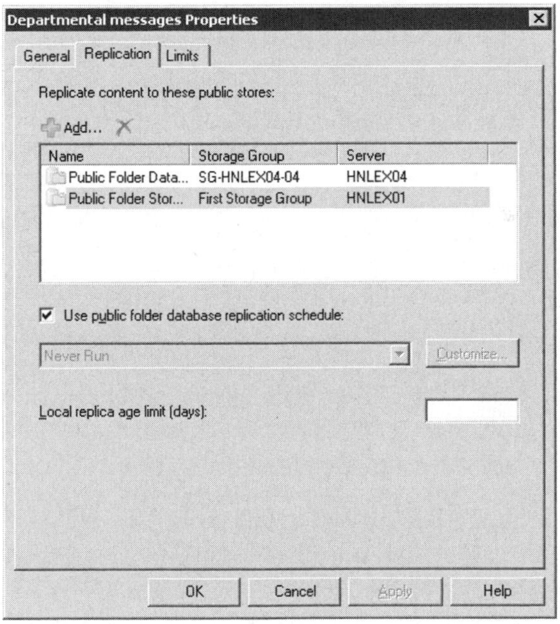

FIGURE 21.6
Viewing the replicas of
a public folder

ADDITIONAL MANAGEMENT TASKS

You may have noticed two additional tasks in the Actions pane. The first is the Update Content task. If you click this task, Exchange will attempt to synchronize any missing or added content in this folder to other replicas.

FIGURE 21.7
Viewing the limits of a
specific public folder

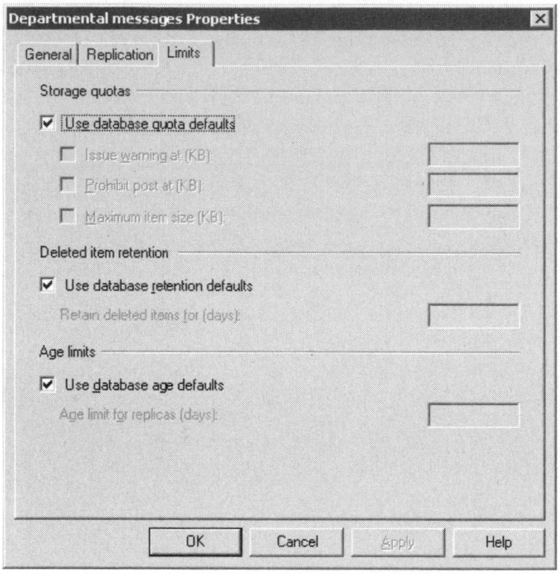

The second task is the Mail Enable task. Just as in earlier versions of Exchange, a public folder can have an email address. By default, public folders are not configured with an email address. However, you can mail-enable a folder so it shows up in your Global Address List (GAL) and has an email address.

Real World Scenario

WHEN PUBLIC FOLDERS PROVIDE EASY BUSINESS SOLUTIONS

Public folders have been around for a while. Organizations of varying sizes have been using public folders to provide easy solutions to sometimes complex problems. Sometimes, it seems that using a public folder is truly the easiest solution to a business requirement. Maybe that is the secret to the longevity of this simple technology.

The simplest aspect of public folders, and one that some companies forget to implement, is the ability to send/receive mail into a public folder. You can mail-enable a public folder and then configure it to receive emails. This solution is typically used for public folders that must receive information from external senders or users that do not use a client application that supports public folder access.

Last year, we encountered a company that needed a solution for collecting resumes for job postings. Resumes needed to be sent from external individuals applying for positions. The specific need was for external individuals to send an email by using the external email address. The solution was easy. All we did was mail-enable a public folder, hence converting the folder into an e-mail recipient. Whenever an email came in to the public folder, the resume was then reviewed by internal HR employees responsible for selecting applicants.

A user must have permissions to post to the folder to successfully send a message to the folder's email address. If you are setting up a mail-enabled public folder that will receive email from outside your organization, make sure that the Anonymous user has Contributor permissions to the public folder. The Contributor role contains two rights: the right to post to a folder and the right to see the folder in a folder list.

Suppose we select a folder called Support Requests in the Results pane and then click the Mail Enable task. This action automatically mail-enables the folder so that it shows up in the Exchange address lists; now the folder has some new properties pages. One of the new properties pages (Exchange General) is shown in Figure 21.8.

FIGURE 21.8
Viewing the Exchange General properties tab of a public folder

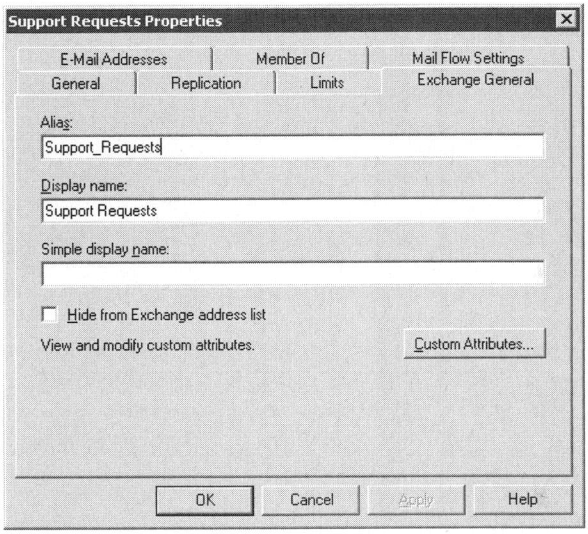

On the Exchange General properties page, you can see the Exchange alias (which is used to generate the SMTP addresses as well as the display name) and the simple display name. You can also access the custom attributes. If you don't want the public folder to show up in the address lists, select the Hide From Exchange Address List check box.

On the E-Mail Addresses properties page (shown in Figure 21.9), you can see and edit the email addresses that are assigned to the folder's Active Directory object.

Anyone can now send email to this folder from outside the organization by addressing mail to support_requests@directory-update.com. One important thing to note is that the default permissions on a folder include allowing the Anonymous user to contribute to a folder. If you remove this permission, the folder will not accept email from outside your organization.

Using the Exchange Management Shell to Manage Public Folders

One of the capabilities in Exchange Server 2010 is the inclusion of the Exchange Management Shell and the ability to manage public folders from the command line. Command-line management of public folders is a feature that has been missing from previous versions of Exchange Server.

ABOUT TYPING LONG LINES IN THE EXCHANGE MANAGEMENT SHELL

In some of the following examples, you'll see lines terminated by a ↵ character. This character tells you that this is supposed to represent a single command line. You can also use the backtick (`` ` ``) character if you want to continue typing on the next line. PowerShell uses the backtick character for line termination; it tells the shell that the logical line of input will be continued on the next physical line. This allows you to break up long lines for display and still ensure that they work correctly when you enter them.

FIGURE 21.9
Email addresses for a
mail-enabled folder

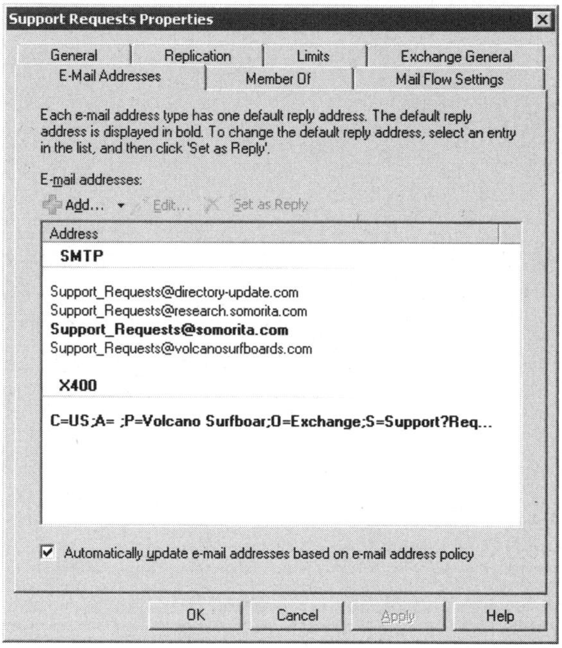

PERFORMING GENERAL PUBLIC FOLDER TASKS

These cmdlets apply to the entire public folder hierarchy at once and provide broad control of your public folder infrastructure:

Get-PublicFolderStatistics   This cmdlet provides a detailed set of statistics about the public folder hierarchy on a given server:

```
Get-PublicFolderStatistics -Server "MBX01"
```

If the -Server parameter is not specified, the cmdlet will default to displaying the statistics on the local server.

Resume-PublicFolderReplication   This cmdlet reenables all public folder content replication when it has been suspended:

```
Resume-PublicFolderReplication
```

Suspend-PublicFolderReplication   This cmdlet suspends all public folder content replication:

```
Suspend-PublicFolderReplication
```

You may want to suspend public folder replication for various reasons. For example, you may suspend replication of the public folder content if an error has occurred in a public folder replica or in the configuration of the public folder hierarchy.

Update-PublicFolderHierarchy   This cmdlet starts the content synchronization process for the public folder hierarchy on the specified server:

```
Update-PublicFolderHierarchy -Server "MBX01"
```

You may want to force a new replication of the public folder hierarchy if one public store in your organization has an out-of-date public folder list.

MANIPULATING INDIVIDUAL PUBLIC FOLDERS

These cmdlets are designed to work with a specific public folder:

Get-PublicFolder   This cmdlet retrieves the properties for the specified public folder. If you don't name a public folder by specifying a value for the -Identity property, it will default to the root public folder:

```
Get-PublicFolder -Identity "\Jobs\Posted" -Server "MBX01"
```

If you want to see system folders, you'll need to set the -Identity property to a value beginning with the string \NON_IPM_SUBTREE:

```
Get-PublicFolder -Identity \NON_IPM_SUBTREE -Recurse
```

New-PublicFolder   This cmdlet creates a new public folder. The -Path property is required and provides the name and location of the new public folder:

```
New-PublicFolder -Name New -Path "\Jobs" -Server "MBX01"
```

Remove-PublicFolder   This cmdlet deletes a public folder. The -Path property is required and provides the name and location of the public folder to be deleted:

```
Remove-PublicFolder -Path "\Jobs\Old" -Server "MBX01"
```

By default, the Get-PublicFolder cmdlet returns the values for only a single folder. The -Recurse switch changes the behavior to report on all subfolders as well:

```
Get-PublicFolder -Identity "\Jobs\Posted" -Server "MBX01" -Recurse
```

By default, the Remove-PublicFolder cmdlet removes only the named public folder. The -Recurse switch will delete all subfolders as well, which is handy for removing an entire group of folders at once.

Set-PublicFolder   This cmdlet allows you to set most of the properties for the named public folder, such as limits, replicas, replication schedules, and more:

```
Set-PublicFolder -Identity "\Jobs\Posted" -Server "MBX01"
```

You cannot use the Set-PublicFolder cmdlet to mail-enable a public folder or to change its mail-related attributes. See the next section, "Manipulating Public Folder Mail Attributes," for the cmdlets to use for these tasks.

Update-PublicFolder   This cmdlet starts the content synchronization process for the named public folder. The -Identity property is required:

```
Update-PublicFolder -Identity "\Jobs\Posted"
```

MANIPULATING PUBLIC FOLDER MAIL ATTRIBUTES

These cmdlets are designed to work with a specific public folder and modify the attributes it receives when it is mail-enabled:

Disable-MailPublicFolder   This cmdlet takes an existing mail-enabled public folder and renders it mail-disabled (what a great term!):

```
Disable-MailPublicFolder -Identity "\Jobs\New"
```

Enable-MailPublicFolder   This cmdlet takes an existing public folder and renders it mail-enabled. The optional -HiddenFromAddressListsEnabled switch allows you to hide the folder from your address lists:

```
Enable-MailPublicFolder -Identity "\Jobs\New"
-HiddenFromAddressListsEnabled ↵
$true -Server "MBX01"
```

You set the mail-related attributes separately using the Set-MailPublicFolder cmdlet.

Get-MailPublicFolder   This cmdlet retrieves the mail-related properties for the specified public folder. If you don't name a public folder by specifying a value for the -Identity property, it will default to the root public folder:

```
Get-MailPublicFolder -Identity "\Jobs\Old" -Server "MBX01"
```

Set-MailPublicFolder   This cmdlet allows you to set the mail-related properties for the named public folder, such as an alias, email addresses, send and receive sizes, permitted and prohibited senders, and so on:

```
Set-MailPublicFolder -Identity "\Jobs\Posted"  -Alias PostedJobs ↵
-PrimarySmtpAddress "Jobs@Ithicos.com"
```

Keep in mind that to be able to modify the mail-related attribute for a public folder, you must first mail-enable it using the Enable-MailPublicFolder cmdlet.

MANAGING PUBLIC FOLDER DATABASES

These cmdlets allow you to manage the public folder databases:

Get-PublicFolderDatabase   This cmdlet provides the functionality used by the EMC and allows you to view the properties of existing public folder databases:

```
Get-PublicFolderDatabase -Server "MBX01"
```

This cmdlet takes one of three parameters: -Identity, -Server, or -StorageGroup. The parameters are not compatible with each other. Use only one of the three to narrow down your selection.

New-PublicFolderDatabase   This cmdlet allows you to create a new public folder database. You can see the New-PublicFolderDatabase cmdlet in action by using the EMC to create a new database; it will show you the exact syntax it used with the cmdlet.

Remove-PublicFolderDatabase   This cmdlet deletes an existing public folder database from the active configuration of the server:

```
Remove-PublicFolderDatabase ' -Identity "Public Folder Database"
```

The corresponding EDB file is not deleted by the Remove-PublicFolderDatabase cmdlet; you have to manually remove it from the hard drive.

Set-PublicFolderDatabase   This cmdlet provides the underlying functionality used by the EMC to update the properties of existing public folder databases:

```
Set-PublicFolderDatabase -Identity "Public Folder Database"↵
-Name "New and Improved PF Database"
```

MANAGING PUBLIC FOLDER PERMISSIONS

These cmdlets allow you to modify and monitor the permissions on your public folders. Administrative and client permissions are handled through two separate sets of nouns. The Exchange 2010 documentation contains the list of specific permissions that you can apply.

Add-PublicFolderAdministrativePermission   This cmdlet lets you add an administrative permission entry to a given public folder:

```
Add-PublicFolderAdministrativePermission -User 'Jlong'
-Identity "\Jobs\Posted"↵
-AccessRights "ViewInformationStore, AdministerInformationStore"
```

You can specify a single access right or list multiple rights at once using the syntax shown in the example for the Add-PublicFolderAdministrativePermission cmdlet.

Add-PublicFolderClientPermission   This cmdlet lets you add a client permission entry to a given public folder:

```
Add-PublicFolderClientPermission -User Cohen.Oliver↵
-Identity "\Jobs\Posted" -AccessRights CreateItems
```

You can specify a single access right or list multiple rights at once using the syntax shown in the example for the Add-PublicFolderAdministrativePermission cmdlet.

Get-PublicFolderAdministrativePermission   This cmdlet lets you view the administrative permission entries on a given public folder:

```
Get-PublicFolderAdministrativePermission  -Identity "\Jobs\Posted"
```

Get-PublicFolderClientPermission   This cmdlet lets you view the client permission entries on a given public folder:

```
Get-PublicFolderClientPermission  -Identity "\Jobs\Posted"
```

Remove-PublicFolderAdministrativePermission   This cmdlet lets you remove an administrative permission entry from a given public folder:

```
Remove-PublicFolderAdministrativePermission -User Cohen.Larry↵
-Identity "\Jobs\Posted" -AccessRights ViewInformationStore
```

You can specify a single access right or list multiple rights at once using the syntax shown in the Remove-PublicFolderAdministrativePermission example.

Remove-PublicFolderClientPermission   This cmdlet lets you remove a client permission entry from a given public folder:

```
Remove-PublicFolderClientPermission -User Bouganim.Mike↵
-Identity "\Jobs\Posted" -AccessRights CreateItems
```

You can specify a single access right or list multiple rights at once using the syntax shown in the Remove-PublicFolderAdministrativePermission example.

USING ADDITIONAL SCRIPTS FOR COMPLICATED TASKS

Although the cmdlets described in the preceding sections are certainly great for single folder operations, performing common operations on entire groups of folders starts getting sticky. Because most of us aren't scripting gurus, Exchange 2010 provides some example EMS scripts that allow you to perform more complicated server and management tasks that affect groups of folders:

- `AddReplicaToPFRecursive.ps1` adds the specified server to the replica list for a given public folder and all folders underneath it.

- `AddUsersToPFRecursive.ps1` allows you to grant user permissions to a folder and all folders beneath it.

- `MoveAllReplicas.ps1` finds and replaces a server in the replica list of all public folders, including system folders.

- `RemoveReplicaFromPFRecursive.ps1` removes the specified server from the replica list for a given public folder and all folders underneath it.

- `ReplaceReplicaOnPFRecursive.ps1` finds and replaces a server in the replica list of a given public folder as well as all subfolders.

- `ReplaceUserPermissionOnPFRecursive.ps1` finds and replaces one user in the permissions on a given public folder and all its subfolders with a second user; the original user permissions are not retained.

- `ReplaceUserWithUserOnPFRecursive.ps1` copies one user's access permissions on a given public folder and all its subfolders to a second user while retaining permissions for the first user; its name is confusing.

- `RemoveUserFromPFRecursive.ps1` removes the given user's access permissions from the given public folder and all its subfolders.

You can find these scripts in the Scripts subfolder of the Exchange 2010 installation folder. Note that with the default Windows PowerShell configuration, you just can't click on these scripts and run them; you must invoke them from within the EMS, usually by navigating to the folder and calling them explicitly.

Using Outlook to Create a Public Folder

Exchange public folders can also be created by mailbox-enabled users in their email clients. Here's how you create a public folder using the Outlook client:

1. Open Outlook and make sure the folder list is displayed.

2. Double-click Public Folders in the folder list, or click the plus icon just in front of Public Folders. Notice that the plus sign becomes a minus sign when a folder is expanded to show the folders within it.
   You've now expanded the top-level folder for public folders, which contains two subfolders: Favorites and All Public Folders.

3. Expand the All Public Folders folder. If your organization uses public folders, you probably have many subfolders listed here.

4. Right-click All Public Folders, select a child folder, and select New Folder from the menu that pops up. This brings up the Create New Folder dialog box (see Figure 21.10).

5. Enter a name for the folder; we've given ours the name Custom Development.
Note that the folder will hold two different kinds of items:

   ◆ Email items that are messages.

   ◆ Posted items that contain a subject and text. You can post an item in a folder designed to hold posts without having to deal with messaging attributes, such as whom the item is sent to. To post an item, click the down arrow near the New icon on the main Outlook window and select Post In This Folder from the drop-down menu.

6. When you're done creating your folder, click OK.
If you're told that you don't have sufficient permissions to create the folder, you need to assign those permissions using one of the other Exchange public folder management tools. If you have Exchange administrative permissions, you can make this change yourself. The new public folder now shows up under the All Public Folders hierarchy. If you can't see the full name of your new folder, make the Folder List pane a little wider.

7. To set additional properties for your folder, right-click your new folder and select Properties from the pop-up menu.

FIGURE 21.10
Naming a new folder

If your Exchange organization has a large number of public folders, you can drag the ones that you use a lot to your Favorites subfolder. This makes them easier to find. Folders in the Favorites folder are also the only ones that are available when you work offline without a connection to your Exchange server. Only public folders that are in your Favorites folder, and that have been selected by the user, will be downloaded when working in local cache mode.

The properties dialog box for the folder is shown in Figure 21.11.

We're not going to spend a lot of time with this dialog box. Among other things, mailbox owners use a public folder's properties dialog box to do the following:

◆ Add a description for other mailbox owners who access the folder

◆ Make the folder available on the Internet

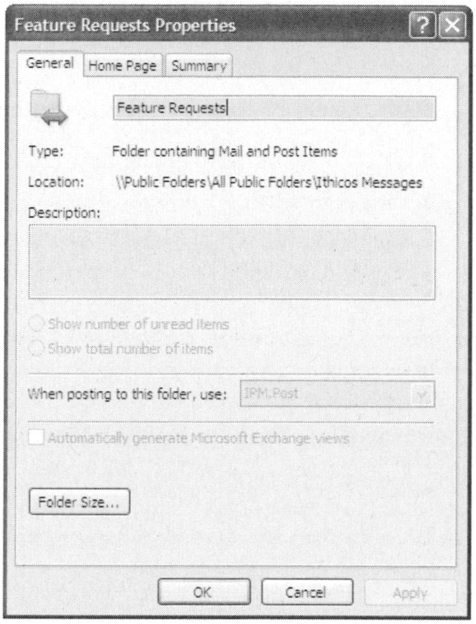

FIGURE 21.11
The Outlook client's
properties dialog box
for a public folder

FIGURE 21.11
The Outlook client's
properties dialog box
for a public folder

- Set up a default view of the folder, including grouping by such things as the subject or sender

- Set up administrative rules on folder characteristics, access, and such

- Set permissions for using the folder

Working with the Public Folder Hierarchy and Replication

A public folder hierarchy, or public folder tree, is a list of public folders and their subfolders that are stored in the default public folder database on the Exchange servers in an Exchange organization. The hierarchy also includes the name of the server on which a copy of each folder resides. The hierarchy does not contain any of the actual items in your various public folders. There is one organization-wide public folder hierarchy object. You cannot create nonvisible public folder trees using the management tools in Exchange 2010. You will have to continue using the Exchange 2003 System Manager if you need to create these objects, and those public folder trees would not be accessible by users that have mailboxes on an Exchange Server 2010 server.

THE THREE PIECES OF THE PUZZLE THAT MAKE UP PUBLIC FOLDERS

Most people start to get confused at about this point, when we introduce the public folder hierarchy. So let's do a little recap to identify the various objects or components that make up public folders.

Public Folder Hierarchy As outlined earlier, the hierarchy is essentially the list of public folder names available in your organization. This list is viewed from the Exchange 2010 Public Folder Management Console or from the Outlook client when viewing all public folders. When you are delegating administrative permissions over Exchange public folders, the hierarchy is the target of the permissions.

Public Folder Content   The content of a public folder is the items that are contained in the folder. These items could be files, emails, posts, or any other content type that is supported by Outlook. When you are delegating client permissions to public folders, the content is the target of the permissions.

Public Folder Recipient Object   When a public folder is mail-enabled, a recipient object is created for the folder. Since the recipient must be added to the Exchange address lists, this object is created in Active Directory. When you delegate recipient management permissions over Exchange objects, the permissions would apply to a public folder recipient object.

Understanding Public Folder Replication

Earlier, you saw the replica list of the public folder; this list controls which servers have a replica of a particular public folder. Why would you want to replicate public folders? Well, this depends on the size of your organization, but we can think of four reasons:

◆ You need to balance public folder access loads on your Exchange servers. Having all of your users connect to a single server for all of their public folder access can quickly result in an overwhelmed server if you have a large number of users or if you have heavy public folder usage.

◆ You have an Exchange server or group of Exchange servers separated from other servers in your organization by low-bandwidth links. In that case, you may be better off having limited replication traffic over your links and allowing users to connect to local replicas, keeping their traffic on the LAN.

◆ Public folder replication is essential when you're planning to remove an Exchange server from your organization (like all those Exchange 2003/2007 servers you're migrating away from). If the server you're removing hosts the only replica for a set of public folders and you don't want to lose those folders, you must replicate them to another Exchange server in your organization and then remove the original copy of the folder.

◆ Additional replicas act as a fault-tolerance mechanism as well, but this should not replace regular backups, since content deletions are replicated just as much as additions.

Replicating Public Folders

In a single Exchange server environment, the hierarchy exists and is stored on the Exchange server. In an environment with multiple public folder databases, each Exchange server that has a public folder database has a copy of the public folder hierarchy. Exchange servers work together to ensure that each Exchange server hosting a public folder database has an up-to-date copy of the public folder hierarchy. This process, called *public folder hierarchy replication*, is automatic. In Exchange 2003, there were certain limitations with this process when replication crossed routing group boundaries. Once you've fully migrated to Exchange 2007 or Exchange 2010, these limitations will be a thing of the past; all Exchange 2010 servers are in a single separate administrative group that has been created for backward compatibility with Exchange 2003 servers in the organization.

Exchange 2010 uses the public folder hierarchy to appropriately display public folder objects in various containers and to retrieve information about public folders, whether that information is stored in the hierarchy or on the server where the public folder physically resides. Email clients such as Outlook and OWA use the hierarchy to display a list of public folders available on all servers in the organization and to access items in a specific folder. Security limits associated with a given public folder, of course, limit the actual access granted to administrators and users.

The public folder hierarchy also includes what are called *system folders*, such as the Schedule+Free Busy folder. We talk about it and the other system folders later in this chapter.

Outlook and Outlook Web App clients look for a public folder server setting on the user's public folder database, which might or might not be on the same Exchange server where the user's mailbox is located. The default public folder database is configured on the General properties page of the properties dialog box for a mailbox database.

If a specific public folder doesn't exist in the default public folder database, the client is directed to a server where the public folder resides. When public folders that contain large items are accessed over a lower-bandwidth network, server and network loads can get pretty heavy; especially when these items are modified often. In these situations, public folder replication becomes especially useful, where you replicate public folder content to multiple servers, therefore making folder content available locally to users.

Configuring Public Folder Replication

Technically, all copies of a public folder, including the one on the Exchange server where the folder was originally created, are called *replicas*. There's a good reason for this. After a folder has been replicated, users will place items into it via the replica on their own default public folders server or on the nearest server as calculated using site link costs. So no replica of the folder can be considered a master copy. The replicas of a folder update each other on a regular basis, reinforcing the idea that there is no master copy.

You can set up replication of a public folder on either the server that will provide the folder or the server that will hold the new replica of the public folder. To replicate a folder, follow these steps:

1. Open the Exchange Server 2010 Public Folder Management Console and expand the Default Public Folders container. You may need to navigate through the public folder tree if you want to manage the replica configuration of a child folder.

2. Select the public folder you want in the Results pane and select Properties from the Actions pane to see the properties of the public folder. Select the Replication properties page. Click Add to open the Select Public Folder Database dialog box and then click OK.

Let's look quickly at some of the other properties that you can set on the Replication properties page. You can set the public folder database replication schedule. Depending on the importance of the contents of the folder and the available network bandwidth, you can accept the default Always Run, select other options from the drop-down list, or create your own custom schedule for replication of this folder. In order to set a schedule, you must clear the Use Public Folder Database Replication Schedule check box.

The Local Replica Age Limit (Days) option allows you to specify the maximum age that an item will be retained in a particular replica of the folder. Once the item reaches that age, Exchange Server will automatically remove it.

Understanding Public Folder Referrals

So we've already determined why and how you would create multiple copies, *replicas*, of a public folder. Now we need to explain how a client determines which public folder replica to use. This process actually has its own name; it's called a *referral*.

If a replica of the public folder content exists on the Exchange server that responds to the client request, the client accesses the local replica of the public folder. When a user connects to a public folder database that does not contain a copy of the public folder content that the user wants, the user is redirected to, or *referred* to, another public folder database that has a copy of the content. When multiple public folder databases contain a replica of the public folder, the client will choose from the list of replicas that were returned by the Exchange server. The client will then attempt to access each replica in the list by connecting to the server, attempting to locate the folder, and then attempting to read the content of the folder.

The order in which the client connects to the Exchange servers is defined by the cost assigned to the Active Directory site links. Connection costs are determined by querying Active Directory for the site link cost information of the other Mailbox servers in the organization on which a public folder database resides. Alternatively, an administrator can specify costs to other servers by providing a custom override list to the public folder database.

To override the use of Active Directory site links for public folder referrals, an administrator can customize the referral list by using the Exchange Management Shell or the Exchange Management Console. From the Exchange Management Console, you can modify the server list from the Public Folder Referral tab on the public folder database. From the Exchange Management Shell, run the following command:

```
Set-PublicFolderDatabase -Identity "MTL-SRV1\Public Folder Database"
-UseCustomReferralServerList $true
-CustomReferralServerList "HNL-SRV1:1","HNL-SRV2:50"
```

This command modifies the referral list for clients that connect to MTL-SRV1 and define that the referrals returned are HNL-SRV1, with a custom cost of 1, and HNL-SRV2, with a custom cost of 50.

Managing Public Folder Permissions

You can manage folder permissions in one of two ways. The simplest is just to use Outlook; navigate to the public folder, right-click to display its properties, and select the Permissions properties page (shown in Figure 21.12).

Of course, when you are using Outlook, your user account must be one of the owners of the folder. Otherwise the Permissions properties page will not be displayed. What you see on the Permissions properties page are the permissions that the groups (mail-enabled groups) or users will have to the folder.

You can use the Permissions properties page to assign specific folder access rights to Exchange users and distribution groups, who can then work with a public folder using their Outlook clients. For emphasis, let's restate what we just said in a somewhat different form: *You grant public folder access permissions to Exchange recipients, not to Active Directory users and groups.* Once access to a public folder is granted, Exchange recipients access the folder in their Outlook client while connected to their mailbox.

For a graphic reinforcement of this point, click Add in the Permissions box to start adding a new user or group that will have access to this public folder. This action opens a dialog box that looks very much like the Outlook address book that you use to select recipients to send a message to. You do not see the dialog box that you use to select Windows 2003 users and groups. (Click Cancel to get out of the Add Users dialog box.)

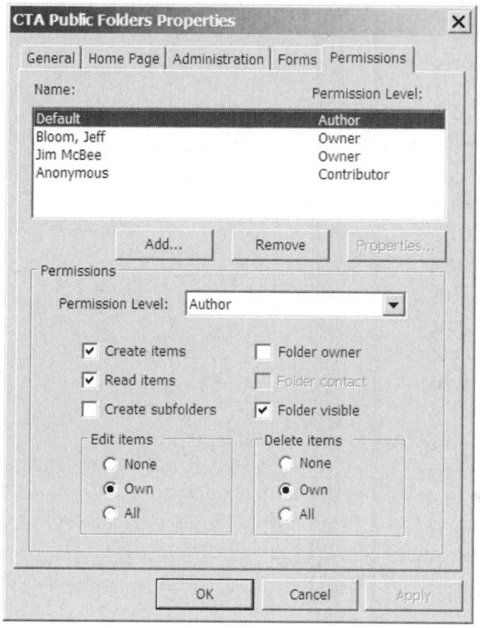

FIGURE 21.12
Managing public folder permissions via Outlook

If a user has the correct permissions on a public folder, that user can change access permissions on the folder for other users. Permissions on a public folder can only be modified from within the Outlook client using the Permissions properties page for a public folder.

There is a group named Default that includes all Exchange recipients not separately added to the Name list box. When the folder is created, this group is automatically given the default role of Author. Authors can edit and delete only their own folder items, and they do not own the folder and cannot create subfolders.

To make assigning permissions easier, Microsoft has created predefined roles. Each role has a specific combination of permissions to the folder. The roles include Owner, Publishing Editor, Editor, Publishing Author, Author, Nonediting Author, Reviewer, Contributor, and Custom — each with a different combination of client permissions.

The Bottom Line

Understand how public folders are supported in Exchange 2010. If you're coming new to Exchange 2010 or don't have a lot of investment in public folders in your current Exchange organization, you probably haven't been too worried about the rumors of the demise of public folders in Exchange 2010. These rumors are fortunately not true; public folders are still supported in Exchange 2010.

Master It You are the administrator of a distributed messaging environment that runs Exchange Server 2010. You plan to deploy a collaboration solution and you are currently evaluating both public folders and SharePoint. You need to identify the limitations of each product and present recommendations to your company's executives. What information should you present to your company's executives?

Manage public folders. By concentrating its effort on providing solid support for public folder management in the Exchange Management Shell, Microsoft has finally provided the missing command-line management interface that can simplify dealing with one-off public folder management tasks. These cmdlets also make it easy to do large-scale scripted and bulk management operations. The new Exchange Public Folder Management Console will also help you when managing public folders, though it does lack some key functionality.

Master It You need to identify the Exchange management tools that must be used to perform the following tasks:

◆ Manage Client permissions

◆ Configure a public folder replica

◆ Modify the location of the public folder database files

Manage replication. An efficient way of providing high availability and increasing capacity for public folders is to replicate the content across Mailbox servers. Public folder replication is scheduled and can therefore be configured for continuous replication or to occur during off-peak hours.

Master It Your Exchange organization contains 100 Mailbox servers. You plan to replicate 100 public folders from one server to all other servers. You want to do this as quickly as possible. What should you do?

## Chapter 22

Getting Started with Email Archiving

Since the rise of archiving systems in business more than a decade ago in response to storage concerns on Exchange Servers, the technology has gone through some very impressive growth and technology improvements. The need for archiving systems is also growing with ever-increasing stringent regulations and litigation procedures.

Messaging systems such as Microsoft Exchange Server 2010 — Microsoft's latest version of Exchange Server — have also seen their share of changes and improvements in archiving and compliance.

In this chapter, you will learn to:

◆ Understand the basic principles of email archiving

◆ Enable Exchange 2010 archiving

◆ Use Exchange 2010 retention policies

◆ Use Exchange 2010 retention hold

Introduction to Archiving

Over time, archiving products have evolved significantly. They have gone from simple storage reduction software to sophisticated enterprise content management systems that not only offer the storage management of Exchange servers, but have moved beyond email to managing file systems, SharePoint, Lotus Notes, GroupWise, and even databases. Don't be intimidated by archiving products; they can resolve many pain points in your organization and in some way they can even be seen as an insurance policy.

One of the main things to understand is that the way business communications are handled has drastically changed over the last 10 or 15 years as well. In the past, most of the communications and even business contracts were done by either fax or paper records. Nowadays over 90 percent of business communications take place by electronic means — email and instant messaging (IM), for instance — and this number is increasing on an annual basis. A couple of famous corporate failures in 2002 sparked massive lawsuits. One of the world's largest accounting firms, Arthur Andersen, collapsed due to evidence that was brought up through email in the Enron scandal.

Citibank nearly suffered a similar fate and was forced to pay some $400 million in penalties after the attorney general of New York State demanded emails that originated from stock analyst Jack Grubman and Citigroup chairman Sanford I. Weill. What had happened is that in 2004 the stock price of insurance broker Marsh & McLennan had dropped a devastating 50 percent after evidence surfaced from emails about investments they publicly praised but internally described as disasters. And the list of these cases goes on, with Merrill Lynch and PriceWaterhouseCoopers having gone through public court cases over information in emails. As a result, eDiscovery (that is, the discovery of electronic information) has become entrenched in current business because of lawsuits/litigations, external compliance investigations, and even internal human resources (HR) investigations. In the United States, all these cases have resulted in the courts finally deciding that organizations now have to retain and be able to recover emails within a "reasonable" time frame, and also to prove, when these records are provided, that the emails have not been tampered with and are complete.

To clarify this process, amendments were made to the Federal Rules of Civil Procedure (FRCP). These amended rules went into effect on December 1, 2006, and require that companies create, document, and enforce policies to retain email or dispose of them as part of operating procedures. As we mentioned earlier, one of the more important parts of the new FRCP rules is that organizations must now discover and disclose relevant information and emails within a reasonable time frame, so stalling tactics no longer work.

Archiving systems are used throughout the world in many different scenarios largely depending on industry and country. Some of the scenarios are as follows:

- Storage management of Exchange Server
- Simple compliance data capture by using journaling
- Complete data capture using journaling and archiving
- eDiscovery and litigation support
- Enterprise content management (beyond just Exchange)

Archiving

Archiving systems generally can be tailored or tweaked for use with specific case scenarios. Archiving generally refers to the process of removing data from one storage location and moving it to another, cheaper storage location.

Retention

These days it is an accepted fact that business email is considered a record or controlled record, and that these records need to be archived by either your corporate policy or government regulatory requirements. A defined email retention policy informs employees as to what email must be archived and for how long. For an email retention policy to be effective, you have to distribute this policy in written format to all employees. A written retention policy should include several of these options:

Effective Date   This leaves no doubt as to whether the policy is currently in effect or is an old one that should be discarded.

Last Change Date and Changes Made   This information confirms the policy's authenticity and appropriateness because regulations change over time.

Person or Department Responsible for the Policy   This gives employees or their managers someone to contact with questions regarding the policy.

Scope/Coverage   This includes the geographic limits of the policy (if any), affected departments and offices, and a definition of what company information is covered.

Purpose of the Policy/Policy Statement   This can include a company philosophy statement about the business, legal, or regulatory reasons for records retention.

Definitions   This area defines what constitutes business records and applicable exceptions.

Responsibilities   This area covers the following:

- Business units, subsidiaries, and special departments (such as the legal department)
- General employees
- Records retention coordinators
- Procedures for retention and deletion of email and attachments (if no automated email archiving system is employed)
- How the emails should be stored (usually in a personal folder storage [PST] file)
- Where those PSTs should be stored, like a network storage target or share drive; however, many would argue that PSTs are not a good form for archiving/compliance
- How often those files should be cleaned out
- How duplicate and convenience copies are treated

Consequences   This describes what happens if the policy isn't adhered to.

Appendix A   This appendix should include litigation hold and stop destruction policies, including a backup procedure.

Appendix B   Appendix B should include a current list of department records retention coordinators and contact information.

A manually managed email retention policy relies on employees understanding and following the email retention policy. The obvious fact is that each employee will interpret the policy a little differently, so in reality organizations will have many different email retention policies. This fact is the main reason you need to adopt an email archiving solution.

The benefits of first writing or developing and then automating your email retention policy are multifold:

Regulatory Compliance   Email retention for regulatory compliance isn't a choice but a requirement. The only choice your company will have is how you meet the requirements: manually or with email archiving automation. Creating and automating your email retention policy lowers your overall risk of noncompliance and ensures that you are keeping your email for the required time period.

Legal Risk Management   When you can show the court that you keep your email retention policy current and enforce it, you can demonstrate retention intent and that you might not have purposely destroyed information in case of litigation.

Document Retention for Corporate Governance   Businesses rely on the generation, use, and reference of data to make ongoing business decisions. The data business generates has a value to the business if that data can be used efficiently. An effective retention policy ensures that valuable information is available for some period of time, and an email archiving system allows for quick search and reference.

Discovery

One of the primary reasons United States–based organizations use archiving software is for the aid of electronic discovery, also known as eDiscovery. This refers to the process of finding electronically stored information for litigation reasons and generally isn't just restricted to searching for email. In 80 percent of eDiscovery cases, email including attachments is requested, but in at least 60 percent of the cases, general office productivity documents are also requested (which means Word and Excel files on your file server and desktops are part of the litigation). Metadata does play an important role in this process and is referred to as "chain of custody." Chain of custody is basically a verifiable process of who had access to the data, and whether the data could have been altered or changed during the eDiscovery process.

Eliminating PST Files

It is our opinion that there are no good reasons at all to have PST files in a corporate environment other than handing them over to a lawyer for review. Starting to see the trend here? Archiving systems can be your friend, but you will start working closely with your HR and legal people. PST files have become popular because of mailbox quotas, which were implemented to help curb the growth of Exchange databases. These easy-to-implement policies were for the longest time the only option an Exchange administrator had to gain some sort of control over this growth. Now the problem is that the quotas have a nasty side effect: end users who are unable to find the Delete key on their keyboards are forced to groom their inboxes for old email messages when they hit their mailbox limit.

They will then naturally create PST files. For the longest time, this approach was encouraged by Exchange administrators. These files then were created either locally on the desktop or laptop or on the file server, where they would take up valuable storage space. PST files use up more storage than the content would have used if you kept the data in Exchange in the first place. However, we could probably write an entire book on just eliminating PST files and we don't have the space for that.

Large mailboxes together with an archiving product can be one of your best allies here, helping you find the PST files and bring them back under control, which ultimately reduces the storage footprint of PST files in your environment.

Reducing Storage

Reducing the storage of production Exchange databases was the first reason archiving systems became popular. In the late 1990s, Standard editions of Exchange still had a 16 GB mailbox store limit, and having a 5 or 10 MB mailbox limit was extremely common. People were looking for other ways to offload content from their mailbox stores, not only to keep the databases in line for storage limits, but also to reduce the backup times. A reduced backup also means a reduced recovery, which is something you start to appreciate once you have gone through a full-blown Exchange disaster recovery. Archiving systems can offload email to the archiving storage system, while either leaving a shortcut behind to open up the archived email or simply removing the entire message. Doing this can reduce the size of your Exchange databases — sometimes up to 90 percent.

Compliance

Compliance makes most people cringe. Compliance, however, is a word that is misused but is something that you will need to understand. The odds are that your company is subject to some regulation that enforces you to retain records. Some industries face stricter and more complex rules than others, especially health care and finance. Regulatory compliance is just something that is either already part of your daily Exchange life or soon will be. Let's briefly go over some of the current laws that might be applicable to your organization:

Federal Rules of Civil Procedure (FRCP)   On December 1, 2006, a number of amendments to the FRCP took effect. These new revisions and additions have an impact on how companies retain, store, and produce electronic data, including email for litigation. The rules that mostly affect organizations are as follows:

Rules 16 and 26   These rules call for organizations to "give early attention to issues relating to electronic discovery, including the frequently-recurring problems of the preservation of the evidence . . . ." This means being ready to discuss a strategy for dealing with electronically stored evidence at the very first meeting with other parties in litigation.

Rule 34(b)   This rule requires organizations to produce electronically stored information in its native format with its metadata intact and to prove chain of custody. While the duty to preserve evidence is narrowed only to relevant data, the potential repercussions are great. For example, if a defensible process is not demonstrated, opponents may be granted access to an organization's network.

Rule 37(f)   This rule provides a "safe harbor" for data destruction. Safe harbor means that organizations face no penalties for deleting electronically stored information in keeping with routine operation of IT systems if the party took "reasonable" steps to preserve it. However, any destruction must be the result of routine operation and done in good faith, a systematic framework must be in place, and this systematic framework must have integrated litigation hold procedures.

Sarbanes-Oxley Act (SOX)   The Sarbanes-Oxley Act was passed mostly in response to the front-page news headlines of corporate corruption and financial scandals (namely Enron and WorldCom) in the early part of the decade. SOX provides severe criminal penalties, including jail sentences, for corporate executives who knowingly destroy business documents and other information that is used in the daily operations of their organization. It also describes specific records that need to be retained and requires a records retention period of seven years.

FINRA (Formerly Known as SEC Rule 17a-3 and a-4)   The FINRA rules focus on brokers and traders and require these people to retain and store specific records, such as customer communications and customer account trading activities, for a specific period of time on nonrewritable electronic media and to make them ready for easy review by the SEC within a reasonable time frame, typically 24 hours.

Health Insurance Portability and Accountability Act (HIPAA)   One part of HIPAA requires that an organization's patient records and related data (including related email) be archived and retained in a secure manner that ensures privacy and content integrity for at least two years after the death of the patient.

ISO 15489 (Worldwide)   This standard offers guidelines on the classification, conversion, destruction, disposition, migration, preservation, tracking, and transfer of records.

Title 17 CFR Part 1   This regulation allows record keepers for futures trading companies to store information either on electronic media or on micrographic media. This regulation also requires that "record keepers store required records for the full five-year maintenance period" while continuing to provide commission auditors and investigators with timely access to a reliable system of records.

FERC Part 125   This rule sets specific retention periods for the public utilities industry and states the records must have a life expectancy equal to or greater than the specified retention periods.

NARA Part 1234   The National Archives and Records Administration (NARA) regulations specify which government agency records are kept, for how long, and in what form and how they are to be accessed.

Freedom of Information Act (FOIA) — for Federal Agencies   FOIA allows for the full or partial disclosure of previously unreleased information and documents controlled by the US government. The act, which relies on the NARA regulations, defines federal agency records subject to disclosure and outlines mandatory disclosure procedures, and under certain circumstances, time frames for response.

The Patriot Act   The Patriot Act requires the Secretary of the Treasury to prescribe regulations "setting forth the minimum standards for financial institutions and their customers regarding the identity of the customer that shall apply in connection with the opening of an account at a financial institution." Broker-dealers must have a fully implemented customer identification program (CIP) that includes procedures for making and maintaining a record of all information obtained.

Federal Employment–Related Regulations   Largely unknown to many Exchange administrators, many federal employment regulations exist that require some sort of records retention, and they apply to all companies with employees. Some of the better known are as follows:

◆   Title VII of the Civil Rights Act of 1964

◆   Age Discrimination in Employment Act

◆   Americans with Disabilities Act

◆   Family and Medical Leave Act

◆   Equal Pay Act of 1963

◆   Vocational Rehabilitation Act

◆   Employee Retirement Income Security Act of 1974

◆   National Labor Relations Act

◆   Fair Labor Standards Act

These employment regulations are good examples of employer requirements, so any company that employs people should at least consider email archiving as a way to meet these regulations.

The regulatory requirements listed are the well-known US federal government drivers for record retention and cover quite a bit, including email data. However, this is not a complete list. There are more than 10,000 records retention regulations effective in the United States alone, and many of these are state-mandated, so a review of the states' regulations your company operates in would be a great idea.

Real World Scenario

IMPLEMENTING ARCHIVING

A city in the Midwest was using Microsoft Exchange for the city's email communication infrastructure. However, due to ever-increasing messaging volume, the network was slowly starting to become unmanageable. One of the reasons was that employees were retaining all of their historical email dating back to the early 1990s outside of their mailbox in PST files. This resulted in backups and storage capacity being strained to the limit. Because many state and local governments do business electronically, and with the paperless initiatives taking off, the problem was only getting worse. Any efforts to bring the PST sprawl back under control manually by asking employees to clean up were futile, and because end users continued to save all their email in local PST files, the problems reached a boiling point when the PST files started to experience corruption and monopolized costly storage space on file shares, desktops, and laptops.

To ensure that data was preserved, retained, and protected properly, the city government decided to move ahead and implement archiving. A project was initiated to locate all the PST files in the environment and bring them back under centralized control. This strategy ensured that Legal, General Counsel and city officials could perform retention management and search all the email content easily for discovery when the city got a request for public records. This allowed the city to comply with the US Department of State Freedom of Information Act (FOIA) requirements.

Disaster Recovery

You are probably wondering what disaster recovery has to do with archiving products. Well, the whole idea is related to storage management. Probably 90 percent of the data stored in Exchange databases is never accessed again by end users; however, this data is backed up daily to either tape or disk and in case of a disaster this data will also have to be restored. Archiving can help us remove this 90 percent of data and therefore reduce not only the backup time but also the amount of time it would take to recover a database.

Industry Best Practices

Organizations that are planning to deploy an archiving system in their environment soon realize that the deployment can be a daunting task. Having been in this industry for many years now, we've seen people doing things right and doing things wrong, and doing something wrong can result in some serious trouble (the worst is jail time). So in this chapter, we want to give you some insight into the industry's best practices (that is, things you should be doing to do things right the first time).

Email archiving is a critical application for driving down the cost of managing email for corporate governance, litigation support, and regulatory compliance.

Storage Management

One of the main reasons that many organizations want to use archiving is storage management. The offloading of old email messages to cheaper storage makes sense, and we always describe this as keeping your IRS tax records on the kitchen table. You don't keep your IRS records on the table forever; you file them away where you have easy access to them. In the years that we've been working with and deploying archiving solutions, one thing has stood out when it comes to storage management: 99.9 percent of email older than six months is never accessed again and then you start to wonder why you keep them on your Exchange server.

Most administrators mistakenly think that the performance of the Exchange database is related to the size of the database or the size of the mailbox. The Knowledgebase article 905803 (http://support.microsoft.com/kb/905803) describes how Microsoft Office Outlook 2003 and 2007 users experience poor performance when they work with a folder that contains many items on a server that is running Exchange Server 2007, Exchange Server 2003, or Exchange 2000 Server. The issue is caused because Outlook must perform several operations against the Exchange server to retrieve the contents of a folder, and the more items there are in a folder, the more time it will take to respond to the requests. The reason for this is restricted views; see http://technet.microsoft.com/en-us/library/cc535025.aspx to learn more about this topic. While the article doesn't particularly mention Exchange 2010, it does apply to this release as well. The number of items per folder at which performance degradation starts to take place has now been raised to around 100,000 items per folder excluding third-party products, so these issues will be a lot less. You can help avoid the performance degradation in Outlook by managing the number of items in heavily used folders, including inbox, sent items, and calendars.

Archiving solutions reduce the storage footprint, but traditionally administrators will only perform archiving because they want to allow end users to have transparent access to data. When that happens, you will run into the item limit counts, because even though the stubbed archived messages are only a few kilobytes in size, they count toward the item limits.

A few storage management options are available, and we'd like to go over two of them that have worked at organizations in the past:

Time Based With this option you perform archive data pretty much from day 1, but you don't create stubs in the mailbox; instead, you delete all data from the mailbox that's older than a specific age. The philosophy behind this approach is so you don't possibly confuse the end user with stubbed or archived messages. The time frame in which you want to delete the older data depends on how users use email in your organization, but deleting anything older than six months or a year is generally a safe time frame. You have to realize that even though you delete it from the mailbox, the data is in the archiving system, so end users can get access to the data if they need to do so. In some situations, however, organizations deploy an organizational archive and do not allow end users to access the data.

Stub and Time Based This option combines the first one — deleting data older than six months or a year — with stubbing or archiving messages. This means that you can squeeze out a bit more storage savings by replacing the larger emails that are younger than six months or so.

We can't tell you exactly what will work in your environment; however, don't create a stubbing policy that acts on data that is younger than a few days. Not only would that create frustration for your end users, but it would also result in data ping-pong as end users would constantly want to restore archived data to their mailbox.

Importing PSTs

PSTs are notoriously bad for your environment. We often compare them to those pesky blackberries in your garden that take over the entire yard if you don't keep them in line. Most administrators know what PST files are because we've been using them daily since we started to use Exchange and Outlook. Archiving these days has almost become a standard practice as part of a process to get the rest of the messaging data under centralized management. It has been nearly 15 years since the first version of Exchange Server (4.0) was released, and many things that we have available nowadays in Exchange we take for granted.

Two versions of PST files are available. The most common and current version, known as the Unicode version, became available with Office 2003 and replaced the "original" PST file version. The main difference is that the first-generation PST file has a 2 GB hardcoded limit and the Unicode file has a theoretical 32 TB file size limit. In the real world, the Unicode PST file could cause performance degradation beyond 5 GB in file size if you do not have adequate performing hardware. Beyond 10 GB, according to Microsoft, you will encounter short pauses on almost all hardware (see `http://support.microsoft.com/?kbid=968009` for more details).

The fact that you didn't have any centralized management tools available played a major role in the sprawl of PST files. For more than a decade, users controlled the creation and location of PST files. As you would expect, this has caused problems. A company we worked with reported that they had close to 300 TB of data in PST files that were spread over desktops, laptops, servers, and backup tapes. The PST file storage far exceeded the storage allocated and available to their messaging system, resulting in major headaches. The company couldn't even bring PST files back into Exchange but had to bring the data under centralized management.

In such a situation, an archiving system can make your life easier. To comply with laws and regulations, you can't simply ignore and delete PST files. It fascinates us that organizations often spend a small fortune on protecting their messaging infrastructure with data leak prevention software to block sensitive data from leaving the organization unchecked. By forgetting about PST files, they might have closed one door, but they have forgotten to close a major security leak. One of the most common ways for end users to take their mailbox data with them is to simply export all the contents of their mailbox to a PST file and store it on a thumb drive or even MP3 player. They then can walk out the door with your company's sensitive information, contracts, and IP, all unchecked.

Even if you have managed to retain the information in your infrastructure, the cost of storing data in PST files is enormous. The file format itself is so bloated that it uses more storage than if the data was kept in the Exchange database.

So how do you eradicate PST files from your environment? We recommend implementing a multistep process:

1. Write a project plan.   For smaller companies, writing a project plan might not be as important, but for larger organizations such a plan will come in handy. A project plan allows you to prepare and think about exceptions that you didn't consider. For instance, what are you going to do with data from employees who have left your organizations? How are you going to handle password-protected PST files? A good plan will save you time.

2. Prevent further growth of the problem.   Microsoft has finally made some good Microsoft system management (Group Policy Object) policies available, which allows you to restrict users from creating PST files. You can download them from `http://go.microsoft.com/fwlink/?LinkId=78161`. Use them. We love, for instance, that you now have the option Prevent Users From Adding New Content To PST Files. This option still allows end users to open their PST files but prevents them from adding any new content.

3. Discover all existing PST files.   This task probably will take up the most time as you will have to find *all* the files on your network. If you run scripts to do this, ensure that you don't do an all-out search as it will saturate your network with network traffic. The reason why it takes such a long time is because you'll find PST files on servers, tapes, laptops, and workstations. Think about how you are going to deal with people who work remotely.

4. Bring PST data into an archive. Bringing PST data into an archive allows you to bring the data back under your control. One of the reasons why you shouldn't bring it into Exchange directly is because there is a good chance that you might not have the required storage available. A big advantage is that if the data is in an archive, it allows you to set retention and gives you additional benefits when it comes to eDiscovery, risk management, and early case assessment.

5. Give end users access to their archived PSTs. Taking away PST files from end users and not giving them access to their own data is the quickest way to start a users' revolt. Give end users access to the archived data — they need access to the data for productivity reasons.

6. Avoid creating excessive stubs. Stub files are shortcuts in the mailbox pointing to the archived item that now resides in the archive and no longer on Exchange. Excessive use of stubs can create problems on Exchange with whitespace, fragmentation, and major I/O overhead.

7. Disable PST file creation. This final step is important because, after all, what good would it do if you bring everything under control and then you do not prevent your users from creating PST files again? Use the policies that we referred to in step 2.

Retention

Deciding on your retention categories or how long you want to retain information within the archive will probably take up the most planning time. This process will involve most of the departments in your organization, from the storage team to the Exchange team, management, legal counsel, and even HR.

Retention controls the creation, filing, storage, and disposal of records in a way that is not only legally correct, but also administratively possible. Retention has to serve multiple purposes, fulfill the operational needs, and provide a way to preserve an adequate historical record of the information. It is very important to implement and practice proper retention management as it allows your organization to accomplish the following:

◆ Reduce compliance and litigation risks by proactively managing the retention and disposition of all potentially discoverable information

◆ Reduce storage costs by only storing important and relevant information in the archive

◆ Have only the relevant information in the archive, which will also make it easier and faster to find relevant information

◆ Increase the reliability of information by managing the appropriate versions of information assets and ensuring that they have high value as evidence if they are needed in a court of law

As we said earlier, you will most likely spend most of your time developing your retention policies, and there are significant benefits to first developing these policies before automating and implementing an archiving solution:

More Effective Regulatory Compliance You don't have a choice when it comes to email retention for regulatory compliance; it is simply an absolute requirement. The only choice your company will have is in how you meet the requirements: manually or with an email archiving automation system. Creating and automating your email retention policy lowers your overall risk of non-compliance and ensures that all required email is kept for the required time period.

Better Legal Risk Management   The ability to show a court an updated and regularly enforced email retention policy can demonstrate retention policy intent and counter the claims of "spoliation" or purposeful destruction of evidence by the plaintiff's attorney.

More Consistent Corporate Governance   Organizations these days rely on the active generation, use, and leverage/reference of data for business processes and decisions. The data that a business generates has a value to the business if that data can be used efficiently. An effective retention policy will ensure that this information will remain available for some period of time, and an email archiving system allows for quick search and reference.

Exchange Server 2010 Email Archiving

One of the major new features that both Microsoft and customers are excited about in Exchange 2010 are the compliance and archiving features. The features available in Exchange 2010 allow you to create retention rules to preserve information regardless of the end user's mailbox management and filing habits.

The following is a list of new messaging and compliance features that have been included in Exchange 2010:

◆   New interface for applying retention policies

◆   Auto-tagging for retention policies by inheriting the default retention tag policy from the parent folder

◆   A GUI that allows nontechnical people to perform cross-mailbox searches

◆   New transport rule predicates and actions

The one thing that does have to be clarified, though, is the target market of Exchange 2010 archiving. By no means should the solution be confused or compared with an "Enterprise" scaled solution like a Symantec Enterprise Vault or Mimosa NearPoint. Microsoft refers to these solutions as "business archives" while Exchange 2010 is more of a "personal archive." We had to set the record straight on this as many people have been confused, and when it comes down to compliance archiving or enterprise records retention, you can't afford to make mistakes.

Personal Archive vs. Organizational Archive

So when should you use the Personal Archive that is available in Exchange 2010 and when should you use an organizational archive solution available through third parties? In essence, the decision has to be made based on the requirements and functionality offered by these solutions. Microsoft positions Exchange 2010 as a personal archive and not as a business archive solution. Microsoft's basic archiving solution enables organizations to get rid of PST files, implement large mailboxes, and provide advanced search. It does not provide records management or preservation of electronic information beyond Exchange and write-once, read-many (WORM) storage. Organizations that have stricter requirements to retain information beyond email or have the need to store information on WORM storage should look at a business archive or organizational archive solution. Organizational archiving goes beyond the scope of the Personal Archive and delivers full mailbox capture for all users, full single-instance storage across all data, and advanced search and case management tools for eDiscovery.

By way of comparison, a typical third-party email archival solution can be expected to deliver all or a portion of the following key functions in addition to the Personal Archive functionality in Exchange 2010:

- Logs, WORM, read only
- Single instancing/compression
- Configuration auditing
- Mailbox auditing
- Regulatory accreditation
- Federated discovery, retention, and reporting across multiple content sources
- Data mining and visualization
- Case management and advanced eDiscovery
- Content monitoring and supervisory tools
- Archive for Bloomberg data and other non-Microsoft IM data
- Archive for both files and SharePoint

Microsoft is positioning the new archiving functionality in Exchange 2010 for basic storage management, PST archiving, and discovery while leaving the door open for third-party vendors to offer additional value that is necessary for organizational archiving. Small organizations will find the basic features of Exchange 2010 satisfactory to reduce the strain on storage growth and eliminate PST files. However, for organizations that require full email retention and advanced eDiscovery, a third-party email archiving solution is the answer for the next few years.

Policies

The technology used in Exchange Server 2010 to maintain records management is called messaging records management (MRM) and helps organizations reduce legal risks associated with email and other communications. It is much easier to make an organization comply with company policies and regulatory needs with MRM, and within Exchange Server 2010 this is accomplished with retention policies. Exchange 2010 has multiple sets of policies available for maintaining and moving data from the primary mailbox to the archive:

Retention Policy Tag   A retention policy tag (RPT) applies retention settings to the default folders (Inbox, Deleted Items, and Sent Items) in a mailbox, and all items that are in these default folders inherit the folders' policy tag. Users are not able to change the tag that is applied to a default folder, but they can apply a different tag to individual items in one of the default folders. You can create RPTs for the following default folders:

- Deleted Items
- Drafts
- Inbox
- Junk Mail
- Outbox

- Sent Items

- Rss Subscriptions

- Sync Issues

- Conversation History

RPTs are not supported for the Calendar, Journal, Notes, and Tasks folders. Currently, you can only use the MoveToArchive retention action with tags of type All and Personal; Microsoft doesn't support using MoveToArchive against specific folders.

Default Policy Tag   Default policy tags (DPTs) are used to apply retention policies to untagged mailbox items. Untagged items are mailbox items that either did not receive a retention tag from the folder that they are located in or didn't get a policy applied explicitly by the user. DPTs are created by specifying the type All. A retention policy should not contain more than one DPT.

Personal Tags   Personal tags are available to users in their mailbox as part of their retention policy, and they can apply these tags to folders they create themselves or to individual items. This allows end users to tag information they consider critical and therefore apply a longer retention period to it.

You can define RPTs with the following actions:

Move To Archive Policy   Automatically moves messages from the primary mailbox to the personal archive. Available options are 1 year, 2 years (default), 5 years, and Never. This policy can help keep the mailbox under quota. The policy works like the Outlook Auto-Archive functionality without creating the PST file and will create a folder name that matches the primary mailbox folder name from which the item was moved.

Move To Deleted Items Policy   Automatically deletes messages and moves them to the Deleted Items folder. Delete policies are global because they remain tied to the message when they move to the archive and they remove unwanted items.

Delete And Allow Recovery   Emulates the behavior when the Deleted Items folder is emptied or the user deletes a message using Shift-Delete. Messages move to the Recoverable Items folder when deleted item retention is configured for either the mailbox database or user. Recoverable Items, also known as the "dumpster," gives the user another chance to recover deleted messages.

Permanently Delete   Permanently deletes a message. A message is purged from the mailbox when this policy is applied; this is similar to a deleted message being removed from Recoverable Items. Once this happens, the user can no longer recover the message (although when single-item recovery or legal hold is enabled, the item is placed in the Purges folder of Recoverable Items and thus can be recovered by administrators).

The priority in which policies take effect is pretty simple. Explicit policies have a higher priority over default policies, and longer policies apply over shorter policies. An important thing to remember is that you can't apply a managed folder policy to a mailbox that has an archive mailbox enabled. The managed folder settings created can't use the MoveToArchive action.

During setup, Exchange Server creates a default archiving policy, which is a retention policy that contains the retention tags shown in Table 22.1.

TABLE 22.1: Default Retention Tags

RETENTION TAG NAME	TAG TYPE	DESCRIPTION
Default 2 Year Move To Archive	Default	Applies to items in the entire mailbox that do not have a retention tag applied explicitly or inherited from the folder. Messages are automatically moved to the archive mailbox after 2 years.
Personal 1 Year Move To Archive	Personal	Messages are automatically moved to the archive mailbox after 365 days.
Personal 5 Year Move To Archive	Personal	Messages are automatically moved to the archive mailbox after 5 years.
Personal Never Move To Archive	Personal	Messages are never moved to the archive mailbox.

The default archiving policy is automatically assigned to each mailbox that has archiving enabled. The tags will be made available to the mailbox user after the mailbox assistant has processed the mailbox. The user can then use these tags and apply them to folders or messages.

MOVING ITEMS BETWEEN FOLDERS

When an item is moved from one folder to another, it inherits the retention tag from the new folder location. If there is no retention policy tag active on that particular folder, the item automatically gets the default policy tag. However, when the item has a specific tag assigned to it, this tag will always take priority over any folder-level tags or the default tag.

SETTING A RETENTION TAG

You can set retention policies to a direct mailbox and distribution group. Keep in mind that new members added to a distribution group do not automatically get the retention policy of that group, and you should run the distribution group policy cmdlet at regular intervals. The following example applies the Finance retention policy to John Doe's mailbox:

```
Set-Mailbox "John Doe" -RetentionPolicy "Finance"
```

The next example applies the Finance retention policy to members of the distribution group Seattle-Finance:

```
Get-DistributionGroupMember -Identity "Seattle-Finance" | Set-Mailbox - ↵
RetentionPolicy "Finance"
```

CHANGING A RETENTION TAG POLICY

You can also change the policy that is applied to mailboxes to a new policy. The following example applies the new retention policy "New-Retention-Policy" to all mailboxes that have the old policy "Old-Retention-Policy":

```
$OldPolicy=(Get-RetentionPolicy "Old-Retention-Policy"}.distinguishedName
Get-Mailbox -Filter {RetentionPolicy -eq $OldPolicy} -Resultsize Unlimited | ↵
Set-Mailbox -RetentionPolicy "New-Retention-Policy"
```

DELETING AND REMOVING A RETENTION TAG

When you remove a retention tag from the retention policy that is applied to the mailbox, it is no longer available to the user and therefore can no longer be applied to items in the mailbox. Items that have been specifically stamped with this tag, however, will continue to be processed by the mailbox assistant with these settings.

Deleting a tag using the Remove-RetentionPolicyTag cmdlet will not only remove the retention tag from being available to the user, but also remove the tag from Active Directory. The next time the mailbox assistant runs, it will restamp all the items that had the removed policy applied and apply the default policy tag. If you removed the tag from a large number of mailboxes and items, this could result in a significant increase in resource consumption on your mailbox servers.

RETENTION HOLD

Retention might take actions on new email messages before end users get to them when they are away or unable to access email due to vacation or other reasons. Depending on the policies that may be active and applied to the user, this could mean that messages may have been moved from the primary mailbox to the archive or even deleted. For these users, you have the option to temporarily suspend the retention policies from processing the mailbox for a set amount of time by placing the mailbox on a retention hold. You can specify a retention comment that will notify and inform the user (or another user who might have access to the mailbox) about this hold, and explain when it begins and ends. These retention holds are only visible in supported Outlook clients, however, and can be localized in the language of the user's preferred language setting.

Applying a retention hold will not modify or change mailbox quota limits if they are applied, and it might be advisable if you have end users leaving for an extended period of time to increase or remove the mailbox quota limits. Also, it might take the user a while to catch up on email after he returns, so give the user some time after he returns to work to go through the messages before removing the retention hold status.

Placing a Mailbox on Retention Hold

In Exchange 2010, when you place a mailbox on retention hold the Mailbox Manager process stops processing the retention policies or the managed folder mailbox policy that might exist on that particular mailbox. End users can log on to their mailbox as they normally would during a legal hold and send, delete, or change emails. However, when the user searches her mailbox during a search, she will not be able to find items that were older than the retention time period because they are stored in the Purges folders of Recoverable Items. You can configure to leave a comment when you place a mailbox on retention hold. This comment will be displayed in supported versions of Outlook.

You have two ways to set retention:

◆ Through the Exchange Management Console (EMC)

◆ Through PowerShell

To place a mailbox on retention hold using the EMC, expand the Recipient option on the left and select mailbox or mailboxes that you would like to put on retention hold. In the Action panes, click Properties and select the Mailbox Settings tab. Then select Messaging Records

Management and click Properties. In the Messaging Records Management dialog, fill in the following fields:

Enable Retention Hold For Items In This Mailbox   Select this check box to place the mailbox on retention hold.

Start Date   Select this check box to enable a start date for retention hold. Use the date and time controls below the check box to set the start date and time.

End Date   Select this check box to enable an end date for retention hold. Use the date and time controls below the check box to set the start date and time.

You can also use PowerShell to place a mailbox on retention hold. The following example places John Doe's mailbox on retention hold:

```
Set-Mailbox "John Doe" -RetentionHoldEnabled $true
```

This example removes the retention hold from John Doe's mailbox:

```
Set-Mailbox "John Doe" -RetentionHoldEnabled $false
```

Litigation or Legal Hold

A litigation or legal hold is a process that an organization uses to preserve all forms of relevant information when litigation is reasonably anticipated. It basically prevents deletions from happening and also preserves record changes to mailbox items in both the user's primary mailbox and archive mailboxes. Retention hold simply disables MRM policies whereas litigation hold keeps the policies enabled but simply does not purge data and is either enabled or disabled (that is, there are no time frames for litigation hold). What is nice is that you can send alerts to the end users that their mailbox data is on hold, which eliminates manually notifying users and telling them that they can't delete data.

Placing a Mailbox on Litigation Hold

In Exchange 2010, when you place a mailbox on litigation hold policies are still acted and applied upon but data is never purged from the mailbox. End users can log on to their mailbox as they normally would during a legal hold and send, delete, or change emails. However, when the user searches her mailbox during a search, she will not be able to find items that are older than the retention time period.

Litigation hold can be set through PowerShell. The following example places John Doe's mailbox on a litigation hold:

```
Set-Mailbox johndoe@archiving101.com -LitigationHoldEnabled $true
```

This example removes the litigation hold from John Doe's mailbox:

```
Set-Mailbox johndoe@archiving101.com -LitigationHoldEnabled $false
```

Enabling Archiving

You have two ways to archive-enable mail:

◆ Through the Exchange Management Console (EMC)

◆ Through PowerShell

To enable an already existing mailbox for archiving within the EMC, you expand the Recipient option on the left and select the mailbox or mailboxes that you would like to enable. Right-click and select the Enable Archiving option to make an archive available for the users selected.

To enable new users that are created through the EMC with the wizard, you simply select the check box Create An Archive Mailbox For This Account (see Figure 22.1).

FIGURE 22.1
Select the Create An Archive Mailbox For This Account option.

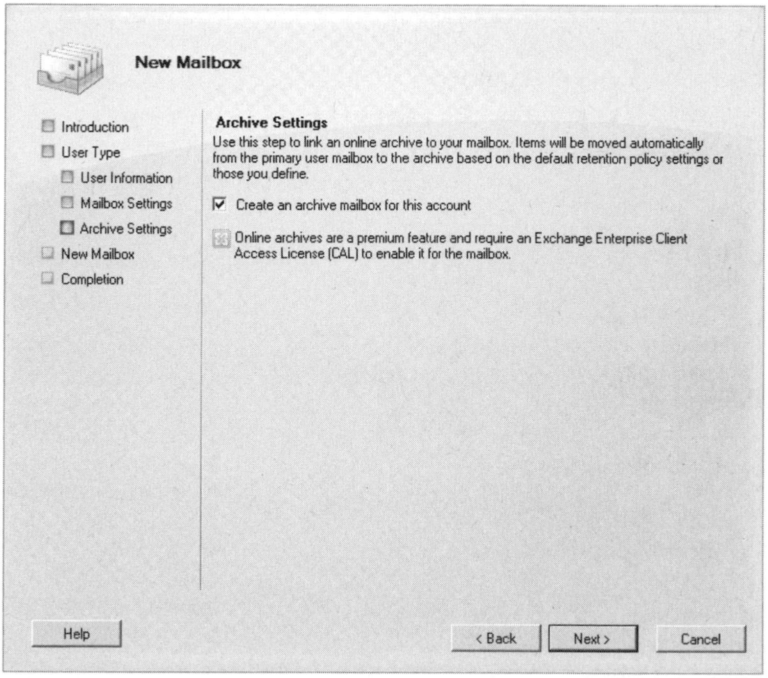

You can use PowerShell to enable it as well, and your cmdlet would look like this:

```
Enable-Mailbox "John Doe" -archive
```

Disabling a mailbox from being archive-enabled can be done in the same way: by right-clicking it in the EMC and selecting Disable Archive or by selecting the Disable Archive option in the right pane of the EMC when you highlight the mailbox. If you want to do it with a cmdlet, the command looks like this:

```
Disable-Mailbox "John Doe" -archive
```

Disabling ensures that the data remains but that no new data can be added. This is basically the same as disconnecting a primary mailbox from an account.

The Remove command will delete the archive mailbox from Exchange, and the command looks like this:

```
Remove-Mailbox "John Doe" -archive
```

Archive Quotas

Many organizations enforce quotas on users' mailboxes, and archive mailboxes are designed to allow users to store historical data outside their primary mailboxes. Mailbox quotas are one of the primary reasons end users have started using PST files. To attempt to remove the desire and need for using PST files by your end users, you must ensure that the archive mailbox has enough storage available for the end users to store all of their data. However, organizations may want to cap the growth of archive mailboxes for cost reasons or storage expansion planning. You can configure an end user's archive mailbox with two options:

ArchiveWarningQuota When an end user's archive mailbox exceeds this limit, an event is logged in the Application event log.

ArchiveQuota When an end user's archive mailbox exceeds this limit, moving data to the archive mailbox is prohibited.

Both options are set to Unlimited by default.

Like most of the archiving functionality in Exchange 2010, you have two ways to configure quotas:

◆ Through the Exchange Management Console (EMC)

◆ Through PowerShell

To set personal archive quotas within the EMC, expand the Recipient option on the left and select the mailbox or mailboxes that you would like to configure. In the Action panes, click Properties and select the Mailbox Settings tab. Then select Archive Quota and click Properties. To enable the warning quota limits, select the check boxes and fill in the storage value in megabytes.

You can configure both the `ArchiveQuota` and `ArchiveWarningQuota` settings with PowerShell. To set an `ArchiveQuota` of 2 GB and an `ArchiveWarningQuota` of 1500 MB for an end user, use this command:

```
Set-Mailbox -Identity "John Doe" -ArchiveQuota 2GB -ArchiveWarningQuota ↵
1500MB
```

Exchange 2010 Discovery Operation Considerations

Microsoft does not use the common industry term *eDiscovery* for its advanced search functionality. Instead, it is called Exchange Server 2010 Discovery and is aimed toward helping organizations with functionality to search for relevant information in Exchange mailboxes, whether they are local or remote on another Exchange 2010 Server. These searches are common practice with organizations that are dealing with litigations and lawsuits or that want to ensure they are in compliance with either organizational rules or rules that are enforced by their business bylaws or rules that are enforced on their business by legislation or laws.

The Discovery functionality uses the existing content indexes created by Exchange Search. Instead of the PowerShell queries used in Exchange 2007 to do cross-mailbox and -server search, there is now an easy search interface, but behind the scenes it is still a PowerShell cmdlet (`search-mailbox`). One of the reasons for this change is that it is fairly rare to find a lawyer or HR person who is fluent in PowerShell, and the GUI is much more suited for them. Since cross-mailbox and -server search is a "powerful" right to have (that is, you technically could look in everyone's mailbox), it is a restricted permission. Use role-based access control (RBAC) to add the Mailbox Search role to give nontechnical people access to this search functionality without disclosing administrative permissions.

When Do You Use Discovery?

There are a few scenarios for which you would use the Discovery option. As we said earlier, Discovery is a powerful search option that allows you to search and collect data across your Exchange organization. The main use scenarios are as follows:

Legal eDiscovery   More and more organizations are forced to provide information to support litigation or lawsuits. Traditionally, you had to manually search multiple servers, and if you were lucky you could use some of the PowerShell cmdlets in Exchange 2007. No matter what you used, it was a time-consuming and costly exercise. Exchange 2010 Discovery fills a niche; you can search across your entire organization without using cmdlets (which is important for HR or legal people).

HR   Responds to requests to research and monitor email content or complaints. For instance, in a case where an employee feels that the email content he or she has received from peers is offensive in content and in violation with HR policies, HR should investigate this matter.

Organizational Investigations   Responds to requests from the internal legal department or management as part of investigations. There are many organizations that are involved in legal matters that involve an external party. In this case the internal legal department will respond to a formal request for information as part of a legal matter and the legal department will have a limited set of time to respond to this request.

How does Exchange 2010 Discovery differ from other solutions? Well, the difference is largely in the expansiveness of the functionality. A quick view of the differences between Exchange 2010 and an enterprise or business archiving eDiscovery solution shows that for reviewing purposes Exchange 2010 requires you to copy the search result set to a target mailbox instead of reviewing the content straight from the application.

Using the Exchange Server 2010 Archive

For an end user to get access to his archived data with Exchange 2010, he will either have to use Outlook Web App or have Outlook 2010 installed (see Figure 22.2 and Figure 22.3). An end user can drag and drop email from his PST files directly into the personal archive, but mail in the primary mailbox can be moved automatically using retention and archive policies that can be set on the mailbox, folder, or item level.

You can set a quota on the personal archive separately from the primary mailbox. (See the section "Archive Quotas" earlier in this chapter.)

Using Exchange 2010 Discovery

To use Exchange Server 2010 Discovery, a user should be added to the Discovery Management role group. By default, this group does not have any members. Administrators who have the Organizational Management role are restricted from doing any Discovery searches without being added to the Discovery Management role group. Discovery is a powerful feature that allows anyone with the appropriate permissions to have potential access to all the email records stored in your entire organization. Therefore, it is critical to control and monitor who gets access to the Discovery Management role and keep a close eye on the Discovery actions.

You can use PowerShell to add a user to the Discovery Management role group. To add, for instance, User John Doe, the cmdlet looks like this:

```
Add-RoleGroupMember "Discovery Management" -User Jdoe
```

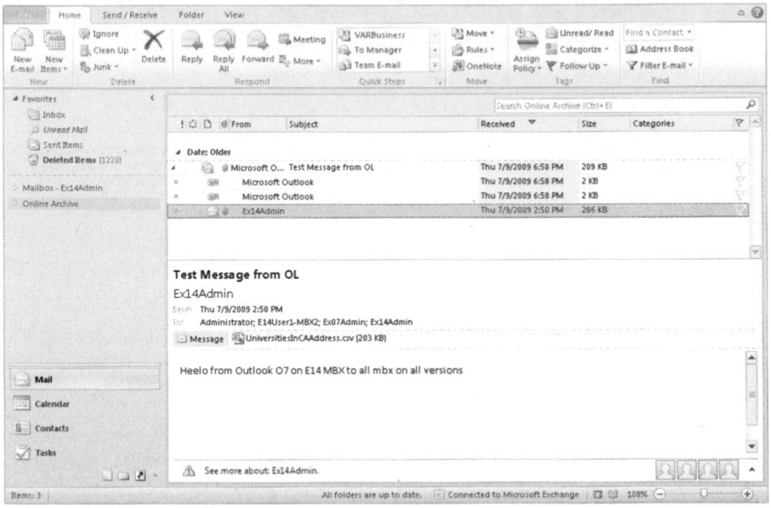

FIGURE 22.2

Accessing a personal archive with Outlook 2010

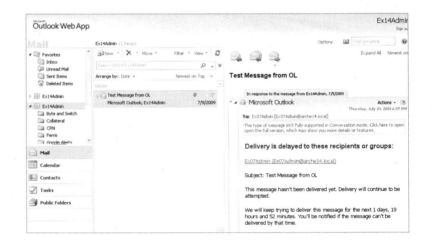

FIGURE 22.3

Accessing a personal archive with OWA

After you have gotten permission, you can open the Discovery Manager console by going to `https://servername.local.com/ecp` and logging in with your credentials (see Figure 22.4).

Once logged in, you can select what you want to search. You have the option to search on Mailboxes, Groups, and External Contacts. In Figure 22.5, we selected Mailboxes and clicked the Search option.

On the Search page, select the keywords, message types, to and from addresses, date range, and mailboxes you want to search on. Before clicking Save, be sure you select a storage location (discovery mailbox) for the search to be saved to as well as a unique search name. It is important to understand exactly what a discovery mailbox is. It should be a special resource mailbox that has been configured with large quotas (50 GB), permissioned so that only discovery role administrators can open it, with email delivery disabled.

FIGURE 22.4

Exchange 2010 Discovery
Manager Console

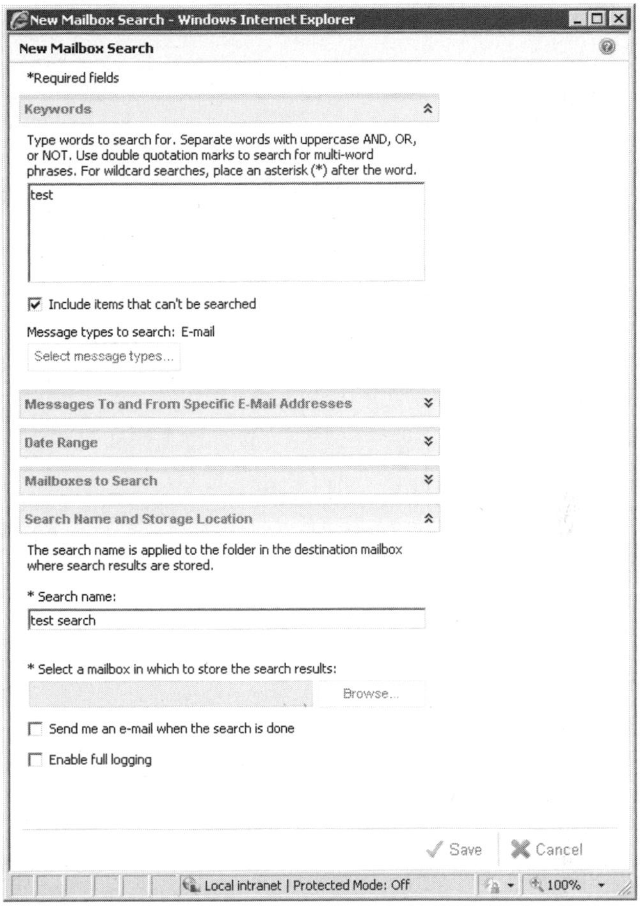

VIEWING THE SEARCH RESULTS

Once the search is completed, the results are copied to the target mailbox that you specified in
the search configuration. The Discovery application will create a new folder in the mailbox that
has the same name you gave to the search, and a subfolder will be created below that for each
mailbox that had information that matches the search query.

Offline Access

Most users have Outlook configured to synchronize their mailbox with Exchange using an
offline folder, or OST, file. This gives users an offline cache so that they can still read their
email when they are not connected to the network. The personal archive is not integrated with
the OST file, which means that when data has been moved from a user's mailbox to their
archive, the data will not be in the offline cache. If the user requires access to this data, she has
two options: get access through OWA or move the data back to her live mailbox. Most people

when they are traveling or flying on an airplane are not looking at old email but most likely processing some of the more recent information they have received.

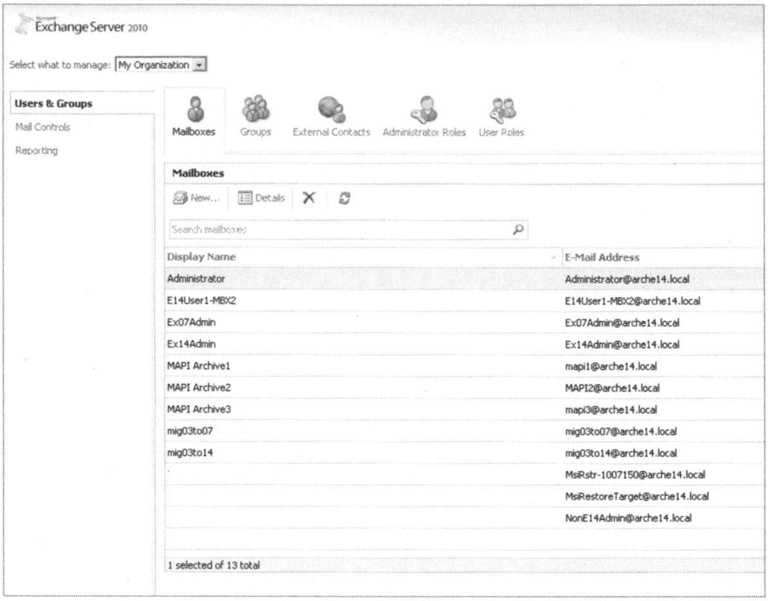

FIGURE 22.5
Selecting Mailboxes in
the Discovery Manager
Console

Requirements and Factors to Consider

There are several important factors to consider when you deploy Exchange 2010 archiving in your organization.

LICENSING

The archiving functionality in Exchange 2010 is marketed as a way that organizations can get archiving for free without purchasing an expensive third-party business archive solution. But as with lots of marketing, you have to lift up the curtains a bit to get the correct answer.

As a starter, the archiving functionality requires an Enterprise client access license also known as eCAL, which adds some cost on top of the regular license cost of Exchange Server. Also, you need at least Outlook 2010. Of course, you can use Outlook Web Access for lots of the functionality, but it's smart to deploy Exchange 2010 in combination with Outlook 2010 since the archiving functionality in Exchange 2010 is only available with the RTM release with Outlook 2010. This isn't in line with the ''free'' marketing theme, but it is embedded within the product.

SERVER STORAGE

When it comes to archiving software, proper storage planning is important. With Exchange 2010 there are a few additional ''curveballs'' you have to work with. Some architectural changes were implemented in the Exchange database structure with Exchange 2010. Single-instance storage (SIS) has been removed in favor of better performance and reduced input/output per second (IOPS) requirements. Single-instance storage refers to storing a single copy of a message or item once, even though it is stored in multiple locations. On average, the SIS savings were about 20 percent. But for an Exchange database that is upgraded from Exchange 2007 to Exchange 2010, this increase has largely been mitigated by the page compression features that were added in the Extensible Storage Engine (ESE) functionality.

Additionally, when you bring in PST files with Exchange 2010, you need to ensure that the additional capacity is available. The problem gets more interesting when you start deploying database availability groups (DAGs) and replicate data. You will not only replicate the primary mailbox but also the archived data in the personal archive. This could mean that your storage requirements grow exponentially. There is a reason why Microsoft put the personal archive in the same database as the primary mailbox it belongs to: Microsoft spent a lot of time making Serial Advanced Technology Attachment (SATA) storage a viable option for Exchange 2010 for both performance and capacity. If you decide to go with SATA, there is no reason to split the personal archive and primary mailbox onto separate databases because you are already on the cheapest disks out there. In addition, keep in mind that disk capacity is continuing to increase while performance isn't; this means that if you continue to split the data onto different drives, you are not maximizing the efficiency of the drives (either capacity or performance). The personal archive is attached to the primary mailbox and can't be split up on two separate databases.

If your organization is going to use the Discovery functionality extensively, be prepared for the additional storage requirements as well. This is, of course, because of the removal of SIS; however, the added page compression that was included in Exchange 2010 does provide some mitigation against this. A rapid increase in storage needs could occur when someone is going to create a large search result set that is copied to the Discovery mailbox. When you quickly export those results and provide them to the legal team, this might only be a short-term problem.

CLIENT REQUIREMENTS

At the time of this writing, only Outlook 2010 and Outlook Web App 2010 give the end user access to the archive. It is still unknown if at a later stage the archiving functionality will be made available to earlier versions of Outlook.

The Bottom Line

Ensure your company complies with regulations that apply to your business It is extremely important that your messaging system is configured in such a way that email data is managed according to laws and regulations.

Master It Which laws and regulations are in effect on your business and what does it mean for your organization?

Understand the basic principles of email archiving. An archiving solution not only provides a way to ease the pain of storage problems on Exchange whether they are with the databases or with PST files, but also assists in helping organizations become compliant and make discovery of email easier.

Master It How can government organizations actively comply with regulations on open records laws to taxpayers?

Enable Exchange 2010 archiving. Exchange 2010 allows for more efficiently managing the primary mailbox of the user by enabling the mailbox for archiving and using policies to move the content between the mailbox and the archive.

Master It How does archiving allow for moving older email content automatically from the primary mailbox to the personal archive?

Use Exchange 2010 retention policies. Retention policies define how long data must be retained before it is automatically removed when the time setting has been met.

Master It You can create as many policies as you need; however in many organizations retention policies will be created per department (for instance, Finance).

Use Exchange 2010 retention hold. In certain situations you possibly need to prevent deletion of email from end users' mailboxes.

Master It Without retention hold, and depending on the policies that may be active and applied to the user, messages may have been moved from the primary mailbox to the archive or even deleted. What is the cmdlet to put a mailbox on retention hold?

Part 4

Server Administration

Chapter 23

Creating and Managing Mailbox Databases

To us, an Exchange server at its core is a database management server. When we remember the days of Exchange 5.0, Exchange Server handled its databases, its Internet connectivity, its own directory service, and its own SMTP connectivity. In Exchange 2000/2003, SMTP became a function of Internet Information Services (IIS). After this brief trip, it is now back under Exchange's umbrella. Also, today all other responsibilities have been passed on to other Windows components, except for one. Database and storage management is what Exchange does best, and in Exchange Server 2010 we find some of the most impressive improvements.

In this chapter, you will learn to:

◆ Identify the core components of Exchange database storage

◆ Plan for disk storage requirements for Exchange databases

◆ Configure Exchange Mailbox servers with the appropriate storage objects

Getting to Know Exchange Database Storage

So we've established that we're old enough to remember the many iterations of Exchange Server prior to Exchange Server 2010. We also remember an expression that goes something like, "Explore the past and you will understand the present." We think this expression is fitting for database management in Exchange Server. So, let's turn on the Exchange Time Machine and explore the essence of mail storage in Exchange Server.

Exchange Server 4.0, 5.0, and 5.5 (First Generation)

Back when a 28.8 modem was considered high-speed Internet, Microsoft released the predecessors of what we now know as Exchange Server 2010. The servers ran an earlier version of the Extensible Storage Engine (ESE) data storage technology. A major benefit of ESE at the time was that it provided Atomic, Consistent, Isolated, Durable (ACID) transactions for Exchange, ensuring that transactions are reliable and recoverable.

Three Exchange database (EDB) files were used to store all Exchange information:

◆ `Dir.edb`, a file for the directory information

◆ `Pub.edb`, a file for public folders

◆ `Priv.edb`, a file for all user mailboxes.

The maximum database file size was 16 GB, and each server could only hold one database for user mailboxes, thus limiting each server storage to 16 GB (for the Standard Edition).

Exchange Server 2000 and 2003 (Second Generation)

ESE proved its stability and efficiency for dynamic storage and graduated to become the data storage technology for Active Directory, starting with Windows 2000 Server. In the world of Exchange, the Exchange directory was replaced by Active Directory. Two database files remained: one for user mailboxes and another for public folders.

Database file sizes were still capped at 16 GB for the Standard Edition (though later increased to 75 GB thanks to an Exchange Server 2003 service pack), but the game changed when administrators were able to create multiple databases (up to 20 and unlimited in Enterprise editions). Databases known as *mailbox stores* were organized in container objects called storage groups. For each database, in addition to the EDB file, Microsoft introduced the streaming database (STM) file. Designed to store content in native MIME format and reduce content conversion requirements, the STM file now lived side by side with the EDB file.

Exchange Server 2007 (Third Generation)

So, the rumors of Exchange moving to a SQL-based storage technology proved untrue. In fact, Microsoft pushed forward with ESE and increased its investment, introducing database replication technologies and essentially providing greater availability options to administrators, now stressed out about their ever-growing databases.

Exchange Server 2007 introduced two major changes in database management. First, the maximum number of available databases, still organized in storage groups, was increased to 50. Second, finally recognizing the need for large mailboxes, Microsoft removed all database hard file size limits. There were many other changes, but a notable one was the graceful removal of the STM file from Exchange, ensuring that the EDB was once again riding solo, storing all content in a single database file.

Exchange Server 2010 (Current Generation)

Exchange Server 2010 now introduces a version of ESE that is reengineered to denote years of customer feedback, experience, and the reality of larger user mailbox requirements. The changes in Exchange Server 2010 are mostly the kind of changes that most administrators would not notice when working with middle-of-the-range servers or hardware. However, for administrators who manage Mailbox servers with 500 or more mailboxes, the importance of the changes becomes very real, very fast.

Online defragmentation running at runtime, new database tables, a larger page size, and an aggressive compression solution, to name just a few, are some of the architectural changes in storage for Exchange 2010. Exchange Server 2010 promises to reduce IOPS (input/output operations per second) requirements by up to 90 percent (when compared to Exchange Server 2003). Since most organizations are still running Exchange Server 2003, we're estimating that this change can make many IOPS-hungry and fast disk–deprived administrators happy.

Basics in Storage Terminology

In this section, let's visit the basics of storage terminology and why these terms should be relevant to you in a discussion on storage.

Mailbox Database

For those of you who came from an Exchange Server 2003 background, this is what we called a mailbox store. In Exchange Server 2010, the mailbox database is the configuration object that provides management for all database settings. From the mailbox database properties, an administrator can configure the location of the database file, the transaction log file settings, and some settings that apply to mailboxes stored in the mailbox database.

Each Exchange Server 2010 server that has the Mailbox Server role installed has a mailbox database named Mailbox Database <GUID> (The GUID suffix is there to ensure that the database name is unique; more on that later in this chapter). This database is created during the installation process and has an EDB file named `Mailbox Database.edb`, stored in the default Mailbox folder in the Exchange Installation directory. (The EDB file may also be stored in an alternate location if you specified one during the Exchange Server installation by using the `/DBFilePath` parameter.) On an Exchange Server 2010 Standard Edition Mailbox Server, an administrator can create up to five mailbox databases. On an Exchange Server 2010 Enterprise Edition Mailbox server, an administrator can create up to 100 mailbox databases (though most administrators will likely *not* want to create so many). Administrators often ask me why they should ever need to create more than one Exchange database, especially since the maximum mailbox database size is *unlimited*. Later in this chapter we will discuss the organizational and business reasons why having multiple mailbox databases may be the right solution for your Exchange environment.

Transaction Logs

Transaction logging is one of those aspects of Exchange that is obscure to most administrators. It is easy to forget about transaction logging, since it all occurs automatically (or *automagically*). For every transaction that enters your messaging server (new email, deleted email, a change to an email message, a modified attachment . . .), the information is written to a transaction log file. When transaction log files are filled up with data, new transaction log files are created in a perpetual fashion that bears resemblance to a factory production line.

Transaction log files always have the same size, 1024 KB. We compare them to milk containers (whether empty or full, they are always one gallon containers, or one liter containers for those using the metric system). Transaction log files are created at the 1024 KB size and then filled to capacity. These files will be persistent on the hardware. Later in this chapter, we will discuss the recommended methods for administrators to purge or remove older transaction log files.

Storage Groups, RIP

Yes, they are finally gone. In your Exchange administration tools, you will no longer find configuration options for Storage Group objects. Microsoft has finally deprecated this object, which seemed mostly inconsequential in Exchange Server 2007. Well, we had to configure it, create it, and modify it, whenever a configuration seemed to be placed in its tabs and pages. However, the recommendation has long been to create only one mailbox database per storage group. So why have the storage group at all? Well, Microsoft answered that question and got rid of this object. All storage group configuration settings (such as Circular Logging and Transaction Log Location) have been moved to the Mailbox Database objects.

Storage in Exchange Server 2010

There have been notable changes in database storage and architecture in Exchange Server 2010. These are real changes that have a far-reaching impact on Exchange deployments and the overall strategy that an organization takes with its messaging infrastructure. Let's outline some of those changes, or at least the ones most relevant to Exchange administrators:

◆ Most write transactions to the Exchange databases are now performed as sequential writes rather than the traditional *random* writes. Why should you care? Well, it means that now the hard disk drive needle does not move; the disk is spinning, but the needle is not moving. This change, which may seem like a detail at first, is significant in reducing the number of required disks or IOPS for Mailbox servers and improving overall database access performance. (Note that some write transactions are still performed as random writes to handle database space compactness or for other specific architectural reasons.)

◆ The database itself has a brand-new schema, and this is the first major change in schema since Exchange 2000. (By the way, this new database schema is the main reason why you cannot perform an in-place upgrade from Exchange Server 2007 to Exchange Server 2010.)

◆ Well, it can't all be good. Single Instance Storage (SIS) was the sacrificial lamb and is no longer a database feature. (Keep in mind that SIS was effectively gone in Exchange Server 2007 when it no longer applied to email attachments.)

◆ The database page (each transaction resulting in new data creates at least one database page) size has increased from 8 KB to 32 KB. In essence, what this means is that a 5 KB message will require a 32 KB block of space in the database. However, a 16 KB message is now stored in a single page, rather than two pages as in previous versions of Exchange Server.

◆ To mitigate the risk of an increased database size, potentially caused by the new larger page size and other new database architectural changes, database pages are compressed.

Real World Scenario

HOW SHOULD I THINK ABOUT STORAGE?

Wouldn't it be great if you could walk into your boss's office and ask for the budget to give every user a 20 GB mailbox so they would never (well, not for a while at least) have to delete anything? Then you could create as many databases on your Exchange server as you could create before your fingers went numb and let the users go to town.

Unfortunately, we all have constraints within which we have to live; that goes for system administrators, end users, and our VIP users. So, thinking about adding more storage and allowing larger mailboxes or databases, what are some of the constraints that we face? Some of these are technological in nature and some are budgetary or political. We're hoping that you already know most of these and can skim right through them:

◆ Exchange Server 2010 Standard Edition supports a maximum of five mailbox databases.

◆ Exchange Server 2010 Enterprise Edition supports a maximum of 100 mailbox databases.

◆ For previous editions of Exchange Server, the disk I/O limitations affected storage design. In Exchange Server 2010, this limitation now has a lessened impact on storage design.

◆ The bigger a mailbox is, the longer it takes to back up and restore. For typical backups of Exchange databases, the restore time will be twice as long as the backup time.

◆ Microsoft recommends a maximum Exchange database of 2 TB when you have two or more copies of your databases. If you have a single copy of your database, the recommended maximum size is 200 GB.

◆ You need to plan for 7 to 10 days' worth of transaction logs; a good starting point for estimating how much space transaction logs will consume is about 9 GB of transaction logs for each 1,000 average users. However, we will discuss later in "Managing Mailbox Databases" how some organizations will want to enable Circular Logging and therefore not require additional disk space to store transaction logs.

◆ If you implement database replication with a database availability group (DAG) and multiple replication partners, remember that log files will only purge after a successful replication (even when Circular Logging is enabled). Therefore, you must account for network outages where replication will fail and transaction log files can queue on your physical disks. Depending on the time necessary to troubleshoot or repair the problem that is preventing successful replication, enough disk space must be available before databases will begin to shut down.

◆ You should assume that each database needs to contain 10 to 15 percent additional space for deleted items (known as the database dumpster) and for database whitespace. Also, note that whitespace can continue to grow if the Online Maintenance process does not get to complete during its scheduled interval. Make sure that your Online Maintenance is large enough to allow a completed process.

An Additional Factor: The Personal Archive

A personal archive is what we call the "Siamese" mailbox to a user's primary mailbox. It's a secondary mailbox that is "joined at the hip" to a user's primary mailbox and provides a second location for storing older, rarely accessed emails. We'll briefly discuss the personal archive in this chapter, since it does have an effect on the overall storage solution. Let's look at some of the features unique to the personal archive:

◆ A personal archive is created by using the `Enable-mailbox <mailbox> -archive` command.

◆ A personal archive and a primary mailbox for a user must be stored in the same mailbox database.

◆ The personal archive cannot be cached locally on an Outlook client through an offline store (OST).

◆ A personal archive can only be accessed by Outlook 2010 or Outlook Web App 2010.

◆ Personal archives allow administrators to provide larger storage solutions for users, while still providing access to all email.

We want to point out two features that have brought about a lot of discussion. First, we often get the question, "Why are Personal Archives relevant if they must be stored in the *same* mailbox database as the user's primary mailbox?" At first glance, one would think that an organization could benefit from Personal Archives by having them stored in a separate mailbox database; and as you now know, it is not the case. There would have been obvious benefits from this, such as separate backup schedules for Personal Archives and smaller databases for primary mailboxes. Microsoft's customers have been vocal about the ability to separate the two, and we would not be too surprised if this functionality becomes available through a future Service Pack release.

So this leads us to the other feature, which comes directly from the other question we often get, "If I can't store the Personal Archive in a separate mailbox database, what is my immediate benefit from implementing Personal Archives?" In our opinion, the biggest benefit of using Personal Archives is the reduction in OST file size. Since the Personal Archive is not available offline, it will reduce OST file bloat, while still providing remote access through Outlook Web App 2010. So for Archive Mailboxes, our opinion is, it's great now, and it will likely get even better.

Disk Size vs. I/O Capacity

Historically, Exchange has been limited by the performance of its disk, rather than by the disk space available on those disks. In Exchange Server 2010, there has been somewhat of a role reversal between those two characteristics. The improvements and reductions in I/O requirements permit administrators to use lower-cost SATA disks (or equivalent) to handle storage.

For many Exchange Server administrators (these authors included), the knowledge of and understanding of disk I/O capacity constraints came slowly. For some reason, we kept thinking that the disk technology far outperformed the database capacity. But as Exchange servers got more heavily loaded with more simultaneous users and larger databases, the demands on the disk grew.

Let's take a look at a quick example. Say you have an 18 GB SCSI disk from the olden days; that disk may be able to support 100 reads and/or writes to the disk each second. That's not a big deal if you have 50 users, but what if you have 500 users? Can the disk subsystem service the I/O requests that those 500 users will put on it? If the disk system is not properly sized — both for capacity and for the required I/O load — then users will see performance problems.

This load is normally measured (and planned) in terms of the IOPS profile of the users who will use the system. The Exchange team at Microsoft has done much research into the type of load that users place on an Exchange server; they have broken that down based on different types of users, from a *light user* who may send 5 messages per day and receive 20, to an *extra heavy* user who may send 40 messages per day and receive 160.

Note that the reductions in IOPS between recent Exchange versions are significant. Initial testing at Microsoft IT demonstrates a reduction in IOPS of 70 percent when compared to Exchange Server 2007.

What's Keeping Me Up at Night?

We spend quite a bit of time wondering if we have our storage configuration optimized. Ask yourself these questions about your own environment:

◆ Am I giving my users enough mailbox space to store enough historical information to do their jobs? Or (*shudder*) too much?

◆ Are users wasting mail storage on personal or non–work-related content such as MPG files of cats playing the piano (http://www.youtube.com/watch?v=npqx8CsBEyk)?

◆ Should I employ an email archival solution to move older content off the mailbox database and on to alternative storage? Should I use the built-in personal archive solution or should I use a third-party solution? If I do, how much "recent" content should be left on the Exchange server versus moved out to the archive?

◆ Do I need to be keeping copies of certain types of messages (such as for regulatory, legal, or business reasons)?

- ◆ Are my databases growing so fast that I may run out of disk space before I notice?

- ◆ Do I have the right balance of databases, size of disk, frequency of backups, and deployment of redundancy?

Mailbox Storage

When estimating mailbox database size for a given configuration, as a worst-case scenario we once estimated that a single database could grow to 1.3 TB in size. Although Exchange Server can technically support a database that large, it would take forever to back up, and worse, it would take forever to restore. (Okay, maybe not "forever," but longer than what would make operational sense.) Even if you are using snapshot technologies, if the snapshot backup software performs database verification, the verification would take far too long. So a database size of 1.3 TB is just not practical in organizations that have not yet implemented a DAG with continuous replication.

Maximum Database Sizes

Microsoft recommends that you keep each mailbox database under about 200 GB if you are not using any type of replication technology. If you are using a DAG and maintaining at least two copies of each database, you can consider allowing a maximum database size of 2 TB.

These numbers are based on some simple principles. Consider that if you *don't* use replication for your mailbox databases, you have to account for the time necessary to restore a database and the impact of a restore operation. A smaller database, in the case of loss or hardware failure, can be restored quickly, ensuring minimal impact on users. When database replication is put in place, the replica of the database in essence acts as a backup and, depending on the number of mailbox database copies, may never be used in a restore operation. In that case, a large database is more efficient, as it simplifies administration by reducing the number of databases in the organization.

We urge you to consider your existing environment when you think about these maximum sizes. Ultimately, you need to consider how much time it will take to restore one of these databases from a tape backup; if the absolute longest time you can take to restore a database from your backup media (for example, a tape) is two hours, and your tape system restores at a rate of 30 GB per hour, then the largest database size you should consider supporting is 60 GB. A company's Recovery Time Objective/Recovery Point Objective (RTO/RPO) will most likely dictate recovery time and therefore will help you in calculating what your maximum database sizes should be.

Replication technologies in Exchange Server 2010 provide options for quicker access to a mailbox database, in the event of a server or disk failure. Naturally, this requires a proper implementation and configuration of a DAG.

Determining the Number of Databases

A common way to improve the scalability of Mailbox servers is to add mailbox databases. Though this might not improve overall server performance or a user's perceived response time, it allows you to break up the amount of data you are storing and place it across multiple smaller mailbox databases. In turn, this enables you to support larger mailboxes. Keep in mind as you increase the number of mailboxes that each Mailbox server supports, increasing the amount of RAM will help improve performance and reduce the disk I/O profile.

Some administrators may want to create multiple mailbox databases to gain underlying performance benefits. Each mailbox database is configured with a 20 MB checkpoint depth.

This means that 20 MB of outstanding transactions can be written to the logs but not immediately committed to the database. If you have one mailbox database, then that database's default checkpoint depth is 20 MB; for databases that are replicated, the default checkpoint depth is 100 MB. Note that in previous versions of Exchange Server, the recommendation was to create multiple storage groups that each had a single mailbox store, rather than a single storage group with multiple mailbox stores. This recommendation was in place to ensure that the checkpoint depth, which was unique to the log stream of the storage group, would not have to be shared by the multiple mailbox stores in the storage group. Instead, you were urged to have only a single mailbox store per storage group. In Exchange Server 2010, this issue no longer has relevance, since all mailbox databases maintain their own checkpoint depth and log stream.

When creating additional mailbox databases that do not use database replication with a DAG, you should plan to place each database's transaction logs on separate disk spindles from the database files. This can help improve performance (due to the nature of the I/O differences), though it mainly improves recoverability. If you are using a DAG and have two copies or more, you can safely place the transaction logs and the database files on the same spindles/disks.

 **Real World Scenario**

PLANNING FOR MAILBOX DATABASES

A company named ABC is planning to migrate their existing messaging infrastructure to Exchange Server 2010. ABC has 1,200 users who connect to a server farm in the company's main office. During their planning process, administrators are attempting to determine the number of databases that will support their requirements.

They have identified the following requirements:

◆ Minimize the time necessary to perform a restore in the event of a single disk failure.

◆ Minimize the time necessary to perform an offline operation on the database files.

◆ Provide all users with at least 1 GB of storage, but support even much larger mailboxes.

When looking at each requirement, ABC has determined that they should design the following storage solution:

Create Multiple Mailbox Databases   By having multiple mailbox databases, ABC feels that they will be able to split up the 1,200 users in the multiple mailbox databases and therefore keep the database files to a smaller size. With smaller database files, database restore and offline database operation times are minimized.

Configure Mailbox Size Limits   To ensure that a user or a group of users do not overrun the amount of disk space used, ABC has decided to implement mailbox size limits on the mailbox databases. Hard disk drives have been purchased to support up to 5 GB of storage for each user. For now, administrators plan to configure users to receive a warning message when their storage reaches 4 GB.

Though a single Mailbox server can support the company's users, ABC has also determined that they should plan for mailbox resiliency by using a DAG and database replication across multiple Mailbox servers.

Note that this scenario did not take into consideration the performance requirement of the mailbox databases. You must also analyze the backup/restore needs, service level agreements, and user profiles, and then recommend a storage configuration that will meet the I/O and performance requirements.

Allocating Disk Drives

The traditional logic for Exchange Server design was to place databases on a set of physical disk drives separate from the transaction log files. As Exchange 2000/2003 servers scaled upward to support thousands of mailboxes, administrators placed the transaction log files for each storage group on separate spindles (or physical disks) and placed the database files for each group on a different set of spindles.

Although placing different files on separate disks is pretty good advice, today many of us use Fiber Channel or iSCSI SANs to store our Exchange data. The SAN is usually some aggregation of a large number of disks in a RAID 5, RAID 1+0, or other redundant configuration. The person who manages the SAN (hereafter known as one of the SAN people) carves up the amount of storage you request from that large aggregation of disk space and assigns it to you as a logical unit (LUN) of disk space. You then configure your Windows server to connect to those LUNs across the iSCSI or Fiber Channel network (or fabric).

We were skeptical at first of putting Exchange databases on a *networked storage* device, but we have come to see the advantages for many medium and large organizations. The ability to combine large numbers of disks together into very large volumes and then allocate pieces of that large volume to the applications (such as Exchange) that need disk space can help reduce your storage costs and allow you take advantage of technologies such as snapshot backups and improved recoverability features. Further, because some of the storage is not physically connected to the server, a disaster that befalls the server hardware may not affect the storage system.

If you are a SAN user, you should ask your SAN people for two LUNs for each mailbox database. One LUN should be sized to hold a mailbox database's transaction log files and the other should be sized to hold that database file — that is, of course, for a Mailbox server role, and does not account for the backup requirements. By putting one database on each LUN and one transaction log on each LUN, you ensure that the granularity of snapshot solutions is per database. Dedicating LUNs to specific tasks helps you isolate I/O for those tasks; you should avoid placing the data for other applications on those LUNs that would affect I/O.

When allocating disk drives, we need to look at both capacity requirements and meeting performance needs, based on requirements. When evaluating those performance needs, you must look at the *worst-case scenario* Exchange environment. That typically means looking at the peak usage periods and maximum user load. We discussed earlier that users can be categorized based on their *profile*, defined by the number of messages they send and receive. However, you may also want to look at other factors that can impact disk performance and overall server load, such as posts to public folders, third-party archival, BlackBerry server interaction, and other factors. When analyzing your disk I/O capacity and reviewing your I/O requirements, you can arrive at a disk solution that will support your existing environment, as well as allow for growth.

A lot of what has been done in Exchange Server 2010 has been to optimize storage for lower-cost disk solutions. A storage configuration that has no built-in redundancy (RAID-less) and mid-range SATA disks is a reality. Microsoft talks about JBOD (Just a Bunch of Disks, a pretty self-explanatory terminology) configurations, providing a solution where storage capacity can dramatically increase, while keeping storage costs very low. (A caveat in this design is that it depends entirely on a high availability solution that uses a DAG for database replication.)

For heavily used Hub Transport server roles, you might also want to put the Hub Transport server database and log files on a SAN or separate disk storage; the transport database and the log files should each go on their own LUN. All database performance improvements discussed in this chapter also affect the Hub Transport server database where message queues are stored.

Those of you who think about disks and disk performance may be wondering about all of those LUNs being carved out of the same logical disk. If your SAN is improperly sized and does not have enough spindles, performance can be a problem. A properly engineered SAN solution should provide enough total I/O capacity for all the LUNs and the applications that will use those LUNs to function correctly.

Managing Mailbox Databases

Although Exchange Server 2010 allows up to 100 mailbox databases, the examples here will be limited to a single mailbox database. As discussed earlier, some Exchange deployments may only require a single mailbox database, since the recommended maximum size is now 2 TB for mailbox databases that have multiple copies.

Viewing Mailbox Databases

You can view the current mailbox database for each server using the EMC, or you can use the Get-MailboxDatabase cmdlet to list all the mailbox databases stored on an Exchange Server:

```
Get-MailboxDatabase -server MTLEXC01
```

Name	Server	Recovery	ReplicationType
Mailbox Database 1	MTLEXC01	False	None
Mailbox Database 2	MTLEXC01	False	None

A new parameter for the Get-MailboxDatabase cmdlet is -includePreExchange2010. This parameter instructs the cmdlet to return information for all mailbox databases in the organization, including those on servers that run previous versions of Exchange Server. For example, the following command will return all mailbox databases in a mixed organization:

```
Get-MailboxDatabase -IncludePreExchange2010
```

Of course, you can narrow the scope of this output to just a specific server or a specific storage group using the Where-Object cmdlet (well, just the Where alias). Here are some examples:

```
Get-MailboxDatabase -IncludePreExchange2010 | Where {$_.Server -eq "HNLEX03"}
Get-MailboxDatabase -IncludePreExchange2010 | Where {$_.StorageGroupName -eq↵
"Executives SG"}
```

Creating Mailbox Databases

To create a new mailbox database, right-click on the Mailbox role in the Organization pane and select New Mailbox Database (or New Public Folder Database, if you plan to store public folders on your server). This launches the New Mailbox Database wizard, shown in Figure 23.1. To create a new mailbox database, provide a name for the database and then enter the name of the server that will store the database; the path will automatically be completed and the database's EDB file will be put in the same path as the transaction logs.

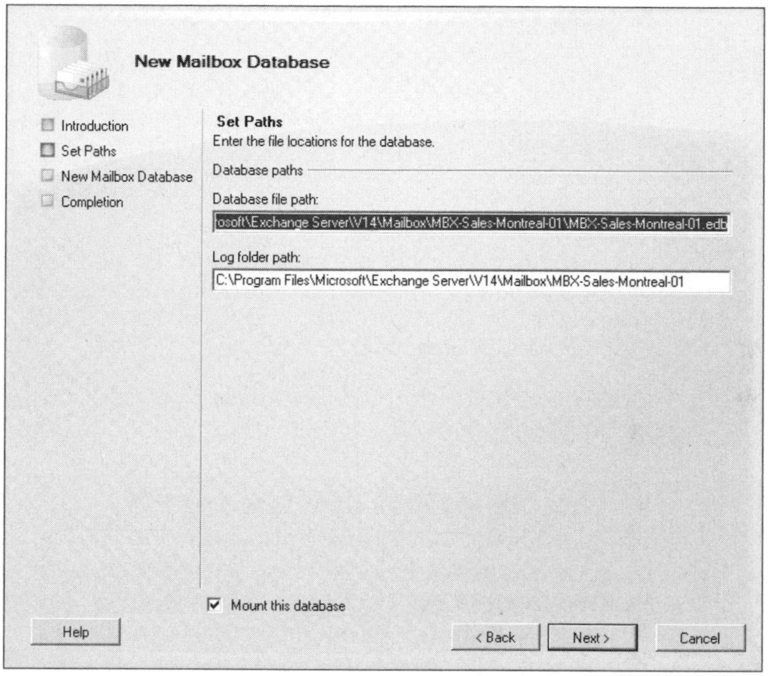

FIGURE 23.1

Creating a new mailbox database using the Exchange Management Console

When creating a new mailbox database, name the database something that is standardized and descriptive, but unique in the entire organization. Note that a mailbox database can be activated and then mounted on any Mailbox server in your organization, given that it is part of the same DAG. This new functionality introduced in Exchange Server 2010 created the requirement for unique mailbox database names within an organization. Also, making sure the filename matches the display name of the database will ensure that it is easier to manage. For example, a database name of *MBX-Sales-Montreal-01* can adequately describe the mailboxes stored in the database, as well as include a numerical trailer to allow for growth in the Sales department.

Normally, you would modify the database file and transaction log paths and select a correct location for the mailbox database now, but we will show you how to move the mailbox database in the next section.

The wizard creates the configuration for the database and then mounts the database. This will initialize a new empty database file. The resulting commands are as follows; the New-MailboxDatabase cmdlet is used in the command to create the database and the Mount-Database cmdlet is used in the command to mount the database:

```
New-MailboxDatabase -Name 'Executives' -EdbFilePath
'F:\executiveslogs\Executives.edb'

Mount-Database -Identity Executives
```

Notice that when the database was created, the distinguished name of the database was not used. This is because we know that the database name is unique, and therefore the location does not need to be specified. All databases are always created in the same location under the Exchange organization.

Moving the Mailbox Database EDB File

We created the database in the default path (see Figure 23.1) so we could illustrate the process of moving it. Using the EMC, you can move the database by choosing the Move Database Path task in the Actions pane. The only thing that needs to be provided in the Move Database Path wizard is the new location of the database file.

When you specify that you are about to move the database, you are warned that the database will be dismounted while the files are being copied and that it will be inaccessible.

The amount of time that it takes to move the database file will depend both on the size of the database file and the speed of the disk subsystem. Once the file is moved, the Completion page of the Move Database Path wizard will show the EMS command that was used to move the database file. Here is an example:

```
Move-DatabasePath -Identity Executives -EdbFilePath
'F:\ExecutivesDB\Executives.edb'
```

Moving the Mailbox Database Log Files

The same method using the EMC outlined in the previous section can be used to move the Transaction Log folder location for a mailbox database. Administrators of previous versions of Exchange Server remember that the Transaction Log folder location was tied to a storage group. By using the EMC in Exchange Server 2010 and selecting the Move Database Path option in the Actions pane, you can also modify the Transaction Log folder path.

The resulting cmdlet that moves the Transaction Log folder has the following syntax:

```
Move-DatabasePath -Identity Executives -LogFolderPath F:\Databases\Logs
```

Properties of a Mailbox Database

Now let's look at some of the properties of a mailbox database. Figure 23.2 shows the General tab of the mailbox database's properties dialog box. At the top is the display name of the mailbox database. From here, you can rename the database if you need to conform to a new database naming standard. The path to the database is shown, but you cannot change the path here; you must use the `Move-DatabasePath` cmdlet or the Move Database Path task.

There is a lot of dynamic state information on the General tab as well, including the following:

Last Full Backup   Indicates the last time a full or normal Exchange-aware VSS backup was performed. Transaction logs would have also been purged at that time.

Last Incremental Backup   Indicates the last time an incremental backup was run. This backup type will back up the database's transaction logs and then purge them.

Master   Indicates if the copy of the database is the master copy in a DAG deployment.

Master Type   Indicates the type of master copy of the database that exists on the server.

Status   Indicates if the database is mounted or dismounted.

Modified   Shows the date and time the database properties in Active Directory were last changed.

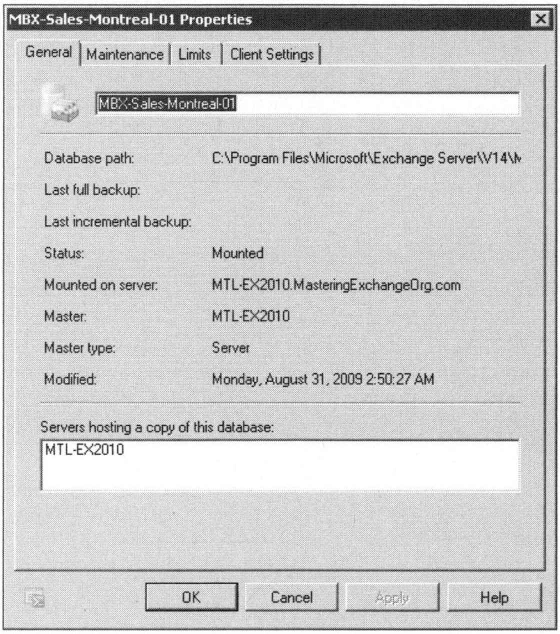

FIGURE 23.2
General tab of the mailbox database's properties dialog box

This information (including the dynamic information) can be retrieved using the -Status option of the Get-MailboxDatabase cmdlet:

```
Get-MailboxDatabase MTL-EX2010 -Status | FL Name,*last*,Mounted
```

```
Name                           : Executives
SnapshotLastFullBackup         : False
SnapshotLastIncrementalBackup  :
SnapshotLastDifferentialBackup :
SnapshotLastCopyBackup         :
LastFullBackup                 : 6/22/2009 1:45:47 AM
LastIncrementalBackup          :
LastDifferentialBackup         :
LastCopyBackup                 :
Mounted                        : True
```

The next tab in the mailbox database's properties dialog box is named Maintenance. Here we find a ''potpourri'' of various configurations that relate to overall database file and content management.

The Journal Recipient option allows you to specify a journaling recipient for all mailboxes located on this mailbox database. If this is enabled, a copy of any message or delivery receipt sent or received by a mailbox on this system will be sent to the journal mailbox.

The Maintenance Schedule drop-down list (and its Customize button) allows you to schedule online maintenance for this particular database. The Enable Background Database Maintenance (24 × 7 ESE Scanning) option, which is enabled by default, ensures that database maintenance occurs at runtime. If you disable this option, database maintenance will only run during the maintenance schedule.

The Do Not Mount This Database At Startup check box allows you to prevent the database from being mounted after the information store service is restarted. This might be useful when you want to make the mailbox databases available one or two at a time rather than all at once.

The This Database Can Be Overwritten By A Restore check box is used when you must restore a database file from a backup.

The Enable Circular Logging check box is used to automatically purge transaction log files on the disk. In a DAG deployment scenario, we recommend that you enable this option if you are using mailbox database replication as a backup solution. For organizations that use VSS-aware backup solutions, Circular Logging should be disabled. In any case, for a stand-alone Mailbox server scenario, Circular Logging should not be enabled, since it will allow you to recover your mailbox database to the exact point of a total failure when combining with an older backup. When Circular Logging is not enabled, transaction log files will only be purged following a successful Full or Incremental backup or when the transaction logs have been successfully copied to another server in a DAG.

The next tab on the properties dialog box is named Limits. The Storage Limits section allows you to specify the amount of storage that the mailbox is allowed to have. Administrators used to previous versions of Exchange will be surprised to learn that newly created mailbox databases have defaults. *Everyone* will be surprised to see the actual default values:

◆ Issue Warning At (KB) is set to 1,991,680 KB. When a mailbox reaches this limit, users will receive an email message informing them that they have reached a limit on their mailbox and they should clean up some data in it.

◆ Prohibit Send At (KB) is set to 2,097,152 KB. Once the mailbox hits this limit, the user will be unable to send new messages or reply to existing messages. Both Outlook and Outlook Web App will inform users if they try to send a message while they are over this limit.

◆ Prohibit Send and Receive At (KB) is set to 2,411,520 KB. When a mailbox exceeds this limit, the mailbox is closed or disabled. Even though the user can access the mailbox, the server will not allow the user to send new messages or reply to existing messages. In addition, the mailbox will not receive any incoming mail from other Exchange users or from outside the organization.

Outlook Web App has a neat new feature that will inform users of how close they are to their limit or if they are over their limit. Simply move your mouse pointer over the top of the mailbox in the folder listing pane of Outlook Web App and you will see a pop-up box similar to one shown in Figure 23.3.

The limit that you see in the messages is the Prohibit Send At (KB) limit, not the Prohibit Send And Receive At (KB) limit.

The Warning Message Interval drop-down list determines the interval at which Exchange generates a warning message informing users that they are over their Issue Warning limit. By default, this is sent once daily at 1:00 a.m. local time. You can customize this to another time, but be careful. The Select Schedule dialog box (shown in Figure 23.4) has a detail view option of either 1 hour or 15 minutes.

When using any schedule box that has both a 1-hour view and a 15-minute view, switch to the 15-minute view to set a schedule. If you select an entire hour, whatever process you are scheduling will run four times per hour. In this case, if you select an entire hour, a warning message will be sent to all mailboxes over their warning limit four times per hour. The users would *not* be amused.

FIGURE 23.3
Size limit messages in Outlook Web App

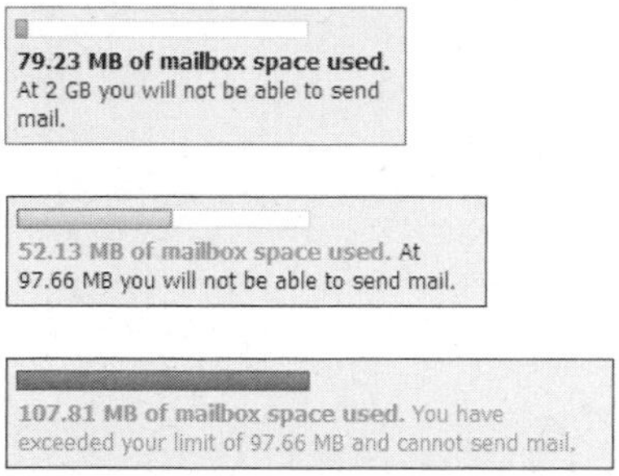

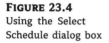

79.23 MB of mailbox space used. At 2 GB you will not be able to send mail.

52.13 MB of mailbox space used. At 97.66 MB you will not be able to send mail.

107.81 MB of mailbox space used. You have exceeded your limit of 97.66 MB and cannot send mail.

FIGURE 23.4
Using the Select Schedule dialog box

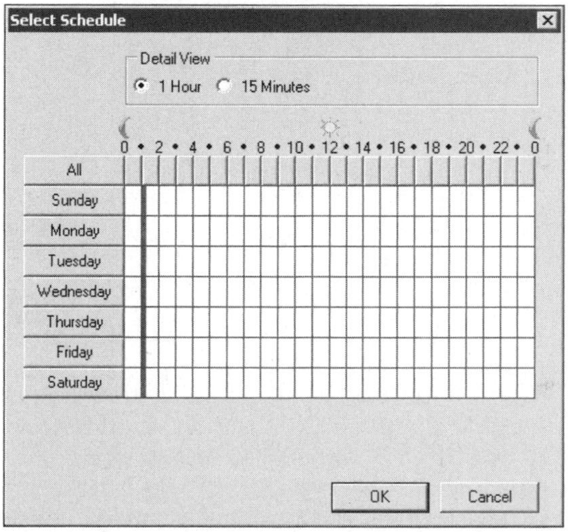

The Deletion Settings section of the Limits tab allows you to configure how long the server will retain deleted items for this mailbox and how long the server will retain a mailbox once it is deleted. The Keep Deleted Items For (Days) option specifies how many days the Exchange server will keep items that have been deleted either from the Deleted Items folder or via a hard delete (Shift+Delete) from another folder. Once a message has been in the deleted item cache for longer than this period (14 days by default for Exchange 2010), the user will no longer be able to retrieve the message using the Recover Deleted Items feature.

The Keep Deleted Mailboxes For (Days) option specifies how long the mailbox database will keep a deleted mailbox before it is permanently purged. The default is 30 days, which is reasonable for most organizations. A mailbox that has been deleted but not purged can be recovered using the EMC's Disconnected Mailbox feature or via the EMS Connect-Mailbox cmdlet.

The Do Not Permanently Delete Items Until The Database Has Been Backed Up check box tells the server that it should not permanently purge an item or a mailbox until the mailbox database has been backed up. This ensures that a copy of the deleted item or deleted mailbox could be recovered from backup media if necessary.

The Client Settings tab (shown in Figure 23.5) allows you to specify two configuration settings that affect the mailboxes on this database. The first is the Default Public Folder Database setting; this field contains the name of the public folder database that MAPI clients should connect to first when retrieving information about public folder hierarchy or content.

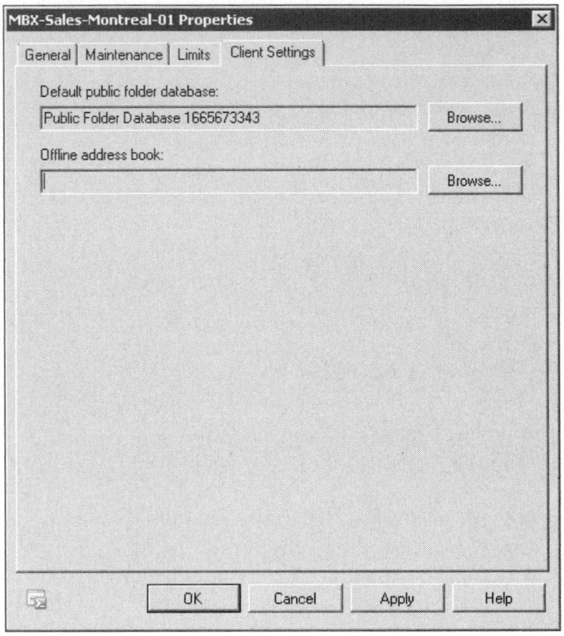

FIGURE 23.5
Client Settings properties of a mailbox database

The Offline Address Book setting affects clients that work in offline mode or local cache mode. Here you specify which offline address book (OAB) a MAPI client should download. The default OAB contains the default global address list and is sufficient for most small and medium-sized businesses.

The properties you have just examined using the graphical user interface can also be examined using the Get-MailboxDatabase cmdlet. The following example retrieves mailbox database properties and sends them to a formatted list:

```
Get-MailboxDatabase 'Database01' | FL
JournalRecipient              :
MailboxRetention              : 30.00:00:00
OfflineAddressBook            :
OriginalDatabase              :
PublicFolderDatabase          : MTL-PF-SERVER\First Storage Group\Default
ProhibitSendReceiveQuota      : 2.3 GB (2,469,396,480 bytes)
Recovery                      : False
ProhibitSendQuota             : 2 GB (2,147,483,648 bytes)
RecoverableItemsQuota         : 30 GB (32,212,254,720 bytes)
RecoverableItemsWarningQuota  : 20 GB (21,474,836,480 bytes)
IndexEnabled                  : True
IsExcludedFromProvisioning    : False
IsSuspendedFromProvisioning   : False
```

```
DataMoveReplicationConstraint    : None
DumpsterStatistics               :
DumpsterServersNotAvailable      :
ReplicationType                  : None
AdministrativeGroup              : Exchange Administrative Group (FYDIBOHF23SPDLT)
AllowFileRestore                 : False
BackgroundDatabaseMaintenance    : True
BackupInProgress                 :
DatabaseCreated                  : True
Description                      :
EdbFilePath                      : C:\Program Files\Microsoft\Exchange↩
Server\V14\Mailbox\Executives\Database01.edb
ExchangeLegacyDN                 : /o=ExchangeOrganization/ou=Exchange↩
Administrative Group (FYDIBOHF23SPDLT)/cn=Configuration/cn=Servers/cn=EX2010/↩
cn=Microsoft Private MDB
DatabaseCopies                   : {Database01\EX2010}
Servers                          : {EX2010}
ActivationPreference             : {[EX2010, 1]}
ReplayLagTimes                   : {[EX2010, 00:00:00]}
TruncationLagTimes               : {[EX2010, 00:00:00]}
RpcClientAccessServer            : Ex2010.ExchangeOrganization.com
MountedOnServer                  :
DeletedItemRetention             : 14.00:00:00
SnapshotLastFullBackup           :
SnapshotLastIncrementalBackup    :
SnapshotLastDifferentialBackup   :
SnapshotLastCopyBackup           :
LastFullBackup                   :
LastIncrementalBackup            :
LastDifferentialBackup           :
LastCopyBackup                   :
DatabaseSize                     :
AvailableNewMailboxSpace         :
MaintenanceSchedule              : {Sun.1:00 AM- Sun.5:00 AM, Mon.1:00 AM-↩
Mon.5:00 AM, Tue.1:00 AM-Tue.5:00 AM, Wed.1:00 AM-Wed.5:00 AM,↩
Thu.1:00 AM-Thu.5:00AM, Fri.1:00 AM-Fri.5:00 AM, Sat.1:00 AM-Sat.5:00 AM}
MountAtStartup                   : True
Mounted                          :
Organization                     : ExchangeOrganization
QuotaNotificationSchedule        : {Sun.1:00 AM-Sun.1:15 AM, Mon.1:00 AM-↩
Mon.1:15 AM, Tue.1:00 AM-Tue.1:15 AM, Wed.1:00 AM-Wed.1:15 AM, Thu.1:00 AM-↩
Thu.1:15 AM, Fri.1:00 AM-Fri.1:15 AM, Sat.1:00 AM-Sat.1:15 AM}
RetainDeletedItemsUntilBackup    : False
Server                           : EX2010
MasterServerOrAvailabilityGroup  : EX2010
MasterType                       : Server
ServerName                       : EX2010
IssueWarningQuota                : 1.899 GB (2,039,480,320 bytes)
EventHistoryRetentionPeriod      : 7.00:00:00
```

```
Name                          : Database01
LogFolderPath                 : C:\Program Files\Microsoft\Exchange↵
Server\V14\Mailbox\Database01
CircularLoggingEnabled        : False
LogFilePrefix                 : E02
LogFileSize                   : 1024
AdminDisplayName              : Database01
ExchangeVersion               : 0.10 (14.0.100.0)
DistinguishedName             : CN=Database01,CN=Databases,CN=Exchange↵
Administrative Group (FYDIBOHF23SPDLT),CN=Administrative↵
Groups,CN=ExchangeOrganization,CN=Microsoft↵
Exchange,CN=Services,CN=Configuration,DC=ExchangeOrganization,DC=com
Identity                      : Database01
Guid                          : 98119b8d-2413-4c07-b418-2d858caf34cf
ObjectCategory                :↵
ExchangeOrganization.com/Configuration/Schema/ms-Exch-Private-MDB
ObjectClass                   : {top, msExchMDB, msExchPrivateMDB}
WhenChanged                   : 13/07/2009 1:25:05 PM
WhenCreated                   : 13/07/2009 1:16:02 PM
WhenChangedUTC                : 13/07/2009 5:25:05 PM
WhenCreatedUTC                : 13/07/2009 5:16:02 PM
OrganizationId                :
OriginatingServer             : DOMAINCONTROLLER.ExchangeOrganization.com
IsValid                       : True
```

Some of these properties can be changed through the EMS using the `Set-MailboxDatabase` cmdlet. For example, to change the Prohibit Send At (KB) quota to 100 MB, you would type this:

```
Set-MailboxDatabase 'Executives' -ProhibitSendQuota:100MB
```

Not all of the properties that you see in the output of the `Get-MailboxDatabase` cmdlet can be changed. Some of them are system properties. The mailbox database location must be changed using the `Move-MailboxDatabase` cmdlet.

The Bottom Line

Identify the core components of Exchange database storage   The ability to identify the components of your Exchange servers that provide storage functionality will provide all the tools necessary for you to properly plan and troubleshoot storage.

Master It   You plan to have redundancy for Mailbox servers. You need to establish how redundancy for databases has changed since Exchange Server 2003. What major change should you identify?

Plan for disk storage requirements for Exchange databases   A major paradigm shift has occurred in the Exchange messaging world. Up to now, administrators have been focused on their IOPS and the capacity of their disks to handle the client requests. Today, administrators have to rethink the way they plan for server storage, though they still need to think about IOPS and capacity, new storage capabilities, and limits. Calculate your IOPS requirements based on the number and profiles of your users. By using Microsoft's user profile guidelines, you can reliably predict your IOPS requirements.

> **Master It**   When planning for storage requirements for Exchange, you must take many factors into consideration. Many of them have to do with storage type, capacity, load, and redundancy. However, many administrators don't always plan for the number of databases that need be created, and opt for a reactionary approach to mailbox database creation.

Configure Exchange Mailbox servers with the appropriate storage objects   Storage groups no longer exist in Exchange Server 2010. All storage group configuration options have been moved to the mailbox database objects.

> **Master It**   You need to prepare your junior administrator to manage the properties of your mailbox databases. Though most administrators have experience managing Exchange, most of their experience was attained in previous versions of Exchange. What are some of the issues you want to be aware of when managing mailbox databases?

Chapter 24

Understanding the Client Access Server

When we went from Exchange Server 2003 to Exchange Server 2007, there were some dramatic changes introduced with the Client Access server role. Now, going into Exchange Server 2010, the Client Access server has been improved to provide additional functionality that enables exciting new scenarios and capabilities.

The Client Access server role now brokers almost all client communications, including Outlook Web App (formerly known as Outlook Web Access), IMAP/POP3, Exchange ActiveSync, and Outlook Anywhere. The new addition to this list is standard Exchange MAPI over RPC connections. Because of this, clients no longer access their mailbox by talking to the Mailbox server. Instead, clients now only talk to the Client Access server. There is one exception, though. The only client component that is not brokered by the Client Access server is public folder access. Clients still talk directly to Mailbox servers when accessing public folders. This model is the next step in Microsoft's plan to abstract all transport and data access functions out of the information store and away from the Mailbox server role. Because of this dramatic change in mailbox access, there are some new capabilities that you will want to explore and some additional knowledge to be gained in understanding Client Access servers.

Many things have not changed, however, including the Web Services model implemented in Exchange Server 2007. For many of the services performed by the Client Access server, everything still works similarly to how it did in Exchange Server 2007. The Web Services model in Client Access servers forms the basis of many features used.

This chapter introduces the new features of the Client Access server role and shows you the steps required to get the most out of them.

In this chapter, you will learn to:

- ◆ Configure Client Access server arrays
- ◆ Generate valid subject alternative name certificates
- ◆ Configure proxying and redirection
- ◆ Transition Client Access servers from previous versions of Exchange

Requirements for the Client Access Server Role

When the Client Access server (CAS) was first introduced in Exchange Server 2007, the hardware requirements were more demanding than its predecessor, the front-end server in Exchange Server 2000/2003. The CAS was given a lot of responsibility because it was doing things that Mailbox servers used to do. In Exchange Server 2010, the CAS has been given even more responsibility, and as a result, the system requirements have again increased.

Client Access Server Operating System Requirements

When we talk to clients, they are sometimes confused about which version of Exchange is required for a particular task. Therefore, we think it is worth clarifying the software requirements of the Client Access server role. The Client Access server role is absolutely fine running on the Standard Edition of Exchange Server 2010, Windows Server 2008 SP2, and Windows Server 2008 R2. Also, like every other role in Exchange Server 2010, the CAS requires a 64-bit processor and 64-bit operating system.

In Exchange Server 2010, there is great benefit to using network load balancing (NLB) to increase the availability of your Client Access servers. There is typically some confusion around whether NLB can be used with Windows Server standard editions, since failover clustering is only available in Enterprise editions. The answer is yes, you can use Windows Server Standard Edition even when you want to use NLB to create a Client Access server array, which we'll cover a little later in this chapter.

Client Access Server Hardware Recommendations

One of the first considerations when planning for your installation of the Client Access server role is what hardware to use. As you can see from the introduction, the CAS has a lot of work to deal with. Since the CAS now processes client MAPI RPC and address book traffic, there is additional load that needs to be accounted for in hardware.

In addition to RPC client access, all of the rendering for Outlook Web App is done on the CAS, as well as all message conversion for non-MAPI clients. These factors remove the load from the Mailbox server (assuming you are running the roles on separate boxes) and help enable Exchange to scale better.

So what does this mean in terms of hardware? This means that the CAS makes heavy use of the processor, memory, and network resources. Disk access is typically not heavy. The recommendations and requirements for processors are as follows:

◆ As with all versions of Exchange Server, x64-capable processors are required.

◆ Two processor cores are required for your implementation to be supported by Microsoft. However, in most implementations, Microsoft recommends that eight processor cores be used for a CAS.

◆ Microsoft recommends a maximum of 12 processor cores when a CAS stands alone. However, when the CAS is combined with the Hub Transport and Mailbox roles on a single server, Microsoft recommends up to 24 processor cores.

◆ For every four Mailbox server processor cores, there should be at least three Client Access server processor cores. So for example, if in one site you have four Mailbox servers with four processor cores in each (with a total of sixteen processor cores), then you should have three Client Access servers with four processor cores (a total of twelve processor cores) as well.

Memory is the second part of your hardware considerations:

◆ The minimum recommendation is 4 GB of RAM when a CAS is the only role on the server, or 8 GB of RAM when it is combined with other roles.

◆ In general, servers should be sized with 2 GB for each CPU core up to a maximum of 16 GB.

◆ The processor and memory used by the Client Access server role has a linear relationship. If you add processors later, remember to increase the amount of memory as well.

◆ When purchasing memory, you want to pack as much memory on a single chip as possible. These chips are generally more expensive, but it gives you the option to scale up later if the load turns out to be heavier than you expected.

The last of the three areas is networking. The Client Access server role puts heavy use on the network, and eliminating network bottlenecks is especially important if you're servicing clients from multiple sites. This is particularly important in Exchange Server 2010, since Client Access servers now handle all RPC client traffic. Therefore, we recommend providing Gigabit Ethernet where possible.

Services Provided by the Client Access Server

Before we start digging deeper into the Client Access server, we want to explain the services that the CAS provides. There are some things added into the Exchange Server 2010 version of the CAS that have a great impact on your Exchange organization. We'll start off by covering the new services: RPC Client Access, mailbox replication, the Address Book service, and Remote PowerShell. We'll then discuss the new version of Outlook Web App and its tight integration with the Exchange Control Panel. After that, we'll cover other services that are provided by the CAS and call out the changes in the Exchange Server 2010 version of the services as we go along.

RPC Client Access

RPC Client Access is probably the most significant change to the CAS in Exchange Server 2010. This service provides RPC connectivity to Outlook clients, performs data validation, creates a compliance log, and provides the infrastructure for connecting to the archive mailbox. The RPC Client Access service runs as a Windows service on your Client Access servers using the Network Service account. The name of the service is Microsoft Exchange RPC Client Access (MSExchangeRPC).

RPC Client Access moves the connection for MAPI-based connections for mailbox data to the Client Access server instead of the Mailbox server. This means that the Outlook clients inside the LAN will no longer connect to Mailbox servers to access their mail. Instead, they talk to the Client Access servers, which in turn broker the connection to the Mailbox servers. This layer of abstraction for client connections is useful and important for a few reasons:

◆ In the past, there was a limit of 65,535 RPC context handles to Mailbox servers. This is no longer an issue. Instead, you can add multiple Client Access servers to a site and each CAS can handle 65,535 RPC context handles. This means that the Mailbox server can support more MAPI client connections.

◆ There is a reduced network load on the Mailbox servers since they maintain fewer connections. Keep in mind, however, that this network load could be replaced by other functions of a Mailbox server, such as data replication.

◆ This architecture has enabled a dramatic improvement in the Mailbox server switchover and failover experience. Since clients connect to the CAS, a failed Mailbox server does not require a reconfiguration of the client connection settings.

◆ Because the connection to the Mailbox server is abstracted, mailboxes can be moved from one Mailbox server to another without client profile reconfiguration. The user simply needs to close Outlook and reopen it.

◆ All client connections connect to Client Access servers now instead of the Mailbox server (except in the case of public folder access). This supplies a consolidated entry point into your Exchange organization.

This enhanced functionality does come at a cost. RPC Client Access is a big factor in driving the hardware requirements for the CAS in Exchange Server 2010 higher than in Exchange Server 2007. There is an increased load on Client Access servers from the perspective of processor utilization, memory utilization, and network utilization.

Your Outlook 2007 and Outlook 2010 clients can natively talk to the RPC Client Access service on the CAS without any changes. However, your Outlook 2003 clients may need a configuration change. The RPC Client Access service enables RPC encryption by default. Outlook 2007 and Outlook 2010 already encrypt RPC in their default configurations. But if you want your Outlook 2003 clients to use RPC Client Access, then you will need to enable the encryption setting for those clients. You can do this through a Group Policy Object or you can reconfigure it manually in Outlook.

Another option you have, which we don't recommend, is to turn off the encryption requirement for RPC Client Access. You have to turn this off on a per–Client Access server basis, so if you are turning it off in your environment, you need to remember to do this when you add new Client Access servers to the Exchange organization. You don't want to run into a situation where you have the RPC encryption requirement enabled for some Client Access servers and disabled for others. If so, Outlook 2003 clients will be able to connect to some servers, but not others. And if you were to do this inside a load-balanced Client Access server array, the problems that arise could be difficult to troubleshoot. We highly recommend that you leave the encryption setting alone, but if you want to do this in a lab or just want to ignore our warning, you can disable the RPC encryption requirement with the following command:

```
Set-RpcClientAccess -Server CAS-1 -EncryptionRequired $False
```

Address Book Service

The Address Book service on Client Access servers replaces the Name Service Provider Interface (NSPI) referral functionality that used to run on Mailbox servers in previous versions of Exchange. The purpose of the NSPI is to either refer Outlook clients to a Global Catalog server or proxy connections to the Global Catalog server for the client. In the past, this service was provided by the System Attendant service on the Mailbox server. It now exists on the CAS as part of the initiative to make this server the primary connection point for clients. In addition to directory referrals, the Address Book service writes changes that are made in Outlook to Active Directory. When the user changes the membership of a distribution group, manages their list of delegates, or manages their certificates from Outlook, the Address Book service calls the appropriate EMS cmdlet to make the change. The Address Book service runs as a Windows service under the context of the Local System account. The name of the service is Microsoft Exchange Address Book (MSExchangeAB), and it only runs on Client Access servers.

The CAS still uses the NSPI to provide directory services to older clients and to provide directory services to mailboxes on legacy versions of Exchange Server. When a user whose mailbox is on an Exchange Server 2003 or an Exchange Server 2007 Mailbox server connects, the Exchange Server 2010 Client Access server issues a referral to the client to contact the Mailbox server instead. If the user's mailbox is on an Exchange Server 2010 Mailbox server, the Exchange Server 2010 Client Access server will either handle the request itself or refer the client to an Exchange Server 2010 Client Access server that is in the same site as the user's mailbox.

The Address Book service uses the following steps to provide the address book to the Outlook client:

1. Outlook contacts the CAS and requests the address book.

2. The CAS uses Active Directory to gather the mailbox location, Exchange version, and the name of the CAS specified in the RPCClientAccessServer property of the mailbox database.

3. The CAS uses the information it gathered to tell Outlook which CAS to use for the address book.

4. The Outlook client connects to the appropriate CAS for accessing the address book.

Mailbox Replication

You may be wondering why we are discussing the topic of mailbox replication in the Client Access server chapter of this book. Mailbox replication is one of the more interesting and welcomed new features of the Exchange Server 2010 Client Access server. Traditionally, when you wanted to move a mailbox from one server to another, you would have to open your Exchange management tool (either the Exchange System Manager or the Move-Mailbox cmdlet in the Exchange Management Shell) and process the mailbox move from the computer that you were logged in at. Unless you scheduled the move to happen later, you would have to remain logged in until the move completed. Not only that, but users couldn't access their mailbox during the move.

In Exchange Server 2010, mailbox moves are executed differently. Instead of the move occurring with the client, the client simply creates a new move request. Once this move request is created, a CAS will find the request and fill it. The Mailbox Replication service actively monitors for move requests and executes them when it finds them. The Mailbox Replication service runs as a Windows service on the Client Access servers. The name of the service is Microsoft Exchange Mailbox Replication Service (MSExchangeMailboxReplication), and it runs under the context of the Local System account.

The mailbox replication that is performed by the Mailbox Replication service is done asynchronously. The service can move mailboxes from Exchange Server 2003/2007/2010 source Mailbox servers to Exchange Server 2003/2007/2010 target Mailbox servers, with two exceptions: Exchange 2003 to Exchange 2003 and Exchange 2007 to Exchange 2007 mailbox moves are not supported.

Remote PowerShell

One of the new features of Exchange Server 2010 is the ability to remotely connect to the Exchange Management Shell (EMS) and issue commands from another computer. This is made possible by the PowerShell virtual directory. The PowerShell virtual directory is installed on every role by default except for the Edge Transport server. In fact, when you open the EMS locally on an Exchange server, it connects to the PowerShell virtual directory that is running on the server itself. As you can see in Figure 24.1, the PowerShell virtual directory shows up in the Internet Information Services (IIS) Manager as a web service, just like the other Exchange virtual directories. You can view the properties of the PowerShell virtual directory using IIS Manager, though Microsoft recommends using the EMS cmdlets to view and make changes to the PowerShell virtual directory when possible.

FIGURE 24.1
Viewing the PowerShell virtual directory on the Exchange server

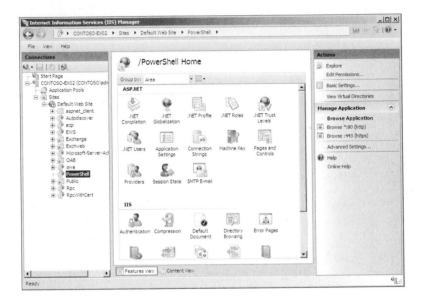

As with other virtual directories in Exchange, the EMS provides a set of cmdlets that can be used for configuring the web service. Exchange includes the following cmdlets for PowerShell:

◆ Get-PowerShellVirtualDirectory

◆ Set-PowerShellVirtualDirectory

◆ New-PowerShellVirtualDirectory

◆ Remove-PowerShellVirtualDirectory

◆ Test-PowerShellConnectivity

Exchange gives you the Test-PowerShellConnectivity cmdlet that you can use to test the connection to the PowerShell virtual directory. You can specify various options with this cmdlet to test things such as the authentication method, the certificate, and the URL of the web service. This following example command will test the PowerShell connection using Basic authentication and ignoring certificate problems:

```
Test-PowerShellConnectivity -TrustAnySSLCertificate ↵
-ConnectionUri https://mail.pacific.contoso.com -Authentication Basic
```

CasServer	LocalSite	Scenario	Result	Latency(MS)	Error
	Honolulu	Logon User	Success	890.45	

As you can see from the output, the test provides some useful information, such as the success of the connection and even the latency encountered.

Outlook Web App

Outlook Web App (OWA) underwent several changes in Exchange Server 2010. The first and most obvious is the name change from Outlook Web Access to Outlook Web App. In addition, there have been many other graphical user interface (GUI) changes. Here are some of the more obvious ones:

◆ Overall theme change

◆ Conversation view on messages

◆ OWA options that use the Exchange Control Panel

◆ Instant Messaging integration through Office Communications Server

There are some great administrative changes in OWA as well. Probably the biggest is the ability to apply a mailbox policy specifically for OWA. You can create and manage Outlook Web App mailbox policies through the Organization Configuration ➢ Client Access node in the EMC. Inside the OWA mailbox policy, you will find the segmentation options such as enabling and disabling certain items and functionality. After you create or edit an OWA mailbox policy, you can apply the policy to one or more users.

Exchange Control Panel

The Exchange Control Panel (ECP) is a new virtual directory added in Exchange Server 2010 that provides access to the configuration data for users. The ECP works in conjunction with OWA to provide full browser-based functionality to users and administrators. To access the ECP, you can browse to it directly, or you can click the Options button in OWA. The default URL for the ECP is `https://servername.domain.com/ecp`. The ECP uses forms-based authentication by default, so if you browse directly to it your logon experience will be similar to your logon experience in OWA.

> ### CONSISTENCY OF THE OWA AND ECP EXPERIENCE
>
> Because the ECP and OWA go hand in hand, you should keep the virtual directory settings similar. For example, don't require SSL on OWA but not ECP. Since the two are integrated, you want the user's experience to flow from OWA to the ECP without any additional authentication prompts or other annoyances.

ECP FOR END USERS

The ECP exposes some new functionality for browser-based access for both users and administrators. Users now have the ability to update their contact information in the Global Address List (GAL) through the ECP. Figure 24.2 demonstrates this capability.

In addition, users can manage their own groups. There are two aspects to group management:

◆ Users can manage which groups they are a part of.

◆ Users can manage groups that they themselves have created and own.

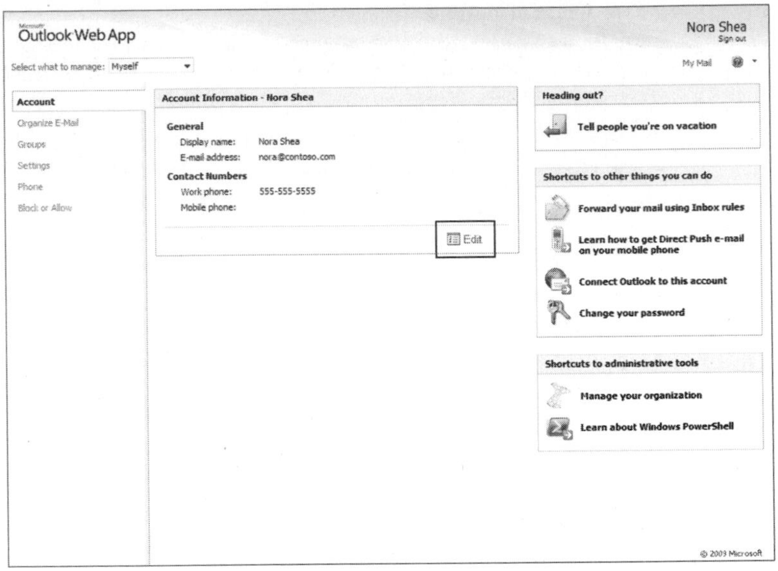

FIGURE 24.2
Users can now update their contact information in OWA using the ECP.

This group management component is a powerful new feature for users. Not only can they create distribution groups, edit their properties, and manage their memberships, but they can also determine how group membership is approved and whether the messages sent to the group are moderated. For example, the user who owns the group can determine that they want the group to require owner approval, meaning that users can only join if the owner approves. This powerful group management component is a significant advancement in browser-based email access. For more information on how this works and to learn how to customize these capabilities, check out Chapter 15, ''Management Permissions and Role-Based Administration (RBAC).''

ECP FOR ADMINISTRATORS

In addition to end-user benefits, the ECP also provides new functionality for administrators. When a user with administrator rights is logged into the ECP, they can choose to manage their organization instead of just their own mailbox. This is demonstrated in Figure 24.3.

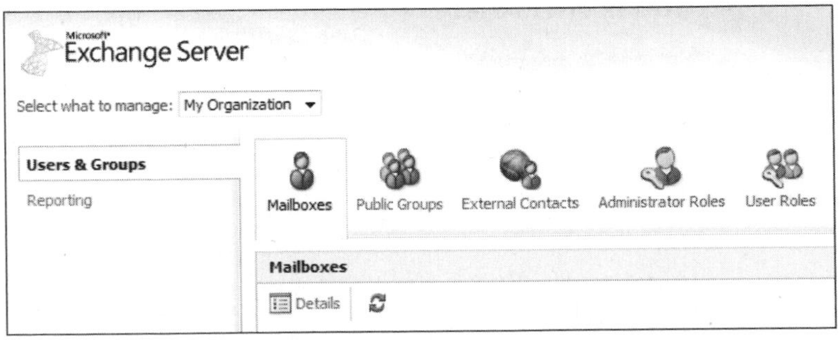

FIGURE 24.3
Users with administrative permissions can manage the organization.

When an administrator uses the ECP to manage the organization, something interesting happens. Only the functionality that the administrator has permissions to administer will appear in the ECP. For example, if the administrator can't perform discovery searches, then the Mailbox Searches tab doesn't appear.

MANAGING ECP SETTINGS

You manage the settings on the Exchange Control Panel in the same way that you manage Outlook Web App settings. You can modify some properties directly in the virtual directory using the IIS Manager tool. However, even though you have access to the virtual directory through IIS Manager, we strongly recommend that you make changes through the EMC or the EMS. The following cmdlets can be used for managing the ECP:

- ◆ New-EcpVirtualDirectory

- ◆ Get-EcpVirtualDirectory

- ◆ Set-EcpVirtualDirectory

- ◆ Remove-EcpVirtualDirectory

TESTING THE ECP

Exchange Server 2010 provides you with the Test-EcpConnectivity cmdlet out of the box for testing the ECP. The following example demonstrates the use of this command:

```
Test-EcpConnectivity

Creating a new session for implicit remoting of "Test-EcpConnectivity"
command...

CasServer   LocalSite    Scenario       Result  Latency(MS) Error
---------   ---------    --------       ------  ----------- -----
CONTOSO...  Baltimore    Reset Creden... Success    4437.50
CONTOSO...  Baltimore    Logon          Success   23390.62
CONTOSO...  Baltimore    WebServiceCall Success       0.00
```

As you can see from the output of the test cmdlet, a series of scenarios is tested.

Outlook Anywhere

As in Exchange Server 2007, Outlook Anywhere provides users with access to their email in Outlook over the Internet. Users who are not accessing their email from inside the domain typically cannot use remote procedure calls (RPC) to access to their mailbox, because RPC uses a wide port range that most firewalls don't allow. Also, RPC performs poorly in high latency scenarios.

Therefore, the Outlook Anywhere service takes the RPCs used by Outlook and wraps them in HTTPS. HTTPS is a commonly used protocol across the Internet, so using HTTPS instead of RPCs allows users to connect to their mailbox. The HTTPS session is terminated at the RPC proxy server (typically a Client Access server) and the CAS then uses standard RPCs to access the mailbox on the behalf of the user.

Enabling Outlook Anywhere

Outlook Anywhere is not enabled by default when you install the Client Access server role. You will need to manually enable Outlook Anywhere to take advantage of its functionality. Before you do, ensure that the RPC over HTTP Proxy feature is installed first. If you used the `Exchange-CAS.xml` or `Exchange-Typical.xml` Server Manager installation package to prepare your server, this feature was installed during that process. If not, you can use the following command to install the RPC over HTTP Proxy feature:

```
ServerManagerCMD -i RPC-over-HTTP-Proxy
```

After the RPC over HTTP Proxy feature is installed, you can enable Outlook Anywhere in the EMC under the Server Configuration ➢ Client Access node. You will need to select the CAS and then choose Enable Outlook Anywhere from the Actions menu.

You can also enable Outlook Anywhere with the `Enable-OutlookAnywhere` command in the EMS. The following example enables Outlook Anywhere with NTLM authentication:

```
Enable-OutlookAnywhere -Server CAS-1 -ClientAuthenticationMethod NTLM ↵
-ExternalHostname mail.contoso.com -SSLOffloading $False
```

SSL Offloading

By default, Outlook Anywhere requires SSL connections. Multiple SSL connections by several clients can sometimes cause a performance bottleneck on servers. With Outlook Anywhere, you have the option of offloading the SSL processing to another server. When you do this, the client establishes a secure SSL connection with the server that you offloaded SSL to. The connection from the server doing the SSL offloading to the CAS is unencrypted.

Outlook Anywhere with Self-Signed Certificates

The default self-signed certificate created by Client Access servers will not work when Outlook clients attempt to use Outlook Anywhere. Instead, you will need to issue a valid certificate to your CAS that is trusted by the client computers.

The Autodiscover Service

The Autodiscover service was introduced in Exchange Server 2007. This valuable service, which runs on Client Access servers, provides automatic configuration of Outlook profiles for Outlook 2007 and newer versions. This provides a way to get users up and running in an easy manner on a new machine without using scripts, running Custom Installation wizard installations, or relying on users to set up their own account (which is always dangerous!). When setting up an Outlook profile while connected to the domain, users only have to click the Next button a few times because Outlook picks up all the relevant information from the account the user logged in with. If not connected to the domain, users are simply asked to enter their email address and password. (Note that users must specify their primary address; otherwise, Autodiscover may not work.)

Aside from the profile configuration, Autodiscover also provides Outlook with the information needed for downloading the offline address book, connecting to Outlook Anywhere, and even for connecting to Exchange Web Services which, among other things, provides calendar availability information.

WINDOWS MOBILE SUPPORT FOR AUTODISCOVER

Originally, Windows Mobile 6 was planned to support Autodiscover for configuring devices for Exchange ActiveSync. Unfortunately, this feature didn't make it into Windows Mobile 6, but it arrived in Windows Mobile 6.1 and continues to exist in Windows Mobile 6.5. It's interesting to note that Windows Mobile devices use Autodiscover differently than Outlook does. While Outlook clients continuously use Autodiscover to ensure that the client is up to date, Windows Mobile only uses it on the initial configuration of the profile.

Autodiscover works in two ways, depending on whether the client is on the internal LAN and a member of the forest where the mailbox is held, or external to the LAN.

INTERNAL AUTODISCOVER

When a computer is connected to the Active Directory domain, the Autodiscover process is different than when the computer is not currently connected to the domain. The method used when Autodiscover is used on a client within the LAN is described here and shown in Figure 24.4:

1. When Outlook is launched, it checks to see if an Outlook profile exists. If there is none, it automatically fills in the user's email address and password from Active Directory.

2. Outlook then searches for a Service Connection Point (SCP) object in Active Directory for Autodiscover. An SCP is a special object that gives computers a mechanism for advertising an application or service that it is hosting. The location of the SCP for Autodiscover is shown in Figure 24.5.

   SCP objects in Active Directory aren't only used for Exchange. Other applications can use SCPs as well to publish information about a service that it provides. For Exchange, the information published in the Autodiscover SCP gives Outlook the FQDN of the servers hosting the Autodiscover service (the Client Access servers).

FIGURE 24.4
The Autodiscover process on the LAN

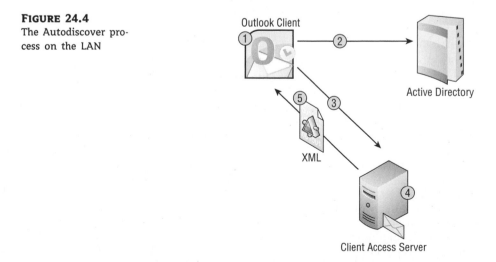

Outlook Client

Active Directory

XML

Client Access Server

FIGURE 24.5
The location of the SCP as seen in Active Directory

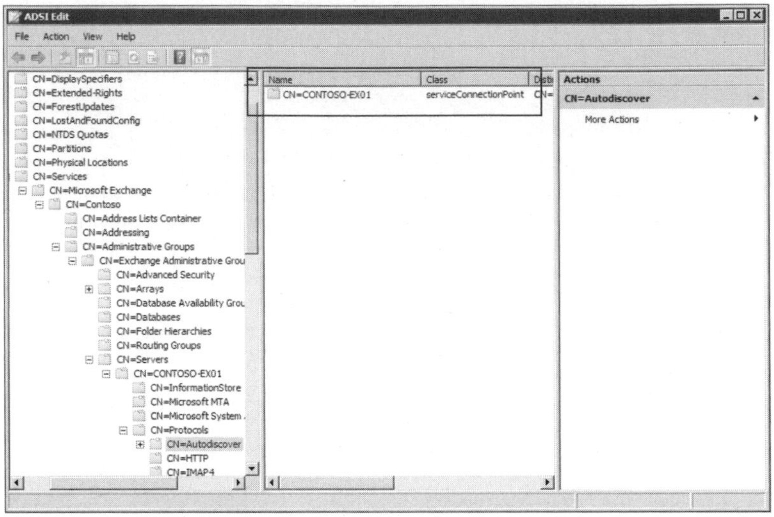

3. Outlook queries the CAS using the FQDN that it got from the SCP.

4. The server prepares an XML file specifically for the user.

5. The Autodiscover XML file is downloaded by the Outlook client, which applies the settings and connects the user to his or her mailbox.

EXTERNAL AUTODISCOVER

If the user is outside the Active Directory forest (for example, on a machine that is not domain joined) or on a machine that is outside the LAN, the internal Autodiscover process is not used. If the client cannot contact the Active Directory domain, then it can't read the SCP. So the Outlook client needs another way to find out where the Autodiscover service is running. This is accomplished using the following process, which is also demonstrated in Figure 24.6.

FIGURE 24.6
The process that Autodiscover uses when the computer cannot contact Active Directory

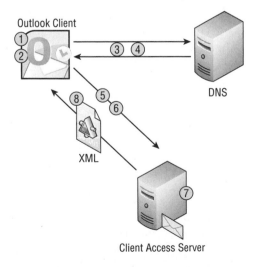

To find a Client Access server that can provide Autodiscover functions externally, the Outlook client will try to connect to one of these two URLs (where the domain is somorita.com):

https://somorita.com/autodiscover/autodiscover.xml

https://autodiscover.somorita.com/autodiscover/autodiscover.xml

For more information on this process, see the following URL:

http://technet.microsoft.com/en-us/library/bb332063.aspx#OutlookAndAD

The following steps are used when Outlook uses Autodiscover to configure the Outlook profile outside the LAN:

1. Outlook prompts the user to enter his name, password, and email address.

2. Outlook extracts the FQDN from the email address.

3. Outlook performs a DNS query for the namespace.

4. Outlook 2007 clients without a service pack will attempt to connect to `https://domain.com/autodiscover/autodiscover.xml`. If this fails, an attempt is made to connect to `https://autodiscover.domain.com/autodiscover/autodiscover.xml`.

5. If the previous two attempts fail, Outlook attempts to connect using an HTTP redirect. Therefore, for the Autodiscover process to work correctly in Outlook with no service pack, one of the URLs must be resolvable in DNS.

6. If using Outlook 2007 SP1 or later, an additional DNS query will be performed, looking for a service locator (SRV) record that advertises Autodiscover. If this record is found, the client uses the hostname in the record to make another connection attempt to the Autodiscover service.

7. Once the connection has been made, the process continues in the same way as for internal connections. Exchange creates a specific XML file containing the relevant details for the user based on the credentials entered in Step 1.

8. Outlook downloads the Autodiscover XML file and uses it to build the profile.

THE AUTODISCOVER XML

Now that we've discussed how Autodiscover works, let's take a look at how we can tune it. First, here's an example of the XML that is passed to the client:

```
<?xml version="1.0" encoding="utf-8"?>
<Autodiscover xmlns="http://schemas.microsoft.com/exchange/autodiscover/
    responseschema/2006">
<Response xmlns="http://schemas.microsoft.com/exchange/autodiscover/outlook/
responseschema/2006a">
  <User>
    <DisplayName>Nathan Winters</DisplayName>
    <LegacyDN>/o=OEXCH015/ou=Exchange Administrative Group (FYDIBOHF23SPDLT)
/cn=Recipients/cn=nathan_nwinters</LegacyDN>
    <DeploymentId>996755d4-d79d-4cf9-94ba-fb91ec8877f8</DeploymentId>
  </User>
```

```
<Account>
  <AccountType>email</AccountType>
  <Action>settings</Action>
  <Protocol>
    <Type>EXCH</Type>
    <Server>EXVMBX015-3.exch015.msoutlookonline.net</Server>
    <ServerDN>/o=OEXCH015/ou=Exchange Administrative Group
(FYDIBOHF23SPDLT)
/cn=Configuration/cn=Servers/cn=EXVMBX015-3</ServerDN>
      <ServerVersion>720082AD</ServerVersion>
      <MdbDN>/o=OEXCH015/ou=Exchange Administrative Group (FYDIBOHF23SPDLT)
/cn=Configuration/cn=Servers/cn=EXVMBX015-3/cn=Microsoft Private MDB</MdbDN>
<ASUrl>https://owa015.msoutlookonline.net/EWS/Exchange.asmx</ASUrl>
<OOFUrl>https://owa015.msoutlookonline.net/EWS/Exchange.asmx</OOFUrl>
  <UMUrl>https://owa015.msoutlookonline.net/UnifiedMessaging/
Service.asmx</UMUrl>
      <OABUrl>Public Folder</OABUrl>
    </Protocol>
    <Protocol>
      <Type>EXPR</Type>
      <Server>owa015.msoutlookonline.net</Server>
      <SSL>On</SSL>
      <AuthPackage>Basic</AuthPackage>
      <OABUrl>Public Folder</OABUrl>
    </Protocol>
    <Protocol>
      <Type>WEB</Type>
      <External>
        <OWAUrl AuthenticationMethod="Fba">https://owa015.msoutlookonline.net/owa
</OWAUrl>
        <Internal>
          <OWAUrl AuthenticationMethod="Basic, Fba">
https://owa015.msoutlookonline.net/owa</OWAUrl>
          <Protocol>
            <Type>EXCH</Type>
<ASUrl>https://owa015.msoutlookonline.net/EWS/Exchange.asmx</ASUrl>
          </Protocol>
        </Internal>
      </External>
    </Protocol>
  </Account>
</Response></Autodiscover>
```

As you can see, a fair amount of information is included, in particular the URLs for the main services. So where does this information come from and how is it set?

When the CAS is installed, a virtual directory called Autodiscover is created in the IIS default website. It is from here that the configuration file is downloaded by the Outlook client. To determine which URLs to include in the XML file, Autodiscover uses the InternalURL and ExternalURL parameters from the various virtual directories. These two parameters are discussed in greater detail later in this chapter.

The Availability Service

The Availability service is installed by default as part of the Client Access server role. The primary job of the Availability service is to retrieve free/busy information about other users. Back in Exchange Server 2003, free/busy information was published in a public folder. When users use Outlook 2007/2010 or Outlook Web App and access free/busy information for mailboxes on Outlook 2007/2010, then the Availability service retrieves that information straight from the user's mailbox. When users use Outlook 2003, the information is always retrieved using public folders. When using newer versions of Outlook, the location of where the data is pulled is dependent on where the mailbox resides. If the mailbox resides on an Exchange Server 2007 or Exchange Server 2010 Mailbox server, the Availability service accesses this information directly from the mailbox.

Here's how the Availability service works:

1. The Outlook client locates the Availability service URL using Autodiscover. The client then connects to the URL (on the Client Access server) given by Autodiscover.

2. If the target mailbox is in another Active Directory site, the CAS will make an HTTPS connection to the target CAS. The target CAS will obtain the free/busy information by communicating, using MAPI, with the Mailbox server and will then send the information back to the source CAS, which passes it on to the client.

3. If the target mailbox is in the same Active Directory site, the CAS will communicate with the Mailbox server (via MAPI) and obtain the free/busy information. The source CAS will then provide the data back to the Outlook or Outlook Web App client.

   You should note that this process may vary if different Exchange versions are involved. For example, if the requesting mailbox is on Exchange 2010 and the target mailbox is on Exchange 2007, then the Exchange 2010 CAS will talk to the Exchange 2007 CAS and retrieve the free/busy information. This happens even if the servers are in the same site.

The Availability service enables some other great functionality. When coupled with the Outlook 2007/2010 scheduling assistant, it provides suggested meeting times, and Exchange suggests the time when all users and resources are available. It also allows users to share their calendar information in more granular ways. For each target person or group, users can choose one of four levels of sharing on the properties page for their calendar, as shown in Figure 24.7.

On the Permissions tab of the Calendar Properties dialog, users can control the following settings:

◆ Whether items can be deleted or modified

◆ Item and detail visibility, such as the subject of a meeting, location, and meeting time

◆ How free/busy information is published

Offline Address List Distribution

The last service that we want to cover is offline address list distribution. Like free/busy information, in Exchange Server 2003, the offline address book (as it was then known) was distributed via public folders. This changed in Exchange Server 2007 and the story remains the same in Exchange Server 2010. The offline address list can be distributed both through a public folder and from a web share.

Because the offline address list is still generated by the System Attendant service on the Mailbox server, you may wonder how the CAS does the distribution. Well, in Exchange Server

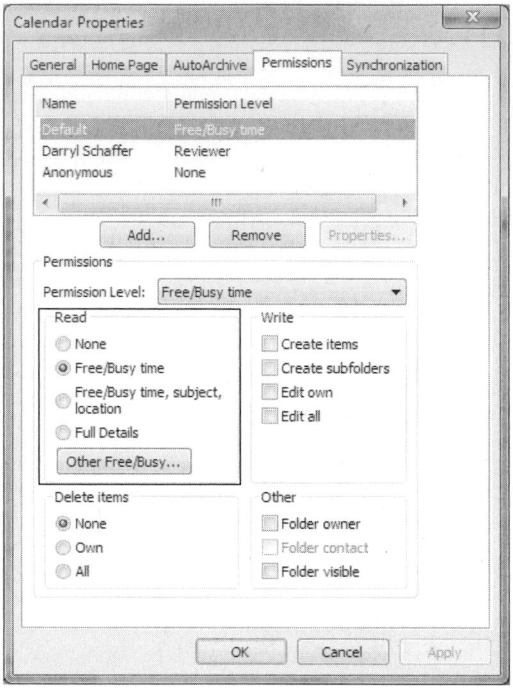

FIGURE 24.7
Specifying the level of detail viewable by free/busy lookups

2007 and Exchange Server 2010, there is a service called the Microsoft Exchange File Distribution service (MSExchangeFDS), which runs on the CAS. Its job is to pick up the files left by the System Attendant service on the Mailbox server in the share \\MBXServ\ExchangeOAB and copy them to the local web directory (`https://serverFQDN/oab`) on the CAS.

One thing to note when setting up the offline address list is that, by default, the distribution share is not configured for HTTPS. The reason that Microsoft does this is because the Background Intelligent Transfer Service (BITS) is used for downloading the offline address list. By default, BITS doesn't support self-signed certificates, which is what the CAS uses for SSL when it is installed. You can rectify this problem when you configure external access by installing a trusted CA-issued certificate and then using the following command:

```
Set-OABVirtualDirectory -Identity "EX-01\OAB (Default Web Site)" ↵
-ExternalURL "https://mail.northwind.co.uk/OAB" -RequireSSL:$true
```

For some excellent troubleshooting information about offline address list distribution, look at the following website:

```
http://blogs.msdn.com/dgoldman/archive/tags/Offline+Address+Book+Related/
default.aspx
```

Positioning the Client Access Server in Your LAN

After you complete your design for the hardware on which the Client Access server role will run, the next step to consider is the positioning of the Client Access server role in your LAN. As a bare minimum, every Active Directory site hosting a Mailbox server also requires a CAS.

As with Exchange Server 2007, you want to avoid placing your Exchange Server 2010 Client Access servers in your perimeter network. This is important because the CAS uses RPCs to connect to the Mailbox server role. Because of this, the number of ports you must open to provide access for your CAS leaves a rather large hole for potential attack. You can either publish a CAS directly to Internet clients or you can use a reverse proxy to provide an additional layer of protection. We strongly urge you to put your Client Access servers on your internal network and use a reverse proxy to publish the servers to the Internet. In fact, placing your Client Access servers in the perimeter network is not a scenario supported by Microsoft. There is a great blog post about this on the Exchange Team Blog at http://msexchangeteam.com/archive/2009/10/21/452929.aspx.

So what are you expected to do? Our recommendation is to place the Client Access server role on your internal LAN and then proxy connections to it using a reverse proxy server like ISA Server 2006 or Microsoft's successor, Forefront Threat Management Gateway (TMG). This gives you many benefits, not the least of which is that the only thing being exposed directly to Internet traffic is the proxy/firewall — which is designed specifically for that exposure. When using ISA or TMG, you also get the benefit of preauthentication, which ensures that only authenticated traffic gets through to your internal LAN. On top of this, all inbound connection requests are inspected to ensure they are valid. This makes things even more secure by closely checking all traffic to your Client Access servers for potential HTML exploits and nonstandard HTML requests before passing it through to your LAN.

Client Access Server Proxying

Let's take a more detailed look at how remote access works and, more specifically, how your placement of Client Access servers and Internet connections affects what happens.

First, you need to understand how Client Access servers talk to Mailbox servers when users try to access their mailboxes. If you have a single Active Directory site (Baltimore) with Exchange servers in it, then you have a fairly simple scenario, as shown in Figure 24.8. You would provide remote access via a reverse proxy or some other type of firewall. In this scenario, the user talks to the CAS (either directly or through the firewall) and the CAS talks to the Mailbox server.

FIGURE 24.8
A simple single-site
Exchange setup

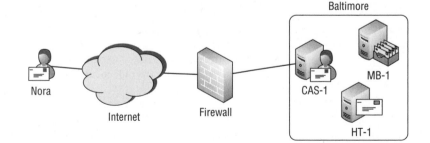

So what about when you introduce another Active Directory site (Honolulu) with Mailbox and Client Access servers? It depends. Let's look at a situation where a user, Nora, has her mailbox on a Mailbox server in Honolulu. If Nora were to use Outlook Web App to access the CAS in Baltimore (CAS-1), the server would look up Nora's mailbox location in Active Directory and find that her mailbox is actually hosted on a Mailbox server in Honolulu (MB-2).

At this point, the CAS in Baltimore (CAS-1) will determine if an external URL is configured for the CAS in Honolulu (CAS-2). If not, CAS-1 will contact CAS-2 and then proxy Nora's request to it. CAS-2 gets the info from Nora's Mailbox server and passes it back to CAS-1. From there the information is returned to Nora. So proxying is nothing more than one CAS telling another CAS to access the user's mailbox because it can't contact the Mailbox server itself. As shown in Figure 24.9, the cross-site traffic between Client Access servers uses HTTPS, and not RPC. HTTPS is better to use than RPC for long-distance connections that are unreliable and susceptible to network latency.

FIGURE 24.9
A simple CAS proxy
scenario

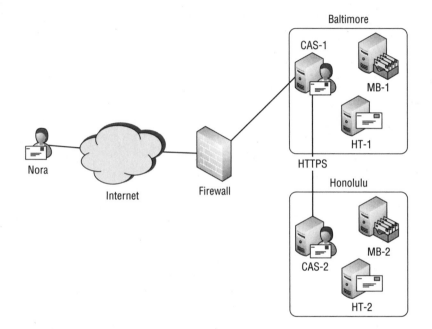

When designing your Exchange topology to include Client Access servers, keep in mind that proxying only works in a point-to-point fashion between the requesting CAS and a CAS in the same site as the Mailbox server. If firewalls are in place that prevents this traffic, the CAS will not negotiate a hop-to-hop route via another site where there is connectivity.

In previous versions of Exchange, there were a couple of cases where proxying could not be used: when connecting via IMAP or POP3. However, Exchange 2010 now provides support for IMAP and POP3 proxying. Client Access servers are configured for proxying IMAP and POP3 by default. Proxying only works for virtual directories configured for Integrated Windows authentication, which means if you want Forms-based authentication (FBA) or Basic Authentication to be used internally, you will need to configure a separate Outlook Web App virtual directory for use when inside your network.

To provide a better understanding of proxying, we want to introduce you to two important parameters. The `InternalURL` and `ExternalURL` parameters can be specified on web-accessible virtual directories, such as Outlook Web App, the Exchange Control Panel, Exchange ActiveSync, and the Offline Address Book distribution web service. These parameters define how the CAS performs proxying and redirection. In many cases, Client Access servers that are Internet facing should have their public, Internet-accessible URL in the `ExternalURL` parameter for the web services that are accessible over the Internet, such as Outlook Web App or Exchange ActiveSync. For example, this URL could be `https://webmail.domain.com/owa`. If you don't specify an `ExternalURL` for your Internet-facing servers, those servers won't be used for client redirection. If you are using a single-site configuration, you don't need the `ExternalURL` specified for OWA. However, if you want to take advantage of using Autodiscover for external client configuration, you will still need to configure `ExternalURL` for Exchange ActiveSync, Offline Address Book distribution, and Exchange Web Services.

In the `InternalURL` parameter, the CAS should have the URL that users inside the network will use to access it. This is important, because when a Client Access server (CAS-1) realizes that the mailbox it's looking for isn't in its site, it looks in Active Directory to find another Client Access server (CAS-2) that is in the same site as the mailbox that it wants to access. When CAS-1 uses CAS-2 as a proxy, CAS-1 uses the `InternalURL` parameter for CAS-2 to figure out how to connect to it. If your `InternalURL` is wrong or missing, that server can't be used for proxying.

Back in Exchange Server 2007, only the `InternalURL` was specified during installation. If your organization had Internet-facing Client Access servers, you had to configure the `ExternalURL` parameters on the virtual directories after Exchange was installed. However, there is a new screen added to the Exchange Setup process in Exchange Server 2010 that allows you to configure your external URL when the CAS is installed and the appropriate virtual directories are configured for you. This screen is shown in Figure 24.10.

FIGURE 24.10
Configuring the external URL for Client Access servers during Exchange setup

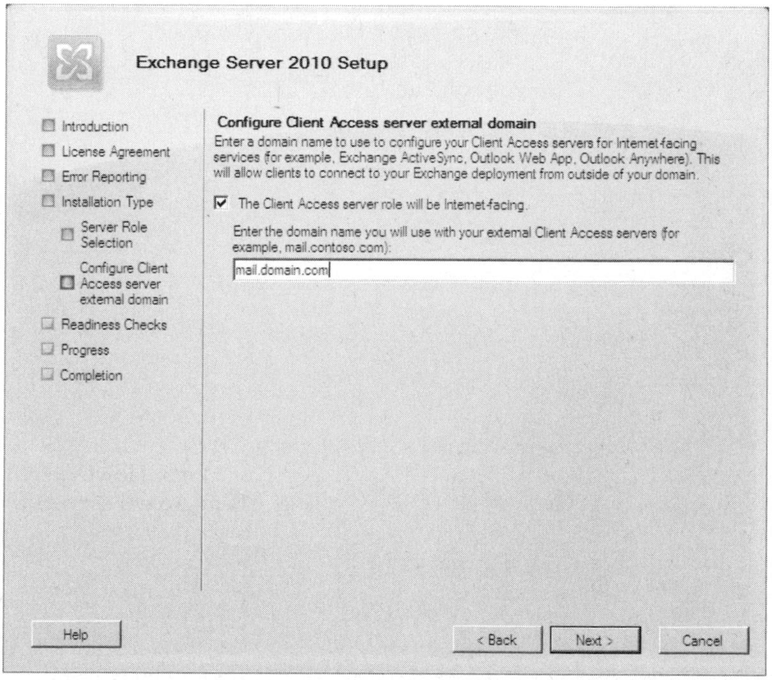

The `InternalURL` is the server's fully qualified domain name (FQDN), which is also what the default self-signed certificate (see the section "Certificates" later in this chapter) uses for its subject name. This could potentially be the name that the clients inside your network will use to access the service on your CAS. If you are configuring a CAS only for internal access (either for use by internal clients or for other Client Access servers that proxy requests to it), you should set the ExternalURL parameter to $Null for the virtual directories listed here:

◆ Outlook Web App

◆ Exchange Control Panel

◆ Offline Address Book

◆ Exchange ActiveSync

◆ Exchange Web Services

◆ PowerShell

Table 24.1 summarizes the recommended InternalURL and ExternalURL configurations. There are some important things that you should note about this information. First, a split-brain DNS architecture is assumed. This means that the namespace used on your internal DNS servers is also the namespace used on your external DNS servers. Technically both zones are authoritative, but the server used will depend on whether the client is coming from inside or outside your network. Second, this information assumes that you are using load-balanced Client Access servers, which we recommend as a standard practice in Exchange 2010. And finally, you should configure the AutoDiscoverServiceInternalUri property to be the FQDN of the load balancer on the CAS and the EWS property called InternalNLBBypassURL should be set to the Client Access server FQDN.

TABLE 24.1: Recommended InternalURL and ExternalURL Configurations

VIRTUAL DIRECTORY	InternalURL	ExternalURL (INTERNET-FACING SERVERS)	ExternalURL (NON-INTERNET-FACING SERVERS)
OWA	CAS Server FQDN	Load-Balancer FQDN	$null
EWS	Load-Balancer FQDN	Load-Balancer FQDN	$null
ActiveSync	Load-Balancer FQDN	Load-Balancer FQDN	$null
Offline Address Book	Load-Balancer FQDN	Load-Balancer FQDN	$null
Unified Messaging	Load-Balancer FQDN	Load-Balancer FQDN	$null
ECP	Load-Balancer FQDN	Load-Balancer FQDN	$null

If you don't specify an external URL for your Client Access servers during Exchange setup, the ExternalURL parameter will already be empty. You only need to go back and clear the parameter if you've specified an external URL for your CAS but don't want every web service available externally. For example, you could disable the ExternalURL parameter for the Outlook Web App service, but keep it enabled for the OAB distribution service. You can only clear the ExternalURL parameter on some of the virtual directories using the Exchange Management Console (EMC). For the rest, you will need to use the Exchange

Management Shell (EMS). Table 24.2 lists each EMS cmdlet that you can use to clear the ExternalURL parameter.

TABLE 24.2: EMS Cmdlets for Setting the ExternalURL Parameters on Different Virtual Directories

VIRTUAL DIRECTORY	EMS CMDLET
Outlook Web App	Set-OwaVirtualDirectory
Exchange Control Panel	Set-EcpVirtualDirectory
Offline Address Book	Set-OabVirtualDirectory
Exchange ActiveSync	Set-ActiveSyncVirtualDirectory
Exchange Web Services	Set-WebServicesVirtualDirectory
PowerShell	Set-PowerShellVirtualDirectory

The following example demonstrates the usage of the Set-OwaVirtualDirectory cmdlet in the EMS to set the default OWA virtual directory ExternalURL parameter to a null value:

```
Set-OwaVirtualDirectory "CAS-1\owa (Default Web Site)" -ExternalURL $Null
```

OUTLOOK WEB APP AND THE EXCHANGE CONTROL PANEL

Outlook Web App and the Exchange Control Panel are closely tied together. Users will be logging into OWA to read their mail and then use the ECP to access their options. If you set an ExternalURL for OWA, but not for ECP, users may not be able to use the Options button in OWA. When setting the ExternalURL parameter on the OWA virtual directory, make sure that you set the ExternalURL parameter on the ECP virtual directory as well.

To demonstrate how the InternalURL and ExternalURL affect proxying, let's take another look at what happens when Nora tries to get to her mail from that Baltimore CAS. Here's what happens when Nora tries to open Outlook Web App:

1. The CAS in Baltimore (CAS-1) locates a CAS in the same Active Directory site as Nora's Mailbox server (Honolulu).

2. The Baltimore CAS determines if the Honolulu CAS has the ExternalURL property configured. If it does, Nora's web session is manually redirected to the Honolulu CAS (more on redirection in the next section of this chapter).

3. If the Honolulu CAS does not have the ExternalURL set, then the Baltimore CAS checks for an InternalURL on the Honolulu CAS.

4. If the InternalURL is configured and the web service is configured to use Integrated Windows authentication, the connection is proxied to the location specified in the InternalURL property.

Client Redirection

Redirection occurs when you set up multiple Internet-facing Client Access servers in different Active Directory sites. If a user connects to a CAS that is not in the same site as their mailbox, and if there is an Internet-facing CAS that is in the same site as the user's mailbox, the user will be redirected to the Internet-facing CAS in the site that their mailbox is in. Redirection is useful because it's generally a good idea to avoid proxying when possible. There's nothing inherently wrong with proxying, but the user will get the best experience when connecting to a CAS in the same site as their Mailbox server. Also, redirection puts less of a toll on WAN utilization.

For Outlook Web App, this redirection comes in the form of a web page redirection, as shown in Figure 24.11. This is simply a web page that tells the user that they would be better off using the CAS closest to their site. This does not happen automatically; the user has to physically click the link to the site that it's being redirected to.

FIGURE 24.11
The Outlook Web App
redirection page

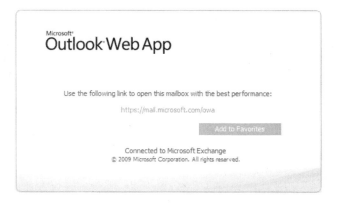

For this process to work, the CAS that the user connects to needs to be able to determine whether the CAS near the user's mailbox is Internet facing. To make this determination, the server uses the `ExternalURL` parameter. If the `ExternalURL` is filled out, the server is considered Internet facing. Our recommendation is to configure your Internet-facing Client Access server web services with different URLs. Since Active Directory sites typically align to physical regions, many organizations use a geographic URL, such as `ne-owa.domain.com` or `mail.europe.domain.com`.

🌐 Real World Scenario

COMPLEXITY IN PROXYING AND REDIRECTION

Over the years, we've picked up several lessons in IT that have stuck with us. We want to share two of those lessons with you right now. Not only are they relevant to proxying and redirection, they are also easy to ignore, especially when you get wrapped up in a particular design. The first lesson is to make sure that you understand how something works before rolling out into production. And the second lesson is to keep your designs as simple as possible.

A couple of years ago, one of the authors worked with a client in a worldwide Exchange Server 2007 deployment. This organization had many sites with Exchange servers and every site was

Internet facing. They didn't want their users to have to remember different URLs for accessing OWA, so they decided to attempt using the same namespace for every site. This client didn't understand that the external URLs were used for redirection. So when all the external URLs for OWA are configured for the same namespace, `mail.contoso.com`, nothing redirects like it's supposed to.

To get around this, they issued regional namespaces to their Client Access servers. They then bought a third-party DNS appliance that can resolve a DNS query differently based on the IP address of the computer performing the query. The idea is that the user would type in `https://mail.contoso.com` and it would resolve to the DNS alias of the regional external URL physically closest to them. This solution works fine for users who are using OWA when they are geographically close to their Mailbox servers; however, when users travel they get a manual redirection anyway. In addition, this solution wreaks havoc when users use `mail.contoso.com` for Outlook Anywhere and Exchange ActiveSync.

The lesson here is that it would have been a lot easier and simpler to just have users use their regional URLs to begin with. Then thousands of dollars would have been saved by not buying the special DNS appliances, and the complexity of the design would have been reduced tremendously.

Client Access Arrays

Now that the RPC client access endpoint has been moved away from the Mailbox server and out to the CAS instead, it's especially important to ensure that your Client Access servers are highly available. You can have a dozen mailbox database replicas in your DAG, replicated off site, but if you have one CAS, you seriously cripple your resiliency capabilities due to this single point of failure. If the CAS that a user is connected to goes down, the user will lose their MAPI connection and their profile will need to be reconfigured to connect to another CAS in that site. To avoid this problem, you can use a load-balanced Client Access array instead of using stand-alone Client Access servers.

The Client Access array object in Active Directory only provides a unified namespace for mailbox databases in the site. To make your Client Access servers resilient, you need to use a load balancer with the array. A variety of products are available for load-balancing your Client Access servers. However, if you only need basic load-balancing functionality with a small number of load-balanced Client Access servers (fewer than eight), we recommend that you check out Microsoft's free Network Load Balancing component, which is built into Windows Server. If you have a heavily used environment and anticipate having more than just a few Client Access servers in an array, you may want to consider going with a third-party load balancer.

It's important to understand that a load-balanced Client Access array is only used to provide resiliency for users connected inside the network with Outlook clients. You can still have resiliency for OWA and other web services on your Client Access servers, but you will need to define those ports independently in the load balancer.

LOAD-BALANCING YOUR CLIENT ACCESS SERVERS

The first step in building a Client Access array is to load-balance your Client Access servers. If you want to load-balance fewer than eight Client Access servers and if you only need basic load-balancing functionality, we recommend looking at the Network Load Balancing (NLB) service in Windows Server 2008 R2. NLB presents a virtual name and IP address for all of your Client Access servers in the array. Each node in the array gets either a multicast

MAC address or the MAC address on one of their network cards replaced with a custom unicast MAC address. Whether unicast or multicast is used depends entirely on how you configure NLB.

When you configure your load balancer, you will need to specify the ports that you want to be load-balanced between the servers. Outlook clients inside your network establish a MAPI connection to your CAS using RPC. Since many different applications and processes on a server use RPC, RPC can't use a single port for communications. Instead, RPC uses an endpoint mapper to negotiate the port to use. The RPC endpoint mapper always uses port 135. The negotiated port is assigned from a pool of ports ranging from port 1024 to port 65535. Therefore, to enable RPC in the load-balanced array, you will need to specify the following ports:

◆ RPC Endpoint Mapper: TCP 135

◆ RPC Dynamic Port Range: UDP/TCP 1024-65535

You don't know which port the RPC endpoint mapper is going to negotiate to use. So you need to use the entire range to ensure that the port that is picked is properly load-balanced. The port assignment in the NLB configuration is shown in Figure 24.12.

FIGURE 24.12
Port range configured for NLB

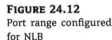

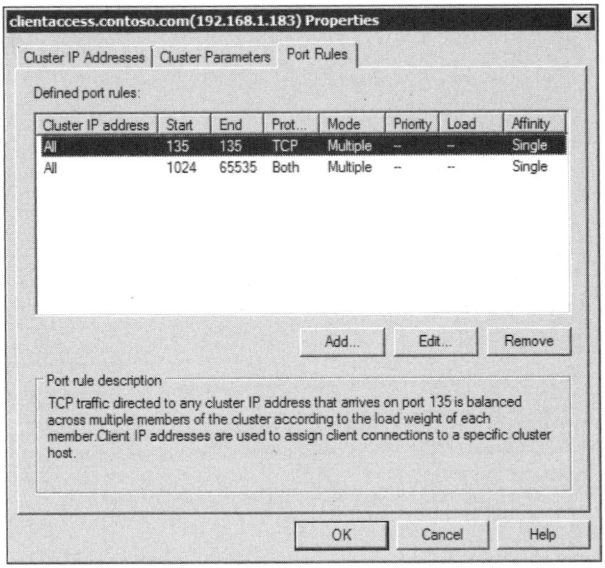

clientaccess.contoso.com(192.168.1.183) Properties

Cluster IP Addresses | Cluster Parameters | Port Rules

Defined port rules:

Cluster IP address	Start	End	Prot...	Mode	Priority	Load	Affinity
All	135	135	TCP	Multiple	--	--	Single
All	1024	65535	Both	Multiple	--	--	Single

Add... Edit... Remove

Port rule description

TCP traffic directed to any cluster IP address that arrives on port 135 is balanced across multiple members of the cluster according to the load weight of each member. Client IP addresses are used to assign client connections to a specific cluster host.

OK Cancel Help

CONFIGURE DNS

After you have your load-balanced Client Access servers up and running, you must ensure that DNS is updated. You will want to create a host record that points the hostname of the load-balanced Client Access servers to the virtual IP address that the load balancer is using. For example, if you named your load-balanced array `outlook.contoso.com`, you must ensure that `outlook.contoso.com` resolves to the virtual IP address of the array.

CONFIGURING THE CLIENT ACCESS ARRAY

The final step is to create the Client Access array object and assign it to a site. You can create the Client Access array using the following command:

```
New-ClientAccessArray -FQDN outlook.domain.com -Site Baltimore ↵
-Name "Baltimore Array"
```

By creating this object, you create a virtual CAS that mailbox databases can use for their `RPCClientAccessServer` parameter. When you create a mailbox database, if a Client Access array object exists in the site, the database automatically uses the array for the `RPCClientAccessServer`. However, if you created a mailbox database before you create the array, the mailbox database will be using the name of the Client Access server itself for the `RPCClientAccessServer`. Therefore, if you have any mailbox databases that existed in the site before array was added, you need to update the `RPCClientAccessServer` parameters on those mailbox databases to point to the array. To do this, you would use the `Set-MailboxDatabase` cmdlet with the `RPCClientAccessServer` parameter. The following command demonstrates how this is done:

```
Set-MailboxDatabase DB01 -RPCClientAccessServer outlook.contoso.com
```

Interoperability with Earlier Versions of Exchange

The interoperability and transition story for Exchange Server 2010 Client Access servers is a little different from the transition story from Exchange Server 2003 to Exchange Server 2007. In this section, we'll examine some of the details around transitioning the Client Access server role from Exchange 2003 and Exchange 2007 to Exchange 2010.

Exchange 2010 Coexistence Behavior

When thinking through your transition plan from your legacy Exchange infrastructure to Exchange 2010, it's important to understand how Exchange 2010 will behave when interacting with your older Exchange servers. For the Client Access server role, specifically, there are several things that you will need to know and keep in mind while you are planning.

The first thing that you should remember is that Exchange 2010 Client Access servers only talk to Exchange 2010 Mailbox servers. The Exchange 2010 CAS will never access an Exchange 2007 or Exchange 2003 Mailbox server directly. However, it will proxy connections to another Exchange 2007 CAS if the CAS doesn't have an external URL defined.

The second thing that you should remember is that your old Exchange 2003 front-end servers and your old Exchange 2007 Client Access servers need to use a different namespace for external access. What we mean by this is that you can't use `mail.contoso.com` for both your Exchange 2010 servers and your Exchange 2003/2007 servers. The reason is that if they use the same namespace, your Exchange 2010 Client Access server can't redirect the connection to the old Exchange server if it needs to. We'll look at this scenario more closely a little later.

The third thing that you should remember is that because your legacy servers require a new namespace, you will probably need to buy a new SAN certificate for them. If you are using wildcard certificates, this shouldn't be an issue.

And the last thing is that you should always transition your Client Access servers from the edge of your network inward. What do we mean by this? First, transition your Internet-facing sites, and then transition your non-Internet-facing sites. Exchange 2010 can handle coexistence scenarios with older versions of Exchange, so you want your users to hit the Exchange 2010 CAS first, and then let the Exchange 2010 CAS redirect or proxy the connection as appropriate.

With these principles in mind, let's take a closer look at the specifics for Exchange 2003 and Exchange 2007.

Coexistence with Exchange Server 2003

As we mentioned earlier, you will want to move your external namespace to your Exchange 2010 Client Access servers and ensure that your clients are touching those servers first when they access their mail from the Internet. Because of this, you will need to determine a new namespace for your old Exchange 2003 Outlook Web Access connections. For example, if your old namespace is mail.contoso.com, you will need to re-point this namespace to your Exchange 2010 servers and use a new namespace, such as e2k3mail.contoso.com, for your Exchange 2003 front-end servers. Don't forget to make the necessary DNS or proxy changes for e2k3mail.contoso.com.

After that, you must ensure that your Exchange 2010 Client Access servers know what URL to use for Exchange 2003 OWA. This is the URL that an Exchange 2010 CAS will use to redirect the Exchange 2003 users to a publicly accessible Exchange 2003 front-end server. It's interesting to note that this redirection is silent (the user won't know it's redirecting) if you have Forms-based authentication configured on your Exchange 2010 CAS and your Exchange 2003 front-end server. You configure this URL on your Exchange 2010 Client Access servers by running the Set-OwaVirtualDirectory cmdlet with the Exchange2003URL parameter, as shown here:

```
Set-OwaVirtualDirectory "CAS-1\owa (Default Web Site)" ↵
-Exchange2003URL https://e2k3mail.contoso.com/exchange
```

When you are ready to switch your infrastructure over and have your Exchange 2010 Client Access servers take over the entry point into your Internet-facing sites, you just need to make the DNS change to point mail.contoso.com to your Exchange 2010 CAS.

There are two other things that you will probably want to do as well. The first is that if you are using ActiveSync, you should ensure that your Exchange 2003 ActiveSync virtual directory is using Integrated Windows authentication. Second, if you are using RPC over HTTP, you can go ahead and move the connection point to the Exchange 2010 servers and turn off the RPC over HTTP on your Exchange 2003 servers.

Coexistence with Exchange Server 2007

When transitioning from Exchange 2007, you still want to stick to the principle of transitioning your Internet-facing sites first. However, with Exchange 2007, you want to transition the site hosting Autodiscover before the other Internet-facing sites. The proxying and redirection story is also different in Exchange 2007. If a user with an Exchange 2007 mailbox accesses a service on the Exchange 2010 CAS, one of the scenarios outlined in Table 24.3 will happen.

As in Exchange 2003, use a different namespace for your Internet-facing Exchange 2007 Client Access servers. You will move your public namespace (such as mail.contoso.com) to Exchange 2010. If the private keys are exportable on your Exchange 2007 SAN certificates, you can reuse them on your Exchange 2010 CAS, though the internal name will not be on the certificate. For external access scenarios, though, this shouldn't matter.

When you are ready for users to start using the Exchange 2010 CAS, update your DNS records for your existing namespace and point them to your Exchange 2010 CAS. Don't forget to update your Autodiscover record in addition to your public namespace. You will also have

TABLE 24.3:   Coexistence with Exchange Server 2007

SERVICE	EXCHANGE 2007 MAILBOX LOCATION	RESULT
OWA	Same site as Exchange 2010 CAS	Silently redirect to Exchange 2007 CAS
	Different Internet-facing site	Manually redirect to Exchange 2007 CAS
	Different non-Internet-facing site	Proxy connection to Exchange 2007 CAS
ActiveSync	Same site as Exchange 2010 CAS	If device supports Autodiscover, redirects device to Exchange 2007 CAS; if device does not support Autodiscover, proxies connection to Exchange 2007 CAS
	A different non-Internet-facing site	Proxy connection to Exchange 2007 CAS
Outlook Anywhere	Anywhere	Direct connection to the Mailbox server

to reconfigure the external URLs on your Exchange 2007 Client Access servers to use the new namespace. You cannot share the namespace between Exchange 2010 and Exchange 2007. If you don't update your external URLs, Exchange 2010 will not properly handle the redirection for Exchange 2007 mailboxes.

Your transition scenario will be unique to your organization, because it's based on how you implemented the previous versions of Exchange. As always, before going public with Exchange 2010 Client Access servers, test, test, and test!

Certificates

In versions of Exchange prior to Exchange Server 2007, the use of certificates was simple. By default there were none installed, so if you wanted to use one, you requested a certificate with the principal name of your external access URL and installed it on the default website. This gave you secure access to OWA and RPC over HTTP. This process changed starting in Exchange Server 2007. In an effort to ensure that an out-of-the-box Exchange server secures traffic, a self-signed certificate is created by default, which is used for SMTP, POP3, IMAP4, and IIS.

Default Certificate Usage

When Exchange is installed, a self-signed certificate is created by default to offer some semblance of secure communications out of the box. In Exchange Server 2007, the expiration for this certificate was one year. In Exchange Server 2007 SP2 and Exchange Server 2010, the default expiration period for self-signed certificates increased to five years.

You might be wondering what a self-signed certificate is. A self-signed certificate is a certificate that is issued by the computer itself. This basically allows the server to vouch for itself. This is akin to you creating your own driver's license to prove who you are. Someone who knows you, like your parents, trusts you already, so they don't need to verify your homemade driver's license with a third party. In the same manner, if you don't trust the server that issued the self-signed certificate, the certificate is considered invalid. You either need to trust the certificate or issue a certificate to the server by a mutually trusted third party. In the case of your homemade driver's license, you would need to get a state-issued license in order for other people to accept it as valid.

Generally speaking, self-signed certificates don't scale well. They aren't trusted by your clients by default, so your users get annoying warnings. Some services, such as Outlook Anywhere, won't even work with self-signed certificates.

To illustrate, take a look at the default certificate and you will notice some important details. Figure 24.13 shows the certification path details. In this case, the certificate is self-signed, so the certification terminates at the Exchange server that issued itself the certificate.

FIGURE 24.13
The Certificate window showing the certification path

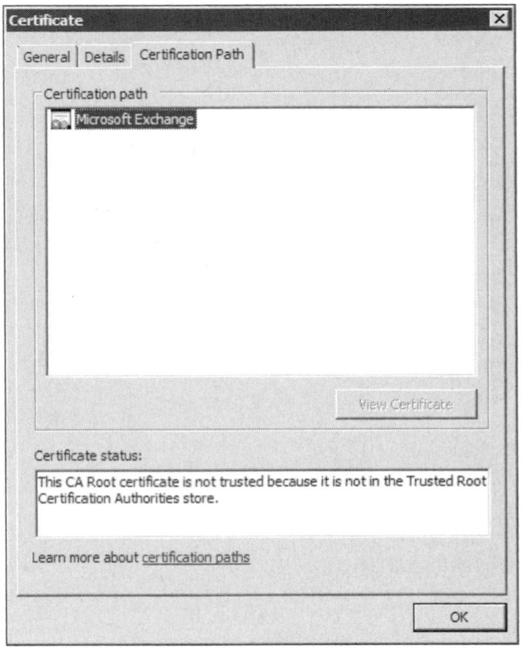

Using Subject Alternative Name (SAN) Certificates

As you've learned by now, Client Access servers can operate under the guise of many names. A few of the ways that you can refer to a CAS is by the hostname, fully qualified internal domain name, fully qualified external domain name, Autodiscover name, and any aliases that you might use. This can be a tricky situation with certificates because certificates require that the subject name in the certificate be the same name that you use to access the server. For example, if you issued your certificate to your CAS with the Subject Name of `cas-1.contoso.com`, then if you were to browse to `https://cas-1.contoso.com/owa`, everything would check out fine. However, if you were to browse to `https://mail.contoso.com/owa`, the certificate would fail validation because the URL has a different name than the Subject Name in the certificate. The way to solve this problem in Exchange is to use a certificate that allows you to use multiple names. Two types of certificates allow you to do this:

◆ Wildcard certificate

◆ Subject Alternative Name (SAN) certificate

Wildcard certificates allow you to specify a wildcard character in the name. For example, a wildcard certificate for *.contoso.com will allow you to use mail.contoso.com, cas-1.contoso.com, mail.europe.contoso.com, and so forth. Wildcard certificates tend to be a more expensive option, so many organizations will opt for the second option, SAN certificates.

SAN certificates have an additional field in the certificate called Subject Alternative Name. You input several other names in this field that you want the server to be accessed with. Certificates that support Subject Alternate Names are also referred to as Unified Communications Certificates. To find certificate authorities that will issue this type of certificate, search the Internet for "Subject Alternate Name" or "Unified Communications Certificates." Microsoft has also provided a list of certificate authorities that it has partnered with to provide Exchange-specific websites for issuing the right certificates. This list is kept at http://support.microsoft.com/kb/929395.

When specifying the common name for a SAN certificate, you should use the name that will most frequently be used from the Internet, such as mail.contoso.com. Figure 24.14 shows a SAN certificate with a couple of entries in the Subject Alternative Name field. Keep in mind that you only need to include names in the certificate that will be used to access the server over SSL. If your users won't be using the NetBIOS name (contoso-ex01) or the server's FQDN (contoso-ex01.contoso.com), those names don't need to be included in the certificate.

FIGURE 24.14
The Subject Alternative
Name field of the default
certificate

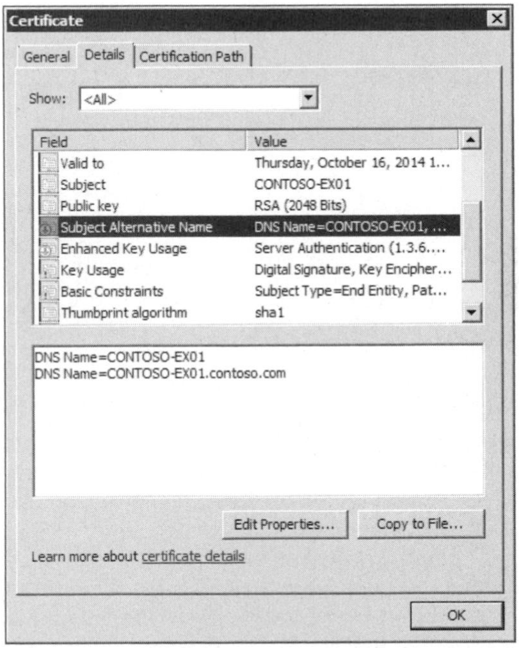

You also need to know where and how you can get one of these SAN certificates. You can get them either from yourself (self-signed) or from a third-party certificate authority like Comodo, DigiCert, and Entrust. One thing to bear in mind is that these certificates can be expensive and sometimes a little hard to obtain; not all third-party certificate authorities will issue you one. Check with the certificate authority you are planning to use.

USING THE EXCHANGE CERTIFICATE WIZARDS

The New Exchange Certificate wizard and the Import Exchange Certificate wizard are new tools in the EMC that help you more easily configure your certificates. The wizards walk you through the process of generating certificate requests and importing existing certificates.

You will find these wizards in the Server Configuration node of the EMC. Select the server that you want to acquire a certificate for and then choose the appropriate wizard from the Actions pane, as shown in Figure 24.15.

FIGURE 24.15
Launching the Exchange Certificate wizards

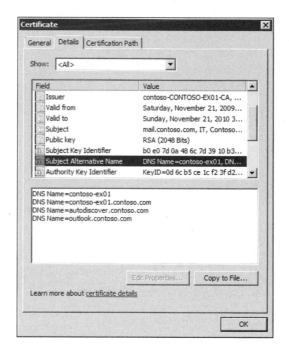

To acquire a new certificate, you first need to use the New Exchange Certificate wizard to walk you through the process of generating your certificate request. The wizard does a nice job of presenting you with relevant certificate options, including the option to generate a request for a wildcard certificate. The Exchange Configuration screen in the wizard presents the entire list of Exchange services that you might like to use the certificate for. You can go through each service and check or uncheck the appropriate options, as well as customize the names in the certificate. Figure 24.16 demonstrates this functionality in the wizard.

After you finish going through the wizard, a certificate request file is generated. You will need to give this certificate request to your certificate authority. They will use this request to issue you the certificate. When they issue the certificate, they will return it to you in the form of another file. This is the file that you will use to complete the certificate request.

After you have your certificate in hand, you can go back into the Server Configuration node in the EMC and complete the certificate installation. Select the server that certificate request is for and the list of outstanding requests is displayed in the bottom pane. Select the request that you previously generated and choose the Complete Pending Request task from

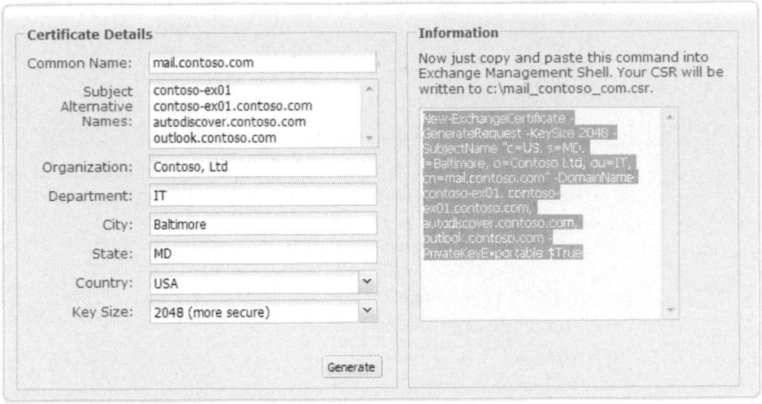

FIGURE 24.16
Configuring the names
for use in the certificate
using the New Exchange
Certificate wizard

FIGURE 24.16
Configuring the names
for use in the certificate
using the New Exchange
Certificate wizard

the Actions pane, as shown in Figure 24.17. Follow the Complete Pending Request wizard to import your certificate.

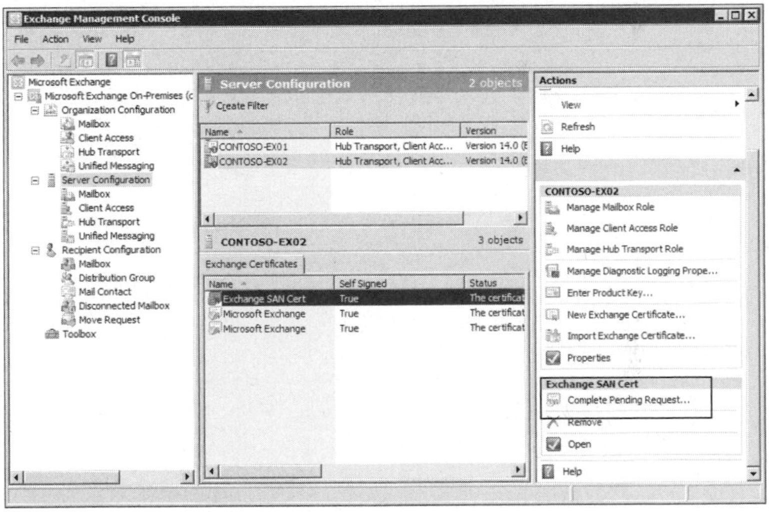

FIGURE 24.17
Completing the certifi-
cate request in the EMC

GENERATING A CERTIFICATE REQUEST IN THE EMS

In addition to using the New Exchange Certificate wizard, you can generate the certificate request using the EMS. Use the following steps to get a SAN certificate using the EMS:

1. First, decide on the external name for your email access (in this case, `email.domain.com`).

2. Next, open the EMS and generate your certificate request using a command like the following (substituting your domain names):

```
New-ExchangeCertificate -GenerateRequest -DomainName email.domain.com, ↵
autodiscover.domain.com,hostname,internaldomain.com, ↵
hostname.internaldomain.com -FriendlyName "Exchange SAN cert" ↵
-PrivateKeyExportable:$true | Set-Content -path c:\ExchSANcert.req
```

Make sure that the first domain you enter is the external one that you will use for Outlook Anywhere and Outlook Web App. This domain goes into the Subject Name field of the certificate and is required by Outlook Anywhere in the Outlook client's configuration.

3. After running the command, you will have a text file in the path specified (in this case, C:\ExchSANcert.req), which you should submit to your certificate authority (your internal one or a certificate authority like DigiCert or VeriSign).

4. Once you receive the certificate back, you need to import it using the following command:

```
Import-ExchangeCertificate -Path c:\certificate.cer
```

5. When you run the `Import-ExchangeCertificate` command, the output will contain a `ThumbPrint`, which is what you will use to refer to the certificate in future commands. Make a note of it.

6. Enable the certificate by using the following command, which will enable use for all Exchange services:

```
Enable-ExchangeCertificate -ThumbPrint [Value] -Services "IIS,SMTP,IMAP,POP"
```

When you check the SAN field after you configure your new certificate, you will see all the entries you specified, as shown in Figure 24.18.

FIGURE 24.18
The SAN entries for a certificate

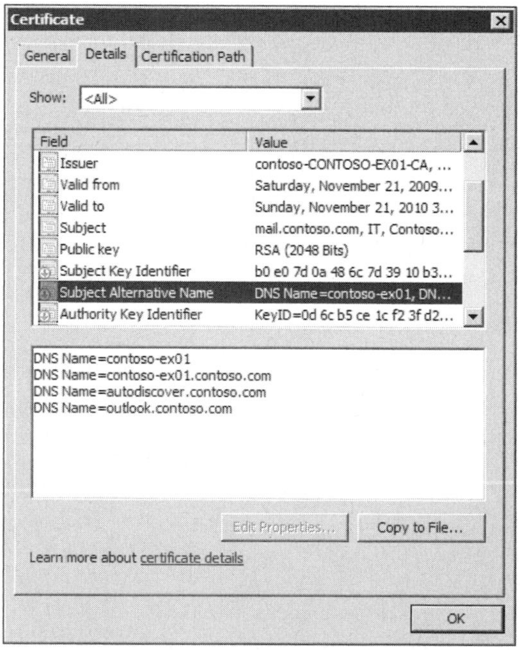

The Bottom Line

Configure Client Access server arrays.   Now that clients connect to Client Access servers for MAPI RPC connectivity, it's even more important that your Client Access servers be highly available. By placing your Client Access servers in load-balanced arrays, you can increase the redundancy and availability of your environment.

> **Master It**   To increase the resiliency of the Client Access servers in your company's main datacenter, you have decided to place them in a Windows NLB cluster. You want to ensure that your users can use Outlook while inside the network to access their email. What ports do you need to ensure are load-balanced in the array?

Generate valid subject alternative name certificates.   Each Client Access server has multiple names that clients use to access it. To secure access to the server using all of the names used, you need to issue Subject Alternative Name certificates to your Client Access servers. SAN certificates allow you to specify multiple names for your server in a single certificate.

> **Master It**   Your company, Contoso Pharmaceuticals, implements a split-brain DNS architecture. Your main campus in Baltimore has an array of six Client Access servers called outlook.contoso.com. Each server in the array is named accordingly, starting at CONTOSO-CAS1 and ending at CONTOSO-CAS6. This same Client Access array also serves Outlook Web App clients and Outlook Anywhere clients under the name of mail.contoso.com. You need to make sure that your Client Access servers have the right certificates to operate correctly when accessed from both inside and outside the organization. What Subject Alternative Names need to be used in the certificate, and which name should be used for the Subject Name field?

Configure proxying and redirection.   For users to access their mailboxes, they need to go through a Client Access server that is in the same Active Directory site as their Mailbox server. Client Access servers need to communicate to the Mailbox server through RPC. If the Client Access servers in the same site as a user's mailbox aren't exposed to the Internet, then Internet-based users will need to access their email from Client Access servers in another site. The Internet-facing Client Access servers will proxy the connection to the non-Internet-facing Client Access servers.

> **Master It**   You have a Client Access server in two primary datacenters, one in Baltimore (cas-bal.contoso.com) and another in Honolulu (cas-hon.contoso.com). You also have a Client Access server in your branch offices in Seattle (cas-sea.contoso.com), Atlanta (cas-atl.contoso.com), and Amarillo (cas-ama.contoso.com).You want to ensure that only the Baltimore and Honolulu Client Access servers can be used over the Internet. You want users in Baltimore, Atlanta, and Amarillo to use mail-east.contoso.com and you want users in Honolulu and Seattle to use mail-west.contoso.com when accessing their email from outside the network. How should you configure your internal and external URLs for each of these Client Access servers to support your desired outcome?

Transition Client Access servers from previous versions of Exchange.   When replacing your legacy Client Access servers, you will want to start from the edge of your network and work your way in. Therefore, you want to transition Internet-facing Client Access servers first. When transitioning from Exchange Server 2003, you will want to use a new namespace for your Exchange Server 2003 URLs and move the old namespace to the Exchange Server 2010 Client Access servers. When transitioning from Exchange Server 2007, you can use the same namespace on your Exchange Server 2010 Client Access servers.

Master It   Your current environment is composed of both Exchange Server 2003 and Exchange Server 2007 servers. You decide to install your Exchange 2010 Client Access servers in an Internet-facing site using the same namespace as your existing Exchange 2007 Client Access servers. You notice that users with mailboxes on Exchange 2007 can no longer access their email through OWA. However, users with Exchange 2010 mailboxes can use OWA just fine. What should you do to fix this problem?

Chapter 25

Managing Connectivity with Hub Transport Servers

Exchange Server's primary purpose is to send, receive, and store messages. In previous versions of Exchange, messages delivered locally (to a user whose mailbox was on your mailbox database or another database on the same server) never actually left that particular server. In fact, they never even left the Information Store service's handle. That changed with Exchange Server 2007 and has been built upon in Exchange Server 2010.

The Hub Transport server role is responsible for moving messages from one mailbox to another. All messages must pass through the Hub Transport server role. This lightens the transport load on the Mailbox server role and centralizes transport to a single server role.

In this chapter, you will learn to:

◆ Create and manage send connectors

◆ Create and manage receive connectors

◆ Design an Exchange routing topology

Transport Improvements in Exchange Server 2010

Before we delve into how internal email routing works, it's worth noting a few of the many improvements Exchange 2010 delivers in comparison to earlier versions of Exchange.

Prior to Exchange Server 2007, all messages were processed by the same server that connected MAPI clients, managed the information store, and hosted Outlook Web Access. This all-in-one approach worked well for many years, but it couldn't scale with the growing needs of organizations that had become increasingly dependent on their messaging systems. To remedy this, Microsoft abstracted all message-processing and delivery functions into the Hub Transport server role. The Hub Transport server role processes all messages regardless of their source or destination — even if they're in the same mailbox database or on the same server. At first blush, this may seem inefficient compared to routing in previous versions of Exchange. But when you take into account features like message classification, transport rules, and journaling, it makes sense for the Hub Transport server to offload some of the Mailbox server role's burden. Actually, those transport features have made it essential for the Hub

Transport server to now handle all messages in flight. Exchange Server 2010 lets you do a lot with a message while it is in transit (see Chapter 26, "Managing Transport and Journaling Rules").

The Hub Transport server role can share a server with any other server role, except for Edge Transport servers. This means that if a Mailbox server does not also host the Hub Transport server, then the entire message is transferred to the Hub Transport server over the network via remote procedure calls (RPCs), categorized, and finally routed to the appropriate location. This is true even if that location is the same mailbox database from which the message originated. This is one of the reasons that it is so critical to have a Hub Transport server in each Active Directory site that contains a Mailbox server. One of the design goals (well, not a goal, but a direct result) was to abstract message transport functions out of the Mailbox server completely. To properly control message flow, all messages should be processed by a standard group of servers, exactly the same way. As long as there are any types of transport functions being run by the Mailbox server role, this goal cannot be met.

Also, the message transport architecture needs to be able to treat all messages equally when processing transport rules and other transport agents. Otherwise, transport rules would apply only to server-to-server messages. By having the entire message sent through the Hub Transport server, you can apply rules or functions not only to the message header, but also to the entire message body and attachments.

Looking back to earlier versions of Exchange, administrators used *routing groups* (called *sites* in Exchange 5.5) to build their email routing systems. Routing groups allowed organizations to engineer a message transport solution unique to their topology, but they were often superfluous to another underlying architecture, Active Directory (AD). Exchange Server 2010 leverages your existing infrastructure by defining an AD site as the natural boundary for the email routing infrastructure. As long as your AD topology (including sites, site links, and site link costs) is correctly designed, Exchange will automatically discover the most efficient way to route email. However, between sites Exchange servers will always initiate a point-to-point connection for message delivery, rather than playing Pass-The-Message-Along with other Exchange servers. More on that later in the section "Message Routing in the Organization."

Many Exchange administrators were puzzled by the fact that Exchange 2000 and 2003 depended on Internet Information Server (IIS) for SMTP services (which was not the case in Exchange 5.5). Happily, Exchange 2007 replaced IIS virtual SMTP servers with send and receive connectors for establishing SMTP connections — all of which is managed from within the Exchange Management Console (or Shell). This means that IIS is no longer required by Exchange Server 2010 Server to perform email routing.

In maintaining the spirit of separating tasks, the Edge Transport server role is the one server dedicated to message delivery and filtering tasks. This hardened Exchange server's purpose is to accept and deliver Internet email and perform *message hygiene* functions (such as antispam, content filtering, and antivirus) on messages before they enter the internal network.

The Edge Transport server is separated from the rest of the Exchange server roles because it does not communicate directly with Active Directory but utilizes an Active Directory Lightweight Directory Services (LDS, previously known as ADAM) directory database stored locally on the server. The Edge Transport server role was designed to exist in a perimeter network/demilitarized zone (DMZ) segregated from the internal network. Both the Edge Transport and the Hub Transport servers facilitate transport in an Exchange organization.

Unlike a front-end server in Exchange Server 2003, an Edge Transport server does not require connectivity to your internal AD infrastructure to route email and only requires minimal ports to be opened from your internal network (where your Hub Transport servers reside) to the DMZ.

Message Routing in the Organization

Let's start with a review of how Exchange 2010 delivers messages in a single Exchange organization. While similar to Exchange Server 2007, the message-routing architecture is sufficiently different from earlier versions of Exchange 2000/2003 (which is the version from which more administrators are moving to Exchange Server 2010) that it deserves additional mention.

You should understand a few important points about the basics of Exchange 2010 message routing:

◆ All messages must go through the Hub Transport server role.

◆ The Active Directory site architecture is used as a boundary for message routing.

◆ All Active Directory sites that contain a Mailbox server must also have a Hub Transport server and a Client Access server.

One of the nice features of Exchange Server 2010 is that as long as your Active Directory site architecture has been properly configured, you will not need to worry about message-routing architecture design.

Basics of Exchange Message Routing

In earlier versions of Exchange, the message-routing architecture was based on a structure that was defined by the administrator. For example, in Exchange 2000/2003, the message-routing architecture was defined by a collection of servers separated by full-time and reasonably good available bandwidth. This collection of servers is called a *routing group*. Prior to Exchange 2000, all servers were grouped together into a single collection of servers called a *site*.

In Exchange 2000/2003, the administrator could define the routing groups and move servers between routing groups based on their message-routing requirements. Messages were then delivered between routing groups using some type of connector. The most common connector for routing groups is a connector called the *routing group connector* (RGC), which uses RPC or SMTP to deliver messages.

Exchange Server 2007 changed this by relying on the Active Directory site architecture rather than requiring administrators to create a separate routing infrastructure for their organization. Exchange Server 2010 builds on this major architectural change and continues to rely on Active Directory sites for message routing. Figure 25.1 shows a simple Active Directory site topology that consists of three Active Directory sites.

In Figure 25.1, each Active Directory site has a Mailbox server and a Hub Transport server. The Hub Transport server will always attempt a direct delivery of a message to a Hub Transport server in a remote Active Directory site even if that remote Active Directory site does not have an Active Directory site link directly to it. If you are still running any Exchange 2003 servers, though, they retain their routing group architecture and have routing group connectors to the Exchange 2010 Hub Transport servers.

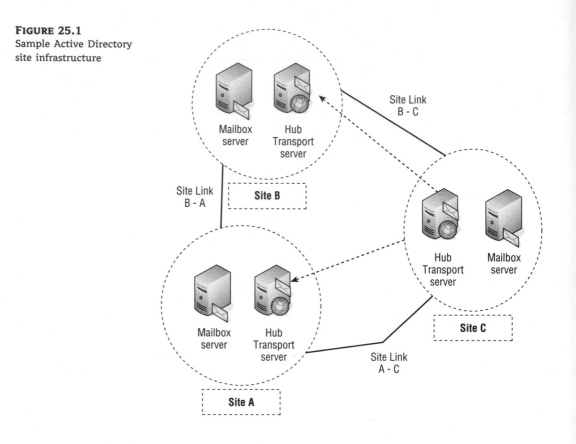

FIGURE 25.1
Sample Active Directory
site infrastructure

CUSTOMIZING ROUTING

For some companies, the default site routing mechanism is not adequate.

Earlier, we briefly described a major architectural change for Exchange Server 2007 that was also adopted by Exchange Server 2010. This change is direct point-to-point connection (notwithstanding the underlining network infrastructure) for email delivery, which basically summarizes the *desire* of an Exchange server to deliver a message to its final destination site. If that delivery is not successful, a Hub Transport server will try to contact another Hub Transport for queuing and later delivery.

By default, Exchange Server 2010 Hub Transport servers always attempt to directly deliver a message to a remote Hub Transport server (in another Active Directory site). This feature ensures the quickest and most direct delivery of email messages to remote sites. The Hub Transport server ignores the Active Directory site link costs (and possibly your underlying network topology) and performs direct delivery. Note that Active Directory site link costs are relevant if the final destination is unavailable, and then the next site along the least cost route is contacted for email queuing. The servers in that site will then attempt to redeliver the message to the final destination based on its configured intervals.

We recently consulted for a company that required all email be delivered through a "hub" site. This is still possible by modifying the behavior of the Hub Transport delivery mechanism using the Set-AdSite Exchange Management Shell cmdlet. To make this functionality work, we followed these steps:

1. Enable the hub site functionality using a command similar to this:

   ```
   Set-AdSite SiteName -HubSiteEnable $True
   ```

2. Ensure that the Active Directory site link costs truly represent a "least cost" route from the remote sites to the hub site. Why? Well, the *override* feature of a hub site *only* works if that hub site is within the least cost path, as defined by the Active Directory Site Link costs. If the Hub Site is not within the least cost path and you don't want to disrupt your Active Directory replication topology, you can also create an Exchange-specific site link cost. The Exchange-specific site link cost is set by using a shell command such as this one:

   ```
   Set-AdSiteLink -Identity SiteLinkName -ExchangeCost CostValue
   ```

Luckily, the environment that we were working with already had the hub site within its least cost path, so that second command was not necessary. After the modifications were made, the Exchange routing topology resembled the underlying network infrastructure of routers and WAN links.

So Microsoft recommends that you implement hub site routing only if your network topology requires it, such as when you have a firewall between all the remote sites.

The Hub Transport server role is at the center of the message-routing architecture for messages being delivered internally as well as messages leaving the organization. All messages are processed by the Hub Transport server role regardless of whether they are being delivered locally or remotely. Figure 25.2 shows an example of the Hub Transport server sitting at the center of the message delivery universe.

The Hub Transport server role handles categorization, rule processing, transport-level journaling, and delivery for mail that is intended for local delivery and Mailbox servers in the same Active Directory site. The Hub Transport server uses the messaging API (MAPI) and RPCs to communicate with the Mailbox server role. If a message is to be delivered to a Mailbox server in a remote Active Directory site, the Hub Transport server delivers the message via SMTP to a Hub Transport server in the remote site; the remote Hub Transport server then delivers the message to the local Mailbox server via RPC.

The Exchange Server 2010 Hub Transport server handles message categorization. The Categorizer component figures out where the message is going next. Messages arrive in the submission queue, and the Categorizer picks up the message and processes it. Here are some of the steps involved in message categorization:

♦ Expand any distribution lists, if applicable, by querying the global catalog.

♦ Resolve recipient addresses to determine which recipients are local, remote, or outside the organization.

♦ Apply message transport rules to the message.

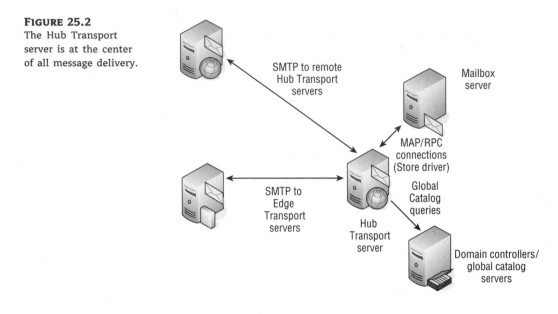

FIGURE 25.2
The Hub Transport server is at the center of all message delivery.

◆ Split the message into multiple parts if the message is going to both local and remote recipients; this process is called *bifurcation*.

◆ Examine the message sender, recipients, message header, body, and attachments and apply message transport rules that apply to that message.

◆ Convert the message to the appropriate message format (Summary-TNEF, MIME, or UUencode) depending on the destination of the message.

◆ Determine the next "hop" for the message.

◆ Place the message into appropriate local or remote delivery queue.

With a few exceptions, such as application transport rules, the Categorizer function has not changed from Exchange 2000/2003.

As messages are moved within your organization's infrastructure, they are protected with different types of encryption. The encryption used is either RPC encryption or Transport Layer Security (TLS) encryption. Figure 25.3 shows different paths the message may take and how it is encrypted.

As messages are transmitted via MAPI over RPC between Mailbox servers and Hub Transport servers, RPC encryption is automatically used. When a message is transmitted from one Hub Transport server to another, the Hub Transport servers transport the message using SMTP, they authenticate using Kerberos, and the data stream is encrypted using TLS. When messages are transmitted from a Hub Transport server to an Edge Transport server, SMTP is used for message transfer, mutual authentication using certificates is used for authentication, and messages are encrypted using TLS. Optionally, an organization that is sending messages to another organization also using Edge Transport services can configure authenticated connections and TLS encryption to these remote organizations.

FIGURE 25.3
Messages are encrypted during transit.

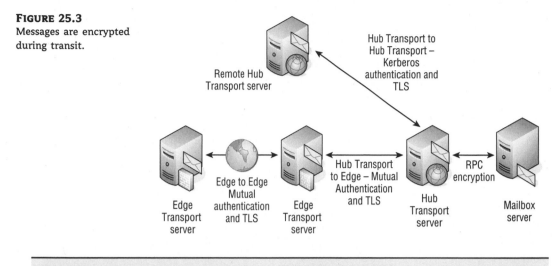

Send and Receive Connectors

In Exchange 2000/2003, each Exchange server had one or more SMTP virtual servers. These SMTP virtual servers received inbound mail from other servers, from outside the organization, or from POP3/IMAP4 clients. The SMTP virtual server could be configured to host an SMTP connector for delivering messages to external SMTP hosts or it could host a routing group connector (RGC) for delivering messages to remote Exchange 2000/2003 routing groups.

Exchange Server 2007/2010 has replaced the SMTP virtual servers and SMTP connectors with send and receive connectors.

Receive Connectors

The receive connector is the point where inbound SMTP mail is received on the Hub Transport server. Receive connectors do not deliver outbound mail (unlike the Exchange 2000/2003 SMTP virtual server). Each Hub Transport server automatically has two receive connectors. These are the Default *servername* connector and the Client *servername* connector. Figure 25.4 shows the Exchange Management Console and the Server Configuration work center. In the Hub Transport subcontainer, you can see each server that hosts the Hub Transport role. The receive connectors for server EX2010 are shown.

FIGURE 25.4

Receive connectors for an Exchange 2010 server

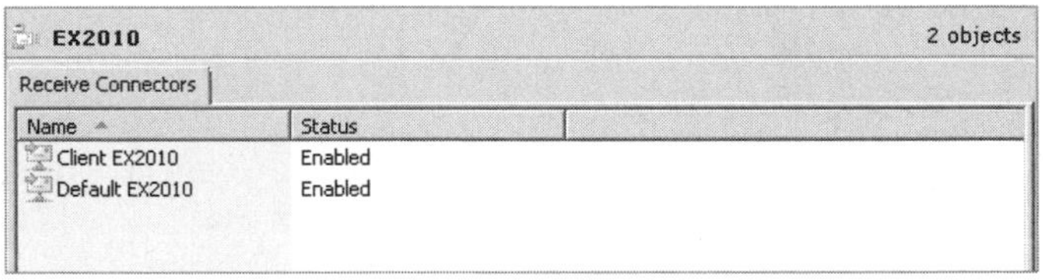

The Client receive connector listens on TCP port number 587, not TCP port 25. TCP port 587 is the alternate port for POP3/IMAP4 clients to access SMTP, as per RFC 2476. The Client receive connector is intended for receiving mail from non-MAPI clients such as POP3 and IMAP4 clients. You would, of course, have to change the non-MAPI client's outbound SMTP port in order to use this connector, though some new POP3/IMAP4 client applications now default to port 587.

The Default receive connector is used to receive inbound SMTP mail from other Exchange 2010 Hub Transport servers in the organization. In Figure 25.5, the Permission Groups properties of the Default EX2010 receive connector are shown. These are the default permissions for the Default receive connector.

FIGURE 25.5

Default receive connector permissions

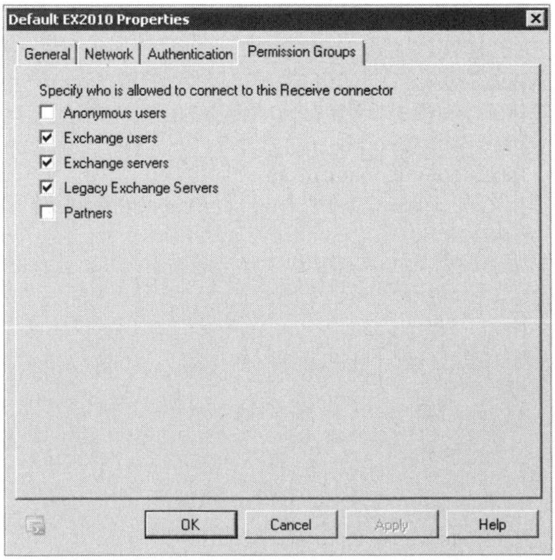

Notice that the Default receive connector does not accept connections from anonymous users. This means that you must modify permissions before you use it to receive email from the Internet; even though the receive connector is listening on TCP port 25. We'll come back to this later when we cover receiving email from the outside in Chapter 27, "Internet and Email."

You can also view the properties of a receive connector using the `Get-ReceiveConnector` cmdlet. Here is an example that displays all the properties of the Default EX2010 receive connector:

```
Get-ReceiveConnector "Default EX2010" | FL
```

```
RunspaceId                             :
f981d6a2-e04e-4fc8-a470-f7377e69e574
AuthMechanism                          :
Tls, Integrated, BasicAuth, BasicAuthRequireTLS, ExchangeServer
Banner                                 :
BinaryMimeEnabled                      : True
Bindings                               : {:::25, 0.0.0.0:25}
ChunkingEnabled                        : True
DefaultDomain                          :
DeliveryStatusNotificationEnabled      : True
EightBitMimeEnabled                    : True
DomainSecureEnabled                    : False
EnhancedStatusCodesEnabled             : True
LongAddressesEnabled                   : False
OrarEnabled                            : False
SuppressXAnonymousTls                  : False
AdvertiseClientSettings                : False
Fqdn                                   : Ex2010.Contoso.com
Comment                                :
Enabled                                : True
ConnectionTimeout                      : 00:10:00
ConnectionInactivityTimeout            : 00:05:00
MessageRateLimit                       : unlimited
MessageRateSource                      : IPAddress
MaxInboundConnection                   : 5000
MaxInboundConnectionPerSource          : unlimited
MaxInboundConnectionPercentagePerSource : 100
MaxHeaderSize                          : 64 KB (65,536 bytes)
MaxHopCount                            : 30
MaxLocalHopCount                       : 8
MaxLogonFailures                       : 3
MaxMessageSize                         : 10 MB (10,485,760 bytes)
MaxProtocolErrors                      : 5
MaxRecipientsPerMessage                : 5000
PermissionGroups                       : ExchangeUsers, ExchangeServers,
ExchangeLegacyServers
PipeliningEnabled                      : True
ProtocolLoggingLevel                   : None
```

```
RemoteIPRanges                      :
{::-ffff:ffff:ffff:ffff:ffff:ffff:ffff:ffff, 0.0.0.0- 255.255.255.255}
RequireEHLODomain                   : False
RequireTLS                          : False
EnableAuthGSSAPI                    : False
LiveCredentialEnabled               : False
Server                              : EX2010
SizeEnabled                         : EnabledWithoutValue
TarpitInterval                      : 00:00:05
MaxAcknowledgementDelay             : 00:00:30
AdminDisplayName                    :
ExchangeVersion                     : 0.1 (8.0.535.0)
Name                                : Default EX2010
DistinguishedName                   : CN=Default EX2010,CN=SMTP Receive
Connectors,CN=Protocols,CN=EX2010,CN=Servers,CN=Exchange Administrative
Group(FYDIBOHF23SPDLT),CN=Administrative Groups,CN=Contoso,CN=Microsoft
Exchange,CN=Services,CN=Configuration,DC=Contoso,DC=com
Identity                            : EX2010\Default EX2010
Guid                                :
e8eb2c53-de0b-4a94-98d1-f5d3965d6d58
ObjectCategory                      :
netlogontech.com/Configuration/Schema/ms-Exch-Smtp-Receive-ConnectorObjectClass:
{top, msExchSmtpReceiveConnector}
WhenChanged                         : 10/07/2009 5:10:38 PM
WhenCreated                         : 10/07/2009 5:10:38 PM
WhenChangedUTC                      : 10/07/2009 9:10:38 PM
WhenCreatedUTC                      : 10/07/2009 9:10:38 PM
OrganizationId                      :
OriginatingServer                   : DC.Contoso.com
IsValid                             : True
```

With few exceptions, you will usually not need to create additional receive connectors, nor will you need to make many changes to the existing receive connectors that are used internally. The only situations that should involve creating new Receive Connectors are when you need to accommodate the needs of a custom application or server that needs to route email through your Exchange servers. For example, you may have a monitoring server that may need to send email internally to your server administrators. In this case, you could use the default Receive connectors, but would then have to customize them for that need. To avoid messing around with the default Receive Connectors, most organization choose to create a new Receive Connector that has a custom IP address range (which would allow only the monitoring server to communicate) and custom permissions (which would allow the monitoring server to relay email through your Receive connector). This solution ensures that you have not, inadvertently, prevented your organization from receiving email because of misconfigurations on your default Receive Connectors.

Send Connectors

Although receive connectors are configured for each server, send connectors are organizational connectors that you can assign to a number of different Hub Transport servers. Each server also has an implicit send connector, but that connector is used only for transferring mail to other

Hub Transport servers. The implicit send connector does not show up either in the Exchange Management Console (EMC) or when you use the Exchange Management Shell (EMS), and there are no properties that can be set for the implicit send connector. In fact, that connector does not exist unless it is needed. It is created in memory whenever a message needs to be sent between Hub Transport servers. The implicit send connector cannot be used to deliver messages to the Internet or to an external host directly.

Send connectors are managed in the EMC under the Hub Transport subcontainer of the Organization Configuration work center. Figure 25.6 shows the Source Server properties for a connector called From Exchange 2010 to the World.

FIGURE 25.6
Managing send connectors

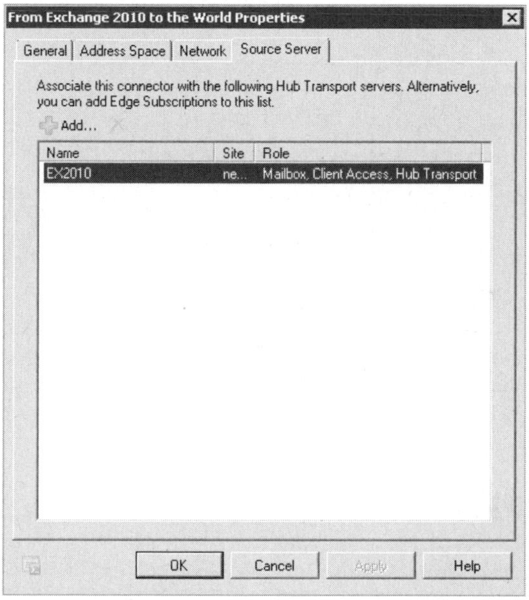

The Source Server properties page is where you designate which Hub Transport servers will deliver messages for this particular send connector. When you assign more than one Hub Transport server as a source server, the outbound messaging load will be load-balanced among the source servers. You can view the properties of this send connector also using the EMS cmdlet `Get-SendConnector`; here is an example:

```
Get-SendConnector "From Exchange 2010 to the World" | FL

AddressSpaces                 : {SMTP:*;1}
AuthenticationCredential      :
Comment                       :
ConnectedDomains             : {}
ConnectionInactivityTimeOut   : 00:10:00
DNSRoutingEnabled             : True
DomainSecureEnabled           : False
Enabled                       : True
ForceHELO                     : False
Fqdn                          :
```

```
HomeMTA                       : Microsoft MTA
HomeMtaServerId               : EX2010
Identity                      : From Exchange 2010 to the World
IgnoreSTARTTLS                : False
IsScopedConnector             : False
IsSmtpConnector               : True
LinkedReceiveConnector        :
MaxMessageSize                : 10 MB (10,485,760 bytes)
Name                          : From Exchange 2010 to the World
Port                          : 25
ProtocolLoggingLevel          : None
RequireTLS                    : False
SmartHostAuthMechanism        : None
SmartHosts                    : {}
SmartHostsString              :
SmtpMaxMessagesPerConnection  : 20
SourceIPAddress               : 0.0.0.0
SourceRoutingGroup            : Exchange Routing Group (DWBGZMFD01QNBJR)
SourceTransportServers        : {EX2010}
UseExternalDNSServersEnabled  : False
```

Because Exchange Server 2010 does not have a default SMTP connector for outbound mail, you will need to create at least one send connector. Most organizations will need to create only a single send connector; this connector will be used to send mail to the Internet, to an Edge Transport server, or to an SMTP smart host system that will deliver mail to the Internet on behalf of the Exchange server.

CREATING A SEND CONNECTOR

This section goes through an example of creating a send connector that will be responsible for sending mail to the Internet. In the Hub Transport subcontainer of the Organization Configuration work center, make sure the Send Connectors tab is highlighted, and then click the New Send Connector task in the Actions pane. This launches the New SMTP Send Connector wizard shown in Figure 25.7. On the Introduction page, you must provide the name of the connector and specify the intended use of the connector.

The wizard will allow you to create four types (intended use options) of send connectors, but these are just predefined configurations and you can always change the properties of the connector you create later. The four types of send connectors you can create are as follows:

◆ The Custom Send connector type allows you to manually configure all the configuration settings at some point after the connector is created.

◆ The Internal Send connector type allows you to configure a connector that connects to Edge Transport servers in your organization or servers in another organization. Because all internal mail routing is automatic, you will usually not need to create an internal send connector to another Hub Transport server in your organization.

◆ The Internet Send connector type is used to send mail to the Internet using DNS MX records.

◆ The Partner Send connector type creates a connector that will be used to send mail to specific Internet domains and will use certificate authentication and TLS encryption.

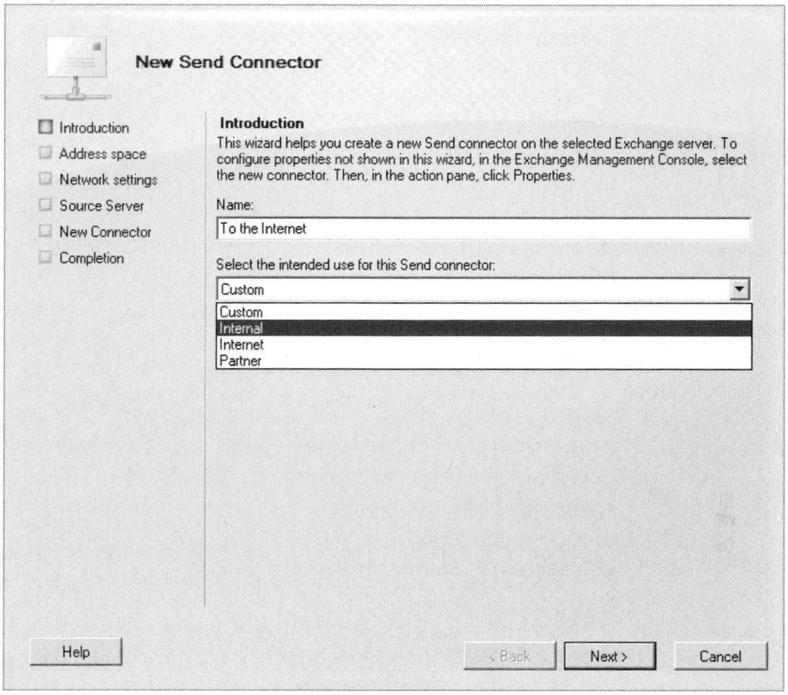

FIGURE 25.7
Introduction page of
the New SMTP Send
Connector Wizard

On the Address Space page of the wizard, you can specify the SMTP domains to which this send connector will deliver email. Because this connector is going to send mail to the Internet, use an address space of * for this example. The * address space represents all SMTP addresses that are not explicitly defined on another connector.

On the Network Settings properties page, you can configure Smart Host if you want mail to be delivered to another SMTP host for external delivery, such as with an Edge Transport server, or you can select Use Domain Name System (DNS) "MX" Records To Route Mail Automatically. If you use DNS for mail delivery, this send connector will be responsible for all outbound mail delivery.

The Source Server page allows you to specify the Hub Transport servers that will deliver mail for this send connector. If you have more than one Hub Transport server, we recommend you use additional Hub Transport servers for redundancy.

Once you click the New button on the New Connector page, the EMC will execute the command necessary to create the new send connector. The following is the EMS command that executes:

```
New-SendConnector -Name 'Internet Connector' -Usage 'Internet'
-AddressSpaces 'smtp:*;1' -DNSRoutingEnabled $true
-UseExternalDNSServersEnabled $false -SourceTransportServers 'EX2010'
```

Once you have created the connector, you should make one additional configuration option. On the General properties page of the send connector, enter the public name of the FQDN for this server, such as **MAIL.NETLOGON.COM**.

This is the name that the send connector uses in the EHLO or HELO command when it connects to a remote SMTP system. If you don't specify an FQDN for the connector to use, the connector will use the default FQDN for the server. Often this is an internal name that is not recognized on the Internet. Some Internet hosts will reject a connection if the name cannot be resolved.

Connectivity to Exchange 2003

When you install Exchange 2010 in an existing Exchange 2003 organization, to allow coexistence and facilitate routing, Setup creates an administrative group, a routing group, and a Windows security group for backward compatibility. (In a native Exchange 2007/2010 organization, routing group connectors are not used. They are necessary only when interoperating with Exchange 2000/2003.) These groups are as follows:

◆ Setup creates an administrative group for the Exchange 2010 servers to be housed in. This administrative group is called Exchange Administrative Group (FYDIBOHF23SPDLT). All Exchange 2010 servers will be in this administrative group; do not move them out of this administrative group.

◆ Setup creates a routing group called Exchange Routing Group (DWBGZMFD01QNBJR). All Exchange 2010 servers will be in this routing group and you must not move them out of this routing group.

◆ Setup creates an Active Directory universal security group called ExchangeLegacyInterop. The ExchangeLegacyInterop group has permissions that allow Exchange 2003 and Exchange 2010 servers to send messages between each other.

The new administrative and routing groups are not visible within the Exchange 2010 Management Console, but you can see them using the Exchange 2000/2003 System Manager console or ADSIEdit (see Figure 25.8).

If you are installing Exchange Server 2010 into an existing Exchange 2000/2003 environment, during the installation of the first Exchange 2010 Hub Transport server role, you are prompted for an Exchange 2000/2003 server to use as a bridgehead. The Setup program will create a routing group connector from the Exchange Routing Group (DWBGZMFD01QNBJR) routing group to the specified server in the remote routing group.

Only the first Hub Transport server is set up as a bridgehead server to Exchange Server 2003; you must use the Set-RoutingGroupConnector cmdlet to add additional bridgeheads.

For example, say an organization has two routing groups: the New York routing group and the San Francisco routing group. Each routing group has two Exchange 2003 servers that function as bridgehead servers for the routing group connector that connects the New York and San Francisco routing groups, as illustrated in Figure 25.9.

When the first Exchange 2010 server is installed, the Exchange Routing Group (DWBGZMFD01QNBJR) is created and the Setup program prompts the installer for a remote Exchange 2003 server to use as a bridgehead. In this example, we're choosing one of the servers in the San Francisco routing group.

The Setup program creates a routing group connector from the Exchange 2010 routing group to the San Francisco routing group. A single local bridgehead and a single remote bridgehead are defined. An identical routing group connector is created from the San Francisco routing group to the Exchange 2010 routing group. Figure 25.10 shows the properties of one of these routing group connectors using the Exchange 2003 System Manager console.

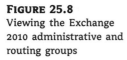

FIGURE 25.8
Viewing the Exchange 2010 administrative and routing groups

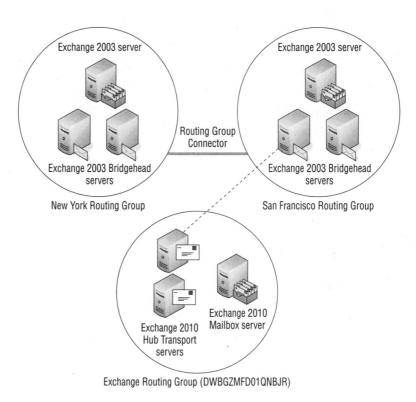

FIGURE 25.9
Message routing between Exchange 2003 and Exchange 2010

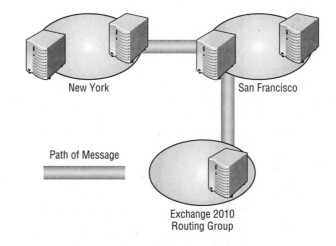

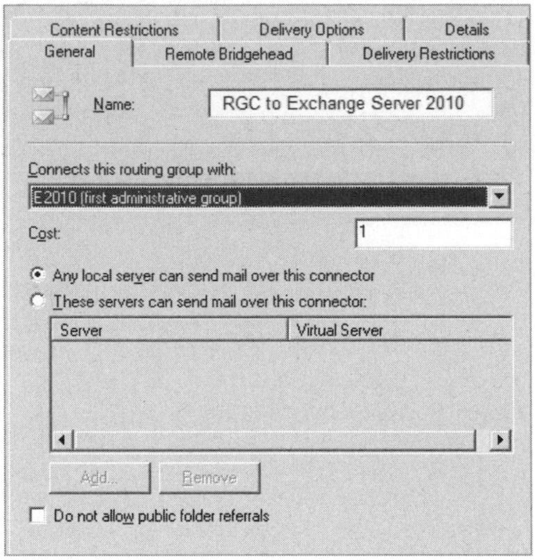

FIGURE 25.10
Properties of a routing group connector as viewed from Exchange 2003 System Manager

If you have multiple routing groups and multiple bridgehead servers, you will want to correct a couple of issues. First, there is no redundancy between the Exchange 2003 servers and the Exchange 2010 servers. If either the Hub Transport server or the Exchange 2003 bridgehead server that is being used for the routing group connector fails, messaging between the Exchange 2003 and Exchange 2010 mailboxes will halt.

Second, you will want to verify that all messages from New York to the Exchange 2010 Mailbox servers (and vice versa) will be sent through the San Francisco Exchange 2003 bridgehead servers.

Routing group connectors between Exchange 2010 and Exchange 2003 cannot be modified using the Exchange 2000/2003 System Manager console or the Exchange 2010 Exchange Management Console. Therefore, you need to correct both of these issues using the Exchange Management Shell and the routing group cmdlets. Table 25.1 lists the most useful cmdlets for managing routing groups between Exchange 2000/2003 and Exchange 2010.

TABLE 25.1: Cmdlets for Managing Routing Groups Between Exchange 2000/2003 and Exchange 2007

CMDLET	DESCRIPTION
Get-RoutingGroupConnector	Retrieves the routing group connectors or properties of specified connectors
New-RoutingGroupConnector	Creates a new routing group connector
Remove-RoutingGroupConnector	Deletes a routing group connector
Set-RoutingGroupConnector	Sets the properties of a routing group connector

Because this is all done from the EMS, let's start with some basics. Here is an example of using the `Get-RoutingGroupConnector` with no parameters to retrieve a list of the routing group connectors:

```
Get-RoutingGroupConnector
Name                    SourceRoutingGroup        TargetRoutingGroup
----                    ------------------        ------------------
Ex2010 to Exc 2003      Exchange Routing Group…    First Routing Group
Exc 2003 to EX2010      First Routing Group        Exchange Routing Group
```

The `SourceRoutingGroup` and `TargetRoutingGroup` columns have been truncated to fit better into the page in case you were wondering where the full name of the Exchange 2010 routing group is. Here is an example of retrieving all the properties:

```
Get-RoutingGroupConnector "Exc2003toEX2010" | FL

TargetRoutingGroup        : Exchange Routing Group (DWBGZMFD01QNBJR)
Cost                      : 1
TargetTransportServers    : {EX2010}
ExchangeLegacyDN          : /o=SnowboardingServers/ou=First
Administrative Group/cn=Configuration/cn=Connections/cn= Exc2003toEX2010
PublicFolderReferralsEnabled : True
SourceRoutingGroup        : First Routing Group
SourceTransportServers    : {EXC2003}
HomeMTA                   : Microsoft MTA
HomeMtaServerId           : EXC2003
MinAdminVersion           : -2147453113
AdminDisplayName          :
ExchangeVersion           : 0.1 (8.0.535.0)
Name                      : Exc 2003 to EX2010
DistinguishedName         : CN= Exc 2003 to EX2010,
CN=Connections,CN=First Routing Group,CN=Routing
Groups,CN=First Administrative Group,CN=Administrative
Groups,CN=SnowboardingServers,CN=Microsoft
Exchange,CN=Services,CN=Configuration,DC=volcanosurfboards,DC=com
Identity                  : Exc 2003 to EX2010
Guid: 4445126d-f275-4f5e-9934-d0048591a59a
ObjectCategory            :
Snowboardingservers.com/Configuration/Schema/
ms-Exch-Routing-Group-Connector
ObjectClass               :
{top, msExchConnector, msExchRoutingGroupConnector}
WhenChanged               : 11/19/2009 6:38:35 PM
WhenCreated               : 11/19/2009 6:38:35 PM
OriginatingServer         : Exc2003.Snowboardingservers.com
IsValid                   : True
```

If you wanted to add another Hub Transport server as an additional target bridgehead server, you would use the `Set-RoutingGroupConnector` cmdlet. But this is going to be a bit tricky because the display names of the routing group connectors are identical. You need to retrieve just the connector that connects from the Exchange 2003 routing group to the Exchange 2010 routing group.

Messages in Flight

By now you get the point that Hub Transport servers are essential to the Exchange organization. You understand that without transport servers, messages from any user to any other user in your organization, regardless of where their mailboxes are located, will simply not be delivered. Well, where are those messages stored on a Hub Transport server? The trusted transport database of course! (Actually, it's the same database file format and database engine as the one used to store all mailboxes on your Mailbox servers.) The Hub Transport servers store all messages in transit in a single database file, often referred to as the queue database. When administrators open the Queue Viewer, they are no longer looking at a flat NTFS file structure (such as the one in Exchange Server 2003), but they are making a query into a database.

You can imagine that for organizations that maintain thousands of mailboxes, and therefore have very busy Hub Transport servers, the queue database can become very large. Although in a healthy transport scenario the messages stored in the database don't reside there very long, the database likely contains sensitive messages where message delivery must be guaranteed.

Backing up the queue database does not seem practical, considering that the data it contains is highly dynamic and will be quite irrelevant within a few minutes of its backed-up state. But in a case of data loss or complete server failure, it is possible, and likely, that the entire queue database may be lost, including all those sensitive messages it contained.

The solution to this problem is shadow redundancy (or also known as shadow transport).

Understanding Shadow Redundancy

Yes, Shadow redundancy is a new technology introduced in Exchange Server 2010, which protects organizations in the event of a Transport server loss. Shadow redundancy is used by Exchange Server Hub Transport servers and Edge Transport servers. The main principle behind shadow redundancy is maintaining a copy of a message on the previous hop until the server verifies that it has successfully delivered it to all hops. In a shadow redundancy scenario, the following occurs:

1. The Hub Transport server delivers a message to another Hub Transport server *or* an Edge Transport server.

2. An SMTP session is opened.

3. The receiving server advertises support for shadow redundancy.

4. The sending server instructs the receiving server to track the discard status.

5. The message is delivered to the receiving server.

6. The receiving server acknowledges receipt of the message and records the sending server name for sending discard information for the message.

7. The sending server moves the message to a shadow queue.

8. The message is delivered to its next hop (in this case, a third-party server).

9. The third-party mail server acknowledges receipt of the message. The delivery is marked as complete.

10. The sending server queries the receiving server for the status of the message.

11. The receiving server checks the local discard status, sends back the list of messages that have been delivered, and removes the discard information.

12. The sending server deletes the list of messages from its shadow queue.

13. In a case of delivery failure, the sending server (in this case a Hub Transport server) would resubmit the message.

Several caveats exist. First, all servers that participate in the process must support shadow redundancy. At this point, that means all Exchange Server 2010 Hub Transport and Edge Transport servers only. If your organization contains Hub Transport servers from previous versions of Exchange Server, they can coexist in the same organization. However, in the event that an Exchange Server 2010 Edge Transport server communicates with an Exchange Server 2007 Hub Transport server, the advertisement of shadow redundancy (XSHADOW) will fall on deaf ears. The message will not be moved to a shadow queue and a delivery attempt occurs immediately.

There are not too many actions that are configurable for shadow redundancy, though you can disable shadow redundancy (it's enabled by default) and you can modify the expiry time-stamp on messages stored in the shadow database (the default is two days, since that is the default amount of time that a message is queued for delivery). For example, the following EMS command will modify the expiry value for messages in the queue to 1 hour.

```
Set-TransportConfig -ShadowMessageAutoDiscardInterval 01:00:00
```

We want to briefly mention that Exchange Server 2010 has provisions in place when communicating with servers other than Exchange Server 2010 Transport servers. The delayed acknowledgment process provides a ''best effort'' attempt at minimizing the possibility of lost messages originating from the Internet. Delayed acknowledgment is a receive connector setting that is designed for submitting SMTP servers that are not configured for shadow redundancy. Delayed acknowledgement *delays* the acknowledgment that a Hub Transport server provides to a sending server, letting it know that the message was accepted. The benefit here is that if the server fails and it had not yet delivered the message internally (and therefore benefited from shadow redundancy), the sending server would *resubmit* the message. As you can imagine, Exchange servers relinquish most of the control in this scenario. The responsibility for redelivering the message to the Exchange organization, when no acknowledgment is sent out, lies solely with the submitting server on the Internet.

Transport Dumpster

With a similar purpose as shadow redundancy, Exchange Server 2007 introduced the Transport Dumpster feature. The Transport Dumpster is a special cache maintained on all Hub Transport servers. The purpose of the Transport Dumpster is to maintain a copy of the recently delivered messages. This feature is used in conjunction with the database replication technologies introduced in Exchange Server 2010 the database availability group (DAG).

In the event that a message was delivered to a Mailbox server that is a member of a DAG and that server fails, the Mailbox server that will become active will then contact the Hub Transport server to verify which messages in its Transport Dumpster have already been replicated to members of the DAG.

During normal mailbox database copy replication, each Hub Transport server obtains the timestamp of the last transaction that is considered to be consistent across all Mailbox database copies. This value tells the Hub Transport server exactly which transactions have been properly replicated to and applied to Mailbox databases within the DAG. (The value that is queried for is the value for the LastLogInspected time.) At that point, the Transport Dumpster knows that it is now safe to delete any messages that have been delivered prior to this timestamp, maintaining only messages that have not been replicated to all Mailbox database copies. In the event that replication status cannot be obtained for one or more mailbox database copies, the Transport Dumpster does not truncate (delete messages) until the replication status for all copies is successfully retrieved.

The Transport Dumpster size, by default, is set to 18 MB per Mailbox database. An administrator can modify the dumpster size by using the `Set-TransportConfig` cmdlet.

The Bottom Line

Create and manage send connectors.   All messages delivered by an Exchange server are routed through these Exchange connectors. Send connectors are always used in communications between Hub Transport servers, and are *never* used when communicating between a Mailbox server and a Hub Transport server.

> **Master It**   You've been called in to deploy Exchange Server 2010 in a "greenfield" deployment, where no messaging system is present. Installing Exchange is pretty easy, even for the least experienced IT consultants.
>
> But... surprise. After your successful installation, you notice that emails cannot be sent to the Internet. You need to connect this new organization to the Internet. What configuration will allow your customer to book his golf games by email?

Create and manage receive connectors.   The second half of the Exchange Server 2003 SMTP virtual server, the receiving piece, is now coined as the receive connector. The many improvements in receive connectors over the SMTP virtual servers are considerable. The management of the connector is straightforward, but keep in mind that when you modify the properties of your receive connectors, you can impact all email flow for your organization

> **Master It**   You need to plan for the deployment of an Exchange Server 2010 organization. You quickly notice that the organization is concerned with reducing the number of physical servers. Of course, virtualized installation of Exchange Server is always possible, but this customer has very little expertise in virtualization technologies.
>
> They ask you a very important question: do they really need an Edge Transport server on their network?

Design an Exchange routing topology.   Once you start sending messages between more than one Exchange server, you must understand how Exchange Server 2010 uses your existing Active Directory infrastructure to route messages between Hub Transport and Mailbox servers. When you begin to discuss server placement and the message routing path with the networking team at your company, you need to understand exactly how messages will flow within your organization.

Master It   You have an Exchange server organization that contains multiple sites, separated by WAN links. Another administrator handles all Active Directory configurations for your organization.

This kind of scenario means that you may want to alter the route that messages take within an Exchange organization. Although Exchange servers always attempt a direct connection to a final destination server, in some cases (Back off and Delayed fan-out) connection is not established directly. This may be a good reason for modifying the site link costs used by Exchange servers when determining the least-cost path. What are your options in modifying these options?

## Chapter 26

Managing Transport and Journaling Rules

As you may have noticed by now, in spite of the extra features it offers, Exchange provides messaging as its core functionality. Messaging systems have been part of the business environment for years — long enough for the novelty of electronic messaging to wear off and for it to become a staple of the office. Email is now ubiquitous; right or wrong, your users think of it in the same class as utilities such as electricity or telephone. Because of this perception, the majority of messaging administrators must now deal with issues such as regulatory compliance that once were the province of only a few types of businesses.

Legacy versions of Exchange were not equipped with the tools and technology to allow administrators to effectively deal with these sorts of issues out of the box. Electronic discovery, regulatory compliance, long-term message data archives, and effective retention policies — the basic Exchange architecture was designed without these needs in mind. But in today's business world, they are very real problems that some administrators may face. The solution has traditionally been the implementation of expensive, complicated, third-party software suites.

When setting the design goals for Exchange Server 2010, Microsoft wanted to ensure that it was better adapted for modern needs and problems. Wisely, the product team didn't try to become compliance experts and bake every possible needed feature into the product; if they had, we'd be seeing the first delivery sometime around 2017. However, we now have some key features that allow administrators to design compliance solutions for the enterprise.

This chapter covers all the elements that work with a transport environment and allow you to control your messages as they flow through your environment. Whether it is to retain message information or to delete messages automatically; the Exchange transport servers provide many options to the administrators.

In this chapter you will learn to:

◆ Create and manage message classifications to control message flow

◆ Control message flow and manipulate messages by using transport rules

◆ Understand and configure message journaling

Introducing the New Exchange 2010 Transport Architecture

In all versions of Exchange from 4.0 through 2003, the message database was an integral part of the message routing and transport architecture. This is in large part because of its use of the MAPI protocol, in which the client's main point of contact with the messaging system is the MAPI session to the user's Mailbox server. This store-centric architecture made it possible for Exchange to perform certain tasks quickly and efficiently, but also made it more difficult to consistently perform certain types of tasks on *all* email messages (inbound, outbound, and internal) necessary to meet regulatory requirements. The role-based architecture in Exchange Server 2010 is a direct answer to many of these difficulties.

To illustrate the problem, take the common requirement in many businesses of ensuring that messaging policies are applied to all messages in the organization. In older versions of Exchange, if you send a message to another user whose mailbox is on the same server your mailbox is on, the message never passes through a transport component. As a result, the code for the message store becomes more complex in order to apply policies at this level, third-party developers have to find ways to hook into this process, and the Mailbox server runs more and more code that has nothing to do with the basic task a Mailbox server is supposed to handle (which is storing and retrieving messages in the most efficient manner possible).

In contrast, the distinction in Exchange Server 2010 between transport servers (two different kinds, in fact: Hub Transport [HT] and Edge Transport) and Mailbox servers permits the Mailbox servers to run only the code that deals with storage and disk I/O. If a message is submitted for delivery, the Mailbox server doesn't have to try to figure out exactly what to do with it; instead, it hands the message off to a local HT role in the site. The HT server can determine which policies apply, which recipients need to get a copy of it, and whether any special actions need to be taken. All messages are now handled consistently, the code is cleaner and more efficient, and third-party applications have a well-defined set of interfaces to hook into. For more details about the specific steps and tasks of the Hub Transport server, see Chapter 25.

All Messages Pass Through Hub Transport

Yes, you read that correctly. Every single message you send in Exchange passes through a Hub Transport server, even when you're sending it to another mailbox in your storage database. Although this might seem inefficient at first glance, the reality is that the resulting benefits make this a great design change. Mainly, and more importantly, it ensures that every single message can be captured by Exchange's transport components and therefore can act upon that message. See Chapter 25 for more information about this design change and the underlying benefit.

This chapter covers three principal transport capabilities in Exchange Server 2010 in detail:

Message Classifications These are annotations to an email message that mark it as belonging to a designated category of information that Exchange and Outlook may need to treat in a special fashion. These annotations are exposed as properties of the message, allowing clients to display them visually for the users as well as permitting them to be exposed to the rules engine for automated processing. As an example, all messages with certain keywords can be classified as being confidential.

Transport Rules These are server-side rules that allow you to create and apply messaging policies throughout the entire Exchange Server 2010 organization. They come in two varieties: Hub Transport rules, which are intended to be used for compliance enforcement and policy application activities, and Edge Transport rules, which are designed to modify messages as they are sent or received from the Internet.

Message Journaling This is the process of capturing complete copies and histories of specified messages within your organization. Journaled message reports are generated and sent to specified recipients, which can be within the Exchange organization or some external entity. Journaling may not be exciting or useful by itself, but it's one of the main ways to get messaging data into an external archival system. Note that Exchange Server 2010 also offers archival of content through the Personal Archive functionality, Retention tags, Retention policies and many other technologies designed around the compliance needs of an organization. These features are discussed in the chapters that focus on Mailbox server and data storage technologies.

Setting Up Message Classifications

At their heart, message classifications are simply labels that are set on certain messages. These labels in turn allow other software, such as Outlook and Outlook Web Access (OWA), to display a visual warning for the user and, optionally, take special action when processing the message with rules.

Message classifications have four principal properties:

◆ The *display name* determines how the classification is displayed in the client user interface and is scanned by the mailbox rules engine.

◆ The *sender description* allows the client interface to tell the sender the purpose of this classification if it isn't clear from the display name alone.

◆ The *recipient description* allows the client interface to tell the recipient the purpose of this classification.

◆ The *locale* is a code that defines the localized version of a classification.

Figure 26.1 illustrates how Outlook 2007 displays a message classification on a message by means of the additional colored field directly above the To line. The text of this message classification states, "R + D Internal Only — This message may contain confidential Ithicos Solutions confidential Research and Development information. Do not forward to external parties without department lead approval."

FIGURE 26.1
A message
classification displayed
in Outlook 2007

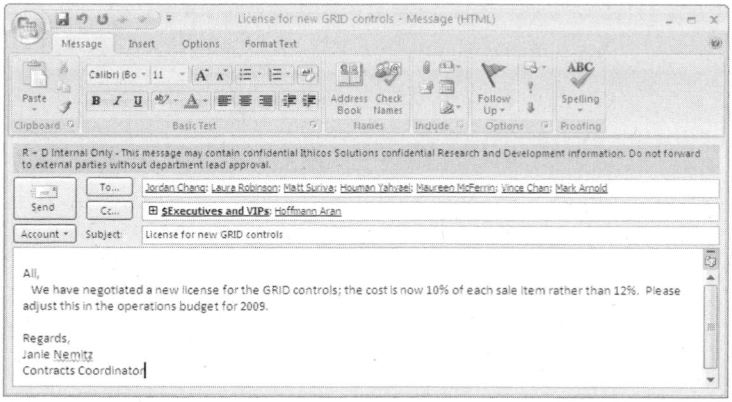

For Outlook end users, this classification was simple to add — all they needed to do was to click the Permissions button and choose from a list of valid classifications. The same classification labels are also included (automatically) with Outlook Web Access.

Out of the box, Exchange Server 2010 comes with six message classifications: A/C Privileged, Attachment Removed, Company Confidential, Company Internal, Originator Requested, Alternate Recipient Mail, and Partner Mail. By default, these classifications are informational only; no associated rules enforce them, and their purpose is simply to display text to recipients. You can modify these default classifications, and create new ones, to suit your business needs, such as the message classifications shown in Figure 26.2. No GUI exists for creating and managing classifications; you must use the Exchange Management Shell (EMS). However, once the classifications are created, you can use the GUI Transport Rule wizard (covered later in this chapter in the section "Creating New Rules with the Exchange Management Console") to apply them using transport rules.

FIGURE 26.2
A list of message classifications

In addition to the basic classification properties, you can optionally set some other properties:

◆ You can specify the precedence, which determines the order that a given classification is applied to a message if multiple classifications are set. You have nine values (Highest, Higher, High, MediumHigh, Medium, MediumLow, Low, Lower, and Lowest) from which to choose.

◆ You can specify whether a given classification should be retained on the message if it is forwarded or replied to; some classifications, such as Attachment Removed, would make little sense when applied to a forwarded copy of a message or to its replies.

◆ You can create localized versions of message classifications if you are working in a multilingual organization. When working with localizations, Outlook 2007 and OWA will display the accurate classification based on the localization settings configured on the client.

By default, OWA supports the display and manual selection of message classifications. To use them in Outlook 2007, you must manually deploy them, which is covered in "Deploying Message Classifications" later in this chapter. Advanced users can control permissions on message classifications and thus restrict the use of some classifications to a subset of users. See the Exchange 2010 help topic "Deploying Message Classifications for Outlook 2007" for instructions if you need this capability.

Modifying and Creating Message Classifications

To create new classifications or customize the properties of existing classifications, you must use the New-MessageClassification, Get-MessageClassification, and Set-MessageClassification cmdlets in the Exchange Management Shell.

Get-MessageClassification This cmdlet shows you the existing message classifications in your organization:

```
Get-MessageClassification
```

Set-MessageClassification This cmdlet modifies the properties of an existing classification. The following example takes an existing classification named NewMC, sets its precedence to High, and sets the RetainClassificationEnabled property so that the classification will be retained across forwards and replies:

```
Set-MessageClassification -Identity NewMC -DisplayPrecedence High ↵
-RetainClassificationEnabled $True
```

New-MessageClassification This cmdlet creates a new message classification in your organization, configuring it on your Exchange 2010 servers and registering it in the Active Directory:

```
New-MessageClassification -Name "RandDInternal" -DisplayName "R+D ↵
    Internal Only"
-RecipientDescription "This message may contain confidential and/or ↵
 proprietary information.  If you have received this message in error, please ↵
 delete it."  -SenderDescription "This message may contain confidential ↵
 Ithicos Solutions confidential R and D information. Do not forward to ↵
    external parties without department lead approval."
```

Deploying Message Classifications

When you create or modify classifications, they are automatically visible to OWA users. In what is a particularly painful oversight, the same is not true for Outlook 2007 users. If you want your Outlook 2007 users to benefit from message classifications, you have two tasks to complete:

1. Export the message classifications from Exchange 2010 to an XML file.

2. Configure Outlook 2007 to use the XML file that contains the classification information.

These steps must be performed every time you add new classifications or modify display properties of existing classifications. Just to make it even more annoying, these tasks are completely manual.

The following sections cover these steps in greater detail.

EXPORTING CLASSIFICATIONS FROM EXCHANGE

If you're looking for an EMS cmdlet to export all your classifications, stop. You have to use EMS, but no built-in cmdlet exists to perform this task. Here's how to do it:

1. Navigate to the Scripts subdirectory of the folder that you installed Exchange Server 2010 to (by default, this folder is located at C:\Program Files\Microsoft\Exchange Server\V14\Scripts).
    Microsoft has provided several useful and complex EMS scripts in this folder; the one you want is named Export-OutlookClassification.ps1. Though you can use the Export-OutlookClassification.ps1 script to export a single classification, you will probably want to export all classifications and configure Outlook to use them.

2. To export all of the classifications to a file called `c:\Classifications.XML`, type the following command:

```
& 'C:\Program Files\Microsoft\Exchange Server\Scripts\Export-↵
OutlookClassification.ps1' > c:\Classifications.xml
```

OUT-OF-SYNC CLASSIFICATIONS

If the XML file that Outlook uses is out of sync with the actual classifications specified on the Exchange server, Outlook will not display the classifications that are missing from the file. It will, however, retain them if they can be retained, and they will still be on the messages (and can be viewed in OWA). Once the file is updated, they will become visible to the user.

IMPORTING CLASSIFICATIONS IN OUTLOOK

This task has two parts: creating the necessary Registry entries and copying over the XML file you just created in the previous step. Once you've created the Registry settings on a given client, you don't need to keep setting them when you update the classifications XML file.

Copying the XML file over is simple; you can do it manually, via a batch script, or through your existing desktop management solution. If you are going to change the classifications on a regular basis, you might want to configure some sort of automated deployment system to minimize the need for manual involvement. For example, you might consider the use of a logon script to ensure that the latest copy of the classifications XML file is pushed out to your clients. If you've deployed Microsoft Systems Management Server (or some third-party equivalent) in your environment, you can also use that mechanism.

Outlook reads the file in when it starts, so if the file is updated while Outlook is open, it will not use the updated information until it is next restarted.

The following Registry key and values must be created on all Outlook 2007 computers whose users have mailboxes on Exchange Server 2010 servers and who are going to be sending message classifications. Until these Registry entries are created, classifications will not be displayed in Outlook, even though they exist on messages.

For Outlook 2007, In the `HKCU\Software\Microsoft\Office\12.0\Common` key, first create a new key named Policy. Within this new key, create the following values:

```
"AdminClassificationPath"="C:\\Path\\To\\Filename.xml"
"EnableClassifications"=dword:00000001
"TrustClassifications"=dword:00000001
```

You should set the values of these keys accordingly:

AdminClassificationPath   Specifies the full path and filename of the XML file you copied from the export process. Though this path can be on a network share, it might cause problems for laptop users or other users who lose network connectivity. The file is small, so there's no harm in copying it to the local hard drive.

EnableClassifications   Allows you to toggle whether message classifications are read and honored in Outlook 2007 on a per-user basis. The value 1 enables classifications, and the value 0 disables them.

TrustClassifications   Allows you to toggle whether Outlook actually trusts classifications on messages that are sent to users on legacy Exchange Mailbox servers. The value 1 enables trust; 0 disables it. Microsoft recommends that you enable this value only for mailboxes on Exchange 2010 servers.

Keep in mind that there are other options as well. The Office 2007 Customization Tool allows you to specify additional Registry keys that will be installed when Office is installed on a machine. If you want to ensure that message classification support is universally deployed and supported in your organization, you might want to include these Registry settings in your configuration when creating your installation scripts.

Setting Up Transport Rules

The two types of transport rules (Edge Transport and Hub Transport rules) in Exchange Server 2010 give you the ability to define and automatically enforce messaging policies within your organization. In Exchange 2010, transport rules are enforced on the Hub Transport and Edge Transport roles. You can use transport rules to append disclaimers to messages, search messages for certain types of content, apply ethical walls, append classifications, insert text into a message, apply Rights Management Service templates, and more.

If you remember (from just a few pages ago), we mentioned that all messages are handled by the Hub Transport server. A major reason for this change was to allow the Hub Transport server to trigger all these powerful transport rules that you will create for your organization.

You can create and manage transport rules in both the Exchange Management Console and the Exchange Management Shell. In the EMC, transport rules are found under the Organization Configuration properties and under the Hub Transport subcontainer, as shown in Figure 26.3.

FIGURE 26.3
Locating the Hub Transport rules in the Exchange Management Console

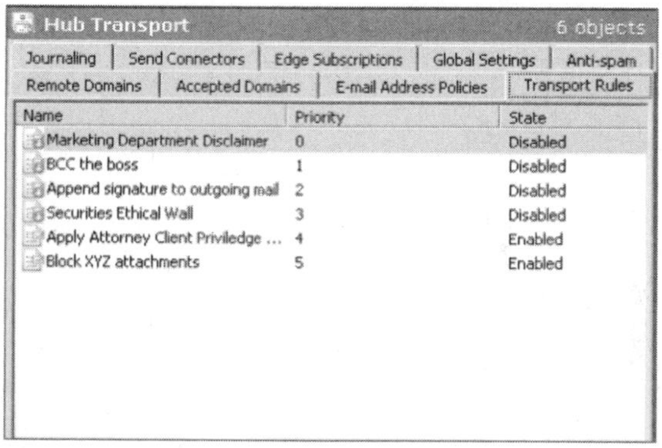

Although you use the same processes to create and manage the rules on both roles, the actions you can take, and the way the rules are stored, are different. Transport rules are similar to mailbox rules, but they are applied at the server level to all traffic that goes through that server.

Like mailbox rules, transport rules have three parts:

◆ Conditions identify the message properties that trigger the application of the rule to a given message. If you define no conditions, the rule will apply to all messages.

◆ Exceptions identify message properties that exempt a given message from being processed by the rule even if it matches the defined conditions. Exceptions, like conditions, are optional.

◆ Actions modify the properties or delivery of messages that match the conditions without matching the exceptions defined by the rule. In a given rule, there must be at least one action, and you can have multiple actions.

Transport rules on a Hub Transport server are defined and stored in the Active Directory; each Hub Transport server in the organization sees the entire set of defined rules and attempts to match them against all messages. This allows you to define a single, consistent set of message policies throughout your organization. Technically, you can define an unlimited amount of transport rules. However, because of management performance issues, Microsoft recommends a total of 1,000 transport rules in your organization. That may seem like a lot, but in large enterprises, you often need hundreds of transport rules to fully define the automated policy restrictions required.

TRANSPORT RECIPIENT CACHE IN EXCHANGE SERVER 2010

Exchange Hub Transport servers maintain a local cache of recipients and group memberships queried from Active Directory. The cache is maintained to minimize further queries to Active Directory. By default, the recipients in the cache are refreshed every 3 hours. This information can be particularly useful when troubleshooting transport rules that are not applied consistently in your organization.

The cache refresh interval can be changed by modifying the AppSettings section of the EdgeTransport.Exe.Config file on each Hub Transport server. You need to modify the value for the Transport_IsMemberOfResolver_ExpandedGroupsCache_ExpirationInterval property. Note that the minimum value for this property is 5 seconds and the maximum is 24 hours. The default maximum size for the cache is 32 MB. This value can also be modified from the EdgeTransport.Exe.Config file.

TRANSPORT RULES COEXISTENCE BETWEEN EXCHANGE 2007 AND 2010

There are some specific issues related to coexistence between Exchange Server 2007 and Exchange Server 2010, when it relates to transport rules. The details of impact and causes are discussed in Chapter 14, "Upgrades and Migration." Essentially, though, Exchange Server 2010 needs to prevent Exchange Server 2007 servers from running rules created on an Exchange Server 2010 server.

Exchange 2007 transport rules created using the Exchange 2007 Management Console or Management Shell are stored in Active Directory under the "Transport" container which is represented under the Configuration name context as CN=Transport, CN=Rules, CN=Transport Settings, CN=<org name>, CN=Microsoft Exchange, CN=Services. Transport rule agents running on Exchange Server 2007 hub transport servers retrieve their rules from this "Transport" container.

To prevent the Exchange 2007 transport rules agents from loading rules created in Exchange Server 2010, a separate Active Directory container is created to separate the transport rules based on the version of Exchange used to create them.

During Exchange 2010 server installation, a new Exchange Server 2010 transport rule container is created. This new container is located in Active Directory under the Configuration name context as CN=TransportVersioned, CN=Rules, CN=Transport Settings, CN=<org name>, CN=Microsoft Exchange, CN=Services.

Provisioning a separate Active Directory container for the new Exchange Server 2010 transport rules prevents legacy Exchange 2007 servers from loading rules that they are unable to read. In the case that an Exchange 2007 organization already has existing transport rules that they need to function in the new Exchange 2010 environment, Exchange Server 2010 provides two methods to migrate existing legacy transport rules to Exchange Server 2010: Automatic and Manual migration.

Automatic migration is performed during Exchange Server 2010 setup. If the setup program detects the existence of legacy rules, those rules are copied to Exchange Server 2010.

Manual migration is performed by exporting and importing transport rules between the two messaging platforms. Automatic migration of transport rules is only performed during the initial installation of an Exchange 2010 server, so new transport rules created after the setup process has run will not be read by Exchange Server 2010 Hub Transport servers. The same problem exists from Exchange Server 2010 to Exchange Server 2007.

To overcome this limitation, Exchange administrators can manually migrate a Transport Rule collection from Exchange Server 2010 to Exchange Server 2007, or from Exchange Server 2007 to Exchange Server 2010 by using the Export and Import PowerShell tasks.

Just as with Exchange Server 2007, the `Import-` and `Export-TransportRuleCollection` cmdlets are used by administrators to migrate or back up transport rules. However, in Exchange Server 2010, these tasks have been updated to allow the migration of transport rules.

The updated tasks must be run from the Exchange Server 2010 Management Shell in order to move/copy transport rules between Exchange Server 2007 and Exchange Server 2010.

You should be aware that importing a transport rule collection will overwrite any preexisting Exchange Server 2010 transport rules, except for one special case: if an existing Exchange Server 2010 transport rule has any 2010 specific predicate or action, that Exchange Server 2010 rule will be left untouched. The remaining Exchange Server 2007 rules will be imported into the Exchange Server 2010 collection.

Transport Rules and Server Design Decisions

A number of factors will come into play when you are sizing and making server design decisions around Transport servers. The number of messages per hour and the number of transport rules will affect your design decisions regarding the amount of RAM and number of processors that are on the Hub Transport servers. An organization that sends 2,000 messages per hour and has 10 transport rules will need far less computing power (and fewer Hub Transport servers in each site) than an organization that sends 10,000 messages per hour and has a few hundred transport rules.

Because rules are stored in the Active Directory, modifications to your transport rules are subject to your normal AD replication. Depending on your site topology, it may take some time before your current changes replicate fully throughout your organization.

If you have Exchange Server 2003 servers in your organization, they will not make use of your transport rules. If acting as bridgeheads, these servers may represent a significant loophole in your messaging policy enforcement. Likewise, Exchange Server 2003 servers do not pass all messages through a Hub Transport server, so you may notice that some policies are not applied consistently until all mailboxes are on Exchange Server 2007 or Exchange Server 2010 servers.

In contrast, transport rules for Edge Transport servers are defined on a per-server basis and stored in the local ADLDS database on the Edge Transport server. Thus, though you have no replication delays to worry about, you do have to manually maintain a consistent set of rules on your Edge Transport servers or you'll find you have some interesting discrepancies to track down at a later date.

If you have multiple Edge Transport servers, I recommend creating an EMS script to manage your transport rule configurations. Not only can you easily reuse this script on each Edge

Transport server to maintain consistency, but the script makes for great documentation on what your current configuration is. Keep in mind that Edge Transport rules do not synchronize to Hub Transport servers during the Edge Synchronization process.

Another design decision point for Exchange Server 2010 Transport rules is one of those features that requires previous implementation of non-Exchange components. Specifically, a Windows Server 2008 server with the Active Directory Rights Management Service role needs to be available to provide enhanced security through message encryption and authorization. Exchange is now RMS (or AD RMS) aware, ensuring that an administrator can create transport rules that can leverage built-in or custom RMS templates.

Selecting Conditions and Exceptions

Because conditions and exceptions are both involved in identifying whether a given message should be processed by the rule, it should be no surprise that they give you the same set of options. Which options you get depends on whether you're creating the rule on a Hub Transport or Edge Transport server. The Exchange 2010 help files contain detailed descriptions of how each of these conditions and exceptions are defined and applied, but the following discussion should help you get an idea of what types of selection criteria you have available at your fingertips.

HUB TRANSPORT CONDITIONS AND EXCEPTIONS

The conditions of the rule define the circumstances under which the rule will apply. Figure 26.4 shows the Conditions page of the Edit Transport Rule wizard and some of the conditions that can be applied to the rule.

FIGURE 26.4
Transport rule
conditions

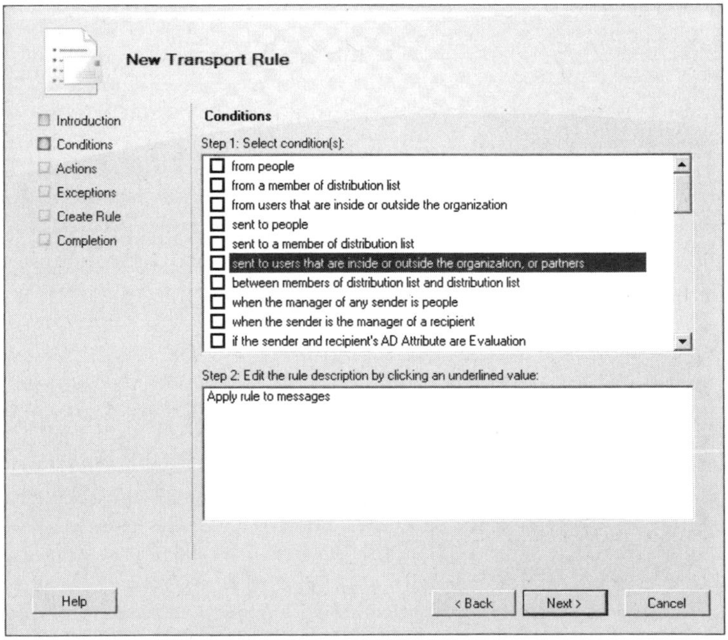

You can select the following transport rule conditions on Hub Transport servers:

◆ From people

◆ From a member of distribution list

◆ From users that are inside or outside the organization

◆ Sent to people

◆ Sent to a member of distribution list

◆ Sent to users that are inside or outside the organization or partners

◆ Between members of distribution list and distribution list

◆ When the manager of any sender is people

◆ When the sender is the manager of a recipient

◆ If the sender and recipient's AD Attribute are Evaluation

◆ When a specific recipient's address contains specific words

◆ When a specific recipient's address contains text patterns

◆ When a recipient's properties contains text patterns

◆ When any of the recipients in the To field is people

◆ When any of the recipients in the To field are a member of distribution list

◆ When any of the recipients in the Cc field is people

◆ When any of the recipients in the CC field is member of distribution list

◆ When any of the recipients in the To or Cc fields are people

◆ When any of the recipients in the To or CC fields is a member of a distribution list

◆ Marked with classification

◆ When the Subject field contains specific words

◆ When the Subject field or the body of the message contains specific words

◆ When a message header contains specific words

◆ When the From address contains specific words

◆ When the Subject field contains text patterns

◆ When the Subject field or the body of the message contains text patterns

◆ When the message header contains text patterns

◆ When the From address contains text patterns

◆ When any attachment file name contains text patterns

◆ With a spam confidence level (SCL) rating that is greater than or equal to limit

◆ When the size of any attachment is greater than or equal to limit

◆ Marked with importance

◆ If the message is Message Type

◆ When the sender's properties contains specific words

◆ When the sender's properties matches text patterns

◆ Not marked with a message classification

◆ When an attachment contains words

◆ When an attachment matches text patterns

◆ When an attachment is unsupported

EDGE TRANSPORT CONDITIONS AND EXCEPTIONS

When creating a transport rule on an Edge Transport server role, you can define the following conditions:

◆ When the Subject field contains specific words

◆ When the Subject field or the body of the message contains specific words

◆ When a message header contains specific words

◆ When the From address contains specific words

◆ When any recipient address contains specific words

◆ When the Subject field contains text patterns

◆ When the Subject field or the body of the message contains text patterns

◆ When the message header contains text patterns

◆ When the From address contains text patterns

◆ When text patterns in any of recipient address match a transport rule

◆ With a spam confidence level (SCL) rating that is greater than or equal to limit

◆ When the size of any attachment is greater than or equal to limit

◆ From users inside or outside the organization

Selecting Actions

As with conditions and exceptions, your choice of possible actions depends on whether you're creating the rule on a Hub Transport server or an Edge Transport server. The Exchange 2010 help files contain detailed descriptions of how each of these actions is defined and applied.

HUB TRANSPORT ACTIONS

The actions of the transport rule specify what the rule will do to the message (or what it will do *about* the message). Figure 26.5 shows the Actions page of the Edit Transport Rule wizard.

FIGURE 26.5
Viewing the Actions
page of the Edit
Transport Rule wizard

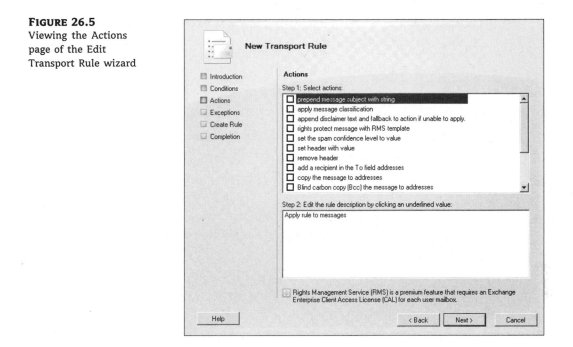

You can select the following actions on Hub Transport servers:

◆ Prepend the subject with string

◆ Apply message classification

◆ Append disclaimer text and fallback to action if unable to apply

◆ Rights protect message with RMS template

◆ Set the spam confidence level to value

◆ Set header with value

◆ Remove header

◆ Add a recipient in the To field addresses

◆ Copy the message to addresses

◆ Blind carbon copy (Bcc) the message to addresses

◆ Add the sender's manager as a specific recipient type

◆ Forward the message to addresses for moderation

◆ Forward the message to the sender's manager for moderation

◆ Redirect the message to addresses

◆ Send rejection message to sender with enhanced status code

◆ Delete the message without notifying anyone

One disappointing omission in the Hub Transport rule actions is the ability to designate that a matching message must be delivered to a specific location in the destination mailbox. Such an action would be extremely useful in conjunction with the Managed Folders functionality described in Chapter 17, "Managing Mailboxes," because it would allow the messaging administrators to automatically file certain messages (perhaps those with a specified classification) into known locations such as a managed custom folder.

HTML DISCLAIMERS IN EXCHANGE SERVER 2010

In Exchange Server 2010, an administrator can create HTML disclaimers, as a Transport Rule action. When using HTML disclaimers, a Hub Transport server inserts disclaimers into email messages using the same message format as the original message. For example, if a message is created in HTML, the disclaimer is added in HTML. If the message is created as plaintext, HTML tags are stripped from the HTML disclaimer text and the resulting disclaimer text is added to the plaintext message.

Exchange 2010 HTML disclaimer text can include HTML tags. This allows you to create messages with rich functionality available in HTML code. For example, HTML tags can include in-line Cascading Style Sheets. Messages sent in the HTML format can then display rich disclaimer messages.

More importantly, in Exchange Server 2010, you can add images to an HTML disclaimer by using IMG tags. You cannot actually drag and drop image files directly into the transport rule, but you have to place the image files on a publicly accessible web server. Once you have verified that the image is available by using a URL, you can add the path to the disclaimer Action in the Transport rule. For example:

```
<IMG src=''http://PublicServer.Netlogon.com/images/logo.gif''
```

EDGE TRANSPORT ACTIONS

You can select the following actions on Edge Transport servers:

- Log an event with a message
- Prepend the subject with a string
- Set the spam confidence level to a value
- Set the header with a value
- Remove the header
- Add a recipient in the To field addresses
- Copy the message to addresses
- Blind carbon copy (Bcc) the message to addresses
- Drop the connection
- Redirect the message to addresses
- Put the message in a spam quarantine mailbox

◆ Reject the message with a status code and response

◆ Delete the message without notifying anyone

Creating New Rules with the Exchange Management Console

To create a new transport rule on your Hub Transport servers using the EMC, launch the EMC. Navigate to Exchange Organization ➤ Organization Configuration ➤ Hub Transport in the left-hand pane, then select the Transport Rules tab in the middle pane. Click the New Transport Rule task in the pane on the right to start the New Transport Rule wizard.

Figure 26.6 shows the Introduction screen of the wizard. Here you provide the name and optional description of the new rule, as well as select whether the rule will be enabled once it is created. The Name field is required. We recommend using the Comment field liberally — otherwise, after you have 50 transport rules you will begin to lose track of what each one does without digging through the rule itself. Click Next to continue once you have configured a name and comment.

FIGURE 26.6
New Transport Rule
wizard Introduction
page

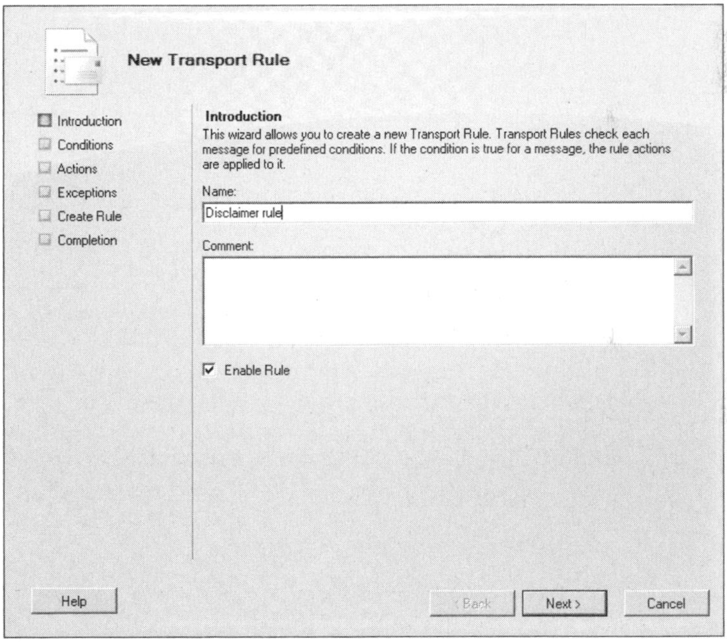

Figure 26.4 (shown previously) shows the Conditions page of the wizard. The default condition is Apply Rule To Messages (there is no check box for this), which will match all messages. If you want to narrow down which messages will be affected, select the check boxes of one or more conditions; they will be added to the lower text field.

To fill in the values of the conditions, click the underlined blue text fields and select the results from the selection dialog boxes that are opened. Once you are satisfied with the selections, click OK to close the selection dialogs. Click Next to continue.

Figure 26.5 (also shown previously) shows the Actions page of the Edit Transport Rule wizard. There are no default actions. Select the check boxes of one or more actions; they will be added to the lower text field.

Figure 26.7 shows the Exceptions screen; essentially this is the same set of conditions that you find on the Conditions page. Unlike the Conditions page, though, there are no default exceptions. Exceptions allow you to specify the conditions under which the transport rule will *not* apply. If you want to create an exception, select the check boxes of one or more exceptions; they will be added to the lower text field.

FIGURE 26.7
New Transport Rule
wizard Exceptions
screen

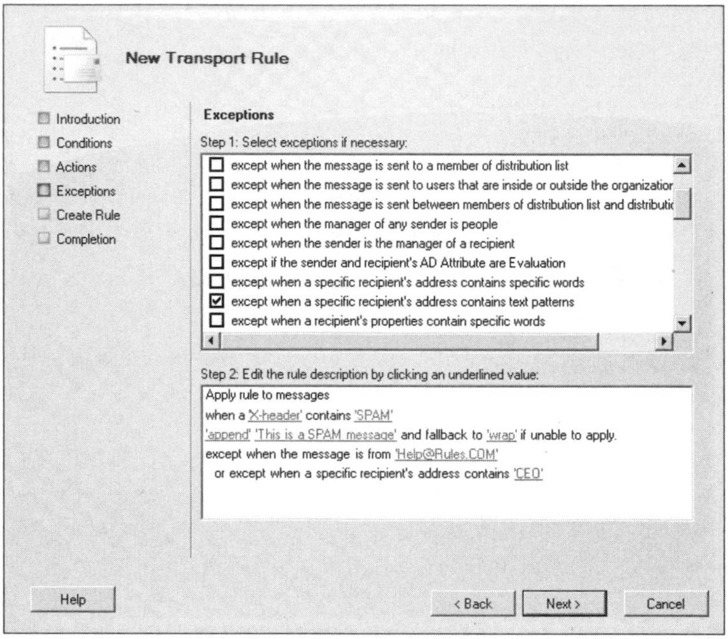

Figure 26.8 shows the Create Rule screen. This screen gives you a summary of the rule that will be created. In this figure, you can see a rule we have created that applies a disclaimer to all messages received that have an X-header value of SPAM. The transport rule states that the messages must have a disclaimer added except if the message is from the email address `Help@rules.com` or if the sender's address contains the string "CEO".

🌐 Real World Scenario

TRANSPORT RULES

Transport rules are always fun to describe to customers, since they have a familiar point of reference. We simply tell them that they are similar in experience to what they create with the Outlook Rules wizard, except that these rules have many more available settings and run completely server-side.

One of the things that we often run into, when we start diving a bit deeper, is the ability to get *creative* around transport rules. Specifically, we had a customer who needed to define a disclaimer based on the user's department. This customer ran Exchange Server 2007 on all Hub Transport servers and had not yet upgraded to Exchange Server 2010. So for users in the legal department, the outbound disclaimer had to state the legal requirements regarding client communication, while the sales department disclaimer had to state the company's warranty information.

So our first reaction was "Sure, basic stuff!" So we fired up the New Transport Rules wizard and chose the "if sender and recipient AD *attributes* are *evaluation*" condition. When we selected *attributes* in the editing pane, we were presented with a list of available Active Directory attributes that could be added to our rule condition. Well... bad news... Department is not one of the AD attributes that were available. We then realized that we do have all the AD Custom Attributes available. We simply ran a script in Active Directory that cloned the value of the department attribute to the Custom Attribute 15, and then selected Custom Attribute 15 for our condition. Done — and we successfully fought and conquered devolution!

Now, what we didn't realize at that time — and what would have helped us back then — is that Exchange Server 2010 now includes pretty much every Exchange recipient attribute as an available Transport Rule condition. So today, in Exchange Server 2010, we can create a new rule for this customer simply by selecting the Department attribute.

FIGURE 26.8
New Transport Rule wizard

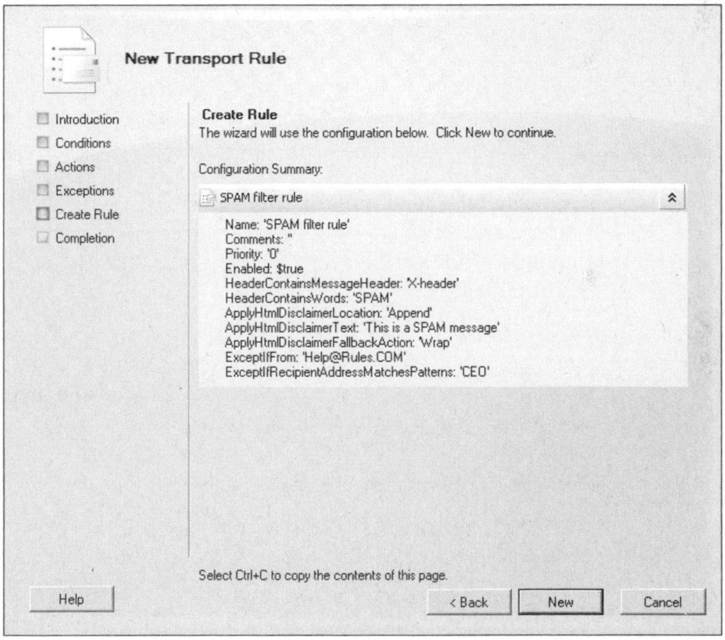

Creating New Rules with the Exchange Management Shell

The following Exchange Management Shell commands let you add, change, remove, enable, or disable transport rules that are used by the Transport Rules agent on a Hub Transport server or an Edge Transport server:

Get-TransportRule This cmdlet shows you the existing transport rules in your organization (if run on an HT server) or Edge server (if run on an ET server):

```
Get-TransportRule
```

Enable-TransportRule This cmdlet sets an existing transport rule as enabled, which means it will be applied to messages:

```
Enable-TransportRule -Identity MyTransportRule
```

Disable-TransportRule This cmdlet sets an existing transport rule as disabled, which means that it will still be present in the configuration but will not be applied to messages:

```
Disable-TransportRule -Identity MyTransportRule
```

The `Disable-TransportRule` cmdlet is useful for troubleshooting problems with transport rules. You can also disable all transport rules with this command:

```
Get-TransportRule | Disable-TransportRule
```

Remove-TransportRule This cmdlet allows you to delete an existing transport rule:

```
Remove-TransportRule -Identity TransportRuleToDelete
```

Set-TransportRule This cmdlet allows you to modify the parameters of an existing transport rule:

```
$Condition = Get-TransportRulePredicate FromMemberOf ↵
$Condition.Addresses = @((Get-DistributionGroup "Sales Group")) ↵
Set-TransportRule -Identity FromSales -Condition @($condition)
```

To make this cmdlet manageable, we made use of variables to create the condition *from a member of the distribution list* and fill its Addresses property with the *Sales Group* distribution list. We then passed the variable into the `Set-TransportRule` cmdlet, modifying the condition of the *FromSales* rule.

New-TransportRule This cmdlet allows you to create a new transport rule. Creating a new rule from the EMS is beyond the scope of this book, but it follows the same principles as the `Set-TransportRule` example. From the EMS, issue the following command for a full description of the cmdlet, including examples:

```
Help New-TransportRule -full
```

You may have noticed in the previous examples of creating or editing a transport rule that when you reference the actions or the conditions, you have to use the object names. You can retrieve a list of the actions by using the `Get-TransportRuleAction` cmdlet and a list of the conditions using the `Get-TransportRulePredicate` cmdlet.

Introducing Journaling

A lot of people confuse *journaling*, which is the process of capturing a set of communications for future use, with *archiving*, which is the practice of removing less frequently accessed or older message data from the message store in favor of a secondary storage location.

Archiving is all about getting stuff — usually older and bulkier messages and attachments — out of your mailboxes, so you can reduce the performance hit on your comparatively expensive Mailbox server storage systems and reduce your backup windows. Archival solutions are discussed in Chapter 23, "Creating and Managing Mailbox Databases," which has some very interesting new archival solutions.

Journaling is record keeping; you're defining a set of users whose traffic you must keep track of, and Exchange dutifully captures faithful copies of every message they send or receive. As stated before, journaling is one of the main strategies that compliance and archival vendors use to get messaging data into their solutions.

Although you may not have any explicit applicable regulatory language that forces you to implement journaling, journaling can still be one of the easiest ways to meet the requirements you do have. As compliance becomes more of an issue, the ability to quickly and easily put your hands on complete and accurate records of messaging communications will become critical.

Exchange Server 2007 journaling capabilities are essentially identical to those in Exchange Server 2010. The base journaling mechanism used by Exchange 2010 is envelope journaling, which captures all recipient information (even Bcc: headers and forwards). However, you have two options for journaling:

◆ Standard journaling (a.k.a. per-mailbox database journaling) uses the Journaling agent on Hub Transport servers to journal all messages sent to and from recipients and senders whose mailboxes are homed on specified mailbox databases.

◆ Premium journaling (a.k.a. per-recipient journaling) also uses the Journaling agent on Hub Transport servers, but it's more granular. It offers you the ability to design journaling rules for groups or even specific users if need be.

You must have an Exchange Enterprise Client Access License (CAL) to use premium journaling.

Implementing Journaling

The Journaling agent, present on your Hub Transport servers, is responsible for detecting whether a given message falls under your journaling rules. When you use standard journaling, you enable it for an entire mailbox database. Any messages sent to or by recipients whose mailboxes are located on a journal-enabled database will be detected by the Journaling agent and copies will be sent to a designated *journal recipient*. This journal recipient can be another recipient in the Exchange organization — if it is an Exchange mailbox it must be dedicated to the purpose — or an SMTP address on another messaging system.

Journaling to an external recipient may seem like a crazy idea at first blush. However, this allows Exchange 2010 to be used with compliance and archival solutions that are not part of the Exchange organization or even with hosted solution providers.

If you use an external journal recipient, you should ensure that your SMTP transport connections to the external system are fully secure and authenticated. Exchange 2010 supports the use of the Transport Layer Security (TLS) protocol; see Chapter 27, "Internet and Email," for details on how to configure TLS connections to specific domains and how to enable SMTP authentication.

When you use premium journaling, you create journal rules that define a subset of the recipients in your organization. Premium journaling rules are stored in the Active Directory and propagated to all Hub Transport servers, depending on the normal AD replication mechanism. The Journaling agent on the Hub Transport server detects that the rule matches a given message and again sends a copy of the message to the journal recipient. Premium journaling rules are found on the Hub Transport subcontainer of the Organization Configuration in the Exchange Management Console.

Journaling rules can have three scopes, which helps the Journaling agent decide whether it needs to examine a given message:

◆ The Internal scope matches messages where all senders and recipients are members of the Exchange organization.

◆ The External scope matches messages where at least one sender or recipient is an external entity.

◆ The Global scope matches all messages, even those that may have already been matched by the other scopes.

To create a new journaling rule, run the New Journal Rule wizard found on the Actions pane.

This same operation can be performed by using the Exchange Management Shell and the following command:

```
New-JournalRule -Name 'Journal VIP mail' -JournalEmailAddress
'volcanosurfboards.com/Users/zz_VIP Mail Archive' -Scope 'Global'
-Enabled $True -Recipient 'VIPs@somorita.com'
```

MANAGING JOURNALING TRAFFIC AND SECURITY

If you are using an internal mailbox as your journaling recipient, you should be aware that it may collect a large amount of traffic. Though you can use the same mailbox for all journal reports generated in your organization, you may need to create multiple mailboxes to control mailbox size and ensure that your backup windows can be maintained. If you are using the Unified Messaging role in your organization, you may not want to journal UM-generated messages such as voicemail because of the large amount of storage space it requires. (On the other hand, you may be required to preserve these types of messages as well as your regular email.)

Journaling mailboxes should be kept very secure and safe from everyday access because they may one day be material evidence in the event that your business is sued or must prove compliance to auditors.

To guard against the loss of journaling reports in the event of trouble within your Exchange organization, you can designate an *alternate journaling mailbox*. This mailbox will receive any nondelivery reports that are issued if your journaling recipient cannot be delivered to.

Unfortunately, you can configure only a single alternate mailbox for your entire organization. Not only can this cause performance and mailbox size issues, but your local regulations may prevent you from mixing multiple types of journal information in one mailbox.

Note that since the introduction of RMS interoperability with messaging and transport rules, it brings up some new issues, notably with journaling. Exchange Server 2010 now has the ability to decrypt and journal an unencrypted version of a message.

Reading Journal Reports

The journaling process creates a special Exchange message known as the *journal report*. This message is essentially a wrapper that contains a summary of the original message properties. It also contains a pristine copy of the original message that generated the report, neatly attached to the journal report.

The journal reports are designed to be human and machine readable, allowing you to automate processing of journal reports via a third-party application as well as perform manual checks on the data.

Table 26.1 shows the fields that Exchange 2010 places in the journal report.

TABLE 26.1:   Exchange 2010 Journal Report Fields

FIELD	WHAT IT CONTAINS
To	The SMTP address of a recipient in the To header or the SMTP envelope recipient. If the message was sent through a distribution list, this field contains the Expanded field. If the message was forwarded, this field contains the Forwarded field.
Cc	The SMTP address of a recipient in the Cc header or the SMTP envelope recipient. If the message was sent through a distribution list, this field contains the Expanded field. If the message was forwarded, this field contains the Forwarded field.
Bcc	The SMTP address of a recipient in the Bcc header or the SMTP envelope recipient. If the message was sent through a distribution list, this field contains the Expanded field. If the message was forwarded, this field contains the Forwarded field.
Recipient	The SMTP address of a recipient who is not a member of the Exchange 2010 organization, such as Internet recipients or recipients on legacy Exchange servers.
Sender	The sender's SMTP address, found either in the From or Sender header of the message.
On Behalf Of	The relevant SMTP address if the Send On Behalf Of feature was used.
Subject	The Subject header.
Message-ID	The internal Exchange Message-ID.

Depending on your routing topology and journal rule configuration, you may receive multiple journal reports for a given message. This is not an error; it reflects the fact that any given Hub Transport server may not have a complete view of the organization, depending on AD replication, recipient caching, and other factors.

The Bottom Line

Create and manage message classifications to control message flow   Message classifications provide a way to visibly tag selected messages and show that they require specific treatment. On their own, they're merely advisory, but combined with transport rules and mailbox rules, they can become powerful selection criteria for managing messages and ensuring policy compliance.

Master It   You need to use message classifications to manipulate messages by using Outlook. You verify that custom message classifications are available from Outlook Web

App. From Outlook, you look around but cannot find any options that relate to the custom message classifications. What do you need to do first?

Configure message flow and manipulate messages by using transport rules Transport rules give you a powerful, centralized method for creating automated policy enforcement in your environment. You can create rules on both Hub Transport and Edge Transport servers, although they serve slightly different purposes.

Master It You need to add a logo to an email disclaimer; you notice that you cannot include an image in New Transport Rules wizard. The availability of adding logos to a disclaimer was a major decision point of your Exchange 2010 implementation. What do you need to do to make the logo visible in the disclaimer?

Master It You need to provide the highest possible level of encryption in Exchange 2010 for mail sent among a group of users in your company. What solution should you identify?

Understand and configure message journaling Journaling is still around and better than ever in Exchange 2010. In addition to journaling to mailboxes within the organization, you can designate external recipients to send reports to. Standard journaling enables journaling on a per-database basis, whereas premium journaling allows you to create journaling rules targeted to specific groups or even individual users.

Master It If you are monitoring the Journaling Rules agent, you may notice that it runs twice on every message. Why the additional overhead?

Chapter 27

Internet and Email

Email has been around for nearly 30 years, but only in the last 10 years has it become a business-essential tool. One of the reasons that email is now so essential is that we can send and receive email with people outside our own organization.

Configuring Exchange to reliably send email to the Internet and to reliably receive email from the Internet is one of your most important configuration tasks. Notice that we used the word "reliably"; simply standing up an Exchange server and creating a send connector is no guarantee you will deliver mail reliably. Further, registering a mail exchanger (MX) record with your Internet DNS is also no guarantee that you will receive all the email you are supposed to receive.

In this chapter, we will help you to get your Exchange servers configured to reliably send email to the Internet and to make sure that email that others send to your users is properly received.

In this chapter, you will learn to:

◆ Configure DNS to ensure email is reliably sent and received

◆ Add an Edge Transport server to handle inbound and outbound email

◆ Configure Exchange Hub Transport servers to send and receive

◆ Configure Exchange 2010 antispam technologies

What Do You Need to Know?

Most of the people reading this chapter are probably already running an older version of Exchange, and you are probably delivering email to the Internet and receiving email just fine. However, a review of best practices is useful not only for experienced Exchange administrators but also for people who are just getting started.

Reliably delivering email to the Internet seems to be becoming increasingly complicated. Most of the reasons why this is complex relate to efforts by small and large organizations alike to block spam and to try to prevent messages from being spoofed.

Much of what you will need to know about your organization when it comes to sending and receiving email will depend on the size of your organization, number of servers, message hygiene solutions, and how many Internet connections your organization has. You should gather or learn about the following information:

◆ Determine who manages the DNS servers that maintain your public-facing domain name.

◆ Determine who manages the DNS PTR (pointer) records for your public-facing IP addresses.

◆ Determine the domains for which you will accept mail.

◆ Determine who will be responsible for setting up mail exchanger (MX), address (A), pointer (PTR), and sender protection framework (SPF) records for your organization.

◆ Document which public-facing IP addresses are used to send mail from your mail servers.

◆ Document which public-facing IP addresses are used to receive mail.

◆ Determine if you have more than one route for inbound or outbound mail, such as if you have Internet connections in more than one office or location through which you may want to deliver or receive email. Once you bring your Exchange 2010 servers online, you probably have more than one route for outbound mail through the co-existence period.

◆ Determine if you route mail directly to the Internet or relay outbound mail through a smart host or managed SMTP services provider.

◆ Document the path your inbound and outbound mail takes during delivery. This is especially important in medium-sized and large organizations where mail may go through three or four different hops as it enters or leaves your organization.

Important Information When Receiving Email

When you are configuring Exchange to receive email from the Internet, what do you need to know? This might not seem like such a hard question, but there are a number of variables that you should consider so that you reliably receive email. Some of these factors include:

◆ You must determine the public- or Internet-facing IP address of all hosts that will accept mail for your organization. In small and medium-sized businesses, this may be only one or two IP addresses at the same location. For large businesses, this may be multiple IPs spread across several physical locations.

◆ If you are using a managed provider or other external service to handle inbound mail for you, contact the provider to determine what you need to know.

◆ You must determine if inbound mail will pass directly through your firewall to your Exchange servers or if inbound mail will be routed to some type of mail relay such as an Edge Transport server or a third-party message hygiene system.

◆ For each host that will accept inbound email for your organization, ensure that your Internet-facing DNS has a public A record registered for that host. For example, if your organization (somorita.com) has two Edge Transport servers that will accept mail for you, create two public A records for those servers. The actual A record names do not need to correspond to the actual host names. Here are some examples:

```
mail1.somorita.com      IN      A      192.168.244.10
mail2.somorita.com      IN      A      192.168.244.11
```

◆ Ensure that your Internet-facing DNS server has mail exchanger (MX) records created for each of the hosts. MX records should point to A records, not CNAME records. For the example of somorita.com, the MX records would look something like this:

```
somorita.com      MX      10      mail1.somorita.com
somorita.com      MX      10      mail2.somorita.com
```

One of the practices mentioned earlier suggests that for each host that will receive mail for your organization, you should create a separate A record and then include an MX record for each A record. This works best when you are trying to set multiple levels of priority so that certain hosts will accept mail only if the servers with the lower preference value are not available. However, this does not necessarily work well if you are trying to load-balance multiple servers that should all have equal value. In the previous example, the domain somorita.com has two MX records that have equal preferences values. Many SMTP servers will not properly load-balance or "round robin" between these two different servers (`mail1.somorita.com` and `mail2.somorita.com`.) Thus, one of these two servers will always be much busier than the other.

If you are trying to allow for round-robin load balancing across multiple inbound mail servers, there is a simple solution that most DNS servers will support, but you will probably have to configure the DNS servers to perform "round robin" name resolution. In the previous example where we have two servers that will accept mail, instead of creating two MX records, create a single MX record like this:

```
somorita.com        MX        10        mail1.somorita.com
```

Then, create a single A record that has two IP addresses; in our example this record would have both 192.168.244.10 and 192.168.244.11 as valid IP addresses.

The MX record resolves to the host `mail1.somorita.com`. When the TCP/IP address of the host `mail1.somorita.com` is resolved, the DNS name server rotates the IP address values that it returns. In this way, DNS guarantees `mail1.somorita.com` hosts are cycled through and used equally for receiving inbound mail. Using this approach means that you take control for cycling through the mail systems: you are not at the mercy of the sender's SMTP server always picking the same A record when sending your mail.

PRACTICE GOOD DNS RECORD MANAGEMENT FOR INBOUND MAIL

Poor DNS management contributes to many of the inbound mail problems organizations experience. Sometimes these things are a matter of simple oversight, and sometimes they are a result of sloppy management. Your Internet-facing DNS servers should be configured to provide all the necessary information for someone who needs to send you email, but they should be maintained so that stale information is removed.

◆ All Internet-facing mail servers should have an A record.

◆ MX records should point to your mail server's A records.

◆ Not all SMTP servers will use the MX record's weighting value. You may think that by setting your mail servers to an equal value that you are load-balancing the inbound mail flow. Creating a single A record with multiple IP addresses (one for each of your inbound mail servers) will provide better inbound mail load balancing.

◆ Keep your MX records up-to-date and remove records that are no longer active.

◆ Don't confuse your external and internal DNS records. For most organizations, internal MX records are not necessary.

Important Information When Sending Email

Making sure that users on the Internet can send you email is fairly simple, but making sure they can receive email you send is a bit more challenging. Many of these challenges are because there are so many different types of antispam and antispoofing systems on the Internet. Unfortunately, these message hygiene systems don't all follow the same set of rules. Why might a remote mail server reject a connection from your public-facing server?

◆ The public IP address of your sending server may be on a real- time block list (RBL). This could be because that IP had been a source of spam at one time, it could have been an open SMTP relay, or the IP address could be listed as part of a DHCP or dial-up IP address range.

◆ The public IP address of your sending server may not have a pointer (PTR) record registered in DNS. Some mail servers will not accept a connection from you unless your public IP has a PTR record.

◆ Your email domain may be missing or have an invalid sender protection framework (SPF) DNS record. Care must be taken during infrastructure changes and when your outbound IP addresses change; you must remember to keep your SPF record up-to-date as well. While outright rejects due to this are not common yet, more organizations are using SPF as a way to protect against spoofing.

◆ The name that your sending server uses to introduce itself in the SMTP HELO or EHLO command may be an invalid domain name.

To ensure that remote servers will accept connections from your email servers, there are a number of things you should do for your connections and in your public-facing DNS servers:

◆ Use a tool such as the Microsoft Remote Connectivity Analyzer (www.testexchangeconnectivity.com) or the DNSBL spam database lookup tool (www.dnsbl.info). If you find that your public-facing IP is on one of spam database lists, the list will usually have information on how to remove your IP. If the reason your IP is on the list is because they consider your IP part of a dial-up or DHCP range (common with cable service providers), you will need to work with your ISP to ensure you are removed from the list.

◆ Ensure that each public-facing IP address has a PTR record associated with it. We recommend trying to use the same name that the server uses for EHLO or HELO commands, such as mail1.somorita.com, but this is usually not necessary and often not practical as different servers deliver outbound mail from the servers that receive mail. The "owner" of the IP address range will need to register the PTR records for you; this is usually the ISP.

◆ Create an SPF record in DNS that identifies the SMTP hosts that are authorized to send email for your domain. For small organizations this will be a simple matter of determining the public-facing IP addresses of your email servers. You can use the Sender ID Framework SPF Record wizard to help you create this record; this wizard can be found at www.microsoft.com/mscorp/safety/content/technologies/senderid/wizard/. If you use a managed provider to deliver all of your outbound mail, you will need to contact the provider to get the information necessary to create SPF records for you. In the previous example for the mail servers for somorita.com, the following SPF record indicates that only the listed host is authorized to send mail for somorita.com:

```
somorita.com    text =   "v=spf1 mx ip4:192.168.244.10 ip4:192.168.244.11 -all"
```

🌐 **Real World Scenario**

INCONSISTENT EMAIL DELIVERY FAILURES

The company LMNO had been reliably sending email to the Internet for a number of years. The users rarely reported nondelivery reports (NDRs) or other outbound email problems.

During an upgrade of the speed of their Internet connection, they also changed their public IP addresses. The mail server and DNS manager dutifully changed the address and MX records on their public-facing DNS server. After the DNS changes took effect, they tested email to and from various domains. All their tests succeeded.

Since the IP address switch-over was so successful, it was quickly forgotten. Therefore, their administrators and their Help Desk were not quick to make a connection between the IP address change and occasional mail delivery problems that the users were experiencing. Most of the NDR messages that the users were receiving were not very helpful and usually very cryptic.

Only after looking at the SMTP logs on their outbound smart host did LMNO determine that a few of the remote systems that were rejecting mail were doing so because there were no PTR records for the IP addresses.

The mail administrator contacted their ISP and asked the ISP to create the necessary PTR records for the IP subnet. This resolved the problem.

AOL and Time Warner are particularly strict on requiring IP addresses to have PTR records, but most organizations will accept mail from you regardless. Since only a small fraction of your outbound email is being rejected, it can make troubleshooting this problem more difficult.

Incorporating a Separate Message Hygiene System

Message hygiene, email hygiene, and content inspection can all be used to describe software that opens an email message and looks at the message body and attachments. The software may be looking for viruses, malware, phishing schemes, spam, spoofed messages, or the use of a rule set that you have defined to prevent certain types of messages from coming into or leaving your mail system. A good example of the last type of content inspection would be a system that examines a message to ensure that confidential or proprietary email messages are not being sent to unauthorized users.

Software is available you can install on an Exchange Mailbox or Hub Transport server to perform message hygiene functions. However, moving the hygiene functions to a separate system can provide additional levels of security and functionality. Providing a message hygiene system that sits between the Exchange server and the Internet has become a best practice for any type of email system.

Typically, this additional server or service sits within your perimeter network and uses antispam, antivirus, and possibly other types of content inspection technologies to protect the mail servers on the inside of the network. This system can be any third-party system (there are dozens of vendors on the market) that provides message content security. Figure 27.1 shows an Exchange Server 2010 system that is protected by two Exchange Edge Transport servers.

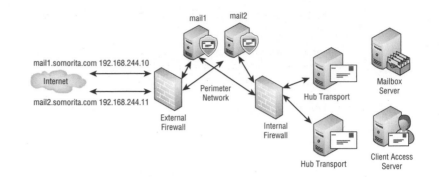

FIGURE 27.1
Implementing an Edge
Transport server for
additional message
security

The Edge Transport servers in Figure 27.1 may have at a minimum the Exchange 2010 anti-spam components but possibly also an antivirus software package that can inspect messages in the Exchange transport pipeline.

By placing the hosts that accept inbound SMTP mail for your organization in your perimeter network and using software that does not require the SMTP servers to be domain members, you can further protect your Exchange servers. The Exchange Hub Transport servers are not directly exposed to the Internet, and all inbound email first goes through the message hygiene system before getting to the Exchange servers.

The Edge Transport server has added benefits, including the ability to accept mail based on a user's "safe senders" list or reject mail based on a blocked senders list, maintain a synchronized list of valid email addresses from your Global Address List (without being a domain member), and perform authenticated connections to internal Hub Transport servers.

In the example in Figure 27.1, the Edge Transport server's Internet IP addresses are 192.168.244.10 and 192.168.244.11. These are the only IP addresses that need to be exposed to the Internet in order to send and receive email. To check the validity of the organization's MX records, you could use the NSLOOKUP utility as in this example:

```
nslookup -q=mx somorita.com
Server:  kilauea1.volcanosurfboards.com
Address:  192.168.254.15

somorita.com    MX preference = 10, mail exchanger = mail1.somorita.com
mail1.somorita.com      internet address = 192.168.244.11
mail1.somorita.com      internet address = 192.168.244.110
```

To verify that the organization's SPF record is set correct, you can use NSLOOKUP in this manner.

```
nslookup -q=txt somorita.com
Server:  kilauea1.volcanosurfboards.com
Address:  192.168.254.15

somorita.com    text =

        "v=spf1 mx ip4:192.168.244.10 ip4:192.168.244.11 -all"
```

To verify that each of the IP addresses has a PTR record, you could use NSLOOKUP like this:

```
nslookup -q=ptr 192.168.244.11
Server:  kilauea1.volcanosurfboards.com
Address:  192.168.254.15


11.244.168.192.in-addr.arpa     name = mail1.somorita.com
```

Using a Managed Provider

A fairly common trend in the email world today is to offload the first layer of your email security to a third-party organization. Figure 27.2 shows how this might be implemented.

FIGURE 27.2
Using a managed provider

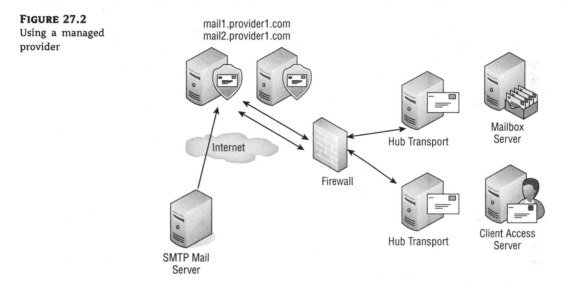

All inbound mail is delivered to the servers at the managed provider. The managed provider then performs message hygiene functions on the messages and may also provide functions such as archiving or backup. The managed provider's SMTP servers are then configured to deliver the mail on to specific servers, such as directly to your Hub Transport servers. In the case of our sample organization, somorita.com, their MX records may look something like this:

```
nslookup -q=mx somorita.com
Server:  kilauea1.volcanosurfboards.com
Address:  192.168.254.15

somorita.com    MX preference = 10, mail exchanger = mail2.provider1.com
somorita.com    MX preference = 10, mail exchanger = mail1.provider1.com
mail2.provider1.com      internet address = 172.16.31.85
mail1.provider1.com      internet address = 172.16.35.87
```

The hosts that you will need to use for your MX records will have to be provided by your managed provider. Further, if you want to use the managed provider for outbound mail delivery, you must get the host information from them that is used for outbound mail so that you can properly configure SPF records for your domain. You need to use their hosts since that is the source of messages sent by your users.

There are a number of advantages to using a managed provider as your first line of defense against spam and viruses:

◆ Managed providers act as your first line of defense and can eliminate most of the junk mail before it hits your mail servers. This can reduce the load placed on your Internet connection by spammers and bot nets that perform dictionary spamming.

◆ Managed providers are generally larger and can provide more scalability and redundancy for accepting and scanning email.

◆ You can secure your firewall so that only the managed provider's SMTP servers can even connect to your mail servers, thus providing a higher degree of security.

◆ Managed providers usually have 24/7 operations and support and can therefore react to emerging and day zero threats more quickly than a typical corporation.

Accepted Domains

An accepted domain is an SMTP domain name (aka SMTP namespace) for which your Exchange 2007 servers will accept mail. The servers will either deliver the mail to Exchange 2010 mailboxes or relay it on to internal or external SMTP mail servers. If you are in the middle of a migration from Exchange 2003, the accepted domains list will include the SMTP domains for your Exchange 2003 mailboxes. Accepted domains must be defined for all email addresses that will be routed into or by your Exchange 2010 servers.

Most small and medium-sized organizations will have only a single accepted domain.

SETTING UP AN ACCEPTED DOMAIN USING THE EMC

Accepted domains are found within the Organization Configuration work center under the Hub Transport subcontainer. When you choose the Accepted Domains tab in the Results pane, you will see a list of the accepted domains that have been defined for your organization, such as those shown in Figure 27.3.

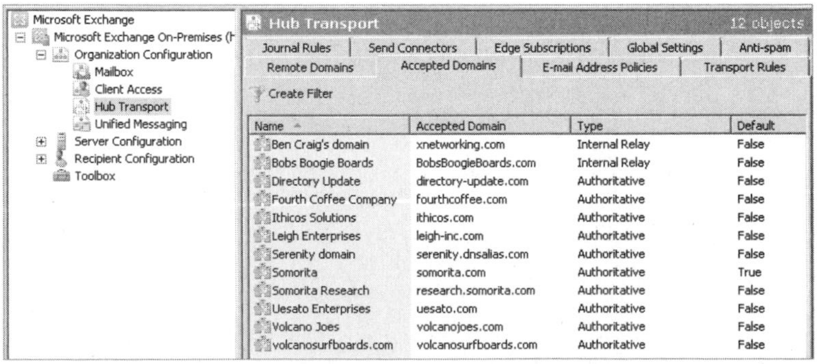

FIGURE 27.3
List of accepted domains

When Exchange 2010 is first installed, a single accepted domain is automatically created and given a name. This is the name of the Active Directory forest root domain; for many organizations this will not be correct because the naming convention for Active Directory domain names and SMTP domain names may be different. For example, your Active Directory name may be somorita.local whereas your public domain name for email is somorita.com.

Accepted domains are simple to create and require little input. To create a new accepted domain using the EMC, click the New Accepted Domain task in the Actions pane to see the New Accepted Domain wizard (shown in Figure 27.4). You only need to provide a descriptive name for the accepted domain, the SMTP domain name, and how messages for this domain should be treated when messages are accepted by Exchange 2010.

Keep in mind that you cannot change the domain name of an accepted domain once it is created. (You can change the domain type, however.)

FIGURE 27.4
Creating a new accepted domain

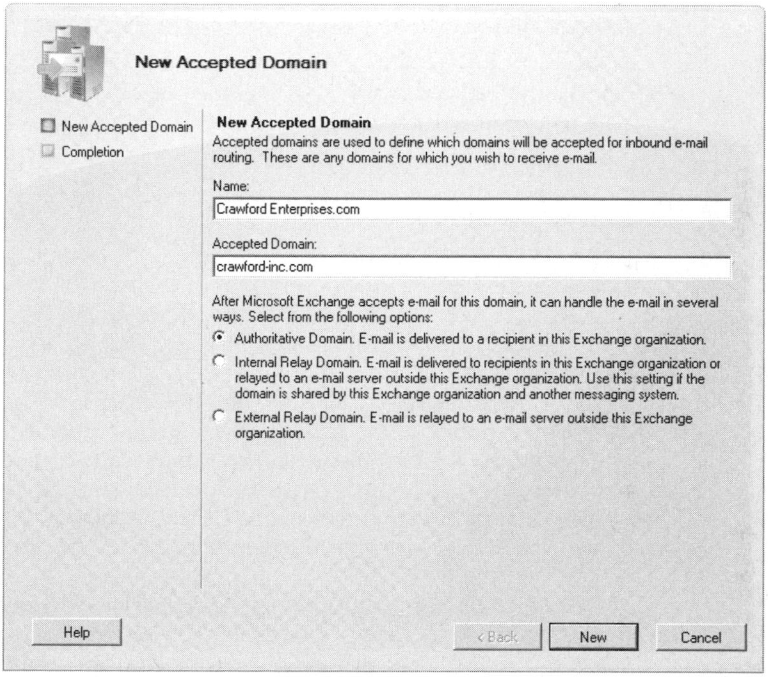

SETTING UP AN ACCEPTED DOMAIN USING THE EMS

You can also manage accepted domains using the following EMS cmdlets:

- New-AcceptedDomain

- Set-AcceptedDomain

- Get-AcceptedDomain

- Remove-AcceptedDomain

For example, to create the new accepted domain shown in Figure 27.4, use the following EMS command:

```
new-AcceptedDomain -Name 'Crawford Enterprises.com' -DomainName ↵
'crawford-inc.com' -DomainType 'Authoritative'
```

ABOUT DOMAIN TYPES

One tricky thing about defining an accepted domain is that you must define how Exchange is to treat a message addressed to that domain. You can choose from three types of domains when creating an accepted domain:

Authoritative Domains   These are SMTP domains for which you accept the inbound message and deliver it to an internal mailbox within your Exchange organization.

Internal Relay Domains   These are SMTP domains for which your Exchange server will accept inbound SMTP mail. The Exchange server must have mail-enabled contacts that specify forwarding addresses for users in those domains. The Exchange server then relays the message on to another internal mail system. Internal relay domains are used when two Exchange organizations are doing Global Address List (GAL) synchronization.

External Relay Domains   These are SMTP domains for which your Exchange organization will accept inbound SMTP mail and then relay that mail on to an external SMTP mail server, usually one that is outside the organization's boundaries. If Edge Transport servers are used, the Edge Transport server handles external relay domains.

Remote Domains

When sending email outside your organization, Exchange Server will make certain assumptions about message formatting and out-of-office replies. These types of settings can be controlled by the Remote Domains feature. For a fresh installation of Exchange Server 2010, there is a single remote domain configuration that is used for all outbound mail for all external domains.

You can find this global configuration information in the Exchange Management Console (EMC) by navigating to the Organization Configuration ➢ Hub Transport subcontainer and then clicking the Remote Domains tab in the Results pane. There is a single remote domain called Default.

If you display the properties of the Default remote domain, you will see on the General tab (see Figure 27.5) how out-of-office messages are handled for the domain specified in the Domain Name field.

By default, out-of-office (OOF) messages will be delivered only if the user has set external out-of-office messages using Outlook 2007 or later or Outlook Web App. Here are the choices available:

Allow None   Allows no out-of-office messages to be sent to the specified domain.

Allow External Out-Of-Office Messages Only   Only sends OOF messages if the user has designed an external message via Outlook Web App or Outlook 2007 or later.

Allow External Out-Of-Office Messages And Legacy Out-Of-Office Messages   Allows Outlook 2007/Outlook Web App external OOF messages as well as Outlook 2003 and earlier OOF messages to be sent out.

Allow Internal Out-Of-Office Messages And Legacy Out-Of-Office Messages   Allows all internal OOF messages to be sent out regardless of client type.

The Message Format tab of the remote domain's properties has a bit more information on it. Here, you can specify how message deliveries, character sets, and rich text formatting are handled. Figure 27.6 shows an example of the Message Format tab.

FIGURE 27.5
Remote domain
General tab

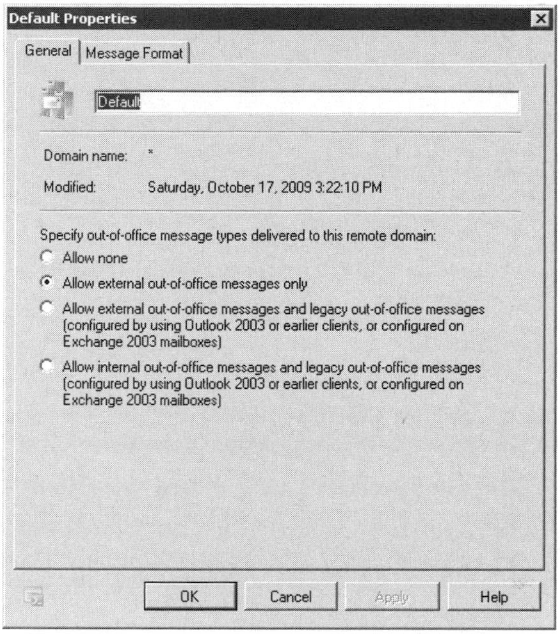

Default Properties

General | Message Format |

Default

Domain name: *

Modified: Saturday, October 17, 2009 3:22:10 PM

Specify out-of-office message types delivered to this remote domain:

○ Allow none
● Allow external out-of-office messages only
○ Allow external out-of-office messages and legacy out-of-office messages (configured by using Outlook 2003 or earlier clients, or configured on Exchange 2003 mailboxes)
○ Allow internal out-of-office messages and legacy out-of-office messages (configured by using Outlook 2003 or earlier clients, or configured on Exchange 2003 mailboxes)

OK | Cancel | Apply | Help

FIGURE 27.6
Message formatting
options for the Remote
Domains feature

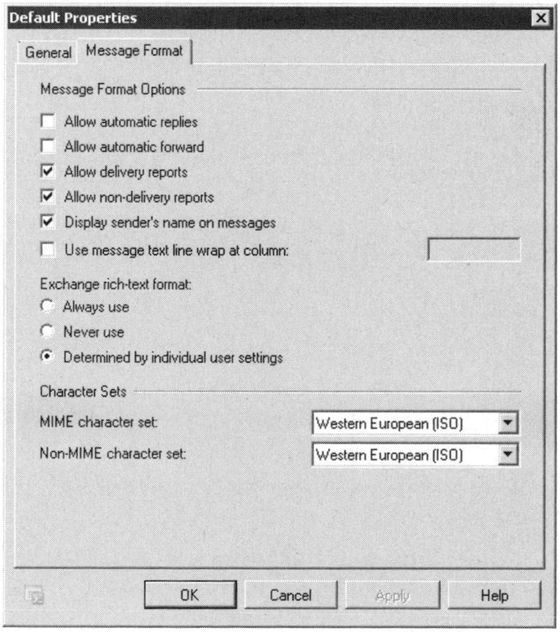

Default Properties

General | Message Format |

Message Format Options

☐ Allow automatic replies
☐ Allow automatic forward
☑ Allow delivery reports
☑ Allow non-delivery reports
☑ Display sender's name on messages
☐ Use message text line wrap at column:

Exchange rich-text format:

○ Always use
○ Never use
● Determined by individual user settings

Character Sets

MIME character set: Western European (ISO)
Non-MIME character set: Western European (ISO)

OK | Cancel | Apply | Help

The options on the Message Format tab are set to specific defaults, usually with security as a consideration. A good example of this is allowing automatic forwards, such as if a user puts a rule on their Outlook client to automatically forward some or all of their email to an external email address. This might allow confidential information to leak out to an external server and in some cases can cause message loops. Options available on Message Format tab include the following:

Allow Automatic Replies   Restricts whether users can set up their Outlook client to send replies automatically to some or all messages sent to them. This is treated differently than the out-of-office feature.

Allow Automatic Forwards   Restricts whether a user can set up Outlook to automatically forward some or all inbound messages to an external address.

Allow Delivery Reports   Allows you to specify whether your servers will return a delivery report to an external domain once a message has been delivered.

Allow Non-Delivery Reports   Allows you to specify whether your servers will return an error if a message was unable to be delivered.

Display Sender's Name On Messages   When unchecked, will not include the user's display name on the outgoing message.

Use Message Text Line Wrap At Column   Automatically wraps messages at a maximum number of characters per column. This option is generally not useful on most modern mail systems.

Exchange Rich-Text Format   Allows you to configure whether to always send rich text formatting, never to use it, or allow users to specify whether they want to use rich text formatting. You should only set the rich-text formatting option to Always if you know that the clients on the other side of a connection are capable of reading rich text messages.

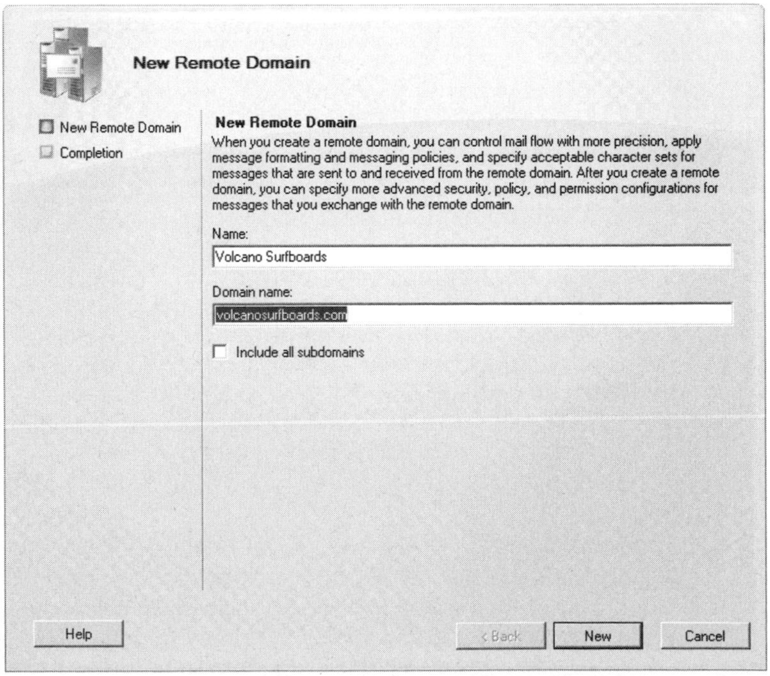

FIGURE 27.7
Creating a new remote domain

Character Sets Allows you to specify which character sets are used for MIME and Non-MIME messages. Unless you have a specific need to change this, leave the settings at Western European (ISO).

The Default remote domain covers all remote email addresses. So, why would you want to define additional remote domains? One good example might be if you have a business partner to whom you want to allow automatic forwards or you always want to send rich-text formatted messages. Creating a new remote domain is simple: merely launch the New Remote Domain wizard, specify a display name for the remote domain, and enter the domain name to which you want this remote domain to apply (see Figure 27.7.)

You can also create the remote domain from an EMS prompt by typing the following command:

```
New-RemoteDomain -Name "Volcano Surfboards" -DomainName "volcanosurfboards"
```

Configuring Hub Transport Servers

Out of the box, Exchange Server 2010 will neither send email outside the organization nor receive email from outside. This is a big change from Exchange Server 2003, where outbound email just worked out of the box and inbound email would work if you got your DNS MX records right.

Many small and medium-sized businesses route their email directly to a single Exchange server or to a single dedicated Hub Transport server. Although this might not be the best approach for an organization with thousands of mailboxes, it works well for small businesses (fewer than 500 users). Figure 27.8 shows an organization that is using this simple configuration.

FIGURE 27.8
Combined function server and Internet mail

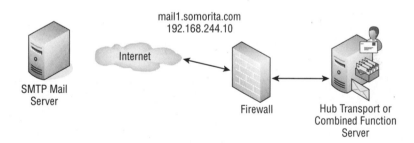

For the Exchange combined function server shown in Figure 27.8, your public MX record would need to point to a single Internet-facing host (such as mail1.somorita.com shown in the figure), and the SPF record for your domain would need to indicate the correct public-facing IP address as being authorized to send mail for your domain.

You should two steps to allow this organization to send mail to and from the Internet. First, you must configure the server to accept anonymous connections from the Internet; second, you must configure the server to know how to send mail to the Internet.

Configuring the Default Receive Connector

An Exchange 2010 Hub Transport server has two receive connectors (Client and Default). You can think of the receive connector as being something similar to the Exchange 2003 SMTP virtual servers except the SMTP services in Exchange 2010 are handled by the Microsoft Exchange Transport service (MSExchangeTransport) rather than the IIS SMTP service.

The Client receive connector is intended to be used by POP3 or IMAP clients; it listens on TCP port 587 and allows only Exchange-enabled users to authenticate (yes, they must provide credentials) to use this connector.

The Default receive connector is intended for use by other SMTP servers, but out of the box it will not accept connections from any SMTP client or other server that does not provide credentials. You can find the Default receive connector for each Hub Transport by using the EMC to navigate to Server Configuration ➢ Hub Transport, select the appropriate server in the details pane (the middle pane), and then select the receive connector in the work pane. Right-click on the receive connector and choose Properties.

On the Permission Groups tab (shown in Figure 27.9), you can see who is allowed to connect to this particular receive connector. The Anonymous Users check box is cleared by default and thus will only allow authenticated connections.

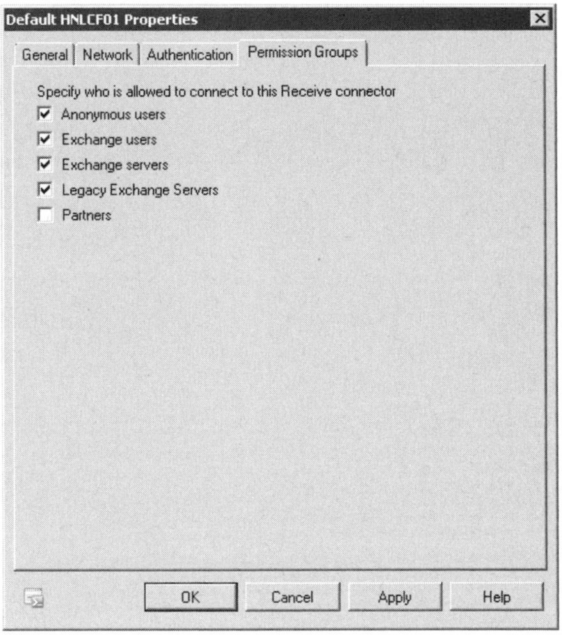

FIGURE 27.9
Configuring the receive connector

For your Hub Transport server to accept mail from the outside world or from a third-party message hygiene system, you must check the Anonymous Users check box.

The General tab (shown in Figure 27.10) for the Default receive connector has some additional options you might want to consider setting. These include the protocol logging level (either None or Verbose), the fully qualified domain name that remote clients will see when connecting, and the maximum message size.

There are few items that we feel are noteworthy on the General tab. The first, and probably the most useful, is the protocol logging level. Sooner or later, you will have to diagnose a problem when receiving inbound email from the outside. You will have to enable protocol logging on each Hub Transport server that receives inbound SMTP mail from outside your organization. You can view each Hub Transport server's receive logging feature using the `Get-TransportServer` cmdlet; here is an example for server HNLEX05:

```
Get-TransportServer HNLEX05 | FL *receiveprotocol*

ReceiveProtocolLogMaxAge          : 30.00:00:00
ReceiveProtocolLogMaxDirectorySize : 250 MB (262,144,000 bytes)
ReceiveProtocolLogMaxFileSize     : 10 MB (10,485,760 bytes)
ReceiveProtocolLogPath            : C:\Program Files\Microsoft
\Exchange Server\V14\TransportRoles\Logs\ProtocolLog\SmtpReceive
```

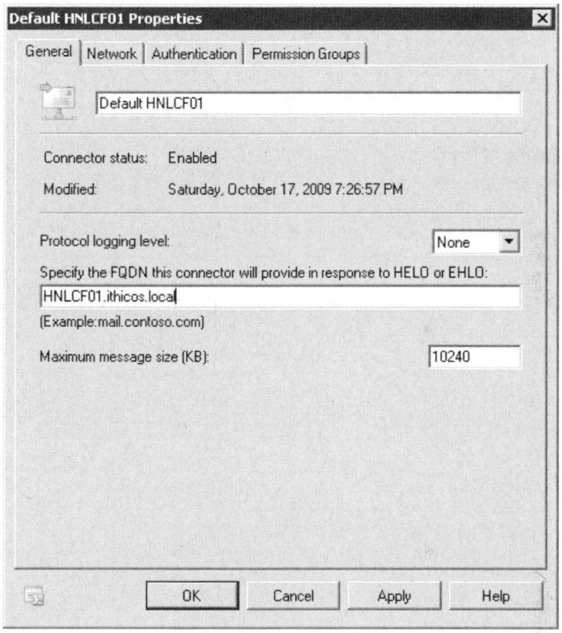

FIGURE 27.10
General tab for
the Default receive
connector

A maximum of 250 MB worth of logs are kept and the log file sizes are no more than 10 MB. The receive log files are stored in the C:\Program Files\Microsoft\Exchange Server\V14\TransportRoles\Logs\ProtocolLog\SmtpReceive folder, though you can change any of these using the Set-TransportServer cmdlet.

Next is the FQDN that will be returned when clients connect to this server. Note in Figure 27.10 that this is currently hnlcf01.ithicos.local; while this should not cause any sort of mail delivery issues for you, it does expose your internal server name and internal domain name. Here is an example of the banner that is presented to a client when it connects to an Exchange server:

```
220 HNLCF01.ithicos.local Microsoft ESMTP MAIL Service ready at Sun,
18 Oct 2009 00:18:10 -0700
```

The third feature that is interesting on this page is the maximum message size that the receive connector will support. The default is 10 MB, which is the same as the global message size limit.

Configuring a Send Connector

For Exchange 2010 to deliver outbound email, a send connector must be created. The send connector is similar to the SMTP connector found in Exchange 2003. When you define a send connector, you specify what SMTP email address spaces that the connector will support, if the connector will use a smart host or DNS to deliver mail, and which servers will be used as a bridgehead (source) server.

Your organization's send connectors are not associated with any single Hub Transport server, so they are an organization-wide resource rather than a per-server resource (like the receive connectors). Using the EMC, navigate to Organization Configuration ➢ Hub Transport and then click the Send Connectors properties page in the Results pane.

To create a new send connector, launch the New Send Connector wizard from the Actions pane. On the Introduction page of the wizard (shown in Figure 27.11), you must specify the name of the connector and its intended use.

FIGURE 27.11
The Introduction page of the send connector wizard

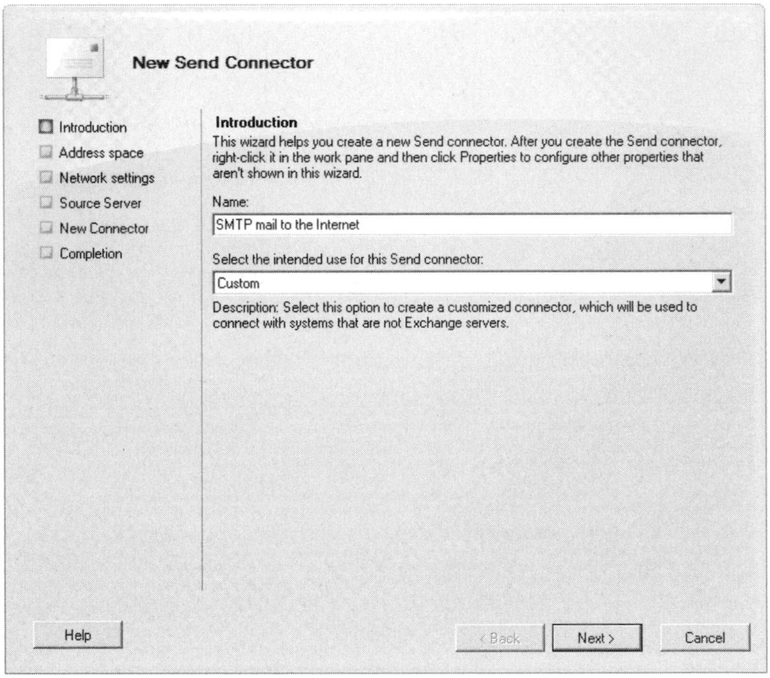

The intended use of the connector is merely an option that helps you to quickly configure some specific settings of the connector; you can change these settings later. We recommend using the Custom option for most send connectors. Here are the options for intended use:

Custom   Allows you the maximum flexibility when creating a send connector that will be used for delivering email outside your organization.

Internal   Configures a send connector that can be used to deliver email to Exchange servers within your organization, such as Exchange 2003 servers that use the SMTP connector's Connected Sites option.

Internet   Configures a send connector that will use DNS to route email outside your organization.

Partner   Configures a send connector that will deliver email to predefined partner organizations; this is part of the configuration necessary for the domain security feature. The connections sent using this type of connector are authenticated using certificates and data is transferred via TLS. You must also define the list of specific domains to be used by using the `Set-TransportConfig` cmdlet.

The next page of the New Send Connector wizard is the Address Space page (Figure 27.12). Here, you define the address spaces you can reach through this connector; for most organizations, the only address space you will have is *, since the connector will be used to deliver mail to all external domains.

FIGURE 27.12

Defining a send connector's address space

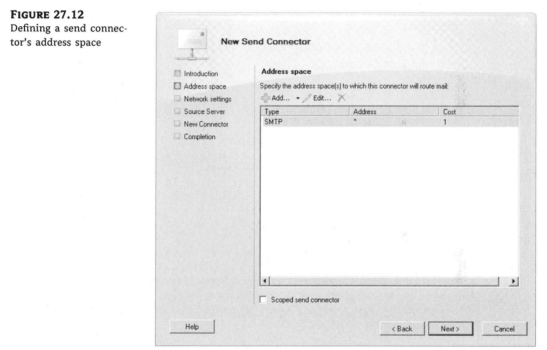

We have found the address spaces feature to be useful in some organizations that need to route email for specific domains through another path or directly to a specific host. In this case, you might have a second send connector with a specific address space and a smart host configured that will accept mail for that specific address space.

If you have a connector that has an address space of * and a second connector that has an address space of partnerdomain.com, any email addressed to recipients at partnerdomain.com will always go through the second connector.

The next page of the wizard is the Network Settings page shown in Figure 27.13; this is where you configure how the Hub Transport server will deliver outbound mail:

Use Domain Name System (DNS) "MX" Records To Route Mail Automatically   When this option is selected, the Hub Transport server will look up a remote domain's MX records, select a server for remote delivery, and deliver the mail directly to the server that was selected via DNS.

Route Mail Through The Following Smart Hosts   This option instructs the Hub Transport server to send all mail (based on the address space for the connector) to the host or hosts specified in the smart host list.

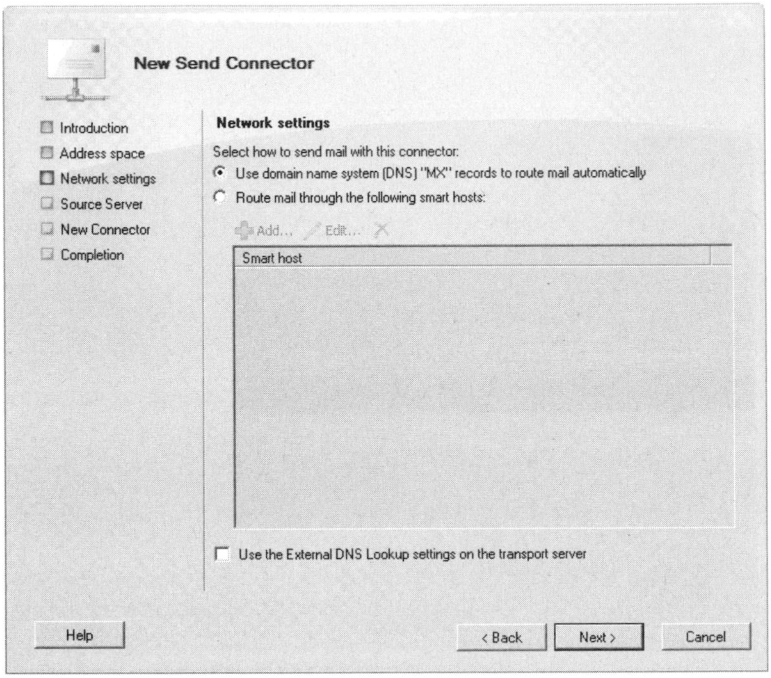

FIGURE 27.13
Configuring the send connector's network settings

Use the Route Mail Through The Following Smart Hosts option if you are planning to use a third-party message hygiene system or a managed provider. Do not use this option if you will be configuring an Edge Transport server or sending mail directly to the Internet via the Hub Transport server.

If your internal DNS servers are not capable of resolving external DNS names properly but you need the Hub Transport server to deliver mail externally, click the Use The External DNS Lookup Settings On The Transport Server check box. Before this will work, however, you must also define valid (and reachable) DNS servers on the External DNS Lookups properties page of the Hub Transport server.

The next page of the wizard is the Source Server page (Figure 27.14). Here, you designate the Hub Transport servers (or Edge Transport servers) that will be used to deliver the outbound mail. In a large environment, this may be only part of your Hub Transport servers.

When you have configured the send connector options properly in the wizard, the New Connector page includes a New button. Click this button to create the connector. Here's the EMS command that created this connector:

```
New-SendConnector -Name 'SMTP mail to the Internet' -Usage 'Custom' ↵
-AddressSpaces 'SMTP:*;1' -IsScopedConnector $false -DNSRoutingEnabled $true ↵
-UseExternalDNSServersEnabled $false -SourceTransportServers 'HNLEX05'
```

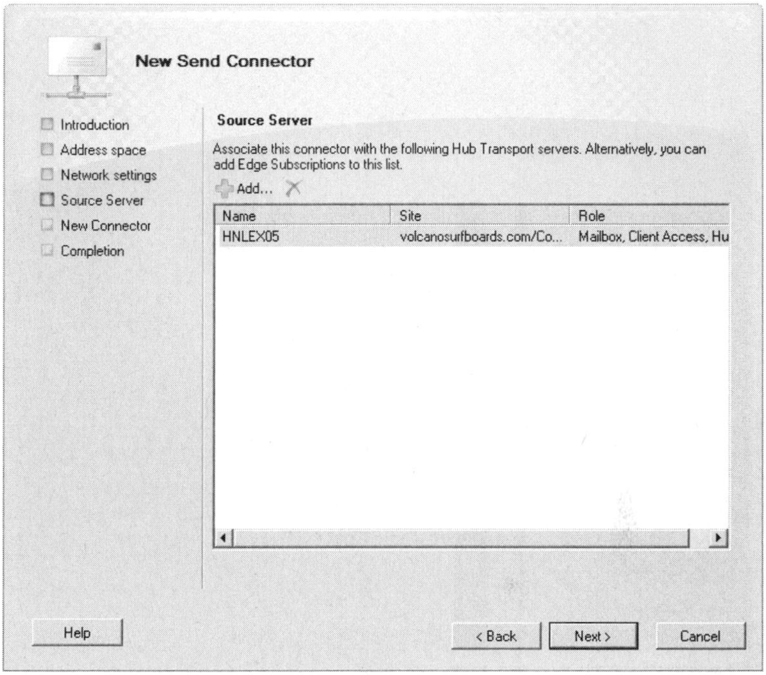

FIGURE 27.14
Defining the source
(bridgehead) servers
that a send connector
will use

Implementing Edge Transport Servers

The Exchange 2010 Edge Transport server role can provide you with an additional layer of email protection between your mail servers and the Internet, with the added advantage of using the same management interface as the rest of Exchange 2010.

Some Background Information on Edge Transport

Microsoft decided shortly after the release of Exchange Server 2003 that the Exchange server platform was not the best place for preliminary virus and spam inspection. Neither was it a good idea to put Active Directory member servers in the perimeter network. After all, an Exchange server is a member of the Active Directory and requires connectivity to other Exchange servers as well as the Active Directory domain controllers and global catalog servers. To build an Exchange 2000/2003 server for handling just message transfer, a number of unnecessary components had to be installed. The Information Store service even had to remain running. If this server were compromised, the entire network could be exposed.

The Edge Transport server was developed with minimal messaging functionality but with a certain amount of "knowledge" of your internal recipients and infrastructure. Essentially, it is nothing more than a message transport engine that allows for the plug-in of additional components such as transport rules, antispam agents, and antivirus software. Edge Transport does not communicate directly with or even require Active Directory; instead, Edge Transport uses the Microsoft Active Directory Lightweight Directory Services (AD LDS) module (formerly known as Active Directory Application Mode Application, or ADAM) database for its configuration.

The Hub Transport server runs a service called Microsoft Exchange EdgeSync that pushes configuration data, recipient information, and safe sender, blocked sender, and safe recipient lists. The EdgeSync process replicates the following data from the internal Active Directory to the AD LDS database:

◆ A list of all Exchange recipient data, including the following:

  ◆ Recipient information, such as the list of recipients in the Exchange organization. Each recipient is identified by the GUID assigned to it in Active Directory. If you configure a recipient's user account to deny receipt of mail from outside the organization, the recipient is not replicated to the AD LDS database. If you disable or delete the mailbox for a recipient, it is not replicated to AD LDS.

  ◆ SMTP email addresses for all valid recipients (mail-enabled users, contacts, groups, and public folders). All proxy addresses assigned to each recipient are replicated to AD LDS as hashed data. This is a one-way hash that uses Secure Hash Algorithm (SHA) 256. SHA-256 generates a 256-bit message digest of the original data. Storing proxy addresses as hashed data helps secure this information in case the Edge Transport server or AD LDS is compromised. Proxy addresses are referenced when the Edge Transport server performs the recipient lookup antispam task.

  ◆ Safe sender, blocked sender, and safe recipient lists for each user

  ◆ Per-user anti-spam settings (configured via the Set-Mailbox cmdlet)

◆ The list of internal accepted domains

◆ The list of remote domains

◆ Configured message classifications

◆ Send connector configuration

◆ TLS Send and Receive Domain Secure lists

◆ The Internal SMTP Servers list

◆ The list of Hub Transport servers in the subscribed Active Directory site

Edge Transport rules are based on SMTP addresses, not Active Directory objects — but you can use the SMTP addresses of mail-enabled groups. For the most part, the Edge Transport rules are a subset of hub rules — the exception is Quarantine, which is available only on the edge, because it is intended for spam.

As an added advantage, the Edge Transport server is managed using the same management tools (the EMC, EMS, Queue Viewer, Best Practices Analyzer, and so on) you use to manage other Exchange 2010 server roles, so no steep learning curve is associated with deploying the Edge Transport server role.

Placement of the Edge Transport Server

To maximize the security benefits, we recommend that the Edge Transport server be deployed in your perimeter network, as shown in Figure 27.15. The organization's DNS MX record directs inbound email to the Edge Transport server that is located in the perimeter network.

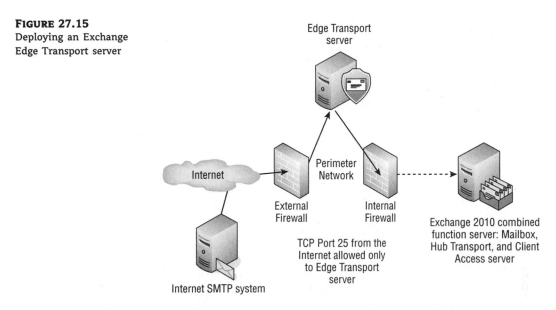

The Edge Transport server performs antispam and antivirus functions and then passes messages on to an internal Hub Transport server. The firewall is configured so that TCP port 25 inbound from the Internet is allowed only to the Edge Transport server. Likewise, the internal firewall only allows inbound TCP port 25 from the Edge Transport server in the perimeter network and only to the Hub Transport server on the internal network.

The Edge Transport server has specific antispam transport agents installed that handle different types of filtering, analysis, and transport rules. Table 27.1 shows the transport agents that are installed on an Edge Transport server. All the transport agents are installed and enabled by default.

TABLE 27.1:   Edge Transport Server Transport Agents

AGENT	FEATURES PROVIDED
Address Rewriting Inbound agent	Messaging policy and compliance
Address Rewriting Outbound agent	Messaging policy and compliance
Attachment Filter agent	Antispam and antivirus
Connection Filter agent	Antispam and antivirus
Content Filter agent	Antispam and antivirus
Edge Rule agent	Messaging policy and compliance
Protocol Analysis agent	Antispam and antivirus
Recipient Filter agent	Antispam and antivirus
Sender Filter agent	Antispam and antivirus
Sender ID agent	Antispam and antivirus

SETTING UP THE EDGE TRANSPORT

This section goes through a sample configuration of the Edge Transport server and the Hub Transport server, as illustrated in Figure 27.16. The internal firewall must first be configured to allow certain types of inbound and outbound connectivity between the internal network and the perimeter network. Specifically, connectivity is required between the Edge Transport server and the Hub Transport server. We have kept this example really simple; you would need to scale this for additional Hub Transport servers and Edge Transport servers.

FIGURE 27.16
Simple Edge Transport deployment

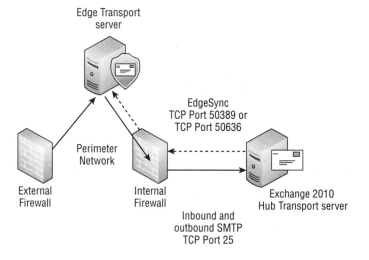

This setup has the following requirements:

♦ The Edge Transport server must be able to send SMTP (TCP port 25) to the Hub Transport server.

♦ The Edge Transport server must have its fully qualified domain name (FQDN) configured.

♦ The Hub Transport server should be able to send SMTP to the Edge Transport server if the Edge Transport server will be used for outbound mail.

♦ The Hub Transport server must also be able to communicate using the ports designated for LDAP synchronization to the AD LDS database.

♦ These are either TCP port 50389 for regular LDAP or TCP port 50636 for secure LDAP. You will usually use port 50389 unless you have configured AD LDS on the Edge Transport to use SSL.

You might need to open additional ports through the internal firewall and to the Edge Transport server if you want to use the Remote Desktop Connection (RDP) client to manage the Edge Transport server remotely. The RDP client uses TCP port 3389.

To configure simple mail flow between an Edge Transport server and a Hub Transport server, you could just configure the necessary send and receive connectors, but you would not be receiving the full benefits of the Edge Transport role. To do so, you need to configure Edge Synchronization (EdgeSync). This process involves five basic steps:

1. Perform prerequisite checks and configuration settings.

2. Create an Edge Subscription file on the Edge Transport server.

3. Copy the Edge Subscription file to the Hub Transport server.

4. Import the Edge Subscription file and create a send connector for the Edge Subscription.

5. Start the Microsoft Exchange EdgeSync service on the Hub Transport server (if it's not already started).

You should perform all these steps within 24 hours because the bootstrap account that is created with the Edge Subscription file is only good for 24 hours from the time it was created.

The Edge Subscription that you are creating will work for all existing Hub Transport servers at the time you create it. However, if you add additional Hub Transport servers into the Active Directory site, you must create a new Edge Subscription for each Hub Transport server that will communicate with the Edge Transport.

CONFIGURING EDGESYNC

Let's go through the preconfiguration checklist and make sure you are ready to configure EdgeSync. Here is a list of tasks you should perform:

◆ Confirm that DNS name resolution between the Hub Transport and the Edge Transport works. In some cases, you may need to create HOSTS files for the two systems if the internal Hub Transport server is not resolvable in DNS by the Edge Transport server, and vice versa.

◆ Ensure that the necessary ports on the firewall are opened.

◆ Configure the accepted domains and remote domains for your organization (on the internal Exchange 2010 servers).

◆ Define the internal SMTP servers so that Sender ID knows which servers are internal to your organization and the connection filters know not to reject connections from your internal IP addresses.

The internal SMTP servers must be configured using the EMS cmdlet `Set-TransportConfig`. In the following example, the internal mail servers are defined as having the IP addresses 192.168.254.102 and 192.168.254.19:

```
Set-TransportConfig -InternalSMTPServers 192.168.254.102,192.168.254.19
```

Next, you need to switch to the console of the Edge Transport server and create the Edge Subscription file. The following command creates a new EdgeSync subscription file called EdgeSync.xml. Note that the confirmation message mentions a couple of the prerequisites:

```
New-EdgeSubscription -FileName "c:\EdgeSync.xml"
```

```
Confirm
Creating an Edge Subscription makes the configuration of this Edge
Transport server ready to be managed via EdgeSync. Any of the
following types of objects that were created manually will be deleted:
accepted domains; message classifications; remote domains; and Send
connectors. Also, the InternalSMTPServers list of the TransportConfig
object will be overwritten during the synchronization process. The
Exchange Management Shell tasks that manage those types of objects will
be locked out on this Edge Transport server. You must manage those
objects from inside the organization and allow EdgeSync to update the
```

Edge Transport server. EdgeSync requires that this Edge Transport
server is able to resolve the fully qualified domain names (FQDN) of
the Hub Transport servers in the Active Directory site to which the
Edge Transport server is being subscribed. Those Hub Transport servers
must be able to resolve the FQDN of this Edge Transport server. You
should complete the Edge Subscription inside the organization in the
next "1440" minutes before the bootstrap account expires.
[Y] Yes [A] Yes to All [N] No [L] No to All [S] Suspend [?] Help
(default is "Y"):y

READY THE SNEAKERNET: TRANSFERRING THE *EDGESYNC.XML* FILE

One of the things that Exchange administrators are often not prepared for is that they must
transfer the edgesync.xml file from the Edge Transport server to the Hub Transport server.
Have a floppy disk or a USB thumb drive handy when you generate this file at the Edge Transport server. Of course, if you allow local disk drives to be mapped through Remote Desktop,
then you can copy the file through that connection.

The file that is created is shown in Figure 27.17. Take special note of the <EdgeServerFQDN>
XML tag. This value will be used by the Hub Transport server when it must transmit data
(SMTP data or EdgeSync replication data) to the Edge Transport server, so this FQDN must
be resolvable by the Hub Transport server.

FIGURE 27.17
The result of the
New-EdgeSubscription
command

Other content you will find in the EdgeSync subscription file includes the Edge server's
certificate, the username, and password information that the Hub Transport server will use
when authenticating to the Edge Transport server, and vice versa.

You need to transport this EdgeSync.xml file to the Hub Transport server now. If all
file-sharing ports between the perimeter and the internal network are locked down, you
may have to use a USB drive, CD-ROM, or a floppy disk (oh, the horror). Once you have
the EdgeSync subscription file on the Hub Transport server, you can import the file into the
Exchange 2010 organization.

In the Organization Configuration work center of the Exchange Management Console, open
the Hub Transport subcontainer and select the Edge Subscriptions tab. To import the new

EdgeSync subscription file, choose the New Edge Subscription task from the Actions pane. This launches the New Edge Subscription wizard (shown in Figure 27.18).

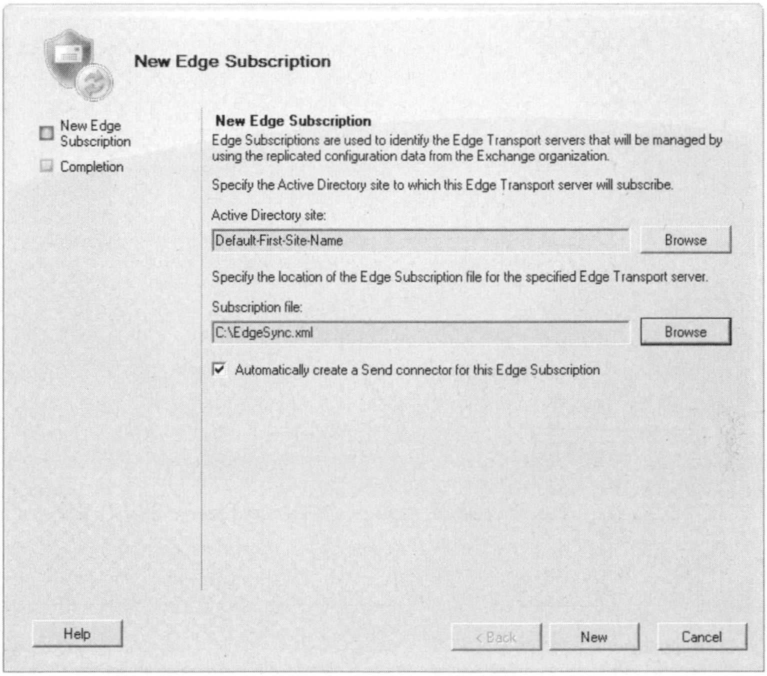

FIGURE 27.18
Creating a new Edge Subscription for the Hub Transport server

You must specify the Active Directory site of which this Edge Transport server will be a member. We recommend that you allow the New Edge Subscription wizard to create the necessary send connector to be used with the Edge Transport server. When you are ready, click the New button. The Completion page will remind you to verify firewall connectivity and name resolution.

The Edge Synchronization process should start almost immediately and will synchronize configuration data once every three hours afterward. Recipient information will be synchronized once every five hours. You can force the synchronization to run by running the EMS cmdlet `Start-EdgeSynchronization` with no parameters.

If you want to include your user's safe sender list in the synchronization, you should also schedule the `Update-SafeList` cmdlet to run periodically (usually once per day is fine). This command should run on the Hub Transport server. Here is an example that will update the safe sender lists for all users so that they are pushed to the Edge Transport via the EdgeSync process:

```
Get-Mailbox | Update-SafeList
```

If you have more than 1,000 recipients in your organization, you will need to tell `Get-Mailbox` to return more than the default 1,000 recipients. You can use this command instead:

```
Get-Mailbox -ResultSize Unlimited | Update-SafeList
```

CONFIRMING THAT EDGESYNC IS RUNNING

Once you have started Edge Synchronization, you can perform a few tasks to confirm that the data is synchronizing to the AD LDS database on the Edge Transport server. The quickest and most accurate way to verify that Edge Synchronization is functioning properly is to use the `Test-EdgeSynchronization` cmdlet. An example of this cmdlet using the -FullCompareMode switch is shown in Figure 27.19.

FIGURE 27.19
Viewing successful
EdgeSync information

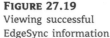

```
Machine: HNLEX05.volcanosurfboards.com
[PS] C:\>Test-EdgeSynchronization -FullCompareMode

RunspaceId                    : b0364b6e-4b61-4442-8437-59ec929a84d7
SyncStatus                    : Normal
UtcNow                        : 2/4/2010 8:20:49 AM
Name                          : HNLET01
LeaseHolder                   : CN=HNLEX05,CN=Servers,CN=Exchange Administrative Group (FYDIBOHF23SP
                                e Groups,CN=Volcano Surfboards,CN=Microsoft Exchange,CN=Services,CN=
                                anosurfboards,DC=com
LeaseType                     : Option
FailureDetail                 :
LeaseExpiryUtc                : 2/4/2010 9:19:02 AM
LastSynchronizedUtc           : 2/4/2010 8:19:02 AM
TransportServerStatus         : Synchronized
TransportConfigStatus         : NotSynchronized
AcceptedDomainStatus          : Synchronized
RemoteDomainStatus            : NotSynchronized
SendConnectorStatus           : Synchronized
MessageClassificationStatus   : Synchronized
RecipientStatus               : Synchronized
CredentialRecords             : Number of credentials 6
CookieRecords                 : Number of cookies 3


[PS] C:\>_
```

Annoyingly, the times listed in 1000 are in GMT rather than in local time, but this is rather minor.

In addition, you can verify that the configuration data has been transferred over to the Edge Transport server's AD LDS database by looking in the EMC on the Edge Transport server. Figure 27.20 shows the EMC and the Edge Transport work center. On the Accepted Domains tab in the Work pane for server HNLET01, you can see the accepted domains that were transferred from the Exchange 2010 organization.

FIGURE 27.20
Viewing the accepted
domains that have
synchronized to an
Exchange 2010 Edge
Transport server

Name ▲	Accepted Domain	Type	Default
Ben Craig's domain	xnetworking.com	Internal Relay	False
Bobs Boogie Boards	BobsBoogieBoards.com	Internal Relay	False
Crawford Enterprises.com	crawford-inc.com	Authoritative	False
Directory Update	directory-update.com	Authoritative	False
Fourth Coffee Company	fourthcoffee.com	Authoritative	False
Ithicos Solutions	ithicos.com	Authoritative	False
Leigh Enterprises	leigh-inc.com	Authoritative	False
Serenity domain	serenity.dnsalias.com	Authoritative	False
Somorita	somorita.com	Authoritative	True
Somorita Research	research.somorita.com	Authoritative	False
Uesato Enterprises	uesato.com	Authoritative	False
Volcano Joes	volcanojoes.com	Authoritative	False
volcanosurfboards.com	volcanosurfboards.com	Authoritative	False

HNLET01 — 13 objects

Anti-spam | Receive Connectors | Send Connectors | Transport Rules | Accepted Domains

Create Filter

Any objects or properties that have synchronized from the internal Exchange Server 2010 organization (such as accepted domains, remote domains, or send connectors) should not be managed on the Edge Transport server. These objects and properties should be managed on the internal Exchange Server 2010 organization; they will be replicated to the Edge Transport server automatically. Note that the Edge Transport's management console cannot be accessed remotely. You must manage Edge Transport servers from their console or using Remote Desktop Connection.

Using Exchange Server 2010 Antispam Tools

Microsoft has continued to improve the antispam capabilities of Exchange over the past few years. This evolution has continued through Exchange Server 2007 and to Exchange Server 2010. Out of the box, many of the antispam agents are enabled and configured; the configuration is usually targeted toward a typical organization. You can make some tweaks to ensure that your organization is effectively filtering spam. You can find the anti-spam features of the Edge Transport server on the Anti-spam tab, as shown in Figure 27.21.

FIGURE 27.21

Customizing anti-spam features of an Edge Transport server

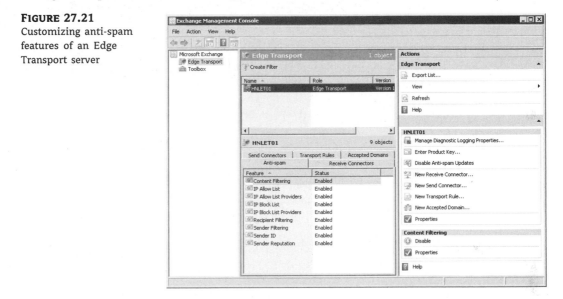

You can see the different antispam configuration options you can configure for the Exchange 2010 Edge Transport server.

🌐 Real World Scenario

OVERWHELMED WITH SPAM

Company DEFG is an 18-person company that had become overwhelmed with spam. In the early days of the Internet, this company had widely posted their employees email addresses on their website; further, many employees participated in online forums and made no effort to mask or obfuscate their email address. The average employee received between 100 and 300 spam messages per day, and they were relying on client-side technologies, such as the Outlook junk email filter to clean up their junk email.

Analyzing the connections on their Exchange 2003 server, you would see between 5 and 40 bot connections at any given time, each trying to deliver to a series of random email addresses.

In one 24-hour period, this small company had more than 18,000 connections and connection attempts, most by spammers.

By using the Exchange 2010 content filter (set to reject everything with an SCL of 7 or above and put everything with an SCL of 4 or above into the user's Junk Email folder) as well as using the Spamhaus ZEN block list, they were able to dramatically reduce the amount of spam making it to the user's mailbox.

After these features were enabled, the average user received fewer than two to three spam messages directly in their Inbox each day, and their Junk Email folder usually had 10 to 15 messages per day.

Enabling Antispam Agents for Hub Transport Servers

Out of the box, the Exchange 2010 Edge Transport server has several useful features that can help you dramatically reduce the amount of spam that you are receiving. If you do not deploy the Edge Transport server role and only use Hub Transport servers, these antispam transport agents can be installed on your Hub Transport servers as well.

You will find two PowerShell scripts (`Install-AntispamAgents.ps1` and `Uninstall-AntispamAgents.ps1`) in the folder `C:\Program Files\Microsoft\Exchange Server\v14\scripts`.

On each of your Hub Transport servers on which you will be using the antispam agents, you will need to run the `Install-AntispamAgents.ps1` script. This script only needs to be run on the Hub Transport servers that will receive inbound email from outside your organization.

To run the installation script, open the EMS, change to the scripts folder listed earlier, and then type this command:

```
.\Install-AntispamAgents.ps1
```

After you run this command, you will need to restart the Microsoft Exchange Transport service, then close and reopen any instances of the EMS and EMC.

Enabling Automatic Updates for the Antispam Signatures

If you want to receive antispam signature updates and IP reputation service updates, you will need to enable antispam updates. You would need to do this on all Hub Transports that receive email from the Internet and Edge Transport servers. To enable all updates to be automatically processed, here is the command we recommend running:

```
Enable-AntispamUpdates -IPReputationUpdatesEnabled $True ↵
-SpamSignatureUpdatesEnabled $True -UpdateMode Automatic ↵
-MicrosoftUpdate RequestScheduled
```

Once you run this command, you should stop and restart the Windows Update service. Note that automatic anti-spam updates depend on the Microsoft Update service function. You can verify the version of the updates that are being downloaded by using the `Get-AntispamUpdates` cmdlet, such in this example:

```
Get-AntispamUpdates

RunspaceId               : 8752c366-c8c7-4304-bf2d-eb0de9cc2808
UpdateMode               : Automatic
```

```
LatestContentFilterVersion   : 3.3.4604.600
SpamSignatureUpdatesEnabled  : True
LatestSpamSignatureVersion   : 3.3.4604.600
IPReputationUpdatesEnabled   : True
LatestIPReputationVersion    : 3.3.4604.001
MicrosoftUpdate              : RequestScheduled
```

Content Filtering

Content filtering is a feature in Exchange Server 2010 that was formerly known as the Intelligent Message Filter. And arguably it is the most useful of the antispam features. The content filter examines the message's content based on keyword analysis, message size, and other factors, and then assigns the message a spam confidence level (SCL) ranking. This ranking is from 0 to 9. A message with a ranking of 0 is the least likely to be spam, and a message with an SCL of 9 is very likely to be spam. Based on the SCL value of the message, you have several actions you can take (see Figure 27.22).

FIGURE 27.22
The Action tab of the Content Filtering object's properties

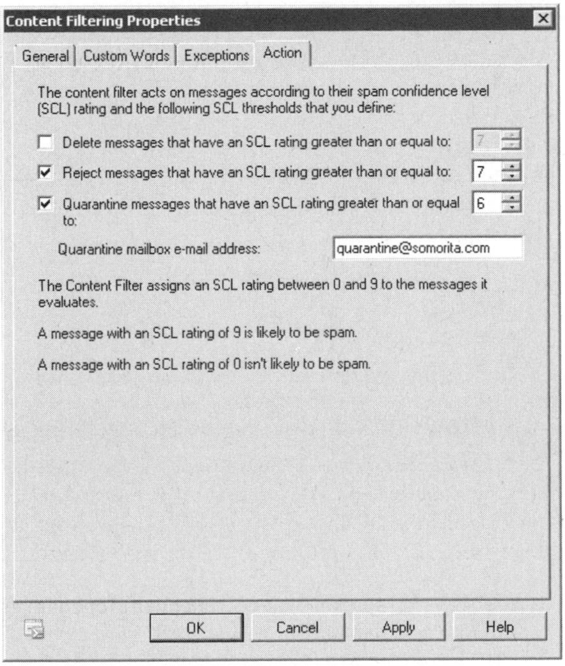

You can take three possible actions, ranked in order of severity:

1. Delete messages that meet or exceed a specific SCL threshold. This is the most drastic of actions. The sender is not notified that this has occurred, and you can't later evaluate whether the message really was spam.

2. Reject messages that meet or exceed a specific SCL threshold. The Edge Transport or Hub Transport server accepts the message, analyzes it, and kicks it back to the sender with text indicating that the message was rejected because it looks like spam.

3. Quarantine messages that meet or exceed a specific SCL threshold. Any messages with the specified SCL value or higher will be sent to an SMTP address where you can then analyze them to determine whether they are truly spam.

NEGATIVE SCL VALUES?

Is it possible to have an SCL value of −1? Yes, actually it is. Any message that is sent to your server via an authenticated connection, or if the sender's email address is on your safe senders list, then the SCL value of the message is set to −1. So if one of your trusted senders is sending you a short message about low-interest rate mortgages and buying cheap Viagra, you will still get the message.

You can activate none, one, two, or all three of the actions, but the SCL values must progress downward in accordance with the severity of the action. For example, you could set a reject value of 8 or higher and a quarantine value of 7 or higher. In that case, any messages with an SCL value of 8 or 9 will be rejected; messages with an SCL value of 7 will be sent to the quarantine email address. However, you cannot set a quarantine value of 9 but then delete everything with an SCL value greater than or equal to 7.

On the inside of your Exchange organization, a global value called the SCL Junk Threshold is set to 4 by default. This instructs the information store to place any messages with a spam confidence level of 4 or higher into the user's Junk Email folder. Users can then review their Junk Email folder to determine whether a message was truly spam. However, if you set the quarantine value on the Edge Transport server to 3, then only messages with an SCL value of 3 will reach the Junk Email folder.

For most organizations, a global SCL Junk Threshold of 4 is probably sufficient, but depending on your business model and the types of mail you receive, you might want to raise it. You can raise the SCL value to 5 or 6. To raise the Junk Email threshold for all users, on one of the Exchange Server 2010 servers in your organization, type this command:

```
Set-OrganizationConfig -SCLJunkThreshold 6
```

You can view the organization configuration using the `Get-OrganizationConfig` cmdlet. Here is an example:

```
Get-OrganizationConfig | FL SCLJunk*
```

```
SCLJunkThreshold : 4
```

In some cases, a specific user may need a different set of SCL values than the Edge Transport server provides. The values the Edge Transport server provides can be customized on a user-by-user basis. In the following command, we have disabled the Quarantine and Reject parameters for a particular user, and we have specified that this user's Junk Email threshold is 4:

```
Set-Mailbox "Matt Paleafei" -SCLRejectEnabled $False -SCLQuarantineEnabled ↵
$False  -SCLJunkThreshold 4 -SCLJunkEnabled $True
```

You can view the resulting configuration for the mailbox with the `Get-Mailbox` cmdlet. Here is an example:

```
Get-Mailbox "Matt Paleafei" | FL Name,*scl*

Name                     : Matt Paleafei
SCLDeleteThreshold       :
SCLDeleteEnabled         :
SCLRejectThreshold       : 7
SCLRejectEnabled         : False
SCLQuarantineThreshold   : 9
SCLQuarantineEnabled     : False
SCLJunkThreshold         : 4
SCLJunkEnabled           : True
```

On the Exceptions tab of the Content Filtering properties, you can configure the SMTP addresses of the internal recipients to which you do not want to apply the content filter. This can be useful when managing a mailbox that is so important you never want any of its messages to be filtered.

🌐 Real World Scenario

WAY TOO MANY VALID EMAILS BEING FLAGGED AS SPAM

Company STUV is a real estate services company. Much of their communication with customers and prospective customers is via email. They found when they started using the content filter that many of their customers' emails were being flagged as spam because of key words in the message body.

They decided to use the content filter's custom words feature to specify some words or phrases that the content filter would not block. This included words and phrases such as "mortgage," "interest rates," "real estate," and "assessment." The thought behind this was that it was better to possibly receive a few extra spam messages that use these words than it was to reject a message from a real customer.

The Custom Words tab of the Content Filtering object's properties enables some interesting features (see Figure 27.23). You can enable two types of word lists. If the message contains words in the first list, even if the message appears to be spam, the message is accepted. If the words in the second list are contained in a message, the message is blocked unless it contains words from the first list.

The list with words and phrases that are always accepted can be particularly useful if legitimate messages to your company will frequently contain a particular word or phrase that might otherwise be filtered.

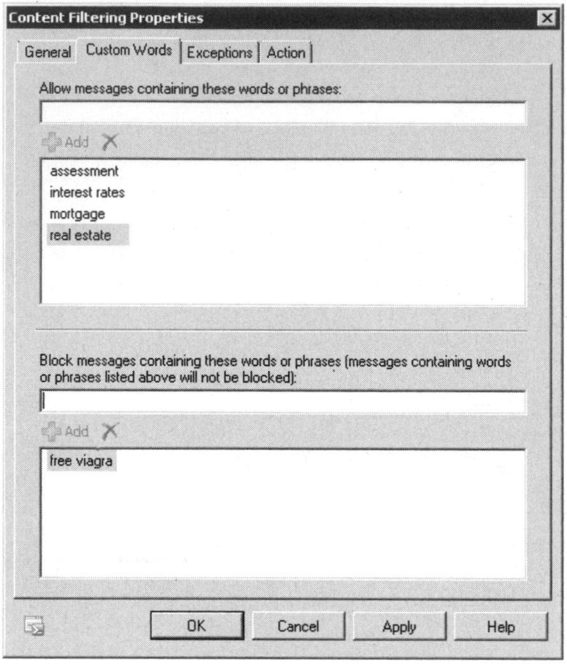

FIGURE 27.23
Configuring custom
words for the
content filter

FIGURE 27.23
Configuring custom
words for the
content filter

IP Block and IP Allow Providers

Arguably, block list providers are one of the most effective ways to prevent spam from reaching your users. The block list is an effective way to block spam, but some mail administrators consider block lists to be one step above evil incarnate. If you have ever had one of your public IP addresses incorrectly listed on one of these lists, you may sympathize with them since getting off some lists can be challenging.

An IP block list provider is better known as a real-time block list (RBL) provider. This is a service that keeps track of known sources of spam, open relays, open proxies, IP addresses used by dial-up connections, and IP addresses used by DHCP ranges. These are all frequent sources of spam. Conversely, an IP allow list provider is a service provider that maintains a list of IP addresses that are likely not to send spam.

The most common configuration is an IP block list provider. When an SMTP client connects to your Edge Transport (or Hub Transport) server, the Edge Transport server issues a DNS query using the reverse format of the IP address along with the DNS suffix of the block list provider. For example, if an SMTP client at IP address 192.168.254.10 connects to an Edge Transport server, it will issue the DNS query `10.254.168.192.zen.spamhaus.org` if it is configured to use the Spamhaus ZEN list.

USING IP BLOCK LIST PROVIDERS

We are fans of block list providers (also known as real-time block lists) and encourage our customers to use them. On average, a typical block list, such as the Spamhaus ZEN list, will help you cut in half or more the amount of spam that you receive.

In one particular situation, we used Exchange Server's performance monitoring tools to determine how many messages per day the Exchange Server content filter considered a spam confidence level of 7 or higher. This particular organization was receiving nearly 40,000 messages per day that had an SCL of 7 or higher.

After enabling the IP block list provider to use the zen.spamhaus.org block list, the average daily count of messages with an SCL of 7 or higher dropped to 16,000. The messages identified by the RBL as spam were dropped at the Hub Transport and were not transferred. This saved on bandwidth as well as Hub Transport processing capacity.

If the IP address is not on the Spamhaus block list, the DNS query will return a Host Not Found message. However, if the entry is on a block list, the DNS query will return an IP address such as 127.0.0.1, 127.0.0.2, and so on. The different return codes have different meanings for different providers.

Figure 27.24 shows the IP Block List Providers Properties dialog; in this figure, one block list provider has been configured.

FIGURE 27.24

Viewing the current IP block list provider

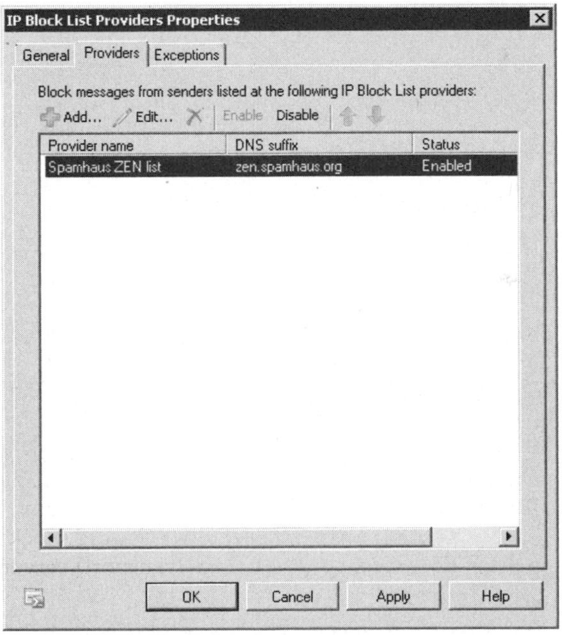

If you click the Add button, you can add RBL providers (there are none configured by default). Figure 27.25 shows part of the Add IP Block List Provider dialog box and the custom error messages screen. The information that is required in the Add IP Block List Provider dialog box is a name for the provider and the DNS suffix or the lookup domain. You get the DNS suffix from the block list provider.

When you add a new IP block list provider, you can also configure it so that it responds only to certain error codes. This could be useful, for example, if the provider returns different error codes for different types of hosts and you only want to block mail for certain error codes.

FIGURE 27.25
Adding a new IP block
list provider

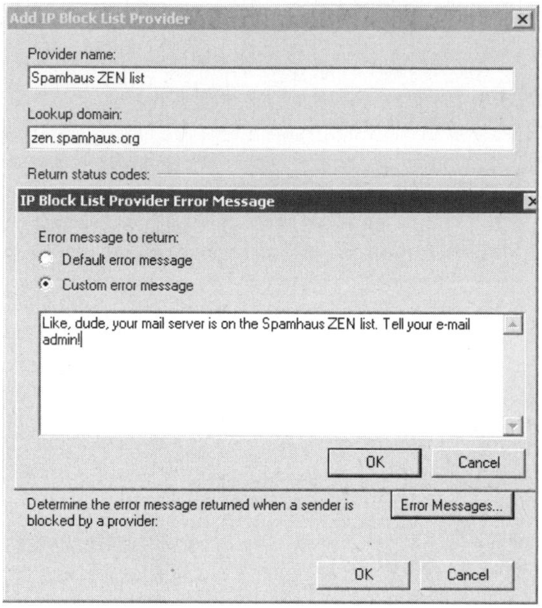

For each block list provider, you can configure a custom error message. This can be useful for administrators whose systems may be on a block list. We recommend configuring a message that would be helpful for the administrator of a system from which you are rejecting mail.

The Exceptions tab is useful if you want to specify SMTP addresses to which the RBL blocking should not apply.

A lot of RBL providers are available on the Internet, and almost all are free. Some of these providers are pretty accurate, and some are not. Some are more aggressive than others. The more aggressive RBLs will often block entire IP subnets or entire IP ranges from regions of the world. Other IP block lists make it difficult to remove your IP address if you get on their list. Table 27.2 lists some of the RBLs we recommend using. We usually recommend choosing two RBLs; in the table, they are listed in order of preference. Our preference is to choose less aggressive RBLs and also use other filtering technologies, such as content filtering or sender reputation.

TABLE 27.2:   Recommended IP Block List Providers

PROVIDER	PROVIDER'S WEBSITE	PROVIDER'S DNS SUFFIX
Spamhaus	www.spamhaus.org	zen.spamhaus.org
Composite Blocking List	cbl.abuseat.org	cbl.abuseat.org
SORBS	www.sorbs.net	dnsbl.sorbs.net
SpamCop	www.spamcop.net	bl.spamcop.net

IP Block and Allow Lists

The IP Block List and IP Allow List features allow you to specify individual IP addresses, sub-nets, or entire ranges of IP addresses from which you will not accept or will always accept mail, respectively. Block lists are configured on a per–Hub Transport or per–Edge Transport basis. Figure 27.26 shows the interface for the IP Block List, but the interface for the IP Allow List is identical.

FIGURE 27.26

Configuring an IP Block List entry

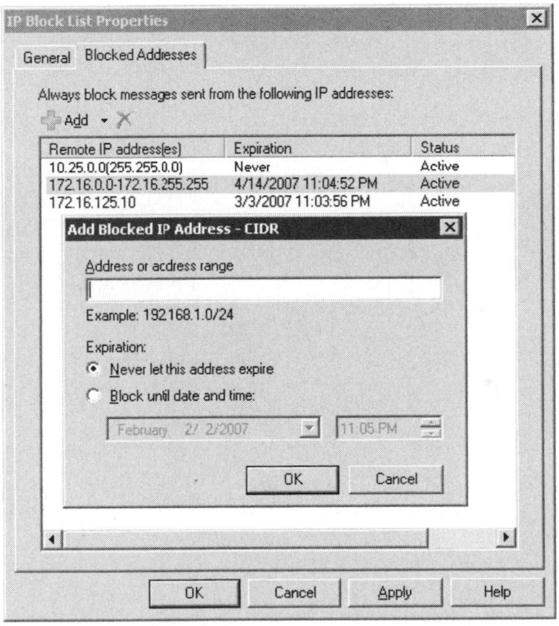

In the foreground of Figure 27.26, you can see the interface for adding a single IP address. A nice feature of this interface is that you can specify that you always want to block an IP address, subnet, or address range or that you want to automatically unblock the address after a date and time.

Recipient Filtering

When recipient filtering is enabled, the Edge Transport is configured to reject mail intended for any SMTP address that is not found in the Active Directory or to reject mail intended for specific SMTP addresses. This will reduce a lot of the garbage messages for which your Exchange server accepts and then has to issue a nondelivery report. Figure 27.27 shows the Blocked Recipients list for the Recipient Filtering object.

We recommend that you select the Block Messages Sent To Recipients Not Listed In The Directory check box. This will help reduce the burden placed on your system by zombie networks of spammers. However, by recommending that you enable this check box, we are assuming that you have EdgeSync enabled and that all valid SMTP addresses are replicated to the Edge Transport server's local AD LDS database.

If you are performing recipient filtering, newly created mailboxes may have their mail rejected by the Edge Transport server until the replication runs again. You can force the synchronization after new mailboxes are created by running the `Start-EdgeSynchronization` cmdlet. Or just make sure that the users do not give anyone their email address for at least four hours after the account is created.

FIGURE 27.27
Configuring recipient filtering

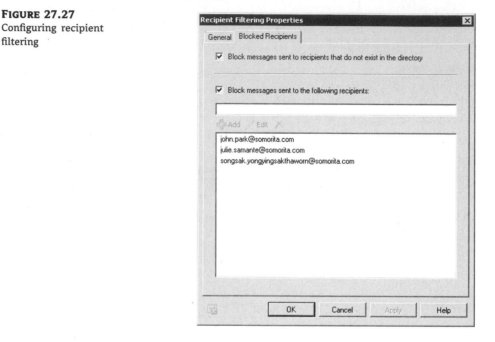

Tarpitting

The Hub Transport and Edge Transport in Exchange Server 2010 implement a feature called a tarpit. The tarpit feature tells the SMTP server to wait a specified number of seconds (five seconds by default) before responding to a request to send a message to an invalid recipient. For example, if the recipient `Luke@somorita.com` is an invalid recipient in your organization, but someone's mail server sends a message to that address, your server will wait five seconds and then respond with this error:

```
550 5.1.1 User unknown
```

Now, you may wonder why this feature is even worth mentioning. Spammers often hijack people's home (or work) computers with agents that send mail on their behalf. These ''bots'' can offer the spammer an almost unlimited supply of SMTP clients, all sending email. They can locate your domain and then go through a dictionary of common names and try to send mail to each one for example, sending to `alicia@somorita.com`, then `amelia@somorita.com`, then `anthony@somorita.com`, and so on. An Exchange server without a tarpit could send back dozens of 550 error messages each second. This makes dictionary spamming more practical.

Another evil part of the dictionary spamming attack is that the spammer can note which addresses were valid and use them in the future. This is called directory harvesting.

A five-second tarpit slows the spammer down by a factor of maybe even 500 (depending on your server's speed and your Internet connection speed) by rejecting all the invalid delivery attempts. Most spammers' software programs can't handle the rejects, and they disconnect after some period of time.

You can view your receive connector's tarpit interval by using the `Get-ReceiveConnector` cmdlet. For example, if you want to change the HNLEX05 Default receive connector's tarpit interval to 30 seconds, you would type this command:

```
Set-ReceiveConnector "HNLEX05 Default" -TarpitInterval 00:00:30
```

We recommend that you do not set this value to more than about 30 seconds on any of your Hub Transport or Edge Transport servers.

Sender Filtering

Sender filtering is one of the oldest antispam features in Exchange; it is probably also the least effective. The premise is that you provide a list of SMTP addresses or domains that should not be able to send your users email. The problem is that most spammers don't use the same email address twice, so this is less than completely effective. Figure 27.28 shows the Blocked Senders tab of the Sender Filtering object's properties.

FIGURE 27.28
Configuring sender filtering

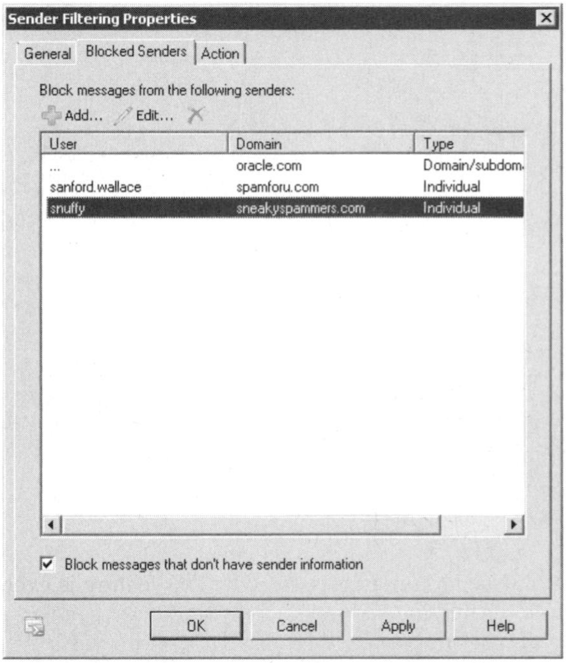

You can block individual senders and you can block all senders in a specific domain. One interesting antispam technique that some organizations employ is to put their own domain in this list. This prevents those spam messages that claim to be from one of your own recipients. However, if you do that on an internal Hub Transport server, make sure that it is not being used for POP3, IMAP4, or other clients that use SMTP to send mail internally.

Another interesting antispam technique that blocks a few pieces of mail is selecting the check box Block Messages That Don't Have Sender Information. If a message does not have a sender (and it should), then this rejects the message.

The interface is a little different than in previous versions of Exchange Server. When you add or edit blocked senders, you have the option of adding an individual user or an entire domain and subdomains.

On the Action tab of the Sender Filtering object's properties, you can specify what action to take. You can either reject the message entirely or stamp the message with a blocked sender and allow it through. If you stamp the message as being from a blocked sender, the content filter will rank it as spam.

Sender ID

Earlier in this chapter, we talked a bit about sender protection framework records and DNS and how to make sure that yours are registered properly. Contrary to popular misconception, Sender ID is not an antispam technology but an antispoofing technology. Quite simply, each organization on the Internet that sends email should register a sender protection framework (SPF) record in their public DNS server. This SPF record contains a list of the servers authorized to send mail on behalf of their domain.

When an STMP server receives a message from a particular domain, it analyzes the message to determine the actual sender and determines which server sent it. If the message originated from an authorized server, it is probably not being spoofed. If it is accepted from a server that is not in the DNS SPF record, the message might be from a spoofed sender.

On the Action tab of the Sender ID object's properties, you can specify which action to take. Figure 27.29 shows the Action tab. You can reject the message, delete the message, or accept it for further processing by the content filter.

FIGURE 27.29
Configuring a Sender
ID action

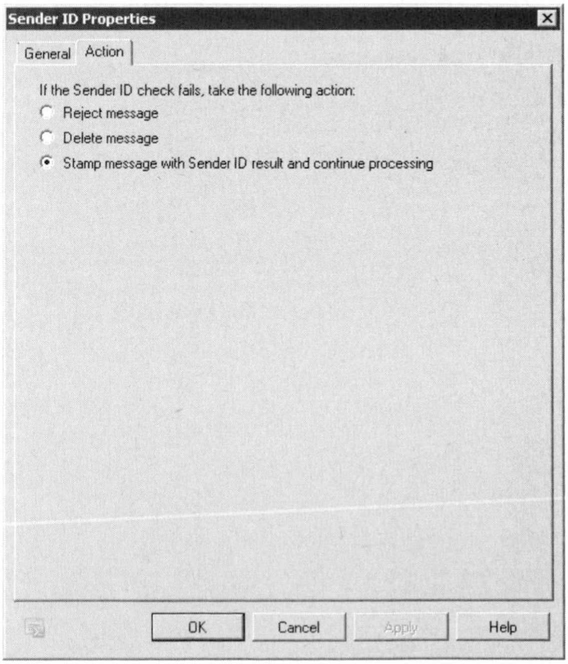

The problem with Sender ID is that fewer than 15 percent of all domains on the Internet have an SPF record, at least by some estimates. And frequently an organization's SPF records get out of date and are therefore wrong. The only thing worse than not having an SPF record is having one that is wrong. Therefore, it is impractical to reject or delete messages that fail the Sender ID test. You should keep this setting configured to Stamp Message With Sender ID Result And Continue Processing.

Sender Reputation

Sender reputation is the most promising feature of Exchange 2010 when it comes to reducing the amount of spam you receive. This is because much of the spam that is received today is sent by bot or zombie networks. Spammers have joined forces with virus writers; the virus writers have written malware that infects hundreds of thousands of users' computers. Periodically, these computers check with the spammer and download a new batch of spam. Blocking a single IP address becomes impractical because the spammers have so many of these computers all over the Internet. However, these zombie networks are usually not using correct SMTP commands and are not RFC compliant. A lot of spammers also use SMTP proxies by sending messages through a proxy on the Internet.

Sender reputation allows Exchange to analyze the connections that are coming in to an Edge Transport or Hub Transport server and look for things such as the number of protocol errors, invalid delivery attempts, and the number of messages from the same sender. These can be used to determine if a specific IP address is sending spam. On the Action tab of the Sender Reputation object's properties (shown in Figure 27.30), you can specify the Sender Reputation Level Block Threshold value; this is a value from 0 to 9 that is used to block senders that exceed a certain "suspicious" threshold.

FIGURE 27.30
Configuring the sender reputation level block threshold

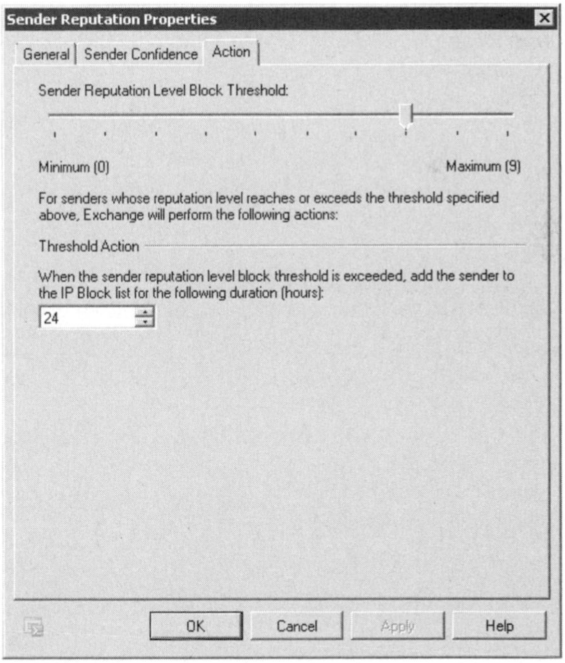

The default for the SRL block threshold is 7; we recommend keeping it at this slightly less aggressive value and then monitoring to see if a lot of spam still gets through. If so, you can increase it slightly, but keep in mind that as you get more aggressive with this value, the possibility of valid connections getting rejected becomes higher.

The Threshold Action section allows you to specify how long a sender is retained on an IP block list once the sender has been determined to be suspicious. The default is 24 hours, and we recommend that you keep that value.

Exchange can test for open proxies and determine if the source of a connection is an open proxy that is probably being used to send spam. On the Sender Confidence tab (Figure 27.31), you can enable the open proxy test. If a connecting SMTP client is determined to be an open proxy, it will be added to the IP block list for the time specified on the Action tab.

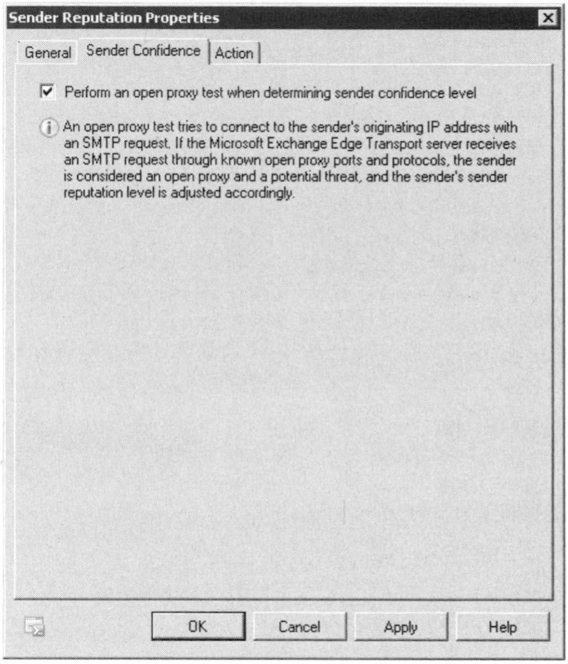

FIGURE 27.31
Configuring the sender reputation filter to perform an open proxy test

CONFIGURING THE EDGE TRANSPORT SERVER TO ENFORCE ORGANIZATION POLICIES

The Edge Transport server has a transport rules feature just as the Exchange 2010 Hub Transport server does. You may find this useful if there are certain types of organizational policies that you wish to enforce on messages that are arriving on the Edge Transport server and before they are delivered on to the Exchange 2010 Hub Transport server.

To illustrate the use of transport rules on the Edge Transport server, let's go through an example that enforces a policy of blocking outbound messages that contain certain confidential words and phrases. Here are the requirements:

1. All messages being sent to a user outside the organization should have this transport rule applied to them.

2. If the message subject or body contains the words *confidential*, *secret formula*, or *secret recipe*, we want to take action on the message.

3. If the message meets the criteria, an error should be recorded in the event log, the message should be dropped, and a copy of the message should be sent to the company audit alias.

For this example, it is assumed that the Edge Transport server is used to relay outbound messages to the Internet as well as to accept inbound messages. This example could also apply to transport rules used inside the organization.

In the Actions pane, select the New Transport Rule task to launch the New Transport Rule wizard. On the Introduction page (shown in Figure 27.32), provide a descriptive name for the policy as well as an accurate description of the function of the transport rule. When finished, click Next to move on to the next page of the wizard.

FIGURE 27.32

Introduction page of the New Transport Rule Wizard

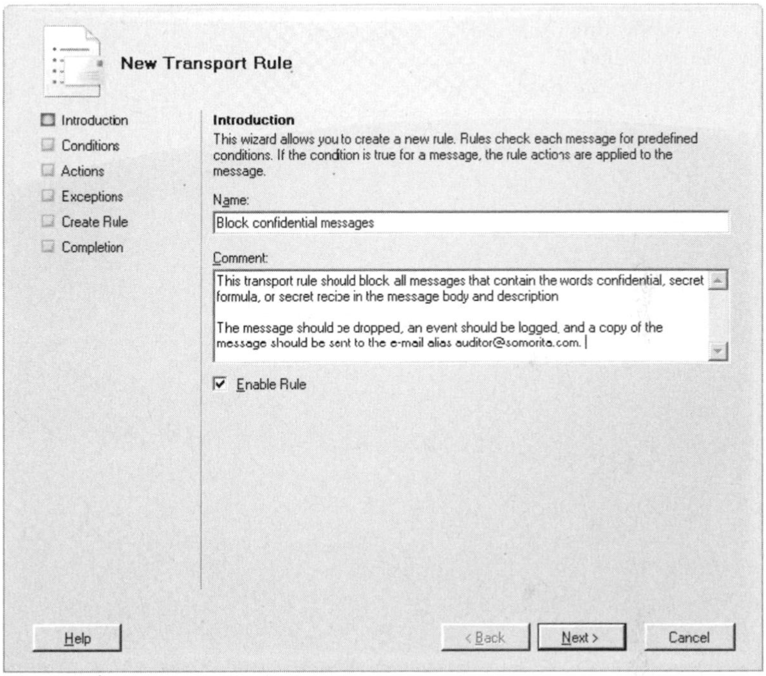

On the Conditions page, specify the conditions of the transport rule. For this rule, two conditions must be met: the message must be from a user inside the organization and there must be specific words in the message body or subject. First, check the condition When The Subject Field Or The Message Body Of The Message Contains Specific Words; this will add that condition to the Step 2 portion of the wizard page. From here you need to click the specific word's link so that you can use the Specify Words dialog. In the Specify Words dialog, you can add or remove words and phrases that are part of the condition.

When finished, click the OK button to close the Specify Words dialog. You now need to select the second condition. Select the From Users Inside Or Outside The Organization check box. This adds that selection to the Step 2 portion of the wizard page. The default is from users inside the organization, but you could change this by clicking the Inside link to see the Select Scope dialog box.

The finished product for the Conditions page looks like Figure 27.33. You can see the conditions selected on the top part of the wizard page (the Step 1 section) and the additional information that was specified for the conditions (Step 2), such as the words to search for and the fact that it applies to message sent by users inside the organization.

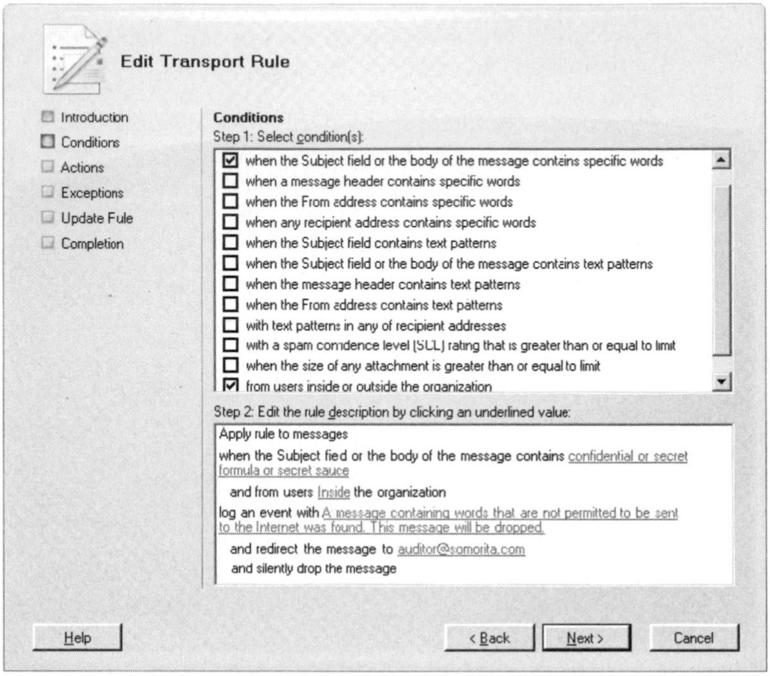

FIGURE 27.33
Conditions page of the
transport rule

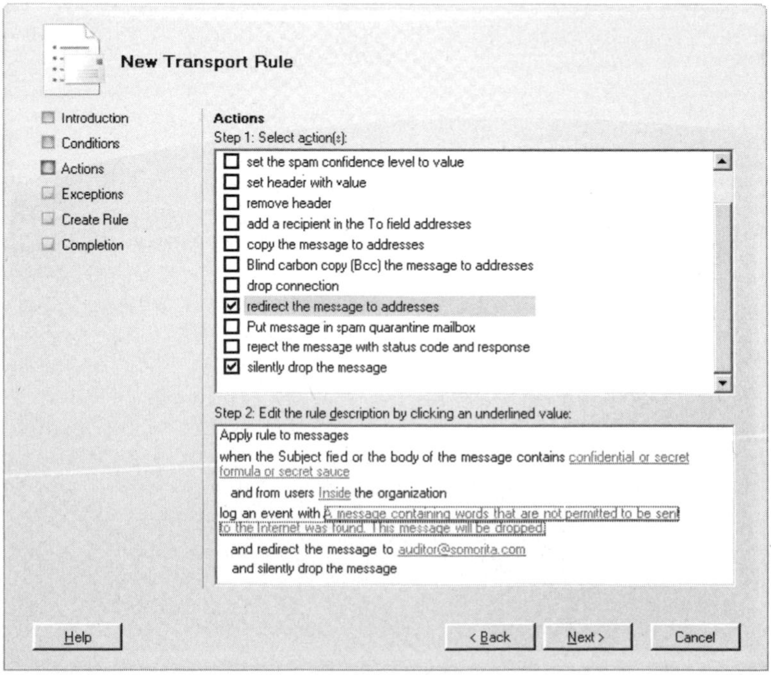

FIGURE 27.34
The Actions page of the
New Transport Rule
wizard

The next page of the wizard is the Actions page. On this page, you specify what you want to do if you find a message that meets the conditions you set on the Conditions page. First, you select the Log An Event With Message action; this adds a message link to the Step 2 section of the page. You click the message link to see the Specify Event Message dialog. Here you enter the information you want entered in the event log.

Next you select the Redirect The Message To Address check box and then click the addresses link that is now in Step 2 of the wizard page. This will display the Specify Recipients dialog. Here you need to add the SMTP address auditor@somorita.com.

After you add the email address to the Specify Recipients dialog, click OK and then select the Silently Drop The Message check box. There is nothing else you need to do for this particular action. Figure 27.34 shows the finished product for the Actions tab.

You can now click Next to see the Exceptions page of the wizard. The Exceptions page allows you to add exceptions to this particular rule. In this example there are none, so you can click Next to move on to the Create Rule configuration summary. From here, you can click the New button to create the new rule.

The Bottom Line

Configure DNS to ensure email is reliably sent and received   Properly configured DNS records are the key to ensuring reliable and timely delivery of not only messages that you send but also that Internet users send to you. You should know who is responsible for your public-facing DNS servers as well as who is responsible for your public-facing IP addresses.

Master It   Some of your users are reporting that they are receiving nondelivery reports when they send email to Internet addresses. This does not happen for all email that users are sending to the Internet, but for a small percentage. Some of the nondelivery errors indicate that your mail server's IP address does not have a reverse lookup record. Your mail server's IP address is 192.168.243.10. What Windows command can you use to verify that the DNS record is correct?

Add an Edge Transport server to handle inbound and outbound email   The Edge Transport server can provide a valuable, additional layer of protection for your internal mail servers. The Edge Transport server role can be configured to accept inbound mail for your domain and to route outbound mail to the Internet. Your internal servers do not need to be exposed to the Internet and only need minimal exposure to the Edge Transport server that is placed in the perimeter network. The Edge Transport server does not need to be a member of your corporate Active Directory.

The Edge Transport server, instead, receives internal configuration about your Exchange organization and recipients via the edge synchronization process. The Edge Transport server stores in an Active Directory Lightweight Directory Services database information such as your recipient's email addresses, accepted domains, and safe sender lists.

Out of the box, the Edge Transport server provides antispam capabilities and can be enhanced with third-party antivirus software or Forefront Security for Exchange.

Master It   You have placed an Edge Transport server into your perimeter network and have opened up TCP ports 25 and 50389 between the Edge Transport server and your internal Hub Transport server. To complete the installation and allow mail flow, what things must you do?

Master It   You need to look up a list of servers that accept inbound mail for your domain, somorita.com. What Windows utility can you use to look up this information?

Configure Exchange Hub Transport servers to send and receive   The most secure way to protect your internal SMTP mail servers is to not expose them to the Internet at all. However, it is possible to allow your Hub Transport servers to directly send and receive Internet mail.

Master It   You need to configure your Hub Transport server to allow it to send email to the Internet and to receive email from the Internet. You have successfully registered a DNS mail exchanger (MX) record that points directly to the Hub Transport server and you have confirmed that the firewall allows inbound SMTP to pass through to the Hub Transport server. What two things do you need to do in order to configure Exchange to send and receive SMTP mail?

Configure Exchange 2010 antispam technologies   Exchange Server 2010 includes a number of technologies that can help you reduce or eliminate the spam that your users receive. The content filter inspects messages based on message content and characteristics. Block list providers can reject an inbound IP connection based on known sources of spam, and sender reputation filters can analyze inbound connections for errors and improperly formatted connections and reject connections from both networks or spammers.

Master It   Your consultant has recommended that you configure the content filter so that messages that contain certain words will be accepted rather than rejected as spam. What should you do?

Part 5

Troubleshooting, Operations, and Monitoring

Chapter 28

Troubleshooting Exchange Server 2010

Despite our care and attention, despite our best efforts to design the perfect Exchange environment, something will inevitably go wrong at some point. Whether it's an unintended configuration setting, faulty hardware, a change to a dependency, or *gasp* a bug in the product, something invariably happens to cause problems for end users and ultimately for us, the administrators.

So what do you do when the lights go out on the Exchange server, figuratively speaking? The goal of this chapter is to outline tried-and-true strategies for recovering an Exchange server as quickly as possible — strategies that work for other technologies as well.

In this chapter, you will learn to:

- ◆ Narrow the scope of an Exchange problem

- ◆ Use basic Exchange troubleshooting tools

- ◆ Troubleshoot Mailbox server problems

- ◆ Troubleshoot mail transport problems

Basic Troubleshooting Principles

In the old days of Exchange, one server could do it all — an Exchange 5.5 or Exchange 2000 server would receive and deliver email, handle client connections, and store user data. There was limited separation of roles between front-end and back-end servers, achieved by selecting the This Is A Front End Server check box in Exchange System Manager. But that didn't enable or disable a role; it merely changed functionality for HTTP, POP3, IMAP4, and NNTP access from redirect to proxy. Exchange Server 2007 saw a significant change in architecture with the separation of functions into server roles, although it wasn't a complete transformation — certain clients (MAPI) would still connect directly to the Mailbox servers for data while all other clients connected through Client Access servers. Now in Exchange Server 2010, even MAPI clients connect to the Client Access servers through the new RPC Client Access functionality.

If you've read the previous chapters, the preceding paragraph should be a quick recap — why reproduce it here? Because it reinforces a key point: in order to troubleshoot Exchange, you have to understand the architecture. Understanding which functions of

Exchange are controlled by which server roles is absolutely critical, or you could spend a lot of time troubleshooting the wrong server.

Troubleshooting Exchange Server 2010 often involves collecting and reviewing information from a series of servers, rather than focusing on one. For example, a user complains that he isn't receiving new email. There are a number of possible causes for this:

- The user's client isn't receiving notifications of new email.

- The user's client can't connect to the Client Access server to retrieve new email.

- All copies of the relevant mailbox database are offline.

- The user's mailbox is full.

- There are no Hub Transports available to deliver his message.

- Transport agents preclude delivery of email to this end user.

A closer look at this list shows an interesting breakdown. The first two issues could loosely be categorized as client access issues, the next two as database issues, and the last as transport issues. Obviously these correspond nicely to the three required server roles, and since that makes a logical breakdown, that's how we'll cover troubleshooting in the following sections. However, before we dive right into the tools, let's take a moment to consider what troubleshooting involves.

When faced with a technical problem, your immediate impulse is often to jump right into the system and start clicking. While this can be successful, particularly when you're resolving a problem you've seen hundreds of times and know like the back of your own hand, it's not necessarily a reproducible strategy. What happens when you encounter a problem you haven't seen before? What do you do when you truly have no idea what the root cause could be?

The first step in troubleshooting a problem, any problem, is to define *what the problem is*. In many cases, this requires asking for more information. When an end user says that she can't send email, does she mean that she can't open Outlook? That she can't generate a new email? That she clicks Send but the email never leaves the Drafts or Outbox folders? Or that she's sent messages that were never received? The end result is the same — the user can't send email — but the root causes are very different.

Once the problem has been defined, the next step is to determine the scope of the problem. This often helps clarify the direction of further troubleshooting. By determining how many users are affected — and more importantly, determining what those users have in common — you can rule out some possibilities and focus on things with a greater impact. For example, if one user can't send email, the root cause could be many things unique to that user, from Outlook configuration to network connectivity to a disabled user account.

However, if a second user has a similar issue, it's more likely to be something they have in common. Are they in the same network segment, perhaps? If 10 users on different floors all report Outlook problems, there may possibly be a problem on an Exchange server. Are all 10 users in the same database, for example, or in the same Active Directory site?

There are a number of clarifying questions that are extremely useful in determining the scope of a particular problem:

- How many users are affected by the outage?

- Do all the affected users access Exchange through the same method, such as Outlook, Outlook Web App, or ActiveSync?

- What exactly are the users trying to do when they encounter the problem?

◆ Are other users able to perform the same task without problems?

◆ Are all of the users in the same database?

◆ Are all of the users in the same site?

◆ Does the problem occur all the time, only some of the time, or rarely?

The answers to these will often rule out possibilities right from the start. If one user can't log into Outlook successfully, but another in the same database can, you know immediately that the relevant database must be mounted and accessible, and you can then concentrate on other things.

Speaking of concentrating on other things, one of the most difficult things in troubleshooting is ignoring the unimportant distracters and focusing on what's causing the issue. It's often difficult to differentiate between what's important and what's not unless you know where to start (which is why defining the problem is so important).

Here's an example: an end user reports that he can't send email to a specific user, and during investigation you also discover that he can't access a particular public folder. Is the public folder problem directly related to the email problem? It might be — if the recipient's mailbox is on a server that also houses the only replica of that public folder, and that server's inaccessible, that would explain both problems. But in many cases it might not — the public folder store might be dismounted, the user might not have permissions, or Exchange may be blocking referrals to the replica due to site link costs. Although there's at least one explanation that covers both problems, many more exist that are unique to the secondary problem. The steps to troubleshoot internal mail flow are dramatically different from those required to troubleshoot public folder access, so if you're trying to resolve a problem with internal email, concentrate on that and leave the public folder issue for later.

General Server Troubleshooting Tools

During troubleshooting, there are some steps that should be the same no matter what the symptoms are. Yes, you need to define the problem, as discussed earlier, and you also need to understand the scope of the issue. But once you've determined that the problem is indeed server based rather than specific to a group of clients, what next? This section will focus on the key tools you should use first.

Event Viewer (Diagnostic Logging)

Troubleshooting a server involves data collection and analysis, and the best ways to collect that data are the same regardless of server role. The Event Viewer includes detailed information about recent system and application errors, and this should always be an administrator's first move in the event of crisis. Once you've determined the scope of a problem, and you've positively identified the root cause as server related, your next step should be to check the event logs on the relevant system. Because Exchange has so many moving parts, so to speak, you'll often find a large number of events clustered together at the time of the reported issue. The default logging level for the majority of services and categories is Lowest, which means that only critical, error, and warnings of logging level 0 will be written to the event log.

If the events generated during the problem aren't quite enough, you might need to increase the logging level for a specific service and category — for example, `MSExchange Transport\Mail Submission` — to Low, Medium, or High. There is another logging level, Expert, but this generates so many events that it should only be used for short periods, typically when working directly with Microsoft support.

As with nearly everything in Exchange Server 2010, you can configure diagnostic logging through either the Exchange Management Console (EMC) or the Exchange Management Shell (EMS).

ENABLING DIAGNOSTIC LOGGING — WELCOME BACK!

In the initial release of Exchange Server 2007, diagnostic logging was removed from the EMC, and the only way you could increase logging for a particular service was by using the `Set-EventLogLevel` cmdlet. Since PowerShell was still new at the time (Exchange Server 2007 was many administrators' first exposure to it), the change wasn't well received, and so Microsoft reintroduced diagnostic logging control to the console in Service Pack 2.

The Manage Diagnostic Logging Properties wizard (shown in Figure 28.1) is available from the Server Configuration node. Select the server role, then the server, and click Manage Diagnostic Logging Properties in the Actions pane. This launches the wizard, which allows you to select one or more services to modify.

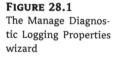

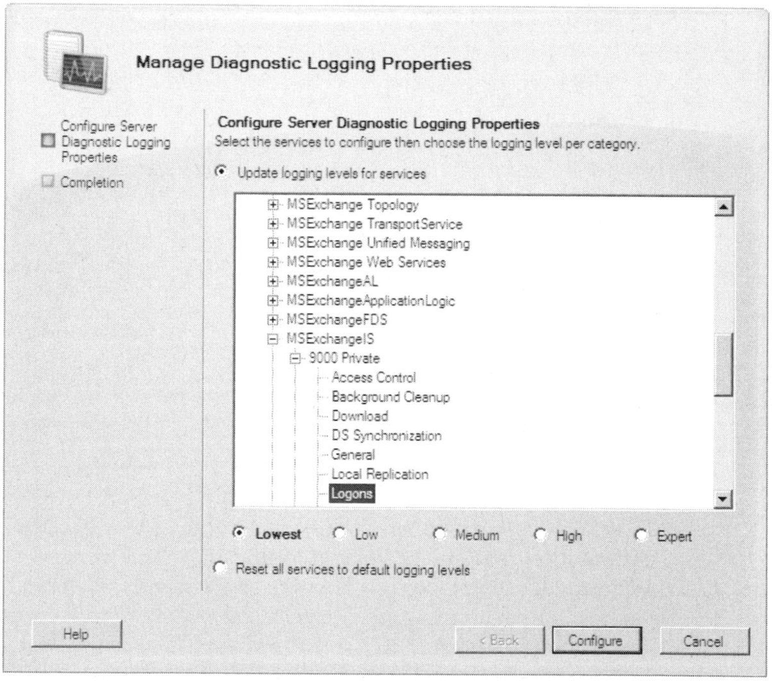

FIGURE 28.1
The Manage Diagnostic Logging Properties wizard

Configuring diagnostic logging with the EMS is a little trickier, because although `Get-EventLogLevel` (which retrieves logging information) can be used remotely, `Set-EventLogLevel` does *not* take a server parameter. In other words, you have to run the command from the shell on the target server to configure logging. The syntax is relatively straightforward:

```
Set-EventLogLevel -Identity "MSExchange Transport\Mail Submission" ↵
-Level Medium
```

It's always a good idea to reset the logging back to Lowest when you're done troubleshooting. Increased logging can add significantly to event log growth, and depending on your settings it might fill up your event log quickly or overwrite events.

Once you've identified the target server and configured logging, you might not see relevant events right away. You may need to reproduce the issue (for example, by having the user send another email or attempt to force a connection for a mail queue) before Exchange logs anything of value. Exchange events themselves will always appear in the Application event log, although some dependencies (clustering, network, disk drives, and so forth) will log their information to the System event log.

Diagnostic events include a wealth of information, but the most important pieces are the following:

Description Although the field is unnamed in Windows Server 2008, it's the equivalent of the legacy Description field from previous versions of Windows. This includes the text of the event, and will in many cases include additional error codes or critical information. For example, the well-known and widely feared "-1018 error" isn't an event — it's a JET error code that appears within the description text of other ESE events, like ESE error 474. The description may also include a link to further information on the Microsoft support site.

Source This tells you which component logged the event. Note that this will typically be the underlying service name rather than the "friendly" name, so expect to see MSExchangeIS rather than Microsoft Exchange Information Store.

Event ID This is the specific event number. Along with the Source, this is the most important information for the event.

Level This reflects the severity of the event, and can range from Informational to Error.

Logged This displays the date and time the event, displayed in local time. This information is stored in the event in UTC, and the Event Viewer displays the equivalent local time — if you're looking at a remote server, make sure you take this into account!

Task Category This is the subcomponent of the service that logged the event. Not all services will provide this additional information, but the majority of Exchange services do. This corresponds to the categories visible in the Manage Diagnostic Logging Properties wizard or via `Set-EventLogLevel`.

Depending on the error, you should see something similar to the event shown in Figure 28.2.

Many Exchange events include detailed diagnostic steps in the Description field, which is extremely convenient in times of trouble. Even if the event doesn't provide too much information, you might be able to find more information on the TechNet Events and Errors Message Center at `www.microsoft.com/technet/support/ee/ee_advanced.aspx`. Simply select the appropriate product (Exchange, obviously); select the appropriate version (14.0 for Exchange Server 2010); enter the event ID, source, or both; and then click Go. Assuming the event appears in the TechNet database, you should see a link for additional information, which then provides a detailed explanation of the issue as well as troubleshooting steps and recommendations. If you can't find information on the specific event here, there's always the Microsoft Knowledge Base (`http://support.microsoft.com/search/?adv=1`) or your favorite search engine.

Test-SystemHealth

PowerShell cmdlets control so much functionality in Exchange Server 2010 that it's not a surprise to see troubleshooting cmdlets as well. One of the most basic is `Test-SystemHealth`, a handy little tool that quickly collects data about the local server and analyzes it according to Microsoft-recommended practices. The standard syntax is mercifully simple: type **Test-SystemHealth**, press Enter, and then wait for the output. Unlike many cmdlets, Test-SystemHealth generates a progress bar at the top of the EMS window. This is a useful visual indicator — it's high contrast so you can see it from several feet away

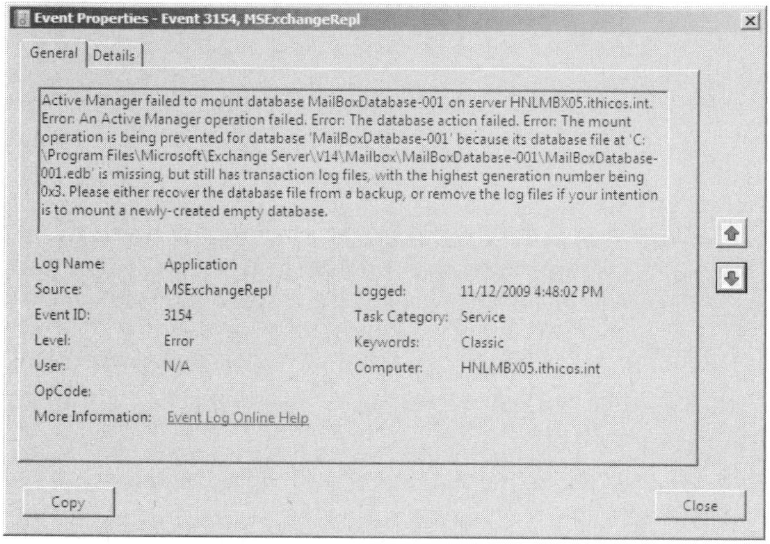

FIGURE 28.2
Viewing an event from the Application log

When the cmdlet finishes, it displays the results in a simple list format (which you could format with the Format-List cmdlet if you wanted to), as shown in Figure 28.3.

FIGURE 28.3
Using the Test-SystemHealth cmdlet

As you can see in the output, the resulting data is a mini-health check for your server. The Test-SystemHealth cmdlet will alert you to many common misconfigurations as well as recommended settings.

Test-ServiceHealth

Another extremely useful cmdlet is Test-ServiceHealth, which does what its name suggests: it checks the health of all required Exchange services on the server. Since the cmdlet recognizes roles as well, it doesn't just check for every service; it only looks for the services the installed roles use. It won't check for MSExchangeRPC on a Hub Transport server, for example, or for MSExchangeMailSubmission on a Client Access server.

This cmdlet also uses a very simple syntax; just type **Test-SystemHealth**, press Enter, and peruse the results. The output from this cmdlet is preformatted into a table and simply reports on the status of the required services; an example of the output is shown in Figure 28.4.

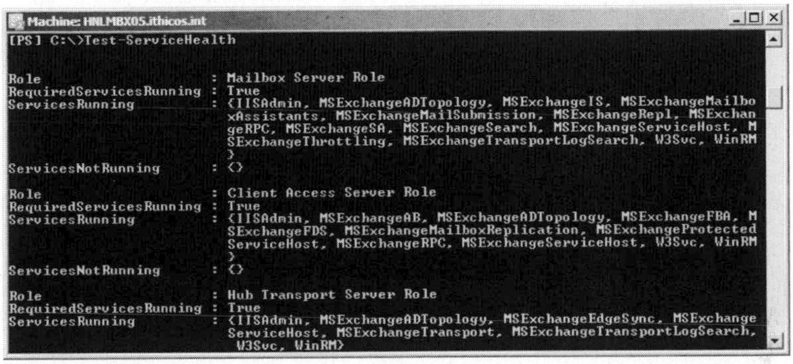

FIGURE 28.4
Using the Test-
ServiceHealth cmdlet

If you want to quickly check the status of a single server, the two preceding cmdlets can save a lot of time and effort. However, neither cmdlet runs against multiple servers at once. To check the configuration of a group of servers, or even every server in the organization, you need a tool that runs at a higher level.

Exchange Best Practices Analyzer

If you've been using Exchange for the last few years, you're probably familiar with the Exchange Best Practices Analyzer (generally known as ExBPA). If not, or if you're new to Exchange, this tool will probably become one of your best friends, particularly during troubleshooting. It's one of the best free tools Microsoft ever produced, and it's no stretch to say that it completely changed the way Exchange administrators work with the product.

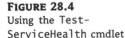 **Real World Scenario**

RUNNING THE EXBPA MONTHLY

Company GHIJ had been having weird errors with their Exchange server. The issues were affecting client connectivity and, like most good, weird errors, were unpredictable and inconsistent. At times the problems affected two or three of their 620 clients and at other times a few dozen. Every time the Exchange administrator would start troubleshooting the problem, the errors would clear up.

For months, they chalked up this problem to merely ghosts in the network or some hard-to-reproduce error. Their administrator decided one day to run the Exchange Best Practices Analyzer; she had not done so since the Exchange server had first been installed. The first time she ran the scanner it reported no issues, but she noted that she did not allow it to update its rule set from the Internet.

> She ran the scanner again with an updated rule set, and it reported several potential issues that should be resolved. She investigated each of the reported issues and found one that would produce inconsistent network issues for Outlook clients. Once she applied the recommended fix, the issue did not return.
>
> This organization learned an important lesson about the ExBPA; run it on a regular basis and make sure that you have updated rule sets.

The Exchange Best Practices Analyzer is, at its heart, a rules-based data collection and display engine (see Figure 28.5). In its most common usage, it connects to a group of servers that you specify, collects a host of data about each of them, and then compares what it finds against a defined set of specific criteria. If it finds a match for a particular value, it displays that information in the form of a recommendation, complete with links to authoritative Microsoft online content. It might not sound too exciting, but it's powerful — *very* powerful.

FIGURE 28.5
Running the ExBPA

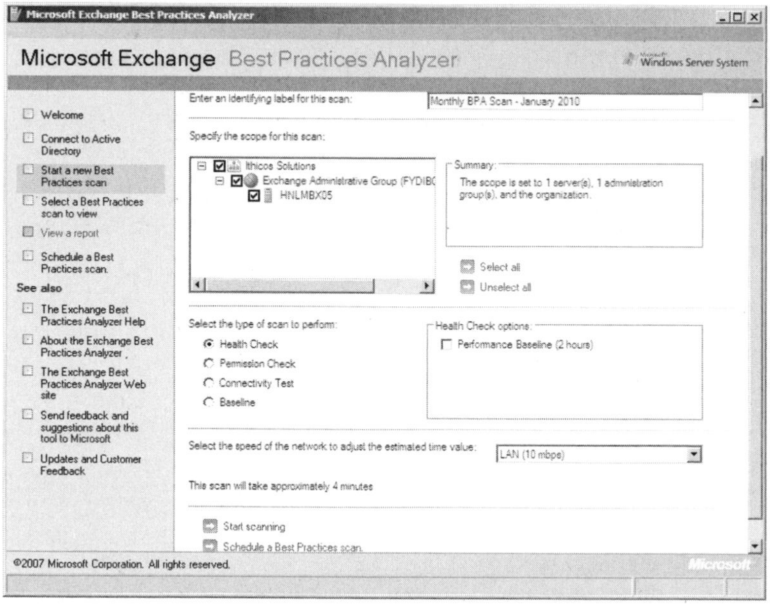

What makes ExBPA so powerful is the collective knowledge base it represents: all of the various Exchange subject matter experts within Microsoft contribute their knowledge to this tool, and the rules reflect their input. Like any other successful tool, it spawned a series of related tools, many of which we'll discuss later in this chapter.

For the ExBPA to be truly useful and up-to-date for your organization, you should ensure that you have updated it with the newest rule sets and definitions prior to using it. To ensure that the ExBPA has the latest rule sets, make sure that the server or workstation from which you are running it has the latest available service packs or rollup fixes for Exchange Server 2010. This is a change from Exchange 2007 and earlier, where you could download the updates separately.

RUN AN ExBPA SCAN PRIOR TO CALLING FOR SUPPORT

Because ExBPA is such an easy and thorough data collection tool, Microsoft support engineers will always ask you to send them an XML output tool when you open a support case. If you do need to open a case for troubleshooting, you can save time by providing an up-to-date ExBPA output file right away.

The Exchange Best Practices Analyzer (see Figure 28.6) is included on every Exchange server as part of the EMC. It's available in the Toolbox along with a number of other tools (many of which we'll review in this chapter). To launch it, simply select Best Practices Analyzer and click Launch Tool in the Actions pane.

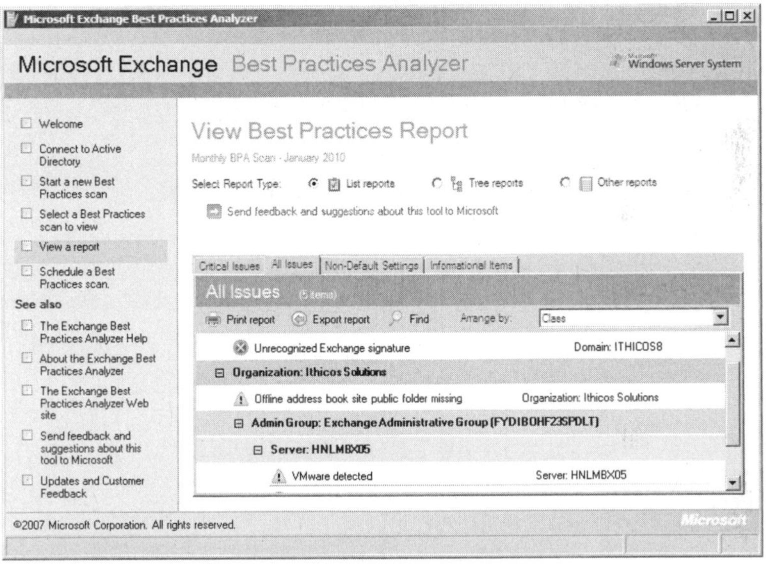

FIGURE 28.6
Viewing a report

If you have any serious configuration or system issues, you will notice the output of the ExBPA and the output of `Test-SystemHealth` will be similar. That's because `Test-SystemHealth` and ExBPA use the same basic configuration information, albeit in different forms. Both tools check configuration, but while `Test-SystemHealth` runs against only one server, ExBPA can scan every system in your environment at once. Of course, the ExBPA will provide a much more detailed report than `Test-SystemHealth`.

ExBPA provides runs in four basic modes:

Health Check This is the mode you'll use the most, and it does the checks we covered earlier: it connects to a group of servers, reads configuration information about those servers, and then alerts you to possible issues arising from that configuration.

Connectivity Check This is a quick scan that's useful for ensuring that all servers in your environment are up and running, that the account you provided has access to them, and that critical system services on the servers are started and accessible; this includes Remote Procedure Call (RPC), Windows Management Instrumentation (WMI), and the Remote Registry.

Baseline Check   This scan allows you to select one server as a reference system and then compare all other servers to it. Differences between the systems are highlighted, allowing you to quickly and easily audit your Exchange environment.

Health Check With Performance   This is a super-set of the Health Check test case listed earlier, with a performance capture bolted onto the end. You probably won't need to run this mode, because there are better tools available for performance analysis. See Chapter 29, "Monitoring and Performance" for more information.

No matter which mode you choose, you'll need to select an appropriate network speed from the drop-down menu. There are four choices: Fast LAN, LAN, Fast WAN, and WAN. These correspond to timeout values built into the tool: ExBPA will wait longer to consider a server unreachable if you select WAN, as it increases the timeout value to 300 seconds (5 minutes). Conversely, it will only wait 30 seconds to declare that system "dead" if you've selected Fast LAN.

Once you've done this, go ahead and click Next to begin the test. The next screen will be a progress screen of sorts, with each server to be scanned listed on the left and progress bars for each on the right.

THE EXBPA AND DOMAIN CONTROLLERS

ExBPA has a little quirk that you should be aware of: when it finishes scanning all the Exchange servers, it attempts to connect to all the domain controllers those servers have accessed via the ADAccess component. In a large environment, that could be literally hundreds of domain controllers. So if you see the main screen progress bar stuck at 99 percent despite the fact that all the Exchange servers have completed, don't worry — it's just checking the domain controllers.

After ExBPA has finished collecting data, it'll let you know that scanning is complete, and it's at this point that the real fun begins. Click Next to have ExBPA analyze the output, and when it's processed all the raw data, it'll present you with the list of issues. The default view only shows you the critical issues, however, so be sure to click All Issues to see the complete list such as the list shown previously in Figure 28.6.

Each issue should include a descriptive title (like "Exchange information store service is not set to start"), a more detailed description that becomes visible when you select the issue, and three additional links: one for more information online, one to hide that instance of the issue, and one to hide that issue permanently. The Tell Me More About This Issue link takes you to some of the best and most descriptive content on the Microsoft site; you can learn an awful lot of stuff about Exchange simply by going through the ExBPA content. The other two links let you clean up your output a bit. If you know that the Information Store service isn't set to start on a specific server, and it's by design, you can simply hide that issue.

DO NOT MAKE CHANGES BLINDLY

The ExBPA is an excellent tool and one that can save you many hours of potential problems or hours on the phone with support. The collective knowledge built in to the ExBPA's rule sets represents literally thousands of hours of field experience and Microsoft product support experience.

> However, these rule sets make recommendations based on typical organizations and typical configurations. Do not blindly make configuration changes or apply patches without understanding the ramifications to your own Exchange environment. The ExBPA may be your consultant-in-a-box, but there is no way that Microsoft can accommodate the variations found in all Exchange organizations in the world. Your own knowledge of your system, research, and personal experiences must still supplement this powerful tool.

Although it was designed primarily as a troubleshooting tool, many administrators use it for other purposes. Some engineers use ExBPA as a validation tool, running it both before and after making changes to the environment, while others use it to discover if any changes were made in the last week or month. However you use it, you'll definitely want to make it a part of your standard troubleshooting toolkit, because it's useful in bringing so many things to light.

Troubleshooting Mailbox Servers

With the shift of mailbox access over to the Client Access server in Exchange Server 2010, the Mailbox server's role now essentially encompasses only data storage and retrieval. The primary focus of troubleshooting Mailbox servers rests on two things: database replication health and server performance. These aren't the only things Mailbox servers do, of course, but they're probably the two most common troubleshooting topics. However, before we get into those, let's recap some of the standard troubleshooting techniques you should apply to a Mailbox server before diving into the situation-specific tasks.

General Mailbox Server Health

Although a Mailbox server is essentially useless without Client Access and Hub Transport servers to provide access and deliver mail, it's still the most important role in an Exchange environment. This is, of course, because the data is stored on the server — in the databases on the associated storage, to be precise. So when dealing with Mailbox server issues, you'll want to perform the basic checks we covered in the general troubleshooting section earlier:

- From the client workstation, can you ping the Mailbox server by NetBIOS name, FQDN, and IP address?

- Are all required Exchange services able to start as necessary?

- Do you see any errors in the event log relating to MSExchangeDatabase, MSExchangeDatabase ➤ Instances, or MSExchangeIS Mailbox?

- Are there any Active Directory issues that might have a negative impact on Exchange?

Obviously, the `Test-SystemHealth` and `Test-ServiceHealth` cmdlets would be useful in detecting basic problems, like a dismounted database or a stopped service. They should always be the first two cmdlets you execute when troubleshooting a Mailbox server, simply because they group together so many common checks.

Using Test-MapiConnectivity

Like its close cousin, `Test-OutlookConnectivity`, `Test-MapiConnectivity` will help you determine problems accessing a specific mailbox. However, unlike the other cmdlet (which tests the end-to-end process), `Test-MapiConnectivity` just focuses on the Mailbox server.

It logs into a target mailbox (which you can specify with the −Identity parameter), the system mailbox in a specific database (which you can specify with −Database), or the system mailbox in every active database on a server (through −Server). The output for all three variants looks like the following:

```
Test-MAPIConnectivity -Server HNLMBX05

MailboxServer       Database          Result     Error
-------------       --------          ------     -----
HNLMBX05            MailboxDatabase... Success
HNLMBX05            MailBoxDatabase... Success


Test-MAPIConnectivity jmcbee

MailboxServer       Database          Result     Error
-------------       --------          ------     -----
HNLMBX05            MailBoxDatabase... Success


Test-MAPIConnectivity -Database MailboxDatabase-001

MailboxServer       Database          Result     Error
-------------       --------          ------     -----
HNLMBX05            MailBoxDatabase... Success
```

This is a useful (and quick) cmdlet for narrowing down the possible scope of a problem; Test-MapiConnectivity essentially tests not only the Exchange information store but also ADAccess and RPCs, so a successful test against any mailbox on a server proves that those three components are at least functioning. If you can log into the system mailbox for a database, but not into a user mailbox in that same database, the problem is clearly something unique to that user.

Checking Poison Mailboxes

One new feature that might lead to confusion for users (and more than a few administrators!) is poison mailbox detection. By default, Mailbox servers will tag any mailbox that causes a thread in the Exchange Information Store service to crash or that is connected to five or more "hung" threads. If a mailbox is tagged three times in two hours, Exchange Server 2010 will block access to that mailbox for up to six hours or until the administrator unblocks it, whichever comes first. If a user reports that she cannot connect to a mailbox, but other users have no difficulty, check to see if there are any quarantined mailboxes on the server. You can do this either through Performance Monitor (through the MSExchangeIS Mailbox\Quarantined Mailbox Count performance counter) or through the Get-MailboxStatistics cmdlet. For example, to find out if mailbox JanieN is quarantined, simply use this command:

```
Get-MailboxStatistics JanieN | Format-List DisplayName, IsQuarantined
```

Exchange Server 2010 will also write an event to the Application log when it quarantines a mailbox.

Checking Database Replication Health

The introduction of continuous replication in Exchange Server 2007 dramatically changed the face of disaster recovery, as administrators could deploy two separate copies of a single database, each on a physically separate server. There were a few limitations, of course; end users still connected to the *server*, not just the database, so problems with the underlying cluster would render both database copies inaccessible. Standby continuous replication (introduced in Exchange Server 2007 Service Pack 1) provided another disaster recovery option, but this had its limits as well — it was purely manual and, depending on the configuration, would require at least a setup "trick" (setup /recovercms) or even wholesale "rehoming" of users. A successful activation of a standby copy was also heavily dependent on replication of both DNS and Active Directory information, so users might still be unable to connect even after the issue was resolved.

Database availability groups (DAGs) in Exchange Server 2010 provide multiple copies of a single database on different servers, even in different datacenters, so a single server failure should have a significantly smaller impact on an Exchange deployment. Other architectural changes — namely RPC Client Access — effectively hide the server object from the end user, so the actual location of the active database is immaterial from the end user's perspective.

Database replication health is, loosely speaking, how successful Exchange is keeping database copies in sync. This depends on server configuration, network health, and a few other things (most of which Exchange checks automatically as part of the Test-SystemHealth and Test-ServiceHealth cmdlets). However, you can check the health of the replication infrastructure quite easily with two cmdlets. The first cmdlet, Test-ReplicationHealth, checks the health of the replication services and alerts you to any errors it finds. The output is extremely easy to read, as shown here:

```
Test-ReplicationHealth

Server          Check                Result    Error
------          -----                ------    -----
HNLMBX05        ClusterService       Passed
HNLMBX05        ReplayService        Passed
HNLMBX05        ActiveManager        Passed
HNLMBX05        TasksRpcListener     Passed
HNLMBX05        TcpListener          Passed
HNLMBX05        DagMembersUp         Passed
HNLMBX05        ClusterNetwork       Passed
HNLMBX05        QuorumGroup          Passed
HNLMBX05        DBCopySuspended      *FAILED*  Failures:...
HNLMBX05        DBCopyFailed         Passed
HNLMBX05        DBInitializing       Passed
HNLMBX05        DBDisconnected       Passed
HNLMBX05        DBLogCopyKeepingUp   Passed
HNLMBX05        DBLogReplayKeepingUp Passed
```

Once you've validated the replication services, you can check the replication status for the databases themselves with Get-MailboxDatabaseCopyStatus. You can focus on a particular database by using the –Identity parameter, or check the status for all mailbox database copies on a specific server by using –MailboxServer. You could even check the status of one specific database on one specific server by including both parameters. Here is an example of using the Get-MailboxDatabaseCopyStatus cmdlet.

```
Get-MailboxDatabaseCopyStatus | Format-List ↵
Name,Status,LastInspectedLogTime,ContentIndexState
```

Name	Status	LastInspectedLogTime	ContentIndex State
----	------	--------------------	----------
MDB001\HNLMBX05	Healthy	11/13/2009 8:44:03 AM	Healthy
MDB002\HNLMBX05	Healthy	11/15/2009 8:03:24 PM	Healthy
MDB003\HNLMBX05	Healthy	11/15/2009 8:12:56 PM	Healthy

There are many possible causes for replication errors, among them:

◆ Transient network connectivity issues

◆ Permissions issues

◆ Insufficient disk space on target server

The general troubleshooting steps we covered in the beginning of this chapter will help you determine the exact cause of a replication problem.

With the reduction in functionality, Mailbox servers have become significantly easier to troubleshoot than in the past. There are a number of useful cmdlets for validating mailbox database availability and mailbox access, among them Test-SystemHealth, Get-MailboxStatistics, and Test-MapiConnectivity. Two additional cmdlets, Test-ReplicationHealth and Get-MailboxDatabaseCopyStatus, provide insight into the replication of those databases across member servers in the organization.

Troubleshooting Mail Flow

Message delivery is arguably the most important piece of Exchange Server 2010, and it's only fitting that Microsoft has provided a formidable arsenal of troubleshooting weapons to deal with pesky delivery failures. You'll have your pick of tools, from self-serve ones, such as message tracking in the Exchange Control Panel, to several forms of tracing, to the inevitable cmdlets.

However, just because you have an array of choices doesn't mean you have to use them right away. Again, it's important to approach a message delivery problem with clear eyes and ask probing questions about what you're facing. Remember the example earlier in the chapter, with the end user who can't send email? There were a number of plausible explanations for this, some of which didn't involve message delivery at all! So it's still important to gather the essential information:

◆ Can the user send any emails at all? Is nondelivery restricted to a subset of users?

◆ Does the user receive a delivery status notification? If so, what is the delivery code?

◆ Is the recipient in the same Exchange organization or in a different organization (presumably on the Internet)?

◆ How close do messages get to their destination?

◆ What is the messaging path between the end user and the recipient?

These questions, though relatively simple, conceal a bewildering list of possible root causes. Consider the impact on message delivery on the following:

DNS Failure   Hub Transport servers can't locate A records and therefore can't reach next-hop servers.

Site Link Failure   No site link exists between sender and recipient.

Transport Failure   All of the Hub Transport servers in the user's site are inaccessible.

Transport Agent   A transport rule prevents this email from reaching the recipient (either because of sender restrictions, content restrictions, or recipient issues).

Mailbox Limits   The recipient's mailbox is full, but nondelivery reports do not reach the sender for whatever reason.

Messages Stuck in Queue   A transient failure has temporarily stopped messages at a back-off location.

Back Pressure   A Hub Transport server is temporarily throttling message delivery due to resource constraints.

This isn't even an exhaustive list, but it includes a wealth of possibilities. Now, there are few listed here that you would probably detect by performing the basic troubleshooting steps we covered earlier in this chapter (like DNS failure or transport failure). We'll begin with a simple cmdlet to check basic mail flow, which is typically the first step in locating undelivered messages, and then move on to message tracking and agent logging.

Using Test-Mailflow

Assuming you've done some of the basic checking (is the user's client connected to a database, are Hub Transports available, and so on), you'll probably want to test that mail is flowing in the organization. There's an aptly named cmdlet for just this job: Test-Mailflow. You could argue that Test-Mailflow doesn't belong in this section, since it's ostensibly testing Mailbox servers. But it's listed as a Transport cmdlet in the Exchange Server 2010 help file, and when you get right down to it, mail flow is the Hub Transport's responsibility.

The cmdlet's basic function is simply to send and receive email from the system mailbox of the target server, but it can do so much more. The syntax is extremely simple: Test-Mailflow followed by the source server, then –TargetMailboxServer, -TargetDatabase, or –TargetEmailAddress. The different options mean that you can start with a Mailbox server, and if that test succeeds, focus on the user's database and then the user's email address. If you've deployed multiple databases in a DAG, you should skip the first step and start with –TargetDatabase.

```
Test-Mailflow hnlmbx05 -TargetEmailAddress Luke.McBee@ithicos.com

RunspaceId          : 0848e0b8-4228-4195-b1ee-c4c967ac9a41
TestMailflowResult  : Success
MessageLatencyTime  : 00:00:02.5631250
IsRemoteTest        : True
Identity            :
IsValid             : True
```

The output from Test-Mailflow doesn't need much interpretation. The most important piece is the TestMailflowResult property. If it reads Success, you know that you can reach that server, database, or email address, and you know that email is flowing, at least for some combination of user and database. The next property, MessageLatencyTime, lets you know the time it took for the message to reach the destination server. The IsRemoteTest property simply indicates whether the message left the server (this will also be True if you use the –TargetEmailAddress parameter).

However, if your test fails, the TestMailflowResult property reads *FAILURE*, and that's unfortunately the only indicator you receive — no messages about where the failure might have occurred, or other useful information. That's when you need to start figuring out where the messages are stopped, and for that we need to move into different tools. We'll start with the Queue Viewer and then look into message tracking.

Queue Viewer in the EMC

The Queue Viewer is located in the Toolbox of the EMC, alongside a number of other useful tools (some of which we'll cover later in this section). A big believer in truth in advertising, the Queue Viewer allows you to, yes, view the contents of the various delivery queues. Obviously, you need to connect to a Hub Transport server to use this tool, but you can open the Queue Viewer from anywhere and then connect to the appropriate Hub Transport server. The interface for the Queue Viewer is shown in Figure 28.7.

FIGURE 28.7
Using the Queue Viewer interface

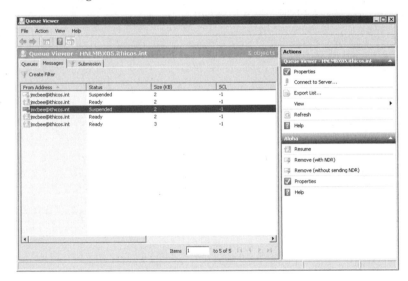

It's largely unchanged from Exchange Server 2007, but it didn't need any enhancements; it tells you the status of the queues, how many messages are pending delivery, and where the mail is heading, among other things. The list of queues is a bit thinner than in previous versions of Exchange (particularly when compared to the positively garrulous Exchange Server 2003), but if there's a problem with a particular queue, it'll be listed here.

Most of the columns in the Queue tab are relatively self-explanatory, but here's a brief rundown of what you'll see on this page:

Next Hop Domain This is where the mail is heading next, whether a Hub Transport in a different site, a Mailbox server in the same site, or an Internet host. You'll also see a Submission queue, which obviously represents incoming mail submission to that Hub Transport.

Delivery Type   This indicates where the messages are heading next in their journey to the recipient.

Status   This simply indicates whether the queue is Active (sending messages at the moment), Suspended (stopped through administrative action), Ready (able to send messages should any arrive), or Retry (unable to send messages). Queues in a Retry state are the most obvious candidates for additional review and analysis, but remember that queues can fail because of the sending server as well as the recipient.

Message Count   This lets you know how many messages are stuck in this queue.

Next Retry Time   This is only applicable to queues in a Retry state, and lets you know the next time Exchange will attempt to "wake up" the queue for delivery.

Last Error   This is the Hub Transport's way of letting you know what might have caused a particular issue: was it an authentication issue, a DNS lookup failure, or simple network connectivity problems?

You can perform a small number of tasks on the queues, including temporarily stopping them (Suspend), forcing them to connect if they've failed (Retry), or deleting all the messages (Remove messages with or without NDR). This can be useful for restarting mail flow after you've resolved a problem somewhere else in the environment, or deleting a quantity of undesired email. The Actions pane at the right of the EMC will display only valid actions for the queue you've selected.

The Messages tab has similar information to the Queues tab, and it's generally most useful when you've clicked a queue and then selected View Messages. You can click the Messages tab right away, but it'll show you every message queued on the server, which might take a little while for a busy system. The columns for the Messages tab are similar to that on the Queues tab:

From Address   This is the address of the sender, taken directly from the SMTP envelope.

Status   This indicates the message status, which is generally the same as the parent queue but is also influenced by administrator action (for example, if the administrator has tried to delete the message while it was being delivered, the message will appear as Pending Remove).

Size (KB)   This is the size of the message, displayed in kilobytes.

SCL   This is the spam confidence level (SCL) rating; the values range from –1 through 9, with –1 representing authenticated email and 9 representing email that is almost certainly unsolicited commercial email (UCE, or spam).

Queue ID   This value indicates the queue in which the message appears. If you chose a specific queue and then selected View Messages, this should be the same for all messages and should reflect the queue you chose on the Queues tab.

Message Source Name   This indicates the Exchange component that delivered the message to this particular queue. Depending on your architecture, this could be a Hub Transport server in another site, a Mailbox server in the same site, or possibly even an application or client submitting a message directly to the Hub Transport via SMTP.

Subject   This is the subject of the email, taken from the SMTP envelope.

Last Error   This indicates the last error experienced when attempting delivery of this message. This typically only appears if the message is in a Suspended, Retry, or Pending state.

There are a couple of good articles on the technical details of the Queue Viewer at
http://technet.microsoft.com/en-us/library/bb629568.aspx and
http://technet.microsoft.com/en-us/library/bb676413.aspx.

The Queue Viewer is useful for locating a message that hasn't been delivered, but the
message-tracking feature is also useful for this in larger environments, and depending on
the Last Error field for the queue or message in question, you may be able to figure out
what your next move should be. However, the one drawback to the Queue Viewer is that,
unless you have a simple topology, you might not necessarily know exactly *how* a message
reached that particular server. For that type of analysis, we need something a little more
detailed (like message tracking, which we'll cover in a moment as well).

Depending on the messages you're seeing (or not seeing) in the queues, it may be an
indication that the Hub Transport server is experiencing back pressure. This is usually
evident in both the Event Viewer (look for MSExchangeTransport events), performance
data (a shortage of available memory or high disk write times), or even Windows
Explorer (insufficient free space on the disks housing the mail database or the associated
logs). There are more details on back pressure in Exchange Server 2010 in the article at
http://technet.microsoft.com/en-us/library/bb201658(EXCHG.140).aspx.

Message Tracking

With end-user message tracking in the Exchange Control Panel, Exchange Server 2010
introduces a new wrinkle into what used to be a purely administrative task. The conscientious
administrator now has three choices for tracking messages:

- Allow the end user to search for messages
- Track messages via the Exchange Management Console
- Track messages via the Exchange Management Shell

These options are listed in order of power and usability, so we'll start with the simplest first:
end-user message tracking.

SELF-SERVICE MESSAGE TRACKING IN THE EXCHANGE CONTROL PANEL

In the past the only way an end user could determine the delivery status of a message was
by requesting delivery receipts, but there were two drawbacks: many companies would
block delivery (and read) receipts from leaving the Exchange organization, and many users
elected to never send them at all. This left a functionality gap that the Exchange Control
Panel (ECP) helps fill. This new option, available in Outlook Web App (OWA), allows end
users to gather information about their own messages (or other people's messages if they
have the permissions). This can be incredibly useful for environments with lots of tech-savvy
users, but would require a little investment in training, documentation, and, above all,
communication. For the security conscious among us, the message-tracking function in the
ECP adheres to the same role-based access control regime as all the other Exchange components, so users couldn't use this interface to just browse their way through random users'
message history.

To access the self-service message-tracking component, simply log into OWA as you normally would, and then select Options. Select Organize E-Mail and then select Delivery Reports
in the center pane. This displays the message tracking screen shown in Figure 28.8.

Although the title of the message tracking pane seems to indicate that it's processing
delivery reports, don't worry: Exchange hasn't been secretly appending delivery reports to

every email your users have been sending! It's simply processing delivery information taken from the message-tracking logs (remember, message tracking is enabled by default in Exchange Server 2010).

FIGURE 28.8
Viewing message tracking in the ECP

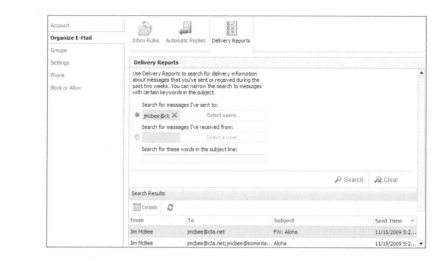

Assuming the logs are still available, users should be able to determine information about their own messages although as in medicine sometimes a little knowledge is a dangerous thing! Users might become so enamored of self-service message tracking that they check the status of all their messages, so any small delay could turn into *more* help desk calls, not fewer. You'll need to balance out the needs of the community with the realistic expectations of delivery performance.

MESSAGE TRACKING VIA THE EXCHANGE MANAGEMENT CONSOLE

The message tracking tool in the Exchange Management Console in Exchange Server 2010 is broadly the same as it was in Exchange Server 2007. Administrators can search for messages from any sender, to any recipient, with any subject line, using wildcards and filters as necessary to focus on the critical data.

To launch message tracking from within the EMC, select the Toolbox in the navigation pane at the left, choose Message Tracking in the display pane, and then select Open Tool in the Message Tracking Actions pane at the right. This launches the web-based message-tracking tool that is the same tool you would use as an end user but with a few additional options. The big difference is that as an administrator you will be able to track everyone's messages and not just your own.

Once you've launched the tool, you'll be presented with what might be a bewildering array of possibilities. You can track on any of a number of fields, including recipients, sender, server, message ID, and subject, as well as date and time. By default, the `EventID` parameter is pre-populated with `Receive`, although you can change this to any valid field via the drop-down control. If you're tracking a message that was never received, it's best to deselect this box (as it only pertains to messages that were actually *received*).

As you add in parameters, notice that the `Get-MessageTrackingLog` cmdlet script is automatically updated to reflect your changes. This behavior is almost unique within the EMC, and it's extremely useful for learning the cmdlet's syntax for later use in more complex tracking operations.

Once you've entered all the relevant criteria, click Next to begin searching for messages. Depending on your search criteria, this process could take a significant amount of time.

The Message Tracking Results page is a little confusing when you first encounter it, but it makes sense after you've visited it a few times. Because messages pass through different stages during the mail transfer process, you should (hopefully) see multiple entries for every message. At a bare minimum, a message should be listed three times, for the original notification to a Hub Transport server in the local site (SUBMIT), the delivery to the database on the receiving Mailbox server (DELIVER), and the ultimate delivery to the recipient (RECEIVE). If the recipient is in a different site, you'll see the delivery (SEND) of the message from one Hub Transport to another, and if there are multiple recipients, you'll probably see a TRANSFER, which indicates that a message was bifurcated en route.

The message-tracking tool in the console can be useful, but it's a lot slower than building your own queries with PowerShell. After you've tracked messages a few times with the EMC, you'll probably be comfortable enough to forgo the GUI and just use the shell.

MESSAGE TRACKING USING THE EXCHANGE MANAGEMENT SHELL

Since the message-tracking tool in the EMC uses the `Get-MessageTrackingLog` cmdlet, there's little to do here but show the actual output of the cmdlet with no input:

```
Get-MessageTrackingLog | Format-table EventID,Source,Sender, ↵
MessageSubject
```

EventId	Source	Sender	MessageSubject
-------	------	------	--------------
NOTIFYMAPI	STOREDRIVER		
SUBMIT	STOREDRIVER	SystemMailbox...	Test-Mailflow.
NOTIFYMAPI	STOREDRIVER		
SUBMIT	STOREDRIVER	jmcbee@ithico...	Aloha
NOTIFYMAPI	STOREDRIVER		
SUBMIT	STOREDRIVER	jmcbee@ithico...	FW: Aloha
RECEIVE	STOREDRIVER	SystemMailbox...	Test-Mailflow.
DELIVER	STOREDRIVER	SystemMailbox...	Test-Mailflow.
DSN	DSN	MicrosoftExch...	Delivered: Te.
DELIVER	STOREDRIVER	MicrosoftExch...	Delivered: Te.
RECEIVE	STOREDRIVER	jmcbee@ithico...	Aloha
TRANSFER	ROUTING	jmcbee@ithico...	Aloha
RECEIVE	STOREDRIVER	jmcbee@ithico...	FW: Aloha
TRANSFER	ROUTING	jmcbee@ithico...	FW: Aloha

There's only one "advantage" to using the shell over the console, and that's the fact that you can specify an unlimited result set (the GUI is limited to a result set of 1,000 messages). However, since there aren't many circumstances when you'd need to process 1,000 messages at a time, this advantage isn't a pronounced one. But it's the only major difference between the two, so it's still worth noting in case the need arises.

Now that we've gone through message tracking, you should be well equipped to determine whether a message was delivered and if not, where it stalled. If you're still unable to determine what's happening, there's one more tool we'll cover here that might help you make sense of what's happening in your environment.

Exchange Mail Flow Troubleshooter

The Mail Flow Troubleshooter section of the Troubleshooting Assistant is shown in Figure 28.9; yet another handy tool found in the Toolbox, it is a close cousin of the Exchange Best Practices Analyzer and is part of the Exchange Troubleshooting Assistant. Its purpose, not surprisingly, is to help you determine what might be causing mail flow issues in an environment. It's useful for many things, not least of which is automating some of the things we've discussed earlier. In fact, it does one particular thing that makes it of huge value for administrators — we'll come to that in a moment.

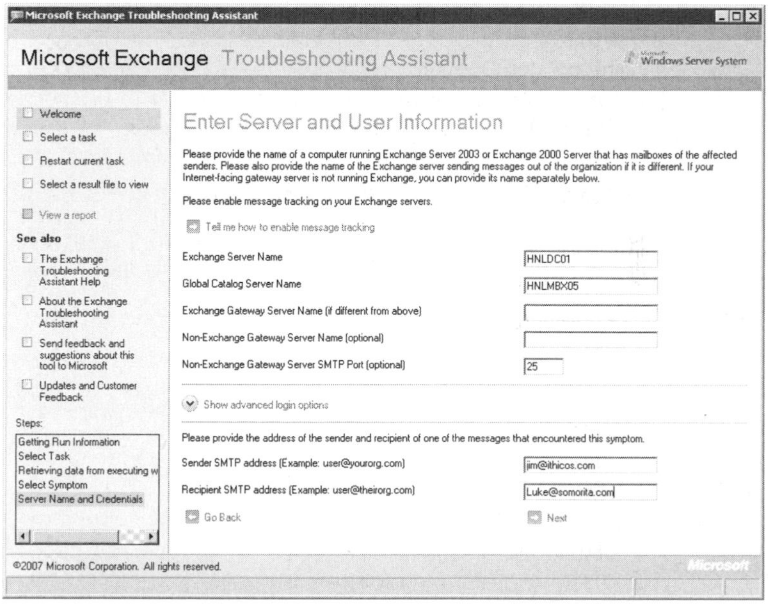

FIGURE 28.9

Using the Mail Flow Troubleshooter in the Exchange Troubleshooting Assistant

Once you've launched the Mail Flow Troubleshooter, the first thing you'll need to do is select the appropriate symptom. Choose wisely! The symptom you choose determines the troubleshooting path the tool will follow, so you want to make sure it doesn't take the wrong path (and lead you with it).

Here are the six symptoms you can choose from:

◆ Users are receiving unexpected nondelivery reports when sending messages.

◆ Expected messages from senders are delayed or are not received by some recipients.

◆ Messages destined to recipients are delayed or are not received by some recipients.

◆ Messages are backing up in one or more queues on a server.

◆ Messages sent by user(s) are pending submission on their Mailbox server(s).

◆ You are experiencing problems with Edge Server synchronization with Active Directory.

The symptoms are pretty clear, but it's worth clarifying two of them: the second and third items are similar, but the expected messages from senders item refers to messages delayed on their *inbound* journey, whereas the messages destined to recipients item refers to messages on their way *out*. In other words, you'll select the Expected Messages From Senders option if one of your users calls and says, "I'm waiting for an email but I haven't received it yet," but you'd select Messages Destined To Recipients if the user calls and says, "I sent an email to someone but he hasn't received it."

No matter which symptom you choose, you'll need to provide the name of the Exchange server in question as well as a global catalog server. After you do so, the Mail Flow Troubleshooter will perform some quick data collection and then display information about the target Exchange server. It's only when you click Next that the real analysis begins.

Earlier we hinted that there's a useful feature in the Mail Flow Troubleshooter, and it's related to the first symptom. Few humans have the Delivery Status Notification codes memorized, and finding them can sometimes be a bit of a chore. Look back at the list to see the first item, users are receiving nondelivery reports when sending messages. Although strictly speaking nondelivery reports are just a subset of delivery status notifications, it's generally only the nondelivery reports that we get worked up about. If you enter the appropriate three-digit code, you'll get a convenient explanation of the NDR and the tool will then search the message-tracking logs for events that match that information. The text in the NDR is often enough to alert you to the problem, and when you combine that with the ability to find the message in the environment, well, that's pretty useful functionality.

One of the other strengths of the Mail Flow Troubleshooter is that it doesn't require any specific knowledge on the part of the administrator: you don't need to know where the message is delayed, or which database a user is in. If Joe Smith is waiting for a message and hasn't received it, you can simply select the appropriate symptom, provide Joe's email address, and then let the Mail Flow Troubleshooter do the rest. Although it won't solve every issue, it's still a powerful and surprisingly underappreciated tool.

Other Tools

If you've used all the tools and techniques we've outlined to troubleshoot a mail issue, you might be facing more than a simple mail flow issue. If you've deployed transport agents in your environment, you may need to enable pipeline tracing, which essentially records every message to disk for later review. However, pipeline tracing is rather complex and is typically only used in conjunction with a Microsoft support case, so we won't cover it here — not to mention that it would deserve its own chapter! If you're curious about what pipeline tracing entails, what it offers, and (if you're brave enough) how to enable it, have a look at `http://technet.microsoft.com/en-us/library/bb125018(EXCHG.140).aspx`.

Troubleshooting Client Connectivity

Many of us subconsciously assume that "client" means Outlook, but it's not the only client software (or device) capable of accessing Exchange Server 2010. Outlook is the most popular, but there's also Outlook Web App and ActiveSync-enabled devices like Windows Mobile smartphones and Apple's iPhone. Despite the obvious differences between these devices, they all rely on the same basic mechanisms to connect — locating the Client Access server and connecting to the appropriate interface. They also depend on the health and proper configuration of network resources, including IP address schemes, site definitions, and DNS records and zones.

Before troubleshooting the server components, it's a good idea to test the following:

◆ Verify that the client can successfully ping the Client Access server by both IP and fully qualified domain name. If the forest includes multiple domains, ping the Client Access server by short (NetBIOS) name as well so that you can verify that NetBIOS names are being resolved correctly.

- For a mobile device, verify that the device can access Internet-based content by browsing to a known website.

- Verify the username and password combination for the mailbox you're attempting to access.

If these tests fail, the problem may not be unique to Exchange.

Troubleshooting Autodiscover

The most important initial consideration for Outlook client connectivity (specifically Outlook 2007 and the upcoming Outlook 2010) is the Autodiscover service. As described earlier in this book, the Autodiscover service generates an XML file with all the appropriate user settings and sends it to Outlook, which then uses that information to connect the user to his or her mailbox. But how does Outlook even know where to find Autodiscover in the first place? Depending on the client's location (on the corporate network or the Internet), the client will either check Active Directory for an appropriate record or look for a specific URL. There are a few different ways to check this, all of them very useful.

INTERNAL CLIENTS

Internal clients connect to Active Directory and check for the service connection point (SCP) records, which are automatically published as part of the setup process. One easy way to validate Autodiscover for internal clients is with Outlook 2007 or 2010's Test E-mail AutoConfiguration option. This useful little feature was introduced in Outlook 2007 and simply goes through the steps for Autodiscover without making changes to current configuration. To access this wizard, simply start Outlook, Ctrl+right-click the Outlook icon in the notification area (system tray), and then select Test E-mail AutoConfiguration from the context menu. You can see a sample of the Test E-mail AutoConfiguration tool in Figure 28.10.

FIGURE 28.10
Using the Test E-mail
AutoConfiguration tool

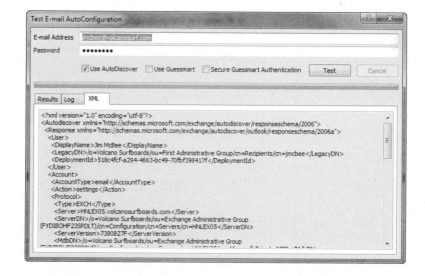

After providing appropriate user credentials and ensuring that only the check box for Use AutoDiscover is selected, click Test to begin the configuration check. The AutoConfiguration test checks for much more than just Autodiscover: it also locates Availability Service, OOF,

Offline Address Book, Unified Messaging, Outlook Web App, and Exchange Control Panel URLs, making this one of the most useful client-based configuration tools.

If the AutoConfiguration test fails, the tool will display an error message. The four most common error codes, along with root causes, are listed in Table 28.1.

TABLE 28.1: Common AutoConfiguration Error Codes

CODE	MEANING
0x80072EE7 – ERROR_INTERNET_NAME_NOT_RESOLVED	This error is usually caused by a missing host record for the Autodiscover service in the Domain Naming service.
0X80072F17 – ERROR_INTERNET_SEC_CERT_ERRORS	This error is usually caused by an incorrect certificate configuration on the Exchange computer that has the Client Access server role installed.
0X80072EFD – ERROR_INTERNET_CANNOT_CONNECT	This error is usually caused by issues that are related to Domain Naming service.
0X800C820A – E_AC_NO_SUPPORTED_SCHEMES	This error is usually caused by incorrect security settings in Outlook.

The AutoConfiguration test also works for external Outlook clients (including those connecting via Outlook Anywhere), so it's useful for the External Clients scenario listed next.

EXTERNAL CLIENTS

If external clients can't connect to Exchange, you may need to ensure that you've configured your environment for external access for the appropriate clients. Hopefully you've already done this, but if you haven't, here's what you need to do for an organization named somorita.com:

- To configure the external Autodiscover name for Outlook Anywhere, the appropriate command is `Enable-OutlookAnywhere -Server CAS01 -ExternalHostname "mail .somorita.com" -ExternalAuthenticationMethod "Basic" -SSLOffloading:$False`.

- The equivalent command for Web Service clients is `Set-WebServicesVirtualDirectory -identity "CAS01\EWS (Default Web Site)" -externalurl https://mail.somorita.com/EWS/Exchange.asmx -BasicAuthentication:$True`. In each case you'll obviously need to substitute your own domain namespace.

- The equivalent command for ActiveSync clients is `Set-ActiveSyncVirtualDirectory -identity "CAS01\Microsoft-Server-ActiveSync (Default Web Site)" -externalurl https://mail.somorita.com/Microsoft-Server-ActiveSync`. In each case, you'll obviously need to substitute your own domain namespace.

- The equivalent command for the Offline Address Book is `Set-OABVirtualDirectory -identity "CAS01\OAB (Default Web Site)" -externalurl https://mail.somorita.com/oab`. In each case, you'll obviously need to substitute your own domain namespace.

The Test E-mail AutoConfiguration option in Outlook 2007 and 2010 works for external Autodiscover as well as internal, and because Autodiscover is a published web address, you can always test it with a web browser (by navigating to `https://somorita.com/autodiscover/autodiscover.xml`, or whatever address you published). For external clients, however, there's a much better solution available online. In 2008 Microsoft quietly released the beta of an extremely useful tool called the Exchange Server Remote Connectivity Analyzer (ExRCA for short), which simulates a number of connectivity scenarios, including Autodiscover, Exchange ActiveSync, Outlook Anywhere, and incoming Internet SMTP email. You can find this tool (shown in Figure 28.11) at `www.testexchangeconnectivity.com`.

FIGURE 28.11
The main page of the Remote Connectivity Analyzer web page

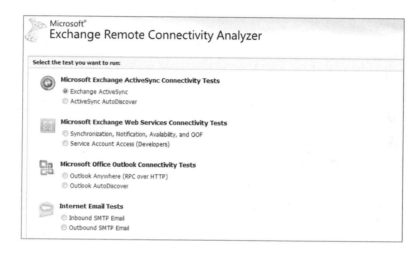

To use ExRCA, simply browse to `www.testexchangeconnectivity.com` and select the appropriate option (in this case we'll choose Exchange ActiveSync Autodiscover). Because you're providing information to a third party (in this case, Microsoft), it's a good idea to create a brand-new test user just for this purpose instead of exposing user credentials. Once you've provided the appropriate details, click OK to launch the test; the resulting output should either confirm that all is well or give you specific feedback on what might be missing. In Figure 28.12, ExRCA determined that the Autodiscover DNS name was not properly registered for the domain.

Test-*Connectivity Cmdlets

One of the most fundamental changes in Exchange Server 2010 sees the final shift of mailbox access away from the Mailbox server role over to the Client Access server role. Of course, Exchange ActiveSync and Outlook Web App clients also access the Client Access server, which means that your Client Access servers are even more critical to an Exchange environment than in the past. In other words, you need to make sure your clients can access the Client Access servers in all situations. Microsoft has long recommended that you deploy at least two Client Access servers in every site that houses a Mailbox server to ensure full redundancy. This recommendation assumes that your site definitions correctly include all appropriate subnets, that your servers' IP addresses are correctly configured, and that all DNS records are properly registered in the appropriate zones.

If your client can access Autodiscover, you know that you can connect to at least one Client Access server, but it's possible to access one service on a Client Access system but not others. How can you tell if other necessary components on the Client Access server are functioning properly? Earlier we talked about two very useful cmdlets — Test-SystemHealth and Test-ServiceHealth — that can help diagnose general issues on a server. However, sometimes you can take a more surgical approach and focus on one protocol. For this, we'll use a series of cmdlets called Test-*Connectivity (where * is the protocol or client you're testing).

FIGURE 28.12
Results of an ActiveSync
Autodiscover test

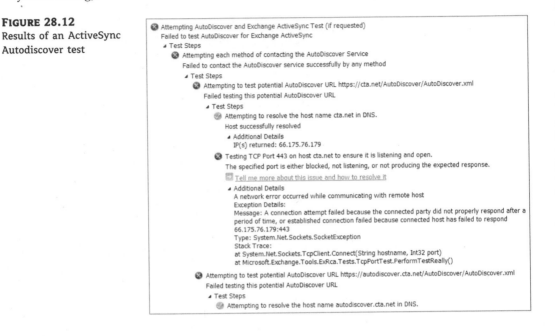

TROUBLESHOOTING USING CMDLETS

You've probably noticed that troubleshooting Exchange Server 2010 involves a lot of cmdlets, and you're right: there are a lot of troubleshooting cmdlets! The Exchange product group worked hard to ensure that administrators had easy-to-use, robust, focused troubleshooting tools right at their fingertips, and the resulting family of cmdlets serves as a testament to those efforts.

Depending on the client you're testing, you'll want to use one of the following cmdlets:

◆ Test-ActiveSyncConnectivity

◆ Test-OutlookConnectivity

◆ Test-PopConnectivity

◆ Test-ImapConnectivity

◆ Test-OwaConnectivity

◆ Test-WebServicesConnectivity

Most of the cmdlets above are all pretty self-explanatory; they correspond to the most popular connectivity models (although it's important to note that the cmdlets to test POP3 and IMAP4 connectivity don't include the version numbers for the protocols — it's just POP and IMAP). The `Test-OutlookConnectivity` cmdlet (shown in Figure 28.13) covers both MAPI and Outlook Anywhere connectivity, so you don't need separate ones (although as you've seen, there is also a separate `Test-MapiConnectivity` cmdlet).

FIGURE 28.13
Example of
Test-Outlook
Connectivity

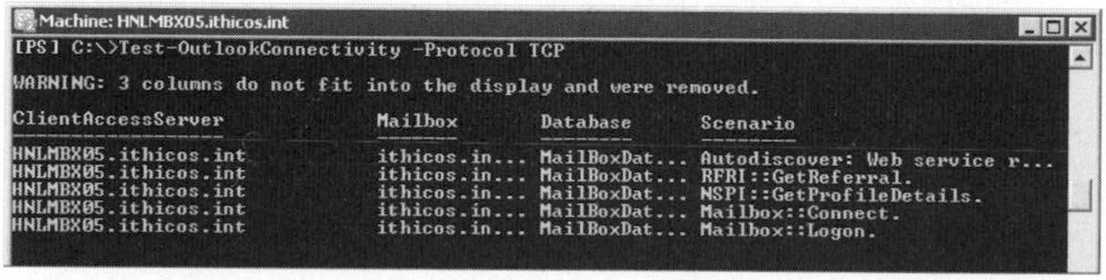

The cmdlets `Test-WebServicesConnectivity` (shown in Figure 28.14) and `Test-OutlookWeb Services` have a lot of overlap, and the essential difference is that the former checks only the web services.

FIGURE 28.14
Using Test-
WebServices
Connectivity

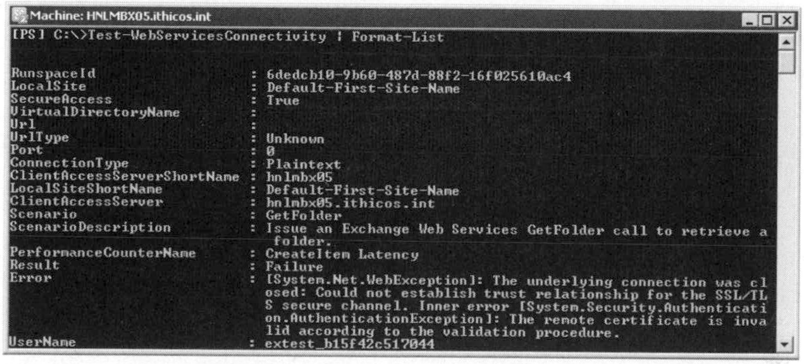

The `Test-OutlookWebServices` cmdlet tests all the web services that the clients might use during normal client activity such as Autodiscover, Availability Service, and Offline Address Book. It's primarily used to troubleshoot Outlook Anywhere clients (for obvious reasons), but is still useful in other environments. Prior to running the cmdlet, though, you should run the `New-TestCasConnectivityUser.ps1` script to create test users for your CAS server or servers.

The suite of cmdlets listed here provides comprehensive coverage for connectivity issues. If you can run these successfully but still can't connect your client, there's a good chance that the problem isn't with Exchange at all.

Client connectivity is a complex and involved process, and the number of troubleshooting tools reflects this. Outlook includes some basic tools, including the Test E-mail AutoConfiguration option, but for more detailed troubleshooting you'll probably need to use one of the incredibly useful `Test-*Connectivity` cmdlets. For external connections, you have the added luxury of the Exchange Remote Connectivity Analyzer (www.testexchangeconnectivity.com). You can also test the other services provided by Client Access servers with the `Test-OutlookWebServices` cmdlet. Taken as a group, these tools should allow you to quickly determine whether client connectivity problems are caused by the Exchange infrastructure.

The Bottom Line

Narrow the scope of an Exchange problem.   One of the most important troubleshooting skills that an Exchange administrator must possess is the ability to quickly and effectively narrow the scope of problem. Determining the commonalities in a problem can help you quickly locate and solve a problem.

> **Master It**   Seven of your 400 users are reporting an error in Outlook that indicates that they cannot connect to the Exchange server. What are some things you would determine to narrow the scope of the problem?

Use basic Exchange troubleshooting tools.   A number of tools are available to you that will help you in troubleshooting Exchange Server problems as well as possibly determining future issues. These include the Windows Event Viewer, the Exchange Best Practices Analyzer, Exchange diagnostics logging, and the `Test-SystemHealth` and `Test-ServiceHealth` cmdlets.

> **Master It**   After installing a recent service pack, you have started noticing intermittent issues with your Exchange server. What tool or tools could you run to help you identify potential issues?

Troubleshoot Mailbox server problems.   The Mailbox server is at the core of your Exchange organization; all Exchange data is located and serviced via this Exchange server role. When the Exchange Mailbox server role is not functioning correctly, this will cause a fast-moving ripple effect through your organization that will affect more and more users. Tools such as the `Test-MapiConnectivity` cmdlet can help you determine whether a mailbox can be reached.

The Exchange Server 2010 database availability group (DAG) high-availability feature will become increasingly prevalent in even small businesses as companies look to find ways to keep their Exchange infrastructure up and running as much as possible. The `Test-ReplicationHealth` and `Get-MailboxCopyStatus` cmdlets can help in testing the health of the DAG replication.

> **Master It**   A user named Luke.Husky is reporting that he cannot use Outlook to access his mailbox, yet he can access it via Outlook Web App. What tool could you use to determine whether the mailbox is accessible via Outlook?

Troubleshoot mail transport problems.   The Exchange Server 2010 Hub Transport role plays the all-important role of delivering all messages that are processed via the Exchange 2010 infrastructure. This is true even if a message is sent from one user to another on the same mailbox database.

A number of useful tools are available to help you and your users determine where a problem may exist. These include the Exchange 2010 Queue Viewer, the `Test-MailFlow` cmdlet, and message tracking.

> **Master It**   A user is reporting that they are sending email but that recipient is never getting the message. The user is convinced your server is not delivering the message. You would like the user to determine whether the message is leaving your organization. What would you advise the user to do?

Chapter 29

Monitoring and Performance

An Exchange server — any version — requires more than just sticking in the installation DVD, clicking Next, Next, Next, Finish, and then walking away. This does not mean that, after initial configuration, you have to fiddle with settings on a day-to-day basis. On the contrary: once initial configuration is complete, outside of recipient management you will likely not have to often make many configuration changes to your Exchange application.

However, Exchange is a complex application, especially as your usage grows. The overall performance of Exchange is also dependent on the performance of the servers on which it runs (that is, Windows Server performance), the performance of Active Directory, the performance of the Domain Name System (DNS), and the performance of the network connecting individual Exchange servers and the Internet. The Exchange application plus these individual pieces — the Exchange infrastructure — make up the Exchange environment (sometimes called the Exchange ecosystem).

It behooves the Exchange administrator to track the performance of her Exchange environment. With tracking, the Exchange administrator can see trends in usage, discover and analyze end-user issues, find peak and minimum usage times, and be alerted to problems before and as they occur.

Performance tracking is a major piece of historical monitoring.

In this chapter, you will learn to:

◆ Examine and interpret key performance monitor counters

◆ Install and configure the Exchange Management Pack

◆ Configure, locate, and examine SMTP connector logs

◆ Configure and evaluate Exchange diagnostic logging

Key Performance Monitor Counters

Each and every server, not just your Exchange servers, has key metrics that you will be interested in. These include the following:

◆ Memory usage and historical memory utilization

◆ Processor usage and historical processor utilization

◆ Disk usage and historical disk utilization

Specifically for Exchange servers, you are also interested in metrics covering these additional items:

◆ Active Directory performance

◆ Network performance

◆ MAPI performance

Unsurprisingly, Windows Server provides us with a mechanism for accessing this information in several ways:

◆ The Performance Monitor tool

◆ The Resource Monitor tool

◆ The Task Manager tool

◆ The .NET Framework API

◆ The Win32 API

The Win32 API and the .NET Framework API are developer-oriented mechanisms and beyond the scope of our discussion. We will cover the other mechanisms in this section.

Types of Monitoring

Monitoring falls into two broad categories:

Real-Time or Instantaneous   In this case, monitoring information is recorded as an event occurs. For example, when a connection is made to an Edge server to begin the process of transferring an email, an entry is written to a log file. This happens in real time, as each event occurs.

Scheduled   In this case, a monitoring "probe" is executed on a regular basis. For example, every 15 minutes you may check the amount of disk space available on the volume hosting a mailbox store.

Both types of monitoring are valuable. Both can produce immediate "This situation needs to be handled right now!" types of alerts. Both can be used to produce historical trendingbreak information.

Real-time monitoring is often used for producing volume reports (for example, how many email messages were received per hour during each day of the preceding month). Real-time monitoring is also often used for diagnosing failures of one type or another (for example, why a message transfer failed between Server A and Server B).

Scheduled monitoring is generally used for probing specific values of a property against a known optimum value. For example, you can specify that you want an alert to be generated if disk space on a volume goes below 10 percent available, if processor utilization over the last five minutes has exceeded 95 percent, or if Average RPC Latency exceeds 50 ms.

If you think about it, it is easy to see that monitoring is trying to tell us two things about our servers. First, is our server performing at an acceptable level? Second, is our server healthy?

WHAT IS A HEALTHY SERVER?

In this case, a healthy server is one that has all of its tested properties fall within ranges that are defined as being acceptable. System Center Operations Manager (OpsMgr) builds hierarchical health for modules on a server (for example, Exchange Server may be one module on a server and the disk may be another, and Exchange Server's health may depend on the disk module being healthy).

Also, you can see that some monitoring measurements may mean nothing by themselves, and become important only when viewed over a period of time to see how they have grown or shrunk. This process is called "trending" and is an important part of server monitoring.

Different roles of Exchange Server will have different optimum values for some things. However, certain considerations apply to all Windows servers, be they Exchange, Active Directory, SQL, File/Print, or (heaven forbid!) some combination of these. The servers require the following:

◆ Sufficient processor power

◆ Sufficient memory

◆ Sufficient disk space

You can consider those to be the "big three" for any server of any type (be it Windows, Linux, Sun, IBM mainframe, or whatever). Most, but certainly not all, performance problems will be traced to a deficiency of one of those items or an improper configuration of software. Any Windows server running Exchange Server will also require the following:

◆ Sufficient network bandwidth

◆ Sufficiently fast disk access

◆ Sufficiently fast Active Directory response

◆ Properly implemented Active Directory

◆ Properly implemented DNS

Now that you know the types of monitoring, let's discuss the detailed performance counters and Windows Management Instrumentation (WMI) classes that are relevant for implementing this type of monitoring.

Memory

Interestingly, in the operating systems of today, memory and disk space will have some overlap. Using so-called virtual memory, when a computer system experiences memory pressure — that is, a need for more memory than what is actually installed on the server — the operating system will begin to page some unused or (less used) memory to disk. This is used to make some of the main memory available for use by other programs.

> ### A Quick Primer on Virtual Memory
>
> Virtual memory works by *paging in* and *paging out*. When the operating system is paging out, it is writing a copy of memory from RAM to disk. When the operating system is paging in, it is reading memory from disk to put into RAM. You can configure a server to have much more virtual memory than physical RAM. However, that will probably not provide the best performance for your server.

For a given workload, a server will always require approximately the same amount of virtual memory. Paging activity is measured in terms of pages per second, which measures the total number of pages either read or written from disk in a given second. However, there is no fixed limit on the value of Memory\Pages/Sec that represents a "problem." In the old days (Windows NT 4.0), a value greater than 20 was considered to indicate that too much paging was going on. However, that value was artificial due to the slow speeds of disk, memory, and processor of the day. To get the best counter value, you need to look at historical data from your Exchange servers to determine what is in range and what is out of range. However, the counter should never exceed a value of 1000.

In general terms, if paging plus other I/O to the volume where the paging file resides causes disk queuing to occur, then too much paging is occurring.

> ### Where Does Paging Happen?
>
> All paging occurs to and from a file known as the paging file. On Windows systems, this file is known as `pagefile.sys` and it resides in the root directory of a paging volume. This file has the hidden and system attributes set on the file. That means it is not normally visible in Windows Explorer or from the command prompt. It is possible to have multiple paging files, one per disk volume. This was fairly common with the 32-bit versions of Windows Server, but on 64-bit versions of Windows Server, you should only use a single paging file.

The Memory\Pages/Sec value is the sum of two other values: Memory\Pages Input/Sec and Memory\Pages Output/Sec. The individual meanings of these values are fairly obvious; the number of pages read from the paging file and the number of pages written to the paging file, respectively.

Use of the Paging File

Another value of interest is the Memory\Commit Limit counter. A little explanation is in order for Memory\Commit Limit. The paging file in Windows has a number of possible settings:

◆ No paging file

◆ System-managed paging file

◆ Fixed-size paging file

As you might suspect, when the Windows computer is configured to have no paging file, the paging file has a size of zero. This setting indicates that the paging file may never be expanded. If you select the option to allow Windows to manage the paging file, the minimum size of the paging file is set to the amount of RAM in your computer plus 300 MB. The maximum size of the paging file is set to three times the amount of RAM in your computer. A fixed-size paging file is just that: you specify the minimum and maximum sizes for the paging file. In general, for Windows clients you should allow the system to manage the paging file. For Windows servers, if you have guidance for your server for a specific role (as you will for Exchange servers), follow that guidance. Otherwise, allow the system to manage the paging file.

ARE YOU SURE ABOUT THOSE VALUES?

The system-managed paging file defaults discussed are accurate for Windows Vista (and above) and for Windows Server 2008 (and above). The values are smaller for earlier versions of both the Windows client and Windows server.

The Memory\Commit Limit counter is the amount of virtual memory that can be allocated without expanding the paging file. When the paging file must be expanded, paging out is a much more "expensive" operation. Strongly related to the Memory\Commit Limit counter is the value of Memory\Committed Bytes. The Memory\Committed Bytes counter defines how many bytes of the paging file are currently in use.

The final paging file counter of interest is a calculated counter based on the two counters just discussed. That counter is Memory\% Committed Bytes In Use. This counter provides the system administrator with an instantaneous value for how much of the paging file is being used. The counter is the ratio of Memory\Committed Bytes to Memory\Commit Limit. The range of this value is between 0 percent and 100 percent. A low value is good; a high value is bad.

AVAILABLE MEMORY

Generally speaking, the more memory a computer has, the better that computer will perform. An efficiency goal for a server is never to use the paging file. This reduces the I/O load on the server as well as reducing the processor overhead of the memory manager on the server. For Exchange Server, there are recommended minimum and maximum values for the amount of memory installed on a server, based on the particular server roles installed on that server. When multiple roles are combined, those values need to be added together to obtain the optimal amount of memory for that server.

Regardless of what programs are installed on a server, it is important to have enough memory on a server to be able to satisfy memory requests, whether those memory requests are large or small. When you do not have sufficient memory installed on a computer, you will have both visible warnings displayed and error entries will be written into the System event log. In Figure 29.1, the Resource Exhaustion Detector has detected that there is very little virtual memory left on a computer and has generated a warning to that effect. Figure 29.2 shows the application pop-up that is displayed to the console user.

It is certainly possible to track memory availability using the counters described so far. Another counter that is of great value is the Memory\Available MBytes counter. This counter contains the amount of physical memory (not virtual memory) that can be immediately allocated to a running process or used by the operating system. In the general case of a memory leak, the Memory\Available MBytes counter would gradually decrease over time. Eventually, no more memory would be available to the system and the system would become unstable (which is just a fancy way to say that programs would begin crashing). The Memory\Available MBytes counter value should never fall below 50 MB.

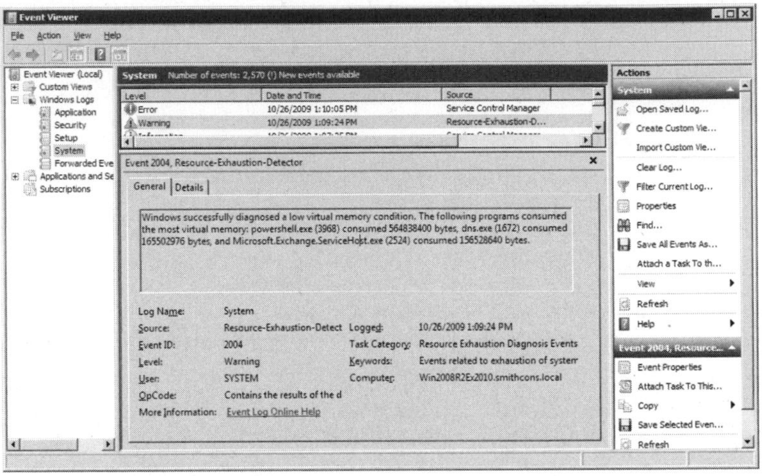

FIGURE 29.1
Resource Exhaustion Detector

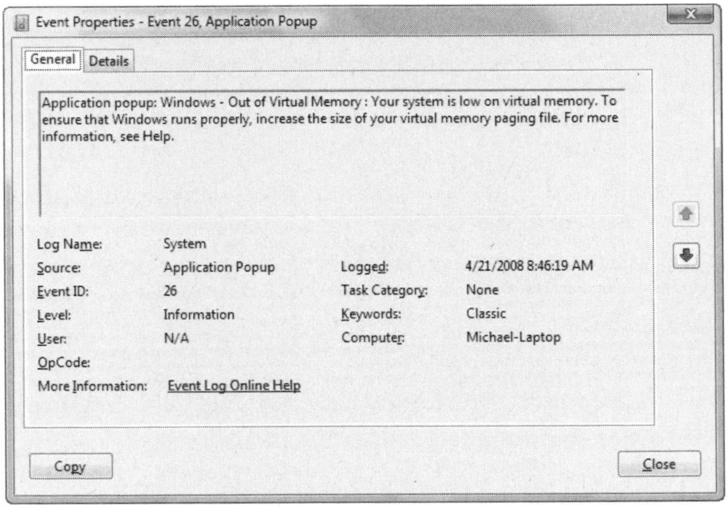

FIGURE 29.2
Out of Virtual Memory event

EXCHANGE SERVER 2010 MEMORY REQUIREMENTS

In general, Exchange Server 2010 is just like almost any other program — the more memory you allow it to use, the better it will run. The Exchange team at Microsoft has produced guidelines that describe which values they consider the minimum and optimal values of memory on an Exchange server. At the time of this writing, 4 GB RAM sticks are common in servers with 8 GB to 16 GB of RAM more expensive but not prohibitively so for server-class machines.

Each of the various Exchange Server 2010 roles (Edge Transport, Hub Transport, Client Access Server, Mailbox, and Unified Messaging) has different recommendations for the amount of memory. See Table 29.1 for these recommendations.

TABLE 29.1: Exchange Server 2010 Memory Information

EXCHANGE 2010 SERVER ROLE	MINIMUM PER SERVER	RECOMMENDED
Edge Transport	4 GB	1 GB per core (4 GB minimum)
Hub Transport	4 GB	1 GB per core (4 GB minimum)
Client Access	4 GB	2 GB per core (8 GB minimum)
Unified Messaging	4 GB	2 GB per core (4 GB minimum, 8 GB maximum)
Mailbox	4 GB	4 GB plus 3–30 MB/mailbox
Multiple roles (combinations of Hub Transport, Client Access, and Mailbox server roles)	10 GB	10 GB plus 3–30 MB per mailbox (4-core server) 14 GB plus 3–30 MB per mailbox (8-core server) 18 GB plus 3–30 MB per mailbox (12-core server) 22 GB plus 3–30 MB per mailbox (16-core server) 30 GB plus 3–30 MB per mailbox (24-core server)

For Exchange Server 2010 RTM: `http://technet.microsoft.com/en-us/library/dd346700(EXCHG.140).aspx`

MEMORY CHANGES SINCE EXCHANGE SERVER 2007

Most of the server role recommendations are on par with their Exchange Server 2007 roles. However, with very large mailbox support, the per-mailbox cache recommendation has increased from 5 MB to 30 MB. As of this writing, specific memory cache recommendations per mailbox size/activity are not available, but they should be available by the time you receive this book. Check for "Mailbox Memory Recommendations" in the Exchange 2010 section on TechNet. For Hub Transport the size of caching in the `mail.que` database has increased significantly as well (from 128 MB to 1024 MB).

 **Real World Scenario**

DO I NEED MORE MEMORY?

As we stated in the beginning of this section, performance issues with memory and disk can be tightly related — and in fact, they may serve to hide issues with each other.

As an example, consider an Exchange 2010 server with 8 GB of RAM. This server is performing slowly both in serving user requests and in performing console interactions. However, processor utilization viewed from Task Manager is low.

Starting Performance Monitor and examining the Avg. Disk Queue Length for each volume and the Page Faults/Sec counters can quickly determine the likely culprit (memory exhaustion or I/O exhaustion). However, these two counters must be considered together. If the Avg. Disk Queue Length on a volume is consistently high, this may mean that too much I/O is occurring to that volume. However, if that volume is a paging volume, the Page Faults/Sec counter also needs to be examined because the problem may be too little memory.

> So, if Page Faults/Sec is high, the issue is likely with inadequate memory and that's where you need to look. If Page Faults/Sec is low, the issue is likely with an inadequate I/O subsystem and that's where you should continue your search.
>
> Note that when an Exchange server is first starting (all servers, but especially Mailbox servers), these counters will be skewed and their values shouldn't be depended on until the server reaches a steady state.

Processor

Monitoring for processor usage is simpler than monitoring for memory, and the concepts are easier to grasp. After all, a processor is in one of only two states, right? Either busy or not busy? Unfortunately, it isn't quite that simple.

A processor can generally be in any of five states:

◆ Idle

◆ Processing an interrupt

◆ Processing a user task

◆ Processing a system task

◆ Waiting

Each of these states can occur during each processor second.

MORE ON PROCESSOR STATES

Windows 7 and Windows Server 2008 R2 introduced a new state for a processor core called "parked." This basically means that a processor core is powered down, as it hasn't been used for a long period of time. For the purposes of our discussion, a parked core is equivalent to an idle core.

MEASURING PROCESSOR STATES

A processor utilization measurement is made every *tick*, where a tick is an interrupt from the system clock. Each tick is exactly 10 milliseconds apart. With today's fast processors, a processor may have been busy at some point during that tick (doing any of the items mentioned previously) and that wouldn't be recorded. Because of this, processor utilization tends to be higher than actually reported and the total of all the individual tasks processor times is often higher than expected.

The processor idle state occurs when, as you might expect, the processor isn't doing anything. The processor is simply waiting for an interrupt to occur. As a result of that interrupt, a system task or a user task (or both) may be scheduled for execution. Very low values of the Processor\% Idle Time counter may indicate that you should add additional processors to your computer. However, before making that decision, examine the other processor counters.

Interrupts are caused by hardware. They literally interrupt the computer from doing whatever it was doing to process an interrupt routine. Interrupt routines are used to do such things as update the system clock, process an I/O complete message, move data into a program's buffer, or wake up another task. Interrupts take priority over any other task running on a processor. Very high values of the Processor\% Interrupt Time counter may indicate faulty hardware.

User tasks are those tasks initiated by normal applications. This includes applications such as Exchange. User mode tasks are restricted in that they cannot access all physical memory, only that memory which is assigned to them by the operating system. They are also restricted in that they cannot access hardware directly; they must use a device driver or other operating system intermediary to access hardware. The Processor\% User Time counter identifies the relative amount of time spent processing user mode tasks. Generally, when a processor is fully utilized, it is being used primarily by user mode tasks.

Privileged tasks, or system tasks, are those tasks identified as being part of the operating system. Privileged tasks can access all physical memory and they can access hardware directly. Usually, the value of the Processor\% Privileged Time counter is quite low. The amount of processor resource consumed by privileged tasks can increase when, for example, garbage collection takes too long and memory resources are low, and when a system is being used as a file server.

Waiting time is counted as a piece of Processor\% Interrupt Time. It indicates that a processor is waiting for some resource and cannot proceed until that resource is available. Generally, this happens when a processor core is waiting on access to a particular piece of memory. When a processor is waiting on memory, it is called memory starved. Reduction of memory starvation is one of the primary reasons that multicore processors are more efficient than multiple single-core processors. Multiple single-core processors have to arbitrate access to the memory bus whereas in a multicore processor there is a single memory controller.

Finally in the Processor object, the Processor\% Processor Time counter is approximately the sum of the counters Processor\% Interrupt Time, Processor\% User Time, and Processor\% Privileged Time. It is measured by subtracting Processor\% Idle Time from 100%, so it will not necessarily be exactly equal to the sum of the counters. The Processor\% Processor Time counter should not normally exceed 80% for extended periods of time. If it does, you should consider upgrading the available processor resources on a server.

When looking at processor usage, another counter comes in quite handy. That counter is the System\Processor Queue Length counter. There is a single queue for any system, regardless of the number of processors. This queue contains all tasks (privileged and user — but not interrupts!) that are "ready to run." That is, if processor time was available on any core to execute them, they would be running. There is only a single processor queue because any task can run on any core. Generally, the value of this counter should average less than one. Spikes up to the number of cores in a system are permissible. However, if on average the value of the counter is greater than one, then the system is processor bound. That is, the system does not have sufficient processor resources to meet the needs of all tasks.

DECODING THE GEEK-SPEAK

Modern processors are discussed in terms of speed, sockets, and cores. Speed is obvious — it is the clock rate at which the processor executes. Although it is not the only indication of a processor's performance, speed is a key indicator of how quickly a processor can process instructions. Sockets indicate the number of physically separate processors contained within a computer. Each socket contains one physical processor. Cores are the number of logical processors within a socket. At the time of this writing, quad-core chips are common, a six-core chip is available, and an eight-core chip is expected soon. Each core is basically another processor contained within the same socket on the same chip.

EXCHANGE SERVER 2010 PROCESSOR REQUIREMENTS

These requirements are similar to the minimum and maximum memory recommendations we presented earlier; in general, Exchange Server 2010 will run faster the more processor you give it to use. The Microsoft Exchange team has also worked out processor recommendations for minimum, maximum, and recommended configurations for each server role. See Table 29.2 for those values.

TABLE 29.2: Processor Configurations for Exchange Server 2010 Roles

EXCHANGE 2010 SERVER ROLE	MINIMUM	MAXIMUM	RECOMMENDED
Edge Transport	1 × processor core	12 × processor cores	4 × processor cores
Hub Transport	1 × processor core	12 × processor cores	4 × processor cores
Client Access	2 × processor cores	12 × processor cores	8 × processor cores
Unified Messaging	2 × processor cores	12 × processor cores	8 × processor cores
Mailbox	2 × processor cores	12 × processor cores	8 × processor cores
Multiple server roles (combinations of Hub Transport, Client Access, and Mailbox server roles)	2 × processor cores	24 × processor cores	8 × processor cores

For Exchange Server 2010 RTM: `http://technet.microsoft.com/en-us/library/dd346699(EXCHG.140).aspx`

When planning for your Exchange Server 2010 solution, remember that the recommendations published by Microsoft do not include any overhead that may be caused by third-party solutions, such as on-server antivirus or antispam solutions.

CHANGES IN PROCESSOR RECOMMENDATIONS SINCE EXCHANGE SERVER 2007

In Exchange Server 2010, all Messaging Applications Programming Interface (MAPI) access was moved from the Mailbox server to the Client Access server (CAS), and a number of new features were added to the CAS (such as MailTips). This has increased the processor recommendation (and the minimum) for the CAS role rather dramatically. Also, new features (for example, archiving and retention) in the mailbox role have increased processor recommendations there as well.

Much work on multicore support was also done in Windows Server 2008 R2. That version of Windows Server supports the situation of having many processor cores much more efficiently than did earlier versions of Windows Server, making it possible to scale both further up and out than you could previously.

Disk

Disk performance is something of an art; some would say it is a "black art," much more than a science. This is especially true where storage area networks (SANs) and network-attached storage (NAS) come into play. Disk performance also impacts memory performance (how much data is cached in main memory) and processor performance (how many I/O requests we have to process), making it even more confusing. In Exchange Server 2010, the confusion has been reined in a bit, since Microsoft's guidance for Exchange servers is now to utilize SATA direct-attached storage (DAS) — that is, disk directly connected to server.

SATA vs. SCSI

SATA is slow. In general, while higher-quality SATA disk is available, SATA disk is workstation-class instead of enterprise-class (that means it fails more often). However, it has the major benefit of being cheap.

SCSI and fiber-channel (FC) disk are fast. In general, SCSI and FC disks are enterprise-class. However, they have the major drawback of being expensive.

Through and including Exchange Server 2007, Microsoft recommended that Exchange Server be hosted on high-performing SCSI disk. In many companies, that meant using expensive SAN solutions. With Exchange Server 2010, Microsoft is now recommending the use of SATA as an acceptable disk platform. This recommendation is causing lots of conversations throughout the Exchange partner ecosystem.

Disk performance is all about IOPS (input-output operations per second). However, we're not here today to tell you how to design your disk subsystem, but instead how to monitor it and determine whether it is performing as well as you desire. Monitoring is complicated enough, but not quite the art that better-performing design is. First, let's explore some background information. Windows breaks disk monitoring into two separate performance monitor objects: LogicalDisk and PhysicalDisk. LogicalDisk is the standard disk drive letter that you are used to, such as C:\ or D:\. Within Windows, a logical disk may consist of one or more physical disk drives (the drives can be spanned across multiple physical disk drives or set up in a software-based RAID array).

From the Windows perspective, PhysicalDisk is a single physical disk. Within Windows (or just about any other operating system), there may be more than one logical disk contained on a physical disk. This uses a technique known as partitioning in order to place multiple logical disks on the physical disk. Note that this can be confusing because Windows may see a single physical disk when, in fact, the disk is composed of multiple spindles aggregated by a hardware RAID controller or host bus adapter for a SAN. In the case of a SAN, the logical unit number (LUN) presented to Windows as a single physical disk may actually be an array split between many systems.

Sounds complicated, doesn't it? Usually, though, it isn't too bad. The take-away from this section is that the relationship between logical disks and physical disks may be complex in some environments. When you are designing storage arrays, the simpler you can design it, the easier your long-term support will be.

EXCHANGE SERVER 2010 DISK NEEDS

An Exchange Server has a number of disk needs, depending on the roles that are installed on it:

◆ Operating system

◆ Log files

◆ Paging file

◆ Event log files

◆ Databases

◆ Database transaction log files

◆ Content indexing

◆ Content conversion

◆ Backup and restore

◆ Replication (optional)

◆ Zero Out Deleted Database Pages

Every Exchange server, no matter the role, will have an operating system and probably a page file. The log files referred to in the second bullet are text-based log files, such as those generated by protocol and activity logging or by IIS on the Client Access server. Databases are mailbox stores and public folder stores on Mailbox servers and queue databases on Hub Transport and Edge servers. Transaction logs are the files used for recovery in the case a database were to crash.

Content indexing is the generation of a fast searchable index for the emails contained within an Exchange database. Content conversion occurs when an email message is received by a Hub Transport server and is translated into a format appropriate for storage in an Exchange database. It's also the reverse — the conversion that takes place when a message is leaving the Exchange organization. Online maintenance is a daily activity that assures the health of an Exchange database. Replication is copying the contents of a database, as it changes, to another location as a high-availability option.

Zero Out Deleted Database Pages is a security option. In Exchange 2007 and before, Zero Out Deleted Database Pages was off by default. In Exchange 2010, the default is for the option to be enabled. Previously, when an Exchange database page was made available (for example, after a message had been deleted and it was time for the message to be purged from the database), the page was simply marked as "available." Now, during normal operations, available pages are gathered together and added to the whitespace in the database that is available for reuse. By zeroing out database pages, a page is not simply marked as available and added to the whitespace tables, but the contents of the page are set to zero and the page is rewritten to disk. In Exchange Server 2010 this has a relatively minor I/O cost, unlike previous versions of Exchange Server. Databases and operating system files are accessed on a random basis. Log files and transaction log files are accessed sequentially (after all, they are written record by record, and if they ever need to be read, they will be read record by record). This difference in usage patterns makes it best, in an ideal situation, to separate each of the disk requirements onto different physical disks and onto separate controllers.

However, in Exchange Server 2010 we have two possible configurations for disk environments: a DAG-based solution and a non-DAG-based (stand-alone) solution.

A COMMON DISK FALLACY

From a performance perspective, there is no benefit to creating multiple logical volumes on a single physical volume. For example, some administrators mistakenly believe that performance will improve if they take a RAID 5 array, partition it into two logical drives, and place databases on one of those logical drives and transaction log files on the other. That is not true. Each usage type should be on separate physical devices for optimum performance.

A Stand-alone Disk Configuration

In a stand-alone disk solution, you probably only have a couple of servers and each is very important. Your configuration is designed to enhance the resiliency of each server to attempt to ensure that the server does not go down.

In this solution, the operating system and database transaction log files go onto separate RAID 1 (mirrored) drive sets. This strategy allows for doubling the read performance and minimizing the write overhead that is associated with RAID. Depending on the importance of text logs to your organization, they should be placed on either a stand-alone disk or another RAID 1 drive set. Database files on Hub Transport servers are pretty easy, too. Except when queues grow to very large sizes, the queue databases remain fairly small. Another set of RAID 1 is just the ticket. For mailbox databases it gets a little more complicated. The ideal situation is a striped set of mirrored disks (that is, RAID 1+0 or RAID 10). However, that approach has a very high disk cost (that is, you must have twice the number of disks as you have usable disk space). The alternatives are RAID 5 (which has a one-disk cost) and RAID 6 (which has a two-disk cost). The problem with both RAID 5 and RAID 6 is that the mechanism they use to stripe the data puts a very high overhead on write operations.

A DAG Disk Configuration

If you are setting up your servers with DAGs, you have at least two Mailbox servers and likely you have multiple Client Access and Hub Transport servers as well. In this case, you are most interested that a failing server will fail seamlessly and send all its users to another server that has enough capacity to take them over. Then, you'll repair or replace the failed server and bring it back online.

In this case, you'll probably have the operating system and paging file on a single volume (still with RAID 1) and transaction log files and the mailbox database(s) on another volume. Everything is replicated from one server to another, and all configurations are standard and documented.

DAG OR STAND-ALONE SOLUTIONS?

Which works better: DAG or stand-alone solutions? The answer in two words: it depends.

Stand-alone solutions are typically better suited to smaller environments where multiple servers are not an option due to cost, configuration, or other concerns. It is worthwhile to note that in Exchange Server 2010 the only Microsoft-supported high-availability solution for the Mailbox server is the DAG. All of the "continuous replication" solutions and "single-copy cluster" solutions that were present in earlier versions of Exchange Server have been removed from Exchange Server 2010.

Although this removal of choice does simplify both configuration and the decision-making process, it comes at a cost. Literally. The DAG uses components of Windows Failover Clustering (WFC). Since WFC components are only available with Windows Server Enterprise Edition, you can only use DAGs on that edition of Windows Server. This leads to DAG-based solutions becoming significantly more expensive than stand-alone solutions.

Cost issues aside, the DAG-based solution works very, very well. Many of the issues associated with failover and failback and user connectivity are gone. Instead of an end user (that is, an Outlook or Outlook Web Access user) connecting directly to a Mailbox server, the end user now connects to a client access array (CAA). The CAA knows immediately when it loses contact with any Mailbox server that is part of a DAG. The database fails over within 30 seconds and the CAA starts contacting the new DAG primary server. If the user is in cached mode, they never notice that anything happened. If the user is on OWA, they get a short period of no response. This is very unlike the failover situation with CCR or SCC, which could take from two to five minutes and then might be required to reauthenticate.

However, implementing this type of solution is not a single-server kind of solution. A DAG consumes a minimum of two servers (up to 16). A CAA consumes a minimum of two servers (based on documentation, there is no set limit). While Exchange Server 2010 allows collocation of the DAG, Client Access, and Hub Transport servers, to have a highly available solution in that scenario requires that your CAS array be front-ended by a redundant hardware-based load balancer.

So, if your tolerance for downtime is very low, a DAG-based solution will work well for your company. If your tolerance for added software expense is very low, then a stand-alone solution may be a better solution for your company.

HOW DO I KNOW IF I HAVE ENOUGH?

As always, in Exchange Server 2010 you should buy the biggest and best Exchange hardware you can afford. Your company will probably grow into it. Refer to the detailed sizing guidelines for Exchange Server 2010 on TechNet.

However, it is also worthwhile to know that Exchange is pretty forgiving. If your disk space configuration isn't exactly right, Exchange will continue to run and will (probably) eventually get all the work done (unless it runs out of disk space); it just may be slow for a while. The term for this is "degrading gracefully." This gives you the opportunity to update your disk subsystem to a better-performing solution. And, in fact, for most companies this is a nonissue. Computers are fast, disks are fairly fast, and memory is cheap; for the small and medium-sized company (500 mailboxes or less), the Exchange server hardware is generally more than those companies need, without going into any detailed design specification.

DISK PERFORMANCE COUNTERS

As described earlier, disk performance tends to be all about IOPS. Therefore, it is not surprising that the most interesting of disk counters are involved with communicating the latency of I/O. After all, regardless of how fast a single I/O operation can be completed, if that operation has to wait a significant amount of time prior to its execution, that can be a problem. I/O operations go into queues, which are more or less first-in, first-out (FIFO). However, Windows will perform some optimization when possible, grouping together I/O that is "close" in disk terms. On a transaction log, this optimization can be significant. On a mailbox database, it probably will not be.

We'll discuss optimum values for specific I/O types on each Exchange server role shortly. First, let's tackle the performance counters themselves. As I/O can be fairly complicated, there are a large number of performance counters that may come into play. We consider these in a tiered fashion. That is, there is a group of counters we consider most important. Based on results from those counters, we may need to investigate other counters.

Tier 1 Disk Performance Counters

Perhaps the most critical of all disk performance counters is LogicalDisk\% Free Space. We say that because, if a disk is full, you are probably in an emergency situation trying to resolve that situation. Also, urban legend has long held that, when the NTFS file system (which must be used on all Exchange disks) falls below 10 percent free space, the disk is in danger of crashing. Although that is not true in modern operating systems, it is certainly true that this is probably not an optimum situation in many environments.

HOW MUCH IS TOO MUCH FREE DISK SPACE?

Today 1.5 TB disks are common and 2.0 TB disks only slightly less so. Larger disks are coming quickly. Ten percent of 1.5 TB is 150 GB, which is a large amount of space. While it is a best practice to keep LogicalDisk\% Free Space at 10 percent or higher, you should temper this with reason in your environment, depending on the size of your disks and arrays. This best practice was originally developed when the normal size of a disk was 9 GB.

A related counter is LogicalDisk\Free Megabytes, which may be a more relevant counter for some installations of Exchange. As described earlier, with large disks it may make sense to set a number of free megabytes of disk space at which the administrator should be alerted. However, unlike LogicalDisk\% Free Space, the LogicalDisk\Free Megabytes counter requires specific knowledge about a given environment to pick an appropriate value.

In a non-SAN environment, the next most important counter is PhysicalDisk\Avg. Disk Queue Length. As you know, I/O operations are processed in queues. If that queue grows too large, your I/O subsystem is not operating quickly enough to service the load. This counter is your number one indicator of that. On average, the PhysicalDisk\Avg. Disk Queue Length counter should not exceed the value of the number of disks in an array. That is, if an Exchange volume is one disk, then the counter shouldn't exceed one, on average. If an Exchange volume is two mirrored disks, the counter shouldn't exceed two, on average, and so on. In a SAN environment, the results obtained from this counter are almost meaningless, and the counter should be ignored.

Two important counters that are related to PhysicalDisk\Avg. Disk Queue Length are PhysicalDisk\Avg. Disk Sec/Write and PhysicalDisk\Avg. Disk Sec/Read. These counters define the average amount of time that it takes for a write I/O and a read I/O to complete, respectively. Long-term trending on these counters can go a long way toward showing you how your I/O subsystem is holding up over time. These counters are also absolutely valid in a SAN environment.

FASTER ISN'T ALWAYS BETTER

Don't let yourself be fooled. A 500 GB Ultra-320 drive is not necessarily all it's cracked up to be. Just because under some situations it can transfer 320 MB of data per second doesn't mean that it will for your Exchange database! Under some situations, a 9 GB SCSI-1 drive will outperform it. Be more concerned with the "average ms per transfer" — this is far more indicative of how a disk will perform with Exchange than what its maximum transfer rate is.

Those two counters define overall input-output latency for a given disk. However, especially if a disk is shared either for multiple applications (not a good idea with Exchange Server) or for multiple roles within Exchange Server, knowing the average latency for the Exchange databases and the Exchange log files is also important. Those counters have longer, but obvious names: MSExchange Database\I/O Database Reads (Attached) Average Latency, MSExchange Database\I/O Database Writes (Attached) Average Latency, and MSExchange Database\I/O Log Writes (Attached) Average Latency. The attached databases are currently active databases. DAG copies have Recovery in parentheses next to them instead of Attached. The MSExchange Database counters should have values that are the same, or lower, than the overall PhysicalDisk counters. If they do not, you may have other applications whose I/O load is causing unacceptable I/O degradation on your Exchange server disk volumes.

In a major break with prior recommendations, with Exchange Server 2010 Microsoft now recommends, or allows, for the transaction logs and database to be contained on a single volume (when you have two or more copies in a DAG configuration). Many people are wary about this concept. However, there is no question that Microsoft has proven that it works in large environments. Whenever that configuration is used, the MSExchange Database counters we just discussed are arguably more important than the LogicalDisk or PhysicalDisk counters, as they express the specific overhead that is being experienced by Exchange, as opposed to the overall experience for the entire volume.

Tier 2 Disk Performance Counters

The "Tier 2" performance counters are those which, if the Tier 1 counters indicate a problem, can assist in further narrowing down problems. They primarily assist in differentiating between types of problems rather than identifying new problems.

Exchange mailbox databases are fairly even in terms of the number of reads versus writes that they execute. To minimize both, Exchange mailbox databases implement caches, which store pages of a database in memory. Accessing memory is much faster than accessing disk. Therefore, the larger that the database cache is, the fewer I/O operations that need to occur (at least theoretically). Output operations in Exchange are flushed to disk by a task known as the

"Lazy Writer" that processes the cache on a regular basis to aggregate and write the output to the database disk. However, transaction log entries are flushed to the disk prior to an entry being committed to the cache. This is what provides recoverability in case of a system crash. It is also one of the major causes of the difference in I/O profiles between transaction logs and databases (the other is random versus sequential I/O).

EXCHANGE 2010 I/O PROFILE CHANGE

In all versions of Exchange prior to Exchange Server 2010, Exchange mailbox databases were "read-heavy" (with Exchange Server 2007 much less read-heavy than Exchange Server 2003). That is, they executed far more read I/O operations than they did write I/O operations.

With Exchange Server 2010, the schema of the Exchange database, along with much of the program logic associated with doing I/O, was changed. The purpose of these changes was to execute fewer overall I/Os by using cache more effectively and by consolidating both read and write operations.

This served to provide an overall I/O reduction in Exchange Server 2010 of approximately 70 percent.

However, caching does have its own potential issues. In large memory systems, it may take an extended period of time to thaw the cache. During that period of time, server performance suffers. Also, if a cache is full, the need to empty a portion of the cache can cause a "stall." A stall is a delay in an I/O operation. During the process of a cache thawing, the I/O subsystem can be severely stressed, especially if the cache is large. When planning an I/O subsystem, be aware of this potential stress, but your general design plan should be for the hot cache, not the frozen cache; otherwise you will far over-provision the I/O subsystem.

DECODING THE GEEK-SPEAK

A cache that is "frozen" is completely empty. This happens when a cache is first created. The process of filling a cache with data is known as "thawing." A cache that is optimally full is a "hot" cache. Some caches have prefill algorithms that load them before the data is actually used. This process is known as "seeding" the cache.

Now that you know everything about the cache, a key performance counter relating to the cache is MSExchange Database\Database Page Fault Stalls/Sec. A page fault stall occurs when something needs to be put into the cache, but the cache is full. On a production Exchange server, except during online maintenance, this value should always be zero. If it isn't, then either the cache is too small (indicating a need for memory on a server) or the I/O write performance of the database volume cannot keep up with the needs of the Exchange database (indicating a need for more spindles or faster spindles in the database volume).

A similar counter, except that it applies to the transaction log files instead of the database files, is MSExchange Database\Log Record Stalls/Sec. This performance counter should also average near zero. If the value of the counter averages one or higher, flushing the transaction log buffer may be a bottleneck for this Exchange server. This can occur when the I/O write performance of the log volume cannot keep up with the needs of the Exchange "Lazy Writer." Similarly to the MSExchange Database\Database Page Fault Stalls/Sec counter, this indicates a need for more spindles or faster spindles in the log volume.

Another counter that helps monitor the performance of the log volumes is MSExchange Database\Log Threads Waiting. This counter indicates the number of update threads that are waiting to write their information to the log. Generally, this is the in-memory log. If there are so many updates that the in-memory log is stalling output to the disk log, there is a performance issue. Again, the issue would typically revolve around the disk subsystem. While it is normal for this counter to be in the single-digit range, if it begins to average over 10, you need to investigate why log files cannot be written quickly enough.

The Paging File\% Usage counter is an in-the-middle performance counter. It has attributes of both memory and of disk. Our primary interest in the counter is how full the paging file is. On average, the Paging File\% Usage counter should stay below 50 percent. If it does not, you may have to either increase the size of your paging file or add more memory. If you have sized your paging file according to the recommendations for Exchange servers discussed previously, paging should be low (note that Exchange itself should not page at all, but related applications and third-party applications may page — this includes such items as content indexing and management agents). Otherwise, just keep this counter in mind as indicating that your server is experiencing memory pressure and may not be able to handle much additional workload before the server requires an upgrade.

If you are experiencing high I/O volumes on a server and it is unclear what program is causing the I/O, it is time to bring the Process performance object under examination. Each running process is tracked within this performance object, and it contains pretty much anything that you may ever want to know about a specific process. The counters that are of high interest in an I/O situation are Process\IO Read Operations/Sec and Process\IO Write Operations/Sec. On an Exchange server, the most common processes that exhibit high values of the I/O operation counters are `store.exe` and System.

The final eight Tier 2 counters are a family of counters that provide specific measurements of the total amount of I/O occurring to a physical disk. We left these for last because they tend to be more important from a trending perspective (that is, how the utilization of this server is changing over time) as opposed to something that provides immediately worthwhile information. However, they are also important for determining whether the I/O subsystem on a server is "fast enough." The counters are shown in Table 29.3.

TABLE 29.3: PhysicalDisk Counters for I/O Size and Speed

DESCRIPTION	READ COUNTER	WRITE COUNTER
Average I/O Request Size	Avg. Disk Bytes/Read	Avg. Disk Bytes/Write
Average I/O Time	Avg. Disk Sec/Read	Avg. Disk Sec/Write
I/O Speed	Disk Read Bytes/Sec	Disk Write Bytes/Sec
I/O Completion Speed	Disk Reads/Sec	Disk Writes/Sec

Source: http://www.microsoft.com/technet/prodtechnol/windows2000serv/reskit/prork/pree_exa_qkkb.mspx

SOME THOUGHTS ON MONITORING EXCHANGE DISK PERFORMANCE

Disk monitoring is fairly complicated, even in the best of environments. It becomes more complicated in an Exchange environment because of the many different types of I/O that the various roles of Exchange will incur, and the fact that the different types of I/O perform differently (that is, they have different usage and utilization profiles). While memory was arguably the most difficult item to tune in Exchange Server 2003 and earlier, the move to 64-bit processing has made that a "yes or no" question: do I have enough memory or not? Processor utilization has primarily always been that way, although memory and processor can have a somewhat incestuous relationship once a system is overloaded and begins thrashing.

When presented with a disk performance issue, pursue the solution using a bottom-down approach. Verify that it's an I/O problem, identify the offending task(s), identify the problem, and then identify the solution. The performance counters presented in the preceding sections will help you follow that process. Finally, consider the following optimum values when investigating primary performance objects:

PERFORMANCE OBJECT	PERFORMANCE COUNTER	DESIRED VALUES
MSExchange Database	I/O Database Writes (Attached) Average Latency	Less than the Read counter below
MSExchange Database	I/O Database Reads (Attached) Average Latency	Less than 20 ms for active databases; less than 200 ms for passive copies
PhysicalDisk (for stand-alone disk configurations)	Avg. Disk Sec/Read	Less than 20 ms for active databases, less than 200 ms for passive copies
PhysicalDisk (for stand-alone disk configurations, logs only)	Avg. Disk Sec/Write	Less than 5 ms
PhysicalDisk	Avg. Disk Queue Length	Less than the number of spindles in the volume
MSExchange Database	Database Page Fault Stalls/Sec	Zero
MSExchange Database	Log Record Stalls/Sec	Less than 10, on average
MSExchange Database	Log Threads Waiting	Less than 10, on average
Paging File	% Usage	Less than 50%

ACTIVE DIRECTORY

To say that Exchange depends on the performance of Active Directory is something of an understatement. Exchange Server is very tightly tied to Active Directory (AD) and cannot function properly if AD is not configured properly. Exchange utilizes the Configuration Naming Context of AD for storing information about all Exchange servers, address lists, policies, and so forth — almost any piece of Exchange information that is not recipient related. Recipient information (contacts, users, distribution lists, etc.) is stored in the Domain Naming

Context of AD. Every Exchange object has a corresponding entry in AD. Even a mailbox, which resides in the Exchange mailbox database, is tied to an AD user and has both a GUID (Globally Unique Identifier) and a legacyExchangeDN (basically an X.500 address). These attributes on the user object point from the AD to the mailbox within the Exchange database.

ACTIVE DIRECTORY NAMING CONTEXTS

The Configuration Naming Context (ConfigNC) of Active Directory is a part of AD called a partition. This partition is replicated to every single domain controller (DC) that is contained within an AD forest. That is, every DC has a copy of the ConfigNC, so every DC has a copy of all information about Exchange Server and organization configuration. However, the Domain Naming Context (DomainNC) partition only resides on DCs that are within a specific domain. Therefore, full recipient information is not on every DC. Exchange identifies certain types of recipient information (such as email addresses) as needing to be more widely available by marking them as a member of the Partial Attribute Set (PAS). Attributes in the PAS are present on every global catalog server in the global catalog partition.

Since Exchange currently stores server and configuration information in the ConfigNC in a specific way, there may be only one Exchange organization installed per AD forest. Exchange will normally use any available DC to obtain information about server and organization configurations. However, that isn't possible for recipient information. To obtain recipient information, Exchange is heavily dependent on global catalog (GC) servers.

Since most of what Exchange does deals with recipients (receiving email for a recipient, sending email from a recipient, expanding a distribution list of recipients, checking out delegate permissions, etc.), most of Exchange Server's interaction with AD on a volume basis is via GCs. This leads to a requirement that every AD domain that contains an Exchange server must have at least one GC within the domain (and preferably a minimum of two for resiliency in the case of a GC failure).

In medium-sized and large organizations with an already established AD environment, the impact of Exchange Server to that environment can be surprisingly high. The AD requirements of Exchange can be so high that it is common for Exchange Server to have a parallel forest stood up just for its needs.

In small and most medium-sized environments, this is a nonissue. However, the Exchange administrator must be aware of the performance of the AD that is supporting Exchange and (if the Exchange administrator is not an AD administrator) when that performance becomes strained, ensure that the AD performance is improved.

Three key counters in Exchange Server 2010 need to be monitored in the MSExchange ADAccess Processes performance object. This object has an instance for each process in the Exchange application that accesses AD, as well as an <All Instances> instance. The interesting counters in the object are

◆ LDAP Read Time

◆ LDAP Write Time

◆ Number of Outstanding Requests

The read and write counters should average below 50 ms. The number of outstanding requests counter should average zero. Generally, tracking <All Instances> is the right place to start in determining a performance issue; then you need to investigate each instance to acquire more detailed data.

Another interesting counter for Active Directory is MSExchange ADAccess Domain Controllers\Local Site Flag. The value of this counter is one if the instance of the counter is a DC in the local site; otherwise the value is zero. A particular Exchange server will perform much better if all DCs are in the same site as the Exchange server. Among other attributes, local sites are assumed to be well connected.

NETWORK

It will come as no surprise that Exchange is a network-intensive application. Good performance of an Exchange server requires fast connectivity between that server and the other servers in the local site, low latency connectivity to AD, low latency responses to DNS queries, and nonsaturated network connections. Not only that — all of this connectivity needs to be free of errors. To that end, there are other performance objects and counters that can help you learn the status of your network connection. These are shown in Table 29.4. In Figure 29.3 and Figure 29.4, you can see examples of Performance Monitor displaying the information contained in Table 29.4. Note especially that one interface does report errors against the Packets Outbound Errors counter, but it does not increase across the captured timeframe.

TABLE 29.4: Network I/O Objects, Counters, and Values

PERFORMANCE OBJECT	PERFORMANCE COUNTER	IDEAL VALUE
Network Interface	Bytes Total/Sec	For 10 Mbps NIC, less than 600 KB/sec; for 100 Mbps NIC, less than 6 MB/sec; for 1 Gbps NIC, less than 60 MB/sec
Network Interface	Packets Outbound Errors	Zero
Network Interface	Packets Received Errors	Zero
TCPv4 or TCPv6	Segments Retransmitted/Sec	Less than 2 percent of Segments Sent/Sec
TCPv4 or TCPv6	Segments Sent/Sec	N/A

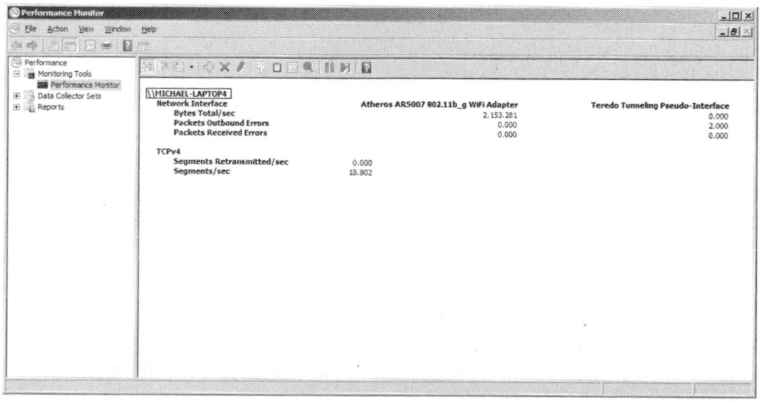

FIGURE 29.3
Performance Monitor report output for counters in Table 29.4

FIGURE 29.4

Performance Monitor
line graph output for
counters in Table 29.4

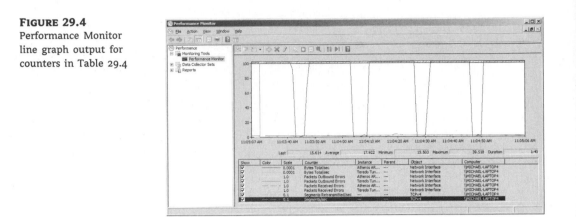

The TCPv4 and TCPv6 protocol objects contain counters that give basic high-level information about TCP connections and packets. TCPv4 is the version of the Transmission Control Protocol (TCP) that we have all known and loved for many years. TCPv6 is enabled by default in Windows Server 2008 and Windows Server 2008 R2. TCPv6 is fully supported by Exchange Server 2010 RTM. The important counter in those objects is Segments Retransmitted/Sec. Unfortunately, that is not available as a percentage directly as a performance counter. However, as you will see in the next section, System Center Operations Manager can calculate the value for us — the % Segments Retransmitted/Sec. Performance Monitor cannot do that for us directly. When Segments Retransmitted/Sec is greater than zero, it indicates that TCP packets are being resent over the wire. This is generally due to a hardware or cabling fault and can cause network performance to be abysmal.

The Network Interface performance object contains counters that record information at a lower level of the OSI model than the TCP counters do. The Network Interface object records the individual packets received and/or sent across the wire before the packets are handed over to a specific protocol stack (such as TCP, UDP, or ARP). At this lower level, it is necessary to be concerned about the physical limitations of the network interface. Also, protocols such as TCP (upon which all of the email protocols such as SMTP, POP3, and IMAP are built) hide lower-level errors by requesting retransmissions of packets that exhibit errors. The upper-level protocols are not even aware that lower-level errors have occurred, unless they are "fatal" — that is, unless they cause the connection between the two computers to be terminated.

Within the Network Interface object, two counters are especially interesting when used to look at errors: Packets Outbound Errors and Packets Received Errors. Nonzero values indicate that errors have occurred "on the wire" since the last initialization of the interface. A few errors are normal (as any Ethernet-based protocol will experience an occasional collision-generated error). These values are much more indicative of an ongoing problem if they continue to increase every second — that is, when they are compared to other counters in the object, such as Packets Sent/Sec and Packets Received/Sec. Again, Operations Manager can perform calculations and use nonzero values of these calculations as alerting criteria. However, Performance Monitor does not have that capability natively.

SOME DEFINITIONS

The OSI model is used in the design of networking protocols, such as TCP/IP. The OSI model separates protocols into seven layers: Physical, Data, Network, Transport, Session, Presentation, and Application.

TCP/IP is a reliable connection-oriented protocol. In other words, the lower protocol layers are supposed to ensure that the data that is passed to the upper layers is error free. The upper layers are allowed to leave error detection and correction to the lower layers, thus simplifying the programming required to support the application. This does, however, make it difficult for the upper layers to be aware of issues that may be occurring at the lower layers.

So, a packet is a group of data that is transmitted at the lower layers. If the packet passes all error checking and detection, it is handed off to the upper layers and is then known as a data segment.

MAPI

MAPI is the native protocol used by Exchange Server to exchange information between Mailbox servers, Hub Transport servers, Client Access servers, and client applications (such as Outlook). MAPI is also encapsulated within SSL to support Outlook Anywhere (which was originally called RPC/HTTP). MAPI is based on remote procedure calls (RPCs), as are many of Microsoft's server protocols. RPC is the foundation of the Distributed Component Object Model (DCOM) on which Microsoft interserver communication is based.

That's a lot of alphabet soup. If you are trying to get certified with Microsoft in enterprise messaging, you'll need to know all that (and much more). For right now, remember these things:

- MAPI is an RPC-based protocol.
- Because MAPI is RPC based, MAPI must be encapsulated to use it on the Internet; this encapsulation is known as Outlook Anywhere.
- MAPI and SMTP are the two primary messaging protocols used by Exchange, regardless of the Exchange role.

The Microsoft Exchange RPC Client Access service, whose short name is MSExchangeRPC, is the endpoint for MAPI RPCs. MAPI requests are handled by MSExchangeRPC using this general process:

1. Receive a MAPI request.
2. Decode the request into an XSO request.
3. Hand the request off to a database server.
4. Receive the result from the database server.
5. Encode the response from XSO to MAPI.
6. Return the MAPI result.

This can be complicated when the result of a database operation cannot be returned within a single MAPI result packet and instead the results must be paged. However, the general process remains the same. As you can imagine, the RPC-encode and RPC-decode process itself can put a significant processor load onto an Exchange server. The length of time taken from the receipt of a MAPI request until the result is returned is known as the RPC latency (end-to-end). The RPC latency is affected by many things, including processor utilization of the server, how long a database request takes, whether a database execution thread is available, whether memory is available to create a response packet, and many other things. Significantly, by default MSExchangeRPC will attempt to process only 100 RPCs at a time. The service is also aware of where packets originate and how many packets have originated from specific sources; it will prioritize packets in order to ensure that a single requestor does not unfairly consume the resources of the Mailbox servers.

WHAT IS AN XSO?

An Exchange System Object (XSO) is the internal format of requests that Exchange Server roles use to communicate with each other. Unlike MAPI, XSO is compatible with managed-code interfaces. Beyond that, little is known about XSO; it is an Exchange-internal proprietary format.

A Client Access server is the endpoint for MAPI communications, except for public folders. Public folder MAPI is processed by the MSExchangeRPC service on a Mailbox server hosting public folders.

The MSExchange RpcClientAccess\RPC Averaged Latency counter measures the average amount of time consumed by the last 1,024 RPC requests, and the value is expressed in milliseconds. This counter should not exceed 50 ms. If the counter begins to increase, this indicates one (or more) of the following:

◆ Additional load is being put on the server.

◆ There is a network problem.

◆ There is a performance problem.

This particular counter will likely be the "first indicator" of a performance problem and is worthy of continuous monitoring and tracking.

The MSExchange RpcClientAccess\RPC Requests counter measures the total number of RPC requests that the Client Access server is currently servicing. It should stay under 30. As described earlier, without specific configuration changes, the limit of this counter is 100. However, if the counter averages over 30, the Exchange administrator should investigate (using many of the other counters already discussed) whether there is a performance requirement spike or if there are growing performance issues in the Exchange environment.

Using System Center Operations Manager

The brief introduction possible in this chapter cannot, of course, cover all the details about using System Center Operations Manager (OpsMgr), even in an Exchange environment. There are many fine books on OpsMgr, including *Monitoring Exchange Server 2007 with System Center Operations Manager 2007*, also from Sybex (2009).

A native-mode management pack (MP) was introduced for Exchange Server 2007 in 2009. Before then, all MPs for Exchange Server were based on Microsoft Operations Manager (MOM, which was the precursor product to OpsMgr), and the OpsMgr MP was migrated from the MOM MP. The MP available for Exchange Server 2010 is native-mode only and an MP for MOM has not been released.

Earlier in this chapter, you learned about several dozen key test points for Exchange Server 2010, based on performance counters. These key pieces of data are the most important items to monitor, but they are only the beginning. As you may have surmised, literally hundreds of factors can come into play when examining performance issues on Exchange servers — many more than can reasonably be tested either manually or built into a manual testing application.

Enter management applications such as OpsMgr. For Exchange alone, OpsMgr will generate over 50 reports and examine 1,000 test points. Once you include test points for Active Directory, Windows Server, Internet Information Services (IIS), and the DNS, OpsMgr will look at more than 2,500 items to ensure that your Exchange environment and its associated infrastructure is healthy. And when it isn't, it ensures that you know about it.

There are two separate MPs for Exchange Server 2010:

♦ The Core MP, Microsoft.Exchange.2010

♦ The Reports MP, Microsoft.Exchange.2010.Reports

The Reports MP is dependent on the Core MP (that is, you can install the Core MP all by itself, but you can't install the Reports MP all by itself). You can download the MPs from the Microsoft Download Center (head over to `http://microsoft.com/downloads` and search for "Exchange 2010 Management Pack").

When you install the MP on your OpsMgr server, it will go into a different folder than you are used to: `C:\Program Files\Microsoft\Exchange Server\V14\Bin`. Check that folder out in Windows Explorer; it should look like Figure 29.5. If you note the two files of type "MP File," those are the actual MPs. All of the other files are supporting DLLs, configuration files, and documentation.

FIGURE 29.5
Contents of the directory where the Exchange Server 2010 MP is located

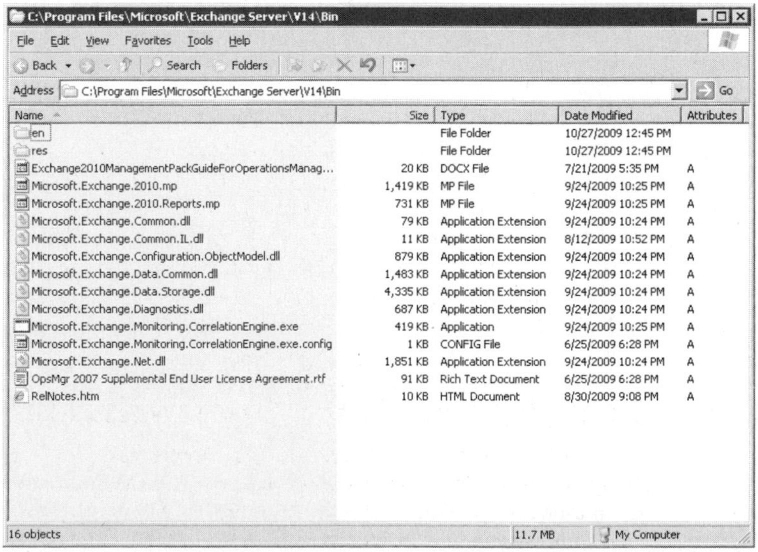

Before Importing the Management Pack

Before you import the MP, you should be aware of a few idiosyncrasies that affect the MP and actions that you should take:

Agentless monitoring is not supported.   The Exchange Server 2010 MP does *not* support agentless monitoring. Every Exchange 2010 server to be monitored must have an OpsMgr agent installed.

You must use Local System.   All monitored Exchange 2010 servers must use *Local System* as the *Agent Action Account*. Low-privilege monitoring has not been tested by Microsoft and is not supported.

All DAG servers must be monitored.   If you are monitoring any servers that host a DAG, you must monitor all servers that host that DAG. Otherwise, you will receive incorrect alerting and performance measurements.

Agent proxying is required.   All monitored Exchange 2010 servers must have agent proxying enabled.

Hotfixes are required.   System Center Operations Manager 2007 with Service Pack 1 is the minimum version of OpsMgr supported for the Exchange Server 2010 MP. You must install the hotfix described in Knowledge Base article 971541 if that is the version of OpsMgr you are using. Your only other version option is System Center Operations Manager 2007 R2. You must install the hotfix described in Knowledge Base article 974144 if that is the version of OpsMgr you are using. You can access these knowledge base articles at http://support.microsoft.com.

Install the Correlation Engine.   A feature of the Exchange 2010 MP is called the Correlation Engine. It attempts to aggregate many detected errors and alert on only the most important ones, to minimize the number of alerts that may be generated when something fails. Installing this as a part of the MP installation is recommended (on the root management server), but is not required.

Additional management packs may be needed.   As discussed previously in this chapter, Exchange Server does not stand alone. For any monitored Exchange server, you should also consider monitoring Windows Server and IIS. For other servers in your Exchange infrastructure, consider monitoring Active Directory and the DNS.

Importing the Management Pack

Before you can begin to use the capabilities of the Exchange Server 2010 MP, you must do two things:

◆   Deploy an agent to each Exchange server.

◆   Import the MP into OpsMgr.

Deploying agents is a normal part of using OpsMgr, so we won't cover it here. However, the detailed list for importing the MP follows this list:

1. Open the Operations Console.

2. In the lower-left pane of the console, click Administration.

3. In the upper-left pane of the console, right-click the Management Packs node, and select Import Management Packs from the context menu.

4. In the Select Management Packs To Import dialog, find the MP folder discussed earlier, then multiselect both of the Exchange MP files, and then click Open.

5. In the Import Management Packs dialog, as shown in Figure 29.6, click Import.

FIGURE 29.6
The Import Management Packs dialog

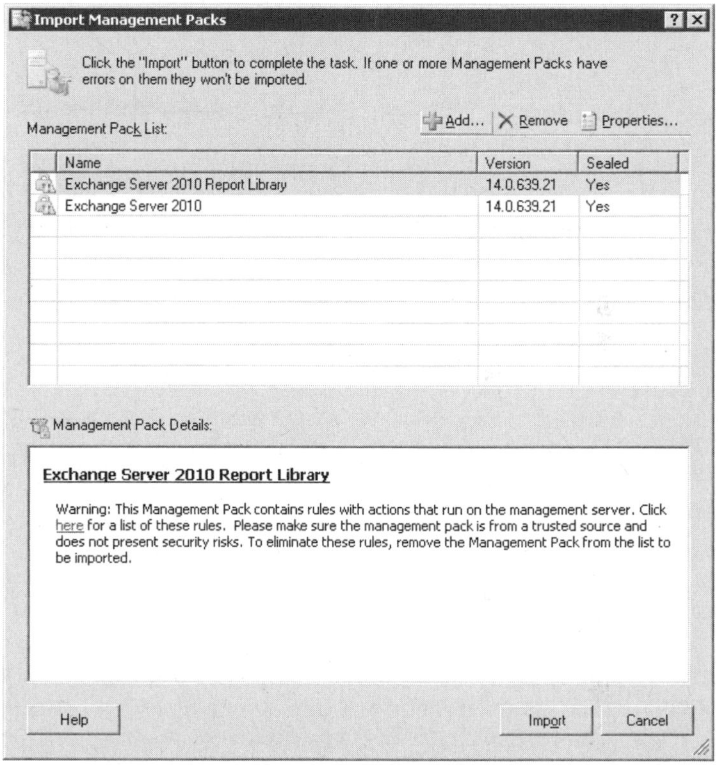

6. In the warning dialog, as shown in Figure 29.7, click Yes (this warning dialog is caused by the MPs using agent proxying).

FIGURE 29.7
Security Risk dialog for Exchange MPs

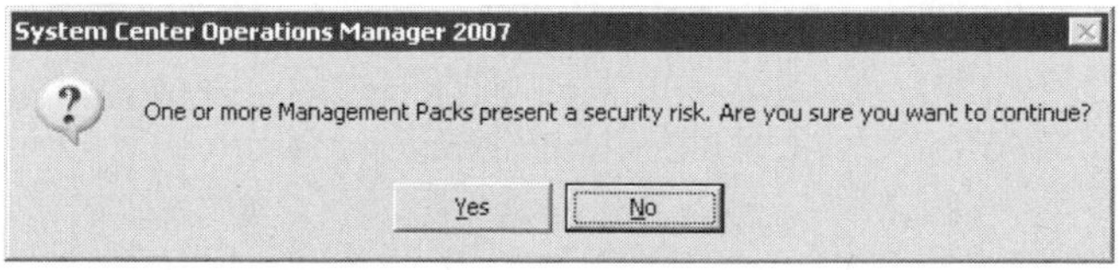

7. Allow the import process to execute — depending on the speed and power of your OpsMgr and SQL servers, it may take as long as 25–30 minutes for the import to occur.

8. Click the Close button in the Import Management Packs dialog.

Now, you will see the Exchange Server 2010 Management Packs in your Operations Console display, as illustrated in Figure 29.8. Note that the version of the MP is 14.0.639.21 — this is the same as the version of Exchange Server 2010 RTM.

FIGURE 29.8
List of MPs after the Exchange MP import is complete

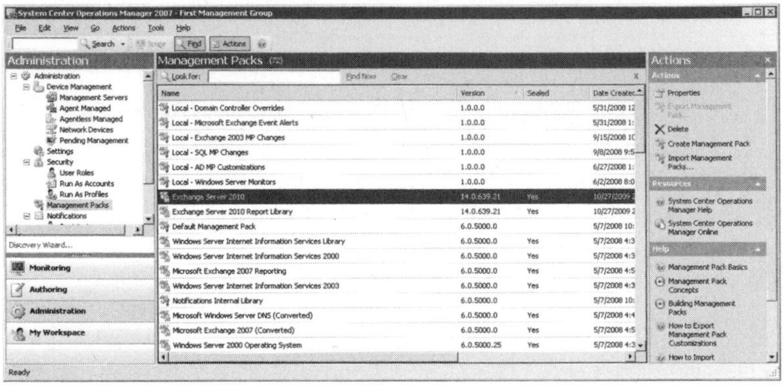

Modifying Management Pack Objects

Although you cannot modify a sealed MP, you have quite a number of options:

Attribute   You can create new attributes to be used by your own custom rules, monitors, tasks, or views. Unfortunately, no mechanism is available to see the contents of an existing attribute or the source from which it is obtained. The purpose of attributes is to store information about an object, such as the object's name, its Active Directory type, other objects that it may connect to, and so on. For a given object type, all attributes are stored together, effectively forming a record in the OpsMgr database for an instance of that object.

Monitor   You can disable the monitor (for any specific computer, any group of computers, or all computers). You may also create your own monitor that applies to any specific computer, any group of computers, or all computers. The purpose of monitors is to collect data and, based on the contents of that data, generate a health report for a given object or a piece of an object. For example, you may have monitors that measure hardware availability, configuration correctness, or the performance of a system's processor.

Rule   You can disable a rule (for any specific computer, any group of computers, or all computers) or you can override specific attributes of a rule (for any specific computer, any group of computers, or all computers). You may also create your own rule that applies to any specific computer, any group of computers, or all computers. The purpose of rules is also to collect data. However, unlike a monitor, a rule cannot be used to affect the health of an object. Rules can generate alerts. A monitor can use a rule as input to its health calculation.

Task   Tasks are used as resources by monitors and rules; they never stand alone. Therefore, disables and overrides do not make sense in their context. However, you can create your own command-line or script-based task to use in the monitors and rules that you create. Tasks may also be executed within the Operations Console by the OpsMgr administrator to report on the current status of objects (such as the health of a domain controller or on replication health). Finally, tasks can be used to implement recovery steps, such as restarting a service.

View   Views are created and managed in the Monitoring pane (since they represent graphical views of monitoring data), not the Authoring pane. We have no idea why they are shown in the Authoring pane other than they are stored as an MP object. Views are basically SQL queries that are based on stored attribute information.

RULES VS. MONITORS: WHAT'S THE DIFFERENCE?

Monitors allow you to calculate and view the health of an object and raise alerts based on that health. You can also use monitors to build a health hierarchy where the health of an upper-level object is based on the health of a lower-level object. Rules, however, do not calculate health, and while you can raise an alert based on the result of a rule, it is not related to the health of an object but simply the result of the rule. However, the result of a rule can be used by a monitor to assist in the calculation of an object's health. The difference between the two is a fine line.

If you modify a sealed MP or create new MP objects, by default the change (called an override) is saved into a system-provided MP called the Default MP. However, this can lead to many overrides, new rules, and monitors all being saved into one place. That is simply a recipe that will lead to confusion. It is considered a best practice to do the following:

◆ Save modifications to a sealed MP into a new MP with a similar (but standard) name.

◆ Group your new MP objects into new MPs and document why they have been created.

ANOTHER GOOD REASON FOR A CUSTOM MANAGEMENT PACK

When you remove an MP, you must first remove all custom MPs that refer to objects within that MP, such as the overrides that you created. So, if you store all overrides within the Default MP, you would have to remove that MP before you could remove any other MP to which you have applied overrides! That could be disastrous.

Creating an Override Management Pack

As discussed previously, we recommend that you create a new MP that should be used to store all your overrides, custom rules, and monitors for each installed MP. This simplifies the process of moving customizations from one environment to another, and it removes the dependency on the Default MP from all other installed MPs.

To create a new MP to store your overrides and customizations for the Exchange Server MP, follow these steps:

1. Open the Operations Console.

2. Click Administration in the lower-left pane.

3. Right-click on Management Packs in the upper-left pane and select Create Management Pack from the context menu. This will start the Create a Management Pack wizard.

4. On the first page of the wizard, in the Name field enter a recognizable custom name for the MP, such as **Local - Exchange MP Customizations**.

5. In the Description field, enter a detailed description of the types of customizations that you have entered in this MP.

6. Click Next.

7. On the second page of the wizard, if you have company information that you want to appear on the override, you can enter it here. Microsoft Word must be installed on the same computer as the Operations Console to edit the information on this page of the wizard.

8. Click Create.

Use this MP to store all customizations and overrides for the Exchange Server MP.

Management Pack Discoveries

Unlike the Exchange Server 2007 native-mode MP, the Exchange Server 2010 MP will automatically process all discoveries. The items specifically discovered by the Exchange Server 2010 MP include the following:

◆ Which instances of Exchange are on a virtual server

◆ All Client Access servers

◆ All Hub Transport servers

◆ All Edge Transport servers

◆ All Mailbox servers

◆ All Unified Messaging servers

◆ All "other" Exchange servers (those that are not Exchange Server 2010)

However, the so-called synthetic transactions are not enabled by default. A synthetic transaction is executed by OpsMgr. This transaction is generally a PowerShell cmdlet that tests a specific function on an Exchange server, such as Test-ActiveSyncConnectivity. To see all the available synthetic transactions, follow this procedure:

1. Open the Operations Console.

2. In the lower-left corner, click Authoring.

3. If it is not already expanded, expand the Management Pack Objects node.

4. Click Rules.

5. In the Rules pane in the middle of the window, click Change Scope, as shown in Figure 29.9.

6. In the Scope Management Pack Objects By Target(s) dialog, click Clear All, as shown in Figure 29.10.

7. In the Look For box (also shown in Figure 29.10), enter **Exchange Server 2010** and then click Select All.

8. Click OK.

9. In the Look For box in the Rules pane of the window, enter **Script event collection** and then click Find Now.

Your result should look like that shown in Figure 29.11. The Look For field and the Find Now button are also shown in that figure.

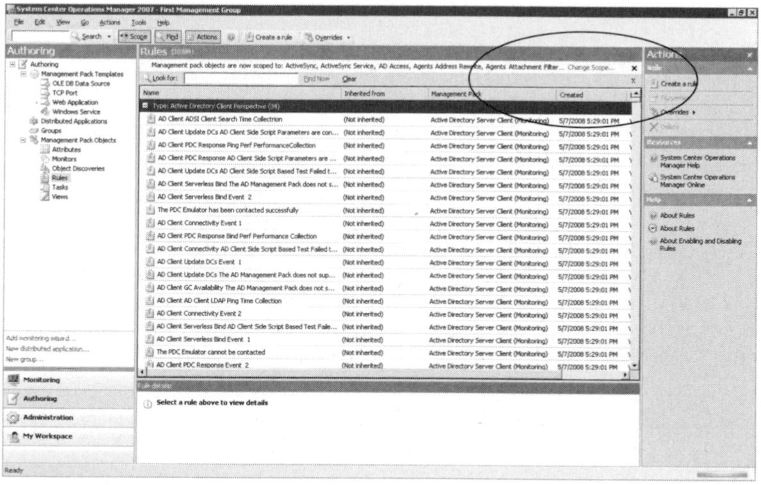

FIGURE 29.9
Changing the scope of
the rules display

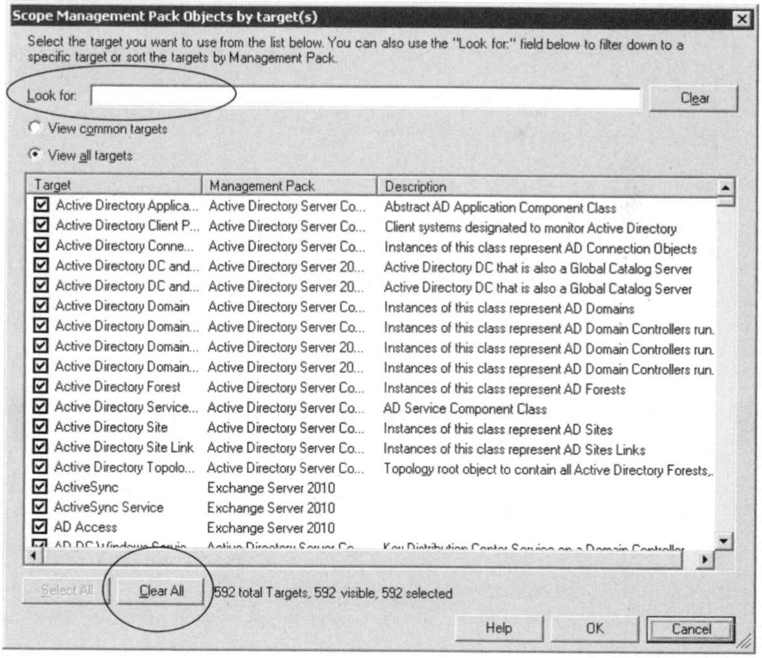

FIGURE 29.10
Scope Management
Pack Objects By
Target(s) dialog

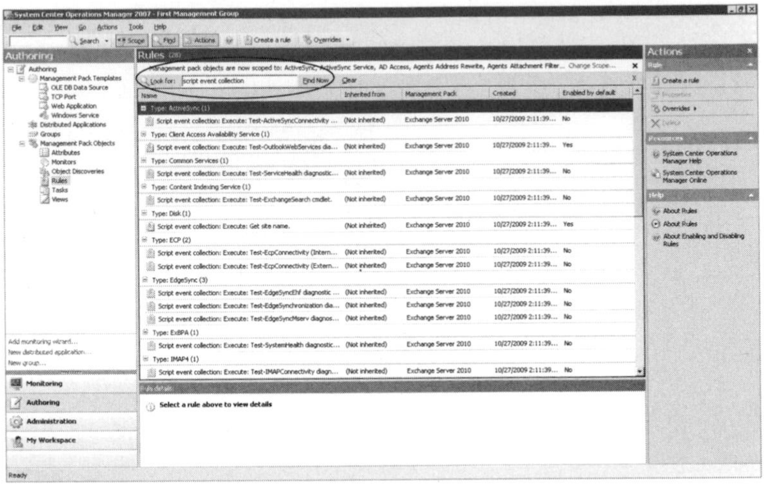

FIGURE 29.11
Result from changing
the rule scope

For each synthetic transaction in this list that you want to enable, follow this procedure:

1. Right-click on the rule.

2. From the first fly-out menu, select Overrides.

3. From the second fly-out menu, select Override The Rule.

4. From the third fly-out menu, select For All Objects Of Type: *<typename>* (see Figure 29.12).

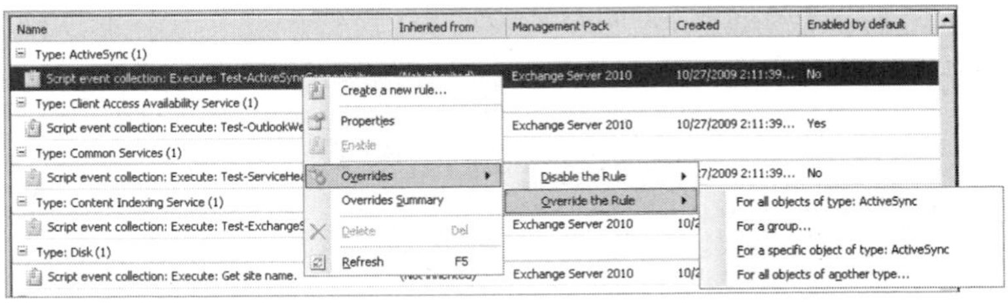

FIGURE 29.12
Finding the proper
Override item

5. In the Override Properties dialog that opens, click the check box underneath the Override heading and change the Override Setting to True.

6. Select the custom destination MP you created earlier (Local - Exchange MP Customizations was our suggestion).

7. Click OK (see Figure 29.13).

Going through each of these can take some time (there are 28 synthetic transactions), but we recommend you enable them all. However, be aware that each synthetic transaction will generate between five and ten Warehouse Database records for each server it is executed on each time it is executed (by default, every five minutes). This can be many records and you should plan for database growth. Note that it can take up to 24 hours for an override change to take effect, so be patient.

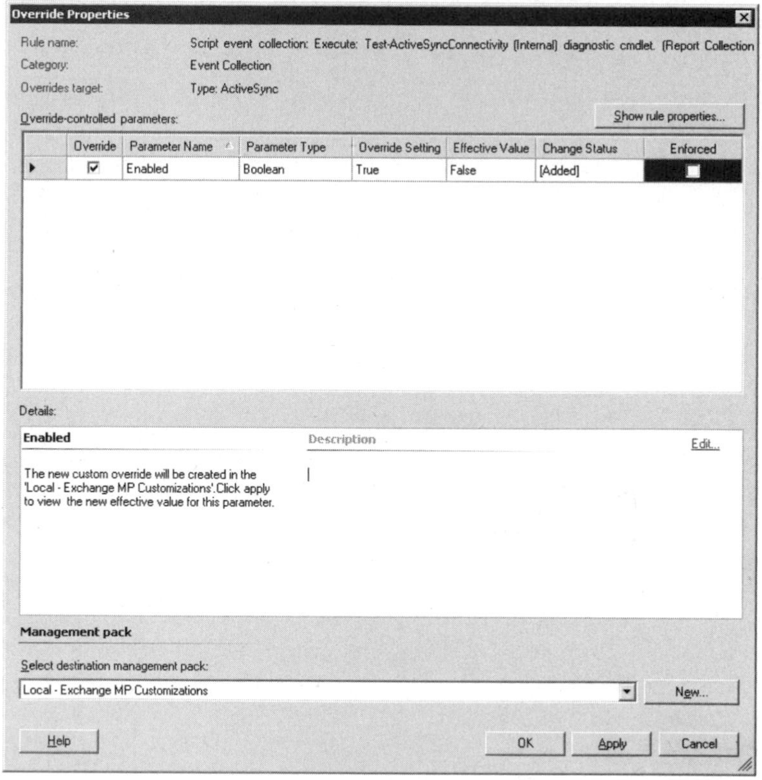

FIGURE 29.13
Changes required for
a proper override

Over 40 reports are available from within the Operations Console:

◆ Organization Status

◆ Organization Performance

◆ Client Access Status

◆ Client Access Performance

◆ ActiveSync DirectPush Latency

◆ IMAP Connectivity Latency

◆ Outlook HTTP Connectivity Latency

◆ Outlook HTTP AutoDiscover Connectivity Latency

◆ Outlook TCP Connectivity Latency

◆ Outlook TCP AutoDiscover Connectivity Latency

◆ OWA External Logon Latency

◆ OWA Internal Logon Latency

- POP3 Connectivity Latency
- EWS CreateItem Latency
- Connection Filter Agent
- Content Filter Agent
- Protocol Analysis Agent
- Recipient Filter Agent
- Sender Filter Agent
- Sender Id Agent
- Edge Transport Performance
- Edge Transport DSN
- Edge Transport Queues
- Hub Transport Performance
- Hub Transport DSN
- Hub Transport Queues
- Hub Transport SMS Agent
- Mailbox Performance
- Client RPC Latency (3 reports)
- Client RPCs Succeeded
- MAPI Connectivity Logon Latency
- I/O Database Performance (5 reports)
- RPC Averaged Latency
- RPC Requests
- Unified Messaging Performance
- Unified Messaging Connectivity Call Latency

An additional nine reports are available from the Reporting Console:

- Service Availability
- Client Access Availability
- Unified Messaging Availability
- SMTP (Client Submission) Availability
- Outlook Client Performance
- Hourly Mailflow Statistics

◆ Daily Mailflow Statistics

◆ Distribution Group Usage

◆ Top Users

Event Logs

Windows Server and Exchange Server can generate a great deal of information regarding their operation to the Windows event logs. Exchange will generate most of its information to the Application event log and, optionally, to the Audit event log.

Items placed in the Audit event log are typically Success/Failure type of items that are in some way related to security. This includes opening a mailbox, opening a folder, and using *SendAs*.

Items placed in the Application event log may contain information of practically any type, but are generally separated into one of three levels: Informational, Warning, or Error.

In Windows Server 2008, the event log subsystem of Windows was rebuilt from scratch. Prior to that release of Windows, the total size of all event logs combined (due to an implementation constraint) should never exceed 300 MB. Beginning with Windows Server 2008, that limitation is gone. Regardless of the removal of that restriction, event logs are shipped with default sizes that are quite small. The default sizes in Windows Server 2008 R2 are shown in Table 29.5.

TABLE 29.5:   Default Windows Event Log Sizes in Windows Server 2008 R2

EVENT LOG	SIZE
Application	20 MB
Security	128 MB
System	20 MB

We recommend that you significantly increase the sizes of your event logs before you need to. When the time comes to diagnose an issue, you will find that difficult (if not impossible) to do if you cannot access all the information that could be available to you.

Viewing the size of a Windows event log (and adjusting it) is a simple matter. Open the Event Viewer in Administrative Tools and expand the Windows Log node. Right-click on a particular event log and select Properties from the context menu. In Figure 29.14, you see the Log Properties dialog for the System event log in the default configuration.

We recommend that you set the sizes of the three primary event logs to the values shown in Table 29.6 as a minimum. If you have busy servers, you may want to increase these values.

You may also (if you haven't already) consider increasing the size of the System and Security event logs on all your domain controllers (if they are on Windows Server 2008 or later).

The Log Properties dialog (see Figure 29.14) includes a setting for controlling the behavior of event logging when the maximum log size is reached. The default is Overwrite Events As Needed. In a security-conscious environment, you may want to set this option to Do Not Overwrite Events (Clear Log Manually). If you set this and the event log fills up before it is either cleared or the maximum number of days is reached, event logging will stop. That is considered a feature — it is designed to prevent intruders or evildoers from covering their tracks by generating additional event logging and thus removing evidence of their evil deeds. However, in the case of the Security log, if the event log fills up the server will Halt. This option is designed to prevent someone from filling up the event log and then continuing activities that would normally generate errors but would not get logged because the file was full.

If you need logging to continue, regardless of the size consumed by event logs and their archives, select Archive The Log When Full (Do Not Overwrite Events).

Event log sizes and event log overwrite settings can be configured manually on a server-by-server basis, or they can be updated using Group Policy. If you have more than a few servers, using Group Policy will be less work. Keep in mind the size limitation that impacts Windows Server 2003 and prior versions of Windows Server. If you try to assign larger event log file sizes on Windows Server 2003, you will cause that server to operate poorly, and it may crash.

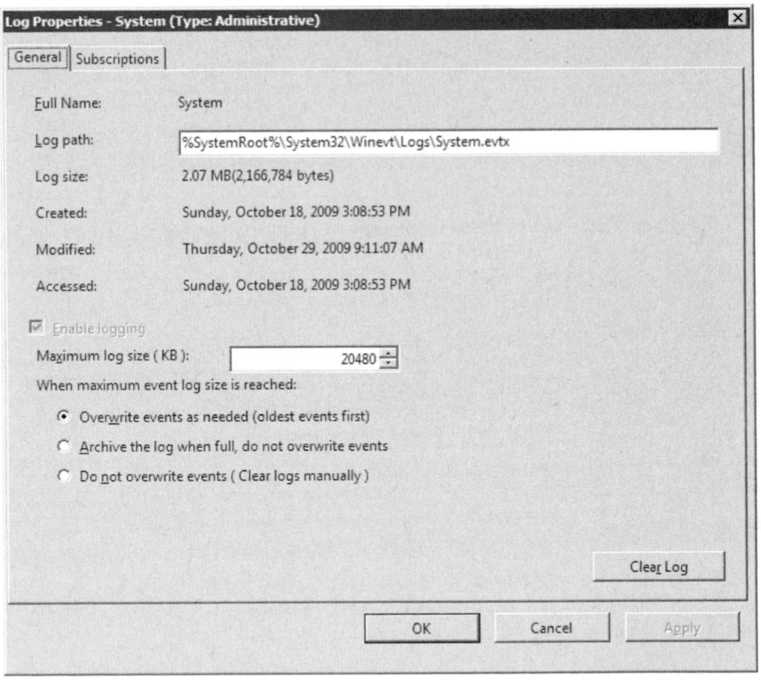

FIGURE 29.14
Default Log Properties dialog for the System event log on Windows Server 2008 R2

TABLE 29.6: Recommended Sizes for Event Logs

EVENT LOG	SIZE
Application	192 MB (196,608 KB)
Security	256 MB (262,144 KB)
System	192 MB (196,608 KB)

WHY THE SIZE LIMITATION IN WINDOWS SERVER 2003?

In Windows Server 2003, the event logs were stored in memory-mapped files, using memory that could not be paged out (that is, nonpaged pool memory). This resulted in less memory available for applications.

The event mechanism rewrite in Windows Server 2008 no longer uses memory-mapped files, and it adds a large number of features (such as eventing and notifications) to the event log subsystem.

System Center Operations Manager 2007, discussed earlier in this chapter, has a submodule called the Microsoft Audit Collection System (MACS). MACS is designed for reading and archiving the contents of the Security event log (and generating reports from those contents). When OpsMgr is in use, the Security event logs can generally be kept quite small.

Defining a Security Audit Policy

Defining a local audit policy in Windows Server is quite simple. Open Local Security Policy in Administrative Tools, expand the Local Policies node, and click Audit Policies. See Figure 29.15 for the default configuration on Windows Server 2008 R2.

FIGURE 29.15
Default audit policies in
Windows Server 2008 R2

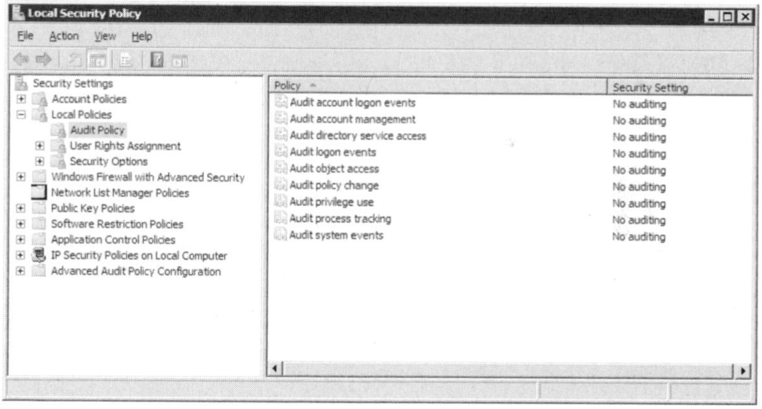

To change an audit policy, simply double-click on the policy and check the box for when you want the audit to occur (Success, Failure, or both). Our recommendations for auditing for a Windows Server 2008 and later member server are shown in Figure 29.16. Events generated by an audit policy appear in the Security event log.

Exchange Event Logging

Exchange Server 2010 generates two separate types of log entries to the event log: diagnostic logging and access auditing. In diagnostic logging, the events appear in the Application event log. In access auditing, the events appear in a new custom event log, which is named Application and Services Logs in the Exchange Auditing folder.

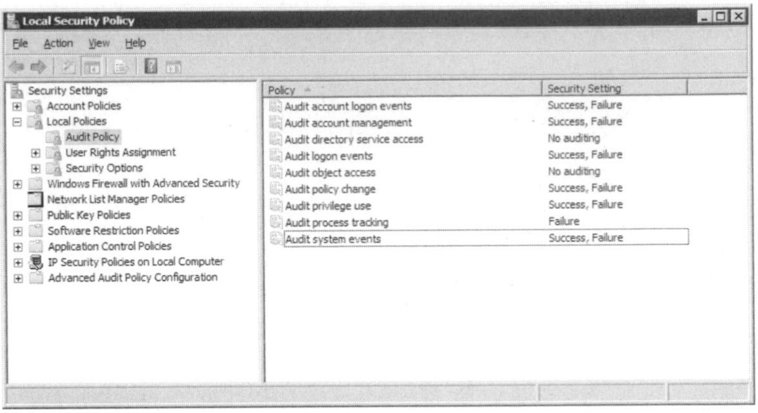

FIGURE 29.16
Recommendations
for audit policy on a
member server

Both types of event logging may be viewed and set either from the Exchange Management Shell (EMS) or from the Exchange Management Console (EMC). In the case of the EMS, you will use the following two cmdlets:

Get-EventLogLevel This cmdlet allows you to access one or many of the levels set on the various logging items from any Exchange server in the organization (Exchange Server 2010).

Set-EventLogLevel This cmdlet allows you to set the value of a logging item on any Exchange server in the organization (Exchange Server 2010).

To view or set the values from the EMC, select a particular server from Microsoft Exchange On-Premises ➤ Server Configuration and then click on Manage Diagnostic Logging Properties in the Actions pane (you can also right-click on the server and make this selection from the context menu).

Both types of event logging support a range of values. However, the meaning of that range differs between the two types of logging and will be discussed next.

EXCHANGE DIAGNOSTICS LOGGING

Exchange Server 2010 enables you to view and modify the values of logging items from the EMC, but it's actually much easier to deal with from the EMS. In Table 29.7, you can see each item available for modification of its diagnostic logging level as well as its default level for logging.

The level of *Lowest* provides, as you might assume, the least level of logging available for a particular item. Most items have a default level of *Lowest*, but a few have a default level of *Low*. In Table 29.8, immediately following Table 29.7, we list five items where we recommend you might want to increase the default event level and what those items concern.

Each diagnostic logging item can have one of five documented values. Those values and their meanings are as follows:

Lowest (0) With a value of Lowest, the diagnostic logging item will produce the minimum amount of output possible for that item. Usually, this means that no output will be produced by that item in terms of Informational events, but that all Warning and Error events will still be generated.

TABLE 29.7:   Exchange Server 2010 Diagnostics Logging Items and Their Default
Event Level

IDENTITY	DEFAULT EVENT LEVEL
MSExchange ActiveSync\Requests	Lowest
MSExchange ActiveSync\Configuration	Lowest
MSExchange Antispam\General	Lowest
MSExchange Assistants\Assistants	Lowest
MSExchange Autodiscover\Core	Lowest
MSExchange Autodiscover\Web	Lowest
MSExchange Autodiscover\Provider	Lowest
MSExchange Availability\Availability Service	Lowest
MSExchange Availability\Availability Service General	Lowest
MSExchange Availability\Availability Service Authentication	Lowest
MSExchange Availability\Availability Service Authorization	Lowest
MSExchange Cluster\Move	Lowest
MSExchange Cluster\Upgrade	Lowest
MSExchange Cluster\Action	Lowest
MSExchange Common\General	Lowest
MSExchange Common\Configuration	Lowest
MSExchange Common\Logging	Lowest
MSExchange Configuration Cmdlet – Management Shell\General	Lowest
MSExchange Configuration Cmdlet – Management Shell\RBAC	Low
MSExchange Configuration Cmdlet – Remote Management\General	Lowest
MSExchange Configuration Cmdlet – Remote Management\RBAC	Lowest
MSExchange Configuration Cmdlet – Control Panel\General	Lowest
MSExchange Configuration Cmdlet – Control Panel\RBAC	Lowest
MSExchange Configuration Cmdlet – Management Web Service\General	Lowest

TABLE 29.7:   Exchange Server 2010 Diagnostics Logging Items and Their Default
Event Level *(CONTINUED)*

IDENTITY	DEFAULT EVENT LEVEL
MSExchange Configuration Cmdlet - Management Web Service\RBAC	Lowest
MSExchange Configuration Cmdlet - Management Console\General	Lowest
MSExchange Configuration Cmdlet - Management Console\RBAC	Lowest
MSExchange Extensibility\Transport Address Book	Lowest
MSExchange Extensibility\MExRuntime	Lowest
MSExchange EdgeSync\Synchronization	Lowest
MSExchange EdgeSync\Topology	Lowest
MSExchange EdgeSync\SyncNow	Lowest
MSExchange TransportService\TransportService	Lowest
MSExchange Web Services\Core	Lowest
MSExchange IMAP4\General	Lowest
MSExchange Messaging Policies\Journaling	Lowest
MSExchange Messaging Policies\AttachFilter	Lowest
MSExchange Messaging Policies\AddressRewrite	Lowest
MSExchange Messaging Policies\Rules	Lowest
MSExchange Messaging Policies\Prelicensing	Lowest
MSExchange Messaging Policies\PolicyApplication	Lowest
MSExchange Messaging Policies\JournalReportDecryption	Lowest
MSExchange Messaging Policies\RightsManagement	Lowest
MSExchange Anti-spam Update\HygieneUpdate	Lowest
MSExchange Mailbox Replication\Service	Lowest
MSExchange Mailbox Replication\Mailbox Move	Lowest
MSExchange Management Application\Shell	Lowest
MSExchange Management Application\Console	Lowest

TABLE 29.7:   Exchange Server 2010 Diagnostics Logging Items and Their Default Event Level *(CONTINUED)*

IDENTITY	DEFAULT EVENT LEVEL
MSExchange Management Application\ProvisioningAgent	Lowest
MSExchange Management Application\ComponentInfoBasedTask	Lowest
MSExchange Management Application\AdminAuditLog	Lowest
MSExchange OWA\FormsRegistry	Lowest
MSExchange OWA\Core	Lowest
MSExchange OWA\Configuration	Lowest
MSExchange OWA\Themes	Lowest
MSExchange OWA\SmallIcons	Lowest
MSExchange OWA\Proxy	Lowest
MSExchange OWA\Transcoding	Lowest
MSExchange OWA\ADNotifications	Lowest
MSExchange OWA\InstantMessage	Lowest
MSExchange POP3\General	Lowest
MSExchange Process Manager\ProcessManager	Lowest
MSExchange Repl\Service	Lowest
MSExchange Repl\Exchange VSS Writer	Lowest
MSExchange Search Indexer\General	Lowest
MSExchange Search Indexer\Configuration	Lowest
MSExchange Store Driver\General	Lowest
MSExchange Store Driver\MeetingMessageProcessing	Lowest
MSExchange Store Driver\OofHistory	Lowest
MSExchange Store Driver\Approval	Lowest
MSExchange Store Driver\ContentAggregation	Lowest
MSExchange Topology\Topology Discovery	Lowest

TABLE 29.7: Exchange Server 2010 Diagnostics Logging Items and Their Default Event Level *(CONTINUED)*

IDENTITY	DEFAULT EVENT LEVEL
MSExchange Unified Messaging\UMWorkerProcess	Lowest
MSExchange Unified Messaging\UMCore	Lowest
MSExchange Unified Messaging\UMManagement	Lowest
MSExchange Unified Messaging\UMService	Lowest
MSExchange Unified Messaging\UMClientAccess	Lowest
MSExchange Unified Messaging\UMCallData	Lowest
MSExchange Unified Messaging\MWI General	Lowest
MSExchange ADAccess\General	Lowest
MSExchange ADAccess\Cache	Lowest
MSExchange ADAccess\Topology	Low
MSExchange ADAccess\Configuration	Lowest
MSExchange ADAccess\LDAP	Lowest
MSExchange ADAccess\Validation	Low
MSExchange ADAccess\Recipient Update Service	Lowest
MSExchange ADAccess\Site Update	Lowest
MSExchange ADAccess\Exchange Topology	Lowest
MSExchange ADAccess\Statistics	Lowest
MSExchangeApplicationLogic\TextMessaging	Lowest
MSExchangeApplicationLogic\ServerPicker	Lowest
MSExchangeAL\Ldap Operations	Lowest
MSExchangeAL\Service Control	Lowest
MSExchangeAL\Attribute Mapping	Lowest
MSExchangeAL\Account Management	Lowest
MSExchangeAL\Address List Synchronization	Lowest

TABLE 29.7: Exchange Server 2010 Diagnostics Logging Items and Their Default Event Level *(CONTINUED)*

IDENTITY	DEFAULT EVENT LEVEL
MSExchangeIS\9000 Private\Transport General	Lowest
MSExchangeIS\9000 Private\General	Lowest
MSExchangeIS\9000 Private\Transport Sending	Lowest
MSExchangeIS\9000 Private\Transport Delivering	Lowest
MSExchangeIS\9000 Private\Transfer Into Gateway	Lowest
MSExchangeIS\9000 Private\Transfer Out Of Gateway	Lowest
MSExchangeIS\9000 Private\MTA Connections	Lowest
MSExchangeIS\9000 Private\Logons	Lowest
MSExchangeIS\9000 Private\Access Control	Lowest
MSExchangeIS\9000 Private\Send On Behalf Of	Lowest
MSExchangeIS\9000 Private\Send As	Lowest
MSExchangeIS\9000 Private\Rules	Lowest
MSExchangeIS\9000 Private\Storage Limits	Lowest
MSExchangeIS\9000 Private\Background Cleanup	Lowest
MSExchangeIS\9000 Private\DS Synchronization	Lowest
MSExchangeIS\9000 Private\Views	Lowest
MSExchangeIS\9000 Private\Download	Lowest
MSExchangeIS\9000 Private\Local Replication	Lowest
MSExchangeIS\9001 Public\Transport General	Lowest
MSExchangeIS\9001 Public\General	Lowest
MSExchangeIS\9001 Public\Replication DS Updates	Lowest
MSExchangeIS\9001 Public\Replication Incoming Messages	Lowest
MSExchangeIS\9001 Public\Replication Outgoing Messages	Lowest
MSExchangeIS\9001 Public\Replication NDRs	Lowest

TABLE 29.7:   Exchange Server 2010 Diagnostics Logging Items and Their Default Event Level *(CONTINUED)*

IDENTITY	DEFAULT EVENT LEVEL
MSExchangeIS\9001 Public\Transport Sending	Lowest
MSExchangeIS\9001 Public\Transport Delivering	Lowest
MSExchangeIS\9001 Public\MTA Connections	Lowest
MSExchangeIS\9001 Public\Logons	Lowest
MSExchangeIS\9001 Public\Access Control	Lowest
MSExchangeIS\9001 Public\Send On Behalf Of	Lowest
MSExchangeIS\9001 Public\Send As	Lowest
MSExchangeIS\9001 Public\Rules	Lowest
MSExchangeIS\9001 Public\Storage Limits	Lowest
MSExchangeIS\9001 Public\Replication Site Folders	Lowest
MSExchangeIS\9001 Public\Replication Expiry	Lowest
MSExchangeIS\9001 Public\Replication Conflicts	Lowest
MSExchangeIS\9001 Public\Replication Backfill	Lowest
MSExchangeIS\9001 Public\Background Cleanup	Lowest
MSExchangeIS\9001 Public\Replication Errors	Lowest
MSExchangeIS\9001 Public\DS Synchronization	Lowest
MSExchangeIS\9001 Public\Views	Lowest
MSExchangeIS\9001 Public\Replication General	Lowest
MSExchangeIS\9001 Public\Download	Lowest
MSExchangeIS\9001 Public\Local Replication	Lowest
MSExchangeIS\9002 System\Recovery	Lowest
MSExchangeIS\9002 System\General	Lowest
MSExchangeIS\9002 System\Connections	Lowest
MSExchangeIS\9002 System\Table Cache	Lowest

TABLE 29.7:   Exchange Server 2010 Diagnostics Logging Items and Their Default Event Level *(CONTINUED)*

IDENTITY	DEFAULT EVENT LEVEL
MSExchangeIS\9002 System\Content Engine	Lowest
MSExchangeIS\9002 System\Performance Monitor	Lowest
MSExchangeIS\9002 System\Move Mailbox	Lowest
MSExchangeIS\9002 System\Download	Lowest
MSExchangeIS\9002 System\Virus Scanning	Lowest
MSExchangeIS\9002 System\Exchange Writer	Lowest
MSExchangeIS\9002 System\Backup Restore	Lowest
MSExchangeIS\9002 System\Client Monitoring	Lowest
MSExchangeIS\9002 System\Event History	Lowest
MSExchangeIS\9002 System\Database Storage Engine	Lowest
MSExchangeMailboxAssistants\Service	Lowest
MSExchangeMailboxAssistants\OOF Assistant	Lowest
MSExchangeMailboxAssistants\OOF Library	Lowest
MSExchangeMailboxAssistants\Resource Booking Attendant	Lowest
MSExchangeMailboxAssistants\Email_Lifecycle_Assistant	Lowest
MSExchangeMailboxAssistants\Junk Email Options Assistant	Lowest
MSExchangeMailboxAssistants\Conversations Assistant	Lowest
MSExchangeMailboxAssistants\Approval Assistant	Lowest
MSExchangeMailboxAssistants\FreeBusy Assistant	Lowest
MSExchangeMailboxAssistants\ELC Library	Lowest
MSExchangeMailSubmission\General	Lowest
MSExchangeMU\General	Lowest
MSExchangeSA\Clean Mailbox	Lowest
MSExchangeSA\OAL Generator	Lowest

TABLE 29.7:   Exchange Server 2010 Diagnostics Logging Items and Their Default
                    Event Level *(CONTINUED)*

IDENTITY	DEFAULT EVENT LEVEL
MSExchangeSA\Proxy Generation	Lowest
MSExchangeSA\RPC Calls	Lowest
MSExchangeSA\RPC-HTTP Management	Lowest
MSExchangeTransport\SmtpReceive	Lowest
MSExchangeTransport\SmtpSend	Lowest
MSExchangeTransport\DSN	Lowest
MSExchangeTransport\Routing	Lowest
MSExchangeTransport\Logging	Lowest
MSExchangeTransport\Components	Lowest
MSExchangeTransport\RemoteDelivery	Lowest
MSExchangeTransport\Pickup	Lowest
MSExchangeTransport\Categorizer	Lowest
MSExchangeTransport\PoisonMessage	Lowest
MSExchangeTransport\MessageSecurity	Lowest
MSExchangeTransport\TransportService	Lowest
MSExchangeTransport\Exch50	Lowest
MSExchangeTransport\Process	Lowest
MSExchangeTransport\ResourceManager	Lowest
MSExchangeTransport\Configuration	Lowest
MSExchangeTransport\Storage	Lowest
MSExchangeTransport\Agents	Lowest
MSExchangeTransport\Transport Address Book	Lowest
MSExchangeTransport\Orar	Lowest
MSExchangeTransport\ShadowRedundancy	Lowest

TABLE 29.7: Exchange Server 2010 Diagnostics Logging Items and Their Default Event Level *(CONTINUED)*

IDENTITY	DEFAULT EVENT LEVEL
MSExchangeTransport\Approval	Lowest
MSExchangeTransport\TransportDumpster	Lowest
MSExchangeFDS\General	Lowest
MSExchangeFDS\FileReplication	Lowest
MSExchangeTransportSyncCommon\General	Lowest
MSExchangeTransportSyncManager\General	Lowest
MSExchangeTransportSyncWorker\General	Lowest
MSExchange OutlookProtectionRules\Outlook Protection Rules	Lowest
MSExchange Provisioning MailboxAssistant\Provisioning Assistant General	Lowest
MSExchangeThrottling\General	Lowest
MSExchangeThrottlingClient\General	Lowest

TABLE 29.8: Some Diagnostic Logging Items to Increase from Default

ITEM	DESCRIPTION
MSExchangeIS\9000 Private\Logons	Audits events relating to mailbox access
MSExchangeIS\9000 Private\Send As	Audits events relating to using the Send-As functionality of the Outlook client
MSExchangeIS\9000 Private\Send On Behalf Of	Audits events relating to using the Send-On-Behalf-Of functionality of the Outlook client
MSExchangeIS\9000 Private\Storage Limits	Audits events related to mailboxes exceeding their storage quotas
MSExchangeIS\9002 System\Move Mailbox	Audits events related to moving mailboxes between servers and mailbox databases

Low (1)   A value of Low indicates that additional warnings and errors may be generated by the diagnostic logging item, plus some Informational details about the processing that occurs for that item.

You should always start your diagnostics with a level of Low and work up from there.

Medium (3)   A value of Medium indicates that more detailed information should be reported than that with Low.

High (5)   More detailed information is reported than with Medium. Also support information (often requested by Microsoft Customer Support Services) begins to be output at the level of High.

Expert (7)   This level of information can be overwhelming with the modules that implement it. The information is rarely of use to anyone other than Microsoft Customer Support Services. Many modules may not implement the Expert level to produce more information over the High level.

Older versions of Microsoft Exchange Server also supported another value, Field Engineering (15), but that always had to be set using a Registry editing tool. It is likely that the level still exists. However, since it isn't documented, it isn't supported.

If you have increased the value of the logging level to assist in diagnosing a problem, you should always restore the value to the default when you are done in order to reduce the overall load on your Exchange server.

Protocol and Connection Logs

Exchange Server 2010 can optionally maintain logs for almost every conversation that takes place between two servers. The exception is end-user MAPI connections — and if you are using Outlook Anywhere, you can get a pretty good feel for those using IIS logs.

There are two primary reasons for enabling protocol and connection logs:

- Diagnosing and correcting problems
- Performance reporting

In the case of problem diagnosis, sometimes nothing is better than being able to point at a particular log file and say, "Yes, you are connecting, but this is what is happening . . . " And likely, the day will come that your management will want to be able to tell how many messages you have incoming, outgoing, heaviest users, and so forth. OpsMgr provides some of those reports for you, but many third-party utilities are available to produce detailed analysis of the comings and goings of your Exchange servers.

A common theme in all Exchange-generated log files (please note that this does not apply to IIS-generated log files — they follow a different standard) is that each line of the log file is reporting some *event*. In this case, Event is a fixed field in each log file, and that field will contain one of the characters in Table 29.9.

Let's take a brief introductory look at each of the protocol logs and what they contain.

IMAP

By default, the IMAP protocol is neither enabled nor running on Exchange Server 2010. To enable the service, run the following PowerShell command:

```
Set-Service MSExchangeIMAP4 -StartupType Automatic
```

TABLE 29.9:   The Events in Protocol Log Files

CHARACTER	MEANING
+	A connection is being established to this computer.
−	A connection has been completed or was disconnected.
>	A message is being sent outbound.
<	An inbound message was received.
*	An informational event has occurred.

However, before you start the service, you may want to review the logon authentication method required. As shown in Figure 29.17, the default method requires TLS to be enabled (that is, IMAP over TLS). While many modern IMAP clients support this, if you simply want to test, you can change that to basic authentication. Here's the PowerShell command for that:

```
Set-ImapSettings -LoginType PlainTextLogin
```

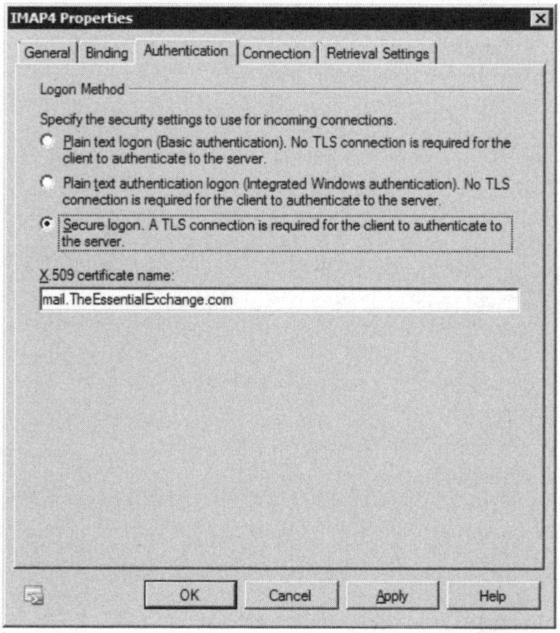

FIGURE 29.17
The Authentication tab
of the IMAP4 Properties
dialog

And finally, to enable IMAP logging, you execute the follow PowerShell command:

```
Set-ImapSettings -ProtocolLogEnabled $true
```

You are now ready to start the IMAP service:

```
Start-Service MSExchangeIMAP4
```

With the exception of setting the `ProtocolLogEnabled` value to `$true`, all these items can also be done in the appropriate GUI.

IMAP log files are comma-separated-value (CSV) format log files, in plaintext. They are located in `C:\Program Files\Microsoft\Exchange Server\V14\Logging\Imap4`. You can see a sample of the information contained within the log file in Figure 29.18.

FIGURE 29.18
Information contained in an IMAP log file

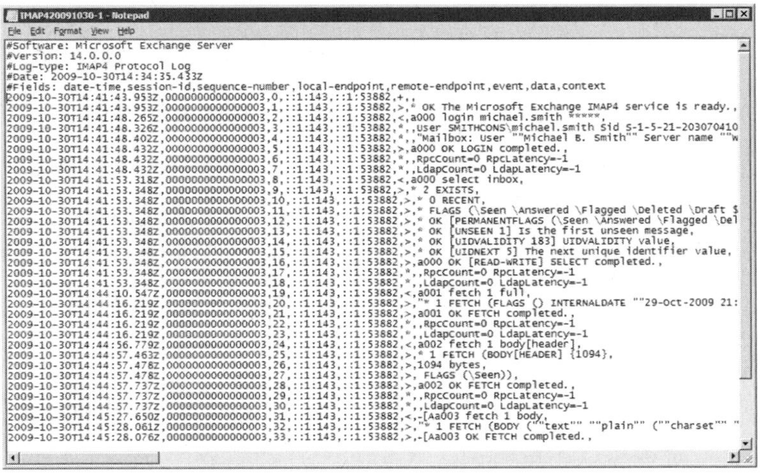

In comparison to the contents of the IMAP log file from prior versions of Exchange, the presence of the Session-id and Sequence-number fields are noteworthy. The session-id value is guaranteed to be unique, and the sequence-number value identifies the order of commands. They are important when you have many users using the service at the same time, as the input and output from the sessions are interleaved in the log files and can be quite confusing.

POP

POP configuration is almost exactly the same as IMAP configuration. By default, the POP protocol is neither enabled nor running on Exchange Server 2010. To enable the service, run the following PowerShell command:

```
Set-Service MSExchangePOP3 -StartupType Automatic
```

However, before you start the service, you may want to review the logon authentication method required. As shown in Figure 29.17 for IMAP (but exactly the same for POP), the default method requires TLS to be enabled (that is, POP over TLS). While many modern POP clients support this, if you simply want to test, you can change that to basic authentication. The PowerShell command for that looks like this:

```
Set-PopSettings -LoginType PlainTextLogin
```

And finally, to enable POP logging, you execute the following PowerShell command:

```
Set-PopSettings -ProtocolLogEnabled $true
```

You are now ready to start the IMAP service:

```
Start-Service MSExchangePOP3
```

With the exception of setting the `ProtocolLogEnabled` value to `$true`, all these items can also be done in the appropriate GUI.

POP log files are CSV format log files in plaintext. They are located in `C:\Program Files\Microsoft\Exchange Server\V14\Logging\Pop3`. You can see a sample of the information contained within the log file in Figure 29.19.

FIGURE 29.19

Information contained in a POP log file

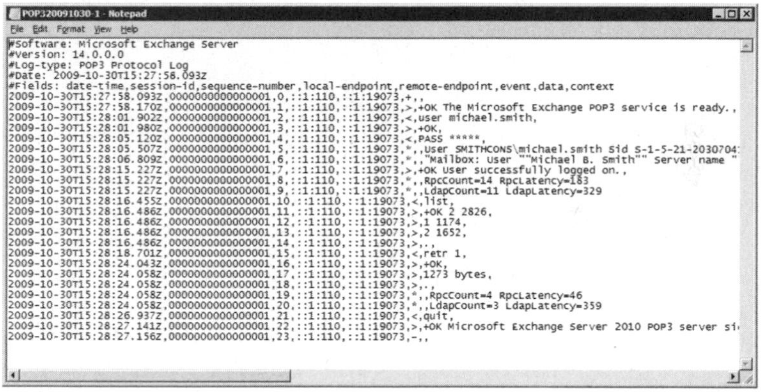

In comparison to the contents of the POP log file from prior versions of Exchange, the presence of the Session-id and Sequence-number fields are noteworthy. The session-id value is guaranteed to be unique, and the sequence-number value identifies the order of commands. They are important when you have many users using the service at the same time, as the input and output from the sessions are interleaved in the log files and can be quite confusing.

Transport

By far in Exchange Server 2010, the most logging choices revolve around SMTP logging on the Transport server. However, most of this logging cannot be configured using the Transport server properties dialog. Figure 29.20 illustrates what can be configured for logging on the Transport server.

PowerShell provides a much richer set of logging options:

```
[PS] C:\>get-transportserver | fl *Log*

ConnectivityLogEnabled          : True
ConnectivityLogMaxAge           : 30.00:00:00
ConnectivityLogMaxDirectorySize : 250 MB (262,144,000 bytes)
ConnectivityLogMaxFileSize      : 10 MB (10,485,760 bytes)
```

```
ConnectivityLogPath                        : C:\Program Files\Microsoft\Exchange
                                             Server\V14\TransportRoles\Logs\Con
                                             nectivity

MessageTrackingLogEnabled                  : True
MessageTrackingLogSubjectLoggingEnabled: True
MessageTrackingLogMaxAge                    : 30.00:00:00
MessageTrackingLogMaxDirectorySize         : 1000 MB (1,048,576,000 bytes)
MessageTrackingLogMaxFileSize              : 10 MB (10,485,760 bytes)
MessageTrackingLogPath                     : C:\Program Files\Microsoft\Exchange
                                             Server\V14\TransportRoles\Logs\Mes
                                             sageTracking

ActiveUserStatisticsLogMaxAge              : 30.00:00:00
ActiveUserStatisticsLogMaxDirectorySize: 250 MB (262,144,000 bytes)
ActiveUserStatisticsLogMaxFileSize         : 10 MB (10,485,760 bytes)
ActiveUserStatisticsLogPath                : C:\Program Files\Microsoft\Exchange
                                             Server\V14\TransportRoles\Logs\Act
                                             iveUsersStats

ServerStatisticsLogMaxAge                  : 30.00:00:00
ServerStatisticsLogMaxDirectorySize        : 250 MB (262,144,000 bytes)
ServerStatisticsLogMaxFileSize             : 10 MB (10,485,760 bytes)
ServerStatisticsLogPath                    : C:\Program Files\Microsoft\Exchange
                                             Server\V14\TransportRoles\Logs\Ser
                                             verStats

IntraOrgConnectorProtocolLoggingLevel : None

ReceiveProtocolLogMaxAge                   : 30.00:00:00
ReceiveProtocolLogMaxDirectorySize         : 250 MB (262,144,000 bytes)
ReceiveProtocolLogMaxFileSize              : 10 MB (10,485,760 bytes)
ReceiveProtocolLogPath                     : C:\Program Files\Microsoft\Exchange
                                             Server\V14\TransportRoles\Logs\Pro
                                             tocolLog\SmtpReceive

RoutingTableLogMaxAge                      : 7.00:00:00
RoutingTableLogMaxDirectorySize            : 50 MB (52,428,800 bytes)
RoutingTableLogPath                        : C:\Program Files\Microsoft\Exchange
                                             Server\V14\TransportRoles\Logs\Rou
                                             ting

SendProtocolLogMaxAge                      : 30.00:00:00
SendProtocolLogMaxDirectorySize            : 250 MB (262,144,000 bytes)
SendProtocolLogMaxFileSize                 : 10 MB (10,485,760 bytes)
SendProtocolLogPath                        : C:\Program Files\Microsoft\Exchange
                                             Server\V14\TransportRoles\Logs\Pro
                                             tocolLog\SmtpSend
```

```
HttpProtocolLogEnabled              : False
HttpProtocolLogFilePath             :
HttpProtocolLogMaxAge               : 7.00:00:00
HttpProtocolLogMaxDirectorySize     : 250 MB (262,144,000 bytes)
HttpProtocolLogMaxFileSize          : 10 MB (10,485,760 bytes)
HttpProtocolLogLoggingLevel         : None

TransportSyncLogEnabled             : False
TransportSyncLogFilePath            :
TransportSyncLogLoggingLevel        : None
TransportSyncLogMaxAge              : 7.00:00:00
TransportSyncLogMaxDirectorySize    : 10 GB (10,737,418,240 bytes)
TransportSyncLogMaxFileSize         : 10 MB (10,485,760 bytes)

TransportSyncHubHealthLogEnabled    : False
TransportSyncHubHealthLogFilePath   :
TransportSyncHubHealthLogMaxAge     : 14.00:00:00
TransportSyncHubHealthLogMaxDirectorySize : 10 GB (10,737,418,240 bytes)
TransportSyncHubHealthLogMaxFileSize  : 10 MB (10,485,760 bytes)


[PS] C:\>
```

FIGURE 29.20
Transport server
logging options

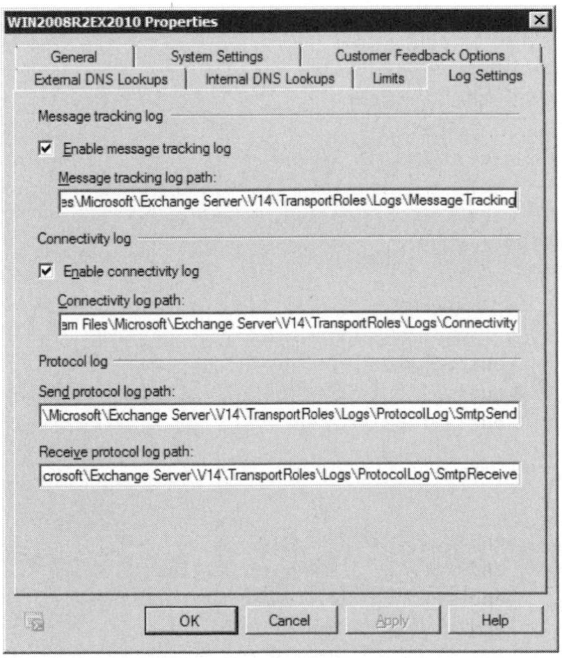

We won't cover each of these in detail, but we will cover concepts. First and foremost: all TransportSync* and HttpProtocol* variables and values are reserved for internal Microsoft use. A reasonable guess (and we have no knowledge on the accuracy of this) is that they are used for Microsoft's Exchange Hosting business.

Any *LogMaxAge variable is used to limit how long a log file is retained in a log file directory. It is the maximum amount of time that the log file will reside in the *LogPath directory. When *LogMaxAge is exceeded, Exchange will automatically remove log files that exceed that age.

Any *LogMaxDirectorySize variable is used to limit how large a log file directory can grow. If a log directory grows larger than *LogMaxDirectorySize, then enough older log files are removed to bring the size of the directory beneath the *LogMaxDirectorySize. Oldest log files are removed first.

Any *LogMaxFilesize variable is used to limit the size of an individual log file. If an in-use log file exceeds that value, it is closed and a new log file is opened. Some logging types (such as the routing table) don't include this value because a new log file is opened every time something needs to be logged.

Any *LogPath variable is used to indicate the directory where that particular type of log file is stored.

Finally, any *LogEnabled variable is used to indicate whether or not that particular type of logging is enabled. Certain log files, such as Active User Statistics and Server Statistics, are always generated and cannot be disabled. Other log files, such as connectivity logging and message tracking, are generated by default but can be disabled. However, the Send Protocol and the Receive Protocol log files are not controlled at the Transport server level but at the connector level.

CONNECTIVITY LOG

The connectivity log shows every connection to the Transport server and some brief information about what happened during that connection. You can see sample output from a connectivity log in Figure 29.21.

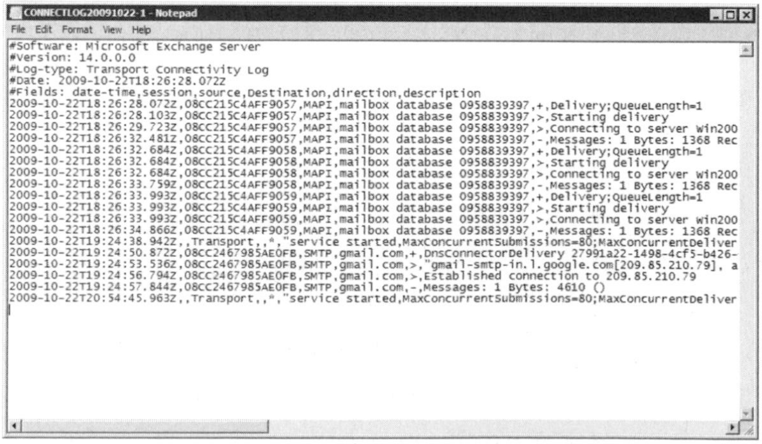

FIGURE 29.21
Connectivity log sample

MESSAGE TRACKING

Message tracking logs and their use are covered, in detail, in Chapter 28, "Troubleshooting Exchange Server 2010." A message tracking log tracks every step that a message follows through a specific Exchange server.

ACTIVE USER STATISTICS

Each day, a Transport server generates a summary of email for each incoming and each outgoing email address. This summary contains the following fields of information in CSV format:

- DateTime
- UserAddress
- MessageScope
- SenderSmtpMessages
- SenderSmtpBytes
- SenderSmtpRecipientCount
- SenderStoreDriverMessages
- SenderStoreDriverBytes
- SenderStoreDriverRecipientCount
- RecipientStoreDriverMessages
- RecipientStoreDriverBytes
- RecipientSmtpMessages
- RecipientSmtpBytes
- RecipientFailMessages
- RecipientFailBytes
- SenderFailMessages
- SenderFailBytes
- SenderExternalSmtpMessages
- SenderExternalSmtpBytes
- SenderExternalSmtpRecipientCount
- RecipientAggregationMessages
- RecipientAggregationBytes
- SenderGatewayMessages
- SenderGatewayBytes
- RecipientPickupMessages

- RecipientPickupBytes
- SenderAgentMessages
- SenderAgentBytes
- RecipientExpandMessages
- RecipientExpandBytes
- TotalEndToEndMessageLatency
- TotalEndToEndMessageLatencyCount

SERVER STATISTICS

Each day a Transport server also generates an overall summary of its activities to a log file, based on its connections to source and destination servers. This summary contains the following fields of information in CSV format:

- DateTime
- ClientHostName
- ServerHostName
- DeliverGatewayMessages
- DeliverGatewayBytes
- DeliverGatewayRecipients
- DeliverAgentMessages
- DeliverAgentBytes
- DeliverAgentRecipients
- DeliverStoreDriverMessages
- DeliverStoreDriverBytes
- DeliverStoreDriverRecipients
- DeliverSmtpIntraOrgMessages
- DeliverSmtpIntraOrgBytes
- DeliverSmtpIntraOrgRecipients
- DeliverSmtpForeignMessages
- DeliverSmtpForeignBytes
- DeliverSmtpForeignRecipients
- ReceiveStoreDriverMessages
- ReceiveStoreDriverBytes
- ReceiveStoreDriverRecipients

- ReceiveSmtpLocalMessages
- ReceiveSmtpLocalBytes
- ReceiveSmtpLocalRecipients
- ReceivePickupMessages
- ReceivePickupBytes
- ReceivePickupRecipients
- ReceiveSmtpIntraOrgMessages
- ReceiveSmtpIntraOrgBytes
- ReceiveSmtpIntraOrgRecipients
- ReceiveSmtpForeignMessages
- ReceiveSmtpForeignBytes
- ReceiveSmtpForeignRecipients
- ReceiveAggregationMessages
- ReceiveAggregationBytes
- ReceiveAggregationRecipients
- ReceiveMailboxRulesMessages
- ReceiveMailboxRulesBytes
- ReceiveMailboxRulesRecipients
- ResubmitDumpsterMessages
- ResubmitDumpsterBytes
- ResubmitRedundancyMessages
- ResubmitRedundancyBytes
- DSNMessages
- DSNBytes
- AgentFailLocalMessages
- AgentFailLocalBytes
- AgentFailForeignMessages
- AgentFailForeignBytes
- RoutingFailLocalMessages
- RoutingFailLocalBytes
- RoutingFailForeignMessages
- RoutingFailForeignBytes

- ◆ EndToEndLatencyPercentile100
- ◆ EndToEndLatencyPercentile99
- ◆ EndToEndLatencyPercentile95
- ◆ EndToEndLatencyPercentile90
- ◆ EndToEndLatencyPercentile80
- ◆ EndToEndLatencyPercentile70
- ◆ EndToEndLatencyPercentile60
- ◆ EndToEndLatencyPercentile50
- ◆ EndToEndLatencyPercentile25
- ◆ EndToEndLatencyPercentileCount
- ◆ LocalLatencyPercentile100
- ◆ LocalLatencyPercentile99
- ◆ LocalLatencyPercentile95
- ◆ LocalLatencyPercentile90
- ◆ LocalLatencyPercentile80
- ◆ LocalLatencyPercentile70
- ◆ LocalLatencyPercentile60
- ◆ LocalLatencyPercentile50
- ◆ LocalLatencyPercentile25
- ◆ LocalLatencyPercentileCount

SEND AND RECEIVE LOGS

While the location of send and receive logs are controlled by the Transport server configuration (see Figure 29.20 earlier), whether or not a particular SMTP transaction is logged is controlled by the individual connector that the transaction passes through.

Each receive connector and send connector has a *Protocol Logging Level* associated with it. That level is either *None* or *Verbose*. The default value for the level is *None*. See Figure 29.22 for a sample showing this on the General tab of a receive connector's properties dialog. The value is in the same place on a send connector.

You can also easily set the value of the Protocol Logging Level from PowerShell. For the receive connector shown in Figure 29.22, the PowerShell command would look like this:

```
Set-ReceiveConnector "Default Win2008R2Ex2010" -ProtocolLoggingLevel Verbose
```

That command enables protocol logging. To disable protocol logging, use this command:

```
Set-ReceiveConnector "Default Win2008R2Ex2010" -ProtocolLoggingLevel None
```

The same `ProtocolLoggingLevel` parameter exists in `Set-SendConnector` and uses the same values.

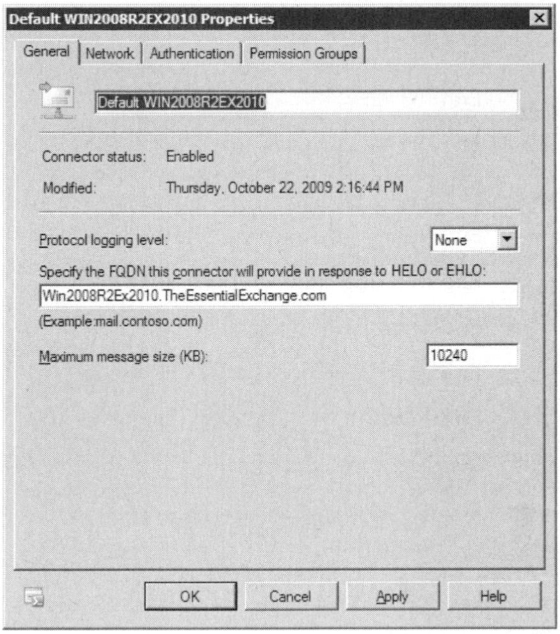

FIGURE 29.22
Receive connector show-
ing default log level
of None

FIGURE 29.22
Receive connector show-
ing default log level
of None

By default, receive connector log files reside in C:\Program Files\Microsoft\Exchange Server\V14\TransportRoles\Logs\ProtocolLog\SmtpReceive and send connector log files reside in C:\Program Files\Microsoft\Exchange Server\V14\TransportRoles\Logs\ ProtocolLog\SmtpSend.

The log files generated by the send and receive connectors will look familiar to you. Figure 29.23 shows the output of a send connector named Internet Send Connector when it sends a single message to a Gmail address from an Exchange 2010 Transport server.

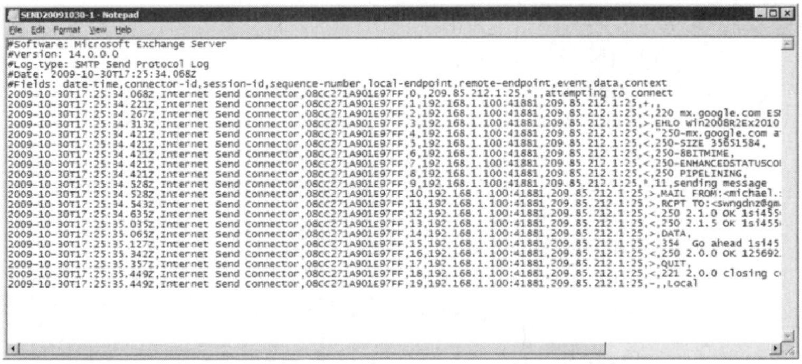

FIGURE 29.23
SMTP send connector
protocol log

IntraOrg Connector

Here's a final note on connectivity and protocol logging. By default, not all communication is logged — only communication that is either entering or exiting the Exchange organization is logged. Every Hub Transport server has an implicit "invisible" bidirectional connector to every other Hub Transport server and Edge Transport server. If you want to see logging for communications across this implicit connector, you have to specifically enable it. And, as the volume of internal traffic may be much higher than external traffic, you may want to keep a close eye on how many system resources are consumed by doing this.

To enable intraorganizational logging, use this command:

```
Set-TransportServer Win2008R2Ex2010 -IntraOrgConnectorProtocolLoggingLevel ↵
  Verbose
```

And to disable it:

```
Set-TransportServer Win2008R2Ex2010 -IntraOrgConnectorProtocolLoggingLevel ↵
  None
```

ROUTING LOGS

Exchange Server 2010 does not have a routing engine per se, but it does maintain logs of the known routes to access other Exchange servers and other message destinations. The log files are written four times a day or when the transport services are restarted. By default, the log files are found in C:\Program Files\Microsoft\Exchange Server\V14\TransportRoles\Logs\Routing.

However, the XML-formatted log file is not particularly easy to follow if you open it in a text editor. In the Exchange Management Console Toolbox work center you'll find the Routing Log Viewer, which will allow you to retrieve these logs and to view information such as servers, connectors, address spaces, and Active Directory site information. An example is shown in Figure 29.24.

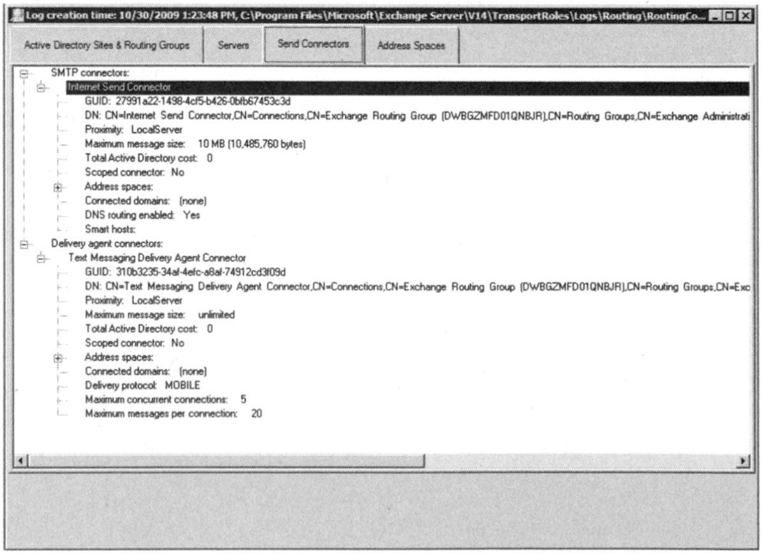

FIGURE 29.24
The Routing Log Viewer

Other Logs

We have not specifically discussed using log files from either IIS or the DNS. However, many facets of Exchange Server 2010 run through IIS:

◆ Outlook Web App

◆ Outlook Anywhere

◆ Exchange Control Panel

◆ Remote PowerShell

◆ Exchange ActiveSync

◆ Exchange Web Services

◆ Public Folders

◆ Offline Address Books

◆ Free/busy

◆ AutoDiscover

◆ . . . plus other things we've probably forgotten

To the Exchange administrator, that means IIS logs can be invaluable tools to determine whether users have been able to connect, what errors may have occurred, what security is required, and so forth. The IIS logs can also be mined for performance data (such as how many Outlook Anywhere sessions are occurring, or how many authentication errors are happening) — so do not ignore them in your search for diagnostic data.

Finally, the DNS servers used by your Exchange servers can also maintain log files about DNS queries, how long those queries take to answer, and errors that may occur in answering those queries. From time to time, those log files can help you answer difficult questions about why a particular piece of email could not be received or transmitted.

The Bottom Line

Examine and interpret key performance monitor counters. Making proper use of your Exchange server requires that you also be able to make fast evaluations of existing performance of that Exchange server using a tool such as Performance Monitor.

Master It Your user community is complaining of poor performance from a particular Exchange server. You need to make a quick best-guess as to what may be causing the issue. You decide to use Performance Monitor. What performance objects will you examine and what are you looking for?

Install and configure the Exchange management pack. While it is possible to manually build a set of test-points for examining Exchange Server 2010 and evaluating its performance and health, using the knowledge that Microsoft already has developed is certainly an easier way to go. This is best done by using the management pack that Microsoft developed for Operations Manager 2007.

> **Master It**   Due to ongoing problems with Outlook Web App on a Client Access server, you need to regularly test to ensure that OWA is working properly.

Configure, locate, and examine SMTP connector logs.   The SMTP connector logs generated by send and receive connectors (and the connectivity logs generated by the Transport server itself) can provide invaluable information when it is time to diagnose message transfer issues for both incoming and outgoing messages in your Exchange organization.

> **Master It**   A client reports that they cannot send email to your Exchange server, but email from every other location seems to be working fine. How do you diagnose the issue?

Configure and evaluate Exchange diagnostic logging.   Exchange can provide much detail about its operation if you increase the levels of diagnostic logging.

> **Master It**   You are receiving an error in your event log relating to the processing of server-side mailbox rules, but you don't have enough information to resolve the problem. What do you do?

## Chapter 30

Backing Up and Restoring Exchange Server

Exchange has come full circle in regard to backing up servers. Originally Exchange could be backed up directly from the Windows server. Then with Exchange 2007 SP2, this option was removed. Exchange 2010 brings this capability back. You now have the ability to back up and restore the Exchange data from Windows 2008.

In this chapter, you will learn to:

- ◆ Back up Exchange

- ◆ Prepare to recover the Exchange server

- ◆ Use Windows Server Backup to back up the server

- ◆ Use Windows Server Backup to recover the data

- ◆ Recover the entire Exchange server

Backing Up Exchange

Exchange gives your organization the ability to store very large amounts of data. In most cases this data is considered mission critical. Your users potentially send and receive hundreds of emails per day. Over time, this amount of email adds up. In some cases the only copy of an email or company data will be in the end user's mailbox.

Before you can successfully perform any backups, you must define your backup strategy. Your organization requirements will drive the strategy that you need to deploy. Deploying a backup strategy without taking in the recovery scenarios or the backup requirements sets you up for failure. Knowing the backup requirements also helps you define the correct tool for the job.

You must understand why you are backing up the data. Once you know this, you will be able to define your goals and requirements. By establishing your goals and requirements, you will also have gathered the necessary information for the backup schedule.

With Exchange 2010, Volume Snapshot Service (VSS) backups are the only option to perform backups. VSS is a technology that allows you to take manual or automatic backup copies or snapshots of data, even if it has a lock, on a specific volume at a specific point in time over regular intervals. Make sure that your backup solution is capable of performing VSS backups.

Performing the backup is the easy part; restoring the data is the tough part. Various backup solutions are available for Exchange. There are hardware options such as hardware-based VSS providers on a Storage Area Network (SAN), or you can use software-based VSS provider solutions. This chapter will focus on the solutions that Exchange provides out of the box.

There is some backup terminology that you may or may not be familiar with as you read this chapter. In regards to VSS, you will read or hear about the following:

Requestor   The application that requests the creation of a shadow copy

Provider   The interface that provides the functionality to make the shadow copy

Writer   Application-specific software that acts to ensure that application data is ready for shadow copy creation

Having functional backups is an extremely important part of the IT administrator's job. The first reason to keep a functional backup is for data recovery; the second (and sometimes forgotten) reason for backups is to provide transaction log truncation. Exchange has always protected itself in case the system was not able to be backed up. As you know, when the transaction log location fills up the mailbox database dismounts. So if you were not able to back up your server for several days, you risked having the server taken offline and thus answering to the end users.

Windows Server 2008 has kept up with the ever-changing backup technology by providing a plug-in that gives you the ability to make VSS backups of the Exchange data. VSS has enabled servers to be backed up in a fraction of the time as traditional tapes. What used to take hours now takes minutes depending on the amount of data being backed up.

When Windows 2008 backs up Exchange data, it also performs checks against that data. These checks make sure the files that have been backed up are in good shape and prepared for the recovery efforts. Once the snapshot has been taken of the Exchange data, verification is run against the data. If there are any issues with the snapshot, you will receive errors and be able to work on the data to figure out where the problem is. Once the issue has been located, you can make adjustments.

Determining Your Strategy

In the past there were several reasons why you needed to back up your databases. Some of the popular reasons were as follows:

◆ Single message recovery

◆ Database recovery

◆ Entire server recovery

Just as there are times when you will want to perform backups, there also will be times when you may not choose to restore an entire server. For example, if you are utilizing DAGs you may not want or need to restore the entire server from your backup. Instead, you may choose to install another mailbox server, join it to the DAG, and then enable a database copy on the new mailbox server.

Why Recover Data?

You are probably familiar with many scenarios in which you need to recover Exchange data. When such a scenario arises, you must know how to handle it. Some will be simple to handle, such as a deleted mailbox or deleted messages, while others will be more in depth and time consuming, such as server or site recovery.

Regardless of the scenario, you need to have a well-documented recovery plan. Practicing recovery is just as important as the recovery plan. We know that practicing is about as much fun as having your teeth pulled. But the wrong time to figure out how to do the recovery is when the recovery becomes necessary. When you are in the middle of a disaster, you don't have time to stumble through figuring it out.

Think of the practice as insurance. You put a lot of money in your insurance in the hopes that you will not need it. But when you need it, you are glad you have it. Don't get caught without insurance in your organization.

ESTABLISHING YOUR RECOVERABILITY GOALS

Once you understand why you want to perform backups, you can determine the goals for your recovery. Think about how you are maintaining your backups, how long you are keeping the backups, and how quickly you need to restore the data. These scenarios will help you determine what your backup architecture should look like. One example is to keep your backups on-site (instead of storing them off-site) to meet your Recovery Time Objective (RTO).

Each scenario could have different recovery objectives. Table 30.1 shows how recoverability goals can be different for each scenario.

TABLE 30.1:   Scenarios for Recovery and Goals

SCENARIO	DATA RETENTION GOAL	DATA RESTORATION GOAL
Corrupted database	Restored database must not be older than 1 day.	Must have dial-tone service up within 1 hour and the database must be restored within 8 hours.
Mailbox deletion	Restored data must be less than 30 days old.	Mailbox must be restored within 1 hour.
Recover a message that was deleted more than 30 days ago	Must be able to restore messages for up to 60 days.	Message must be restored within 1 business day.

The key is to determine the minimum and maximum lengths of time that backed-up data must be kept and select a backup methodology that allows you to restore the data within your target restoration goal.

SETTING A BACKUP SCHEDULE

Knowing what you are backing up is just as important as the other factors. To determine your backup schedule, you must know how much data you are going to back up and what the backup rate is for your specific environment. Look at the databases you are backing up, where you will place the data once it is backed up, and how the data will get there. All of these concerns factor into the design of your backup window. Once you put numbers to this information, you can do the simple math to figure out your backup window. Not only will you be able to determine your window, but you will also understand what your backup schedule will look like.

Your backup schedule will take into account the backup strategy you have identified, the recoverability goals, and the organizational requirements for the backups. You may also hear terms like Recovery Point Object (RPO) and RTO.

The RPO is the maximum acceptable amount of data loss after an unscheduled outage. The RPO is defined as a measurement of time. This is generally the point in time before the event at which the data could be successfully recovered. The RPO varies from organization to organization. Some businesses might only need a backup since the most recent close of business, while other businesses may require a backup from the point of failure.

The RTO is the maximum acceptable length of time that Exchange can be down after a failure or disaster. It is a function of the extent to which the interruption disrupts normal operations. The RTO is measured in seconds, minutes, hours, or days, and is an important consideration in disaster recovery planning. Next, you need to determine a schedule that will map to your requirements.

If you have to back up 2.5 TB of Exchange data and you can back up and restore 500 GB per hour, then you are looking at 5 hours for the process to complete. If you need to restore your data in 4 hours, you are not going to make it. In this case, you would have to decrease the amount of Exchange data. You can decrease the data by adjusting the settings for deleted item retention or adding an additional Exchange server into the environment. By adding an additional server, you will be able to move some of mailboxes, level out the amount of data per server and fit your backup into your backup window. These numbers are completely random and are just used an example of what could be done.

Let's look at the example from Table 30.1. You see that the databases must be less than one day old, which tells you that the Exchange databases must be backed up daily. You also will note that you should be able to recover messages for a maximum of 60 days, which tells you that you must keep the database backups for 60 days. That means that no matter what solution you decide to implement, you must have enough tapes or disk space to hold the 60 backups that you will be keeping.

Keep in mind that database backups should not be the primary recovery mechanism. The recommended solution would be to implement database copies. Having multiple copies online are much quicker to implement. You also don't have to worry about corruption during a restore of the database(s).

BACKUP ALTERNATIVES WITH EXCHANGE

So far we have talked about the need for a successful backup of your data. Now, let's look at another possibility. With Exchange 2010, Microsoft introduced an alternative to the standard backup methodology. Think about an environment in which you don't perform backups and you don't have to store backups. Microsoft chose this solution for the internal deployment of Exchange 2010. By doing this they were able to eliminate the backup and maintenance cost.

This is a lifestyle change for most IT shops. Imagine the conversation you will have with the CIO when you tell him that you are not going to be backing up his Exchange mailbox. Naturally this method will not be the most welcoming topic to begin with. We have all run across situations that we wanted to change, but can't because it has always been done a certain way. Backups are just the next topic in that conversation. Even after you have had the discussion, you still may not be the most popular person in the room. The proof is in the pudding. As you know Exchange 2010 has brought about new technical capabilities that will help fill in the gap. Here are some of the most common issues and their solutions:

Individual Message Recovery   No more need for a third-party solution. Exchange gives you the ability to recover an individual item — just enable and configure.

Corrupted Mailbox Database   If you know when the corruption occurred, you can use the transaction log replay lag on the DAG to recover the database minus the log that caused the corruption in the original database.

Mailbox Recovery   By default, Exchange is set to keep deleted mailboxes for 30 days. This is an adjustable setting that can be specified based on the organization requirements.

Hard Drive Failure   Multiple copies of the database placed in the DAG help protect against drive failures.

Complete Server Failure   Placing the databases from the server in a DAG replicates data and provides protection for the server.

Site Failure   Stretch the DAG across to a remote data center instead of performing off-site backups.

Microsoft recommends that you have a minimum of three copies in your DAG before you implement this backup alternative. How many times have you been told not to use circular logging unless you are performing a migration or in a situation where recovery is not a high priority? Well, here is one of those situations. Since you are not performing a standard backup, you will not allow Exchange to truncate the logs. Because of this, circular logging is a must. If you don't enable circular logging, you will most certainly fill up the transaction logs and bring down the databases.

Preparing to Recover the Exchange Server

Preparing the server and the environment is the first step to making sure that you are able to recover the server in case the worst happens. It is also one of the easiest things that you will do. Making sure that you have protected your servers and have a documented recovery plan will help you when the need arises for a recovery. It is not a matter of *if* you will need it, but *when* you will need it.

Before you can perform a supported backup of your Exchange servers, you must prepare the operating system. Windows Server 2008 comes with the features to back up Exchange, file systems, and other applications. These features are not installed during the normal setup of the server; you must manually install them. You can perform the installation from the command line or from Server Manager. The easiest way to do this is to open an elevated command prompt and type the following command:

```
ServerManagerCmd -i Backup-Features
```

With the introduction of Windows Server 2008 R2, some of the command-line commands have changed. The one that we are concerned with is the `ServerManagerCMD` command. When you run this command from a Windows 2008 R2 server, you will get the following warning:

```
Servermanagercmd.exe is deprecated, and is not guaranteed to be supported ↵
in future releases of Windows. We recommend that you use the Windows ↵
PowerShell cmdlets that are available for Windows Server Manager.
```

The TechNet article "Overview of Server Manager Commands," at http://technet .microsoft.com/en-us/library/cc732757.aspx, provides information on the new commands and shows you how to work with PowerShell cmdlets to manage a server. If you are using Windows Server 2008 R2, you will enable the backup features with the following commands. Be sure to open PowerShell in an elevated session.

```
Import-Module Servermanager
```

```
Add-WindowsFeature Backup-Features
```

You should receive the following when the command has completed:

```
Success Restart Needed Exit Code Feature Result
------- -------------- --------- --------------
True    No             Success   {Windows Server Backup}
```

Your server is now configured to allow you to back up your Exchange data. You can verify that the backup features installed correctly by opening Administrative Tools and looking for Windows Server Backup. If you see this item, then you are ready to go. If you don't, look in the event logs and see if an error in the logs can tell you what happened. Once you have resolved the issues (if there are any), run the installation again.

There is the option to install the Windows Server backup command-line tools. You should not install these tools. Those tools require an older version of PowerShell. This older version is not compatible with Exchange 2010. A command-line tool, WBAdmin.exe, is installed when you install the Windows Server backup features. This tool can be run against Exchange 2010 from the command prompt, cmd.exe.

Using Windows Server Backup to Back Up the Server

To back up the Exchange server from within Windows, you don't just hit a few buttons and walk away. You need to select the correct settings for the backup to work, so that it can be restored and so that it's supported by Microsoft.

Since you have chosen to use the Windows 2008 server to perform the backups for your Exchange environment, we need to look at what the requirements are and what will make your backups and restores successful. Before you start configuring your backups, let's see what is required before and during the backup process.

All backups must be performed on the Windows 2008 or Windows 2008 R2 servers locally. You are not able to back up a remote server. For example, you are not able to install the backup features on a Windows 2008 R2 Domain Controller named DC01 and then backup the Exchange mailbox server named EX-MBX01. In this scenario, the backup must be run from the server EX-MBX01.

Your account must also be delegated rights to either the local Backup Operators group or the local Administrator group. You cannot pick and choose the information that you want to back up. Your only option is to back up an entire volume. All of the Exchange data must be on the same dataset so you can restore the Exchange data.

You can either run a onetime backup or use the Task Scheduler to perform a recurring backup. Your backup strategy will help you determine which is best for your environment. Either way, the same basic information is needed. Remember, to truncate the transaction logs you must perform a full backup.

Most of the Exchange servers in your organization will have multiple databases. One thing to keep in mind is that you cannot restore a single database by using the Windows Server 2008 backups. All databases in the backup set will be restored. Keep this in mind because you will need enough space to perform the restores and you don't want to be fooled into believing that you can piecemeal a restore together.

Exchange provides the option to back up a passive copy of the database(s). However, this option is not available to you if you are using the Windows Server 2008 backup features. Since Windows Server 2008 and Exchange 2010 are "talking" to each other, the system knows if the database is not the active copy. You are only able to perform backups on the active copy of the database.

Backup copies of the Exchange database can be stored either locally on the server or on a separate storage device. You can use drive letters or a UNC path as the destination for the backup. You will have the opportunity to specify the location as you move through the backup wizard.

Performing the Backup

So, we know that you can perform a onetime backup or schedule the backups. We are going to look at everything involved with both options and then perform the backups.

VERIFYING THAT THE BACKUP FEATURES ARE INSTALLED

Make sure that you have installed the backup features on the server. You can run a command from an elevated command prompt to verify. The following command will give you the information. Just because you see the application icon for Windows Server Backup does not mean that you have installed the feature.

```
Servermanagercmd -query
```

After this command runs, you will see a long list of features and roles for the server. The items in gray have not been installed; the items in green with an [X] beside them have been installed. Look for the line shown in Figure 30.1 in the `features` section close to the bottom (see Figure 30.1).

FIGURE 30.1
Command-line verification of backup features

```
[X] Windows Server Backup Features   [Backup-Features]
```

If you are not a fan of the command line, you can follow these steps:

1. Click Start ➤ Administrative Tools ➤ Windows Server Backup (see Figure 30.2).

2. If you have already installed the Windows Server Backup Features, you will see the window shown in Figure 30.3.

   If you have not installed Windows Server Backup Features, you will see the window shown in Figure 30.4.

ONETIME BACKUP

Now that you have verified that the backup features are installed, it is time to perform the onetime backup of the data volume.

1. Click Start ➤ Administrative Tools ➤ Windows Server Backup.

2. In the Actions pane, click Backup Once. The Backup Once wizard appears.

FIGURE 30.2
Choosing Start ➤ Administrative Tools ➤ Windows Server Backup

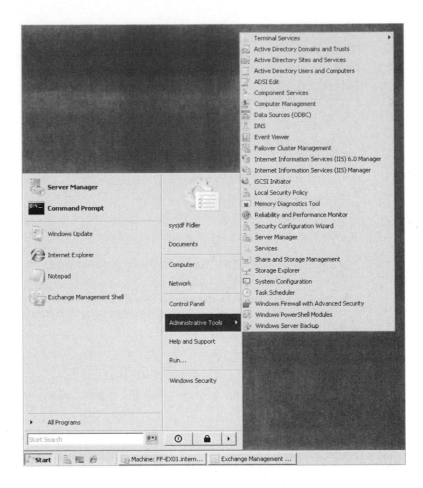

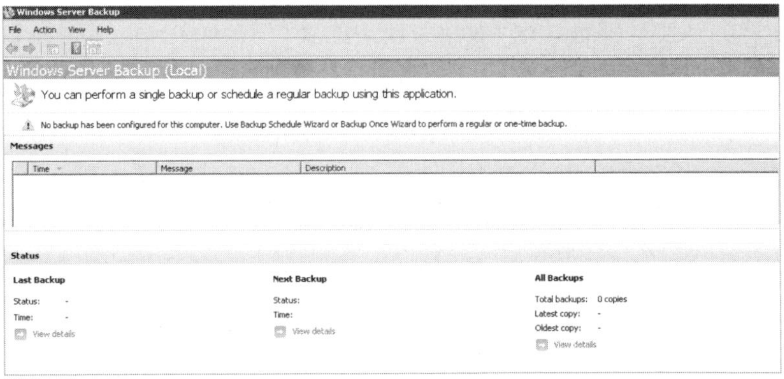

FIGURE 30.3
Windows Server Backup has been installed.

FIGURE 30.4
Windows Server Backup
has not been installed.

FIGURE 30.4
Windows Server Backup
has not been installed.

3. On the Backup Options screen, select Different Options and click Next.

4. On the Select Backup Configuration screen, select Custom and click Next.

   The reason for selecting the Custom option is so that you can select only the volumes that contain the Exchange data. Remember that drives containing the OS components or applications will be included in the backup set. These volumes cannot be excluded.

5. Select the volume or volumes to backup.

6. On the Select Backup Items screen, click Next.

   This screen lets you decide which volumes to back up. Make sure you have selected the correct volumes for the location of the Exchange data.

7. On the Specify Destination screen, type **windows**, and then select the proper location for your backup. For this scenario, we are backing up to a local drive. Click Next.

8. On the Select Backup Destination screen, select the correct location from the Backup Destination drop-down list and click Next.

9. On the Specify Advanced Option screen, select VSS Full Backup and click Next.

   The VSS Full Backup option is the only Microsoft supported option when using the Windows Server 2008 backup features. Don't let this frighten you; you can choose only the Exchange data during the restoration process.

10. At the Confirmation screen, select Backup.

AUTOMATED BACKUPS

If you are going to be using the Windows Server 2008 backup mechanism, you can automate the process. Follow these steps:

1. Click Start ➤ Administrative Tools ➤ Windows Server Backup.

2. In the Actions pane, click Backup Schedule. The Backup Schedule wizard appears.

3. On the Select Backup Configuration screen, select Custom and click Next.

   The reason for selecting the Custom option is so that you can select only the volumes that contain the Exchange data. Remember that drives containing the OS components or applications will be included in the backup set. These volumes cannot be excluded.

4. On the Select Backup Items screen, click Next.

   This screen lets you decide which volumes to back up. Make sure you have selected the correct volumes for the location of the Exchange data.

5. On the Specify Backup Time screen, select Once A Day, specify the time that you want to perform the backup, and click Next.

Make sure you are not selecting a backup time that will occur during the online maintenance.

6. On the Select Backup Destination screen, click Show All Available Disks.

7. Place a check mark in the box beside the drive you are backing up to, and then click OK (see Figure 30.5).

You are now back to the Select Destination Disk screen. Notice that the Next button is unavailable; that's because you must place a check mark in the box beside the volume that you will be using, just as you did in the previous step.

8. Place a check mark in the box, and click Next.

9. You will see a warning dialog reminding you that Windows Server Backup will be formatting the disk. Click Yes after verifying there is no data on the volume you will be using (see Figure 30.6).

10. Click Next on the Label Destination Disk screen.

11. Click Finish on the Confirmation screen.

12. Once the processing has completed, the Summary screen appears; click Close.

FIGURE 30.5
Selecting the backup location

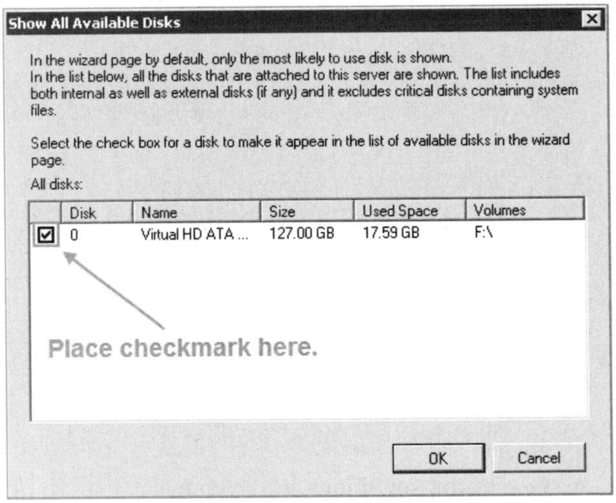

Show All Available Disks

In the wizard page by default, only the most likely to use disk is shown.
In the list below, all the disks that are attached to this server are shown. The list includes both internal as well as external disks (if any) and it excludes critical disks containing system files.

Select the check box for a disk to make it appear in the list of available disks in the wizard page.

All disks:

	Disk	Name	Size	Used Space	Volumes
☑	0	Virtual HD ATA ...	127.00 GB	17.59 GB	F:\

Place checkmark here.

OK   Cancel

FIGURE 30.6
Warning dialog

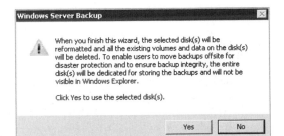

Windows Server Backup

⚠ When you finish this wizard, the selected disk(s) will be reformatted and all the existing volumes and data on the disk(s) will be deleted. To enable users to move backups offsite for disaster protection and to ensure backup integrity, the entire disk(s) will be dedicated for storing the backups and will not be visible in Windows Explorer.

Click Yes to use the selected disk(s).

Yes   No

Your server is now backing up your Exchange data. At this point you are able to use the onetime method or the recurring method. Windows Server Backup will allow you to write to internal or external disks. You can also have a mixture of disks. You may choose to have your daily backups sent to an external storage device, while the onetime backups are backed up to a local disk for quick and easy recovery. Just make sure you have enough space on the destination drive, no matter where you write the backup.

The length of time the backup will take depends on several factors, such as the size of the Exchange databases and transaction logs that are being backed up. Another factor is the location of the data being copied and the location to which it is being written. If you choose to back up to a remote location, you need to think about the network bandwidth and latency from the server and the storage. Different types of storage make a difference as well. If you are using a SAN, your server may have a 4 GB connection to the storage. If you are using an iSCSI device, you may have only a 1 GB connection to the network and then to the storage. No matter what storage you are writing to, consider the type and speed of the drives that are writing the data. As you know, there is a big difference in performance between 15k RPM drives in a SAN compared to 7,200 RPM SATA drives.

Using Windows Server Backup to Recover the Data

Now that you have backed up your Exchange data, let's perform a restore of that data. There are several ways to recover the data for the users and the organization.

Users Can Recover Email

Although the ability has been around for several generations of Exchange, many users don't realize they can recover their own email. The easiest way for users to recover deleted email is to use the Recover Deleted Items option in Outlook. We know this seems simple, but don't let the simplicity fool you. Education of the help desk and in turn the end users will go a long way. Once you train the users to recover their own messages within the allotted time, you will hopefully decrease the number of calls that you get.

Recovering the Database

Just because you backed up the entire volume during the backup sequence does not mean you need to restore the entire volume to recover your Exchange data. You are able to recover only the Exchange application data. At this point, you also have the opportunity to decide where you want the data restored. Do you want it restored to its original location or to an alternate location?

One of the key things to remember is that you cannot pick and choose the database(s) you want to recover. When you use Windows Server Backup to restore the database, all the databases in the backup set will be restored. Think about this before you give the command to restore the backup and overwrite all your data when you only needed a portion of the data.

RECOVERING TO THE ORIGINAL LOCATION

By restoring the data to the same location, you are recovering the data and overwriting the current Exchange data. You need to do this in case of database corruption. Only restore the data to the original location if you truly don't need the data. If you overwrite the data, you will not be able to recover it. When you are restoring to the original location, you can leave the database in a dirty shutdown. The recovery will perform the proper steps to get the database healthy. There are occasions where the database cannot be cleaned up without help. You can either perform more in-depth troubleshooting and maintenance with the `eseutil.exe` command, or you can pick a different backup to restore. You can make that call as you move through your restore.

To restore from a specific volume:

1. Open Windows Server Backup.

2. In the Actions pane on the right, select Recover

3. On the Getting Started screen, select This Server (*ServerName*), and then click Next.

4. On the Select Backup Date screen, select the date from which you want to restore data. If there are multiple backups for that date, select the time of the backup that you want to use. Click Next when you have selected the backup date and time that you want.

5. On the Select Recovery screen, type **dialog**, select Applications, and then click Next.

6. On the Select Application screen, make sure Exchange is highlighted and click Next.

   By default, if you are recovering the last backup, Exchange will replay the log files for the backup. You must tell the backup application if you do not want to perform the log replay.

7. On the Specify Recovery Options screen, the option Recover To Original Location should be selected; if not, select it and click Next.

8. The Confirmation screen gives you a recap of the recovery you are getting ready to perform. Click Recover.

9. Once the recovery is complete, click Close.

The recovery application will now start performing the recovery. You will be able to see the status throughout the recovery. If you told the backup application you did not want to perform the log replay, you can test the recovery by sending an email to an account on the system. Once you do, perform a backup and then make a change to the data in the account. When you have restored the Exchange database and logs, log into the account and look at the contents. You should be see the information that was there before the backup. If there is any discrepancy, check the event log for any errors and then run the complete test again. If you kept the default settings and let the recovery play the transaction logs, your Exchange server will be restored and up-to-date.

RECOVERING TO AN ALTERNATE LOCATION

When you recover to an alternate location, you can extract data from the restored data. Before you can perform any work on the restored database, you need to put it in a clean state. You will use the `eseutil.exe` command to accomplish this task.

1. Open Windows Server Backup.

2. In the Actions pane on the right, select Recover.

3. On the Getting Started screen, select This Server (*ServerName*), and then click Next.

4. On the Select Backup Date screen, select the date from which you want to restore data. If there are multiple backups for that date, select the time of the backup that you want to use. Click Next.

5. On the Select Recovery screen, type **dialog**, select Applications, and then click Next.

6. On the Select Application screen, make sure Exchange is highlighted and click Next.

By default, if you are recovering the last backup, Exchange will replay the log files for the backup. You must tell the backup application if you do not want to perform the log replay.

7. On the Specify Recovery Options screen, select the option Recover To Another Location. Click Browse and browse to the location where you want to place the recovered files; click Next.

8. The Confirmation screen gives you a recap of the recovery you are about to perform. Click Recover.

9. Once the recovery is complete, click Close.

10. Open a command prompt and change to the location of the restore.

11. Run the `eseutil.exe` command against the database with the base name of the database.

The base name is the first three characters of the log files for the restored database. If your log file is named E0500000004.log, your base name will be E05. Your command will look like this: `Eseutil /r BaseName /L<path to logs>`. You may receive the following error message:

```
Operation terminated with error -1216 (JET_errAttachedDatabaseMismatch. ↵
An outstanding database attachment has been detected at the start or end ↵
of recovery, but database is missing or does not match attachment info) ↵
after xx seconds.
```

If you receive this message, run the command with the /i switch so that it will ignore any inconsistencies in the database:

```
Eseutil.exe /r E05 /i
```

Now your database should be in a consistent state. You can redirect the original database and use the restored database. Run the `Move-DatabasePath` cmdlet from the Exchange Management Shell. You will also and use the `ConfigurationOnly` parameter. Your command should look like this:

```
Move-DatabasePath -EdbFilePath C:\RestoredExchange\DB05.edb ↵
-LogFolderPath C:\RestoredExchange -ConfigurationOnly
```

Your Exchange database is not ready yet because you must mount the database. You can mount the database Exchange Management Shell via EMS or EMC.

USING BACKUPS FOR TESTING

You can test your backup by performing a recovery of the data to an alternate location. You use real Exchange data for testing. You may be testing mailbox recovery or single item recovery scenarios.

Restoring to an alternate location gives you a perfect situation to test the recovery to verify that all the data is accessible. A successful backup does not mean that the successful recovery will give you good, usable data. By restoring the database(s) to an alternate location, you can run through a number of recovery options to verify that the data is there and that your staff is well equipped to handle restores when the pressure is on. By running through the recovery process when times are good, you and your staff will become familiar with the recovery steps and options needed to restore any of the server roles, configuration, and data. This will help you notice something that may be out of the ordinary if you are performing the emergency restoration.

DELETED MAILBOX RETENTION

A mailbox becomes disconnected when it is no longer associated with an account in Active Directory. By default, all of the disconnected mailboxes are kept for 30 days before they are purged from the system. During this time the disconnected mailbox can be reconnected to a valid Active Directory account by using the Connect-Mailbox cmdlet or the Connect Mailbox wizard from the EMC. This allows you to clean up from an accidental user deletion. Since the disconnected mailbox is not associated with any Active Directory account, you must have a way to identify the mailbox. There are three ways to identify the mailbox:

◆ Display name of the mailbox

◆ Legacy Distinguished Name (LegacyDN)

◆ Globally Unique Identifier (GUID)

The following command shows you the list of disconnected mailboxes. You can see that we have also included a date command. This should help narrow your search for the specific mailbox.

```
Get-MailboxStatistics -Server CONTOSO-EX01 | where ↵
{$_.DisconnectDate -ne $null} | fl DisplayName, MailboxGUID, LegacyDN, ↵
DisconnectDate
```

Once you have the mailbox identifier, you can reconnect the mailbox to an account with the following command:

```
Connect-Mailbox MailboxID -Database DatabaseName -User UserToConnectTo ↵
-Alias MailboxAlias
```

At any point in time, you have the ability to permanently delete the disconnected mailbox. The Remove-Mailbox cmdlet from the EMS will delete the mailbox. You must set the Permanent parameter to $True when you use this command.

By using the StoreMailboxIdentity parameter with the Remove-Mailbox cmdlet, you can permanently delete the data within the mailbox database of a disconnected mailbox. Use the Get-MailboxStatistics cmdlet with the StoreMailboxIdentity parameter to determine the values you need to supply for this cmdlet.

You can also adjust the number of days that you must keep the mailboxes. This setting will affect all the mailboxes in the database. However, it will only affect the database that is specified in the cmdlet. To change the retention time from 30 to 60 days, you would run a command like this:

```
Set-MailboxDatabase DB05 -MailboxRetention 60.00:00:00
```

You can also configure this setting using the EMC:

1. Browse to the Organization Configuration ➢ Mailbox node in the Console tree.

2. Click the Database Management tab to view the databases in the organization.

3. Select the database you want to adjust and click Properties in the Actions pane.

4. In the Database Properties dialog, select the Limits tab.

5. In the Keep Deleted Mailboxes For (Days) field, enter the number of days that you want to keep deleted mailboxes.

6. Click OK to save the changes and close the Properties dialog.

Recovery Database

You are probably familiar with the Recovery Storage Group feature from earlier versions of Exchange. Exchange 2010 has changed that as well. We know have a Recovery Database (RDB). The basic concept is the same in that you can mount a database and extract data from it. The RDB allows you mount a restored database and extract mailbox data from it via the `Restore-mailbox` cmdlet. After the data has been removed, it can be exported or merged into an existing mailbox.

You are able to restore an existing database to a recovery database in one of two ways. If you already have a recovery database, Exchange can dismount the active database, restore it on the recovery database and log files, and then mount the database. You can also restore the database to an alternate location. Once Exchange has brought the database up to date, you can configure the recovery database to point to the recovered database.

Either method allows you to mount the database and perform a recovery and extraction of the target data. You can only use databases from Exchange 2010, not from previous versions of Exchange. If you need to extract data from previous versions of Exchange, you will have to use the Recovery Storage Group function on an Exchange 2007 server. The target mailbox you will be using must be located in the same Active Directory forest as the database that will be mounted in the recovery database.

When you use the recovery database, there is no preservation of the folder access control lists. Due to the nature of the recovery database, there is no need to preserve any access control list information.

MAILBOX AND RECOVERY DATABASE DIFFERENCES

The recovery database is not the same as the standard mailbox database; here are the differences:

◆ Recovery databases are created in the EMS.

◆ Mail cannot be sent or received from the recovery database.

◆ The recovery database cannot be used to insert information into the Exchange environment.

◆ No client access is available to the recovery database through any protocols.

◆ No systems or mailbox policy settings are applied.

◆ A single recovery database can be mounted at a time and does not count against the 100-database limit.

◆ You cannot use the recovery database to recovery Pubic Folder data.

◆ You cannot perform a backup against the recovery database.

◆ Any mailboxes that are in the recovery database are not connected to the original mailboxes in any way.

There are several situations where a recovery database would be the proper selection for the restore:

◆ Dial Tone recovery (same server)

◆ Dial Tone recovery (alternate server)

◆ Mailbox recovery

◆ Individual item recovery

There are instances when a recovery database should not be used. You already know that you cannot use the recovery database to recover the Public Folder database. If you have to rebuild your Active Directory topology, thus restoring multiple Exchange databases, or you need to restore the entire server, you would not choose to use a recovery database.

Recovering Single Messages

One recovery scenario that Exchange has never been able to handle easily is the recovery of a single message once the user has deleted it. Third-party companies have developed software to help organizations with this problem. Exchange 2010 now provides this ability out of the box. You no longer have to purchase a third-party application to perform this task.

Here is a breakdown of what happens to an email message:

1. The email is delivered to the user's Inbox.

2. The user deletes the email.

3. The email is moved from the Deleted Items folder to Dumpster 2.0 automatically.

4. The email is purged by the user.

5. The email is removed from Exchange in 14 days (see Figure 30.7).

As you can see, things have changed from the previous versions of Exchange. By moving the email messages to Dumpster 2.0, you now have an added safety feature to help your organization and users. In previous versions of Exchange, once a user removed the message from the Deleted Items Recovery or the age of the message has surpassed the Deleted Items limit, it was gone forever.

New steps have been implemented in Exchange to handle Dumpster 2.0. When a user removes an email item using the Recover Deleted Items tool, it is moved to a Purges folder that lives in the dumpster. This new feature is available only if single item recovery has been enabled. Neither the Purges folder nor the messages within the folder can be seen by the end user. Any administrators that have been delegated the right to perform Discovery Searches can search the Purges folder and perform a recovery of the email items for the end users. By doing this, your standard administration staff can help the end users without needing the permission

FIGURE 30.7
Dumpster 2.0

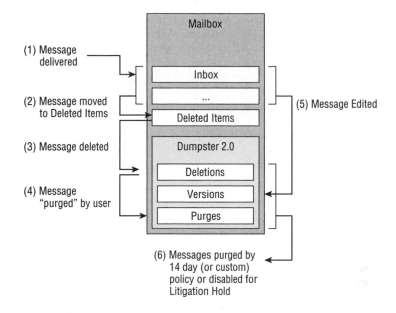

to restore and mount the user's database. Since the database does not need to be restored, the process is much easier.

The only individuals who can perform the Discovery Searches are those who have been granted the Discovery Management RBAC role.

All items in the Recoverable Items folder will be indexed and can be searched by using the discovery cmdlets. The Recoverable Items folder is located in the NON_IPM_Subtree of the user's mailbox. There are three folders in the Recoverable Items folder:

Deletions All soft deleted items from the Deleted Items folder within the mailbox end up here. The user can see these items when they access the Recover Deleted Items feature in Outlook or OWA.

Versions The original item and any modifications of the item are placed here, when either a litigation hold or single item recovery is enabled. This folder is not visible to the end user.

Purges All hard-deleted items end up here, when either legal hold or single item recovery is enabled. This folder is not visible to the end user.

Recoverable items are not counted against the user's quota. These messages are instead counted against the recoverable items size limits. There is a 20 GB soft limit for the recoverable items. At the 20 GB point, administrators are notified of the size by an event in the event log and by an Operations Manager alert if Operations Manager is in the environment. The alert fires as soon as the 20 GB limit is reached and once a day until it has been addressed. There is a hard limit of 30 GB on the recoverable items. You can run two EMS commands to set the warning level and the quota sizes:

```
Set-Mailbox -Identity MailboxName -RecoverableItemsWarningQuota 12GB

Set-Mailbox -Identity MailboxName -RecoverableItemsQuota 15GB
```

Earlier, we said email is removed from Exchange at the 14-day mark. This is the default setting for Exchange. If you have installed Exchange 2010 and have not made any changes, then your system is set up for the 14 days. You can change the amount of time that the messages will stay in the dumpster before they are removed. There are good and bad points to making this change. If you make the change to keep the messages for 30 days, you can recover a user's mail for the extra 16 days time; that is the good part. The not-so-good part is that now you have increased your storage requirements. Depending on the size of your organization and the amount of email that is sent and received, this may not be a huge problem. But if you have a large organization and your users send and receive a lot of email, this may end up being a large problem. Each organization is different — just be sure that before you make a change to the default settings you fully understand the impact on the environment.

Another thing to consider is the number of times that you have to perform these single item restores of messages that are older than the default settings. If you find your organization is not performing this type of restore often or that the data is within the 14 days, then there is no reason to change the defaults. This information will help you decide if changing the defaults is the right way to go. If you are performing the restores past the 14 days but only a few times a year, what is the impact? Changing the defaults would "fix" the problem but at what cost? Would it have been just as easy to perform a restore of the database for those few cases? That is something you will need to research. Table 30.2 shows the breakout for the single item recovery features. It will help you see what the settings will provide you in the end.

TABLE 30.2:   Single Item Recovery Features

FEATURE STATE	SOFT DELETED ITEMS KEPT IN DUMPSTER	MODIFIED (VERSIONS) AND STORE HARD DELETED ITEMS KEPT IN DUMPSTER	USER CAN PURGE ITEMS FROM DUMPSTER	MRM AUTOMATICALLY PURGES ITEMS FROM DUMPSTER
Item recovery disabled	Yes	No	Yes	Yes, 14 days by default and 120 days for calendar items
Single-item recovery enabled	Yes	Yes	No	Yes, 14 days by default and 120 days for calendar items
Litigation hold enabled	Yes	Yes	No	No

CONFIGURING FOR SINGLE-ITEM RECOVERY

Since we know we can change the default number of days from 14 to a new number, let's look at how we need to do that. For this example, we will change the limit to 30 days. A simple command from the EMS enables Single Item Recover for a specific mailbox.

ENABLING SINGLE ITEM RECOVERY

The following command will enable Single Item Recovery on a specific user's mailbox:

```
Set-Mailbox MailboxName -SingleItemRecoveryEnabled $True
```

Once you have enabled Single Item Recovery you must specify the amount of time that the items will be recoverable:

```
Set-Mailbox MailboxName -RetainDeletedItemsFor NumberofDays
```

You can combine both of these commands into a single command. To enable all the mailboxes on the same database and set the number of days to 30, type the following command:

```
Get-Mailbox -Database DatabaseName | Set-Mailbox ↵
-SingleItemRecoveryEnabled $True -RetainDeletedItemsFor 30
```

You can also set all mailboxes on a single server by changing the -Database switch to the -Server switch, as in the following command. You must enable single item recovery first.

```
Get-Mailbox -Server ServerName | Set-Mailbox ↵
-SingleItemRecoveryEnabled $True -RetainDeletedItemsFor 30
```

You have enabled the mailboxes for single item recovery; now perform the recovery. You will use the Discovery Search tool to locate the message that needs to be recovered. Once you have located the message, you will export it from the Discovery Search mailbox into the user's mailbox.

You must know what item you are looking for in the Discovery Search mailbox. You can use date ranges or keywords. First, you need to create the Discovery Search.

1. Open a web browser and navigate to the ECP URL on one of your Client Access servers. For example, the ECP URL would be https://mail.contoso.com/ecp.

2. If you get a certificate error, you may still be using a nontrusted self-signed certificate. Click the option Continue To This Website.

3. Log into the web interface with an account that has access to create and execute Discovery Searches.

4. Select My Organization in the drop-down list in the upper left; if you don't see this drop-down list, you don't have permissions to perform Discovery Searches.

5. Select Reporting.

6. Select the Mailbox Searches tab.

7. Click the New button in the Multi-Mailbox Search tool.

   The New Mailbox Search dialog will open.

8. In the New Mailbox Search dialog, enter the search criteria.

9. Click the Search Name And Storage Location category. In the Search Name field, enter a name for this search. Other individuals with search permissions will be able to view your search, so make sure that you use a descriptive name.

10. In the field Select A Mailbox In Which To Store The Search Results, click the Browse button and choose the Discovery mailbox. Any search results in this mailbox will be deleted.

    Searches may take a long time to complete. If you select the Send Me An E-mail box, you will receive an email notification when the search is complete.

11. When you are finished filling out the search options, click the Save button.

Now you can open the Discovery Search mailbox and view the results for the search. Once you have located the message(s), you can create a directory in which to place these items. All you need to do is drag the messages from the Recoverable Items folder to the folder you just created.

The Discovery Search mailbox is a resource mailbox. As such, it does not have an owner. You will only be able to view the Discovery Search mailbox if you have permission to do so. When you ran the discovery search, all the email that fit the criteria was copied to this mailbox. To view the results of the search, click the Open link in the properties pane on the right. The Discovery Search mailbox will open via OWA and you will see the results. The results will be under a folder with the same name as the search you created. If you searched multiple mailboxes, you will see as separate folders each mailbox containing messages that meet the criteria. You will notice the Primary Mailbox folder and the Recoverable Items folder. The Primary Mailbox folder contains the undeleted mail items. The Recoverable Items contains the mail items that the user had deleted and that are still in the retention window.

Now you need to run the `Export-Mailbox` cmdlet from EMS. This command will be run against the Discovery Search mailbox. You will only be able to run the `Export-Mailbox` cmdlet on a computer that has the 64-bit version of Outlook 2010 and the Exchange Management Tools installed. The user running the command should be assigned the Discovery Management RBAC role. The following command will export the mail items from the Recovered Mail folder in the Discovery Search mailbox to the Recovered Mail folder inside John's mailbox:

```
Export-Mailbox "Discovery Search Mailbox" -IncludeFolders ↵
"John's Recovered Mail" -TargetMailbox abe -TargetFolder "Recovered Mail"
```

John's mail items have been recovered to the Recovered Mail directory in his active Exchange mailbox. At this point he is able to do anything that he needs to do with these mail items.

Recovering the Entire Exchange Server

There will be times (hopefully not many) that you will need to restore an entire server. We say not many because you should have engineered a good Exchange solution that includes proactive monitoring, good supporting resources for the services (people), and a well-thought-out and tested disaster recovery plan. These pieces will not ensure that you will never need to recover any of your Exchange servers, but it does place you in a better position to deal with such a situation.

Recovering an Exchange server is a relatively straightforward task. Since almost all the configuration settings for the Exchange servers are kept in Active Directory, you will use the `setup /m:recoverServer` command. This method can be used for all Exchange 2010 server roles except the Edge Transport server role. You also cannot use this command for a Mailbox server that was part of a DAG.

There are prerequisites to recovering an Exchange server this way:

♦ The server on which recovery is being performed must be running the same operating system as the lost server. You cannot recover an Exchange 2010 server that was running Windows Server 2008 on a server running Windows Server 2008 R2, or vice versa.

♦ The server on which recovery is being performed should have the same performance characteristics and hardware configuration as the lost server.

◆ The following procedure can be run on an Exchange 2010 server that has the Client Access, Hub Transport, Mailbox, and/or Unified Messaging role installed. You cannot recover an Edge Transport server using `setup /m:RecoverServer`.

Client Access, Hub Transport, and Unified Messaging Roles

We know that you have deployed multiple Client Access and Hub Transport servers in your organization. So losing one of the servers should not result in a service outage to the user community. Because of the multiple Client Access Servers and the proper load balancers you have in place, all of your users will still be able to access their email using any method they choose: OWA, mobile, or Outlook Anywhere. You will also be able to send and receive email since you have multiple Hub Transport servers. In most cases, it is just as quick to reinstall the OS and use the `setup /m:RecoverServer` command for these roles. Don't forget that your servers need to be at the same code level for the OS before you run this command. You must have the correct service pack and hotfixes or updates that were in use on the server before proceeding. After Exchange has been installed via the `setup /m:RecoverServer` command, update Exchange to the latest service pack to include any hotfixes or updates that have been approved by your organization.

Since you have the ability to configure OWA pages on your Client Access Servers, be sure to back up any customizations. When you perform a restore with the `/m:RecoverServer` switch, the server will only have the configuration pieces that are stored in Active Directory. Make sure that you have a method for backing up your certificates and any other IIS customizations that you have performed.

Before you can begin to recover the Exchange server, make sure that you have the correct permissions. To successfully perform the restore, you will need the Server Management permission. Here are the steps for performing the recovery:

1. Reset the computer account for the lost server through Active Directory Users and Computers.

2. Reinstall the operating system. The operating system and NetBIOS name must be the same as for the server you are replacing. If the name is not the same, the recovery will fail.

3. Join the server to the same domain as the lost server.

4. Install the necessary prerequisites and operating system component.

5. Log on to the server being recovered and open a command prompt.

6. Navigate to the Exchange 2010 installation files and run the following command:

```
setup /m:RecoverServer
```

The `/m:RecoverServer` parameter is not new and operates under the same assumptions as previous versions of Exchange. The replacement server will be running the same OS as the server that you are recovering. The replacement server should have the same performance specifics as the server you are recovering. The NetBIOS name and the IP address must be the same as well.

When you run a setup function with the `/m:RecoverServer` parameter, the setup program will ask Active Directory for the relevant configuration information. This information will be pulled from Active Directory and used during the reinstallation of the server.

In Exchange 2007 when you lost your Hub Transport server, you lost any messages that were still in the queue, including redelivery. This has changed in Exchange 2010. All Hub Transport servers have a new feature called shadow redundancy. This provides end-to-end redundancy for messages.

You can also use the `Export-TransportRuleCollection` cmdlet to export the transport rules from the Hub Transport server. This data can be used to help document your environment in case you need to rebuild this information from scratch in a green-field scenario. The `Export-TransportRuleCollection` cmdlet will be covered next.

EDGE TRANSPORT SERVER

Obviously Edge Transport servers cannot pull configuration information from Active Directory. But there are two options for recovering your Edge Transport server. The first option is to use the Edge Transport clone method. When you clone the Edge Transport server, the information is exported from the "good" server to an XML file to be imported on the new Edge Transport server. The certificate information is not cloned in the process; only the settings are cloned. The following information is captured in the cloning process.

- `ReceiveProtocolLogPath`.

- `SendProtocolLogPath`.

- `MessageTrackingLogPath`.

- `PickupDirectoryPath`.

- `RoutingTableLogPath`.

- Transport agent-related information that includes the status and priority settings of each transport agent.

- All send connector–related information. If any send connectors are configured to use credentials, the password is written to the intermediate XML file as an encrypted string. You can use the `-key` parameter with the `ImportEdgeConfig.ps1` and `ExportEdgeConfig.ps1` scripts to specify the 32-byte string to use for password encryption and decryption. If you do not use the `-key` parameter, a default encryption key is used.

- Receive connector–related information. To modify the local network binding and port properties, you must modify the configuration information in the answer file that is created in the validate configuration step.

- Accepted domain configuration.

- Remote domain configuration.

- Anti-spam features configuration settings. The following information is imported:

    - IP Allow list information. Only the IP Allow list entries that were manually configured by the administrator are exported.

    - IP Block list information.

    - Content filter configuration.

    - Recipient filter configuration.

    - Address rewrite entries.

    - Attachment filter entries.

The second method for recovering the Edge Transport servers is to back up the transport rules that are currently on another server. You will want to use this method when you only need the rule set and not the full configuration from the other Edge Transport servers. Use the `Export-TransportRuleCollection` and `Import-TransportRuleCollection` cmdlets for this. You must export the rules set to a variable and then use the `Set-Content` cmdlet to write the rule set to an XML file. The following shows the command in use. This can easily be put into a PowerShell script and run against all the Edge or Hub Transport servers. This command sets the `$file` variable and then uses the `Set-Content` cmdlet to write the data to the XML file `C:\MyDocs\Rules.xml`:

```
$file = Export-TransportRuleCollection Set-Content -Path "C:\Rules.xml" ↵
-Value $file.FileData -Encoding Byte
```

When you look at the XML file, you will see something similar to Figure 30.8. The information in the figure is from a server that has a single transport rule. The rule is named Test Rule 1 and will append the text "This is the disclaimer text." to all messages originating from internal users.

FIGURE 30.8
Transport rules XML

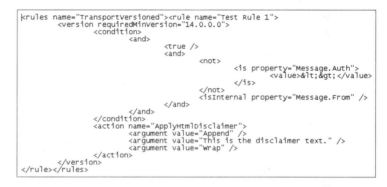

```
<rules name="Transportversioned"><rule name="Test Rule 1">
        <version requiredMinVersion="14.0.0.0">
            <condition>
                <and>
                    <true />
                    <and>
                        <not>
                            <is property="Message.Auth">
                                <value>&lt;&gt;</value>
                            </is>
                        </not>
                        <isInternal property="Message.From" />
                    </and>
                </and>
            </condition>
            <action name="ApplyHtmlDisclaimer">
                <argument value="Append" />
                <argument value="This is the disclaimer text." />
                <argument value="Wrap" />
            </action>
        </version>
</rule></rules>
```

When you want to import the transport rules, use the `Import-TransportRuleCollection` cmdlet. It will read the information from the specified XML file and input the information into Exchange. They will allow you to import any transport rules that you have stored in the `rules.xml` file. If you have not been keeping your XML data up-to-date after changes, then your import may be stale data. The commands will look like the following.

```
[Byte[]]$Data = Get-Content -Path ↵ "C:\Rules.xml" -Encoding Byte ↵
-ReadCount 0 Import-TransportRuleCollection -FileData $Data
```

Now when you look at the transport rules through the EMC or EMS, you should see the correct rules. If you have the EMC open to the transport rules already, you may need to refresh the screen to view the updates.

The Bottom Line

Back up Exchange.   Performing backups is the somewhat easy part of the equation. The more difficult part is defining the requirements for the backup.

Master It   Document the goals for your backup solution.

Prepare to recover the Exchange server. Before you are able to perform any backups from Windows Server 2008, you must install the backup features.

Master It What do you need to do to install the backup features on Windows 2008?

Use Windows Server Backup to back up the server. There is always a need to back up your server(s). Since you have the requirements, you need to perform the backup.

Master It Perform a recurring backup utilizing the Windows Server 2008 backup features.

Use Windows Server Backup to recover the data. You may need to perform a restore of your Exchange data for several reasons. One of the reasons is that you need to give a user email that had been deleted but that is still recoverable.

Master It Perform a single item restore for a user.

Recover the entire Exchange server. There may be occasions that you need to reinstall the entire Exchange server. You have the ability to perform a reinstallation to any of the roles.

Master It How do you recover the Client Access Server?

Appendix

The Bottom Line

Each of The Bottom Line sections in the chapters suggest exercises to deepen skills and understanding. Sometimes there is only one possible solution, but often you are encouraged to use your skills and creativity to create something that builds on what you know and lets you explore one of many possible solutions.

Chapter 1: Introducing Exchange Server 2010

Understand new high-availability options. Exchange Server now provides replication technology that keeps databases synchronized between an active copy of the database and one or more passive copies. In the event of failure of the active database, one of the passive copies can be brought online. Storage groups have been eliminated and now each Exchange database has its own set of transaction logs.

An Exchange Mailbox server can belong to a database availability group (DAG). Exchange databases can be synchronized to one or more members of a DAG. Failovers between servers can now be handled at the database layer rather than a single database failure having to cause an entire cluster node to fail over.

Master It You have been asked to provide a high-availability solution for your organization's 1,000 mailboxes. Describe the Exchange Server 2010 feature that will allow you to provide high availability for your Exchange 2010 mailboxes.

Solution The Exchange Server 2010 feature DAG allows you to include two or more Exchange 2010 mailbox servers in a group. The databases on those servers can be replicated to one or more of the DAG members. At any given time, the database is "active" on one of the members of the DAG and "passive" on the other members. In the event of a failure on the active copy of the DAG, the database will automatically be failed over to a passive copy.

Understand new recipient management features. The underlying management components for all Exchange server and mail recipient administration have been completely rewritten from scratch. All management tools are built on top of the Windows PowerShell and are included in the EMS. Exchange administration can now be performed from either a graphical user interface (the EMC) or the EMS. The EMS often includes functions that are not available from the management interface.

Master It You support 8,000 mailboxes in your Exchange Server 2010 organization. You have been asked to perform a management task on mailbox-enabled users in your organization. This task consists of setting the Outlook Web App policy to a new policy name. What is the quickest way to assign all of your users the new policy?

Solution   Use the EMS to perform the bulk recipient management tasks.

Recognize Exchange architecture changes.   Significant changes were made to the Exchange Server 2010 architecture to improve the scalability, security, and stability. This includes providing only an x64 edition of Exchange Server 2010. Requiring an x64-based operating system and hardware dramatically improves the scalability and performance of Exchange Server 2010. The x64 architecture means that Exchange Server 2010 can now access more than 3 GB of physical memory. Microsoft has tested server configurations with up to 64 GB of physical memory. The additional physical memory means that data can be cached and written to disk more efficiently. This greatly improves the Exchange Server 2010 disk I/O profile over previous versions.

Unlike Exchange Server 2003 and earlier where a server's roles and functions were configured after installation, Exchange Server roles allow the Exchange administrator to define the functions of the server during installation.

Master It   You are planning your Exchange Server 2010 infrastructure to provide basic messaging functionality (email, shared calendars, and Windows Mobile phones). Which Exchange Server roles will you need to deploy?

Solution   The Mailbox, Client Access, and Hub Transport server roles are required for basic messaging functionality.

Chapter 2: Introduction to Email Administration

Understand email fundamentals.   To gain the best advantage from Exchange Server 2010, you should have a good grounding in general email applications and principles.

Master It   What two application models have email programs traditionally used? Which one does Exchange Server use? Can you name an example of the other model?

Solution   The two models are *shared files*, in which a central shared file system is used to store messages and each client has access to those files; and *client/server*, where the central email server and clients communicate using a distinct protocol. The client/server model allows the system to provide stronger safeguards and permissions, better performance, and greater integrity for the data. Exchange Server has always used a client/server model. Its predecessor, Microsoft Mail, was a shared file system.

List email administration duties.   Installing an Exchange Server system is just the first part of the job. Once it's in place, it needs to be maintained. Be familiar with the various duties and concerns that will be involved with the care and feeding of Exchange.

Master It   What are the various types of duties that a typical Exchange administrator will expect to perform?

Solution   Recipient management tasks, basic monitoring tasks, daily troubleshooting tasks, security-related tasks, client administration tasks, and application integration tasks.

Explain Exchange Server history.   Exchange Server 2010 is the seventh and latest version of Exchange, starting from Exchange 4.0 in 1996. Although it introduces some new concepts and makes some radical changes from previous versions, several core concepts have stayed the same.

Master It   The Extensible Storage Engine (ESE) is the heart of Exchange mailbox storage. Describe its basic architecture. Describe one past feature of the ESE that is no longer present in Exchange Server 2010.

Solution   The ESE has two main parts: the *mailbox database* and the *transaction logs*. The mailbox database file stores the permanent copies of user mailboxes. The transaction log files capture every transaction written to the database, and are later replayed back into the mailbox database. Previous versions of Exchange grouped mailbox databases by storage groups; Exchange 2010 removes storage groups and provides a separate set of transaction logs for each mailbox database.

Chapter 3: Standards and Protocols

Understand the components of an email system.   As we begin to take a deeper look at the Exchange 2010 system, we examine how the different roles and components work together. To understand these pieces, it is necessary to understand the purpose each one fulfills.

Master It   How many components are in an email system? What are they called and how could they be described in an analogy to the traditional postal system?

Solution   The mail user agent is roughly the equivalent of your local mailbox; the mail retrieval agent (MRA) is typically a set of additional routines in the MUA; the mail transport agent (MTA) corresponds to the network of post offices in various cities; the mail submission agent (MSA) is a specialized form of MTA adapted to accept mail submissions from clients; and the mail delivery agent (MDA) is the equivalent of a local neighborhood post office or corporate mail room.

Identify the three major components of Active Directory.   Exchange depends heavily on the Windows Active Directory service. Many Exchange design, deployment, and administrative tasks depend on a mastery of Active Directory concepts and technologies.

Master It   There are three major components and technologies that make up Active Directory. What are they, and what purpose do they serve?

Solution   The Domain Name Service (DNS) provides a hostname-to-IP address lookup service, allowing each computer to find critical services in the Active Directory forest. The Lightweight Directory Access Protocol (LDAP) component provides a standard, hierarchical directory service capable of storing and indexing extensive amounts of data on services, users, computers, and other applications and objects. The Kerberos service provides a secure way for computers and services to authenticate each other without exposing credentials to attack or unauthorized release.

Understand common protocols and standards used by Microsoft Exchange.   Exchange doesn't just depend on Microsoft standards and technologies. There's a whole range of protocols and standards that are used by multiple applications, and Exchange Server 2010 provides support for them in order to allow interoperability.

Master It What are the major standard protocols used by Exchange to interact with other mail servers and clients, and what are they commonly used for?

Solution The Simple Mail Transfer Protocol (SMTP), the common protocol used by Internet message transports to exchange messages back and forth; the Messaging Application Programming Interface (MAPI), which is the primary protocol used between Exchange Server and Outlook to offer the full range of functionality including mail, contacts, calendaring, and more; POP3 and IMAP, two mailbox access protocols with limited functionality compared to MAPI and used by generic email systems and clients; and SSL and TLS, encryption protocols based on X.509 digital certificates that are used to protect other transport protocols.

Chapter 4: Understanding Availability, Recovery, and Compliance

Distinguish between availability, backup and recovery, and disaster recovery. When it comes to keeping your Exchange 2010 deployment healthy, you've got a lot of options provided out of the box. Knowing which problems they solve is critical to deploying them correctly.

Master It You have been asked to select a backup type that will back up all data once per week but on a daily basis will ensure that the server does not run out of transaction log disk space.

Solution Create a backup schedule that performs a full backup once per week and an incremental backup once per week.

Determine the best option for your disaster recovery. When creating your disaster recovery plans for Exchange 2010, you have a variety of options to choose from. Exchange 2010 includes an improved ability to integrate with external systems that will widen your recovery possibilities.

Master It What are the different types of disaster recovery?

Solution The two main types of disaster recovery are on-premise and off-premise. On-premise solutions include the use of out-of-the-box functionality such as database availability groups, appliances, remote managed services, or some combination. Off-premise solutions are supplied by hosted service providers, who can offer other types of services.

Distinguish between the different types of availability meant by the term *high availability*. The term high availability means different things to different people. When you design and deploy your Exchange 2010 solution, you need to be confident that everyone is designing for the same goals.

Master It What types of availability are there?

Solution Service availability is the overall availability of the Exchange service as a whole, rather than focusing on specific pieces of the Exchange organization. This includes needing to consider the availability of services that Exchange depends on but may be outside the control of your Exchange team.

Network availability is the ability to ensure that incoming client or server connections can still be processed even if an Exchange server or component is down.

Data availability is ensuring that there are multiple copies of Exchange mailbox data that can be accessed, automatically if possible, by the Exchange system.

Storage availability concerns the design of the storage system to protect against individual disk failures and other single points of failure.

Implement the four pillars of compliance and governance activities.   Ensuring that your Exchange 2010 organization meets your regular operational needs means thinking about the topics of compliance and governance within your organization.

Master It   What are the four pillars of compliance and governance as applied to a messaging system?

Solution   Discovery is the ability to quickly and efficiently search your messaging system for specific message data. This is often critical for auditing or legal reasons.

Compliance is the ability to define, manage, and monitor how the policies and regulations that govern your organization are applied to your messaging system.

Archival is the protection of key data that has entered the messaging system, often for a period of several years. Archival is useful for several purposes.

Retention is the ability to define and distinguish between messaging data that is critical to keep and messaging data that can be safely removed from the system.

Chapter 5: Message Security and Hygiene

Secure messages through the transport protocols.   Some of the easiest and most effective email security measures you can take involve keeping the various protocols secure. Rather than use a separate security mechanism for each protocol, Exchange uses two versatile, standards-based security protocols that can protect virtually all client-to-server and server-to-server traffic from hop to hop.

Master It   What is the major difference between SSL and TLS?

What type of certificate does Exchange use to secure transport protocols out of the box?

Which Exchange protocol is not secured by SSL or TLS?

Solution   SSL and TLS are in essence the same protocol, with some minor differences. The biggest difference is that TLS can be used on a nonsecured protocol connection to negotiate the security layer in-band with the protected protocol and bootstrap the connection to a secure status. As a result, TLS allows both secure and nonsecure traffic over the same port; SSL requires separate ports for secure and nonsecure traffic.

Out of the box, each Exchange 2010 server issues a self-signed X.509v3 certificate for use with SSL and TLS. These certificates are typically only trusted by other Exchange 2010 and 2007 servers, so are of limited use except for testing.

Exchange uses either SSL or TLS to secure every client-to-server or server-to-server protocol except for MAPI-RPC when run over TCP; MAPI includes its own encryption mechanisms. However, if MAPI is tunneled through Outlook Anywhere, the HTTP tunnel typically uses SSL.

Secure messages from end to end. While transport security has become more ubiquitous and suffices for many organizations, there are times when messages must be secured every step of the way, from the sender's client to the recipient's client — no intermediate systems or entities must be able to read or open the message, even if they are trusted entities used to transport the message.

Master It What options does Exchange 2010 provide for end-to-end message security?

Why don't these options include the common PGP suite?

Solution The two main options that Exchange offers for message security are the S/MIME standard and integration with Rights Management Service. S/MIME uses X.509v3 digital certificates to digitally sign and encrypt messages using either Outlook or Outlook Web Access; these certificates can be issued and managed through Active Directory Certificate Services or other compatible PKIs. RMS provides even more granular control, allowing per-message and even per-document definition of the particular access rights recipients can have. It can also be integrated with Windows Live to allow the distribution of RMS-protected messages outside your organization.

PGP is a great solution for the same kind of problem, but it doesn't come with out-of-the-box enterprise support in any major messaging system or client. Those clients that do support PGP or the open source alternative GPG don't provide support for enterprise key management or policy application; they require each user to manage their keys. Additionally, PGP doesn't use standard X.509v3 certificates, which means that you can't use the same public or private PKI that you use to manage the rest of your certificates.

Ensure the email hygiene of your organization. Ensuring that your messaging system doesn't accept improper messages, such as spam, phish, and virus messages, improves the health of the overall organization and makes each user's mail experience better.

Master It What options do you have for deploying a mail hygiene solution with Exchange 2010?

Solution The Exchange Server 2010 Edge Transport role includes a wide variety of message hygiene agents that can perform connection filtering, sender and recipient filtering, content filtering, IP allow and block lists, and support for additional techniques such as DNS realtime block lists (RBLs), Sender ID, and domain reputation services. Many of these agents can also be installed on the Hub Transport role. Additionally, you can use a third-party messaging server to perform antispam functions, a hosted service, or even some combination of these. You can install virus-scanning software on the Edge Transport, Hub Transport, and Mailbox roles, as well as on the clients.

Chapter 6: Introduction to PowerShell and the Exchange Management Shell

Use PowerShell command syntax. The PowerShell is an easy-to-use, command-line interface that allows you to manipulate many aspects of the Windows operating system, Registry, and file system. The Exchange Management Shell extensions allow you to manage all aspects of an Exchange organization and many Active Directory objects.

PowerShell cmdlets consist of a verb (such as `Get`, `Set`, `New`, or `Mount`) that indicates what is being done and a noun (such as `Mailbox`, `Group`, `ExchangeServer`) that indicates on which object the cmdlet is acting. Cmdlet options such as `-Debug`, `-Whatif`, and `-ValidateOnly` are common to most cmdlets and can be used to test or debug problems with a cmdlet.

> **Master It**   You need to use the Exchange Management Shell cmdlet `Set-User` to change the telephone number (the `phone` property) to (808) 555-1234 for user Matt.Cook, but you want to first confirm that that the command will do what you want to do without actually making the change. What command should you use?
>
> **Solution:**   `Set-User Matt.Cook -Phone "(808) 555-1234" -WhatIf`

Understand object-oriented use of PowerShell.   Output of a cmdlet is not simple text but rather objects. These objects have properties that can be examined and manipulated.

> **Master It**   You are using the `Set-User` cmdlet to set properties of a user's Active Directory account. You need to determine the properties that are available to use with the `Set-User` cmdlet. What can you do to view the available properties?
>
> **Solution**   `Set-User | Get-Member -MemberType Property`

Employ tips and tricks to get more out of PowerShell.   The PowerShell (as well as extensions for PowerShell, such as the Exchange Management Shell) is a rich, powerful environment. Many daily administrative tasks can be performed via the PowerShell as well as tasks that previously may have been difficult to automate.

One of the most powerful features of the PowerShell is the ability to pipe the output of one cmdlet to another cmdlet to use as input. While this is not universally true, cmdlets within the same family can usually be used, such as cmdlets that manipulate or output mailbox information.

> **Master It**   You need to set the custom attribute 2 to have the text "Marketing" for all members of the Marketing department. There is a distribution group called Marketing that contains all of these users. How could you accomplish this using a single command (a one-liner)?
>
> **Solution:**   `Get-DistributionGroupMember "Marketing" | Set-Mailbox -CustomAttribute2 "Marketing"`

Get help with using PowerShell.   Many options are available when you are trying to figure out how to use a PowerShell cmdlet, including online help and the Exchange documentation. PowerShell and the EMS make it easy to "discover" the cmdlets that you need to do your job.

> **Master It**   How would you locate all the cmdlets available to manipulate a mailbox?
>
> You are trying to figure out how to use the `Set-User` cmdlet and would like to see an example. How can you view examples for this cmdlet?
>
> **Solution**   `Get-ExCommand *mailbox*`

`Get-Help Set-User -Examples`

Chapter 7: Exchange Autodiscover

Work with Autodiscover. Autodiscover is a key service in Exchange 2010, both for ensuring hassle-free client configuration as well as keeping the Exchange servers in your organization working together smoothly. Autodiscover can be used by Outlook 2007, Outlook 2010, Entourage, and Windows Mobile 6.1 and later.

Master It You are configuring Outlook 2007 to connect to Exchange server and you want to diagnose a problem that you are having when connecting. What tool can you use?

Solution Use the Outlook 2007 Test E-mail AutoConfiguration tool.

Domain-joined Windows clients will make use of the Service Connection Points in Active Directory. All other clients, and domain-joined Windows clients outside the firewall, will use DNS A and CNAME records. Some clients can also use DNS SRV records.

CNAME records are considered a redirect, and will display a warning dialog to the end user.

SRV records are considered a redirect, and will display a warning dialog to the end user. Additionally, they are not fully supported by many clients and DNS hosts.

Configure site affinity. In a large organization with multiple Active Directory sites, it is important to consider the question of which CAS instances will receive Autodiscover traffic.

Master It What is a method you can use to set site affinity on an Autodiscover SCP object?

Solution Use the Get-ClientAccessServer and Set-ClientAccessServer cmdlets in EMS to view and configure the SCP objects. Or, you can also edit them directly with Active Directory editing utilities such as the ADSI Edit MMC snap-in or LDP.EXE.

Manage Exchange certificates. Exchange 2010 servers rely on functional X.509v3 digital certificates to ensure proper SSL and TLS security.

Master It Which tools will you need to create and manage Exchange certificates?

Solution Typically, you will use one or more of the following EMS cmdlets including New-ExchangeCertificate, Get-ExchangeCertificate, Import-ExchangeCertificate, and Enable-ExchangeCertificate. You can also use the EMC Server Configuration node in Exchange 2010.

Chapter 8: Virtualizing Exchange Server 2010

Evaluate the possible virtualization impacts. Knowing the impacts that virtualization brings to the table will help you make the virtualization a success. Failure to realize how virtualization will impact your environment can end up making virtualization a poor choice.

Master It What kind of impact would be caused by virtualizing Exchange in your environment?

Solution Gather performance information from your current email servers. After you have gathered the information, use the ROI calculation tools and a tool such as Microsoft

Hyper-Green to give you an idea of where your organization may be once you have finished virtualizing Exchange.

Evaluate the existing Exchange environment.   Before you can determine the feasibility of a virtualized Exchange environment, you must first know how your current systems are performing.

Master It   Are your Exchange servers good candidates for virtualization?

Solution   Run the numbers. Verify that your servers are currently underutilized and can be virtualized successfully. Once you have verified that virtualizing is a positive solution, make sure the requirements will be upheld. Verify that you will be able to meet your SLAs, recovery point objectives, and recovery time objectives. Set the expectations for all stakeholders around the possibilities of the virtualization solution.

Determine which roles to virtualize.   There are going to be times when virtualization of one or more roles would be successful and there are going to be times when virtualization of roles is not going to be successful.

Master It   What roles will you virtualize?

Solution   Define what the virtual guests will be and how they will map to the virtual hosts. During this mapping include disk space, RAM, virtual processors, and network information. Validate that you have enough physical resources for the virtual guests. Verify that the performance of the virtualized roles will meet the requirements of the organization.

Chapter 9: Exchange Server, Email, and SharePoint 2007

Connect to SharePoint using Outlook as a client.   Outlook lets you connect to SharePoint and manage its content while either connected or offline. When using Outlook, working with SharePoint calendars, contacts, tasks, alerts, and document libraries is usually faster and more intuitive for users. You can also create new meeting workspace websites right from Outlook.

Master It   Outlook is not able to connect to all types of SharePoint lists. Name a few list types that cannot be connected.

Solution   Announcements, surveys, links, and custom lists, among others

Configure outgoing and incoming email in SharePoint.   Outgoing email from SharePoint is how SharePoint notifies users that content they are monitoring has changed in some way. It is also used to notify users that they have been granted permissions to a new area of SharePoint. Configuring it is as easy as telling SharePoint which SMTP server to use.

Incoming email allows internal or external users to email messages and documents directly to SharePoint. Configuring incoming email involves two steps: enabling incoming email in Central Administration and then enabling email on the desired lists and libraries.

Master It   You are a consultant and one of your customers is an insurance company. They want to have their third-party agents email new policy contracts directly into a document library within SharePoint. The insurance company's mail routing plan is to create an MX record in their external-facing DNS server that points to the IP address of their internal SharePoint server. What are some of the advantages and disadvantages of this design?

Solution   The primary advantage is that it is easy to configure. However, it assumes that the internal SharePoint server is using an externally accessible IP address, which is unlikely. Other disadvantages are that you will not get spam filtering or virus scanning. A better design is to route the message through Exchange and then forward to SharePoint using a send connector.

Set up SharePoint to enable searching on an Exchange public folder.   By configuring SharePoint to crawl Exchange public folders, users can more easily find content located here. This also helps unify content regardless of where it is located. Keep in mind that your public folder store must be located on an Exchange 2003 or 2007 server. To enable searching, you need to create an Exchange Public Folder content source in SharePoint and supply the web URL to the path where you want the crawl to start.

Master It   You are setting up SharePoint and Exchange to crawl public folders. How can you find the account SharePoint will use when crawling this source? Also, what minimum permission level to the public folder store will this account need?

Solution   To identify the Default Content Access account, which is the account used to call into Exchange when crawling public folders, log on to Central Administration. In the navigation menu on the left, select your active Shared Services Provider under Shared Services Administration. In the Search section, select Search Settings. On the resulting screen, click Default Content Access Account.

The minimum (and recommended) permission level to grant the Default Content Access account is Reviewer.

Chapter 10: Exchange Server 2010 Quick Start Guide

Quickly size a typical server.   Having a properly equipped server for testing can yield a much more positive experience. Taking the time to get the right hardware will avoid problems later.

Master It   What parameters must be kept in mind when sizing a lab/test server?

Solution   CPU, memory, and storage are all critical. Storage must be allocated for binaries, mailboxes, transaction logs, and tracking logs.

Install the necessary Windows Server 2008 R2 prerequisites.   Certain configuration settings must be performed before installing Exchange 2010.

Master It   What is involved in installing and configuring the prerequisites?

Solution   Verify that domain and forest functional levels are correct using Active Directory Domains and Trusts.

Install the filter pack, and use PowerShell and the `ServerManagerCmd.exe` program to quickly import the configuration settings via XML files and configure the newly installed services.

Install a multi-function Exchange Server 2010 server.   You should provide a basic, bare-bones server for testing and evaluation.

Master It What installation methods are available for installing Exchange 2010?

Solution Use the `setup.exe` GUI to walk through the wizard and install Exchange 2010.

Use the `setup.com` command-line option to specify all parameters on a single line for a quick unattended installation.

Configure Exchange to send and receive email.

Master It What are the configuration requirements for sending and receiving email?

Solution Create send and receive connectors to configure mail flow for both internal and external (Internet-based) messages.

Configure recipients, contacts, and distribution groups. Add mailboxes, distribution groups, resource accounts, and mail contacts to Exchange.

Master It How are recipients created, and what's the difference between them?

Solution Mailboxes are for mailbox-enabled users; distribution groups are for lists of people who can be addressed as one; resource accounts are for conference rooms, projectors, and so forth; and mail contacts are for external recipients you'd like to appear in your Global Address List.

Use `New-Mailbox`, `New-DistributionGroup`, and `New-MailContact` in the Exchange Management Shell to create these recipients, or use the Exchange Management Console to do the same.

Chapter 11: **Understanding Server Roles and Configurations**

Understand the importance of server roles. For medium-sized and large organizations, server roles allow more flexibility and scalability by providing you with the ability to isolate specific Exchange Server 2010 functions on different Windows servers. By installing only the necessary Exchange server roles on a Windows server, there is less likelihood that one set of functions will consume all the server's resources and interfere with the operation of the other functions.

Installing less actual Exchange server binaries reduces the amount of software running on the Windows server and thereby reduces the attack surface of the server.

Server complexity is reduced since only specific functions must be configured on servers hosting segmented server roles.

Master It You are the administrator for an Exchange organization with 1,700 mailboxes. Your design calls for a dedicated Mailbox server. Your boss has asked you to explain some of the reasons why you need to segment the Mailbox role to a dedicated server.

Solution

1. Reduce the complexity of the Windows Server by installing only the necessary functions to perform the task at hand. This can improve security and reliability.

2. Simplify the configuration and setup of the Mailbox server role.

3. Reduce the overall load on the Exchange Mailbox server by removing other components that might interfere with the Mailbox server functions.

Understand Exchange Server 2010 server roles. Exchange Server 2010 supports five unique server roles.

The Mailbox server hosts the Exchange server database engine, which in turn provides access to mailbox and public folder databases.

The Client Access server provides access to email data for Outlook MAPI clients, POP3, IMAP4, Outlook Web App, and ActiveSync (mobile) clients.

The Hub Transport server moves messages between the sender and the recipient (even if they are on the same server), routes mail to Hub Transport servers in other Active Directory sites, interacts with the Edge Transport server role, and can even send or receive Internet mail. The Hub Transport server is also responsible for message journaling and transport rules.

The Unified Messaging server acts as an organization's voicemail system by recording voicemail and delivering it to the user's mailbox (via the Hub Transport servers). Users can call the Unified Messaging server (via VOIP access) and listen to their voicemails, have their emails read, review their calendar, or even make changes to their calendar.

The Edge Transport server role is similar to the Hub Transport server, but resides in the perimeter network and requires no connectivity to the Active Directory. The Edge Transport server provides message hygiene (antispam and possible antivirus functions) was well as Internet message routing.

Master It Which Exchange server role provides access to the mailbox database for Outlook Web App and Outlook clients?

Solution The Client Access server role.

Explore possible server role configurations. Server roles can be mixed and matched to meet most configuration requirements. Roles can be mixed and matched as necessary depending on an organization's requirements.

For small organizations, a combined function server that hosts the Mailbox, Client Access, and Hub Transport roles will suffice provided it has sufficient hardware even if it needs to support 500 or more mailboxes.

We do not recommend installing Exchange Server 2010 on a domain controller.

Scalability, fault tolerance, and high availability can be achieved by adding additional Windows servers and splitting server roles across many servers.

Client Access, Hub Transport, and Unified Messaging servers can be virtualized. Depending on the client load, Mailbox servers may also be virtualized as long as you remain within Microsoft's support boundaries.

Master It Your company has approximately 400 mailboxes. Your users will only require basic email services (email, shared calendars, Outlook, and Outlook Web App). You already have two servers that function as domain controllers / global catalog servers. What would you recommend to support the 400 mailbox?

Solution Install an additional Windows Server 2008 SP2 or R2 server that supports the Exchange Server 2010 Mailbox, Hub Transport, and Client Access servers.

Do not install Exchange Server 2010 on a domain controller/global catalog server.

Chapter 12: Exchange Server 2010 Requirements

Use the right hardware for your organization.   Properly sizing the hardware that will support your Exchange servers is one of the most important decisions you will make with respect to ensuring the stability of your Exchange organization and the satisfaction of your end users.

Size the memory required for Exchange Mailbox server roles based on the number of active mailboxes and the usage profile. Estimate the amount of RAM required based on your user community's usage profiles or the mailbox sizes so that your server has sufficient memory.

Ensure that the processor core ratio for Hub Transport and Client Access servers to Mailbox servers is adequate to keep up with the load clients will place on these servers. For Hub Transport servers, use a ratio of five Hub Transport processor cores for each Mailbox server. For Client Access servers, use a ratio of three processor cores for every four mailbox processor cores.

> **Master It**   You must estimate the minimum amount of RAM required for an Exchange 2010 Mailbox server that will support 1000 mailboxes that have been designated as heavy users and 500 mailboxes that are designated as average users. What is the minimum amount of RAM this server should have?

> **Solution**   The server should have a minimum of 4GB of RAM to support the operating system and Exchange components plus 6GB of RAM (6MB per mailbox times 1000) plus 2GB of RAM (4MB per mailbox times 500) or 12GB of RAM.

Configure Windows Server 2008 to support Exchange Server 2010.   Windows Server 2008 requires that additional software be downloaded and installed as well as adding some roles and features. You should always start with at least Windows Server 2008 Service Pack 2 or Windows Server 2008 R2 plus the latest updates and patches.

> **Master It**   How would you use the ServerManagerCmd.exe command-line utility to quickly add the necessary additional roles and features.

> **Solution**

> ```
> ServerManagerCmd -i Web-Server Web-Metabase Web-Lgcy-Mgmt-Console Web-Basic-Auth
> Web-Windows-Auth Web-Net-Ext RSAT-ADDS -restart
> ```

Confirm that Active Directory is ready.   Avoid frustration during installation or potential problems in the future that may result from domain controllers or global catalog servers running older versions of the software.

> **Master It**   You must verify that your Active Directory meets the minimum requirements to support Exchange Server 2010. What should you check?

> **Solution**   The Active Directory forest must be at Windows Server 2003 Forest Functional level.

> All domain controllers should be running a minimum of Windows Server 2003 Service Pack 2.

Verify that previous versions of Exchange can interoperate with Exchange Server 2010. Exchange Server 2010 will only interoperate with specific previous versions of Exchange.

Master It You must verify that the existing legacy Exchange Servers in your organization are running the minimum versions of Exchange required to interoperate with Exchange Server 2010. What should you check?

Solution Exchange 2003 servers should be at a minimum of Exchange Server 2003 Service Pack 2.

Exchange 2007 servers should be at a minimum of Exchange Server 2007 Service Pack 2.

Chapter 13: Installing Exchange Server 2010

Implement important steps before installing Exchange Server 2010. One of the things that slows down an Exchange Server installation is finding out you are missing some specific Windows component, feature, or role. Reviewing the necessary software and configuration components will keep your installation moving along smoothly.

Server hardware should match the minimum requirements, including at least 10 GB of free space and 4 GB of RAM for most server roles. Ensure that you are using Windows Server 2008 SP2 or R2 with the most recent updates. Install the Windows Server 2008 roles and features necessary for the Exchange server's role requirements.

Master It You are working with your Active Directory team to ensure that the Active Directory is ready to support Exchange Server 2010. What are the minimum prerequisites that your Active Directory must meet in order to support Exchange Server 2010?

Solution All domain controllers must be running Windows Server 2003 Service Pack 1 or later.

The Active Directory forest must be at Windows Server 2003 Forest Functional level or higher.

Prepare the Active Directory forest for Exchange Server 2010 without actually installing Exchange Server. In some organizations, the Exchange administrator or Exchange installer may not have the necessary Active Directory rights to prepare the Active Directory schema, the forest, or a child domain.

◆ A user account that is a member of the Schema Admins group is necessary to extend the Active Directory schema.

◆ A user account that is a member of the Enterprise Admins group is necessary to make all the changes and updates necessary in the forest root.

◆ A user account that is a member of the Enterprise Admins group or the child domain's Domain Admins group is necessary to prepare a child domain.

◆ The Exchange Server 2010 setup.com program allows the schema to be prepared without installing Exchange by using the /PrepareSchema command-line option.

◆ The Exchange Server 2010 setup.com program allows the forest root domain and the Active Directory configuration partition to be prepared without installing Exchange by using the /PrepareAD command-line option.

Master It   You have provided the Exchange 2010 installation binaries to your Active Directory team so that the forest administrator can extend the Active Directory schema. She wants to know what she must do in order to extend only the schema to support Exchange Server 2010. What must she do?

Solution   From the command line and in the same folder as the Exchange Server 2010 `setup.com` program, run this command:

```
Setup.com /prepareschema
```

Use the graphical user interface to install Exchange Server 2010.   The graphical user interface can be used for most Exchange Server installations that do not require specialized prestaging or nonstandard options. The GUI will provide all the necessary configuration steps, including Active Directory preparation.

The GUI allows you to install the Mailbox, Client Access, Hub Transport, Unified Messaging, or Edge Transport roles on a server.

Master It   You are using the GUI for the Exchange Server 2010 installation program to install the Hub Transport and Client Access server roles onto the same Windows Server R2 system. You must install both of these roles. Which setup option must you choose?

Solution   During setup, specify the Custom setup option, and then on the Custom Setup screen, select the Hub Transport and Client Access server roles.

Determine the command-line options available when installing Exchange.   The Exchange 2010 command-line installation program has a robust set of features that allow all installation options to be chosen from the command line exactly the same as if you were installing Exchange Server 2010 using the graphical user interface.

Master It   You are attempting to use the command line to install an Exchange Server 2010 Mailbox server role. What is the command line necessary to install this role?

Solution   The command line looks like this:

```
setup.com /mode:install /role:mailbox
```

Chapter 14: Upgrades and Migrations

Choose between an upgrade and a migration.   The migration path that you take is going to depend on a number of factors, including the amount of disruption that you can put your users through and the current version of your messaging system.

Master It   Your company is currently running Exchange Server 2003 and is supporting 3,000 users. You have a single Active Directory forest. You have purchased new hardware to support Exchange Server 2010. Management has asked that the migration path you choose have minimal disruption on your user community. Which type of migration should you use? What are the high-level events that should occur?

Solution   You should pick a transition migration to Exchange Server 2010.

1. Evaluate and meet the prerequisites.

2. Install the Exchange 2010 servers.

3. Move email transport, messaging, and client access services to the new servers.

4. Remove the old servers from service.

Determine the factors you need to consider before doing your upgrade.   Organizations frequently are delayed in their expected deployments due to things that they overlook when preparing for their migration.

Master It   You are planning your Exchange Server 2010 migration from an earlier version. What are some key factors that you must consider when planning the migration?

Solution

◆ Confirm that all domain controllers are running Windows Server 2003 SP1 or later.

◆ Ensure that there are no Exchange 5.5 or Exchange 2000 servers.

◆ Review all third-party products currently in use and that interoperate with your messaging system. Confirm that you have versions that will work with Exchange Server 2010.

◆ Examine your current backup procedures, backup storage, and processes; determine if these need to change and, if so, what you will need to purchase.

Coexist with legacy Exchange servers.   Coexistence with earlier versions if Exchange Server is a necessary evil unless you were able to migrate all your Exchange data and functionality at one time. Coexistence means that you must keep your old Exchange servers running for one of a number of functions, including message transfer, email storage, public folder storage, or mailbox access. One of the primary goals of any transition migration should be to move your messaging services (and mailboxes) over to new servers as soon as possible.

Master It   You are performing a transition migration from Exchange 2003 to Exchange Server 2010. Your desktop clients are a mix of Outlook 2003 and Outlook 2007. You quickly moved all your mailbox data and public folder data to Exchange Server 2010. Why should you leave your Exchange 2003 mailbox servers online for a few weeks after the mailbox moves have completed?

Solution   Outlook 2003 clients that do not use Autodiscover are not capable of automatically determining the correct Mailbox server for a mailbox. The Exchange 2003 Mailbox servers should be left online for two to three weeks to ensure that all users have started Outlook at least once and connected to their mailbox. Outlook will contact the old server and automatically determine that the mailbox has been moved to a new server. The Outlook profile will be updated automatically upon first use of the mailbox after it has been moved.

Perform an interorganization migration.   Interorganization migrations are by far the most difficult and disruptive migrations. These migrations move mailboxes as well as other messaging functions between two separate mail systems. User accounts and mailboxes usually have to be created for the new organization; user attributes such as email addresses, phone numbers, and so forth must be transferred to the new organization. Metadata such as "reply-ability" of existing messages as well as folder rules and mailbox permissions must also be transferred.

Although simple tools are provided to move mailboxes from one Exchange organization to another (such as the New-MoveRequest Exchange Management Shell cmdlet), large or complex migrations may require third-party migration tools.

Master It   You have a business subsidiary that has an Exchange 2003 organization with approximately 2,000 mailboxes; this Exchange organization is not part of the corporate Active Directory forest. The users all use Outlook 2003. You must migrate these mailboxes to Exchange Server 2010 in the corporate Active Directory forest. What options are available to you to move email to the new organization?

Solution

◆   Use third-party migration tools.

◆   Issue the Exchange 2010 New-MoveRequest cmdlet.

◆   Export the mailbox in the source organization to a PST file and then import using Import-Mailbox.

Chapter 15: Management Permissions and Role-Based Administration (RBAC)

Determine what built-in roles and role groups provide you with the permissions you need. Exchange Server 2010 includes a vast amount of built-in management roles out of the box. Many of these roles are already assigned to role groups that are ready for you to use. To use these built-in roles, figure out which roles contain the permissions that you need. Ideally, determine which role groups you can use to gain access to these roles.

Master It   As part of your recent email compliance and retention initiative, your company hired a consultant to advise you on what you can do to make your Exchange implementation more compliant. The consultant claims that he needs escalated privileges to your existing journal rules so he can examine them. Since you tightly control who can make changes to your Exchange organization, you don't want to give the consultant the ability to modify your journal rules, though you don't mind if he is able to view the configuration details of Exchange. What EMS command can you run to find out what role the consultant can be assigned to view your journal rules but not have permissions to modify them or create new ones? What role do you want to assign to the consultant?

Solution   To determine which role has permissions to run the Get-JournalRule cmdlet, run the following command:

```
Get-ManagementRoleEntry "*\Get-JournalRule"
```

The two roles discovered with this command are the Journaling role and the View-Only Configuration role. To satisfy the consultant's requirements and satisfy your desire to not give him anymore permissions than what is necessary, you can assign the View-Only Configuration role to the consultant.

Manage RBAC through both the Exchange Management Shell and the Exchange Control Panel. Exchange provides you with the ability to manage RBAC through both the EMS and the ECP. The ECP is a less powerful interface than the EMS, but it has a visual layout that could be useful when browsing roles and it gives you the ability to manage a subset of the RBAC features through a web browser.

Master It One of your junior administrators on staff isn't as well versed in Exchange Server 2010 as you are. He is refusing to learn how to use the EMS because he claims that he can just use the ECP to manage RBAC. To convince your junior administrator that he needs to learn to use the EMS, you should come up with three things that you can't do in the ECP that you need the EMS for.

Solution There are many things that you can't do in the ECP that you need to use the EMS for. The only RBAC management tasks that you can perform in the ECP are modifying the memberships of role groups and adding or removing roles from role assignment policies. You must use the EMS to manage every other aspect of RBAC. Here is a noncomprehensive list of RBAC management tasks that you can't complete in the ECP:

◆ Create, delete, or modify custom roles

◆ Create or delete role groups

◆ Assign roles to role groups

◆ Modify the scope of role assignment

◆ Assign a role directly to a user account

Assign permissions to administrators using roles and role groups. When assigning permissions to administrators, the preferred method is to use assign management roles to role groups and then add the administrators account to the appropriate role group. However, Exchange allows you to assign management roles directly to the administrator's account if you want.

Master It Earlier in the day, you determined that you need to assign a certain role to your email compliance consultant. You've created a role group called Email Compliance Evaluation and you need to add your consultant to this role group. What command would you use in the EMS to add your consultant, Sam, to this role group?

Solution To add Sam to the role group, you would run the following command:

```
Add-RoleGroupMember "Email Compliance Evaluation" -Member "Sam"
```

Grant permissions to end users for updating their address list information. RBAC doesn't just apply to Exchange administrators. You can also use RBAC to assign roles to end-user accounts, so users can have permissions to update their personal information, Exchange settings, and their distribution groups.

Master It You've decided that you want to give your users the ability to modify their contact information in the Global Address List. You want to make this change as quickly as possible and have it apply to all existing users and new users coming into your Exchange organization immediately. You determine that using the ECP would be the easiest way to make this change. What would you modify in the ECP to make this change?

Solution In the ECP, you open the User Roles tab and modify the Default role assignment policy. Check the option to assign the My Profile Information role to the policy. This is the default policy for the organization, so making the change on this policy would update all the existing mailboxes and ensure that new mailboxes also get that role.

Create custom administration roles and assign them to administrators.   If you can't find an existing role that meets your needs, don't worry! You can create a custom role in Exchange Server 2010 and assign the permissions you need to the custom role.

Master It   Your company's legal team is asking you for permissions to export mail from people's mailboxes. However, you operate a highly secure environment and want to ensure that they only have the ability to export mail and not import it as well. You've decided that you need to create and assign a custom role to your legal team that only grants them the ability to export mail. What are the high-level steps for making this happen?

Solution   To create a custom role and assign the role to a role group, perform these steps:

1. Determine what parent role you should use for your custom role.

2. Create the custom role with the appropriate parent.

3. Remove the necessary management role entries to give the role the permissions that you want it to have.

4. If desired, create a custom role group that the custom role will have a role assignment for.

5. Create a role assignment to assign the custom role to a role group.

6. Add your legal team to the role group that has the custom role assigned to it.

Chapter 16: Basics of Recipient Management

Identify the various types of recipients.   Most recipient types that we find today in Exchange Server 2010 have been around since the early days of Exchange. Each serves a specific different purpose and all have objects that reside in Active Directory.

Master it   Your company has multiple Active Directory domains that exist in a single forest. You must make sure that the following needs for your company are met:

◆ Group managers cannot, by mistake, assign permissions to a user by adding someone to a group.

◆ Temporary consultants for your company must not be able to access any internal resource.

Solution   Create only distribution groups in your company. Ensure that security groups are never mail-enabled.

Create mail-enabled contacts for each of the temporary consultants. Do not create any mail-enabled users for the temporary consultants.

Use the Exchange management tools to manage recipients.   Historically, Exchange administrators mainly used a combination of Active Directory tools and Exchange-native tools to manage Exchange servers and objects. That all changed with Exchange 2007 and Exchange 2010, mainly with the advent of the Exchange Management Shell, but also with the now more powerful Exchange Management Console.

Master It You are responsible for managing multiple Exchange organizations and you need to apply identical configurations to servers in all organizations. Since you are just starting out with Exchange Server 2010 and you are not yet familiar with the Exchange Management Shell, you need some guidance regarding the commands that must be used. What should you do?

Solution One of our favorite features of the Exchange Management Console is the *summary* page. The final page that appears once a task has been run, the summary page contains the PowerShell command that executed. A simple Ctrl+C will put that command in your clipboard and away you go with some simple Notepad editing. Though that is a great way to get insight on some of the most advanced Exchange-related PowerShell commands, most administrators will find that the online Help files available with Exchange are simply invaluable as well.

Configure accepted domains and define email address policies. The concept of accepted domains and email address policies was once a single concept in Exchange Server 2000/2003, the recipient policy. Now that this concept has been broken up, it gives us more flexibility in managing email address suffixes and SMTP domains that will be accepted by your Hub Transport servers.

Master It You plan to accept mail for multiple companies inside your organization. Once accepted, the mail will be rerouted to the SMTP servers responsible for each of those companies. What do you need to create in your organization?

Solution Create an external relay domain for each of the SMTP domains. Ensure that all transport configurations and permissions have been set to be able to deliver mail to those SMTP servers.

Chapter 17: Managing Mailboxes and Mailbox Content

Create and delete user mailboxes. Exchange Server 2010 supports the same types of mail-enabled users as previous versions of Exchange. These are mailbox-enabled users which have a mailbox on your Exchange server and the mail-enabled user account. The mail-enabled user account is a security principal within your organization (and would appear in your Global Address List), but their email is delivered to an external email system.

For mailbox-enabled user accounts, there are four different types of accounts: the User mailbox, a Room Resource mailbox, an Equipment Resource mailbox, and a Linked mailbox. Mailbox management tasks can either be performed via the Exchange Management Console or the Exchange Management Shell.

Master It Your Active Directory forest has a trust relationship to another Active Directory forest that is part of your corporate IT infrastructure. The administrator in the other forest wants you to host their email. What type of mailboxes should you create for the users in this other forest?

Solution Create linked mailboxes. Linked mailboxes create a disabled user account in the forest with the Exchange server and assign external account permissions for a user account in the trusted forest.

Master It   You must modify user Nikki.Char's office name to say Honolulu. You want to do this using the Exchange Management Shell. What command would perform this task?

Solution   You would use the following command:

```
Set-User Nikki.Char -Office "Honolulu"
```

Master It   You need to change the maximum number of safe senders allows for user Jeff.Bloom's mailbox to 4096. You want to make this change using the Exchange Management Shell. What command would you use?

Solution   You would use the following command:

```
Set-Mailbox Jeff.Bloom -MaxSafeSenders:4096
```

Manage mailbox permissions.   A newly created mailbox only allows the owner of the mailbox to access the folders within that mailbox. An end user can assign someone else permissions to access individual folders within their mailbox or to send mail on their behalf using the Outlook client. The administrator can assign permissions to the entire mailbox for other users. Further, the administrator can assign a user the Send As permission to a mailbox.

Master It   All executives within your organization share a single administrative assistant whose username is Chris.Rentch; all of the executives belong to a mail distribution group called #Executives. All of the executives want user Chris.Rentch to be able to access all of the folders within their mailboxes. What are some different ways you can accomplish this?

Solution

◆ Use the Exchange Management Console's Manage Full Access Permissions wizard to assign user Chris.Rentch permission to each mailbox one at a time.

◆ Use the `Add-MailboxPermission` cmdlet to assign the `FullAccess` permissions one executive user at a time.

◆ Use the `Get-DistributionGroupMember` cmdlet to retrieve the membership of the #Executives group and pipe the output of that to the `Add-MailboxPermission` cmdlet, as shown here:

```
Get-DistributionGroupMember #Executives | Add-MailboxPermission -User ↵
Chris.Rentch -AccessRights FullAccess
```

Move mailboxes to another database.   Exchange Server 2010 implements an entirely new way to move mailbox content from one mailbox database to another. The administrative tools (the Exchange Management Console and the `New-MoveRequest` cmdlet) are no longer responsible for moving mailbox data. The Microsoft Exchange Mailbox Replication service that runs on each Client Access server role handles mailbox moves.

Master It   You want to use the Exchange Management Shell to move mailbox Brian.Desmond from mailbox database MBX-001 to MBX-002. The move should ignore up to three bad messages before it fails. What command should you use?

Solution   You would use the following command:

```
New-MoveRequest Brian.Desmond -TargetDatabase MBX-002 -BadItemLimit:3
```

Master It   You have submitted a move request for user Brian.Desmond. You want to check the status and statistics of the move request to see if it has completed; you want to use the Exchange Management Shell to do this. What command would you type?

Solution   You would use the following command:

```
Get-MoveRequestStatistics Brian.Desmond
```

Perform bulk manipulation of mailbox properties.   Perhaps the most powerful and useful feature of Exchange Server 2007 and 2010 has been the inclusion of the Exchange Management Shell. Even a new Exchange administrator can quickly take advantage of the basic shell features. As an administrator gains more experience, she can use piping to use the object(s) that are output from one cmdlet as input for another cmdlet.

By taking advantage of piping and the EMS, bulk manipulation of users and mailboxes can performed in a single command that previously might have taken hundreds of lines of scripting code.

Master It   You want to move all of your executives to a single mailbox database called MBX-004. All of your executives belong to a mail distribution group called #Executives. How could you accomplish this task with a single command?

Solution   You would use the following command:

```
Get-DistributionGroupMember #Executives | New-MoveRequest ↵
-TargetDatabase:MBX-004 -Confirm:$False
```

Use messaging records management to manage mailbox content.   Messaging records management provides you with control over the content of user's mailbox. Basic MRM features allow you to automatically purge old content such as Deleted Items or Junk E-mail. You can create new managed folders within the user's mailbox as well as move content to these folders.

Master It   You are managing an Exchange organization that was transitioned from Exchange Server 2003. You have found that many of your users are not emptying the contents of their Deleted Items and Junk E-mail folders. You want to automatically purge any content in these folders after 14 days. What are the steps you should take to do this?

Solution

1. Notify your users of the new policy and the date/time on which it will go in to effect.

2. Create a new managed content setting on the Deleted Items folder that automatically purges items 14 days after they are moved to this folder.

3. Create a new managed content setting on the Junk E-mail folder that automatically purges items 14 days after they are moved to this folder.

4. Create a new managed folder mailbox policy that includes the Deleted Items and Junk E-mail folders.

5. Assign the newly created managed folder mailbox policy to each user account.

Master It   You have a newly created managed folder mailbox called E-mail Purge Policy. You now need to assign this to all 900 of your existing mailboxes. What is the quickest and most efficient way to perform this task?

Solution   Use the Exchange Management Shell and execute a command similar to this:

```
Get-Mailbox | Set-Mailbox -ManagedFolderMailboxPolicy ↵
"Email Purge Policy"
```

Chapter 18: Managing Mail-Enabled Groups

Choose the appropriate type and scope of mail-enabled group.   Though you can modify your group scope or group type at any time after the group has been created, it's always a best practice to create all groups as universal groups in an environment that contains Exchange servers.

Master It   Your company needs to ensure that if an administrator adds a user to a distribution list, that user will not get any unnecessary access to resources on the network. How should you ensure that this type of administrative mistake does not impact the security of your networking environment?

Solution   Ensure that security groups are not mail enabled, and use only mail-enabled distribution groups. This separation prevents an unfortunate addition to "a distribution list" when in fact a user that is added to a group inherits access rights. The information to which he may be given access could be sensitive information.

Create and manage mail-enabled groups.   Creating and managing distribution groups can mostly be done from the Exchange Management Console, with only limited options that require the Exchange Management Shell.

Master It   You want to simplify the management of groups in your organization. You recently reviewed the functionalities of dynamic distribution groups and decided that this technology can provide the desired results. You need to identify the tools that should be used to manage dynamic distribution groups. What tool should you identify?

Solution   Dynamic distribution groups provide the ability to update membership automatically based on the Active Directory attributes defined on member recipients. Because this is a solution that is specific to Exchange, you can only create dynamic distribution groups by using the Exchange Management tools. Active Directory Users and Computers cannot be used.

Explore the moderation features of Exchange Server 2010.   Moderation and moderated groups is one of the new features of Exchange Server 2010. As part of the new self-service focus of Exchange Server 2010, moderation allows a user to review messages sent to an email address on your server.

Master It   If you want to use moderated groups in a mixed organization that contains both Exchange Serve 2007 and an Exchange Server 2010 Hub Transport server, what group feature should you configure?

Solution   In an organization that contains older versions of Exchange, you must specify an Exchange 2010 Hub Transport server as the expansion server for moderated groups. If a message that is sent to a moderated distribution group or dynamic distribution group is expanded on an Exchange Server 2007 Hub Transport server, it will be delivered to all members of that distribution group, bypassing the moderation process. By specifying an

Exchange 2010 Hub Transport server as the expansion server, you ensure that all messages are moderated.

Chapter 19: Managing Mail-Enabled Contacts and Users

Create and mail-enable contact objects. Mail-enabled contacts can be used to provide easy access to external email contacts by using your internal address lists. Mail-enabled users can be used to provide convenient access to internal resources for workers who require an externally hosted email account.

Master It You periodically update the email addresses for your Active Directory contacts. However, some users report that they are not seeing the updated contact address and that they receive NDRs when sending mail to some contacts. What should you do?

Solution A problem could arise if a user has added the recipient to a local address book; the result is that the local object is not updated and can therefore result in NDRs. In that case, the user must delete and then copy again the recipient to the local address book.

Manage mail-enabled contacts and mail-enabled users in a messaging environment. All Exchange-related attributes for mail-enabled users and contacts are not available from Active Directory Users and Computers. To manage all Exchange-related attributes, you must use the EMC or EMS tools.

Master It Whether you want to manage users in bulk, need to create multiple users in your domain or multiple mail-enabled contacts in your organization, or simply want to change the delivery restrictions for 5,000 recipients, what tool should you use?

Solution Administrators who have experience with Exchange Server 2000/2003 may be familiar with bulk management tools such as `LDIFDE.exe` and Visual Basic Scripting. However, in Exchange Server 2010, you can achieve identical results by first using the `Get-object_type` command and then piping the results to a `Set-object_type` command. Those are PowerShell commands available in the Exchange Management Shell. You *must* get comfortable with PowerShell if you plan to manage an Exchange messaging environment.

Implement coexistence between Exchange on-premises and Outlook Live deployments. When an organization goes through the decision process of moving to a "cloud computing" solution, the design may involve moving the messaging infrastructure to the cloud. This decision may require coexistence and GAL synchronization.

Master It You have implemented OLSync and started synchronizing mailbox-enabled users to your Outlook Live domain. You notice that for each mailbox in your on-premises organization, a corresponding mailbox is created in the Outlook Live domain. You need to ensure that only mail-enabled users are created in the corresponding Outlook Live domain.

Solution You can modify the properties of the management agents — in this case the Outlook Live Management agent — and specify the properties of the target of the mailbox-enabled users.

Chapter 20: Managing Resource Mailboxes

Understand how Resource mailboxes differ from regular mailboxes.   Resource mailboxes serve a different purpose in Exchange 2010 than standard User mailboxes, and thus have different features and capabilities. Understanding how Resource mailboxes are different, including what added features are provided, can help improve the end-user experience and increase adoption rate.

> **Master It**   You are planning to create Resource mailboxes to support conference room and other resource scheduling. Identify how the Resource mailboxes are different from regular User mailboxes.

> **Solution**   Resource mailboxes, such as conference rooms, show up in the All Rooms address list. Room and Equipment mailboxes have a different icon when viewing them in address lists and the Exchange Management Console.

> Resource mailboxes can have additional properties defined, such as capacity and features.

Create Resource mailboxes.   Creating Resource mailboxes is easy using various tools in Exchange. Users need Resource mailboxes for conference rooms and equipment like vehicles to allow for easier, more informative scheduling.

> **Master It**   What tools are available to create Resource mailbox and to define additional schema properties for resource mailboxes?

> **Solution**   Use the EMC, use the New Mailbox wizard and specify room or equipment when creating the mailbox. Using the EMS, use New-Mailbox with the -room or -equipment parameter to create a Resource mailbox. Use Set-ResourceConfig in the EMS to define additional schema properties, and use the EMC or EMS to define capacity and features for each Resource mailbox.

Configure Resource mailbox booking and scheduling policies.   Properly configured resource mailboxes help users find the correct resource that is available when needed. When the resource mailbox is properly configured, users need to quickly and easily find conference rooms that have the proper capacity and features needed to hold a meeting.

> **Master It**   You need to configure a resource mailbox to handle automatic scheduling. What tools can you use?

> **Solution**   Use the Resource tabs in the EMC, the Resource settings in Outlook Web App, or the Set-ResourceConfig, Set-CalendarProcessing, and Set-MailboxCalendar Configuration cmdlets in the EMS to configure resource accounts correctly.

Migrate Resource mailboxes.   Moving Resource mailboxes from legacy versions of Exchange require proper planning an execution to ensure that Exchange 2010 features and capabilities for Resource mailboxes are available. Resource mailboxes in Exchange versions prior to 2007 were standard user accounts, and need to be migrated and converted to Resource mailboxes.

Master It You have moved a resource mailbox from an Exchange 2003 mailbox server to an Exchange 2010 mailbox server. You need to convert this resource to an Exchange 2010 Resource mailbox. What steps should you take?

Solution

1. Disable any automate processing or scripts that were previously enabled in Exchange 2003.

2. Use the EMS Set-Mailbox cmdlet with the –Room option to convert the mailbox type.

3. Use Outlook Web App, the EMC, or the EMS to define the resource rules and to enable the automatic processing of schedule requests.

Chapter 21: Public Folder Management

Understand how public folders are supported in Exchange 2010. If you're coming new to Exchange 2010 or don't have a lot of investment in public folders in your current Exchange organization, you probably haven't been too worried about the rumors of the demise of public folders in Exchange 2010. These rumors are fortunately not true; public folders are still supported in Exchange 2010.

Master It You are the administrator of a distributed messaging environment that runs Exchange Server 2010. You plan to deploy a collaboration solution and you are currently evaluating both public folders and SharePoint. You need to identify the limitations of each product and present recommendations to your company's executives. What information should you present to your company's executives?

Solution The following are disadvantages of public folders:

◆ Although public folder databases can exist on servers that are members of a DAG, the public folder databases can be replicated across member servers through the clustering services. A high availability solution depends on public folder replication.

◆ Public folders cannot be accessed by POP3 and IMAP4 clients.

◆ Storing large files is not an efficient use of public folders.

The following are disadvantages of SharePoint technologies:

◆ Additional infrastructure is needed to support and administrator learning curve.

◆ When using Office SharePoint Portal Server products, additional licensing costs may be incurred.

◆ Outlook can only be used to read files in SharePoint document libraries. Modifications to files require the use of a web-based interface or SharePoint Workspace 2010.

Manage public folders. By concentrating its effort on providing solid support for public folder management in the Exchange Management Shell, Microsoft has finally provided the missing command-line management interface that can simplify dealing with one-off public folder management tasks. These cmdlets also make it easy to do large-scale scripted and bulk management operations. The new Exchange Public Folder Management Console will also help you when managing public folders, though it does lack some key functionality.

Master It   You need to identify the Exchange management tools that must be used to perform the following tasks:

◆   Manage Client permissions

◆   Configure a public folder replica

◆   Modify the location of the public folder database files

Solution   To manage client permissions, you must use the Outlook client.

To configure a public folder replica, you can use the Public Folder Management Console or the Exchange Management Shell.

To modify the location of the Public Folder database files, you can use the Exchange Management Console or the Exchange Management Shell.

Manage replication.   An efficient way of providing high availability and increasing capacity for public folders is to replicate the content across Mailbox servers. Public folder replication is scheduled and can therefore be configured for continuous replication or to occur during off-peak hours.

Master It   Your Exchange organization contains 100 Mailbox servers. You plan to replicate 100 public folders from one server to all other servers. You want to do this as quickly as possible. What should you do?

Solution   The quickest way to achieve this goal is by running the `AddReplicaToPFRecursive.ps1` PowerShell script. There are a number of scripts available in the Exchange installation folder, used mainly to facilitate management tasks.

Chapter 22: Getting Started with Email Archiving

Ensure your company complies with regulations that apply to your business.   It is extremely important that your messaging system is configured in such a way that email data is managed according to laws and regulations.

Master It   Which laws and regulations are in effect on your business and what does it mean for your organization?

Solution   Work with your legal and HR departments to determine with laws and regulations you need to comply with. Once you have these policies, use Exchange 2010 retention management policies to configure email retention and manage content as defined by the regulations.

Understand the basic principles of email archiving.   An archiving solution not only provides a way to ease the pain of storage problems on Exchange whether they are with the databases or with PST files, but also assists in helping organizations become compliant and make discovery of email easier.

Master It   How can government organizations actively comply with regulations on open records laws to taxpayers?

Solution   The Freedom of Information Act or (FOIA) allows for the full or partial disclosure of previously unreleased information and documents controlled by the U.S. Government.

Enable Exchange 2010 archiving. Exchange 2010 allows for more efficiently manage the primary mailbox of the user by enabling the mailbox for archiving and using policies to move the content between the mailbox and the archive.

Master It How does archiving allow for moving older email content automatically from the primary mailbox to the personal archive?

Solution You can archive enable the mailbox by using the following PowerShell example:

```
Enable-Mailbox "John Doe" -archive
```

Use Exchange 2010 retention policies. Retention policies define how long data must be retained before it is automatically removed when the time setting has been met.

Master It You can create as many policies as you need, however in many organizations retention policies will be created per department (for instance, Finance).

Solution You can archive enable the mailbox by using the following PowerShell example:

```
Set-Mailbox "John Doe" -RetentionPolicy "Finance"
```

Use Exchange 2010 retention hold. In certain situations you possibly need to prevent deletion of email from end users mailboxes.

Master It Without retention hold, and depending on the policies that may be active and applied to the user, messages may have been moved from the primary mailbox to the archive or even deleted. What is the cmdlet to put a mailbox on retention hold?

Solution You have the option to temporarily suspend the retention policies from processing the mailbox for a set amount of time by placing the mailbox on a retention hold. You can archive enable the mailbox by using the following PowerShell example:

```
Set-Mailbox "John Doe" -RetentionHoldEnabled $true
```

Chapter 23: Creating and Managing Mailbox Databases

Identify the core components of Exchange database storage. The ability to identify the components of your Exchange servers that provide storage functionality will provide all the tools necessary for you to properly plan and troubleshoot storage.

Master It You plan to have redundancy for Mailbox servers. You need to establish how redundancy for databases has changed since Exchange Server 2003. What major change should you identify?

Solution Placing your database and transaction log files on separate disks has been, and continues to be, the method of choice for administrators to ensure a complete data restore when mailbox database replication is not used. By using Exchange Server 2010 mailbox resiliency, complete data redundancy is achieved through replication and no longer requires separate spindles for transaction logs. Note also that transaction log files are automatically purged on Mailbox servers that are members of a DAG. After replication has completed successfully, the truncation lag time has expired, Circular Logging is enabled, or a full database backup has been performed.

Plan for disk storage requirements for Exchange databases.   A major paradigm shift has occurred in the Exchange messaging world. Up to now, administrators have been focused on their IOPS and the capacity of their disks to handle the client requests. Today, administrators have to rethink the way they plan for server storage, though they still need to think about IOPS and capacity, new storage capabilities, and limits. Calculate your IOPS requirements based on the number and profiles of your users. By using Microsoft's user profile guidelines, you can reliably predict your IOPS requirements.

Master It   When planning for storage requirements for Exchange, you must take many factors into consideration. Many of them have to do with storage type, capacity, load, and redundancy. However, many administrators don't always plan for the number of databases that need be created, and opt for a reactionary approach to mailbox database creation.

Solution   As more mailboxes are supported on a single Exchange Mailbox server, scaling the server upward to support more storage is important. Creating more mailbox databases will help you support larger mailboxes and more data while preventing any single database from growing too large. Smaller mailbox databases are faster to back up and manage.

Configure Exchange Mailbox servers with the appropriate storage objects.   Storage groups no longer exist in Exchange Server 2010. All storage group configuration options have been moved to the mailbox database objects.

Master It   You need to prepare your junior administrator to manage the properties of your mailbox databases. Though most administrators have experience managing Exchange, most of their experience was attained in previous versions of Exchange. What are some of the issues you want to be aware of when managing mailbox databases?

Solution   To minimize loss of email and the necessity for restore operations, modify the Deleted Item retention settings. A high setting will have limited impact on your organization and can be advantageous.

Maximum mailbox size limit can be set at the mailbox database level, but also at the individual mailbox level. When set at both levels, the mailbox-level configuration is the effective configuration.

When moving mailbox database files, always ensure that a recent backup of the mailbox database is available.

Chapter 24: Understanding the Client Access Server

Configure Client Access server arrays.   Now that clients connect to Client Access servers for MAPI RPC connectivity, it's even more important that your Client Access servers be highly available. By placing your Client Access servers in load-balanced arrays, you can increase the redundancy and availability of your environment.

Master It   To increase the resiliency of the Client Access servers in your company's main datacenter, you have decided to place them in a Windows NLB cluster. You want to ensure that your users can use Outlook while inside the network to access their email. What ports do you need to ensure are load-balanced in the array?

Solution Internal Outlook users will use MAPI over RPC to access their mailboxes through Client Access servers. You will need to ensure that the RPC Endpoint Mapper on TCP port 135 and the dynamic RPC port range of 1024–65535 are included in the load-balanced array.

Generate valid subject alternative name certificates. Each Client Access server has multiple names that clients use to access it. To secure access to the server using all of the names used, you need to issue Subject Alternative Name certificates to your Client Access servers. SAN certificates allow you to specify multiple names for your server in a single certificate.

Master It Your company, Contoso Pharmaceuticals, implements a split-brain DNS architecture. Your main campus in Baltimore has an array of six Client Access servers called `outlook.contoso.com`. Each server in the array is named accordingly, starting at CONTOSO-CAS1 and ending at CONTOSO-CAS6. This same Client Access array also serves Outlook Web App clients and Outlook Anywhere clients under the name of `mail.contoso.com`. You need to make sure that your Client Access servers have the right certificates to operate correctly when accessed from both inside and outside the organization. What Subject Alternative Names need to be used in the certificate, and which name should be used for the Subject Name field?

Solution SAN certificates need to include each name that a Client Access server can be contacted with. Since certificates validate the name of the server, the validation will fail if the name that the server is accessed by is different than the name on the certificate. Outlook anywhere clients require that the subject name in the certificate match the name in the Outlook configuration. Therefore, the Subject Name of the certificate should be `mail.contoso.com`. Here is the list of Subject Alternative Names:

- `outlook.contoso.com`
- `autodiscover.contoso.com`

Configure proxying and redirection. For users to access their mailboxes, they need to go through a Client Access server that is in the same Active Directory site as their Mailbox server. Client Access servers need to communicate to the Mailbox server through RPC. If the Client Access servers in the same site as a user's mailbox aren't exposed to the Internet, then Internet-based users will need to access their email from Client Access servers in another site. The Internet-facing Client Access servers will proxy the connection to the non-Internet-facing Client Access servers.

Master It You have a Client Access server in two primary datacenters, one in Baltimore (`cas-bal.contoso.com`) and another in Honolulu (`cas-hon.contoso.com`). You also have a Client Access server in your branch offices in Seattle (`cas-sea.contoso.com`), Atlanta (`cas-atl.contoso.com`), and Amarillo (`cas-ama.contoso.com`). You want to ensure that only the Baltimore and Honolulu Client Access servers can be used over the Internet. You want users in Baltimore, Atlanta, and Amarillo to use `mail-east.contoso.com` and you want users in Honolulu and Seattle to use `mail-west.contoso.com` when accessing their email from outside the network. How should you configure your internal and external URLs for each of these Client Access servers to support your desired outcome?

Solution   The `InternalURL` and `ExternalURL` values for each of the virtual directories on the Client Access servers should be configured as follows:

◆   Baltimore `InternalURL`: `cas-bal.contoso.com`

◆   Baltimore `ExternalURL`: `mail-east.contoso.com`

◆   Honolulu `InternalURL`: `cas-hon.contoso.com`

◆   Honolulu `ExternalURL`: mail-west.contoso.com

◆   Seattle `InternalURL`: `cas-sea.contoso.com`

◆   Seattle `ExternalURL`: empty

◆   Atlanta `InternalURL`: `cas-atl.contoso.com`

◆   Atlanta `ExternalURL`: empty

◆   Amarillo `InternalURL`: `cas-ama.contoso.com`

◆   Amarillo `ExternalURL`: empty

Transition Client Access servers from previous versions of Exchange.   When replacing your legacy Client Access servers, you will want to start from the edge of your network and work your way in. Therefore, you want to transition Internet-facing Client Access servers first. When transitioning from Exchange Server 2003, you will want to use a new namespace for your Exchange Server 2003 URLs and move the old namespace to the Exchange Server 2010 Client Access servers. When transitioning from Exchange Server 2007, you can use the same namespace on your Exchange Server 2010 Client Access servers.

Master It   Your current environment is composed of both Exchange Server 2003 and Exchange Server 2007 servers. You decide to install your Exchange 2010 Client Access servers in an Internet-facing site using the same namespace as your existing Exchange 2007 Client Access servers. You notice that users with mailboxes on Exchange 2007 can no longer access their email through OWA. However, users with Exchange 2010 mailboxes can use OWA just fine. What should you do to fix this problem?

Solution   The reason that this problem is occurring is because you are trying to use the same namespace as your existing Exchange 2007 servers. Both the Exchange 2007 Client Access servers and the Exchange 2010 Client Access servers are using the same external URL. When an Exchange 2007 user accesses Outlook Web App on Exchange 2010, they are redirected to the external URL specified on the Exchange 2007 Client Access server.

To fix this problem, you need to configure a new namespace for your existing Exchange 2007 Client Access servers and configure the external URLs on those servers to use the new namespace.

Chapter 25: Managing Connectivity with Hub Transport Servers

Create and manage send connectors.   All messages delivered by an Exchange server are routed through these Exchange connectors. Send connectors are always used in communications between Hub Transport servers, and are *never* used when communicating between a Mailbox server and a Hub Transport server.

Master It   You've been called in to deploy Exchange Server 2010 in a "greenfield" deployment, where no messaging system is present. Installing Exchange is pretty easy, even for the least experienced IT consultants.

But . . . surprise. After your successful installation, you notice that emails cannot be sent to the Internet. You need to connect this new organization to the Internet. What configuration will allow your customer to book his golf games by email?

Solution   By default, there are no send connectors. When you install a new Exchange organization, you will not be able to send mail to the Internet until you create your first connector.

Administrators can manage and modify the send connectors by using the `Set-Send Connector` cmdlet on any Hub Transport server. If you need to enable outbound SMTP logging, this is where you will want to do it. Treat your send connectors with respect; they deliver!

Create and manage receive connectors.   The second half of the Exchange Server 2003 SMTP virtual server, the receiving piece, is now coined as the receive connector. The many improvements in receive connectors over the SMTP virtual servers are considerable. The management of the connector is straightforward, but keep in mind that when you modify the properties of your receive connectors, you can impact all email flow for your organization

Master It   You need to plan for the deployment of an Exchange Server 2010 organization. You quickly notice that the organization is concerned with reducing the number of physical servers. Of course, virtualized installation of Exchange Server is always possible, but this customer has very little expertise in virtualization technologies.

They ask you a very important question: do they really need an Edge Transport server on their network?

Solution   For small organizations, a single Hub Transport server is truly all you need. The receive connector is flexible enough and has practically all available filtering agents and tools necessary for most companies. There are downsides to having only a single Hub Transport server, such as the lack of redundancy for Transport services and the possibility of overloading your server. However, for organizations that are trying to limit software and hardware costs, you can definitely get away with a single Hub Transport server.

When you are looking for more flexibility in configuring inbound mail flow, look at the options available for the receive connectors — especially the remote IP address ranges configuration, which allows you to have multiple SMTP listeners with a single IP address and a single listening port.

Design an Exchange routing topology.   Once you start sending messages between more than one Exchange server, you must understand how Exchange Server 2010 uses your existing

Active Directory infrastructure to route messages between Hub Transport and Mailbox servers. When you begin to discuss server placement and the message routing path with the networking team at your company, you need to understand exactly how messages will flow within your organization.

Master It   You have an Exchange server organization that contains multiple sites, separated by WAN links. Another administrator handles all Active Directory configurations for your organization.

This kind of scenario means that you may want to alter the route that messages take within an Exchange organization. Although Exchange servers always attempt a direct connection to a final destination server, in some cases (Back off and Delayed fan-out) connection is not established directly. This may be a good reason for modifying the site link costs used by Exchange servers when determining the least-cost path. What are your options in modifying these options?

Solution   Stay away from the Exchange-specific site link costs and the hub sites, unless you absolutely need to configure them to meet requirements. In fact, the more complexity that you incorporate into your Exchange design, the more complicated it will become to troubleshoot any kind of problem. Of course, if you opt against Exchange-specific site link costs, there is always the possibility of modifying the costs of the Active Directory site links directly. This may, however, result in an impact on normal Active Directory replication.

The moral of the story? Unless you have some truly mitigating reasons for changing AD or Exchange link costs, don't. If you do have those reasons, then keep it as simple as possible, and document your changes adequately.

And don't forget that for redundancy, install two Hub Transport servers within your site. (Two Hub Transport servers will never communicate with each other, by the way.) Have your Mailbox servers simply select a Hub Transport server by making an Active Directory query for email delivery.

Chapter 26: Managing Transport and Journaling Rules

Create and manage message classifications to control message flow.   Message classifications provide a way to visibly tag selected messages and show that they require specific treatment. On their own, they're merely advisory, but combined with transport rules and mailbox rules, they can become powerful selection criteria for managing messages and ensuring policy compliance.

Master It   You need to use message classifications to manipulate messages by using Outlook. You verify that custom message classifications are available from Outlook Web App. From Outlook, you look around but cannot find any options that relate to the custom message classifications. What do you need to do first?

Solution   The catch is that although message classifications work out of the box with OWA, using them with Outlook requires you to get your hands dirty copying files and adding Registry entries.

Configure message flow and manipulate messages by using transport rules.   Transport rules give you a powerful, centralized method for creating automated policy enforcement in your environment. You can create rules on both Hub Transport and Edge Transport servers, although they serve slightly different purposes.

Master It   You need to add a logo to an email disclaimer; you notice that you cannot include an image in New Transport Rules wizard. The availability of adding logos to a disclaimer was a major decision point of your Exchange 2010 implementation. What do you need to do to make the logo visible in the disclaimer?

Solution   You can include HTML code that points to an image file that is stored on a web server on the Internet. The key here is that the image file is publicly available on a server on the Internet.

Master It   You need to provide the highest possible level of encryption in Exchange 2010 for mail sent among a group of users in your company. What solution should you identify?

Solution   Install and configure a Rights Management Service infrastructure, and publish additional RMS templates to your organization. By using RMS templates, you can define RMS-based transport rules and secure emails as they are delivered within and without your network.

Understand and configure message journaling.   Journaling is still around and better than ever in Exchange 2010. In addition to journaling to mailboxes within the organization, you can designate external recipients to send reports to. Standard journaling enables journaling on a per-database basis, whereas premium journaling allows you to create journaling rules targeted to specific groups or even individual users.

Master It   If you are monitoring the Journaling Rules agent, you may notice that it runs twice on every message. Why the additional overhead?

Solution   Well, journaling makes a concerted effort in ensuring the journaled information is accurate and up-to-date. The journaling rules agent runs a second time *after* all other rules and agents have acted on a message — ensuring that it will get the information from the last-modified version of the message.

Chapter 27: Internet and Email

Configure DNS to ensure email is reliably sent and received.   Properly configured DNS records are the key to ensuring reliable and timely delivery of not only messages that you send but also that Internet users send to you. You should know who is responsible for your public-facing DNS servers as well as who is responsible for your public-facing IP addresses.

Master It   Some of your users are reporting that they are receiving nondelivery reports when they send email to Internet addresses. This does not happen for all email that users are sending to the Internet, but for a small percentage. Some of the nondelivery errors indicate that your mail server's IP address does not have a reverse lookup record. Your mail server's IP address is 192.168.243.10. What Windows command can you use to verify that the DNS record is correct?

Solution   From a computer that uses an Internet-facing DNS server, type `nslookup -q=ptr 192.168.243.10`.

Add an Edge Transport server to handle inbound and outbound email. The Edge Transport server can provide a valuable, additional layer of protection for your internal mail servers. The Edge Transport server role can be configured to accept inbound mail for your domain and to route outbound mail to the Internet. Your internal servers do not need to be exposed to the Internet and only need minimal exposure to the Edge Transport server that is placed in the perimeter network. The Edge Transport server does not need to be a member of your corporate Active Directory.

The Edge Transport server, instead, receives internal configuration about your Exchange organization and recipients via the edge synchronization process. The Edge Transport server stores in an Active Directory Lightweight Directory Services database information such as your recipient's email addresses, accepted domains, and safe sender lists.

Out of the box, the Edge Transport server provides antispam capabilities and can be enhanced with third-party antivirus software or Forefront Security for Exchange.

> **Master It** You have placed an Edge Transport server into your perimeter network and have opened up TCP ports 25 and 50389 between the Edge Transport server and your internal Hub Transport server. To complete the installation and allow mail flow, what things must you do?
>
> **Solution**
>
> 1. On the console of the Edge Transport server, create an EdgeSync subscription file using the `New-EdgeSubscription` cmdlet.
>
> 2. On the Hub Transport server, using the EdgeSync subscription file you created on the Edge Transport, create a new EdgeSync subscription.
>
> **Master It** You need to look up a list of servers that accept inbound mail for your domain, somorita.com. What Windows utility can you use to look up this information?
>
> **Solution** From a computer that uses an Internet-facing DNS server, type `nslooup -q=mx somorita.com`.

Configure Exchange Hub Transport servers to send and receive. The most secure way to protect your internal SMTP mail servers is to not expose them to the Internet at all. However, it is possible to allow your Hub Transport servers to directly send and receive Internet mail.

> **Master It** You need to configure your Hub Transport server to allow it to send email to the Internet and to receive email from the Internet. You have successfully registered a DNS mail exchanger (MX) record that points directly to the Hub Transport server and you have confirmed that the firewall allows inbound SMTP to pass through to the Hub Transport server. What two things do you need to do in order to configure Exchange to send and receive SMTP mail?
>
> **Solution**
>
> 1. Configure the Permissions Groups on the Default receive connector on the Hub Transport server to allow anonymous users.
>
> 2. Create a send connector that uses the Hub Transport as a source server and that has an address space of *.

Configure Exchange 2010 antispam technologies. Exchange Server 2010 includes a number of technologies that can help you reduce or eliminate the spam that your users receive. The content filter inspects messages based on message content and characteristics. Block list providers can reject an inbound IP connection based on known sources of spam, and sender reputation filters can analyze inbound connections for errors and improperly formatted connections and reject connections from both networks or spammers.

Master It Your consultant has recommended that you configure the content filter so that messages that contain certain words will be accepted rather than rejected as spam. What should you do?

Solution Add the specified words to the list of words or phrases that will be allowed on the content filter's custom words list.

Chapter 28: Troubleshooting Exchange Server 2010

Narrow the scope of an Exchange problem. One of the most important troubleshooting skills that an Exchange administrator must possess is the ability to quickly and effectively narrow the scope of problem. Determining the commonalities in a problem can help you quickly locate and solve a problem.

Master It Seven of your 400 users are reporting an error in Outlook that indicates that they cannot connect to the Exchange server. What are some things you would determine to narrow the scope of the problem?

Solution

1. Are the users on the same database?

2. Do they use the same Outlook client version?

3. Are they on the same network or switch?

Use basic Exchange troubleshooting tools. A number of tools are available to you that will help you in troubleshooting Exchange Server problems as well as possibly determining future issues. These include the Windows Event Viewer, the Exchange Best Practices Analyzer, Exchange diagnostics logging, and the `Test-SystemHealth` and `Test-ServiceHealth` cmdlets.

Master It After installing a recent service pack, you have started noticing intermittent issues with your Exchange server. What tool or tools could you run to help you identify potential issues?

Solution You could use the Exchange Best Practices Analyzer and the `Test-ServiceHealth` cmdlet.

Troubleshoot Mailbox server problems. The Mailbox server is at the core of your Exchange organization; all Exchange data is located and serviced via this Exchange server role. When the Exchange Mailbox server role is not functioning correctly, this will cause a fast-moving ripple effect through your organization that will affect more and more users. Tools such as the `Test-MapiConnectivity` cmdlet can help you determine whether a mailbox can be reached.

The Exchange Server 2010 database availability group (DAG) high-availability feature will become increasingly prevalent in even small businesses as companies look to find ways to keep their Exchange infrastructure up and running as much as possible. The `Test-ReplicationHealth` and `Get-MailboxCopyStatus` cmdlets can help in testing the health of the DAG replication.

> **Master It**   A user named Luke.Husky is reporting that he cannot use Outlook to access his mailbox, yet he can access it via Outlook Web App. What tool could you use to determine whether the mailbox is accessible via Outlook?
>
> **Solution**   You can issue the following command:
>
> `Test-MAPIConnectivity   Luke.Husky`

Troubleshoot mail transport problems.   The Exchange Server 2010 Hub Transport role plays the all-important role of delivering all messages that are processed via the Exchange 2010 infrastructure. This is true even if a message is sent from one user to another on the same mailbox database.

A number of useful tools are available to help you and your users determine where a problem may exist. These include the Exchange 2010 Queue Viewer, the `Test-MailFlow` cmdlet, and message tracking.

> **Master It**   A user is reporting that they are sending email but that recipient is never getting the message. The user is convinced your server is not delivering the message. You would like the user to determine whether the message is leaving your organization. What would you advise the user to do?
>
> **Solution**   The user can use the Delivery Reports feature of the Exchange Control Panel to track the message and determine if it was delivered to the Internet.

Chapter 29: Monitoring and Performance

Examine and interpret key performance monitor counters.   Making proper use of your Exchange server requires that you also be able to make fast evaluations of existing performance of that Exchange server using a tool such as Performance Monitor.

> **Master It**   Your user community is complaining of poor performance from a particular Exchange server. You need to make a quick best-guess as to what may be causing the issue. You decide to use Performance Monitor. What performance objects will you examine and what are you looking for?
>
> **Solution**   The objects are Memory, Processor, and Disk (either LogicalDisk or PhysicalDisk). A first estimation on performance problems will examine whether the server has enough memory (based on total memory used, total memory available, and paging), enough processor (based on processor utilization), and disk (based on free disk and the average disk queue length). Most performance problems can be identified by examining those "big three" elements.

Install and configure the Exchange management pack.   While it is possible to manually build a set of test-points for examining Exchange Server 2010 and evaluating its performance and health, using the knowledge that Microsoft already has developed is certainly an easier way to go. This is best done by using the management pack that Microsoft developed for Operations Manager 2007.

Master It   Due to ongoing problems with Outlook Web App on a Client Access server, you need to regularly test to ensure that OWA is working properly.

Solution   Override the rule to enable the Test-OwaConnectivity synthetic transaction.

Configure, locate, and examine SMTP connector logs.   The SMTP connector logs generated by send and receive connectors (and the connectivity logs generated by the Transport server itself) can provide invaluable information when it is time to diagnose message transfer issues for both incoming and outgoing messages in your Exchange organization.

Master It   A client reports that they cannot send email to your Exchange server, but email from every other location seems to be working fine. How do you diagnose the issue?

Solution   First, you must obtain the IP address of their sending server (if they don't know it offhand, you can ask them to log on to their sending email server and visit a website such as http://WhatIsMyIp.com). Next, you examine your connection logs. If that IP is connecting to your Exchange server, proceed to the receive connector logs. At that point you can review the entire SMTP transaction. Very likely, your client's message is being bounced because a transport agent is calling it spam.

Configure and evaluate Exchange diagnostic logging.   Exchange can provide much detail about its operation if you increase the levels of diagnostic logging.

Master It   You are receiving an error in your event log relating to the processing of server-side mailbox rules, but you don't have enough information to resolve the problem. What do you do?

Solution   Change the level of MSExchangeIS\9000 Private\Rules to Medium. Knowing the specific diagnostic level is less important than knowing how to search the list of available diagnostic items and increase the diagnostic level to a higher value.

Chapter 30: Backing Up and Restoring Exchange Server

Back up Exchange.   Performing backups is the somewhat easy part of the equation. The more difficult part is defining the requirements for the backup.

Master It   Document the goals for your backup solution.

Solution   Interview the key stakeholders for the organization and determine what the requirements are for the organization. Define the RTO and RPO for the backup solution. Document the amount of Exchange data that will be backed up. Understand the various scenarios that you will be supporting.

Prepare to recover the Exchange server.   Before you are able to perform any backups from Windows Server 2008, you must install the backup features.

Master It   What do you need to do to install the backup features on Windows 2008?

Solution   Installing the Backup-Features is a simple process. Either open an elevated command prompt or PowerShell prompt. After you agree to the elevation of permissions, type **servermanagercmd -i backup-features**. You can also install the features using Server Manager.

Use Windows Server Backup to back up the server.   There is always a need to back up your server(s). Since you have the requirements, you need to perform the backup.

Master It   Perform a recurring backup utilizing the Windows Server 2008 backup features.

Solution   Setup the Windows backup to perform a daily full backup of the Exchange data. Configure the backup to run every day at 10 p.m. Monitor the amount of time the backup is taking to verify that you are not performing the backup during scheduled online maintenance.

Use Windows Server Backup to recover the data.   You may need to perform a restore of your Exchange data for several reasons. One of the reasons is that you need to give a user email that had been deleted but that is still recoverable.

Master It   Perform a single item restore for a user.

Solution   Pick a user in the organization who has single item recovery enabled and restore the volume that contains his Exchange data. Once you have restored the data, run through the steps to recover some of the email that he has deleted. Export this email to his email account and verify that he can perform operations with the restored email messages.

Recover the entire Exchange server.   There may be occasions that you need to reinstall the entire Exchange server. You have the ability to perform a reinstallation to any of the roles.

Master It   How do you recover the Client Access Server?

Solution   Since Active Directory holds information about the Client Access Server recovering this role is not difficult. You will need to perform the recovery by using the `setup.exe /RecoverServer` command. Once the setup has finished, apply all necessary patches and updates to the system. If any specific configurations have to be changed, make those changes.

Index

Note to the Reader: Throughout this index **boldfaced** page numbers indicate primary discussions of a topic. *Italicized* page numbers indicate illustrations.